ELEVENTH EDITION

CONTEMPORARY MARKETING

Louis E. Boone
University of South Alabama

David L. Kurtz
University of Arkansas

THOMSON
SOUTH-WESTERN

Australia · Canada · Mexico · Singapore · Spain · United Kingdom · United States

Contemporary Marketing Interactive Text
Louis E. Boone and David L. Kurtz

VP/Editorial Director:
Jack W. Calhoun

VP/Editor-in-Chief:
Michael P. Roche

Senior Publisher:
Melissa S. Acuña

Senior Acquisitions Editor:
Steve Hazelwood

Senior Developmental Editor:
Rebecca von Gillern

Marketing Manager:
Nicole Moore

Production Editor:
Chris Hudson

Manufacturing Coordinator:
Diane Lohman

Production House:
Orr Book Services

Compositor:
Parkwood Composition Service

Printer:
QuebecorWorld
Dubuque, Iowa

Design Project Manager:
Michael H. Stratton

Printed in the United States of America
1 2 3 4 5 07 06 05 04

Package ISBN: 0-324-29010-1
Text only: 0-324-29008-X
Xtra! access certificate: 0-324-29009-8
InfoTrac: 0-534-55853-4

Library of Congress Control Number:
2003117133

For more information contact South-Western,
5191 Natorp Boulevard,
Mason, Ohio 45040.
Or you can visit our Internet site at:
http://www.swlearning.com

To the two million students around the globe who began their marketing studies using ***Contemporary Marketing*** *in their classes*

and

to the Text and Academic Authors Association, which awarded
Contemporary Marketing
the William Holmes McGuffey Award for Excellence and Longevity, the only basic marketing text to receive this prestigious award.

Gene Boone was born about the time World War II began and had a relatively quiet childhood until 1956 when he received a 45 rpm RCA Victor recording of "Heartbreak Hotel" by Elvis Presley. Within a year he had discovered Buddy Holly, Little Richard, and Chuck Berry—and he wanted more. So he decided to combine high school with a two-year gig as a part-time DJ at a local radio station. Talk about soft jobs! Play music you wanted to hear and get paid for it. Play lists didn't exist in those days, and as long as irate listeners didn't call in and demand that the station manager fire you, you could play anything you liked.

But few people spend a lifetime career spinning tunes at a small-time radio station, and, following graduation, he started looking for something fun that paid a bit more. College professor sounded like a cool occupation that would keep him indoors and, perhaps, help him meet women (assuming they considered tweed jackets attractive). Nobody told him until it was too late that it was going to take another eight years in college to achieve his ambition—eight more years!—but he struggled through it. He's happy he did because he was able to affect (at least a little) the lives of thousands of his young, middle age, and older students in a half-dozen universities throughout the United States, as well as in Australia, England, and Greece. These gigs proved to be almost as much fun as the first. Oh, yes, his hobby is writing marketing books.

During his high-school days, no one in Salisbury, Maryland, would have mistaken **Dave Kurtz** for a scholar. In fact, he was a mediocre student, so bad that his father felt he could convince him that an educated life was preferable to a series of day jobs by finding him a succession of back-breaking summer jobs. Thankfully, most of them have been erased from his memory, but a few linger, including picking peaches, loading watermelons on trucks headed for market, and working as a pipe fitter's helper. The work made him physically strong, but had zero impact on his academic standing. Worse yet, it made him no better than average as a high-school athlete in football and track.

But a four-year stint at Davis & Elkins College in Elkins, West Virginia, turned him around. Excellent instructors like Dr. Gloria Payne helped get Dave on a sound academic footing. His grade point average soared—enough to get him accepted by the Graduate School at the University of Arkansas, where he met Gene Boone. After graduate school, the two became career coauthors, with 48 books between them.

Today, Dave is back teaching at the University of Arkansas after duty tours in Ypsilanti, Michigan, Seattle, and Melbourne, Australia. He is the proud grandfather of five "perfect" kids and a sportsman with a golfing handicap too high to mention. Dave, his wife Diane, and their aging Yorkie live in Rogers, Arkansas, where he holds a university professorship at the University of Arkansas in nearby Fayetteville.

BRIEF CONTENTS

CONTENTS

PART 2

MANAGING TECHNOLOGY AND INFORMATION TO ACHIEVE MARKETING SUCCESS 109

PART 3

MARKET SEGMENTATION AND CUSTOMER BEHAVIOR 175

PART 4

PRODUCT STRATEGY 245

CHAPTER 11
Product Strategies 246

CHAPTER 12
Category and Brand Management, Product Identification, and New-Product Planning 267

PART 5

PRICING STRATEGY 289

PART 6

DISTRIBUTION STRATEGY 331

WHY WE WROTE *CONTEMPORARY MARKETING*

The first course Dave Kurtz and I taught at our first fulltime academic position was Principles of Marketing. I was a member of the marketing faculty at Auburn University and Dave was teaching at Eastern Michigan University. As a neophyte instructor, I found it to be a fascinating, often frustrating, and constantly challenging assignment. Questions were posed about every aspect of marketing and students wanted to know the strategies behind current popular ads as well as the impact of broader political and economic events on marketing, causing me to often respond with "I don't know the answer to that question, but I'll find out and let you know." It was a memorable experience, one that played an important role in my decision to remain in academia.

In fact, I liked everything about teaching the class except the textbook. It was one of the market leaders at the time, almost 900 pages long, filled with lists and definitions, and appeared to cover the subject adequately. What it lacked was the heartbeat of marketing—it's vitality, its ability to solve societal and ethical problems, its importance in determining the standards of living we enjoy, and its choices of meaningful careers in which each student could achieve personal and professional goals and contribute to society. I hoped that one day I would have the opportunity to create a book that would convey this to college and university students.

Dave and I talked about this need for a number of years and eventually we formed a writing partnership that began with academic papers and journal articles and culminated in the publication of *Contemporary Marketing*—a book that vaulted to market leadership and has never wavered from its position as the unquestioned market leader. At last count, 2 million students have begun their academic careers using *Contemporary Marketing* as their text. We are also especially proud that our U.S. and Canadian colleagues who write college textbooks recently honored our text with the McGuffey Award as one of the best business texts published in the past 50 years.

Dave and I understood and practiced the concept of continuous improvement years before it became a management buzzword. We are convinced that leadership of any industry is accompanied by a commitment to make each new edition better than its predecessor. Rather than resting on the laurels of the success of the current edition, we practice the philosophy embodied in the statement, "First, we will be best. Then we will be first."

The process of making each new edition better than the last involves inputs from a variety of sources: Our own classrooms become real-life laboratories in which to experiment with new chapter materials, new teaching approaches, and new assignments. Although Dave and I visit dozens of classrooms on college campuses throughout the nation and use market research feedback, check-off questions on mail questionnaires can never replace the immediacy of conducting classroom sessions and receiving feedback firsthand from students and other faculty members.

The result of this classroom experimentation, combined with feedback from students and marketing professors and numerous other colleges and universities, is the new eleventh edition. The new edition responds to these requests:

- "We want more emphasis on business ethics and social responsibility in the new edition."
- "All the leading marketing texts are too long to cover in a single term. We want a shorter text."
- "We want a text that is more strategic in focus than the overly descriptive nature of so many marketing texts."
- "We want an up-to-the-minute text that deals with such major issues as the current recession, the terrorist attacks on America, and the shocking ethical scandals that are devastating the image of business and marketing."
- "We want a book with more emphasis on technology, the most complete teaching package, the largest—and highest quality—test bank, two cases at the end of each chapter, and more experiential, hands-on assignments for our students."

As Dave and I will demonstrate in the following pages, we have worked hard to serve our instructor and student customers by addressing these requests. We are confident that you will be delighted with the results.The world of work is changing rapidly.

WHAT IS *INTERACTIVE TEXT?*

Contemporary Marketing Interactive Text by Louis E. Boone and David L. Kurtz offers a new and innovative approach for learning and teaching marketing. By combining the benefits of a traditional textbook and the power of rich, multimedia resources, *Interactive Text* integrates active learning experiences throughout the chapters to give students immediate application of marketing concepts. To shorten preparation time for instructors, *Interactive Text* offers a complete teaching solution that integrates all of the media together in one seamless package – no "assembly" is required.

To achieve a truly interactive learning experience, the Print Component and Online Companion work together to deliver a comprehensive and powerful teaching tool. Using the most innovative resources available, students will experience a unique method for learning marketing concepts using time-tested multimedia resources. Features of the *Interactive Text* include the following:

Learning through Interactive Self-assessment Every chapter begins with a Pre-Test to introduce students to the chapter topics and identify content areas requiring special focus. Because of their tutorial nature, the Pre-Tests provide students with comprehensive feedback for incorrect answers and a final score to gauge their progress. Post-Tests serve a similar role helping students test their chapter knowledge and guide them, by topic, to specific areas of the chapter in which they need further study.

Learning through Customized, Interactive Study As students read the text in the Online Companion, they can annotate the text using the Notes feature. The Notes feature enables students to place a marker in the text indicating a note, and then type in further explanations, questions, comments, or ideas. Instructors can also create annotations and send these notes to every student in the class. In essence, every student and instructor can customize *Interactive Text* with additional hints, questions, and comments to create a personalized study tool.

Learning through Interactive Exploration Unique features in the Online Companion, such as Interactive Examples, provide links to the Web's richest marketing resources. These features, identified by icons throughout the Print Companion, direct students to the Web at a point in their reading when it is most relevant for them to explore the Web resources. This interactivity allows students to use the dual power of print and multimedia to experience a whole new learning environment.

COMBINING THE BEST OF PRINT AND THE WEB

To achieve the interactive learning experience, *Contemporary Marketing Interactive Text* includes two components—a Print Companion and an Online Companion—seamlessly integrated to provide an easy-to-use teaching and learning experience.

Print Companion The Print Companion is a paperback textbook that includes the core content from the original textbook, *Contemporary Marketing,* eleventh edition, by Louis E. Boone and David L. Kurtz. All time-sensitive pedagogical features and materials at the end of chapters have been moved from the printed textbook to the Online Companion. This approach to interactive learning allows for the following:

- A briefer paperback textbook that includes core content.
- A clear roadmap for students directing them from the Print Companion to the Online Companion with easy-to-understand icons placed throughout each chapter.
- A Web-based, real-time learning experience.

Online Companion (http://interactivetext.swlearning.com) The Online Companion for *Contemporary Marketing Interactive Text* is available from a dedicated Web site featuring unique views for instructors and students. The Online Companion includes the following:

- All of the core content from the Print Companion.
- The most interactive, multimedia learning resources available for the marketing course.
- Self-assessment activities with options for tracking scores and monitoring student progress.
- Note-taking features that enable students to bookmark and index specific content.
- Course-management tools that offer the ability to manage the syllabus, track student test scores, broadcast notes to students, and send electronic messages to students.
- InfoTrac College Edition, an online library with articles from over 3,800 scholarly and popular periodicals.

INTERACTIVE LEARNING TOOLS

Contemporary Marketing Interactive Text includes the following interactive learning tools:

Pre- and Post-Test Self-assessment tools give students the power and motivation to test and retest their knowledge of key chapter concepts. The *Interactive Text Online Companion* has a built-in self-assessment system that encourages students to evaluate their knowledge before and after reading each chapter. The Pre- and Post-Tests provide exam-style questions addressing the main topics and concepts of the chapter. At the completion of each test, students receive a score and instructive feedback for incorrect answers as well as direct links to the topics in the chapter addressed in each question. Students can take the tests as often as they need to—a record of their progress for each attempt is kept for them to revisit and gauge their improvement. In addition, instructors have access to these progress reports.

Lecture Enhancements Through PowerPoint Lecture Review Slides, students have full access to instructional material that complements the classroom lecture or facilitates independent study. Because these materials span entire chapters, these are collected in a unique location for easier access. The Lecture Enhancements are provided only in the Online Companion.

End-of-Chapter Materials All of the End-of-Chapter review materials are available in the Online Companion, many enhanced with tools that enable students to deliver answers to their instructors. The end-of-chapter materials in this textbook include:

- Summary of Chapter Objectives
- Chapter Outline
- Key Terms
- Review Questions
- Projects and Teamwork Exercises
- 'netWork
- Crossword Puzzles
- Case

InfoTrac College Edition With each new textbook purchase, students receive a free, exclusive subscription to InfoTrac College Edition. InfoTrac is an online library, updated daily, featuring over ten million articles from 3,800 full-text journals and periodicals. These articles, available 24 hours a day, 7 days a week, range over 23 years, from 1980 until the present.

Interactive Example Interactive Examples offer real-life demonstrations of the key concepts and ideas in the text. Often these examples are drawn from periodical articles, Web resources, and interviews with academics and practitioners, among other sources. These Interactive Examples include:

- Marketing Miss
- Marketing Hit
- Right/Wrong: Solving an Ethical Controversy

Interactive Exercise Interactive Exercises provide opportunities to apply the concepts and ideas in the chapter through structured activities. Typically, these draw upon resources from the Web and other information sources. These Interactive Exercises include:

- 'netEx

Interactive Video Case Interactive Video Cases provide real-life examples of businesses and managers. Each video is accompanied by a written case with several questions for students to answer. Students may email the answers to these questions to their instructor. Interactive Video Cases include:

- Video Case
- Krispy Kreme Continuing Video Case

Interactive Game Interactive Games offer students a fun and interesting way to test their understanding of key concepts. Interactive Games include:

- Quiz Bowl

Interactive Learning Goal Interactive Learning Goals provide the opportunity, at various points in the chapter, to review a high-level overview of the relevant learning goal.

Interactive Review The Interactive Review provides a concise explanation of the chapter learning goals through a dynamic multimedia presentation, complete with audio narration.

FLEXIBLE COURSE MANAGEMENT TOOLS

The *Interactive Text* provides course management tools that help facilitate on-site or distance learning courses. A variety of course management tools are available and include tools to track students' progress through Pre- and Post-Test scores, customize content with additional notes, provide a unique course syllabus, broadcast messages, and bookmark the text. Because each instructor has unique teaching goals, the *Interactive Text* provides flexibility in using these goals and in determining what students view. A convenient "student view" button is always available to instructors so they can review exactly what the student sees. Here is a listing of the course tools found in *Interactive Text.*

Syllabus Instructors can create a syllabus for their course directly in *Interactive Text.* This tool enables instructors to provide course information, such as course name, title, and policies, as well as add custom information. Further, instructors can create a course schedule that provides students with assignments, homework, and other information based around the course calendar. The course schedule is completely customizable.

If instructors already have a syllabus or wish to use another tool to build a course syllabus, the *Interactive Text* Syllabus tool provides the option to link directly to this syllabus. If instructors do not want students to have access to a syllabus, the Syllabus tool may be turned off.

Messages The Messages tool enables instructors to broadcast text messages to individual students, groups of students, or to every student in the class. Instructors can create a message and send it immediately, or they can indicate a future date at which time to broadcast the message. The Messages tool will remember this request and send the message automatically at the specified time. These messages are visible upon logging into the Online Companion of the *Interactive Text.*

Notes The Notes tool enables students and instructors to place a marker in the text and then type in further explanations, questions, comments, or ideas. Instructors also can create annotations and send these notes to every student in the class. Specifically, with the Notes tool students and instructors can do the following:

- Read notes that were previously recorded.
- Change or delete notes that were previously recorded.
- Read notes that the instructor has broadcast.
- View all notes (student and instructor notes) for the entire chapter, and then download these notes to a file to print or revise further in a word processing program.

View Progress Students who take the Pre- and Post-Tests have their scores recorded within the View Progress grade book. After students complete the tests, the test results and accompanying feedback are reported. This feedback also includes a direct link to the content in the chapter where answers to questions may be found. Scores are saved within the View Progress grade book.

Instructors have the ability to change the presentation of these scores in the View Progress grade book, either presenting all test scores for a student by chapter, or all test scores for a chapter by student. Instructors also have the option to download the scores in their grade book into a spreadsheet-ready format to aid in organizing and managing student scores.

Bookmarking The Bookmarking tool enables students and instructors to "bookmark" or create a direct link to the last topic visited in *Interactive Text.* This link is then presented at the start of the next visit into the product, to jump back to where the instructor or student left off.

Find a Topic and Resource Index The Find a Topic tool is a useful way to quickly locate and jump to a specific topic in the *Interactive Text.* A content expert has carefully compiled all of the topics in the text, as well as alternate ways in which the typical students would search for the topic. These topics and alternate topics are then indexed alphabetically.

The Resource Index lists all of the major features of the text, such as Interactive Updates and Interactive Videos. It's a quick way to find specific types of resources that are located throughout the *Interactive Text.*

Technical Support Technical support for *Interactive Text* is available through Thomson Learning Academic Resource Center and Technology Services. To contact a technical support representative, call 1-800-423-0563 or email tl-support@thomson.com.

ACKNOWLEDGMENTS

We are grateful for the many suggestions and contributions of dozens of people who teach the introductory marketing course on a regular basis and are in the best position to comment on what works best—and what doesn't work at all. Every recommendation made a difference in the creation of the new 11th edition. Our special thanks go out to Focus Group attendees at Summer Educators Conference of the American Marketing Association at the August 2001 Washington, D.C., meetings:

Elise Sautter
New Mexico State University

Oscar Deshields, Jr.
California State University–Northridge

Brian Larson
Widener University (PA)

Rama Yelkur
University of Wisconsin–Eau Claire

Michael Tsiros
University of Miami (FL)

Chick Kasouf
Worcester Polytechnic Institute (MA)

Michael Little
Virginia Commonwealth University

David Urban
Virginia Commonwealth University

Janet Parish
University of Alabama

Sue Mantel
University of Toledo

Don Roy
Middle Tennessee State University

Bill Kehoe
University of Virginia

Guangping (Walter) Wang
Pennsylvania State University

A large number of marketing colleagues made major contributions to the 10th edition. Our special thanks go out to:

Keith Absher
University of North Alabama

Alicia T. Aldridge
Appalachian State University

Amardeep Assar
City University of New York

Tom F. Badgett
Angelo State University

Joe K. Ballenger
Stephen F. Austin State University

Michael Bernacchi
University of Detroit Mercy

David Blanchette
Rhode Island College

Barbara Brown
San Jose State University

Reginald E. Brown
Louisiana Tech University

Marvin Burnett
St. Louis Community College–Florissant

Scott Burton
University of Arkansas

Howard Cox
Fitchberg State University

James Coyle
Baruch College

William Demkey
Bakersfield College

Michael Drafke
College of DuPage

Joanne Eckstein
Macomb Community College

John Frankel
San Juan College

Robert Georgen
Trident Technical College

Robert Googins
Shasta College

Arlene Green
Indian River Community College

Joel Haynes
State University of West Georgia

Mabre Holder
Roane State Community College

Andrew W. Honeycutt
Clark Atlanta University

Dr. H. Houston
California State University–Los Angeles

John Howe
Santa Ana College

Tom Jensen
University of Arkansas

Stephen C. King
Keene State College

Kathleen Krentler
San Diego State University

Laddie Logan
Arkansas State University

Kent Lundin
College of the Sequoias

Patricia Macro
Madison Area Tech College

Frank Markley
Arapahoe Community College

Tom Marshall
Owens Community College

Dennis C. Mathern
The University of Findlay

Lee McGinnis
University of Nebraska

Michael McGinnis
Pennsylvania State University

Norma Mendoza
University of Arkansas

Mohan Menon
University of South Alabama

Anthony Miyazaki
University of Miami

Jerry W. Moorman
Mesa State College

Linda Morable
Richland College

Diane Moretz
Ashland University

Eugene Moynihan
Rockland Community College

Margaret Myers
Northern Kentucky University

Nita Paden
Northern Arizona University

George Palz
Erie Community College–North

George Prough
University of Akron

Warren Purdy
University of Southern Maine

Salim Qureshi
Bloomsburg University

Thomas Read
Sierra College

Joel Reedy
University of South Florida

Dominic Rella
Polk Community College

Ken Ridgedell
Southeastern Louisiana University

Lillian Roy
McHenry County College

Arthur Saltzman
California State–San Bernardino

Elise T. Sautter
New Mexico State University

Jonathan E. Schroeder
University of Rhode Island

Farouk Shaaban
Governors State University

John Sondey
South Dakota State University

James Spiers
Arizona State University

David Starr
Shoreline Community College

Bob Stassen
University of Arkansas

Sue Taylor
Belleville Area College

Lars Thording
Arizona State University–West Campus

Rajiv Vaidyanathan
University of Minnesota

Charles Vitaska
Metro State College of Denver

Cortez Walker
Baltimore City Community College

Roger Waller
San Joaquin Delta College

Mary M. Weber
Emporia State University

Vicki L. West
Southwest Texas State University

Elizabeth White
Orange County Community College

David Wiley
Anne Arundel Community College

William Wilkinson
Governors State University

James Williams
Richard Stockton College of New Jersey

Mary Wolfindarger
California State University–Long Beach

Joyce Wood
North Virginia Community College

Earlier reviewers of *Contemporary Marketing* include:

Keith Absher
Kerri L. Acheson
Zafar U. Ahmed
M. Wayne Alexander
Bruce Allen
Linda Anglin
Allen Appell
Paul Arsenault
Dub Ashton
Amardeep Assar
Tom F. Badgett
Joe K. Ballenger
Wayne Bascom
Richard D. Becherer
Tom Becker
Richard F. Beltramini
Robert Bielski
Carol C. Bienstock
Roger D. Blackwell
Jocelyn C. Bojack
Michele D. Bunn
James Camerius
Les Carlson
John Carmichael
Robert Collins
Elizabeth Cooper-Martin
Deborah L. Cowles
Howard B. Cox
Jacob Chacko
John E. Crawford
Michael R. Czinkota
Kathy Daruty
Grant Davis
Gilberto de los Santos
Carol W. DeMoranville
Fran DePaul
Gordon Di Paolo
John G. Doering
Jeffrey T. Doutt
Sid Dudley
John W. Earnest
Philip E. Egdorf
Michael Elliot
Amy Enders
Bob Farris
Lori Feldman
Sandra M. Ferriter
Dale Fodness
Gary T. Ford
Michael Fowler
Edward Friese
Sam Fullerton
Ralph M. Gaedeke
G.P. Gallo
Nimish Gandhi
Sheryl A. Gatto
Robert Georgen
Don Gibson
David W. Glascoff
James Gould
Donald Granbois
John Grant
Paul E. Green
William Green
Blaine Greenfield
Matthew Gross
Robert F. Gwinner
Raymond M. Haas
John H. Hallaq
Cary Hawthorn
E. Paul Hayes
Hoyt Hayes
Betty Jean Hebel
Debbora Heflin-Bullock
John (Jack) J. Heinsius
Sanford B. Helman
Nathan Himelstein
Robert D. Hisrich
Ray S. House
George Housewright
Donald Howard
Michael D. Hutt
Gregory P. Iwaniuk
Don L. James
James Jeck
Candida Johnson
David Johnson
Eugene M. Johnson
James C. Johnson
Harold H. Kassarjian
Bernard Katz
Stephen K. Keiser
Michelle Keller
J. Steven Kelly
James H. Kennedy
Charles Keuthan

Maryon King
Randall S. Kingsbury
Donald L. Knight
Linda S. Koffel
Philip Kotler
Terrence Kroeten
Russell Laczniak
Martha Laham
L. Keith Larimore
Edwin Laube
Ken Lawrence
Francis J. Leary, Jr.
Mary Lou Lockerby
James Lollar
Paul Londrigan
David L. Loudon
Dorothy Maass
James C. Makens
Lou Mansfield
Warren Martin
James McCormick
Carl McDaniel
Michael McGinnis
James McHugh
Faye McIntyre
H. Lee Meadow
Mohan Menon
William E. (Gene) Merkle
John D. Milewicz
Robert D. Miller
Laura M. Milner
Banwari Mittal
Harry J. Moak
J. Dale Molander
John F. Monoky
James R. Moore
Thomas M. Moran
Susan Logan Nelson
Colin F. Neuhaus
Robert T. Newcomb
Jacqueline Z. Nicholson
Tom O'Connor
Robert O'Keefe
Sukgoo Pak
Eric Panitz
Dennis D. Pappas
Constantine Petrides
Barbara Piasta
Dennis D. Pitta
Barbara Pletcher
Carolyn E. Predmore
Arthur E. Prell
Bill Quain
Rosemary Ramsey
Thomas C. Reading
Gary Edward Reiman
Glen Riecken
Arnold M. Rieger
C. Richard Roberts
Patrick J. Robinson
William C. Rodgers
William H. Ronald
Bert Rosenbloom
Barbara Rosenthal
Carol Rowery
Ronald S. Rubin
Don Ryktarsyk
Rafael Santos
Duane Schecter
Dennis W. Schneider
Larry J. Schuetz
Bruce Seaton
Howard Seigelman
Jack Seitz
Steven L. Shapiro
F. Kelly Shuptrine
Ricardo Singson
Norman Smothers
Carol S. Soroos
James Spiers
Miriam B. Stamps
William Staples
David Steenstra
Bruce Stern
Robert Stevens
Kermit Swanson
G. Knude Swenson
Cathy Owens Swift
Clint B. Tankersley
Ruth Taylor
Donald L. Temple
Vern Terpstra
Ann Marie Thompson
Howard A. Thompson
John E. Timmerman
Frank Titlow
Rex Toh
Dennis H. Tootelian
Fred Trawick
Richard Lee Utecht
Rajiv Vaidyanathan
Toni Valdez
Peter Vanderhagen
Dinoo T. Vanier
Gayle D. Wasson
Donald Weinrauch
Fred Weinthal
Susan B. Wessels
John J. Whithey
Debbora Whitson
Robert J. Williams
Nicholas C. Williamson
Cecilia Wittmayer
Van R. Wood
Julian Yudelson
Robert J. Zimmer

We would also like to express our appreciation to our research and editorial assistants Jeanne Bartimus, Karen Hill, and Mikhelle Taylor. Their untiring efforts on our behalf are most appreciated.

In addition, we applaud the contributions of the high-quality instructors who participated in making the *Contemporary Marketing* supplements an outstanding and innovative teaching and learning package:

Douglas Hearth
University of Arkansas

Stephen M. Peters
Walla Walla Community College

Tom O'Connor
The University of New Orleans

Dona Hightower
UpStream Press

Finally, this book would never have become a reality without the outstanding efforts of the South-Western/Thomson editorial, production, and marketing teams. Our Acquisitions Editor Steve Hazelwood, Developmental Editor Rebecca von Gillern, Marketing Manager Nicole Moore, and Production Editor Chris Hudson all did a wonderful job. We also thank Karen Hill at Elm Street Press for her contributions to making this exciting new 11th edition.

Louis E. Boone & David L. Kurtz

PROLOGUE

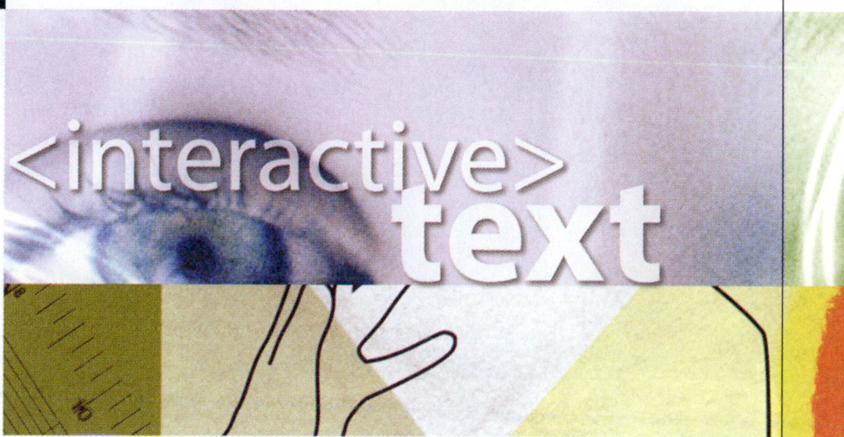

Planning a Career in Marketing

At this point, you should be congratulated on your decision to take this course. After all, marketing is a pervasive element in our lives. In one form or another, it reaches every person. As you begin this course, you should be aware of three important facts about marketing.

> **Briefly Speaking**
>
> If I had my life to live over again, I would elect to be a trader of goods rather than a student of science. I think barter is a noble thing.
>
> *Albert Einstein (1879–1955) American physicist*

MARKETING COSTS ARE A BIG COMPONENT OF YOUR TOTAL BUDGET

Approximately 50 percent of the total costs of products you buy are marketing costs. In short, half of the $20 you pay for that chart-topping compact disc goes not for the plastic disc, protective sleeve, paper jacket, or the physical act of burning the tracks onto the disk, but for marketing costs. The same is true of your purchase of a new flat-screen monitor for your desktop, your first DVD player, and the $22,000 price tag on that PT Cruiser you want so badly.

But costs alone do not indicate the value of marketing. The high living standard your family, friends, and you enjoy in large part is a function of our nation's efficient marketing systems. When considered in this perspective, the costs of marketing seem more reasonable. For example, marketing expands overall sales, thereby spreading fixed production costs over more units of output and reducing total output costs.

MARKETING PROVIDES AN OPPORTUNITY TO CONTRIBUTE TO SOCIETY AS WELL AS TO AN INDIVIDUAL COMPANY

Marketing decisions affect everyone's welfare. How much quality should be built into a product? Will people buy a safer product if it costs twice as much as the current version? Should every community adopt recycling programs? Because ethics and social responsibilities are critical factors for marketers in a business environment tarnished by both ethical and legal failings of a number of well-known companies and their leaders, it is essential that marketers strive to exceed customer and government expectations of ethical behavior. Reading the *Solving an Ethical Controversy* exercises included in every chapter will increase your awareness of the role of high ethical standards in every dimension of marketing and allow you to examine the not always black-and-white ethical issues such as prescription drug pricing, online privacy, advertising to children, promotion of liquor and tobacco products, and invasive practices such as spam, pop-up ads, and telemarketing.

Not only does marketing influence numerous facets of our daily lives, decisions regarding marketing activities affect everyone's welfare. Opportunities to advance to more responsible decision-making positions come sooner in marketing than in most occupations. This combination of challenges and opportunities has made marketing one of the most popular fields of academic study.

A recent survey by executive recruiter Korn/Ferry International revealed that the best route to the top of the corporate ladder begins in a company's marketing division. Three of every eight CEOs are chosen from a company's marketing division because the growing global economy demands proven market leaders in winning the fight to increase a firm's worldwide market shares. Finance, which had long dominated as the top career path for senior executives, fell to third place, and executives who had completed international assignments—many of the assignments being marketing related—came in second.

Colon polyps. Stop them before they go bad.
Colon cancer almost always starts with a polyp. Get the polyp early and stop colon cancer before it even starts. And that's for both men and women. Just get a test from your doctor. 1-800-ACS-2345 or cancer.org
Colon cancer. Get the test. Get the polyp. Get the cure.
Ad Council

Managers of not-for-profit organizations like The American Cancer Society use on-staff specialists and outside agencies to develop marketing strategies designed to strengthen commitments to early detection of all types of cancer. In addition to communicating the overall mission, promotional messages like this are intended to prompt concerned readers to make donations to the organization.

YOU MAY CHOOSE A CAREER IN MARKETING

When asked about their conception of an ideal entry-level job following graduation, most students mention salary and opportunity for professional growth and advancement. While compensation is almost always an issue, the 21st century job seeker also wants to feel recognized for his or her achievements, be assigned new responsibilities, and work in continuous-learning environments. Many will also include as an important issue working for a family-friendly organization that offers a high quality of life.

Of the many career paths chosen by business graduates, marketing is the single largest employment category in the U.S. labor force, and job growth in the field is expected to accelerate. The U.S. Bureau of Labor Statistics estimates that the number of jobs in marketing, advertising, and public relations management will grow much faster through 2010 than the average for all occupations. Every successful organization—profit-seeking or not-for-profit—recognizes the necessity of effective marketing in accomplishing its goal of providing customer satisfaction by hiring highly motivated, professionally educated marketing specialists to design and implement these customer-driven programs.

Marketing-related occupations account for 25 to 30 percent of jobs in the typical highly industrialized nation. History has shown that the demand for effective marketers is not affected by cyclical economic fluctuations.

YOUR QUEST FOR A SUCCESSFUL, REWARDING CAREER

Selecting a career may be the most important decision you will ever make. That's why *Contemporary Marketing* begins by discussing the best way to approach career decisions and how to prepare for an *entry-level position*—your first permanent employment after leaving school. We then look at a range of marketing careers and discuss employment opportunities in fields related to each major part of the text.

Entry-level positions have been more difficult to find recently. As the economy suffered after September 11, 2001, so did the job market. As a result, students have to be even more creative in their employment searches. But, as you know, creativity has never been in short supply on the nation's campuses.

Today, economic conditions are improving, and job prospects are brighter for most students. Still, you need to do everything you can to enhance your career opportunities. You've already taken an important first step by enrolling in a class using this textbook.

During the next few months, you will be introduced to all of the key functional areas of marketing. As you learn about marketing concepts, you will also be able to identify areas of employment that you may wish to pursue.

Education will improve your prospects of finding and keeping the right job. Last year, the average full-time employee 18 or older with a high school diploma earned just under $23,000. By contrast, the average employee with a bachelor's degree earned $40,000-plus annually—one and three-fourths more than the pay of the high school grad. Applying yourself in class, expanding your experiences through career-directed volunteer efforts, part-time and summer jobs, and effective internships—and selecting the right major—will put you well on your way to improving these salary statistics when you launch your career.

In addition to taking classes, try to gain related experience either through a job and/or by participating in campus organizations. Internships, carefully selected summer and part-time jobs, and volunteer activities on campus and in your community can also give you invaluable hands-on experience while you pursue your education. During the tight job market of the recent recession when youth unemployment has soared to 12 percent and even college-educated young people with little or no job experience have had difficulty in securing job offers, these work experiences will often set you apart from other job seekers in the eyes of recruiters.[1] They are invaluable for traditional students who entered college immediately following graduation from high school and who possess little or no work experience.

This career-focused Prologue provides you with a brief look at the trends and opportunities available for future marketers in an increasingly diversified professional field. It describes essential elements of an effective résumé and discusses the latest trends in electronic job searches. Finally, it provides a listing of primary marketing information sources that contain answers to many of the questions typically asked by applicants. This information will provide valuable career-planning assistance in this and other future courses, whether your career plans involve marketing or you decide to major in another field.

Many of the marketing positions you read about throughout the text are described here. Specifically, the job summaries describe the job and the responsibilities and duties that are typically required as well as the usual career path for each of the eight marketing-related positions.

An ideal job is one that makes you want to go to work every morning. It's working at something you enjoy and for which you get rewarded handsomely for performing at your typically superior level.

Marketing your skills to a prospective employer is much the same as marketing a product to a consumer. Increasingly, job seekers are selling their skills online, eliminating the intermediary and leveling the playing field between applicant and potential employer. The greatest challenge for online job seekers is learning how to market themselves.

Despite the vast databases and fancy tools of the giant career sites such as Monster.com and CareerMosaic (http://www.careermosaic.com), which may receive hundreds of thousands of visits each day, savvy job seekers often find their time better spent zeroing in on niche boards offering more focused listings. For example, sales applicants can check out Salesgiant.com.

In many instances, students desiring interviews with specific employers or in certain geographical locations will go directly to the employer's or region's Web site to learn of available positions. Most employers include an employment site as part of their home page. Some offer virtual tours of what it is like to work for the firm. For example, the Enterprise Rent-a-Car Web site features profiles of young assistant managers as they perform daily work activities.

After spending $1.8 million in a single year to hire between 12,000 and 14,000 people, Lockheed Martin decided to make better use of its corporate Web site in recruiting job candidates. The defense contractor hired the same number of new employees during 2002, but its cost-cutting approach made it possible to fill its vacancies and spend only $750,000 on boards.[2]

Your online job search can focus on positions in a specialized field or location, or these positions can be posted on meta-sites like Monster.com with few if any particular limitations on company or location. In either case, the key to getting the job you want is letting the market know who you are and what you can do. While few college graduates are hired directly based on their response to an online listing, this approach is often an important first step in zeroing in on specific employers of interest and then soliciting interviews that may lead to subsequent job offers.

As you begin your career, you will apply many of the principles and concepts discussed in the text, including how to do the following: target a market, capitalize on brand equity, position a product, and use marketing research techniques. Even in jobs that seem remote from the marketing discipline, this knowledge will help you stay focused on the most important aspect of business: the consumer.

Briefly Speaking

True terror is to wake up one morning and discover that your high school class is running the country.

Kurt Vonnegut, Jr. (b. 1922) American author

6FigureJobs.com is just one of the 3,000-plus online career sites available for use by online job seekers.

STANDING OUT FROM THE CROWD OF JOB SEEKERS

In a tight job market, employers can afford to be choosy in deciding which applicants will make the cut, be interviewed, and, possibly, be offered a position. And often the applicant's accumulated job and leadership experiences will be key decision criteria in determining whether he or she is given serious consideration as a potential employee.

Students often choose to continue their studies following graduation and pursue an MBA degree or enter a master's program specially suited to their career goals. For example, students interested in a marketing research career may decide to study for a specialized master's degree in this field offered by a growing number of universities. A student who wishes to extend formal education in a specialized degree program should seek advice on specific programs from instructors who teach in that area. For example, a marketing research professor is likely to have information on master's programs in that field at different universities.

Other activities that enhance your personal worth are internships and volunteering. Internships have been described as a critical link in bridging the theory–practice educational gap. They help to carry students between the academic present and the professional future. They provide students with an opportunity for learning how classroom theory is applied in real-world business environments.

An internship is a partnership between the student, the university, and the agency or internship site. All of these parties assume definite responsibilities, perform specific functions, and achieve benefits as a result of their involvement. In addition, internships can serve as critical networking and job-hunting tools. In some instances, internships are precursors for specific employment opportunities, allowing students to demonstrate technical proficiency while providing cost-effective employee training for the company or not-for-profit organization.[3]

Excellent sources of information about the nation's outstanding internships can be found at your local bookstore. One particularly useful publication by Mark Oldman and Samer Hamadeh is *America's Top 100 Internships,* published annually by Villard Books in New York.

Your Résumé

Writing a résumé is a task that almost every job seeker dislikes—and one that is often postponed until the last minute. "After all," the thinking usually goes, "I won't be involved in interviewing for another year." However, this task is made less daunting with the help of your faculty advisor or career counselor, a growing number of books and articles on résumé writing, and numerous computer software packages that require little more than filling in the blanks.

A résumé is probably the most important document that a job seeker can provide to a potential employer because it frequently is the only written record of credentials available with which an evaluation and the selection of a job candidate can be made. It is a concise summary of academic, professional, and personal accomplishments that makes focused statements about the job applicant.

Three basic formats are used in preparing a résumé. *Chronological résumés* arrange information in reverse chronological order, emphasizing job titles and organizations and describing responsibilities held and duties performed. This format highlights continuity and career growth. A *functional résumé* accents accomplishments and strengths, placing less emphasis on job titles and work history, and often omits job descriptions. A functional résumé prepared by a recent graduate is shown in Figure 1. Some applicants use a *combined résumé* format, which emphasizes skills first, followed by employment history. This format

Résumé Blunders

The following list of errors appeared in job résumés, applications, and cover letters received by Robert Half, the late founder of Accountemps:

- "I have worked in a fairy wide range of industries."
- "Great eye for derail."
- "I have incredibly entertaining hair."
- "I am accustomed to being in the hot seat."
- "EDUCATION: Some."

highlights a candidate's potential and suits students who often have little experience directly related to their desired positions.

Most résumés include full names as well as mail and e-mail addresses. If the username of your e-mail address is "MachoDude" or "SnowboardDoll," replace it with one related to your real name or location to convince employers to take you seriously.

A statement of career objectives typically follows. Academic information is provided next, followed by experience and work history. Applicants with limited work histories and no internship experiences typically focus on relevant personal activities and interests. Any and all professional and extracurricular activities, as well as academic, work, and internship experiences, should be included on your résumé. Most résumés close with lists of references.

Whether yours is a traditional résumé on paper or posted on an Internet résumé listing, the important thing to remember in creating an effective résumé is to present the most relevant information in a clear, concise manner that emphasizes your best attributes.

FIGURE 1

Functional Résumé

Jorge Paz
Two Seaside Drive, Apt. 3A
Los Angeles, CA 90026
215-555-7092
JPAZ@hotmail.com

Objective
Joining a growth-oriented company that values highly productive employees. Seeking an opportunity that leads to senior merchandising position.

Professional Experience
Administration
Management responsibilities in a major retail buying office included coordinating vendor relation efforts. Supervised assistant buyers.

Category Management
Experience in buying home improvement and sport, recreation, and fitness categories.

Planning
Leader of a team charged with reviewing the company's annual vendor evaluation program.

Problem Solving
Successfully developed a program to improve margins in the tennis, golf, and fishing product categories.

Work Experience
Senior Buyer
Southern California Department Stores 2000–Present

Merchandiser
Pacific Discount Stores, a division of Southern California Department Stores 1998–2000

Education
Bachelor of Science degree in business
Double major in marketing and retailing
California State University–San Bernardino 1994–1998

Computer Skills
Proficient with IBM-compatible computers and related software, including spreadsheets, graphics, desktop publishing, and word processing.
Packages: Excel, Lotus 1-2-3, Harvard Graphics, PowerPoint, Microsoft Word 7.0

Familiar with Adobe PageMaker and the Macintosh.

Language Skills
Fluent in speaking and writing Spanish.

Cover Letter

An employer is typically first introduced to a job applicant through a cover letter. Like gift wrapping on a present, a cover letter should attract attention and interest about what is inside and should be addressed to a specific person. The cover letter must provide specifically targeted information, state the particular position you are applying for, where you learned about the position, and why you are interested in it. It should also describe attributes of your personality, such as dependability, responsibility, energy level, and technical skills, without sounding overly boastful or arrogant.

Next, your cover letter should specifically state when you will follow up with a phone call or letter. Your cover letter then should close with an expression of appreciation for being considered for the position. Make certain that your cover letter is neat and grammatically correct, since employers often use it to evaluate written communication skills. Finally, sign the letter in blue or black ink.

Mark your calendar and follow up your cover letter and résumé when you stated you would. If you indicated that you would call, then use this opportunity to ask any additional questions and set a possible date for an interview.

Briefly Speaking

A résumé is a balance sheet without any liabilities.

Robert Half (1918–2001) American personnel agency executive

Letters of Recommendation

Letters of recommendation serve as testimonials to your performance in academic and work settings. The best references provide information relevant to the desired industry or marketing specialty, as well as opinions of your skills, abilities, and character. References may be obtained from former or current employers, supervisors from volunteer experiences, professors, and others who can attest to your academic and professional competencies.

An effective letter of recommendation typically contains the following elements:

1. Statement of the length and nature of the relationship between the writer and the job candidate.
2. Description of the candidate's academic and career growth potential.
3. Review of important achievements.
4. Evaluation of personal characteristics (what kind of colleague the candidate will make).
5. Summary of the candidate's outstanding strengths and abilities.

Because letters of recommendation take time and effort, it helps to provide a résumé and any other information relevant to the recommendation, along with a stamped, addressed (typed) envelope. When requesting letters of recommendation, you should allow ample time for your references to compose them—as long as a month is not unusual.

In addition to including a cover letter, résumé, and letters of recommendation, candidates should include photocopies of transcripts, writing samples, or other examples of work completed. For example, if you are applying for a position in public relations, advertising, or sports marketing, you may want to include examples of professional writing, graphics, and audio/visual tapes and DVDs to support written evidence of your credentials. Research and service projects that resulted in published or unpublished articles may also enhance your portfolio.

Briefly Speaking

Put it to them briefly so they will read it; clearly, so they will appreciate it; picturesquely, so they will remember it—and, above all, accurately, so they will be guided by its light.

Joseph Pulitzer (1847–1911) American journalist

Dealing with Automated Systems

Employers are quickly moving to automated (paperless) résumé processing and applicant-tracking systems. As a result, if you prepare a technology-compatible résumé and cover letter, you'll enjoy an edge over applicants whose résumés and cover letters can't be added to the firm's database. Also, remember that résumés are often transmitted electronically. Figure 2 contains a number of tips for creating an effective, technology-compatible résumé.

Employers who review electronic résumés and those posted on some of the 3,000 Web sites currently carrying job postings frequently save time by using computers to search for keywords in job titles, job descriptions, or résumés to narrow the search. In fact, *manager* is the number one word for which companies search. Regardless of the position you seek, the key to an effective electronic résumé is to use exact words and phrases, emphasizing nouns rather than the action verbs you are likely to use in a printed résumé. For example, a company looking for a marketing account manager with experience in Lotus 1-2-3, Microsoft Word, and Microsoft Excel programs is likely to conduct computer searches for only those résumés that include the job title and the three software programs.

FIGURE 2

Tips for Preparing an Electronic Résumé

Tips for Preparing an Electronic Résumé

- Use a plain font. Use a standard serif typeface, such as Courier, Times, Arial, Univers, or Futura. Simplicity is key.
- Use 11- to 14-point type sizes.
- Keep your line length to no more than 65 characters (letters, spaces, and punctuation).
- Do not use graphics, bullets, lines, bold, italics, underlines, or shading.
- Use capital letters for your headings.
- Justify your text to the left.
- Use vertical and horizontal lines sparingly. Lines may blur your type.
- Omit parentheses and brackets, even around telephone numbers. These can blur and leave the number unreadable.
- Use white paper and black type.
- Use a laser-quality printer.
- Print on one side of the paper only.
- Don't compress space between letters. Use a second page rather than pack everything into one page and have it scan unclearly.
- Do not staple pages of a résumé together.
- Use industry buzzwords. Keyword searches often look for industry jargon.
- Place your name as the first text on the résumé. Do not put anything else on that line.
- Fax résumés on the *fine mode* setting. It is much easier to read than the *standard mode* setting.
- Do not fold your résumé. A crease makes scanning—and retrieving—difficult.
- If you are sending your résumé in the body of an e-mail transmission, do not distinguish between pages, as the full e-mail will download into the database as one sheet.
- Don't send a résumé as an e-mail attachment unless you are specifically instructed to do so. Many employers discard unsolicited attachments.

Source: Mary Dixon Werdler, "Translate Your Résumé for Electronic Eyes," http://www.jobweb.com, accessed February 1, 2002. © National Association of Colleges and Employers. Used by permission.

LEARNING MORE ABOUT JOB OPPORTUNITIES

You should carefully study the various employment opportunities you have identified. Obviously, you will like some more than others, but you should examine a number of factors when assessing each job possibility:

1. Actual job responsibilities
2. Industry characteristics
3. Nature of the company
4. Geographic location
5. Salary and opportunities for advancement
6. How the job is likely to contribute to your long-range career opportunities

Too many job applicants consider only the most striking features of a job, perhaps its location or the salary offer. However, a comprehensive review of job openings should provide a balanced perspective of the overall employment opportunity, including both long-run and short-run factors.

Job Interviews

The first objective of your job search is obtaining an interview with a prospective employer. This interview demands considerable planning and preparation on your part. You want to enter the interview equipped with a good understanding of the company, its industry, and its competitors. Prepare yourself by researching the following basic information about the firm:

- When was the company founded?
- What is its current position in the industry?
- What is its financial status?
- In which markets does it compete?

- How is the firm organized?
- Who are its competitors?
- How many does it employ?
- Where are its production facilities and office located?
- Does it have a written code of ethics? How is it administered?

This information is useful in several ways. First, knowing so much about the firm should give you a feeling of confidence during the interview. Second, it can help you avoid making an unwise employment decision. Third, it may help you to impress an interviewer, who may well try to determine how much you know about the company as a means of evaluating your interest level. A job applicant who fails to make an effort to obtain such information often risks elimination from further consideration.

But where do you find this company information? First, your college's or university's career center is likely to have detailed information on prospective employers. Your marketing and business professors may also provide tips. In addition, the university's reference librarian can direct you to sources to use in investigating a firm. Also, you can write directly to the company. Most medium- and large-sized companies maintain informative Web sites; others publish career brochures. Finally, ask friends and relatives for input. Either they or people they know may have had experience with the company.

Interviewers usually cite poor communication as the main reason for an unsuccessful job interview. The job seeker either is inadequately prepared for the interview or lacks confidence. Remember that the interviewer will certainly make a determination of whether you can communicate directly based on the question-and-answer sequence that comprises this meeting. You should be specific in answering and asking questions, and you should clearly and positively express your concerns. The questions that interviewers ask most often include the following:

- "Why do you want this job?"
- "Where do you see yourself ten years from now?"
- "What are your strengths?"
- "What are your weaknesses?"
- "Why should I hire you?"

It is important to know the name of the person (or persons) who will conduct the interview, what the interviewer's regular job responsibilities are, and who will make the final hiring decisions. In many cases the people who conduct initial job interviews work in the human resources division of their company. These interviewers typically make recommendations to line managers about which applicants appear most suitable for the vacancy. Line managers who head the units in which the applicant would be employed will get involved later in the hiring process. Some hiring decisions result from joint interviews conducted by both human resources personnel and the immediate supervisor of the prospective employee. Most often, however, immediate supervisors make the decision alone or in combination with input from senior employees in the department who will be colleagues of the new hire. Rarely does the human resources department have sole hiring authority.

In a typical format, the interviewer talks little during the interview. This approach, referred to as an *open-ended interview,* forces you to talk about yourself and your career goals. If you appear unorganized, the interviewer may eliminate you on that basis alone. When faced with this type of interview, be sure to express your thoughts clearly and keep the conversation on target. Talk for about 10 minutes, then ask some specific question of the interviewers. (Come prepared with questions to ask.) Listen carefully to the responses. Remember that if you prepare for a job interview, it will become a mutual exchange of information.

A successful first interview will probably result in an invitation to return for another interview. In some cases, this invitation will include a request to take a battery of tests. Most students do very well on these tests because they have had plenty of practice during the previous years in class!

It is not uncommon for applicants to receive an attractive job offer only after being rejected one or more times previously. Students at an Arizona university once pooled their rejection letters from would-be employers, reviewed them, and then voted on the company that had written the worst rejection letter. Here are excerpts from the five finalists:

- "After most careful consideration of your qualifications and background, we are unable to identify anything you can do for us . . ."
- "We're certain you could be more useful someplace else . . ."
- ". . . but we're sure you will find something you can do."
- "My conscience doesn't allow me to encourage you . . ."
- "Unfortunately, we have to be selective . . ."[4]

Employment Decisions

Employers still considering you to be a viable job candidate now know a lot about you. You should also know a lot about the company. The primary purpose of further interviews is to determine whether you can work effectively within the organization.

Briefly Speaking

The future belongs to those who believe in the beauty of their dreams.

Eleanor Roosevelt (1884–1962) First Lady of the United States (1933–1945)

TABLE 1

Text Chapters Describing Responsibilities of Different Marketing Positions

Marketing Position	*Contemporary Marketing* Chapter(s) Most Directly Related to the Marketing Position
Marketing, Advertising, Product, and Public Relations Managers	Chapters 1–2 (marketing) Chapters 11–12 (product) Chapters 17–18 (advertising and public relations)
Sales Representatives and Sales Managers	Chapter 19
Advertising Specialists	Chapters 17–18
Public Relations Specialists	Chapters 17–18
Purchasing Agents and Managers	Chapter 10
Retail and Wholesale Buyers and Merchandise Managers	Chapter 16
Marketing Research Analysts	Chapter 7
Logistics: Material Receiving, Scheduling, Dispatching, and Distributing Occupations	Chapter 15

If you continue to create a positive impression during subsequent interviews, you may be offered a position with the firm. Again, your decision to accept the offer should depend on how well the opportunity matches your career objectives. Make the best entry-level job decision you can, and learn from it. Learn your job responsibilities as quickly and thoroughly as possible; then start looking for ways to improve your performance and that of your employer.

Marketing Positions

The basic objective of any firm is to market its goods or services. Marketing responsibilities vary among organizations and industries. In a small firm, the owner or president may assume many of the company's marketing responsibilities. A large firm needs a staff of experienced marketing, advertising, and public relations managers to coordinate these activities. Some typical marketing positions are described in the following sections. Table 1 identifies the text chapters directly related to the responsibilities of each position. Note also that specific titles of different marketing positions may vary among firms. For example, the person holding the senior marketing position in a company may hold such titles as vice president of marketing, marketing director, or marketing manager. Job descriptions and typical career paths of eight major marketing positions are included in Table 2.

TABLE 2

Job Descriptions and Career Paths for Eight Major Marketing Positions

MARKETING, ADVERTISING, PRODUCT, AND PUBLIC RELATIONS MANAGERS

Marketing management spans a range of positions, including vice president of marketing, marketing manager, sales manager, product manager, advertising manager, promotion manager, and public relations manager. The vice president directs the firm's overall marketing policy, and all other marketers report through channels to this person. Sales managers direct the efforts of sales professionals by assigning territories, establishing goals, developing training programs, and supervising local sales managers and their personnel. Advertising managers oversee account services, creative services, and media services departments. Promotion managers direct promotional programs that combine advertising with purchase incentives designed to increase the sales of the firm's goods or services. Public relations managers are responsible for communicating with the firm's various publics, conducting publicity programs, and supervising the specialists who implement these programs.

TABLE 2

(Continued)

Job Description
As with senior management positions in production, finance, and other areas, top marketing management positions often involve long hours and extensive travel. Work under pressure is also common. For sales managers, job transfers between headquarters and regional offices may disrupt one's personal life. Approximately 460,000 marketing, advertising, product, and public relations managers are currently employed in the U.S. The Bureau of Labor Statistics estimates for the first decade of this century show strong growth of 168,000 new positions in these categories, the seventh-largest growth category.[5]

Career Path
A degree in business administration, preferably with a concentration in marketing, is usually required for these positions. In highly technical industries, such as computers, chemicals, and electronics, employers typically prefer bachelor's degrees in science or engineering combined with master's degrees in business administration. Liberal arts students can also find many opportunities, especially if they have business minors. Most managers are promoted from positions such as sales representatives, product or brand specialists, and advertising specialists within their organizations. Skills or traits that are most desirable for these jobs include high motivation levels, maturity, creativity, resistance to stress, flexibility, and the ability to communicate persuasively.

SALES REPRESENTATIVES AND SALES MANAGERS

Millions of items are bought and sold every day. The people in the firm who carry out this activity may have a variety of titles—sales representative, account manager, manufacturer's representative, sales engineer, sales agent, retail salesperson, wholesale sales representative, and service sales representative. Sales managers are typically selected from people in the current sales force who have demonstrated that they possess the managerial skills needed to lead teams of sales representatives. In addition, many organizations require that all marketing professionals spend some time in the field to experience the market firsthand and to understand the challenges faced by front-line personnel.

Job Description
Salespeople are usually responsible for developing prospective client lists, meeting with current and prospective customers to discuss the firm's products, and then following up to answer questions and supply additional information. By knowing the business needs of each customer, the sales representative can identify products that best satisfy these needs. Following a customer purchase, they are likely to revisit their customers to ensure that the products are meeting the customers' needs and to explore further business opportunities or referrals provided by satisfied buyers. Some sales of technical products involve lengthy interactions. In these cases, a salesperson may work with several clients simultaneously over a large geographical area. Those responsible for large territories may spend most of their workdays on the phone, receiving and sending e-mail messages, or on the sales floor. Recent compensation data revealed that top-level professional salespeople received total annual pay of $140,000 on average, a nine-percent increase over the previous year—even in the midst of a recession.[6]

Work as a sales representative or sales manager can be rewarding for those who enjoy interacting with people, those invigorated by competition, and those who feel energized by the challenge of expanding sales in their territories. Successful sales professionals—both individual sales reps and sales managers—should be goal-oriented, persuasive, self-motivated, and independent. In addition, patience and perseverance are important qualities.

Many newly graduated marketing majors begin their careers in advertising agencies. These members of the Joker Ad Agency were responsible for a notable anti-AIDS campaign.

Briefly Speaking

The best way to get what you want is to help other people get what they want.

Zig Ziglar (b. 1927) American motivational speaker

TABLE 2

(Continued)

> **Briefly Speaking**
>
> Anyone who keeps learning stays young.
>
> *Henry Ford (1863–1947) American automobile manufacturer*

CAREER PATH

The background needed for a sales position varies according to the product line and market. Most professional sales jobs require a college degree, and many companies run their own formal training programs that can last up to two years for sales representatives in technical industries. This training may take place in a classroom, in the field with a mentor, or most often using a combination of both methods. Sales managers are usually promoted from the field; they are likely to include successful sales representatives who exhibit managerial skills and promise. Sales management positions begin at a local or district level, then advance to positions of increased authority and responsibility such as area, regional, national, and international sales manager.

ADVERTISING SPECIALISTS

Most companies, especially firms serving consumer markets, maintain small groups of advertising specialists who serve as liaisons between the marketer and its outside advertising agencies. The leader of this liaison function is sometimes called a *marketing communications manager.* Positions in an advertising agency include specialists in account services, creative services, and media services. Account services functions are performed by account executives, who work directly with clients. An agency's creative services department develops the themes and presentations of the advertisements. This department is supervised by a creative director, who oversees the copy chief, art director, and their staff members. The media services department is managed by a media director, who oversees the planning group that selects media outlets for ads.

JOB DESCRIPTION

Advertising can be one of the most glamorous and creative fields in marketing. Because the field combines the best of both worlds—that is, the tangible and scientific aspects of marketing along with creative artistry—advertising attracts people with a broad array of abilities.

Thousands of retailers such as May Department Stores—parent of such widely known and highly regarded retailers as Lord & Taylor, Robinsons-May, Filene's, Foley's, Kaufmann's, Famous-Barr, and Hecht's—employ hundreds of thousands of college graduates who have decided on a career in retailing.

CAREER PATH

Most new hires begin as assistants or associates for the position they hope to acquire, such as copywriter, art director, and media buyer. Often, a newly hired employee must receive two to four promotions before becoming manager of these functions. College degrees in liberal arts, graphic arts, communications, psychology, or sociology, in addition to marketing training, are preferred for entry-level positions in advertising.

PUBLIC RELATIONS SPECIALISTS

Specialists in public relations strive to build and maintain positive relationships with various publics. They may assist management in drafting speeches, arranging interviews, overseeing company archives, responding to information requests, and handling special events, such as sponsorships and trade shows, that generate promotional benefits for the firm.

JOB DESCRIPTION

While public relations specialists normally work a standard 40-hour week, they will occasionally rearrange their normal schedules to meet deadlines or prepare for major events. Occasionally, they are required to be on the job or on call around the clock to respond to an emergency or crisis. About 110,000 public relations specialists are currently employed in the U.S., two-thirds of them in service industries. Public relations positions tend to be concentrated in large cities near major press services and communications facilities. However, this centralization is changing with the increased popularity of new communications technologies, such as satellite uplinks, wireless technologies, and the Internet, which allow more freedom of movement. Most public relations consulting firms are concentrated in New York, Los Angeles, Chicago, and Washington, D.C.

Essential characteristics for a public relations specialist include creativity, initiative, good judgment, and the ability to express thoughts clearly and simply—both verbally and in writing. An outgoing personality, self-confidence, and enthusiasm are also recommended traits.

(Continued)

Career Path

A college degree combined with public relations experience, usually gained through one or more internships, is considered excellent preparation for public relations. Many entry-level public relations specialists hold degrees with majors in advertising, marketing, public relations, or communications. New employees in larger organizations are likely to participate in formal training programs; those who begin their careers at smaller firms typically work under the guidance of experienced staff members. Entry-level positions carry such titles as research assistant or account assistant. A potential career path includes a promotion to account executive, account supervisor, vice president, and eventually senior vice president.

PURCHASING AGENTS AND MANAGERS

In the 21st century business world the two key marketing functions of buying and selling are performed by trained specialists. Just as every organization is involved in selling its output to meet the needs of customers, so too must all companies make purchases of goods and services required to operate their businesses and turn out items for sale.

Modern technology has transformed the role of the purchasing agent. The transfer of routine tasks to computers now allows contract specialists, or procurement officers, to focus on products, suppliers, and contract negotiations. The primary function of this position is to purchase the goods, materials, component parts, supplies, and services required by the organization. These agents ensure that suppliers deliver quality and quantity levels that match the firm's needs; they also secure these inputs at reasonable prices and make them available when needed.

Purchasing agents must develop good working relationships both with colleagues in their own organizations and with suppliers. As the popularity of outsourcing has increased, the selection and management of suppliers have become critical functions of the purchasing department. In the government sector, this role is dominated by strict laws, statutes, and regulations that change frequently.

Job Description

Purchasing agents can expect a standard work week with some travel to suppliers' sites, seminars, and trade shows. Over 600,000 people are employed in purchasing positions in the U.S., most of them in manufacturing and government.

Career Path

Organizations prefer college-educated candidates for entry-level jobs in purchasing. Strong analytical and communication skills are required for any purchasing position. New hires often begin their careers by enrolling in extensive company training programs in which they learn procedures and operations. Training may include assignments dealing with production planning. Professional certification is becoming an essential criterion for advancement in both the private and the public sectors. A variety of associations serving the different categories of purchasing confer certifications on agents, including Certified Purchasing Manager, Professional Public Buyer, Certified Public Purchasing Officer, Certified Associate Contract Manager, and Certified Professional Contract Manager.

RETAIL AND WHOLESALE BUYERS AND MERCHANDISE MANAGERS

Buyers working for retailers and wholesale businesses purchase goods for resale. Their goal is to find the best possible merchandise at the lowest prices. They also influence the distribution and marketing of this merchandise. Successful buyers must understand what appeals to consumers and what their establishments can sell. Product bar codes and point-of-purchase terminals allow organizations to accurately track goods that are selling and those that are not; buyers frequently analyze this data to improve their understanding of consumer demand. Buyers also check competitors' prices and sales activities and watch general economic conditions to anticipate consumer buying patterns.

Job Description

Approximately 260,000 people are currently employed in the U.S. as retail and wholesale buyers and merchandise managers. These jobs often require substantial travel, as many orders are placed on buying trips to shows and exhibitions. Effective planning and decision- making skills are strong assets in this career. In addition, the job involves anticipating consumer preferences and ensuring that the firm keeps needed goods in stock. Consequently, the people filling these positions must possess such qualities as resourcefulness, good judgment, and self-confidence.

Career Path

Most retail and wholesale buyers begin their careers as assistant buyers or trainees. Larger retailers seek college-educated candidates, and extensive training includes job experience in a variety of positions. Advancement often comes when buyers move to departments or new locations with larger volumes—or become merchandise managers to coordinate or oversee the work of several buyers.

TABLE 2

(Continued)

MARKETING RESEARCH ANALYSTS

These marketing specialists provide information that assists marketers in identifying and defining opportunities. They generate, refine, and evaluate marketing actions and monitor marketing performance. Marketing research analysts devise methods and procedures for obtaining needed, decision-oriented data. Once they compile data, analysts evaluate it and then make recommendations to management.

Job Description

Firms that specialize in marketing research and management consulting employ the majority of the nation's marketing research analysts. These positions are often concentrated in larger cities, such as New York, Los Angeles, and Chicago. Those who pursue careers in marketing research must be capable of working accurately with detail, display patience and persistence, work effectively both independently and with others, and operate objectively and systematically. Significant computer and analytical skills are essential for success in this field.

Career Path

A bachelor's degree with an emphasis in marketing provides sufficient qualifications for many entry-level jobs in marketing research. Because of the importance of quantitative skills and the need for competence in using analytical software packages, this education should include courses in calculus, linear algebra, statistics, sampling theory and survey design, computer science, and information systems. Students should try to gain experience in conducting interviews or surveys while still in college. A master's degree in business administration or a related discipline is advised for improving advancement opportunities.

LOGISTICS: MATERIAL RECEIVING, SCHEDULING, DISPATCHING AND DISTRIBUTING OCCUPATIONS

Logistics offers a myriad of career positions. Job titles under this broad heading include material receiving, scheduling, dispatching, materials management executive, distribution operations coordinator, distribution center manager, and transportation manager. The logistics function includes responsibilities for production and inventory planning and control, distribution, and transportation.

Job Description

Approximately 3.8 million people are currently employed in logistics positions in the U.S., including material receiving, scheduling, dispatching, and distribution. These positions demand good communication skills and the ability to work effectively under pressure.

Career Path

Computer skills are highly valued in these jobs. Employers look for candidates with degrees in logistics and transportation. However, graduates in marketing and other business disciplines may succeed in this field.

ADDITIONAL INFORMATION SOURCES

A wealth of helpful career information is continually updated for you at the Boone & Kurtz Web site: http://boone.swlearning.com. You'll find a complete *Marketing Careers* section located under the heading *Marketing Topics* on the left-hand navigation bar. Here you'll learn more about marketing careers and be able to locate currently posted job opportunities. The site provides a vast number of career resources such as links to job sites, career guidance sites, U.S. newspaper job ads, and company information. It also provides ways for researching cities of special interest to you.

In addition, the *Personal Development* section of the Web site contains career guidance tips, including interviewing techniques and résumé writing advice. The site is updated regularly.

PART 1

Designing Customer-Oriented Marketing Strategies

CHAPTER 1

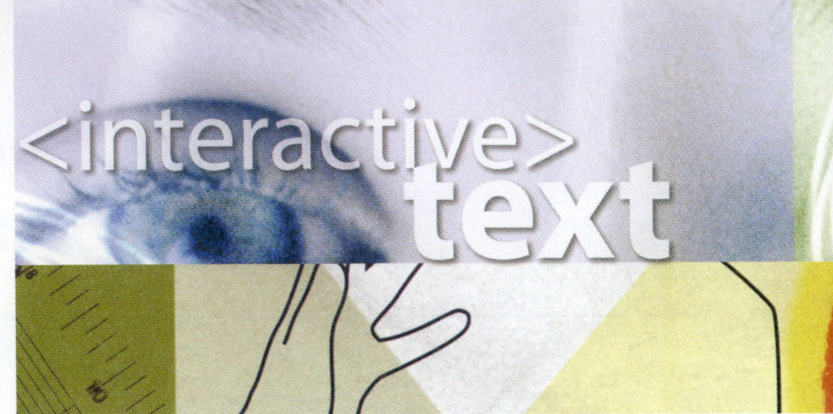

Customer-Driven Marketing

Chapter Objectives

1. Explain how marketing creates utility through the exchange process.
2. Contrast marketing activities during the four eras in the history of marketing.
3. Define the marketing concept and its relationship to marketing myopia.
4. Describe the characteristics of not-for-profit marketing.
5. Describe the five types of nontraditional marketing.
6. Outline the changes in the marketing environment due to technology.
7. Explain the shift from transaction-based marketing to relationship marketing.
8. Identify the universal functions of marketing.
9. Demonstrate the relationship between ethical business practices and marketplace success.

CUSTOMER LOYALTY IS THE ULTIMATE GOAL

The essence of marketing isn't about goods and services. It isn't about selling. It isn't even about profits or beating the competition. It's about developing a relationship with customers so that they will grow loyal to a company's goods and services. It's about developing trust between customers and the firms from which they purchase goods and services. This idea is not a recently developed marketing concept; it has been around for a long time. When Henry J. Heinz began traveling around the country to county fairs and expositions in 1875 to stage demonstrations of his mustard, pickles, and vinegar, he also showed slides of his Pittsburgh factory. By 1890, he was giving daily tours of the factory. Why? He believed that consumers would be more apt to trust the quality of packaged foods—a new idea—if they could see firsthand that the factory was clean and well managed. "We keep our shingle out and then let the public blow our horn, and that counts," said Heinz. Today, Heinz products rake in about $9 billion in sales each year because consumers have grown loyal to them.

Today's marketing environment is fraught with even more challenges as marketers strive to attract and keep customers. The average U.S. business loses half its customers in five years. Generating a new customer costs five times as much as keeping a current one, so firms pay a steep price when customers stray to other brands. And in a slower economy, customers are looking for greater value when they spend their hard-earned dollars. Loyalty is the result of customer service, treating the customer as an individual, and creating the best value for the customer. Jeff Multz, director of sales and marketing at Firstwave Technologies Inc., a Web-based customer relationship management firm in Atlanta, says, "It's so basic, its scary. We find out what our customers' needs and wants are, and then we overdeliver." Firstwave, whose customers are other businesses, routinely does small—but noticeable—favors for its customers, whether it is fulfilling orders early or upgrading software even before it is requested. Firstwave's customers remember these little niceties and come back for more. Multz also notes that in a slower economy, value is crucial to cultivating loyalty. "To keep our customers, we need to make them feel like they're getting a dollar fifty back for every dollar they spend."

Sometimes, national or world events can change the factors involving customer loyalty. Since the tragedy of September 11, 2001, airlines have struggled to keep travelers flying. According to a survey conducted by New York–based Brand Keys, the single most important factor driving loyalty is now safety; after that, it's in-flight comfort, airline experience, and booking and boarding efficiency. "Airlines won't attract loyal customers with trifles like scented soap in bathrooms barely roomy enough for a Schnauzer and nobody will fly in their super-comfy armchairs with built-in 250-channel entertainment if they fear the plane may slam into a mountain," says Robert Passikoff, president of Brand Keys. Delta ranked best among the airlines, but none of them—including Delta—ranked high in comfort.

Finally, there's the challenge of developing loyalty among consumers who shop online. "E-tailing is 24 hours, so customer service should be 24 hours," says Stratis Morfogen, CEO of FultonStreet.com, an online retail fish market based in Westbury, New York. "Otherwise, it's like having a 7-Eleven store with no one at the counter from midnight to 7 A.M." Customers can log on anytime, anywhere, and order their lobsters to go. "Customer support is very important to closing the deal," explains Morfogen. "If it were just an answering machine, we would have no orders at night." And that's no fish story.[1]

Pre-Test

Take the Pre-Test to assess your initial knowledge of the key ideas in this chapter. The Pre-Test provides exam-style questions addressing the main topics and concepts of the chapter. At the completion of each Pre-Test, you will receive a score and instructive feedback on how you answered each question, and a direct link to the part of the chapter addressed in the question. Take the Pre-Test as often as you need to—a record of your progress for each attempt is kept for you to revisit and gauge your improvement.

CHAPTER OVERVIEW

- "They're the best."
- "I always eat there."
- "I only fly with that airline."
- "I buy my electronics at that store."

These words are music to a marketer's ears. Customer loyalty is the watchword of 21st century marketing. Customer loyalty has always been important to businesses; Henry Heinz knew that. But today, individual consumers and business purchasers have so many goods and services from which to choose—and so many different ways to purchase them—that marketers must continually seek out new—and better—ways to attract and keep customers. Advances in communications

Briefly Speaking

Increasingly, the center of the marketing universe is the customer. It's the customer who sets the rules and the marketer who responds.

Robert Wientzen
CEO, Direct Marketing Association

technology allow information to be exchanged between buyers and sellers faster, cheaper, and through more media channels than ever before, including broadcast media, print, telecommunications, online computer services, and the Internet. Companies can now offer consumers more product choices and more places to buy. Today's savvy shoppers can visit a brick-and-mortar shopping mall, hire a personal shopper, order from catalogs, watch television home shopping channels, and browse virtual stores accessed through online services.

The technology revolution is changing the rules of marketing during this first decade of the 21st century. The combined power of telecommunications and computer technology creates inexpensive, global networks that transfer voice messages, text, graphics, and data within seconds. These sophisticated technologies create new types of products, and they also demand new approaches to marketing existing products. Communications technology contributes as well to the globalization of today's marketplace, where businesses manufacture, buy, and sell across national borders. You can eat a Big Mac or drink Coca-Cola almost anywhere in the world; your DVD or CD player was probably manufactured in China or Korea. Both Mercedes-Benz and Hyundai sport utility vehicles are assembled in Alabama, while many Volkswagens are imported from Mexico. Products and components routinely cross international borders, but successful global marketing also requires knowledge to tailor products to regional tastes. An Asian food store in Austin, Texas, may also sell popular Hispanic foods such as tortillas to satisfy local tastes of shoppers who like both.

Rapidly changing business landscapes create new challenges for companies, whether they are giant multinational firms or small boutiques, profit-oriented or not-for-profit. Organizations must react quickly to shifts in consumer tastes, competitive offerings, and other market dynamics. Fortunately, information technologies give organizations fast, new ways to interact and develop long-term relationships with their customers and suppliers. In fact, such links have become a core element of marketing today.

Every company must serve customer needs—create customer satisfaction—to succeed. Two customer satisfaction researchers described its value this way: "Customer satisfaction has come to represent an important cornerstone for customer-oriented business practices across a multitude of companies operating in diverse industries."[2] Marketing strategies provide the tools by which businesspeople identify and analyze customers' needs and then inform these customers about how the company can meet those needs. Tomorrow's market leaders will be companies who can effectively harness the vast amounts of customer feedback and respond with solutions to their needs.

This new edition of *Contemporary Marketing* focuses on the strategies that allow companies to succeed in today's interactive marketplace. This chapter sets the stage for the entire text, examining the meaning of customer-driven marketing and its importance for all organizations. Initial sections describe the development of marketing, from early times to today's focus on relationship marketing and its contributions to society. Later sections introduce the technology revolution, the universal functions of marketing, and the relationship between ethical business practices and marketplace success.

WHAT IS MARKETING?

Production and marketing of goods and services are the essence of economic life in any society. All organizations perform these two basic functions to satisfy their commitments to society, their customers, and their owners. They create a benefit that economists call **utility**—the want-satisfying power of a good or service. Table 1.1 describes the four basic kinds of utility—form, time, place, and ownership.

<interactive>**learning goal**

CHAPTER OBJECTIVE #1: EXPLAIN HOW MARKETING CREATES UTILITY THROUGH THE EXCHANGE PROCESS.

Form utility is created when the firm converts raw materials and component inputs into finished goods and services. By combining glass, plastic, metals, circuit boards, and other components, Toshiba creates a television set and Sony makes a camcorder. With fabric, thread, wood, springs, and down feathers, Ethan Allen produces a sofa. MTV's hit television comedy show *The Osbournes*—starring heavy metal superstar Ozzy Osbourne, his wife, and their teenagers pink-haired Kelly and spiky-haired Jack—starts with writers, artists, actors, scripts, a director, producers, technical crew, and a sound stage.[3] Although the marketing function determines consumer and audience preferences, the organization's production function is responsible for the actual creation of form utility.

Marketing creates time, place, and ownership utilities. Time and place utility occur when consumers find goods and services available when and where they want to purchase them. Overnight courier services like FedEx and Airborne Express emphasize time utility; vending machines focus on providing place utility for people buying newspapers, snacks, and soft drinks. The transfer of title to goods or services at the time of purchase creates ownership utility.

The Osbourne family portrait shown in Figure 1.1 illustrates the result of a combination of efforts by both production and marketing to achieve this marketplace success. While production is responsible for

TABLE 1.1

Four Types of Utility

Type	Description	Examples	Organizational Function Responsible
Form	Conversion of raw materials and components into finished goods and services	Citibank checking account; Nissan Pathfinder; Ramen Noodles (nutrition for students who are hungry, broke, and can't—or won't—cook)	Production*
Time	Availability of goods and services when consumers want them	One-hour photographs; LensCrafters eyeglass guarantee; U.S. Priority Mail	Marketing
Place	Availability of goods and services at convenient locations	Soft-drink machines outside gas stations; on-site day care; ATM machines in shopping malls	Marketing
Ownership (possession)	Ability to transfer title to goods or services from marketer to buyer	Retail sales (in exchange for currency or credit-card payment)	Marketing

*Marketing provides inputs related to consumer preferences, but the actual creation of form utility is the responsibility of the production function.

creating form utility, marketing's ability to create time, place, and ownership utility also contributes to the success of this rock 'n' roll sitcom. The choice of cable channel MTV as the delivery vehicle is particularly appropriate in reaching the *The Osbournes'* core audience of teenagers and young adults.

FIGURE 1.1

Production and Marketing at the Osbourne Household: Generating a Surprise Cable TV Success by Creating Form, Time, Place, and Ownership Utility

All organizations must create utility to survive. Designing and marketing want-satisfying goods, services, and ideas are the foundation for the creation of utility. Organizations recently have begun to elevate the function of marketing in their hierarchies; top marketing executives may be promoted to senior vice presidential positions. But where does the process start? In the toy industry, manufacturers try to come up with items that children will want to play with—creating utility. But that's not as simple as it sounds. At the Toy Fair held each February in New York, retailers pore through the different booths of manufacturers and suppliers, looking for the next Barbie or scooter—trends that turn into classics, generating millions of dollars of revenues over the years. They also try to identify which toys will be the hottest items for the coming year; often figures or games tied to the latest film release in the *Star Wars, Hobbit,* and *Harry Potter* series. If their decisions are on target, everyone wins—retailers, manufacturers, and children. But if parents and kids don't buy what the retailers stock in their stores, everyone loses.[4] If a toy creates utility, manufacturers and retailers have created customers.

In general, how does an organization create a customer? Professors Joseph Guiltinan and Gordon Paul explain it this way:

> Essentially, "creating" a customer means identifying needs in the marketplace, finding out which needs the organization can profitably serve, and developing an offering to convert potential buyers into customers. Marketing managers are responsible for most of the activities necessary to create the customers the organization wants. These activities include:
>
> - Identifying customer needs
> - Designing goods and services that meet those needs
> - Communicating information about those goods and services to prospective buyers
> - Making the goods or services available at times and places that meet customers' needs
> - Pricing goods and services to reflect costs, competition, and customers' ability to buy
> - Providing for the necessary service and follow-up to ensure customer satisfaction after the purchase[5]

Briefly Speaking

We're always looking to see what we can do to make our customers' lives easier or save them money. It pervades every part of the company.

Michael Dell (b. 1965) founder and CEO, Dell Computer

A Definition of Marketing

The word *marketing* encompasses such a broad scope of activities and ideas that settling on one definition is often difficult. Ask five people to define it, and five different definitions are likely to follow. Continuous exposure to advertising and personal selling leads most respondents to link marketing and selling or to think that marketing activities start once goods and services have been produced. But marketing also involves analyzing customer needs, securing information needed to design and produce goods or services that match buyer expectations, and creating and maintaining relationships with customers and suppliers. It applies not only to profit-oriented firms but also to thousands of not-for-profit organizations that offer goods and services.

Today's definition takes all these factors into account. **Marketing** is the process of planning and executing the conception, pricing, promotion, and distribution of ideas, goods, services, organizations, and events to create and maintain relationships that will satisfy individual and organizational objectives.

The expanded concept of marketing activities permeates all organizational functions. It assumes that the marketing effort will proceed in accordance with ethical practices and that it will effectively serve the interests of both society and the organization. The concept also identifies the marketing variables—product, price, promotion, and distribution—that combine to provide customer satisfaction. In addition, it assumes that the organization begins by identifying and analyzing the consumer segments that it will later satisfy through its production and marketing activities. In other words, the customer, client, or public determines the marketing program. The concept's emphasis on creating and maintaining relationships is consistent with the focus in business on long-term, mutually satisfying sales, purchases, and other interactions with customers and suppliers. Finally, it recognizes that marketing concepts and techniques apply to not-for-profit organizations as well as to profit-oriented businesses.

Today's Global Marketplace

Several factors have forced countries to extend their economic views to events outside their own national borders. First, international agreements are being negotiated in attempts to increase trade among nations. Second, the growth of electronic commerce and related computer technologies brings previously isolated countries into the marketplace for buyers and sellers around the globe. Third, the interdependence of the world's economies is a reality since no nation produces all of the raw materials and finished goods purchased by its citizens or consumes all of its output without some exporting to other countries. Evidence of this interdependence is illustrated by the introduction of the euro as a common currency to facilitate trade among the nations of the European Union and the creation of trade alliances such as NAFTA.

A recession in Europe affects business strategies in North America and the Pacific Rim. To remain competitive, companies must continually search for the most efficient manufacturing sites and most lucrative markets for their products. Marketers now find tremendous opportunities serving customers not only in traditional industrialized nations but also in Latin America and emerging economies in eastern Europe and Asia, where rising standards of living create increased customer demand for the latest goods and services.

Expanding operations beyond the U.S. market gives domestic companies access to 6 billion international customers. This explains why over 80 percent of Coca-Cola sales are generated outside the United States. Japan alone accounts for nearly 20 percent of Coke's profit.[6] For Colgate-Palmolive, a whopping 70 percent of its revenue comes from abroad, and three-fourths of Exxon's revenues are from non–U.S. customers.

Service firms also play a major role in today's global marketplace. The New York Stock Exchange, illustrated in Figure 1.2, advertises itself as the "gateway to the global economy." Although the organization is based in New York City, investors trade over $50 billion worldwide every day over the exchange.[7] Manpower Temporary Services, a worldwide firm that provides temporary and permanent workers in a broad range of jobs, earns almost 70 percent of its profits from foreign contracts. Technology products are also popular U.S. exports. Compaq's Digital Equipment subsidiary sells two-thirds of its computer products outside the United States, while Apple Computer generates half its revenues from non–U.S. sales.

The U.S. is also an attractive market for foreign competitors because of its size and the high standard of living that American consumers enjoy. Companies like Nissan, Sony, and Sun Life of Canada operate production, distribution, service, and retail facilities in the U.S. Foreign ownership of U.S. companies has increased as well. Pillsbury and MCA are two well-known firms with foreign parents. Even American-dominated industries like computer software must contend with foreign competition. While U.S. firms still hold about 75 percent of the market, European companies are quickly gaining market share. They currently supply about 18 percent of the $100 billion worldwide market for packaged software.

In many cases, global marketing strategies are almost identical to those used in domestic markets. Rather than creating a different promotional campaign for each country where they sell Pringles potato chips, Procter & Gamble marketers used the same ad—with spectacular results. Nearly everything in the U.S.-made ads was the same—the rap music themes, the young people dancing, and the tag line, "Once you pop, you can't stop." As a result, P&G had to boost production to handle the global demand.[8]

In other instances, domestic marketing strategies may need significant changes to adapt to unique tastes or different cultural and legal requirements abroad. It is often difficult to standardize a brand name on a global basis. The Japanese, for example, like names of flowers or girls for their car models, such as Bluebird, Bluebonnet, Violet, and Gloria. Americans, on the other hand, prefer rugged outdoorsy names like Mountaineer, Explorer, Sierra, and Yukon.[9]

FIGURE 1.2

The New York Stock Exchange: "Gateway to the Global Economy"

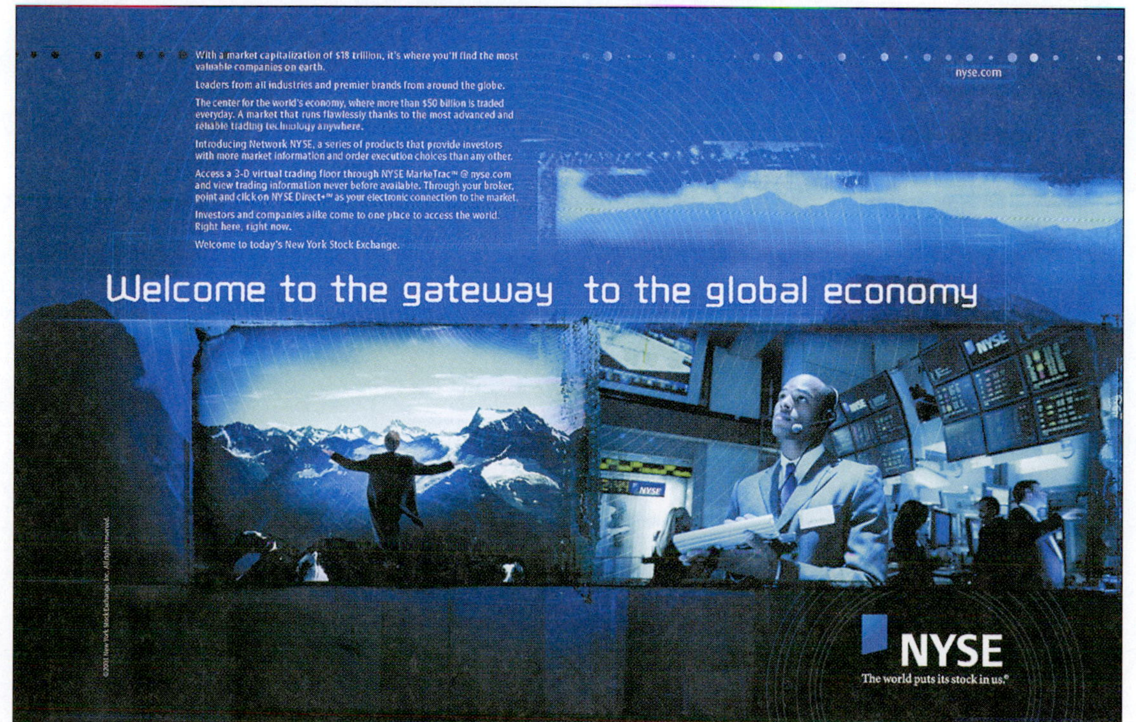

FOUR ERAS IN THE HISTORY OF MARKETING

The essence of marketing is the **exchange process,** in which two or more parties give something of value to each other to satisfy felt needs. In many exchanges, people trade money for tangible goods, such as CDs, clothes, or cars. In others, they trade for intangible services like child care, haircuts, or concerts. In still others, people may donate funds or time for a cause, such as a Red Cross blood drive, a new gymnasium for a church or school, or a campaign to clean up the environment.

<interactive>**learning goal**

CHAPTER OBJECTIVE #2: CONTRAST MARKETING ACTIVITIES DURING THE FOUR ERAS IN THE HISTORY OF MARKETING.

Although marketing has always been a part of business, its importance has varied greatly. Figure 1.3 identifies four eras in the history of marketing: (1) the production era, (2) the sales era, (3) the marketing era, and (4) the relationship era.

The Production Era

Prior to 1925, most firms—even those operating in highly developed economies in western Europe and North America—focused narrowly on production. Manufacturers stressed production of quality products and then looked for people to purchase them. The history of Pillsbury provides an excellent example of a production-oriented company. The late Robert J. Keith, who was once the company's chief executive officer, described Pillsbury during its early years:

> We are professional flour millers. Blessed with a supply of the finest North American wheat, plenty of water power, and excellent milling machinery, we produce flour of the highest quality. Our basic function is to mill high-quality flour, and, of course, we must hire [salespeople] to sell it, just as we hire accountants to keep our books.[10]

FIGURE 1.3

Four Eras of Marketing History

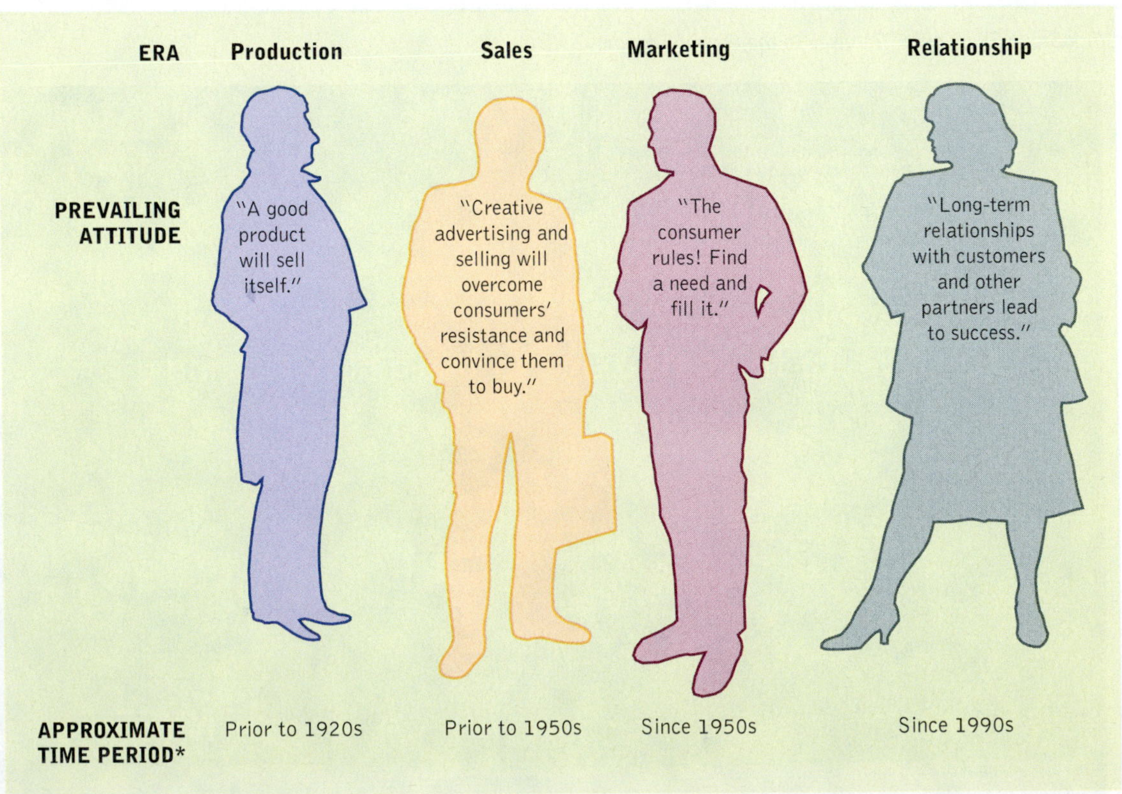

ERA
Production
Sales
Marketing
Relationship
PREVAILING ATTITUDE
"A good product will sell itself."
"Creative advertising and selling will overcome consumers' resistance and convince them to buy."
"The consumer rules! Find a need and fill it."
"Long-term relationships with customers and other partners lead to success."
APPROXIMATE TIME PERIOD*
Prior to 1920s
Prior to 1950s
Since 1950s
Since 1990s

*In the United States and other highly industrialized economies

The prevailing attitude of this era held that a good product (one with high physical quality) would sell itself. This **production orientation** dominated business philosophy for decades; indeed, business success was often defined solely in terms of production victories.

The production era did not reach its peak until the early part of the 20th century. Henry Ford's mass-production line exemplifies this orientation. Ford's slogan, "They [customers] can have any color they want, as long as it's black," reflected the prevalent attitude toward marketing. Production shortages and intense consumer demand ruled the day. It is easy to understand how production activities took precedence.

The essence of the production era resounds in a statement made over 100 years ago by the philosopher Ralph Waldo Emerson: "If a man writes a better book, preaches a better sermon, or makes a better mousetrap than his neighbor, though he builds his house in the woods, the world will make a beaten path to his door." However, a better mousetrap is no guarantee of success, and marketing history is full of miserable failures despite better mousetrap designs. In fact, over 80 percent of new products fail. Inventing the greatest new product is not enough. That product must also solve a perceived marketplace need. Otherwise, even the best-engineered, highest-quality product will fail. Even the horseless carriage took a while to catch on. People were afraid of motor vehicles, which spit out exhaust, stirred up dust on dirt roads, got stuck in mud, and tied up horse traffic. Besides, at the wild speed of seven miles per hour, they caused all kinds of accidents and disruption. It took savvy marketing by some early salespeople—and eventually a widespread perceived need—to change people's minds about the product.[11]

The Sales Era

Production techniques in the United States and Europe became more sophisticated, and output grew from the 1920s into the early 1950s. Thus, manufacturers began to increase their emphasis on effective sales forces to find customers for their output. In this era, firms attempted to match their output to the potential number of customers who would want it. Companies with a **sales orientation** assume that customers will resist purchasing goods and services not deemed essential and that the task of personal selling and advertising is to convince them to buy.

Although marketing departments began to emerge from the shadows of production, finance, and engineering during the sales era, they tended to remain in subordinate positions. Many chief marketing executives held the title of sales manager. Here is how Pillsbury described itself during the sales era:

> We are a flour-milling company, manufacturing a number of products for the consumer market. We must have a first-rate sales organization which can dispose of all the products we can make at a favorable price. We must back up this sales force with consumer advertising and marketing intelligence. We want our sales representatives and our dealers to have all the tools they need for moving the output of our plants to the consumer.[12]

But selling is only one component of marketing. As Harvard University marketing professor Theodore Levitt has pointed out, "Marketing is as different from selling as chemistry is from alchemy, astronomy from astrology, chess from checkers."[13]

The Marketing Era

Personal incomes and consumer demand for goods and services dropped rapidly during the Great Depression of the early 1930s, thrusting marketing into a more important role. Organizational survival dictated that managers pay close attention to the markets for their goods and services. This trend ended with the outbreak of World War II, when rationing and shortages of consumer goods became commonplace. The war years, however, created only a pause in an emerging trend in business: a shift in the focus from products and sales to satisfying customer needs.

Emergence of the Marketing Concept

The marketing concept, a crucial change in management philosophy, can be explained best by the shift from a **seller's market**—one in which there were more buyers for fewer goods and services—to a **buyer's market**—one in which there were more goods and services than people willing to buy them. When World War II ended, factories stopped manufacturing tanks and ships and started turning out consumer products again, a type of activity that had, for all practical purposes, stopped in early 1942.

CHAPTER OBJECTIVE #3: DEFINE THE MARKETING CONCEPT AND ITS RELATIONSHIP TO MARKETING MYOPIA.

The advent of a strong buyer's market created the need for **consumer orientation** in businesses. Companies had to market goods and services, not just produce and sell them. This realization has been identified as the emergence of the marketing concept. The recognition of this concept and its dominant role in business dates from 1952, when General Electric heralded a new management philosophy:

> [The concept] introduces the [marketer] at the beginning rather than at the end of the production cycle and integrates marketing into each phase of the business. Thus, marketing, through its studies and research, will establish for the engineer, the designer, and manufacturing [person], what the customer wants in a given product, what price he [or she] is willing to pay, and where and when it will be wanted. Marketing will have authority in product planning, production scheduling, and inventory control, as well as in sales, distribution, and servicing of the product.[14]

Marketing would no longer be regarded as a supplemental activity performed after completion of the production process. Instead, the marketer would play a leading role in product planning. Marketing and selling would no longer be synonymous terms.

The fully developed **marketing concept** is a *company-wide consumer orientation* with the objective of achieving long-run success. All facets of the organization must contribute first to assessing and then to satisfying customer wants and needs. Marketers are not the only people working on this. Accountants in the credit office and engineers designing products also play important roles. Focusing on the objective of achieving long-run success differentiates the concept from policies of short-run profit maximization. Since the firm's continuity is an assumed component of the marketing concept, company-wide consumer orientation will lead to greater long-run profits than managerial philosophies geared toward reaching short-run goals.

A strong market orientation—the extent to which a company adopts the marketing concept—generally improves market success and overall performance. It also has a positive effect on new-product development and the introduction of innovative products. Companies that implement market-driven strategies are better able to understand their customers' experiences, buying habits, and needs. These companies can, therefore, design products with advantages and levels of quality compatible with customer requirements. Customers more quickly accept the new products. This is the beginning of customer-driven marketing.

The Relationship Era

The fourth era in the history of marketing emerged during the last decade of the 20th century, and continues today into the 21st century. Organizations now carry the marketing era's customer orientation one step further by focusing on establishing and maintaining relationships with both customers and suppliers. This effort represents a major shift from the traditional concept of marketing as a simple exchange between buyer and seller. **Relationship marketing,** by contrast, involves long-term, value-added relationships developed over time with customers and suppliers. Strategic alliances and partnerships among manufacturers, retailers, and suppliers often benefit everyone. Ryder System—owner of those yellow rental trucks—has made alliances with such firms as Delphi Automotive, America's largest auto parts supplier, and Toyota Tsusho America, which provides iron, steel, and textiles to automotive companies. Ryder and Toyota formed a joint venture called TTR Logistics, in which Toyota Tsusho provides the materials and Ryder manages the flow and warehousing of other materials such as plastics and wires.[15] Ryder expects the alliance to generate $22 million in its first year and hundreds of millions in the future. Participants in collaborative relationships generate an estimated 25 percent more sales than independent firms. Teaming up with potential buyers of their products also reduces the risks of new-product introductions. The concept of relationship marketing, which is the current state of customer-driven marketing, is discussed in detail later in this chapter.

Converting Needs to Wants

Every consumer must acquire goods and services on a continuing basis to fill certain needs. Everyone must satisfy the fundamental needs for food, clothing, shelter, and transportation by purchasing things or, in some instances, temporarily using rented property and hired or leased transportation. By focusing on the benefits resulting from these goods and services, effective marketing converts needs to wants. A need for clothing may be translated into a desire (or want) for designer clothes. The need for a vacation may become the desire to take a Caribbean cruise or to backpack in the Rocky Mountains.

As easier-to-use software has enabled millions of nontechnical consumers to operate personal computers, and as falling retail prices make these computers affordable to most households, computers have become fixtures in many schools, offices, and homes. Thousands of tiny and large PC makers have pushed prices below $1,000, and this once-prestigious possession has been reduced to a commodity. Best Buy, the electronics discount retailer shown in Figure 1.4, has achieved major sales success during the past five years by offering PCs from companies like HP for less than $600 and e-machines for under $400. Because computers are now viewed as a common household need, much like a television or a cell phone, retailers and manufacturers must find new ways to compete for consumer attention.

Companies that adopt the marketing concept focus on providing solutions to customer problems. They stress product benefits rather than features to show the added value that customers will receive from the

FIGURE 1.4

Best Buy: Attracting Consumer Attention and Sales Growth by Offering PCs at Rock-Bottom Prices

product. Auto marketers emphasize powerful engines, ABS brakes, and air bags as safety benefits, while office products dealers promote reliable, high-speed copiers and printers for the time savings and low maintenance costs they offer to business purchasers.

AVOIDING MARKETING MYOPIA

The emergence of the marketing concept has not been devoid of setbacks. One troublesome problem led Theodore Levitt to coin the term marketing myopia. According to Levitt, **marketing myopia** is management's failure to recognize the scope of its business. Product-oriented rather than customer-oriented management endangers future growth. Levitt cites many service industries—dry cleaning, electric utilities, movies, and railroads—as examples of marketing myopia.

To avoid marketing myopia, companies must broadly define organizational goals oriented toward consumer needs. This approach can help a company stand out from others in highly competitive environments, such as the communications industry. The evolution of AT&T in the information age has created the largest telecommunications company in the U.S. and a world leader in communication services.

AT&T has undergone drastic changes since the demise of the regulated telephone monopoly in 1984. It began by focusing on offering long-distance service but gradually escaped the myopic view of itself as merely a telephone company. In the decades since deregulation, AT&T added Internet, wireless, cable, and local telephone services, transforming itself into a much broader role as a provider of communication services. Intense competition coupled with declining long-distance rates prompted AT&T to divide into separate companies so that specific marketing and other specialists could devote their creative efforts to become market leaders in each product category.[16]

Revlon founder and president Charles Revson understood the need for a broader focus on benefits rather than on products. As Revson described it, "In our factory we make perfume; in our advertising we sell hope." Table 1.2 illustrates how firms in a number of other industries have overcome myopic thinking by developing broader marketing-oriented business ideas that focus on consumer need satisfaction.

EXTENDING THE TRADITIONAL BOUNDARIES OF MARKETING

Today's organizations—both profit-oriented and not-for-profit—recognize universal needs for marketing and its importance to their success. During a television commercial break, viewers might be exposed to an advertisement for a Subaru Outback, an appeal to help children in foreign countries, a message by a political

TABLE 1.2

Avoiding Marketing Myopia by Focusing on Benefits

Company	Myopic Description	Marketing-Oriented Description
Verizon	"We are a telephone company."	"We are a communications company."
JetBlue Airways	"We are in the airline business."	"We are in the transportation business."
Merrill Lynch	"We are in the stock brokerage business."	"We are in the financial services business."
Nintendo	"We are in the video game business."	"We are in the entertainment business."

candidate, and a 30-second music-oriented ad featuring Britney Spears for a soft drink—all in the space of about two minutes.

Marketing in Not-for-Profit Organizations

The more than 1 million not-for-profit organizations across the U.S. employ nearly 15.1 million people and generate revenues of more than $620 billion each year.[17] In addition, 109 million volunteers do $255 billion worth of work every year.[18] That makes not-for-profit organizations big business.

Not-for-profit organizations operate in both public and private sectors. Federal, state, and local government units and agencies derive revenues from tax collection to pursue service objectives that are not keyed to profitability targets. The U.S. Department of Defense, for example, protects the nation from foreign aggression; a state's department of natural resources regulates conservation and environmental programs; the local animal-control officer enforces ordinances that protect people and animals.

The private sector has an even more diverse array of not-for-profit organizations, including art institutes, the University of Miami football team, labor unions, hospitals, private schools, the American Cancer Society, and the YMCA. Some, like University of Miami's football team, may generate surplus revenues that can pay for other athletic activities, but the organization's primary goal is to win football games.

In some not-for-profit organizations, adopting the marketing concept means forming a partnership with a for-profit company to promote the not-for-profit's message or image. The organization Save the Children Federation—which provides food, clothing, and shelter to impoverished children around the world—has 27 licensees, or for-profit companies that use the name of the organization on various products, and donate portions of the proceeds to Save the Children. Discount retailer T.J. Maxx recently introduced a line of clothing called Save the Children in a five-year licensing deal. Pepsi ran a holiday promotion offering greeting cards with children's artwork on them, donating $1 from each purchase to Save the Children. Licensing fees and royalties raise about $2 million a year for the organization.[19]

Generally, the alliances formed between not-for-profit organizations and commercial firms benefit both. The reality of operating with multimillion-dollar budgets requires not-for-profit organizations to maintain a focused business approach. Consider some current examples:

- McDonald's Ronald McDonald House Charities work with several local and national not-for-profit organizations to help critically ill children and their families through difficult times.
- The fight against breast cancer has generated donations from many organizations, including the U.S. Postal Service, Avon, JCPenney, and Ford Motor Co., among others.
- The Children's Miracle Network, a $172 million organization that raises money for children's hospitals across the country, gets about $70 million from contributions from corporations like Wal-Mart, Toys "R" Us, and Delta Air Lines.
- General Motors throws its charitable funding behind the United Negro College Fund.

The diversity of not-for-profit organizations suggests the presence of numerous organizational objectives other than profitability. In addition to organizational goals, not-for-profit organizations differ from profit-seeking firms in other ways.

Characteristics of Not-for-Profit Marketing

The most obvious distinction between not-for-profit organizations and for profit—commercial—firms is the financial *bottom line,* business jargon that refers to the overall profitability of an organization. For-profit organizations measure profitability in terms of sales and revenues, and their goal is to generate revenues above and beyond their costs in order to make money for all stakeholders involved, including employees, shareholders, and the organization itself. Not-for-profit organizations hope to generate just as much revenue to support their causes, whether it is feeding children, preserving wilderness, or helping single mothers find work. Historically, not-for-profits have had less exact goals and marketing objectives than for-profit firms, but in recent years many of these groups have recognized that in order to succeed, they must develop more cost-effective ways to provide services, and they must compete with other organizations for donors' dollars. Marketing can help them accomplish these tasks.

<interactive>**learning goal**

CHAPTER OBJECTIVE #4: DESCRIBE THE CHARACTERISTICS OF NOT-FOR-PROFIT MARKETING.

There are other distinctions between the two types of organizations as well, which influence marketing activities. Like profit-seeking firms, not-for-profit organizations may market tangible goods and/or intangible services. The Chicago Art Institute offers items in its gift shop and through direct-mail catalogs (tangible goods), as well as the special exhibits and educational classes (intangible services). But profit-seeking businesses tend to focus their marketing on just one public—their customers. Not-for-profit organizations, however, must often market to multiple publics, which complicates decision making regarding the correct markets to target. Many deal with at least two major publics—their clients and their sponsors—and often many other publics, as well. Political candidates, for example, target both voters and campaign contributors. A college targets prospective students as clients of its marketing program, but it also markets to current students, parents of students, alumni, faculty, staff, local businesses, and local government agencies.

A customer or service user of a not-for-profit organization may wield less control over the organization's destiny than would be true for customers of a profit-seeking firm. The children who are fed and sheltered by Save the Children, Childreach, and other such organizations have less influence on the organization's direction than do affluent American children who buy CDs at the local mall. Not-for-profit organizations also often possess some degree of monopoly power in a given geographic area. An individual contributor might object to United Way's inclusion of a crisis center among its beneficiary agencies, but that agency still receives a portion of the person's total contribution.

In another potential problem, a resource contributor—whether it is a cash donor, a volunteer, or someone who provides office space—may try to interfere with the marketing program in order to promote the message that he or she feels is relevant. Or a donor might restrict a contribution in certain ways that make it difficult for the organization to use. During a capital campaign to raise funds for a new science center, a college alumnus might make a restricted gift to the college theater instead.

NONTRADITIONAL MARKETING

As marketing has gained acceptance as a generic activity, its application has broadened far beyond its traditional boundaries. In some cases, broader appeals focus on causes, events, individuals, organizations, and places in the not-for-profit sector. In other instances, they encompass diverse groups of profit-seeking individuals, activities, and organizations. Table 1.3 lists and describes five major categories of nontraditional marketing: person marketing, place marketing, cause marketing, event marketing, and organization marketing.

<interactive>**learning goal**

CHAPTER OBJECTIVE #5: DESCRIBE THE FIVE TYPES OF NONTRADITIONAL MARKETING.

Person Marketing

One category of nontraditional marketing, **person marketing,** refers to efforts designed to cultivate the attention, interest, and preferences of a target market toward a celebrity or authority figure. Celebrities can be real people; Olympic skier Picabo Street promotes Chapstick; former boxing great George Foreman can be seen in Meineke muffler ads as well as commercials for his indoor barbecue grill; actor Jason Alexander runs around the television screen carrying buckets of Kentucky Fried Chicken. Celebrities can be fictional characters, such as Snoopy, who encourages people to buy MetLife insurance. Or they can be widely recognized authority figures, such as former presidential candidate Bob Dole—who spoke out for cancer awareness and promoted Viagra. Campaigns for political candidates and the marketing of celebrities are examples of person marketing. In political marketing, candidates target two markets: They attempt to gain the recognition and preference of voters and the financial support of donors.

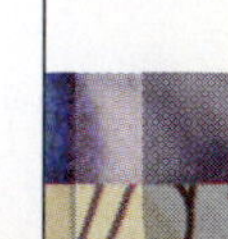

TABLE 1.3

Categories of Nontraditional Marketing

Type	Brief Description	Examples
Person marketing	Marketing efforts designed to cultivate the attention and preference of a target market toward a person	Celebrity Britney Spears; athlete Tiger Woods; political candidates
Place marketing	Marketing efforts designed to attract visitors to a particular area; improve consumer images of a city, state, or nation; and/or attract new business	Georgia: Experience the Soul of Georgia; Belize: Catch the Adventure; Tennessee: Sounds Good to Me
Cause marketing	Identification and marketing of a social issue, cause, or idea to selected target markets	"Welfare to Work. It works." "Friends don't let friends drive drunk."
Event marketing	Marketing of sporting, cultural, and charitable activities to selected target markets	NASCAR Pepsi 400; American Cancer Society Relay for Life
Organization marketing	Marketing efforts of mutual-benefit organizations, service organizations, and government organizations that seek to influence others to accept their goals, receive their services, or contribute to them in some way	U.S. Army: An Army of One. United Way brings out the best in all of us. Tech Corps: America needs to know.

FIGURE 1.5

City Harvest: Generating Increased Public Awareness and Contributions from Person Advertising

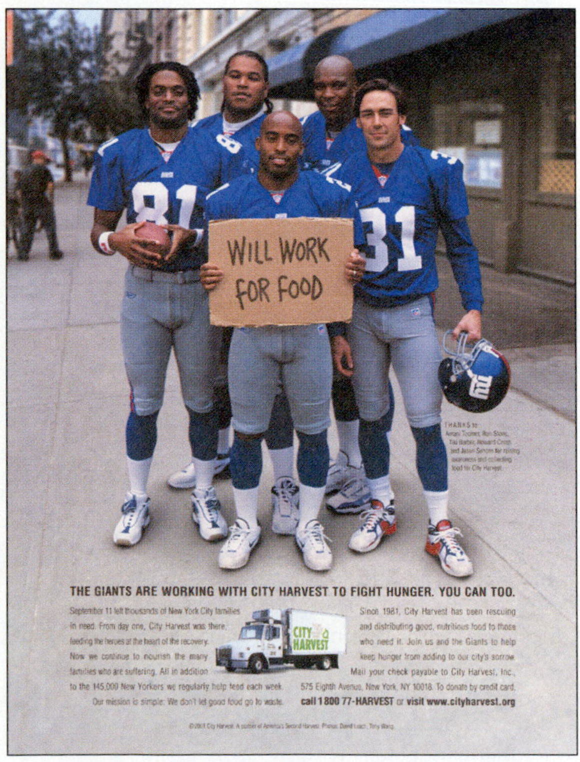

The big winners among celebrity endorsers are professional athletes. Basketball legend Michael Jordan earns as much as $40 million each year endorsing such products as Oakley sunglasses and Hanes underwear; tennis stars Venus and Serena Williams have agreements with Avon and other companies; and golfer Tiger Woods lends his celebrity to products ranging from Nike to American Express.[20] Sometimes, professional athletes lend their names and images to ads promoting not-for-profit organizations, like the one in Figure 1.5. Five New York Giants football players posed for this advertisement for City Harvest, an organization that picks up fresh food from restaurants and supermarkets and distributes it to those in need.

Jimmy Buffett is the most unlikely sort of celebrity. His only top-ten single hit the charts back in 1977. But here in the 21st century, he is packing in thousands of concertgoers who make his summer tours one of the top draws each year. His hard-core fans, known as Parrot Heads, often show up in full tropical attire—foam parrot hats, green and yellow grass skirts, and coconut-shell bras.

The fans are eager to participate in an illusion—those landlocked pillars of their community pretending they are finally going to cash in their chips and set sail for uncharted waters. And the man they have come to see is Jimmy Buffett. They spend over $50 million a year on his concert tickets, albums, books, T-shirts, trinkets, and food. The Buffett "brand" is carved from over 30 albums, eight movies, a clothing line, a series of Margaritaville Cafes, a custom record label, three best-selling novels, and hundreds of gift-shop trinkets.

Buffett works hard at perpetuating this image. He launched a Web site to sell his merchandise and was among the first stars to land a corporate sponsor—Corona Beer. His books, including *Tales from Margaritaville* and *A Pirate Looks at Fifty*, add to the carefree, beach-bum lifestyle legend. In addition, he gives freely to environmental causes, donating $1 from every concert ticket to local causes of the cities where he tours. He has served as chairman of the Save the Manatee society. Buffett's three-decades-long career is a textbook example of how to cross-market books, music, restaurants, and retailing.[21]

Top-grossing entertainer Jimmy Buffett practices person marketing with a combination of CD releases, concert tours, restaurants, and merchandise sales.

Place Marketing

Another category of nontraditional marketing is **place marketing,** which attempts to attract customers to particular areas. Cities, states, and countries publicize their tourist attractions to lure vacation travelers. They also promote themselves as good locations for businesses. Place marketing has become more important in the world economy, where localities compete for economic advantage, increased employment, trade, and investment. Organizations as varied as the San Diego Zoo, the Alamo in San Antonio, state bureaus of tourism and conventions, and the Seattle Port Authority apply place marketing techniques to attract visitors, residents, and new businesses to their areas. Their strategies include promoting positive images; marketing special attractions like The Great Wall of China, India's Taj Mahal, and Niagara Falls; highlighting efficient transportation infrastructures and communication systems; and stressing the quality of available education, low crime rates, clean air and water, and cultural and recreational opportunities. Place marketing also fills promotional messages with positive perceptions of visitors as well as people who live in the area. But place marketing can't be successful if the place advertised simply can't fulfill the wants and needs of potential travelers, as the Interactive Example "Marketing Misses" illustrates.

MARKETING MISS: IS AN AFGHANISTAN VACATION IN YOUR FUTURE?

Cause Marketing

A third category of nontraditional marketing, **cause marketing,** refers to the identification and marketing of a social issue, cause, or idea to selected target markets. Cause marketing covers a wide range of issues, including literacy, physical fitness, gun control, family planning, prison reform, control of overeating, environmental protection, elimination of birth defects, child-abuse prevention, and punishment of drunk drivers.

An increasingly common marketing practice is for profit-seeking firms to link their products to social causes. The San Francisco Giants baseball team dedicates several dates each season to raising awareness—and funds—for a worthy cause. In one recent season, the team used several game days at their home park to focus on AIDS research, blood donations, and prevention of domestic violence. The team also sponsors book and food drives.[22] The Coca-Cola Co. sponsors TigerJam, Tiger Woods's annual fundraiser, which can run the company as much as $1 million. Other corporate sponsors of the event who spend as much as $100,000 include American Airlines, Williams Energy, Cirque du Soleil, Southern Wine and Spirits, and NetJets. The proceeds from the event go to the Tiger Woods Foundation, which supports various youth organizations.[23]

Surveys show strong support for cause-related marketing by both consumers and company employees. Two-thirds of those surveyed say they are more likely to switch to a civic-minded brand or retailer if price and quality are equal. The top three issues consumers would like marketers to address are public education, crime, and the environment.[24] Of course, supporting good causes is good publicity for corporations.

To entice more visitors to its historic city, the San Antonio Convention & Visitors Bureau uses promotions such as this striking photo of the Alamo, the 18th century mission that ranks as one of the most recognized and revered structures in the U.S.

An empty seat
is a lost opportunity.
Give a cancer patient a lift.
So near, yet so far.
There are thousands of kids and adults with cancer. Many have an opportunity for treatment that can help win their battle. The problem is, critical treatment centers aren't across the street. They're often across the country. And many of these patients and their families need help in bridging the miles between home and critically needed treatment.
Without any cost,
your company can help.
These patients are going your way, and you don't have to go out of your way to help them win their battle.
We're the Corporate Angel Network, a public charity with only one mission—to arrange passage for cancer patients traveling to treatment centers using the empty seats on corporate aircraft flying the same routes as part of normal business. We handle all the logistics. You just provide the seat.
A perfect opportunity
to avoid lost opportunities.
Join 500 major corporations, including 56 of the top 100 in the Fortune 500®, that are currently Corporate Angels. To date, they've given more than 15,000 cancer patients a lift to treatment centers—as a seamless part of their regular business travel. With your help, cancer patients feel that somebody cares. You enable them to fly with dignity, in comfort, and at no cost to the patient or your company.
Join 500 of the world's best corporations in giving cancer patients a lift. Become a Corporate Angel.
CAN
Corporate Angel Network
Corporate Angel Network, Inc.
Westchester County Airport, One Loop Road, White Plains, NY 10604
Phone (914) 328-1313 Fax (914) 328-3938
Patient Toll Free — (866) 328-1313
Info@CorpAngelNetwork.org www.CorpAngelNetwork.org

Corporate Angel Network supports cancer patients who need to travel for their treatment.

Event Marketing

Event marketing refers to the marketing of sporting, cultural, and charitable activities to selected target markets. It also includes the sponsorship of such events by firms seeking to increase public awareness and bolster their images by linking themselves and their products to the events. Sports sponsorships have gained effectiveness in increasing brand recognition, enhancing image, boosting purchase volume, and increasing popularity with sports fans in demographic segments corresponding to sponsor business goals.

Some people might say that the premier sporting event is the World Series. Others might argue that it's the Super Bowl. But there is a special place in everyone's heart for the Olympics, both summer and winter. Countries the world over compete for the privilege of hosting the games. Television networks bid for the right to cover them. Marketers pour millions into special campaigns tied to the events. Home Depot and UPS, which proudly count a number of athletes among their own employees, create advertisements featuring Olympians such as speed skater Derek Parra. Hallmark recently sponsored the 2002 Winter Games in Salt Lake City and plans to continue its sponsorship of the U.S. Olympic team through the 2006 Games in Turin, Italy. In addition to a flurry of TV commercials, the giant card marketer offered Olympic visitors at Salt Lake City the opportunity to send a complimentary greeting card with a unity theme free of charge to friends or family members and furnished the flower bouquets presented to medalists. Hallmark marketers chose the Olympics carefully as an event to sponsor. "When you look at the values of the Olympics—celebration, support, family being behind everyone—all the emotional elements of the Games fit quite neatly with Hallmark," explained Kylie Watson-Wheeler, director of advertising at Hallmark.[25]

Organization Marketing

The category of nontraditional marketing called **organization marketing** involves attempts to influence others to accept the goals of, receive the services of, or contribute in some way to an organization. Organization marketing includes mutual-benefit organizations (churches, labor unions, and political parties), service organizations (colleges and universities, hospitals, and museums), and government organizations (military services, police and fire departments, and the U.S. Postal Service).

As cultural organizations encounter declining public funding for the arts and rising competition from other entertainment forms, they respond by actively marketing their programs. Like profit-seeking businesses, the Detroit Museum of Art must generate funds to cover its operating expenses. Revenues come from a number of sources, including individual donations, memberships, government grants, gift-shop sales, and special fund-raising drives. The organization also has a Web site and uses such business techniques as marketing research, advertising, and publicity. Special events, such as a recent exhibition of one of the largest number of works ever exhibited in the U.S. by the Dutch Post-Impressionist master Vincent van Gogh, provide added value to museum members and attract thousands of occasional and first-time visitors who may become members.

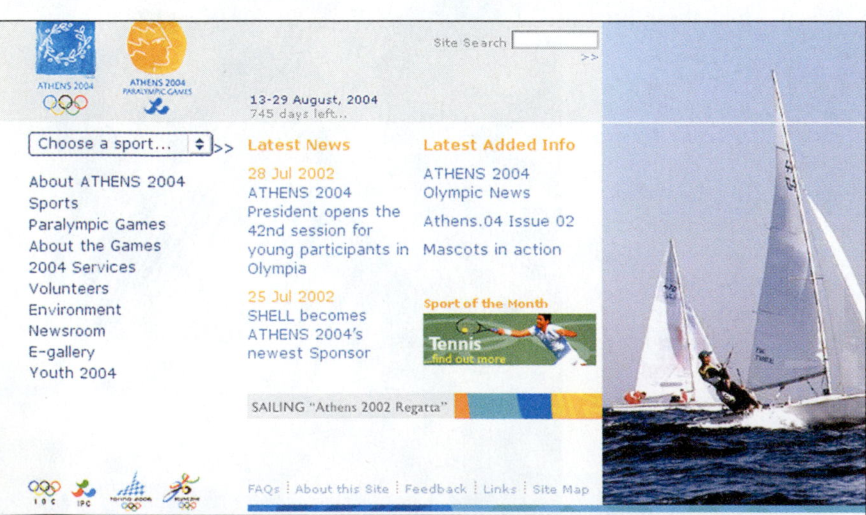

Likely sponsors for the 2004 Summer Olympics in Athens include beer marketers, a major credit-card company, an auto maker, and a fast-food franchise. Such global events are effective in attracting huge audiences that include prime targets for these firms' product offerings.

Organization marketers don't just make appeals for money. They must also reassure donors that the money is being handled correctly and ethically. After the tragedy of the September 11 terrorist attacks, millions wanted to donate funds to charities and relief organizations in an effort to help the victims and their families recover. In fact, so much money flowed into organizations that it became a huge task for administrators to identify who should receive the money and to distribute it in a manner that everyone deemed fair. Even the American Red Cross suffered some damage to its reputation when it announced that some of the $500 million collected would be kept in reserve for possible future terrorist attacks and other disasters. But within weeks of the announcement, the organization reversed its stance and agreed that all the contributions would be directed to victims and relief efforts related to September 11.[26] The advertisement in Figure 1.6 emphasizes that donors can trust these organizations to handle their contributions correctly; a quote from President George W. Bush lends the ad credibility.

FIGURE 1.6

Request for Donations to Help the Relief Efforts Related to September 11, 2001

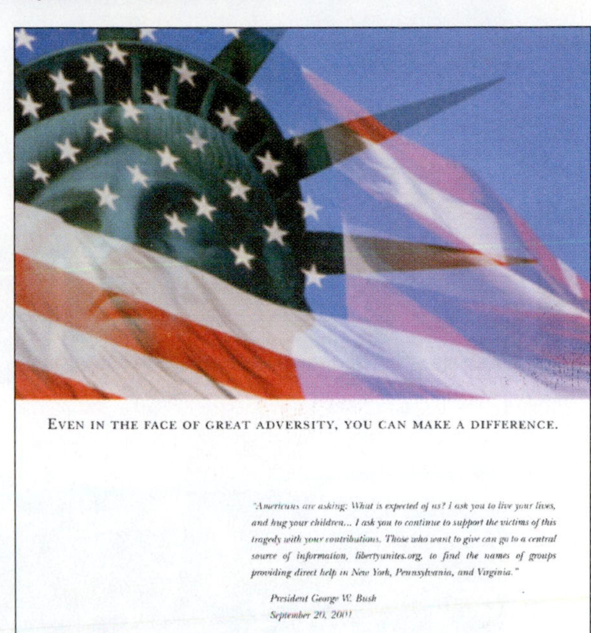

EVEN IN THE FACE OF GREAT ADVERSITY, YOU CAN MAKE A DIFFERENCE.
"Americans are asking: What is expected of us? I ask you to live your lives, and hug your children... I ask you to continue to support the victims of this tragedy with your contributions. Those who want to give can go to a central source of information, libertyunites.org, to find the names of groups providing direct help in New York, Pennsylvania, and Virginia."
President George W. Bush
September 20, 2001

FOR MORE INFORMATION, OR TO MAKE A DONATION NOW TO ONE OR MORE TRUSTED RELIEF ORGANIZATIONS, PLEASE VISIT WWW.LIBERTYUNITES.COM

CRITICAL THINKING AND CREATIVITY

The challenges presented by today's complex and technologically sophisticated marketing environment require critical-thinking skills and creativity from marketing professionals. *Critical thinking* refers to the process of determining the authenticity, accuracy, and worth of information, knowledge, claims, and arguments. Critical thinkers do not take information at face value and simply assume that it is accurate; they analyze the data themselves and develop their own opinions and conclusions.

Creative government bureaucracy might sound like an oxymoron, but it is an accurate description of the U.S. Mint since Philip N. Diehl became director. After years of fighting entrenched political resistance, Diehl was able to transform this $1 billion government agency into a close approximation of a private sector, profit-seeking business. The organization chart was reorganized, jobs were redesigned and positions added, state-of-the-art computerized information systems were installed, bureaucratic workers were trained to become customer-responsive employees, and new products were introduced. The 50-state quarter program, launched during Diehl's tenure, proved highly successful. The Mint decided to release five quarters a year, through 2008, each featuring a different state. As a result, kids—and adults—are clamoring to collect the new quarters as they are released. Despite slowdowns in consumer purchases during the recent economic downturn, these creative changes contributed in a big way in bringing about a government agency that shines, as they say, like a brand-new penny.[27]

Creativity is a human activity that produces original ideas or knowledge, frequently by testing combinations of ideas or data to produce unique results. It is an extremely valuable skill for marketers. Creativity helps them to develop novel solutions to perceived marketing problems. Creativity has been a part of human endeavor since the beginning of time. Leonardo da Vinci conceived his idea for a helicopter after watching leaves twirl in the wind. Swiss engineer George de Mestral, noticing that burrs stuck to his wool socks because of their tiny hooks, invented Velcro. Many people think that creativity is the domain of only the young. But famed architect I. M. Pei designed the Rock and Roll Hall of Fame in Cleveland when he was 78 years old. Tom Peters, who wrote the business and marketing best-seller *In Search of Excellence* at age 40, launched a five-book series at age 57. "Creativity is being in one setting and seeing something strange someplace else," he says. "To me, books on butterflies or baseball are more legitimate in terms of thinking about business strategy issues than books on business strategy."[28] Peters' remark is particularly applicable to the creation of promotional messages. Figure 1.7 demonstrates the use of creativity to communicate that Duke Energy has the power to become a global energy leader, no matter which way the wind blows.

THE TECHNOLOGY REVOLUTION IN MARKETING

As we move through the opening decade of the 21st century, we also enter a new era in communication, considered by some as unique as the 15th-century invention of the printing press or the first radio and television broadcasts early in the 20th century. *Technology* is the business application of knowledge based on scientific discoveries, inventions, and innovations. Interactive multimedia technologies such as computer networks, video conferencing, online services and the Internet, interactive kiosks, CD-ROM catalogs, and personal digital assistants (PDAs) have revolutionized the way people store, distribute, retrieve, and present information. Computer networks and other telecommunications technologies link employees, suppliers, and customers in different locations through the Internet or in-house intranets.

FIGURE 1.7

Demonstrating Duke Energy's Creativity and Ability to Become a Global Energy Leader

<interactive>learning goal

CHAPTER OBJECTIVE #6: OUTLINE THE CHANGES IN THE MARKETING ENVIRONMENT DUE TO TECHNOLOGY.

Satellite radio giants Sirius and XM offer subscribers 100 commercial-free channels of music, news, talk, and sports for their cars at about the same price that cable viewers pay to tune in weekly installments of The Sopranos *and similar fare on HBO. Market growth is being aided by the growing number of automakers who offer this feature in their new models.*

These technological advances are revolutionizing marketing. Companies can reach specific groups of customers in a variety of ways: from hotels' in-house television channels targeting guests to toll-free telephone numbers and in-store videos with point-of-purchase product demonstrations. Now that half of all U.S. households have personal computers, online services and the Internet offer a new medium over which companies can market products and offer customer service. Marketing and sales departments can quickly access vast databases with information about customers and their buying patterns. They can develop targeted marketing campaigns and zoned advertising programs for consumers located within a certain distance from a store and even within specific city blocks.

Shoppers can visit kiosks in shopping malls that feature video displays, discount coupons, and product information for a variety of merchants. They can browse through a CD-ROM product catalog on their computers or conduct specific searches to quickly find desired items. Surfing the Web or online services is another way to get product information and order merchandise from catalogs. Firms can quickly update this information at minimal costs. Online retail spending in the U.S. is growing at an astounding rate—from $7.8 billion in 1998 to $100 billion in 2003. Consumers' willingness to spend online is growing—as is the amount they spend on each visit, despite the sluggish economy. More women are now shopping online than men, and shoppers are now looking for a greater range of products. "In the past, online shopping was all about books, videos, and music," observes Rob Solomon of Yahoo! "Now shoes, watches, and all sorts of apparel items are moving into the top categories."[29] Still, the most popular items at MSN's eShop include digital cameras, personal digital assistants, and MP3 players. All of these changes represent opportunities for marketers.

Interactive Marketing

Interactive media technologies combine computers and telecommunications resources to create software that users can direct themselves. They allow people to digitize reports and drawings and transmit them, quickly and inexpensively, over phone lines, coaxial cables, or fiber-optic cables. People can subscribe to personalized news services that deliver article summaries on specified topics directly to their fax machines or computers. They can telecommunicate via e-mail, voice mail, fax, videoconferencing, and computer networks; pay bills using online banking services; and use online resources to get information about everything from investments to a local retailer's special sale, day-care facilities, and local entertainment activities for the upcoming weekend.

Companies are now using interactivity in their marketing programs. **Interactive marketing** refers to buyer-seller communications in which the customer controls the amount and type of information received from a marketer. This technique provides immediate access to key product information when the consumer wants it. Interactive techniques have been used for more than a decade; point-of-sale brochures and coupon dispensers are a simple form of interactive advertising. Want to go skiing tomorrow? Log on to the Web site of your favorite mountain and you may be offered a coupon for a free lift ticket. Want to try a new restaurant? Check the Web site for a coupon offering a free appetizer. Interactive marketing also includes two-way electronic communication using a variety of media such as the Internet, CD-ROMs, and virtual reality kiosks.

Interactive marketing allows marketers and customers to customize their communication. Customers may come to companies for information, creating opportunities for one-to-one marketing. Interactive marketing can also allow many-to-many exchanges, where consumers can communicate with one another using e-mail or electronic bulletin boards. These electronic conversations establish innovative relationships between users and the technology, providing customized information based on users' interests and levels of understanding. Interactive technologies support almost limitless exchanges of information.

One of the busiest areas of interactive marketing is online auctions and name-your-own-price vendors. Ebay, the online auction house, connects sellers and buyers directly—millions of them daily. Consumers who want to name their own price for airline tickets, hotel rooms, cruises, and rental cars can do so at a variety of sites. Budget Car Rental was the first in the car rental industry to establish an interactive price bidding feature, the BidBudget program. Online bidders simply fill out a form indicating the desired dates and airport pickup location, preferred car type, contact information, a major credit-card number, and the price they are willing to pay. Budget notifies the bidder within 24 hours whether a bid is accepted and offers a money-back guarantee up to 48 hours before the pick-up time.[30]

Interactive promotions put the customer in control. Consumers can easily get tips on product usage and answers to customer service questions, they can also tell the company what they like or dislike about a product, and they can just as easily click the exit button and move on to another area. As interactive promotions grow in number and popularity, the challenge will be attracting and holding consumer attention.

The Internet

Most of today's discussion of interactive marketing centers on the Internet. The **Internet** is an all-purpose global network composed of some 50,000 different networks around the globe that, within limits, lets anyone with access to a personal computer send and receive images and text anywhere.

The Internet provides an efficient way to find and share information, but until the last decade, most people outside universities and government agencies found it difficult to use and learn. This changed in 1993 with the advent of browser technology that provides point-and-click access to the **World Wide Web (WWW** or **Web).** The Web is actually an interlinked collection of graphically rich information sources within the larger Internet. Web sites provide hypermedia resources, a system allowing storage of and access to text, graphics, audio, and video in so-called pages linked to each other in a way that integrates these different media elements. When a user clicks on a highlighted word or picture (icon), the browser converts the click to computer commands and brings the requested new information—text, photograph, chart, song, or movie clip—to the user's computer.

Compared with traditional media, the hypermedia resources of the Web offer a number of advantages. Data moves in seconds, without the user noticing that several computers in different locations combine to

Briefly Speaking

An irate banker demanded that Alexander Graham Bell remove "that toy" from his office. That toy was the telephone. A Hollywood producer scrawled a rejection note on a manuscript that became *Gone with the Wind.* Ford's largest original investor sold all his stock in 1906. Roebuck sold out to Sears for $25,000 in 1895. Today, Sears may sell $25,000 of goods in 16 seconds.

United Technologies Corp. Advertisement

fulfill a request. Interactive control allows users to quickly access other information resources through related pages, either at the same or other sites, and easily navigate through documents. Because it is dynamic, Web site sponsors can easily keep information current. Finally, multimedia capacities increase the attractiveness of these documents.

Broadband

Broadband technology—an always-on Internet connection that runs at a speed of 200 kilobytes per second or higher—can deliver large amounts of data at once, making online marketing even faster and easier than it was a few years ago. Consumers can access Web pages and sites can process credit card purchases much quicker via broadband. The number of households with broadband connections is increasing rapidly, as people grow impatient with the old, slower "dial-up" Internet connections. By 2003, more than 18 million U.S. households (nearly 30 percent of all online U.S. households) used a broadband Internet connection, even though subscription costs remained about double that of traditional dial-up connections. "These technologies are going to be moving from novelties to integrated tools," predicts Glenn McClanan, director of broadband initiatives for Edmunds.com, a California-based auto shopping information site that offers free downloads of informational video clips.[31]

Wireless

More and more consumers now have *wireless* Internet connections for their laptop computers and personal digital assistants, which is both a challenge and an opportunity for marketers. By 2003, the number of U.S. consumers with these connections had passed the 30 million mark, a 100 percent increase in a single year. Although wireless advertising is still in its infancy, industry watchers predict that wireless ad revenues will reach $700 million by 2005.[32] This high-tech form of advertising has been slower to catch on with marketers because of the relatively high cost—$40 to $50 per thousand impressions, compared with $2 to $3 for a banner ad on the Web. But wireless ads offer tremendous potential to target certain audiences. And since these ads appear by themselves on a PDA user's screen, they command more attention than a banner ad would. Currently, wireless carriers put a limit on how much wireless advertising they allow, for fear of alienating their own customers if they are bombarded with unneeded—and unwanted—information. Also, the speed of data transfer via wireless Internet service is not quite where it needs to be in order to handle this type of communication on a regular basis. But marketers would do well to prepare for this next generation of advertising.

The Web is a powerful, affordable way to reach consumers anywhere, anytime.

Interactive Television Service

Interactive Television (iTV) service is another new technology for marketers and consumers alike to embrace. Interactive television service is a package that includes a return path for viewers to interact with programs or commercials by clicking their remote controls. The 18 million U.S. TV viewers who have iTV can request additional information about products or actually purchase them without having to dial their phones. Companies such as Ford have already incorporated iTV into their marketing programs.[33]

How Marketers Use the Web

The Web offers marketers a powerful, yet affordable way to reach customers across town or overseas, at almost any time, with interactive messages. The online techniques that companies use to market their businesses fall into four broad categories: virtual storefronts, interactive brochures, online newsletters, and customer service tools.

- The virtual storefront allows customers to view and order merchandise. Amazon.com and eBay are two of the largest such sites. Web stores can be stand-alone operations or grouped in cybermalls with links to 30 to 100 participating retailers. The Internet service provider Yahoo! operates such a mall.

  After the initial rush to establish a virtual storefront, many retailers are backing off because they have discovered that their customers are either not interested in shopping for their products online or their product offerings just don't lend themselves to online shopping. Ames Department Stores learned that customers would rather run into the store to pick up the small items it sells; Ikea reasoned that the shipping costs it would have to charge to send its furniture items to online shoppers would undermine the store's low prices. Such companies instead set up Web sites that act as information clearinghouses, providing in-depth product information. Shoppers can ask questions and get online answers, and companies can hold virtual meetings (online conferences) and sponsor discussion groups. Not-for-profit organizations use this tool as well. The World Wildlife Fund (WWF) maintains a Web site that provides information about the organization and its conservation activities. With 4.7 million supporters and a global network active in over 100 countries, WWF's primary mission is to protect nature. Site visitors can obtain membership information and learn about publications, fund-raising campaigns, educational programs, and current conservation issues facing the world today.

- Interactive brochures that provide company and product information are popular Internet marketing applications. These range from simple, one-page electronic flyers to multimedia presentations. When American Airlines' travelers need information, they can simply log on to AA.com to get instant access to their AAdvantage account, browse programs and services, make reservations, and check out special benefits available to them as members of American's frequent flyer programs.
- Online newsletters provide current news, industry information, and contacts and links for internal and external customers. *Web Commerce Today,* a monthly online newsletter, helps merchants plan, design, manage, and promote retail or business-to-business Web stores.
- The Web is also a customer service tool. Consumers can order catalogs, refer to lists of frequently asked questions with answers, place orders online, and send questions to company representatives. For instance, they can access many Kraft Foods Web sites, such as jell-o.com, to obtain information on Kraft's many products, learn new recipes, ask questions about cooking, and even buy merchandise online.

A colorful, dynamic, user-friendly Web site is not enough to ensure cyberspace success. The online marketer must convince potential customers to visit the site. A common method of generating traffic is to advertise on heavy-traffic sites like directories and search engines such as Yahoo! and AOL.

The Web is probably the most significant innovation affecting marketing and business in the past 50 years. Properly used, it should prove an indispensable tool in promoting connections, building associations, delivering information, and creating online communities.

However, to date, few companies have made money on the Internet—and many have lost a bundle. The primary beneficiaries have been firms marketing Net-related goods or services—for example, computer networking equipment; software such as access, browser, Web page authoring, and e-mail programs; consultants and Web page creators; Internet access and online service providers like PsiNet, Netcom, Amèrica Online, and CompuServe; and companies offering sites where businesses can advertise.

As fast as the first tidal wave of Internet-based companies—dot.coms—rose, it crashed, drowning most of the firms that thought they were going to ride the wave to riches. Even companies that became household names, like Pets.com and eToys, fell victim to the flood. The online auction house eBay was the only major online merchant to show a profit, while Monster.com and E*Trade survived but remained in the red. As the Web evolves, marketers need to explore its capabilities and learn the best ways to use it effectively in combination with other distribution channels and communications media. Among the questions marketers need to ask are the following:

- What types of goods and services can be successfully marketed on the Web?
- What characteristics make a successful Web site?
- Does the Internet offer a secure way to process customer orders?
- How will Internet sales affect traditional store-based and non-store retailing and distribution?
- What is the best use of this technology in a specific firm's marketing strategy: promotion, image building, or sales?

The importance of the Internet is reflected throughout this text, and as forthcoming chapters discuss specific marketing topics, we will revisit the Internet and its related technologies to look for answers to the preceding questions.

'NET EX: HOW MARKETERS USE THE WEB

FROM TRANSACTION-BASED MARKETING TO RELATIONSHIP MARKETING

As marketing progresses through the 21st century, a significant change is taking place in the way companies interact with customers. The traditional view of marketing as a simple exchange process, or *transaction-based marketing,* is being replaced by a different, longer-term approach. Traditional marketing strategies focused on attracting customers and closing deals. Today's marketers realize that, although it's important to attract new customers, it's even more important to establish and maintain a relationship with

them so they become loyal repeat customers. These efforts must expand to include suppliers and employees, as well.

<interactive>**learning goal**

CHAPTER OBJECTIVE #7: EXPLAIN THE SHIFT FROM TRANSACTION-BASED MARKETING TO RELATIONSHIP MARKETING.

As defined earlier in this chapter, relationship marketing refers to the development, growth, and maintenance of long-term, cost-effective exchange relationships with individual customers, suppliers, employees, and other partners for mutual benefit. It broadens the scope of external marketing relationships to include suppliers, customers, and referral sources. In relationship marketing, the term *customer* takes on a new meaning. Employees serve customers within an organization as well as outside it; individual employees and their departments are customers of and suppliers to one another. They must apply the same high standards of customer satisfaction to intradepartmental relationships as they do to external customer relationships. Relationship marketing recognizes the critical importance of internal marketing to the success of external marketing plans. Programs that improve customer service inside a company also raise productivity and staff morale, resulting in better customer relationships outside the firm.

Relationship marketing gives a company new opportunities to gain a competitive edge by moving customers up a loyalty hierarchy from new customers to regular purchasers, then to loyal supporters of the firm and its goods and services, and finally to advocates who not only buy its products but recommend them to others, as shown in Figure 1.8.

By converting indifferent customers into loyal ones, companies generate repeat sales. As pointed out earlier in this chapter, the cost of maintaining existing customers is far below the cost of finding new ones, and these loyal customers are profitable ones. In fact, creating loyal customers can mean the difference between flying and remaining grounded. Air travel plummeted in the aftermath of September 11, 2001, causing the nation's air carriers to suffer tremendous losses, despite a federal bail-out. While most airlines chose the cost-cutting path, eliminating onboard meals and in-flight movies, closing ticket offices and airport clubs, and suspending any construction projects, Continental decided to push ahead. CEO Gordon M. Bethune reasoned that cabin comforts and customer service, part of building relationships with passengers, were more important than making a couple of extra bucks from each passenger. Understanding and acknowledging passenger safety concerns, Continental added security checkpoints and self-service check-in kiosks. The airline offered free in-flight movies and free drinks at its airport clubs—which it kept open. Bethune authorized more than a month of overtime pay to construction workers in order to complete an expanded terminal at Newark International Airport, which was vital to Continental's presence in the New York area. Then Continental launched a commuter-train service, making it easier for New York passengers to get to the new terminal. Within a couple of months, the results of this relationship building were evident. While all the big U.S. airlines incurred billions in losses during those difficult times, Continental's losses were minimal compared with its competitors. And by the end of the year, its planes carried a higher percentage of passengers than those of its rivals, who had grounded many of their nearly empty flights.[34]

Programs to encourage customer loyalty are not new. Frequent purchaser rewards for everything from clothing to groceries are popular examples. Firms in the service industries are among the leaders in building such relationships. Visa teams up with Holiday Inn resorts and hotels during peak vacation months. Holiday Inn advertisements target families, offering a "kids eat free, stay free" program. In addition, travelers who use their Visa cards to stay at one of over 1,000 participating hotels receive a Kids' Activity Book with valuable coupons. Customers who use their Holiday Inn Visa for any purchase receive points for upgrades and free nights at Holiday Inns.

FIGURE 1.8

Converting New Customers to Advocates

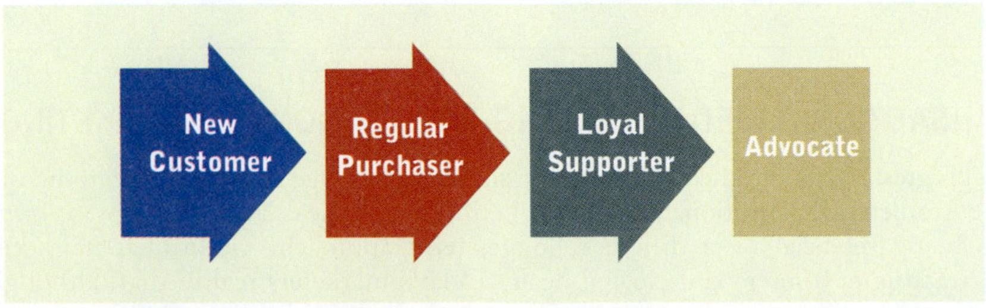

Effective relationship marketing relies heavily on information technologies such as computer databases that record customers' tastes, price preferences, and lifestyles. This technology helps companies become one-to-one marketers who gather customer-specific information and provide individually customized goods and services. The firms target their marketing programs to appropriate groups, rather than having to rely on mass-marketing campaigns. Companies who study customer preferences and react accordingly gain distinct competitive advantages.

Developing Partnerships and Strategic Alliances

Relationship marketing does not apply just to individual consumers and employees, however. It also affects a wide range of other markets, including business-to-business relationships with the firm's suppliers and distributors as well as other types of corporate partnerships. In the past, companies have often viewed their suppliers as adversaries against whom they must fiercely negotiate prices, playing one off against the other. But this attitude has changed radically, as both marketers and their suppliers discover the benefits of collaborative relationships.

The formation of **strategic alliances**—partnerships that create competitive advantages—is also on the rise. These take many forms, from product development partnerships that involve shared costs for research and development and marketing to vertical alliances in which one company provides a product or component to another firm who then distributes or sells it under its own brand. Starbucks follows its customers' tastes by forming alliances with other businesses. Several years ago, the coffee giant made a deal with Dreyer's Ice Cream to create five coffee-flavored ice creams. Then it formed an alliance with PepsiCo to create the leading bottled coffee drink, Frappuccino. Shoppers can find Starbucks products in Marriott's airport hotels, Albertson's supermarkets, and Barnes & Noble bookstore cafes—all the result of strategic alliances. These partnerships now rake in an additional $20 million a year in earnings for Starbucks.[35]

FIGURE 1.9

Stride Rite and Save the Children: Working Together to Market Shoes and Raise Money for Needy Children

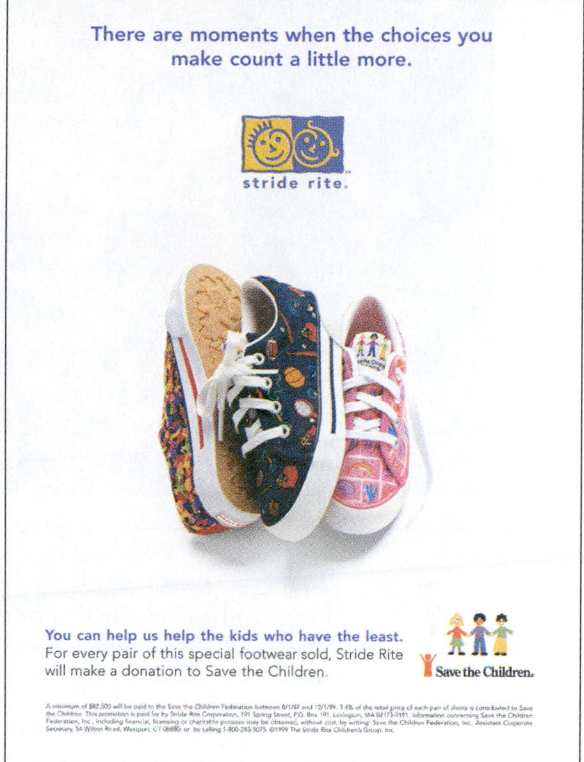

Not-for-profit organizations often make use of strategic alliances in order to raise awareness and funds for their causes. In Figure 1.9, Stride Rite and Save the Children have teamed up in a combined effort to increase shoe sales and raise money for needy children.

Clearly, relationship building begins early in the marketing process and applies to many areas. It begins with the development of quality products that meet customer needs and continues with the provision of excellent customer service during and after the purchase process. Relationship building also includes programs that encourage repeat purchases and foster customer loyalty.

Briefly Speaking

I get by with a little help from my friends.

John Lennon (1940–1980) and Paul McCartney (b. 1942)
English songwriters

COSTS AND FUNCTIONS OF MARKETING

Firms must spend money to create time, place, and ownership utilities. Numerous attempts have been made to measure marketing costs in relation to overall product costs, and most estimates have ranged between 40 and 60 percent of total costs. On the average, one-half of the costs involved in a product, such as a Subway sandwich, an ounce of Safari perfume, a pair of Steve Madden shoes, or even a European vacation, can be traced directly to marketing. These costs are not associated with fabrics, raw materials and other ingredients, baking, sewing, or any of the other production functions necessary for creating form utility. What, then, does the consumer receive in return for this 50 percent marketing cost? What functions does marketing perform?

<interactive>**learning goal**

CHAPTER OBJECTIVE #8: IDENTIFY THE UNIVERSAL FUNCTIONS OF MARKETING.

As Figure 1.10 reveals, marketing is responsible for the performance of eight universal functions: buying, selling, transporting, storing, standardizing and grading, financing, risk taking, and securing marketing information. Some functions are performed by manufacturers, others by retailers, and still others by marketing intermediaries called *wholesalers.*

FIGURE 1.10

Eight Universal Marketing Functions

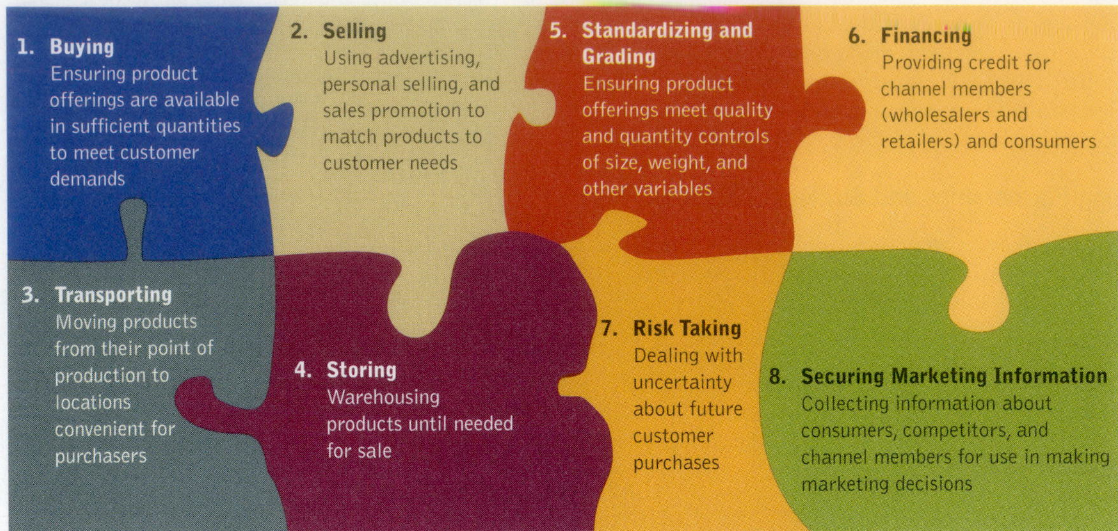

1. Buying
Ensuring product offerings are available in sufficient quantities to meet customer demands
2. Selling
Using advertising, personal selling, and sales promotion to match products to customer needs
5. Standardizing and Grading
Ensuring product offerings meet quality and quantity controls of size, weight, and other variables
6. Financing
Providing credit for channel members (wholesalers and retailers) and consumers
3. Transporting
Moving products from their point of production to locations convenient for purchasers
4. Storing
Warehousing products until needed for sale
7. Risk Taking
Dealing with uncertainty about future customer purchases
8. Securing Marketing Information
Collecting information about consumers, competitors, and channel members for use in making marketing decisions

Buying and selling, the first two functions shown in Figure 1.10, represent *exchange functions. Buying* is important to marketing on several levels. Marketers must determine how and why consumers buy certain goods and services. To be successful, they must try to understand consumer behavior. In addition, retailers and other intermediaries must seek out products that will appeal to their customers. Since they generate time, place, and ownership utilities through these purchases, marketers must anticipate consumer preferences for purchases to be made several months later. *Selling* is the second half of the exchange process. It involves advertising, personal selling, and sales promotion in an attempt to match the firm's goods and services to consumer needs.

Transporting and storing are *physical distribution functions. Transporting* involves the physical movement of goods from the seller to the purchaser. Storing involves warehousing goods until they are needed for sale. Manufacturers, wholesalers, and retailers all typically perform these functions.

The final four marketing functions—standardizing and grading, financing, risk taking, and securing marketing information—are often called *facilitating functions* because they assist the marketer in performing the exchange and physical distribution functions. Quality and quantity control *standards* and grades, frequently set by federal or state governments, reduce the need for purchasers to inspect each item. Specific tire sizes, for example, permit buyers to request needed sizes and to expect uniform sizes.

Financing is another marketing function because buyers often need access to funds in order to finance inventories prior to sales. Manufacturers often provide financing for their wholesale and retail customers. Some types of wholesalers perform similar functions for their retail customers. Finally, retailers frequently permit their customers to buy on credit.

The seventh function, *risk taking,* is part of most ventures. Manufacturers create goods and services based on research and their belief that consumers need them. Wholesalers and retailers acquire inventory based on similar expectations of future consumer demand. Entrepreneurial risk takers accommodate these uncertainties about future consumer behavior when they market goods and services.

The final marketing function involves *securing marketing information.* Marketers gather information to meet the need for decision-oriented input about customers—who they are, what they buy, where they buy, and how they buy. By collecting and analyzing marketing information, marketers also try to understand why consumers purchase some goods and services and reject others.

ETHICS AND SOCIAL RESPONSIBILITY: DOING WELL BY DOING GOOD

While most companies do their best to abide by an ethical code of conduct, sometimes organizations and their leaders fall short. In recent years, headlines have publicized unethical conduct by several well-known businesses. In 1999, Microsoft Corp., which owns more than 90 percent of the PC operating-systems software market, was convicted of violating antitrust laws by abusing its monopoly to stifle competition and harm consumers. In late 2001, the Texas-based energy giant Enron collapsed, taking with it the retirement savings of its employees and investors. Enron's accounting firm, Arthur Andersen, was accused of shredding documents related to the fall of the company. And in 2002, chemical manufacturer Monsanto was convicted not only of polluting water sources and soil in a rural Alabama area for decades, but of ignoring evidence its own scientists had gathered indicating the extent and severity of the pollution.

interactive>learning goal

CHAPTER OBJECTIVE #9: DEMONSTRATE THE RELATIONSHIP BETWEEN ETHICAL BUSINESS PRACTICES AND MARKETPLACE SUCCESS.

Despite these and other alleged breaches of ethical standards, most businesspeople do follow ethical practices. Over half of all major corporations now offer ethics training to employees, and most corporate mission statements include pledges to protect the environment, contribute to communities, and improve workers' lives. Unfortunately though, in some cases, only media attention and pressure from consumers motivate companies to implement social responsibility programs. The tobacco industry paid for an anti-smoking commercial during the 2002 Super Bowl, but the agreement to do so was part of a $205 billion settlement with 46 state attorneys general in 1998.[36] Sometimes marketers walk a fine line with the public when it comes to advertising their company's good deeds, as shown in the Interactive Example "Marketing Hits."

MARKETING HIT: HOW CAN MARKETING HELP IN THE MIDST OF DISASTER?

These programs often produce such benefits as improved customer relationships, increased employee loyalty, marketplace success, and improved financial performance. The National Basketball Association has a partnership with Reading Is Fundamental, in which the NBA holds NBA Reading Month and produces and airs public service announcements for reading. This socially responsible program helps develop relationships with the general public.[37] Timberland Co., the New Hampshire– based manufacturer of boots and other outdoor clothing featured in Figure 1.11, is well-known for its high ethical standards and socially responsible programs. The company donates large sums of money to charities each year, and its employees are given paid time off to volunteer for their favorite organizations—from the animal shelter to the local preschool.

FIGURE 1.11

Timberland: Reminding Readers of Everyone's Capabilities

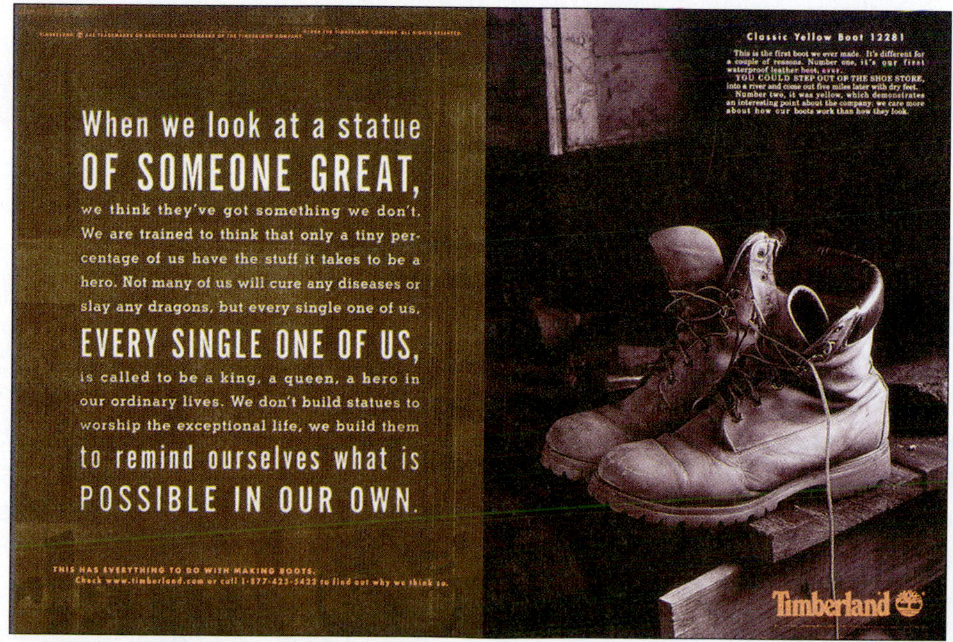

Many companies of all types and sizes sponsor community-based programs. Phillips Petroleum expresses its commitment to reducing air pollution by reducing sulfur emissions in its refining processes. In its communications to shareholders, employees, customers, and the general public, the energy giant stresses its belief that not only does the human race benefit, but so do animals and vegetation.[38]

Because ethics and social responsibility are important topics to marketers, each chapter in this book includes an Interactive Example called "Solving an Ethical Controversy." This chapter's controversy deals with some companies capitalizing on patriotism and American symbols in the wake of September 11, 2001.

RIGHT/WRONG: SOLVING AN ETHICAL CONTROVERSY—HOW MUCH IS TOO MUCH PATRIOTISM?

STRATEGIC IMPLICATIONS OF MARKETING IN THE 21ST CENTURY

Unprecedented opportunities have emerged out of electronic commerce and computer technologies in business today. These advances and innovations have allowed organizations to reach new markets, reduce selling and marketing costs, and enhance their relationships with customers and suppliers. Business-to-business e-commerce has grown into a global market thanks to the Internet.

As a new universe for consumers and organizations is created, it demands new marketing approaches to meet changing environments and avoid being left behind in a desolate business world. Profit-seeking and not-for-profit organizations must broaden the scope of their activities to prevent myopic results in their enterprises.

As we begin the rapid journey on a course paved by information technology that leads to a global economy, many aspects of business will become extinct while others will be born. It seems everything is electronic these days: marketing, communications, entertainment, the economy, commerce, and business in general. While some have predicted the demise of traditional marketing and brick-and-mortar retailing, the majority feel that the world of electronic commerce will not eliminate but enhance the systems that exist today.

Marketers must be aware of today's customer-oriented environment and employ computer technologies to satisfy individual needs. One outcropping of this new electronic era is mass customization—providing unique product offerings to match the specific needs of individual buyers while also retaining the production efficiencies of mass-produced items. Five key trends that will influence consumer behavior include an environment ranging from do-it-yourself, no-service to full-service organizations; a strong emphasis on healthy, better-for-you purchases; more leisure activities with less effort and physical exertion; a shift to entrepreneurship; and a search for goods and services that save time in a multitasking society.

Marketers must understand that although consumers are empowered with unlimited accessibility to information, they still require quality and satisfaction in the products they purchase. Marketers must overcome barriers facing one-to-one interactive relations with their customers, be faster than the competition, and be able to adapt to changes when necessary. The future is in the Internet, using data, voice, optical, and wireless communications to help bring buyers and sellers together. After all, communication is the basis of all marketing activities.

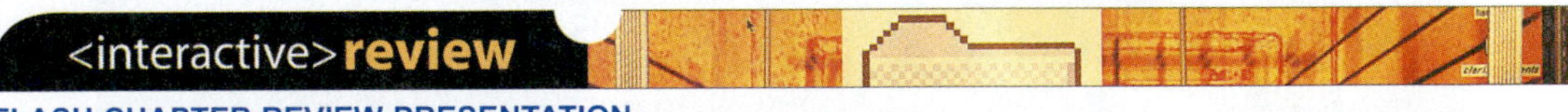

FLASH CHAPTER REVIEW PRESENTATION

HOW BURTON SNOWBOARDS BUILT A SPORT—AND A CUSTOMER BASE

- **Summary of Chapter Objectives**
- **Chapter Outline**
- **Key Terms**
- **Review Questions**
- **Projects and Teamwork Exercises**
- **'netWork**
- **Crossword Puzzles**
- **Case 1.1: Dracula Park Wants You**

Take the Post-Test to assess your overall understanding of the key ideas in this chapter. The Post-Test provides a comprehensive selection of exam-style questions addressing the main topics and concepts of the chapter. At the completion of each Post-Test, you will receive a score and instructive feedback on how you answered each question, and a direct link to the part of the chapter addressed in the question. Take the Post-Test as often as you need to—a record of your progress for each attempt is kept for you to revisit and gauge your improvement. And each Post-Test is randomly generated, so every attempt is new.

Post-Test

CHAPTER 2

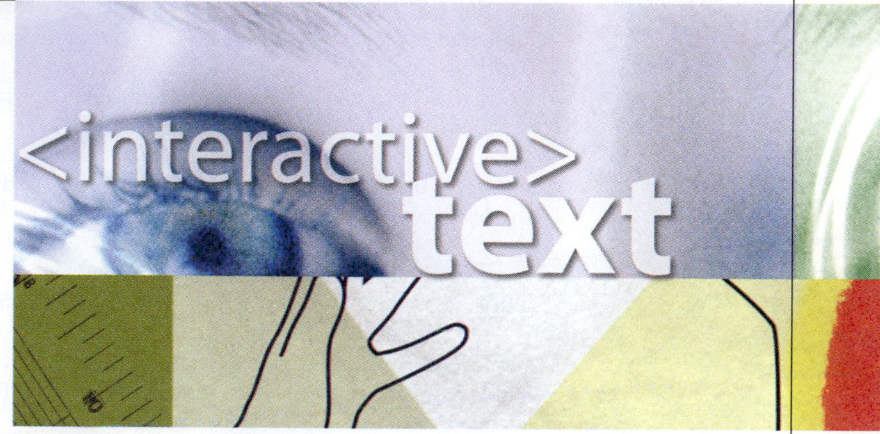

Strategic Planning and the Marketing Process

Chapter Objectives

1. **Distinguish between strategic planning and tactical planning.**
2. **Explain how marketing plans differ at various levels in an organization.**
3. **Identify the steps in the marketing planning process.**
4. **Describe the concept of SWOT analysis and its major elements.**
5. **Discuss how a strategy can be implemented through marketing plans.**
6. **Identify the basic elements of a marketing strategy.**
7. **Describe the environmental characteristics that influence strategy decisions.**
8. **Explain how the strategic business unit concept, the market share/market growth matrix, the market attractiveness/business strength matrix, and spreadsheet analysis can be used in marketing planning.**

Take the Pre-Test to assess your initial knowledge of the key ideas in this chapter. The Pre-Test provides exam-style questions addressing the main topics and concepts of the chapter. At the completion of each Pre-Test, you will receive a score and instructive feedback on how you answered each question, and a direct link to the part of the chapter addressed in the question. Take the Pre-Test as often as you need to—a record of your progress for each attempt is kept for you to revisit and gauge your improvement.

MICROSOFT VERSUS AOL TIME WARNER: A STRATEGIC BATTLE

Learning to share is a lifelong process. It starts in the sandbox and continues through personal relationships and into career relationships. The problem is, strategic marketing planning involves finding ways not to share; instead, it seeks ways to capture as much of the market as possible. Two of today's biggest companies—Microsoft and AOL Time Warner—are locked in a fierce strategic battle to create loyal customers. They've even dragged their cases to court.

Just a few years ago, Microsoft and AOL were focused on different markets. Microsoft's domain was software. In fact, the company grew so powerful in its control of operating systems and other software that were installed on computers by PC makers that it was ruled a monopoly by a federal court, and it was forced to forge an antitrust settlement. AOL, on the other hand, virtually owned the Internet service provider (ISP) market when consumers were just discovering the power of the Internet. Despite highly publicized mistakes, including a widely publicized price drop that drew so many new customers to AOL that the provider couldn't handle them all, the company managed to dominate. But the lines between the two markets eventually became blurred as Microsoft made its entry into the ISP field with its MSN service; then AOL acquired Time Warner and all of its entertainment content.

Each company has tried different strategies for capturing customers' interest—and dollars—but more and more often, they have found themselves in the same arena duking it out with bare fists. When Microsoft launched its new Windows XP operating system, touting it as a boost to the computer industry (which has been flagging the last few years), AOL Time Warner made a deal with PC maker Compaq to appear as the preferred Internet service provider on its machines. Microsoft, despite its antitrust troubles, didn't like the deal and insisted that computer manufacturers include the MSN icon if they were offering AOL (or another service provider) as well. Then AOL Time Warner slapped Microsoft with another antitrust suit, claiming that Microsoft had undermined AOL's Netscape Navigator browser by using its Windows presence to get people onto its own Explorer browser. Since this was an important issue in the federal antitrust case, AOL Time Warner figured it had a powerful case; if nothing else, the company could win billions of dollars in damages.

The contest is basically between software (Microsoft) and content (AOL Time Warner). Microsoft's strategy is based on the strength of its Windows operating system—including the new XP—and its lock on loyal software developers. Microsoft is hoping that its new .Net technology, which allows PC software programs and Web sites to communicate with each other, will entice consumers to sign up for a number of one-click services. AOL Time Warner's strategy is based on its control over a huge amount of entertainment and informational content as well as the loyalty of its online subscribers, who want access to that content. AOL Time Warner already has 30 million online subscribers who are willing to try whatever new services the company has to offer, whether it is online music or interactive TV. So the company is focusing on television, Sony's Playstation, and other Internet-connected devices that provide entertainment. At the end of the race, predicts Mike Homer, a former Netscape executive, "AOL will win in the living room, and Microsoft will continue to march forward on the PC."

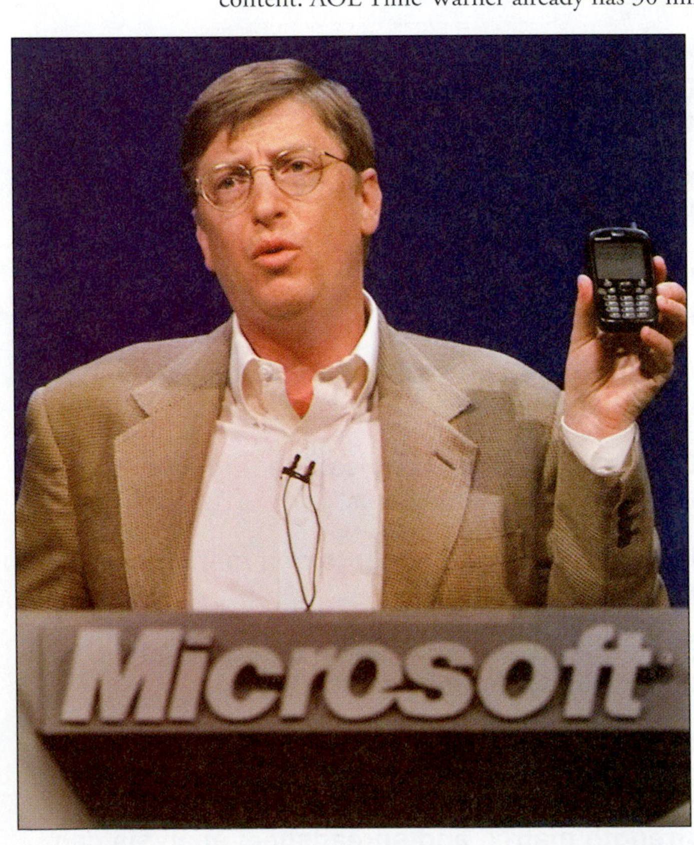

So why do the two companies keep taking shots at each other? "Neither will cede dominance in any market," observes John Corcoran, Internet analyst at CIBC World Markets. "They're saying: 'I'm keeping my fingers in all your pies, and you're keeping a finger in all mine.'" AOL Time Warner recently formed a strategic alliance with Bertelsman and EMI to offer MusicNet (music over the Internet), and Microsoft teamed up with Sony to offer PushPlay. In the rapidly changing tech sector to win is to win big—and to lose spells disaster. The Internet represents the biggest technological advance in decades; it has changed the way companies and consumers conduct business. Perhaps the battle can be summed up best by Neil MacDonald, vice president and research director at Gartner Group, a technology research firm. In his comments about the AOL Time Warner lawsuit against Microsoft over Netscape he says, "This is about future control of the Internet." Marc Rotenberg of the Electronic Privacy Information Center (EPIC) would agree. "They're two giants who want to rule the world." And neither one will give up.[1]

CHAPTER OVERVIEW

- Given the success of recent retro models, should we add a similar model to our line of cars?
- Our lines of detergent are not moving according to the marketing plans. Should we seek lower entry-level price points from our vendors?
- Recent marketing research shows we are not reaching our customer target—women aged 30 to 50 with household incomes over $60,000. Should we reconsider our advertising agency pick?

These are strategic issues that marketers face every day. The marketplace changes continually in response to changes in consumer tastes and expectations, technological developments, competitors' actions, economic trends, and political and legal events, as well as product innovations and pressures from channel members. Although the causes of these changes often lie outside a marketer's control, effective planning can anticipate many of these changes. In fact, effective planning often means the difference between success and failure, something that marketers at both Microsoft and AOL Time Warner understand well.

This chapter provides an important foundation for thinking about all aspects of marketing by demonstrating the necessity for effective planning and gathering reliable information. These activities provide a structure within which a firm can take advantage of its unique strengths. Marketing planning identifies the markets a company can best serve as well as the most appropriate mix of approaches to satisfy the customers in those markets. This chapter examines marketing planning. Later, Chapter 7 discusses marketing research, the way marketers use the information they gather to make decisions, and sales forecasting—all of which are based on planning.

Briefly Speaking

Someone's sitting in shade today because someone planted a tree a long time ago.

Warren E. Buffett (b. 1930) American investor

WHAT IS MARKETING PLANNING?

Everyone plans. We plan which courses we want to take, which movie we want to see, which outfit to wear to a party. We plan where we want to live, what career we want to pursue. Businesspeople engage in planning as well. **Planning** is the process of anticipating future events and conditions, and of determining the best way to achieve organizational objectives. Of course, before marketing planning can even begin, an organization must define its objectives. Planning is a continuous process that includes identifying objectives and then determining the actions through which a firm can attain these objectives. The planning process creates a blueprint for marketers, executives, production staff, and everyone else in the organization to follow for achieving organizational objectives. It also defines checkpoints so that people within the organization can compare actual performance with expectations to indicate whether current activities are moving the organization toward its objectives.

Marketing planning—implementing planning activities devoted to achieving marketing objectives—establishes the basis for any marketing strategy. Product lines, pricing decisions, selection of appropriate distribution channels, and decisions relating to promotional campaigns all depend on plans formulated within the marketing organization.

An important trend in marketing planning centers on relationship marketing. You will recall from Chapter 1 that this term refers to a firm's attempt to develop long-term, cost-effective links with individual customers and suppliers for mutual benefit. Good relationships with customers can arm a firm with vital strategic weapons. Many companies now include relationship-building goals and strategies in their plans. Nordstrom, the Seattle-based chain of fashion specialty retail stores illustrated in Figure 2.1, is legendary for its relationship marketing; in fact, the company has focused most of its marketing efforts in that direction. Sales staff routinely send thank-you notes to customers; they call customers when sought-after items arrive in the store; they answer the telephone within three rings; they lead customers to fitting rooms instead of just pointing them in the right direction. None of this activity takes place at random; it is all part of a plan to develop strong relationships with customers, and it works. Building relationships with consumers online requires planning, as well. On the company's Web site, keywords (words that customers have typed in to do a search) are analyzed to figure out what customers are looking for, in order to make the site easier for shoppers to navigate.[2]

FIGURE 2.1

Nordstrom's: Famous for Strong Customer Relationships

Relationship marketers frequently maintain databases to track customer preferences. These marketers may also manipulate spreadsheets, discussed later in the chapter, to answer what-if questions related to prices and marketing performance.

Strategic Planning versus Tactical Planning

Planning is often classified on the basis of its scope or breadth. Some extremely broad plans focus on long-range organizational objectives that will significantly affect the firm for a period of five or more years. Other, more targeted plans cover the objectives of individual business units over shorter periods of time. The "Marketing Hit" Interactive Example describes how Marriott used both strategic and tactical planning to recover from 9/11 losses.

<interactive>**learning goal**

CHAPTER OBJECTIVE #1: DISTINGUISH BETWEEN STRATEGIC PLANNING AND TACTICAL PLANNING.

<interactive>**example**

MARKETING HIT: HOW MARRIOTT RECOVERED FROM DISASTER

Strategic planning can be defined as the process of determining an organization's primary objectives and then adopting courses of action that will eventually achieve these objectives. This process includes, of course, allocation of necessary resources. The word *strategy* dates back to a Greek term meaning "the general's art." Strategic planning has a critical impact on a firm's destiny because it provides long-term direction for its decision makers.

Strategic planning is complemented by **tactical planning,** which guides the implementation of activities specified in the strategic plan. Unlike strategic plans, tactical plans typically address shorter-term actions that focus on current and near-future activities that a firm must complete to implement its larger strategies.

Mistakes in strategic decisions and in tactical planning are usually costly. Once-trendy Gap has been criticized for the past couple of years for some goofy styles—like flared capri pants—that shoppers aren't buying. Sales have dropped dramatically, but the company has continued with plans for expansion and long-term leases, making it difficult to cut costs. The company's long-term debt has mushroomed to $2 billion, damaging Gap's credit and stock ratings. The company's bankers and investors are not happy with the situation. "They'll have to give up something," says Gerald Hirschberg, an analyst at Standard & Poor's.[3]

PLANNING AT DIFFERENT ORGANIZATIONAL LEVELS

Planning is a major responsibility for every manager, so managers at all organizational levels devote portions of their workdays to planning. However, the amount of time spent on planning activities and the types of planning typically vary.

<interactive>**learning goal**

CHAPTER OBJECTIVE #2: EXPLAIN HOW MARKETING PLANS DIFFER AT VARIOUS LEVELS IN AN ORGANIZATION.

Top management—the board of directors, chief executive officers (CEOs), chief operating officers (COOs), and functional vice presidents, such as chief marketing officers—spend greater proportions of their time engaged in planning than do middle-level and supervisory-level managers. Also, top managers usually focus their planning activities on long-range strategic issues. In contrast, middle-level managers—such as advertising directors, regional sales managers, and marketing research managers—tend to focus on operational planning, which includes creating and implementing tactical plans for their own departments. Supervisors often engage in developing specific programs to meet goals in their areas of responsibility. Table 2.1 summarizes the types of planning undertaken at various organizational levels.

To be most effective, the planning process includes input from a wide range of sources—employees, suppliers, and customers. Monica Luechtefeld, head of Office Depot's online business, obtains information and feedback from a variety of people, in a variety of ways. She calls on customers and potential customers in person to learn what they might need or want. She communicates with purchasing managers, who are typically the people in companies who buy office equipment, supplies, and services. She studies customer-satisfaction surveys and e-mails. "I learn the most from the ones that challenge me," Luechtefeld comments. One thing she discovered from reading the surveys is that her customers care more about how easy the Office Depot Web site is to use than they do about cutting-edge technology. Based on this knowledge, she badgered Office Depot's tech staff to design an online network that even the most inexperienced customer could use.[4]

STEPS IN THE MARKETING PLANNING PROCESS

The marketing planning process begins at the corporate level with the development of objectives. It then moves to develop procedures for accomplishing those objectives. Figure 2.2 shows the basic steps in the process. First, a company must define its mission. It then determines its objectives, assesses its resources, and evaluates environmental risks and opportunities. Guided by this information, marketers then formulate a marketing strategy, implement the strategy through operating plans, and gather feedback to monitor and adapt strategies when necessary.

<interactive>**learning goal**

CHAPTER OBJECTIVE #3: **IDENTIFY THE STEPS IN THE MARKETING PLANNING PROCESS.**

Defining the Organization's Mission

The planning process begins with activities to define the firm's **mission,** the essential purpose that differentiates the company from others. The mission statement specifies the organization's overall goals and operational scope and provides general guidelines for future management actions. Adjustments in this statement reflect changing business environments and management philosophies.

Bass Pro Shops was founded in 1972 by tournament bass fisherman John L. Morris because he couldn't find a consistent source for the top-quality bass fishing gear he needed to pursue his sport. Since then, the company has been serving the more than 35 million U.S. anglers—nearly 70 percent of whom are men. The company sells everything for freshwater and saltwater fishing—from rods, reels, and flies to apparel. They also sell a complete line of hunting, camping, and biking equipment and casual clothing. The company's mission statement is as follows: "To be the leading merchant of outdoor recreational products, inspiring people to love, enjoy, and conserve the great outdoors."[5]

Bass Pro Shops' mission is more than selling fishing gear; it is to inspire people to enjoy outdoor recreational activities and to preserve the natural environment. To that end, the company has made major

TABLE 2.1

Planning at Different Management Levels

Management Level	Types of Planning Emphasized at This Level	Examples
Top Management		
Board of directors Chief executive officer (CEO) Chief operating officer (COO) Divisional vice presidents	Strategic planning	Organization-wide objectives; fundamental strategies; long-term plans; total budget
Middle Management		
General sales manager Marketing research manager Advertising director	Tactical planning	Quarterly and semiannual plans; divisional budgets; divisional policies and procedures
Supervisory Management		
District sales manager Supervisors in staff Marketing departments	Operational planning	Daily and weekly plans; unit budgets; departmental rules and procedures

FIGURE 2.2

The Marketing Planning Process

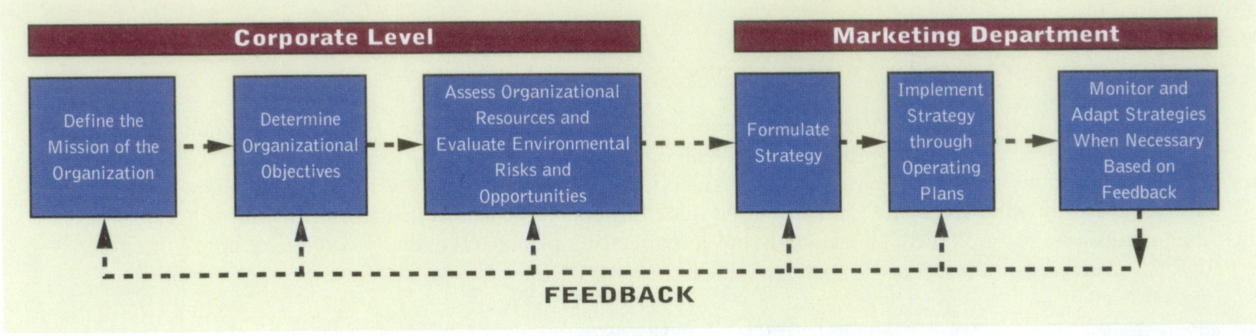

contributions to, and has been honored by, various wildlife conservation organizations and causes, including a $100,000 commitment to the National Fish and Wildlife Foundation a couple of years ago. In addition, the company's Outdoor World retail stores, located in states across America, try to offer visitors a true "outdoor environment" while they are shopping for products.

Determining Organizational Objectives

An organization lays out its basic objectives, or goals, in its mission statement. These objectives in turn guide development of supporting marketing objectives and plans. Soundly conceived objectives should state specific intentions (for example, generate a 12 percent increase in profits over last year, attain a 20 percent share of the market by 2008, or increase sales 15 percent over last year). In addition, these objectives should specify the time periods for specific achievements.

Assessing Organizational Resources and Evaluating Environmental Risks and Opportunities

The third step of the marketing planning process involves a back-and-forth assessment of an organization's strengths, weaknesses, and available opportunities. Organizational resources include the capabilities of the firm's production, marketing, finance, technology, and employees. An organization's planners pinpoint its strengths and weaknesses. Strengths help them to set objectives, develop plans for meeting those objectives, and take advantage of marketing opportunities. Malden Mills, maker of Polarfleece and Polartec fabrics, can identify several strengths: 200 percent growth in the past decade; customers in more than 50 countries; U.S. factory operations; high visibility, with appearances in *People,* on *Dateline,* and in the Lands' End catalog; and customer *and* employee retention above 95 percent. Its weaknesses include the high cost of manufacturing in the U.S.; a devastating factory fire; and an increase in competition.[6]

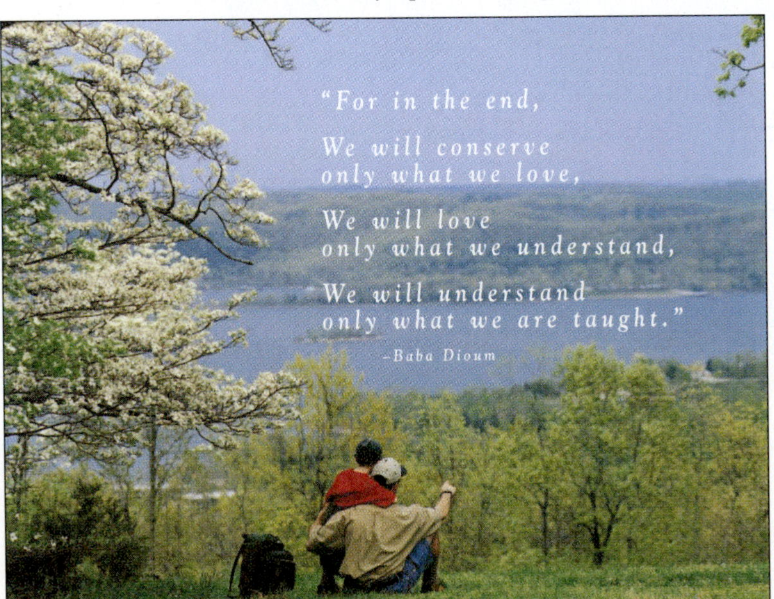

This Bass Pro Shops ad promotes not only outdoor recreation but also environmental conservation.

Chapter 3 will discuss environmental factors that affect marketing opportunities. Environmental effects can emerge both from within the organization and from the external environment. For example, the World Wide Web has transformed the way people communicate and do business.

SWOT Analysis An important strategic planning tool, the **SWOT analysis,** helps planners to compare internal organizational strengths and weaknesses with external opportunities and threats. (SWOT is an acronym for strengths and weaknesses, opportunities, and threats.) This form of analysis provides managers with a critical view of the organization's internal and external environments and helps them to evaluate the firm's fulfillment of its basic mission.

<interactive>**learning goal**

CHAPTER OBJECTIVE #4: DESCRIBE THE CONCEPT OF SWOT ANALYSIS AND ITS MAJOR ELEMENTS.

A company's strengths reflect its *core competencies*—what it does well. Core competencies are capabilities that customers value and competitors find difficult to duplicate.[7] As Figure 2.3 shows, matching an internal strength with an external opportunity produces for the organization a situation known as leverage. Marketers face a problem when environmental threats attack their organization's weaknesses. Planners anticipate constraints when internal weaknesses or limitations prevent their organization from taking advantage of opportunities. These internal weaknesses can create vulnerabilities for a company—environmental threats to its organizational strength.

The Strategic Window Professor Derek Abell has suggested the term **strategic window** to define the limited periods during which the key requirements of a market and the particular competencies of a firm best fit together.[8] The view through a strategic window shows planners a way to relate potential opportunities to company capabilities. Such a view requires a thorough analysis of (1) current and projected external environmental conditions, (2) current and projected internal company capabilities, and (3) how, whether, and when the firm can feasibly reconcile environmental conditions and company capabilities by implementing one or more marketing strategies.

Apple Computer took advantage of a strategic window when it introduced its new iMac, which contains its new operating system, the Mac OS X. The new computer appears in the ad in Figure 2.4, which shows a highly streamlined machine that allows users to perform a number of cutting- edge tasks, including getting the most out of their digital cameras. When a digital camera is plugged into iMac's USB port, software called iPhoto automatically imports the photos, catalogs them, stores them, and displays them on the computer screen. Apple planners noted that while people were buying digital cameras, they were having trouble storing, sending, and displaying the photos. So they leapt through the strategic window with a software product—iPhoto—linked to the capabilities of its new hardware product—the iMac.

Polartec and Polarfleece: Featured in Catalogs Like Lands' End

Formulating a Marketing Strategy

Opportunity analysis culminates in the formulation of marketing objectives designed to achieve overall organizational objectives and to help planners develop a marketing plan. The marketing plan revolves around a resource-efficient, flexible, and adaptable marketing strategy.

A marketing strategy is an overall, companywide program for selecting a particular target market and then satisfying consumers in that market through a careful balance of the elements of the marketing mix—product, price, distribution, and promotion—each of which is a subset of the overall marketing strategy.

Implementing a Strategy through Marketing Plans

In the two final steps of the marketing-planning process, marketers use operating plans to put the marketing strategy into action; then they monitor performance to ensure that objectives are being achieved. Sometimes strategies need to be modified if the product's or company's actual performance is not in line with expected results.

<interactive>**learning goal**

CHAPTER OBJECTIVE #5: DISCUSS HOW A STRATEGY CAN BE IMPLEMENTED THROUGH MARKETING PLANS.

Consider what happened at Cisco Systems. Just a couple of years ago, the company was riding high on the wave of a surging economy. Deregulation of the U.S. telecommunications industry, along with a

FIGURE 2.3

SWOT Analysis

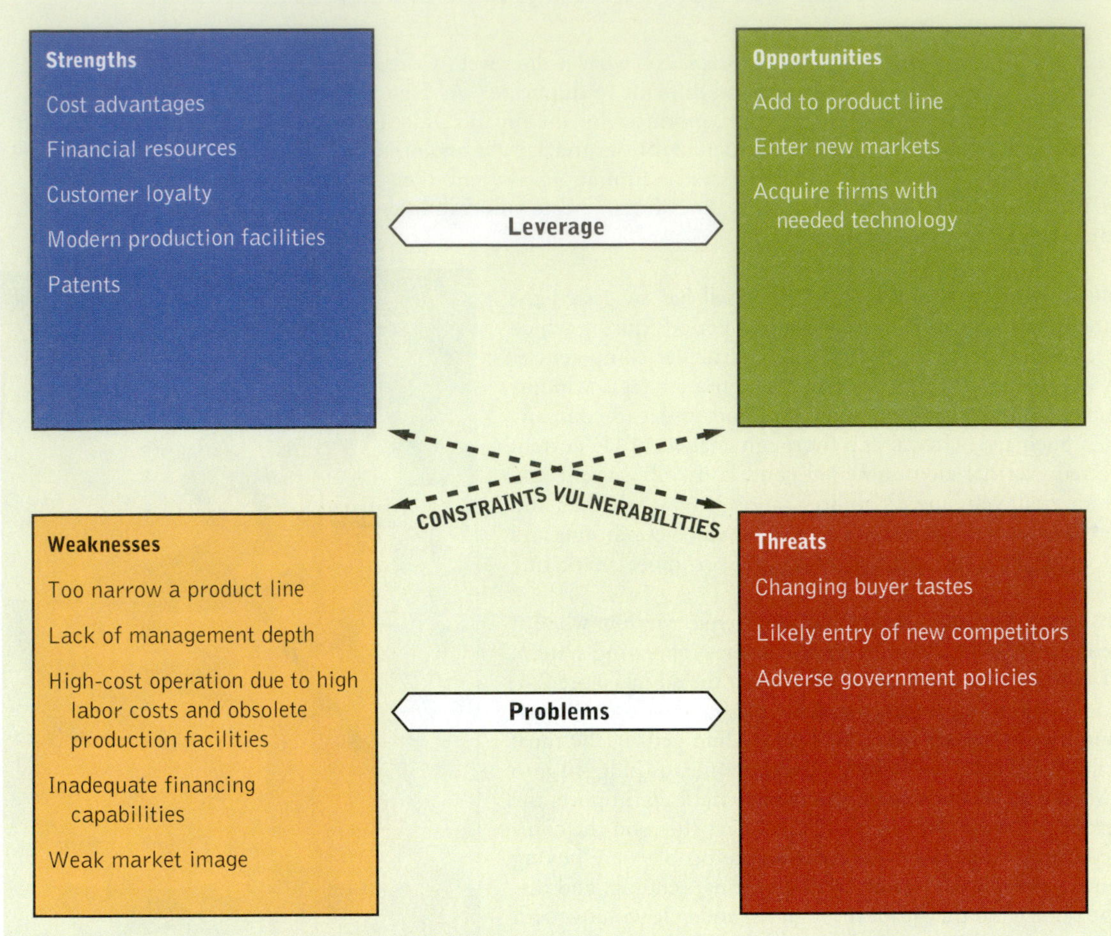

healthy stock market and the boom of the Internet, propelled Cisco and hundreds of other companies into a whole new industry and economy. Cisco's core business is selling software and hardware used in powering Internet networks. But Cisco's bold strategy of pursuing new service providers as customers turned out to be the wrong move. As each of these new companies began to stumble and fall, Cisco suffered a loss. By now, not only have these companies slowed their spending on products that Cisco provides, but many have also simply gone under. Meanwhile, Cisco ignored or alienated some of the larger, "old economy" phone companies. In addition, planners were overly optimistic about the demand for Cisco's equipment, and the company was stuck with inventory it couldn't sell. Today, Cisco is focusing its attention on the more established telecommunications companies and is dedicating more sales and technical support staff to give better service to a smaller number of customers. The strategy now is to focus on helping existing phone companies develop value-added services that their own corporate customers desire. Senior Vice President William Nuti says, "We're going to get back to basics in terms of listening to our customers and responding to what their needs are."[9]

As Cisco's experience shows, the overall strategic marketing plan serves as the basis for a series of operating plans necessary to move the organization toward accomplishing its objectives. Marketing planning affects activities discussed throughout this text, including analysis and selection of a target market and development of a marketing mix designed to satisfy that market.

ELEMENTS OF A MARKETING STRATEGY

Although the product at the center of a marketing campaign may consist of a tangible good or an intangible service, cause, event, person, place, or organization, success in the marketplace always depends on an effective marketing strategy. The basic elements of a marketing strategy consist of (1) the target market and (2) the marketing mix variables of product, distribution, promotion, and price that combine to satisfy the needs of the target market. The outer circle in Figure 2.5 lists environmental characteristics that provide the framework within which marketing strategies are planned.

<interactive>**learning goal**

CHAPTER OBJECTIVE #6: IDENTIFY THE BASIC ELEMENTS OF A MARKETING STRATEGY.

The Target Market

A customer-driven organization begins its overall strategy with a detailed description of its *target market:* the group of people toward whom the firm decides to direct its marketing efforts, and ultimately its goods and services. For instance, Kohl's serves a target market consisting of consumers purchasing for themselves and their families. Other companies, such as Boeing, market most of their products to business buyers like American Airlines and government purchasers. Still other firms provide goods and services to retail and wholesale buyers. In every instance, however, marketers should pinpoint their target markets as specifically as possible. Although the concept of actually dividing markets into segments is discussed in more detail in Chapter 8, it's important to understand the idea of targeting a market from the outset. Consider the following examples:

- Just My Size targets plus-size women (who account for over half of U.S. women) by designing casual wear, lingerie, hosiery, and jeans in sizes 16 and up.
- Build-a-Bear Workshop is a unique retailer in that it provides a setting for people of all ages to make their own stuffed bears. Founder Maxine Clark jokingly says her target market is aged 3 to 103.[10]
- The target market for Overseas Adventure Travel is well-educated, healthy individuals with household incomes over $50,000 who want a high-adventure vacation experience. When the Cambridge, Massachusetts–based travel company started 20 years ago, its target market was people in their twenties and thirties; today, OAT focuses on older customers who are retired, have the time and money to travel, and want adventure. The company now offers shorter trips with more amenities.

Diversity plays an ever-increasing role in targeting markets. According to the U.S. Census Bureau, the rapidly growing Hispanic population in the U.S. is now nearly even with African Americans. The census reports about 35 million Hispanics in America, an increase of 58 percent in one decade; the African American population is roughly the same. "It's a little surprising," notes Hans Johnson, demographer with the Public Policy Institute of California in San Francisco. "But still, we've known the trends for some time. We know eventually Hispanics will become the largest minority group in the United States."[11] With this phenomenal growth, marketers would be wise to pay attention to these and other markets—including women, seniors, and children of baby boomers—as they develop goods and services to offer to consumers. Food manufacturers like General Mills and Bestfoods have enlisted the help of consultants to help them understand and develop products for the Hispanic market. Under their advice, the division that produces General Mills's Trix cereal sponsored a 17-city tour of an all-Hispanic circus, Trix Circo Mundial. Similarly, Bestfoods's grocery division took several of its brands that were already popular in the Hispanic market (including Mazola and Best Foods Mayonnaise) to Fiesta Broadway, an annual festival in Los Angeles.[12]

FIGURE 2.4

Apple Computer's New iMac

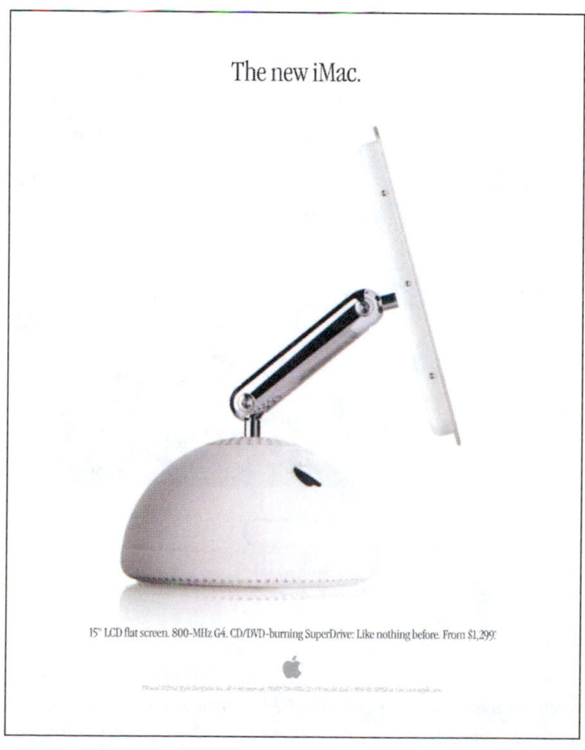

The new iMac.
15" LCD flat screen. 800-MHz G4. CD/DVD-burning SuperDrive: Like nothing before. From $1,299.

Marketing Mix Variables

After marketers select a target market, they direct their company's activities toward profitably satisfying that segment. Although they must manipulate thousands of variables to reach this goal, marketing decision making can be divided into four strategies: product, pricing, distribution, and promotion strategies. The total package forms the **marketing mix**—the blending of the four strategic elements to fit the needs and preferences of a specific target market. While the fourfold classification is useful to study and analyze, remember that the marketing mix can—and should—be an ever-changing combination of variables to achieve success.

Figure 2.5 illustrates the focus of the marketing mix variables on the central choice of the target market. In addition, decisions about

FIGURE 2.5

Elements of a Marketing Strategy and Its Environmental Framework

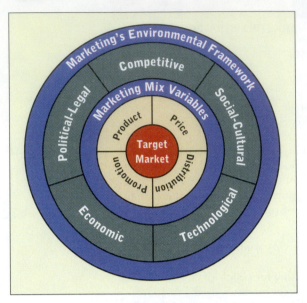

Marketing's Environmental Framework
Competitive
Social-Cultural
Technological
Economic
Political-Legal
Marketing Mix Variables
Product
Price
Distribution
Promotion
Target Market

product, price, distribution, and promotion are affected by the environmental factors in the outer circle of the figure. The environmental variables may play a major role in the success of a marketing program, and marketers must consider their probable effects.

Product Strategy In marketing, the word *product* means more than a good, service, or idea. Product is a broad concept that also encompasses the satisfaction of all consumer needs in relation to a good, service, or idea. So **product strategy** involves more than just deciding what goods or services the firm should offer to a group of consumers. It also includes making decisions about customer service, package design, brand names, trademarks, patents, warranties, the life cycle of a product, positioning the product in the marketplace, and new product development. Figure 2.6 illustrates some of these elements. The ad for Lean Cuisine emphasizes Stouffer's ability to provide high quality, healthful food fast, as a way for the consumer to "do something good for yourself." The product is aimed at the busy person who wants to eat well but doesn't have time to cook. The ad even provides a Web address for consumers to learn more about Stouffer's Lean Cuisine foods. Lean Cuisine is a well-known, trademarked brand, and the packaging includes a photograph of a tasty-looking meal.

The growing number of female business travelers has prompted the travel industry to modify its offerings by adding a number of services designed to increase satisfaction among women hotel guests. Based on suggestions by Wyndham Hotels & Resorts' Advisory Board of Women Business Travelers, the chain added a number of features in its product strategy:

- special amenities such as loofah mitts and skirt hangers in hotel rooms
- networking tables set aside in hotel restaurants for solo travelers who prefer to eat with others
- a warning call five minutes before room-service delivery to alert guests before a meal is delivered
- jogging partners and chilled bottled water, fresh fruit, and plush towels upon return from a run.

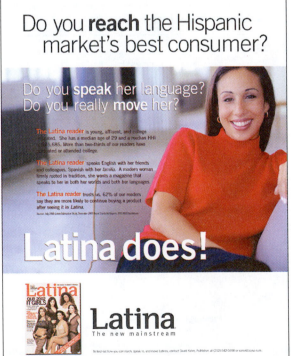

Demographers predict that Hispanics will soon be the largest minority group in the U.S. A growing number of marketers use magazines such as Latina *to reach this audience.*

This strategy lets Wyndham offer improved customer satisfaction for this growing market. As recently as 1970, women accounted for only 1 percent of all business travelers; today the number has grown to 50 percent.[13]

Some companies adopt the *first-mover strategy*, which is exactly that—being the first company to offer a product in a market. This strategy hopes to link that company's goods or services permanently in customers' minds when they consider what to buy. The strategy can work if you are Kimberly-Clark and you own the trademark to Kleenex, or if you happen to be Microsoft and manage to get your operating system onto just about every personal computer. But being the first mover into a market can have its pitfalls. If a company invests too much money too fast in a product for a new market, it can end up with a flop, which is what happened to Apple Computer with its pioneering handheld computer, Newton. Yes, there was a new market for handheld computers, but Apple failed to consider a variety of factors and set too-high performance goals for the Newton, too soon.[14]

Distribution Strategy Marketers develop **distribution strategies** to ensure that consumers find their products in the proper quantities at the right times and places. Distribution decisions involve modes of transportation, warehousing, inventory control, order processing, and selection of marketing channels. Marketing channels are made up of institutions such as retailers and wholesalers—all those involved in a product's movement from producer to final consumer.

Technology is opening new channels of distribution in many industries. For example, software, a product made of digital data files, is ideally suited to electronic distribution. Major players like Microsoft and IBM already distribute their programs and upgrades directly over the Internet. Electronic commerce holds great promise for providing quick response to purchasers while markedly reducing prices by slashing packaging and shipping costs, cutting out many intermediaries, and allowing online shoppers to look for the best prices from both domestic and international suppliers.

Distribution is the perfect place for many companies to form alliances. Sony's music division formed an agreement with Universal Music Group to form Duet, an online music service that will make thousands of songs available to consumers over the Internet—without the royalty issues confronted by Napster. Georgia-Pacific Group, best known for manufacturing paper goods, formed an alliance with Amazon.com to exclusively provide the corrugated boxes for shipping books.[15]

Promotional Strategy **Promotion** is the communication link between sellers and buyers. Organizations use varied ways to send messages about their goods, services, and ideas. They may communicate messages directly through salespeople or indirectly through advertisements and promotions. Figure 2.7 shows a new promotion for Oreo cookies that have a new center that turns blue when dunked in milk. Sometimes firms face an ethical decision about whether to use the image of a spokesperson who has passed away, as discussed in the "Solving an Ethical Controversy" Interactive Example.

RIGHT/WRONG: SOLVING AN ETHICAL CONTROVERSY—AFTER A SPOKESPERSON'S DEATH, SHOULD A PROMOTIONAL STRATEGY CHANGE?

In developing a promotional strategy, marketers blend the various elements of promotion to communicate most effectively with their target market. Many companies use an approach called *integrated marketing communications (IMC)* to coordinate all promotional activities so that the consumer receives a unified and consistent message. Consumers might receive newsletters, e-mail updates, discount coupons, catalogs, invitations to company-sponsored events, and any number of other types of marketing communications about a product.

Pricing Strategy One of the most difficult areas of marketing decision making, **pricing strategy,** deals with the methods of setting profitable and justifiable prices. It is closely regulated and subject to considerable public scrutiny.

One of the many factors that influence a marketer's pricing strategy is competition. The computer industry has become all too familiar with price cuts by both current competitors and new market entrants. After years of steady growth, the market has become saturated with low-cost computers, driving down profit margins even farther. Big PC makers such as Dell and IBM are trying to compensate by focusing more on business customers. Meanwhile, start-ups like eMachines are giving the large competitors a run for their money. EMachines prices its computers at least $100 lower than competing models—from $399 to $699 after a $75 rebate. Customers have responded, placing the company at the number 3 spot at retail, right behind Hewlett-Packard and Compaq.[16]

While price wars are well-known in industries such as air travel and automobile manufacturing, price fixing is another type of practice altogether. It is both illegal and unethical. For example, A. Alfred Taubman, the former head of the elite Sotheby's auction house, was convicted of price fixing—by meeting secretly with Sir Anthony Tennant, the former chairman of Christie's auction house, to set identical rates for sellers' commissions, which would effectively cut out fair pricing competition. After the guilty verdict was announced, jury foreman Mike D'Angelo said, "You've got to have competition. Competition is what makes the world go around."[17]

FIGURE 2.6

Stouffer's Lean Cuisine: Low-Fat, Easy-to-Prepare Meals in Attractive Packaging

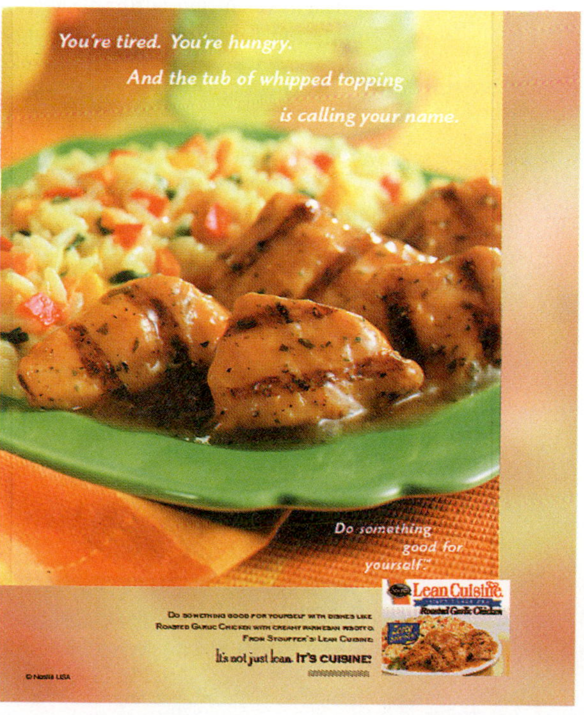

The Marketing Environment

Marketers do not make decisions about target markets and marketing mix variables in a vacuum. They must take into account the dynamic nature of the five dimensions of the marketing environment

FIGURE 2.7

Combining Promotions in One Advertisement

shown back in Figure 2.5: competitive, political-legal, economic, technological, and social-cultural factors. Environmental concerns have led to new regulations concerning air and water pollution. Automobile engineers, for instance, have turned public concerns and legal issues into opportunities by developing hybrid cars. These new models are fueled by dual energy: a gasoline engine and an electric motor. Toyota was the first to enter the market with its Prius, which depends primarily on the electric motor but includes a backup gasoline engine. The Prius currently sells in Japan for about $19,000. Changes in the legal environment regarding automobile emissions alerted automobile designers to make these changes. By accommodating future needs of consumers and meeting the more stringent legal requirements, they created a new market segment. It did not take long for competitors to follow Toyota's lead. Honda's new VV model, a hybrid version of the Civic, runs primarily on its gasoline engine with the electric motor as its secondary energy source. Honda plans to hit the showrooms with a vehicle that offers a lower price and better gas mileage. Nissan and Fuji Heavy Industries also have models on the drawing boards for launches scheduled within the next two years. European and U.S. automakers, however, have not jumped at the chance to enter the race with their version of a hybrid car. Ford and DaimlerChrysler plan to have their versions ready by 2005.[18] However, U.S. automakers may have missed the boat when it comes to maintaining the competitive advantage against foreign rivals in the manufacture of popular trucks and SUVs, as described in the "Marketing Miss" Interactive Example.

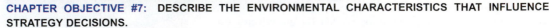

<interactive>**learning goal**

CHAPTER OBJECTIVE #7: DESCRIBE THE ENVIRONMENTAL CHARACTERISTICS THAT INFLUENCE STRATEGY DECISIONS.

<interactive>**example**

MARKETING MISS: WHAT'S AHEAD FOR THE AMERICAN SUV?

Businesses are increasingly looking to foreign shores for new growth markets. General Mills has been manufacturing everything from cereal to snack foods for decades. But when the company wanted to expand overseas, instead of starting from scratch it decided to partner with Nestlé in a venture called Cereal Partners Worldwide. General Mills was the cereal expert and Nestlé already had a presence in Europe. So far, the strategy has been successful. Since its formation, CPW has expanded its operations into 75 different markets and captured 21 percent of the international cold cereal business.[19]

Technology has changed the marketing environment as well, partly with the advent of the Internet. Throughout this text, you will encounter examples of the way the Internet and other technological developments are continuously altering the way firms do business. And as technology forces these changes, other aspects of the environment must respond. Naturally, there are legal disputes over who owns which innovations. Amazon.com recently won a court battle barring its rival Barnes & Noble.com from using Amazon's patented "one-click" checkout system, which allows shoppers to place their orders with a single click of the mouse instead of re-keying in billing information when they are ready to complete a sale.

Interestingly, technology moves much more quickly than patenting procedures, which can leave some businesses behind. Amazon founder and chief executive Jeff Bezos has suggested that software and Internet patents should have a shorter life span than other patents—perhaps because of the rapid changes in technology—and that they should be open to public comment before being issued. "I now believe it's possible that the current rules governing business methods and software patents could end up harming all of us," says Bezos.[20]

Two other important characteristics in the contemporary marketing environment include cultural diversity and ethical concerns. Every chapter in this book contains detailed examples that explore the impact of these factors, like the ones in the section in this chapter on targeting markets. The "Solving an Ethical Controversy" Interactive Examples in each chapter discuss in detail one ethical issue.

The marketing environment is important because it provides a framework for all marketing activity. Marketers consider the environmental dimensions when they develop strategies for segmenting and targeting their markets, and when they study consumer and organizational buying behavior.

Briefly Speaking

America is not like a blanket—one piece of unbroken cloth, the same color, the same texture, the same size. America is more like a quilt—many pieces, many colors, many sizes, all woven and held together by a common thread.

Rev. Jesse Jackson (b. 1941)
American civil rights leader

TOOLS FOR MARKETING PLANNING

As growing numbers of companies have discovered the benefits of effective marketing planning, they have developed planning tools to assist in this important function. This section discusses four specific tools: the strategic business unit concept, the market share/market growth matrix, the market attractiveness/business strength matrix, and spreadsheet analysis.

<interactive>**learning goal**

CHAPTER OBJECTIVE #8: EXPLAIN HOW THE STRATEGIC BUSINESS UNIT CONCEPT, THE MARKET SHARE/MARKET GROWTH MATRIX, THE MARKET ATTRACTIVENESS/BUSINESS STRENGTH MATRIX, AND SPREADSHEET ANALYSIS CAN BE USED IN MARKETING PLANNING.

Strategic Business Units (SBUs)

Although a relatively small company may offer only a few items to its customers, a larger organization frequently produces and markets numerous offerings to widely diverse markets. Top managers at these larger firms need some method for spotting promising product lines that warrant investments of additional resources, as well as those lines that they should weed out from the firm's product portfolio. This is where the concept of an SBU comes in.

Strategic business units (SBUs) are key business units within diversified firms. Each SBU has its own managers, resources, objectives, and competitors. A division, product line, or single product may define the boundaries of an SBU. Each SBU pursues its own distinct mission, and each develops its own plans independently of other units in the organization.

Strategic business units focus the attention of company managers so that they can respond effectively to changing consumer demand within limited markets. Companies redefine their SBUs as market conditions dictate. An example of this redefinition is Maine-based outfitter L.L. Bean, a longtime family-run enterprise. In fact, its current president, Leon Gorman, is a grandson of L.L. himself and has run the company since 1967. To counter recent sagging sales, Gorman reorganized the company's hierarchical management structure to create SBUs that focus on specific merchandise areas, such as men's and women's clothing, hunting and fishing product lines, travel clothing and accessories, and home furnishings. The catalog shown in Figure 2.8 features the SBU of women's outdoor and fitness clothing.[21]

FIGURE 2.8

Women's Outdoor & Fitness: An SBU of L. L. Bean

<interactive>**exercise**

'NET EX: STRATEGIC BUSINESS UNITS

Market Share/Market Growth Matrix

To evaluate their organization's strategic business units, marketers need some type of portfolio performance framework. A widely used framework was developed by the Boston Consulting Group. This **market share/market growth matrix** places SBUs in a four-quadrant chart that plots market share—the percentage of a market that a firm controls—against market growth potential. The position of an SBU along the horizontal axis indicates its market share relative to those of competitors in the industry. Its position along the vertical axis indicates the annual growth rate of the market. After plotting all of a firm's business units, planners divide them according to the matrix's four quadrants. Figure 2.9 illustrates this matrix by labeling the four quadrants cash cows, stars, dogs, and question marks. Firms in each quadrant require a unique marketing strategy.

Stars represent units with high market shares in high-growth markets. These products or businesses are high-growth market leaders. Although they generate considerable income, they need inflows of even more cash to finance further growth. Microsoft's Windows operating system requires ongoing expenditures on research and development to stay current, but the outlay pays off by maintaining the company's dominant position in the global personal computer market. It is estimated that Microsoft spent $500 million in marketing and launch costs alone to present its new Windows XP to the world.[22]

Cash cows command high market shares in low-growth markets. Marketers for such an SBU want to maintain this status for as long as possible. The business produces strong cash flows, but instead of investing heavily in the unit's own promotions and production capacity, the firm can use this cash to finance the growth of other SBUs with higher growth potentials.

FIGURE 2.9

Market Share/Market Growth Matrix

		Relative Market Share: High	Relative Market Share: Low
Industry Growth Rate	High	**Stars** Generate considerable income **Strategy:** Invest more funds for future growth	**Question Marks** Have potential to become stars or cash cows **Strategy:** Either invest more funds for growth or consider disinvesting
	Low	**Cash Cows** Generate strong cash flow **Strategy:** Milk profits to finance growth of stars and question marks	**Dogs** Generate little profits **Strategy:** Consider withdrawing

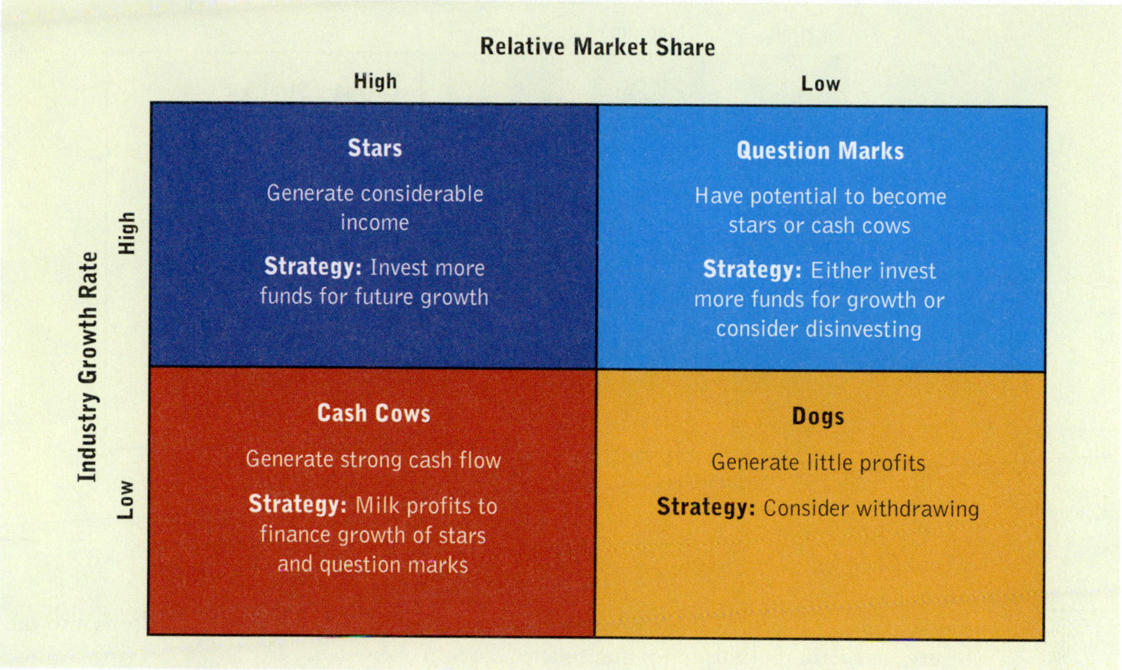

Question marks achieve low market shares in high-growth markets. Marketers must decide whether to continue supporting these products or businesses since question marks typically require considerably more cash than they generate. If a question mark cannot become a star, the firm should pull out of the market and target other markets with greater potential. Early Toyota and Honda minivans actually failed because they were too small for Americans.[23] With design adjustments, they became the staple of the average American family.

Dogs manage only low market shares in low-growth markets. SBUs in this category promise poor future prospects, and marketers should withdraw from these businesses or product lines as quickly as possible. For example, after Stroh's beer sales had languished for several years, managers finally decided to sell the company to Miller and Pabst.[24]

Market Attractiveness/Business Strength Matrix

Another model that can aid marketing planning is the **market attractiveness/business strength matrix,** a portfolio analysis technique that rates SBUs according to the attractiveness of their markets and their organizational strengths, as illustrated in Figure 2.10. Market attractiveness criteria include market share, growth, size, and stability; potential profitability; extent of government regulation; potential environmental and social impacts; and competitive conditions.[25] Managers must also take into account the organization's specific strengths and areas of competence, including its financial resources, image, relative cost advantages, customer base, and technological capabilities, along with the skills of its personnel.

Based on these criteria, managers create composite evaluations of SBUs. The most promising units in the upper-left area of the matrix offer strong business positions in attractive markets. These initiatives should receive the most company support. Those in the lower-right corner, on the other hand, offer little potential since they hold weak business positions in unattractive markets. Managers may choose to reduce funding for these operations or discontinue them altogether. In between, other SBUs rank from low to medium on market attractiveness and business strength. Decisions about allocating resources to these borderline SBUs depend on the strengths and weaknesses of the firm's entire business portfolio.

Planners apply this matrix when they are analyzing both their company's core competencies and their industry's environments. Using a matrix like this can help them direct investments to more profitable areas.

Evaluating the Matrix Approach to Planning The market share/market growth matrix emphasizes the importance of creating market offerings that will help a company gain a competitive advantage. It also acknowledges changes in successful SBUs as they move through their life cycles. A successful product or

FIGURE 2.10

Market Attractiveness/Business Strength Matrix

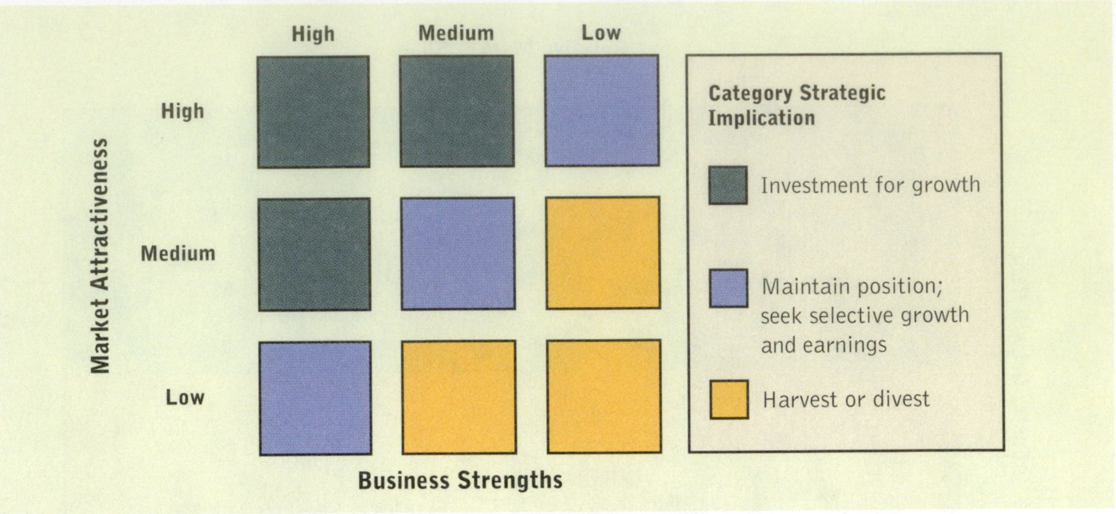

> **Briefly Speaking**
>
> Success is simply a matter of luck. Ask any failure.
>
> *Earl Wilson (1907–1987) American newspaper columnist*

business typically begins as a question mark, then becomes a star, and eventually drops into the cash-cow category, generating surplus funds that finance the firm's new stars.

The market attractiveness/business strength matrix is a useful tool for identifying SBUs with the greatest and least potential. It can also help managers identify a firm's need for new sources of growth while indicating its most and least attractive markets.

Spreadsheet Analysis

Spreadsheet analysis lays out a rigid grid of columns and rows that organize numerical information in a standardized, easily understandable format. It helps planners to answer what-if questions. Electronic spreadsheets, such as the popular Microsoft Excel, are the computerized equivalent of an accountant's hand-prepared worksheet.

Spreadsheet analysis helps planners anticipate marketing performance given specified sets of circumstances. For example, a spreadsheet might project the outcomes of different pricing decisions for a new product, as shown in Table 2.2.

In this example, the item will be sold for $10 per unit and can be produced for $5 in variable costs. The total fixed costs of $310,000 include $100,000 for manufacturing-overhead outlays, such as salaries, general office expenses, rent, utilities, and interest charges; $120,000 for marketing expenditures; and $90,000 for research and development to design the product. The spreadsheet calculation, using the basic model on line 1, reveals that the product would have to achieve sales of 62,000 units to break even.

But what if someone convinces other members of the marketing team to increase marketing expenditures to $230,000? In line 2 of Table 2.2 the $120,000 marketing expenditure changes to $230,000, and the newly calculated break-even point is 84,000 units. As soon as an amount in one or more cells changes, the software automatically recalculates all affected amounts.

Line 3 of Table 2.2 demonstrates the impact of a reduction in variable costs to $4 (perhaps the result of switching to lower-cost materials) coupled with a $1 reduction in the product's selling price. The new break-even point is 62,000 units.

This figure demonstrates the ease with which a marketing manager can use a computer spreadsheet program to determine the potential results of alternative decisions. More complex spreadsheets may include 50 or more columns of data and formulas but can complete new calculations as quickly as the manager changes the variables.

STRATEGIC IMPLICATIONS OF MARKETING IN THE 21ST CENTURY

Never before has planning been as important to marketers as the 21st century speeds ahead with technological advances. Marketers need to plan carefully, accurately, and quickly if their companies are going to gain a competitive advantage in today's global marketplace. They need to define their organization's mission and understand the different methods for formulating a successful marketing strategy. They must consider a changing, diverse population and the boundaryless business environment created by the Internet.

TABLE 2.2

How Spreadsheet Analysis Works

Fixed Costs				Per-Unit Variable Cost	Sales Price	Break-Even Point
Manufacturing	Marketing	R & D	Total			
$100,000	$120,000	$90,000	$310,000	$5	$10	62,000
$100,000	$230,000	$90,000	$420,000	$5	$10	84,000
$100,000	$120,000	$90,000	$310,000	$4	$ 9	62,000

They must be able to evaluate when it's best to be first to get into a market, and when it's best to wait. They need to recognize when they've got a star and when they've got a dog; when to hang on and when to let go. As daunting as this seems, planning can reduce the risk and worry of bringing new goods and services to the marketplace.

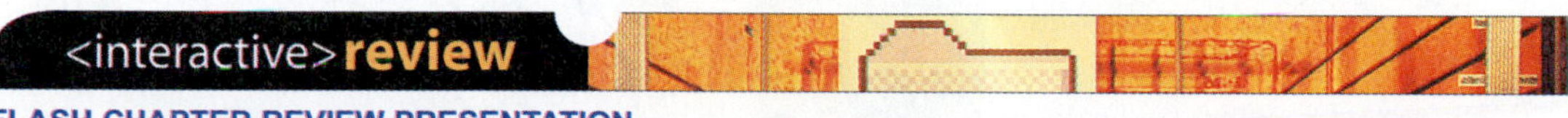

FLASH CHAPTER REVIEW PRESENTATION

CARIBOU COFFEE BREWS UP A FINE CUP OF STRATEGY

endofchaptermaterial

- **Summary of Chapter Objectives**
- **Chapter Outline**
- **Key Terms**
- **Review Questions**
- **Projects and Teamwork Exercises**
- **'netWork**
- **Crossword Puzzles**
- **Case 2.1: Every Company Needs a Disaster Plan**

Take the Post-Test to assess your overall understanding of the key ideas in this chapter. The Post-Test provides a comprehensive selection of exam-style questions addressing the main topics and concepts of the chapter. At the completion of each Post-Test, you will receive a score and instructive feedback on how you answered each question, and a direct link to the part of the chapter addressed in the question. Take the Post-Test as often as you need to—a record of your progress for each attempt is kept for you to revisit and gauge your improvement. And each Post-Test is randomly generated, so every attempt is new.

Post-Test

CHAPTER 3

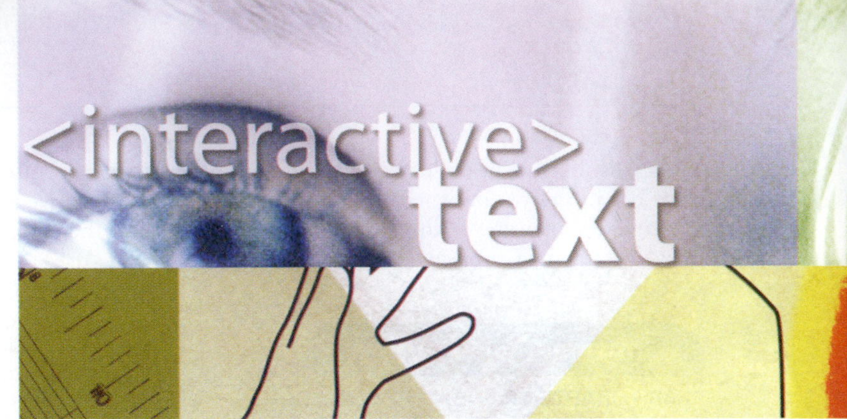

The Marketing Environment, Ethics, and Social Responsibility

Chapter Objectives

1. Identify the five components of the marketing environment.
2. Explain the types of competition marketers face and the steps necessary for developing a competitive strategy.
3. Describe how government and other groups regulate marketing activities and how marketers can influence the political-legal environment.
4. Outline the economic factors that affect marketing decisions and consumer buying power.
5. Discuss the impact of the technological environment on a firm's marketing activities.
6. Explain how the social-cultural environment influences marketing.
7. Describe the role of marketing in society and identify the two major social issues in marketing.
8. Identify the four levels of the social responsibility pyramid.

Take the Pre-Test to assess your initial knowledge of the key ideas in this chapter. The Pre-Test provides exam-style questions addressing the main topics and concepts of the chapter. At the completion of each Pre-Test, you will receive a score and instructive feedback on how you answered each question, and a direct link to the part of the chapter addressed in the question. Take the Pre-Test as often as you need to—a record of your progress for each attempt is kept for you to revisit and gauge your improvement.

TERRORISM LANDS A BODY BLOW TO THE AIRLINE INDUSTRY

Even before the terrorist attacks of September 11, 2001, the airline industry was headed for trouble. During a five-year period of giddy prosperity that ended with the dawn of the 21st century, profits had soared above $23 billion. Yet as the global economy slid into recession during the first years of the new century, the airlines were caught short. Despite government attempts to boost consumer spending through tax cuts and multiple interest rate reductions, by the summer of 2001 the airlines reported the lowest performance levels in a decade. By September, they had lost $2.5 billion. Worst of all, business travel was down by almost a third—corporations sought to ride out the slowdown by trimming their own expenses. Extremely tight operating margins, heavy debt loads, powerful unions, and terrible labor relations combined to make the major airlines extremely vulnerable if the recession should deepen. They had virtually no defenses against an all-out emergency.

Then, out of crystal-clear skies over Manhattan, Washington, D.C., and western Pennsylvania, a crisis of unprecedented gravity hit. Commercial aircraft slammed into the World Trade Towers, the Pentagon, and into the earth in rural Pennsylvania, sending the nation—and the economy—reeling. Air traffic halted for four days, planes sat idle, and stranded passengers made their way home by bus, train, or rental car.

Within days, major carriers, including United Airlines, American Airlines, Delta, Continental, and US Airways, announced layoffs in the tens of thousands. Ticketing slumped to all-time lows as businesses curtailed nonessential travel and security-conscious consumers stayed home. Even after air-traffic restrictions were lifted, the skies remained eerily quiet. Hundreds of flights were cancelled due to lack of passengers.

The Bush administration quickly came to the rescue of the industry with a multibillion-dollar bailout. The airlines received a cash injection of $5 billion—with virtually no strings attached. A further $10 billion in loan guarantees were available if the airlines created an operating plan that would revitalize their competitive and financial health and—at the same time—help stimulate the economy. Banks were expected to reschedule loans, suppliers to lower prices, and unions to accept pay cuts. The rescue plan managed to keep the major airlines in business, at least in the short term. Reducing personnel, eliminating a third of pre–September 11 flights, and substantially increasing the number of passengers on the remaining flights helped curb operating losses. Massive fare sales, extra frequent-flyer incentives, and extensive advertising campaigns gradually coaxed reluctant flyers onto planes. Improved security measures—mandated by the Aviation Security Act of 2001—eased safety concerns. To cut costs still further, the airlines eliminated millions of dollars in commissions previously paid to travel agencies. Although monthly passenger volume during early 2002 totaled 6 million less per month than during the previous year, the drop-off was significantly less than the steep declines experienced in the first months following the attacks. By 2003, such carriers as Delta and United had begun hiring back displaced workers as air traffic returned to normal. The first signs of recovery were evident.

For the major carriers, the government bailout was a lifeline, without which they may have been forced out of business after September 11. Yet some players were better positioned than others to weather the crisis. While rivals like Continental, United, and America West were deeply in debt, and U.S. Airways filed for bankruptcy protection, Delta Airlines—though incurring losses as high as $354 million per quarter—had cash reserves and credit lines of $3.1 billion and was able to continue its flights at near-normal levels. A long-time champion of labor relations, Southwest Airlines refused to lay off employees. With the best management team in the industry, the airline boasted 29 consecutive years of profitability. Despite the bad economy and despite September 11, profits topped $500 million in 2001.[1]

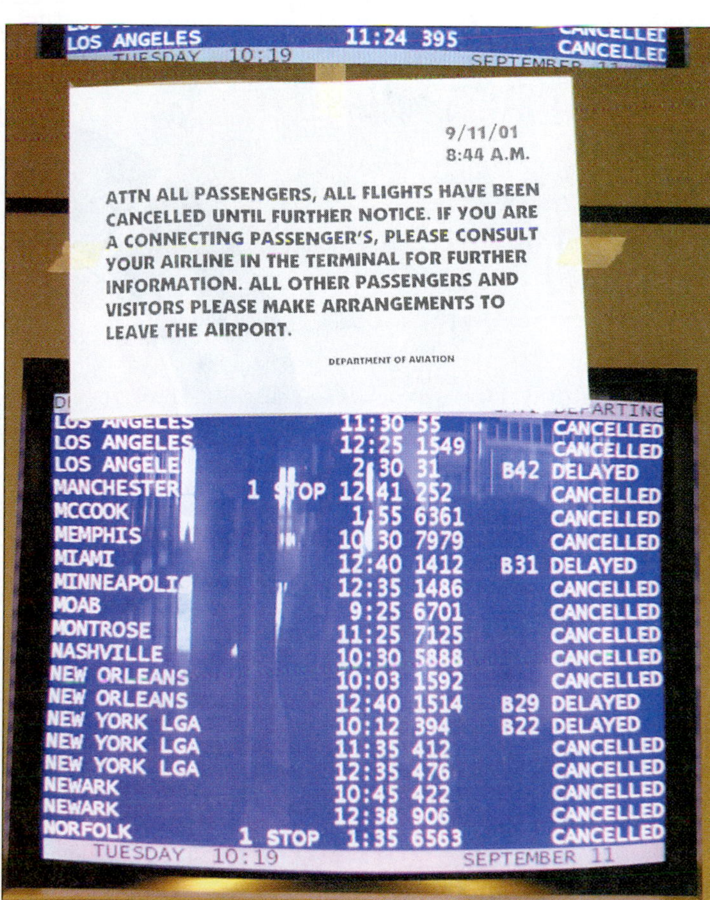

CHAPTER OVERVIEW

The government bailout of the airline industry depended on effective and immediate collaboration between airlines, banks, labor unions, regulatory bodies, security forces, and other agencies. To survive the sudden shift in the environment in which they operated, the airlines needed to adapt operations at all levels. Their ability to respond to change kept them in business. Southwest Airlines' sound management strategies and solid balance sheet enabled it to recover quickly, even when disaster struck.

Change may be the result of crises, but more often it is gradual. For example, not a video rental outlet could be found in America in 1975, but by 2003, over 21,000 were open for business—with as much shelf space devoted to DVDs as to videotapes. During the same period, computer retail outlets exploded in number, increasing twelvefold. Mobile phones replaced car phones—and transformed from plain gray into a rainbow of colors and styles. Beauty salons reinvented themselves as day spas. The prosperity of recent years led consumers to outsource their domestic drudgery, contributing to growth in industries ranging from restaurants and hotels to amusement parks and lawn-care services.

In addition to planning for change, marketers must set goals to meet concerns of customers, employees, shareholders, and members of the general public. Industry competition, legal constraints, the impact of technology on product designs, and social concerns are some of the many important factors that shape the business environment. All potentially have impact on a firm's goods and services. Although external forces frequently are outside the marketing manager's control, decision makers must still consider those influences together with the variables of the marketing mix in developing—and occasionally modifying—marketing plans and strategies that take these environmental factors into consideration.

This chapter begins by describing five forces in marketing's external environment—competitive, political-legal, economic, technological, and social-cultural. Figure 3.1 identifies them as the foundation for making decisions involving the four marketing mix elements and the target market. These forces provide the frame of reference within which all marketing decisions are made. The second focus of this chapter is marketing ethics and social responsibility. This section describes the nature of marketers' responsibilities, both to business and to society at large.

ENVIRONMENTAL SCANNING AND ENVIRONMENTAL MANAGEMENT

Marketers must carefully and continually monitor crucial trends and developments in the business environment. **Environmental scanning** is the process of collecting information about the external marketing environment to identify and interpret potential trends. The goal is to analyze the information and decide whether these trends represent opportunities or threats to the company. The firm is then able to determine the best response to a particular environmental change.

FIGURE 3.1

Elements of the Marketing Mix within an Environmental Framework

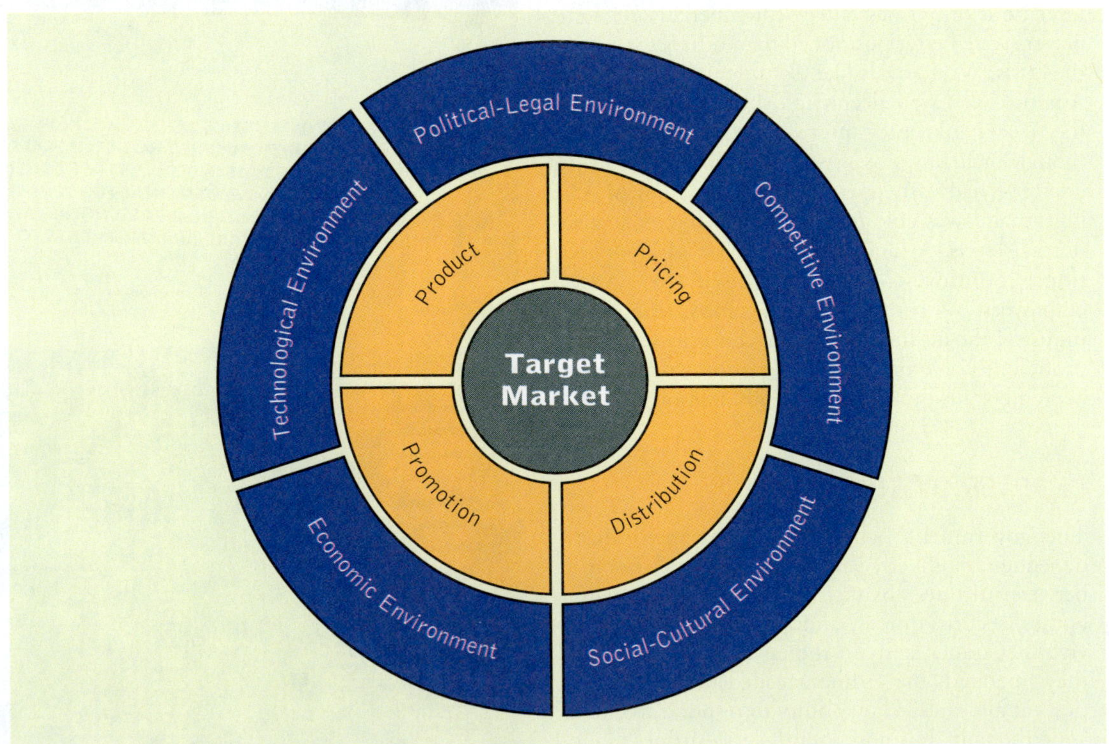

<interactive>**learning goal**

CHAPTER OBJECTIVE #1: IDENTIFY THE FIVE COMPONENTS OF THE MARKETING ENVIRONMENT.

All across America, consumers have discovered that there is money to be made in online auctions. Bidding on everything from Beanie Babies to sports memorabilia, over a third of all U.S. online retail customers made at least one online auction purchase during the first four years of the 21st century. With over 2 million registered users, eBay is the industry giant among approximately 1,000 auction Web sites. Yet the Federal Trade Commission links almost half of all scams on the Web to online auctions. Counterfeit items, failure to deliver (or pay for) products sold at auction, and manipulation of bids by sellers are common complaints. Even though eBay claims that fraud accounts for a minuscule 1 in every 3,000 transactions, the company takes steps to overcome consumer fears. It offers free insurance coverage for transactions up to $200. Rival Auction Universe provides up to $3,000 of insurance for $19.95.[2]

Environmental scanning is a vital component of effective **environmental management.** Environmental management involves marketers' efforts to achieve organizational objectives by predicting and influencing the competitive, political-legal, economic, technological, and social-cultural environments. In the political-legal environment, managers who are seeking modifications of regulations, laws, or tariff restrictions may join political action committees (PACs) to lobby legislators or contribute to the campaigns of sympathetic politicians. After a multimillion-dollar lobbying campaign that lasted more than 18 months, the U.S. Department of Transportation granted United Parcel Service (UPS) a new air route into China, the most recent member of the World Trade Organization. The route is potentially worth $300 million in annual revenues.[3]

For many domestic and international competitors, competing with established industry leaders frequently involves *strategic alliances*—partnerships with other firms in which the partners combine resources and capital to create competitive advantages in a new market. A recent alliance between MasterCard International and Dallas-based Hotel Reservations Network allows cardholders to book rooms online and take advantage of exclusive offers and rebates. MasterCard benefits from extra exposure in the network's print and online advertising. Amazon marketers decided to jump-start their move into online auctions by forming an alliance with Sotheby's, the world's largest international auction house for fine art. Amazon benefits from the instant credibility associated with Sotheby's name, along with access to its clients. Sotheby's gains entry into the market for lower-end collectibles.[4]

Strategic alliances are especially common in international marketing, where partnerships with local firms provide regional expertise for a company expanding its operations abroad. Members of such alliances share risks and profits. Alliances are essential in countries such as China and Mexico, where local laws require foreign firms doing business there to work with local companies.

Through successful research and development efforts, firms may influence changes in their own technological environments. A research breakthrough may lead to reduced production costs or a technologically superior new product.

While the dynamic marketing environment may exceed the confines of the firm and its marketing mix components, effective marketers continually seek to predict its impact on marketing decisions and to modify operations to meet changing market needs. Even modest environmental shifts can alter the results of those decisions.

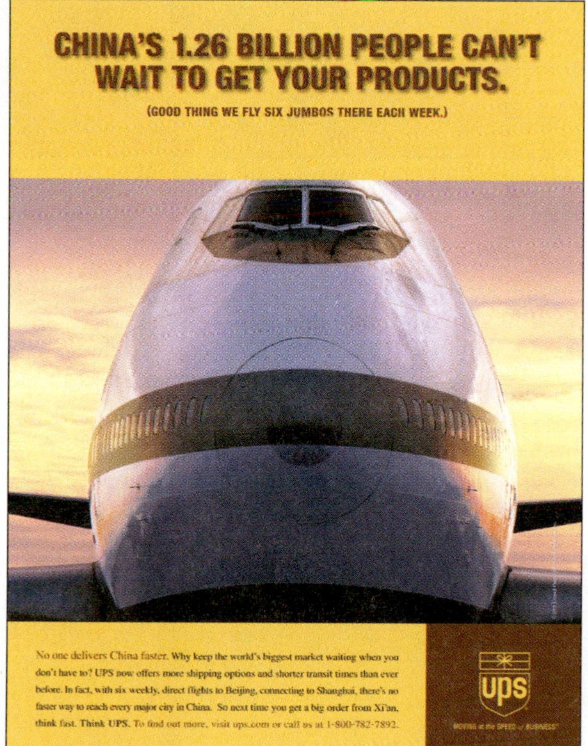

Environmental management played a major role in United Parcel Service's receipt of the air package delivery rights between the U.S. and China. Today, UPS offers the fastest delivery of packages between the two countries—with direct six-times-a-week flights to Beijing.

THE COMPETITIVE ENVIRONMENT

As organizations vie to satisfy customers, the interactive exchange creates the **competitive environment.** Marketing decisions by each individual firm influence consumer responses in the marketplace. They also affect the marketing strategies of competitors. As a consequence, decision makers must continually monitor competitors' marketing activities—their products, channels, prices, and promotional efforts.

Few organizations enjoy *monopoly* positions as the sole supplier of a good or service in the marketplace. Utilities, such as natural

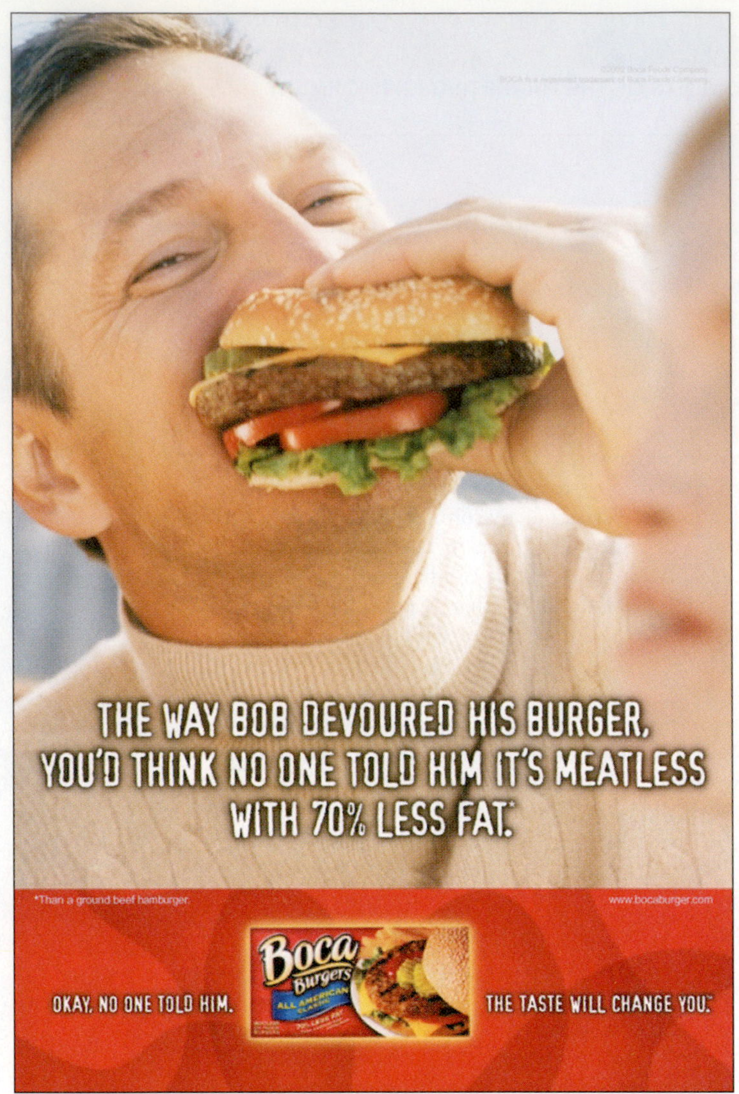

Although Kraft's Boca Burgers brand targets the market niche of shoppers choosing meatless dishes, it still competes directly with other menu options in the packaged foods category.

gas, electricity, water, and cable TV service, have traditionally accepted considerable regulation from local authorities who controlled such marketing-related factors as rates, service levels, and geographic coverage. In exchange, the utilities gained exclusive rights to serve a particular group of consumers. The *deregulation movement* of the past three decades has ended total monopoly protection for most utilities. Today's shoppers can choose from alternative cable TV and Internet providers, cell phone and long-distance telephone carriers, and even gas and electric utilities. The constant stream of solicitations from long-distance telephone companies provides almost daily evidence of increased competition in this formerly monopolized industry.

Some marketers, such as pharmaceutical firms Merck and Pfizer, are able to achieve temporary monopolies from patents on drugs they invest millions to develop. When the Food and Drug Administration approves a new antiarthritis drug, improved blood pressure medicine, or even a pill to stimulate hair growth, the manufacturers are typically granted exclusive rights to produce and market the product during the life of the patent. By being first to market and holding on to their leadership positions, some firms have achieved virtual monopolies. De Beers owns more than 70 percent of the diamond market; Intel has the lion's share of the market for microprocessors; four out of five flights out of Charlotte, N.C., are operated by U.S. Airlines; and baseballs made by Rawlings Sporting Goods are practically the only game in town.[5]

Through industry megamergers, often on a global scale, some companies seek to dominate markets without ceding the controls that regulated monopolies forfeit. As a result of mergers, the auto, tobacco, accounting, and telecommunications industries are all dominated by just three or four giants. Rather than seeking sole dominance of a market, corporations increasingly prefer to share the pie with just a few rivals. Referred to by economists as an *oligopoly,* this industry structure of a limited number of sellers in an industry where high start-up costs form barriers to keep out new competitors deters newcomers from breaking into markets, while ensuring that corporations remain innovative. In the ongoing antitrust trial, Microsoft Corp. is fighting allegations that it first attempted to create an oligopoly by sharing the Internet browser market with Netscape Communications. When Netscape balked, Microsoft allegedly attempted to destroy the fledgling Internet company.[6]

Types of Competition

Marketers face three types of competition. The most *direct* form occurs among marketers of similar products, as when a Shell station opens across the street from BP or Marathon. Telecommunications giant Motorola, battered by Finland's Nokia when the market for cell phones exploded, recently fought back with the release of a new line of sleek and stylish phones that serve as fashion accessories as well as communication devices. Motorola hopes that its aggressive design offensive, coupled with the launch of its new 3G handsets—an innovative technology that offers instant access to the Internet—will win back lost market share. In the race for teen dollars, chain store Hot Topic is beating out youth retailers like Gap and American Eagle. Offering funky fashions and oddball gifts—like the glow-in-the-dark tongue ring—the store caters to tastes of almost a fifth of high-school students who consider themselves "alternative." Located in easy-to-access suburban malls, Hot Topic keeps in touch with customers' fashion choices, inviting comments and suggestions. Buyers also check out cutting-edge trends at rock concerts and rave parties.[7]

<interactive>**learning goal**

CHAPTER OBJECTIVE #2: EXPLAIN THE TYPES OF COMPETITION MARKETERS FACE AND THE STEPS NECESSARY FOR DEVELOPING A COMPETITIVE STRATEGY.

A second type of competition is *indirect* and involves products that are easily substituted. In the business document delivery industry, overnight express mail services and messenger services compete with e-mail and voice mail. In the fast-food industry, pizza competes with chicken, hamburgers, and tacos. In transportation, Greyhound bus lines compete with auto rental services, airlines, and train services. Unable to compete directly with substitute transportation services, Amtrak decided to team up with their cruise ship and airline competitors by offering custom-designed vacation packages. With a single phone call, Amtrak can make travel arrangements to get vacationers where they want to go by air, land, and sea.

Six Flags and Universal Studios amusement parks—the traditional hot spots for family vacations—now compete with outdoor adventure trips. One of every two U.S. adults now substitutes a tranquil week at the beach or a trip to Disney World for something more adventurous—thrill-filled experiences such as skydiving, white-water rafting, or climbing Mount Rainier. A decade after it was slammed for ignoring local culture and travel habits in its Disneyland Paris theme park, Walt Disney Co. opened a more Eurocentric resort nearby. The new Euro Disney park combines traditional Hollywood-style entertainment with features that are distinctly European. Restaurants, theaters, rides, and montages are all designed to appeal to the multiple indigenous cultures throughout Europe.[8]

A change such as a price increase or an improvement in a product's attributes can also affect demand for substitute products. A major drop in the cost of solar energy would not only increase the demand for solar power but also adversely affect the demand for such energy sources as heating oil, electricity, and natural gas.

The final type of competition occurs among all organizations that compete for consumers' purchases. Traditional economic analysis views competition as a battle among companies in the same industry (direct competition) or among substitutable goods and services (indirect competition). Marketers, however, are aware that all firms compete for a limited amount of discretionary buying power. Competition in this sense means that a PT Cruiser competes with a Colorado ski vacation. For the buyer's entertainment dollar, a Korn compact disc competes with two tickets to a San Antonio Spurs' game.

Because the competitive environment often determines the success or failure of a product, marketers must continually assess competitors' marketing strategies. New product offerings with technological advances, price reductions, special promotions, service requirements, or other competitive variations must be monitored. Then, marketers must decide whether to adjust one or more marketing mix components to compete with the new market entry.

Developing a Competitive Strategy

Every firm's marketers must develop an effective strategy for dealing with the competitive environment. One company may compete in a broad range of markets in many areas of the world. Another may specialize in particular market segments, such as those determined by customers' geographical location, age, or income characteristics. Determining a *competitive strategy* involves answering the following three questions:

1. Should we compete?
2. If so, in what markets should we compete?
3. How should we compete?

The answer to the first question depends on the firm's resources, objectives, and expected profit potential. A firm may decide not to pursue or continue operating a potentially successful venture that does not mesh with its resources, objectives, or profit expectations. Semiconductor manufacturer Texas Instruments

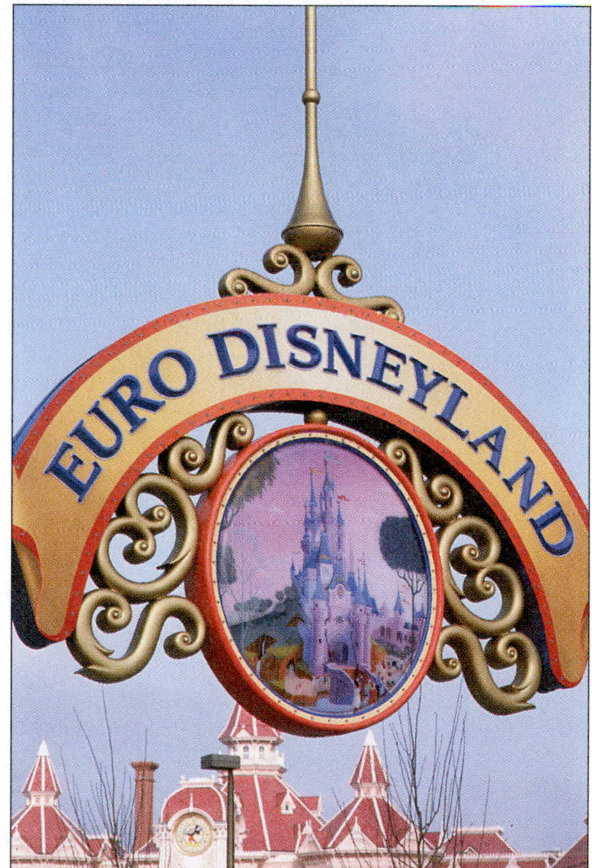

Euro Disneyland competes for vacation dollars. The resort mingles Disney-style fun with attractions that are distinctly European—including daredevil stunts in a mock car race through a model of Saint-Tropez.

Briefly Speaking

If you set aside Three Mile Island and Chernobyl, the safety record of nuclear [energy] is really very good.

Paul O'Neill (b. 1935) U.S. Treasury Secretary, 2001–2002

shed its defense electronics business unit, which makes missile sensors and radar and night-vision systems, to an aircraft company where this unit was a better fit. In a recent move to spin off Medco, its profitable pharmacy-benefits-management subsidiary, Merck cited its needs to concentrate on its core business—the development of breakthrough medicines.[9]

Answering the second question—In what markets should we compete?—requires marketers to acknowledge their firm's limited resources (sales personnel, advertising budgets, product development capability, and the like). They must accept responsibility for allocating these resources to the areas of greatest opportunity.

Some companies gain access to markets or new technologies through acquisitions and mergers. The merger of Hewlett-Packard and Compaq created an $87 billion company, an instant world leader in PCs, computer servers, handheld devices, and printers. Moreover, the elimination of overlapping units was expected to trim operating costs by $2.5 billion a year. The emergence of international petroleum giant ChevronTexaco through the merger of the world's two leading oil companies resulted in annual savings of at least $1.2 billion—and the opportunity to create breakthrough technologies by combining strengths and expertise.[10]

Answering the third question—How should we compete?—requires marketers to make product, pricing, distribution, and promotional decisions that give the firm a competitive advantage in the marketplace. Firms can compete on a variety of bases, including product quality, price, and customer service. For example, retailer Neiman Marcus has gained a competitive advantage by providing superior customer service, while retailer Target competes by providing quality goods at low prices. As Figure 3.2 shows, the ultra-hip clothing company FUBU has an extensive Web site. FUBU brings a competitive edge to the hip-hop clothing market by offering shoppers the ability to purchase their clothing online, but supports the retail sales of the company's signature stores by also directing online shoppers to the nearest FUBU clothing retailer in their area of the country.

Time-Based Competition

With increased international competition and rapid changes in technology, a steadily growing number of firms are using time as a strategic competitive weapon. **Time-based competition** is the strategy of developing and distributing goods and services more quickly than competitors. The flexibility and responsiveness of time-based competitors enables them to improve product quality, reduce costs, and expand product offerings to satisfy new market segments and enhance customer satisfaction.

Time was a key factor that recently won Lockheed Martin Aeronautics the biggest Defense Department contract ever—$200 billion to build a new fleet of supersonic stealth fighter planes. By collaborating via the Internet with more than 80 suppliers scattered worldwide using a complex system of Web software tools, the Lockheed proposal won over government procurement specialists by demonstrating its ability to get the first plane in the air in just four years.[11]

In the computer industry, time-based competition is critical. Consumer demands for speed push developers to work on several generations of their technology simultaneously. In the mid-1990s, high-speed 3-D graphics capability came at a cost exceeding $300,000 and was reserved for high-tech applications such as medical imaging or flight simulations. Today, far more sophisticated graphics programs are available on Sony's PlayStation 2 or Microsoft's Xbox for less than $200. Less than five years ago, a new PC typically came with 20 gigabytes of storage; now a single drive has a terabyte—or 1,000 gigabytes. That's enough space to hold about 400 movies. The speed at which changes occur in the Internet arena is so great that marketers count time in "Internet years," actually time periods of only several weeks or months.[12]

THE POLITICAL-LEGAL ENVIRONMENT

Before you play the game, learn the rules! It is absurd to start playing a new game without first understanding the rules, yet some businesspeople exhibit a remarkable lack of knowledge about marketing's **political-legal environment**—the laws and their interpretations that require firms to operate under certain competitive conditions and to protect consumer rights. Ignorance of laws, ordinances, and regulations or noncompliance with them can result in fines, embarrassing negative publicity, and expensive civil damage suits.

<interactive>**learning goal**

CHAPTER OBJECTIVE #3: DESCRIBE HOW GOVERNMENT AND OTHER GROUPS REGULATE MARKETING ACTIVITIES AND HOW MARKETERS CAN INFLUENCE THE POLITICAL-LEGAL ENVIRONMENT.

The existing U.S. legal framework was constructed on a piecemeal basis, often in response to issues that were important at the time individual laws were enacted. Businesspeople need considerable diligence to

FIGURE 3.2

The Internet: Important Sales Component of FUBU's Competitive Strategy

understand its relationship to their marketing decisions. Numerous laws and regulations affect those decisions, many of them vaguely stated and inconsistently enforced by a multitude of different authorities.

Regulations enacted at the federal, state, and local levels affect marketing practices, as do the actions of independent regulatory agencies. These requirements and prohibitions touch on all aspects of marketing decision making—designing, labeling, packaging, distribution, advertising, and promotion of goods and services. To cope with the vast, complex, and changing political-legal environment, many large firms maintain in-house legal departments; small firms often seek professional advice from outside attorneys. All marketers, however, should be aware of the major regulations that affect their activities.

Government Regulation

The history of U.S. government regulation can be divided into four phases. The first phase was the antimonopoly period of the late 19th and early 20th centuries. During this era, major laws such as the Sherman Antitrust Act, Clayton Act, and Federal Trade Commission Act were passed to maintain a competitive environment by reducing the trend toward increasing concentration of industry power in the hands of a small number of competitors. Laws enacted more than 100 years ago still affect business in the 21st century.

The recent Microsoft case is a good example of antitrust legislation at work. The U.S. Justice Department accused the software powerhouse of predatory practices designed to crush competition. By bundling its own Internet Explorer browser with its Windows operating system (which runs 90 percent of the world's personal computers), Microsoft grabbed significant market share from rival Netscape. It also bullied firms as large as America Online to drop Netscape Navigator in favor of the Microsoft browser. Microsoft's supporters countered that consumers have clearly benefited from the integrated features in Windows. Its bundling decisions were simply efforts to offer customer satisfaction through added value. As one critic joked, "In the U.S. government's fight with Bill Gates, I'm for the federal government. I always like to root for the little guy."[13]

The second phase, aimed at protecting competitors, emerged during the Depression Era of the 1930s, when independent merchants felt the need for legal protection against competition from larger chain stores. Among the federal legislation enacted was the Robinson-Patman Act. The third regulatory phase focused on consumer protection. Although the objective of consumer protection underlies most laws—

Sony's PlayStation 2 brings sophisticated technology to the fingertips of game players. PlayStation 3, now in development, promises even better performance.

with good examples including the Sherman Act, FTC Act, and Federal Food and Drug Act—many of the major consumer-oriented laws have been enacted during the past 40 years. The fourth phase, industry deregulation, began in the late 1970s and continues to the present. During this phase, government has sought to increase competition in such industries as telecommunications, utilities, transportation, and financial services by discontinuing many regulations and permitting firms to expand their service offerings to new markets.

The newest regulatory frontier is cyberspace. Federal and state regulators are investigating ways to police the Internet and online services. For example, the FTC has devoted a Web site to publicizing *e-fraud,* schemes such as meta-tags that falsely lure browsers to sites they have not requested or start-your-own business scams. Another popular con is to send consumers a check, apparently with no strings attached. When the check is cashed the consumer has signed up for a long-term Internet access agreement, usually with an unreliable and overpriced operator. Although the federal government has been slow to regulate spam—junk e-mail—many states have enacted legislation and many more have introduced bills to protect consumers and punish offenders. Yet the effectiveness of state campaigns is limited. The Internet is, after all, global, not local.[14]

Privacy and child protection issues are another difficult enforcement challenge. With the passage of the Children's Online Privacy Protection Act, Congress took the first step in regulating what children are exposed to on the Internet. The primary focus is a set of rules regarding how and when marketers need to get parental permission before obtaining marketing research information from children over the Web.

Many Internet marketers are taking proactive steps to protect the consumer. Microsoft is developing technology that lets people automatically skip sites that do not meet their privacy standards. Citigroup has teamed up with the U.S. Secret Service to develop a pilot program to combat identity theft.[15]

Table 3.1 lists and briefly describes the major federal laws affecting marketing. Legislation covering specific marketing practices, such as product development, packaging, labeling, product warranties, and franchise agreements, is discussed in later chapters.

Marketers must also monitor state and local laws that affect their industries. Many states, for instance, allow hard liquor to be sold only in liquor stores; such laws limit the distribution of low-alcohol cocktails made with rum, vodka, whiskey, and bourbon. California's stringent regulations for automobile emissions require special pollution control equipment on cars sold in the state.

Government Regulatory Agencies

Federal, state, and local governments have established regulatory agencies to enforce laws. At the federal level, the Federal Trade Commission (FTC) wields the broadest powers of any agency to influence marketing activities. It has the authority to enforce laws regulating unfair business practices and can take action to stop false and deceptive advertising. The Federal Communications Commission regulates communication by wire, radio, and television. Other federal regulatory agencies include the Food and Drug Administration, the Consumer Products Safety Commission, the Federal Power Commission, and the Environmental Protection Agency.

The FTC uses several procedures to enforce laws. It may issue a consent order through which a business accused of violations can agree to voluntary compliance without admitting guilt. If a business refuses to comply with an FTC request, the agency can issue a cease-and-desist order, which gives a final demand

TABLE 3.1

Major Federal Laws Affecting Marketing

Date	Law	Description
A. Laws Maintaining a Competitive Environment		
1890	Sherman Antitrust Act	Prohibits restraint of trade and monopolization; identifies a competitive marketing system as national policy goal
1914	Clayton Act	Strengthens the Sherman Act by restricting such practices as price discrimination, exclusive dealing, tying contracts, and interlocking boards of directors where the effect "may be to substantially lessen competition or tend to create a monopoly"
1914	Federal Trade Commission Act (FTC)	Prohibits unfair methods of competition; establishes the Federal Trade Commission, an administrative agency that investigates business practices and enforces the FTC Act
1938	Wheeler-Lea Act	Amends the FTC Act to outlaw additional unfair practices; gives the FTC jurisdiction over false and misleading advertising
1950	Celler-Kefauver Antimerger Act	Amends the Clayton Act to include major asset purchases that will decrease competition in an industry
2001	Air Transportation Safety and System Stabilization Act	Enacted in response to terrorist attacks that crippled the airline industry; granted airlines $5 million in cash and $10 million in loan guarantees to keep them in business
B. Laws Regulating Competition		
1936	Robinson-Patman Act	Prohibits price discrimination in sales to wholesalers, retailers, or other producers; prohibits selling at unreasonably low prices to eliminate competition
1993	North American Free Trade Agreement (NAFTA)	International trade agreement between Canada, Mexico, and the United States designed to facilitate trade by removing tariffs and other trade barriers among the three nations
C. Laws Protecting Consumers		
1906	Federal Food and Drug Act	Prohibits adulteration and misbranding of foods and drugs involved in interstate commerce; strengthened by the Food, Drug, and Cosmetic Act (1938) and the Kefauver-Harris Drug Amendment (1962)
1970	National Environmental Policy Act	Establishes the Environmental Protection Agency to deal with various types of pollution and organizations that create pollution
1971	Public Health Cigarette Smoking Act	Prohibits tobacco advertising on radio and television
1972	Consumer Product Safety Act	Created the Consumer Product Safety Commission, which has authority to specify safety standards for most products
1998	Children's Online Privacy Protection Act	Empowers FTC to set rules regarding how and when marketers must obtain parental permission before asking children marketing research questions
2000	Cybersquatting Law	Bans the bad-faith purchase of domain names that are identical or confusingly similar to existing registered trademarks
2001	Electronic Signature Act	Gives electronic signatures the same legal weight as handwritten signatures
2001	Aviation Security Act	Requires airlines to take extra security measures to protect passengers, including the installation of cockpit doors, improved baggage screening, and increased security training for airport personnel
D. Laws Deregulating Specific Industries		
1978	Airline Deregulation Act	Grants considerable freedom to commercial airlines in setting fares and choosing new routes
1980	Motor Carrier Act and Staggers Rail Act	Significantly deregulates trucking and railroad industries by permitting them to negotiate rates and services
1996	Telecommunications Act	Significantly deregulates the telecommunications industry by removing barriers to competition in local and long-distance phone and cable and television markets

to stop an illegal practice. Firms often challenge cease-and-desist orders in court. The FTC can require advertisers to provide additional information about products in their advertisements, and it can force firms using deceptive advertising to correct earlier claims with new promotional messages. In some cases, the FTC can require a firm to give refunds to consumers misled by deceptive advertising.

The FTC and U.S. Justice Department can stop mergers if they believe the proposed acquisition will reduce competition by making it harder for new companies to enter the field. In recent years, these agencies have taken a harder line on proposed mergers, especially in the computer, telecommunications, financial services, and health-care sectors.

Removing regulation also changes the competitive picture considerably. Following deregulation of the telecommunications and utilities industries, suppliers no longer have exclusive rights to operate within a territory. Natural gas utilities traditionally competed with electric companies to supply homeowners and businesses with energy needs. Because of deregulation, they now also compete with other gas companies. Customers of KN Energy in southeastern Wyoming can choose from among 12 competing gas companies, some of which deliver gas through out-of-state pipelines. Deregulation also allows new opportunities for start-up companies. GreenMountain.com differentiates itself as an environmentally conscious energy supplier, claiming to offer a cleaner electricity product. Moreover, its 100,000 customers, mostly in California and Pennsylvania, earn discounts whenever they engage in environmentally beneficial activities, such as walking to work instead of driving.[16]

Restructuring of the utility industry after 90 years of monopoly will affect many different sectors. If power costs drop the expected 20 percent due to deregulation of the generation process, businesses and individuals will have more money to spend on other things. Competition will improve efficiency in what had become a complex and inefficient market. Consolidation of the industry will increase due to mergers between utility companies.

The latest round of deregulation brought the passage of the Telecommunications Act of 1996. This law removed barriers between local and long-distance phone companies and cable companies. It allowed the so-called "Baby Bells"—the seven regional Bell operating companies—to offer long-distance service; at the same time, long-distance companies—such as AT&T, WorldCom, and Sprint, which control over 90 percent of this market—were able to offer local service. Satellite television providers such as DISH and DirectTV and cable companies like Comcast and Time Warner Cable can offer phone service, and phone companies can get into the cable business. The change promises huge rewards for competitive winners. Just capturing 20 percent of the local calling market, for example, is worth $15 billion to $20 billion per year to AT&T.

However, deregulation is not without its critics. Although the previous decade witnessed a flurry of moves by state authorities to deregulate utilities, California's near disaster from their recent deregulatory moves prompted dozens of states to postpone further consideration of deregulations. Following allegations of financial malpractice at Houston's Enron Corp.—once the poster child of deregulation—the courts recently decided to split the bankrupt company apart and sell it off in pieces. Skyrocketing prices due to gas shortages led the Georgia legislature to try to reform the state's deregulated gas market. One bill would re-regulate prices under state rules; another would create a state-regulated supplier to which consumers could switch from privately owned, unregulated gas companies.[17]

Other Regulatory Forces

Public and private consumer interest groups and self-regulatory organizations are also part of the legal environment. Consumer interest organizations have mushroomed in the past 25 years, and today hundreds of groups operate at national, state, and local levels. The National Coalition Against Misuse of Pesticides seeks to protect the environment. People for Ethical Treatment of Animals (PETA) opposes the use of animals for product testing. Other groups attempt to advance the rights of minorities, elderly Americans, and other special-interest causes. The power of these groups has also grown. Pressure from antialcohol groups has resulted in proposed legislation requiring health warnings on all alcohol ads and stricter regulations of alcoholic beverage advertising. (See the Interactive Example "Solving an Ethical Controversy" for a discussion of the pros and cons of alcohol advertising on television.)

RIGHT/WRONG: SOLVING AN ETHICAL CONTROVERSY—LIQUOR ADVERTISING AND NETWORK TELEVISION: SOCIALLY UNACCEPTABLE OR FAIR PLAY?

Self-regulatory groups represent industries' attempts to set guidelines for responsible business conduct. The Council of Better Business Bureaus is a national organization devoted to consumer service and business self-regulation. The Council's National Advertising Division (NAD) is designed to promote truth and accuracy in advertising. It reviews and advocates voluntary resolution of advertising-related complaints between consumers and businesses. If NAD fails to resolve a complaint, an appeal can be made to the National Advertising Review Board, which is composed of advertisers, ad agency representatives, and public members. In addition, many individual trade associations set business guidelines and codes of conduct and encourage members' voluntary compliance.

In an effort to protect consumer privacy and curb unwanted mail or phone solicitations, the Direct Marketing Association (DMA) recently approved new rules requiring customers to be notified if information about them—including their name and address—was being shared with other marketers. Companies must also tell consumers that they have the option not to have their information shared. The new rules apply to nearly 4,500 DMA member firms and include 2,600 Internet companies, catalogs, banks, financial institutions, publishers, not-for-profits, and book and music clubs.

As mentioned earlier, regulating the online world poses a challenge. Favoring self-regulation as the best starting point, the FTC sponsored a Privacy Initiative for consumers, advertisers, online companies, and others as a way to develop voluntary industry privacy guidelines. The Interactive Services Association is also working on its own privacy standards.

Controlling the Political-Legal Environment

Most marketers comply with laws and regulations, since noncompliance can scar a firm's reputation and hurt profits. Yet most also fight regulations they consider unjust. The regional Bell operating companies filed lawsuits to protect their turf against competition from long-distance carriers and cable companies, while GTE claimed the deregulation of local phone service was unconstitutional. Other companies have jumped in to take advantage of new opportunities. Furst Group, a long-distance phone company with no lines or equipment, buys blocks of long-distance time from major carriers at greatly reduced rates and resells it by the minute at a discount. Now the regional Bells and long-distance carriers are competing aggressively to keep their customers. They are also working with *switchless resellers* like Furst to retain small business customers that they would otherwise lose.

Consumer groups and political action committees within industries may try to influence the outcome of proposed legislation or change existing laws by engaging in political lobbying or boycotts. Lobbying groups frequently enlist the support of customers, employees, and suppliers to assist their efforts.

THE ECONOMIC ENVIRONMENT

The overall health of the economy influences how much consumers spend and what they buy. This relationship also works the other way. Consumer buying plays an important role in the economy's health; in fact, consumer outlays perennially make up some two-thirds of overall economic activity. Since all marketing activity is directed toward satisfying consumer wants and needs, marketers must understand how economic conditions influence consumer purchasing behavior.

<interactive>**learning goal**

CHAPTER OBJECTIVE #4: OUTLINE THE ECONOMIC FACTORS THAT AFFECT MARKETING DECISIONS AND CONSUMER BUYING POWER.

Marketing's **economic environment** consists of forces that influence consumer buying power and marketing strategies. They include the stage of the business cycle, inflation, unemployment, income, and resource availability.

Stages in the Business Cycle

Historically, the economy has tended to follow a cyclical pattern consisting of four stages: prosperity, recession, depression, and recovery. No depressions have occurred in the U.S. since the 1930s, and many economists argue that society is capable of preventing future depressions through intelligent use of various economic policies. Good decision making should ensure that a recession would give way to a period of recovery, rather than sinking further into depression.

Consumer buying differs in each stage of the *business cycle*, and marketers must adjust their strategies accordingly. In times of prosperity, consumer spending maintains a brisk pace and buyers are willing to spend more for premium versions of well-known brands. Marketers respond by expanding product lines, increasing promotional efforts and expanding distribution to raise market share, and raising prices to widen profit margins. Figure 3.3 illustrates how marketers appeal to shoppers' desires to indulge themselves with luxury items during prosperous times—such as the TAG Heuer watch embedded with "alter ego diamonds."

FIGURE 3.3

Increased Spending for Luxury Products during Times of Prosperity

During the recent recession, consumers shifted their buying patterns to emphasize basic, functional products that carry low price tags. They limited travel, restaurant meals, entertainment, and convenience purchases, preferring to spend money on video rentals and home cooking. In recessionary periods, sales of lower-priced brands of grocery and household-goods products and private-label goods rise. To compete, marketers consider lowering prices, eliminating marginal products, improving customer service, and increasing promotional outlays to stimulate demand. They may also launch value-priced products likely to appeal to cost-conscious buyers.

Consumer spending sinks to its lowest level during a depression. The last true depression in the U.S. occurred during the 1930s. Although a severe depression could occur again, most experts see it as a slim possibility. Through its monetary and fiscal policies, the federal government attempts to control extreme fluctuations in the business cycle that lead to depression.

In the recovery stage, the economy emerges from recession and consumer purchasing power increases. But while consumers have money to spend, caution often restrains their willingness to buy. During the recovery of the early 1990s, for instance, U.S. consumers paid down their car loans and bank loans and borrowed less on their credit cards. With lower principal and interest payments, they actually had higher levels of disposable income to spend; however, they continued to spend cautiously. Usually, as a recovery strengthens, consumers become more indulgent, buying more convenience products and higher-priced goods and services.

In the 1990s, the U.S. economy surpassed the performance of the previous quarter-century. The nation experienced strong productivity growth, as measured by the gross domestic product (GDP), low inflation, a strong labor market, and profits that more than doubled. Sales of new single-family homes and cars were up, reflecting an increasing confidence in the economy. These major purchases had a ripple effect in related sectors, such as home appliances, furnishings, and lawn care. Not only did consumers spend more, but they also charged more purchases. As the economy showed signs of slowdown in 2001, growth stalled. In attempts to cut costs and hold on to profits, corporations made massive layoffs. Telecommunications company Motorola shed a third of its worldwide workforce. Consumer debt rose faster than income, delinquent credit-card payments reached new highs, and personal bankruptcy filings increased fivefold over the previous year.[18] By 2003, following federal interest rate cuts and tax cuts aimed at stimulating the economy, the worst was over.

Recovery remains a difficult stage for businesses just climbing out of a recession since it requires them to earn profits while trying to gauge uncertain consumer demand. Many cope by holding down costs. Some trim payrolls and close branch offices. Others cut back on business travel budgets. DaimlerChrysler pared spending on airline tickets by two-thirds during a single year. Teleconferencing and videoconferencing took the place of nonessential travel. Some industries struggle more than others during recovery periods. Among the hardest hit after the recent recession were the airline and lodging industries and the nation's major theme parks. Not only were consumers reluctant to fly following the terrorist attacks of September 11, but they viewed such services as travel and entertainment as unnecessary luxuries.[19]

Despite the recent slowdown, economic growth is expected to continue at an annual rate of 3 percent for the remainder of this decade. Inflation should continue to level off, and the standard of living will rise. During the first decade of this century, established industries such as finance, media, wholesale, and retail will change dramatically and new industries will be created at an astounding pace.

Business cycles, like other aspects of the economy, are complex phenomena that seem to defy the control of marketers. Success depends on flexible plans that can be adjusted to satisfy consumer demands during the various business cycle stages.

Inflation

A major constraint on consumer spending, which can occur during any stage of the business cycle, is *inflation*—rising prices caused by some combination of excess demand and increases in the costs of raw materials, component parts, human resources, or other factors of production. Inflation devalues money by reducing the products it can buy through persistent price increases. Inflation would restrict purchases less severely if income were to keep pace with rising prices, but often it does not. These rising prices increase marketers' costs, such as expenditures for wages and raw materials, and the resulting higher prices may therefore negatively affect sales.

High inflation makes consumers conscious of prices, leading to three possible outcomes: (1) consumers elect to buy now, in the belief that prices will be higher later (a popular argument in advertisements from automobile dealers); (2) they decide to alter their purchasing patterns; or (3) they postpone certain purchases.

In 1980, the U.S. rate of inflation had jumped to a heart-stopping 13.6 percent. Nearly a quarter-century later, it is almost zero, depending largely on whether the price of imported oil rises or falls. Many economists predict that low levels of inflation will continue throughout this decade. As long as these low levels continue, inflation is unlikely to affect the economy as strongly in the future as it has in the past.

Unemployment

Unemployment is defined as the proportion of people in the economy who do not have jobs and are actively looking for work. Unemployment rises during recessions and declines in the recovery and prosperity stages of the business cycle. Like inflation, unemployment affects marketing by modifying consumer behavior. Unless unemployment insurance, personal savings, and union benefits effectively offset lost earnings, unemployed people have relatively little income to spend. Even if these protections completely compensate people for lost earnings, their buying behavior is still likely to change. Instead of buying, they may choose to build their savings.

The relationship between unemployment and stages in the business cycle was illustrated the past dozen years. After peaking near 8 percent during the recession of 1992, it declined steadily since then in the midst of the extended period of prosperity from the mid-1990s to the early years of this century, reaching a low of 3.9 percent in 2001. It crept back up to the 6 percent mark when the nation experienced a double blow of an economic downturn combined with the terrorist attacks.[20] Since that time, unemployment has declined in the wake of an improved economy.

Internet job boards are cutting into the job-search market once controlled by matchmaking agencies and newspaper advertising. The Web now accounts for about 15 percent of employment advertising, up from only 2 percent just three years ago. Thousands of large and medium-sized employers include an "Available Positions" section on their Web sites. Online recruiters like HotJobs.com and Monster.com are both popular with job seekers and growing rapidly. HotJobs.com, one of the big success stories in online recruiting, is a regular advertiser on annual Super Bowl telecasts. It maintains a database of more than 9.8 million registered job seekers—and has in excess of 70,000 job listings.[21]

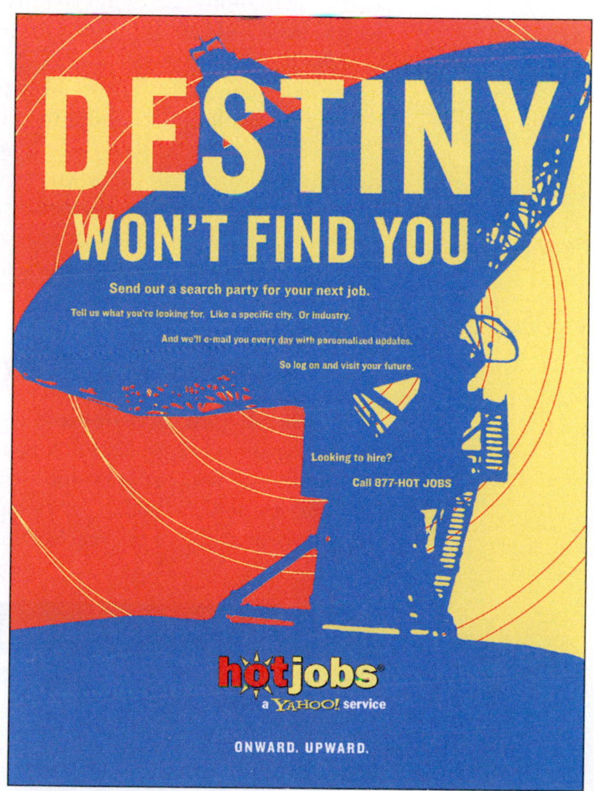

HotJobs.com is one of the major firms that help job seekers and employers find each other online.

Income

Income is another important determinant of marketing's economic environment because it influences consumer buying power. By studying income statistics and trends, marketers can estimate market potential and develop plans for targeting specific market segments. For example, U.S. household incomes have grown in recent years. Coupled with a low rate of inflation, this increase has boosted purchasing power for millions of consumers. A rise in income represents a potential for increasing overall sales. However, marketers are most interested in *discretionary income,* the amount of money people have to spend after buying necessities such as food, clothing, and housing.

Changes in average earnings powerfully affect discretionary income. Historically, periods of major innovation have been accompanied by dramatic increases in living standards and rising incomes. During the first half of the 20th century—a period of unprecedented innovations in transportation from the railroads to supersonic jets—real per-capita incomes tripled and even quadrupled, fueled by rising productivity. The 21st century could see similar income gains with the growth of electronic technologies. Some predictions indicate a 9 percent rise in real wages, a more than 50 percent rise in corporate earnings, and interest rates below 4 percent. These rapidly climbing income rates could lead to a 25 percent growth in the overall economy.

Resource Availability

Resources are not unlimited. Shortages—temporary or permanent—can result from several causes, including lack of raw materials, component parts, energy, or labor. A continuing concern of both business executives and government officials is the nation's dependence on imported oil and the risk that these imports might be curtailed by exporting countries attempting to influence U.S. foreign policy. Also, brisk demand may bring in orders that exceed manufacturing capacity or outpace the response time required to gear up a production line. Regardless of the cause, shortages require marketers to reorient their thinking.

One reaction is **demarketing,** the process of reducing consumer demand for a product to a level that the firm can reasonably supply. Oil companies publicize tips on how to cut gasoline consumption and utility companies encourage homeowners to install more insulation to reduce heating costs. Many cities discourage central business-district traffic by raising parking fees and violation penalties and promoting mass transit and carpooling.

A shortage presents marketers with a unique set of challenges. They may have to allocate limited supplies, a sharply different activity from marketing's traditional objective of expanding sales volume. Shortages may require marketers to decide whether to spread limited supplies over all customers or limit purchases by some customers so that the firm can completely satisfy others.

Marketers today have also devised ways to deal with increased demand for fixed amounts of resources. Reynolds Metal Co. addresses the dwindling supply of aluminum through its recycling programs, including cash-paying vending machines. Such "reverse" vending machines allow people to insert empty cans into the machines and receive money, stamps, and/or discount coupons for merchandise or services.

The International Economic Environment

In today's global economy, marketers must also monitor the economic environment of other nations. Just as in the U.S., a recession in Europe or Japan changes buying habits. Changes in foreign currency rates compared with the U.S. dollar also affect marketing decisions. The strong dollar and the problems in Asia hurt companies such as BP Amoco, whose foreign sales fell nearly 20 percent in just two years. Even beverage giant Coca-Cola Co. is not immune. With 75 percent of its operating profit generated overseas, currency fluctuations risk damaging overall performance. Rival PepsiCo gets only a fifth of its earnings from international sales.[22]

For the most part, however, U.S. companies have posted higher revenue gains in overseas operations. Technology companies are the biggest beneficiaries. Combined, Lucent Technologies, Dell Computer, and Seagate Technology accounted for well over $12 billion in sales from outside the U.S.

In China, where the market for cell phones shows growth at the phenomenal rate of 50 percent while demand in Europe slows down, technology companies foresee a similarly explosive market for wireless Internet access. A recent partnership between Chinese Internet commerce platform Best-of-China.com, Motorola, IBM/China, direct marketer R. R. Donnelley, and Internet company Roundpoint seeks to enable e-commerce opportunities for businesses and Internet consumers. The alliance will create an Internet gateway into China.[23]

THE TECHNOLOGICAL ENVIRONMENT

The **technological environment** represents the application to marketing of knowledge in science, inventions, and innovations. Technology leads to new goods and services for consumers; it also improves existing products, offers better customer service, and often reduces prices through new, cost-efficient production and distribution methods. Technology can quickly make products obsolete—e-mail, for example, quickly eroded the market for fax machines—but it can just as quickly open new marketing opportunities.

<interactive>**learning goal**

CHAPTER OBJECTIVE #5: DISCUSS THE IMPACT OF THE TECHNOLOGICAL ENVIRONMENT ON A FIRM'S MARKETING ACTIVITIES.

As we discussed in Chapter 1, technology is revolutionizing the marketing environment, transforming the way companies promote and distribute goods. Technological innovations create not just new products and services but also entirely new industries. Among the new businesses developing as a result of the

Internet are Web-page designers, new types of software firms, interactive advertising agencies, and companies like VeriSign that allow customers to make secure financial transactions over the Web. Industrial and medical use of lasers, superconductor transmission of electricity, wireless communications products, seeds and plants enhanced by biotechnology, and genetically engineered proteins that fight disease are just a few more examples of technological advances.

Phillips Petroleum Co. has revamped its manufacturing operations with new software applications. A new planning and optimization program, designed to help refinery operations comply with stiff federal environmental regulations that took effect in 2004, also cut supply chain and manufacturing costs.[24]

Technology can sometimes address social concerns. In response to pressure from the World Trade Organization and the U.S. government, Japanese automakers were first to use technology to develop more fuel-efficient vehicles and reduce dangerous emissions with offerings like the Toyota Prius and a hybrid version of the Honda Civic. A new wave of "hybrid vehicles" that combine a conventional gasoline engine with a battery-powered electric motor will be released in 2005 by the Big Three automakers. Ford Motor Co.'s hybrid Escape sport-utility vehicle (SUV) promises up to 40 mpg in the city and DaimlerChrysler is offering a hybrid Durango SUV. In 2004, General Motors launched a hybrid powertrain for its big pickups and SUVs.[25] Figure 3.4 shows the Prius, Toyota's successful hybrid vehicle capable of achieving up to 52 miles per gallon in highway driving.

Industry, government, colleges and universities, and other not-for-profit institutions all play roles in the development of new technology—but not always with the best results. Energy-efficiency improvements for home appliances, mandated by Congress, will do little to help the environment or give consumers value for the money. For instance, after 2006, all new air-conditioning systems must be designed to meet higher efficiency standards. The systems will save consumers money only if they are used at maximum capacity for 18 years, even though the average American moves every 7 years and, depending on climate, turns on the air conditioning only in the summertime. Even worse, most homeowners will have to install new ductwork and interior walls to fit the new units. Rather than take on this expense, they're likely to just keep fixing existing appliances, negating the energy savings initiative.[26]

Research and development efforts by private industry represent a major source of technological innovation. Pfizer, a U.S.-based global pharmaceutical company, discovers, develops, manufactures, and markets innovative medicines, spending billions each year on research. Among its most publicized breakthroughs are the cholesterol-lowering drug Lipitor, which ranks as the biggest-selling prescription drug in the U.S.; Viagra, a revolutionary treatment for erectile dysfunction; and Trovan, one of the most prescribed antibiotics in the U.S. Pfizer Animal Health develops animal vaccines, feed additives, and the first arthritis medication in the U.S. specifically for dogs. To maximize the strength of its product lines, Pfizer invests nearly $3 billion in research and development annually. Its U.S. sales force, which doubled in just three years, has ranked number one in overall quality for the last four years.

FIGURE 3.4

The Toyota Prius: One of the First Hybrid Automobiles Available for U.S. Auto Buyers

Another major source of technology is the federal government, including the military. Air bags originated from Air Force ejection seats, digital computers were first designed to calculate artillery trajectories, and the microwave oven is a derivative of military radar systems. The technology and styling behind Hummer trucks, featured in Figure 3.5, comes from U.S. military vehicles.

Although the United States has long been the world leader in research, competition from rivals in Japan and Europe is intense. While U.S. companies spearheaded the technologies behind personal computers, networking systems, and the Internet, Japanese firms capitalized on their ability to transfer those technologies into commercial products. For instance, Sony and JVC commercialized videocassette recorders—an American technology—into one of the most successful new products of the past two decades. Chinese companies, which traditionally operated as subcontractors for U.S. firms, are working to build their own international brands—much like current Japanese competitors did 30 years ago.[27]

Applying Technology

The technological environment must be closely monitored for a number of reasons. For one, creative applications of new technologies not only give a firm a definite competitive edge but can also benefit society. Kenmore's energy-efficient refrigerator uses less

FIGURE 3.5

Adapting Military Technology and Styling to Create a Successful Product for the Consumer Market

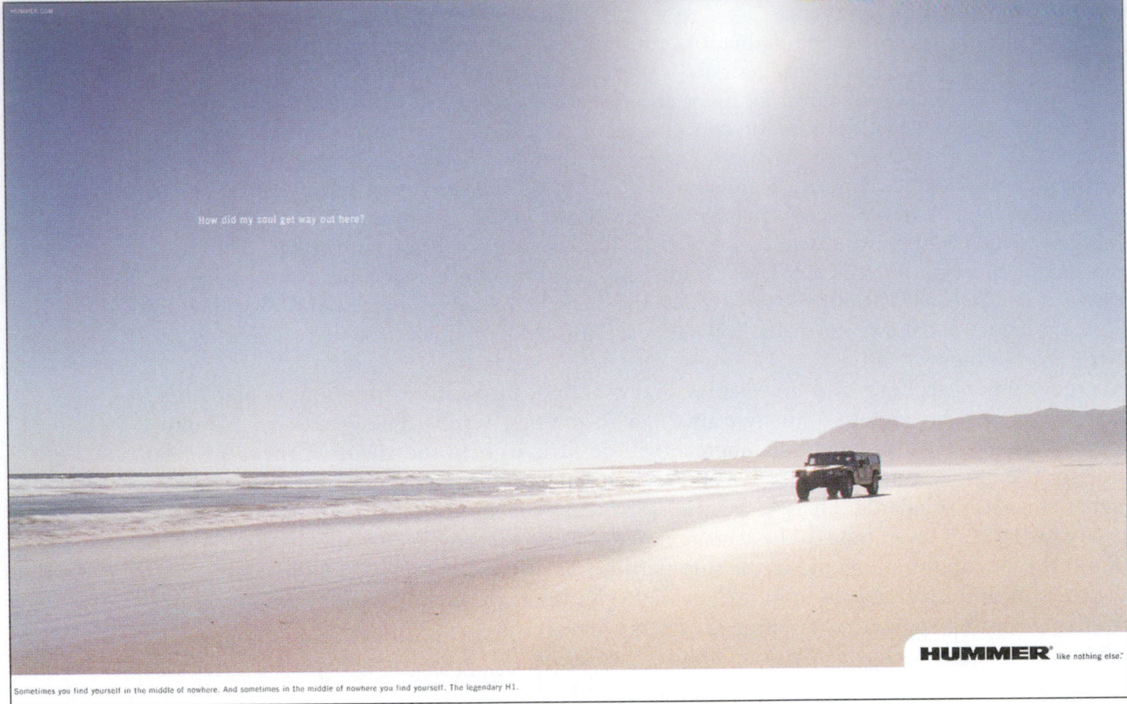

energy than a light bulb, while delivering all custom features and the sleek styling buyers require. As the message from the Council for Biotechnology Information in Figure 3.6 explains, advances in biotechnology help Hawaiian crop farmers resist viruses—and increase production.

How did my soul get way out here?
HUMMER like nothing else.
Sometimes you find yourself in the middle of nowhere. And sometimes in the middle of nowhere you find yourself. The legendary H1.

Marketers who monitor new technology and successfully apply it may also enhance customer service. Breakthroughs in electronic communications have brought consumers the convenience of in-home shopping and 24-hour banking at automated teller machines and via the Internet. Some restaurants provide faster service by equipping serving staff with palmtop computers that transmit patrons' orders to the kitchen staff.

When boutique online brokers such as Ameritrade, E*Trade Group, and Scott created a new market of small Internet traders, Merrill Lynch & Co, Wall Street's largest brokerage firm, decided to get in on the act. Transferring its reputation for financial services expertise to its online capabilities, Merrill Lynch was able to compete on price with discount rival Charles Schwab Corp., charging a fraction of the cost of its traditional transaction fees. However, online trading has fallen dramatically since 2001 as the stock market was buffeted by the blows of recession and widespread investor concerns following the collapse of Enron and other former high-flyers. The resulting slowdown took its toll on brokerages that did not enjoy the protection of a larger umbrella organization.[28]

FIGURE 3.6

How Biotechnology Advances Reduce Prices, Increase Production, and Benefit Hawaii's Economy

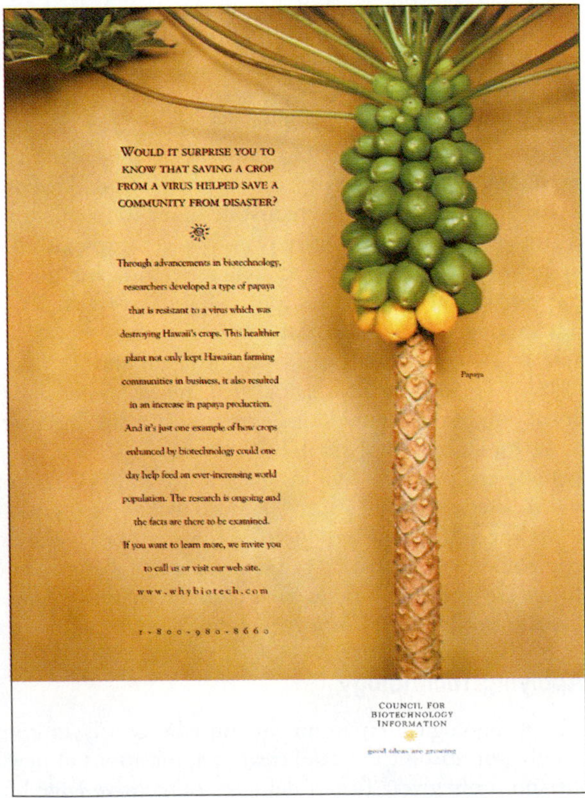

WOULD IT SURPRISE YOU TO KNOW THAT SAVING A CROP FROM A VIRUS HELPED SAVE A COMMUNITY FROM DISASTER?
Through advancements in biotechnology, researchers developed a type of papaya that is resistant to a virus which was destroying Hawaii's crops. This healthier plant not only kept Hawaiian farming communities in business, it also resulted in an increase in papaya production. And it's just one example of how crops enhanced by biotechnology could one day help feed an ever-increasing world population. The research is ongoing and the facts are there to be examined. If you want to learn more, we invite you to call us or visit our web site.
www.whybiotech.com
1-800-980-8660
Papaya
COUNCIL FOR BIOTECHNOLOGY INFORMATION
good ideas are growing

As Merrill Lynch learned, implementing technology involves considerable expense, and there is no guarantee of unbridled success. Subsequent chapters discuss in more detail how companies apply technologies—such as databases, electronic data interchange, and interactive promotional techniques—to create a competitive advantage.

THE SOCIAL-CULTURAL ENVIRONMENT

As a nation, the U.S. is becoming older, more affluent, and more culturally diverse. The birthrate is falling, and subculture populations are rising. People express concerns about the environment, buying ecologically friendly products that reduce pollution. They value the time at home with family and friends, watching videos and eating microwavable snacks. These aspects of consumer lifestyles help to shape marketing's **social-cultural environment**—the relationship between marketing and society and its culture.

<interactive>**learning goal**

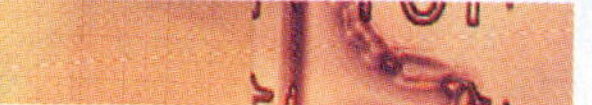

CHAPTER OBJECTIVE #6: EXPLAIN HOW THE SOCIAL-CULTURAL ENVIRONMENT INFLUENCES MARKETING.

To remain competitive, marketers must be sensitive to society's demographic shifts and changing values. These variables affect consumers' reactions to different products and marketing practices. College students—the core market for new releases on compact disc or DVD—have found new ways to get hold of popular music and movies. While Napster, the song-swapping service that allowed friends to trade pirated music over the Web, has been silenced by litigation, a wave of new products that promise "free" entertainment have recently flooded the market. Microsoft, Sony, TiVo, and others offer devices that can download video through high-speed Net connections. A software program, Morpheus, enables video piracy via PC and claims over 20 million users. In response, five major film studios—MGM, Sony, Paramount, Warner Bros., and Universal—recently initiated Moviefly, a joint venture through which they will deliver movies via the Internet. The move may have lasting impact on the buying behavior of movie fans.[29]

Creative marketers of products for the U.S. population of the 21st century must take into consideration all the segments of their market. In addition to its original Quaker Oats and its spin-off brands targeted to children, Quaker now offers a product targeted specifically to women. Figure 3.7 shows the company's new Nutrition for Women offering, which promises a breakfast fortified with calcium, iron, and all the vitamins women need to stay healthy.

Another social-cultural consideration is the increasing importance of cultural diversity. The U.S. is a mixed society composed of various submarkets, each with its unique values, cultural characteristics, consumer preferences, and purchasing behaviors. Advertising firm Dieste Harmel specializes in targeting the Hispanic market. When research showed that Hispanic consumers ate only half as many salty snacks as non-Hispanic consumers, Dieste went to work. The resulting campaign featured two Latin music stars and created a fun, party atmosphere around the client's product, Doritos. Sales shot up by 25 percent. Even better, a campaign tie-in showcased Pepsi, whose sales in Hispanic markets tripled.[30]

The social-cultural context often exerts a more pronounced influence on marketing decision making in the international sphere than in the domestic arena. Learning about cultural and societal differences among countries is paramount to a firm's success abroad. Marketing strategies that work in the U.S. often fail when directly applied in other countries, and vice versa. In many cases, marketers must redesign packages and modify products and advertising messages to suit the tastes and preferences of different cultures.

French firm Alcatel badly misjudged the effects of its recent marketing campaign in the U.S. Its ads featuring the late Martin Luther King, Jr., not only raised eyebrows but some tempers as well, as the "Marketing Misses" Interactive Example discusses. Chapter 4 explores the social-cultural aspects of international marketing.

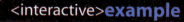

<interactive>**example**

MARKETING MISS: ALCATEL TURNS AMERICAN ICON INTO SALES PITCHMAN

Consumerism

Changing societal values have led to **consumerism,** defined as a social force within the environment that aids and protects the buyer by exerting legal, moral, and economic pressures on business. Today everyone—marketers, industry, government, and the public—is acutely aware of the impact of consumerism on the nation's economy and general well-being.

FIGURE 3.7

Nutrition for Women: A New Breakfast Alternative for Quaker Oats Designed Especially for Women

In recent years, marketers have witnessed increasing consumer activism. No organization or industry is immune. Marketers of canned tuna have been criticized for promoting sales of tuna caught by nets that also trap and kill dolphins. Private airport security firms have been replaced by federal employees in response to heightened concerns over the threat of terrorist attacks. Protesters oppose moves to allow oil drilling in the Alaska wildlife refuge. Boycotts, another means through which consumers make their objections known, have increased in recent years to include companies from almost every industry: Nike, McDonald's, Disney, Monsanto, and British Airways have all been targeted in recent years. Even the threat of a boycott can bring results.

Firms, however, do not always give in to consumer demands. The economic system cannot work if excessive demands prevent firms from achieving reasonable profit objectives. This choice between pleasing consumers and remaining viable defines one of the most difficult dilemmas facing society today. Given these constraints, what should buyers have the right to expect from the competitive marketing system?

The most frequently quoted answer came from a speech made by President John F. Kennedy in 1962. While this list does not amount to a definitive statement, it offers good rules of thumb that explain basic **consumer rights:**

1. *The right to choose freely.* Consumers should be able to choose from among a range of goods and services.
2. *The right to be informed.* Consumers should be provided with enough education and product information to enable them to be responsible buyers.
3. *The right to be heard.* Consumers should be able to express their legitimate displeasure to appropriate parties—that is, sellers, consumer assistance groups, and city or state consumer affairs offices.
4. *The right to be safe.* Consumers should be assured that the goods and services they purchase are not injurious with normal use. Goods and services should be designed in such a way that the average consumer can use them safely.

These rights have formed the conceptual framework of much of the legislation passed in the first 40 years of the consumer rights movement. However, the question of how best to guarantee them remains unanswered. Sometimes, state or federal authorities step in. California's "lemon law" gives car dealers only three chances to repair a defective auto. Following the terrorist attacks of September 11, airlines were immediately required to install titanium cockpit doors. Food labeling regulations force disclosure of such details as expiration date, ingredients, and nutritional values on packaged foods. Though not required to do so, fast-food chain Subway now includes similar information on its menus. Often, marketers such as Subway who see a genuine consumer benefit in their products use advertising to communicate it. Recently, the FDA, which already permitted marketers to advertise the disease-fighting benefits of foods rich in dietary fiber, allowed marketers of foods with more than 51 percent whole-grain ingredients to make the same claims. General Mills's whole-grain cereals Cheerios, Total, and Wheaties can now promise consumers health benefits for breakfast—a diet high in whole-grain foods and low in fat may reduce the risk of heart disease and certain cancers.[31]

The social-cultural environment for marketing decisions at home and abroad is expanding in scope and importance. Today, no marketer can initiate a strategic decision without considering the society's norms, values, culture, and demographics. Understanding how these variables affect decisions is so important that some firms have created a new position—typically, manager of public policy research—to study the changing societal environment's future impact on their organizations. And consumer groups are finding that sometimes progress can be made more quickly if they work with marketers, instead of against them, as the "Marketing Hits" Interactive Example explains.

MARKETING HIT: ALLIANCES WIN OUT WHEN ACTIVISM FAILS

ETHICAL ISSUES IN MARKETING

The five environments described so far in this chapter do not completely capture the role that marketing plays in society and the consequent effects and responsibilities of marketing activities. Because marketing is closely connected with various public issues, it invites constant scrutiny by the public. Moreover, since marketing acts as an interface between an organization and the society in which it operates, marketers often carry much of the responsibility for dealing with social issues that affect their firms.

<interactive>**learning goal**

CHAPTER OBJECTIVE #7: DESCRIBE THE ROLE OF MARKETING IN SOCIETY AND IDENTIFY THE TWO MAJOR SOCIAL ISSUES IN MARKETING.

Marketing operates in an environment external to the firm. It reacts to that environment and, in turn, is acted upon by environmental influences. Relationships with customers, employees, the government, vendors, and society as a whole form the basis of the social issues that confront contemporary marketers. While these concerns often grow out of the exchange process, they produce effects coincidental to the primary sales and distribution functions of marketing. Marketing's relationship to its external environment has a significant effect on the firm's eventual success. It must continually find new ways to deal with the social issues facing the competitive system.

The diverse social issues that marketers face can be divided into two major categories: marketing ethics and social responsibility. While the overlap and classification problems are obvious, this simple framework provides a foundation for systematically studying these issues.

Environmental influences have directed increased attention toward **marketing ethics,** defined as the marketer's standards of conduct and moral values. Ethics concern matters of right and wrong: the responsibility of individuals and firms to do what is morally right. As Figure 3.8 shows, each element of the marketing mix raises its own set of ethical questions. Before any improvements to the marketing system can be made, each of them must be evaluated.

Increased recognition of the importance of marketing ethics is evident from the more than 600 full-time corporate ethics officers in firms ranging from Dun & Bradstreet, Dow Corning, and Texas Instruments to even the Internal Revenue Service. The Federal Sentencing Guidelines for Organizations provides a framework for evaluating misconduct in business activities, such as fraud or price fixing. The sentencing guidelines act as an incentive for corporations to implement effective ethics compliance

FIGURE 3.8

Ethical Questions in Marketing

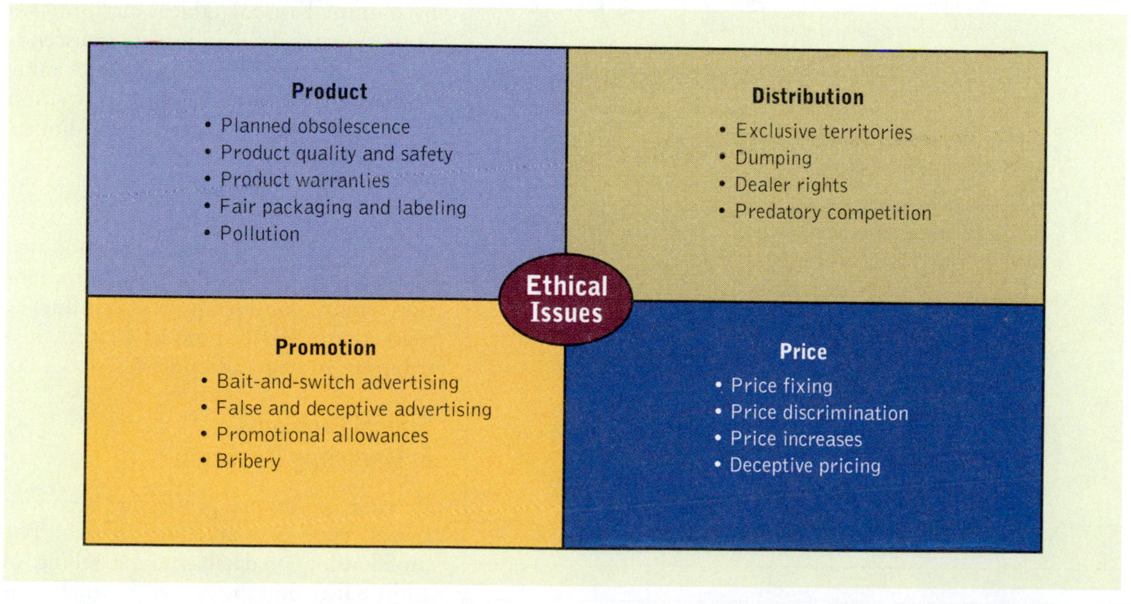

programs—if they are hauled into court, the existence of such a program can help reduce fines or sentences. A step-by-step framework for building an effective program is shown in Figure 3.9.

When Tyson Foods paid $6 million to settle accusations that it made illegal gifts to build political favor, the company was also required to set up an ethics compliance program. However, since then, Tyson has had a checkered ethical track record, facing allegations of violating antipollution laws and child labor laws and of racial discrimination in its hiring practices. Recently, six Tyson employees were indicted on charges of accepting false immigration documents and smuggling illegal workers into the U.S.[32]

Ensuring ethical practices means promising customers and business partners not to sacrifice quality and fairness for profit. In exchange, organizations hope for increased customer loyalty toward their brands. Yet issues involving marketing ethics are not always clear-cut. The issue of cigarette advertising, for example, has divided the ranks of advertising executives. Is it right for advertisers to promote a product that, while legal, has known health hazards?

For years, charges of unethical conduct have plagued the tobacco industry. In the largest civil settlement in U.S. history, tobacco manufacturers agreed to pay $206 billion to 46 states. Four other states—Florida, Minnesota, Mississippi, and Texas—had separate settlements totaling another $40 billion. The settlement frees tobacco companies from state claims for the cost of treating sick smokers. For their part, cigarette makers can no longer advertise on billboards or use cartoon characters in ads, nor can they sell non-tobacco merchandise containing tobacco brands or logos. A University of Michigan study credits the lawsuits and the resulting advertising restrictions—especially the elimination of the teen-oriented Joe Camel campaign—with recently reducing teen smoking by up to 9 percent in a single year. Aggressive state-run anti-smoking campaigns, paid for out of the tobacco settlements, was another key factor. However, researchers reported a fourfold rise in smoking among college students over a recent 5-year period. Consumer groups are also pointing their fingers at cigarette marketers. Says one analyst, "Tobacco is still a highly profitable business and companies are going to remain competitive with each other. You may not be able to put up a 50-foot sign on the street, but you can still send it in the mail to smokers. I would expect to see more emphasis on direct-to-consumer marketing."[33]

People develop standards of ethical behavior based on their own systems of values, which help them deal with ethical questions in their personal lives. However, the workplace may generate serious conflicts when individuals discover that their ethical beliefs are not necessarily in line with those of the employer. For example, while employees may think that shopping online during lunch break using a work computer is fine, the company may decide otherwise. The quiz in Figure 3.10 highlights other everyday ethical dilemmas.

How can these conflicts be resolved? In addition to individual and organizational ethics, individuals may also be influenced by a third basis of ethical authority—a professional code of ethics that transcends both organizational and individual value systems. A professional peer association can exercise collective oversight to limit a marketer's individual behavior.

Any code of ethics must anticipate the variety of problems that marketers are likely to encounter. While promotional matters tend to receive the greatest attention, ethical considerations also influence marketing research, product strategy, distribution strategy, and pricing.

Ethical Problems in Marketing Research

Invasion of personal privacy has become a critical issue in marketing research. The proliferation of databases, the selling of address lists, and the ease with which consumer information can be gathered through Internet technology have all

Briefly Speaking

There's no incompatibility between doing the right thing and making money.

William Clay Ford, Jr. (b. 1958)
CEO, Ford Motor Co.

FIGURE 3.9

Ten Steps for Corporations to Improve Standards of Business Ethics

1. Appoint a senior-level ethics compliance officer.
2. Set up an ethics code capable of detecting and preventing misconduct.
3. Distribute a written code of ethics to employees, subsidiaries, and associated companies and require all business partners to abide by it.
4. Conduct regular ethics training programs to communicate standards and procedures.
5. Establish systems to monitor misconduct and report grievances.
6. Establish consistent punishment guidelines to enforce standards and codes.
7. Encourage an open-door policy, allowing employees to report cases of misconduct without fear of retaliation.
8. Prohibit employees with a track record of misconduct from holding positions with substantial discretionary authority.
9. Promote ethically aware and responsible managers.
10. Continually monitor effectiveness of all ethics-related programs.

Source: Adapted from O. C. Ferrell, John Fraedrich, and Linda Ferrell, *Business Ethics* (Boston, MA: Houghton Mifflin, 2002), pp. 179–184.

FIGURE 3.10

Test Your Workplace Ethics

Workplace Ethics Quiz

The spread of technology into the workplace has raised a variety of new ethical questions, and many old ones still linger. Compare your answers with those of other Americans at the end of the chapter.

Office Technology

1. Is it wrong to use company e-mail for personal reasons?
   ❑Yes ❑No
2. Is it wrong to use office equipment to help your children or spouse do schoolwork?
   ❑Yes ❑No
3. Is it wrong to play computer games on office equipment during the workday?
   ❑Yes ❑No
4. Is it wrong to use office equipment to do Internet shopping?
   ❑Yes ❑No
5. Is it unethical to blame an error you made on a technological glitch?
   ❑Yes ❑No
6. Is it unethical to visit pornographic Web sites using office equipment?
   ❑Yes ❑No

Gifts and Entertainment

7. What's the value at which a gift from a supplier or client becomes troubling?
   ❑$25 ❑$50 ❑$100
8. Is a $50 gift to a boss unacceptable?
   ❑Yes ❑No
9. Is a $50 gift from the boss unacceptable?
   ❑Yes ❑No
10. Of gifts from suppliers: Is it OK to take a $200 pair of football tickets?
    ❑Yes ❑No
11. Is it OK to take a $120 pair of theater tickets?
    ❑Yes ❑No
12. Is it OK to take a $100 holiday food basket?
    ❑Yes ❑No
13. Is it OK to take a $25 gift certificate?
    ❑Yes ❑No
14. Can you accept a $75 prize won at a raffle at a supplier's conference?
    ❑Yes ❑No

Truth and Lies

15. Due to on-the-job pressure, have you ever abused or lied about sick days?
    ❑Yes ❑No
16. Due to on-the-job pressure, have you ever taken credit for someone else's work or idea?
    ❑Yes ❑No

Source: *The Wall Street Journal,* October 21, 1999, p. B1, from Ethics Officer Association, Belmont, Massachusetts; Leadership Group, Wilmette, Illinois; surveys sampled a cross-section of workers at large companies and nationwide.

increased public concern. The issue of privacy will be explored in greater detail in Chapter 5. From an ethical standpoint, a marketing research practice that is particularly problematic is the promise of cash rewards or free offers in return for marketing information that can then be sold to direct marketers. Consumers commonly disclose their demographic information in return for an e-mail newsletter or a favorite magazine. Recently, California-based marketing research company Free-PC.com offered consumers a new desktop PC in exchange for revealing personal information, such as age, income, and spending habits. Says Jupiter Media Metrix analyst Rob Leathern, "Consumers are very schizophrenic. They want their privacy, but they're willing to give out information for entry into an online sweepstakes."[34]

Privacy issues have grown as rapidly as companies on the Web, and consumers are fighting back. Following a recent investigation by the Federal Trade Commission (FTC) into its consumer research practices, online advertiser DoubleClick.com paid out $1.8 million to settle federal and state class-action suits. In addition, DoubleClick will send out more than 300 million consumer-privacy banner ads, inviting consumers to learn more about protecting their privacy online.[35]

Several agencies, including the FTC, offer assistance for Internet consumers. To find information on how to stop junk mail and telemarketing calls, a good place to start is at http://www.ftc.gov/privacy. The Direct Marketing Association also offers services, such as the Mail, Telephone, and E-Mail Preference Services, to help consumers get their names removed from marketers' targeted lists. UnlistMe.com and Junkbusters are free Web services that also help consumers remove their names from direct mail and telemarketing mailing lists.

Ethical Problems in Product Strategy

Product quality, planned obsolescence, brand similarity, and packaging questions are of critical importance to the success of a brand. Not surprisingly, competitive pressures have forced some marketers into packaging practices that may be considered misleading, deceptive, or unethical. Larger packages help gain shelf space and consumer exposure in the supermarket. Oddly sized packaging makes price comparisons difficult. Bottles with concave bottoms give the impression that they contain more liquid than they actually do. Are these practices justified in the name of competition or can they be considered deceptive? Growing regulatory mandates appear to be narrowing the range of discretion in this area.

Product endorsement is another area that raises ethical concerns. To convince consumers of quality, product-packaging prominently displays "seals of approval," such as the Good Housekeeping Seal of

Approval or the American Heart Association seal. The seals do not promise that the product is the best one on the market nor even that it has been tested against competing brands. Yet since they can be purchased for fees ranging from $10,000 to $1 million, is their use misleading?[36]

Ethical Problems in Distribution Strategy

Two ethical issues influence a firm's decisions regarding channel strategy:

1. What is the appropriate degree of control over the channel?
2. Should a company distribute its products in marginally profitable outlets that have no alternative source of supply?

The question of channel control typically arises in relationships between manufacturers and franchise dealers. For example, should an automobile dealership, a gas station, or a fast-food outlet be coerced to purchase parts, materials, and supplementary services from the parent organization?

The second question concerns marketers' responsibility to serve unsatisfied market segments even if the profit potential is slight. Should marketers serve retail stores in low-income areas, serve users of limited amounts of the firm's product, or serve a declining rural market? These problems are difficult to resolve because they often involve individuals rather than broad segments of the general public. An important first step is to ensure that the firm consistently enforces its channel policies.

Ethical Problems in Promotional Strategy

Promotion is the component of the marketing mix that gives rise to the majority of ethical questions. Personal selling has always been a target of criticism. Early traders, pack peddlers, drummers, and today's used-car salespeople have all been accused of marketing malpractices that range from exaggerating product merits to outright deceit. Gifts and bribes are common ethical abuses.

In the realm of brand advertising, the means through which marketers target specific demographic groups sometimes falls short of ethical standards. A recent campaign for Merisant's top brand, Equal, for example, targets the artificial sweetener to aging baby boomers with weight or health problems such as diabetes. The campaign, running in such magazines as *Diabetes Digest* and *Voice of the Diabetic,* features custom-created dessert recipes using Equal as a sugar alternative. Critics question the wisdom of persuading people who need to avoid sugar to indulge in cakes and cookies.[37]

The pharmaceutical industry has frequently attracted attention for its questionable advertising practices. Increasingly, television advertising directed at consumers suggests that viewers take a proactive role in family health care by requesting that their doctors prescribe the medications they see advertised. Opponents allege that such advertising puts undue pressure on physicians to prescribe costly branded drugs rather than nondrug remedies or over-the-counter alternatives. Not only may consumer-driven prescriptions lead to unnecessary or even harmful drug use, but it also ratchets up the cost of insurance coverage. The pharmaceutical industry argues that direct-to-consumer advertising educates patients while leaving physicians in control of treatment.[38]

Pfizer talks directly to consumers, recommending that they ask their doctors about cholesterol-lowering Lipitor.

The methods pharmaceutical advertisers use to target doctors has also sounded ethical alarms. Stories are rife of prominent advertisements in medical journals and company-paid seminars in popular vacation spots intended to influence prescription decisions. Recently, an intense campaign by Genzyme Corp. sought to persuade doctors to recommend its $12-a-day-drug Renagel to counter excess phosphorus levels common in kidney-dialysis patients. The alternative? Over-the-counter Tums, at $1-a-day or less. Competitors allege that advertisements for Renagel unfairly claim that calcium-based compounds like Tums cause a condition akin to hardening of the arteries. So far, there is no hard evidence that Tums can aggravate the problem—nor that the costly Renagel can remedy it. Sales of Renagel doubled in 2002, making it one of the year's hottest biotechnology stocks.[39]

As the effectiveness of the Internet as an advertising medium increases, marketers have run afoul of regulations that protect the rights of consumers to full disclosure of product information. For instance, the U.S. Department of Transportation recently investigated five Internet travel agencies who failed to disclose a fuel-surcharge in ticket prices they advertised on the Web. Since marketers have only seconds to communicate their messages on the

Web before consumers click to a new site, the length and placement of disclosures is also at issue. While it may be easiest for consumers to see disclosure statements if they are at the very top of the Web page, advertisers prefer to save that prominent spot for interest-grabbing promotional messages. So far, the Federal Trade Commission has not made any hard rules but instead has offered guidelines on how to make disclosures convenient for consumers to find.[40]

Ethical Problems in Pricing

Pricing is probably the most regulated aspect of a firm's marketing strategy. As a result, most unethical price behavior is also illegal. Schering-Plough Corp., for example, is under investigation for offering pharmaceuticals at no cost or at extremely deep discounts to managed-care plans that include Schering-Plough drugs on HMO lists of drugs for which companies are reimbursed.[41] Some aspects of pricing, however, are still open to ethics abuses. For example, should some customers pay more for merchandise if distribution costs are higher in their areas? Do marketers have an obligation to warn customers of impending price, discount, or return policy changes? All these concerns must be dealt with in developing a professional ethic for pricing products. The ethical issues involved in pricing for today's highly competitive and increasingly computerized markets are discussed in greater detail in Chapters 13 and 14.

SOCIAL RESPONSIBILITY IN MARKETING

As several of the examples in this chapter demonstrate, companies can benefit from their contributions to society and at the same time minimize the negative impact they have on the natural and social environment. **Social responsibility** demands that marketers accept an obligation to give equal weight to profits, consumer satisfaction, and social well-being in evaluating their firm's performance. They must recognize the importance of relatively qualitative consumer and social benefits as well as the quantitative measures of sales, revenue, and profits by which firms have traditionally measured marketing performance.

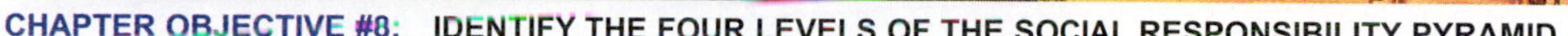

<interactive>learning goal

CHAPTER OBJECTIVE #8: IDENTIFY THE FOUR LEVELS OF THE SOCIAL RESPONSIBILITY PYRAMID.

Social responsibility allows for easier measurement than marketing ethics. Government legislation can mandate socially responsible actions. Consumer activism can also promote social responsibility by business. Actions alone determine social responsibility, and a firm can behave responsibly, even under coercion. Government requirements may force firms to take socially responsible actions in matters of environmental policy, deceptive product claims, and other areas. Also, consumers, through their power to repeat or withhold purchases, may force marketers to provide honest and relevant information and fair prices. Ethically responsible behavior, on the other hand, requires more than appropriate actions; ethical intentions must also motivate those actions. The four dimensions of social responsibility—economic, legal, ethical, and philanthropic—are shown in Figure 3.11. The first two dimensions have long been recognized, but ethical obligations and the need for marketers to be good corporate citizens have increased in importance in recent years.

The locus for socially responsible decisions in organizations has always been an important issue. Who should accept specific accountability for the social effects of marketing decisions? Responses range from the district sales manager to the marketing vice president, the firm's CEO, and even the board of directors. Probably the most valid assessment holds that all marketers, regardless of their stations in the organization, remain accountable for the social aspects of their decisions.

<interactive>exercise

'NET EX: SOCIAL RESPONSIBILITY IN MARKETING

Marketing's Responsibilities

The concept of business's social responsibility traditionally has concerned managers' relationships with customers, employees, and stockholders. Managers felt responsible for providing quality products at reasonable prices for customers, adequate wages and decent working environments for employees, and acceptable profits for stockholders. Only occasionally did the concept extend to relations with the government and rarely with the general public.

FIGURE 3.11

The Four-Step Pyramid of Corporate Social Responsibility

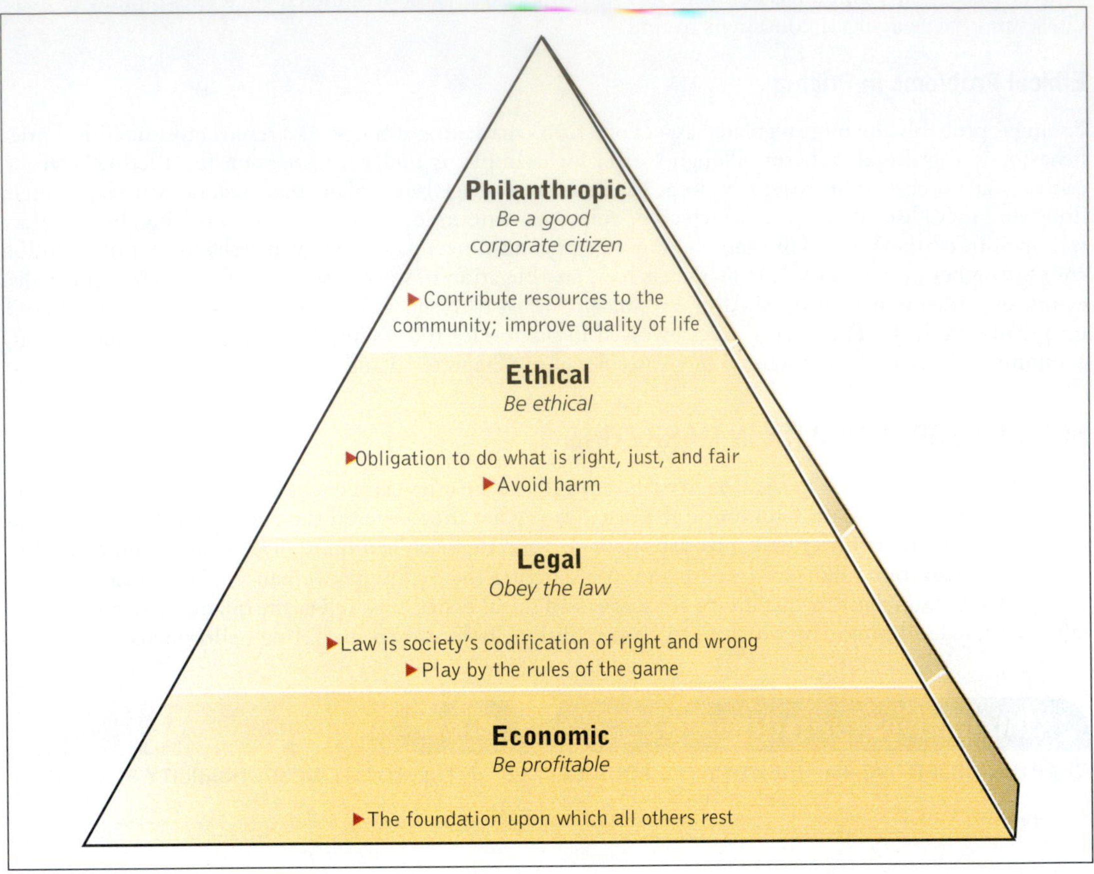

Source: Reprinted fronm *Business Horizon.* Used with permission.

Today, corporate responsibility has expanded to cover the entire societal framework. A decision to temporarily delay the installation of a pollution-control device may satisfy the traditional sense of responsibility. Customers would continue to receive an uninterrupted supply of the plant's products, employees would not face layoffs, and stockholders would still receive reasonable returns on their investments. Contemporary business ethics, however, would not accept this choice as socially responsible.

Similarly, a firm that markets foods with low nutritional value may satisfy the traditional concept of responsibility, but such behavior is questionable in contemporary perspective. This is not to say that all firms should distribute only foods of high nutritional value; it means merely that the previous framework for evaluation is no longer considered comprehensive in terms of either scope or time.

Contemporary marketing decisions must consider the entire societal framework, not only in the U.S. but throughout the world. Recently, apparel manufacturers and retailers have come under fire for buying from foreign suppliers who force employees to work in dangerous conditions or who violate child-labor laws. Drug companies, for example, that refuse to allow the development of low-cost versions of their patented drugs to combat epidemics like AIDS, malaria, or tuberculosis have been accused of ignoring the global reach of corporate responsibility. Merck's pricing policy for a year's supply of its AIDS-fighting drugs ranges from $6,000 in rich countries to $600 in less-developed nations.[42] Marketers must also take into account the long-term effects of their decisions and the well-being of future generations. Manufacturing processes that negatively impact the environment or that use up natural energy resources are easy targets for criticism.

There are several methods through which marketers can help their companies behave in socially responsible ways. Chapter 1 discussed cause marketing as just one channel through which companies can promote social causes. Socially responsible marketing involves campaigns that encourage people to adopt socially beneficial behaviors, whether they be safe driving, eating more nutritious food, or improving the working conditions of people half a world away. Not only can campaigns like these help society, but they can affect the firm's bottom line as well.

Marketing and Ecology

Ecology—the relationship between organisms and their natural environments—has become a driving force in influencing the ways in which businesses operate. Many industry and government leaders rank the protection of the environment as the biggest challenge for today's corporations. From water pollution, garbage disposal, and acid rain to depletion of the ozone layer and global warming, environmental issues are global. They influence all areas of marketing decision making from product planning to public relations, spanning such topics as planned obsolescence, pollution control, recycling waste materials, and resource conservation.

In creating new-product offerings that respond to consumer demands for convenience by offering extremely short-lived products, such as disposable diapers, ballpoint pens, razors, and cameras, marketers occasionally find themselves accused of intentionally offering products with limited durability—in other words, of practicing *planned obsolescence.* In addition to convenience-oriented items, other products become obsolete when rapid changes in technology allow for better alternatives. In the software industry, upgrades that make still-new products obsolete are the name of the game. While companies insist that upgrades are inevitable to meet increasingly sophisticated consumer demands, opponents have countered that new releases are frequently only polished versions of existing technologies, intended to stimulate sales.[43]

Public concern about pollution of such natural resources as water and air affects some industries, such as pharmaceuticals or heavy-goods manufacturing, more than others. However, the marketing system annually generates billions of tons of packaging materials such as glass, metal, paper, and plastics that add to the world's growing piles of trash and waste. Recycling such materials for reuse is another important aspect of ecology. Recycling can benefit society by saving natural resources and energy as well as by alleviating a major factor in environmental pollution—waste disposal.

The impact of powerful, highly creative promotional messages on changing consumer attitudes was never demonstrated more powerfully than in Figure 3.12. First introduced over 30 years ago by advertising agency Marstellar Inc. for the Ad Council, the industry's public service group, a Native American—the very symbol of dignity and respect for the natural world—is brought to tears by pollutants in the air, water, and land. The message made the image of Iron Eyes Cody, the tear-shedding model for the ad, an advertising icon and shamed Americans into accepting responsibility for their environment.[44]

Lawmakers in California, Massachusetts, Nebraska, and South Carolina have proposed legislation to force manufacturers to take back "e-waste"—used PCs and other technology products that contain toxic chemicals. When electronics end up in landfills, the chemicals inside them can poison groundwater, posing health risks. Manufacturers claim that recycling is prohibitively expensive and will likely add about $20 to the cost of a PC.[45]

As the saying goes, one person's trash is another's treasure. Yokohama Metals mines used cell phones, digging out the gold, platinum, and silver embedded there. It takes 125,000 phones to produce a single gold bar worth $10,000. Swedish-owned Metech International turns discarded computer hardware into gold. In just one year, the firm recovered 120,000 ounces of gold worth $35 million, as well as other precious metals including silver, platinum, and palladium.[46]

The disposal of nuclear waste is an ongoing public safety issue. Nevada recently lost its long fight against government plans to open a national storage site in the bowels of isolated Yucca Mountain, about 100 miles outside Las Vegas. The September 11 terrorist attacks gave supporters of the proposed national repository an

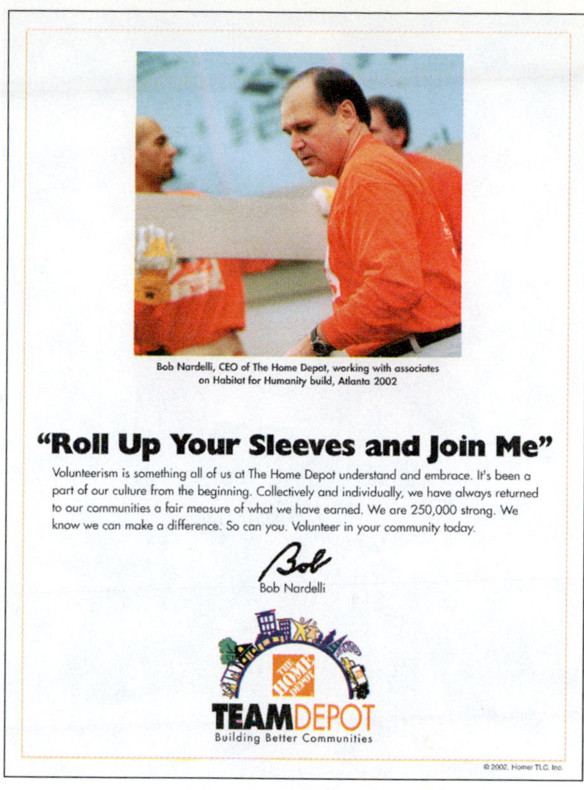

Home Depot is one of thousands of firms addressing philanthropic responsibilities by giving back to the communities in which it operates through a movement called volunteerism. *In this case, the firm's CEO and his Atlanta-based associates are working on a Habitat for Humanity project to build homes for the community's neediest citizens.*

FIGURE 3.12

Iron Eyes Cody: Teaching Generations of Americans to Become Concerned About Their Environment

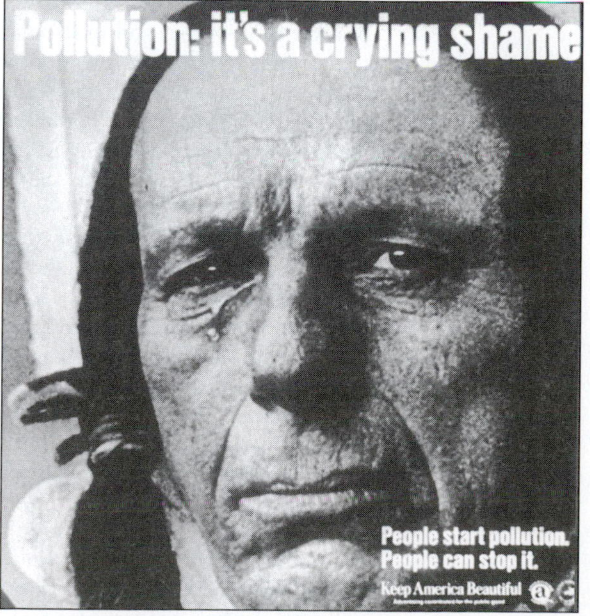

Source: Advertisement created by Marstellar Inc. for the Ad Council. Reprinted by permission of the Ad Council.

The nuclear-storage depository at Yucca Mountain, Nevada, has already cost taxpayers $4 billion.

unexpected boost. Housed at more than 100 power plants nationwide, radioactive materials pose a considerable national security risk—as possible terrorist targets. Supporters of the Nevada storage site also argue that Yucca Mountain is critical to building America's nuclear-power capacity—the means through which the nation may one day meet its own energy needs.[47]

Many companies respond to consumers' growing concern about ecological issues through **green marketing**—production, promotion, and reclamation of environmentally sensitive products. In the green marketing revolution of the early 1990s, marketers were quick to tie their companies and products to ecological themes. Yet recent trends demonstrate that consumers will not pay more at the checkout to support the environment. After finding that 70 percent of baby food shoppers prefer the convenience of plastic, Gerber Products Co. recently traded glass jars for plastic packaging. A recent poll revealed that more than 40 percent of shoppers say that they won't buy green products because they don't work as well as their competitors.[48]

STRATEGIC IMPLICATIONS OF MARKETING IN THE 21ST CENTURY

Management of the nation's businesses is affected by and must respond to a large number of important trends that are shaping business in the 21st century. The marketing decisions they make will influence and be influenced by changes in the competitive, political-legal, economic, technological, and social-cultural environments. Marketing ethics and social responsibility will continue to play important roles in business transactions in your hometown and around the globe.

As the Internet and the rapid changes in technology that it represents are fully absorbed into the competitive environment in coming years, competition will become even more intense than it is today. Respondents to a recent survey report that competitive forces will come from every sector of business. A full third believe the most serious competition will come from U.S. companies who are not yet listed in the Fortune 500. Thirty percent expect foreign marketers to pose the most formidable competitive threat. By a larger than four-to-one majority, most CEOs believe that expanding their markets is a more important priority than increasing their share of current markets.[49]

Much of the competition will result from innovations in technology and scientific discoveries. Business in the 21st century will be propelled by information technologies and sustained by creativity and entrepreneurial activity. Biotechnology—an industry whose growth was fueled in response to terrorist threats of bio-war in 2001—is still in its infancy. It is expected to explode in the next decade. Scientists will be able to create materials atom by atom, replicating much that nature can do and more.

In the 20th-century economy, the major industrial sectors included retail, financial services, and manufacturing. But today, those old sectors frequently do not fit the networked economy. The idea of what it means to be a retail company will change in five years when a billion people are logged on to the Internet. The bundling of services on the Internet will bypass many of the financial services we take for granted today. For example, when a 14-year-old buys a digital CD off the Internet, digital cash will be transferred from her hard drive to that of the recording artist, thereby eliminating the need for a bank or credit-card company. Money will eventually be relegated to encrypted numbers on disk drives and digital wallets.

Dynamic growth cannot be left entirely to self-regulation. The next ten years will produce a plethora of rules and regulations to control the marketing environments that will force businesses to change aspects of their operations. For example, new legislation to control dangerous emissions that deplete the ozone layer will lead to energy-efficient manufacturing processes and a new wave of alternative energy automobiles.

Consumers will feel the impact of environmental changes in every aspect of their lives. The new century is ushering in new generations of consumers who expect high-quality, low-cost products readily available on demand. Every company will be forced to build relationships to attract and retain loyal customers to succeed.

Underlying all the changes in the business environments and marketing mix elements is a requirement for companies to act ethically and in socially responsible ways. Marketers will have to go beyond what is legally right and wrong by integrating ethical behavior in all of their actions. Forward-looking companies will reap the benefits tomorrow of socially responsible behavior today.

<interactive>review

FLASH CHAPTER REVIEW PRESENTATION

<interactive>video case

EQUAL EXCHANGE: FAIR PAY IS FAIR PLAY

endofchaptermaterial

- Summary of Chapter Objectives
- Chapter Outline
- Key Terms
- Review Questions
- Projects and Teamwork Exercises
- 'netWork
- Crossword Puzzles
- Case 3.1: Boca Burgers—The Taste Will Change You

Ethics Quiz Answers

Quiz is on page 77.

1. 34% said personal e-mail on company computers is wrong
2. 37% said using office equipment for schoolwork is wrong
3. 49% said playing computer games at work is wrong
4. 54% said Internet shopping at work is wrong
5. 61% said it's unethical to blame your error on technology
6. 87% said it's unethical to visit pornographic sites at work
7. 33% said $25 is the amount at which a gift from a supplier or client becomes troubling, while 33% said $50, and 33% said $100
8. 35% said a $50 gift to the boss is unacceptable
9. 12% said a $50 gift from the boss is unacceptable
10. 70% said it's unacceptable to take the $200 football tickets
11. 70% said it's unacceptable to take the $120 theater tickets
12. 35% said it's unacceptable to take the $100 food basket
13. 45% said it's unacceptable to take the $25 gift certificate
14. 40% said it's unacceptable to take the $75 raffle prize
15. 11% reported they lied about sick days
16. 4% reported they have taken credit for the work or ideas of others

Briefly Speaking

Air pollution is turning Mother Nature prematurely gray.

Irv Kupcinet (b. 1912) American newspaper columnist

Take the Post-Test to assess your overall understanding of the key ideas in this chapter. The Post-Test provides a comprehensive selection of exam-style questions addressing the main topics and concepts of the chapter. At the completion of each Post-Test, you will receive a score and instructive feedback on how you answered each question, and a direct link to the part of the chapter addressed in the question. Take the Post-Test as often as you need to—a record of your progress for each attempt is kept for you to revisit and gauge your improvement. And each Post-Test is randomly generated, so every attempt is new.

Post-Test

CHAPTER 4

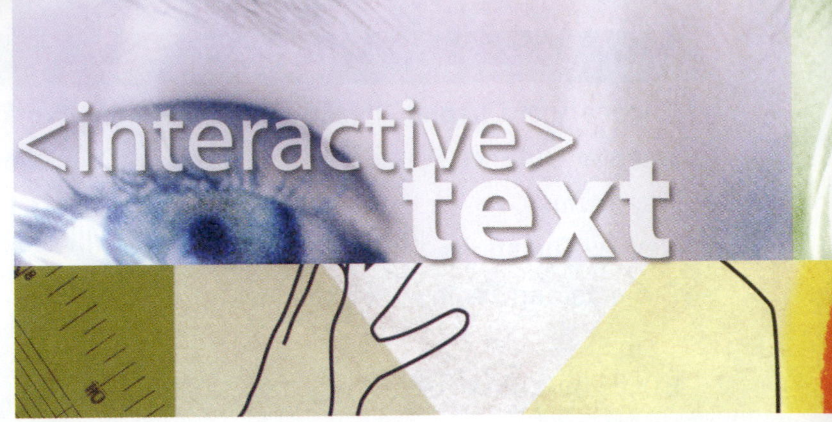

Global Dimensions of Marketing

Chapter Objectives

1. Describe the importance of international marketing from the perspectives of the individual firm and the nation.
2. Identify the major components of the environment for international marketing.
3. Outline the basic functions of GATT, WTO, NAFTA, the proposed FTAA, and the European Union.
4. Compare the alternative strategies for entering international markets.
5. Differentiate between a global marketing strategy and a multidomestic marketing strategy.
6. Describe the alternative marketing mix strategies used in international marketing.
7. Explain the attractiveness of the U.S. as a target market for foreign marketers.

E-MARKETING IS NO PICNIC IN EUROPE

When the World Wide Web opened up to the online public, American marketers began salivating over the possibility of boundless commerce. Just think: With the click of a mouse, a shopper in Geneva could order a T-shirt from a company in Chicago. A homebound New Orleans consumer could pick up fine china from London. A customer in Hong Kong could order a surfboard from Honolulu. Of course, they might encounter some distribution hurdles, maybe some tax-related headaches, a few language barriers, but worldwide e-commerce seemed like a sure bet.

But boundless e-commerce has been trickier than many first thought it would be, especially in Europe. The problem isn't even whether consumers have access to computers. Instead, the struggle centers on laws and regulations. "The legal and regulatory environment is a thicket for Internet companies, and things will get worse," warns Noah Doyle, senior vice president of business development for Mypoints.com, which set up business in the United Kingdom. Regulations governing consumer privacy and data transfers among European Union (EU) countries have made establishing a presence there more time consuming and expensive than for similar operations in the U.S.

Consider what happened to Lands' End, a mail-order retailer based in Dodgeville, Wisconsin. Company managers reasoned that their casual American clothes and accessories—khakis, cotton sweaters, windbreakers, canvas totes—would sell well over the Internet, especially in Great Britain and Germany. After all, there are plenty of Americans living in both those countries who would love a little taste of the homeland, not to mention Europeans who like American goods. But Lands' End ran up against legal roadblocks everywhere. The company's advertisement of unconditional lifetime guarantee is a violation of German law, as are other marketing promotions, such as rebates, that are considered "unconventional" by the government. Recently the Center for the Fight Against Unfair Competition, a German consumer group, took action to stop Lands' End from *honoring* the guarantee to German customers. "The law says when you sell something you can't give anything [else] away," explains group spokesperson Reiner Muenker. "Competition is supposed to focus on the product, not gimmicks."

And those are just the headaches facing international online marketers in Germany. To be fair, many of the EU's regulations are designed to protect the consumer, from privacy laws to consumer contracts. But there are so many of them—and some seem to be so extreme—that they create a quagmire for both consumers and marketers who are trying to reach each other. For instance, France requires that all contracts be completed in French whether or not goods are being transported to France. The Netherlands bans advertising claims about fuel consumption or environmental features of vehicles, while Finland will not permit marketers to advertise speed as a feature. Italy bans all forms of tobacco advertising. Sweden bans any television commercials aimed at children under twelve. Greece bans advertising for toys.

Then there's the question of whether U.S. firms need to comply with the consumer privacy laws as dictated by the European Commission. President George W. Bush has rejected the European privacy plan, saying it would be too burdensome for U.S. companies, particularly those in the financial industry who routinely transfer customer data. Instead, the Bush administration has proposed— unsuccessfully—that American companies abide by U.S. privacy laws.

Some marketers have found a solution to the tangled mess by partnering with European companies. Mentor Communications Group, creator of multimedia training applications, lined up local distributors for its products in Belgium, England, Luxembourg, and the Netherlands. "Our only barriers were language barriers," says president and CEO Dan Gallo. Which seem minor by comparison.[1]

CHAPTER OVERVIEW

Despite the difficulties encountered by marketers who try to use the Internet as a bridge across national boundaries, U.S. and foreign companies are crossing national boundaries in unprecedented numbers in search of new markets and profits. International trade now accounts for at least 25 percent of the U.S. gross domestic product (GDP), compared with 5 percent thirty years ago. As Figure 4.1 shows, ten nations account for more than 70 percent of U.S. imports and almost two-thirds percent of U.S. exports.

International trade can be divided into two categories: **exporting,** marketing domestically produced goods and services abroad, and **importing,** purchasing foreign goods and services. International trade is vital to a nation and its

Pre-Test

Take the Pre-Test to assess your initial knowledge of the key ideas in this chapter. The Pre-Test provides exam-style questions addressing the main topics and concepts of the chapter. At the completion of each Pre-Test, you will receive a score and instructive feedback on how you answered each question, and a direct link to the part of the chapter addressed in the question. Take the Pre-Test as often as you need to—a record of your progress for each attempt is kept for you to revisit and gauge your improvement.

FIGURE 4.1

Top Ten U.S. Trading Partners

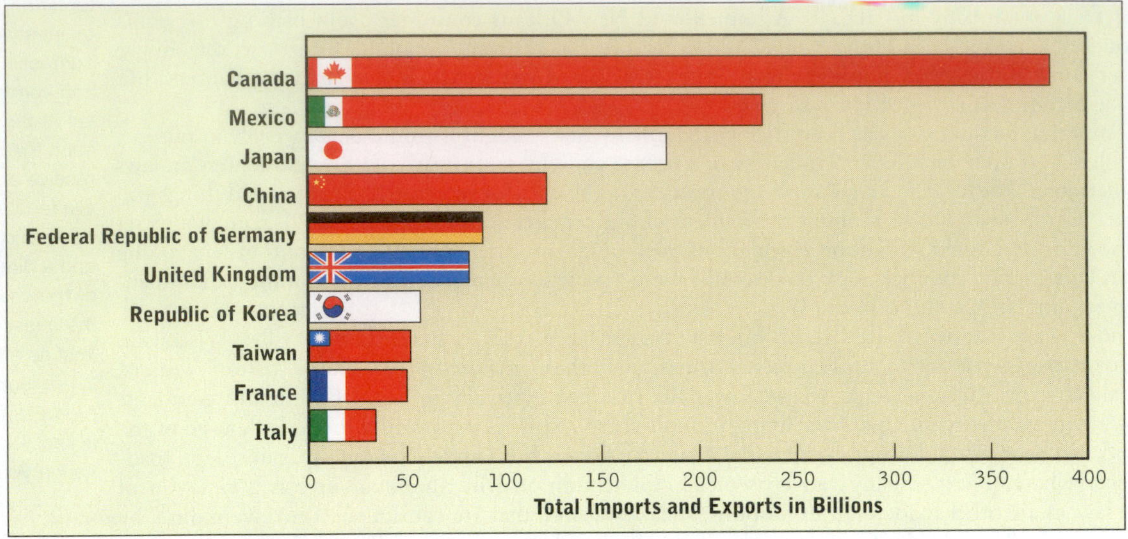

Source: U.S. Census Bureau, "Top Ten Countries with Which the U.S. Trades." Downloaded from http://www.census.gov, May 29, 2002.

marketers for several reasons. It expands markets, makes production and distribution economies possible, allows companies to explore growth opportunities in other nations, and makes them less dependent on economic conditions in their home nations. Many also find that global marketing and international trade can help them meet customer demand, reduce costs, and provide valuable information on potential markets around the world.

For North American marketers, international trade is especially important because the U.S. and Canadian economies represent a mature market for many products. Outside North America, however, it is a different story. Economies in many parts of sub-Saharan Africa, Asia, Latin America, Europe, and the Middle East are growing rapidly. This opens up new markets for U.S. products as consumers in these areas have more money to spend and as the need for American goods and services by foreign companies expands. Exports of high-tech products account for more than one-fourth of U.S total exports worldwide—the largest segment at a whopping $181 billion. International trade also builds employment. The world's 50 largest businesses keep 7.3 million people gainfully employed.[2] Your next job, in fact, might involve global marketing, since export-related jobs play an important role in the U.S. economy.

International marketers carefully evaluate the marketing concepts described in earlier chapters. However, transactions that cross national borders involve additional considerations. For example, different laws, varying levels of technological capability, economic conditions, cultural and business norms, and consumer preferences often require new strategies. Companies that want to market their products worldwide must reconsider each of the marketing variables (product, price, distribution, and promotion) in terms of the global marketplace. To succeed in global marketing, today's marketers answer questions such as: How do our products fit into a foreign market? How can we turn potential threats into opportunities? Which strategic alternatives will work in global markets?

Many of the answers to these questions can be found by studying techniques used by successful international marketers. This chapter first considers the importance and characteristics of the global marketplace. It then examines the international marketing environment, the trend toward multinational economic integration, and the steps that most firms take to enter the global marketplace. Next, the importance of developing an international marketing mix is discussed. The chapter closes with a look at the U.S. as a target market for foreign marketers.

THE IMPORTANCE OF GLOBAL MARKETING

As the list of the world's 10 largest corporations shown in Table 4.1 reveals, half of them are headquartered in the U.S. For most U.S. companies—both large and small—global marketing is rapidly becoming a necessity. The demand for foreign products in the fast-growing economies of Asia and other Pacific Rim nations offers one example of the benefits of thinking globally. In a recent year, U.S. exports to Asia rose 37 percent to about $200 billion—almost twice its exports to Europe. This surge is partly because Asian consumers believe American goods are higher quality and a better value than those made in their own countries. International marketers recognize how the slogan "Made in the USA" yields tremendous selling power throughout the world. As a result, overseas sales are important revenue sources for many U.S. firms.

<interactive>**learning goal**

CHAPTER OBJECTIVE #1: DESCRIBE THE IMPORTANCE OF INTERNATIONAL MARKETING FROM THE PERSPECTIVES OF THE INDIVIDUAL FIRM AND THE NATION.

Over the last 15 years, U.S. exports have grown an average of 10 percent each year, with the number one export during this time period being agricultural products. Other products included among the top five U.S. exports were electrical machinery, computers and office equipment, general industrial machinery, and motor vehicle parts. Among the leading U.S. firms in terms of the portion of their revenues generated from exports were Boeing, Intel, Motorola, Caterpillar, and Sun Microsystems.

Wal-Mart currently ranks as the biggest retailer in the U.S., Canada, and Mexico. And although it recently passed longtime leaders ExxonMobil and General Motors as America's largest corporation, its sights are clearly aimed at global dominance. The retail giant is currently devoting billions of dollars in expansion efforts abroad in Great Britain, the European mainland, Japan, and South America. After some early stumbles with foreign languages, customs, and regulations, the Bentonville, Arkansas–based company is beginning to gain its stride overseas, planning at least 120 new store openings annually during the next few years. "As a global organization, they've become more savvy," says Ira Kalish, director of global retail intelligence at PricewaterhouseCoopers.[3]

The rapid globalization of business and the boundless nature of the Internet have made it possible for every marketer to become an international marketer. However, as the opening vignette illustrates, becoming an Internet international marketer is not necessarily easy. While larger firms have the advantage of more resources and wider distribution systems, smaller companies can build Web sites for as little as a few hundred dollars and can bring products to market quickly. Beth and Lou Drucker began their wedding supplier referral service in 1996 with $3,000. Recently, the couple took their business online at http://NewYorkMetroWeddings.com. The site was an instant hit and remains so, with about 300,000 visitors per month. In one 12-month period, the company tripled in size.[4]

Just as some firms depend on foreign and Internet sales, others rely on purchasing raw materials abroad as input for their domestic manufacturing operations. A North Carolina furniture manufacturer may depend on purchases of South American mahogany, while 21st century furniture retailers are taking advantage of increased Chinese-made styling and quality and their traditionally low prices. The top five U.S.

TABLE 4.1

The World's 10 Largest Marketers

Rank	Company	Country of Origin
1	Wal-Mart Stores	United States
2	ExxonMobil	United States
3	General Motors	United States
4	British Petroleum	Britain
5	Ford Motor Co.	United States
6	DaimlerChrysler	Germany
7	Royal Dutch/Shell	Britain/Netherlands
8	General Electric	United States
9	Toyota Motor	Japan
10	Citicorp	United States

Source: Paola Hjelt, "Fortune Global Hundred," *Fortune,* July 22, 2002.

The global coverage and international reputation of the Hilton name combine to generate additional sales revenues both in the U.S. and around the world as both business and vacation travelers from the U.S. and other countries select accommodations for their stays. Hilton's affiliated hotels offer different services to meet specific traveler needs and the Hilton HHonors frequent-stay card seeks to enhance customer loyalty through rewards for heavy users.

imports are computers and office equipment, crude oil, clothing, telecommunications equipment, and agricultural products. Over the past 15 years, U.S. imports have grown about 7 percent annually.

Service and Retail Exports

In addition to agricultural products and manufactured goods, the U.S. is also the world's largest exporter of services and retailing. Of the approximately $210 billion in annual U.S. service exports, over half comes from travel and tourism—money spent by foreign nationals visiting the U.S. Tourism is the third-largest U.S. industry, contributing $430 billion to its economy each year, and is responsible for creating more than $6 billion in travel and tourism-related jobs. With 102 million tourists per year, the U.S. ranks second only to China in visitors. By 2020, tourists will spend $2 trillion during their international travels. Vacation marketers look to attract and serve customers on a global basis. Hilton Hotels' HHonors program allows travelers to earn hotel points and airline miles for the same stay at any Hilton or affiliate—including Doubletree, Homewood Suites, and Conrad hotels—around the world. If customers book their trip online, they earn 1,000 bonus points toward upgrades and free stays.[5]

The most profitable U.S. service exports are business and technical services, such as engineering, financial, computing, legal services, and entertainment. Worldwide Internet services revenues grew an enormous 71 percent to almost $8 billion during a recent 12-month period. Even more surprising is that the growth is expected to continue at a 60 percent annual rate. The U.S. continues to be the largest market for Internet service providers.[6]

The financial services industry, already a major presence outside North America, is expanding globally via the Internet. Nearly half of the world's active Web population visits a finance Web site at least once a month, with online stock trading and banking leading the way. And more than one of every four Europeans with Internet access currently banks online. By 2005, nearly 60 million French, German, British, Italian, and Spanish consumers will bank online.[7] A glance at the increasing number of foreign companies listed on the New York Stock Exchange illustrates the importance of global financial services.

A number of global service exporters are household names in the U.S.: American Express, AT&T, Citicorp, Disney, and Allstate Insurance. Many earn a substantial percentage of their revenues from international sales. Others are smaller firms, such as the many software firms that have found overseas markets receptive to their products. Still others are nonprofit organizations such as the United States Postal Service, which is attempting to increase overall revenues by operating a worldwide delivery service, as illustrated in Figure 4.2. The service competes with for-profit firms like DHL, UPS, and Federal Express.

The entertainment industry is another major service exporter. Movies, TV shows, and music groups often travel to the ends of the earth to find their audience. Almost a century of exposure to U.S.-made films, television programs, and—more recently—music video clips have made international viewers more familiar with American culture and geography than any other nation on earth. However, some markets are more receptive to American entertainment than others, depending on their own culture and language barriers. India and some Asian countries have their own entertainment industries, complete with stars, and are not necessarily interested in American products. Still, when Warner Bros. released *Lethal Weapon 4* in Hong Kong, it hired a popular local heavy metal band to create a promotional music video in the hope of attracting viewers to the movie.

American retailers ranging from Victoria's Secret, Foot Locker, and The Gap to Office Depot, Toys "R" Us, and Costco, are opening stores around the world at rapid paces. U.S. retailers do especially well in Asia, where consumers like the convenience and wide selection of American-made products. They are also attracted to products associated with American lifestyles. Seattle-based Recreational Equipment Inc. (REI) recently opened a Tokyo store featuring an indoor rock-climbing wall and in-store Starbucks coffee shop. A footwear test trail lets Japanese customers try out hiking boots and trail running shoes; the Kids' Camp area will let children have fun in a "play" campsite; and a family of life-sized bronze bears welcomes shoppers to the new store.[8]

During the last three decades, U.S. fast-food franchises have been opening outlets in foreign countries at a phenomenal rate. To meet local demands for U.S. pizza styles in Brazil, Tricon Global opened 60 Pizza

FIGURE 4.2

The U.S. Postal Service's Global Delivery Service: Increasing Revenues by Offering High-Speed International Delivery Service

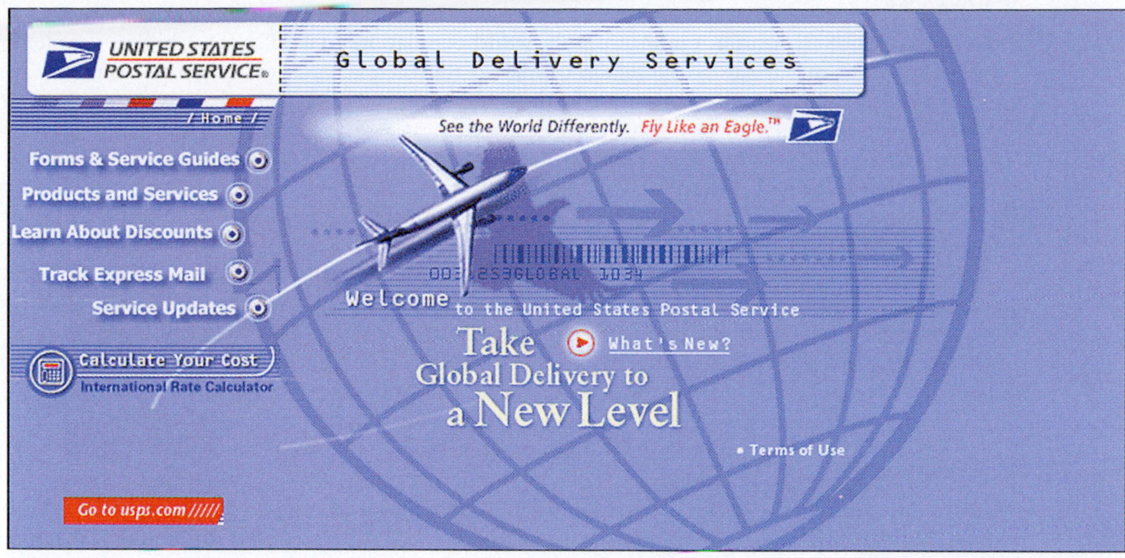

Hut restaurants there by 2003. Pizza Hut competitor Domino's countered by opening 48 new outlets there. McDonald's currently operates over 6,000 outlets internationally in 91 countries. Domino's Pizza now serves its pies to customers in 1,200 outlets in 46 countries. Arby's parent company, Florida-based Triarc Restaurant Group, operates over 3,000 outlets in the U.S. and has recently signed an agreement with Sybra Restaurants UK to take the roast-beef sandwich chain to London. Over 100 Arby's restaurants are expected to open in the U.K. during the next 10 years.[9]

Benefits of Going Global

Besides generating additional revenue, firms expand their operations outside their home country to gain other benefits, including new insights into consumer behavior, alternative distribution strategies, and advance notice of new products. By setting up foreign offices and production facilities, marketers may learn new marketing techniques and gain invaluable experience.

Global marketers are typically well-positioned to compete effectively with foreign competitors. A major key to achieving success in foreign markets is a firm's ability to adapt its products to local preferences. It's important for a fast-food marketer to know that Venezuelans like their fries with mayonnaise, not ketchup; Chileans want an avocado on their burger instead of a tomato; and Europeans prefer the word "light" to "diet" on their cola drinks.[10]

Another method used by international marketers before entering foreign markets is to conduct transcontinental product testing. Procter & Gamble is a veteran of global marketing but only recently began to develop truly global products. Swiffer, a lightweight mop with disposable cleaning cloths that use static electricity to attract dust and dirt, was successfully test marketed in Cedar Rapids, Iowa, and in Sens, France, before its global launch. As one P&G spokesperson explained, "The more that we truly explore consumers on a global basis, the more we find that they're really more alike than they are dissimilar."[11]

Since firms must perform the marketing functions of buying, selling, transporting, storing, standardizing and grading, financing, risk taking, and obtaining market information in both domestic and global markets, some may question the wisdom of treating international marketing as a distinct subject. After all, international marketing is marketing; a firm performs the same functions and works toward the same objectives in domestic or international marketing. As the chapter will explain, however, both similarities and differences influence strategies for international and domestic marketing.

THE INTERNATIONAL MARKETPLACE

Today, it is rare to find a U.S. firm that never ventures outside its domestic market. Even if it focuses almost entirely on the domestic market, which is huge in its own right, it may look overseas for raw materials or component parts or it may face foreign competition in its home market. Those who venture abroad may find the international marketplace far different than the domestic one they are accustomed to. Market sizes, buyer behavior, and marketing practices all vary. To be successful, international marketers must do their homework, capitalize on similarities, and carefully evaluate all market segments in which they expect to compete.

Market Size

From the dawn of civilization until the 1800s, world population grew to about 1 billion people. It almost doubled by 1900, and today over 6 billion people inhabit the planet. According to Census Bureau projections, world population will increase to nearly 8 billion by 2025. Ninety-six percent of the increase in world population occurs in less-developed regions such as Africa, Asia, and Latin America. Population growth rates in affluent countries, however, have slowed to 0.4 percent annually—one-fifth the annual growth of less-developed countries. What this all means is that, over the next quarter-century, firms will have to adapt their goods and services to meet the needs and wants of growing numbers of young consumers in developing countries.

One-fifth of the world's population—1.2 billion people—lives in China. Africa is growing fastest at 2.8 percent a year, followed by Latin America at 1.9 percent and Asia at 1.7 percent. Average birth rates are dropping around the world due to family planning efforts, but death rates are declining even more rapidly and people are living longer. Although African birth rates are still high—6 children per woman—European birth rates have fallen considerably, with couples averaging only 1 or 2 children.12 All of this information is important to marketers as they try to target these markets for their goods and services.

The global marketplace is increasingly an urban one. Today, almost 50 percent of its people live in large cities. As a result, city populations are swelling: 39 cities currently have a population of 5 million or more. Mexico City, whose population of 18 million ranks it as the world's largest city, is expected to grow to 31 million by 2010. Increased urbanization will expand the need for transportation, housing, machinery, and services.

The growing size and urbanization of the international marketplace does not necessarily mean all foreign markets offer the same potential. Another important influence on market potential is a nation's economic development stage. In a subsistence economy such as Nepal, most people engage in agriculture and earn low incomes, supporting few opportunities for international trade of any magnitude. In a newly industrialized country, such as Brazil or South Korea, growth in manufacturing creates demand for consumer products and industrial goods such as high-tech equipment. Industrial nations, including the U.S., Japan, and countries in western Europe, trade manufactured goods and services among themselves and export to less-developed countries. Although these wealthy countries account for just a small percentage of the world's population, they produce over half of its output.

FIGURE 4.3

High-Speed Bullet Trains: Sophisticated Transportation Component of the Japanese Infrastructure

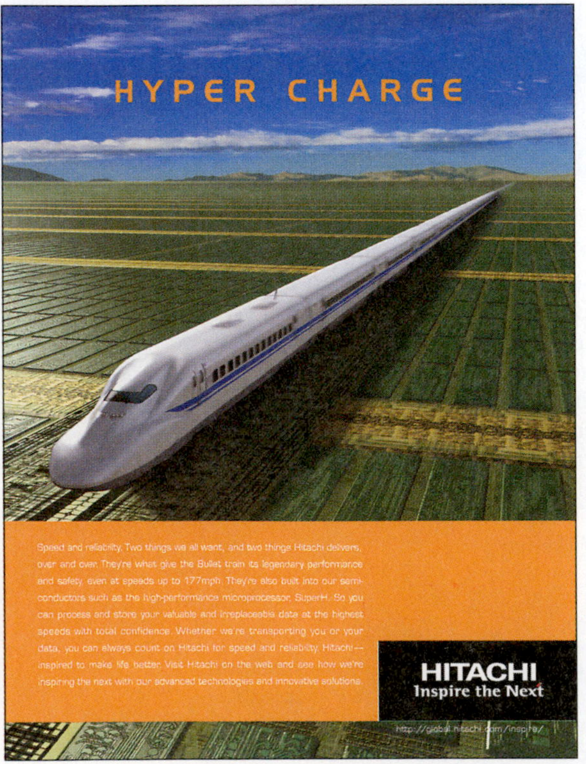

As a nation develops, an increasingly affluent, educated, and cosmopolitan middle class emerges. India's middle class includes nearly 300 million people, a number larger than the entire U.S. population. India's processed-food producers and marketers are now facing global competition as a result of economic reforms and market liberalization. But marketers in India must overcome an underdeveloped **infrastructure,** the underlying foundation for modern life and efficient marketing that includes transportation and communications networks, banking, utilities, and public services. In addition, cultural differences and language barriers frequently exist. On the other end of the scale is Japan, a highly industrialized, educated country with a sophisticated infrastructure that includes such high-speed transportation modes as the bullet trains shown in Figure 4.3. However, in both cases, significant opportunities can be found through joint ventures and strategic alliances.

International marketers see much growth in middle-income households occurring in the booming East Asian economies such as China, Thailand, Singapore, South Korea, and Hong Kong, as well as in Mexico, South America, and sub-Saharan Africa. These new middle-class consumers have both the desire for consumer goods, including luxury and leisure goods and services, and money to pay for them.

Buyer Behavior

Buyer behavior differs among nations and often among market segments within a country. Marketers must carefully match their marketing strategies to local customs, tastes, and living conditions. Even the Coca-Cola Co. can't go to the bank on its name alone in foreign countries. That's because, although Americans consume an average of 872 servings of soft drinks a year, Germans drink only 344 and Chinese a mere 23.[13] Still, Coke commands about half of the global soft-drink market and generates 60 percent of its sales from international markets by varying its product emphasis in different parts of the world. In Japan, it heavily promotes Leaf, a new canned-tea product that has become a hot seller there. The reason for the shift: Soft drinks make up only 20 percent of nonalcoholic beverage sales in Japan.[14]

Meanwhile, Coke's rival PepsiCo is concentrating much of its efforts on the snack foods that its Frito-Lay division produces. In Mexico, the firm's Sabritas brand snacks have captured 81 percent of the salty snack market. PepsiCo plans to export its Mexican marketing strategy—which includes installing colorful "Power of One" displays of Pepsi products in small neighborhood groceries—to other developing nations such as China and India. PepsiCo marketers recognize that to be successful in these countries where personal incomes are low, they must attract consumers by keeping prices low and increasing the availability of snack foods and soft drinks.[15]

In some instances, international marketers succeed in changing local buyer behavior by introducing new marketing strategies that have been well-received in other countries. Johnson & Johnson (J&J) recently debuted RoC, a 40-year-old French line of skincare products, in an attempt to leverage its strong European brand in the U.S. market. J&J marketers are positioning RoC as a major alternative to both the mass-market brand of L'Oréal and prestige department-store brands such as Clinique.[16]

Failure to adapt to local preferences can create costly problems. The French discount retailer Promodes recently expanded into other countries such as Turkey, only to discover that almost everything—from the atmosphere in its huge hypermarkets to the color of meat—had to be modified to meet the specific expectations of Turkish consumers. Shoppers there don't like the large, orderly, brightly lit Promodes store that was recently opened in Mersin, Turkey. They prefer the clutter of their own retail chain, Cetinkaya, which places metal baskets filled with inexpensive goods that customers can dig through to find bargains, like they would at a traditional open-air market. They also want fresh beef to have a light pink color. If it is too dark, they won't buy it. Promodes managers know that they are going to have to make some adjustments if the French discounter is going to be successful in Turkey.[17]

Differences in buying patterns require marketing executives to complete considerable research before entering a foreign market. Sometimes the marketer's own organization or a U.S.-based research firm can provide needed information. In other cases, only a foreign-based marketing research organization can tell marketers what they need to know. Regardless of who conducts the research, investigators must focus on six different areas before advising a company to enter a foreign market:

1. *Demand.* Do foreign consumers need the company's good or service?
2. *Competitive environment.* How do supplies currently reach the market?
3. *Economic environment.* What is the state of the nation's economic health?
4. *Social-cultural environment.* How do cultural factors affect business opportunities?
5. *Political-legal environment.* Do any legal restrictions complicate entering the market?
6. *Technological environment.* To what degree are technological innovations used by consumers in the market?

THE INTERNATIONAL MARKETING ENVIRONMENT

As in domestic markets, the environmental factors discussed in Chapter 3 have a powerful influence on the development of international marketing strategies. Marketers must pay close attention to economic, social-cultural, political-legal, and technological influences as they venture abroad.

<interactive>**learning goal**

CHAPTER OBJECTIVE #2: IDENTIFY THE MAJOR COMPONENTS OF THE ENVIRONMENT FOR INTERNATIONAL MARKETING.

International Economic Environment

A nation's size, per-capita income, and stage of economic development determine its prospects as a host for international business expansion. Nations with low per-capita incomes may be poor markets for expensive industrial machinery but good ones for agricultural hand tools. These nations cannot afford the technical equipment that powers an industrialized society. Wealthier countries may offer prime markets for many U.S. industries, particularly those producing consumer goods and services and advanced industrial products.

In India, for example, the median annual household income is only $480. Economic reforms have improved the country's standard of living somewhat, but most Indians have very few Western conveniences. Only 2 percent own cars, 4 percent have running hot water, and 7 percent have phones. Color television and refrigerator ownership run a bit higher at 12 percent.

FIGURE 4.4

Korea: A Newly Industrialized Nation with a Sophisticated Infrastructure, Employee Skills, and Sufficient Per-Capita Incomes Needed to Attract New Businesses and International Retailers

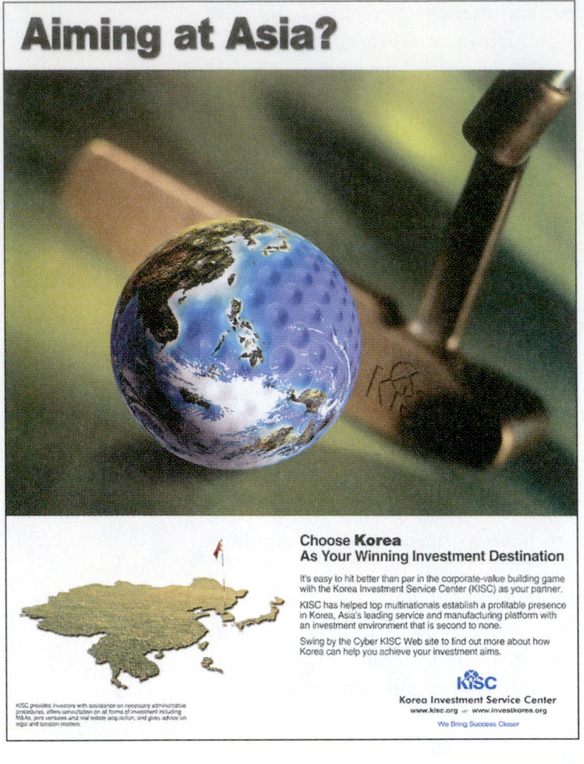

Successful marketing in India requires an understanding of how the economy affects Indian consumers. Both rich and poor Indians practice frugal buying habits and spend as little as possible at one time. They prefer small packages with low prices, even though larger packages may offer more economical purchases. Even the wealthy are price-conscious consumers. Nestlé S.A. improved its market penetration in India by reducing package sizes and then pricing more than half of its food products under 25 rupees (about 70 cents). For example, sales of Maggi instant noodles tripled after Nestlé reduced the price from 19 cents to 14 cents a package. Recycling, a way of life for many Indians, is another issue U.S. marketers must keep in mind before entering the Indian marketplace. Although that country is the world's largest market for razor blades, disposable razors sell very poorly because the idea of throwing them away mystifies typical Indians.[18]

Infrastructure, discussed earlier in the chapter, is another important economic factor to consider when planning to enter a foreign market. An inadequate infrastructure may constrain marketers' plans to manufacture, promote, and distribute goods and services in a particular country. People living in countries blessed by navigable waters often rely on them as inexpensive, relatively efficient alternatives to highways, rail lines, and air transportation. Thai farmers use their nation's myriad rivers to transport their crops. Their boats even become retail outlets in so-called floating markets like the one located outside the capital city of Bangkok.

Marketers expect developing economies to have substandard utility and communications networks. China encountered numerous problems in establishing a 21st-century communications industry infrastructure. The Chinese government's answer was a huge investment in wireless technology. China's cell phone market is the largest in the world now, with Nokia, Motorola, and local providers all vying for places next to Chinese ears. In one year alone, 60 million cell phones were sold there, and the number will grow to 200 million subscribers by 2010. But Chinese cell phone users pay only a nickel a minute, one of the cheapest rates in the world.[19] The South Korean business recruitment message shown in Figure 4.4 is based on the reality that people who live in most newly industrialized countries have established a strong enough infrastructure to begin attracting customers from around the world.

Changes in exchange rates can also complicate international marketing. An **exchange rate** is the price of one nation's currency in terms of another country's currency. Fluctuations in exchange rates can make a nation's currency more valuable or less valuable compared with those of other nations. Argentina plunged into a deep recession for several years, during which it devalued its currency, the peso, which was previously tied to the U.S. dollar. This made Argentina and some of its neighbors a less attractive trade partner for many international businesses.[20] Argentina's struggles are discussed in more detail in the "Marketing Misses" Interactive Example.

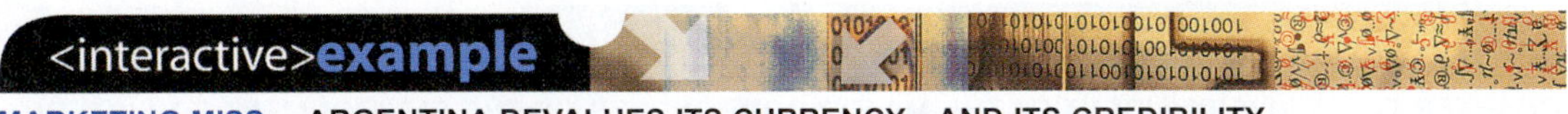

MARKETING MISS: ARGENTINA DEVALUES ITS CURRENCY—AND ITS CREDIBILITY

In 2002, the European Union introduced a new, uniform currency called the euro. The long-range idea behind the new currency is that switching to a single currency will actually strengthen Europe's competitiveness in the global marketplace.[21] Russian and many eastern European currencies are considered *soft currencies* that cannot be readily converted into such hard currencies as the dollar, euro, or Japanese yen. Rather than taking payment in soft currencies, international marketers doing business in these countries may resort to barter, accepting such commodities as oil or timber as payment for exports. U.S. currency continues to be one of the strongest in the world; in fact, demand for American dollars is higher than ever.

International Social-Cultural Environment

Before entering a foreign market, marketers should study all aspects of that nation's culture, including language, education, religious attitudes, and social values. Indian executives are accustomed to interrupting each other. Europeans feel as if they are being treated like children when asked to wear name tags. Israelis prefer fast-paced meetings, without small talk. Malaysian and Japanese managers expect six-second pauses for silence during negotiations. Italians, Germans, and French believe that it is manipulative to soften someone up before offering criticism.[22]

Language plays an important role in international marketing. Table 4.2 lists the world's eight most frequently spoken languages. Marketers must make sure not only to use the right language for a country but also ensure that the message is translated and conveys the intended meaning. Abbreviations and slang words and phrases may also cause misunderstandings when marketing abroad. Among the most humorous—and disastrous—language faux pas by marketers are the following:

- The mailbox icon used for e-mail messages is confusing to most Europeans. To them it looks like a loaf of bread.
- Clocks are out as gifts in China. They're considered by Chinese to be symbols of death.
- Speaking of death, Koreans refer to the Pentium IV chip as the "chip of death."
- Kentucky Fried Chicken's "finger lickin' good" slogan translates literally to "eat your fingers off" in China.
- The "Bakin" brand logo used on some Nike shoes proved offensive in several Muslim countries because it resembles the word *Allah* in Arabic.
- The well-known baby-food brand Gerber translates as "vomit" in French.[23]

Briefly Speaking

An Argentine is an Italian who speaks Spanish and thinks he is British.

Lydia Chavez (b. 1952) American journalist and educator

International Technological Environment

More than any innovation since the telephone, Internet technology has made it possible for both large and small firms to be connected to the entire world. The Internet transcends political, economic, and cultural barriers, reaching to every corner of the globe. As the "Marketing Hits" Interactive Example illustrates, the Internet has helped traditional brick-and-mortar retailers add new e-commerce alternatives. It also assists developing nations in becoming competitive with industrialized nations.

Consider the following facts regarding the Internet:

- The world's online population currently stands at more than 300 million, with the most users in North America and the fewest in the Middle East.
- Business-to-consumer e-commerce grew $120 billion in 2004.
- Advertising on the Web already surpasses $4 billion.
- By 2005, more than 700 million Internet users will be non-English-speaking; only 250 million will be English-speaking Internet users.[24]

MARKETING HIT: SAFEWAY AND TESCO TEAM UP FOR ONLINE GROCERY SHOPPING

The Internet is truly a global medium that allows seamless communications and business transactions between individual consumers and multinational companies. It is critical that 21st-century marketers understand how the Web is reshaping social and cultural values, as discussed in this chapter's opening vignette.

Technology presents challenges for international marketers that extend beyond the Internet and other telecommunications innovations. A major issue involving food marketers competing in Europe is genetic reengineering. Although U.S. grocery shelves are filled with foods grown with genetically modified organisms (GMOs), most Americans do not know they are eating GMO foods, since no labeling disclosures are required. In Britain and other European countries, the story is quite different. Referred to in these countries as "Frankenfoods,"

TABLE 4.2

The World's Most Frequently Spoken Languages

Rank	Language	Number of Speakers
1	Chinese (Mandarin)	1.2 billion
2	English	478 million
3	Hindi	437 million
4	Spanish	392 million
5	Russian	284 million
6	Arabic	225 million
7	Portuguese	184 million
8	French	125 million

Source: Reported in "Vital Statistics," *U.S. News & World Report*, July 2, 2001, p. 9.

The global reach of the Internet and the size of the Asian marketplace are the main reasons for the startling speed at which marketers are adopting this innovation and using it to their advantage.

activists are pushing for labeling laws to inform shoppers that these foods are "not naturally grown" or to ban them altogether. Marketers of agricultural commodities and packaged goods are already taking actions in response to these concerns. Gerber recently reformulated its baby foods to remove all ingredients containing GMOs.[25]

International Political-Legal Environment

Global marketers must continually stay abreast of laws and trade regulations in each country in which they compete. Some laws, such as *les Soldes* (the Sales) in France, are uncommon to U.S. marketers. By law, retail sales can be held only twice a year—in January or February and again during autumn. At least 30 percent of French clothing sales occur during these two sales seasons.[26]

Political conditions often influence international marketing, as well. Political unrest in places like the Middle East, Afghanistan, Africa, eastern Europe, and South America sometimes results in acts of violence, such as destruction of a firm's property. As a result, many Western firms have set up internal *political risk assessment (PRA)* units or turned to outside consulting services to evaluate the political risks of the marketplaces in which they operate. In addition, the fall of communism and the transformation of state-dominated industries into privately owned and managed profit-seeking enterprises has been accompanied by a trend toward freer trade among nations.

The political environment also involves labor conditions in different countries. Chinese officials do not respond well to labor unrest, particularly when it spills into the streets in protest. As recently as 1998, government officials jailed labor activist Zhang Shangguang for ten years for "endangering state security." A year later, 1,000 miners blocked a railway over delayed pay, and 2,000 retired steelworkers barricaded a road after their pensions were cut. In 2002, tens of thousands of factory workers surrounded government buildings, demanding that city officials resign because of unpaid employment benefits and back pay. Protests like these seem to provoke the government's old tactics of rounding people up, arresting them, silencing them with bribes, and the like. All of this makes for an uncertain climate for foreign businesses and investors. Still, many choose to pursue their investment in such a large potential market. The situation "hasn't deterred us," says Michael Dell, founder and CEO of Dell Computer Corp. "We [understand] the risk."[27]

The legal environment for U.S. firms operating abroad results from three forces: (1) international law, (2) U.S. law, and (3) legal requirements of host nations. International law emerges from the treaties, conventions, and agreements that exist among nations. The U.S. has many *friendship, commerce, and navigation (FCN) treaties* with other governments. These agreements set terms for various aspects of commercial relations with other countries, such as the right to conduct business in the treaty partner's domestic market. Other international business agreements concern worldwide standards for various products, patents, trademarks, reciprocal tax treaties, export control, international air travel, and international communication.

Since the 1990s, Europe has pushed for mandatory *ISO (International Standards Organization) 9000 certification*—internationally recognized standards that ensure a company's goods and services meet established quality levels. Today, many U.S. companies follow these certification standards as well. The International Monetary Fund, another major player in the international legal environment, lends foreign exchange to nations that require it to conduct international trade. These agreements facilitate the whole process of world marketing. However, there are no international laws for corporations, only for governments. So marketers include special provisions in contracts, such as which country's courts have jurisdiction.

The second dimension of the international legal environment, U.S. law, includes various trade regulations, tax laws, and import/export requirements that affect international marketing. One important law, the Export Trading Company Act of 1982, exempts companies from antitrust regulations so they can form export groups that offer a variety of products to foreign buyers. The law seeks to make it easier for foreign buyers to connect with U.S. exporters. A controversial 1996 law, the Helms-Burton Act, tried to impose trade sanctions against Cuba. Under this law, U.S. corporations and citizens can sue foreign companies and their executives for using expropriated U.S. assets to do business in Cuba. The Foreign Corrupt Practices Act, which makes it illegal to bribe a foreign official in an attempt to solicit new or repeat sales abroad, has had a major impact on international marketing. The act also mandates that adequate accounting controls be installed to monitor internal compliance. Violations can result in a $1 million fine for the firm and a $10,000 fine and five-year imprisonment for the individuals involved. This law has been controversial, mainly because it fails to clearly define what constitutes bribery. The 1988 Trade Act amended the law to include more specific statements of prohibited practices.

Finally, legal requirements of host nations affect foreign marketers. International marketers generally recognize the importance of obeying legal requirements since even the slightest violation could set back the future of international trade. As discussed in the opening vignette, marketers must navigate a maze of international and foreign laws pertaining to conducting business on the Internet. Sometimes foreign governments allow practices that are not accepted worldwide, as discussed in the "Solving an Ethical Controversy" Interactive Example. Most European laws governing e-commerce have to do with consumer privacy. The U.S. and European Commission are still at odds over whose consumer privacy laws should reign supreme.[28]

Briefly Speaking

The new trade routes of the [21st century] are laser flashes and satellite beams. The cargo is not silk or spices, but technology, information, and ideas.

Renato Ruggiero (b. 1930)
Italian-born director general, World Trade Organization

RIGHT/WRONG: SOLVING AN ETHICAL CONTROVERSY—CHINA'S CREDIBILITY IN THE WORLD MARKETPLACE IS PLAGUED BY PIRACY

A number of European countries have also enacted stringent laws restricting marketing aimed at children. Sweden limits all TV and radio marketing to children age 12 and under, and direct marketing to children under 16. The British Codes of Advertising and Sales Promotion specify that marketing to children may not encourage them to eat or drink near bedtime, or to replace regular meals with snacks or candy. Most European countries also restrict the use of famous cartoon or comic characters, actors, athletes, or other celebrities to attract children to products.[29]

Legal requirements of host countries can create unexpected hurdles. Under new city laws in Beijing, China's capital city, all companies must remove advertising signs that have been posted in pavement or on rooftops. That includes McDonald's famous golden arches, which have risen above Beijing for the past decade. McDonald's has been a huge success in Beijing, particularly with children and teens. But middle-aged and elderly Chinese citizens often view the fast-food chain as a victory of capitalism over traditional Chinese cooking. And city officials, intent on sprucing up Beijing's image by the time it hosts the 2008 Summer Olympics, have decided that the arches "are not in harmony with the surroundings and affect the architectural ambience." Cai Weiqian, deputy general manager of Beijing McDonald's, is concerned about the effects of the new regulation on his business. "Seventy percent of our business comes from people who see our signs," he argues. "Fast food is an instant consumption, and sign-boards are important to attract customers." But a Chinese official in the public relations office of Beijing McDonald's demurs. "We are a law-abiding company. Since the city government has adjusted its rules, we will follow the new regulations."[30]

Trade Barriers

Assorted trade barriers also affect global marketing. These barriers fall into two major categories: **tariffs**—taxes levied on imported products—and administrative, or nontariff, barriers. Some tariffs impose set taxes per pound, gallon, or unit; others are calculated according to the value of the imported item. Administrative barriers are more subtle than tariffs and take a variety of forms such as customs barriers, quotas on imports, unnecessarily restrictive standards for imports, and export subsidies. Because the GATT and WTO agreements (discussed later in the chapter) eliminated tariffs on many products, countries frequently use nontariff barriers to boost exports and control the flows of imported products. The U.S. and other nations are constantly negotiating tariffs and other trade agreements. Recently, the U.S. signed an agreement with Vietnam—a quarter century after the war between the two countries ended—under which Vietnamese goods and services can now be sold in U.S. markets under the same low tariffs that most U.S. trade partners enjoy.[31]

Tariffs The U.S. has long been the champion of free trade throughout the world, but recently with shrinking economies of industrialized foreign nations and a growing number of developing countries that are struggling to stabilize their economies, U.S. legislators have been pressured to protect domestic industries from troubles abroad. But moves designed to protect business at home are frequently a double-edged sword. They also frequently end up penalizing domestic consumers, since prices typically rise under protectionist regulations. For example, the U.S. recently slapped a 30 percent import tax on frozen orange juice concentrate; duties on imported glassware, porcelain, and china as high as 38 percent; rubber boots and shoes, 20 percent; luggage, 16 percent; and canned tuna, 12.5 percent. While this may or may not create a competitive environment for domestic producers, it seldom reduces product prices for the consumer.

Tariffs can be classified as either revenue or protective tariffs. *Revenue tariffs* are designed to raise funds for the importing government. Most early U.S. government revenue came from this source. *Protective tariffs,* which are usually higher than revenue tariffs, are designed to raise the retail price of an imported product to match or exceed that of a similar domestic product. Some countries use tariffs in a selective manner to discourage certain consumption practices and thereby reduce access to their local markets. For example, the U.S. has tariffs on luxury items like Rolex watches and Russian caviar.

Recently, the U.S. government placed a 19.3 percent protective percent tariff on softwood timber imported from Canada because it believes that Canada subsidizes its lumber industry to the point that prices are too low for American timber companies to compete. Some experts predicted that the tariff would add about $1,500 to the cost of building a new home, but U.S. lumber companies welcomed the tariff, saying that it would help level the playing field.[32]

In 1988, the U.S. passed the Omnibus Trade and Competitiveness Act to remedy what it perceived as unfair international trade conditions. Under the so-called Super 301 provisions of the law, the U.S. can now single out countries that unfairly impede trade with U.S. domestic businesses. If these countries do not open their markets within 18 months, the law requires retaliation in the form of U.S. tariffs or quotas on the offenders' imports into this country.

Some nations limit foreign ownership in the business sectors. In the U.S., for example, non-U.S. citizens cannot own more than 25 percent of the voting stock in a U.S.-based airline; they cannot hold controlling interest in a U.S. television station or network; nor can they fish for mackerel—the only fish in surplus in U.S. waters.[33] Tariffs also can be used to gain bargaining clout with other countries, but they risk adversely affecting the fortunes of domestic companies.

In recent years, scores of trading nations have agreed to abolish tariffs on 500 high-technology products such as computers, software, calculators, fax machines, and related goods. Elimination of such tariffs means as much as $100 million in annual savings to communication giants like IBM.

Administrative Barriers In addition to direct taxes on imported products, governments may erect a number of other barriers ranging from special permits and detailed inspection requirements to quotas on foreign-made items to stem the flow of imported goods—or halt them altogether. European shoppers pay about twice the price for bananas that North American shoppers pay. The reason for these high prices? Through a series of import license controls, Europe allows fewer bananas to be imported than people want to buy. Even worse, the European countries set up a system of quotas designed to support banana growing in former colonies in Africa and Asia, which hurt imports from Latin American countries.

Other forms of trade restrictions include import quotas and embargoes. **Import quotas** limit the number of units of products in certain categories that can cross a country's border. The quota is supposed to protect domestic industry and employment and to preserve foreign exchange, but it doesn't always work that way. Since the late 1950s, the U.S. has had quotas affecting the apparel industry—whether they involve certain textiles or the manufacturing of the clothes themselves. However, foreign companies often find loopholes in the quota systems and wind up not only with huge profits but also plenty of jobs for their own workers. Hong Kong billionaire William Fung makes no apologies for his company's success through quotas. "Everybody got rich through holding quotas," he says. "The U.S. artificially restricted supply. So when demand rises, prices rise. That's the quota premium."[34]

The ultimate quota is the *embargo*—a complete ban on the import of a product. Since 1960, the U.S. has maintained an embargo against Cuba in protest of Fidel Castro's dictatorship and policies such as expropriation of property and disregard for human rights. Not only do the sanctions prohibit Cuban exports (cigars and sugar are the island's best-known products) to enter the country, but they also apply to companies that profit from property that Cuba's communist government expropriated from Americans following the Cuban revolution.[35] However, many leading U.S. executives oppose the embargo. They know that they are losing the opportunity to develop the Cuban market while foreign rivals establish production and marketing facilities there.

Other administrative barriers include *subsidies.* Airbus, the French, German, British, and Spanish aircraft consortium, often comes under attack from U.S. trade officials because it is so heavily subsidized. The Europeans, on the other hand, argue that Boeing and Lockheed Martin benefit from research done by NASA, the Pentagon, and other U.S. agencies. And still another way to block international trade is to simply create so many regulatory barriers that it is almost impossible to reach target markets. The European Union, for example, enforces more than 2,700 different sets of trade requirements by states, counties, cities, and insurance providers. Indian law contains even more complex requirements.

Foreign trade can also be regulated by exchange control through a central bank or government agency. *Exchange control* means that firms that gain foreign exchange by exporting must sell foreign currencies to the central bank or other foreign agency and importers must buy foreign currencies from the same organization. The exchange control authority can then allocate, expand, or restrict foreign exchange according to existing national policy.

Dumping

The practice of selling a product in a foreign market at a price lower than what it commands in the producer's domestic market is called *dumping*. Critics of free trade often argue that foreign governments give substantial support to their own exporting companies. Government support may permit these firms to extend their export markets by offering lower prices abroad. In retaliation for this kind of interference with free trade, the U.S. adds import tariffs to products that foreign firms dump on U.S. markets to bring their prices in line with those of domestically produced products. That is the current situation in the U.S. steel industry. However, businesses often complain that charges of dumping must undergo a lengthy investigative and bureaucratic procedure before the government assesses import duties. U.S. firms that claim dumping threatens to hurt their business can file a complaint with the U.S. International Trade Commission (ITC), which tends to reject about half the claims it receives.

Briefly Speaking

WE ARE ALL AMERICANS

Headline in the French newspaper Le Monde *following the September 11, 2001, terrorist attacks*

MULTINATIONAL ECONOMIC INTEGRATION

A noticeable trend toward multinational economic integration has developed since the end of World War II. Multinational economic integration can be set up in several ways. The simplest approach is to establish a **free-trade area** in which participating nations agree to the free trade of goods among themselves, abolishing all tariffs and trade restrictions. A *customs union* establishes a free-trade area plus a uniform tariff for trade with nonmember nations. A *common market* extends a customs union by seeking to reconcile all government regulations affecting trade. Despite the many factors in its favor, not everyone is enthusiastic about free trade, particularly Americans who think their jobs may be affected. So it is important to consider both sides of the issue. Although productivity and innovation are said to grow more quickly with free trade, American workers face pay-cut demands and potential job loss as more companies move their operations overseas.[36]

GATT and the World Trade Organization

The **General Agreement on Tariffs and Trade (GATT),** a 117-nation trade accord that has sponsored several rounds of major tariff negotiations, substantially reducing worldwide tariff levels, celebrated its 50th birthday in 1997. In 1994, a seven-year series of GATT conferences, called the Uruguay Round, culminated in one of the biggest victories for free trade in decades. The new accord's partial opening of trade helped the U.S. economy grow by $1 trillion and created some 2 million new jobs.

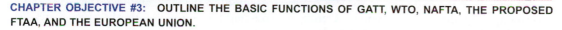

<interactive>**learning goal**

CHAPTER OBJECTIVE #3: OUTLINE THE BASIC FUNCTIONS OF GATT, WTO, NAFTA, THE PROPOSED FTAA, AND THE EUROPEAN UNION.

The Uruguay Round cut average tariffs by one-third, or more than $700 billion. Among its major victories are the following:

- Reduction of farm subsidies, which opened new markets for U.S. exports
- Increased protection for patents, copyrights, and trademarks
- Inclusion of services under international trading rules, creating opportunities for U.S. financial, legal, and accounting firms
- Phasing out import quotas on textiles and clothing from developing nations, a move that benefits U.S. retailers and consumers because quotas increase clothing prices by $15 billion

A key outcome of the GATT talks was establishment of the **World Trade Organization (WTO),** a 136-member organization that succeeds GATT. The WTO oversees GATT agreements, mediates disputes, and continues the effort to reduce trade barriers throughout the world. Unlike GATT, WTO decisions are binding.

To date, however, the WTO has made only slow progress toward its major policy initiatives—liberalizing world financial services, telecommunications, and maritime markets. Trade officials have not agreed on the direction for the WTO. Its activities have focused more on complaint resolution than on removing global trade barriers. The U.S. has been the most active plaintiff in WTO dispute courts. Recently, the WTO announced a decision about U.S. tax breaks for companies like Microsoft and Boeing, which have significant operations overseas, essentially granting the European Union permission to impose billions of dollars in punitive tariffs on U.S. imports. However, both the European Union and the U.S. immediately engaged in discussions to resolve the situation and avert a trade war, which would have been harmful to both.[37]

Big differences between developed and developing areas create a major roadblock to WTO progress. These conflicts became apparent at the first WTO meeting in Singapore in the late 1990s. Asian nations want trade barriers lifted on their manufactured goods, but they also want to protect their own telecommunications companies. In addition, they oppose monitoring of corruption and labor practices by outsiders. The U.S. wants free trade for telecommunications, more controls on corruption, and establishment of international labor standards. Europe wants standard rules on foreign investments and removal of profit repatriation restrictions but is not as concerned with worker rights.

China is the world's largest nation with an economy that has grown 10 percent annually for the last two decades. As a market, it holds the promise of enormous potential for exporters. But China's exports show less than a 2 percent annual growth as a result of the multitude of barriers and red tape that make it extremely difficult for foreign firms to operate there. Recently, however, the release of trade rights allowed new enterprises to engage in importing and exporting, and the nation was admitted to the WTO.

'NET EX: TRADE DISPUTES

The NAFTA Accord

A heated controversy continues almost a decade after the passage of the **North American Free-Trade Agreement (NAFTA),** an agreement between the U.S., Canada, and Mexico that removes trade restrictions among the three nations over a 14-year period. Proponents claim that NAFTA has been good for the American economy; critics charge that U.S. and Canadian workers have lost their jobs to cheap Mexican labor. The NAFTA accord brings together more than 415 million people and a combined gross domestic product of $7.9 trillion, making it by far the world's largest free-trade zone.

The NAFTA accord was approved despite serious concerns about job losses from the relatively high-wage industries in the U.S. and Canada as manufacturers relocated their production facilities in lower-wage Mexico. However, NAFTA supporters point out that imports of components and intermediate goods that require further refinements before becoming part of products "Made in the USA" actually hold down the cost of U.S.-made output and support local jobs. And even though imports of such products as autos assembled in Mexico have risen, these vehicles now include a high percentage of components manufactured in the U.S.[38]

To date, NAFTA seems to have succeeded in promoting greater trade between the U.S. and Mexico, and actually boosted jobs and cut inflation without hurting wages. Canada has long been the United States' leading trade party. In recent years, however, Mexico passed Japan as our No. 2 trade partner—despite the fact that Japan's GDP is 10 times larger than that of Mexico.

But nine of every ten dollars in Mexican exports are shipped to the U.S., and its recent recession has had an impact on the Mexican economy. During that economic downturn, exports of electronics, textiles, chemicals, and auto parts dropped sharply. Not surprisingly, Mexico's unskilled labor is now more expensive than China's, which means that companies are looking to Asia for production facilities. Despite the fact that China was admitted to the WTO, Mexico lagged in forming a bilateral trade agreement with that country.[39]

NAFTA is not the only Western Hemisphere trade bloc. Canada and Chile have a free-trade agreement. The MERCOSUR customs union, comprising Brazil, Argentina, Paraguay, Uruguay, Chile, and Bolivia, is another group with whom the U.S. may have to negotiate.

The Free Trade Area of the Americas

NAFTA was actually the first step toward creating a **Free Trade Area of the Americas (FTAA),** stretching the length of the entire Western Hemisphere, from the Bering Strait to Cape Horn, encompassing 34 countries, a population of 800 million, and a combined gross domestic product of more than $11 trillion. The FTAA would be the largest free-trade zone on earth and would offer low or nonexistent tariffs, streamlined customs, and no quotas, subsidies, or other barriers to trade. Figure 4.5 identifies the countries expected to be members of the proposed FTAA, their levels of economic output, and recent levels of foreign trade. The Bush administration is a staunch supporter of the FTAA, which still has many hurdles to overcome as countries wrangle for conditions that are most favorable to them. Caterpillar Inc., the largest manufacturer of earth-moving equipment in the world, stands to gain a hefty slice of the profit pie. Removal of tariffs and customs delays are expected to increase sales of construction equipment as much as $4.5 billion over the first ten years.[40]

The European Union

The best-known example of a multinational economic community is the **European Union (EU).** Fifteen countries belong to the EU: Finland, Sweden, Denmark, United Kingdom, Ireland, Netherlands, Belgium,

FIGURE 4.5

Proposed Free Trade Area of the Americas

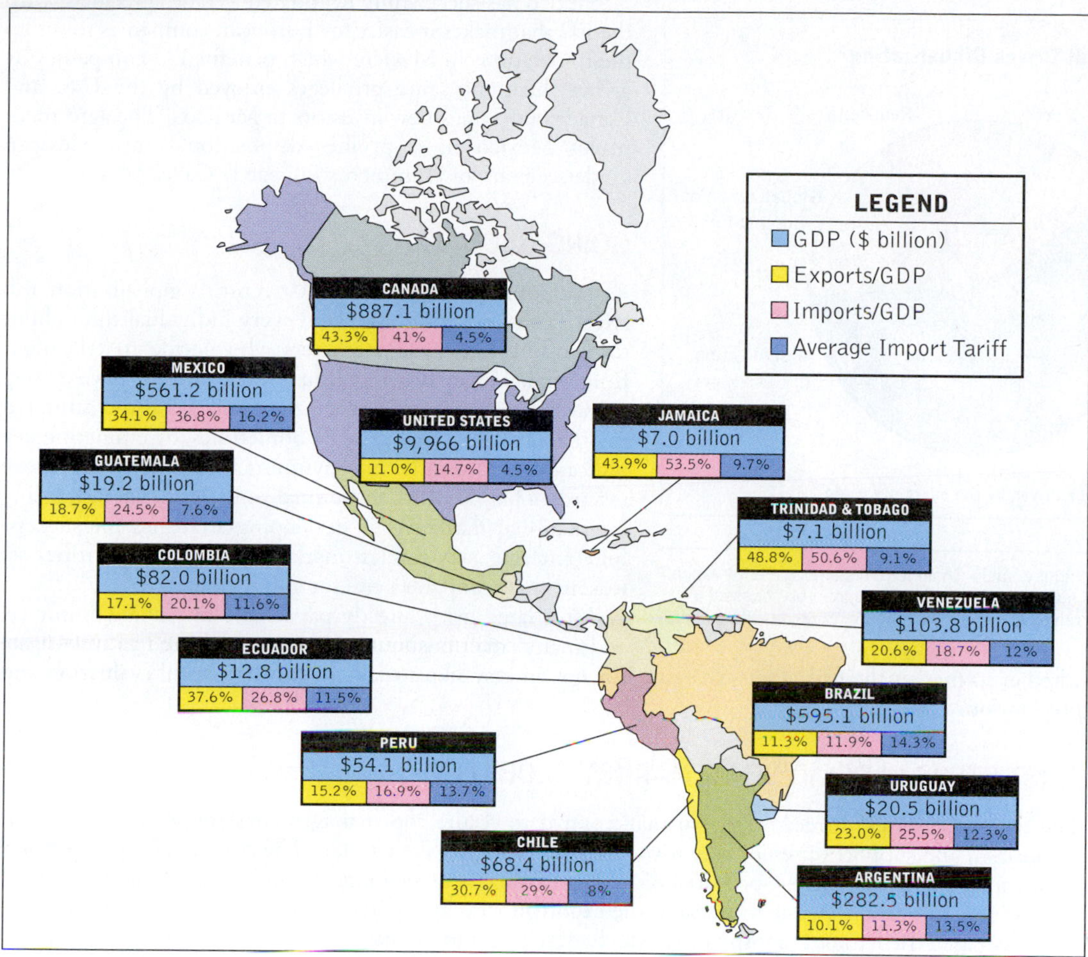

Source: Data from Economist Intelligence Unit, Inter-American Development Bank, found in "Betting on Free Trade," *BusinessWeek*, April 23, 2001, p. 62.

Germany, Luxembourg, France, Austria, Italy, Greece, Spain, and Portugal. With 350 million people, and a combined gross domestic product of $5 trillion, the EU forms a huge common market. In addition to the 15-member nations from Western Europe, several former Soviet republics and other Eastern European countries have applied for admission to the EU.

The goal of the EU is to eventually remove all barriers to free trade among its members, making it as simple and painless to ship products between England and Spain as it is between New Jersey and Pennsylvania. Also involved is the standardization of regulations and requirements that businesses must meet. Instead of having to comply with 15 sets of standards and 15 different currencies, companies will have to deal with just one. This simplification should lower the costs of doing business in Europe by allowing firms to take advantage of economies of scale.

In some ways, the EU is making definite progress toward its economic goals. We have already seen that it is drafting standardized eco-labels to certify that products are manufactured according to certain environmental standards, as well as creating guidelines governing marketers' uses of customer information. Marketers can also protect trademarks throughout the entire EU with a single application and registration process through the Community Trademark (CTM), which simplifies doing business and eliminates having to register with each member country. It is, however, sometimes difficult to obtain approval for trademark protection.

Yet marketers still face challenges when selling their products in the EU. Customs taxes differ, and there is no uniform postal system. Mail between countries is extremely slow. In fact, the Federation of European Direct Marketing is pushing for modernization and integration of postal systems. Using one toll-free number for several countries will not work, either, because each country has its own telephone system for codes

FIGURE 4.6

Why Marketers Decide to Go Global

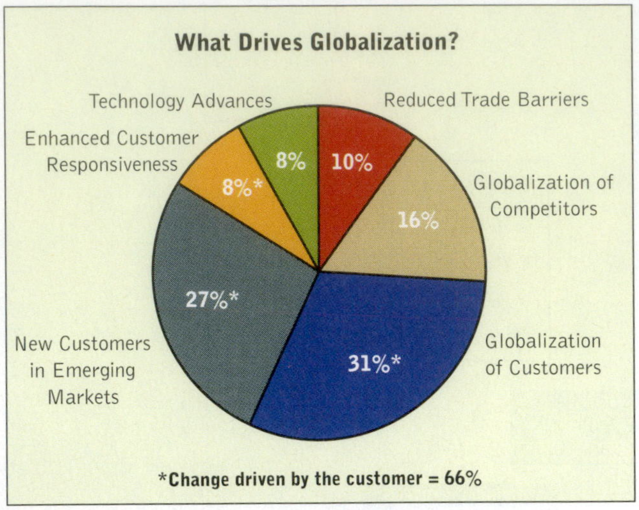

Source: Data from "Shaping the Value Chain for Outstanding Performance," PricewaterhouseCoopers survey of 200 leading European businesses, found in *Fortune*, special advertising section, June 26, 2000, p. S8.

and numbers. Furthermore, when the euro was introduced by the European Union, three EU nations decided to retain their own national currencies, at least temporarily.

Mexico has successfully negotiated a trade agreement with the EU that makes it easier for European companies to set up their operations in Mexico, which benefits EU companies by giving them the same privileges enjoyed by the U.S. and Canada and brings new investors to Mexico. "The agreement places Mexico in a privileged position," says Mexican Undersecretary of Commerce Luis de la Calle.[41]

GOING GLOBAL

As we move further into the 21st century, globalization will affect almost every industry and every individual throughout the world. Traditional marketers who decide to take their firms global may do so because they already have strong domestic market shares or their target market is too saturated to offer any substantial growth. Sometimes, by evaluating key indicators of the marketing environment, marketers can move toward globalization at an optimal time. A critical task facing international marketers is developing strategies for successfully entering new foreign markets. Figure 4.6 identifies six reasons that companies cite for going global.

Most large firms already participate in global commerce, and many small businesses recognize the need to investigate whether to market their products overseas. It is not an easy step to take, requiring careful evaluation and preparation.

FIRST STEPS IN DECIDING TO MARKET GLOBALLY

The first step toward successful global marketing is to secure top management's support. Without the enthusiasm and support of senior executives, export efforts are likely to fail. The advocate for going global must explain and promote the potential of foreign markets and facilitate the global marketing process.

The next important step is to research the export process and potential markets. Burt Cabanas, CEO of Texas-based Benchmark Hospitality, which develops and manages conference centers, hotels, and resorts, explains the consequences of failing to research a market when going global: "We went into Thailand initially without doing research and that was a mistake. We made many assumptions about how we would do marketing in ways that were a few degrees off target. We were told by U.S. companies that if we were going to do business in Thailand, we should be in Bangkok, and we spent a tremendous amount of time getting a presence there. We then found out we could have been just as successful outside the city. Taking someone else's word for it rather than doing the research set us back a year and a half."[42] Benchmark Hospitality has since expanded to Japan and the Philippines and is now researching six additional markets in foreign countries.

The U.S. Department of Commerce sponsors a toll-free hotline that describes the various federal export programs that are currently available. Trade counselors at 68 district offices offer export advice, computerized market data, and names of contacts in over 60 countries. Some services are free, while others are available at a reasonable cost. Table 4.3 describes five important resources for marketers who want to analyze foreign markets.

Strategies for Entering International Markets

Once marketers have completed their research, they may choose from among three basic strategies for entering international markets: importing and exporting; contractual agreements like franchising, licensing, and subcontracting; and international direct investment. As Figure 4.7 shows, the level of risk and the firm's degree of control over international marketing increase with greater involvement. Firms often use more than one of these entry strategies. L.L. Bean subcontracts with a Japanese company to handle its product returns, and it also maintains a direct investment in several Japanese retail outlets in partnership with Matsushita.

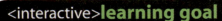

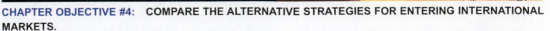

<interactive>learning goal

CHAPTER OBJECTIVE #4: COMPARE THE ALTERNATIVE STRATEGIES FOR ENTERING INTERNATIONAL MARKETS.

TABLE 4.3

Sources for Analyzing Foreign Markets

Source	Description
U.S. Department of Commerce	Maintains the National Trade Data Bank (market reports on foreign demand for specific products), produces catalogs and video shows and participates in trade shows.
Tradepoint USA	A not-for-profit service with print and online resources. Its Internet service, I-Trade, offers country data, international news, the National Trade Data Bank, and other reports.
The Green Book	Published by the American Management Association, this guide lists all market research firms and those with international capabilities.
Esomar	The European Society of Opinion and Market Research maintains a worldwide listing by company.
U.S. State Department	Offers commercial guides compiled by local embassies to almost every country in the world.

A firm that brings in goods produced abroad to sell domestically or to be used as components in its products is an importer. In making import decisions, the marketer must assess local demand for the product, taking into consideration such factors as the following:

- ability of the supplier to maintain agreed-to quality levels
- capability of filling orders that might vary considerably from one order to the next
- response time in filling orders
- total costs—including import fees, packaging, and transportation—in comparison with costs of domestic suppliers

Exporting, another basic form of international marketing, involves a continuous effort in marketing a firm's merchandise to customers in other countries. Many firms export their products as the first step in reaching foreign markets. Success in exporting often encourages them to try other entry strategies.

First-time exporters can reach foreign customers through one or more of three alternatives: export-trading companies, export-management companies, or offset agreements. An export-trading company

FIGURE 4.7

Levels of Involvement in International Marketing

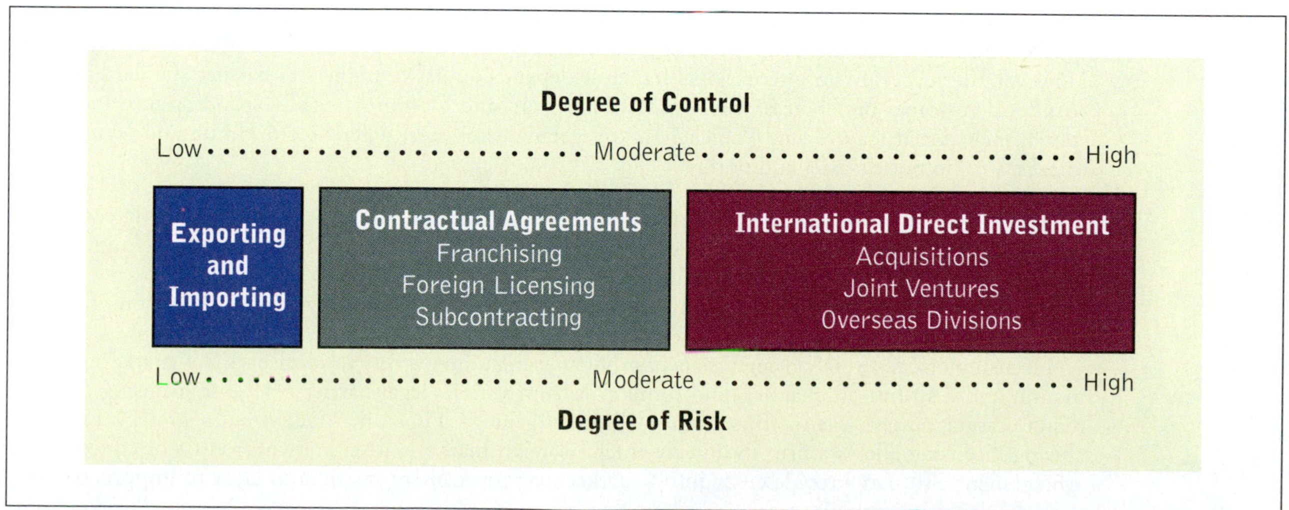

(ETC) buys products from domestic producers and resells them abroad. While manufacturers lose control over marketing and distribution to the ETC, it helps them export through a relatively simple and inexpensive channel, in the process providing feedback about the overseas market potential of their products.

The second option, an export-management company (EMC), provides the first-time exporter with expertise in locating foreign buyers, handling necessary paperwork, and ensuring that its goods meet local labeling and testing laws. However, the manufacturer retains more control over the export process when it deals with an EMC than if it were to sell the goods outright to an export-trading company. Smaller firms can get assistance with administrative needs such as financing and preparation of proposals and contracts from large EMC contractors.

The final option, entering a foreign market under an offset agreement, teams a small firm with a major international company. The smaller firm essentially serves as a subcontractor on a large foreign project. This entry strategy provides new exporters with international experience, supported by the assistance of the primary contractor in such areas as international transaction documentation and financing.

As every international traveler knows, Oak Brook, Illinois–headquartered McDonald's has expanded its franchised fast-food operations around the globe. The "smile" logo of the firm's Golden Arches ranks among the world's ten most valuable brands.

Contractual Agreements

As a firm gains sophistication in international marketing, it may enter contractual agreements that provide several flexible alternatives to exporting. Both large and small firms can benefit from these methods. Franchising and foreign licensing, for example, are good ways to take services abroad. Subcontracting may set up either production facilities or services. Sponsorships are another form of international contractual marketing agreements. When Nintendo CEO Hiroshi Yamauchi bought the Seattle Mariners baseball team a decade ago, skeptics worried about the wisdom of selling "America's pastime" to another nation. But the relationship, which includes sponsorships as well as foreign licensing deals, has been beneficial to Seattle, Major League Baseball, and Japanese baseball fans, who are as passionate about the sport as American fans are. "It's been great for everybody," says baseball commissioner Bud Selig. Major League Baseball has pursued sponsorship deals in Japan with Kirin Brewery Co. and Sumitomo Forestry Co., who have paid out millions to use the Major League Baseball logo in their marketing. In addition, Major League Baseball has a five-year deal with the Japanese television networks for international rights to broadcast the games.[43]

Franchising A **franchise** is a contractual arrangement in which a wholesaler or retailer (the franchisee) agrees to meet the operating requirements of a manufacturer or other franchiser. The franchisee receives the right to sell the products and use the franchiser's name, as well as a variety of marketing, management, and other services. As mentioned earlier, fast-food companies such as McDonald's have been active franchisers around the world.

One advantage of franchising is risk reduction by offering a proven concept. Standardized operations typically reduce costs, increase operating efficiencies, and provide greater international recognizability. However, the success of an international franchise depends on its willingness to balance standard practices with local customer preferences. McDonald's, Pizza Hut, and Domino's are all expanding into India with special menus that feature lamb, chicken, and vegetarian items, in deference to Hindu and Muslim customers who do not eat beef and pork.

Foreign Licensing A second method of going global through the use of contractual agreements is **foreign licensing,** as described in the example about the Seattle Mariners. Such an agreement grants foreign marketers the right to distribute a firm's merchandise or use its trademark, patent, or process in a specified geographic area. These arrangements usually set certain time limits, after which agreements are revised or renewed.

Licensing offers several advantages over exporting, including access to local partners' marketing information and distribution channels and protection from various legal barriers. Because licensing does not require capital outlays, many firms, both small and large, regard it as an attractive entry strategy. Like franchising, licensing allows a firm to quickly enter a foreign market with a known product or concept. The arrangement also may provide entry into a market that government restrictions close to imports or international direct investment.

Subcontracting A third strategy for going global through contractual agreements is *subcontracting,* in which the production of goods or services is assigned to local companies. Using local subcontractors can prevent mistakes involving local culture and regulations. Manufacturers might subcontract with a local company to produce their goods or use a foreign distributor to handle their products abroad or provide customer service. Manufacturing within the country can provide protection from import duties and may be a lower-cost alternative that makes it possible for the product to compete with local offerings. Sears subcontracts with local manufacturers in Mexico and Spain to produce many of the products—especially clothing—sold in its department stores.

International Direct Investment

Another strategy for entering global markets is international direct investment in foreign firms, production, and marketing facilities. As the world's largest economy, the U.S.'s foreign direct investment inflows and outflows—total of American firm investments abroad and foreign firm investments in the U.S.—are nearly 32 percent greater than Germany's and 100 percent greater than Japan's, its two largest competitors. By the beginning of this century, U.S. direct investment abroad was nearly $2.2 trillion, with a high number of acquisitions in the United Kingdom, the Netherlands, and Canada. On the other hand, foreign direct investment in the U.S. had grown to over $2.1 trillion. Three of every four dollars of foreign investment in the U.S. came from Europe and Canada.[44]

Although high levels of involvement and high-risk potential are characteristics of investments in foreign countries, firms choosing this method often have a competitive advantage. Direct investment can take several forms. A company can acquire an existing firm in a country where it wants to do business, or it can set up an independent division outside its own borders with responsibility for production and marketing in a country or geographic region. Recently, European firms have been acquiring U.S. companies as a way to enter the American marketplace. Vodafone Group and Deutsche Telekom bought AirTouch Communications and VoiceStream for a combined $114 billion. Purchases like this open up the wide American market to European firms.[45]

Foreign sales offices, overseas marketing subsidiaries, and foreign offices and manufacturing facilities of U.S. firms all involve direct investment. Motorola has had offices in Israel since 1964 and continues to strengthen its presence in the Middle East. Currently, Motorola has more than 5,000 employees in its manufacturing, design, and marketing facilities in Israel, which generate $1.3 billion in revenue for the company. "The market in Israel in the last ten years shows great potential, and it is very active in the communications area," says Yardena Astel of Motorola Israel. More than 40 percent of the Israeli population has a cell phone, which is far greater than the 20 percent of Americans.[46]

Companies may also engage in international marketing by forming joint ventures, in which they share the risks, costs, and management of the foreign operation with one or more partners. These partnerships join the investing companies with nationals of the host countries. While some companies choose to open their own facilities overseas, others share with their partners. Service companies often find that joint ventures provide the most efficient way to penetrate a market.

Although joint ventures offer many advantages, foreign investors have encountered problems in several areas throughout the world, especially in developing economies. Lower trade barriers, new technologies, lower transport costs, and vastly improved access to information means that many more partnerships will be involved in international trade.

FROM MULTINATIONAL CORPORATION TO GLOBAL MARKETER

A **multinational corporation** is a firm with significant operations and marketing activities outside its home country. Examples of multinationals include General Electric, Siemens, and Mitsubishi in heavy electrical equipment, and Timex, Seiko, and Citizen in watches. Some companies, like Tyco International, are widely diversified in both the industries and the countries they serve. Tyco, whose headquarters are in New Hampshire, has 220,000 employees in more than 100 countries in fields that include medical products, fire safety, fiber optics, and even commercial lending. Despite recent cutbacks resulting in some layoffs, Tyco is looking to strengthen its international presence by selecting directors from Europe and Asia to serve on its board.[47]

Since they first became a force in international business in the 1960s, multinationals have evolved in some important ways. First, these companies are no longer exclusively U.S. based. Today it is as likely for a multinational to be based in Japan, Germany, or Great Britain as in the U.S. Second, multinationals no longer think of their foreign operations as mere outsourcing appendages that carry out the design, production, and engineering ideas conceived at home. Instead, they encourage constant exchanges of ideas, capital, and technologies among all the multinational operations.

Multinationals often employ huge foreign workforces relative to their American staffs. Over half of all Ford and IBM personnel are located outside the U.S. These workforces are no longer seen merely as sources of cheap labor. On the contrary, many multinationals center technically complex activities in locations throughout the world. Texas Instruments does much of its research, development, design, and manufacturing in East

Asia. In fact, it is increasingly common for U.S. multinationals to bring product innovations from their foreign facilities back to the States.

Multinationals have become global corporations that reflect the interdependence of world economies, the growth of international competition, and the globalization of world markets. An increasing number of acquisitions include U.S. multinationals as targets for takeover. In one recent year, Germany's Deutsche Bank acquired Bankers Trust; British Petroleum took over Amoco; and Chrysler became part of Germany's Daimler-Benz.

DEVELOPING AN INTERNATIONAL MARKETING STRATEGY

In developing a marketing mix, international marketers may choose between two alternative approaches: a global marketing strategy or a multidomestic marketing strategy. A **global marketing strategy** defines a standard marketing mix and implements it with minimal modifications in all foreign markets. This approach brings the advantage of economies of scale to production and marketing activities. Procter & Gamble (P&G) marketers follow a global marketing strategy for Pringles potato chips, their leading export brand. P&G sells one product with a consistent formulation in every country. Unlike Frito-Lay's Cheetos snacks, which come in flavors geared to local tastes, P&G meets 80 percent of worldwide demand with only six flavors of Pringles. The brand relies on one package design throughout the world. This standardized approach saves money since it allows large-scale production runs and reinforces the brand's image. Also, similar advertising around the world builds brand awareness by featuring the slogan, "Once you pop, you can't stop." P&G intends all of these tactics to build strong global brand equity for Pringles.

<interactive>learning goal

CHAPTER OBJECTIVE #5: DIFFERENTIATE BETWEEN A GLOBAL MARKETING STRATEGY AND A MULTIDOMESTIC MARKETING STRATEGY.

A global marketing perspective can effectively market some goods and services to segments in many nations that share cultures and languages. This approach works especially well for products with strong, universal appeal, such as McDonald's, luxury items like Rolex watches, and high-tech brands like Microsoft. Global advertising outlets, such as international editions of popular consumer and business magazines and international transmissions of such TV programs as CNN, MTV, and the CNBC financial network, help marketers deliver a single message to millions of global viewers. International satellite television channels such as StarTV reach 260 million Asian viewers through a host of sports, news, movie, music, and entertainment channels programmed in eight languages.

Marketers of luxury watches such as Rolex rely on the images of exclusiveness and extremely high quality to deliver a universal message.

A global marketing strategy can be highly effective for luxury products that target upscale consumers everywhere. Marketers of diamonds and luxury watches, for instance, typically use advertising with little or no copy—just a picture of a beautiful diamond or watch with the name discreetly displayed at the bottom.

A major benefit of a global marketing strategy is its low cost to implement. Most firms, however, find it necessary to practice market segmentation outside their home markets and tailor their marketing mixes to fit the unique needs of customers in specific countries. This **multidomestic marketing strategy** assumes that differences between market characteristics and competitive situations in certain nations require firms to customize their marketing decisions to effectively reach individual marketplaces. (This strategy is sometimes mistakenly called *multinational* marketing. In fact, a multinational corporation may combine both strategies in its international marketing plans.)

Many marketing experts feel that most products demand multidomestic marketing strategies to give them realistic global marketing appeals. Cultural, geographic, language, and other differences simply make it impractical to try to send one message to many countries. Specific situations may allow them to standardize some parts of the marketing process but customize others. Pillsbury wanted to offer its Progresso brand of Italian-style foods to markets in nations outside the U.S. But Pillsbury marketers discovered that in some South American countries, "progress" could mean many different things, including financial services. So they came up with a made-up name, Frescarini, meaning "fresh dough and pasta," to use as the global brand name.[48]

International Product and Promotional Strategies

International marketers can choose from among five strategies for selecting the most appropriate product and promotion strategy for a specific foreign market—straight extension, promotion adaptation, product adaptation, dual adaptation, and product invention. As Figure 4.8 indicates, the strategies center on whether to extend a domestic product and promotional strategy into international markets or adapt one or both to meet the target market's unique requirements.

<interactive>**learning goal**

CHAPTER OBJECTIVE #6: DESCRIBE THE ALTERNATIVE MARKETING MIX STRATEGIES USED IN INTERNATIONAL MARKETING.

A firm may follow a one-product, one-message straight extension strategy as part of a global marketing strategy, like Pepsi Cola's. This strategy permits economies of scale in production and marketing. Also, successful implementation creates universal recognition of a product for consumers from country to country.

Other strategies call for product adaptation, promotion adaptation, or both. While bicycles, motorcycles, and outboard motors primarily form part of the market for U.S. recreational vehicles, they may represent important basic transportation modes in other nations. Consequently, producers of these products may adapt their promotional messages even if they sell the product without changes. Coca-Cola executives in Atlanta have recently loosened their grip on the company's international marketing efforts in order to adapt to local markets around the world. "We used to make TV commercials in Atlanta for China," notes CEO Douglas Daft. "That's not appropriate."[49]

Sometimes, international marketers must change both the product and the promotional message in a dual adaptation strategy to meet the unique needs of specific international markets. As part of its overall efforts to adapt to local markets, Coca-Cola developed new drink flavors. In Turkey, the firm now offers a pear-flavored drink, while in Germany consumers are treated to a berry-flavored Fanta. Both new drinks are designed to appeal to the tastes of people in those countries.[50]

Finally, a firm may select product invention to take advantage of unique foreign market opportunities. To match user needs in developing nations, an appliance manufacturer might introduce a hand-powered washing machine even though such products became obsolete in industrialized countries years ago.

Although Chapter 12 discusses the idea of branding in greater detail, it is important to note here the importance of a company's recognizable name, image, product, or even slogan around the world. Figure 4.9 identifies the world's ten most valuable brands, as rated by Interbrand. Other than Mercedes and Nokia, all are brands owned by U.S.-based companies.[51]

International Distribution Strategy

Distribution is a vital aspect of overseas marketing. Marketers must set up proper channels and anticipate extensive physical distribution problems. Foreign markets may offer poor transportation systems and

FIGURE 4.8

Alternative International Product and Promotional Strategies

Promotion Strategy	Product Strategy: Same Product	Product Adaptation	New Product
Same Promotion	**Straight Extension** Wrigley's gum Coca-Cola Eastman Kodak cameras and film	**Product Adaptation** Campbell's soup Exxon gasoline	**Product Invention** Nonelectric sewing machines Manually operated washing machines
Different Promotion	**Promotion Adaptation** Bicycles/motorcycles Outboard motors	**Dual Adaptation** Coffee Some clothing	

FIGURE 4.9

The World's 10 Most Valuable Global Brands

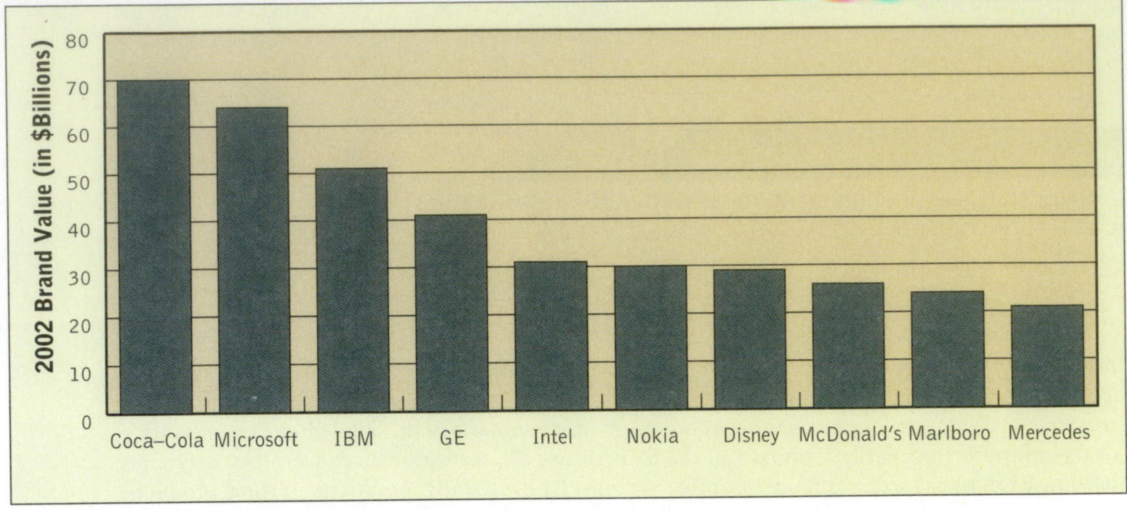

Source: Data from Interbrand Corp., J.P. Morgan Chase & Co.; found in "The Best Global Brands," *BusinessWeek*, August 5, 2002, p. 93.

warehousing facilities—or none at all. International marketers must adapt promptly and efficiently to these situations in order to profit from overseas sales.

A distribution decision involves two steps. First, the firm must decide on a method of entering the foreign market. Second, it must determine how to distribute the product within the foreign market through that entry channel.

Distribution decisions balance many factors, including the nature of the firm's products, consumer tastes and buying habits, market competition, and transportation options. Even though music may be considered a universal language, U.S.-based global Internet music company SonicNet believes that the traditional MTV one-world-sound approach turned off as many viewers as it served. After all, young people do not share the same lifestyles and cultures. SonicNet's strategy involves working with foreign partners who supply rock, pop, rap, and other music video clips, live concerts, and breaking news to local cyberspace surfers. For example, it turned to telecommunications provider Swisscom to create German, French, and Italian editions of its Web-based music entertainment programming. MTV has responded by increasing its focus on country-specific artists and video DJs to address more specifically the music interests of viewers in different countries. But by developing local language editions that reflect that area's taste in music, SonicNet has also succeeded in growing local audiences all around the world for advertisers.[52]

Pricing Strategy

Pricing can critically affect the success of an overall marketing strategy for foreign markets. Considerable competitive, economic, political, and legal constraints often limit pricing decisions. Global marketers can succeed if they thoroughly understand these requirements.

Companies must adapt their pricing strategies to local markets and change them when conditions change. Until recently, foreign shipments carried premium prices without assurance that the package would be delivered on time in good condition—or even delivered at all. After the air-freight and overnight-delivery services boomed in the 1980s, delivery became more reliable but costs were exorbitant to many areas. To compete in this crowded market without losing market share, the United States Postal Service (USPS) began advertising International Express Mail services to over 175 countries at set delivery rates. Global Priority Mail, for example, provides prompt delivery to over 30 key business countries for as little as $3.75.

An important development in pricing strategy for international marketing has been the emergence of commodity marketing organizations that seek to control prices through collective action. The Organization of Petroleum Exporting Countries (OPEC) is a good example of this kind of collective export organization, but many others exist.

Countertrade

In a growing number of nations, the only way a marketer can gain access to foreign markets is through **countertrade**—a form of exporting in which a firm barters products rather than selling them for cash. Less-developed nations sometimes impose countertrade requirements when they lack sufficient foreign currency to attain goods and services they want or need from exporting countries. These countries allow sellers to exchange their products only for domestic products as a way to control their balance-of-trade problems.

Countertrade became popular two decades ago, when companies wanted to conduct business in eastern European countries and the former Soviet Union. Those governments did not allow exchanges of hard currency, so this form of barter facilitated trade. PepsiCo made one of the largest countertrades ever when it exchanged $3 billion worth of Pepsi Cola for Russian Stolichnaya vodka, a cargo ship, and tankers from the former Soviet Union.

Estimating the actual volume of countertrade as percentage of world trade is difficult, but the American Countertrade Association puts the figure at about 25 percent. Countertraders include large multinational firms like General Electric and PepsiCo. Almost half of the *Fortune* 500 companies now practice countertrade in response to increasing global competition. Although countertrade is still growing at about 10 percent a year, its rate of increase has slowed.

THE U.S. AS A TARGET FOR INTERNATIONAL MARKETERS

Foreign marketers regard America as an inviting target. It offers a large population, high levels of discretionary income, political stability, a generally favorable attitude toward foreign investment, and a relatively well-controlled economy.

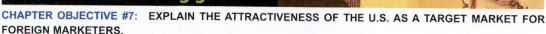

<interactive>learning goal

CHAPTER OBJECTIVE #7: EXPLAIN THE ATTRACTIVENESS OF THE U.S. AS A TARGET MARKET FOR FOREIGN MARKETERS.

Among the best-known industries in which foreign manufacturers have established U.S. production facilities is automobiles. Most of the world's leading auto companies have built assembly facilities in the U.S.: Honda, Hyundai, and Mercedes-Benz in Alabama, BMW in South Carolina, Toyota in Kentucky, Nissan in Tennessee, and Honda in Mississippi and Ohio.

Many foreign executives are transforming their companies' mission statements to reflect their move toward globalization. Fusao Sekiguchi, president and CEO of Venture Safenet, a Japanese firm that provides professional engineers to companies on a temporary basis, wants to expand his company's reach around the world. "With the chance of developing this company profile, I am also in hope of sharing useful business hints with investors who are interested in the Japanese human resource market, as well as looking forward to all the opportunities of expanding my business to a global scale," he writes in an open letter on the firm's Web site.[53] Sekiguchi expanded his reach to America when the racehorse he owned, Fusaichi Pegasus, won the 2000 Kentucky Derby.

As we discussed earlier, foreign investment continues to grow in the U.S. Foreign multinationals will probably continue to invest in U.S. assets as they seek to produce goods locally and control distribution channels. Major U.S. companies owned by foreign firms include Columbia Pictures and Universal Studios, owned by Sony Corp. (Japan); Pillsbury, Heublein, Pearle Vision, and Pet Inc., owned by Grand Metropolitan (United Kingdom); and Maybelline and Cosmair cosmetics, owned by L'Oréal (a French subsidiary of the Swiss conglomerate Nestlé SA); and Citgo Petroleum, owned by Petróleos de Venezuela (Venezuela). European firms poured $250 billion into the U.S. in one recent 12-month period, accounting for 80 percent of all direct foreign investment.[54]

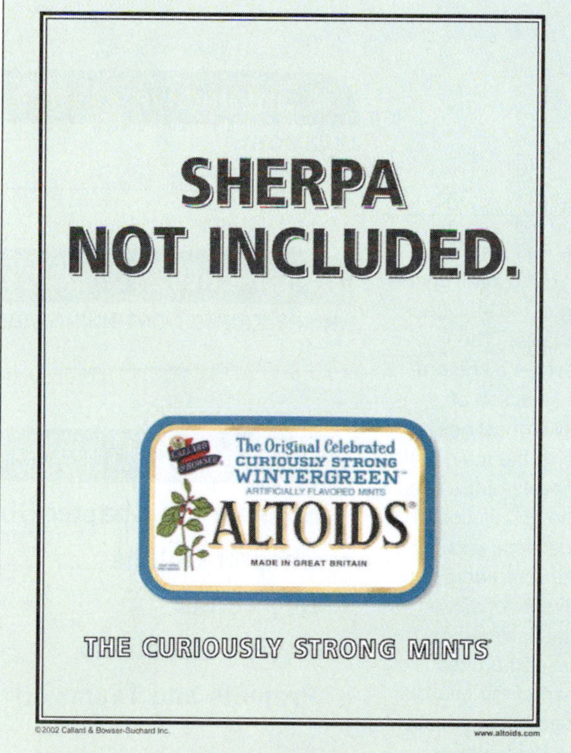

The huge U.S. success of strongly flavored Altoids mints explains why British marketer Callard & Bowser-Suchard views America as an attractive market. The product's packaging, in traditional—even old-fashioned—tins, also contributes to the image of a brand of mints totally different from current U.S. product offerings.

STRATEGIC IMPLICATIONS OF MARKETING IN THE 21ST CENTURY

This first decade of the new century is marking a new era of truly global marketing, where nearly every marketer can become a global marketer. The previous eras of domestic markets are largely being

relegated to niche marketing. The Internet has played a major role in these changes in the traditional marketing practices of the last century. Marketers in both small, localized firms and giant businesses need to reevaluate the strengths and weaknesses of current marketing practices and realign their plans to meet the new demands of the information age.

Marketers are the pioneers in bringing new technologies to developing nations. Their successes and failures will determine the direction global marketing will take and the speed with which they will be embraced. Actions of international marketers will influence every component of the marketing environments: competitive, economic, social-cultural, political-legal, and technological.

The greatest competitive advantages will belong to those marketers who capitalize on the similarities of their target markets and adapt to the differences. In some instances, the actions of marketers today help determine the rules and regulations of tomorrow.

Marketers need flexible and broad views of an increasingly complex customer. Goods and services will become more customized as they are introduced in foreign markets. New and better products in developing markets will create and maintain relationships for the future. Specialization will once again be a viable business concept.

Marketing has just entered a new frontier of limitless opportunities. Much like the first voyages into space, the world looks more different than anyone could have ever imagined. The impact of the Web and other new computer and communications technologies will be discussed in greater detail in the next chapter.

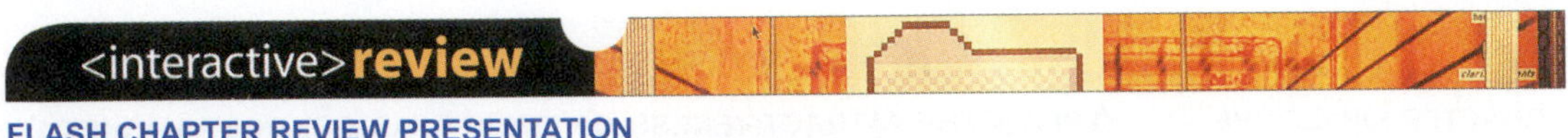

FLASH CHAPTER REVIEW PRESENTATION

<interactive>video case

FALLON WORLDWIDE: GOING GLOBAL, TARGETING LOCAL

<interactive>game

QUIZ BOWL

<interactive>video case

KRISPY KREME CONTINUING VIDEO CASE: CONSUMERS ARE SWEET ON KRISPY KREME

endofchaptermaterial

- Summary of Chapter Objectives
- Chapter Outline
- Key Terms
- Review Questions
- Projects and Teamwork Exercises
- 'netWork
- Crossword Puzzles
- Case 4.1: It's a Small World—Disney Says Going Global Is Crucial

Take the Post-Test to assess your overall understanding of the key ideas in this chapter. The Post-Test provides a comprehensive selection of exam-style questions addressing the main topics and concepts of the chapter. At the completion of each Post-Test, you will receive a score and instructive feedback on how you answered each question, and a direct link to the part of the chapter addressed in the question. Take the Post-Test as often as you need to—a record of your progress for each attempt is kept for you to revisit and gauge your improvement. And each Post-Test is randomly generated, so every attempt is new.

Post-Test

PART 2

Managing Technology and Information to Achieve Marketing Success

CHAPTER

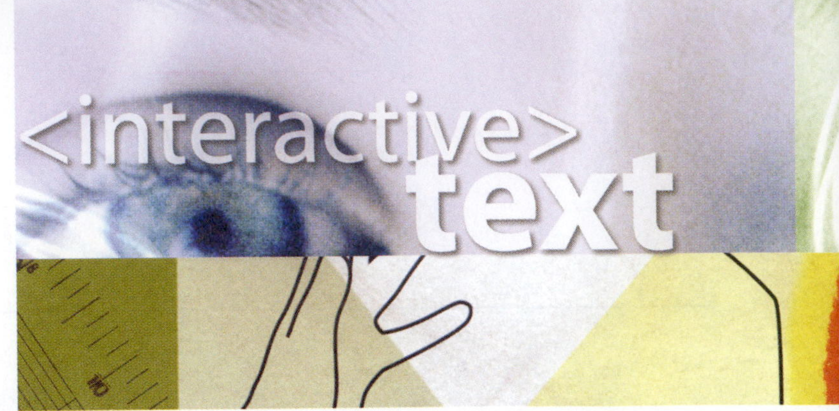

E-Commerce: Electronic Marketing and the Internet for Dot.com and Brick-and-Mortar Marketers

Chapter Objectives

1. Define e-commerce and give examples of each function of the Internet.
2. Describe how marketers use the Internet to achieve their firm's objectives.
3. Explain how online marketing benefits organizations, marketers, and consumers.
4. Identify the goods and services marketed most often on the Internet.
5. Identify the primary online marketing channels.
6. Explain how marketers use interactive tools as part of their online marketing strategies.
7. Discuss how an effective Web site can enhance customer relationships.
8. Describe how to measure the effectiveness of online marketing efforts.

Pre-Test

Take the Pre-Test to assess your initial knowledge of the key ideas in this chapter. The Pre-Test provides exam-style questions addressing the main topics and concepts of the chapter. At the completion of each Pre-Test, you will receive a score and instructive feedback on how you answered each question, and a direct link to the part of the chapter addressed in the question. Take the Pre-Test as often as you need to—a record of your progress for each attempt is kept for you to revisit and gauge your improvement.

SHOPPERS BEAT A PATH TO THE WEB

Online shopping, or B2C e-commerce, got off to a rocky start. Just a couple of years ago, few shoppers ventured online, most of them male looking for videos and music CDs. Then the hype began and a small wave of cybershoppers poured in, creating havoc with sites that weren't ready for the surge, and many holiday gifts weren't delivered on time, much to the frustration of parents who had to scramble at the last minute to put gifts under the tree. Not long after that, some of the first purely online retailers—such as Furniture.com, eToys, and Pets.com—began to fold. Then came September 11 and the economy's slide into recession. The stock market wobbled and thousands lost their jobs. No one knew what to expect next. Some predicted more troubles ahead for online shopping.

Well, B2C e-commerce appears to have confounded the pundits again. During a recent holiday season, one-third of all Americans shopped online and, for the first time, there were more women online shoppers than men (60 percent to 40 percent). Previously, books, videos, and music were the mainstays of online sales. Now, shoes, watches, apparel items, and home electronics are moving into the top categories. Over 6 million more consumers shopped online during the holiday period after the September 11 terrorist attacks, compared with the previous holiday season, and online sales grew by around 15 percent. (Overall retail sales grew by less than 5 percent.) Even Amazon.com—a poster child for B2C e-commerce, both the good and the bad—reported its first ever profit as a result of strong holiday sales. Not bad results in a weak economy.

What happened to turn around the fortunes of online retailing? Some point to the terrorist attacks. People started staying home. Many didn't even want to go to the malls since they might be tempting targets for terrorists. With all that was going on, for many people it was just easier to shop online for gifts and have the retailers ship them. Another factor that helps explain the surge in online shopping is familiarity—today, more people are comfortable with computers and the Internet. Online shopping no longer seems as exotic as it once did.

Perhaps the most important factor, however, is the simple fact that online shopping has become easier. The surviving e-tailers learned some hard lessons over the past few years. Sites now contain easy-to-use shopping tools such as the personal clothing model at Lands' End, and a better categorization of goods, making it simpler for consumers to find what they want. Many sites have added live customer service and have installed sophisticated programs that allow shoppers to track orders and shipments. Moreover, most e-tailers have made it far easier to return merchandise. B2C e-commerce firms have made other improvements as well. Amazon.com, for instance, uses new software to more accurately forecast regional demand, allowing it to reduce inventory costs by over 15 percent.

So e-tailing appears to have finally grown up. Future challenges await, however. The overall growth in online usage has slowed dramatically, raising questions about whether the recent growth in online shopping is sustainable over the long run. Moreover, many of the new online shoppers may start returning to the malls as the economy improves and the memory of September 11 begins to fade.[1]

CHAPTER OVERVIEW

Dramatic changes in global economies and societies in the last ten years have grabbed the attention of almost every person in every industry, from banking and air travel to communications. Marketing now holds the key to creating a competitive advantage. Demographic and lifestyle changes have transformed homogenous mass markets into personalized, one-on- one interactions. Deregulation, rapid technological changes, and the relative stability of its economy has made the U.S. the world leader in e-commerce.

During the past ten years, marketing has become the cutting-edge tool for success on the Internet. Profit-seeking organizations are not the only benefactors of the Internet; organizations of all kinds are beginning to emphasize marketing's role in achieving set goals. Colleges and universities, charities, museums, symphony orchestras, and hospitals now employ the marketing concept discussed in Chapter 1: providing customers the goods and services they want to buy when they want to buy them. Marketing continues to perform its function of bringing buyers and sellers together; it just does it faster and more efficiently than ever before.

With just a few ticks of the clock and a few clicks of a mouse, the Internet revolutionizes every aspect of life. New words have emerged, such as software, Internet, extranet, and intranet; and old words have new meanings never imagined a few years ago: Web, Net, surfer and server, banner and browsers, online and offline. E-commerce has turned virtual reality into reality. With a computer and a telephone, a virtual marketplace is open twenty-four hours, seven days a week to provide almost anything anywhere to anyone, including clothes, food, information, entertainment, and medicine. You can do your banking, make travel reservations, send out a résumé online, or even buy a car—perhaps at a lower price than you could in person.

Internet marketers can reach individual consumers or target organizations worldwide through a vast array of computer and communications technologies. In just a few short years, almost a half million companies large and small have been connected to electronic marketing channels. Goods and services sold to consumers total close to $50 billion per year.[2]

This chapter examines the nature of electronic commerce and explores the many ways it is transforming marketing. After defining e-commerce and e-marketing, this chapter proceeds with a discussion of the Internet and the World Wide Web. It further explains the transition of industrial economies to electronic economies, the benefits online marketing provides, and the challenges it presents. The chapter also looks at the buyers and sellers who populate the Web and how marketers build online relationships with customers. Next, the chapter discusses the various digital marketing tools and the ways marketers use Web sites to achieve organizational goals. Finally, it examines the promises and challenges associated with online marketing.

Briefly Speaking

Remember, America: I gave you the Internet and I can take it away.

Al Gore (b. 1948) Vice President of the United States (1993–2001) (on Late Show with David Letterman, *mocking his overstatement that he "took the initiative in creating the Internet")*

WHAT IS ELECTRONIC COMMERCE?

A number of terms have been used to describe marketing activities that take place on the Internet or through such electronic tools as computer modems, telephones, fax machines, and CD-ROMs. Among the most popular is **electronic commerce (e-commerce)**—targeting customers by collecting and analyzing business information, conducting customer transactions, and maintaining online relationships with customers by means of telecommunications networks. E-commerce provides a foundation for launching new businesses, extending the reach of existing companies, and building and retaining customer relationships.

<interactive>learning goal

CHAPTER OBJECTIVE #1: DEFINE E-COMMERCE AND GIVE EXAMPLES OF EACH FUNCTION OF THE INTERNET.

The component of e-commerce of particular interest to marketers is **electronic marketing (e-marketing),** the strategic process of creating, distributing, promoting, and pricing goods and services to a target market over the Internet or through such **digital tools** as fax machines, computer modems, telephones, and CD-ROMs. E-marketing is the means by which e-commerce is achieved. It encompasses such activities as:

- Ordering a best-seller from Barnes & Noble with the expectation that it will arrive within a few days.
- Placing a bid for a vintage Rolex watch on eBay.
- Purchasing downloaded copies of *New York Times* and *The Economist's* articles on European retailing to use as source material for a research paper.

The application of these electronic tools to 21st century marketing has the potential to greatly reduce costs and increase customer satisfaction by increasing the speed and efficiency of marketing interactions. Just as e-commerce is a major function of the Internet, e-marketing is an integral component of e-commerce.

A closely related but somewhat narrower term than e-marketing is online marketing. While electronic marketing can involve noncomputer digital technologies ranging from fax machines to telephones, online marketing refers to marketing activities that connect buyers and sellers electronically through interactive computer systems.

Regardless of what you are selling or buying, what kind of business you are in, or whether your company has hundreds of employees or just you, e-commerce offers almost limitless opportunities. However, the traditional marketing strategies, such as pricing and distribution, inventory, advertising, promotion, and customer service, must still be dealt with. Each organization needs to develop new business models that adapt to the large volumes of traffic inherent with online transactions. New communities of buyers and sellers are created through e-commerce. In ways not thought of just a few years ago, organizations are utilizing Internet technology to set up businesses and successfully conduct trade over the Web.

E-commerce offers countless opportunities for marketers to reach consumers. This radical departure from traditional bricks-and-mortar operations provides the following benefits to contemporary marketers, as shown in Table 5.1.

- *Global reach.* The Net eliminates the geographic protections of local business. Car dealers selling online, for example, have attracted buyers from hundreds of miles away.
- *One-to-one marketing (personalization).* Only a handful of Dell computers are waiting for customers at any one time. The production process begins when an order is received and ends a day or two later when the PC is shipped to the customer.
- *Interactive marketing.* Customers and suppliers negotiate prices online in much the same manner as they do at a local flea market or car dealership. The result is the creation of an ideal product at the right price that satisfies both parties.
- *Right-time marketing.* Web companies, such as Amazon.com and Buy.com, can provide products when and where customers want them.
- *Integrated marketing.* The Internet enables the coordination of all promotional activities and communication to create a unified, customer-oriented promotional message.

In addition to the benefits listed here, there is increasing evidence that an effective online presence improves the performance of traditional brick-and-mortar operations. For instance, a study by e-commerce research firm Jupiter Media Metrix found that half of customers use a retailer's Web site primarily for research before buying a product in the retailer's physical store.[3]

INTERACTIVITY AND E-COMMERCE

The e-commerce approach to buying and selling has been embraced by millions worldwide because it offers substantial benefits over traditional marketing practices. The two-way, back-and-forth communications enable marketers to supply the precise items desired by their customers. At the same time, purchasers can continue to refine their product specifications to create an opportunity that fills their precise needs.

One of the largest e-tailers is Amazon.com. It uses a concept called **interactive marketing.** This approach, which consists of buyer-seller communications in which the customer controls the amount and type of information received from a marketer, has been used by marketers for over a decade. Point-of-sale brochures and coupon dispensers located in supermarkets are simple forms of interactive marketing. However, when digital tools such as the Internet are included in interactive marketing efforts, the results are infinitely improved for the seller and buyer alike.

TABLE 5.1

E-Commerce Capabilities

Capability	Description	Example
Global reach	The ability to reach anyone connected to a PC anywhere in the world.	Major car makers, such as Ford, Nissan, and Volvo, use the Web to reach car buyers around the world.
One-to-one marketing	Creating products to meet customer specifications, also called personalization.	Customers can order customized clothing—from jeans to shirts to shoes—online.
Interactive marketing	Buyer-seller communications through such channels as the Internet, CD-ROMs, toll-free telephone numbers, and virtual reality kiosks.	Intouch Group's iStations are interactive kiosks placed in retail music stores that allow customers to listen to 30-second music clips before they purchase compact discs.
Right-time marketing	The ability to provide a good or service at the exact time needed.	FedEx customers can place service orders online and track shipments 24 hours a day.
Integrated marketing	Coordination of all promotional activities to produce a unified, customer-focused promotional message.	Nike marketers use the familiar Swoosh logo and "Just Do It" slogan in both online and offline promotions.

Briefly Speaking

Wow! They've got the Internet on computers now!

Homer Simpson
The Simpsons

Say, for example, you want to buy an espresso machine. If you have a computer, Amazon.com has you covered. You don't have to get in the car and drive to the mall. Just visit Amazon.com, where you can search by brand or price, compare features, and read customer ratings. With a few mouse clicks, your order is placed and will be shipped to you. You can even track the status of your shipment online. But Amazon.com doesn't stop there. You can sign in with Amazon.com, permanently registering your shipping information and credit card information. Based on your past purchases and personal preferences, Amazon.com will even send you personalized recommendations of new products. The company wants you to feel that your shopping experience is as personal as it would have been at a brick-and-mortar store.

The Internet

Although two-way communications between buyers and sellers describe most personal sales and have been taking place electronically since the invention of the telephone, the Golden Age of interactivity began a few decades ago. Its beginnings can be traced to the creation of the **Internet (Net),** a global collection of computer networks linked together for the purpose of exchanging data and information. The Net originally served scientists and government researchers, but it has since evolved into a multifaceted and popular medium of communication for individual households and business users. Users can exchange data with other computer users around the world in such formats as text, graphic images, audio, and video.

Even in small, niche markets, the Internet helps build e-commerce capabilities. For instance, Neoforma, a California-based medical supplies distributor, markets its products globally through its Web sites. Among some of its best customers are foreign governments—such as the government of Oman. If this small company had depended only on traditional marketing efforts, it would have had a difficult time serving international markets.[4]

Growth of the Internet In less than 10 years, the Internet has grown from a mere 18 million American users to over 173 million today. The number of Americans online is expected to rise to over 200 million by 2006.[5] This growth has opened more channels for consumers to find a wide array of information. The appeal of the new approach to shopping is obvious. E-commerce shifts the balance of power to the buyer. The online shopper knows that an alternative supplier is just a click away. Consumers today can easily compare prices on such products as new or used automobiles, notebook computers, and airline tickets. Travel sites, for instance, can search through hundreds of airfares, hotel rates, and cruise packages, finding you the best deals.

Intranets and Extranets Internet technologies provide a platform for **intranets,** internal corporate networks that allow employees within a firm to communicate with each other and gain access to corporate information. **Extranets,** on the other hand, are corporate networks that allow communication between a firm and selected customers, suppliers, and business partners outside the firm. Companies that use both extranets and intranets benefit even further from online communication. Intelsat, which operates global communications satellites, has an extranet called Intelsat Business Network (IBN). The more than 2,300 users of IBN log on from 400 organizations to check the availability of satellite capacity, view satellite maps, download corporate documents, and participate in discussion groups. Users can personalize their IBN account so that it shows information about only the services they use.

The World Wide Web

The Internet provides an efficient way to find and share information, but initially, most people outside of universities and government agencies found it difficult to use. This changed in the mid-1990s, when Tim Bernes-Lee at the European Center for Nuclear Research in Geneva, Switzerland, developed the *World Wide Web.* Originally thought of as an internal document-management system, the Web quickly grew to become a collection of tens of thousands of interlinked computers, called Web servers, that function together within the Internet. These computers are located all over the world and rely on high-speed Internet circuits and software to allow users to hop from server to server, providing the illusion that the Web is one big computer. The Web, along with the development of specialized software called Web browsers—such as Netscape and Microsoft Internet Explorer—made the Internet accessible to millions.

The Web can handle so much information in so many different media that it has become the premier means for marketers to reach consumers in their target markets. Close to 50 percent of all online households make a purchase through the Web. Millions of other visitors, though not actually buying online, use the Web to help them make purchasing decisions.

How do people use the Web? Figure 5.1 illustrates how a typical consumer might spend time online during a day. Many of these interactions occur as a means of communicating—such as sending electronic mail or posting messages on electronic bulletin boards. Still other interactions involve gathering information—about airfares, gifts for friends or family members, a new home, a mortgage, or a credit card. Still other interactions—such as L.L. Bean clothing purchases or an order for printer supplies from Staples—would be considered electronic commerce. The Web's entertainment function might be performed reading reviews of a best-selling book on Amazon.com or watching a trailer for an upcoming movie.

FIGURE 5.1

A Typical Day on the Web

11:30 A.M. American Airlines (http://www.aa.com) sends you an e-mail with a special rate on your usual business route.

12 P.M. Amazon.com (http://www.amazon.com) sends you an e-mail telling you the new John Grisham thriller is now available. You click on the site and order the book.

2 P.M. You remember that your aunt's birthday is next week. At the InternetMall.com site, http://www.internetmall.com, you find the perfect gift.

4:30 P.M. You are thinking of moving to another town but don't have time to drive by every home the Realtor has to show. So you check the listings at http://www.realtor.com.

7 P.M. You want to see how mortgage rates are doing and apply for a platinum Visa. So you log on to your bank at http://www.wingspanbank.com to get the information you need.

8 A.M. The kids need new clothes. You order jeans and jackets from Lands' End at http://www.landsend.com.

9 A.M. At the office, you're running low on fax paper. Order it from Office Depot at http://www.officedepot.com.

Four Web Functions

As Figure 5.2 shows, there are four primary functions of the Web: communication, information, entertainment, and e-commerce. Let's consider the role of each in contemporary marketing.

Communication For both households and businesses, one of the most popular applications of the Internet in the U.S. is e-mail. In fact, e-mails now outnumber regular mail by over ten to one. Its popularity is easy to understand: E-mail is simple to use, travels quickly, and can be read at the receiver's convenience. Also, files—such as Microsoft Office documents—can be easily sent as attachments to e-mail messages.

A more recent adaptation of e-mail is **instant messaging.** With this application, when someone sends a message, it is immediately displayed on the recipient's computer screen. As sender and recipient reply to one another, they can communicate in real time. However, unlike regular e-mail messages, instant messages have to be relatively short—a few sentences at the most.

Other popular ways to communicate are chat rooms and bulletin boards. These methods provide a forum in which a group of people can share information. When someone sends a message, it is displayed for all to see. Users join chat sessions, or messages on bulletin boards, on topics that interest them. The resulting online communities are not only personally satisfying but an important force for business. Many companies sponsor such communication as part of their overall customer service. For instance, Symantec's Web site contains several bulletin boards. When a customer has a question or a problem with one of Symantec's products, he or she can send an e-mail directly to Symantec. A technician or customer support representative replies by e-mail to the customer. The original question, as well as the answer, are automatically posted on the appropriate bulletin board. Visitors to the Symantec Web site can search the bulletin boards by entering various key words.

Information For many users, getting information is one of the main reasons they go online. Internet users can begin by consulting commercial search engines—such as Google or AskJeeves—which search for information on topics entered by the user. Or they may visit the online editions of publications like the *Los Angeles Times* or *Forbes*. Government sites provide a wealth of free data in the public domain. Another fast-growing area of the Internet consists of sites providing online educational services. Over one-third of U.S. colleges now offer some sort of accredited degree online.

Entertainment Internet users find lots of entertainment online, including everything from concert Webcasts to online gaming. Online providers of entertainment can offer competitive prices, speed, and boundless services. Games, radio programming, short movies, and music clips are available online, sometimes for free, with the costs borne by advertising on the Web site. Sometimes entire songs, movies, and books are available on the Net. Online gaming has attracted a great deal of interest recently. Both Microsoft and Sony are betting heavily that online gaming is the next big thing for video games. Microsoft's Xbox game console, for instance, has an Ethernet port making it a snap to connect to the Internet.

The availability of free content poses some ethical and business issues, including copyright issues. For instance, a federal judge ordered Video Pipeline to stop posting streaming clips and creating online previews of Disney films, ruling that such actions may violate Disney's copyrights. The judge agreed with Disney's contention that while Video Pipeline had the company's permission to sell video clips to

FIGURE 5.2

Four Functions of the Internet

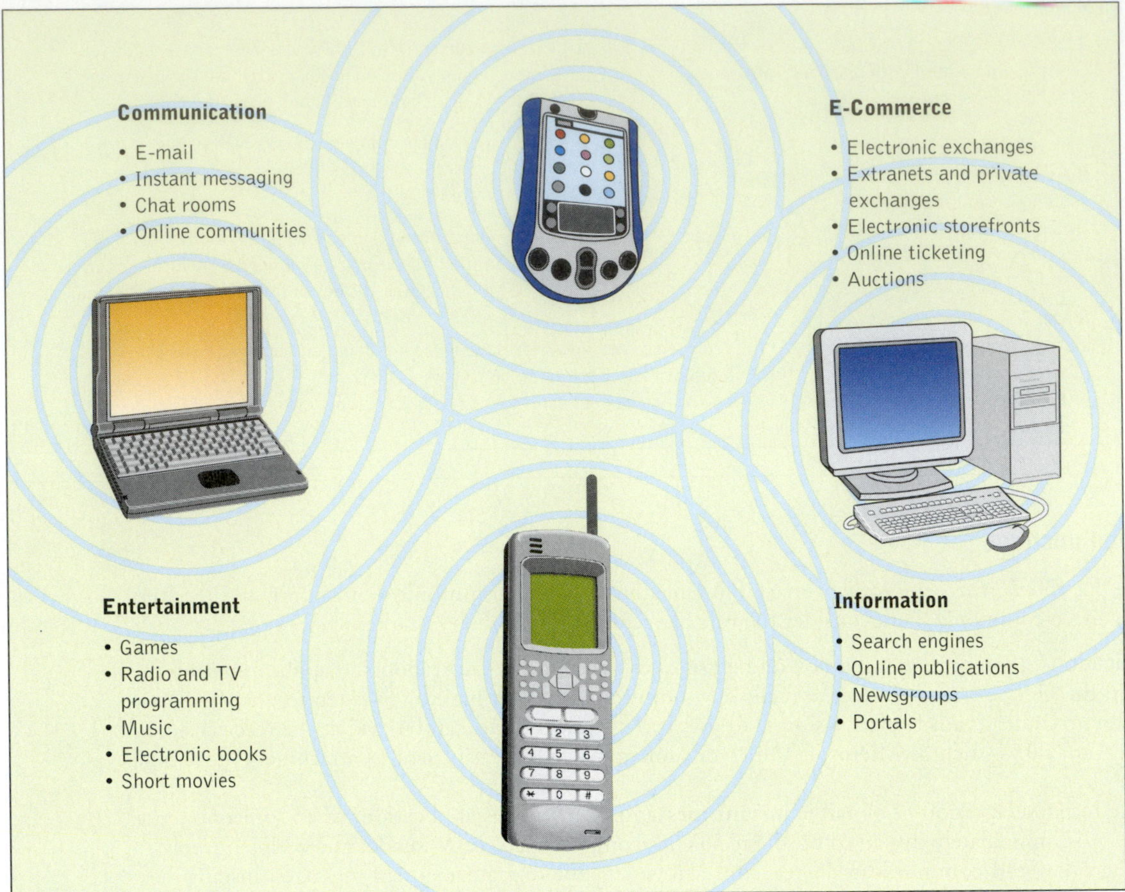

brick-and-mortar retailers, Video Pipeline wasn't allowed to disseminate the same content online.[6] However, copyright and other legal and ethical issues are unlikely to chase entertainment off the Internet.

E-Commerce Today e-commerce is the primary function of the Web. According to recent statistics, almost 80 percent of all Web sites are devoted to some aspect of e-commerce.[7] Almost every organization has some sort of Web presence, from multinational corporations to individual entrepreneurial ventures, and from sellers of goods to service providers. Organizations ranging from the not-for-profit Nature Conservancy to world-famous Tiffany's are vying for space on the Web and for consumers' attention. Upscale retailer Nordstrom recently created the world's largest online shoe store.

The Web facilitates marketing activities, including buying and selling goods and services, building relationships, increasing market size, and reducing the costs of intermediaries. This chapter focuses on the e-commerce function of the Internet since it fuels the growth of electronic marketing. The Web is the most popular area of the Internet, with more than 400 million users worldwide.[8] As the Web becomes easier to use and attracts more participants, it will become a pervasive part of modern life.

Most people generally think of the Web as a giant cybermall of retail stores selling millions of goods online. However, service providers are also important participants in e-commerce. These include providers of financial services. Brick-and-mortar banks—such as Bank of America—and brokerage firms—such as Charles Schwab—have greatly expanded their online services. In addition, many new online service providers are rapidly attracting customers who want to do more of their own banking and investment trading on whatever time and day that suits them. Figure 5.3 illustrates some of the benefits of banking online. Airlines, too, have discovered the power of the Web. Southwest Airlines, for example, generates over $1 billion annually from online ticket sales.

The Web also provides tremendous opportunities for business-to-business e-commerce. Over one-quarter of all B2B transactions are estimated to take place online, amounting to almost $1 trillion. This penetration of e-commerce is predicted to increase to more than 40 percent of B2B sales by 2006.[9] These sales are spread out across many businesses. The number of U.S. businesses engaged in B2B e-commerce is expected

FIGURE 5.3

The Benefits of Online Banking

to grow to more than 90 percent within a year or two.[10] Cisco Systems, IBM, and Intel are among the firms that generate billions of dollars in revenues online each year.

Needless to say, however, not every e-commerce idea worked out. The online landscape is littered with dozens of dot.com failures. Figure 5.4 describes some of the most notorious dot.com busts.

Accessing the Internet

In the same way an explorer relies on a compass and a map to seek out a desired destination, marketers and their customers must depend on navigation instruments to locate Web sites and find information in a database. The basic pathway for going online is through an **Internet service provider (ISP).** An ISP, such as Earthlink and Prodigy, provides individuals and organizations with direct access to the Internet. ISP giants such as America Online (AOL) let the user access the Internet through their own specially designed online sites. Such sites can be thought of as doors opening to a giant communication center called the Internet.

The early gateways for Internet access were *search engines.* Over time, these Internet entrances became portals by adding to their site contents, shopping services, and software applications like e-mail and online calendars. In addition to AOL, Earthlink, and Prodigy, major portals include MSN, Terra Lycos, and Yahoo! A more recent trend is the creation of portals built around specific services or communities. These include ESPN, CNN.com, and CBS Market Watch. Their aim is to draw in Web surfers and keep their interest with specific types of content or transactions.

In addition to serving as gateways for Internet access, portals are pushing to become the grand entrance for consumer business. At present, most portal revenue comes from advertising. Online shopping generates only a small percentage of portal site revenue, but this percentage is increasing. For instance, with around 25 million subscribers, AOL is the world's largest commercial online service. Its virtual shopping mall consists of over 400 merchant partners who pay rent for "real estate" on AOL's shopping pages.

E-COMMERCE AND THE ECONOMY

The last years of the 20th century and the early years of the 21st century witnessed the change from a century-old industrial economy to its electronic successor—an economy based on the Internet and other related online technologies. Many people see e-commerce as the fuel for the rest of the 21st century. Since the Web first opened for commercial activity in 1993, e-commerce has become a leading force in changing the way the world lives and breathes. It is estimated that in the U.S. e-commerce is currently over 2 percent of GDP. This figure is expected to increase to over 5 percent by 2006. The Web is now being

FIGURE 5.4

Some Notorious Dot.com Busts

Name	What It Did	Why It Failed
iHarvest.com	Company offered a browser plug-in that allowed users to store copies of Web pages.	Both Netscape and Internet Explorer already have the same feature; why would anyone pay for something they could get for free?
Furniture.com	Online furniture store.	Since UPS and FedEx wouldn't ship large, bulky items—like furniture—products were shipped using much more expensive common carriers; shipping costs often exceeded cost of product.
Kozmo.com	Single movie rental service; movies messengered to your front door.	Costs overwhelmed revenues; no way the business model could make money.
SwapIt.com	People could trade in used CDs and video games, receiving "swap-it bucks" that they could use to buy other people's used CDs and videos.	Could make money only on shipping and handling charges;people mostly "sold" CDs and videos no one else wanted to buy.
MySpace.com	Gave away free disk space on company servers for people and businesses to store files.	Tried to make money by selling ads; when that didn't work,the company started charging for the service. Only 6,000 out of the company's 9 million customers were willing to pay for the service.

Source: "Fiercely Stupid," Newsweek, March 25, 2002, p. 52. Article excerpted from Philip Kaplan, *F'd Company,* New York: Simon and Schuster, 2002.

explored by small, previously unheard-of companies as well as large, multinational corporations. Consider the following successes:

- Catalog retailer Lands' End's Web site generates more than $200 million a year in sales, or over 15 percent of the firm's total sales; three years earlier, online sales amounted to less than five percent of total sales.
- Startup airline JetBlue sells over half of its tickets online, the highest of any airline.
- Dell Computer is the world's largest maker of personal computers. The Internet accounts for well over half of the company's $30 billion in annual sales.
- After learning that a significant number of the nation's 3 million farmers use the Internet, Ben Zaitz created Farms.com, an online cattle and farm equipment auction site, as well as a general source of agricultural information. Annual sales are approaching $5 million, and the firm was recently cited by *Forbes* magazine as one of the top B2B e-commerce sites.[11]

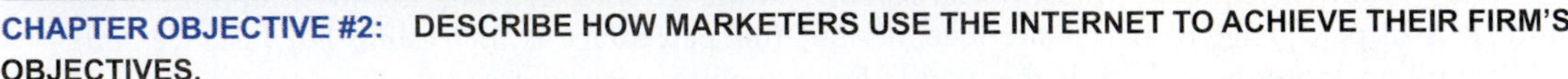

CHAPTER OBJECTIVE #2: DESCRIBE HOW MARKETERS USE THE INTERNET TO ACHIEVE THEIR FIRM'S OBJECTIVES.

But conducting business on the Net is more than just creating a Web site. State-of-the-art graphics and pages of information do not spell success any more than fancy business cards or company brochures do. A Web site must provide a platform for communication between organizations, customers, and suppliers. Businesses now hold auctions for utilities, banks partner with computer companies, and authors sell directly to their readers. New businesses and new ways of conducting business on the Web have contributed to overall economic growth. The following sections in this chapter illustrate the explosion of business-to-business (B2B) transactions. B2B e-commerce has grown to over $800 billion and is expected to top $2.4 trillion by 2005. By some estimates, B2B transactions amount to over 80 percent of e-commerce.[12]

Business-to-Business Online Marketing

CSX's Web site is nothing flashy. No fancy graphics, catchy songs, or state-of-the-art video clips—just lots of practical information, and that's just fine with the railroad's customers. The site enables customers to obtain price quotes, schedule shipments, and examine a map of the railroad's network to see where their shipments are at any given moment. This information is vital to CSX's business customers, who access the site hundreds of thousands of times each month.

Unlike the business-to-consumer (B2C) segment of the online market, B2B interactions involve professional buyers and sellers—people whose performances are evaluated by their purchasing and selling decisions. Consequently, B2B online marketing usually does not need the same glitz and glamour as the B2C segment.

Although most people are familiar with such B2C online marketers as eBay and Amazon.com, these transactions are dwarfed by their B2B counterparts, which are buying and selling both business services and commodities like paper, plastics, and chemicals. The earliest B2B e-commerce usually consisted of a company setting up a Web site and offering products to any buyer willing to make online purchases. More recently, businesses are buying and selling through **electronic exchanges,** Web-based marketplaces that cater to a specific industry's needs. An example of an electronic exchange is FreeMarkets, where suppliers compete for the business of organizational buyers who might be purchasing anything from gears to printed circuit boards. FreeMarkets was founded by Glen Meakem, a former General Electric executive. Meakem understood that manufacturers spend roughly $5 trillion each year on industrial parts and that the purchase process is usually very inefficient. He developed a system whereby suppliers promise to deliver parts on standardized schedules, with identical payment terms and inventory arrangements. The only variable is price. FreeMarkets consults with buyers and screens suppliers so that, by the time an auction takes place, each is familiar with the process. The auction itself usually takes less than an hour. FreeMarkets has proven quite popular, and large manufacturing firms such as General Motors, United Technologies, Raytheon, Emerson Electric, and Quaker Oats regularly participate. H.J. Heinz Company concluded that its relationship with FreeMarkets saved the company at least $50 million.[13]

As noted earlier, B2B e-commerce totals over $800 billion worldwide and is expected to grow to over $2.4 trillion by 2005. The U.S. is expected to remain the largest market for B2B e-commerce over the next few years, with transactions increasing at an annual rate of around 68 percent. However, B2B e-commerce is expected to grow even faster in Western Europe (increasing at an annual rate of 91 percent) and the Asia-Pacific region, where B2B e-commerce transactions are expected to increase at an annual rate of over 100 percent by 2005.[14]

Durable goods manufacturers alone account for almost half of all B2B e-commerce sales. Wholesalers of business products such as office supplies, electronic goods, and scientific equipment are a close second in B2B e-commerce market share. Even though they still provide many of their services in person, professionals such as doctors, attorneys, and accountants are finding new ways to use the Internet to reach existing and potential clients as well as communicate with others in their fields.

Companies large and small have developed the systems and software necessary to make B2B online marketing a reality. Many have even created new business units to serve the needs of customers and suppliers online. Jet-engine maker Pratt & Whitney created a special Web site that collects detailed performance records from its customers to help determine when engine service is required.[15] In addition, a whole new industry has been created to design and manage e-commerce sites for companies who wish to outsource these tasks. While there are many small, start-up companies in this industry, larger, more established firms also have a significant presence. IBM, for instance, provides e-commerce services to hundreds of other companies. In a recent year, e-commerce services generated almost $30 billion in revenue, or more than a third of IBM's total revenue.[16]

Many firms are also finding entirely new markets for their goods and services—markets that either did not exist or were inaccessible without the benefits of the Internet. Network Associates, for example, limited the marketing of its products to the U.S. for years because marketers believed their products were too expensive for foreign consumers. That all changed a few years ago when a Spanish bank downloaded a product from the firm's Web site. No additional marketing expenses were involved, and the message reached the right customers thousands of miles away.[17]

An important objective of both online and offline marketing is to distinguish a firm and its products from competitive offerings. Purchasing managers for companies can search the Web looking for the best deals on everything from office supplies to steel, selecting from hundreds of different vendors. But what about the vendors themselves? How do they position themselves on the Web so that corporate buyers notice them, let alone make a purchase? A first step is to list themselves with the major search engines—such as Terra Lycos and Google. But that is not enough. A single search for an item—say laser printer supplies—could yield thousands of sites, some of which might not even be relevant. Marketers also need to list their firms with Internet yellow pages such as Verizon's SuperPages.com, which operate just like their printed counterparts. A purchasing manager can look up "laser printer supplies" at the SuperPages.com Web site and get listings of relevant sites. Many industries have their own online references, such as the *Thomas Register of American Manufacturers.*

FIGURE 5.5

Lands' End Web Site

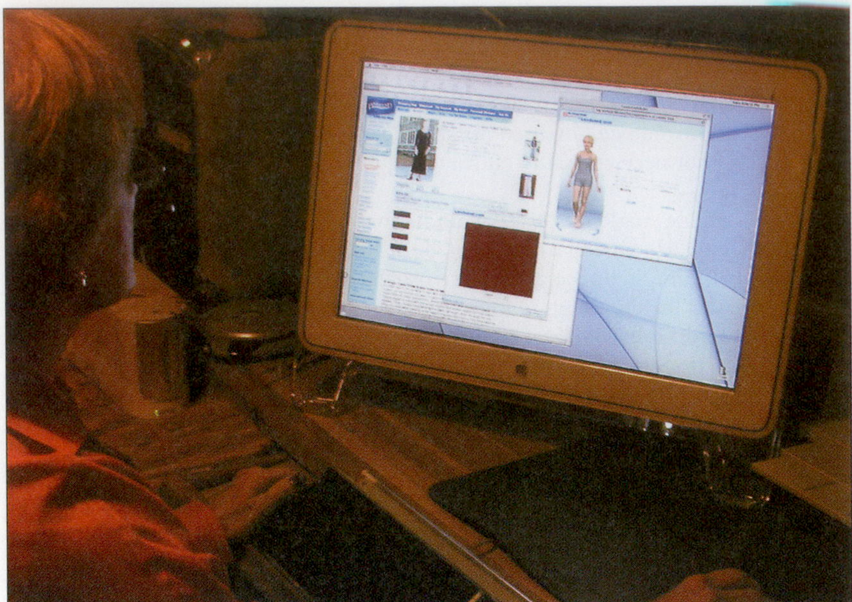

Successful online B2B marketers serve their customers by thinking like a buyer. They interview their regular customers to find out how these customers use the Internet and where they find information they need in making purchase decisions. This information can be used to devise strategies to attract new customers and improve relationships with existing ones.

Benefits of B2B Online Marketing The advantages of business-to-business online marketing strategies over traditional methods are only beginning to be realized. Online marketers can find new markets and customers. They also produce cost savings in every aspect of the marketing strategy as electronic marketing replaces the traditional bricks-and-mortar approach. Some argue that the cost savings from B2B online marketing can add at least a couple of points to the typical firm's profit margin.[18] Finally, online marketing greatly reduces the time involved in reaching target markets. Many business writers label e-commerce as easy commerce, since online marketing tools allow the direct exchange of information, such as order fulfillment and customer service, in a seamless fashion without involvement of marketing intermediaries. Communicating with suppliers, customers, and distributors over the Web is much more cost-effective and efficient than letters, phone calls, faxes, and personal sales calls that were the conventional methods of the pre-Internet era.

The number of Web sites increases daily, with most of the growth being new corporate sites. A home page creates a company's online storefront where consumers go for product and corporate information. A Web site should capture the personality of the company and serve as an effective public relations tool. The Web enhances an organization's operations by reducing distances and removing time zones. Both not-for-profit and profit-seeking organizations are enjoying these benefits. For instance, MunicipalNet Inc. is a growing e-procurement business based in Boston. It focuses on services to state and local governments, and the businesses that supply them. The city of Evanston, Illinois, recently put its procurement process online using the services of MunicipalNet Inc. According to Chad Walton, the city's purchasing manager, one advantage of e-procurement is that "it lessens the cost of responding to solicitations from the city for businesses, which in turn should translate to lower costs for us as well." Both sides, he believes, can save time and money by cutting out some of the red tape from the process. MunicipalNet can also help governments set up Web sites at which citizens can register cars, pay taxes, or look for government jobs. By one estimate, 15 percent of federal, state, and local taxes will be collected online by 2006.[19]

Online Consumer Marketing

Just as e-commerce is a major function of the Internet, online marketing is an integral component of e-commerce. Lands' End used to generate virtually all of its orders by telephone. A few years ago the company decided to turn to online marketing to boost sales and reduce costs. With ads such as the one shown in Figure 5.5, Lands' End marketers alert consumers to its new online services, such as its virtual model that allows consumers to "try on" clothes before they buy. Online customers can communicate with customer service representatives in real time. Two customers can even shop on the site simultaneously—just as if they were shopping together in a brick-and-mortar store. As the following sections explain, both consumers and marketers alike enjoy the benefits of online marketing.

CHAPTER OBJECTIVE #3: EXPLAIN HOW ONLINE MARKETING BENEFITS ORGANIZATIONS, MARKETERS, AND CONSUMERS.

Online marketing is inherently interactive marketing. While it obviously expands the reach of marketers in connecting with consumers, to be effective it must be part of an overall marketing strategy before it can create value for customers. A point to remember is that just as quickly as a firm can rise to become a star in cyberspace, if its online site is not launched properly and operated efficiently, it can just as quickly burn out.

Consumers who shop online can point to a number of advantages to online marketing. Figure 5.6 shows the results of a recent survey in which consumers were asked why they seek out or avoid online transactions.

The benefits online shoppers obtain from Web purchases fall into three categories: lower prices, convenience, and personalization. Marketers should ensure that their Web sites offer consumers these basic advantages over traditional shopping experiences. In addition, Web sites should be easy to navigate, offer a high level of security and privacy, and provide information that consumers can use in making product comparisons and purchase decisions. Moreover, it is important for e-tailers to listen to their customers and be willing to make changes to their Web sites. Online auction site eBay—perhaps the most successful B2C e-commerce firm—has a history of responding quickly to customer needs and concerns. Its approach to e-commerce is profiled in the "Marketing Hits" Interactive Example.

MARKETING HIT: LISTENING TO YOUR CUSTOMERS

Lower Prices Many products actually cost less online. Many of the best deals on airfares and hotels, for instance, can often be found at travel sites on the Internet. Visitors to BN.com—the online store of bookseller Barnes & Noble—find many bestsellers are discounted by up to 40 percent. At the brick-and-mortar stores bestsellers are marked down by only 30 percent. It comes as no surprise to anyone who has ever searched the Web for the best price for software or a newly issued CD that three out of four Web shoppers cited lower prices as a primary motivation for shopping online.

The Web is an ideal method for savvy shoppers to compare prices from dozens—even hundreds—of sellers. Online shoppers can compare features and prices at their leisure, without being pressured by a salesperson or having to conform to the company's hours of operation. Say, for instance, you're in the market for a new computer monitor. One of the newer e-commerce tools, **bots,** aid consumers in comparison shopping. Bots—short for robots—are search programs that check hundreds of sites, gather and assemble information, and bring it back to the sender. At the CNET Web site, you can specify the type and size of

FIGURE 5.6

Determinants of Online Purchasing Behavior

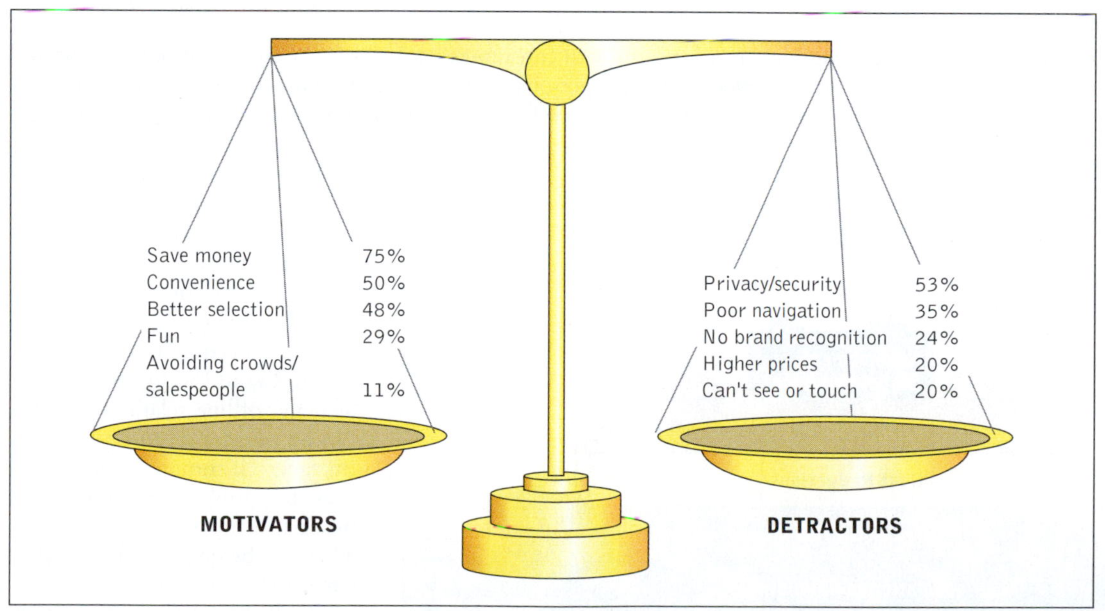

monitor you're looking for and the Web site displays a list of the highest-ranked monitors along with the e-tailer offering the best price on each. The Web site even ranks the e-tailers by customer experience and tells you whether or not a particular model is in stock.

'NET EX: SHOPPING BOTS

Convenience A second important factor in prompting online purchases is shopper convenience. Cybershoppers can order goods and services from around the world at any hour of the day or night. Many e-tailers allow customers to register their credit-card and shipping information for quick use in making future purchases. Registered customers are asked to type in a password when they place another order. E-tailers typically send an e-mail message confirming an order, its shipping date, and the amount charged to the buyer's credit card. Online ordering tracking is also commonplace today.

Many Web sites offer customized products to match individual customer requirements. Nike offers online shoppers the opportunity to customize a running shoe, personalizing such features as the outsole, the amount of cushioning, and the width. The personalized shoe costs about $10 more than buying it off the shelves. Consumers are also able to personalize men's and women's dress pants and men's dress shirts at Landsend.com.[20]

Personalization While electronic marketing often operates with little or no human interaction, cyberspace marketers know how important personalization is to the quality of the shopping experience. Customer satisfaction is greatly affected by the marketer's ability to offer service tailored to many customers. But each person expects a certain level of customer service. Consequently most leading online retailers currently offer customized features on their Web sites.

The early years of e-commerce saw Web marketers casting their nets broadly in an effort to land as many customers as possible. Today, the emphasis has turned toward one-to-one marketing, creating loyal customers who are likely to make repeat purchases. How does personalized marketing work online? Say you buy a book at Amazon.com and register with the site. The site will welcome you back for your next purchase by name. Using special software that analyzes your previous purchases, it will also suggest several other books you might like. You even have the option of receiving periodic e-mails from Amazon.com informing you of new products.

Benefits of Online Consumer Marketing

Many of the same benefits achieved by B2B online marketers are also realized by marketers of consumer products who rely on the Web in their businesses. As Figure 5.7 indicates, marketers can use their Web sites to build strong relationships, reduce costs, increase efficiency, create a more level playing field, and achieve a global presence.

Relationship Building Building relationships with consumers is crucial to the success of both offline and online marketing. As an earlier section explained, personalization is an important component of online relationship building. If a shopper visits a Web site that sells accessories and buys a dress and a purse, the next time she visits the site, she may be greeted with an attractive ad showing a belt or shoes that can be coordinated with her previous purchase. In this way, marketers create a one-on-one shopping experience that often leads to customer satisfaction and repeat purchases. Brand loyalty forms a part of many offline relationships that can be transferred to online sites. In fact, customers expect Web sites to emulate the traditional brick-and-mortar retail world. They like being greeted when they enter a store or a Web site.

Small businesses, with even smaller budgets, can use the Internet to find customers in

FIGURE 5.7

Benefits of Business-to-Consumer Online Marketing

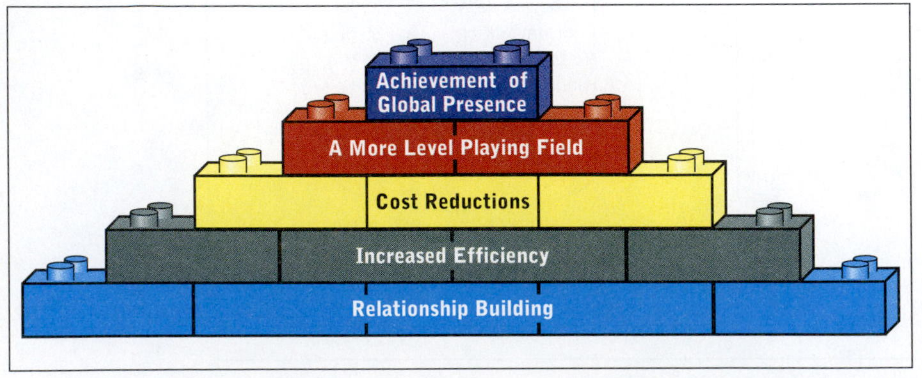

unexpected places and build relationships with them. Rick Brown, president of Newspaper Collectors Society of America, holds online auctions to sell historic papers to collectors. A few years ago, he sold a 19th-century receipt from a drugstore in Canton, Maine. Ordinarily, this would not be a big seller, but it proved highly desirable to residents of Canton who were establishing a local historical society. Another antiques dealer had difficulty at first selling a 1903 bicycle-parts catalog from France, but it sold quickly after French collectors discovered Brown's Web site (now at http:// www.historybuff.com).[21] Once customers have received quick and efficient service from online dealers, they often return in search of other rare objects for which they might be looking.

Customer service is the key to building strong customer relationships, in both traditional and online marketing. Because the Web has the power to create two-way communications between companies and their customers instantly, many people get a good feeling about shopping online, believing that someone is on the other end with immediate answers to their questions and solutions to their problems. Unfortunately, this is too often not the case. Consumers sometimes report waiting hours and even days for a reply; others get no reply at all. A recent survey by Jupiter Media Metrix found that the online travel industry needs to improve customer service if it is going to continue to grow. A majority of respondents, 79 percent, said that they would be less likely to use an online travel site again after a dissatisfying customer service experience.[22]

Increased Efficiency For large corporations and small businesses, sales made entirely through a Web site have a much greater profit margin than sales from traditional channels such as catalogs, retail outlets, or phone centers. However, even if the sale does not close online, marketers who educate their customers online ultimately save money because salespeople no longer have to spend their time answering routine questions.

Cost Reductions Marketers have found that e-commerce can markedly reduce the costs of starting and operating a business. Scott Smith, manager of inventory at Ace Hardware, says that since his company installed a Web-enabled collaborative-commerce program, the cost of picking goods off warehouse shelves has fallen about 18 percent and receiving costs dropped by 20 percent.[23]

A More Level Playing Field Minority business owners believe that the anonymity provided them by the Internet has allowed them to succeed on their own merits in a world where discrimination still exists. Roosevelt Gist, an African-American car dealership owner, often had white customers who would ask for another salesperson when he would approach them. Today, Gist is still in the car business but in cyberspace. He runs AutoNetwork.com, an online forum for researching, buying, and selling cars. The site hosts over 40,000 visitors a month, none of whom have had the chance to prejudge Gist on the basis of race.[24]

Online Marketing Is International Marketing

Another advantage to both online consumer and business-to-business marketers is the Internet's global reach, enabling inexpensive communication with consumers in faraway places. A U.S. marketer who wants to contact consumers in Australia, for example, may find express mail or long-distance telephone rates prohibitive, but the low cost and speed of such online marketing tools as fax machines and e-mail make global marketing a reality. Thirty percent of Australian households have computers, and the typical Australian spends more time accessing Web pages than anyone except Americans.

Culture can prove to be a barrier that hampers online marketing overseas, however. Marketers, particularly those in Asia, face such barriers. Today, most e-commerce sites are still in English, which often restricts access by Asian consumers. Although Asia contains a significant portion of the world's population and the number of Internet users there is increasing, the region still only accounts for less than 20 percent of Internet users worldwide. (The U.S. and Canada make up over one-third of all Internet users worldwide.)[25] Finally, many Asian consumers are less familiar and comfortable with catalog or telephone purchases than are U.S. and Canadian shoppers. Consequently, they are more reluctant to accept online shopping as a safe and secure way of purchasing products.

Even though over 50 million Europeans are online, they use the Internet for shopping much less than American consumers. The European wired set is much more likely to value the Internet as a way to work from home, catch up on local politics, choose vacation destinations, and take courses. Even in Norway, Sweden, and Denmark, where Net penetration is Europe's highest at around half of all households, e-commerce takes a back seat to such uses as e-mail and information services.[26]

As noted in earlier chapters, business is becoming increasingly global. E-commerce allows companies like Pacific Internet and Europe Online to create a regional framework for business transactions. Pacific Internet joined with Internet Initiative and Sumitomo (both based in Japan) and the Hong Kong Supernet, using Hong Kong and Singapore as hubs. Figure 5.8 lists a sampling of international Web sites that call the world their domestic market. Marketers must not forget that although the Internet has no geographical boundaries, countries do. Issues of infrastructure, economy, and politics all come into play when marketers try to enter international markets. While astute marketers think globally, they should also remember that e-commerce is a local experience in each country.

FIGURE 5.8

Examples of Companies with Global Web Sites

http://www.starmedia.com	Spanish- and Portuguese-language StarMedia Network; launched in November 1998 in the United States.
http://www.uol.com.br	Universo Online, the largest portal serving Brazilians.
http://www.sina.com.tw	Sinanet.com, which targets the approximately 60 million Chinese living outside China and Taiwan.
http://www.sify.com	Sify.com, offering users of Indian ancestry "all the India you want to know."

Even though e-commerce is growing rapidly, global online commerce still lags behind the pace of online marketing in the U.S. Web advertising revenues in Europe will not reach current U.S. levels for at least another five years. Some countries have infrastructure barriers. For instance, most telephone calls in Europe, including local calls, are metered and charged based on the length of the call, which makes it much more expensive for European consumers to spend time on the Internet if they use a dial-up connection. Moreover, a smaller percentage of Europeans use broadband connections to get online compared with Americans and Canadians.[27] Nevertheless, marketers should recognize the tremendous potential of international Internet markets, and many are scrambling to expand their international online presence. For instance, eBay has over 20 different country-specific Web sites.

Security and Privacy Issues of E-Commerce

Consumers worry that information about them will become available to others without their permission. In fact, marketing research indicates that privacy is the top concern of Internet users and may be an impediment to the growth of e-commerce.[28] For example, concern about the privacy of credit card numbers has led to the use of secure payment systems. To add to those security systems, e-commerce sites require passwords as a form of authentication—that is, to determine that the person using the site is actually the one authorized to have access to the account. More recently, **electronic signatures** have become a way to enter into legal contracts, such as home mortgages and insurance policies, online. With an e-signature, an individual obtains a form of electronic identification and installs it in his or her Web browser. Signing the contract involves looking up and verifying the buyer's identity with this software.

Thanks to automatic data collection methods, Web users leave electronic trails of personal information about their buying and viewing habits. The way that companies use cookies has the potential both to make visits to the Web site more convenient and to invade computer users' privacy. DoubleClick abandoned a plan to merge its data on Web use with a database of catalog orders, which would have given the company the ability to target online advertising to individual consumers based on their shopping habits.[29] Similarly, Amazon.com received such bad press over its plan to publicize customer shopping information by company or group, called Purchase Circles, that it now allows customers to request removal of their names. With over 23 million customers, Amazon's customer database is one of the largest, and keeping its customers happy is critical to its success.[30]

FIGURE 5.9

TRUSTe: Ensuring Internet Privacy

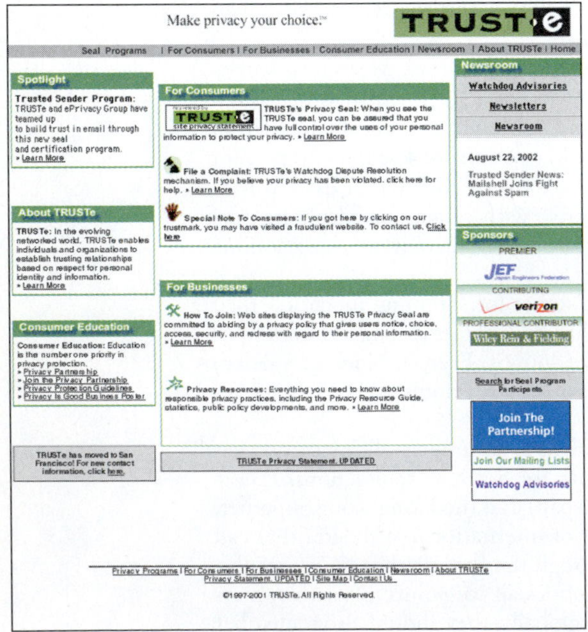

Most consumers want assurances that any information they provide won't be sold to others without their permission. In response to these concerns, online merchants have been taking steps to protect consumer information. For example, many Internet companies have signed on with Internet privacy organizations like TRUSTe, shown in Figure 5.9. By displaying the TRUSTe logo on their Web sites, they indicate that they have promised to disclose how they collect personal data and what they do with the information. Prominently displaying a privacy policy is an effective way to build customers' trust.

A policy is only as good as the company publishing it, though. Consumers have no assurances about what happens if a company is sold or goes out of business. Now-defunct Toysmart.com promised customers that it would never share their personal data with a third party. But when the company landed in bankruptcy court, it considered selling its database, one of its most valuable assets. And Amazon.com has told customers openly that if it or part of its business is purchased at some point, its database would be one of the transferred assets.[31] With these concerns, it is no wonder that some companies are profiting by selling software designed to protect privacy. For example, a program called Freedom enables the user to set up an anonymous online identity. Another package called PersonaValet allows users to determine which personal data to reveal when they visit Web sites that have installed software that works with PersonaValet.[32]

Such privacy features may become a necessary feature of Web sites if consumer concerns continue to grow. They also may become legally necessary. Already in the U.S., the Children's Online Privacy Protection Act (COPPA) requires that Web sites targeting children younger than 13 years of age obtain "verifiable parental consent" before collecting any data that could be used to identify or contact individual users, including names and e-mail addresses. Congress has also begun considering laws to protect the privacy of adult users. The "Solving an Ethical Controversy" Interactive Example debates whether or not additional legislation is needed to protect the privacy of Internet users.

RIGHT/WRONG: SOLVING AN ETHICAL CONTROVERSY—IS THE WEB SPYING ON YOU?

WHO ARE THE ONLINE BUYERS AND SELLERS?

As the growth of e-commerce continues, it becomes easier to use and much broader in its appeal to consumers. Over the past couple of years, online spending has more than doubled. Leading the charge were two primary groups of consumers: people who had never bought online before and consumers over the age of 50. These shoppers spent an average of around $125 per online purchase during a recent holiday period.[33] The actual and projected growth in online consumer spending is shown in Figure 5.10.

Online Buyers

The U.S. Department of Commerce has identified the demographics of Internet users—the target market for e-commerce marketers. The heaviest Internet users make $75,000 or more a year and live in urban areas; conversely, low-income rural dwellers account for less than 3 percent of Internet users. States with the highest percentage of Internet users include Alaska, New Hampshire, Washington, Utah, and Colorado. Americans of Asian and Pacific Island origin are the racial group most likely to use the Internet. In fact, they are twice as likely as African Americans and Hispanics to own PCs and three times more likely to be online. About 75 percent of employed people use the Internet at work, and more than 87 percent of college graduates do so. Over half of all people currently looking for jobs go online to send out résumés and check for job openings.[34]

While the typical Internet user is still relatively young and affluent, there is evidence that online demographics are changing. According to Jupiter Media Metrix, tomorrow's online shoppers will be older and less affluent. As the number of online shoppers doubles over the next five years, the new shoppers will more likely be over 35 and have annual household incomes of between $30,000 and $75,000. Marketers must adapt to these changing demographics. Ken Cassar of Jupiter puts it this way: "The next generation of

FIGURE 5.10

Actual and Projected Online Consumer Spending

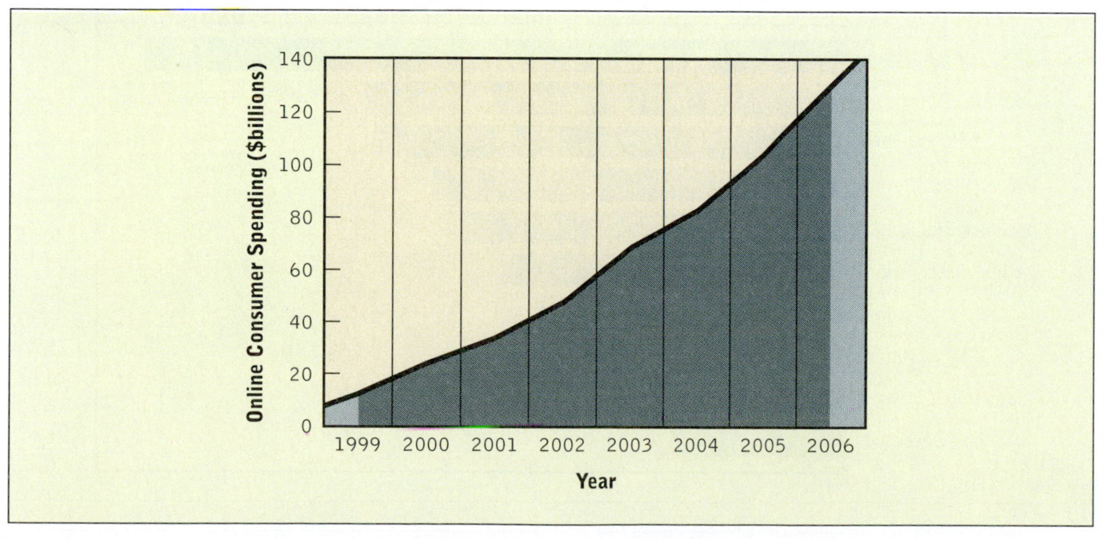

Sources: CyberAtlas and U.S. Department of Commerce.

online shoppers will be quite a bit different. . . . They will be more representative of middle-class America. Retailers who want to appeal to these new shoppers must constantly study the changing composition of their customer base."[35]

Marketers must also continually be aware of the ways in which e-commerce is actually changing customers. For one thing, online marketing reaches people who do not normally watch television and read magazines. For another, online marketing is educating consumers in ways that traditional marketing cannot—by offering more information (often personalized) more rapidly than a retail salesperson, product brochure, or 30-second television commercial. Customers are more knowledgeable—and sometimes more demanding—than they used to be. Once consumers discover how easy it is to learn about wines at winespectator.com, they may be disappointed with the wine-shopping experience in a supermarket.

Online Sellers

Realizing that customers would have little or no opportunity to rely on many of the sense modes—smelling the freshness of direct-from-the-oven bread, touching the soft fabric of a new cashmere sweater, or squeezing fruit to assess its ripeness—early online sellers focused on offering products that consumers were familiar with and tended to buy frequently, such as books and music. Other popular early online offerings included computer hardware and software, and airline tickets.

<interactive>**learning goal**

CHAPTER OBJECTIVE #4: IDENTIFY THE GOODS AND SERVICES MARKETED MOST OFTEN ON THE INTERNET.

Figure 5.11 lists the ten most popular goods and services sold online during a recent two-month holiday shopping period. While airline tickets and computer hardware remained the most popular items sold online, apparel and food and beverages also rank in the top ten. Moreover, online sales of apparel, food and beverages, and other products Web sellers initially avoided selling are growing faster than online sales of books and music.

A recent study by Jupiter Media Metrix predicts that apparel, prescription drugs, and home products will be hot online sellers in the years ahead as the demographics of Web users changes. Once women—who spend more money on apparel than men do—become a larger share of Internet users, online apparel sales are likely to climb. Similarly, as the population of online users over 55 grows, so will the online sales

FIGURE 5.11

What's Selling on the Internet

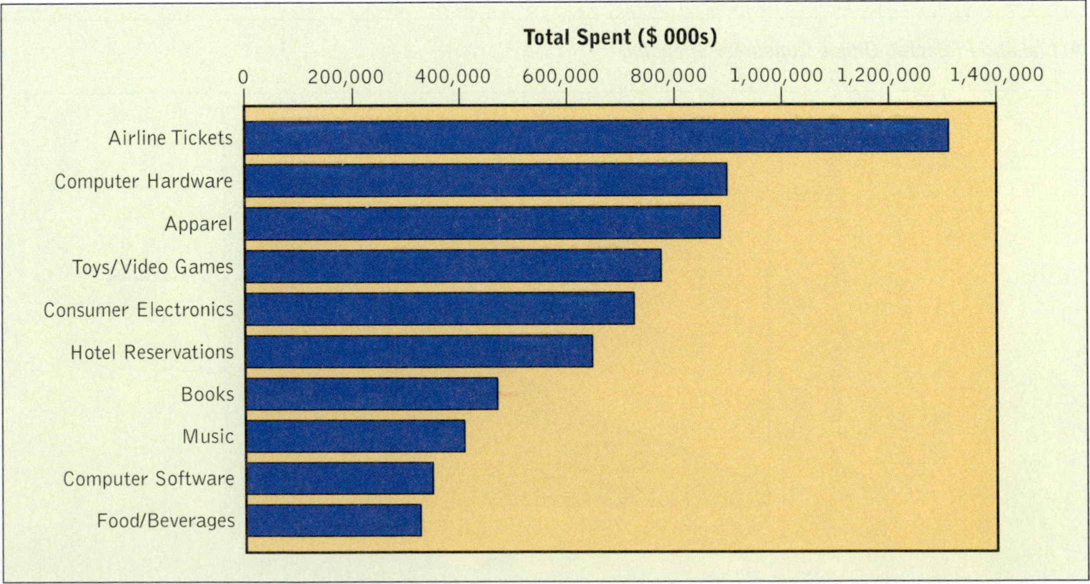

The data shown are for a recent two-month holiday shopping period.
Source: NRF/Forrester Online Retail Index, accessed from the CyberAtlas Web site, http://cyberatlas.internet.com, April 19, 2002.

of prescription drugs. Jupiter also predicts that kitchen products, small appliances, and large appliances—which typically are bought more frequently by women and older consumers—will experience strong growth over the next five years. According to Ken Cassar of Jupiter, "With the online shopping population expected to change dramatically, retailers must adopt a proactive merchandising strategy, anticipating changes in their customer base rather than reacting to changes in sales patterns. In order to measure these changes, retailers must track transaction data, survey customers, analyze the evolving customer base and quickly make appropriate changes."[36]

INTERACTIVE ONLINE MARKETING CHANNELS

Both manufacturers and marketing intermediaries frequently turn to online channels to market their goods and services. Want Dell to build a notebook computer that meets your computing needs? Click on http://www.dell.com. Need a student loan? Click on http://www.lendingtree.com. Looking for a better deal on car insurance? Click on http://www.progressive.com.

<interactive>**learning goal**

CHAPTER OBJECTIVE #5: **IDENTIFY THE PRIMARY ONLINE MARKETING CHANNELS.**

Each of these marketers—and thousands more like them—has turned to online marketing as a faster, less expensive, and more efficient alternative to the traditional approach of setting up brick-and-mortar retail stores. As Figure 5.12 shows, businesses deciding to market their products online can do so through one or a combination of primary online alternatives: company Web sites, online advertisements on other sites, and online communities. Other interactive marketing links include Web kiosks, smart cards, and virtual coupons and samples.

Company Web Sites

Virtually all online marketers have their own Web site that offers general information, electronic shopping, and promotions such as games, contests, and online coupons. Type in the firm's Internet address, and the Web site's home page will appear on your computer screen.

Two types of company Web sites exist. Many firms have established **corporate Web sites** to increase their visibility, promote their goods and services, and provide information for other interested parties. Rather than selling products directly, these sites attempt to build customer goodwill and assist channel members in their marketing efforts. For example, the Web site for Levi's jeans offers product information and a chance to view recent commercials. Consumers who want to actually buy jeans can link to the Web sites of retailers such as Kohl's and JCPenney.

Although marketing Web sites often include information about company history, products, locations, and financial information, their goal is to increase purchases by site visitors. For instance, Starbucks's Web site contains all of the information traditionally found on a corporate Web site, but it also includes an online store selling everything from coffee to espresso machines. Many marketing Web sites try to engage consumers in interactions that will move them closer to a demonstration, trial visit, purchase, or other marketing outcome. Some marketing Web sites, such as Sony.com, are quite complex. Visitors can link to pages for Sony Pictures Entertainment (with movie trailers and sweepstakes), Sony Music (audio and video clips plus news about recordings), and Sony Online Entertainment (online games plus information about games and gaming systems), among other possibilities.

Electronic Storefronts and Cybermalls Clicking on http://www.jcpenney.com takes you on a virtual visit to the store. This **electronic storefront** is just what its name implies—an online store where customers can view and order merchandise much like shopping at brick-and-mortar retail establishments. The JCPenney online shopper is offered a store finder, electronic forms for ordering a catalog or subscribing to promotional e-mail, a gift registry, thousands of inventory items, and secure online shopping. The shopper has the option of having purchases delivered or picking them up at the local JCPenney store.

Whether a supplement to existing brick-and-mortar retail outlets or as a virtual replacement, electronic storefronts can offer

FIGURE 5.12

Online Marketing Channels

Company Web Sites – corporate Web sites – marketing Web sites – virtual storefronts – cybermalls	**Online Communities** – online forums – newsgroups – electronic bulletin boards
Advertisements on Other Web Sites – banner ads – pop-up windows	**Other Interactive Marketing Links** – interactive kiosks – smart cards – virtual coupons and samples

marketers a number of advantages. These include the ability to expand operations in different cities, states, or countries without the major capital investments typically required for such growth. Also there is evidence that an electronic storefront can enhance the performance of brick-and-mortar operations. In addition, virtual stores provide great flexibility since the business is open 24 hours a day, thus removing time-zone barriers. Inventory locations can be centralized and orders can be filled promptly. Moreover, the image of the electronic storefront is controlled by the quality, creativity, and originality of the Web site and the ability of the Web marketers to offer customer satisfaction.

As noted in the chapter's opening vignette, online shopping got off to a rocky start. Many of the original e-tailers went out of business and those that survived learned some hard lessons about how to satisfy customers. While many of the surviving e-tailers have successful brick-and-mortar operations, a few exist only in cyberspace. One of these successful pure e-tailers is Buy.com, which is profiled in the "Marketing Hits" Interactive Example.

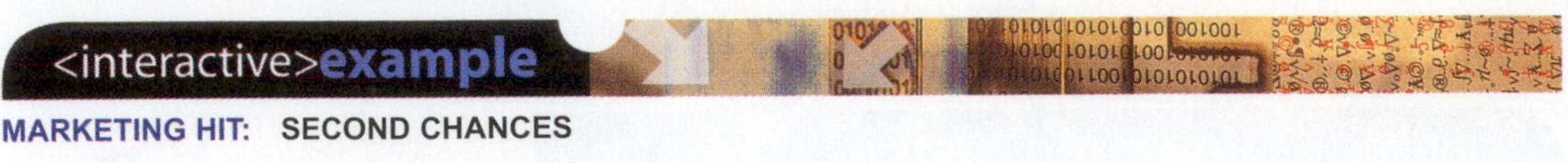

MARKETING HIT: SECOND CHANCES

A common approach is to group electronic storefronts into **cybermalls,** some of which can link as many as 400 participating online retailers. Like concrete shopping malls, cybermalls typically feature a popular national retailer with high customer traffic as an anchor tenant. Other stores included in the mall are selected to produce a good match of merchandise offerings for the shopper. The operators of cybermalls charge each individual storefront operator a fee—either a flat monthly charge or a sliding scale depending on the number of visits to the storefront. Cybermalls are also operated by the major Internet portals and ISPs. In fact the world's largest cybermall is operated by AOL.

Advertising on Other Web Sites

Rather than relying completely on their Web sites to attract buyers, online marketers frequently expand their reach in the marketplace by placing ads on sites their prospective customers are likely to visit. *Banner ads,* the most common form of Internet advertising, are typically small, strip messages placed in high-visibility areas of frequently visited Web sites. *Pop-up ads* are separate windows that pop up. Examples of both types of ads are shown in Figure 5.13.

FIGURE 5.13

Example of Banner Ad and Pop-up Ad

Many online marketers advocate using a variety of online and offline advertising combined with other forms of interactive promotion for better results. Lands' End created its "My Virtual Model" interactive tool to give customers a way of "trying on" clothes and accessories while sitting at their computers. The customer enters some basic information—such as height, weight, and hair color—and the software creates a customized model. The model can even be saved for future use. The firm's marketers also use banners placed on popular Web sites and portals to target its customer base.

Online Communities

In addition to such direct channels as marketing merchandise through a firm's Web site, many firms use Internet forums, newsgroups, electronic bulletin boards, and Web communities that appeal to people who share common interests. All of these take advantage of the communication power of the Internet which, as noted earlier in the chapter, is still a main reason people go online. Members congregate online and exchange views and information on topics of interest. These communities may be organized for commercial or noncommercial purposes.

Online communities can take several forms, but all offer specific advantages to users and marketers alike. Online forums, for instance, are Internet discussion groups located on commercial online services. Users log in and participate by sending comments and questions or receiving information from other forum members. Forums may operate as electronic bulletin boards, as libraries for storing information, or even as a type of classified ad directory.

Marketers often use forums to ask questions and exchange information with customers. Adobe, which designs such software as Acrobat and Photoshop, operates a "user-to-user" forum on its Web site as a support community for its customers. Customers who share common personal and professional interests can congregate, exchange industry news and practical product tips, share ideas, and—equally important—create publicity for Adobe products.

Newsgroups are noncommercial Internet versions of forums. Here people post and read messages on specific topics. Tens of thousands of newsgroups are on the Internet, and the number continues to rise. **Electronic bulletin boards** are specialized online services that center on a specific topic or area of interest. For instance, white-water rafters might check online bulletin boards to find out about the latest equipment, new places to raft, or current rafting conditions on particular waterways. While newsgroups resemble two-way conversations, electronic bulletin boards are more like announcements. Marketers often place banner or pop-up ads on newsgroups and electronic bulletin boards.

Online communities are not limited to consumers. They also facilitate business-to-business marketing. Participating in extranets or business communities like Farms.com helps small businesses develop relationships that transcend the former limits of their real-world, local communities. Using the Internet to build communities helps companies find other organizations to benchmark against, including suppliers, distributors, and competitors that may be interested in forming an alliance. Business owners who want to expand internationally frequently seek advice from other members of their online community.

Briefly Speaking

The 'Net is a waste of time, and that's exactly what's right about it.

William Gibson (b. 1948) American writer

Other Interactive Marketing Links

A variety of high-tech interactive tools are used by today's marketers to reach targeted market segments. These buyer-seller links include interactive kiosks, smart cards, and virtual coupons and samples. **Web kiosks** are freestanding computers, often located in retail showrooms or shopping centers. They are versatile multimedia devices that deliver information on demand. Shoppers can stop by a kiosk and get discount coupons or product information. Web kiosks are a marriage of traditional kiosks and Internet connections. Officially dubbed "in store, Web-assisted selling," the goal of these kiosks is to keep customers from leaving empty-handed and provide new levels of selection, especially for customers who may not otherwise have Internet access.

<interactive>**learning goal**

CHAPTER OBJECTIVE #6: EXPLAIN HOW MARKETERS USE INTERACTIVE TOOLS AS PART OF THEIR ONLINE MARKETING STRATEGIES.

Some Web kiosks can even take the place of online shopping. For instance, all Best Buy stores have a "Computer Creation Station," a Web kiosk that lets customers design their own PC, with or without the assistance of a salesperson. The customer's custom-built PC is usually ready within a week and can be picked up at the store or sent to the customer's home or business. Best Buy's Computer Creation Station allows it to compete with direct sellers of custom-made computers, such as Dell and Gateway.

Another e-commerce innovation involves **smart cards**—plastic cards similar to credit cards that are embedded with computer chips that store personal and financial information. To buy an item, the card is inserted into a card scanner or reader, which electronically debits the purchase amount. The card can be "reloaded" periodically with cash from a checking or savings account. Smart cards were the first step toward electronic currency—a system of exchange in which a consumer can set up accounts at Web sites and transfer money into the accounts.

Although smart cards have been popular in Europe and Asia for years, they have been slower to catch on in the U.S. A few years ago, American Express began offering Blue—one of the first smart credit cards. American Express marketed Blue as a card that provided an added layer of security when shopping on the Web. Each card contains a unique digital certificate that acts much like a key. Those who want extra security online can swipe their cards through a special reader attached to their PCs. After the cardholder enters a PIN, the certificate is read, and the necessary information to complete the purchase is transmitted securely. Blue also contains a magnetic strip so it can be used like an ordinary credit card.

Recently, many traditional direct marketing companies began going online with *virtual coupon* and *online sample* offerings. Customers can find virtual coupons on their PCs by such criteria as business name, location, and keyword and can download them on a home computer. Online consumers can also register to have coupons e-mailed directly to them. ValPak Direct Marketing Systems, a longtime leader in the paper coupon industry, now offers the online equivalent at its Web site, http://www.valpak.com.

Other Web sites offer free product samples. Members of FreeSampleClub (accessible at http://www.sunflowergroup.com) complete interactive profiles that include information such as age, family data, and pet ownership. Based on the profiles, the system creates a personal sample menu from merchants who are targeting that profile. Members click on their choices and receive products within a week.

CREATING AN EFFECTIVE WEB PRESENCE

One of the preliminary tasks of starting a business or entering a new market is performing marketing research. Marketers evaluate every proposed e-commerce venture to ensure it benefits the firm by cutting costs, improving customer satisfaction, and increasing revenues. To have a successful e-commerce business, it is also essential that marketing activities remain customer-oriented. Other areas that must be assessed include the competitive environment and the costs of updating the firm's technological infrastructure. An effective Internet strategy should create sustainable shareholder value by increasing profits, accelerating growth, reducing time-to-market for products, improving customer service, and improving the public perception of the organization.

<interactive>**learning goal**

CHAPTER OBJECTIVE #7: DISCUSS HOW AN EFFECTIVE WEB SITE CAN ENHANCE CUSTOMER RELATIONSHIPS.

Building an Effective Web Site

Most Web experts agree: "It is easier to build a bad Web site than a good one." To be effective, a firm's strategies must focus on building relationships through the use of company Web sites. Because of the high costs associated with going online, marketers must get the highest possible return on their Web site investments. Building an effective Web site involves three basic steps: establish a mission for the company's site, identify the purpose of the site, and satisfy customer needs and wants through a clear site design.

The first step is to establish a mission for the site. A site mission involves the creation of a statement that explains the organization's overall goals. Without a mission to guide decision makers, the technology will be aimless. Dell Computer describes its mission in three clicks: to make it easier for customers to do business with them, to reduce the cost of business for Dell and its customers, and to enhance Dell's relationship with it customers.[37]

Next, marketers must identify the purpose of the site. Is it primarily to provide information or entertainment, or is it intended to solely connect buyers and sellers? Priceline.com, which auctions such things as airline tickets and hotel rooms, operates by the phrase "Name your price" and prominently displays this phrase throughout its Web site. Visitors know exactly what they are supposed to do. In addition, marketers should educate themselves—not so much about the details of technology but about how Web sites enhance customer communications and how those communications benefit the company.

Marketers should also be clear about how the purpose of the site fits in with the company's overall marketing strategy. For instance, Mattel, well-known for producing toys such as Barbie, Cabbage Patch dolls, and Matchbox cars, sells most of its products in toy stores and toy departments of other retailers, like Target and Wal-Mart. The company wants an Internet presence, but it would cut the retailers out of this important source of revenue if it sold toys online to consumers. Mattel cannot afford to lose the goodwill and purchasing power of these giant retailers. So the company sells only specialty products online, such as the pricey American Girl dolls, that are not carried in most retail stores.

Finally, identifying customer needs and wants is critical to marketers both online and offline. However, online marketers must consider how their strategies will need to be adjusted to continue satisfying customers through online transactions. Well-designed Web sites are straightforward, provide security and privacy, and, most important, are easy to navigate. Successful sites follow accepted Internet conventions and familiar screen layouts so customers will not get lost on the site. They also use the right color combinations. Many organizations outsource their Internet services entirely, from building Web sites to designing intranets and extranets.

Managing a Web Site

Once a site is up and running, it has to be managed effectively. Marketers must update the site frequently, flagging new merchandise and services, and eliminating items that did not sell well and references to past events. Some marketers recommend avoiding dates on site pages so the site always appears current. Web site management involves constant attention not only to content but to technical presentation. Frequent software updates may be necessary to take advantage of new technologies that permit increasing levels of customer interaction. Marketers should keep track of costs associated with Web sites. Profitability has still been erratic. If costs exceed revenues, marketers need to reevaluate whether the site is meeting expected goals or whether changes need to be implemented to boost the site's effectiveness.

<interactive>**learning goal**

CHAPTER OBJECTIVE #8: DESCRIBE HOW TO MEASURE THE EFFECTIVENESS OF ONLINE MARKETING EFFORTS.

Amazon.com, one of the world's largest e-tailers, found profitability elusive. Consequently, it kept tinkering with its Web site. It expanded its offerings from books and music to electronics, toys, and housewares. Amazon.com was also the first commercial site to use software that could analyze a customer's purchases and suggest other related items—a terrific way of targeting a market. In order to keep up with future technology needs, Amazon.com acquired Junglee Corporation, a developer of comparison-shopping technologies, and PlanetAll, a computerized register of customer information ranging from addresses to birthdays. Amazon.com marketers use this personalized marketing tool to send e-mail reminders to customers.

Measuring Effectiveness of Online Marketing

How does a company gauge the return from investing in a Web site? Measuring the effectiveness of a Web site is a tricky process and often depends on the purpose of the Web site. Figure 5.14 lists some measures of effectiveness. Profitability is relatively easy to measure in firms that generate revenues directly from online product orders, advertising, or subscription sales. However, a telephone order resulting from an ad on a Web site still shows the sale as a phone sale, not a Web site sale, even though the order originated at the site.

For many companies, revenue is not a major Web site objective. Only about 15 percent of large companies use their Web sites to generate revenue; the rest use them to showcase their products and to offer information about their organizations. For such companies, success is measured by increased brand awareness and brand loyalty, which presumably translates into greater profitability offline.

Some standards guide efforts to collect and analyze traditional consumer purchase data, such as how many Ohio residents bought new Honda Accords the previous year, watched HBO's award-winning *The Sopranos,* or tried Arby's deli-style sandwiches. Still, the Internet presents several challenges for marketers. Although information sources are getting better, it is difficult to be sure how many people use the Internet, how often, and what they actually do online. Some Web pages display counters that measure the number of visits. However, the counters can't tell whether someone has spent time on the page or skipped over it on the way to another site, or whether that person is a first-time or repeat viewer.

Advertisers typically measure the success of their ads in terms of **click-through rate,** meaning the percentage of people presented with a banner ad who click on it, thereby linking to a Web site or a pop-up page of information related to the ad. Recently, the average click-through rate has been declining to about half of 1 percent of those viewing an ad. This rate is much lower than the 1.0 to 1.5 percent response rate for direct-mail advertisements. Low click-through rates have made Web advertising less attractive than it was when it was novel and people were clicking on just about anything online. Selling advertising has therefore become a less reliable source of e-commerce revenues.[38]

As e-commerce gains popularity, new models for measuring its effectiveness are being developed. A basic measurement is the **conversion rate,** the percentage of Web site visitors who make purchases. A conversion rate of 3 to 5 percent is average by today's standards.[39] A company can use its advertising cost, site traffic, and conversion rate data to find out the cost to capture each customer. For instance, a company that spends $10,000 to attract 5,000 visitors to a Web site with a 4 percent conversion rate is obtaining 200 transactions, $.04 \times 5{,}000$. It spent $10,000 for those 200 transactions, so the advertising cost is $50 per transaction, meaning each of those customers cost $50 to acquire through the advertising campaign.

E-commerce businesses are trying to boost their conversion rates by ensuring their sites download quickly, are easy to use, and deliver on their promises. For instance, Lexmark International turned to Web consultants WebCriteria to help it improve the overall performance of its Web site. Analysis of the traffic on Lexmark.com indicated that visitors used the site primarily for product and pre-sales support. The site was large and difficult to navigate. WebCriteria assisted Lexmark.com by simplifying the site and better enabling customers to reach their goals. According to Patti Lybrook of Lexmark.com, "We're in constant change mode. We are constantly monitoring and updating the site design."[40]

Besides measuring click-through and conversion rates, companies can study samples of consumers. Research firms such as PC-Meter and Relevant Knowledge recruit panels of computer users to track Internet site performance and evaluate Web activity. This service works in much the same way that television rating firm AC Nielsen—a major marketing research firm—monitors television audiences. The WebTrends service provides information on Web site visitors, including where they come from, what they

FIGURE 5.14

Measures of Web Site Effectiveness

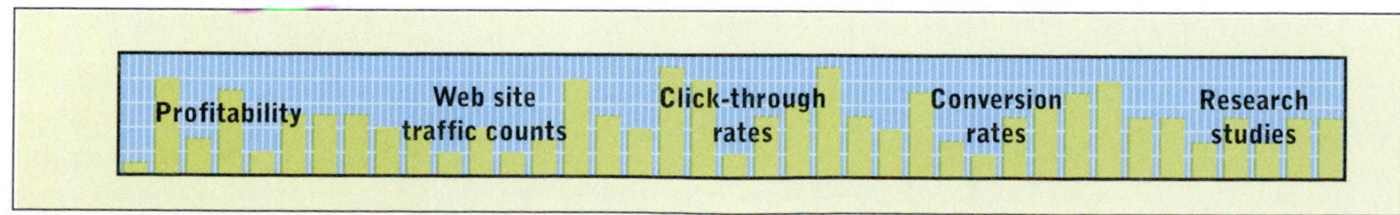

see, and how many "hits," or visits to the site, are logged during different times of the day. Other surveys of Web users investigate their brand awareness and their attitudes toward Web sites and brands.

STRATEGIC IMPLICATIONS OF MARKETING IN THE 21ST CENTURY

The future is bright for marketers who continue to take advantage of the tremendous potential of e-commerce. Online channels that seem cutting edge today will be eclipsed within the next decade by newer technologies, some of which haven't even been invented yet. First and foremost, e-commerce empowers consumers. For instance, already a significant percentage of car buyers show up at a dealership armed with information on dealer costs and option packages—information they obtained online. And the percentage of informed car buyers is only going to increase. This trend isn't about being market led or customer focused; it is about consumer control. Some argue that the Internet represents the ultimate triumph of consumerism.

Since the end of World War II, there has been a fundamental shift in the retailing paradigm from Main Street to malls to superstores. Each time the paradigm shifted, a new group of leaders emerged. The old leaders often missed the early warning signs because they were easy to ignore. When the first Wal-Mart Stores and Home Depots appeared, how many really understood what the impact of superstores and category killers would be on supply chain management? Similarly, marketers must understand the potential impact of the Web.

Initially some experts predicted the death of traditional retailing. This hasn't happened yet, and it may never happen. Rather, what has occurred has been a marketing evolution for organizations that embrace Internet technologies as essential parts of their marketing strategies. E-commerce is fueled by information; marketers who effectively use the wealth of data available will not only survive but thrive in cyberspace.

FLASH CHAPTER REVIEW PRESENTATION

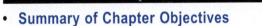

TOWER RECORDS USES BRICKS—AND CLICKS—TO SURVIVE TROUBLED TIMES

endofchaptermaterial

- **Summary of Chapter Objectives**
- **Chapter Outline**
- **Key Terms**
- **Review Questions**
- **Projects and Teamwork Exercises**
- **'netWork**
- **Crossword Puzzles**
- **Case 5.1: The Evolution of E*Trade**

Take the Post-Test to assess your overall understanding of the key ideas in this chapter. The Post-Test provides a comprehensive selection of exam-style questions addressing the main topics and concepts of the chapter. At the completion of each Post-Test, you will receive a score and instructive feedback on how you answered each question, and a direct link to the part of the chapter addressed in the question. Take the Post-Test as often as you need to—a record of your progress for each attempt is kept for you to revisit and gauge your improvement. And each Post-Test is randomly generated, so every attempt is new.

Post-Test

CHAPTER 6

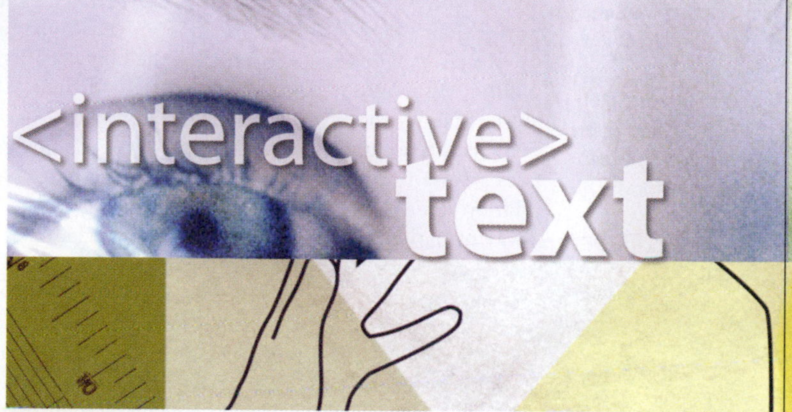

Relationship Marketing and Customer Relationship Management (CRM)

Chapter Objectives

1. Contrast transaction-based marketing with relationship marketing.
2. Identify and explain each of the core elements of relationship marketing.
3. Explain the steps in the development of a marketing relationship and how they lead to enhanced customer satisfaction.
4. Explain customer relationship management (CRM) and the role of technology in building customer relationships.
5. Describe the buyer-seller relationship in business-to-business marketing.
6. Compare the different types of business partnerships and explain how they contribute to relationship marketing.
7. Describe how relationship marketing incorporates national account selling, electronic data interchange, vendor-managed inventories, and collaborative planning, forecasting, and replenishment techniques.
8. Identify and evaluate the most common measurement and evaluation techniques within a relationship marketing program.

Pre-Test

Take the Pre-Test to assess your initial knowledge of the key ideas in this chapter. The Pre-Test provides exam-style questions addressing the main topics and concepts of the chapter. At the completion of each Pre-Test, you will receive a score and instructive feedback on how you answered each question, and a direct link to the part of the chapter addressed in the question. Take the Pre-Test as often as you need to—a record of your progress for each attempt is kept for you to revisit and gauge your improvement.

HOW CUSTOMER RELATIONSHIP MANAGEMENT POWERS THE NATION'S NO. 1 BIKE MAKER

The story is legendary of how Harley-Davidson transformed the image of motorcycle riders and expanded its market beyond outlaw bikers to leather-clad business execs. In doing so, Harley built a fiercely loyal customer base. Its 650,000-member Harley Owner's Group (HOG) has grown into the world's largest biker club. Harley rallies draw half a million riders each year, while a lavishly produced catalog encourages them to buy every part and accessory imaginable.

Big, brawny, and beautiful, a Harley-Davidson bike is a passion not only for its rider but for everyone involved with it—the engineers who build it, the suppliers they rely on, and the dealers who sell it. Half the company's 8,000 employees ride a Harley—and they all buy through dealers. That way, they can relay the customer's-eye-view back to Harley. At rallies, they pick up ideas on how riders customize or accessorize their bikes. All that information feeds right back into product development.

Recently, when recession rocked the *Fortune* 500, Harley defied the odds. Sales grew 15 percent to $3.3 billion. At a time when automakers slashed their own profits to offer zero-percent financing, Harley sold every bike it made—and dealers charged up to $4,000 above sticker price.

Clearly, the biggest challenge for Harley is not generating demand, but meeting it. While scarcity creates a certain cachet, it also erodes market share. Not only is the market shrinking—the average age of a Harley rider is 46, up from 37 ten years ago—but competitors like Honda are designing bikes that lure away impatient buyers. Says James Ziemer, Harley's chief financial officer, "We don't need new customers today, we don't need them tomorrow, but we may 10 years from now."

To keep up with demand, Harley overhauled its supply chain. Modeling on Japan's *keiretsu*—huge vertically integrated companies that foster deep, trusting relationships with suppliers—Harley formed strategic alliances with top-performing vendors. The supplier base was cut from 4,000 to 800, a number that could be effectively managed. All had access to Harley's intranet, making them an integral part of its design and planning processes. Harley quickly learned that bringing suppliers into the design process had multiple benefits. Not only did shared knowledge lead to innovative processes, design efficiencies, and increased insight into competitive moves, but it cut development costs by a third. Better still, defect levels plummeted. Partners benefited, too—for one preferred supplier, sales to Harley increased tenfold to more than $20 million in a year.

Recently, Harley-Davidson signed a deal with E.piphany to drive its fast-evolving customer relationship management system. Working with consulting giant Accenture, E.piphany is creating contact-center software to be integrated into Harley's existing technology. The new system will give Harley employees the right knowledge about customers so that they can reduce the time it takes to resolve issues and eliminate repeat calls. The software will also help Harley analyze information that can play a role in new product development.

As production efficiencies increase, Harley is also tackling the problem of shifting demographics. A new bike—the V-Rod—has all the looks and speed of a Harley, but it is designed and priced for younger riders. It also appeals to women, who currently represent only 9 percent of Harley's market. With the aging rider in mind, designers reengineered the Fat Boy to reduce vibrations. But since vibrations are what make the bike feel like a Harley, the company spent two years developing a counterbalance system that leaves some of the buzz but takes away unpleasant jolts. A 25-hour instruction program offered by dealers aims to attract first-time buyers. So far, 5,200 new bikers have graduated and close to a third of them purchased a bike within four months. Most chose a Harley.[1]

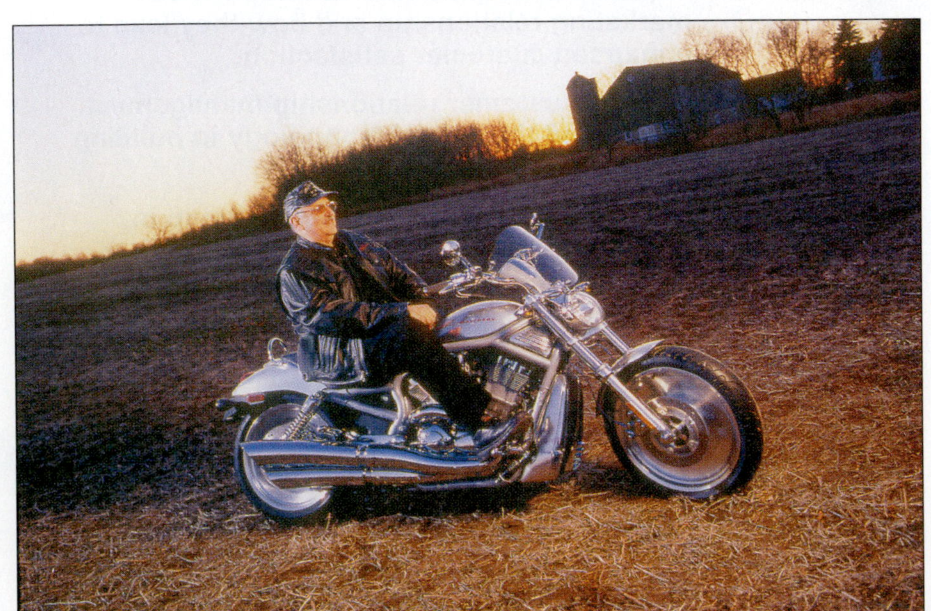

CHAPTER OVERVIEW

As the success of Harley-Davidson demonstrates, marketing revolves around relationships, not only with customers but with everyone involved in creating a product and bringing it to market. The shift away from **transaction-based marketing,** which focuses on short-term, single exchanges, to customer-focused relationship marketing is one of the most important trends in marketing today. Companies recognize that they cannot prosper simply by identifying and attracting new customers; to succeed, they must build loyal, mutually beneficial relationships with existing customers, suppliers, distributors, and employees. This strategy benefits the bottom line, because retaining customers costs much less than acquiring new ones.

Building and managing long-term relationships between buyers and sellers is the hallmark of relationship marketing. **Relationship marketing** is the development, growth, and maintenance of cost-effective, high-value relationships with individual customers, suppliers, distributors, retailers, and other partners for mutual benefit over time. Emerging from and closely linked to relationship marketing, **customer relationship management (CRM)** is the combination of strategies and tools that drive relationship programs, reorienting the entire organization to a concentrated focus on satisfying customers. It leverages technology as a means to manage customer relationships and to integrate all stakeholders into a company's product design and development, manufacturing, marketing, sales, and customer service processes.

Building long-term relationships with consumers and other businesses involves four basic elements. First, database technology helps a company to identify current and potential customers with selected demographic, purchase, and lifestyle characteristics. Second, through database marketing, the firm analyzes this information and can modify its marketing mix to deliver differentiated messages and customized marketing programs to individual consumers. Third, through relationship marketing, the firm is able to monitor each relationship. The company can calculate the cost of attracting one new customer and figure out how much profit that customer will generate during the relationship. The company is also able to assess the customer's level of satisfaction or dissatisfaction with its service. Information is fed back to the firm, which is then able to seek ways to add value to the buyer-seller transaction so that the relationship will continue. Finally, customer relationship management uses intimate knowledge of customers and customer preferences to orient every part of the organization, including its external partners, toward building a unique company differentiation that is based on strong, unbreakable bonds with customers. Sophisticated technology and the Internet are the tools that make that happen.[2]

As Figure 6.1 illustrates, relationship marketing emphasizes cooperation rather than conflict between all of the parties involved. This ongoing collaborative exchange creates value for both parties and builds customer loyalty. Customer relationship management goes a step further, integrating the customer's needs into all aspects of the firm's operations and its relationships with suppliers, distributors, and strategic partners. It combines people, processes, and technology with the long-term goal of maximizing customer value through mutually satisfying interactions and transactions.[3]

This chapter begins by examining the reasons organizations are moving toward relationship marketing and customer relationship management, exploring the impact this move has on producers of goods and services and their customers.

Briefly Speaking

In every instance we found that the best-run companies stay as close to their customers as humanly possible.

Thomas J. Peters (b. 1942) American business writer

THE SHIFT FROM TRANSACTION-BASED MARKETING TO RELATIONSHIP MARKETING

Since the Industrial Revolution, most manufacturers have run production-oriented operations. They have focused on making products and then promoting them to customers in the hope of selling enough to cover costs and earn profits. The emphasis has been on individual sales or transactions.

<interactive>**learning goal**

CHAPTER OBJECTIVE #1: CONTRAST TRANSACTION-BASED MARKETING WITH RELATIONSHIP MARKETING.

In transaction-based marketing, buyer and seller exchanges are characterized by limited communications and little or no ongoing relationships. The primary goal is to entice a buyer to make a purchase through such inducements as low price, convenience, or packaging. The goal is simple and short term: Sell something—now.

Some marketing exchanges remain largely transaction based. In residential real estate sales, for example, the primary goal of the agent is to make a sale and collect a commission. While the agent may seek to maintain the appearance of an ongoing, buyer-seller relationship, in most cases, the possibility of future transactions is limited. The best an agent can hope for is to represent the seller again in a subsequent real-estate deal that may be several years down the line or, more likely, to gain positive referrals to other buyers and sellers. To a lesser extent, automobile purchases are transaction-based—many customers shop around for each new car rather than buy from one dealer exclusively.

FIGURE 6.1

Forms of Buyer-Seller Interactions on a Continuum from Conflict to Integration

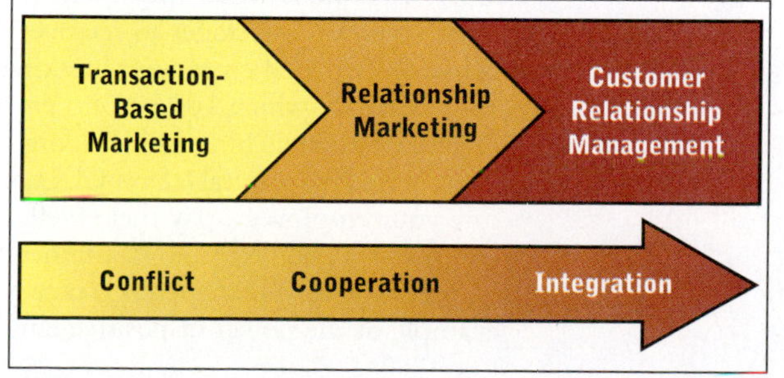

Briefly Speaking

The team that trusts—their leader and each other—is more likely to be successful.

Mike Krzyzewski (b. 1947) Duke basketball coach

Today, many organizations are trying an alternate approach. Relationship marketing looks at customers as equal partners in buyer-seller transactions. By motivating customers to enter a long-term relationship in which they repeat purchases or buy multiple brands from the firm, marketers are able to obtain a clearer understanding of customer needs. This process leads to improved products or customer service, which pays off through better sales and lower marketing costs.

The move from transactions to relationships is reflected in the changing nature of the interactions between customers and sellers. In transaction-based marketing, exchanges with customers are generally sporadic, often disrupted by conflict. As interactions become relationship oriented, however, conflict changes to cooperation, and infrequent contacts between buyers and sellers become ongoing exchanges. Firms now understand they must do more than simply create products and then sell the items. With so many goods and services to choose from, customers look for added value from their marketing relationships.

As a means of providing added value through superior service, Enterprise Rent-A-Car set up each of its 4,800 branch offices worldwide as a separate entrepreneurial entity. Employees were encouraged to find new ways to boost customer referrals and retention. Personalized service scores big. If a customer forgets her driver's license, an agent will take her home to pick it up. If the license has expired, Enterprise will take her to obtain a new one. Recently, Enterprise revenue grew at twice the rate of rival companies.[4]

Internal Marketing

The concept of customer satisfaction is usually discussed in terms of *external customers*—people or organizations that buy or use a firm's goods or services. But, as noted in Chapter 1, marketing in organizations concerned with quality must also address *internal customers*—employees or departments within the organization whose success depends on the work of other employees or departments. A person processing an order for a new piece of equipment is the internal customer of the salesperson who completed the sale, just as the person who bought the product is the salesperson's external customer. Although the order processor might never directly encounter an external customer, his or her performance can have a direct impact on the overall value the firm is able to deliver.

Internal marketing involves managerial actions that enable all members of an organization to understand, accept, and fulfill their respective roles in implementing a marketing strategy. Good internal customer satisfaction helps organizations to attract, select, and retain outstanding employees who appreciate and value their role in the delivery of superior service to external customers. Consider how National City Corp. enriched the banking experience for its customer base. A dual approach involved upgrading the bank's services to better suit customer needs in tandem with a major employee training program. The retraining was intended not only to stem staff turnover but to reduce defections by customers. Within the first year, 3,000 employees—a tenth of the workforce—graduated from National City Institute, a training program that focused on service. New hires now receive three weeks of training rather than three days. Salary increases and major investments in technology also served to boost employee morale. National City credits its customer-focused initiative with reducing turnover by 20 percent.[5]

An organizational culture that is steeped in customer orientation enables employees to achieve the firm's objectives—when employees are loyal, some of that loyalty rubs off on customers. When terrorist attacks on the World Trade Center coated New York's J&R Music World with grit and dust, forcing the retailer to close its doors for six weeks, all 800 employees were kept on at full pay. Recognizing that its employees are its biggest asset, J&R sought to maintain sales levels by cutting prices and adding free shipping rather than eliminating jobs. Many customers responded by deciding to wait to buy music until the store reopened.[6]

Employee knowledge and involvement are important goals of internal marketing. Companies that excel at satisfying customers typically place a priority on keeping employees informed about corporate goals, strategies, and customer needs. Employees must also have the necessary tools to address customer requests and problems in a timely manner. As we discussed in Chapter 5, companywide intranets aid the flow of communications between departments and functions. Several companies—like Harley-Davidson—also include key suppliers on their intranets as a means of speeding and easing communication of all aspects of business from product design to inventory control.

Employee satisfaction is another critical objective of internal marketing. Employees can seldom, if ever, satisfy customers when they themselves are unhappy. Dissatisfied employees are likely to spread negative word-of-mouth messages to relatives, friends, and acquaintances, and these reports can affect purchasing behavior. Satisfied employees buy their employer's products, sending a powerful message to customers. In an industry in which 100 percent employee turnover is common, The Container Store—which sells home organizers such as bins and shelving—boasts a level as low as 15 percent. Almost half of new hires come from employee referrals. Says CEO Kip Tindell, "A funny thing happens when you take the time to educate your employees, pay them well, and treat them as equals. You end up with extremely motivated and enthusiastic people." The Container Store credits its people-management strategies with sustaining sales increases of up to 25 percent each year.[7] The "Marketing Hits" Interactive Example discusses another example of the power of positive employee attitudes—at U.S. Cellular.

<interactive>**example**

MARKETING HIT: U.S. CELLULAR SPINS SUPERIOR SERVICE INTO SALES

Relationship Marketing

In rapidly increasing numbers, producers of goods and services have shifted away from transaction-based systems of marketing to longer-term, more customer-focused relationship systems. Table 6.1 summarizes the differences between the narrow focus of transaction marketing and the much broader view that relationship marketing takes.

Every marketing transaction involves a relationship between the buyer and seller. In a transaction-based situation, the relationship may be quite short in duration and narrow in scope. Few if any social relationships may develop. For example, a traveler running low on gas in an unfamiliar town will likely stop at the first gas station she encounters, regardless of whether it carries ExxonMobil, her preferred brand. When the driver gets back home, however, she is likely to return to her previous practice of buying at ExxonMobil. In short, the single emergency transaction is unlikely to affect future gasoline purchase patterns.

The customer-seller bonds developed in a relationship marketing situation, on the other hand, last longer and cover a much broader scope than those developed in transaction marketing. Customer contacts are generally more frequent. A companywide emphasis on customer service contributes to customer satisfaction. Figure 6.2 shows the need to blend quality and customer service with traditional elements of the marketing mix. When a company integrates customer service and quality with marketing, the result is a relationship marketing orientation.[8]

Relationship marketing creates a new level of interaction between buyers and sellers. Rather than focusing exclusively on attracting new customers, marketers have discovered that it pays to retain customers they already have. Moreover, customers who are satisfied with one of the firm's brands may be persuaded to try others. Consider the popularity of TV's new wave of celebrity chefs. Once confined to restaurant kitchens, the people who create great meals are beginning to leverage their success by becoming their own brands. Chefs like Emeril LaGasse, Wolfgang Puck, and a host of others first connected with national audiences through TV's Food Network. In lively in-the-kitchen demonstrations, LaGasse quickly developed an easy camaraderie with mass audiences with whom he shared food, tastes, and a sense of humor. Then, like fellow chefs, he leveraged that intimate relationship with viewers by offering multiple lines of products under his name. From franchise restaurants, cookbooks, and cookware to spices, marinades, and packaged meals,

TABLE 6.1

Comparing Transaction-Based Marketing and Relationship Marketing Strategies

Characteristic	Transaction Marketing	Relationship Marketing
Time orientation	Short-term	Long-term
Organizational goal	Make the sale	Emphasis on retaining customers
Customer service priority	Relatively low	Key component
Customer contact	Low to moderate	Frequent
Degree of customer commitment	Low	High
Basis for seller-customer interactions	Conflict manipulation	Cooperation; trust
Source of quality	Primarily from production	Companywide commitment

Source: Adapted from Martin Christopher, Adrian Payne, and David Ballantyne, *Relationship Marketing.* Oxford, UK: Butterworth-Heineman Ltd., 1993, p. 4.

FIGURE 6.2

Relationship Marketing Orientation

Customer Service

Relationship Marketing

Quality

Marketing

top chefs have built extensive businesses around their on-air personalities. Customers are enticed with free recipes on the chef's Web sites, where they can buy knives, gift sets, gift certificates, clothing, and other branded merchandise online. Figure 6.3 shows how celebrity chefs Paul Prudhomme and Charlie Trotter count on their mass appeal to bring more and more products to the same core customers who watch their shows.[9]

FIGURE 6.3

Celebrity Chefs: Offering Multiple Products to a Core Base of Customers

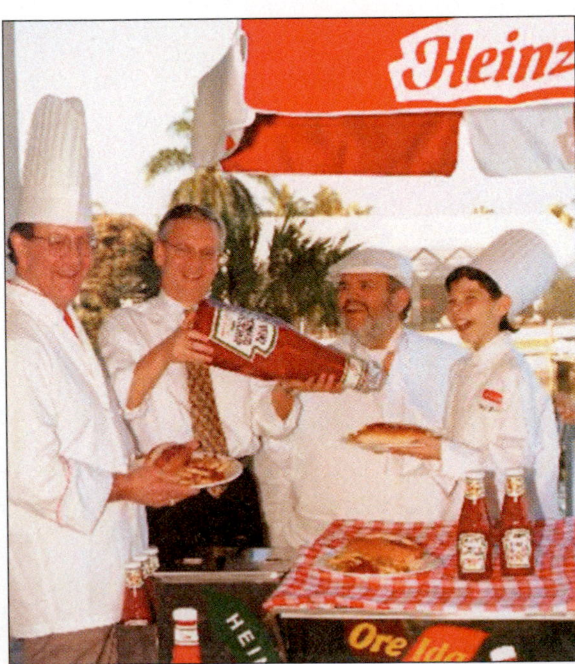

BASIC FOUNDATIONS OF MODERN BUYER-SELLER RELATIONSHIPS

Relationship marketing depends on the development of close ties between the buyer—whether an individual or a company—and the seller. This section considers the core elements of the buyer-seller relationship and how promises form the basis of relationship marketing.

Promises in Relationship Marketing

Relationship marketing is based on promises from organizations that go beyond obvious assurances that potential customers expect. A network of promises—outside the organization, within the organization, and between buyer and seller interactions—determines whether a marketing encounter will be positive or negative and will either enhance or detract from an ongoing buyer-seller relationship.[10]

<interactive>**learning goal**

CHAPTER OBJECTIVE #2: IDENTIFY AND EXPLAIN EACH OF THE CORE ELEMENTS OF RELATIONSHIP MARKETING.

Making Promises Most firms make promises to potential customers through *external marketing*. As discussed earlier in the book, this term refers to the marketing efforts that a company directs toward customers, suppliers, and other parties outside the organization. These promises communicate what a customer can expect from the firm's goods or services.

For example, the NBC television network might run an advertisement for its upcoming coverage of the National Basketball Association finals, touting the great games, great coverage, and great entertainment viewers will experience if they tune in. In this ad, the network would make a promise to its potential viewers and advertisers about what to expect and what the network would deliver. Similarly, in Figure 6.4, Lexus promises customers that its pre-owned vehicles come with a solid warranty that even includes a loaner when their car is in for service.

External marketing goes beyond advertising, however. Special sales promotions, the physical design of a business facility, its cleanliness and comfort, and the service process all provide other ways that companies make promises to potential customers. Tucson Electric Power Co., the electric utility for Tucson, Arizona, recently started a guaranteed cost and comfort program. Building contractors submit their plans to the utility, make recommended design and equipment changes, and undergo regular inspections during construction. In return, Tucson Electric promises flat heating and cooling costs for three years—regardless of jumps in the price of electricity or the owners' carelessness. Tucson Electric has guaranteed large custom-built homes and modest Habitat for Humanity houses. The guarantee results in upgraded building standards, competitive energy rates for consumers, and long-term customers for Tucson Electric.[11]

The promises that companies communicate to potential customers must be both realistic and consistent with one another. A firm that makes unrealistic promises can create a disappointed customer who may not buy the product again. For example, an infomercial for a new weight-loss product promises to work quickly. If after six weeks and considerable expense, you have not lost any weight, you are likely to be very disappointed.

Enabling Promises A company can follow through on promises made to potential customers by external marketing only if it enables these promises through internal marketing. Internal marketing includes recruiting talented employees and providing them with the tools, training, and motivation they need to do their jobs effectively. The firm's structure itself must facilitate rather than hinder the provision of quality offerings. Efficient systems and processes, empowered front-line workers, and flat organizational hierarchies all contribute to a company's ability to provide quality goods and services.

FIGURE 6.4

Making a Promise to Customers

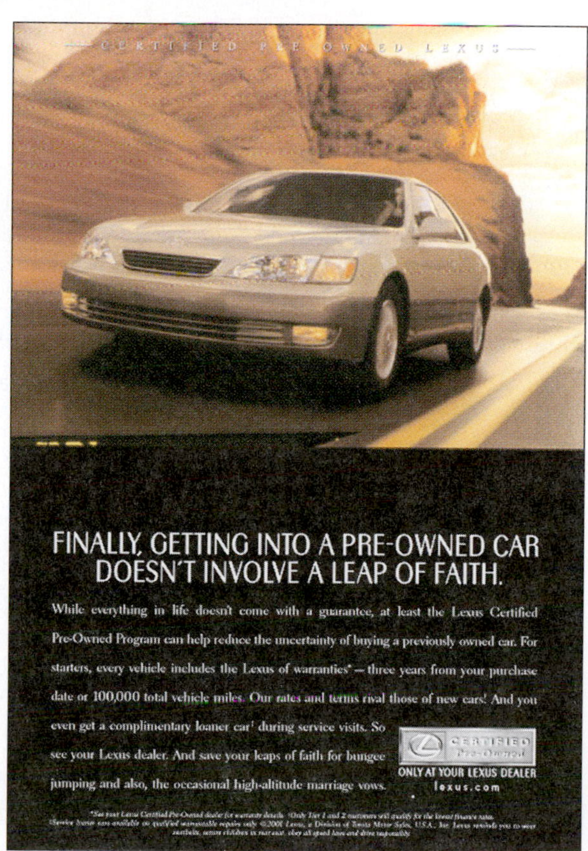

It takes FedEx's entire 200,000-plus workforce to keep its promise to deliver 3.3 million packages to 210 countries—"Absolutely, Positively Overnight." The company invests over $100 million a year in training every employee how to play his or her role in meeting its high-speed, high-performance guarantee. Career development, leadership training, succession planning, organizational development, executive development, and safety training all work toward enabling FedEx's finely tuned, internal-marketing network.[12]

Keeping Promises Every customer interaction with a business reaches the moment of truth when a product is provided to the customer. This action was defined in Chapter 1 as the exchange process. This exchange, the third stage in the buyer-seller relationship following external and internal marketing, defines the point at which a company keeps its promises.

The exchange also provides the place where long-term relationships develop between buyers and sellers. Positive encounters help to build long-term relationships, with the added benefit of possible positive word-of-mouth recommendations from satisfied customers to other potential customers. On the other hand, a company that fails to keep its promises at the exchange point in the marketing process may destroy any hope of continuing buyer-seller relationships. Even a single negative encounter can have a devastating effect.

THE RELATIONSHIP MARKETING CONTINUUM

Like all other interpersonal relationships, buyer-seller relationships function at a variety of levels. As an individual or firm progresses from the lowest level to the highest level on the continuum of relationship marketing, as shown in Table 6.2, the strength of commitment between the parties grows. The likelihood of a continuing, long-term relationship, as well, grows. Whenever possible, marketers want to move their customers along this continuum, converting them from Level 1 purchasers, who focus mainly on price, to Level 3 customers, who receive specialized services and value-added benefits that may not be available from another firm.[13]

<interactive>**learning goal**

CHAPTER OBJECTIVE #3: EXPLAIN THE STEPS IN THE DEVELOPMENT OF A MARKETING RELATIONSHIP AND HOW THEY LEAD TO ENHANCED CUSTOMER SATISFACTION.

First Level—Focus on Price

Interactions at the first level of relationship marketing are the most superficial and the least likely to lead to a long-term relationship. In the most prevalent examples of this first level, relationship marketing efforts rely on pricing and other financial incentives to motivate customers to enter into buying relationships with a seller. General Motors MasterCard rewards cardholders with credits for every dollar charged toward purchases of GM products. McDonald's sometimes offers two Big Macs for the price of one. CleanSweep Homewood Suites offers a "spring cleaning" weekend away. Guests who take a suite for four days receive coupons from ServiceMaster Clean and MerryMaids so that their homes are spotless when they return.[14]

TABLE 6.2

Three Levels of Relationship Marketing

Characteristic	Level 1	Level 2	Level 3
Primary bond	Financial	Social	Structural
Degree of customization	Low	Medium	Medium to high
Potential for sustained competitive advantage	Low	Moderate	High
Examples	American Airlines' AAdvantage program	Harley-Davidson's Harley Owners Group (HOG)	Federal Express's PowerShip Program

Source: Adapted from information in Leonard L. Berry, "Relationship Marketing of Services—Growing Internet, Emerging Perspectives," *Journal of the Academy of Marketing Science,* Fall 1995, p. 240.

A collaboration between Priority Club Rewards and Visa allows guests who choose participating hotels for a second stay to gain their choice of double points or double miles.

Although its owners' club has only 1,000 members, Indian's top brand, American Spirit, appeals to the bike-rider's desire for individuality. This distinctly American product enjoys a cult status similar to that of Harley-Davidson.

Although these programs can be attractive to users, they may not create long-term buyer relationships. Because the programs are not customized to the needs of individual buyers, they are easily duplicated by competitors. When McDonald's runs its two-for-one special on Big Macs, there is a chance that Burger King will respond with a similar offer on its Whopper sandwiches. Within three years after American Airlines introduced its AAdvantage frequent-flyer program, some 23 other airlines enacted similar programs. The lesson here is that it takes more than a low price or other financial incentive to create a long-term relationship between buyer and seller.

Second Level—Social Interactions

As buyers and sellers reach the second level of relationship marketing, their interactions develop on a social level—one that features deeper and less superficial links than the financially motivated first level. Sellers have begun to learn that social relationships with buyers can be very effective marketing tools. Customer service and communication are key factors at this stage.

The NFL builds on its already loyal fan bases through e-mail newsletters that reach 1.5 million subscribers. Not only are they customized for each of its 31 league teams, but they are even tailored toward each fan's special interests or favorite players. By monitoring the "click-through" behavior of avid fans, NFL marketers tailor merchandising to appeal to them.[15]

Third Level—Interdependent Partnership

At the third level of relationship marketing, relationships are transformed into structural changes that ensure buyer and seller are true business partners. As buyer and seller work more closely together, they develop a dependence on one another that continues to grow over time.

Although car manufacturers do not sell through the Internet, their Web strategies are structured to develop leads and provide support for dealers. By advertising on independent research sites like Kelley Blue Book (http://www.kbb.com) or Carpoint.com (http://www.carpoint.com), manufacturers such as Saturn entice browsers to their sites. Since there is no chance of being cornered by a salesperson before they are ready to buy, some customers find Web research a less stressful process than walking into a showroom. At the carmaker's site, customers can configure the exact car they want to buy, feature by feature. Saturn offers price and affordability calculators that help buyers figure out monthly payments. From there, Saturn buyers can find their local dealer and continue the sales process there at the price quoted on the Web site. DaimlerChrysler posts dealer inventory on its site, allowing buyers to find a perfect match for their dream car. Within the first few months of its "dealer inventory transparency" program, 70,000 people sent price requests to dealers—and almost a fifth of visitors to the site ended up buying a DaimlerChrysler vehicle.[16]

Through their Web strategies, Saturn and DaimlerChrysler strengthen relationships with dealers. Not only does this type of collaboration lead directly to increased sales through dealerships, but it enhances the entire buying experience, increasing customer satisfaction.

Briefly Speaking

If we are going to be leaders, we're going to have to make decisions with maybe 75 percent of the facts that we'd like to have. If you wait for 95 percent, you are going to be a follower.

Lawrence A. Weinbach
Chairman and CEO, Unisys

ENHANCING CUSTOMER SATISFACTION

Marketers monitor customer satisfaction through various methods of marketing research discussed in more detail in Chapter 7. As part of an ongoing relationship with customers, marketers must continually measure and improve how well they meet customer needs. As Figure 6.5 shows, three main steps are involved in this process: understanding customer needs, obtaining customer feedback, and instituting an ongoing program to ensure customer satisfaction.

Understanding Customer Needs

Knowledge of what customers need, want, and expect is a central concern of companies focused on building long-term relationships. This information is also a vital first step in setting up a system to measure *customer satisfaction.* Marketers must carefully monitor the characteristics of their product that really matter to customers. They also must remain constantly alert to new elements that might affect satisfaction.

Satisfaction can be measured in terms of the gaps between what customers expect and what they perceive they have received. Such gaps can produce favorable or unfavorable impressions. A product may be better than expected or worse than expected. To avoid unfavorable gaps, marketers need to keep in touch with the needs of current and potential customers. They must look beyond traditional performance measures and explore the factors that determine purchasing behavior in order to formulate customer-based missions, goals, and performance standards.

Obtaining Customer Feedback

The second step in measuring customer satisfaction is to compile feedback from customers regarding present performance. Increasingly, marketers try to improve customers' access to their companies by including toll-free 800 numbers or Web site addresses in their advertising. Most firms rely on reactive methods of collecting feedback. Rather than solicit complaints, they might, for example, monitor Usenet and other online discussion groups as a means of tracking customer comments and attitudes about the value received. Some companies hire mystery shoppers, who visit or call businesses posing as customers, to evaluate the service they receive. Their unbiased appraisals are usually conducted semiannually or quarterly to monitor employees, diagnose problem areas in customer service, and measure the impact of employee training.

HomeMadeSimple, a Web site sponsored by packaged-goods giant Procter & Gamble, counts on input from customers as a means of improving relationships with users of its products. The site features an ideas forum and a monthly poll, both providing direct customer feedback on such brands as Febreze, Dawn, and Swiffer. A monthly e-newsletter is responsive to customer comments and shares ideas on using P&G products.[17]

FIGURE 6.5

Three Steps to Measure Customer Satisfaction

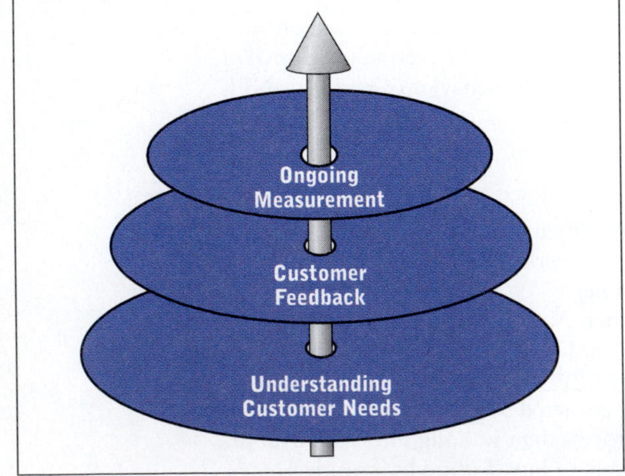

Any method that makes it easier for customers to complain benefits a firm and may be considered a blessing in disguise. Customer complaints offer firms the opportunity to overcome problems and prove their commitment to service. Customers often have greater loyalty to a company after a conflict has been resolved than if they had never complained at all.

Many organizations also use proactive methods to assess customer satisfaction, including visiting, calling, or mailing out written surveys to clients to find out their level of satisfaction. Xerox gathers information by mailing approximately 60,000 customer satisfaction surveys per month to its customers, and AT&T's Universal Credit Card division calls 2,500 customers every month to measure quality in the company's nine most important areas of service performance. Pizza Hut calls 50,000 customers each week to ask about their experiences at the restaurant chain's units. Many car dealers call or send surveys to customers asking them to rate the service they received, either in a purchase situation or service visit.

BUILDING BUYER-SELLER RELATIONSHIPS

Marketers of consumer goods and services have discovered that they must do more than simply create products and then sell them. With a dizzying array of products to choose from, many customers are seeking ways to simplify both their business and personal lives, and relationships provide a way to do this.

One reason consumers form continuing relationships is their desire to reduce choices. Through relationships, they can simplify information gathering and the entire buying process as well as decrease the risk of dissatisfaction. They find comfort in brands that have become familiar through their ongoing relationships with companies. Such relationships may lead to more efficient decision making by customers and higher levels of customer satisfaction.

A key benefit to consumers in long-term, buyer-seller relationships is the perceived positive value they receive. Relationships add value through increased opportunities for frequent customers to save money through discounts, rebates, and similar offers; via special recognition from the relationship programs; and through convenience in shopping. Figure 6.6 shows how e-tailer Amazon seeks to encourage online buyers to spend more—by offering free shipping to its best customers.

Marketers should also understand why consumers end relationships. Computerized technologies and the Internet have made consumers better informed than ever before by giving them unprecedented abilities to compare prices, products, and customer service. If they perceive that a competitor's products or customer service are better, customers may switch loyalties. Many consumers dislike feeling that they are locked into a relationship with one company, and that is reason enough for them to try a competing item next time they buy. Some customers simply become bored with their current providers and decide to sample the competition.

How Marketers Keep Customers

One of the major forces driving the push from transaction-based marketing to relationship marketing is the realization that retaining customers is far more profitable than losing them. Customers usually enable a firm to generate more profits with each additional year of the relationship. In fact, one marketing expert notes that a 5 percent gain in customer retention can pay off with an 80 percent increase in profits.[18]

A good example of this is the Marriott Rewards program, which now boasts 17 million members. Members spend an average of 2.5 times more at Marriott hotels than nonmembers and account for 40 percent of Marriott's total sales. Marriott has three elite levels in the program: Silver, Gold, and Platinum. Each offers special benefits and perks for Marriott's most frequent guests. Marriott Rewards is just one way in which the company seeks to invest in even stronger relationships from its high-value customers. Figure 6.7 illustrates another recent Marriott Rewards offer—visitors who stay for any three weekend nights get one weekend night free. Marriott periodically offers similar promotions to add value to the program and retain these important customers.[19]

An example of **frequency marketing,** programs like Marriott's reward top customers with cash, rebates, merchandise, or other premiums. Buyers who purchase an item more often earn higher rewards. Frequency marketing focuses on a company's best customers with the goal of increasing their motivation to buy even more of the same or other products from the seller.

Many different types of companies use frequency programs, from fast-food restaurants to retail stores, telecommunications companies, and travel firms. Popular programs include airline frequent-flyer programs, such as United Airlines' Mileage Plus, and retail programs, such as Hallmark's Gold Crown Card.

The Internet is proving a fertile medium for frequency-marketing initiatives. Borrowing from the airlines' frequent-flyer model, Harrah's Casino has created a Web-based program to reward frequent gamblers. Loyalty cards are swiped on the casino floor to monitor time spent at slot machines or card tables and to total up the sums gambled. A Web site allows members to view their points and learn how to earn more benefits as they gamble their way up to platinum or diamond status. The program is also able to identify which so-called "high-rollers" yield the highest profits.[20]

In addition to frequency programs, companies use **affinity marketing** to retain customers. Each of us holds certain things dear. Some may feel strongly about Eastern Michigan University, while others admire the New York Yankees. These symbols, along with an almost unending variety of others, are subjects of affinity programs. An affinity program is a marketing effort sponsored by an organization that solicits involvement by individuals who share common interests and activities. With affinity programs, organizations create extra value for members and encourage stronger relationships.

FIGURE 6.6

The Benefit of Becoming a High-Value Customer

Pizza's reign on free delivery
has come to an end.
amazon.com
INTRODUCING
FREE SHIPPING
ON ORDERS OVER $99
Use Super Saver Shipping. Some restrictions apply. See Web site for details.

FIGURE 6.7

Rewards for High-Frequency Customers

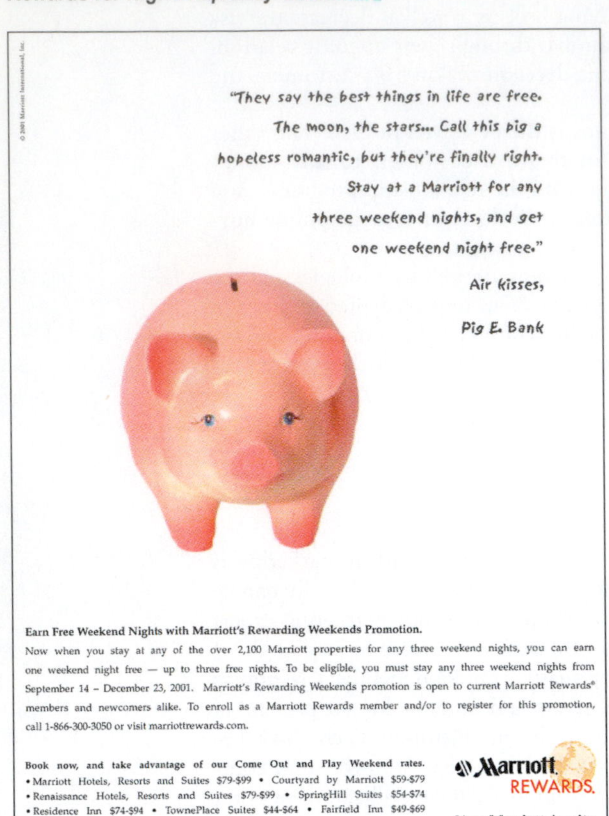

"They say the best things in life are free.
The moon, the stars... Call this pig a
hopeless romantic, but they're finally right.
Stay at a Marriott for any
three weekend nights, and get
one weekend night free."
Air kisses,
Pig E. Bank
Earn Free Weekend Nights with Marriott's Rewarding Weekends Promotion.
Now when you stay at any of the over 2,100 Marriott properties for any three weekend nights, you can earn one weekend night free — up to three free nights. To be eligible, you must stay any three weekend nights from September 14 – December 23, 2001. Marriott's Rewarding Weekends promotion is open to current Marriott Rewards® members and newcomers alike. To enroll as a Marriott Rewards member and/or to register for this promotion, call 1-866-300-3050 or visit marriottrewards.com.
Book now, and take advantage of our Come Out and Play Weekend rates.
• Marriott Hotels, Resorts and Suites $79-$99 • Courtyard by Marriott $59-$79
• Renaissance Hotels, Resorts and Suites $79-$99 • SpringHill Suites $54-$74
• Residence Inn $74-$94 • TownePlace Suites $44-$64 • Fairfield Inn $49-$69
Marriott REWARDS.
Your Marriott Awaits.

Affinity credit cards are a popular form of this marketing technique. The sponsor's name appears prominently in promotional materials, on the card itself, and on monthly statements. For example, the National Association for Female Executives, a professional networking organization, offers qualified members a Gold Visa or MasterCard with no first-year fee and with low interest rates. A not-for-profit organization such as a charity or educational institution, such as the Smithsonian Institution, may sponsor a card if the issuer donates a percentage of user purchases to the group. Not all affinity programs involve credit cards. KETC, the St. Louis public television station, thanks members who contribute more than $50 annually with a diner's card that entitles them to discounts at participating restaurants.

Database Marketing

The use of information technology to analyze data about customers and their transactions is referred to as **database marketing.** The results form the basis of new advertising or promotions targeted to carefully identified groups of customers. Database marketing is a particularly effective tool for building relationships because it allows sellers to sort through huge quantities of data from multiple sources on the buying habits or preferences of thousands or even millions of customers. Companies are then able to track buying patterns, develop customer relationship profiles, customize their offerings and sales promotions, and even personalize customer service to suit the needs of targeted groups of customers. Properly used, databases can help companies in several ways, including these:

- Identifying their most profitable customers
- Calculating the lifetime value of each customer's business
- Creating a meaningful dialogue that builds relationships and encourages genuine brand loyalty
- Improving customer retention and referral rates
- Reducing marketing and promotion costs
- Boosting sales volume per customer or targeted customer group

Where do organizations find all the data that fill these vast marketing databases? Everywhere! Credit card applications, software registration, and product warranties all provide vital statistics of individual customers. Cash register scanners, customer opinion surveys, and sweepstakes entry forms may offer not just details of name, address, and income, but information on preferred brands and shopping habits. Web sites offer free access in return for personal data, allowing companies to amass increasingly rich marketing information. DaimlerChrysler recently developed a partnership with videogame maker Terminal Reality to create a new game that incorporates "cheats"—special codes players need to win. To find the codes, players need to log on to the DaimlerChrysler Web site. The personal details they provide—name, address, income, and other data—are captured for future database marketing use. In its recent Rocket Cash sweepstakes promotion for Sprite, The Coca-Cola Company used a hand-held touch-screen device to swipe the driver's licenses of teens and young adults gathered at rock concerts and other popular events. Not only was the firm able to capture names, addresses, and other valuable data, they also instantly verified the ages of all sweepstakes entrants.[21]

Interactive television promises to deliver even more valuable data—information on real consumer behavior and attitudes toward brands. Linked to digital television, sophisticated set-top boxes like TiVo and Replay TV are already able to collect vast amounts of data on television viewer behavior, organized in incredible detail. Once the technology makes its way into more homes, marketers will have firsthand knowledge of what kind of programming and products their targeted customers want. In addition, rather than using television to advertise to the masses, they will be able to talk directly to those viewers most interested in their products. At a click of a button, viewers will be able to skip ads, but they'll also be able to click to a full-length infomercial on any brand that captures their interest.[22]

As database marketing has become more complex, a variety of software tools and services will enable marketers to target consumers more and more narrowly while enriching their communications to selected groups. *Application service providers (ASPs)* assist marketers in capturing, manipulating, and analyzing masses of consumer data. For example, retail chain Blinds to Go, Inc., based in Iselin, New Jersey, uses an online service to sort and query customer information from 120 stores for use in direct marketing campaigns. Customer-specific purchasing records and buying-frequency data are immediately accessible via secure Internet connections. The Legal Aid Society for Washington Fund uses an ASP to manage extensive donor profile information, maximizing the effectiveness of personalized fundraising campaigns.[23]

CUSTOMER RELATIONSHIP MANAGEMENT

Emerging from relationship marketing, customer relationship management (CRM) is the combination of strategies and technologies that empowers relationship programs, reorienting the entire organization to a concentrated focus on satisfying customers. Made possible by technological advances, it leverages technology as a means to manage customer relationships and to integrate all stakeholders into a company's product design and development, manufacturing, marketing, sales, and customer service processes.

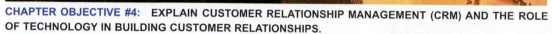

<interactive>**learning goal**

CHAPTER OBJECTIVE #4: EXPLAIN CUSTOMER RELATIONSHIP MANAGEMENT (CRM) AND THE ROLE OF TECHNOLOGY IN BUILDING CUSTOMER RELATIONSHIPS.

CRM represents a shift in thinking for everyone involved with a firm—from the CEO down through and encompassing all other key stakeholders, including suppliers, dealers, and other partners. All recognize that solid customer relations are fostered by similarly strong relationships with other major stakeholders.[24] Since CRM goes well beyond traditional sales, marketing, or customer services functions, it requires a top-down commitment and must permeate every aspect of a firm's business. Technology makes that possible, allowing firms—regardless of size and no matter how far-flung their operations—to manage activities across functions, locations, and among their internal and external partners.

CRM software systems are capable of making sense of the vast amounts of customer data that technology allows firms to collect. After several years of trying to patch together its existing technology to automate functions like customer service and sales lead management, IBM decided to seek a CRM solution. A custom-created software application was implemented at IBM's 26 customer service centers and connected employees worldwide. The impact was huge and immediate: Most customer inquiries were quickly and efficiently resolved, and the number of abandoned calls fell dramatically. Since customer service personnel spent significantly less time with each call, IBM was able to handle the same volume of calls with 450 fewer people.[25] Great Plains software by Microsoft, featured in Figure 6.8, is an example of widely used customer relationship management software. With Great Plains, Microsoft enables companies of all sizes to serve customers better, faster, and with ease.

FIGURE 6.8

Great Plains Software: A Customer Relationship Software Solution

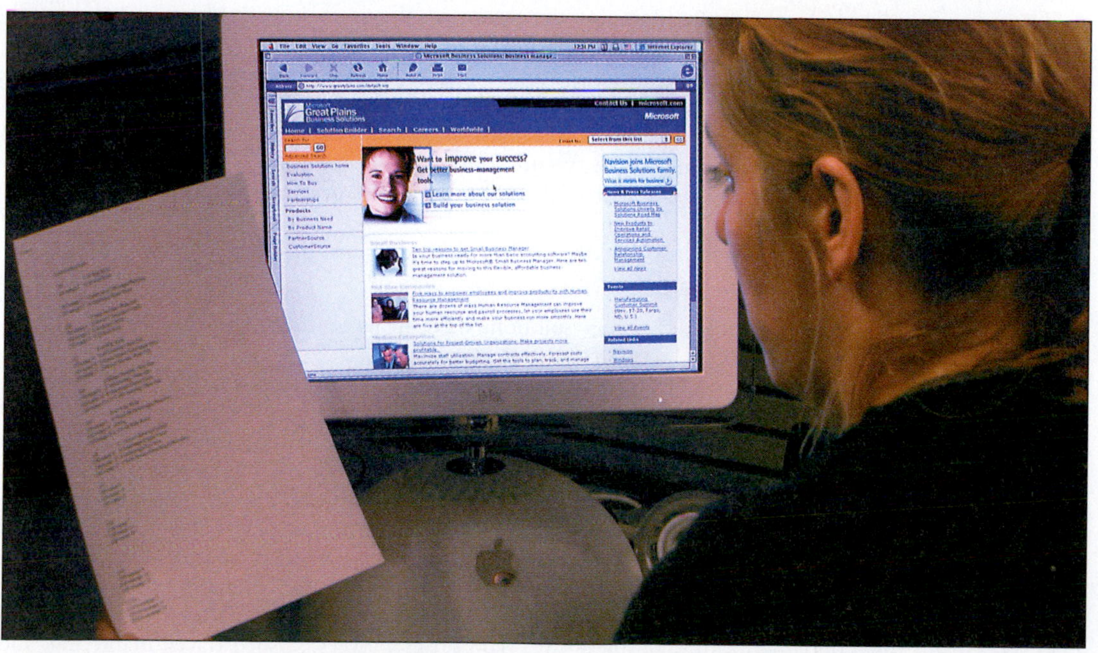

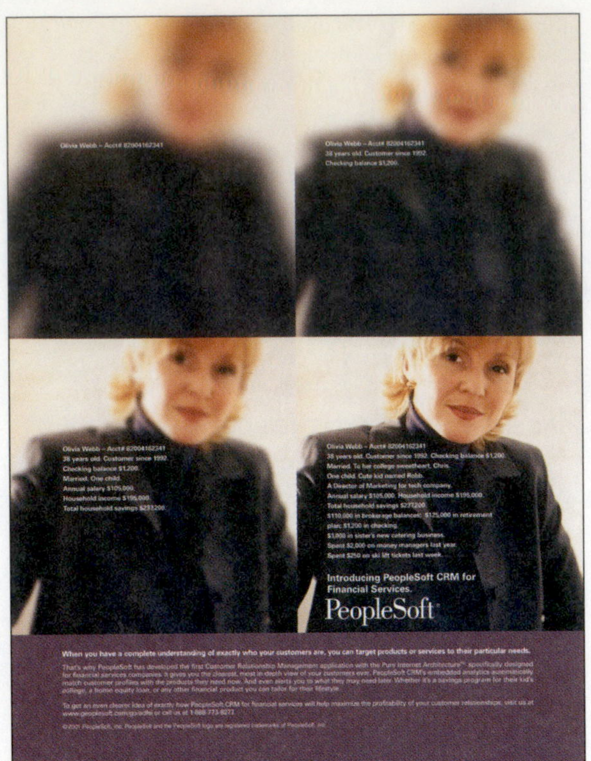

Customer relationship management technology offers marketers more information than traditional customer databases can provide.

Another key benefit of customer relationship management systems is that they are able to simplify complex business processes while keeping the best interests of customers at heart. Biotechnology company Amgen runs about 100 new drug trials each year, involving thousands of doctors and patients and hundreds of clinics. "Protocols" or rules for administering the drugs were so complicated that a third of doctors who signed up for a trial refused to participate again. On top of that, Amgen's system of paying doctors was abysmally inefficient. The result was a huge loss in terms of both money and knowledge, as doctors and patients defected from the trials. As part of its commitment to CRM, Amgen worked with Siebel Systems to create software that would make it easy for customers—in this case, physicians—to manage drug trials. The software is able to keep digital logs of each protocol, as well as each patient's progress. Not only is Amgen able to receive more reliable test results, but physicians get paid faster and are more willing to take part in new trials. Moreover, administration for the trials takes Amgen staff only a fifth of the time it took in the past. Here, a commitment to improve relationships with doctors has led to improved efficiency and real cost savings.[26]

Yet software solutions are just one component of a successful CRM initiative. Like Harley-Davidson, whose successes are described at the beginning of this chapter, and Green Hills Farms, the subject of the end-of-chapter case, the most effective companies approach customer relationship management as a complete business strategy, in which people, processes, and technology are all organized around delivering superior value to customers. Successful CRM systems share the following qualities:

- They are results driven. It is important that the firm decide on specific goals and benefits before attempting to implement a CRM strategy.
- They are implemented from the top down. The CEO and senior-level executives must be committed to changing the firm to a new focus on customers.
- They require investment in training. Remember that firms do not nurture customer relationships—their people do. Training must be companywide so that everyone knows that the firm is transforming itself. Training must also upgrade the skill sets of employees so that they are able to handle new tools.
- They communicate effectively across functions. Effective customer relationship management depends on cross-disciplinary teams that work together to solve customer problems. It shouldn't make any difference whether the customer interacts with the company directly through the sales force, over the Web, or indirectly through a reseller (or is accessing all of these channels simultaneously).
- They are streamlined. A concentrated focus on the customers allows firms to weed out wasteful business practices. If any function or process does not help the firm better serve its customers, it probably is not necessary. Streamlining also eliminates the need for costly customization when it comes to creating software solutions.
- They involve end users in creation of software solutions. Input from employees, suppliers, distributors, and any other partners who will use the systems is essential. It not only ensures that the systems meet the needs of all those who will implement them, but it encourages everyone to support the transition to customer relationship management.
- They constantly seek improvement. By tracking and measuring results, firms are able to continuously improve relationships with customers.[27]

Once the groundwork has been laid, technology solutions drive firms toward a clearer understanding of each customer and his or her needs.

Tom Siebel, who founded one of the first companies to develop CRM systems, credits customer relationship management with saving his sales-automation software firm. In 2000, Siebel Systems held a 70 percent share of its core market. Sales had doubled for the seventh straight year and were set to double again in 2001. A month before the recent recession began, Siebel's up-to-the-minute data on pending sales, gathered from 1,500 field agents, showed customers backing out of deals at an unprecedented rate. With a few clicks of his mouse, Siebel was able to see that this was no mere coincidence—all across the nation, companies were tightening their belts. To Siebel, there was just one possible explanation—the high-tech sector was about to crash. Within hours, Siebel's sales teams were visiting key accounts, closing as many deals as possible. Siebel changed the focus of the company from an aggressive growth strategy to a survival plan. He cut off three underperforming business units, laid off employees, slashed travel, marketing, and hiring budgets, and even cut executive salaries by 20 percent. When recession hit, Silicon Valley reeled and hundreds of dot.coms went under. Siebel Systems stayed financially healthy.[28]

BUYER-SELLER RELATIONSHIPS IN BUSINESS-TO-BUSINESS MARKETS

Customer relationship management and relationship marketing are not limited to consumer goods and services. Building strong buyer-seller relationships is a critical component of business-to-business marketing as well.

nteractive>learning goal

CHAPTER OBJECTIVE #5: DESCRIBE THE BUYER-SELLER RELATIONSHIP IN BUSINESS-TO-BUSINESS MARKETING.

Business-to-business marketing involves an organization's purchase of goods and services to support company operations or the production of other products. Buyer-seller relationships between companies involve working together to provide advantages that benefit both parties. These advantages might include lower prices for supplies, quicker delivery of inventory, improved quality and reliability, customized product features, and more favorable financing terms.

A **partnership** is an affiliation of two or more companies that assist each other in the achievement of common goals. Partnerships cover a wide spectrum of relationships from informal cooperative purchasing arrangements to formal production and marketing agreements. Such links can involve a single function or activity of production and marketing—for example, distribution—or all functions, such as product development, manufacturing, and marketing of a new product. In business-to-business markets, partnerships form the basis of relationship marketing.

A variety of common goals motivate firms to form partnerships. Companies may want to protect or improve their positions in existing markets, gain access to new domestic or international markets, or quickly enter into new markets. Expansion of a product line—to fill in gaps, broaden the product line, or differentiate the product—is another key reason for joining forces. Other motives include sharing resources, reducing costs, warding off threats of future competition, raising or creating barriers to entry, and learning new skills. The Interactive Example "Solving an Ethical Controversy" describes the rocky partnership between video-rental giant Blockbuster and the major film studios.

RIGHT/WRONG: SOLVING AN ETHICAL CONTROVERSY—WHEN STRATEGIC ALLIANCES TURN SOUR

Choosing Business Partners

How does an organization decide which companies to select as partners? The first priority is to locate firms that can add value to the relationship—whether through financial resources, contacts, extra manufacturing capacity, technical know-how, or distribution capabilities. The greater the value added, the greater the desirability of the partnership. In many cases, the attributes of each partner complement those of the other; each firm brings something to the relationship that the other party needs but cannot provide on its own. Some partnerships join firms with similar skills and resources, however, perhaps motivated to reduce costs.

Organizations must share similar values and goals for a partnership to succeed in the long run. Walt Disney Records forged a partnership with Kellogg Cereals that builds sales of Disney CDs while moving newer cereal brands like Mickeys' Magix, Buzz Blasts, and Hunny B's off grocery store shelves. Free on-the-pack sampler CDs encourage families to buy the cereals, and $2-off coupons for full-length CDs spur sales at Disney. Since both marketers target the same group of customers—families with young children—the ongoing campaign succeeds in generating excitement for two distinct products in a single promotion.[29]

Types of Partnerships

Companies form four key types of partnerships in business-to-business markets: buyer, seller, internal, and lateral partnerships. The following section briefly examines each category.

CHAPTER OBJECTIVE #6: COMPARE THE DIFFERENT TYPES OF BUSINESS PARTNERSHIPS AND EXPLAIN HOW THEY CONTRIBUTE TO RELATIONSHIP MARKETING.

In a *buyer partnership*, a firm purchases goods and services from one or more providers. For example, a company may contract with a certified public accountant (CPA) to conduct annual audits of its accounting system and to file federal and state income tax returns. Another company might purchase pens, pencils, and other office supplies exclusively from Office Depot.

When a company assumes the buyer position in a relationship, it has a unique set of needs and requirements that vendors must meet to make the relationship successful over a long period of time. While buyers want sellers to provide fair prices, quick delivery, and good quality, a lasting relationship often requires more effort. To induce a buyer to form a long-term partnership, a supplier must also be responsive to the purchaser's unique needs. If the buyer has a rush job that must be done in one hour, a vendor will score highly if it can perform. Similarly, buyers want reliable partners. Suppose a caterer contracts with a new food broker to provide ingredients for a major charity fund-raising dinner. The supplier, however, fails to perform satisfactorily. The caterer is not likely to use this food broker again, and no relationship results.

Seller partnerships set up long-term exchanges of goods and services in return for cash or other valuable consideration. Sellers, too, have specific needs as partners in ongoing relationships. Most prefer to develop long-term relationships with their partners. Sellers also want prompt payment.

The importance of *internal partnerships* is widely recognized in business today. The classic definition of the word *customer* as the buyer of a good or service is now more carefully defined in terms of external customers. However, customers within an organization also have their own needs. In a company that manufactures cell phones, the unit that assembles the phones is a customer of the firm's purchasing department. In essence, the manufacturing plant "buys" cell phone parts from the purchasing department, and the purchasing department supplies these parts to the plant. In this partnership, the purchasing department must continue to fulfill the needs of manufacturing by selecting vendors that can provide the parts needed with the price, quality, and time-frame characteristics specified by manufacturing. Similarly, the payroll department is a customer of all company employees; data processing is a customer of the accounting department; and a supervisor may be considered the customer of his or her employees.

Internal partnerships are the foundation of an organization and its ability to meet its commitments to external entities. If the purchasing department selects a parts vendor that fails to ship on the dates required by manufacturing, production will halt, and phones will not be delivered to customers as promised. As a result, external customers will likely seek other, more reliable suppliers. Without building and maintaining internal partnerships, an organization will have difficulty meeting the needs of its external partnerships.

Lateral partnerships include strategic alliances with other companies or with not-for-profit organizations, and research alliances with universities and colleges. The relationship is focused on external entities—such as customers of the partner firm—and involves no direct buyer-seller interactions. Strategic alliances are discussed in a later section of this chapter.

IMPROVING BUYER-SELLER RELATIONSHIPS IN BUSINESS-TO-BUSINESS MARKETS

Organizations that know how to find and nurture partner relationships, whether through informal deals or contracted partnerships, can enhance revenues and increase profits. Partnering often leads to lower prices, better products, and improved distribution, resulting in higher levels of customer satisfaction. Partners who know each other's needs and expectations are more likely to satisfy them and forge stronger long-term bonds.

<interactive>**learning goal**

CHAPTER OBJECTIVE #7: DESCRIBE HOW RELATIONSHIP MARKETING INCORPORATES NATIONAL ACCOUNT SELLING, ELECTRONIC DATA INTERCHANGE, VENDOR-MANAGED INVENTORIES, AND COLLABORATIVE PLANNING, FORECASTING, AND REPLENISHMENT TECHNIQUES.

In the past, business relationships were conducted primarily in person, over the phone, or by mail. Today, businesses are using the latest electronic, computer, and communications technology to link up. E-mail, the Internet, and other telecommunications services allow businesses to communicate anytime and anyplace. Chapter 5 discussed the business role of the Internet in detail. The following sections explore other ways that buyers and sellers cooperate in business-to-business markets.

National Account Selling

Some relationships are more important than others due to the large investments at stake. Large manufacturers like Procter & Gamble pay special attention to the needs of major retailers such as Wal-Mart, Target, and others, which sell many millions of dollars of products each year. Manufacturers use a technique called *national account selling* (discussed in detail in Chapter 19) to serve their largest, most profitable customers. The cluster of vendor offices in northwestern Arkansas—near Wal-Mart's home office—suggests how national account selling might be implemented.

The advantages of national account selling are many. By assembling a team of individuals to serve just one account, the seller demonstrates the depth of its commitment to the customer. The buyer-seller relationship is strengthened as both collaborate to find solutions that are mutually beneficial. Finally, cooperative buyer-seller efforts can bring about dramatic improvements in both efficiency and effectiveness for both partners. These improvements find their way to the bottom line in the form of decreased costs and increased profits.[30]

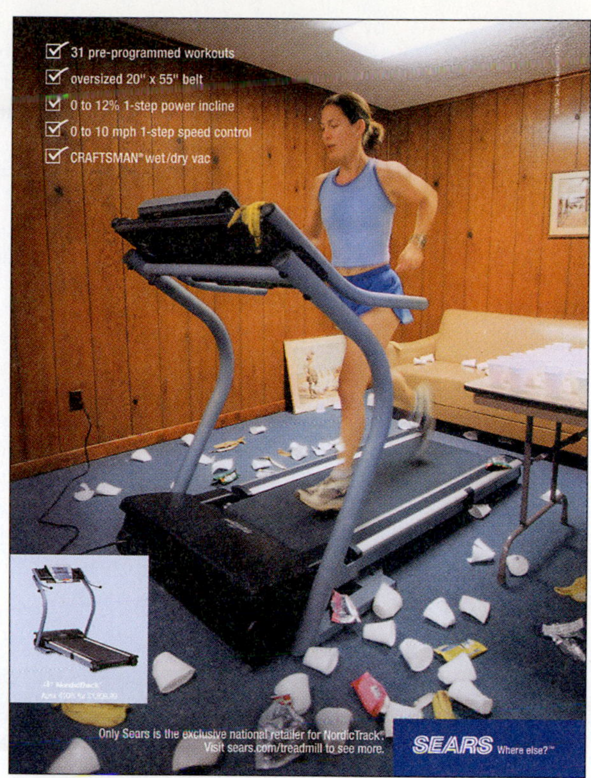

Sears's relationship with its vendors allows for improved inventory control and cost savings across its 900 stores.

Business-to-Business Databases

As noted earlier, databases are indispensable tools in relationship marketing. They are also essential in building business-to-business relationships. Using information generated from sales reports, scanners, and many other sources, sellers can create databases that help to guide their own efforts and those of buyers who resell products to final users. Quaker Oats teamed with San Francisco–based ThirdAge Media, which operates an Internet site geared to older adults, to build a database of health information. The Heart Smart Challenge offered 1,500 ThirdAge members a free bowl of oatmeal every day for a month in exchange for information on their cholesterol levels. Quaker tracked and tabulated the responses and used them in a promotional campaign documenting the link between good nutrition and cardiovascular health. At the same time, ThirdAge acquired valuable data about the health and interests of its members.[31]

Electronic Data Interchange

Technology has transformed the ways in which companies control their inventories and replenish stock. Gone are the days when a retailer would notice stocks were running low, call the vendor, check prices, and reorder. Today's **electronic data interchanges (EDIs)** automate the entire process. EDI involves computer-to-computer exchanges of invoices, orders, and other business documents. It allows firms to reduce costs and improve efficiency and competitiveness. Retailers like Wal-Mart, Dillard's, and Lowe's all require vendors to use EDI as a core **quick-response merchandising** tool. Quick response merchandising is a just-in-time strategy that reduces the time merchandise is held in inventory, resulting in substantial cost savings. An added advantage of EDI is that it opens new channels for gathering marketing information that is helpful in developing long-term business-to-business relationships.

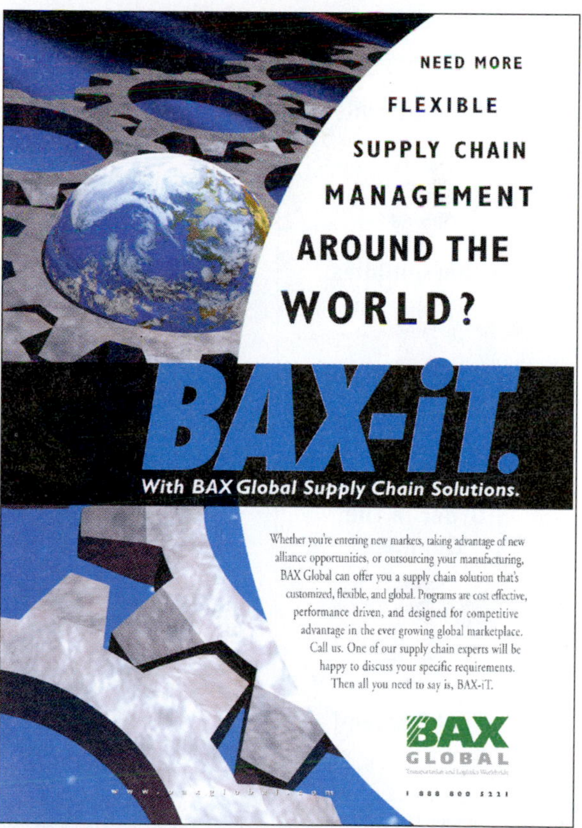

Several software applications and services are available that promise to simplify the supply chain for companies large and small.

Vendor-Managed Inventory

The proliferation of electronic data interchange and the constant pressure on suppliers to improve response time has led to another way for buyers and sellers to do business. **Vendor-managed inventory (VMI)** has replaced buyer-managed inventory in many instances. It is an inventory management system in which the seller—based on an existing agreement with the buyer—determines how much of a product a buyer needs and automatically ships new supplies to that buyer.[32]

Sears collaborates with its appliance vendors to manage inventory in its 900 stores nationwide. Supply-chain management software collects data both from Sears's vendor network and across multiple stores. The application alerts Sears to any potential shortages or overstocks before they have a chance to create a problem. Since vendors also have access to information in the system, they have the opportunity to resolve possible issues, thereby maintaining good relationships with the buyer. While the system currently manages only Sears's appliance vendor relationships, the company expects that if rolled out to Sears's entire vendor network, it could result in inventory savings of tens of millions of dollars.[33]

Some firms, such as Wal-Mart, have modified VMI to an approach called collaborative planning, forecasting, and replenishment (CPFAR). This is a planning and forecasting technique involving collaborative efforts by both purchasers and vendors. Ford Motor Company's sophisticated system manages not just inventory levels of auto parts but factors in transportation routes to assembly plants, freight costs, and many other variables.[34]

Managing the Supply Chain

Good relationships between businesses require careful management of the **supply chain** (sometimes called the *value chain*), which is the entire sequence of suppliers that contribute to the creation and delivery of a product. This process affects both upstream relationships between the company and its suppliers and downstream relationships with the product's end users. Figure 6.9 illustrates the supply chain for Dell Computer. Raw materials go into making subassemblies. When Dell receives an order, these subassemblies are put together into a finished computer that is then shipped to the buyer. The first two steps shown in Figure 6.9 are Dell's upstream relationships, and the final two steps are its downstream relationship with its customers.

<interactive>**exercise**

'NET EX: SUPPLY CHAIN MANAGEMENT

FIGURE 6.9

The Dell Computer Supply Chain

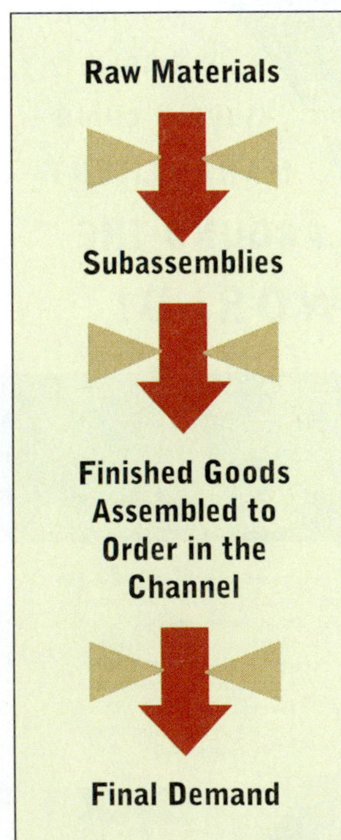

Sources: Charles H. Fine, "The Primary of Chains," *Supply Chain Management Review*, Spring 1999, p. 80. Excerpt from Charles H. Fine, *Clockspeed: Winning Industry Control in the Age of Temporary Advantage* (Perseus Books, 1998).

Effective supply-chain management can provide an important competitive advantage for a business marketer that results in the following:

- Increased innovation
- Decreased costs
- Improved conflict resolution within the chain
- Improved communication and involvement among members of the chain

By coordinating operations with the other companies in the chain, boosting quality, and improving its operating systems, a firm can improve speed and efficiency. Because companies spend considerable resources on goods and services from outside suppliers, cooperative relationships can pay off in many ways.[35]

Business-to-Business Alliances

Strategic alliances are the ultimate expression of relationship marketing. Recall from Chapter 1 that a *strategic alliance* is a partnership formed to create a competitive advantage. These more formal long-term partnership arrangements improve each partner's supply-chain relationships and enhance flexibility in operating in today's complex and rapidly changing marketplace. The size and location of strategic partners is not important. Strategic alliances include businesses of all sizes, of all kinds, and in many locations; it is what each partner can offer the other that is important.

Companies can structure strategic alliances in two ways. Alliance partners can establish a new business unit in which each takes an ownership position. In such a joint venture, one partner might own 40 percent, while the other owns 60 percent. Alternatively, the partners may decide to form a cooperative relationship that is less formal and does not involve ownership—for example, a joint new-product design team. The cooperative alliance can operate more flexibly and can change more easily as market forces or other conditions dictate. In either arrangement, the partners agree in advance on the skills and resources, such as those listed in Table 6.3, that each will bring into the alliance to achieve their mutual objectives and gain a competitive advantage.

Companies form many types of strategic alliances today. Some create horizontal alliances between firms at the same level in the supply chain; others define vertical links between firms at adjacent stages. The firms may serve the same or different industries. Alliances can involve cooperation among rivals who are market leaders or between a market leader and a follower.

Strategic alliances can also be domestic or international. SkyTeam is an international airline network that includes Delta Airlines, Aeromexico, Alitalia, Air France, CSA Czech

TABLE 6.3

Resources and Skills That Partners Contribute to Strategic Alliances

RESOURCES		SKILLS
Patents	Customer base	Marketing skills
Product lines	Marketing resources	• Innovation and product development
Brand equity	• Marketing infrastructure	• Positioning and segmentation
Reputation	• Sales force size	• Advertising and sales promotion
• For product quality	Established relationship with:	Manufacturing skills
• For customer service	• Suppliers	• Miniaturization
• For product innovation	• Marketing intermediaries	• Low-cost manufacturing
Image	• End-use customers	• Flexible manufacturing
• Companywide	Manufacturing resources	Planning and implementation skills
• Business unit	• Location	R&D skills
• Product line/brand	• Size, scale economies, scope economies, excess capacity, newness of plan and equipment	Organizational expertise, producer learning, and experience effects
Knowledge of product-market	Information technology and systems	

Source: Adapted from P. Rajan Varadarajan and Margaret H. Cunningham, "Strategic Alliances: A Synthesis of Conceptual Foundations," *Journal of the Academy of Marketing Science,* Fall 1995, p. 292.

Airlines, and Korean Air. A recent global advertising campaign, "Caring Hands," is built around the consumer and focuses on amenities offered to passengers.[36]

EVALUATING CUSTOMER RELATIONSHIP PROGRAMS

One of the most important measures of relationship marketing programs, whether in consumer or business-to-business markets, is the **lifetime value of a customer:** the revenues and intangible benefits such as referrals and customer feedback that a customer brings to the seller over an average lifetime, less the amount the company must spend to acquire, market to, and serve the customer. Long-term customers are usually more valuable assets than new ones, because they buy more, cost less to serve, refer other customers, and provide valuable feedback. The "average lifetime" of a customer relationship depends on industry and product characteristics. Customer lifetime for a consumer product like microwave pizza or breath mints may be very short, while that for a computer system will last longer.

<interactive>**learning goal**

CHAPTER OBJECTIVE #8: IDENTIFY AND EVALUATE THE MOST COMMON MEASUREMENT AND EVALUATION TECHNIQUES WITHIN A RELATIONSHIP MARKETING PROGRAM.

For a simple example of a lifetime value calculation, assume that a Chinese takeout restaurant determines that its average customer buys dinner twice a month at an average cost of $25 per order over a lifetime of five years. That business translates this calculation to revenues of $600 per year and $3,000 for five years. The restaurant can calculate and subtract its average costs for food, labor, and overhead to arrive at the per-customer profit. This figure serves as a baseline against which to measure strategies to increase the restaurant's sales volume, customer retention, or customer referral rate.

Another approach is to calculate the payback from a customer relationship, or the length of time it takes to break even on customer acquisition costs. Assume that an Internet-service provider spends $75 per new customer on direct mail and enrollment incentives. Based on average revenues per subscriber, the company takes about three months to recover that $75. If an average customer stays with the service 32 months and generates $800 in revenues, the rate of return is nearly 11 times the original investment. Once the customer stays past the payback period, the provider should make a profit on that business.

In addition to lifetime value analysis and payback, companies use many other techniques to evaluate relationship programs, including:

- Tracking rebate requests, coupon redemption, credit-card purchases, and product registrations
- Monitoring complaints and returned merchandise and analyzing why customers leave
- Reviewing reply cards, comment forms, and surveys
- Monitoring "click-though" behavior on Web sites to identify why customers stay and why they leave

These tools give the organization information about customer priorities so that managers can make changes to their systems, if necessary, and set appropriate, measurable goals for relationship programs.

A hotel chain may set a goal of improving the rate of repeat visits from 44 percent to 52 percent. A mail-order company may want to reduce time from 48 to 24 hours to process and mail orders. If a customer survey reveals late flight arrivals as the number-one complaint of an airline's passengers, the airline might set an objective of increasing the number of on-time arrivals from 87 percent to 93 percent.

Companies large and small are able to implement technology to aid in measuring the value of customers and the return on investment from expenditures developing customer relationships. They are able to choose from among a growing number of software products, many of which are tailored to specific industries or that are flexible enough to suit companies of varying sizes. The "Marketing Hits" Interactive Example explains how e-marketers have tried to pin down the value of their Internet customers.

MARKETING HIT: IMPROVING INTERNET RESEARCH BY MEASURING RELATIONSHIPS, NOT JUST EYEBALLS

STRATEGIC IMPLICATIONS OF MARKETING IN THE 21ST CENTURY

Clearly, a focus on relationship marketing helps companies create better ways to communicate with customers and to develop long-term relationships. A company's relationship marketing efforts challenge managers to develop strategies that closely integrate customer service, quality, and marketing functions. This goal usually requires changes in organizational philosophy, structure, and processes in order to be effective. By leveraging technology—both through database marketing and through customer relationship management applications—companies are able to compare the costs of acquiring and maintaining customer relationships with the profits received from these customers. This information allows managers to evaluate the potential returns from investing in relationship marketing programs.

Relationships are not limited to customers but are a way of doing business with partners—including vendors, suppliers, and other companies—outside the firm. Partners can structure relationships in many different ways to improve performance, and these choices will vary for consumer and business markets. In business-to-business relationships such as vendor-retailer partnerships, it is especially important to build shared trust. This goal may require both parties to provide detailed financial information—data some may prefer to keep confidential. However, as the Harley-Davidson case at the beginning of the chapter demonstrates, successful partnerships start with the premise that both parties need to make reasonable profits, and cooperation can pay off in lower costs and higher sales for all concerned.

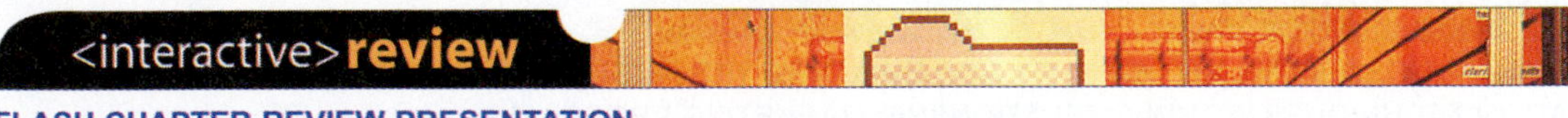

FLASH CHAPTER REVIEW PRESENTATION

DUNKIN' DONUTS AND HILL, HOLLIDAY: A RECIPE FOR GOOD RELATIONSHIPS

endofchaptermaterial

- Summary of Chapter Objectives
- Chapter Outline
- Key Terms
- Review Questions
- Projects and Teamwork Exercises
- 'netWork
- Crossword Puzzles
- Case 6.1: Green Hills Farms—Leveraging Loyalty to Compete with Giants

Take the Post-Test to assess your overall understanding of the key ideas in this chapter. The Post-Test provides a comprehensive selection of exam-style questions addressing the main topics and concepts of the chapter. At the completion of each Post-Test, you will receive a score and instructive feedback on how you answered each question, and a direct link to the part of the chapter addressed in the question. Take the Post-Test as often as you need to—a record of your progress for each attempt is kept for you to revisit and gauge your improvement. And each Post-Test is randomly generated, so every attempt is new.

Post-Test

CHAPTER 7

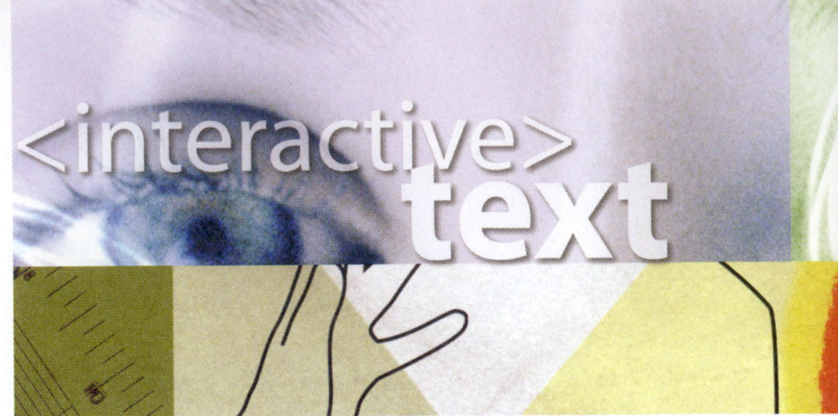

Marketing Research, Decision-Support Systems, and Sales Forecasting

Chapter Objectives

1. **Describe the development of the marketing research function and its major activities.**
2. **List and explain the steps in the marketing research process.**
3. **Differentiate between the types and sources of primary and secondary data.**
4. **Explain the different sampling techniques used by marketing researchers.**
5. **Identify the methods by which marketing researchers collect primary data.**
6. **Discuss the challenges of conducting marketing research in global markets.**
7. **Outline important uses of computer technology in marketing research.**
8. **Identify the major types of forecasting methods and explain the steps in the forecasting process.**

USING MARKETING RESEARCH TO SELECT POST–SEPTEMBER 11 ADVERTISING THEMES

There's an unwritten law in the airline industry—in the event of a fatal crash, airlines must yank all ads for at least a week if they are to avoid offending the flying public. Following the deadly attacks of September 11, all but one U.S. airline disappeared from TV screens for more than a month. A single maverick company—Southwest Airlines—was back on the airwaves by September 15.

But the advertising was different. Gone were the witty, lighthearted ads that had won awards for the upstart airline. In a matter of days, Southwest's agency—GSD&M of Austin, Texas—was ready to roll out messages that played to the altered environment in which the airline would operate following the attacks.

Just two days earlier, on the NFL's opening Sunday, Southwest had aired the first ad in its new fall roster, a hilariously funny campaign that poked fun at America's obsession with football. Within hours, the entire series was deep-sixed. Execs at GSD&M wasted no time. Starting with their own gut-checks, they immediately applied a battery of marketing research methods to figure out if and when America would be ready for an airline to be funny again. Review of past marketing research, analysis of TV ratings, and—most importantly—focus groups were used in the rapid development of new advertising.

The idea for the first campaign emerged quickly as GSD&M staffers, stranded in Annapolis during the grounding of all flights, raced home in a rental van. The strategy was based on the hypothesis that the attacks would inspire Americans to rally around the flag. Poll results, conversations with clients, and focus group sessions bore this out—and indicated that Americans were already yearning for a return to normalcy. The research further revealed that people were reassessing their priorities, seeking to reconnect with traditional values of family, community, and charity.

Created and screened in record time, GSD&M's new ads featured airline employees delivering a message of reassurance and resolve. Identifying the airline as a "company of Americans," the spots managed to tap into the altered public mood. By broadcasting when patriotic fervor was at fever pitch—and while its competitors were still off the air—Southwest was able to position itself in the eyes of travelers as an industry leader. Ad Track—*USA Today's* weekly consumer poll—reported that almost a third of respondents liked the ads a lot, well above the survey average of 22 percent. Only 4 percent disliked them.

A follow-up series of ads was equally low-key. Since research showed that the patriotic theme would not last forever, Southwest stayed ahead of the curve with a campaign that promised to connect people with family and friends: "When you're ready to fly, we're here." By September 29, before its rivals were back on TV, Southwest announced its first fare sale. In October, the airline flew 3.7 billion passenger miles—about the same as the previous October.

By January, Southwest's famed funny ads were ready to make a comeback. While a study conducted six months after the attacks showed that four out of five people still felt their lives were affected by September 11, Americans were ready for advertising—even airline spots—to be fun again.[1]

Pre-Test

Take the Pre-Test to assess your initial knowledge of the key ideas in this chapter. The Pre-Test provides exam-style questions addressing the main topics and concepts of the chapter. At the completion of each Pre-Test, you will receive a score and instructive feedback on how you answered each question, and a direct link to the part of the chapter addressed in the question. Take the Pre-Test as often as you need to—a record of your progress for each attempt is kept for you to revisit and gauge your improvement.

CHAPTER OVERVIEW

Southwest Airlines' ad agency, GSD&M, was forced to adapt overnight to a radically altered business environment. To do so, the agency relied heavily on marketing research. Marketers must not only solve problems as they arise but also anticipate and prevent those that may occur in the future. To avoid surprises and to make the best decisions possible, the right information in sufficient quantities is required in choosing effective solutions.

Marketing research is the process of collecting and using information for marketing decision making. Data comes from a variety of sources. Some results from well-planned studies designed to elicit specific information. Other valuable information comes from sales force reports, accounting records, and published reports. Still other data emerges from controlled experiments and computer simulations. Marketing research, by presenting pertinent information in a useful format, aids decision makers in analyzing data and in suggesting possible actions.

This chapter deals with the marketing research function,

Briefly Speaking

You can give people responsibility and authority, but without information they are helpless. Knowledge is the ultimate power tool.

Bill Gates (b. 1954)
Cofounder, Microsoft Corp.

which is closely linked with the other elements of the marketing planning process. The chapter also explains how marketing research techniques are used to make accurate sales forecasts, a critical component of the strategic plan.

Information collected through marketing research underlies much of the material on market segmentation in Chapter 8. Clearly, the marketing research function is the primary source of the information needed in making effective marketing decisions.

THE MARKETING RESEARCH FUNCTION

Before looking at how marketing research is conducted, we must first examine its historical development, the people and organizations it involves, and the activities it entails. Since an underlying purpose of the research is to find out more about consumers, it is clear that research is central to effective customer satisfaction and customer relationship programs. Media technologies such as the Internet and virtual reality are opening up new channels through which researchers can tap into consumer information.

Development of the Marketing Research Function

More than a century has passed since N. W. Ayer conducted the first organized marketing research project in 1879. A second important milestone in the development of marketing research occurred 32 years later, when Charles C. Parlin organized the nation's first commercial research department at Curtis Publishing Company.

<interactive>**learning goal**

CHAPTER OBJECTIVE #1: DESCRIBE THE DEVELOPMENT OF THE MARKETING RESEARCH FUNCTION AND ITS MAJOR ACTIVITIES.

Parlin got his start as a marketing researcher by counting soup cans in Philadelphia's garbage. Here is what happened. Parlin, an ad salesman, was trying to sell space in the *Saturday Evening Post* to the Campbell Soup Company. Campbell Soup resisted, believing that the *Post* reached primarily working-class readers, who preferred to make their own soup. Campbell Soup was targeting higher-income people who could afford to pay for the convenience of soup in a can. To prove Campbell wrong, Parlin began counting soup cans in the garbage collected from different neighborhoods. His research revealed that working-class families bought more soup than wealthy ones, who had servants to cook for them. Campbell Soup soon became a *Saturday Evening Post* client. It is interesting to note that garbage remains a good source of information for marketing researchers today. Prior to the recent cutbacks in food service, some airlines studied the leftovers from onboard meals to determine what to serve passengers.

Most early research gathered little more than written testimonials from purchasers of firms' products. Research methods became more sophisticated during the 1930s as the development of statistical techniques led to refinements in sampling procedures and greater accuracy in research findings.

In recent years, advances in computer technology have significantly changed the complexion of marketing research. Besides accelerating the pace and broadening the base of data collection, computers have aided marketers in making informed decisions about problems and opportunities. Simulations, for example, allow marketers to evaluate alternatives by posing what-if questions. Marketing researchers at many consumer goods firms simulate product introductions through computer programs to determine whether to risk real-world product launches or even to subject products to test marketing.

Who Conducts Marketing Research?

The size and organizational form of the marketing research function is usually tied to the structure of the company. Some firms organize research units to support different product lines, brands, or geographic areas. Others organize their research functions according to the types of research they need performed, such as sales analysis, new-product development, advertising evaluation, or sales forecasting.

Many firms depend on independent marketing research firms.[2] These independent organizations might handle just part of a larger study, such as conducting consumer interviews. Firms can also contract out entire research studies.

Marketers usually decide whether to conduct a study internally or through an outside organization based on cost. Another major consideration is the reliability and accuracy of the information collected by an outside organization. Because collecting marketing data is what these outside organizations do full time, the information they gather is often more thorough and accurate than that collected by inexperienced in-house staff. A marketing research firm can provide technical assistance and expertise not available within the contracting firm. Interaction with outside suppliers also helps to ensure that a researcher does not conduct a study only to validate a favorite personal theory or preferred option.

Marketing research companies range in size from sole proprietorships to national and international firms such as A. C. Nielsen, Information Resources Inc., and Arbitron. Recently, the 25 largest marketing research firms earned total revenues of $8.8 billion—an increase of almost 9 percent from the year before. Almost 50 percent of these revenues were generated outside the firms' home countries.[3]

Marketing research suppliers can be classified as syndicated services, full-service suppliers, or limited-service suppliers, depending on the primary thrust of their methods. Some full-service organizations are also willing to take on limited-service activities.

Syndicated Services An organization that regularly provides a standardized set of data to all customers is called a *syndicated service.* Mediamark Research Inc., for example, operates a syndicated product research service based on personal interviews with adults regarding their exposure to advertising media. Clients include advertisers, advertising agencies, magazines, newspapers, broadcasters, and cable TV networks.

Full-Service Research Suppliers An organization that contracts with clients to conduct complete marketing research projects is called a *full-service research supplier.* Roper Starch Worldwide, shown in Figure 7.1, is a full-service firm specializing in brand strategies and in building customer loyalty. A full-service supplier becomes the client's marketing research arm, performing all of the steps in the marketing research process (discussed later in this chapter).

Limited-Service Research Suppliers A marketing research firm that specializes in a limited number of activities, such as conducting field interviews or performing data processing, is called a *limited-service research supplier.* Working almost exclusively for clients in the movie industry, The National Research Group specializes in rating entertainment facilities through input from moviegoers. The firm also prepares studies to help clients develop advertising strategies and to track awareness and interest. Syndicated services can be considered a type of limited-service research supplier. Vertis Direct Marketing Services recently commissioned specialty research on the fragrance industry. A telephone survey of 2,000 adults showed that shoppers like to try out scents before buying them. The survey concluded that scent strips that accompany fragrance ads in magazines appeal to 75 percent of Generation Y noses.[4] The "Solving an Ethical Controversy" Interactive Example describes one other group that conducts marketing research—competitive analysis teams, better known as corporate spies.

FIGURE 7.1

Full-Service Marketing Research Firm

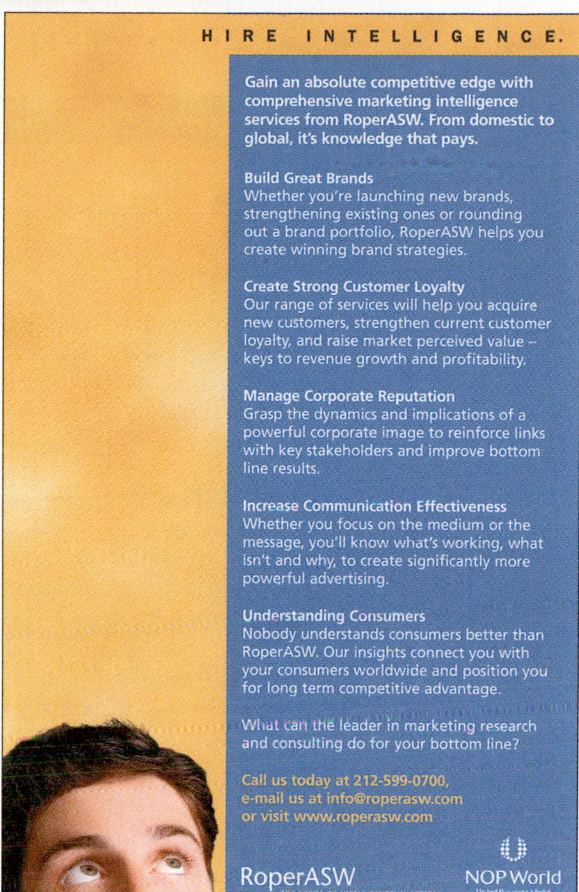

<interactive>**example**

RIGHT/WRONG: SOLVING AN ETHICAL CONTROVERSY—DUMPSTER DIVING AT UNILEVER

Customer Satisfaction Measurement Programs

In their marketing research, firms often focus on tracking the satisfaction levels of current customers. But some companies have gained valuable insights by tracking the dissatisfaction that leads customers to abandon certain products for those of competitors. Some customer defections are only partial; customers may remain somewhat satisfied with a business but not completely satisfied. Such attitudes could lead them to take their business elsewhere. Studying the underlying causes of customer defections, even partial defections, can be useful for identifying problem areas that need attention. Cunningham Field & Research Service, Inc., featured in Figure 7.2, promises to use a variety of research methods to find out exactly how satisfied consumers will be with a firm's products.

THE MARKETING RESEARCH PROCESS

As discussed earlier, businesspeople rely on marketing research to provide the information they need to make effective decisions regarding their firm's current and future activities. The chances of making good decisions improve when the right information is provided at the right time during decision making. To achieve this goal, marketing researchers often follow the six-step process shown in Figure 7.3. In the initial stages, researchers define the problem, conduct exploratory research, and formulate a hypothesis to be tested. Next, they create a design for the research study, followed by the collection of data. Finally, researchers interpret and present the research information The following sections take a closer look at each step of the marketing research process.

<interactive>**learning goal**

CHAPTER OBJECTIVE #2: LIST AND EXPLAIN THE STEPS IN THE MARKETING RESEARCH PROCESS.

Define the Problem

A popular anecdote advises that well-defined problems are half-solved. A well-defined problem permits the researcher to focus on securing the exact information needed for the solution. Clearly defining the question that research needs to answer increases the speed and accuracy of the research process.

Researchers must carefully avoid confusing symptoms of a problem with the problem itself. A symptom merely alerts marketers that they have a problem. For example, suppose that a maker of frozen pizzas sees its market share drop from 8 percent to 5 percent in six months. The loss of market share is a symptom of a problem the company must solve. To define the problem, the firm must look for the underlying causes of its market share loss.

A logical starting point in identifying the problem might be to evaluate the firm's marketing mix elements and target market. Suppose, for example, a firm has recently changed its promotional strategies. Research might then seek to answer the question "What must we do to improve the effectiveness of our marketing mix?" The firm might also look at possible environmental changes. Perhaps a new competitor entered the firm's market. Decision makers will need information to help answer the question "What must we do to distinguish our company from the new competitor?"

Tom Stemberg, CEO of office-supply retailer Staples, values marketing research so highly that he often does his own. Stemberg makes a habit of visiting a different competitor's store at least once a week. During these visits, he pushes himself to answer what he views as the most important question: In what ways are they doing a better job than Staples? Stemberg views every shopping visit as an opportunity to learn from his competition.[5]

FIGURE 7.2

Research to Help Assess Levels of Customer Satisfaction

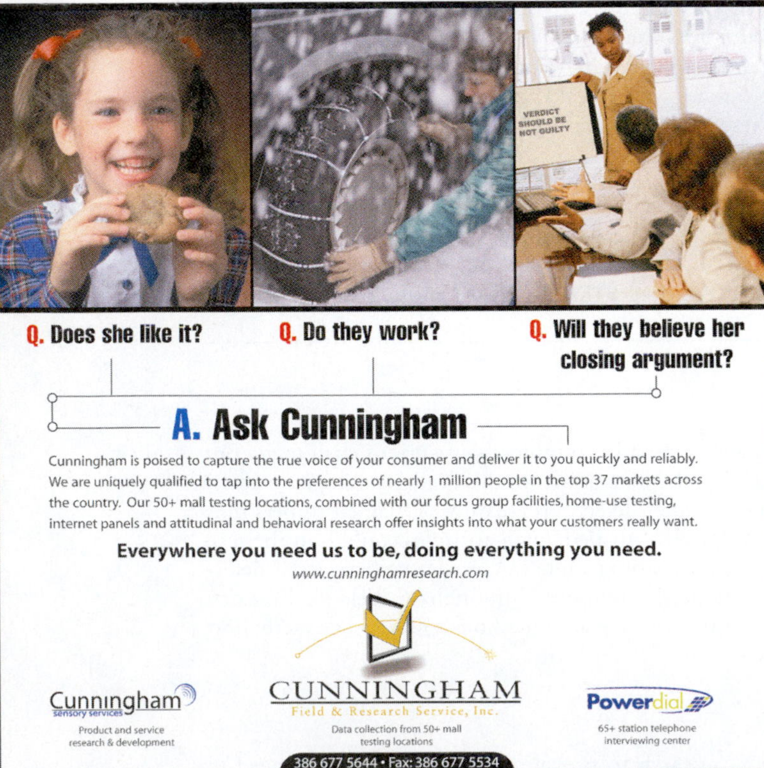

Conduct Exploratory Research

Once a firm has defined the question it wants to answer, researchers can begin exploratory research. **Exploratory research** seeks to discover the cause of a specific problem by discussing the problem with informed sources both within and outside the firm and by examining data from other information sources. The pizza firm, for example, might talk with its wholesalers, retailers, and customers. Executives might also ask for input from the sales force or look for overall market clues.

Staples chairman Stemberg enlists family members as undercover researchers. When a new Office Depot store opened in south Florida, for example, Stemberg asked his mother-in-law to investigate its competitive potential by buying items, noting how long delivery took, and then reporting on the ease of returning these items. She obtained even more valuable insights into the efficiency of the new store's delivery operations by talking to the experts—delivery truck drivers.[6]

In addition to talking with employees, exploratory research can include evaluation of company records, such as sales and profit analyses, and available competitive data. Marketing researchers often refer to internal data collection as situation analysis. The term *informal investigation* is often used for exploratory interviews with informed persons outside the researchers' firms.

Using Internal Data Marketers can find valuable data in their firm's own internal records. Typical sources of internal data are sales records, financial statements, and marketing cost analyses. Marketers analyze sales performance records to gain an overall view of company efficiency and to find clues to potential problems. Easily prepared from company invoices or a computer database system, this sales analysis can provide important details to management. The study typically compares actual and expected sales based on a detailed sales forecast by territory, product, customer, and salesperson. Once the sales quota—the level of expected sales to which actual results are compared—has been established, it is a simple process to compare actual results with expected performance.

Other possible breakdowns for sales analysis separate transactions by customer type, product, sales method (mail, telephone, or personal contact), type of order (cash or credit), and order size. *Sales analysis* is one of the least expensive and most important sources of marketing information available to a firm.

Accounting data, as summarized in the firm's financial statements, can be another good tool for identifying financial issues that influence marketing. Using ratio analysis, researchers can compare performance in current and previous years against industry benchmarks. These exercises may hint at possible problems, but only more detailed analysis would reveal specific causes of indicated variations.

A third source of internal information is marketing cost analysis—evaluation of expenses for tasks such as selling, warehousing, advertising, and delivery to determine the profitability of particular customers, territories, or product lines. Firms most commonly examine the allocation of costs to products, customers, and territories or districts. Marketing decision makers then evaluate the profitability of particular customers and districts on the basis of the sales produced and the costs incurred in generating those sales.

Like sales performance and financial research, marketing cost analysis is most useful when it provides information linked to other forms of marketing research. A later section of this chapter will address how computer technologies can accomplish these linkages and move information among a firm's units.

Formulate a Hypothesis

After defining the problem and conducting an exploratory investigation, the marketer needs to formulate a *hypothesis*—a tentative explanation for some specific event. A hypothesis is a statement about the relationship among variables that carries clear implications for testing this relationship. It sets the stage for more in-depth research by further clarifying what researchers need to test.

The chapter opening vignette explains how executives at ad agency GSD&M quickly developed a theory about the effects of terrorist attacks on consumer attitudes toward lifestyles, advertising, and flying. Marketing research supported the hypothesis and led to the creation and release of a new campaign to put its client, Southwest Airlines, back on the TV airwaves ahead of competitors.

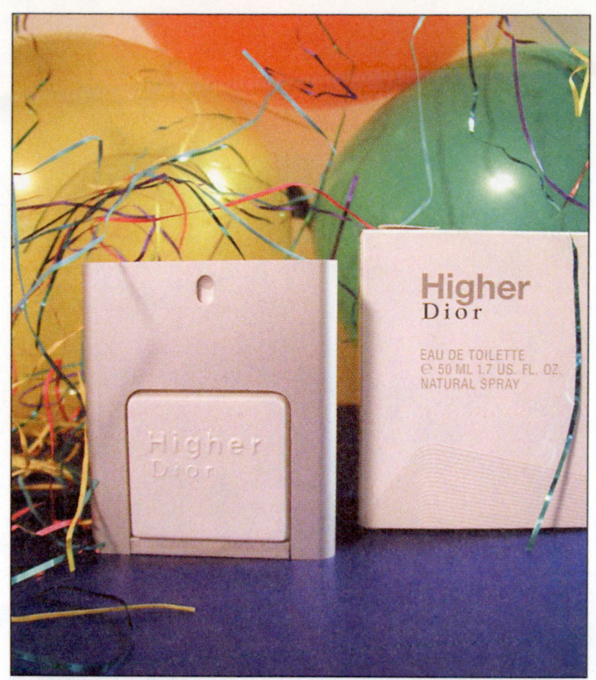

A commissioned survey into the fragrance-selection habits of shoppers revealed that younger buyers like "scratch and sniff" strips.

FIGURE 7.3

The Marketing Research Process

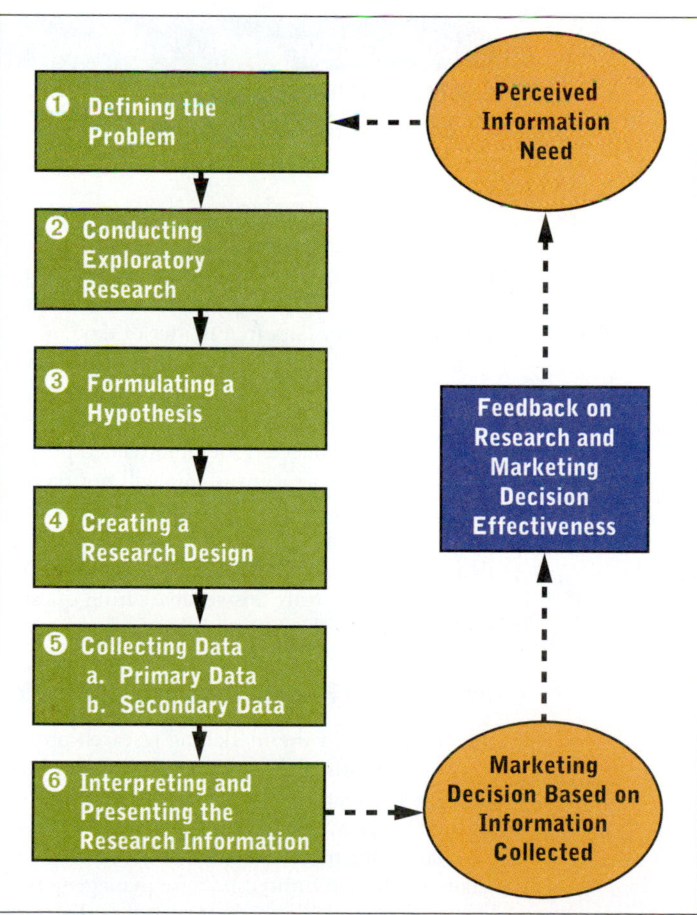

After September 11, exploratory research revealed a profound shift in consumer attitudes. Several organizations, including the Air Force Reserve, used advertising to deliver messages of support and reassurance to a grieving American public.

Not all studies test specific hypotheses. However, a carefully designed study can benefit from the rigor introduced by developing a hypothesis before beginning data collection and analysis.

Create a Research Design

To test hypotheses and find solutions to marketing problems, a marketer creates a *research design,* a master plan or model for conducting marketing research. In designing a research project, marketers must be sure that the study will measure what they intend to measure. A second important research design consideration is the selection of respondents. Marketing researchers use sampling techniques (discussed later in the chapter) to determine which consumers to include in their studies.

Some of the nation's biggest food companies employ a sample research design to test new products. They offer items to Wal-Mart first. The nation's largest retailer doesn't charge producers a fee—called a *slotting fee*—to stock their merchandise. Then, if the item sells at Wal-Mart, other retailers will take notice and drop their slotting fees.[7]

Collect Data

Marketing researchers gather two kinds of data: secondary data and primary data. **Secondary data** is information from previously published or compiled sources. Census data is an example. **Primary data** refers to information collected for the first time specifically for a marketing research study. An example of primary data is statistics collected from a survey that asks current customers about their preferences for product improvements.

<interactive>**learning goal**

CHAPTER OBJECTIVE #3: DIFFERENTIATE BETWEEN THE TYPES AND SOURCES OF PRIMARY AND SECONDARY DATA.

Secondary data offers two important advantages: (1) It is almost always less expensive to gather than primary data, and (2) researchers usually must spend less time to locate and use secondary data. A research study that requires primary data may take three to four months to complete, while a researcher can often gather secondary data in a matter of days.

Secondary data does have limitations that primary data does not. First, published information can quickly become obsolete. A marketer analyzing the population of various areas may discover that the most recent census figures are already out of date because of rapid growth and changing demographics. Second, published data collected for an unrelated purpose may not be completely relevant to the marketer's specific needs. For example, census data will not reveal the brand preferences of consumers in a particular region.

Although research to gather primary data can cost more and take longer, the results can provide richer, more detailed information than secondary data offers. The choice between secondary and primary data is tied to cost, validity, and effectiveness. In reality, many marketing research projects combine secondary and primary data to fully answer marketing questions. This chapter examines specific methods for collecting both secondary and primary data in later sections.

Interpret and Present Research Information

The final step in the marketing research process is to interpret the findings and present them to decision makers in a format that allows management to make effective judgments. Figure 7.4 illustrates possible differences between marketing researchers and their audiences in interpretations of research results due to differing backgrounds, levels of knowledge, and experience.

Marketing researchers and research users must cooperate at every stage in the research process. Too many studies go unused because management fears restrictions on the results after hearing lengthy discussions of research limitations or unfamiliar terminology. Marketing researchers must remember to direct their reports toward management and not to other researchers. They should spell out their conclusions in clear and concise terms that can be put into action. Reports should confine technical details of the research methods to an appendix, if they are included at all. By presenting research results to all key executives at a single sitting, researchers can ensure that everyone will understand the findings. Decision makers can then quickly reach consensus on what the results mean and what actions are to be taken.[8]

Briefly Speaking

Getting the facts is the key to good decision making. Every mistake that I made—and we all make mistakes—came because I didn't take the time. I didn't drive hard enough. I wasn't smart enough to get the facts.

Charles F. Knight (b. 1936)
Chairman, Emerson Electric

MARKETING RESEARCH METHODS

Clearly, data collection is an integral part of the marketing research process. One of the most time-consuming parts of collecting data is determining what method the marketer should use to obtain the data. This section discusses the most commonly used methods by which marketing researchers find both secondary and primary data.

Secondary Data Collection

Secondary data comes from many sources. The overwhelming quantity of secondary data available at little or no cost challenges researchers to select data that is pertinent.

Secondary data consists of two types: internal and external data. Internal data, as discussed earlier, includes sales records, product performance reviews, sales force activity reports, and marketing cost reports. External data comes from a variety of sources, including government records, syndicated research services, and industry publications. Computerized databases provide access to vast amounts of data from both inside and outside an organization. The following sections on government data, private data, and online sources focus on databases and other external data sources available to marketing researchers.

Government Data The federal government is the nation's most important source of marketing data. Census data provides the most frequently used government statistics. A census of population is conducted every ten years and is made available at no charge in local libraries, on computer disks, and through the Internet. The Bureau of the Census also conducts a periodic census of housing, population, business, manufacturers, agriculture, minerals, and governments.

The census of population contains a wealth of valuable information for marketers. It breaks down the population by very small geographic areas, making it possible to determine population traits by city block or census tract in large cities. It divides the populations of nonmetropolitan areas into block-numbering areas (BNAs). The BNAs and census tracts are important for marketing analysis because they highlight populations with similar traits, avoiding diversity within political boundaries such as county lines. This data helps marketers such as local retailers and shopping center developers to gather vital information about customers in an immediate neighborhood without spending time or money to conduct comprehensive surveys. The Census Bureau uses a variety of statistical techniques to group households into homogeneous clusters of people who have similar lifestyles and spending habits, who listen to similar kinds of programming, and who watch similar television shows.[9]

FIGURE 7.4

The Research Report and Presentation: Linking the Study and the Research User

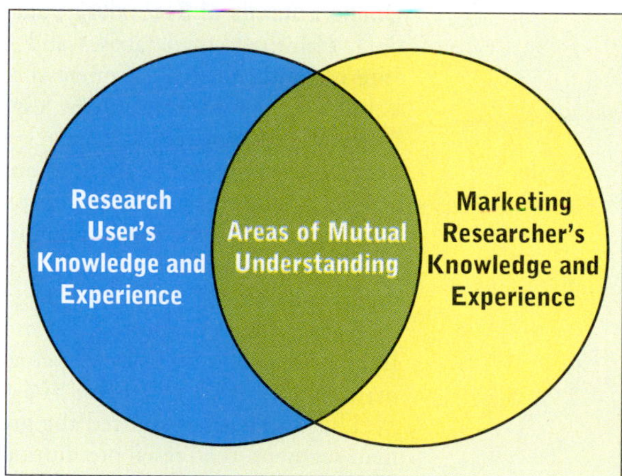

Marketing researchers find even more valuable resources in the government's computerized mapping database called the TIGER system, for Topographically Integrated Geographic Encoding and Referencing system. This system combines topographic features such as railroads, highways, and rivers with census data such as household income figures. TIGER data is available on DVD, making the Census Bureau one of the first federal agencies to use the technology to publish huge amounts of digital data. The DVDs contains both database management software and mapping software, making TIGER data highly accessible to marketers.[10]

Marketers often get other information from the federal government, such as the following:

- *Monthly Catalog of the United States Government Publications* and *Statistical Abstract of the United States,* published annually
- *Survey of Current Business,* updated monthly
- *County and City Data Book,* typically published every three years, providing data on each county and city of over 25,000 residents

Even with the wealth of information available from the Census Bureau, the data gathered is not necessarily comprehensive, as the "Marketing Misses" Interactive Example explains.

<interactive>**example**

MARKETING MISS: WHY THE LATEST FEDERAL CENSUS FAILED TO COUNT ARAB AMERICANS

State and city governments serve as additional important sources of information on employment, production, and sales activities. In addition, university bureaus of business and economic research frequently collect and disseminate valuable information.

Briefly Speaking

When you are drowning in numbers, you need a system to separate the wheat from the chaff.

Anthony Adams (b. 1940) Vice president, Campbell Soup Co.

Private Data Many private organizations provide information for marketing decision makers. A trade association may be an excellent source of data on activities in a particular industry. Gale Publishing's *Encyclopedia of Associations,* available in many libraries, can help marketers to track down trade associations that may have data pertinent to their company. Also, the advertising industry continuously collects data on audiences reached by various media.

Business and trade magazines also publish a wide range of valuable data. Ulrich's *Guide to International Periodicals,* another common library reference, can point researchers in the direction of trade publications that conduct and publish industry-specific research. General business magazines can also be good sources. *Sales & Marketing Management,* for instance, publishes an annual *Survey of Media Markets* that combines statistics for population, effective buying income (EBI), and retail sales into buying power indexes that indicate each market's ability to buy.

Since few libraries carry specialized trade journals, the best way to gather data from them is either directly from the publishers or through online periodical databases like Dialog's *ABI/Inform,* available at many libraries, or CompuServe's *Knowledge Index.* Increasingly, trade publications maintain Web home pages that allow archival searches. Larger libraries can often provide directories and other publications that can help researchers find secondary data. For instance, Find/SVP's *FindEx, the Directory of Market Research Reports, Studies, and Surveys* lists a tremendous variety of completed research studies that are available for purchase.

Several national firms offer information to businesses by subscription. *Roper Starch Worldwide* is a global database service with consumer attitudes, lifestage, and behavior information for 30 countries. Roper also provides *Starch Readership Reports* that measure more than 20,000 ads in 400 magazines.

Electronic systems that scan UPC bar codes speed purchase transactions, and they also provide data for inventory control, ordering, and delivery. Scanning technology is widely used by grocers and other retailers, and marketing research companies, such as A. C. Nielsen and Information Resources Inc., store this data in commercially available databases. These scanner-based information services track consumer purchases of a wide variety of UPC-coded products. Retailers can use this information to target customers with the right products at the right time.

A. C. Nielsen SalesNet uses the Internet to deliver scanner data quickly to clients. Data is processed as soon as it is received from supermarkets and is then forwarded to market researchers so they can perform more in-depth analysis. At the same time, Nielsen representatives summarize the data in both graphic and spreadsheet form and post it on the Internet for immediate access by clients. Recently, retail giant Wal-Mart decided to withhold its scanner data from research services. Nielsen, backed by rival stores, responded by refusing to sell any scanner data to the world's largest retailer.[11]

Online Sources of Secondary Data The tools of cyberspace sometimes simplify the hunt for secondary data. Hundreds of databases and other sources of information are available online, both through the Internet and through commercial services such as America Online. A well-designed, Internet-based marketing research project can cost less yet yield faster results than offline research. For instance, Lego needed to make a quick decision on rereleasing some of its classic sets. The company posted a bulletin board at Lego.com, inviting its 2 million monthly visitors to share opinions and to comment on their favorite Lego classics. Using software from Recipio, results were gathered and analyzed in real time. Within two weeks, the company had the information it needed. Almost 40 percent of respondents aged 18 and under—Lego's "sweet spot"—favored rereleasing Guarded Inn and Metroliner. Within six weeks Metroliner sales topped the annual sales of comparable Lego sets.[12]

A recent survey reported that more than 70 percent of marketing research firms conduct some form of Internet research, up from 50 percent a year earlier. Today, industry experts estimate that about half of all marketing research could easily be done online.[13]

The Internet has spurred the growth of research aggregators—companies that acquire, catalog, reformat, segment, then resell premium research reports that have already been published. Aggregators put valuable data within reach of marketers who lack the time or the budget to commission custom research. Since Web technology makes their databases easy to search, aggregators are able to compile detailed, specialized reports quickly and cost-effectively.[14]

Internet search tools such as Google and Yahoo! can find specific sites that are rich with information. Discussion groups may also provide information and insights that can help answer some marketing questions. Additionally, a post to a chat room or newsgroup may draw a response that uncovers previously unknown sources of secondary data. Usenet, the largest newsgroup network, boasts 500 million messages posted since 1995. Unlike chat-room postings, these opinions are unsolicited and uncensored. Online services like Survey.com and PlanetFeedback gather data from multiple sources, organized according to demographic, industry, product, or multiple other characteristics. A quick search through PlanetFeedback alerted Procter & Gamble to complaints that the tape on its Pampers brand diapers came loose too easily. The company was able to fix the problem before it had thousands of annoyed parents.[15]

Researchers must, however, carefully evaluate the validity of information they find on the Internet. People without in-depth knowledge of the subject matter may post information in a newsgroup. Similarly, Web pages might contain information that has been gathered using questionable research methods. The saying *caveat emptor* (buyer beware) should guide Internet searches for secondary data.

'NET EX: ONLINE INFORMATION SOURCES

Sampling Techniques

Before undertaking a study to gather primary data, researchers must first identify which participants to include in the study. **Sampling** is the process of selecting survey respondents or research participants. It is one of the most important aspects of research design because if a study fails to involve consumers who accurately reflect the target market, the research will likely yield misleading conclusions.

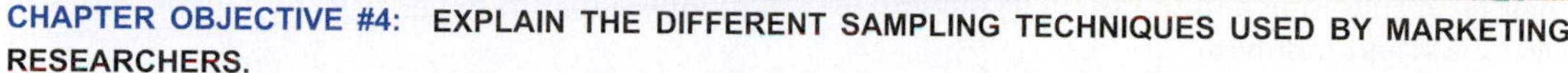

CHAPTER OBJECTIVE #4: EXPLAIN THE DIFFERENT SAMPLING TECHNIQUES USED BY MARKETING RESEARCHERS.

The total group of people that the researcher wants to study is called the *population* or *universe.* For a political campaign study, the population would be all eligible voters. For research about a new cosmetics line, it might be all women in a certain age bracket. The sample is a representative group from this population. Researchers rarely gather information from a study's total population, resulting in a census. Unless the total population is small, the costs of a census are too high.

Samples can be classified as either probability samples or nonprobability samples. A **probability sample** is one that gives every member of the population a chance of being selected. Types of probability samples include simple random samples, stratified samples, and cluster samples.

In a *simple random sample,* every member of the relevant universe has an equal opportunity of selection. The draft lottery of the Vietnam era is an example. The days of the year were drawn and set into an array. The placement of a person's birthday in this list determined his likelihood of being called for service. In a *stratified sample,* randomly selected subsamples of different groups are represented in the total sample. Stratified samples provide efficient, representative groups for such studies as opinion polls, in which groups of individuals share various divergent viewpoints. In a *cluster sample,* researchers select areas (or clusters) from which they draw respondents. This cost-efficient type of probability sample may be the best option where the population cannot be listed or enumerated. A good example is a marketing researcher identifying various U.S. cities and then randomly selecting supermarkets within those cities to study.

In contrast, a **nonprobability sample** is an arbitrary grouping that does not permit the use of standard statistical tests. Types of nonprobability samples are convenience samples and quota samples. A *convenience sample* is a nonprobability sample selected from among readily available respondents. Broadcast news "on-the-street" interviews are a good example. Marketing researchers sometimes use convenience samples in exploratory research but not in definitive studies. A *quota sample* is a nonprobability sample that is divided to maintain representation for different segments or groups. It differs from a stratified sample, in which researchers select subsamples by some random process; in a quota sample, they hand-pick participants. An example would be a survey of owners of imported autos that includes two Hyundai owners, six Honda owners, four Volvo owners, and so on.

Primary Research Methods

Marketers use a variety of methods for conducting primary research. The principal methods for collecting primary data are observation, surveys, and controlled experiments. The choice among these methods depends on the issues under study and the decisions that marketers need to make. In some cases, researchers may decide to combine techniques during the research process.

<interactive>learning goal

CHAPTER OBJECTIVE #5: IDENTIFY THE METHODS BY WHICH MARKETING RESEARCHERS COLLECT PRIMARY DATA.

Observation Method In observational studies, researchers view the overt actions of the subjects. Marketers trying to understand how consumers actually behave in certain situations find observation to be a useful technique. Observation tactics may be as simple as counting the number of cars passing by a potential site for a fast-food restaurant or checking the license plates at a shopping center to determine where shoppers live. Research companies like Ipsos, featured in Figure 7.5, use observation methods to create psychological and sociological profiles of potential market segments.

Technological advances provide increasingly sophisticated ways for observing consumer behavior. The television industry relies on data from people meters, which are electronic remote-control devices that record the TV-viewing habits of individual household members to measure the popularity of TV shows. Traditional people meters require each viewer to punch a button each time he or she turns on the TV, changes channels, or leaves the room.

Marketers have long worried that some viewers do not bother to push people meter buttons at appropriate times, skewing research findings. In response, Arbitron recently tested a portable people meter (PPM) that participants keep with them at all times. Throughout the day, the PPM picks up and stores codes embedded in radio and TV programming. At night, the participant puts the PPM into a docking station, from which the data is uploaded to Arbitron. The PPM even has a built-in motion detector to ensure that it is not abandoned midtest.[16]

Videotaping consumers in action is also gaining acceptance as a research technique. Cookware manufacturers may videotape consumers cooking in their own kitchens to evaluate how they use their pots and pans. A toothbrush manufacturer asked marketing research firm E-Lab to videotape consumers brushing their teeth and using mouthwash in its quest to develop products that would leave behind the sensation of cleanliness and freshness.

When French electronics maker Thomson developed a new digital technology for storing, accessing, and playing music, the company also hired E-Lab to study how, when, and where people listen to music. To get the information, E-Lab researchers issued beepers to consumers. At certain times of the day, E-Lab researchers beeped study participants and asked them to make a note of the music they were listening to, who chose it, and their mood. Researchers also followed people as they moved around their homes, recording where they kept their stereos and how they organized their music collections.[17]

In an effort to understand what makes teenagers tick, advertising agency Bates USA mailed disposable cameras to 36 teens around the U.S. and asked them to document their favorite possessions, locations, and people. Back came snapshots of everything imaginable, including (literally) a kitchen sink. One ninth-

FIGURE 7.5

Observation Methods Leading to Profiles of Target Segments

grader photographed her hockey stick and enclosed a note explaining that making the hockey team was her way of showing she was as good an athlete as her brothers. Bates senior vice president Janice Figueroa notes that information like this is valuable because it goes beyond mere statistics, which document that more girls are participating in sports, and reveals these girls' underlying motivations. Athletics may actually relate to self-confidence—a powerful motivator that marketers can use.[18]

Ethnography—also known as interpretive research or "going native"—is a method of observational research that has attracted considerable interest in recent years. Developed by social anthropologists as a method for explaining behavior that operates below the level of conscious thought, ethnography can provide insights into consumer behavior and the ways in which consumers interact with brands. Ethnography is often used to interpret consumer behavior within a foreign culture, where language, ideals, values, and expectations are all subject to different cultural influences.[19]

Survey Method Observation alone cannot supply all of the desired information. Researchers must ask questions to get information on attitudes, motives, and opinions. It is also difficult to get exact demographic information—such as income levels—from observation. To discover this information, researchers can use either interviews or questionnaires.

Telephone Interviews Telephone interviews are a quick and inexpensive method for obtaining a small quantity of relatively impersonal information. Simple, clearly worded questions are easy for interviewers to pose over the phone and are effective at drawing appropriate responses. Telephone surveys have relatively high response rates, especially with repeated calls; calling a number once yields a response rate of 50 to 60 percent, but calling the same number five times raises the response rate to 85 percent. To maximize responses and save costs, some researchers use computerized dialing and digitally synthesized voices that interview respondents.

However, phone surveys have several drawbacks. Most importantly, about 44 percent of all people now invited to take part in them refuse, compared with only 15 percent 20 years ago. Their reasons include concern for data privacy, a negative association of phone surveys with telemarketing, and the lack of financial rewards for participating.[20]

Many respondents are hesitant to give personal characteristics about themselves over the telephone. Results may be biased by the omission of typical households where adults are off working during the day. Other households, particularly market segments such as single women and physicians, are likely to have unlisted numbers. While computerized random dialing can give access to unlisted numbers, it is restricted in several states.

The popularity of caller-ID systems to screen unwanted calls is another obstacle for telephone researchers. Some legal experts believe caller-ID violates the caller's right to privacy; in one case, the Pennsylvania state courts ruled it unconstitutional. Still, state laws on caller-ID vary. Some require vendors to offer a blocking service to callers who wish to evade the system.

Other obstacles restrict the usefulness of telephone surveys abroad. In areas where telephone ownership is rare, survey results will be highly biased. Telephone interviewing is also difficult in countries that lack directories or where call volumes congest limited phone line capacity.

Personal Interviews The best means for obtaining detailed information about consumers is usually the personal interview since the interviewer can establish rapport with respondents and explain confusing or vague questions. Although slow and expensive to conduct, personal interviews offer a flexibility and a return of detailed information that often offsets the limitations of mail questionnaires. Marketing research firms can conduct interviews in rented space in shopping centers, where they gain wide access to potential buyers of the merchandise they are studying. These locations sometimes feature private interviewing space, videotape equipment, and food-preparation facilities for taste tests. Interviews conducted in shopping centers are typically called *mall intercepts.* Downtown retail districts and airports provide other valuable locations for marketing researchers.

Focus Groups Marketers also gather research information through the popular technique of focus groups. A **focus group** brings together 8 to 12 individuals in one location to discuss a subject of interest. Unlike other interview techniques that elicit information through a question-and-answer format, focus groups usually encourage a general discussion of a predetermined topic. Focus groups can provide quick and relatively inexpensive insight into consumer attitudes and motivations. As the chapter opening vignette described, within days of the September 11 terrorist attacks, Southwest Airlines was able to roll out a campaign that reflected the changed mood of the American public. Focus groups were a key technique used to quickly evaluate consumer attitudes toward the airlines in the wake of the attacks.

In a focus group, the leader, or moderator, typically explains the purpose of the meeting and suggests an opening topic. The moderator's main purpose, however, is to stimulate interaction among group members to encourage their discussion of numerous points. The moderator may occasionally interject questions as catalysts to direct the group's discussion. The moderator's job is difficult, requiring preparation and group facilitation skills.

FIGURE 7.6

Focus Groups: Insights into Consumer Perceptions

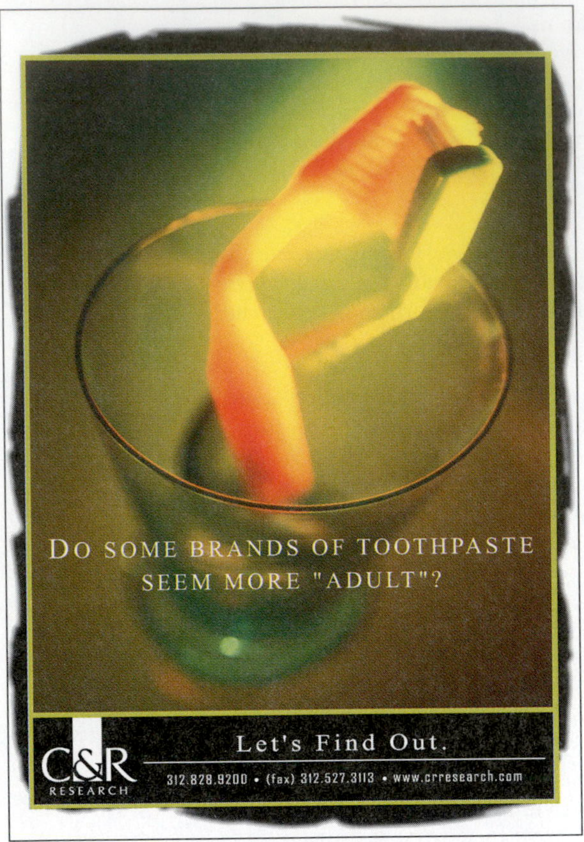

DO SOME BRANDS OF TOOTHPASTE
SEEM MORE "ADULT"?
C&R
RESEARCH
Let's Find Out.
312.828.9200 • (fax) 312.527.3113 • www.crresearch.com

Focus group sessions often last one or two hours. Researchers usually record the discussion on tape, and observers frequently watch through a one-way mirror. Some research firms also allow clients to view focus groups in action through videoconferencing systems.

Marketers use focus groups for a variety of purposes. In Figure 7.6, C&R Research conveys a projective technique that might be used with a focus group to find out how brands of toothpaste are perceived by customers. Teenage Research Unlimited conducts focus groups for a variety of clients to explore aspects of adolescent life. The research firm has found that indirect questions can be the best way to elicit information from teens. For instance, the moderator may display a cartoon drawing of a young woman and ask focus group participants to describe her clothes, accessories, and favorite magazines and music. Rather than inquiring into fast-food preferences directly, the moderator might ask participants to match a list of restaurants with the celebrities most likely to eat at each one. Another favorite ploy, especially for gaining insight into modern teen fashion trends, is to ask teens to pretend they are costume designers for a hit TV show and describe how they would dress the show's characters. Recently, Teen Research Unlimited launched its first syndicated online product, Omnibuzz, a monthly teen survey. Each sample of 850 respondents is weighted to match the national teen population in terms of gender, region, and ethnicity. Questions are custom-designed to meet client needs and results are survey results are available within three weeks.[21]

Focus groups are a particularly valuable tool for exploratory research, developing new product ideas, and preliminary testing of alternative marketing strategies. They can also aid in the development of well-structured questionnaires for larger-scale research.

Focus groups do have some drawbacks, however. Some researchers fear that the focus group setting is sterile and unnatural and may not produce honest responses to questions. Participants may, for example, feel a need to identify with other members of the group and so provide less-than-truthful answers. Other researchers feel that the sample sizes are too small to be truly representative of larger population groups. Still others question the consistency of the interviewing process.[22]

Researchers are finding ways to re-create the focus group environment over the Internet. With experienced moderators who have the technical skills to function fluently online, it is possible to gain valuable qualitative information at a fraction of the cost it takes to run a traditional focus group session.

Research firm Greenfield Online used an online focus group to test reactions to a redesigned Web site for Captain Morgan Original Spiced Rum. Participants "gathered" in Greenfield's private chat room. A moderator posed questions and responded to answers on one side of a split screen, while participants typed their comments on the other side. How can researchers tell if online participants are being truthful? Greenfield staff members cross-checked participants' answers to earlier screening questionnaires against the information they entered later when they registered for the database. The company then cross-checked a second time before the focus group began and found substitutes for respondents whose answers appeared inconsistent.

FocusVision Worldwide in Figure 7.7 advertises some of the benefits Internet-based focus groups can offer. FocusVision technology promises to enable clients to view focus group sessions around the world through videoconferencing and Internet videostreaming. Multiple camera systems, picture-in-picture enhancements, and simultaneous language translation deliver reliable, qualitative data saving staff travel time and expenses. The "Marketing Hits" Interactive Example further explains how researchers are hosting real-time focus groups over the Internet.

MARKETING HIT: COLLECTING QUALITATIVE RESEARCH ONLINE

Mail Surveys Although personal interviews can provide very detailed information, cost considerations usually prevent an organization from using personal interviews in a national study. A mail survey can be a cost-effective alternative. Mail surveys also provide anonymity that may encourage respondents to give candid answers.

Mail surveys help marketers track consumer attitudes through ongoing research. Corning conducts a semiannual survey of consumers to measure customer awareness and satisfaction and to gather information for new-product development. Mail surveys can also provide demographic data that may be helpful in market segmentation.

Mail questionnaires do, however, have several limitations. First, response rates are typically much lower than for personal interviews. Because researchers must wait for respondents to complete and return questionnaires, mail surveys also usually take a long time to conduct. A third limitation, questionnaires cannot answer unanticipated questions that occur to respondents as they complete the forms. Complex questions may not be suitable for a mail questionnaire. Finally, unless they gather additional information from nonrespondents, researchers must worry about bias in the results stemming from differences between respondents and nonrespondents.

Researchers try to minimize these limitations by paying careful attention in developing and in pretesting questionnaires. Researchers can boost response rates by keeping questionnaires short and by offering incentives to respondents who complete and return the survey documents.

Fax Surveys The low response rates and long follow-up times associated with mail surveys have spurred interest in the alternative of faxing survey documents. In some cases, faxes may supplement mail surveys; in others, it may be the primary method for contacting respondents.

Online Surveys and Other Internet-Based Methods The growing population of Internet users has spurred researchers to conduct online surveys. Using the Web, they are able to speed the survey process, increase sample sizes, ignore geographic boundaries, and dramatically reduce costs. While a standard research project can take up to eight weeks to complete, a thorough online project may take two weeks or less. Less intrusive than telephone surveys, online research allows participants to respond at their leisure. The novelty and ease of answering online may even encourage higher response rates. Additional questions and longer responses have only a slight effect, if any, on an online study's cost, enabling researchers to gather detailed information through surveys. Furthermore, since online research is already in digital form, it generally requires less preparation—such as retyping into a database—before analysis.[23]

FIGURE 7.7

Benefits of Online Focus Groups

Businesses are increasingly including questionnaires on their Web pages to solicit information about consumer demographics, attitudes, and comments and suggestions for improving goods and services or improving marketing messages. Circuit City's online survey aims to gather feedback from customers regarding their in-store shopping experiences. It takes just minutes to complete, and participants are automatically registered to win cash prizes in Circuit City's Customer Satisfaction Sweepstakes.[24]

Marketers are also experimenting with electronic bulletin boards as an information-gathering device. On a password-protected Web site, moderators pose questions to selected respondents—usually just 15 to 25—over a predetermined period of time. Respondents have the chance to try out a product and are able to submit feedback at their leisure. Unlike focus group sessions, there are no group dynamics, so some researchers feel that responses are more truthful. Bulletin boards are particularly effective when targeting respondents who are unable to commit to real-time group sessions or for topics that are highly sensitive or complex.[25]

The growth of the Internet is creating a need for new research techniques to measure and capture information about Web-site visitors. At present, no industrywide standards define techniques for measuring Web use. Some sites ask users to register before accessing the pages; others merely keep track of the number of "hits" or number of times a visitor accesses a page. Marketers have tried to place a value on a site's "stickiness" (longer-lasting site visits) as a means of measuring effectiveness. Others use "cookies," which are electronic identifiers deposited on viewers' computers, to track click-through behavior—the paths users take as they move through the site. However, since some consumers change their Internet service providers frequently, cookies have lost some of their effectiveness.

Some software can monitor the overall content that a person is viewing and display banner advertisements likely to be of interest. For example, a search using the keyword "car" might call up a banner ad for General Motors or Ford. CMG Information Services offers a service called Engage.Knowledge, which collects profiles of Web users from numerous sites and organizes the data into 800 categories, including sports and hobbies. Researchers can use this information to develop marketing strategies. The popularity of video games has led to the emergence of a new advertising platform, "advergames." YaYa LLC streams three-dimensional console-quality games over the Internet. A promotional e-mail, for example, invites users to play a Honda-sponsored racing game, driving a replica of a new-model car through an exciting virtual racetrack. A marketing research tool in disguise, players must register before starting their engines—submitting details of their age, address, occupation, and hobbies. They are rewarded with free entry into a contest to win a Honda CR-V. Four out of five users register—and many pass the game along to friends. Of course, Honda gains market data on a key demographic group—potential young car buyers.[26]

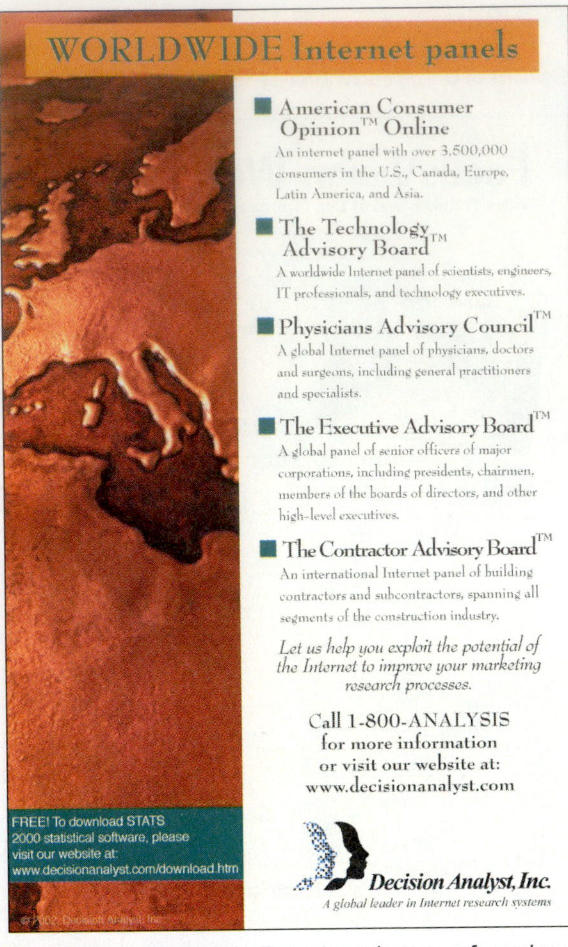

Research companies offer a broad range of services that harness Internet technology to deliver research results on a global scale.

The Experimental Method The least-used method for collecting primary data is the *controlled experiment.* A marketing research experiment is a scientific investigation in which a researcher controls or manipulates a test group (or groups) and compares the results with those of a control group that did not receive the experimental controls or manipulations.

The most common use of this method by marketers is *test-marketing,* or introducing a new product in a specific area and then observing its degree of success. Up to this point, a product development team may have gathered feedback from focus groups. Other information may have come from shoppers' evaluations of competing products. Test-marketing is the first stage at which the product performs in a real-life business environment.

Test-marketing introduces a new product supported by a complete marketing campaign to a selected city or TV coverage areas. Marketers look for a location with a manageable size, where residents match their target market's demographic profile. After the test has been under way for a few months and sales and market share in the test market have been calculated, marketers can estimate the product's likely performance in a full-scale rollout.

After September 11, Hollywood test-marketed upcoming movies in an attempt to gauge the psychological effects of the tragedy on moviegoers. In recruited screenings, viewers were asked whether they saw anything offensive in movies that featured acts of terrorism or scenes filmed in Manhattan. Based on test-market responses, studios decided whether to release their new films, delay them, or reshoot offending scenes.[27]

Anheuser-Busch test-marketed its low-carbohydrate Michelob Ultra in Denver, Tucson, and central Florida. Enthusiastic response led to an earlier-than-expected national rollout. Teasers ads, featuring the famous Michelob red ribbon, promise that the new brand will make diet-conscious consumers "look at beer in a whole new light."[28]

Some firms omit test-marketing and move directly from product development to full-scale production. These companies cite four problems with test-marketing:

1. Test-marketing is expensive. A firm can spend more than $1 million, depending on the size of the test-market city and the cost of buying media to advertise the product.
2. Competitors quickly learn about the new product. By studying the test market, competitors can develop alternative strategies.
3. Some products are not well-suited to test-marketing. Few firms test-market long-lived, durable goods such as cars because of the major financial investments required for their development, the need to establish networks of dealers to distribute the products, and requirements for parts and servicing.

Companies that decide to skip the test-marketing process can choose several other options. A firm may simulate a test-marketing campaign through computer-modeling software. By plugging in data on similar products, it can develop a sales projection for a new product. Another firm may offer an item in just one U.S. region or in another country, adjusting promotions and advertising based on local results before going to other geographical regions. Another option may be to limit a product's introduction to just one retail chain in order to carefully control and evaluate promotions and results.

Conducting International Marketing Research

As corporations expand globally, they need to gather correspondingly more knowledge about consumers in other countries. Although marketing researchers follow the same basic steps for international studies as for domestic ones, they do face some different challenges.

<interactive>**learning goal**

CHAPTER OBJECTIVE #6: DISCUSS THE CHALLENGES OF CONDUCTING MARKETING RESEARCH IN GLOBAL MARKETS.

U.S. organizations can tap many secondary resources as they research global markets. One major information source is the U.S. government, particularly the Department of Commerce. The Commerce Department regularly publishes two useful reports, *Foreign Economic Trends and Their Implications for the United States* (semiannual) and *Overseas Business Reports* (annual), that discuss marketing activities in more than 100 countries. The Department of State offers commercial guides to almost every country in the world, compiled by the local embassies. Other government sources include state trade offices, small business development centers, and U.S. embassies in various nations.

When conducting international research, companies have to be prepared to deal with both language issues—communicating their message in the most effective way—and cultural issues—capturing local citizens' interests while avoiding missteps that could unintentionally offend them. Companies also need to take a good look at a country's business environment, including political and economic conditions, local trade regulations, and the potential for short- and long-term growth. Many marketers recommend tapping local researchers to investigate foreign markets.

Businesses may need to adjust their data collection methods for primary research in other countries because some methods do not easily transfer across national frontiers. Face-to-face interviewing, for instance, remains the most common method for conducting primary research outside the U.S.

While mail surveys are a common data collection method in developed countries, they are useless in many other nations because of low literacy rates, unreliable mail service, and a lack of address lists. Telephone interviews may also not be suitable in other countries, especially those where many people do not have phones.

Marketers sometimes use foreign countries as test markets prior to global product rollouts. Citicorp chose Japan to test the use of mobile phones for electronic commerce because of the high penetration of cellular technology in that country.[29]

Businesses entering new markets often contract with marketing research firms based in the countries they want to study. Also, a growing number of international research firms offer experience in conducting global studies. For example, through alliances between leading U.S. and European research companies, NOP World offers access to integrated information from multiple sources. As Figure 7.8 shows, clients receive custom research specific to industries ranging from automotive and healthcare to finance and high-tech.

COMPUTER TECHNOLOGY IN MARKETING RESEARCH

In a world of rapid change, the ability to quickly gather and analyze business intelligence can create a substantial strategic advantage. As noted earlier, computer databases provide a wealth of data for marketing research, whether they are maintained outside the company or designed specifically to gather important facts about its customers. Chapter 6 explored how companies are leveraging internal databases and customer relationship management technology as a means of developing long-term relationships with customers. This section addresses three important uses of computer technology related to marketing research—the marketing information system (MIS), marketing decision support system (MDSS), and data mining.

<interactive>**learning goal**

CHAPTER OBJECTIVE #7: OUTLINE IMPORTANT USES OF COMPUTER TECHNOLOGY IN MARKETING RESEARCH.

The Marketing Information System (MIS)

In the past, many marketing managers complained that their information problems resulted from too much rather than too little information. Reams of data were difficult to use, not always relevant, and almost impossible to find. Modern technological advances have made constraints like these obsolete.

A *marketing information system (MIS)* is a planned, computer-based system designed to provide decision makers with a continuous flow of information relevant to their areas of responsibility. A component of the organization's overall management information system (also often called an *MIS*), a marketing information system deals specifically with marketing data and issues.

A well-constructed MIS serves as a company's nerve center, continually monitoring the market environment—both inside and outside the organization—and providing instantaneous information. Marketers are able to store data for later use, classify and analyze that data, and retrieve it easily when needed.

The Marketing Decision Support System (MDSS)

A *marketing decision support system (MDSS)* consists of software that helps users quickly obtain and apply information in a way that supports marketing decisions. Taking MIS one step further, it allows managers to explore and make connections between such varying information as the state of the market, consumer behavior, sales forecasts, competitors' actions, and environmental changes. An MDSS can create simulations or models to illustrate the likely results of changes in marketing strategies or market conditions.

While an MIS provides raw data, an MDSS develops this data into business intelligence—information useful for decision making. For example, an MIS might provide a list of product sales from the previous day. The manager could use an MDSS to transform this raw data into graphs illustrating sales trends or reports estimating the impacts of specific decisions, such as raising prices or expanding into new regions.

FIGURE 7.8

Marketing Research on a Global Scale

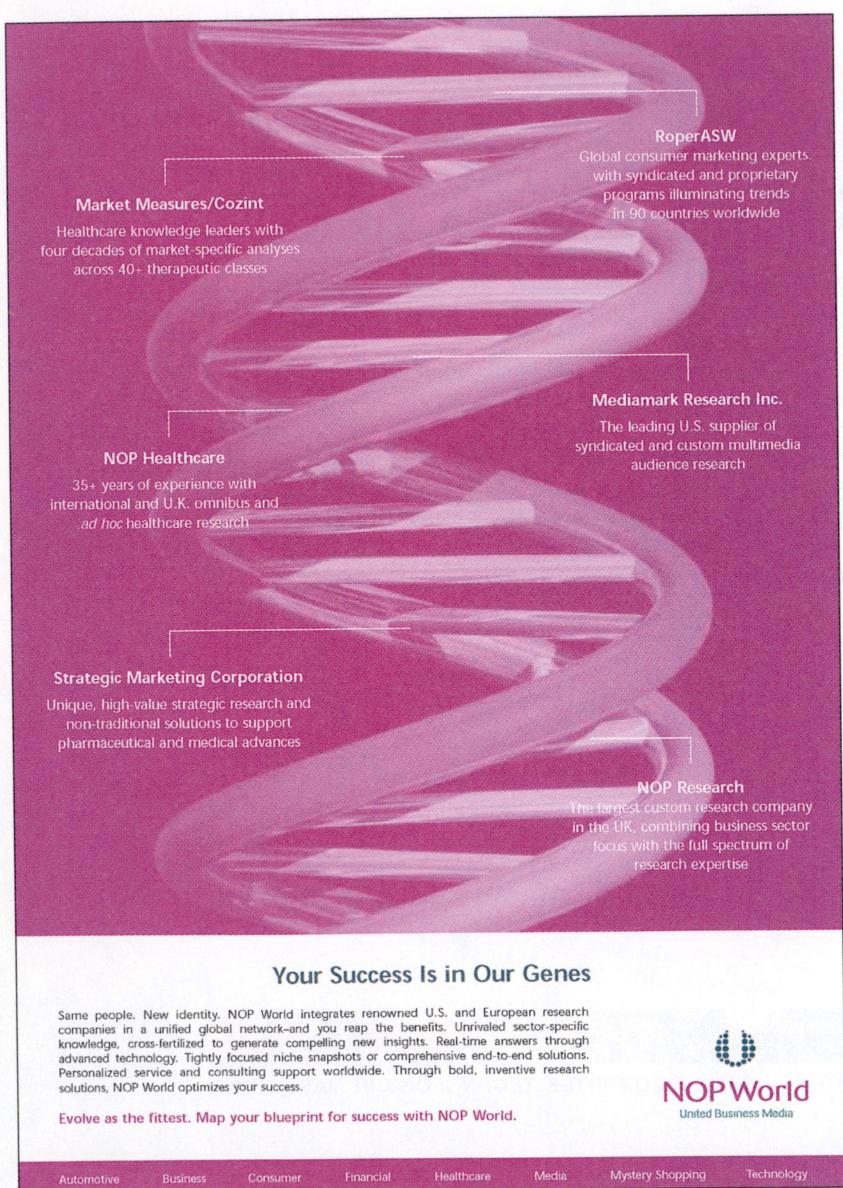

Data Mining

Data mining is the process of searching through customer files to detect patterns. The data is stored in a huge database called a data warehouse. Software for the marketing decision support system is often associated with the data warehouse and is used to mine data. Once marketers identify patterns and connections, they use this intelligence to check the effectiveness of strategy options.

Data mining is an efficient way to sort through huge amounts of data and to make sense of that data. It helps marketers create customer profiles, pinpoint reasons for customer loyalty or the lack thereof, analyze the potential returns on changes in pricing or promotion, and forecast sales. Wal-Mart, for example, mines its point-of-sale data for insights into shoppers' buying habits. By examining data, the retailer can tell which products are purchased together and drive up sales of both items through store placement or special offers.[30]

Advances in data mining applications allow for real-time analysis of data flows. NonObvious Relationship Awareness (NORA) software from Systems Research & Development (SRD) was devised to help casinos identify nonobvious relationships between data from multiple sources. For example, using real-time analysis, the software might discover that a job applicant shares a telephone number with a known criminal and issue an immediate alert to the hiring manager. Given an unexpected boost due to the September 11 terrorist attacks, NORA recently received funding from the CIA to create plug-ins that would help identify potential terrorists. Using streaming technology that scans data in real time, the software might discover that a passenger buying a ticket at an airline counter recently purchased controlled explosive materials. An alert would go out before the passenger could board a plane.[31]

Sometimes the associations revealed by data mining can be unexpected as well as enlightening. Camelot Music Holdings identified a group of customers aged 65-plus who tended to buy lots of classical music, jazz tunes, and movies. Surprisingly, though, Camelot found that a large percentage of them were also buying rap and alternative music. Further analysis of the data revealed that they were buying gifts for their grandchildren.[32]

SALES FORECASTING

A basic building block of a marketing plan is a **sales forecast,** an estimate of a firm's revenue for a specified future period. Sales forecasts play major roles in new-product decisions, production scheduling, financial planning, inventory planning and procurement, distribution, and human-resource planning. An inaccurate forecast may lead to incorrect decisions in each of these areas. Marketing research techniques are used to deliver effective sales forecasts. A sales forecast is also an important tool for marketing control because it sets standards against which to measure actual performance. Without such standards, no comparisons can be made.

<interactive>**learning goal**

CHAPTER OBJECTIVE #8: IDENTIFY THE MAJOR TYPES OF FORECASTING METHODS AND EXPLAIN THE STEPS IN THE FORECASTING PROCESS.

Planners rely on short-run, intermediate, and long-run sales forecasts. A short-run forecast usually covers a period of up to one year, an intermediate forecast covers one to five years, and a long-run forecast extends beyond five years. Although sales forecasters practice dozens of techniques to divine the future—ranging from computer simulations to studying trends identified by futurists—their methods fall into two broad categories: qualitative and quantitative forecasting.

Qualitative forecasting techniques rely on subjective data that reports opinions rather than exact historical data. *Quantitative forecasting* methods, by contrast, use statistical computations such as trend extensions based on past data, computer simulations, and econometric models. As Table 7.1 shows, each method has benefits and limitations. Consequently, most organizations combine techniques.

Qualitative Forecasting Techniques

Planners apply qualitative forecasting methods when they want judgmental or subjective indicators. Qualitative forecasting techniques include the jury of executive opinion, Delphi technique, sales force composite, and survey of buyer intentions.

Jury of Executive Opinion The technique called the **jury of executive opinion** combines and averages the outlooks of top executives from such areas as finance, production, marketing, and purchasing. Top managers bring the following capabilities to the process: experience and knowledge about situations that influence sales, open-minded attitudes toward the future, and awareness of the bases for their judgments. This quick and inexpensive method generates good forecasts for sales and new-product development. It works best for short-run forecasting.

Delphi Technique Like the jury of executive opinion, the **Delphi technique** solicits opinions from several people, but it also gathers input from experts outside the firm, such as university researchers and scientists, rather than relying completely on company executives. It is most appropriately used to predict long-run issues, such as technological breakthroughs, that could affect future sales and the market potential for new products.

The Delphi technique works as follows: A firm selects a panel of experts and sends each a questionnaire relating to a future event. After combining and averaging the answers, the firm develops another questionnaire based on these results and sends it back to the same people. The process continues until it identifies a consensus of opinion. Although firms have successfully used Delphi to predict future technological breakthroughs, the method is both expensive and time-consuming.

TABLE 7.1

Benefits and Limitations of Various Forecasting Techniques

TECHNIQUES	BENEFITS	LIMITATIONS
Qualitative Methods		
Jury of executive opinion	Opinions come from executives in many different departments; quick; inexpensive	Managers may lack sufficient knowledge and experience to make meaningful predictions
Delphi technique	Group of experts can accurately predict long-term events such as technological breakthroughs	Time-consuming; expensive
Sales force composite	Salespeople have expert customer, product, and competitor knowledge; quick; inexpensive	Inaccurate forecasts may result from low estimates of salespeople concerned about their influence on quotas
Survey of buyer intentions	Useful in predicting short-term and intermediate sales for firms that serve only a few customers	Intentions to buy may not result in actual purchases; time-consuming; expensive
Quantitative Methods		
Market test	Provides realistic information on actual purchases rather than on intent to buy	Alerts competition to new product plans; time-consuming; expensive
Trend analysis	Quick; inexpensive; effective with stable customer demand and environment	Assumes the future will continue the past; ignores environmental changes
Exponential smoothing	Same benefits as trend analysis, but emphasizes more recent data	Same limitations as trend analysis, but not as severe due to emphasis on recent data

Sales Force Composite The **sales force composite** technique develops forecasts based on the belief that organization members closest to the marketplace—those with specialized product, customer, and competitor knowledge—offer the best insights concerning short-term future sales. It typically works from the bottom up. Management consolidates salespeople's estimates first at the district level, then at the regional level, and finally nationwide to obtain an aggregate forecast of sales that reflects all three levels.

The sales force composite approach has some weaknesses, however. Since salespeople recognize the role of their sales forecasts in determining sales quotas for their territories, they are likely to make conservative estimates. Moreover, their narrow perspectives from within their limited geographic territories may prevent them from considering the impact on sales of trends developing in other territories, forthcoming technological innovations, or the major changes in marketing strategies. Consequently, the sales force composite gives the best forecasts in combination with other techniques.

Survey of Buyer Intentions A *survey of buyer intentions* gathers input through mail-in questionnaires, online feedback, telephone polls, and personal interviews to determine the purchasing intentions of a representative group of present and potential customers. This method suits firms that serve limited numbers of customers. This method often proves impractical for those with millions of customers. Also, buyer surveys gather useful information only when customers willingly reveal their buying intentions. Moreover, customer intentions do not necessarily translate into actual purchases. These surveys may help a firm to predict short-run or intermediate sales, but they employ time-consuming and expensive methods.

Quantitative Forecasting Techniques

Quantitative techniques attempt to eliminate the subjectiveness of the qualitative methods. They include such methods as market tests, trend analysis, and exponential smoothing.

Market Tests One quantitative technique, the *market test,* frequently helps planners in assessing consumer responses to new-product offerings. The procedure typically begins by establishing a small number of test markets to gauge consumer responses to a new product under actual marketplace conditions. Market tests also permit experimenters to evaluate the effects of different prices, alternative promotional strategies, and other marketing mix variations by comparing results among different test markets.

Verizon Communications recently conducted a limited test in the Boston area to find out whether it could increase overall revenues from pay phones by charging 10 cents rather than 50 cents for a one-minute call. Verizon wanted to see if it could win back business from cell phones if the price was right.[33]

The primary advantage of market tests is the realism that they provide for the marketer. On the other hand, these expensive and time-consuming experiments may also communicate marketing plans to competitors before a firm introduces a product to the total market.

Trend Analysis **Trend analysis** develops forecasts for future sales by analyzing the historical relationship between sales and time. It implicitly assumes that the collective causes of past sales will continue to exert similar influence in the future. When historical data is available, planners can quickly and inexpensively complete trend analysis. Software programs can calculate the average annual increment of change for the available sales data. This average increment of change is then projected into the future to come up with the sales forecast. So, if the sales of a firm have been growing $15.3 million on average per year, this amount of sales could be added to last year's sales total to arrive at next year's forecast.

Of course, trend analysis cannot be used if historical data is not available, as in new-product forecasting. Also, trend analysis makes the dangerous assumption that future events will continue in the same manner as the past. Any variations in the determinants of future sales will cause deviations from the forecast. In other words, this method gives reliable forecasts during periods of steady growth and stable demand. If conditions change, predictions based on trend analysis may become worthless. For this reason, forecasters have applied more sophisticated techniques and complex, new forecasting models to anticipate the effects of various possible changes in the future.

Exponential Smoothing A more sophisticated method of trend analysis, the **exponential smoothing** technique, weighs each year's sales data, giving greater weight to results from the most recent years. Otherwise, the statistical approach used in trend analysis is applied here. For example, last year's sales might receive a 1.5 weight, while sales data from two years ago could get a 1.4 weighting. Exponential smoothing is considered the most commonly used quantitative forecasting technique.

STRATEGIC IMPLICATIONS OF MARKETING IN THE 21ST CENTURY

Marketing research can help an organization develop effective marketing strategies. Approximately 75 percent of new products eventually fail to attract enough buyers to remain viable. Why? A major reason is the seller's failure to understand market needs.

Consider, for example, the hundreds of dot-com companies that have gone under. A characteristic shared by all of those failing businesses is that virtually none of them were founded on sound marketing research. Very few used marketing research techniques to evaluate product potential and even fewer studied consumer responses after the ventures were initiated. While research might not have prevented every dot-com meltdown, it may have helped a few of those businesses survive the waning economy in which they were launched.[34]

Marketing research ideally matches new products to potential customers. Marketers also conduct research to analyze sales of their own and competitors' products, to gauge the performance of existing products, to guide the development of promotional campaigns and product enhancements, and to develop and refine products. All of these activities enable marketers to fine-tune their marketing strategies and reach customers more effectively and efficiently.

Marketing researchers have at their disposal a broad range of techniques with which to collect both quantitative and qualitative data on customers, their lifestyles, behaviors, attitudes, and perceptions. Vast amounts of data can be rapidly collected, accessed, interpreted, and applied to improve all aspects of business operations. Because of customer relationship management technology, that information is no longer generalized to profile groups of customers—it can be analyzed to help marketers understand each and every customer.

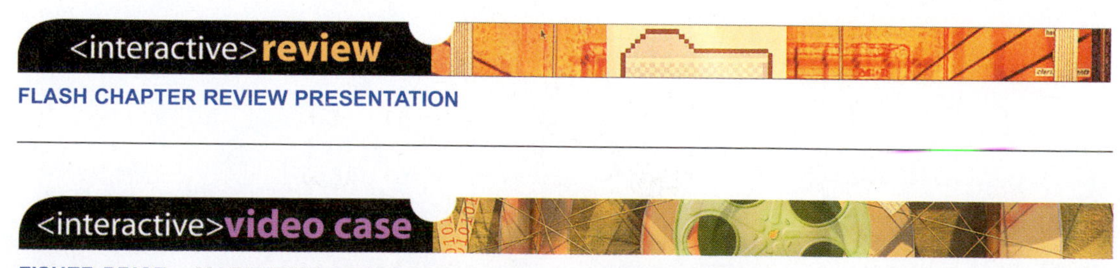

FLASH CHAPTER REVIEW PRESENTATION

FISHER-PRICE: MARKETING RESEARCH IS MORE THAN CHILD'S PLAY

<interactive>game

QUIZ BOWL

<interactive>video case

KRISPY KREME CONTINUING VIDEO CASE: TECHNOLOGY HELPS KRISPY KREME SERVE UP TREATS

endofchaptermaterial

- Summary of Chapter Objectives
- Chapter Outline
- Key Terms
- Review Questions
- Projects and Teamwork Exercises
- 'netWork
- Crossword Puzzles
- Case 7.1: Using Demand Management Software to Predict What Customers Want and When

Take the Post-Test to assess your overall understanding of the key ideas in this chapter. The Post-Test provides a comprehensive selection of exam-style questions addressing the main topics and concepts of the chapter. At the completion of each Post-Test, you will receive a score and instructive feedback on how you answered each question, and a direct link to the part of the chapter addressed in the question. Take the Post-Test as often as you need to—a record of your progress for each attempt is kept for you to revisit and gauge your improvement. And each Post-Test is randomly generated, so every attempt is new.

Post-Test

PART 3

Market Segmentation and Customer Behavior

CHAPTER 8

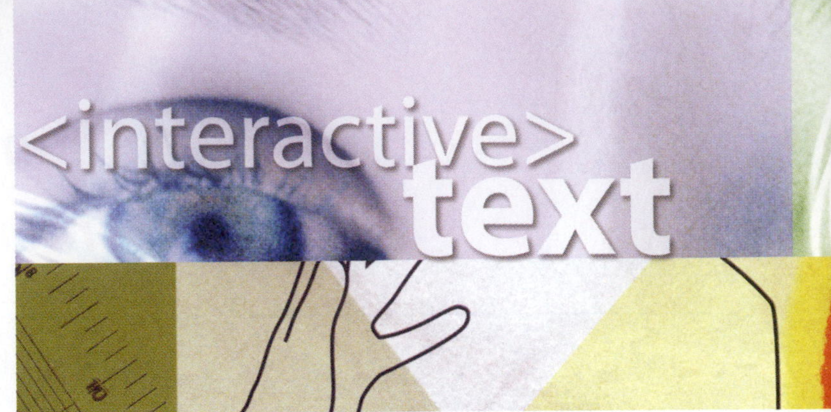

Market Segmentation, Targeting, and Positioning

Chapter Objectives

1. Identify the essential components of a market.
2. Outline the role of market segmentation in developing a marketing strategy.
3. Describe the criteria necessary for effective segmentation.
4. Explain each of the four bases for segmenting consumer markets.
5. Identify the steps in the market segmentation process.
6. Discuss four basic strategies for reaching target markets.
7. Summarize the types of positioning strategies.
8. Explain the reasons for positioning and repositioning products.

Take the Pre-Test to assess your initial knowledge of the key ideas in this chapter. The Pre-Test provides exam-style questions addressing the main topics and concepts of the chapter. At the completion of each Pre-Test, you will receive a score and instructive feedback on how you answered each question, and a direct link to the part of the chapter addressed in the question. Take the Pre-Test as often as you need to—a record of your progress for each attempt is kept for you to revisit and gauge your improvement.

MEN AND WOMEN TEE OFF WITH THE PRECEPT MC LADY

Golf is a favorite pastime of many men and women—young and old. Golfers spend a lot of money on their sport. They buy golf clubs (some golf devotees buy a new set every couple of years), bags, gloves, golf carts, and lots of golf apparel. But perhaps the most important purchase for those who take golf seriously (and few long-term golfers do not) is a golf ball.

So let's consider the hottest golf ball to come along in recent years. A couple of years back, Precept/ Bridgestone Sports developed a golf ball it called the Precept MC Lady. Advertised as a "longer, softer" ball, it was targeted for women golfers—just like women's clubs, apparel, and other gear. But it sat on pro shop shelves until a couple of top players—pro Bill Loeffler and amateur Sam Farlow—won some significant tournaments with the ball. Now shops can't keep them in stock, and it's not just because women are clamoring for the balls. Men have discovered their qualities also. Golfers have also discovered that "The Lady"—as the ball is now called—is more affordable than some of the other top balls—roughly half of what Titleist Pro V1's go for. Interestingly, 98 percent of sales of the MC Lady are now to men.

The demand for "The Lady" is so great that Precept has had four factories manufacturing balls around the clock, and the company still has a monthlong backorder list. Previously, about 14,000 balls sold in a year; today, it's more like 150,000 a month, which represents an increase of 500 percent in one year, mostly owing to word of mouth through the golf community. This crossover selling is significant in a sport with a history of segregating everything from courses to gear. Pro golfer Bill Loeffler wants everyone to know that he uses a ball designed for women because he thinks it's the best. "I put a pink dot above the MC [on the ball] just to let people know where I stood," he says about his use of the ball in tournament play. For those male golfers who can't quite go with the pink dot, Precept sells the Extra Distance—the same ball in "a nice, manly blue box," says marketing director Stephen Graham. A hallmark of good marketing is giving the customer what he or she wants.[1]

CHAPTER OVERVIEW

Each of us is unique. We come from different backgrounds, have different household makeups, different interests and goals. Even best friends may shop at different stores, attend different sporting or cultural events, take different courses. Consider sports, as we did in the opening vignette. A wide variety of sports is available—from golf to hang gliding, basketball to billiards, skiing to snorkeling. Some of us like to participate in our favorite sports; others prefer to be spectators. Depending on where you live, you may be loyal to certain teams—say, the Boston Red Sox or the Seattle Mariners. Your geographic location may also dictate which sports you are exposed to. If you live in Colorado, you might like to hike or ski. If you live in Hawaii, you might be an excellent swimmer or surfer. All of these factors make up a market. A **market** is composed of people or institutions with sufficient purchasing power, authority, and willingness to buy. And marketers must use their expertise to understand the market for a good or service, whether it's tickets for a baseball game—or golf balls, as illustrated in the chapter opening vignette.

<interactive>**learning goal**

CHAPTER OBJECTIVE #1: IDENTIFY THE ESSENTIAL COMPONENTS OF A MARKET.

Most markets likely include consumers with different lifestyles, backgrounds, and income levels. It is unusual for a single marketing mix strategy to attract all sectors of a market. By identifying, evaluating, and selecting a target market to pursue, marketers are able to develop more efficient and effective marketing strategies. The **target market** for a product is the specific segment of consumers most likely to purchase a particular product.

As Chapter 4 illustrated, marketing now takes place on a global basis more than ever, incorporating many target markets. To identify those markets, marketers must determine useful ways for segmenting different populations and communicating with them successfully. This chapter discusses useful ways to accomplish this, explaining the steps of the market segmentation process, and surveying strategies for reaching target markets. Finally, it will look at the role of positioning in developing a marketing strategy.

TYPES OF MARKETS

Products are usually classified as either consumer products or business products. **Consumer products** are those bought by ultimate consumers for personal use. **Business products** are goods and services purchased for use either directly or indirectly in the production of other goods and services for resale. Most goods and services purchased by individual consumers—books, cleaning services, and clothes, for example—are considered consumer products. Rubber and raw cotton are examples of items generally purchased by manufacturers and are, therefore, classified as business products. Goodyear buys rubber to manufacture tires; textile manufacturers such as Burlington Industries convert raw cotton into cloth.

Sometimes a single product can serve different uses. Tires purchased for the family car constitute consumer products; but tires purchased by General Motors to be mounted during production of its Chevy Suburban truck are business products because they become part of another product destined for resale. (Some marketers add another term, *commercial products,* for business products like legal services that do not contribute directly to the production of other goods.) If you want to determine the classification of items, just think about who is going to buy the product and why (or how it will be used). Chapters 8 and 9 focus on segmentation and buying behavior in consumer markets. Chapter 10 will cover business-to-business markets.

THE ROLE OF MARKET SEGMENTATION

In today's business world, the diversification of people causes too many variables in consumer needs, preferences, and purchasing power to attract all consumers within a single marketing mix. That's not to say that firms must actually change products to meet the needs of different market segments—although they often do—but they must attempt to identify the factors that affect purchase decisions and then group consumers according to the presence or absence of these factors. Finally, they adjust marketing strategies to meet the needs of each group.

<interactive>learning goal

CHAPTER OBJECTIVE #2: OUTLINE THE ROLE OF MARKET SEGMENTATION IN DEVELOPING A MARKETING STRATEGY.

Consider cars. Unlike nearly a century ago, when Henry Ford pronounced that customers could order any color of car they liked—as long as it was black—there is a make, model, and color for every taste and budget. But auto manufacturers need to adjust their messages for different markets. And smart marketers are looking toward markets that show growth, such as the U.S. Hispanic population. In recent years, automakers such as Toyota and DaimlerChrysler have created ad campaigns directed specifically to the Hispanic community, especially in the Hispanic media, as illustrated in Figure 8.1.[2]

The division of the total market into smaller, relatively homogeneous groups is called **market segmentation.** Both profit-oriented and not-for-profit organizations practice market segmentation.

'NET EX: MARKET SEGMENTATION

Criteria for Effective Segmentation

Segmentation doesn't automatically guarantee success in the marketing arena; instead, it is a tool for marketers to use. Effectiveness depends on the following four basic requirements.

<interactive>**learning goal**

CHAPTER OBJECTIVE #3: DESCRIBE THE CRITERIA NECESSARY FOR EFFECTIVE SEGMENTATION.

> **Briefly Speaking**
>
> In every instance, we found that the best-run companies stay as close to their customers as humanly possible.
>
> *Thomas J. Peters (b. 1942) American business writer*

First, the market segment must present measurable purchasing power and size. A perfect example is women. With jobs, incomes, and decision making power, women consumers represent a hefty amount of purchasing power. According to some experts, women make up half the potential market for many new electronic products.[3]

Second, marketers must find a way to promote effectively to and serve the market segment. Since women are more likely than men to think twice about a technology purchase—and often care about style and color as well as functionality—marketers need to find different ways to appeal to women. Catherine Markman, director of Evins Communications' technology division, asserts that nearly any electronic device could be sold to women with the right kind of marketing.[4]

Third, marketers must then identify segments that are sufficiently large to give them good profit potential. As mentioned earlier, citizens of Hispanic descent make up one of the fastest-growing populations in the U.S. Forty-two percent of the population of New Mexico and 32 percent of California's and Texas's populations are Hispanic.[5] General Mills pays special attention to this market not only with advertising and promotion but also with Betty Crocker products targeted for Hispanic tastes. Some of these foods include *arroz con leche* (rice pudding) and *flan* (caramel custard), as illustrated in Figure 8.2. "We developed these products with the Latino palate in mind," says Michelle Freedman, marketing manager. "Our strategy is now to put more resources behind ethnic-specific products." Kraft and Nabisco also sell similar products such as Kraft's Jell-O American Flan and Nabisco's Royal Flan.[6]

FIGURE 8.1

Toyota's Attempt to Attract Hispanic Consumers

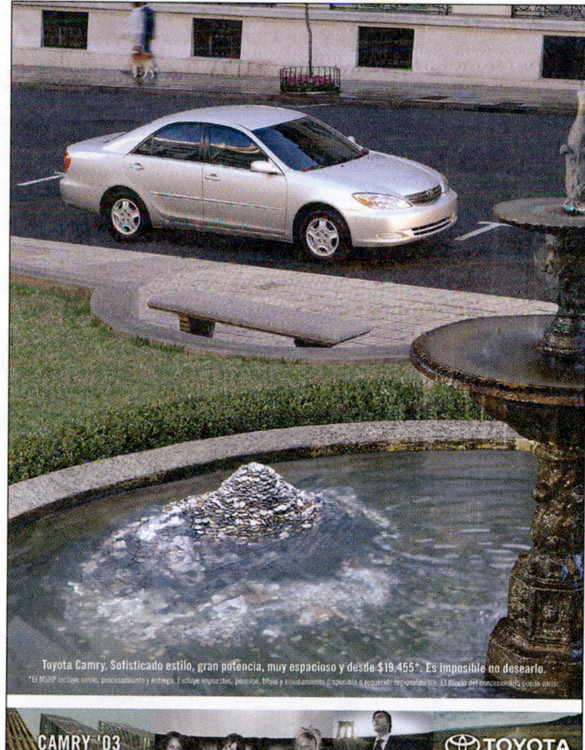

And fourth, the firm must aim for segments that match its marketing capabilities. Targeting a large number of niche markets can be an expensive, complex, and inefficient strategy; so smaller firms may decide to stick with a particular niche, or target market. Zephwear.com creates footwear for children's and youth sports teams. Its special appeal is that consumers can go online to design their own logo cards that slide inside a plastic insert in the tongue flap of each shoe. Kids love it, and the cost of this customization is low to the company; it is also part of the firm's marketing strategy. Furthermore, the shoes themselves are relatively inexpensive at about $35 a pair.[7]

SEGMENTING CONSUMER MARKETS

Market segmentation attempts to isolate the traits that distinguish a certain group of consumers from the overall market. An understanding of the group's characteristics—such as age, sex, geographical location, income, and expenditure patterns—plays a vital role in developing a successful marketing strategy. In most cases, marketers seek to pinpoint a number of factors affecting buying behavior in the target segment. For example, toy manufacturers such as Ideal, Hasbro, Mattel, and Kenner consider not only birthrate trends but also changes in income levels and expenditure patterns to successfully market their products. In trying to attract new students, colleges and universities are affected by the number of graduating high-school seniors and also by changing attitudes toward the value of a college education and trends in enrollment of older adults. Also, few, if any, marketers identify totally homogeneous segments, in which all potential customers are alike; they always encounter some differences among members of a target group.

<interactive>**learning goal**

CHAPTER OBJECTIVE #4: EXPLAIN EACH OF THE FOUR BASES FOR SEGMENTING CONSUMER MARKETS.

The four common bases for segmenting consumer markets are geographic segmentation, demographic segmentation, psychographic segmentation, and product-related segmentation. These segmentation

FIGURE 8.2

Betty Crocker Food Products Targeted for Hispanic Tastes

approaches can give important guidance for marketing strategies, provided they identify significant differences in buying behavior.

Geographic Segmentation

Marketers have practiced **geographic segmentation**—dividing an overall market into homogeneous groups on the basis of their locations—for hundreds of years. Geographic location does not ensure that all consumers in a location will make the same buying decisions, but this segmentation approach does help in identifying some general patterns. The 286 million people who live in the U.S. are not scattered evenly across the country. Instead, they are concentrated in major metropolitan areas. New York City is the largest U.S. city, with 8 million citizens. Los Angeles, Chicago, Houston, and Philadelphia follow. The states with the most residents are California (34 million), Texas (21 million), New York (19 million), Florida (16 million), and Illinois (12 million). By contrast, only about 1 million citizens live in New Hampshire, with about half that in Vermont.[8]

As discussed in Chapter 4, a look at the worldwide population distribution illustrates why so many firms are pursuing customers around the globe. As in the U.S., many of these people live in urban environments. The two metropolitan areas with the world's largest populations, Tokyo and Mexico City, dwarf New York City.

Population size alone, however, may not be reason enough for a business to expand into a specific country. Businesses also need to look at a wide variety of economic variables. Some businesses may decide to cluster together countries that share similar population and product-use patterns instead of treating each country as an independent segment. This grouping is taking place with greater frequency throughout the European Union as the currency and trade laws are unified.

While population numbers indicate the overall size of a market, other geographic indicators such as job growth can also give useful guidance to marketers, depending on the type of products they sell. Food companies might look for geographic segments with large populations because food is an essential product used by everyone. Automobile manufacturers, on the other hand, might segment geographic regions by household income because it is an important factor in the purchase of a new car.

Geographic areas also vary in population-migration patterns. The U.S., for example, has traditionally been a mobile society. About one of every six Americans moves each year. However, this figure is down from one out of five a few decades ago. The slowdown has resulted from changes such as increased home ownership.

U.S. census data also indicates two major population shifts: migration toward the Sunbelt states of the Southeast and Southwest and toward the West. Researchers expect this trend to continue. Between now and 2020, the states expected to experience the fastest population growth are Nevada, Hawaii, California, and Washington.[9]

As people migrate from one geographic area to another, regional consumer tastes often change. Catfish, a longtime staple in the diet of the southern U.S., is now popular in all parts of the country. By contrast, cornbread and other popular southern recipes using cornmeal are considered exotic in Great Britain, where cornmeal is available mainly through health-food stores.

The move from urban to suburban areas after World War II created a need to redefine the urban marketplace. This trend radically changed cities' traditional patterns of retailing and led to disintegration in many downtown shopping areas. It also rendered traditional city boundaries almost meaningless for marketing purposes.

In an effort to respond to these changes, the government now classifies urban data using three categories.

- A *Metropolitan Statistical Area (MSA)* is a freestanding urban area with a population in the urban center of at least 50,000 and a total MSA population of 100,000 or more. Buyers in MSAs exhibit social and economic homogeneity. They usually border on nonurbanized counties. Examples include Rochester, New York; Odessa-Midland, Texas; and Kalamazoo-Battle Creek, Michigan.[10]
- The category of *Consolidated Metropolitan Statistical Area (CMSA)* includes the country's 25 or so urban giants such as Detroit-Ann Arbor-Flint, Michigan; Los Angeles-Riverside-Orange County, California; and Philadelphia-Wilmington-Atlantic City. (Note that in the third example, three states are involved—Pennsylvania, Delaware, and New Jersey.)[11] A CMSA must include two or more Primary Metropolitan Statistical Areas, discussed next.
- A *Primary Metropolitan Statistical Area (PMSA)* is an urbanized county or set of counties with social and economic ties to nearby areas. PMSAs are identified within areas of 1-million- plus populations. Olympia, Washington, is part of the Seattle-Tacoma-Bremerton PMSA. Bridgeport, Connecticut, is part of the New York-Northern New Jersey-Long Island PMSA and Riverside-San Bernardino, California, is a PMSA within the Los Angeles-Riverside-Orange County PMSA.[12]

Using Geographic Segmentation Demand for some categories of goods and services can vary according to geographic region, and marketers need to be aware of how these regions differ. Most major brands get 40 to 80 percent of their sales from what are called *core regions;* elsewhere in the national marketplace, such a product is essentially a specialty brand.

Residence location within a geographic area is an important segmentation variable. City dwellers often get along fine without automobiles, whereas those who live in the suburbs or the country depend on their vehicles. Also, those who live in the suburbs spend more on lawn and garden care products than people in the city.

Climate is another important segmentation factor. Consumers in chilly, northern states, for example, eat more soup than residents in warmer, southern markets. But here's a surprise—they also eat a great deal of ice cream!

Geographic segmentation provides useful distinctions when regional preferences or needs exist. A consumer might not *want* to invest in a snowblower or flood insurance but *may* have to because of the location of his or her home. But it's important for marketers not to stop at geographic location as a segmentation method, because distinctions among consumers also exist within a geographic location. Consider those who relocate from one region to another for work or family reasons. They may bring along with them their preferences from other parts of the country. In one recent year, 19 percent of those who relocated moved to another state.[13] Using multiple segmentation variables will probably be a much better strategy for targeting a specific market.

Suburbanites spend the most on lawn and garden products.

Geographic Information System (GIS) At Domino's Pizza, Super Bowl Sunday is more than a sporting event—it is also the company's single biggest sales day of the year. As the pro football teams face off, Domino's tackles its own challenge: planning and executing timely delivery of more than 900,000 pizzas to residences throughout the country. Domino's has built its reputation as the

Oprah Winfrey lends her support to Oxygen Media.

number-one pizza delivery company in the world, which means that its delivery system must be as streamlined and efficient as possible.

Companies like Domino's traditionally obtained much of their geographic data for deliveries from statistical databases and reports. These sources do provide valuable information, but not in a format that is quick and easy to use. So Domino's invested in a geographic information system. Once used mainly by the military, a **geographic information system (GIS)** simplifies the job of analyzing marketing information by placing data in a spatial format. The result is a geographic map overlaid with digital data about consumers in a particular area.

Thanks to its GIS, Domino's delivery drivers can map in advance the best route to reaching each customer's address. Managers use the GIS to pinpoint the best locations for stores, based on purchase data and driving distances, and identify areas that are promising candidates for new stores. The system also helps them to allocate inventory more efficiently.[14]

The earliest geographic information systems were prohibitively expensive for all but the largest companies. Recent technological advances, however, have made GIS software available at a much lower cost, increasing usage among smaller firms. Like Domino's, a growing number of companies benefit from using a GIS to locate new outlets, assign sales territories, and plan distribution centers and delivery routes. Marketing researchers agree, however, that firms have not yet realized the full potential of GIS technology.

Demographic Segmentation

The most common method of market segmentation—**demographic segmentation**—defines consumer groups according to demographic variables such as gender, age, income, occupation, education, household size, and stage in the family life cycle. This approach is also sometimes called *socioeconomic segmentation.* Marketers review vast quantities of available data to complete a plan for demographic segmentation. One of the primary sources for demographic data in the U.S. is the Bureau of the Census. Marketers can obtain many of the Census Bureau's statistics online at http://www.census.gov. The following discussion considers the most commonly used demographic variables.

Segmenting by Gender Gender is an obvious variable that helps to define the markets for certain products. When segmenting by gender, marketers need to be sure they are targeting consumers correctly. As discussed earlier, women now make up about half the potential market for consumer electronics. Furthermore, during a recent holiday season, a significant percentage of women indicated that computers topped their gift wish list. But a survey conducted by the Consumer Electronics Marketing Association (CEMA) revealed that typical marketing of most technical products leaves women cold. According to Angela Gunn, a columnist for *Yahoo! Life,* women make a distinction between "appliance" technology and "accessory" technology. When shopping for an electronic appliance such as a high-end entertainment center, women want to shop around, learn the specifications, and get the best price. But when it comes to an accessory like a cell phone, color counts.[15]

Some companies market the same product successfully to both genders. Gillette markets its disposable razor Slim Twist in two colors—one for men, one for women—but it's the same razor nonetheless. "The only difference is the color," says a company product specialist.[16]

Other marketers may start by targeting one gender and then later switch to both. In fact, Gillette began producing men's razors first and then added a women's razor in 1915. While the disposable razors remain unisex in design, the nondisposables have distinctive features for each gender. The women's razors typically have larger handles and moisturizers behind the blade, whereas men's are smaller and do not contain lubricants.[17]

Even if marketers think they have targeted a gender market correctly, a product may not reach its audience. After a splashy launch, the cable-TV and Web site operator Oxygen Media failed to catch its breath—or its audience. Oxygen proclaimed that it would offer an intelligent media outlet for women and an online community of women with common interests. But initially, the project fizzled, partly because the station couldn't penetrate enough cable systems. After a year or so of languishing, Oxygen debuted on an important cable system in New York City, delivering the kinds of programs it had promised in the beginning, and reaching its target market—women. Prominent women such as Oprah Winfrey lent their support to the cable channel, and it began to turn around.[18]

Segmenting by Age Many firms identify market segments on the basis of consumers' ages. In fact, they develop some products specifically to meet the needs of people in certain age groups. Gerber Food focuses on food for infants and toddlers. Del Webb Corp. creates Sun Cities retirement communities. Warner-Lambert developed Halls Juniors cough drops for children 5 years and over. Age distribution and projected changes in each age group are important to marketers because consumer needs and wants differ notably among age groups.

Clothing retailer Limited Too targets girls between the ages of 8 and 17 by offering hip clothes and accessories that appeal to the age bracket—including fashion jewelry, glitter cosmetics, and room decorations. The company offers a range of discounts and promotions, including an offer of $5 off any purchase when a customer brings in a current report card with all passing grades. The catalog often shows groups of girls engaged in activities as friends—whether it's sports, trips to the beach, or sleepovers.

Sociologists attribute some of these differences to the *cohort effect*—the tendency of members of a generation to be influenced and bound together by significant events occurring during their key formative years, roughly 17 to 22 years of age. These events help to define the core values of the age group that eventually shape consumer preferences and behavior. Marketers have already labeled people who were in the 17–22 age bracket at the time of the terrorist attacks the *9/11 Generation.* Clearly, this group's previous priorities and values have changed. How the cohort effect for the 9/11 Generation will play out in later years remains uncertain—at least in a marketing sense.

Now let's look at two age groups whose unique characteristics have proved to be of particular importance to marketers: the boomers and the seniors. Let's start with the boomers.

Baby Boomers So-called *baby boomers*—people born from 1946 until 1965—are a popular segment to target because of their numbers. Nearly 42 percent of U.S. adults were born in this period. The values of this age group were influenced both by the Vietnam War era and the career-driven era that followed.

There is no doubt that baby boomers are a lucrative market. Experts predict that baby boomers over the age of 50 will have a total disposable income of $1 trillion within the next few years, which is why businesses like Arby's are trying to woo this group, as illustrated in the "Marketing Hits" Interactive Example. Members of the group, however, do not always behave as expected, complicating segmentation and targeting strategies. For instance, although pundits have predicted the demise of movie theaters, boomers are flocking to the cinema in record numbers.

MARKETING HIT: ARBY'S SERVES UP MARKET FRESH FOOD TO AN OLDER-TARGET MARKET

Different subgroups within this generation also complicate segmentation and targeting strategies. Some boomers put off starting families until their 40s, while others of their age have already become grandparents. Boomer grandparents are healthier and more physically active than their own grandparents were, and they expect to take an active role in their grandchildren's lives. When buying toys, for instance, they often purchase items that focus on a shared experience—games they can play with their grandchildren or craft sets they can assemble together.

Nostalgic references that remind baby boomers of their own childhood and adolescence are a popular way to target this segment. Retro toys such as Sock Monkey, a stuffed-sock simian, are big sellers at home-furnishings retailer Restoration Hardware. The catalog merchant even sells frames for record-album covers so that boomers can decorate their homes with their favorite old album covers, as shown in Figure 8.3.

Seniors Marketers also recognize a trend dubbed *the graying of America.* By 2025, Americans who are over age 65 will make up nearly 20 percent of the population. As Americans continue to live longer, the median age of the U.S. population has dramatically increased. The current median age is now 35.2 years, up from 32.8 years a decade ago.[19] And the average life expectancy in the U.S. has increased for both genders—to age 74 for men and to age 79 for women.[20] In addition, people aged 65 can expect to live an average of nearly 18 more years—to age 83.[21] It is believed that these increases in life spans are due to better medicines, healthier lifestyles, and lower infant mortality rates.[22] And instead of settling down to quiet pursuits, some seniors are opting for adventure travel trips to places like Nepal and South America.

Seniors are a powerful economic force. In the U.S., heads of households aged 55-plus control about three-quarters of the country's total financial assets. Their discretionary incomes and rates of home ownership are higher than those of any other age group. These statistics show why many marketers are targeting this group. Some refer to these prosperous consumers as WOOFS—Well-Off Older Folks. Although many seniors live on modest, fixed incomes, those who are well-off financially have both time and money to spend on leisure activities such as travel and golf. They may also be looking to purchase and furnish a retirement home.

One privilege that seniors have looked forward to since the 1950s is the senior discount—whether it's at McDonald's or on the ski slopes. But in today's slower economy, with more and more people entering the senior age group, companies are rolling back those discounts. Airlines, ski resorts, and travel companies

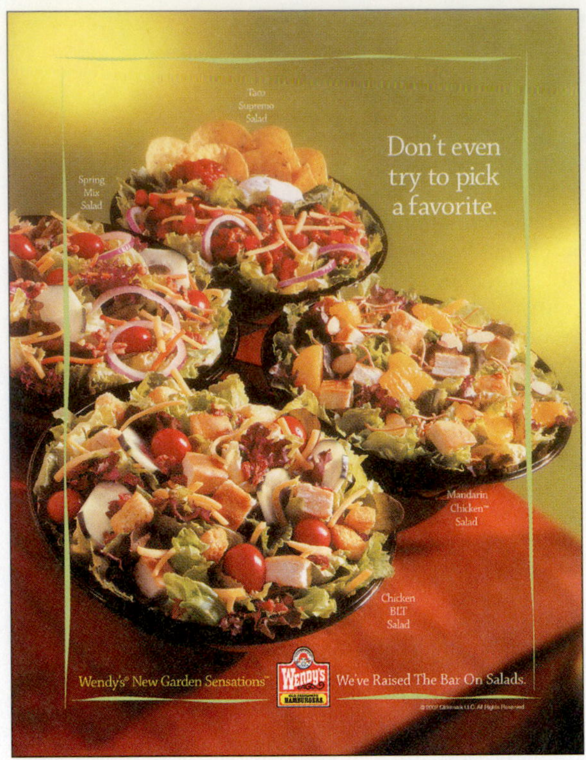

Menus at fast-food restaurants such as Wendy's, Burger King, and Arby's have changed as their marketing efforts have focused more on adults and less on children. Increased emphasis on healthy dining, coupled with an aging U.S. population, has prompted fast-food restaurants to depend less on high-calorie, high-fat mainstays such as fries and burgers.

have curtailed or discontinued senior discounts. Cable TV provider AT&T Broadband recently axed its 10 percent discount for Florida seniors. Some public utilities are reevaluating their senior discount policies. Philadelphia Gas Works estimates that it could save as much as $18 million a year if it cuts out its 20 percent senior discount. But not all marketers agree with this money-saving approach, because seniors make up such a large, affluent group. "There's a saying that today's seniors clip coupons and drive Cadillacs—they'll spend money, but only if they get a good deal," explains Sharon Brooks, an expert in senior marketing. "Discounts are still a very attractive marketing tool."[23]

Segmenting by Ethnic Group According to the Census Bureau, America's racial and ethnic makeup is changing. Because of comparatively high immigration and birthrates among some minority groups, the Census Bureau projects that by 2050, nearly half of the population will belong to nonwhite minority groups. Figure 8.4 shows the breakdown of minority populations in the U.S. in 2000.

The three largest and fastest-growing racial/ethnic groups are African Americans, Hispanics, and Asian Americans. From a marketer's perspective, it is important to note that spending by these groups is rising at a faster pace than for U.S. households in general.

African Americans and Hispanics are currently the largest racial/ethnic minority groups in the U.S.—some 13 percent of the U.S. population each. African-American numbers are projected to grow to 45 million by 2020.[24] But the Hispanic population's growth rate is four times that of the African-American population and nine times the growth rate for whites. During the 1990s, nearly 2 million people immigrated to the U.S. from Mexico alone. Census projections predict that Hispanics will continue to widen their lead over African Americans through 2020.[25]

Many marketers have focused their efforts on the Hispanic population in the U.S. during the last few years, from fast-food restaurants to toy manufacturers, as discussed in the "Marketing

FIGURE 8.3

Album Frames: Marketing Nostalgia to Baby Boomers

FIGURE 8.4

Breakdown of U.S. Minority Populations

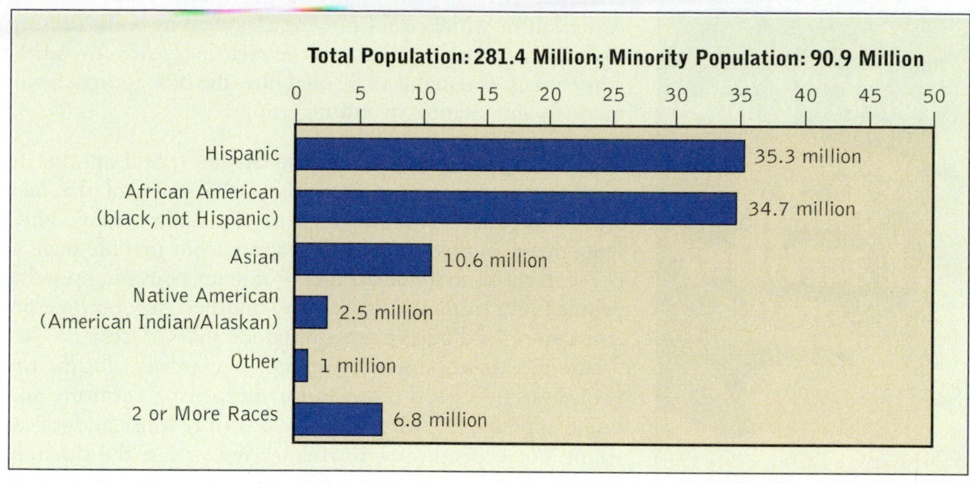

Note: Numbers have been rounded. Information taken from the 2000 Census.
Source: Data from Roger Simon and Angie Cannon, "An Amazing Journey," *U.S. News & World Report,* August 6, 2001, p. 12.

Hits" Interactive Example titled "Marketers Make a Hit with Hispanics." Food manufacturers and supermarkets such as General Mills, Bestfoods, and Pathmark have not only tailored certain products to Hispanic tastes, they have sponsored cultural events designed to draw Hispanics into the marketplace. Last year Bestfoods grocery division took several of its best-selling brands to Fiesta Broadway in Los Angeles. Integrating with its parent company's sponsorship of Major League Soccer (a popular sport among the Hispanic population), promotion of the foods featured soccer themes and interactive games.[26] Knorr Foods has sponsored sweepstakes contests as one way of making its products better known in the Hispanic community. As shown in Figure 8.5, the grand-prize winner won a trip for four to the Bahamas.

MARKETING HIT: MARKETERS MAKE A HIT WITH HISPANICS

Although Asian Americans and Pacific Islanders represent a smaller segment than either the African-American or Hispanic populations, they are the fastest-growing segment of the U.S. population. The Census Bureau estimates that this group will grow to 23 million by 2020. Asian Americans are an attractive target for marketers because they also have the fastest-growing income. Their average income per household is considerably higher than that of any other ethnic group, including whites.[27]

The Asian-American population is concentrated in fewer geographic areas than are other ethnic markets. A particularly high concentration of Asian Americans live in California. Companies can lower their costs of reaching Asian-American consumers by advertising in appropriate local markets rather than on a national scale. Honda's first Asian-American advertising campaign, called "Calligraphy," was launched in Los Angeles.[28]

Another important minority group is Native Americans, whose current population numbers about 2 million. Native American groups have begun to establish economic and political clout, which marketers take seriously. One way these groups have gained economic power is through the establishment of entertainment centers like Foxwoods—a huge resort and casino in Connecticut that is owned and operated by the Mashantucket Pequot Tribal Nation (*Pequot* means "the fox people"). Thousands of tourists visit Foxwoods each year to stay in the 1,400 guest rooms and suites, play golf, enjoy live entertainment, and gamble.[29] The entertainment centers that Native Americans own often are economic dynamos in some of the more rural locations in which they operate.

Researchers have identified differences in consumer preferences, motivations, and buying habits among different ethnic and racial segments. Increasingly, businesses are targeting their marketing strategies to more closely match those differences. All three of the major greeting-card manufacturers have launched ethnically oriented card lines. Chapter 9 will take a closer look at how ethnic and racial culture affects consumer behavior.

U.S. residents now have the option of identifying themselves as more than one racial category. Marketers need to be aware of this change. In some ways, it benefits marketers by making racial statistics

FIGURE 8.5

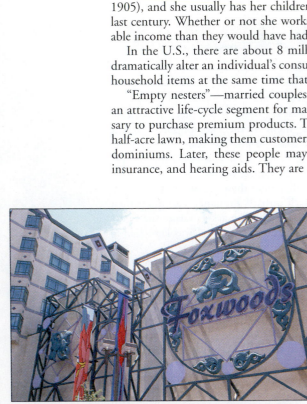

Using Celebrities to Market to the Hispanic Community

more accurate—respondents are no longer forced to place themselves in arbitrary categories. On the other hand, marketers may find it difficult to compare the new statistics with data from earlier censuses. For example, families previously reported as African American or white could now be classified as both, causing them to be tabulated separately from the exclusively African-American or white totals. It remains to be seen how the new approach will affect market segmentation by ethnic groups.

EN ESTAS FIESTAS,
PARTICIPA EN EL CONCURSO
Disfruta y Gana con el Sabor Familiar de Knorr
Knorr
Gran Premio
Un crucero a las Bahamas para 4 personas
30 Primeros Premios
Tarjetas de $100 para llamadas telefónicas de larga distancia
50 Segundos Premios
Subscripciones de un año a "TVyNovelas" y "Vanidades"
FORMULARIO DE PARTICIPACION
CONCURSO Disfruta y Gana con el Sabor Familiar de Knorr
Gran Premio: Un crucero a las Bahamas para 4 personas

Segmenting by Family Life Cycle Stages Still another form of demographic segmentation employs the stages of the *family life cycle*—the process of family formation and dissolution. The underlying theme of this segmentation approach is that life stage, not age per se, is the primary determinant of many consumer purchases. As people move from one life stage to another, they become potential consumers for different types of goods and services.

An unmarried person setting up an apartment for the first time is likely to be a good prospect for inexpensive furniture and small home appliances. This consumer probably must budget carefully, ruling out expenditures on luxury items. On the other hand, a young, single person who is still living at home will probably have more money to spend on goods such as sporting and entertainment equipment, personal-care items, and clothing. As couples marry, their consumer profiles change. Couples without children are frequent buyers of personalized gifts, power tools, furniture, and homes. Eating out and travel may also be part of their lifestyles.

The birth of a first child changes any couple's consumer profile considerably; parents must buy cribs, changing tables, baby clothes, baby food, car seats, and similar products. Parents usually spend less on the children who follow the first because they have already bought many essential items for the first child. Today, the average woman gives birth to two children (as opposed to four children in 1905), and she usually has her children at a later age—about 35, as opposed to 22 in the early part of the last century. Whether or not she works outside the home, she and her spouse probably have more disposable income than they would have had a century ago.[30]

In the U.S., there are about 8 million divorced men and 11 million divorced women.[31] Divorce can dramatically alter an individual's consumer profile. As the household breaks up, the partners may need new household items at the same time that their income levels drop.

"Empty nesters"—married couples whose children have grown up and moved away from home—are an attractive life-cycle segment for marketers. Empty nesters may also have the disposable incomes necessary to purchase premium products. These couples may struggle to maintain a four-bedroom home and a half-acre lawn, making them customers for lawn-care and home-care services, as well as townhouses or condominiums. Later, these people may become customers for retirement centers, supplemental medical insurance, and hearing aids. They are also a prime target market for travel and leisure products.

One trend noted by researchers in the past decade is an increase in the number of grown children who have returned home to live with their parents. Some of these grown children bring along families of their own.

Foxwoods Casino and Resort, owned by the Native American Mashantucket Pequot Tribal Nation, is one of many Native American–owned casinos in the U.S.

Segmenting by Household Type The first U.S. census in 1790 found an average household size of 5.8 persons. By 1960, this number had fallen to 3.4 persons, and today that number is below 3. The U.S. Department of Commerce cites several reasons for the trend toward smaller households: lower fertility rates, young people's tendency to postpone marriage or to never marry, the increasing tendency among younger couples to limit the number of children or to have no children at all, the ease and frequency of divorce, and the ability and desire of many young singles and the elderly to live alone.

An important U.S. trend over the past decades has been the decline of the so-called traditional family, consisting of two parents and their children living in one household. In 1900, 4 of 5 Americans lived within these families; today, only 50 percent do.

Meanwhile, three other segments—single-parent families, single-person households, and nonfamily group households—have increased dramatically during the same time period. Conversely, the numbers of large, extended families living together has fallen dramatically—from 50 percent to 10 percent.[32]

Marketers at Dodge are targeting mothers, whose lives are increasingly hectic—whether they work inside or outside the home.

While the percentage of married-couple families has fallen, the number of unmarried individuals living together has risen. Consequently, the Bureau of the Census created another category, POSSLQ, an acronym for unmarried "persons of the opposite sex in the same living quarters," to describe this trend. In addition, there has been a rise in the number of gay and lesbian couples establishing homes. Companies from auto manufacturers to media outlets have been scrambling to attract loyal customers from within this market, which represents more than $450 billion in buying power. When research showed that lesbian women had a high rate of purchasing its Outback vehicles, Subaru marketers began to tailor its marketing efforts toward lesbians.[33] The "Solving an Ethical Controversy" Interactive Example discusses the gay and lesbian segment further.

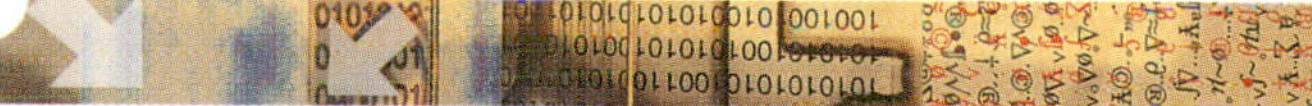

RIGHT/WRONG: SOLVING AN ETHICAL CONTROVERSY—SEGMENTING BY SEXUAL ORIENTATION

Finally, one of the most actively pursued market segments are DINKs—dual-income couples with no kids. With high levels of spendable income, such couples are big buyers of gourmet foods, luxury items, and travel.

Segmenting by Income and Expenditure Patterns Part of the earlier definition of *market* described people or institutions with purchasing power. Not surprisingly, then, a common basis for segmenting the consumer market is income. For instance, marketers often target geographic areas known for the high incomes of their residents. *Sales & Marketing Management* magazine conducts a periodic *Survey of Buying Power*, which lists metropolitan markets by income. Metropolitan markets that rise dramatically in effective buying income often make promising targets for income-related segmentation. Cessna targets consumers and business owners who are wealthy enough to purchase their own aircraft, as shown in Figure 8.6.

FIGURE 8.6

Targeting Wealthier Consumers and Business Owners

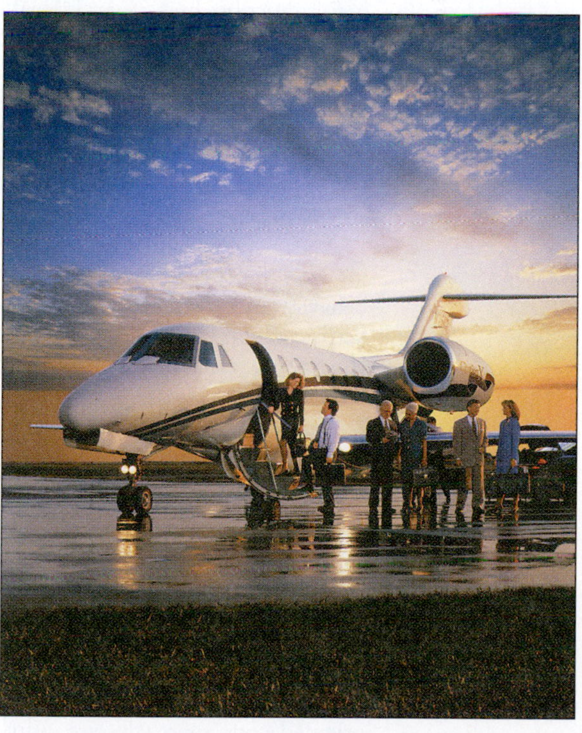

Engel's Laws How do expenditure patterns vary with income? Over a century ago, Ernst Engel, a German statistician, published what became known as *Engel's laws*—three general statements based on his studies of the impact of household income changes on consumer spending behavior. According to Engel, as family income increases, the following will take place:

1. A smaller percentage of expenditures go for food.
2. The percentage spent on housing and household operations and clothing remains constant.
3. The percentage spent on other items (such as recreation and education) increases.

Are Engel's laws still valid? Newer studies say essentially yes, with a few exceptions. Researchers note a steady decline in the percentage of total income spent on food, beverages, and tobacco as income increases. Although high-income families spend greater absolute amounts on food items, their purchases represent declining percentages of their total expenditures as compared with low-income families. The second law remains partly accurate since the percentage of expenditures for housing and household operations remains relatively unchanged in all but the very lowest income groups. The percentage spent on clothing, however, rises with increased income. The third law is also true, with the exception of medical and personal-care costs, which appear to decline as a percentage of increased income.

Engel's laws provide the marketing manager with useful rules about the types of consumer demand that evolve with increased income. These laws can also help marketers to evaluate a foreign country as a potential target market.

Demographic Segmentation Abroad Marketers often face a difficult task in obtaining the data necessary for demographic segmentation abroad. Many countries do not operate regularly scheduled census programs. For instance, the most recent count of the Dutch population is now over two decades old. Germany skipped counting from 1970 to 1987, and France conducts a census about every seven years. By contrast, Japan and Canada conduct censuses every five years; however, the mid-decade assessments are not as complete as the end-of-decade counts.

Also, some foreign data includes demographic divisions not found in the U.S. census. Canada collects information on religious affiliation, for instance. On the other hand, some of the standard segmentation data for U.S. markets are not available abroad. Many nations do not collect income data. Great Britain, Japan, Spain, France, and Italy are examples. Similarly, family life cycle data is difficult to apply in global demographic segmentation efforts. Ireland acknowledges only three marital statuses—single, married, and widowed—while Latin American nations and Sweden count their unmarried cohabitants.

One source of global demographic information is the International Programs Center (IPC) at the U.S. Bureau of the Census. The IPC provides a searchable online database of population statistics for many countries on the Census Bureau's Web page. Another source is the United Nations, which sponsors national statistical offices that collect demographic data on a variety of countries. In addition, private marketing research firms can supplement government data.

Psychographic Segmentation

Marketers have traditionally referred to geographic and demographic characteristics as the primary bases for dividing consumers into homogeneous market segments. Still, they have long recognized the need for fuller, more lifelike portraits of consumers in developing their marketing programs. As a result, psychographic segmentation can be a useful tool for gaining sharper insight into consumer purchasing behavior.

What Is Psychographic Segmentation? **Psychographic segmentation** divides a population into groups that have similar psychological characteristics, values, and lifestyles. *Lifestyle* refers to a person's mode of living; it describes how an individual operates on a daily basis. Consumers' lifestyles are composites of their individual psychological profiles, including their needs, motives, perceptions, and attitudes. A lifestyle also bears the mark of many other influences, such as family, job, social activities, and culture.

The most common method for developing psychographic profiles of a population is to conduct a large-scale survey that asks consumers to agree or disagree with a collection of several hundred AIO statements. These *AIO statements* describe various activities, interests, and opinions. The resulting data allows researchers to develop lifestyle profiles. Marketers can then develop a separate marketing strategy that closely fits the psychographic makeup for each lifestyle segment.

Marketing researchers have conducted psychographic studies on hundreds of goods and services, ranging from beer to air travel. Hospitals and other health-care providers use such studies to assess consumer behavior and attitudes toward health care in general, to learn the needs of consumers in particular marketplaces, and to determine how consumers perceive individual institutions. Many businesses turn to psychographic research in an effort to learn what consumers in various demographic and geographic segments want and need.

VALS2 A quarter century ago, the research and consulting firm SRI International developed a psychographic segmentation system called VALS. The name stands for "values and lifestyles," and the original VALS scheme categorized consumers by their opinions regarding social issues. A decade later, SRI revised the system to link it more closely with consumer-buying behavior. The revised system, VALS2, is based on two key concepts: resources and self-motivation. *VALS2* divides consumers into eight psychographic categories. Figure 8.7 details the profiles for these categories and their relationships.

The VALS network chart in the figure displays differences in resources as vertical distances, while self-orientation is represented horizontally. The resource dimension measures income, education, self-confidence, health, eagerness to buy, and energy level. Self-orientations divide consumers into three groups: principle-oriented consumers who have a set of ideas and morals—principles—that they live their lives by; status-oriented consumers who are influenced by what others think; and action-oriented consumers who seek physical activity, variety, and adventure.

SRI has created several specialized segmentation systems based on this approach. GeoVALS, for instance, estimates the percentage of each VALS type in each U.S. residential zip code. JapanVALS was developed to help companies understand Japanese consumers, and iVALS focuses on Internet sites and users.[34]

SRI uses the VALS2 segmentation information in conjunction with marketers in consulting projects and on a subscriber basis. Product, service, and media data are available by VALS-types from companies' databases.

Several other commercially available psychographic profile systems offer their own insights to marketers. One is MONITOR, available from Yankelovich Partners.[35] A newer syndicated psychographic service, from marketing research firm Odyssey, focuses on the psychographics of people who use new technologies, such as the Internet.

FIGURE 8.7

VALS2 Network

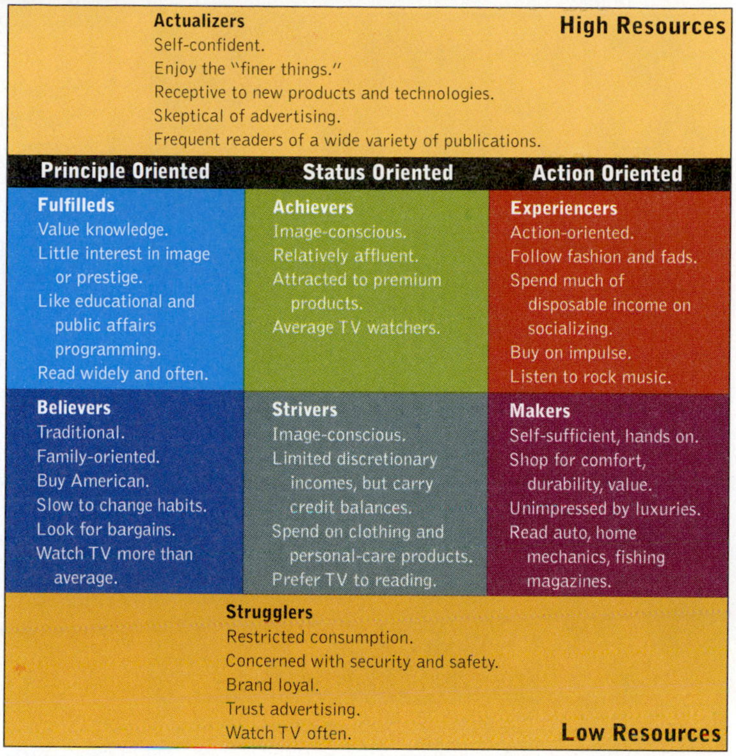

Principle Oriented	Status Oriented	Action Oriented
Actualizers (High Resources) Self-confident. Enjoy the "finer things." Receptive to new products and technologies. Skeptical of advertising. Frequent readers of a wide variety of publications.		
Fulfilleds Value knowledge. Little interest in image or prestige. Like educational and public affairs programming. Read widely and often.	**Achievers** Image-conscious. Relatively affluent. Attracted to premium products. Average TV watchers.	**Experiencers** Action-oriented. Follow fashion and fads. Spend much of disposable income on socializing. Buy on impulse. Listen to rock music.
Believers Traditional. Family-oriented. Buy American. Slow to change habits. Look for bargains. Watch TV more than average.	**Strivers** Image-conscious. Limited discretionary incomes, but carry credit balances. Spend on clothing and personal-care products. Prefer TV to reading.	**Makers** Self-sufficient, hands on. Shop for comfort, durability, value. Unimpressed by luxuries. Read auto, home mechanics, fishing magazines.
Strugglers (Low Resources) Restricted consumption. Concerned with security and safety. Brand loyal. Trust advertising. Watch TV often.		

Source: VALS2 is a trademark of SRI International.

Psychographic Segmentation of Global Markets

As JapanVALS suggests, psychographic profiles can cross national boundaries. Roper Starch Worldwide, a marketing research firm, recently surveyed 7,000 people in 35 countries. From the resulting data, Roper identified six psychographic consumer segments that exist in all 35 nations, although to varying degrees:

- *Strivers,* the largest segment, value professional and material goals more than the other groups. One-third of the Asian population and one-fourth of Russians are strivers. They are slightly more likely to be men than women.
- *Devouts* value duty and tradition. While this segment comprises 22 percent of all adults, they are most common in Africa, the Middle East, and developing Asia. They are least common in Western Europe and developed Asian countries. Worldwide, they are more likely to be female.
- *Altruists* emphasize social issues and societal well-being. Comprising 18 percent of all adults, this group shows a median age of 44 and a slightly higher percentage of women. Altruists are most common in Latin America and Russia.
- *Intimates* value family and personal relationships. They are divided almost equally between males and females. One-fourth of people in America and Europe are intimates, but only 7 percent of consumers in developing Asia fall into this category.
- *Fun seekers,* as you might guess from their name, focus on personal enjoyment and pleasurable experiences. They comprise 12 percent of the world's population, with a male-female ratio of 54 to 46. Many live in developed Asia.
- *Creatives,* the smallest segment, account for just 10 percent of the global population. This group seeks education, technology, and knowledge, and their male-female ratio is roughly equal. Many creatives live in Western Europe and Latin America.

Roper researchers note that some principles and core beliefs apply to more than one psychographic segment. For example, consumers in all 35 countries cite "family" as one of their five most important values, and "protecting the family" ranks as one of the top 10.[36]

Using Psychographic Segmentation Psychographic profile systems like those of Roper and SRI can paint useful pictures of the overall psychological motivations of consumers. These profiles produce much richer descriptions of potential target markets than other techniques can achieve. The enhanced detail aids in matching a company's image and product offerings with the types of consumers who use its products.

Identifying which psychographic segments are most prevalent in certain markets helps marketers plan and promote more effectively. Often, segments overlap. For instance, the advertisement for MasterCard in Figure 8.8 would be attractive both to altruists and intimates.

Psychographic segmentation is a good supplement to segmentation by demographic or geographic variables. For example, marketers may have access to each consumer type's media preferences in network television, cable television, radio format, magazines, and newspapers. Psychographic studies may then refine the picture of segment characteristics to give a more elaborate lifestyle profile of the consumers in the firm's target market.

FIGURE 8.8

Using Psychographic Segmentation

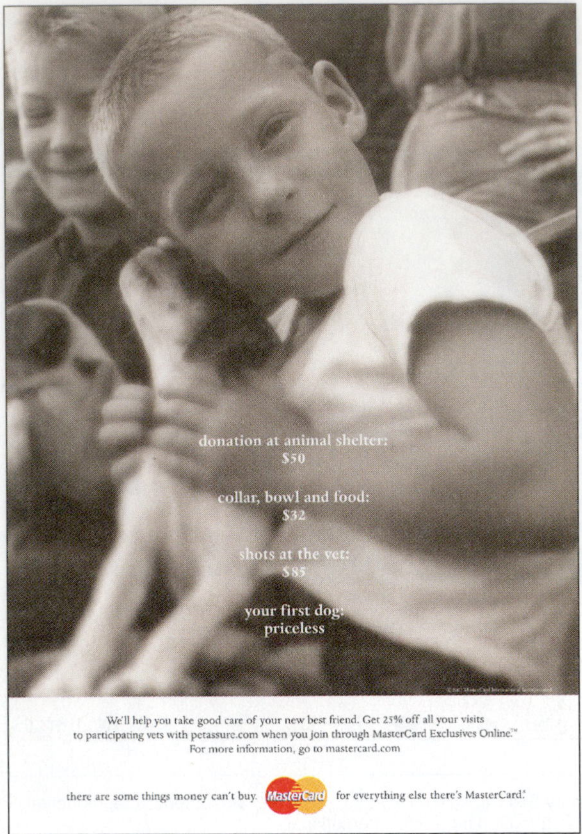

donation at animal shelter:
$50
collar, bowl and food:
$32
shots at the vet:
$85
your first dog:
priceless
We'll help you take good care of your new best friend. Get 25% off all your visits to participating vets with petassure.com when you join through MasterCard Exclusives Online.℠
For more information, go to mastercard.com
there are some things money can't buy.
MasterCard
for everything else there's MasterCard.

Some advertisers, such as cosmetics companies, segment by the benefits consumers seek by using their products.

Product-Related Segmentation

Product-related segmentation involves dividing a consumer population into homogeneous groups based on characteristics of their relationships to the product. This segmentation approach can take several forms:

1. Segmenting based on the benefits that people seek when they buy a product
2. Segmenting based on usage rates for a product
3. Segmenting according to consumers' brand loyalty toward a product

Segmenting by Benefits Sought This approach focuses on the attributes that people seek in a good or service and the benefits they expect to receive from that good or service. It groups consumers into segments based on what they want a product to do for them.

Consumers who quaff Starbucks' premium coffees, for example, are not just looking for a dose of caffeine. They are willing to pay extra to savor a pleasant experience, one that makes them feel pampered and appreciated. Women who use Maybelline cosmetics want to look their best and be able to put their makeup on quickly. People who feed their pets Iams believe that they are giving their animals the best tasting, healthiest pet food.

Even if a business offers only one product line, however, marketers must remember to consider product benefits. Two people may buy the same product for very different reasons. A box of Arm & Hammer baking soda could end up serving as a refrigerator freshener, a toothpaste substitute, an antacid, or a deodorizer for a cat's litter box.

Segmenting by Usage Rates Marketers may also segment a total market by grouping people according to the amounts of a product that they buy and use. Markets can be divided into heavy-user, moderate-user, and light-user segments. The *80/20 principle* holds that a big percentage of a product's revenues—roughly 80 percent—comes from a relatively small, loyal percentage of total customers—perhaps 20 percent. The 80/20 principle is sometimes referred to as "Praedo's Law." While the percentages need not exactly equal these figures, the general principle often holds true: Relatively few heavy users of a product can account for much of its consumption.

Depending on their goals, marketers may target heavy, moderate, or light users as well as nonusers. A company may attempt to lure heavy users of another product away from their regular brands to try a new brand. Nonusers and light users may be attractive prospects because other companies are ignoring them. Usage rates can also be linked to other segmentation methods such as demographic and psychographic segmentation.

Segmenting by Brand Loyalty A third product-related segmentation method groups consumers according to the strength of the brand loyalty they feel toward a product. Despite its nearly 250-year history, the Irish brewer Guinness needed to update the way consumers viewed its brand. So the company revamped its outmoded visitors' center in Dublin, Ireland, to attract more tourists and locals. The new Guinness Storehouse features everything from historic exhibits to a fully stocked gift shop, where loyal Guinness guzzlers can purchase all kinds of company paraphernalia. "The goal was for Storehouse to evolve, adapt, and grow up," explains the company's director of marketing and strategic planning, Ralph Ardill. "Places like Storehouse bring consumers and employees together and open the doors to the community."[37]

A classic example of brand loyalty segmentation is airline frequent-flyer programs. Originally targeted at heavy users—business travelers—frequent-flyer programs now help to tie even occasional travelers to specific airlines. The success of these programs has resulted in similar efforts in the hotel industry, bookstores, and elsewhere. Other companies attempt to segment their market by developing brand loyalty over a period of time, through consumers' stages of life, as shown by Oral-B toothbrushes in Figure 8.9.

THE MARKET SEGMENTATION PROCESS

To this point, the chapter has discussed various bases on which companies segment markets. How does a marketer decide which segmentation base to use? As Figure 8.10 shows, marketers follow a five-step decision process.

<interactive>**learning goal**

CHAPTER OBJECTIVE #5: IDENTIFY THE STEPS IN THE MARKET SEGMENTATION PROCESS.

Stage I: Identify Market Segmentation Process

Segmentation begins when marketers determine the bases on which to identify markets. They follow two methods for achieving this goal. In the first, management-driven method, segments are predefined by managers based on their observation of the behavioral and demographic characteristics of likely users. The market-driven method defines segments by asking customers which attributes are important to them, and then clusters responses to identify potential segments. Both methods try to develop segments that group customers who respond similarly to specific marketing-mix alternatives. For example, Procter & Gamble cannot simply target Crest toothpaste to large families. Management must first confirm that most large families are concerned about preventing tooth decay and will be receptive to the Crest marketing offer.

Sometimes marketers have trouble isolating a preferred segment, or may serve several overlapping segments. Sears serves a variety of segments—families, men or women, children, and seniors. So the company isolates its segments by running a series of advertisements in the same format, but showcasing different products, like the ad in Figure 8.11. While this ad focuses on household appliances, another features women's shoes and Samsonite luggage; still another centers on power tools.

Stage II: Develop a Relevant Profile for Each Segment

After identifying promising segments, marketers should understand the customers in each one. This in-depth analysis of customers helps managers to accurately match customers' needs with the firm's marketing offers. The process must identify characteristics that both explain the similarities among customers within each segment and account for differences among segments.

The task at this stage is to develop a profile of the typical customer in each segment. Such a profile might include information about lifestyle patterns, attitudes toward product attributes and brands, product-use habits, geographic locations, and demographic characteristics.

Stage III: Forecast Market Potential

In the third stage, market segmentation and market opportunity analysis combine to produce a forecast of market potential within each segment. Market potential sets the upper limit on the demand that competing firms can expect from a segment. Multiplying by market share determines a single firm's maximum sales potential. This step should define a preliminary go or no-go decision from management since the total sales potential in each segment must justify resources devoted to further analysis.

An example of a segment that shows tremendous market potential is U.S. children ages 4 to 12. Aggregate spending by consumers in this age group or on their behalf doubled every decade between the 1960s and 1980s and tripled during the 1990s to reach its current level of $24 billion a year. Thirty years ago children spent most of their money on candy. Today, only one-third is spent on food and beverages; the rest goes toward clothing, movies, games, and toys.

FIGURE 8.9

Creating Brand Loyalty through Different Life Stages

FIGURE 8.10

Market Segmentation Decision Process

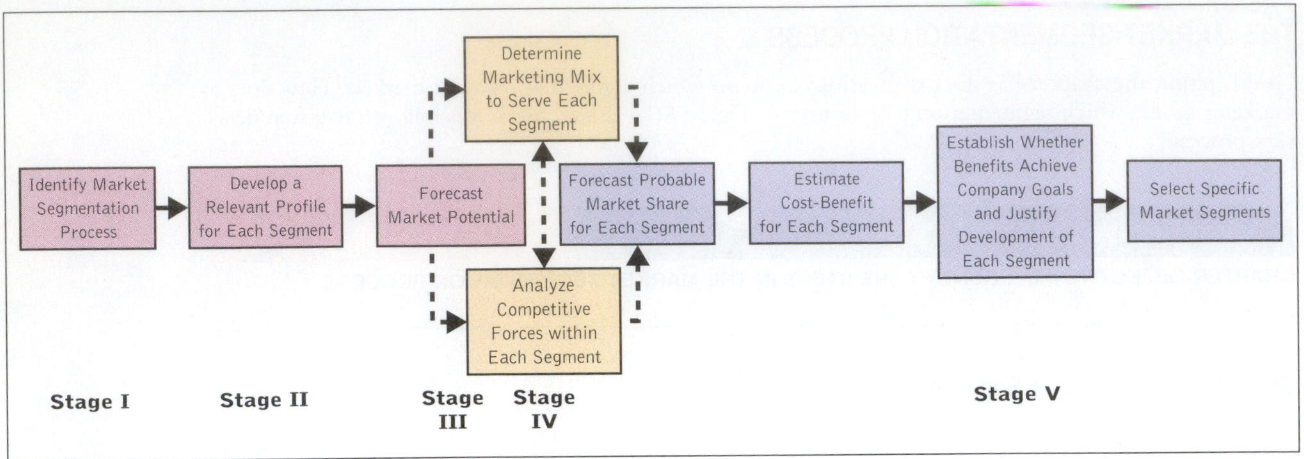

Source: M. Dale Beckman and John M. Rigby, *Foundations of Marketing,* 7th Edition (Toronto: Nelson, 2001).

Clothing retailers, noting this trend, have opened new stores that specialize in fashions for this age segment. An example is the Limited Too, which now has more than 300 stores nationwide as well as a catalog and Web site. Competitors Abercrombie & Fitch and Gymboree have also opened separate outlets for preteens.

Stage IV: Forecast Probable Market Share

Once market potential has been estimated, a firm must forecast its probable market share. Competitors' positions in targeted segments must be analyzed and a specific marketing strategy must be designed to reach these segments. These two activities may be performed simultaneously. Moreover, by settling on a marketing strategy and tactics, a firm determines the expected level of resources it must commit, that is, the costs that it will incur to tap the potential demand in each segment.

Kinko's currently has more than 1,100 photocopying outlets in Asia, Australia, Europe, and North America. The company used to be viewed (and used to view itself) as simply a copy shop at which customers could get quick turnaround for their reports, flyers, or manuscripts. But Gary Kusin, CEO of the company, made a trip around the U.S. to talk to his customers and learned that they are now looking "more for ongoing business partners. They want to know that they can partner with us for digital solutions for bigger jobs." So Kusin and his managers needed to figure out how to meet these needs and capture as much of this segment of the market as possible. "Right now," he says, "the biggest service we can sell is competence: the ability to listen to our customers, to understand their problems, and to apply our knowledge to come up with creative solutions."[38]

FIGURE 8.11

Sears Targets a Variety of Consumer Segments

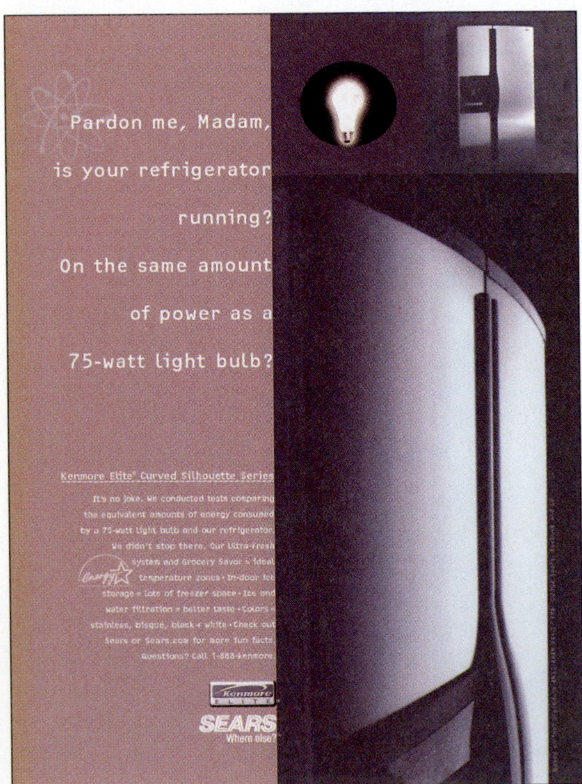

Stage V: Select Specific Market Segments

The information, analysis, and forecasts accumulated throughout the entire market segmentation decision process allows management to assess the potential for achieving company goals and to justify committing resources in developing one or more segments. Demand forecasts together with cost projections determine the profits and the return on investment (ROI) that the company can expect from each segment. Marketing strategy and tactics must be designed to reinforce the firm's image, yet keep within its unique organizational capabilities.

At this point in the analysis, marketers weigh more than monetary costs and benefits; they also consider many difficult-to-measure but critical organizational and environmental factors. The firm may lack experienced personnel to launch a successful attack on an attractive market segment. Similarly, a firm with 60 percent of the market faces possible legal problems with the Federal Trade Commission if it increases its market concentration. This assessment of both financial and nonfinancial factors is a difficult but vital step in the decision process.

STRATEGIES FOR REACHING TARGET MARKETS

Considerable marketing efforts are dedicated to developing strategies that will best match the firm's product offerings to the needs of particular target markets. An appropriate match is vital to the firm's marketing success. Marketers have identified four basic strategies for achieving consumer satisfaction: undifferentiated marketing, differentiated marketing, concentrated marketing, and micromarketing.

<interactive>**learning goal**

CHAPTER OBJECTIVE #6: DISCUSS FOUR BASIC STRATEGIES FOR REACHING TARGET MARKETS.

Undifferentiated Marketing

A firm may produce only one product or product line and promote it to all customers with a single marketing mix; such a firm is said to practice **undifferentiated marketing,** sometimes called *mass marketing.* Undifferentiated marketing was much more common in the past than it is today.

While undifferentiated marketing is efficient from a production viewpoint, the strategy also brings inherent dangers. A firm that attempts to satisfy everyone in the market with one standard product may suffer if competitors offer specialized units to smaller segments of the total market and better satisfy individual segments. In fact, firms that implement strategies of differentiated marketing, concentrated marketing, or micromarketing may capture enough small segments of the market to defeat another competitor's strategy of undifferentiated marketing.

Differentiated Marketing

Firms that promote numerous products with differing marketing mixes designed to satisfy smaller segments are said to practice **differentiated marketing.** By providing increased satisfaction for each of many target markets, a company can produce more sales by following a differentiated marketing strategy than undifferentiated marketing would generate. Oscar Mayer, a marketer of a variety of meat products, practices differentiated marketing. It increased its sales by introducing a new product—Lunchables—aimed at children. In general, however, differentiated marketing also raises costs. Production costs usually rise because additional products and variations require shorter production runs and increased setup times. Inventory costs rise because more products require added storage space and increased efforts for record keeping. Promotional costs also rise because each segment demands a unique promotional mix.

Despite higher marketing costs, however, an organization may be forced to practice differentiated marketing to remain competitive. The travel industry now recognizes the need to target smaller groups of travelers with specialized interests. Elderhostel, for instance, targets seniors with specialized trips that may focus on history, hiking, golf, cooking, or other special interests. Old Sturbridge Village in Massachusetts targets people who are interested in American history.

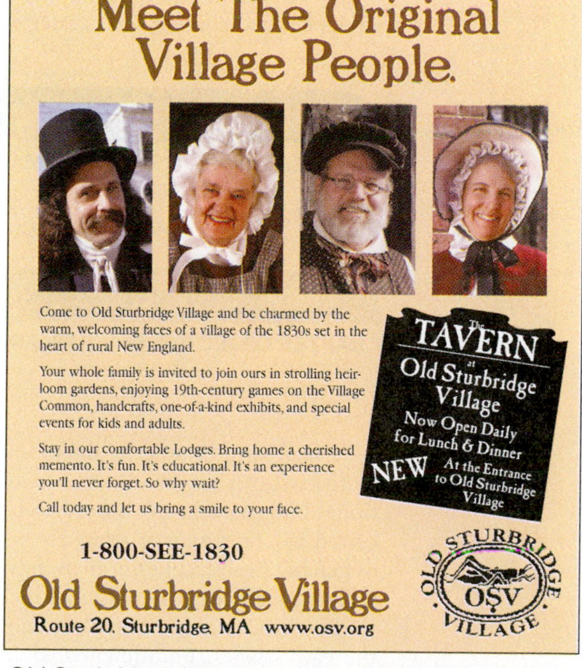

Old Sturbridge Village museum in Massachusetts targets individuals who are interested in American history.

Concentrated Marketing

Rather than trying to market its products separately to several segments, a firm may opt for a concentrated marketing strategy. With **concentrated marketing** (also known as *niche marketing*), a firm focuses its efforts on profitably satisfying only one market segment. This approach can appeal to a small firm that lacks the financial resources of its competitors and to a company that offers highly specialized goods and services. The Petco chain appeals to most owners of small animals—fish, cats, dogs, hamsters, birds—with its array of pet care products and accessories. But a small, Boston-based firm called anguswear.com targets a much narrower audience with tiny cashmere dog sweaters (at $56 apiece), fragrances, and custom-made wooden sleigh beds (for $1,000).[39]

Magazine publishers have discovered that niche markets can be highly lucrative. New niche publications *Jane* and *O* (Oprah Winfrey's magazine) are making the wider-audience magazines reevaluate their strategies. And although conventional wisdom has always declared that young men didn't care about magazines, *Maxim, FHM,* and *Stuff* have been hugely successful during their first few years. Highly specialized spin-offs such as *Sports Illustrated Women* and *Travel & Leisure Golf* are doing better than their more generalized parents.[40]

But along with its benefits, concentrated marketing has its dangers. Since the strategy ties a firm's growth to a specific segment, sales can suffer if new competitors appeal successfully to the same target. Furthermore, errors in forecasting market potential or customer buying habits lead to severe problems, particularly if the firm has spent substantially on product development, advertising, and promotion. "Segmentation can take a marketer only so far before it begins to lose its effectiveness," says Bruce Hall, partner and vice president of marketing research for Howard Merrell & Partners, a marketing and advertising agency in Raleigh, North Carolina.[41]

Briefly Speaking

Put all your eggs in one basket, and watch the basket.

Mark Twain (1835–1910) American author

Micromarketing

The fourth targeting strategy, still more narrowly focused than concentrated marketing, is **micromarketing,** which involves targeting potential customers at a very basic level, such as by zip code, specific occupation, or lifestyle. Ultimately, micromarketing can target even individuals themselves. The salesperson at your favorite clothing boutique may contact you when certain merchandise that she thinks you might like arrives at the store. The Internet may allow marketers to make micromarketing even more effective. By tracking specific demographic and personal information, marketers can send e-mail directly to individual consumers who are most likely to buy their products. If you purchase a book via Amazon.com, the company will offer to send you e-mail notices about other books that may be of interest to you.

But micromarketing, like niche marketing, can turn out to be too much of a good thing if companies spend too much time, effort, and marketing dollars to unearth a market that is too small and specialized to be profitable. In addition, micromarketing may cause a company to lose sight of other, reachable markets. "It may be that only 5 percent to 6 percent of a particular [direct marketing] list may fit the true target criteria, but one cannot rule out the other 94 or 95 percent, because it's still difficult to predict a full range of human behavior," notes marketing researcher Bruce Hall.[42]

Selecting and Executing a Strategy

Although most organizations adopt some form of differentiated marketing, no single, best choice suits all firms. Any of the alternatives may prove most effective in a particular situation. The basic determinants of a market-specific strategy are (1) company resources, (2) product homogeneity, (3) stage in the product life cycle, and (4) competitors' strategies.

<interactive>**learning goal**

CHAPTER OBJECTIVE #7: SUMMARIZE THE TYPES OF POSITIONING STRATEGIES.

<interactive>**learning goal**

CHAPTER OBJECTIVE #8: EXPLAIN THE REASONS FOR POSITIONING AND REPOSITIONING PRODUCTS.

A firm with limited resources may have to choose a concentrated marketing strategy. Small firms may be forced to select small target markets because of limitations in their financing, sales force, and promotional budgets. On the other hand, an undifferentiated marketing strategy suits a firm selling items perceived by consumers as relatively homogeneous. Marketers of grain, for example, sell standardized grades of generic products rather than individual brand names. Some petroleum companies implement undifferentiated marketing to distribute their gasoline to the mass market.

The firm's strategy may also change as its product progresses through the stages of the life cycle. During the early stages, undifferentiated marketing might effectively support the firm's effort to build initial demand for the item. In the later stages, however, competitive pressures may force modifications in products and in the development of marketing strategies aimed at segments of the total market.

The strategies of competitors also affect the choice of a segmentation approach. A firm may encounter obstacles to undifferentiated marketing if its competitors actively cultivate smaller segments. In such instances, competition usually forces each firm to adopt a differentiated marketing strategy.

Having chosen a strategy for reaching their firm's target market, marketers must then decide how best to position the product. The concept of **positioning** seeks to put a product in a certain position, or place, in the minds of prospective buyers. Marketers use a positioning strategy to distinguish their firm's offerings from those of competitors and to create promotions that communicate the desired position.

To achieve this goal, marketers follow a number of positioning strategies. Possible approaches include positioning a product according to the following categories:

1. *Attributes*—Jeep wants you to "think of it as a 4,000-lb. guardian angel."
2. *Price/quality*—Rolex watches are high-quality, high-priced timepieces; Timex watches are low priced but long lasting.
3. *Competitors*—Formula 409 claims that "409 Is Better."
4. *Application*—Crest Whitestrips "reveal your whiter smile."
5. *Product user*—Visa's ads target consumers who are concerned about the security of making purchases on line.
6. *Product class*—Wendy's has "raised the bar on salad."

Some marketers position their products directly against those of major competitors.

Whatever the strategy they choose, marketers want to emphasize a product's unique advantages and to differentiate it from competitors' options. Companies may even promote similar products by stressing different advantages. Managers at Sprint, for instance, feel that their long-distance carrier's prices offer a competitive advantage over AT&T's. So Sprint ads tend to stress price and value. Meanwhile, marketers for AT&T think that their company has a positive image with customers based on its longevity and experience in telecommunications. AT&T ads, therefore, often emphasize reliability and the high quality of its overall service.

A *positioning map* provides a valuable tool in helping managers position products by graphically illustrating consumers' perceptions of competing products within an industry. Marketers can create a competitive positioning map from information solicited from consumers or from their accumulated knowledge about a market. A positioning map might present two different characteristics—price and perceived quality—and show how consumers view a product and its major competitors based on these traits. The hypothetical positioning map in Figure 8.12 compares selected retailers based on possible perceptions of their prices and quality of their offerings.

FIGURE 8.12

Hypothetical Competitive Positioning Map for Selected Retailers

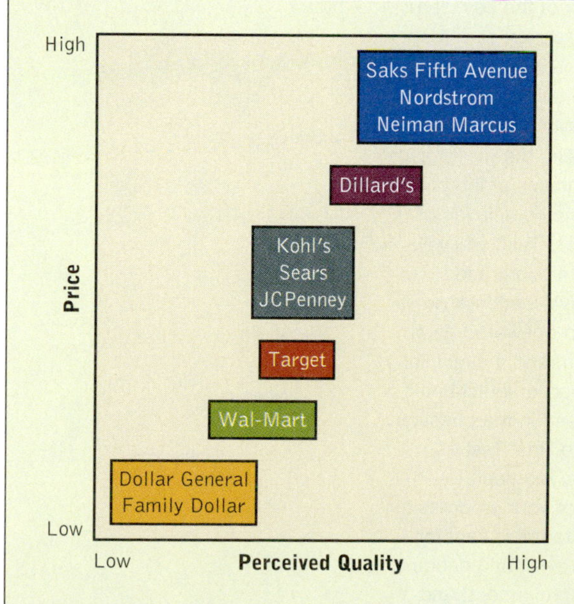

Sometimes, changes in the competitive environment force marketers to *reposition* a product—changing the position it holds in the minds of prospective buyers relative to the positions of competing products. Repositioning may become necessary even for highly successful products. Disney used to pitch its Disney World and Disneyland parks as great places for family vacations. As successful as that positioning was, in recent years the company began to advertise its parks as great places for empty nesters to take a second honeymoon. Bayer aspirin used to get by on its reputation for relieving headaches; now the company is allowed to advertise the aspirin's usefulness in reducing the chances of potential heart attacks. By repositioning their products, these companies reach new markets that they might not otherwise have tapped.

STRATEGIC IMPLICATIONS OF MARKETING IN THE 21ST CENTURY

To remain competitive, today's marketers must be able to accurately identify potential customers for their goods and services.

They can use a variety of methods to accomplish this, from segmenting markets by gender to segmenting by geographic location. The trick is to figure out the best combination of methods for segmentation to identify the most lucrative, long-lasting potential markets. Marketers must also be able to remain flexible, responding to markets as they change—for instance, following a generation as it ages or reaching out to new generations by revamping or repositioning products.

The greatest competitive advantage will belong to firms that can pinpoint and serve markets without segmenting them to the point where they are too small or specialized to garner profits. "In the broadest possible sense, one wants to develop a sense of the key target audience in terms that reach beyond the basic demographics but not so far as to be beyond the ability of media to reach that audience," explains strategic media consultant Jane Hendrickson. "The trick, ideally, is that you end up with a cluster, a target, that you actually can reach and communicate with in some fashion."[43] Marketers who can reach and communicate with the right customers have a greater chance of attracting and keeping those customers than those who are searching for the wrong customers, in the wrong place.

FLASH CHAPTER REVIEW PRESENTATION

<interactive>video case

ANNIE'S HOMEGROWN: A NATURAL SUCCESS

endofchaptermaterial

- Summary of Chapter Objectives
- Chapter Outline
- Key Terms
- Review Questions
- Projects and Teamwork Exercises
- 'netWork
- Crossword Puzzles
- Case 8.1: Getting Ahead by Clipping Kids' Heads

Take the Post-Test to assess your overall understanding of the key ideas in this chapter. The Post-Test provides a comprehensive selection of exam-style questions addressing the main topics and concepts of the chapter. At the completion of each Post-Test, you will receive a score and instructive feedback on how you answered each question, and a direct link to the part of the chapter addressed in the question. Take the Post-Test as often as you need to—a record of your progress for each attempt is kept for you to revisit and gauge your improvement. And each Post-Test is randomly generated, so every attempt is new.

Post-Test

CHAPTER 9

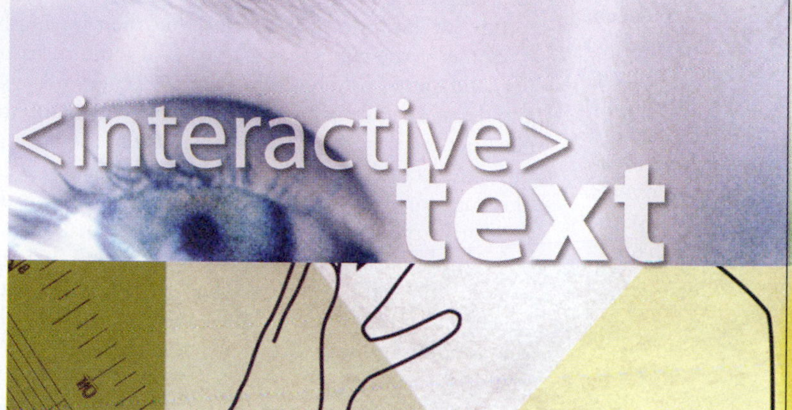

Consumer Behavior

Chapter Objectives

1. Differentiate between customer behavior and consumer behavior.
2. Explain how marketers classify behavioral influences on consumer decisions.
3. Describe cultural, group, and family influences on consumer behavior.
4. Explain each of the personal determinants of consumer behavior: needs and motives, perceptions, attitudes, and self-concept theory.
5. Discuss the difference between high-involvement and low-involvement purchase decisions.
6. Outline the steps in the consumer decision process.
7. Differentiate among routinized response behavior, limited problem solving, and extended problem solving by consumers.

Pre-Test

Take the Pre-Test to assess your initial knowledge of the key ideas in this chapter. The Pre-Test provides exam-style questions addressing the main topics and concepts of the chapter. At the completion of each Pre-Test, you will receive a score and instructive feedback on how you answered each question, and a direct link to the part of the chapter addressed in the question. Take the Pre-Test as often as you need to—a record of your progress for each attempt is kept for you to revisit and gauge your improvement.

PURCHASING HABITS OF THE SEPTEMBER 11 GENERATION

How have American consumers behaved since September 11? According to Unity Marketing, a firm that specializes in consumer psychology and its impact on shopping behavior, consumer spending—after necessities—can be divided into three categories: discretionary purchases (things that people buy that they don't necessarily need but that they believe will make their lives better in a practical sense, such as 100 percent cotton sheets or a down comforter); indulgences (products that provide emotional satisfaction, like candles or fresh flowers); and luxury purchases (Rolex watches or Tiffany jewelry). Since the tragedy, consumers have sought relief from stress in their purchases. "When men get stressed, they go to bars, and women go shopping," says Pam Danziger of Unity. "Our research finds a substantial amount of U.S. household spending is driven by emotional, not physical needs. This is largely the realm of discretionary spending. In the face of crisis, women, who do the bulk of American household shopping, will continue to buy for emotional satisfaction, but their buying behavior will change."

Some of the changes have involved a return to tradition. Parents have been drawn to "back to basics" toys and games for children—such as Legos and jigsaw puzzles—instead of electronics. Home furnishings and decor, including holiday decorations, tabletop items and dinnerware for entertaining, candles and fireplace accessories, as well as family games have been popular. Products with nostalgic themes such as greeting cards, scrapbooks, and stationery are making a comeback. Items made in America—whether patriotic, like flags, or not—are flying off the shelves. Consumers want to feather their nests with picture frames, decorative pillows, and throws instead of making major appliance or furniture purchases. Sewing stores, knitting shops, and craft supply stores are reporting increases in business. In addition, people are turning to comfort foods—soup cookbooks and cooking supplies have become steady sellers. Of course, people haven't entirely abandoned their televisions and VCRs—after all, this is the 21st century. DVD sales and video rentals are up—but that's because consumers would rather have their entertainment at home than go out.

Naturally, these consumer behaviors represent more than one age group. It may be years before we are able to track the full effect of September 11 on the group of young people who were in their formative years at the time of the tragedy. But it's important for marketers to keep in mind the impact of an event on the developing minds and habits of a group of consumers. Perhaps Burton Jablin, president and general manager of cable channel HGTV (Home and Garden Television), describes the response of consumers best: "Americans have been looking for a way to slow down for a long time," he says, noting that the audience for his cable station's decorating and craft shows had been climbing long before September 11. "But what was a subconscious desire is now a conscious one. It's the new intimacy."[1]

CHAPTER OVERVIEW

Why do people buy one product over another? Answering this question is the goal of every marketer. The answer directly affects every aspect of the marketing strategy, from product development to pricing and promotion. Discovering that answer requires an understanding of customer behavior, the process by which consumers and business-to-business buyers make purchase decisions. **Customer behavior** includes both individual consumers who buy goods and services for their own use and organizational buyers who purchase business products.

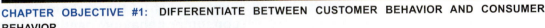

<interactive>**learning goal**

CHAPTER OBJECTIVE #1: DIFFERENTIATE BETWEEN CUSTOMER BEHAVIOR AND CONSUMER BEHAVIOR.

CHAPTER OBJECTIVE #2: EXPLAIN HOW MARKETERS CLASSIFY BEHAVIORAL INFLUENCES ON CONSUMER DECISIONS.

A variety of influences affect both individuals buying items for themselves and professional buyers purchasing products for their firms. This chapter focuses on individual purchasing behavior, which applies to all of us. **Consumer behavior** is the process through which the ultimate buyer makes purchase decisions, from toothbrushes to autos to vacations. Chapter 10 will shift the focus to business buying decisions.

The study of consumer behavior builds on an understanding of human behavior in general. In their efforts to understand why and how consumers make buying decisions, marketers borrow extensively from the sciences of psychology and sociology. The work of psychologist Kurt Lewin, for example, provides a useful classification scheme for influences on buying behavior. (The same concept also sheds light on motivation theory discussed in your management courses.) Lewin's proposition is:

$$B = f(P,E)$$

This statement means that behavior (B) is a function (f) of the interactions of personal influences (P) and pressures exerted by outside environmental forces (E).

This statement is usually rewritten to apply to consumer behavior as follows:

$$B = f(I,P)$$

Consumer behavior (B) is a function (f) of the interactions of interpersonal influences (I)—such as culture, friends, classmates, coworkers, and relatives—and personal factors (P)—such as attitudes, learning, and perception. In other words, inputs from others and an individual's psychological makeup both affect his or her purchasing behavior. Before looking at how consumers make purchase decisions, we first consider how both interpersonal and personal factors affect consumers.

INTERPERSONAL DETERMINANTS OF CONSUMER BEHAVIOR

You don't make purchase decisions in a vacuum. You might not be consciously aware of it yet, although you will be after this course, but every buying decision you make is influenced by something, whether it's external or internal. This section focuses on external, interpersonal influences. Consumers often decide to buy goods and services based on what they believe others expect of them. They may want to project positive images to peers or to satisfy the unspoken desires of family members. Marketers recognize three broad categories of interpersonal influences on consumer behavior: cultural, social, and family influences.

<interactive>**learning goal**

CHAPTER OBJECTIVE #3: DESCRIBE CULTURAL, GROUP, AND FAMILY INFLUENCES ON CONSUMER BEHAVIOR.

Cultural Influences

Culture can be defined as the values, beliefs, preferences, and tastes handed down from one generation to the next. Culture is the broadest environmental determinant of consumer behavior. Marketers need to understand its role in consumer decision making, both in the U.S. and abroad. They must also monitor trends in cultural values as well as recognize changes in these values.

Marketing strategies and business practices that work in one country may be offensive or ineffective in another. Strategies may even have to be varied from one area of a country to another. Sears has 30 of its stores in areas of the U.S. with large Asian populations, so the retailer has created a promotional campaign to coincide with the Asia Moon Festival, a traditional harvesting celebration. While the retail giant reports success with the effort, one major challenge is the diversity of Asian languages. "The main countries [of origin for Asian-American consumers] are China, Korea, Vietnam, Japan, and the Philippines," says Gilbert Davila, vice president of multicultural and relationship marketing, "and they all speak different languages." So Sears has to focus on promotions that rely less on language and more on cultural similarities, like traditional dance performances featuring puppets depicting animals and mythological creatures.[2]

It is also important to recognize the concept of *ethnocentrism,* or the tendency to view your own culture as the norm, as it relates to consumer behavior. Marketers must remember that each culture they are trying to reach views its own values, beliefs, and customs as the norm.

FIGURE 9.1

Reflecting Core Values in Contemporary Advertising

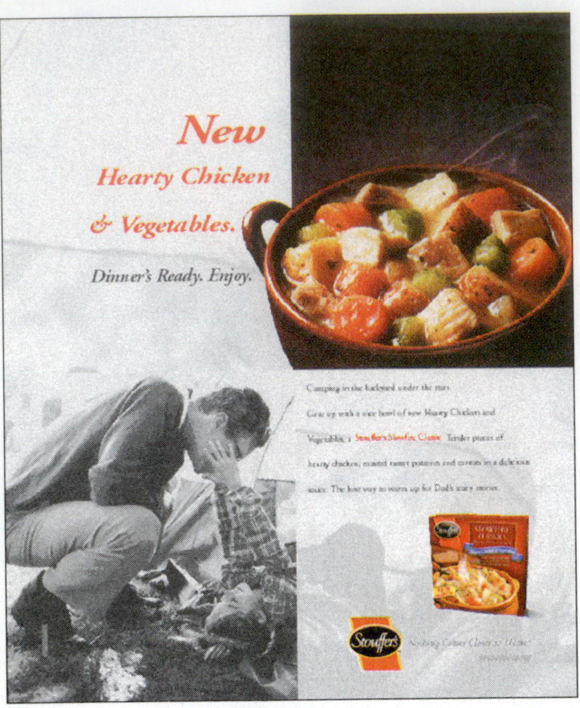

Core Values in U.S. Culture While some cultural values change over time, basic core values do not. The work ethic and the desire to accumulate wealth are two such core values in American society. Even though the typical family structure and family members' roles have changed in recent years, American culture still emphasizes the importance of family and home life. This value has been further strengthened in the wake of the events of September 11, as illustrated by the Stouffer's ad for its Slowfire Classics in Figure 9.1. Stouffer's slogan even reflects this core value: "Nothing comes closer to home."

Other core values include education, individualism, freedom, youthfulness, activity, humanitarianism, efficiency, and practicality. Each of these values influences consumer behavior. As Figure 9.2 emphasizes, Target hopes to attract customers with its pharmacy campaign for St. Jude's Children's Hospital. One percent of each pharmacy purchase goes to the internationally recognized children's hospital.

Values that change over time also have their effects. The Internet has created a generation of sophisticated, globally aware teens who have access to a greater diversity of information and products. They also have considerable purchasing power. Sony recognizes the importance of this group and plans to make extra efforts to build loyal consumers among them. One strategy is to use a comprehensive consumer database to make frequent contact with teens. According to the company's Consumer Segment Marketing Division's mission, the goal is to "develop an intimate understanding of Sony's end consumers . . . from cradle to grave."[3]

International Perspective on Cultural Influences Cultural differences are particularly important for international marketers. Marketing strategies that prove successful in one country often cannot extend to other international markets because of cultural variations. Europe is a good example, with nine different languages and a wide range of lifestyles and product preferences. Even though the continent is becoming a single economic unit, cultural divisions continue to define multiple markets.

FIGURE 9.2

Humanitarianism: A Core Value for Many Americans

Sometimes cultural differences can work to a marketer's advantage. Hog farmers Dale and Lisa Siebrecht have been able to make a profit during a time when more than half of Iowa's pork producers have gone out of business. The Siebrechts decided to begin raising Berkshire hogs, which are big and slow-growing (and thus unappealing to large corporate farming operations) because the meat produced by this breed of hog is fat, sweet, and juicy—and preferred by Japanese consumers. With the reduction of trade barriers and new CryoVac packaging, an improved sealant that keeps meat fresh for the long trip from Iowa to Tokyo, the Siebrechts can get their product to market quickly, much to the delight of Japanese importers.[4]

Subcultures Cultures are not homogeneous entities with universal values. Each culture includes numerous **subcultures**—groups with their own distinct modes of behavior. Understanding the differences among subcultures can help marketers develop more effective marketing strategies.

The U.S., like many nations, is composed of significant subcultures that differ by ethnicity, nationality, age, rural versus urban location, religion, and geographic distribution. The Southwestern lifestyle emphasizes casual dress, outdoor entertaining, and active recreation. Mormons refrain from buying or using tobacco and liquor. Orthodox Jews purchase and consume only kosher foods. Understanding these and other differences among subcultures contributes to successful marketing of goods and services.

As Chapter 8 indicated, America's ethnic mix is changing. By 2050, marketers will no longer easily spot the "typical" American. Ethnic and racial minority groups will constitute much larger percentages of the population. Marketers will need to be sensitive to these changes and to the differences in shopping patterns and buying habits among ethnic segments of the population. Businesses will no longer succeed by selling one-size-fits-all products; they will need to consider consumer needs, interests, and concerns when developing their marketing strategies.

Nearly one-third of Hispanic Americans are younger than age 17, and many are "bilingual and bicultural in their day-to-day lives and able to choose the best of what each world has to offer," says Monica Gadsby, director of Hispanic media for Starcom Worldwide. According to Starcom's Internet-based surveys of this group, they tend to watch general-market television during the day with their friends but Spanish-language programs with their families in the evening. So, Univision Communications, the leading Spanish-language broadcaster in the U.S., developed a prime-time miniseries called *Sonadoras,* which was a huge success among teens and young adults. Now the network is working on several more such series.[5]

Marketing concepts may not always cross cultural boundaries without changes. For example, new immigrants may not be familiar with cents-off coupons and contests. Marketers may need to provide specific instructions when targeting such promotions to these groups.

According to the U.S. Census Bureau, the three largest and fastest-growing U.S. ethnic subcultures are African Americans, Hispanics, and Asians. Figure 9.3 shows the proportion of the U.S. population made

FIGURE 9.3

Ethnic and Racial Minorities as a Percentage of the Total U.S. Population

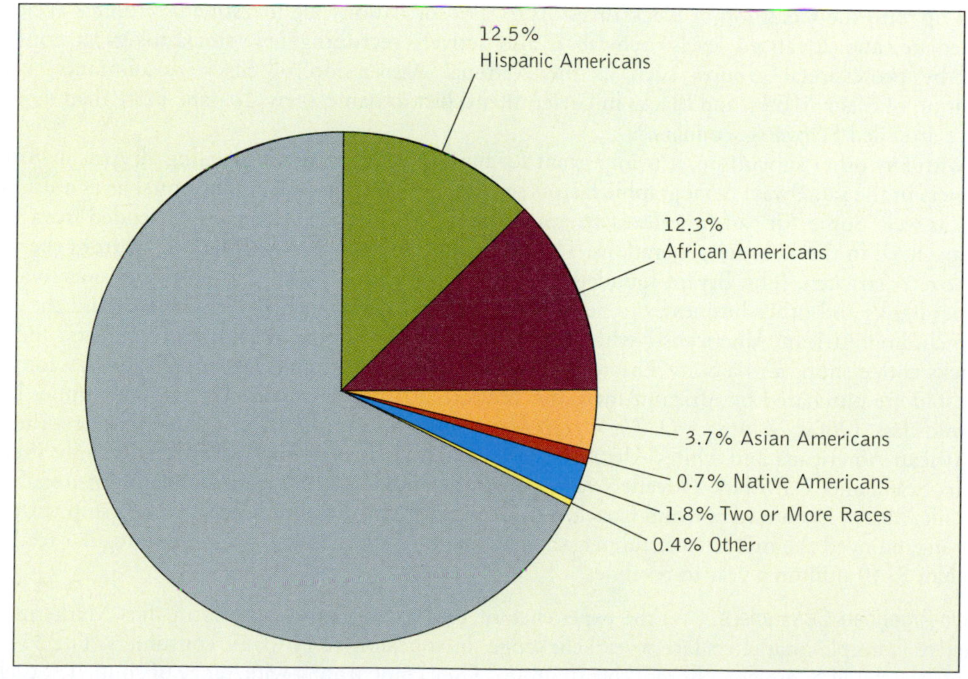

Note: Percentages have been rounded.
Source: Data from Roger Simon and Angie Cannon, "An Amazing Journey," *U.S. News & World Report,* August 6, 2001, p. 12.

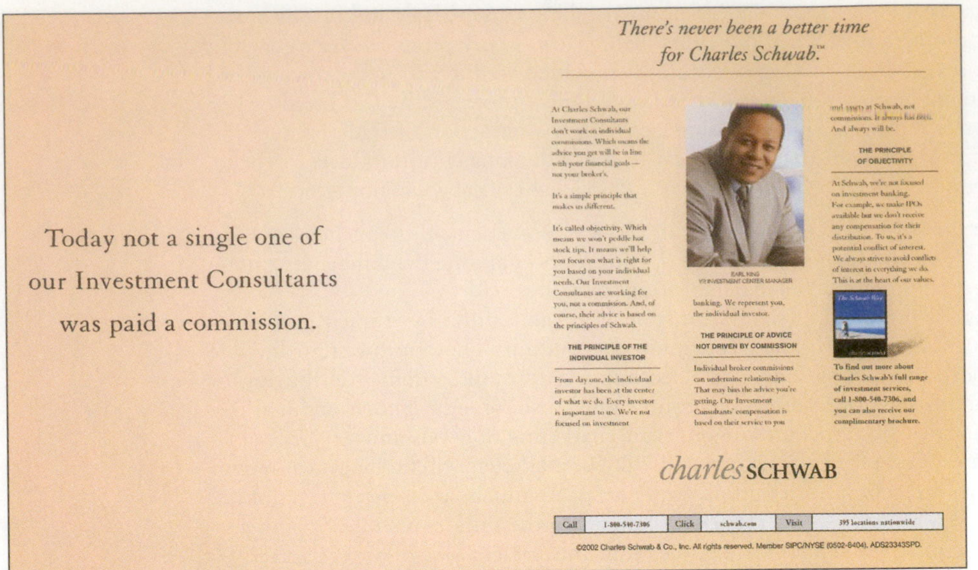

The rising affluence and growing numbers of African Americans prompted Charles Schwab & Co., Inc., to better serve this important market segment by offering services such as retirement workshops at many of their nationwide offices.

up of minority groups. While no ethnic or racial subculture is entirely homogeneous, researchers have found that each of these three ethnic segments have identifiable consumer behavior profiles.

African-American Consumers A recent study shows African-American buying power rose 73 percent during the past ten years, compared with 57 percent for U.S. consumers in general. The growing African-American market offers a tremendous opportunity for marketers who understand its buying patterns.

Family structures may differ for African-American consumers. The median age of the typical African-American household is about five years younger than that of the average white family. This creates differences in preferences for clothing, music, cars, and many other products. Also, African-American households are twice as likely as non–African-American households to be headed by women who make the majority of the purchase decisions.

Successful firms try to reach African-American consumers through various approaches. For example, the Ariel/Schwab Black Investor Survey, sponsored in part by Charles Schwab & Co., Inc., revealed that many African-American investors feel insecure about their investment knowledge and do not fully trust financial advisors. Adding to the credibility issue is a perceived lack of African-American financial professionals. Perhaps as a result, African Americans tend to invest more conservatively than other groups. They are more likely to choose real estate and life insurance as investments and are less likely to put their money in the stock market. However, the latest survey found that the number of high-income African Americans who invest in the stock market is up 30 percent since 1998, while stock ownership among whites rose only 4 percent.

Schwab used this information to design programs specifically for African Americans and believes that these programs helped to increase the percentage of African Americans in the stock market. The company teamed up with the Coalition of Black Investors to sponsor nationwide investment seminars at beginner, intermediate, and advanced levels. Schwab is also actively recruiting new stockbrokers at conferences hosted by professional groups, such as the National Association of Black Accountants, National Association of Black MBAs, and Blacks in Government, just to name a few. To date, more than 4,500 people have attended Schwab's seminars.[6]

As with any other subculture, it is important for marketers to avoid approaching all African-American consumers in the same way; demographic factors such as age, language, and educational level must be considered as well. Some African Americans are recent immigrants, while others are descended from families who have lived in the U.S. for generations. They are members of all economic groups—from the well-to-do to poverty stricken. John Bryant founded Operation Hope after the 1992 Los Angeles riots in an effort to attract banks and other businesses to South Central Los Angeles to revitalize the area and the minorities—including African Americans—who lived there. Because of the organization's efforts, today two Starbucks coffee shops and a Sony Theater operate in the neighborhood, where one of every four movie tickets sold are purchased by African Americans. Still other African Americans occupy the upper levels of economic class. Oprah Winfrey's *O, The Oprah Magazine,* reaches a wealthier group of readers (including both African Americans and whites) than does her daily talk show, whose advertisers include Procter & Gamble, Sears, and Wal-Mart. *O* readers earn an average annual income of $63,000 and generally prefer brands like Lexus, Donna Karan, and Coach. The magazine, which is produced in partnership with Hearst Publishing, enjoyed the most successful magazine launch ever and now has 2.5 million regular readers and more than $140 million a year in revenues.[7]

Hispanic-American Consumers As the experience of Procter & Gamble shows in the "Marketing Hits" Interactive Example, marketers face several challenges in appealing to Hispanic consumers. The 35 million Hispanics in the U.S. are not a homogeneous group. They come from a wide range of countries, each with its own culture. Some 64 percent come from Mexico, about 15 percent from Central and South America,

10.5 percent from Puerto Rico, and approximately 4.7 percent from Cuba. Cultural differences among these segments often affect consumer preferences.

<interactive>**example**

MARKETING HIT: PROCTER & GAMBLE TAPS THE HISPANIC MARKET

The term "Hispanic" is a broad concept that includes a wide spectrum of national identities. "There are white, black, and brown Hispanics," notes Esteban Torres, a former Congressman from California. "You are what you think you are." Even the word *Hispanic* is not universal; Puerto Ricans and Dominicans in New York and Cubans in South Florida refer to themselves as Hispanic, but many Mexican and Central Americans in the Southwest U.S. prefer to be called Latinos.

More important than differences in national origin are differences in *acculturation,* or the degree to which newcomers have adapted to U.S. culture. Acculturation plays a vital role in consumer behavior. For instance, marketers should not assume that all Hispanics understand Spanish. By the third generation after immigration, most Hispanic Americans speak only English.

Hispanics can be divided into three major acculturation groups:

- *Largely unacculturated Hispanics* (about 28 percent of the U.S. Hispanic population) were typically born outside the U.S. and have lived in the country for less than 10 years. They tend to have the lowest income of the three groups and depend almost exclusively on Spanish-language media.
- *Partially unacculturated Hispanics* (approximately 59 percent) were born in the U.S. or have lived there for more than 10 years. Most are bilingual, speaking English at work and Spanish at home. Many are middle income, and marketers can reach them through both Spanish- and English-language media.
- *Highly acculturated Hispanics* (13 percent) enjoy the highest income of the three groups. Usually born and raised in the U.S., they are English speaking but retain many Hispanic cultural values and traditions.

Research indicates several other important points:

- The Hispanic market is large and fast growing. Already the U.S. is home to the fifth-largest Hispanic population in the world; only the populations of Argentina, Colombia, Mexico, and Spain are bigger.
- Hispanics tend to be young, with a median age of 25 compared with a median age of 35 for the general U.S. population.
- Hispanic consumers are geographically concentrated in the following states: California, Florida, New Mexico, New York, and Texas. In fact, 42 percent of New Mexico's population is Hispanic. Almost half of all Hispanics living in the U.S. reside in five cities: Chicago, Los Angeles, Miami, New York, and San Francisco.

Hispanics tend to have larger households than non-Hispanics, making them good customers for products sold in bulk. They spend more on their children than do parents in other subcultures, especially on clothing. Hispanics also place great importance on keeping in touch with relatives in other countries, making them excellent customers for long-distance phone service, air travel, and wire transfers of money. In addition, Hispanics make more visits to pizza and chicken chain restaurants than do general-market consumers and bring along with them a larger group of family members and friends. "Fast-food marketers think about this segment more and more as the opportunity for growth lies within this fast-growing segment," says Andy Barish, a restaurant analyst with Robertson Stephens. "They've barely scratched the surface right now."[8]

Asian-American Consumers Marketing to Asian Americans presents many of the same challenges as reaching Hispanics. Like Hispanics, Asian Americans are spread among culturally diverse groups, many retaining their own languages. The Asian-American

Being aware of subcultures is critical to marketing success. Sears's promotions for the Asia Moon Festival are tailored to the makeup of the local community where its stores are located—whether they are Mandarin, Cantonese, Vietnamese, or Korean.

Briefly Speaking

A father is a banker provided by nature.

French proverb

subculture actually consists of more than two dozen ethnic groups, including Chinese, Filipinos, Indians, Japanese, Koreans, and Vietnamese. Each group brings its own language, religion, and value system to purchasing decisions. As mentioned earlier in the chapter, Sears has been working on attracting Asian-American consumers to its stores by conducting promotions in conjunction with the Asia Moon Festival. Depending on the cultural makeup of the community surrounding a particular Sears store, the company advertises the Festival in Mandarin, Cantonese, Vietnamese, or Korean. The programs within each store are conducted in English. Sixty-eight Chinese language newspapers and 20 magazines are currently published in the U.S.; 34 Vietnamese newspapers and 45 magazines; 46 Korean newspapers and 16 magazines; 37 Filipino newspapers and 18 magazines; and 20 Japanese newspapers and 18 magazines.[9]

Regardless of which Asian subgroup they target, marketers should take care to avoid sounding patronizing; in fact, this advice holds true for any subculture. In addition, Asian-American consumers like gift-with-purchase promotions; again, this is true of many other groups. But marketers should be careful to select gifts that are appropriate. Sears gives out traditional pastries called moon cakes in Chinese communities during its Moon Festival promotion. In other Asian communities, shoppers receive decorative lanterns. "It's a celebration," says Sears vice president of multicultural and relationship marketing Gilbert Davila. "We always run out of gifts."[10]

Social Influences

Every consumer belongs to a number of social groups. A child's earliest group experience comes from membership in a family. As children grow older, they join other groups such as friendship groups, neighborhood groups, school groups, and organizations such as Girl Scouts and Little League. Adults are also members of various groups, at work and in the community.

Group membership influences an individual's purchase decisions and behavior in both overt and subtle ways. Every group establishes certain norms of behavior. *Norms* are the values, attitudes, and behaviors that a group deems appropriate for its members. Group members are expected to comply with these norms. Members of the National Rifle Association, Nature Conservancy, American Medical Association, and local country club tend to adopt their organization's norms of behavior. Norms can even affect nonmembers. Individuals who aspire to membership in a group may adopt its standards of behavior and values.

Differences in group status and roles can also affect buying behavior. *Status* is the relative position of any individual member in a group; *roles* define behavior that members of a group expect of individuals who hold specific positions within that group. Some groups (such as Rotary Club or Lion's Club) define formal roles, and others (such as friendship groups) impose informal expectations. Both types of groups supply each member with both status and roles; in doing so, they influence that person's activities—including his or her purchase behavior.

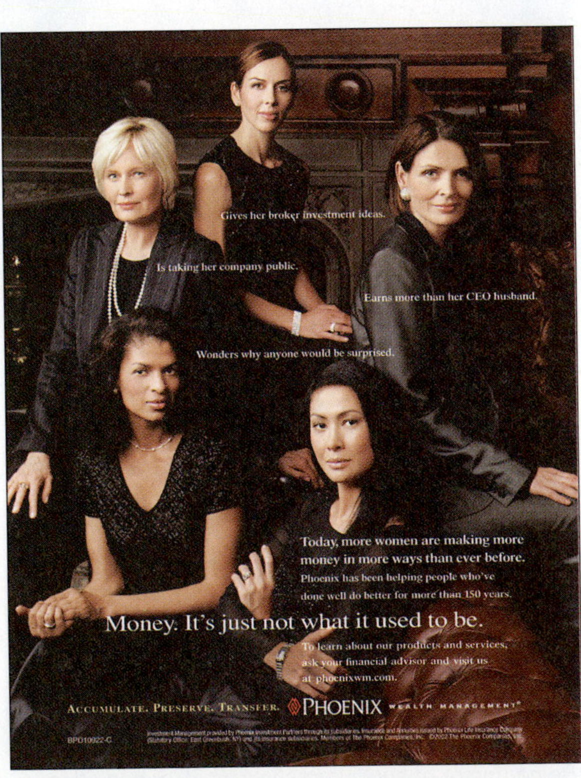

Dual-income households and increases in the number of highly paid and high-profile professional women have made female household members more influential in U.S. social class rankings.

The Internet provides an opportunity for individuals to form and be influenced by new types of groups. Usenet mailing lists and chat rooms allow groups to form around common interests. Some of these online "virtual communities" can develop norms and membership roles similar to those found in real-world groups. For example, to avoid criticism, members must observe rules for proper protocol in posting messages and participating in chats.

The Asch Phenomenon

Groups often influence an individual's purchase decisions more than is realized. Most people tend to adhere in varying degrees to the general expectations of any group that they consider important, often without conscious awareness of this motivation. The surprising impact of groups and group norms on individual behavior has been called the *Asch phenomenon,* named after social psychologist S. E. Asch, who through his research first documented characteristics of individual behavior.

Asch found that individuals would conform to majority rule, even if that majority rule went against their beliefs. The Asch phenomenon can be a big factor in many purchase decisions, from major choices such as buying a house or car to deciding whether to buy a pair of shoes on sale.

Reference Groups

Discussion of the Asch phenomenon raises the subject of **reference groups**—groups whose value structures and standards influence a person's behavior. Consumers usually try to coordinate their purchase behavior with their perceptions of the values of their reference groups. The extent of reference-group influence varies widely among individuals. Strong influence by a group on a member's purchase requires two conditions:

1. The purchased product must be one that others can see and identify.
2. The purchased item must be conspicuous; it must stand out as something unusual, a brand or product that not everyone owns.

Reference-group influence would significantly affect the decision to buy a Jaguar, for example, but it would have little or no impact on the decision to purchase a loaf of bread. The status of the individual within a group produces three subcategories of reference groups: a membership group to which the person actually belongs, such as a political party, an aspirational group with which the person desires to associate, and a dissociative group with which the individual does not want to be identified.

Children are especially vulnerable to the influence of reference groups. They often base their buying decisions on outside forces—what they see on television, popular choices among friends, fashionable products among adults. Advertising, especially endorsements by celebrities, can have much bigger impacts on children than on adults, in part because children want so badly to belong to aspirational groups.

Reference-group influences appear in other countries, as well. Many young people in Japan aspire to American culture and values. Buying products decorated with English words and phrases—even if inaccurate—helps them to achieve this feeling.

Social Classes Research augmented many years ago by sociologist W. Lloyd Warner identified six classes within the social structures of both small and large U.S. cities: the upper-upper, lower-upper, upper-middle, and lower-middle classes, followed by the working class and lower class. Class rankings are determined by occupation, income, education, family background, and residence location. Note, however, that income is not always a primary determinant; pipe fitters paid at union scale earn more than many college professors, but their purchase behavior may be quite different. Thus, marketers are likely to disagree with the old adage that "a rich man is a poor man with more money."

Family characteristics, such as the occupations and incomes of one or both parents, have been the primary influences on social class. As women's careers and earning power have increased over the past few decades, marketers have begun to pay more attention to their position as influential buyers.

People in one social class may aspire to a higher class and therefore exhibit buying behavior common to that class rather than to their own. For example, middle-class consumers often buy items they associate with the upper classes. Although the upper classes themselves account for a very small percentage of the population, many more consumers treat themselves to prestigious products, such as designer clothing or luxury cars, as illustrated in Figure 9.4.

FIGURE 9.4

A Product for Those Aspiring to a Higher Social Class

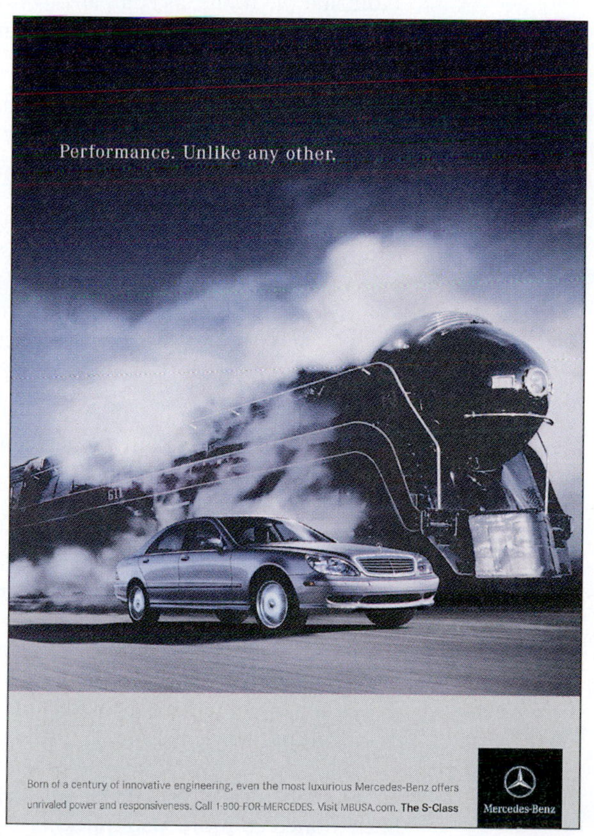

Opinion Leaders In nearly every reference group, a few members act as **opinion leaders.** These trendsetters are likely to purchase new products before others in the group and then share their experiences and opinions via word of mouth. As others in the group decide whether to try the same product, they are influenced by the reports of opinion leaders.

Generalized opinion leaders are rare; instead, individuals tend to act as opinion leaders for specific goods or services based on their knowledge of and interest in those products. Their interest motivates them to seek out information from mass media, manufacturers, and other sources and, in turn, transmit this information to associates through interpersonal communications. Opinion leaders are found within all segments of the population.

Information about goods and services sometimes flows from the Internet, radio, television, and other mass media to opinion leaders and then from opinion leaders to others. In other instances, information flows directly from media sources to all consumers. In still other instances, a multistep flow carries information from mass media to opinion leaders and then on to other opinion leaders before dissemination to the general public. Figure 9.5 illustrates these three types of communication flow.

Some opinion leaders influence purchases by others merely through their own actions, which is particularly true in the case of fashion decisions. When actress Sarah Jessica Parker began wearing a horseshoe necklace studded with diamonds during her television series *Sex in the City,* the necklace style suddenly became the rage among women and girls of all ages. Jewelry manufacturers reproduced the necklace in a variety of materials, ranging from platinum and diamonds to silvertone metal and crystals.

FIGURE 9.5

Alternative Channels for Communications Flow

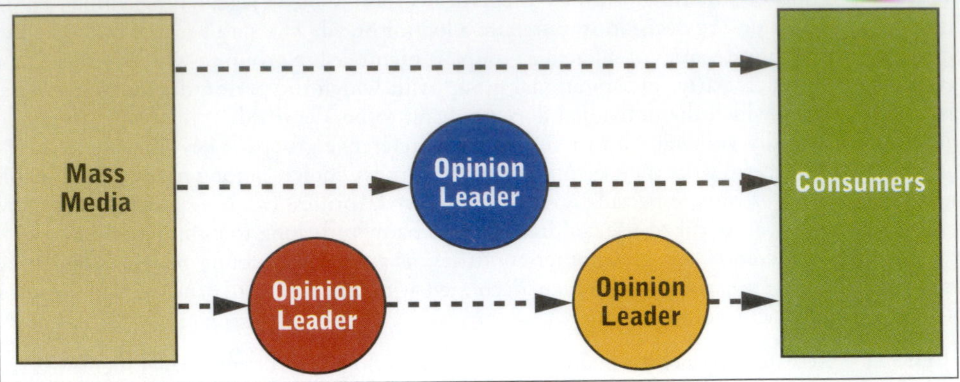

Family Influences

Most people are members of at least two families during their lifetimes—the ones they are born into and those they eventually form later in life. The family group is perhaps the most important determinant of consumer behavior because of the close, continuing interactions among family members. Like other groups, each family typically has norms of expected behavior and different roles and status relationships for its members.

The traditional family structure consists of a husband, wife, and children. However, according to the U.S. Census Bureau, this structure has been steadily changing over the last century. In 1900, 80 percent of households were headed by married couples; today, only 53 percent are. A century ago, half of all households consisted of extended families, with six or more people living under one roof; today, only 10 percent of such households exist. Today, three of every five married women and 69 percent of single women work outside the home, as compared with 6 percent of married women and 44 percent of single women in the year 1900.[11] These statistics have important implications for marketers, because they indicate a change in who makes buying decisions. Still, marketers describe the role of each spouse in terms of these four categories:

1. *Autonomic role* is when the partners independently make equal numbers of decisions. Personal-care items would fall into the kinds of purchase decisions each would make for themselves.
2. *Husband-dominant role* is when the husband makes most of the decisions. Life insurance is a typical example.
3. *Wife-dominant role* is when the wife makes most of the decisions. Children's clothing is a typical wife-dominant purchase.
4. *Syncratic role* is when both partners jointly make most decisions. The purchase of a house or car usually follows a syncratic pattern.

The emergence of the two-income family has changed the role of women in family purchasing behavior. In the 1950s and early 1960s, women exercised only limited control of family purchasing decisions. A woman might make buying decisions about groceries and household items, but she was likely to defer to her husband on larger expenditures. Today, however, women have more say in large-ticket family purchases such as automobiles and computers. Studies of family decision making have also shown that households with two wage earners are more likely than others to make joint purchasing decisions.

Men's roles are also changing. More and more men are now major food purchasers, shopping either alone or with their spouse. Members of two-income households often do their shopping in the evening and on weekends.

Shifting family roles have created new markets for time-saving goods and services. The desire to save time is not new. As early as 1879, Heinz advertised its ready-made ketchup "for the blessed relief of mother and other women of the household"—but it has taken on new urgency as growing numbers of parents juggle multiple roles: raising families, building careers, and managing household operations. This time crunch explains the growing market for home-meal replacement, as more and more grocery stores prepare and sell complete meals to go. As Figure 9.6 shows, Oscar Mayer offers precooked bacon for people who want old-fashioned comfort food quickly.

Busy consumers are looking for ways to save shopping and purchase time as well. Internet and catalog shopping are natural time-savers for frantic families, but brick-and-mortar stores are catching on as well.

Banks, fast-food restaurants, and even drugstores have completely changed the way they serve today's families by adding drive-through windows and call-ahead services.[12]

Children and Teenagers in Family Purchases As parents have become busier, they have delegated some family purchase decisions to children, specifically teenagers. Children learn about the latest products and trends because they watch so much television and cruise the Internet, often becoming the family experts on what to buy. As a result, children have gained sophistication and assumed new roles in family purchasing behavior.

Children and teenagers represent a huge market—over 50 million strong—and they influence what their parents buy, from cereal to automobiles. According to James McNeal, a retired professor from Texas A&M University, children had an influence on an estimated $290 billion in family spending in a recent year. "That's kids actually pointing fingers and making demands," he says. But there's also the "nag factor," in which youngsters had an indirect impact on another $320 billion of household spending. "The real story of kids' market power is not their spending," says John Geraci, vice president of youth research at Harris Interactive. "It's their influence on the household."[13]

The Nickelodeon cable network is a favorite advertising outlet for marketers trying to reach parents through the younger set, in addition to reaching kids themselves. Recently Nickelodeon partnered with Gateway, Ford, and even Embassy Suites Hotels, which began offering a "Nick Trip Pack" with a disposable camera, travel journal, and *Rugrats* "Tommy" doll. In just one month, hotel visits tied directly to the advertising campaign boosted weekend bookings by 34 percent.[14] Even after they grow up, children continue to play roles in family consumer behavior, often by recommending products to their parents. Advertisers try to influence these relationships by showing adult children interacting with their parents.

FIGURE 9.6

Oscar Mayer's Appeal to Busy Families

Of course, children have their own purchasing power as well. In one recent year, children between the ages of 4 and 12 spent $29 billion of their own allowances, baby-sitting and odd-jobs earnings, and handouts from parents on various goods and services.[15]

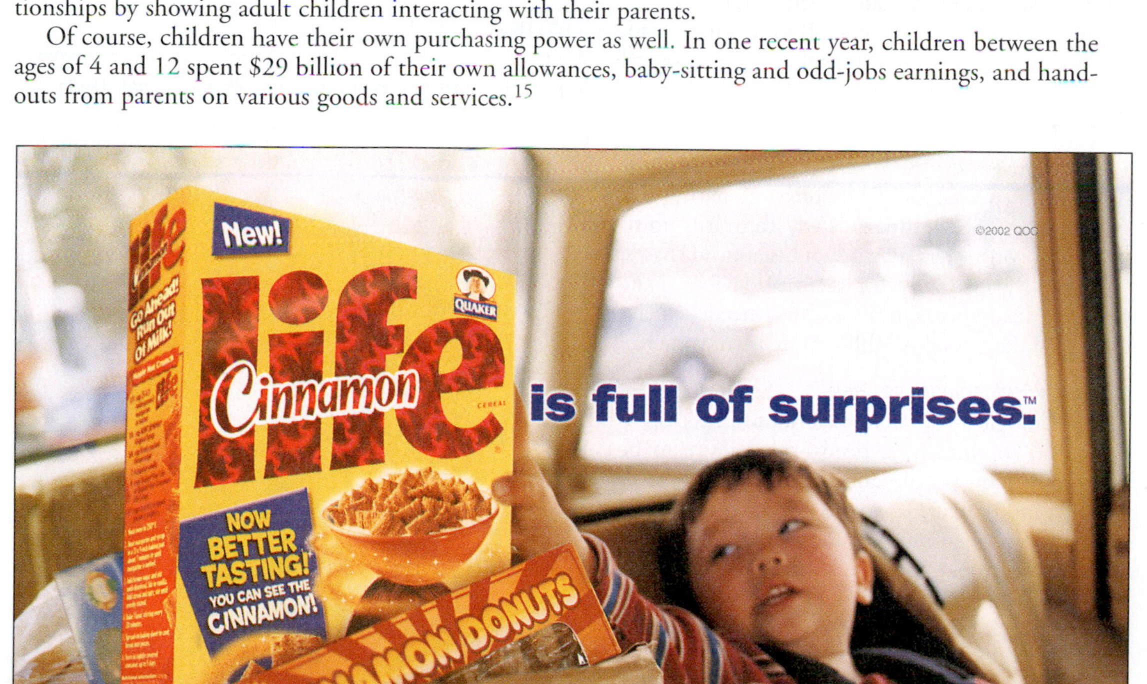

Children often influence what their parents buy. Cereal is a classic example.

Briefly Speaking

Happy is the child whose father dies rich.

Anonymous

PERSONAL DETERMINANTS OF CONSUMER BEHAVIOR

Consumer behavior is affected by a number of internal, personal factors, in addition to interpersonal ones. Each individual brings unique needs, motives, perceptions, attitudes, learned responses, and self-concepts to buying decisions. This section will look at how these factors influence consumer behavior.

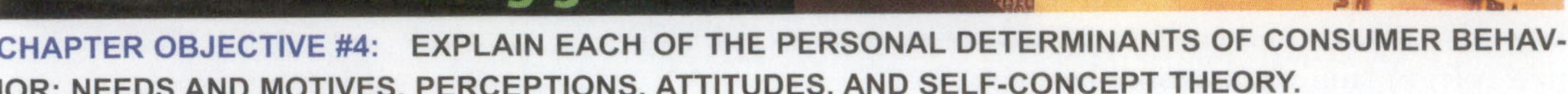

CHAPTER OBJECTIVE #4: EXPLAIN EACH OF THE PERSONAL DETERMINANTS OF CONSUMER BEHAVIOR: NEEDS AND MOTIVES, PERCEPTIONS, ATTITUDES, AND SELF-CONCEPT THEORY.

Needs and Motives

Individual purchase behavior is driven by the motivation to fill a need. A **need** is an imbalance between the consumer's actual and desired states. Someone who recognizes or feels a significant or urgent need then seeks to correct the imbalance. Marketers attempt to arouse this sense of urgency, that is making a need "felt," and then influence consumers' motivation to satisfy their needs by purchasing specific products.

Motives are inner states that direct a person toward the goal of satisfying a felt need. The individual takes action to reduce the state of tension and return to a condition of equilibrium.

Maslow's Hierarchy of Needs Psychologist A. H. Maslow developed a theory that characterized needs and arranged them in a hierarchy to reflect their importance. Maslow identified five levels of needs, beginning with physiological needs and progressing to the need for self-actualization. A person must at least partially satisfy lower-level needs, according to his theory, before higher needs can affect behavior. In developed countries, where relatively large per-capita incomes allow most people to satisfy the basic needs on the hierarchy, higher-order needs may be more important to consumer behavior. Table 9.1 illustrates products and marketing themes designed to satisfy needs at each level.

Physiological Needs Needs at the most basic level concern essential requirements for survival, such as food, water, shelter, and clothing. Pepperidge Farm French Toast Swirl Bread, shown in Figure 9.7, appeals to physiological needs by stating in its advertisements that, "It doesn't go with breakfast. It is breakfast."

Safety Needs Second-level needs include security, protection from physical harm, and avoidance of the unexpected. To gratify these needs, consumers may buy mutual fund shares, disability insurance, or security devices. State Farm Insurance appeals to these needs by saying, "Like a good neighbor State Farm is there."

Social/Belongingness Needs Satisfaction of physiological and safety needs leads a person to attend to third-level needs—the desire to be accepted by people and groups important to that individual. To satisfy this need, people may join organizations and buy goods or services that make them feel part of a group. The ad for Olive Garden restaurants in Figure 9.8 actually appeals to two needs—physiological (food) and social/belongingness. The ad's tagline is "When you're here, you're family."

Esteem Needs The desire for a sense of accomplishment and achievement, to gain the respect of others, and even to exceed the performance of others is a universal human trait that emerges after lower-order needs are satisfied.

Self-Actualization Needs At the top rung of Maslow's ladder of human needs is people's

FIGURE 9.7

Pepperidge Farm's Direct Appeal to Physiological Needs

TABLE 9.1

Marketing Strategies Based on Maslow's Hierarchy of Needs

Physiological Needs	Products	Vitamins, herbal supplements, medicines, food, exercise equipment, fitness clubs
	Marketing themes	Church's Fried Chicken—"Gotta love it."; Campbell's Healthy Request Soups—"M'm! M'm! Good! . . . and Healthy!"; Bausch & Lomb—"See the wonder."
Safety Needs	Products	Cars and auto accessories, burglar alarm systems, retirement investments, insurance, smoke and carbon-monoxide detectors, medicines
	Marketing themes	Fireman's Fund Insurance—"License to get on with it."; American General Financial Group—"Live the life you've imagined." Shell Oil—"Count on Shell."; Bayer—"Changing the world with great care."; Volvo—"Protect the body. Ignite the soul."
Belongingness	Products	Beauty aids, entertainment, clothing, cars
	Marketing themes	Dell Computer—"Hey Dude, you're getting a Dell."; Blue Ridge Knives—"Follow the leader."; Lawson Software—"Leading-edge technology without the attitude."; Egift online retailer—"Great gifts for everyone . . . starting with you."
Esteem Needs	Products	Clothing, cars, jewelry, liquors, hobbies, beauty spa services
	Marketing themes	Saks Fifth Avenue—"Defining Style."; Van Cleef & Arpels—"The pleasure of perfection."; Accutron watches—"Perhaps it's worthy of your trust."; Jenn-Air kitchen appliances—"The sign of a great cook."
Self-Actualization	Products	Education, cultural events, sports, hobbies, luxury goods, technology, travel
	Marketing themes	Gatorade—"Is it in you?"; Baccarat Crystal—"Beauty has its reasons."; Grand Lido Resorts—"Lost and found for the soul."; Gauthier jewelry—"Wear art."

desire to realize their full potential and to find fulfillment by fully expressing their talents and capabilities. Companies specializing in exotic adventure vacations aim to satisfy consumers' needs for self-actualization. Other travel providers, such as Smithsonian Study Tours, offer specialized educational trips that appeal to consumers' desires for a meaningful experience as well as a vacation. Elderhostel tailors similar trips for baby boomers and seniors. These trips usually involve an informal course of study—whether it's cooking, history, anthropology, or golf.

Maslow noted that a satisfied need no longer motivates a person to act. Once the physiological needs are met, the individual moves on to pursue satisfaction of higher-order needs. Consumers are periodically motivated by the need to relieve thirst and hunger, but their interests soon return to focus on satisfaction of safety, social, and other needs in the hierarchy.

Critics have pointed out a variety of flaws in Maslow's reasoning. For example, some needs can be related to more than one level. However, the hierarchy of needs continues to occupy a secure place in the study of consumer behavior.

Perceptions

Perception is the meaning that a person attributes to incoming stimuli gathered through the five senses—sight, hearing, touch, taste, and smell. Certainly a buyer's behavior is influenced by his or her perceptions of a good or service. Only recently have researchers come to recognize that people's perceptions depend as much on what they want to perceive as on the actual stimuli. It is for this reason that Saks Fifth Avenue and Godiva chocolates are perceived so differently from Wal-Mart and Hershey, respectively.

FIGURE 9.8

Olive Garden's Appeal to Social and Belongingness Needs

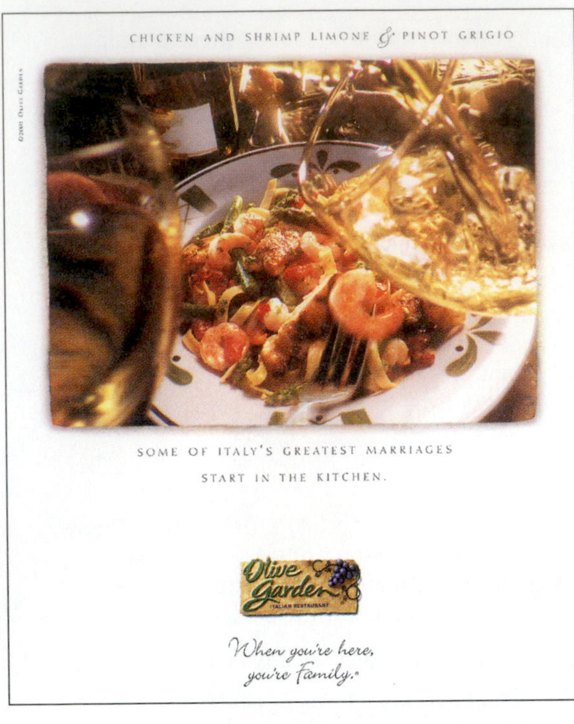

CHICKEN AND SHRIMP LIMONE & PINOT GRIGIO
SOME OF ITALY'S GREATEST MARRIAGES
START IN THE KITCHEN.
Olive Garden
ITALIAN RESTAURANT
When you're here,
you're Family.

A person's perception of an object or event results from the interaction of two types of factors:

1. Stimulus factors—characteristics of the physical object such as size, color, weight, and shape
2. Individual factors—unique characteristics of the individual, including not only sensory processes but also experiences with similar inputs and basic motivations and expectations

Perceptual Screens The average American today is constantly bombarded by marketing messages. According to the Food Marketing Institute, a typical supermarket now carries 30,000 different packages, each serving as a miniature billboard vying to attract consumers' attention. Over 6,000 commercials a week are aired on network TV. Prime-time TV shows carry more than 15 minutes of advertising every hour. Thousands of businesses have set up World Wide Web sites to tout their offerings. Marketers have also stamped their messages on everything from popcorn bags in movie theaters to airsickness bags on planes.

This unceasing marketing clutter has caused consumers to ignore many promotional messages. People respond selectively to attend only to messages that manage to break through their *perceptual screens*—the mental filtering processes through which all inputs must pass.

All marketers struggle to determine which stimuli evoke responses from consumers. They must learn how to capture a customer's attention long enough to read an advertisement, listen to a sales representative, or react to a point-of-purchase display. In general, marketers seek to make a message stand out and to gain the attention of prospective customers. One way marketers can draw attention to their messages is through appeals to consumers' fears, as the "Solving an Ethical Controversy" Interactive Example discusses.

RIGHT/WRONG: SOLVING AN ETHICAL CONTROVERSY—MARKETING TO CONSUMERS' FEARS

One way to break through clutter is to run large ads. Doubling the size of an ad in printed media increases its attention value by about 50 percent. Advertisers use color to make newspaper ads contrast with the usual black-and-white graphics, providing another effective way to penetrate the reader's perceptual screen. Other methods for enhancing contrast include arranging a large amount of white space around a printed area or placing white type on a dark background. Vivid illustrations and photos can also help to break through clutter in print ads.

The psychological concept of closure also helps marketers create a message that stands out. Closure is the human tendency to perceive a complete picture from an incomplete stimulus. Advertisements that allow consumers to do this often succeed in breaking through perceptual screens. During a Kellogg campaign promoting consumption of fruit with cereal, the company emphasized the point by replacing the letters *ll* in Kellogg with bananas. In a campaign featuring a 25-cent coupon offer, Kellogg reinforced the promotional idea by replacing the letter *o* in the brand name with the image of a quarter.

Word-of-mouth marketing can be a highly effective way of breaking through consumers' perceptual screens. Take the early *Harry Potter* books. Although the series featuring the orphaned English schoolboy who is sent to wizardry school is now a huge international success, early popularity of the first two books was based on word of mouth. Before American marketers even got wind of the bespectacled young wizard from England, kids were requesting the books at their local bookstores, reading them, and passing them along to friends.

A new tool that marketers are exploring is the use of virtual reality. Some companies have created presentations based on virtual reality that display marketing messages and information in a three-dimensional format. Eventually, experts predict, consumers will be able to tour resort areas via virtual reality before booking their trips or to walk through the interiors of homes they are considering buying via virtual reality. Virtual reality technology may allow marketers to penetrate consumer perceptual filters in a way not currently possible with other forms of media.

<interactive>**exercise**

'NET EX: VIRTUAL REALITY AND CONSUMER BEHAVIOR

With selective perception at work screening competing messages, it is easy to see the importance of marketers' efforts in developing brand loyalty. Satisfied customers are less likely to seek information about competing products. Even when competitive advertising is forced on them, they are less apt than others to look beyond their perceptual filters at those appeals. Loyal customers simply tune out information that does not agree with their existing beliefs and expectations.

Subliminal Perception Almost 50 years ago, a New Jersey movie theater tried to boost concession sales by flashing the words *Eat Popcorn* and *Drink Coca-Cola* between frames of actress Kim Novak's image in the movie *Picnic.* The messages flashed on the screen every five seconds for a duration of one three-hundredth of a second each time. Researchers reported that these messages, though too short to be recognizable at the conscious level, resulted in a 58 percent increase in popcorn sales and an 18 percent increase in Coke sales. After the findings were published, advertising agencies and consumer protection groups became intensely interested in *subliminal perception*—the subconscious receipt of incoming information.

Subliminal advertising is aimed at the subconscious level of awareness to circumvent the audience's perceptual screens. The goal of the original research was to induce consumer purchases while keeping consumers unaware of the source of the motivation to buy. All later attempts to duplicate the test findings, however, have been unsuccessful.

Although subliminal advertising has been universally condemned as manipulative, it is exceedingly unlikely that it can induce purchasing except by people already inclined to buy. Three reasons ensure that this fact will remain true:

1. Strong stimulus factors are required just to get a prospective customer's attention.
2. Only a very short message can be transmitted.
3. Individuals vary greatly in their thresholds of consciousness. Messages transmitted at the threshold of consciousness for one person will not be perceived at all by some people and will be all too apparent to others. The subliminally exposed message, "Drink Coca-Cola," may go unseen by some viewers, while others may read it as "Drink Pepsi-Cola," "Drink Cocoa," or even "Drive Slowly."

Despite early fears, research has shown that subliminal messages cannot force receivers to purchase goods that they would not consciously want without the messages.

In recent years, subliminal communication has spread to programming for self-help tapes. These tapes play sounds that listeners hear consciously as relaxing music or ocean waves; subconsciously, imperceptibly among the other sounds, they hear thousands of subliminal messages. Americans spend millions of dollars a year on subliminal tapes that are supposed to help them stop smoking, lose weight, or achieve a host of other goals. Unfortunately, the National Research Council recently concluded that the subliminal messages do little to influence personal behavior.

The bright, vivid, swirling colors make this ad stand out and increase the likelihood that it will be noticed by readers.

Attitudes

Perception of incoming stimuli is greatly affected by attitudes. In fact, a consumer's decision to purchase an item is strongly based on his or her attitudes about the product, store, or salesperson.

Attitudes are a person's enduring favorable or unfavorable evaluations, emotions, or action tendencies toward some object or data. As they form over time through individual experiences and group contacts, attitudes become highly resistant to change.

Because favorable attitudes likely affect brand preferences, marketers are interested in determining consumer attitudes toward their offerings. Numerous attitude-scaling devices have been developed for this purpose.

Attitude Components An attitude has cognitive, affective, and behavioral components. The *cognitive* component refers to the individual's information and knowledge about an object or concept. The *affective* component deals with feelings or emotional reactions. The *behavioral* component involves tendencies to act in a certain manner. For example, in deciding whether to shop at a warehouse-type food store, a consumer might obtain information about what the store offers from advertising, trial visits, and input from family, friends, and associates (cognitive component). The consumer might also receive affective input by listening to others about their shopping experiences at this type of store. Other affective information might lead the person to make a judgment about the type of people who seem to shop there—whether they represent a group with which he or she would like to be associated. The consumer may ultimately decide to buy some canned goods, cereal, and bakery products there but continue to rely on his regular supermarket for major food purchases (behavioral component).

All three components maintain a relatively stable and balanced relationship to one another. Together they form an overall attitude about an object or idea.

Changing Consumer Attitudes Since a favorable consumer attitude provides a vital condition for marketing success, how can a firm lead prospective buyers to adopt such an attitude toward its products? Marketers have two choices: (1) attempt to produce consumer attitudes that will motivate purchase of a particular product or (2) evaluate existing consumer attitudes and then make the product features appeal to them.

If consumers view an existing good or service unfavorably, the seller may choose to redesign it or offer new options. American automakers have struggled for years to change consumers' attitudes about the way American cars are built, perform, and look. General Motors has spent decades—and millions—working to overcome quality problems, and has succeeded in many areas. But "hard quality"—making sure things don't break—is only a step toward changing consumers' attitudes. "Hard quality is simply not enough to be competitive," says William Shikany, a GM quality specialist. "Perceived quality is vital." Although GM's new Cadillac Escalade SUV is selling well, the Lexus LX470 SUV is doing better, even though the Lexus is a smaller, less powerful vehicle than the Escalade and costs more. Why? Lexus invested more in the look and feel of the vehicle's interior, which makes it look and feel like a more luxurious truck than the Escalade. Under a new "perceived quality" initiative, General Motors will be upgrading the interiors of several of its models, including the Escalade.[16]

Modifying the Components of Attitude Attitudes frequently change in response to inconsistencies among the three components. The most common inconsistencies result when new information changes the cognitive or affective components of an attitude. Marketers can work to modify attitudes by providing evidence of product benefits and by correcting misconceptions. The makers of A1 steak sauce, shown in Figure 9.9, want consumers to think about their sauce as a necessity to meals, not just an optional condiment. Marketers may also attempt to change attitudes by getting buyers to engage in new behavior. Free samples, for instance, can change attitudes by getting consumers to try a product.

Sometimes new technologies can encourage consumers to change their attitudes. Many people, for example, are reluctant to purchase clothing by mail-order mainly because they are afraid it will not fit properly. To address these concerns, e-retailer Lands' End (now part of Sears) introduced a "personal model" feature on its Web site. Women who visit the site answer a series of questions about height, body proportions, and hair color, and the software creates a three-dimensional figure reflecting their responses. Consumers can then adorn the electronic model with Lands' End garments to get an idea of how various outfits might look on them. Of course, for the electronic model to be correct, women must enter information about their bodies accurately, instead of simply relying on their perception of themselves.

Marketers may rely on new innovations to help change components of consumer attitudes. The Ortho Biotech Products ad in Figure 9.10 attempts to change the attitude of cancer patients that chemotherapy will cause anemia or make them feel tired by offering a new drug, Procrit, to counteract this particular side effect of their treatment.

FIGURE 9.9

Attempts to Change Consumer Attitudes Concerning the Use of Steak Sauce

Learning

Marketing is concerned as seriously with the process by which consumer decisions change over time as with the current status of those decisions. **Learning**, in a marketing context, refers to immediate or expected changes in consumer behavior as a result of experience. The learning process includes the component of *drive,* which is any strong stimulus that impels action. Fear, pride, desire for money, thirst, pain avoidance, and rivalry are examples of drives. Learning also relies on a *cue,* that is, any object in the environment that determines the nature of the consumer's response to a drive.

FIGURE 9.10

Ortho Biotech Products, the Maker of Procrit, Using Persuasive Advertising to Change Attitudes about Anemia

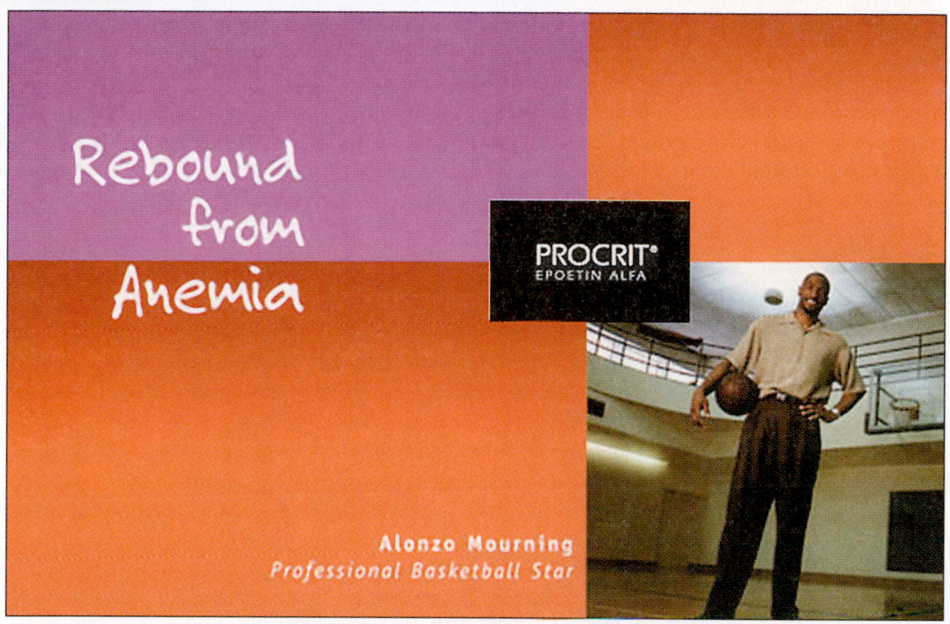

Examples of cues are a newspaper advertisement for a new Thai restaurant—a cue for a hungry person—and a Shell sign near an interstate highway—a cue for a motorist who needs gasoline.

A *response* is an individual's reaction to a set of cues and drives. Responses might include such reactions as purchasing Frontline flea and tick prevention for pets, dining at Pizza Hut, or deciding to enroll at a particular community college or university.

Reinforcement is the reduction in drive that results from a proper response. As a response becomes more rewarding, it creates a stronger bond between the drive and the purchase of the product, likely increasing future purchases by the consumer. Reinforcement is the rationale that underlies frequent-buyer programs, which reward repeat purchasers for their loyalty. These programs may offer points for premiums, frequent-flyer miles, and the like. The OneWorld ad in Figure 9.11 demonstrates a frequent-flyer program for eight participating airlines. Members that earn miles on one of the airlines can redeem the miles on any of the other seven, reinforcing the customer's choice of those airlines.

FIGURE 9.11

Reinforcement Provided for Loyalty to the OneWorld Frequent-Flyer Program

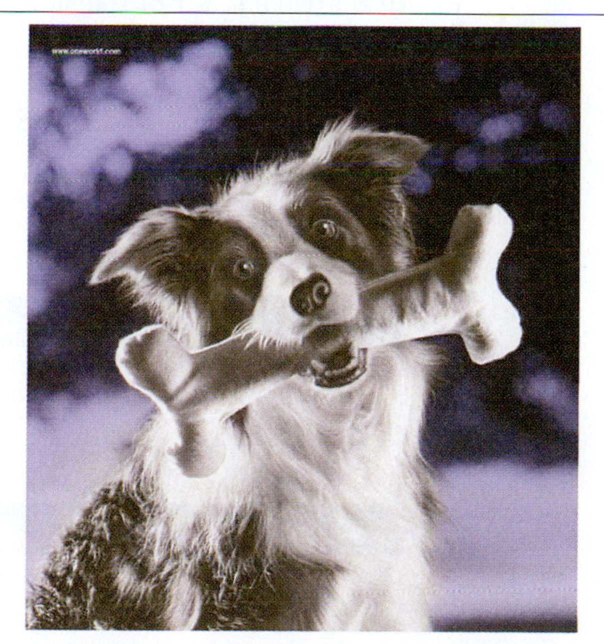

It's natural to want to be rewarded.
oneworld

Applying Learning Theory to Marketing Decisions Learning theory has some important implications for marketing strategists, particularly those involved with consumer packaged goods. Marketers must find a way to develop a desired outcome such as repeat purchase behavior gradually over time. *Shaping* is the process of applying a series of rewards and reinforcements to permit more complex behavior to evolve over time.

Both promotional strategy and the product itself play a role in the shaping process. Marketers want to motivate consumers to become regular buyers of a certain product. Their first step in getting consumers to try the product might be to offer a free-sample package that includes a substantial discount coupon for the next purchase. This example uses a cue as a shaping procedure. If the product performs well, the purchase response is reinforced and followed by another inducement—the coupon.

Briefly Speaking

A man who carries a cat by the tail learns something he can learn in no other way.

Mark Twain (1835–1910) American author

The second step is to entice the consumer to buy the item with little financial risk. The discount coupon enclosed with the free sample prompts this action. Suppose the package that the consumer purchases has still another, smaller discount coupon enclosed. Again, satisfactory product performance and the second coupon provide reinforcement.

The third step is to motivate the person to buy the item again at a moderate cost. A discount coupon accomplishes this objective, but this time the purchased package includes no additional coupon. The only reinforcement comes from satisfactory product performance.

The final test comes when the consumer decides whether to buy the item at its true price without a discount coupon. Satisfaction with product performance provides the only continuing reinforcement. Repeat purchase behavior is literally shaped by effective application of learning theory within a marketing strategy context.

Self-Concept Theory

The consumer's **self-concept**—a person's multifaceted picture of himself or herself—plays an important role in consumer behavior. Say a young woman views herself as bright and ambitious, headed for a successful marketing career. She'll want to buy good clothes and jewelry to reflect that image of herself. Say an older man views himself as young for his age—he may purchase a sports car and stylish clothes to reflect his self-concept.

The concept of self emerges from an interaction of many of the influences—both personal and interpersonal—that affect buying behavior. The individual's needs, motives, perceptions, attitudes, and learning lie at the core of his or her conception of self. In addition, family, social, and cultural influences affect self-concept.

The self-concept has four components: real self, self-image, looking-glass self, and ideal self. The *real self* is an objective view of the total person. The *self-image*—the way an individual views himself or herself—may distort the objective view. The *looking-glass self*—the way an individual thinks others see him or her—may also differ substantially from the self-image because people often choose to project different images to others than their perceptions of their real selves. The *ideal self* serves as a personal set of objectives, since it is the image to which the individual aspires. In purchasing goods and services, people are likely to choose products that move them closer to their ideal self-images. Marketers appeal to the components of self-concept all the time. Nowhere is this more apparent than in the health and beauty industry, which constantly appeals to consumers' ideal self, as discussed in the "Marketing Hits" Interactive Example.

<interactive>example

MARKETING HIT: BOTOX MARKETERS WANT CONSUMERS TO LIKE WHAT THEY SEE

THE CONSUMER DECISION PROCESS

Consumers complete a step-by-step process in making purchasing decisions. The length of time and the amount of effort they devote to a particular purchasing decision depend on the importance of the desired good or service to the consumer.

<interactive>learning goal

CHAPTER OBJECTIVE #5: DISCUSS THE DIFFERENCE BETWEEN HIGH-INVOLVEMENT AND LOW-INVOLVEMENT PURCHASE DECISIONS.

<interactive>learning goal

CHAPTER OBJECTIVE #6: OUTLINE THE STEPS IN THE CONSUMER DECISION PROCESS.

Purchases with high levels of potential social or economic consequences are said to be *high-involvement purchase decisions.* Buying a new car or deciding where to go to college are two examples of high-involvement decisions. Routine purchases that pose little risk to the consumer are *low-involvement decisions.* Purchasing a candy bar from a vending machine is a good example.

Consumers generally invest more time and effort in buying decisions for high-involvement products than in those for low-involvement products. A home buyer will visit a number of homes, compare asking prices, apply for a mortgage, have the selected house inspected, even have friends or family members visit the home before signing the final papers. Few buyers invest that much effort in choosing between Nestlé's and Hershey's candy bars. Believe it or not, though, they will still go through the steps of the consumer decision process—but on a more compressed scale.

Figure 9.12 shows the six steps in the consumer decision process. First, the consumer recognizes a problem or unmet need and then searches for goods or services that will fill that need and evaluates the alternatives before making a purchase decision. The next step is the actual purchase act. After completing the purchase, the consumer evaluates whether he or she made the right choice. Much of marketing involves steering consumers through the decision process in the direction of a specific item.

Consumers apply the decision process in solving problems and taking advantage of opportunities. Such decisions permit them to correct differences between their actual and desired states. Feedback from each decision serves as additional experience in helping guide subsequent decisions.

Briefly Speaking

It is only in our decisions that we are important.

Jean-Paul Sartre (1905–1980) French philosopher, dramatist, and novelist

Problem or Opportunity Recognition

During the first stage in the decision process, the consumer becomes aware of a significant discrepancy between the existing situation and a desired situation. Perhaps the consumer realizes that there is no food in the refrigerator when he or she would rather have a full refrigerator. By identifying the problem—an empty refrigerator—the consumer can begin to prepare for a possible solution, such as a trip to the grocery store. Sometimes, the problem is more specific. The consumer might have a full refrigerator but no mustard or mayonnaise with which to make sandwiches. This problem requires a solution, as well.

Suppose the consumer is unhappy with a particular purchase—say, a brand of cereal. Or maybe he or she just wants a change from the same old cereal every morning. This is the recognition of another type of problem or opportunity—the desire for change.

What if our consumer just got a raise at work? He or she might want to try some of the prepared gourmet take-home dinners offered by the local supermarket. These dinners are more expensive than the groceries our consumer has purchased in the past, but now they are within financial reach. The marketer's main task during this phase of the decision-making process is to help prospective buyers identify and recognize potential problems or needs. This task may take the form of advertising, promotions, or personal sales assistance. A supermarket employee might suggest appetizers or desserts to accompany our grocery shopper's gourmet take-home dinner.

Search

During the second step in the decision process, the consumer gathers information about the attainment of a desired state of affairs. This search identifies alternative means of problem solution. High-involvement purchases may elicit extensive information searches, while low-involvement purchases require little search activity.

FIGURE 9.12

Integrated Model of the Consumer Decision Process

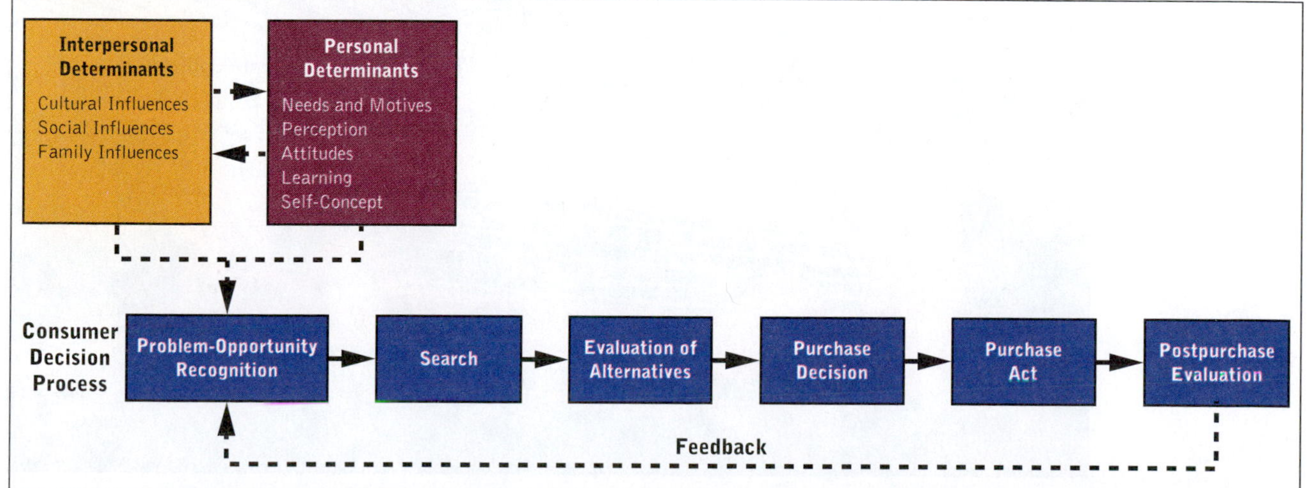

Source: Roger Blackwell, Paul W. Miniard, and James F. Engel, *Consumer Behavior,* 10th Edition (Mason, OH: South-Western, 2004).

Briefly Speaking

Please find me a one-armed economist so we will not always hear "on the other hand."

Herbert Hoover (1874–1964) 31st president of the United States

The search may cover internal or external sources of information. Internal search is a mental review of stored information relevant to the problem situation. Maybe the consumer recalls past experiences with or observations of a certain type of product. Or perhaps it is just recollection of a commercial or magazine advertisement. On an external search, the consumer gathers information from outside sources, which may include family members, friends, associates, store displays, sales representatives, brochures, and product-testing publications such as *Consumer Reports.* The Internet has become a popular source of information as well. Since conducting an external search requires time and effort, consumers often use an internal search to make purchase decisions.

The search identifies alternative brands for consideration and possible purchase. The number of alternatives that a consumer actually considers in making a purchase decision is known in marketing as the **evoked set.** In some searches, consumers already know of the brands that merit further consideration; in others, their external searches develop such information. The actual number of brands included in the evoked set vary depending on both the situation and the person. For example, an immediate need might limit the evoked set, while someone who has more time to make a decision might expand the evoked set to choose from a broader range of options.

Consumers now choose among more alternative products than ever before. This variety can confuse and complicate the analysis necessary to narrow the range of choices for consumers. Instead of comparing one or two brands, a consumer often faces a dizzying array of brands and sub-brands. Products that once included only one or two categories—regular coffee versus decaffeinated—are now available in many different forms—cappuccino, latte, tall skinny latte, flavored coffee, espresso, and iced coffee, just to name a few possibilities.

Marketers try to influence buying decisions during the search process by providing persuasive information about their goods or services in a format useful to consumers. As discussed earlier, marketers encounter a difficult challenge in breaking through the clutter that distracts customers. The marketer must find creative ways to get into a consumer's evoked set of alternatives.

Evaluation of Alternatives

The third step in the consumer decision process is to evaluate the evoked set of options identified during the search step. Actually, it is difficult to completely separate the second and third steps since some evaluation takes place as the search progresses; consumers accept, discount, distort, or reject incoming information as they receive it.

The outcome of the evaluation stage is the choice of a brand or product in the evoked set or possibly a decision to renew the search for additional alternatives, should all those identified during the initial search prove unsatisfactory. To complete this analysis, the consumer must develop a set of evaluative criteria to

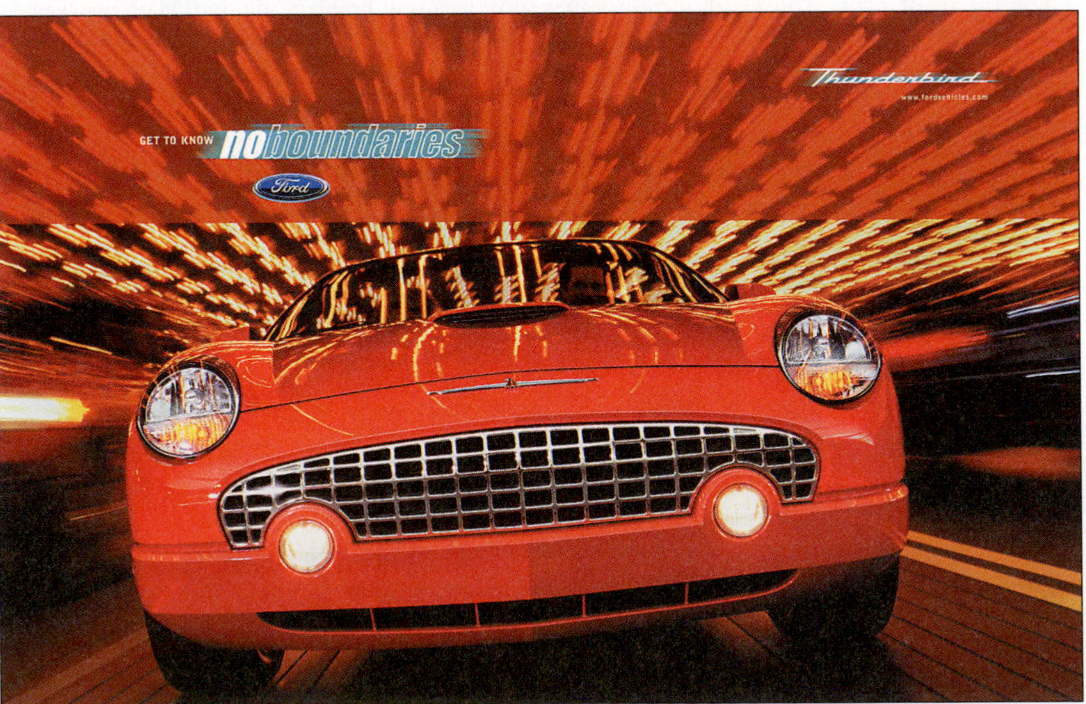

To provide a favorable impression in consumers, Ford demonstrates the appeal of its sleek, redesigned retro-style Thunderbird. The new style has struck a chord with consumers—even with a $40,000-plus sticker price, dealers have a hard time keeping up with demand.

guide the selection. **Evaluative criteria** are the features that a consumer considers in choosing among alternatives. These criteria can either be objective facts (government tests of an automobile's miles-per-gallon rating) or subjective impression (a favorable view of DKNY clothing). Common evaluative criteria include price, brand name, and country of origin. Evaluative criteria can also vary with the consumer's age, income level, social class, and culture. Auto shoppers planning to select one of the so-called "retro" cars introduced in recent years may include such popular models as the Chrysler PT Cruiser, Ford Thunderbird, or the recent entry by BMW of the British Morris MiniCar popularized in the *Austin Powers* movies. The T-Bird has proven so popular that Ford dealers frequently ask buyers to sign a pledge not to resell the vehicle for at least six months.

Marketers attempt to influence the outcome of this stage in three ways. First, they try to educate consumers about attributes that they view as important in evaluating a particular class of goods. They also identify which evaluative criteria are important to an individual and attempt to show why a specific brand fulfills those criteria. Finally, they try to induce a customer to expand the evoked set to include the product being marketed.

A travel agent might ask a client about the family's budget and recreational preferences. The agent might also explain the differences between two destinations that the client had not considered, pointing out important considerations, such as weather and activities. Finally, the agent might suggest other destinations or resorts, increasing the client's range of choices.

Purchase Decision and Purchase Act

The search and alternative evaluation stages of the decision process result in the eventual purchase decision and the act of making the purchase. At this stage, the consumer has evaluated each alternative in the evoked set based on his or her personal set of evaluative criteria and narrowed the alternatives down to one.

The consumer then decides the purchase location. Consumers tend to choose stores by considering such characteristics as location, price, assortment, personnel, store image, physical design, and services. In addition, store selection is influenced by the product category. Some consumers choose the convenience of in-home shopping via telephone or mail order rather than traveling to retail stores to complete transactions. Marketers can smooth the purchase decision and purchase act phases by helping customers arrange for financing or delivery.

Postpurchase Evaluation

The purchase act produces one of two results. The buyer feels either satisfaction at the removal of the discrepancy between the existing and desired states or dissatisfaction with the purchase. Consumers are generally satisfied if purchases meet their expectations.

Sometimes, however, consumers experience some postpurchase anxieties, called **cognitive dissonance.** This psychologically unpleasant state results from an imbalance among a person's knowledge, beliefs, and attitudes. A consumer may experience dissonance after choosing a particular automobile over several other models when some of the rejected models have desired features that the chosen one does not provide.

Dissonance is likely to increase (1) as the dollar values of purchases increase, (2) when the rejected alternatives have desirable features that the chosen alternatives do not provide, and (3) when the purchase decision has a major effect on the buyer. In other words, dissonance is more likely with high-involvement purchases than with those that require low involvement. The consumer may attempt to reduce dissonance by looking for advertisements or other information to support the chosen alternative or by seeking reassurance from acquaintances who are satisfied purchasers of the product. The individual may also avoid information that favors a rejected alternative. Someone who buys a Toyota is likely to read Toyota advertisements and avoid Nissan and Honda ads.

Marketers can help buyers to reduce cognitive dissonance by providing information that supports the chosen alternative. Automobile dealers recognize the possibility of "buyer's remorse" and often follow up purchases with letters or telephone calls from dealership personnel offering personal attention to any customer problems. Advertisements that stress customer satisfaction also help to reduce cognitive dissonance.

A final method of dealing with cognitive dissonance is to change product options, thereby restoring the cognitive balance. The consumer may ultimately decide that one of the rejected alternatives would have been the best choice and vows to purchase that item in the future. Marketers may capitalize on this with advertising campaigns that focus on the benefits of their products or with taglines that say something like, "If you're unhappy with them, try us."

Classifying Consumer Problem-Solving Processes

As mentioned earlier, the consumer decision processes for different products require varying amounts of problem-solving efforts. Marketers recognize three categories of problem-solving behavior: routinized response, limited problem solving, and extended problem solving.[17] The classification of a particular purchase within this framework clearly influences the consumer decision process.

<interactive>learning goal

CHAPTER OBJECTIVE #7: DIFFERENTIATE AMONG ROUTINIZED RESPONSE BEHAVIOR, LIMITED PROBLEM SOLVING, AND EXTENDED PROBLEM SOLVING BY CONSUMERS.

Routinized Response Behavior Consumers make many purchases routinely by choosing a preferred brand or one of a limited group of acceptable brands. This type of rapid consumer problem solving is referred to as **routinized response behavior.** A routine purchase of a regular brand of soft drink is an example. The consumer has already set evaluative criteria and identified available options. External search is limited in such cases, which characterize extremely low-involvement products.

Limited Problem Solving Consider the situation in which the consumer has previously set evaluative criteria for a particular kind of purchase but then encounters a new, unknown brand. The introduction of a new shampoo is an example of a **limited problem-solving** situation. The consumer knows the evaluative criteria for the product, but he or she has not applied these criteria to assess the new brand. Such situations demand moderate amounts of time and effort for external searches. Limited problem solving is affected by the number of evaluative criteria and brands, the extent of external search, and the process for determining preferences. Consumers making purchase decisions in this product category are likely to feel involvement in the middle of the range.

Extended Problem Solving **Extended problem solving** results when brands are difficult to categorize or evaluate. The first step is to compare one item with similar ones. The consumer needs to understand the product features before evaluating alternatives. Most extended problem-solving efforts involve lengthy external searches. High-involvement purchase decisions usually require extended problem solving.

STRATEGIC IMPLICATIONS OF MARKETING IN THE 21ST CENTURY

Marketers who plan to succeed with today's consumers will understand how their potential market behaves. Consider the new generation spawned by the tragic events of September 11 and the ensuing war on terrorism, during which consumers tended to engage in cocooning, or staying close to home.

Cultural influences will play a big role in marketers' relationships with consumers, particularly as firms attempt more and more to conduct business on a global or international scale, but also as they try to reach diverse populations in the U.S. Since 40 percent of U.S. consumers fit a niche that does *not* include the white, heterosexual, middle-class consumers who were once defined as the marketing mainstream, marketers must pedal hard to catch up with the 70 million U.S. residents who identify with other racial, ethnic, social, or economic groups.[18]

In addition, family characteristics are changing—more women are in the workforce, people are working longer—which forecasts a change in the way families make purchasing decisions. Perhaps the most surprising shift in family spending is the amount of power—and money—children and teenagers now wield in the marketplace. These young consumers are becoming more and more sophisticated, and in some cases know more about certain products, like electronics, than their parents do, and very often influence purchase decisions. This holds true even with high-involvement purchases like the family auto. "In [an automobile] showroom, kids will run to the vehicle they like," says Jim Townsend, brand manager for Ford's Windstar minivan. "And if they run to your vehicle, you know you'll be sitting close to the deal."[19]

Marketers will constantly work toward changing or modifying components of consumers' attitudes about their products in order to gain a favorable attitude and purchase decision. Finally, they will refine their understanding of the consumer decision process in order to use their knowledge to design effective marketing strategies.

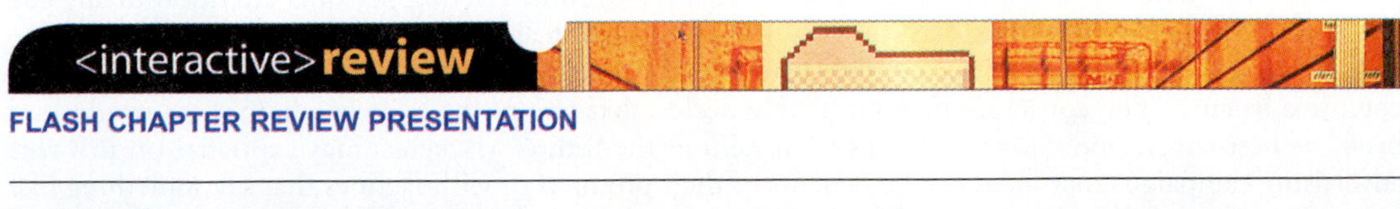

FLASH CHAPTER REVIEW PRESENTATION

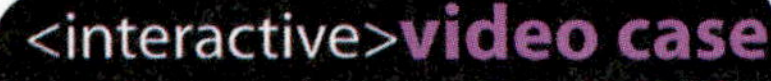

WBRU SOUNDS GOOD TO LISTENERS

endofchaptermaterial

- Summary of Chapter Objectives
- Chapter Outline
- Key Terms
- Review Questions
- Projects and Teamwork Exercises
- 'netWork
- Crossword Puzzles
- Case 9.1: CVS and Walgreen Cater to Consumer Convenience

Take the Post-Test to assess your overall understanding of the key ideas in this chapter. The Post-Test provides a comprehensive selection of exam-style questions addressing the main topics and concepts of the chapter. At the completion of each Post-Test, you will receive a score and instructive feedback on how you answered each question, and a direct link to the part of the chapter addressed in the question. Take the Post-Test as often as you need to—a record of your progress for each attempt is kept for you to revisit and gauge your improvement. And each Post-Test is randomly generated, so every attempt is new.

Post-Test

CHAPTER 10

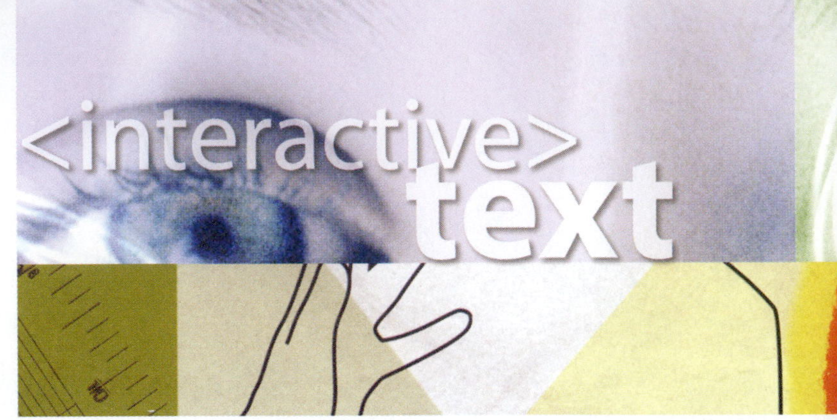

Business-to-Business (B2B) Marketing

Chapter Objectives

1. **Explain each of the components of the business market.**
2. **Describe the major approaches to segmenting business-to-business markets.**
3. **Identify the major characteristics of the business market and its demand.**
4. **Describe the major influences on business buying behavior.**
5. **Outline the steps in the organizational buying process.**
6. **Classify organizational buying situations.**
7. **Explain the buying center concept.**
8. **Discuss the challenges of marketing to government, institutional, and international buyers.**

WILL B2B ONLINE EXCHANGES REPLACE RELATIONSHIP MARKETING?

Close relationships among vendors, clients, and supplier networks have long been a hallmark of business-to-business—often called B2B—companies. B2Bs were the driving force behind electronic data interchanges (EDIs), networked systems that allowed sharing of critical information on purchases, payments, or logistics. It seemed a natural next step for B2B firms to embrace Internet exchanges, or online marketplaces, too.

Companies like FreeMarkets Online, developed by Glen Meakem (shown), help businesses make complex buying decisions by prescreening hundreds of potential suppliers and then conducting an online "reverse auction," in which suppliers make successively lower bids until the auction ends at the lowest possible price, resulting in a contract. When the deal is closed, FreeMarkets collects service fees from the buyer and a sales commission from the seller. FreeMarkets has conducted close to 15,000 online auctions, with cost savings to client companies averaging 15 to 20 percent.

Specializing in chemical products, ChemConnect serves as a central hub in a huge and fragmented industry. Its online auctions take hours instead of weeks, with bids and approvals flying back and forth through the Internet. ChemConnect hooks up buyers with reliable, pre-approved vendors they did not even know existed. Electronic networks like these not only cut costs, but give buyers more power—they get better information and are able to pit suppliers against each other in direct competition.

Yet while online exchanges offer definite benefits, they have failed to corner the market in B2B procurement. A compelling reason is that they introduce an intermediary between the client and the vendor, depriving each of the close-knit relationships on which B2B businesses thrive. Moreover, since online auctions are public, companies risk sharing sensitive proprietary information, such as detailed product specifications, with rivals.

Concerns like these have given rise to a new breed of Internet exchanges—the private exchange. Rather than use the Web to drum up new suppliers or drive down prices, companies are leveraging the Internet to set up their own private marketplaces whose objective is to strengthen ties with existing vendors. Dell Computer, for example, uses its exchange to connect its operations to about 60 parts suppliers. Every 15 minutes they receive updated production schedules, helping Dell trim inventory to the point where parts are held for just six hours before assembly. The Burlington Coat Factory is creating a network that will allow instant ordering and approvals from more than 4,000 suppliers, increasing efficiency across the board.

Yet the popularity of private exchanges has not cut companies like FreeMarkets out of the picture. FreeMarkets, which employs 600 people, has amassed valuable information on supplier networks and has first-hand experience in conducting complex auctions online. It also offers its QuickServe auction software that runs on its Web computer servers for customers. Clients such as industrial equipment maker Eaton Corp. use its technology and expertise to run private auctions with approved trading partners. This eliminates the risk of striking deals with unreliable firms, minimizes security concerns, and reduces procurement costs. Another exchange, Neoforma, which set out to be a single-source online provider of hospital supplies, changed its business model. It now offers private links between hospitals and established vendors, reducing the cost and the paperwork involved in ordering supplies. More than 500 hospitals have signed three-year contracts for its services.

Rather than disrupting the buyer-seller relationship, exchanges like FreeMarkets and Neoforma have the potential to become valued business partners, facilitating collaboration between the firm and its supply-chain network.[1]

Pre-Test

Take the Pre-Test to assess your initial knowledge of the key ideas in this chapter. The Pre-Test provides exam-style questions addressing the main topics and concepts of the chapter. At the completion of each Pre-Test, you will receive a score and instructive feedback on how you answered each question, and a direct link to the part of the chapter addressed in the question. Take the Pre-Test as often as you need to—a record of your progress for each attempt is kept for you to revisit and gauge your improvement.

CHAPTER OVERVIEW

Although the average person is well aware of the consumer market, the business-to-business marketplace is, in fact, significantly larger. U.S. companies pay more than $300 billion each year just for office and maintenance supplies. Government agencies inflate the business-to-business market even further; the Department of Defense budget for 2003 was almost $390 billion.[2] Whether conducted through face-to-face transactions, via telephone, or over the Internet, every day business marketers deal with complex purchasing decisions involving multiple decision makers. They range from simple reorders of previously purchased goods or services to complex buys for which materials are sourced from all over the world.

As you will recall from Chapter 9, attitudes, perceptions, family and social influences, and other factors affect consumer buying behavior. This chapter will discuss buying behavior in the business or organizational market. **Business-to-business,** or **B2B, marketing** deals with organizational purchases of goods and services to support production of other products, to facilitate daily company operations, or for resale.

NATURE OF THE BUSINESS MARKET

Firms generally sell fewer standardized products to organizational buyers than to ultimate consumers. Customer service is extremely important to buying organizations. Advertising plays a much smaller role in the business market than in the consumer market. Business marketers advertise primarily to enhance their company images and the images of their products and to attract new prospects, who are then contacted directly by salespeople. Personal selling plays a much bigger role in business markets than in consumer markets, distribution channels are shorter, customer relationships tend to last longer, and purchase decisions can involve multiple decision makers. Table 10.1 shows significant differences between B2B and consumer-goods marketing.

<interactive>**learning goal**

CHAPTER OBJECTIVE #1: EXPLAIN EACH OF THE COMPONENTS OF THE BUSINESS MARKET.

Like final consumers, an organization purchases products to fill needs. However, its primary need—meeting the demands of its own customers—is similar from firm to firm. A manufacturer buys raw materials to create the company's product, while a wholesaler or retailer buys products to resell. Companies also buy services from other businesses. Institutional purchasers such as government agencies and nonprofit organizations buy things to meet the needs of their constituents.

Environmental, organizational, and interpersonal factors are among the many influences in B2B markets. Budget, cost, and profit considerations all play parts in business buying decisions. In addition, the business buying process typically involves complex interactions among many people. An organization's

TABLE 10.1

Comparing Business-to-Business Marketing and Consumer Marketing

	BUSINESS-TO-BUSINESS MARKETING	CONSUMER MARKETING
Product	Relatively technical in nature, exact form often variable, accompanying services very important	Standardized form, service important but less than for business products
Price	Competitive bidding for unique items, list prices for standard items	List prices
Promotion	Emphasis on personal selling	Emphasis on advertising
Distribution	Relatively short, direct channels to market	Product passes through a number of intermediate links en route to consumer
Customer Relations	Relatively enduring and complex	Comparatively infrequent contact, relationship of relatively short duration
Decision-Making Process	Diverse group of organization members makes decision	Individual or household unit makes decision

goals must also be considered in the B2B buying process.[3] Later sections of the chapter will explore these topics in greater detail.

Some firms focus entirely on business markets. For instance, Hoechst sells chemicals to manufacturers, who use them in a variety of products. Advanced Micro Devices makes flash memory chips for the cellular phone and Internet-provider markets. Manpower Inc., provides temporary personnel services to firms that need extra workers. Computer Associates, Oracle, and Sybase are software vendors specializing in business applications. Chevy Express, featured in Figure 10.1, markets vans designed to meet the needs of businesses.

Other firms sell to both consumer and business markets. The J. M. Smucker Co., for example, sells jellies and preserves to consumers and also sells filling mixes to companies that manufacture yogurt and dessert products. Netscape, best known for selling its Navigator Web browser to consumers, actually gets about 80 percent of its revenues from corporate customers. It offers a complete line of sophisticated networking software for companies like 3M and Chrysler. Similarly, Eastman Kodak sells film to consumers, and it also sells photofinishing paper, chemicals, and services to wholesale photofinishing companies.

Note also that marketing strategies developed in consumer marketing are often appropriate for the business sector, too. As the "Marketing Hits" Interactive Example demonstrates, final consumers are often the end-users of products sold into the business market and, as explained later in the chapter, can influence the buying decision.

Briefly Speaking

We call them naked chickens just because they are naked.

Dr. Avigdor Cahaner, on the new breed of featherless chicken he developed to save on plucking costs

MARKETING HIT: A DUCK RULES THE ROOST IN B2B INSURANCE MARKETING

The B2B market is diverse. Transactions can range from orders as small as a box of paper clips or copy-machine toner for a home-based business to transactions as large as thousands of parts for an automobile manufacturer or massive turbine generators for an electric power plant. Businesses are also big purchasers of services, such as telecommunications, computer consulting, and transportation services. Four major categories define the business market: (1) the commercial market, (2) trade industries, (3) government organizations, and (4) institutions.

Components of the Business Market

The **commercial market** is the largest segment of the business market. It includes all individuals and firms that acquire products to support, directly or indirectly, the production of other goods and services. When Lufthansa buys aircraft built by the European consortium Airbus Industrie, when Sara Lee purchases wheat to mill into flour for an ingredient in its cakes, and when a plant supervisor orders light bulbs and cleaning supplies for a factory in Tennessee, these transactions all take place in the commercial market. Some products aid in the production of other items (the new airplane). Others are physically used up in the production of a good or service (the wheat). Still others contribute to the firm's day-to-day operations (the maintenance supplies). The commercial market includes manufacturers, farmers, and other members of resource-producing industries; construction contractors; and providers of such services as transportation, public utilities, financing, insurance, and real-estate brokerage.[4]

The second segment of the organizational market, *trade industries,* includes retailers and wholesalers, known as *resellers,* who operate in this sector. Most resale products, such as clothing, appliances, sports equipment, and automobile parts, are finished goods that the buyers sell to final consumers. In other cases, the buyers may complete some processing or repackaging before reselling the products. For example, retail meat markets may carry out bulk purchases of sides of beef and then cut individual pieces for their customers. Lumber dealers and carpet retailers may purchase in bulk and then provide quantities and sizes to meet customers' specifications. In addition to resale products, trade industries buy such things as computers, display shelves, and other products they need to operate their businesses. These goods, as well as maintenance items, and specialized services such as scanner installation, newspaper inserts,

FIGURE 10.1

The Chevy Express: Catering to the Business-to-Business Market

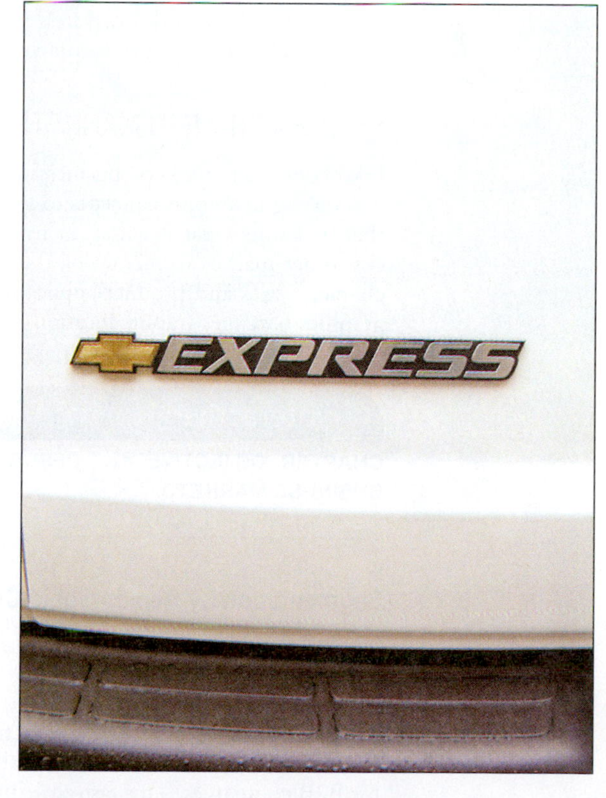

FIGURE 10.2

Composition of B2B Online Sales

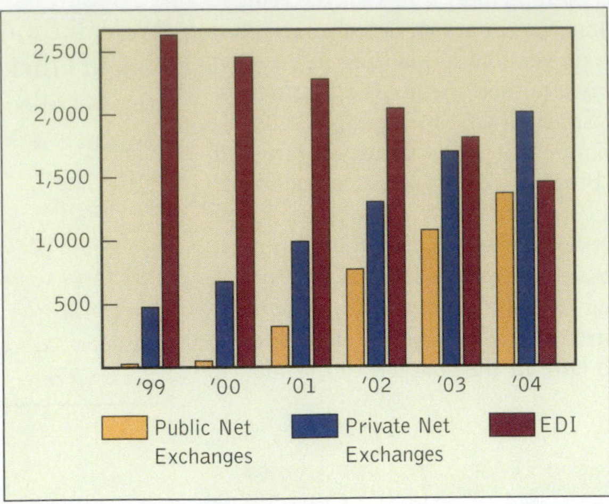

Source: Giga Information Group.

and radio advertising all represent organizational purchases. Chapter 16 provides detailed discussions of the trade industries.

Government organizations, the third category of the business market, include domestic units of government—federal, state, and local—as well as foreign governments. This important market segment makes a wide variety of purchases, ranging from highways to social services. The primary motivation of government purchasing is to provide some form of public benefit, such as national defense or pollution control.

Institutions, both public and private, are the fourth component of the business market. This category includes a wide range of organizations, such as hospitals, churches, skilled care centers, colleges and universities, museums, and not-for-profit agencies. Some institutions—state universities, for instance—must rigidly follow standardized purchasing procedures, while others have less formal buying practices. Business-to-business marketers often benefit by setting up separate divisions to sell to institutional buyers.

B2B Markets—The Internet Connection While consumers' use of Internet markets receives the bulk of public attention, about 70 percent of all Internet sales are, in fact, B2B transactions. Internet-based trade hit $2.4 trillion in 2004.[5] As described in the opening vignette at the beginning of the chapter, many business-to-business marketers have set up private portals that allow their customers to buy needed items. Service and customized pages are accessed through passwords provided by B2B marketers. Online auctions and virtual marketplaces offer other ways for buyers and vendors to connect with each other over the Internet. Figure 10.2 shows the composition of B2B online sales.

Differences in Foreign Business Markets

Business markets in other countries may differ due to variations in government regulations and cultural practices. Some business products need modifications to succeed in foreign markets. In Australia, Japan, and Great Britain, for instance, motorists drive on the left side of the road. Modifications need to be made to automobiles to accommodate such differences. As another example, the electrical wiring of a European building differs from that of a building in the United States. Again, modifications are necessary.

Business marketers must be willing to adapt to local customs and business practices when operating in foreign markets. They should also research cultural preferences. Factors as deceptively simple as the time of a meeting and methods of address for associates can make a difference. A company even needs to consider what ink colors to use for documents because colors can have different meanings in different countries.

SEGMENTING B2B MARKETS

Like consumer markets, business-to-business markets include wide varieties of customers. By applying market segmentation concepts to groups of business customers, a firm's marketers can develop a strategy that best suits a particular segment's needs. The overall process of segmenting business markets resembles consumer market segmentation, but it divides markets based on different criteria, usually organizational characteristics and product applications. Among the major ways to segment business markets are demographics (size, geographic location), customer type, end-use application, and purchasing situation.[6]

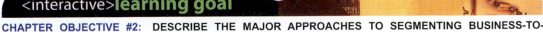

CHAPTER OBJECTIVE #2: DESCRIBE THE MAJOR APPROACHES TO SEGMENTING BUSINESS-TO-BUSINESS MARKETS.

Segmentation by Demographic Characteristics

As with consumer markets, demographic characteristics define useful segmentation criteria for business markets. For example, firms can be grouped by size, based on sales revenues or number of employees. Marketers may develop one strategy to reach *Fortune* 500 corporations with complex purchasing procedures and another strategy for small firms where decisions are made by one or two people. Despite the dot-com bust, small businesses—especially firms with fewer than 100 employees—constitute a major market for B2B companies. This fast-growing segment of about 20 million firms offers tremendous potential.[7] To win their business, American Express created its Small Business Services unit, providing information and assistance for entrepreneurs and small business owners. The ability to print fast, high-quality color is a desired goal in business, regardless of the size of the business. Xerox targets all business users, with an emphasis on small business, with ads like the one in Figure 10.3.

FIGURE 10.3

Targeting the Small Business Segment

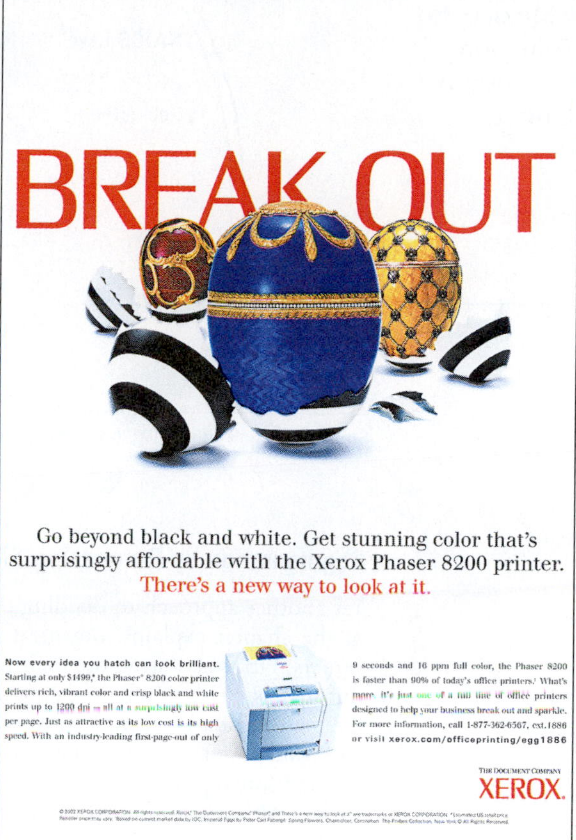

Segmentation by Customer Type

Another useful segmentation approach groups prospects according to type of customer. Marketers can apply this concept in several ways. They can group customers by broad categories—manufacturer, service provider, government agency, not-for-profit organization, wholesaler, or retailer—and also by industry. These groups may be further divided using other segmentation approaches discussed in this section.

Customer-based segmentation is a related approach often used in the business-to-business marketplace. Organizational buyers tend to have much more precise product requirements than ultimate consumers do. As a result, business products often fit narrower market segments than consumer products do. This fact leads some firms to design business goods and services to meet detailed buyer specifications, creating a form of market segmentation.

North American Industrial Classification System (NAICS) In the 1930s, the U.S. government set up a uniform system for subdividing the business marketplace into detailed segments. The Standard Industrial Classification (SIC) system standardized efforts to collect and report information on U.S. industrial activity.

SIC codes divided firms into broad industry categories: agriculture, forestry, and fishing; mining and construction; manufacturing; transportation, communication, electric, gas, and sanitary services; wholesale trade; retail trade; finance, insurance, and real-estate services; public administration; and nonclassifiable establishments. The scheme assigned each major category within these classifications its own two-digit number. Three-digit and four-digit numbers further subdivided each industry into smaller segments.

For almost 70 years, B2B marketers used SIC codes as a tool for segmenting markets and identifying new customers. The system, however, became outdated with implementation of the North American Free Trade Agreement (NAFTA). Each NAFTA member—the United States, Canada, and Mexico—had its own system for measuring business activity. The new North American Free Trade Area required a joint classification system that would allow marketers to compare business sectors among the member nations. In effect, marketers required a segmentation tool they could use across borders.

Established in 1999 and updated every five years, the **North American Industrial Classification System (NAICS)** replaces the SIC and provides more detail than was previously available. NAICS created new service sectors to better reflect the economy of the 21st century. They include information; health care and social assistance; and professional, scientific, and technical services.

Table 10.2 demonstrates the more detailed NAICS system for software. NAICS uses six digits, compared with the four digits used in the SIC. The first five digits are fixed among the members of NAFTA. The sixth digit can vary among U.S., Canadian, and Mexican data. In short, the sixth digit accounts for specific data needs of the member nation.[8]

Segmentation by End-Use Application

A third basis for segmentation, **end-use application segmentation,** focuses on the precise way in which a business purchaser will use a product. For example, a printing equipment manufacturer may serve markets ranging from a local utility to a bicycle manufacturer to the U.S. Department of Defense. Each end use of the equipment may dictate unique specifications for performance, design, and price. Praxair, a supplier of industrial gases, for example, might segment its markets according to user. Steel and glass manufacturers might buy hydrogen and oxygen, while food and beverage manufacturers need carbon dioxide. Praxair also sells krypton, a rare gas, to companies that produce lasers, lighting, and thermal windows. Many small- and medium-sized companies also segment markets according to end-use application. Instead of competing in markets dominated by large firms, they concentrate on specific end-use market segments.

Briefly Speaking

Poor Mexico. So far from God and so close to the United States.

Porfirio Diaz (1830–1915) President of Mexico

TABLE 10.2

Example of the NAICS: Computer Software

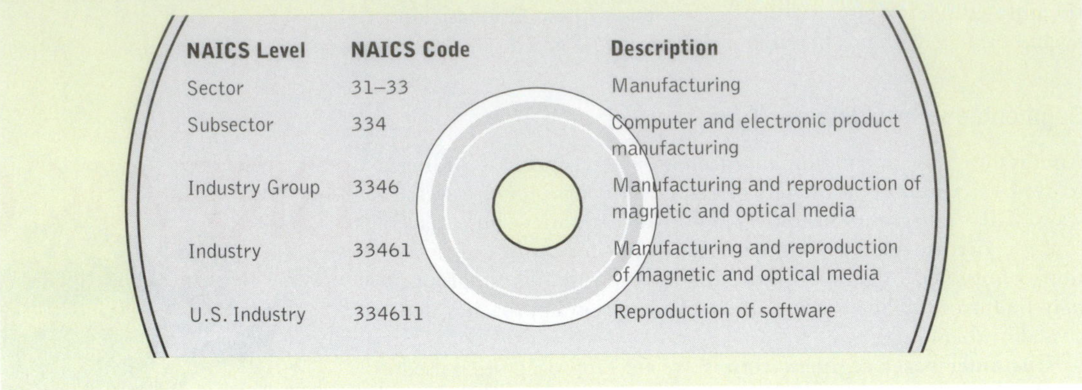

NAICS Level	NAICS Code	Description
Sector	31–33	Manufacturing
Subsector	334	Computer and electronic product manufacturing
Industry Group	3346	Manufacturing and reproduction of magnetic and optical media
Industry	33461	Manufacturing and reproduction of magnetic and optical media
U.S. Industry	334611	Reproduction of software

Source: Reprinted from http://www.census.gov/epcd/www/naics.html, downloaded October 2, 2002.

Segmentation by Purchasing Situation

Yet another approach to dividing business markets centers on the purchasing situation. As a later section of the chapter explains, organizations use more complicated purchasing procedures than those of consumers. Firms also structure their purchasing functions in specific ways, and for some business marketers, this may be the best way to segment the market. Some companies designate centralized purchasing departments to serve the entire firm, while others allow each unit to handle its own buying. A supplier may deal with one purchasing agent or several decision makers at various levels. Each of these structures results in different buying behavior.

When the buying situation is important to marketers, they typically consider whether the customer has made previous purchases or if this is the customer's first order. For example, IBM's Integrated Systems Solutions Corp. subsidiary might use a different marketing approach to sell to Lucent Technologies, an existing customer of its computer support services, than to a potential new customer who is unfamiliar with its offerings.

Increasingly, businesses that have developed customer relationship management (CRM) systems are able to segment customers in terms of the stage of the relationship between the business and the customer. A B2B company, for example, might develop different strategies for newly acquired customers than it would for existing customers to which it hopes to cross-sell new products. Similarly, building loyalty among satisfied customers requires a different approach than developing programs to "save" at-risk customer relationships.[9] CRM was covered in more depth in Chapter 6.

CHARACTERISTICS OF THE B2B MARKET

Businesses that serve both B2B and consumer markets must understand the needs of their customers. However, several characteristics distinguish the business market from the consumer market: (1) geographic market concentration, (2) the sizes and numbers of buyers, (3) purchase decision procedures, and (4) buyer-seller relationships. The next sections will consider how these traits influence business-to-business marketing.

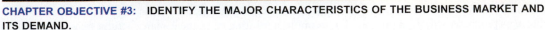

<interactive>**learning goal**

CHAPTER OBJECTIVE #3: IDENTIFY THE MAJOR CHARACTERISTICS OF THE BUSINESS MARKET AND ITS DEMAND.

Geographic Market Concentration

As noted in the previous section, the U.S. business market is more geographically concentrated than the consumer market. Manufacturers converge in certain regions of the country, making these areas prime targets for business marketers. For example, the Midwestern states that make up the East North Central region—Ohio, Indiana, Michigan, Illinois, and Wisconsin—lead the nation in industrial concentration, followed by the Middle Atlantic and the South Atlantic regions.

Certain industries locate in particular areas in order to be close to customers. Firms may choose to locate sales offices and distribution centers in these areas to provide more attentive service. For example, the Washington, D.C., area is favored by companies that sell to the federal government. One survey showed that federal spending on goods and services accounted for about one of every four new jobs created in the Washington, D.C., area.[10]

In the automobile industry suppliers of components and assemblies frequently build plants close to their customers. Ford recently established a first-of-its-kind campus for suppliers, located near its Chicago assembly plant. The campus will allow suppliers to produce or assemble products in close proximity to the plant, reducing costs, controlling parts inventory, and increasing flexibility.[11] Other industries establish facilities near power sources (chemical plants near Niagara Falls) or populations of skilled workers (high-tech firms in California's Silicon Valley).

As Internet-based technology continues to improve, allowing companies to transact business even with distant suppliers, business markets may become less geographically concentrated. Much of government spending, for example, is now directed through the Internet.

Sizes and Numbers of Buyers

In addition to geographic concentration, the business market features a limited number of buyers. Marketers can draw on a wealth of statistical information to estimate the sizes and characteristics of business markets. The federal government is the largest single source of such statistics. Every five years it conducts both a Census of Manufacturers and a Census of Retailing and Wholesaling, which provide detailed information on business establishments, output, and employment. Many government units and trade organizations also operate Web sites that contain helpful information.

Many buyers in limited-buyer markets are large organizations. The international market for jet engines is dominated by three manufacturers: United Technology's Pratt & Whitney unit, General Electric, and Rolls-Royce. These firms sell engines to Boeing and the European consortium, Airbus Industrie. These aircraft manufacturers compete for business from passenger airlines like Delta Airlines, British Airways, KLM, and Singapore Airlines, along with cargo carriers such as Federal Express and United Parcel Service. The case at the end of the chapter describes the intense rivalry between two companies in the limited-buyer market for small regional passenger jets.

Trade associations and business publications provide additional information on the business market. Private firms such as Dun & Bradstreet publish detailed reports on individual companies. This data serves as a useful starting point for analyzing a business market. Finding data in such a source requires an understanding of the NAICS, which identifies much of the available statistical information.

The Purchase Decision Process

To market effectively to other organizations, businesses must understand the dynamics of the organizational purchase process. Suppliers who serve business-to-business markets must work with multiple buyers, especially when selling to larger customers. Decision makers at several levels may influence final orders, and the overall process is more formal and professional than the consumer purchasing process. Purchases typically require a longer time frame because B2B involves more complex decisions. Suppliers must evaluate customer needs and develop proposals that meet technical requirements and specifications. Also, buyers need time to analyze competing proposals. Often, decisions require more than one round of bidding and negotiation, especially for complicated purchases.

Buyer-Seller Relationships

An especially important characteristic of B2B marketing is the relationship between buyers and sellers. Such relationships are more intense than consumer relationships, and they require better communication among the organizations' personnel.

As Chapter 6 explained, relationship marketing involves developing long-term, value-added customer relationships. A primary goal of business-to-business relationships is to provide advantages that no other vendor can provide—for instance, lower price, quicker delivery, better quality and reliability, customized product features, or more favorable financing terms. For the business marketer, providing these advantages means expanding the company's external relationships to include suppliers, distributors, and other organizational partners. For example, John Deere & Co. has built strong relationships with its worldwide network of 5,000 dealerships that sell the company's agricultural products to farmers. Deere recently created a new distribution system that electronically connects the dealers' sales reports to a centralized warehouse that replenishes products as the dealers need them.

Close cooperation, whether through informal contacts or under terms specified in contractual partnerships and strategic alliances, enables companies to meet buyers' needs for quality products and customer service. This holds true both during and after the purchase process. Goodyear, which equips law enforcement

vehicles with its Goodyear Eagle tires, uses its advertising to promote its customers' objectives, thus building the buyer-seller relationship.

Close buyer-seller relationships help companies in good times—and in bad. The "Solving an Ethical Controversy" Interactive Example demonstrates how a crisis can derail even the most long-standing B2B ties.

RIGHT/WRONG: SOLVING AN ETHICAL CONTROVERSY—THE FAILED RELATIONSHIP BETWEEN FORD AND BRIDGESTONE/FIRESTONE

Evaluating International Business Markets

Business purchasing patterns differ from one country to the next. Researching these markets poses a particular problem for B2B marketers. Of course, as explained earlier, NAICS is correcting this problem in the NAFTA countries.

In addition to quantitative data such as the size of the potential market, companies must also carefully weigh its qualitative features. This involves considering cultural values, work styles, and generally the best ways to enter overseas markets. For example, after winning a campaign to fly its aircraft into China, international shipper UPS promoted the introduction of its first flights with media briefings, TV advertising, print and billboard ads, and direct mail. The messages are delivered using Chinese characters that represent such attributes as speed and reliability. The company's Web site uses Mandarin.

Liftomatic Materials Handling, a small company that makes equipment to handle barrels on factory floors, estimates that the Chinese market accounts for a quarter of its revenue. The company found that the Chinese are unwilling to invest in new products without having seen them demonstrated, so Liftomatic depends heavily on in-person or video demonstrations. Trade shows, print advertising, and a Chinese-enabled Web site all aim to improve communications between the American company and its Chinese customers.[12]

In today's international marketplace, companies often practice **global sourcing,** which involves contracting to purchase goods and services from suppliers worldwide. This practice can result in substantial cost savings. FedEx, for example, estimates that it saves over 30 percent on the prices of computer hardware and software by soliciting bids worldwide. Applica is a business-to-business company that manufactures small appliances such as irons and hair dryers for large retailers like Wal-Mart. Applica uses Internet-based technology to link sales data from Wal-Mart directly to the factory floor in Mexico, where irons are made to order. By connecting manufacturing operations directly with customer sales, Applica is able to slash inventories while producing in low-cost regions of the world.[13]

Global sourcing requires companies to adopt a new mind-set; some must even reorganize their operations. Among other considerations, businesses sourcing from multiple multinational locations should streamline the purchase process and minimize price differences due to labor costs, tariffs, taxes, and currency fluctuations.

BUSINESS MARKET DEMAND

The previous section's discussion of business market characteristics demonstrated considerable differences between marketing techniques for consumer and business products. Demand characteristics also differ in these markets. In business markets, the major categories of demand include derived demand, joint demand, volatile demand, and inventory adjustments.

Derived Demand

The term **derived demand** refers to the linkage between consumer demand for a company's output and its purchases of business products such as machinery, components, supplies, and raw materials. For example, demand for microprocessor chips within a computer's central processing unit is derived from the demand for personal computers from both business and individual consumers. Worldwide slowdowns in sales of personal computers have reduced demand for chips. Dell Computer attempts to offset fluctuations in demand by keeping its inventories low and by using falling prices resulting from reduced demand to drive down the cost of computer components, including chips. Dell then passes these savings along to its customers in the form of lower PC prices, thus stimulating sales. Recently, Intel slashed prices of its high-end Pentium 4 processors in half, due to drastically lower demand and excess capacity.[14] Advertisements like the one in Figure 10.4 seek to increase demand.

While demand for computer chips has decreased, demand for embedded chips—microprocessors built into other consumer devices ranging from rice cookers to automobiles—has not. For every personal computer shipped, companies ship approximately 30 toasters, pagers, watches, and other items that rely on built-in chips. As businesses and consumers become increasingly security-conscious, smart cards that store personal information, including passwords, frequent flyer miles, and more, represent a potentially huge new market for embedded chips.[15]

Organizational buyers purchase two general categories of business products: capital items and expense items. Derived demand ultimately affects both. Capital items are long-lived business assets that must be depreciated over time. (Depreciation is an accounting term that refers to charging a portion of a capital item's cost as a deduction against the company's annual revenue for purposes of determining its net income.) Examples of capital items include major installations such as new plants, office buildings, and computer systems.

Expense items, in contrast, are items consumed within short time periods. Accountants charge the cost of such products against income in the year of purchase. Examples of expense items include the supplies necessary to operate the business, ranging from paper clips to machine lubricants.

Briefly Speaking

It doesn't matter if a cat is black or white, so long as it catches mice.

Deng Xiaoping (1904–1997) Chinese prime minister

Joint Demand

Another important influence on business market demand is **joint demand,** which results when the demand for one business product is related to the demand for another business product used in combination with the first item. For example, both coke and iron ore are required to make pig iron. If the coke supply falls, the drop in pig iron production will immediately affect the demand for iron ore.

Another example is the joint demand for electrical power and large turbine engines. If consumers decide to conserve power, demand for new power plants drops, as does the demand for components and replacement parts for turbines.

Volatile Demand

Derived demand creates volatility in business market demand. As an example, assume that the sales volume for a chain of gasoline stations is increasing at an annual rate of 5 percent. Now suppose that the demand for this gasoline brand slows to a 3 percent annual increase. While not a dramatic drop, this slowdown might convince the firm to keep its current gasoline pumps and replace them only when market conditions improved. In this way, even modest shifts in consumer demand for a gasoline brand would greatly affect the pump manufacturer. This disproportionate impact of changes in consumer demand on business market demand is referred to as the *accelerator principle.*

Inventory Adjustments

Adjustments in inventory and inventory policies can also affect business demand. Assume that manufacturers in a particular industry consider a 60-day supply of raw materials to be the optimal inventory level. Now suppose that economic conditions or other factors induce these firms to increase their inventories to a 90-day supply. The change will bombard the raw-materials supplier with new orders.

Further, innovative *just-in-time (JIT)* inventory policies seek to boost efficiency by cutting inventories to absolute minimum levels and by requiring vendors to deliver inputs as the production process needs them. JIT allows companies to better predict which supplies they will require and the timing for when they will need them, markedly reducing their costs for production and storage. While JIT inventory and delivery systems suffered disruptions following the September terrorist attacks, the overall benefits in supply chain savings outweigh the adverse impact of delays to shipments resulting from cross-border conflicts or other international crises.[16] Widespread implementation of JIT has had a substantial impact on organizations' purchasing behavior. Firms that practice JIT tend to order from relatively few suppliers. In some cases, JIT may lead to *sole sourcing* for some items—in other words, buying a firm's entire stock of a product from just one supplier. Electronic data interchange (EDI) and quick-response inventory policies have produced similar results in the trade industries.

The latest inventory trend, *JIT II,* leads suppliers to place representatives at the customer's facility to work as part of an integrated, on-site customer-supplier team. Suppliers plan and order in consultation with the customer. This streamlining of the inventory process improves control of the flow of goods.

FIGURE 10.4

Microprocessors: An Example of Derived Demand

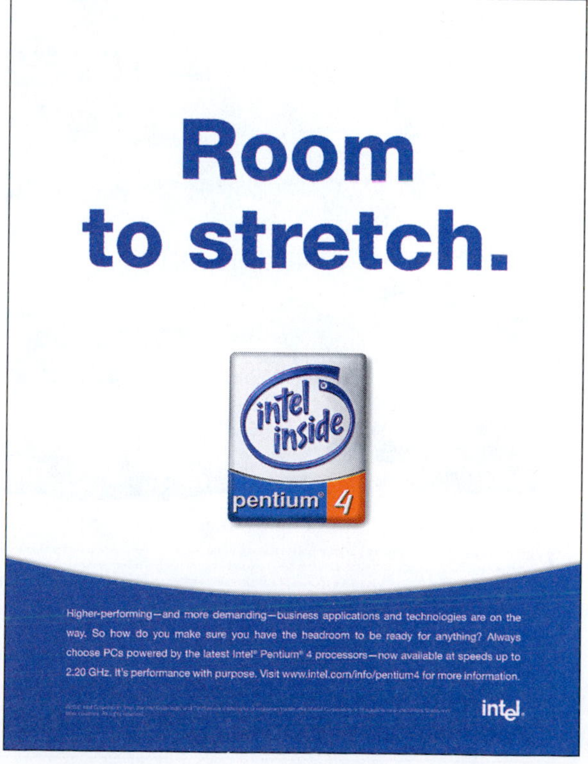

THE MAKE, BUY, OR LEASE DECISION

Before a company can decide what to buy, it should decide whether to buy at all. Organizational buyers must figure out the best way to acquire needed products. In fact, a firm considering the acquisition of a finished good, component part, or service has three basic options:

1. Make the good or provide the service in-house.
2. Purchase it from another organization.
3. Lease it from another organization.

Manufacturing the product itself, if the company has the capability to do so, may be the best route. It may save a great deal of money if its own manufacturing division does not incur costs for overhead that an outside buyer would otherwise charge.

On the other hand, most firms cannot make all of the business goods they need. Often, it would be too costly to maintain the necessary equipment, staff, and supplies. Therefore, purchasing from an outside vendor is the most common choice. Companies can also look outside their own plants for goods and services that they formerly produced in-house, a practice called *outsourcing* that the next section will describe in more detail.

In some cases, however, a company may choose to lease inputs. This option spreads out costs compared with lump-sum costs for up-front purchases. The company pays for the use of equipment for a certain time period. For example, a small business may lease a copy machine for a few years, making monthly payments. At the end of the lease term, the firm can buy the machine at a prearranged price or replace it with a different model under a new lease. This option can provide useful flexibility for a growing business, allowing it to easily upgrade as its needs change.

Companies can also lease sophisticated computer systems and heavy equipment. For example, some airlines prefer to lease airplanes rather than buy them outright because short-term leases allow them to adapt quickly to changes in passenger demand.

The Rise of Outsourcing

Packaged goods giant Procter & Gamble recently announced plans to hire an outside firm to handle parts of its back-office operations, a deal that could be worth approximately $8 billion over 10 years. The top candidate was Affiliated Computer Services (ACS). By farming out such operations as finance and accounting, human resources, and information technology—functions that employ over 8,000 people—P&G can concentrate its efforts on what it does best: manufacturing and marketing top consumer brands. At the same time, P&G can take advantage of the technological and professional expertise of ACS.[17]

In their rush to improve efficiency, firms look outside for just about everything from mailroom management, customer service, human resources, and accounting, to information technology, manufacturing, and distribution.

Outsourcing allows firms to concentrate their resources on their core business. It also allows access to specialized talent or expertise that does not exist within the firm. The most frequently outsourced business functions include information technology, human resources, and facilities management. Many hospitals and managed-care organizations spend more than a third of their IT budgets on outsourced consulting and support services.[18] The ad in Figure 10.5 highlights the benefits of outsourcing even complex office functions, such as payroll administration.

FIGURE 10.5

Benefits of Outsourcing Services

About 60 percent of all outsourcing is done by North American–based companies. However, the practice is rapidly becoming commonplace in Asia and Europe; European firms' expenditures for outsourcing are growing by an impressive 34 percent annually.

Heightened awareness of security following the terrorist attacks of September 11 led companies like Sun Microsystems to focus on e-security as a reason why businesses should outsource computer networking systems. The ad in Figure 10.6 promises improved firewall protection as well as reliability and flexibility.

Outsourcing can be a smart strategy if a company chooses a vendor that can provide high-quality products and perhaps at a lower cost than could be achieved on the company's own. This priority allows the outsourcer to focus on its core competencies. Successful outsourcing requires companies to carefully oversee contracts and manage relationships. Some vendors now provide performance guarantees to assure their customers that they will receive high-quality service that meet their needs.

FIGURE 10.6

Outsourcing Networking Needs for Increased Security

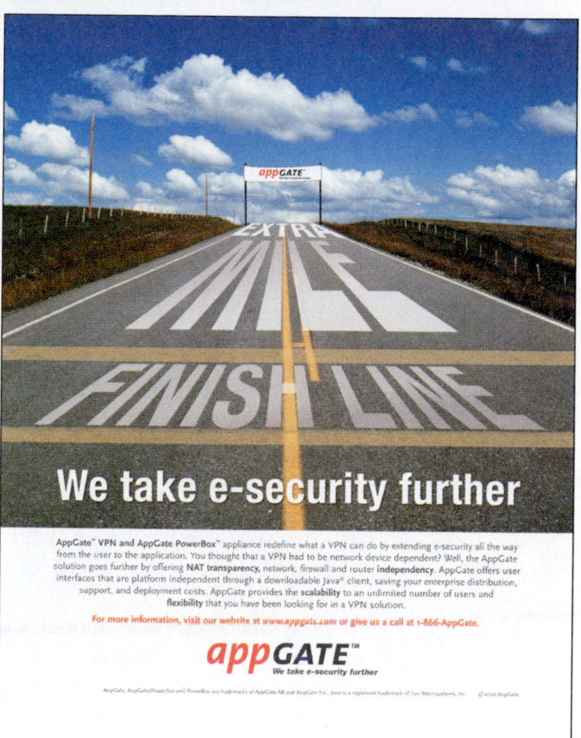

Problems with Outsourcing

Outsourcing is not without its downside. Many companies discover that their cost savings average closer to 10 percent than the 20 to 40 percent that vendors sometimes promise. Also, companies who sign multiyear contracts may find that their savings drop after a year or two. When proprietary technology is an issue, outsourcing raises security concerns. Similarly, companies that are protective of customer data and relationships may think twice about entrusting functions like customer service to outside sources.

In some cases, outsourcing can reduce a company's ability to respond quickly to the marketplace or it can slow efforts in bringing new products to market. Suppliers who fail to deliver goods promptly or provide required services can adversely affect a company's reputation with its customers. General Electric had to delay the introduction of a new washing machine because of a contractor's production problems. Similarly, Southern Pacific Rail had problems with an outsourced computer network.

Another major danger of outsourcing is the risk of losing touch with customers. When Telecom giant Sprint realized that customer data from its outsourced technology providers was not being put to work fast enough, the company decided to pull the plug on its outside vendors. In their place, customized customer relationship management (CRM) software was able to pull data on more than 10 million business accounts, saving Sprint $1 million in the first year.[19]

Outsourcing is a controversial topic with unions, especially in the auto industry, as the percentage of component parts made in-house has steadily dropped. Outsourcing can create conflicts between nonunion outside workers and in-house union employees, who fear job loss from outsourcing. Management initiatives to outsource jobs can lead to strikes and plant shutdowns. Even if it does not lead to disruption in the workplace, outsourcing can have a negative impact on employee morale and loyalty.

THE BUSINESS BUYING PROCESS

Suppose that CableBox Inc., a hypothetical manufacturer of cable television decoder boxes, decides to upgrade its manufacturing facility with $1 million in new automated assembly equipment. Before approaching equipment suppliers, the company must analyze its needs, determine goals that the project should accomplish, develop technical specifications for the equipment, and set a budget. Once it receives vendors' proposals, it must evaluate them and select the best one. But what does *best* mean in this context? The lowest price or the best warranty and service contract? Who in the company is responsible for such decisions?

<interactive>**learning goal**

CHAPTER OBJECTIVE #4: DESCRIBE THE MAJOR INFLUENCES ON BUSINESS BUYING BEHAVIOR.

Clearly, the business buying process is more complex than the consumer decision process described in Chapter 9. Business buying takes place within a formal organization's budget, cost, and profit considerations. Furthermore, B2B and institutional buying decisions usually involve many people with complex interactions among individuals and organizational goals. To understand organizational buying behavior, business marketers require knowledge of influences on the purchase decision process, the stages in the organizational buying model, types of business buying situations, and techniques for purchase decision analysis.

Influences on Purchase Decisions

B2B buying decisions react to various influences, some external to the firm and others related to internal structure and personnel. In addition to product-specific factors such as purchase price, installation, operating and maintenance costs, and vendor service, companies must also consider broader environmental, organizational, and interpersonal influences.

Environmental Factors Environmental conditions such as economic, political, regulatory, competitive, and technological considerations influence business buying decisions. For example, CableBox may wish to defer purchases of the new equipment in times of slowing economic activity. During a recession, sales to cable companies might drop because households hesitate to spend money on cable service. The company would look at the derived demand for its products, possible changes in its sources of materials, employment trends, and similar factors before committing to such a large capital expenditure.

Political, regulatory, and competitive factors also come into play in influencing purchase decisions. For example, passage of a law freezing cable rates would affect demand, as would an introduction of a less expensive decoder box by a competitor. Finally, technology plays a role in purchase decisions. For example, cable-ready televisions decreased demand for set-top boxes, and smaller, more powerful satellite dishes have cut into the market for cable TV, reducing derived demand. CableBox can benefit from technological advances, too. As more homes want fast Internet connections, adding cable modems to its product line may present a growth opportunity.

Organizational Factors Successful business-to-business marketers understand their customers' organizational structures, policies, and purchasing systems. A company with a centralized procurement function operates differently than one that delegates purchasing decisions to divisional or geographic units. Trying to sell to the local store when head office merchandisers make all the decisions would clearly waste salespeople's time. Buying behavior also differs among firms. For example, centralized buying tends to emphasize long-term relationships, while decentralized buying focuses more on short-term results. Personal selling skills and user preferences carry more weight in decentralized purchasing situations than in centralized buying.

How many suppliers should a company patronize? Because purchasing operations spend over half of each dollar their companies earn, consolidating vendor relationships can lead to large cost savings. However, a fine line separates maximizing buying power from relying too heavily on a few suppliers. Many companies engage in *multiple sourcing*—purchasing from several vendors. Spreading orders ensures against shortages if one vendor cannot deliver on schedule. However, dealing with many sellers can be counterproductive and take too much time. Each company sets its own criteria for this decision.

Interpersonal Influences Many people may influence B2B purchases, and considerable time may be spent obtaining the input and approval of various organization members. Both group and individual forces are at work here. When committees handle buying, they must spend time to gain majority or unanimous approval. Also, each individual buyer brings to the decision process her individual preferences, experiences, and biases.

Business marketers should know who will influence buying decisions in an organization for their products and should know each of their priorities. To choose a supplier for an industrial press, for example, a purchasing manager and representatives of the company's production, engineering, and quality control departments may jointly decide on a supplier. Each of these principals may have a different point of view that the vendor's marketers must understand.

Boise Cascade in collaboration with a training and consulting company ran an innovative marketing campaign to encourage organizations to use its catalog and online service as a single source for office supplies. A color flyer was included with its direct-mail catalog, which reached 300,000 potential business buyers. The flyer was designed to appeal to Boise's end users—administrative assistants, a group typically composed of women aged 18 to 54 with a high-school diploma. A focal point of the campaign was an online personality assessment that had been developed using cues that would be popular with this demographic group. The quiz allowed catalog users to gain a better understanding of themselves and their coworkers by "color-typing" themselves, then gave tips on how best to work with other color types. The flyer was so popular that administrative assistants passed it around the office, along with the Boise catalog—creating an informal network of people who influenced the purchase of office supplies. In addition, an interactive quiz on the Boise Web site won more new customers through pass-along e-mails.[20]

To effectively address the concerns of all people involved in the buying decision, sales representatives must be well-versed in the technical features of their products. They must also interact well with employees of the various departments involved in the purchase decision. Sales representatives for medical products, for example, are frequent visitors to hospitals and surgery centers, where they discuss their product line with clinical staff and demonstrate new devices.

The Role of the Professional Buyer Most organizations attempt to make their purchases through systematic procedures employing professional buyers. In the trade industries, these buyers, often referred to as *merchandisers,* are responsible for securing needed products at the best possible prices. Unlike ultimate consumers, who incorporate periodic buying decisions with other activities, a firm's purchasing department devotes all of its time and effort in determining needs, locating and evaluating alternative suppliers, and making purchase decisions.

Purchase decisions for capital items vary significantly from those for expense items. Firms often buy expense items routinely with little delay. Capital items, however, involve major fund commitments and usually undergo considerable review.

One way in which a firm may attempt to streamline the buying process is through *systems integration,* or centralization of the procurement function. One company may designate a lead division to handle all purchasing. Another firm may choose to designate a major supplier as the systems integrator. This vendor then assumes responsibility for dealing with all of the suppliers for a project and for presenting the entire package to the buyer. In trade industries, this vendor is sometimes called a *category captain.*

A business marketer may set up a sales organization to serve national accounts that deals solely with buyers at geographically concentrated corporate headquarters. A separate field sales organization may serve buyers at regional production facilities.

As noted earlier in the chapter, corporate buyers often use the Internet to identify supplier sources. They view online catalogs and Web sites to compare vendors' offerings and to obtain product information. Some use Internet exchanges to extend their supplier networks.

The chapter opening vignette, featuring FreeMarkets.com, explains how Internet exchanges are able to save businesses money as well as locating quality suppliers. The "Marketing Misses" Interactive Example demonstrates that there is a downside to entrusting the buyer-seller relationship to Internet intermediaries.

MARKETING MISS: THE FAILURE OF B2B EXCHANGES

Model of the Organizational Buying Process

An organizational buying situation requires a sequence of activities similar to the six-step consumer decision model presented in the previous chapter. Figure 10.7 illustrates an eight-stage model of a complex organizational buying process. The additional steps arise because business purchasing introduces new complexities that do not affect consumers. Not every buying situation will follow these precise steps, but this model presents a useful overview of the general process.

CHAPTER OBJECTIVE #5: OUTLINE THE STEPS IN THE ORGANIZATIONAL BUYING PROCESS.

Stage 1: Anticipate or Recognize a Problem/Need/Opportunity and a General Solution Both consumer and business purchase decisions begin when the recognition of problems, needs, or opportunities triggers the buying process. Perhaps a firm's computer system has become outdated or a sales representative demonstrates a new good or service that could improve the company's performance.

Companies may decide to hire an outside marketing specialist when their sales stagnate. This was the case for a large building-products manufacturer, which had traditionally sold its products through a catalog mailed to approximately 45,000 building contractors. When its mail-order business stalled, the purchasing manager interviewed several marketing firms, including Milwaukee-based Hunter Business Direct, to create new ways for the company to increase sales.[21]

FIGURE 10.7

Stages in the B2B Buying Process

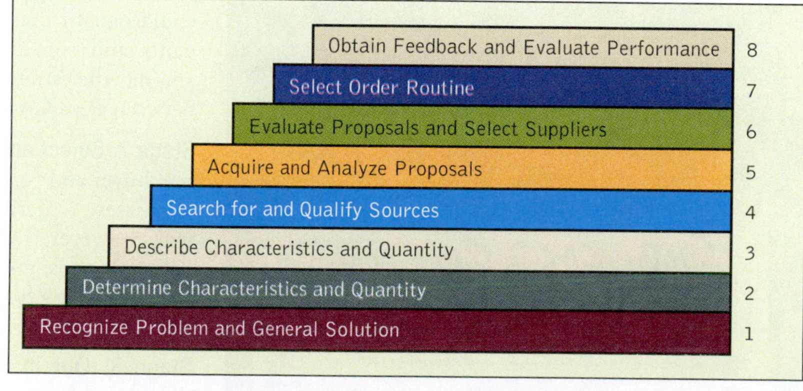

Source: Based on Michael P. Hutt and Thomas W. Speh, *Business Marketing Management,* 8th Edition (Mason, OH: South-Western Publishing, 2004).

Stage 2: Determine the Characteristics and Quantity of a Needed Good or Service The problem described in Stage 1 translated into a service opportunity for Hunter Business Direct. To stimulate the manufacturer's sales, Hunter executive vice president Mark Peck suggested a database marketing strategy.

Peck quickly assembled a marketing team, consisting of employees from both Hunter and the manufacturer's marketing department, to determine what was needed. The team ranked the manufacturer's customers into 10 groups according to total sales. Peck decided to focus on the top three groups, a total of approximately 1,000 contracting businesses. Customers in the top 10 percent of this group placed an average of 18 orders per year, approximately $20,000 per order; the other 90 percent averaged about six orders per year at $5,500 each.

Stage 3: Describe Characteristics and the Quantity of a Needed Good or Service After determining the characteristics and quantity of needed products, B2B buyers must translate these ideas into detailed specifications. For his manufacturer client, Peck prepared a detailed proposal that described how Hunter would implement a database marketing program for his client. His goals were to increase the frequency of target customers' orders, the amount they ordered, and the number of repeat purchases.

Depending on the type of purchase, a company's technical personnel can play an important role in this early stage of the B2B buying process. For instance, a quality control engineer might establish certain specifications for a product that only a few suppliers could meet. This type of decision could have a big impact on the ultimate evaluation and selection of vendors.

Stages 2 and 3 apply mostly to organizations rather than individual consumers. While consumers may perform these steps, they would use a much more superficial analysis.

Stage 4: Search for and Qualify Potential Sources Both consumers and businesses search for good suppliers of desired products. The choice of a supplier may be relatively straightforward; the manufacturer's purchasing manager decided within a few days to hire Hunter Business Direct.

Other searches may involve more complex decision making. A company that wants to buy a group life and health insurance policy, for example, must weigh the varying provisions and programs of many different vendors.

Stage 5: Acquire and Analyze Proposals The next step is to acquire and analyze suppliers' proposals, which are generally submitted in writing. If the buyer is a government or public agency, this stage of the purchase process may involve competitive bidding. During this process, each marketer must develop its bid, including a price, that will satisfy the criteria determined by the customer's problem, need, or opportunity. While competitive bidding is less common in the business sector, a company may follow the practice to purchase nonstandard materials, complex products, or products that are made to its own specifications.

FIGURE 10.8

Price—Not Always the Key Criterion in Selecting a Supplier

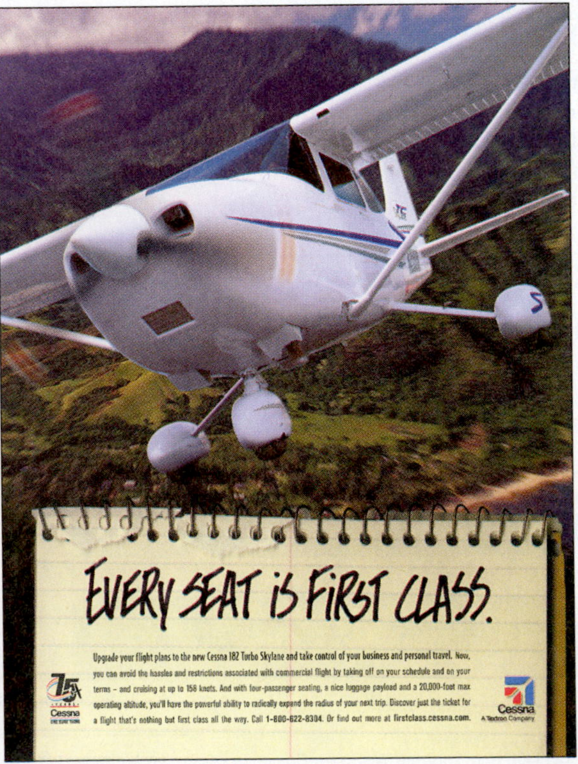

Stage 6: Evaluate Proposals and Select Suppliers Next in the buying process, buyers must compare vendors' proposals and choose the one that seems best suited to their needs. Proposals for sophisticated equipment, such as a large computer networking system, can include considerable differences among product offerings, and the final choice may involve tradeoffs.

Price is not the only criterion for the selection of a vendor. Relationship factors like communication and trust may also be important to the buyer. Other issues include reliability, delivery record, time from order to delivery, quality, and order accuracy. As the ad in Figure 10.8 suggests, reducing the headaches and delays of business travel in the security-conscious post–September 11 world is the reason businesses might invest in the Cessna Turbo.

Recently, United Airlines broke its decades-long pact with The Coca-Cola Company and decided to switch to Pepsi as its inflight soft-drinks supplier. While the financial package was a key motivator, the two companies also explored ways in which the partnership could benefit their businesses. Marketing sessions for flight attendants and soft-drink promotions with air tickets as prizes are among the strategies designed to strengthen the relationship between PepsiCo and United.[22]

Stage 7: Select an Order Routine Once a supplier has been chosen, buyer and vendor must work out the best way to process future purchases. Ordering routines can vary considerably. Most orders will, however, include product descriptions, quantities, prices, delivery terms, and payment terms. Today, companies have a variety of options for submitting orders: written documents, phone calls, faxes, or electronic messages (EDI).

Stage 8: Obtain Feedback and Evaluate Performance At the final stage, buyers measure vendors' performances. Sometimes this judgment may involve a formal evaluation of each supplier's product quality, delivery performance, prices, technical knowledge, and overall responsiveness to customer needs. At other times, vendors may be measured according to whether they have lowered the customer's costs or reduced its employees' workloads.

In general, large firms are more likely to use formal evaluation procedures, while smaller companies lean toward informal evaluations. Regardless of the method used, buyers should tell vendors how they are going to be evaluated.

Returning to the example of Hunter Business Direct, evaluation of the database marketing program showed it was highly successful. During the first six months of the program, 380 of the targeted customers purchased supplies from the manufacturer. The number of orders they placed rose by an impressive 112 percent, and the average size of individual orders also increased. Hunter's client spent approximately $50,000 to implement the program but increased its revenues by nearly $3 million.[23]

<interactive>**exercise**

'NET EX: STAGES IN THE B2B BUYING PROCESS

Classifying Business Buying Situations

As discussed earlier, business buying behavior responds to many purchasing influences such as environmental, organizational, and interpersonal factors. This buying behavior also involves the degree of effort that the purchase decision demands and the levels within the organization where it is made. Like consumer behavior, marketers can classify organizational buying situations into three general categories, ranging from least to most complex: (1) straight rebuying, (2) modified rebuying, and (3) new-task buying. Business buying situations may also involve reciprocity. The following sections look at each type of purchase by a company like CableBox.

<interactive>**learning goal**

CHAPTER OBJECTIVE #6: CLASSIFY ORGANIZATIONAL BUYING SITUATIONS.

Straight Rebuying The simplest buying situation is a *straight rebuy,* a recurring purchase decision in which an existing customer places a new order for a familiar product that has performed satisfactorily in the past. This organizational buying situation occurs when a purchaser likes the product and the terms of the sale. Therefore, the purchase requires no new information. The buyer sees little reason to assess other options and so follows a routine repurchase format. A straight rebuy is the business market equivalent of routinized response behavior in the consumer market.

Purchases of low-cost items such as paper clips and pencils for an office are typical examples of straight rebuys. If the products and their prices and terms satisfy the organization, it will treat future purchases as straight rebuys from the current vendor. For instance, CableBox probably has an account with an office supply firm that provides prompt service.

A marketer who wants to ensure continuing straight rebuys should concentrate on maintaining a good relationship with the buyer by providing excellent service and delivery performance. Competitors will then find it difficult to present unique sales proposals that would break this chain of repurchases.

Modified Rebuying In a *modified rebuy,* a purchaser is willing to reevaluate available options. The decision makers see some advantage in looking at alternative offerings using established purchasing guidelines. They might take this step if a marketer allows a straight rebuy situation to deteriorate because of poor service or delivery performance. Perceived quality and cost differences can also provoke modified rebuys. Modified rebuys resemble limited problem solving in consumer markets.

B2B marketers want to induce current customers to make straight rebuys by responding to all of their needs. Competitors, on the other hand, try to induce buyers to make modified rebuys by raising issues that will convince these buyers to reconsider their decisions. Suppose that CableBox wants to upgrade its computer equipment to optimize business performance. In addition to requesting proposals from its current supplier, IBM, the firm might investigate other computer manufacturers such as Dell and Hewlett-Packard by using an analytic software such as ProClarity. Figure 10.9 shows an ad for ProClarity in which the copy is very brief but the emphasis is on making good decisions quickly. Each vendor will promote its computers' technological advantages and other unique features.

New-Task Buying The most complex category of business buying is *new-task buying*—first-time or unique purchase situations that require considerable effort by the decision makers. The consumer market equivalent of new-task buying is extended problem solving. A recent copy-intensive ad from Hewlett-Packard gave a

FIGURE 10.9

Reducing the Complexity of New-Task Buying

ProClarity Corporation delivers analytic software and services that accelerate the speed at which organizations make informed decisions to optimize business performance. ProClarity has been delivering innovative analytic solutions to Global 3000 companies since 1995. ProClarity ensures maximum return on investment and widespread user adoption by delivering solutions tailored around business processes and decision-making workflows. Headquartered in Idaho, with regional sales offices in Europe and Asia-Pacific, ProClarity currently supports over 500 customers globally including AT&T, CompUSA, Ericsson, Hewlett-Packard, Nordstrom, and Verizon.. (PRNewsFoto/ProClarity Corporation)

detailed explanation of how Hewlett-Packard will help solve the problem of information storage, despite the complexities of shrinking budgets, reduced staff, and the difficulties of predicting future storage needs.

A new-task buy often requires a purchaser to carefully consider alternative offerings and vendors. For example, a company entering a new field must seek suppliers of component parts that it has never before purchased. If CableBox was to decide to manufacture cable modems, it would have to buy new equipment and component parts. This new-task buying would require several stages, each yielding a decision of some sort. These decisions would include developing product requirements, searching out potential suppliers, and evaluating proposals. Information requirements and decision makers can complete the entire buying process, or they may change from stage to stage.

Reciprocity **Reciprocity**—a practice of buying from suppliers that are also customers—is a controversial practice in a number of organizational buying situations. For example, an office equipment manufacturer may favor a particular supplier of component parts if the supplier has recently made a major purchase of the manufacturer's products. Reciprocal arrangements traditionally have been common in industries featuring homogeneous products with similar prices, such as the chemical, paint, petroleum, rubber, and steel industries.

Reciprocity suggests close links among participants in the organizational marketplace. It can add to the complexity of B2B buying behavior for new suppliers who are trying to compete with preferred vendors. Although buyers and sellers enter into reciprocal agreements in the U.S., both the Justice Department and the Federal Trade Commission view them as attempts to reduce competition.

Outside the U.S., however, governments may take more favorable views of reciprocity. Business-to-business buyers in Canada, for instance, see it as a positive, widespread practice. In Japan, close ties between suppliers and customers are common.

Analysis Tools

Two tools that help professional buyers in improving purchase decisions are value analysis and vendor analysis. **Value analysis** examines each component of a purchase in an attempt to either delete the item or replace it with a more cost-effective substitute. For example, airplane designers have long recognized the need to make planes as light as possible. Value analysis supports using DuPont's synthetic material Kevlar in airplane construction because it weighs less than the metals it replaces. The resulting fuel savings are significant for the buyers in this marketplace.

Vendor analysis carries out an ongoing evaluation of a supplier's performance in categories such as price, EDI capability, back orders, delivery times, liability insurance, and attention to special requests. In some cases, vendor analysis is a formal process. Some buyers use a checklist to assess a vendor's performance. A checklist quickly highlights vendors and potential vendors that do not satisfy the purchaser's buying requirements.

THE BUYING CENTER CONCEPT

The buying center concept provides a vital model for understanding organizational buying behavior. A company's **buying center** encompasses everyone who is involved in any aspect of its buying action. For example, a buying center may include the architect who designs a new research laboratory, the scientist who works in the facility, the purchasing manager who screens contractor proposals, the chief executive officer who makes the final decision, and the vice president for research who signs the formal contracts for the project. Buying-center participants in any purchase seek to satisfy personal needs, such as participation or status, as well as organizational needs.

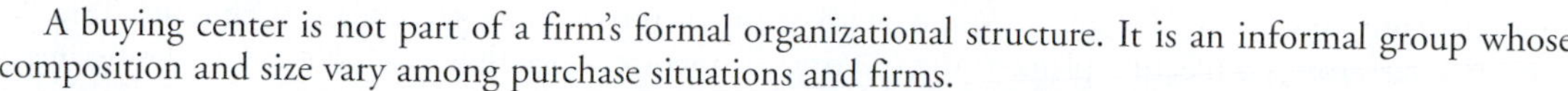

CHAPTER OBJECTIVE #7: EXPLAIN THE BUYING CENTER CONCEPT.

A buying center is not part of a firm's formal organizational structure. It is an informal group whose composition and size vary among purchase situations and firms.

Buying Center Roles

Buying-center participants play different roles in the purchasing decision process. Users are the people who will actually use the good or service. Their influence on the purchase decision may range from negligible to extremely important. Users sometimes initiate purchase actions by requesting products, and they may also help to develop product specifications. Users, for example, often influence the purchase of office equipment. Steelcase promotes its Montage brand of affordable office furniture by featuring the end user prominently in its ads, as shown in the ad in Figure 10.10.

Gatekeepers control the information that all buying center members will review. They may exert this control by distributing printed product data or advertisements or by deciding which salespeople will speak to which individuals in the buying center. For example, a purchasing agent might allow some salespeople to see the engineers responsible for developing specifications but deny others the same privilege.

FIGURE 10.10

End Users: Buying Center Participants

Influencers affect the buying decision by supplying information to guide evaluation of alternatives or by setting buying specifications. Influencers are typically technical staff such as engineers or quality control specialists. Sometimes a buying organization hires outside consultants, such as architects, who influence its buying decisions.

The *decider* actually chooses a good or service, although another person may have the formal authority to do so. The identity of the decider is the most difficult role for salespeople to pinpoint. For example, a firm's buyer may have the formal authority to buy, but the firm's chief executive officer may actually make the buying decision. A decider might be a design engineer who develops specifications that only one vendor can meet.

The *buyer* actually has the formal authority to select a supplier and to implement the procedures for securing the good or service. The buyer often surrenders this power to more influential members of the organization, though. The purchasing manager often fills the buyer's role and executes the administrative functions associated with a purchase order.[24]

B2B marketers face a critical task of determining the specific role and the relative decision-making influence of each buying-center participant. Salespeople can then tailor their presentations and information to the precise role that an individual plays at each step of the purchase process. Business marketers have found that their initial—and, in many cases, most extensive—contacts with a firm's purchasing department often fail to reach the buying-center participants who have the greatest influence, since these people may not work in that department at all.

Consider the selection of meeting and convention sites for trade or professional associations. The primary decision maker could be an association board or an executive committee, usually with input from the executive director or a meeting planner; the meeting planner or association executive might choose meeting locations, sometimes with input from members; finally, the association's annual-meeting committee or program committee might make the meeting location selection. Because officers change annually, centers of control may change from year to year. As a result, destination marketers and hotel operators are constantly assessing how an association makes its decisions on conferences.

International Buying Centers

Two distinct characteristics differentiate international buying centers from domestic ones. First, marketers may have trouble identifying members of foreign buying centers. In addition to cultural differences in decision-making methods, some foreign companies lack staff personnel. For example, in less-developed countries, line managers may make most purchase decisions.

Second, a buying center in a foreign company often includes more participants than U.S. companies involve. International buying centers employ from one to 50 people, with 15 to 20 participants being commonplace. Global B2B marketers must recognize and accommodate this greater diversity of decision makers.

International buying centers can change in response to political and economic trends. Many European firms, for instance, once maintained separate facilities in each European nation in order to avoid tariffs and customs delays. When the European Community lowered trade barriers between member nations, however, many companies closed distant branches and consolidated their buying centers. The Netherlands has been one of the beneficiaries of this trend.

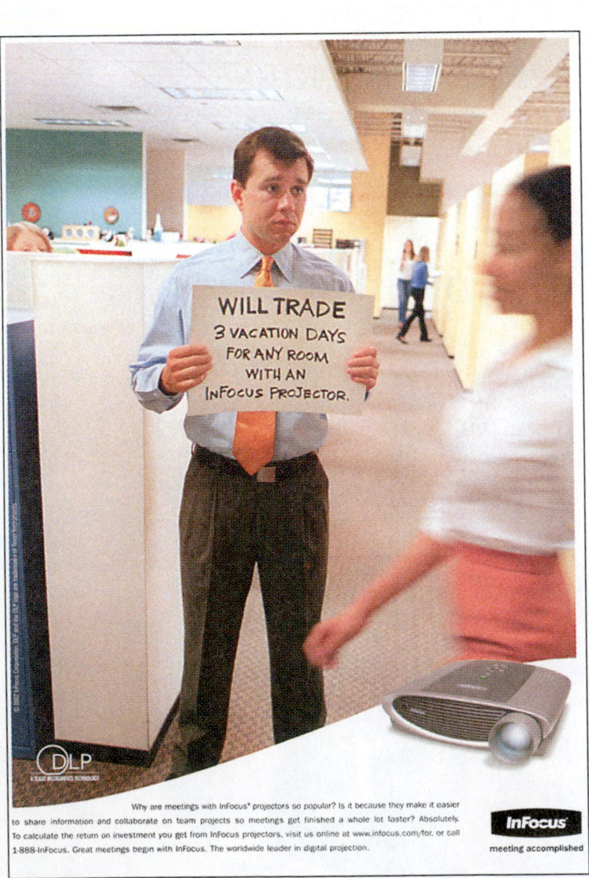

The end user may sometimes feel left out of the buying decision.

Team Selling

To sell effectively to all members of a firm's buying center, many vendors use *team selling,* combining several sales associates or members of the organization to assist the lead sales representative in reaching all those who influence the purchase decision. Fibre Containers, a company that sells corrugated paperboard for making boxes, considers team selling particularly helpful in building chemistry between the buyer and seller. If a salesperson learns, for example, that a prospect's two biggest concerns are box design and payment schedules, a meeting that includes the head designer and the director of finance can help develop a relationship of trust.[25]

Team selling may be extended to include members of the seller firm's own supply network into the sales situation. Consider, for example, the case of small resellers of specialized computer applications whose clients require high levels of product knowledge and access to training. By working with its supply network, for example by forming alliances with suppliers to provide training or ongoing service to end-clients, resellers are able to offer a higher degree of support.

DEVELOPING EFFECTIVE BUSINESS-TO-BUSINESS MARKETING STRATEGIES

A business marketer must develop a marketing strategy based on a particular organization's buying behavior and on the buying situation. Clearly, many variables affect organizational purchasing decisions. This section will examine three market segments whose decisions present unique challenges to B2B marketers: units of government, institutions, and international markets. Finally, it will summarize key differences between consumer and business marketing strategies.

<interactive>**learning goal**

CHAPTER OBJECTIVE #8: DISCUSS THE CHALLENGES OF MARKETING TO GOVERNMENT, INSTITUTIONAL, AND INTERNATIONAL BUYERS.

Challenges of Government Markets

Government agencies—federal, state, and local—together make up the largest customer in the U.S. Over 85,000 government units buy a wide variety of products, including office supplies, furniture, concrete, vehicles, grease, military aircraft, fuel, and lumber, to name just a few.

To compete effectively, business marketers must understand the unique challenges of selling to government units. One challenge results because government purchases typically involve dozens of interested parties who specify, evaluate, or use the purchased goods and services. These parties may or may not work within the government agency that officially handles a purchase.

Government purchases are also influenced by social goals, such as minority subcontracting programs. Government entities such as the U.S. Postal Service strive to maintain diversity in their suppliers, often making a special effort to purchase goods and services from small firms and companies owned by minorities and women. The government also relies on its prime suppliers to subcontract to minority businesses.[26]

Contractual guidelines create another important influence in selling to government markets. The government buys products under two basic types of contracts: fixed-price contracts, in which seller and buyer agree to a set price before finalizing the contract, and cost-reimbursement contracts, in which the government pays the vendor for allowable costs, including profits, incurred during performance of the contract. Each type of contract has advantages and disadvantages for B2B marketers. While the fixed-price contract offers more profit potential than the alternative, it also carries greater risks from unforeseen expenses, price hikes, and changing political and economic conditions.

Government Purchasing Procedures Many U.S. government purchases go through the General Services Administration (GSA), a central management agency involved in such areas as procurement, property management, and information resources management. The GSA buys goods and services for its own use and for use by other government agencies. In its role as, essentially, the federal government's business manager, it purchases billions of dollars worth of products. The Defense Logistics Agency (DLA) serves the same function for the Department of Defense.

By law, most federal purchases must be awarded on the basis of bids, or written sales proposals, from vendors. As part of this process, government buyers develop specifications—detailed descriptions of needed items—for prospective bidders. U.S. government purchases must comply with the Federal Acquisition Regulation (FAR), a 30,000-page set of standards originally designed to cut red tape in government purchasing. FAR standards have been further complicated by numerous exceptions issued by various government agencies. Numerous additional restrictions are designed to prevent overspending, corruption, and favoritism. Recent reforms have attempted to speed purchasing and increase flexibility. They include an increased reliance on fast, easy-to-use, prenegotiated contracts with multiple vendors; elimination of detailed specifications for readily available commercial products; paperwork reduction; and the use of government-issued credit cards to make small buys.[27]

As an indicator of the government's success in making its acquisition system more responsive and effective, consider the following sample of what the GSA purchased for the New York and Pentagon relief efforts within just days of the September 11 attacks: 65,000 protective suits, 5,000 face masks, 3,000 respirators, 400 vehicles, 250 cell phones, 2,000 computers, 300 fax machines, and more than 1,200 items of office equipment.[28]

State and local government purchasing procedures resemble federal procedures. Most states and many large cities have created buying offices similar to the GSA. Detailed specifications and open bidding are common at this level as well. Many state purchasing regulations typically give preference to in-state bidders. For example, the state of Ohio allows a 5 percent preference to businesses with a presence in that state. The preference increases the price upon which the out-of-state bid is evaluated by 5 percent. (This regulation does not apply to bordering states.)

Government spending patterns may differ from those in private industry. Because the federal government's fiscal year runs from October 1 through September 30, many agencies spend much of their procurement budgets in the fourth quarter (July 1 to September 30). They hoard their funds to cover unexpected expenditures, and if they encounter no such problems, they find themselves with money to spend in late summer. Companies understand this system and keep their eyes on government bulletins, so they can bid on the listed agency purchases, which often involve large amounts of money.

Online with the Federal Government Like their colleagues in the private sector, government procurement professionals are streamlining purchasing procedures with new technology. Rather than paging through piles of paper catalogs and submitting handwritten purchase orders, government buyers now prefer online catalogs that help them to compare competing product offerings. In fact, vendors find business with the government almost impossible unless they embrace electronic commerce.

Vendors can sell products to the federal government through three electronic options. Web sites provide a convenient method of exchanging information for both parties. Government buyers locate and order products, paying with a federally issued credit card, and the vendors deliver the items within about a week. Another route is through government-sponsored electronic ordering systems, which help to standardize the buying process. GSA Advantage, shown in Figure 10.11, allows federal employees to order products directly over the Internet at the preferred government price. The Electronic Posting System sends automatic notices of opportunities to sell to the government to more than 29,000 registered vendors. The Phoenix Opportunity System, set up by the Commerce Department, provides a similar service for minority-owned companies. A pilot program at the Treasury is testing an electronic check-payment system to speed up the settling of vendor invoices.[29]

Despite these advances, many government agencies remain less sophisticated than private-sector businesses. The Pentagon, for instance, is still coping with procurement procedures that were developed over the last 50 years. However, it is introducing a streamlined approach to defense contracting that reduces the time necessary to develop specifications and select suppliers. Spurred by the events of September 11, the Department of Defense is taking a lead role reinventing the federal procurement system. The government expenditures on upgrading technology are expected to grow by 65 percent by 2007.[30]

FIGURE 10.11

Goods and Services Sold Online to the U.S. Government

EDS aids the U.S. Chamber of Commerce in upgrading its infrastructure.

Challenges of Institutional Markets

Institutions constitute another important market. Institutional buyers include a wide variety of organizations, such as schools, hospitals, libraries, foundations, clinics, churches, and not-for-profit agencies.

Institutional markets are characterized by widely diverse buying practices. Some institutional purchasers behave like government purchasers because laws and political considerations determine their buying procedures. Many of these institutions, such as schools and prisons, may even be managed by government units. Other, privately managed institutions may, however, implement buying procedures that resemble those of private companies.

Buying practices can differ even between institutions of the same type. For instance, in a small hospital, the chief dietitian may approve all food purchases, while in a larger medical facility, food purchases may go through a committee consisting of the dietitian and a business manager, purchasing agent, and cook. Other hospitals may belong to buying groups, perhaps health maintenance organizations or local hospital cooperatives. Still others may contract with outside firms to prepare and serve all meals.

Within a single institution, multiple-buying influences may affect decisions. Many institutions, staffed by professionals such as physicians, nurses, researchers, and instructors, may also employ purchasing managers or even entire purchasing departments. Conflicts may arise among these decision makers. Professional employees may prefer to make their own purchase decisions and resent giving up control to the purchasing staff. This conflict can force a business marketer to cultivate both professionals and purchasers. For instance, a sales representative for a pharmaceutical firm must convince physicians and nurses of the value to patients of a certain drug while simultaneously convincing the hospital's purchasing department that the firm offers superior prices, delivery schedules, and service.

Group purchasing is an important factor in institutional markets since many institutions join cooperative associations to pool purchases for quantity discounts. Universities may join the Education and Institutional Purchasing Cooperative; hospitals may belong to regional associations; and chains of profit-oriented hospitals like HCA Healthcare can also negotiate quantity discounts. Central headquarters staff usually handles purchasing for all members of such a chain.

Diverse practices in institutional markets pose special challenges for B2B marketers. They must maintain flexibility in developing strategies for dealing with a range of customers, from large cooperative associations and chains to medium-sized purchasing departments and institutions to individuals. Buying centers can work with varying members, priorities, and levels of expertise. Discounts and effective distribution functions play important roles in obtaining—and keeping—institutions as customers.

Challenges of International Markets

To sell successfully in international markets, business marketers must consider buyers' attitudes and cultural patterns within areas where they operate. In Asian markets, for example, a firm must maintain a local

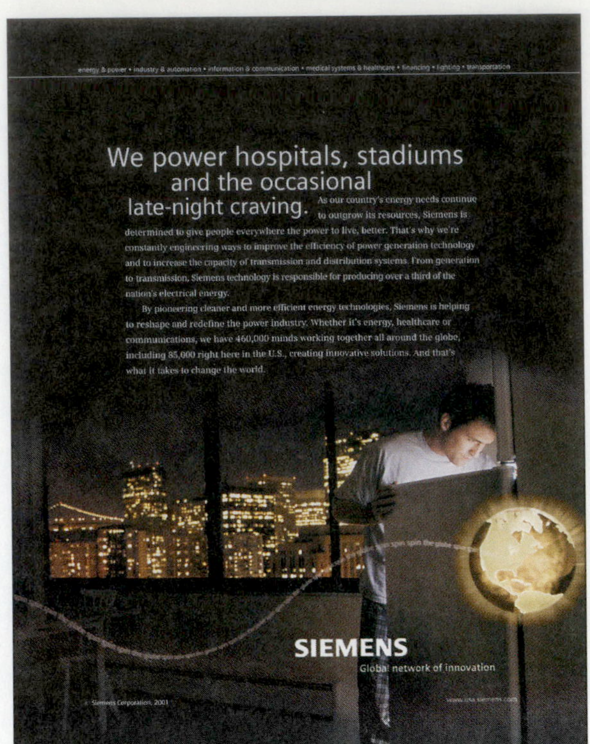

Munich, Germany–based Siemens provides power generation technology to institutional customers, including hospitals and public stadiums.

presence to sell products. Personal relationships are also important to business deals in Asia. Companies that want to expand globally often need to establish joint ventures with local partners.

International marketers must be poised to respond to shifts in cultural values. Consider Taiwan. Government laws mandated that advertisers had to use the official language of Beijing, Mandarin, instead of Taiwan's native dialect. However, as Taiwan has renewed its efforts to break free of Chinese rule, a rise in patriotism has brought the native Taiwanese culture back to the fore. In response, advertisers such as Japan's Kirin Brewery quickly developed new ads with Taiwanese songs and dialog. Booksellers are asking their suppliers to locate works on Taiwanese history; music stores are seeking recordings by native artists; and art stores are ordering record numbers of posters featuring Taiwan's former world champion Little League baseball players.[31]

Local industries, economic conditions, geographic characteristics, and legal restrictions must also be considered in international marketing. For instance, many local industries in Spain specialize in food and wine; therefore, a maker of forklift trucks might market smaller vehicles to Spanish companies than to German firms, which require bigger, heavier trucks to serve the needs of that nation's large automobile industry.

Remanufacturing—production to restore worn-out products to like-new condition—can be an important marketing strategy in a nation that cannot afford to buy new products. Developing countries often purchase remanufactured factory machinery, which costs 35 to 60 percent less than new equipment.

Foreign governments represent another important business market. In many countries, the government or state-owned companies dominate certain industries, such as construction and other infrastructure sales. Additional examples include airport and highway construction, telephone system equipment, and computer networking equipment. Sales to a foreign government can involve an array of regulations. For example, many governments, like that of the U.S., limit foreign participation in their defense programs. Joint ventures and countertrade are common, as are local content laws, which mandate domestic production of a certain percentage of a business product's components.

STRATEGIC IMPLICATIONS OF MARKETING IN THE 21ST CENTURY

To develop marketing strategies into the organizational sector, marketers must first understand the buying practices that govern the segment they are targeting, whether it is the commercial market, trade industries, government, or institutions. Similarly, when selling to a specific organization, strategies must take into account the many factors that influence purchasing. B2B marketers must identify people who play the various roles in the buying decision. They must also understand how these members interact with one another, other members of their own organizations, and outside vendors. Marketers must be careful to direct their marketing efforts to their organization, to broader environmental influences, and to individuals, who operate within the constraints of the firm's buying center.

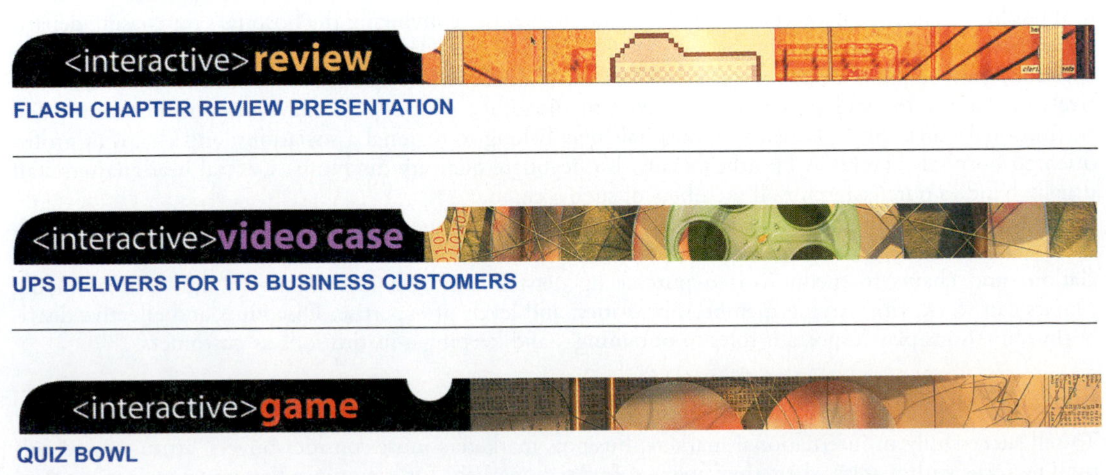

FLASH CHAPTER REVIEW PRESENTATION

UPS DELIVERS FOR ITS BUSINESS CUSTOMERS

QUIZ BOWL

<interactive>video case

KRISPY KREME CONTINUING VIDEO CASE: WHO IS EATING ALL THOSE KRISPY KREME DOUGHNUTS?

endofchaptermaterial

- Summary of Chapter Objectives
- Chapter Outline
- Key Terms
- Review Questions
- Projects and Teamwork Exercises
- 'netWork
- Crossword Puzzles
- Case 10.1: Bombardier vs. Embraer—Trade War at 30,000 Feet

Take the Post-Test to assess your overall understanding of the key ideas in this chapter. The Post-Test provides a comprehensive selection of exam-style questions addressing the main topics and concepts of the chapter. At the completion of each Post-Test, you will receive a score and instructive feedback on how you answered each question, and a direct link to the part of the chapter addressed in the question. Take the Post-Test as often as you need to—a record of your progress for each attempt is kept for you to revisit and gauge your improvement. And each Post-Test is randomly generated, so every attempt is new.

Post-Test

PART 4

Product Strategy

CHAPTER

11

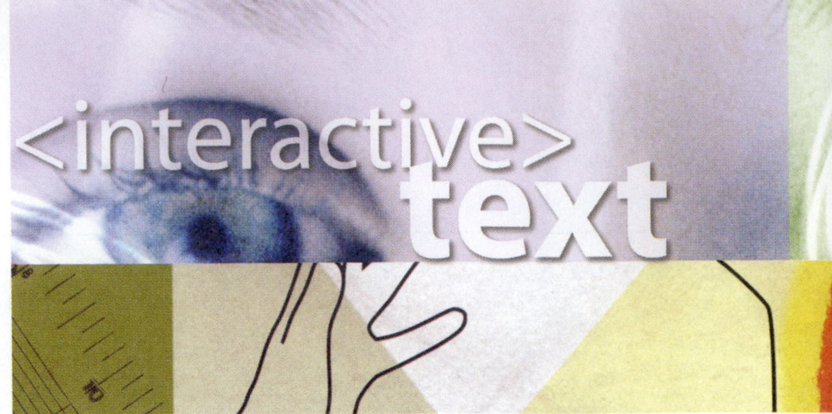

Product Strategies

Chapter Objectives

1. Define the term *product* and distinguish between goods and services.
2. List the classifications of consumer goods and services, and briefly describe each category.
3. Describe each of the types of business goods and services.
4. Discuss how total quality management (TQM) is implemented.
5. Explain the role benchmarking plays in achieving continuous improvement.
6. Explain why firms develop lines of related products rather than marketing individual items.
7. Identify the major product mix decisions that marketers must make.
8. Explain the concept of the product life cycle and how a firm can extend a product's life cycle.

APPLE COMPUTER MAKES EVERYTHING OLD NEW AGAIN

It's easy to get excited about a new product. If it appears to fill an existing consumer need and is hyped enough ahead of time, buyers should be lining up outside the stores to be first to get their hands on it. But it's not so easy to get worked up over a revamped product, except perhaps among high-technology diehards. In fact, marketers may have a tough time getting anyone to notice at all. Apple Computer is used to facing this problem as it has worked to come up with new and better versions of its Mac line of computers ever since it introduced the original model. And sometimes it's difficult to make a change in computer design seem as chic to the buying public as a new car or a really cool new fashion in clothing. In fact, when Apple introduced its PowerMac Cube, the new computer bombed. Although technology experts raved over it, no one bought it, perhaps because it was just too expensive, or perhaps because not enough consumers understood what was so unique about it.

All that may be about to change, however, with the launch of Apple's iMac. The strategy of designing and redesigning a product that the public already loves, and the involvement of top management in ensuring quality—CEO Steve Jobs seems to have his finger in every design pie at Apple—make a good foundation for the iMac's success. In addition, what is "new" about the iMac is something that consumers can quickly see and understand: Mostly, it's the ergonomic screen and unique round base, although there are other features like a digital hub and new software for handling music, pictures, videos, and DVDs. The new screen sits atop an adjustable, patent-pending neck that rotates 360 degrees horizontally and pivots 90 degrees vertically. So users can position it any way they want, whether it's tipped slightly backward for casual reading or perfectly vertical for writing tasks. Those who have tested the screen say it's easy to use and more comfortable on the eyes than conventional screens, potentially reducing eye strain and stiff necks.

Why is an innovation that appears as simple as this so important? Because it makes the computer easier to use for the average consumer, whom various marketers hope will spend more and more time with it—shopping, listening to music, watching movies, chatting with friends, not to mention working. And Jon Rubenstein, Apple's senior vice president for hardware confides that the redesign "was a lot harder than it looks." Sometimes, it takes more effort to achieve a simple, elegant design than it does to come up with a complex one.

Since its launch, the iMac has attracted more first-time Apple buyers than ever before; about 40 percent of the people purchasing computers in Apple's company-owned stores are buying Macs for the first time, reports the company. Other retailers say that new buyers are flocking around the iMac. And in a recent 30-day period, the company received 150,000 orders for the new machine, more than any other Apple product—and more than it could manufacture quickly, which meant that some customers had to wait several weeks for their computers. Despite the production lag, Apple remains optimistic about the success of its new sprout. "It's the best thing we've ever done," claims Steve Jobs. Although critics smile at this remark because Jobs says that about every new Apple product, they concede that Apple's new ideas are often the shape of things to come.[1]

Take the Pre-Test to assess your initial knowledge of the key ideas in this chapter. The Pre-Test provides exam-style questions addressing the main topics and concepts of the chapter. At the completion of each Pre-Test, you will receive a score and instructive feedback on how you answered each question, and a direct link to the part of the chapter addressed in the question. Take the Pre-Test as often as you need to—a record of your progress for each attempt is kept for you to revisit and gauge your improvement.

CHAPTER OVERVIEW

We've discussed how marketers conduct research to determine their markets, how customers behave during the purchasing process, and how firms expand their horizons overseas. Now our attention shifts to a company's **marketing mix,** the blend of four elements of a marketing strategy—product, price, distribution, and promotion—to satisfy the target market. This chapter focuses on how firms select and develop the goods and services they offer. Planning efforts begin with the choice of goods or services to offer. The other variables of the marketing mix—pricing discussions, distribution channels, and promotional plans—must accommodate the product strategy selected.

Briefly Speaking

Competition brings out the best in products and the worst in people.

David Sarnoff (1891–1971) Founder and president of RCA

Marketers develop strategies to promote both goods and services in the same manner. Any such program begins with investigation, analysis, and selection of a particular target market, and it continues with the creation of a marketing mix designed to satisfy that segment. But whereas the designs of tangible goods and intangible services both intend to satisfy consumer wants and needs, their marketing efforts may be vastly different.

This chapter examines both the similarities and the differences in marketing goods and services. It then presents basic concepts—classifications of products, development of product lines, and the product life cycle—that marketers apply in developing successful products. Finally, the chapter discusses product deletion and product mix decisions.

WHAT IS A PRODUCT?

At first, you might think of a product as an object you hold in your hand. But that doesn't take into account the idea of a service as a product. Nor does it consider the idea of what the product is used for. So a television is more than a black box with a screen and a remote control. It's really a means of providing entertainment—your favorite movies or shows. And if something goes wrong with the TV, you can call a repair person to fix it for you—that service is also a product. Marketers acknowledge this broader conception of product; they realize that people buy *want satisfaction* rather than objects. You might feel a need for a television in order to satisfy a want for entertainment. You might not know a lot about how the machine itself works, but you understand the results.

CHAPTER OBJECTIVE #1: DEFINE THE TERM *PRODUCT* AND DISTINGUISH BETWEEN GOODS AND SERVICES.

Marketers think in terms of a product as a compilation of package design and labeling, brand name, warranty, and customer-service activities that add value for the customer. Consequently, a **product** is a bundle of physical, service, and symbolic attributes designed to satisfy a customer's wants and needs.

WHAT ARE GOODS AND SERVICES?

Services are products. A general definition identifies **services** as intangible tasks that satisfy the needs of consumer and business users. But you can't hold a service in your hand the way you can **goods,** which are tangible products that customers can see, hear, smell, taste, or touch like the television just described. Most service providers cannot transport or store their products; customers simultaneously buy and consume these products, like haircuts, car repairs, and visits to the dentist. One way to distinguish services from goods is the *goods-services continuum,* as shown in Figure 11.1.

This spectrum helps marketers to visualize the differences and similarities between goods and services.[2] A car is a pure good, but the dealer may also offer repair and maintenance services or include the services in the price of a lease. Cinema complexes provide pure services, but they also sell goods such as soft drinks and popcorn. The car falls at the pure-good extreme of the continuum because the customer values the repair service less than the car itself, just as movie patrons consider refreshments less important than the entertainment that the theater provides. In the middle range of the continuum, dinner at an exclusive

FIGURE 11.1

Goods-Services Continuum

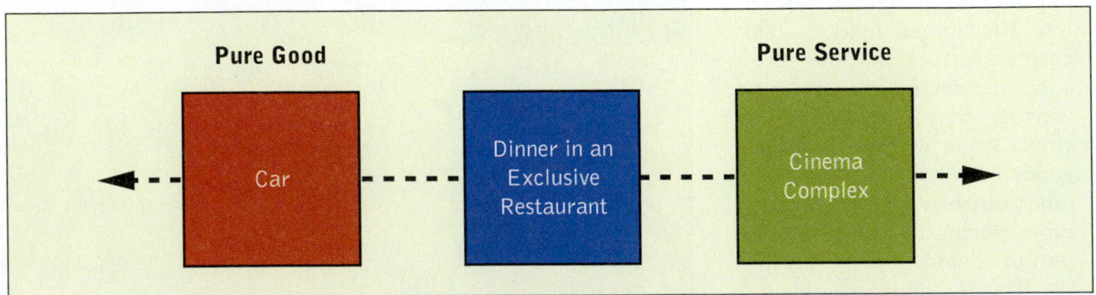

restaurant has equally important good and service components. Customers derive satisfaction not only from the food and beverages but also from services rendered by the restaurant's staff.

You can begin to see how diverse services can be. In fact, they are more diverse than pure goods. Services can be distinguished from goods in several ways:

1. *Services are intangible.* Services do not have physical features that buyers can see, hear, smell, taste, or touch prior to purchase. Service firms essentially ask their customers to buy a promise.
2. *Services are inseparable from the service providers.* Consumer perceptions of a service provider become their perceptions of the service itself. A good haircut will give you the perception that your hairstylist is excellent; a bad haircut will give the opposite perception.
3. *Services are perishable.* Providers cannot maintain inventories of their services. During times of peak demand, prices may rise, only to fall drastically when demand declines. For instance, hotels often raise room rates during special events and lower them to normal levels after the end of the events.
4. *Companies cannot easily standardize services.* However, many firms are trying to change this. Most fast-food chains promise that you'll get your meal within a certain number of minutes. Hotel chains often use the same room decor or offer the same dining menu at all of their hotels.
5. *Buyers often play roles in the development and distribution of services.* Service transactions frequently require interaction between buyer and seller at the production and distribution stages. Marriott International uses a customer management software program to interact with customers and coordinate their visits to Marriott hotels. Several weeks in advance of a visit, a Marriott planning coordinator may contact a visitor to ask whether he or she wants to play golf, eat at certain restaurants, or attend a concert. When the guest arrives, the arrangements have been made.[3]
6. *Service quality shows wide variations.* New York City's posh Le Cirque and your local Pizza Hut are both restaurants. Their customers, however, experience considerably different cuisine, physical surroundings, service standards, and prices.

Always keep in mind that often a product blurs the distinction between services and goods, as when a service provides a good. Avis is a service that provides rental cars, which are goods. Pearle Vision Centers provide eye examinations—services through optometrists—while Pearle sells eyeglasses and contact lenses (goods).

Importance of the Service Sector

You would live a very different life without service firms to fill many needs. You could not place a telephone call, log on to the Internet, flip a switch for electricity, or even take a college course if organizations did not provide such services. During an average day, you probably use many services without much thought, but these products play an integral role in your life.

The service sector makes a crucial contribution to the U.S. economy. Consider that there are more than 1 million retail trade establishments in the U.S., and they produce almost $2.5 trillion annually in sales receipts. While there are fewer finance and insurance service firms—approximately 400,000—their annual sales of over $2.2 billion come close to the retail figure.

Services account for four out of five jobs in the U.S. While manufacturing firms employ a total of 17 million Americans, many more people work for a service provider. The biggest service employers are retail—more than 14 million employees—and health care—more than 13 million employees.[4]

Services also play a crucial role in the international competitiveness of U.S. firms. While the U.S. runs a continuing trade deficit in goods, it has maintained a trade surplus in services for every year since 1970. This trade surplus continues to rise from its current total of roughly $70 billion. Some economists think that more precise measurements of service exports would reveal an even larger surplus.

Observers cite several reasons for the growing economic importance of services, including consumer desire for speed and convenience and technological advances that allow firms to fulfill this demand. Services that involve wireless communications, data backup and storage, and even meal preparation for busy families are on the rise. In the wake of a weak economy and poor stock market performance, consumers are looking to financial advisors for help in managing their investments.

Most service firms emphasize marketing as a significant activity for two reasons. First, the growth potential of service transactions represents a vast marketing opportunity. Second, increased competition is forcing traditional service industries to emphasize marketing in order to compete in the marketplace.

CLASSIFYING GOODS AND SERVICES FOR CONSUMER AND BUSINESS MARKETS

A firm's choices for marketing a good or service depend largely on the offering itself and on the nature of the target market. Product strategies differ for consumer and business markets. Consumer products are those destined for use by ultimate consumers, while business or B2B products (also called *industrial* or *organizational products*) contribute directly or indirectly to the output of other products for resale. Marketers further subdivide these two major categories into more specific categories, as discussed in this section.

It is important to note that some products fall into both categories. A case in point is prescription drugs. Traditionally, pharmaceutical companies marketed prescription drugs to doctors, who then made the purchase decision for their patients by writing the prescription. Thus, the medications could be classified as a business product. However, many drug companies now advertise their products in consumer-oriented media, including magazines and television. In fact, in a recent year, pharmaceutical giant Merck & Co. spent a whopping $135.5 million on advertising for its anti-inflammatory drug Vioxx, which included TV spots featuring Olympic figure-skating champion Dorothy Hamill.[5] As patients begin to behave more like customers, they may request prescriptions for certain medications they have seen advertised in the media, making a classification of consumer product more appropriate.

Types of Consumer Products

Several classification systems divide consumer goods and services in different ways. One basic distinction focuses on the buyer's perception of a need for the product. *Unsought products* are marketed to consumers who may not yet recognize any need for them. Examples of unsought products are life insurance and funeral services. Figure 11.2 takes this classification to another level by suggesting to pet owners that they need veterinary insurance for their pets.

CHAPTER OBJECTIVE #2: LIST THE CLASSIFICATIONS OF CONSUMER GOODS AND SERVICES, AND BRIEFLY DESCRIBE EACH CATEGORY.

In contrast, most consumers recognize their own needs for various types of consumer purchases. The most common classification scheme divides consumer goods and services into three groups: convenience, shopping, and specialty. These categories are based on customers' buying behavior. Figure 11.3 illustrates samples of these three categories, together with the unsought classification.

FIGURE 11.2

Pet Insurance: An Unsought Product

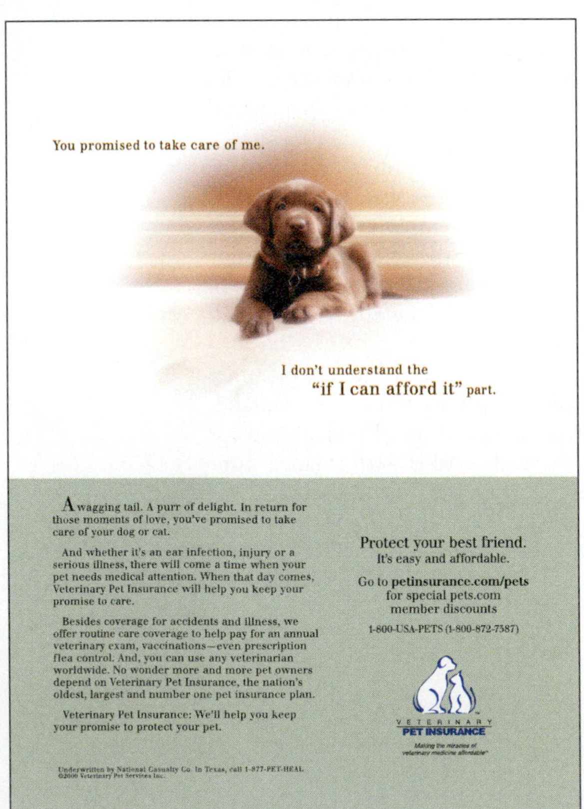

Convenience Products **Convenience products** refer to goods and services that consumers want to purchase frequently, immediately, and with minimal effort. Milk, bread, and soft drinks are examples of these products, as are chewing gum, candy, and most vending-machine items. Convenience services include 24-hour quick-stop stores, walk-in hair salons, copy shops, and dry cleaners.

Marketers further subdivide the convenience category into impulse items, staples, or emergency items:

- *Impulse goods and services* are purchased on the spur of the moment, such as a visit to a car wash or a pack of gum tossed in at the register. Some marketers have even come up with ways to make impulse shopping on the Internet attractive. Marc Malaga, founder of GiftBaskets.com, a site that provides gift and food baskets, flowers, and other gifts, decided to set up a special Gift Emergency Center on his Web site's home page. The Emergency Center allows customers to purchase gift baskets that will be sent the same day, which actually encourages impulse buying. "People might be coming to the site for one thing, and then they see they can send something the same or next day, so they may choose to buy it," Malaga explains.[6]
- *Staples* are convenience goods and services that consumers constantly replenish to maintain a ready inventory—for instance, gasoline and dry cleaning.
- *Emergency goods and services* are bought in response to unexpected and urgent needs. An ice scraper purchased during a snowstorm and a visit to a hospital emergency room to treat a sprained ankle are examples.

Since consumers devote little effort to these purchase decisions, marketers must strive to make these exchanges as convenient as possible. Store location can boost a convenience product's visibility. Marketers compete vigorously for prime locations, which can make all the difference between a consumer choosing one gas sta-

FIGURE 11.3

Classification of Consumer Products

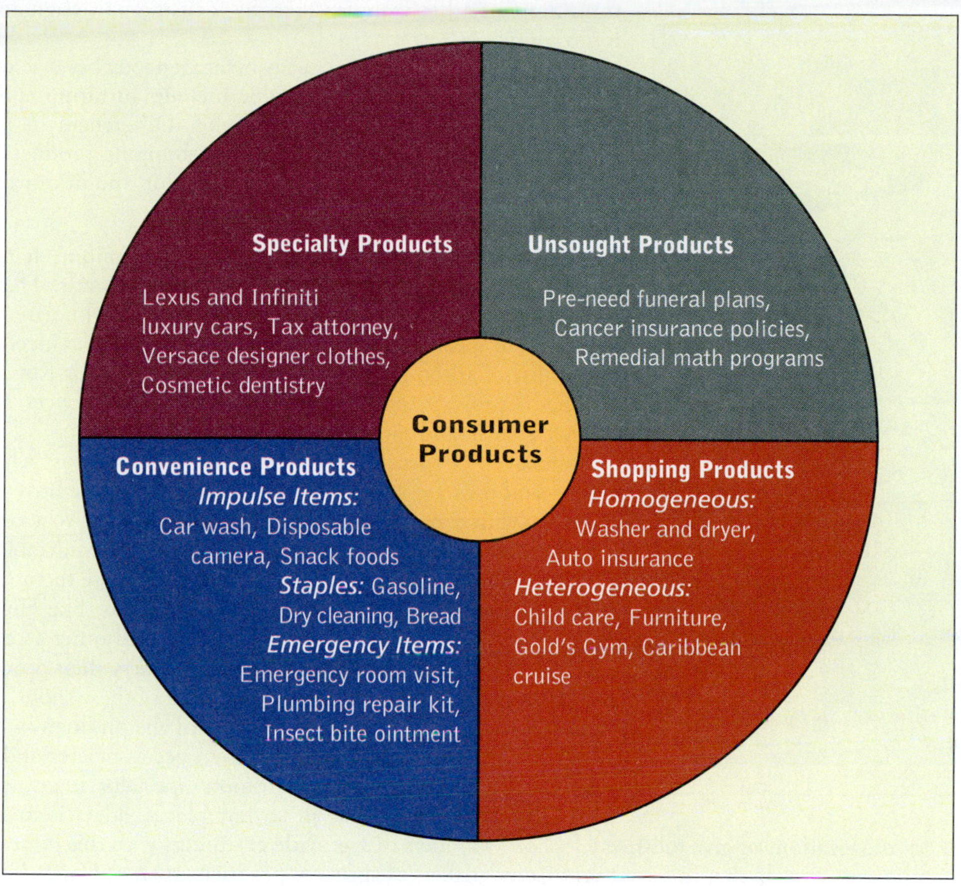

tion, vending machine, or dry cleaner over another. In addition, location *within* a store can make the difference between success and failure of a product, which is why manufacturers fight so hard for the right spot on supermarket shelves. Typically, the larger and more powerful grocery manufacturers get the most visible spots. For instance, Kraft Foods has eight or ten special displays in many supermarkets. Brands like Miracle Whip, Ritz crackers, Philadelphia cream cheese, Kool-Aid, and Oreo cookies all belong to Kraft—and enjoy prime shelf space. But visibility to consumers comes at a price, often through a practice called *slotting allowances,* money paid to retailers to guarantee prominent display. The standard slotting price for a new product in a major supermarket can run as much as $25,000, which could put a small manufacturer of one product line, say yogurt or salsa, out of business before it even gets started. For this reason, the Federal Trade Commission (FTC) has begun to look at the practice of paying for shelf space. "The practice raises questions about whether the big dog not only eats first, but also decides who gets the table scraps," notes U.S. Senator Christopher Bond (Missouri), the ranking member of the Senate Small Business Committee.[7]

Shopping Products In contrast to their purchases of convenience items, consumers buy **shopping products** only after comparing competing offerings on such characteristics as price, quality, style, and color. Shopping products typically cost more than convenience purchases. This category includes tangible items such as clothing, furniture, and appliances and services such as child care, home remodeling, auto repairs, and insurance. The purchaser of a shopping product lacks complete information prior to the buying trip and gathers information during the buying process.

Several important features distinguish shopping products: physical attributes, service attributes such as warranties and after-sale service terms, prices, styling, and places of purchase. A store's name and reputation have considerable influence on people's buying behavior. The personal selling efforts of salespeople provide important promotional support.

Buyers and marketers treat some shopping products, such as refrigerators and washing machines, as homogeneous products. To the consumer, one brand seems largely the same as another. Marketers may try to differentiate homogeneous products from competing products in several ways. They may emphasize

FIGURE 11.4

Distinguishing One Shopping Product from Another

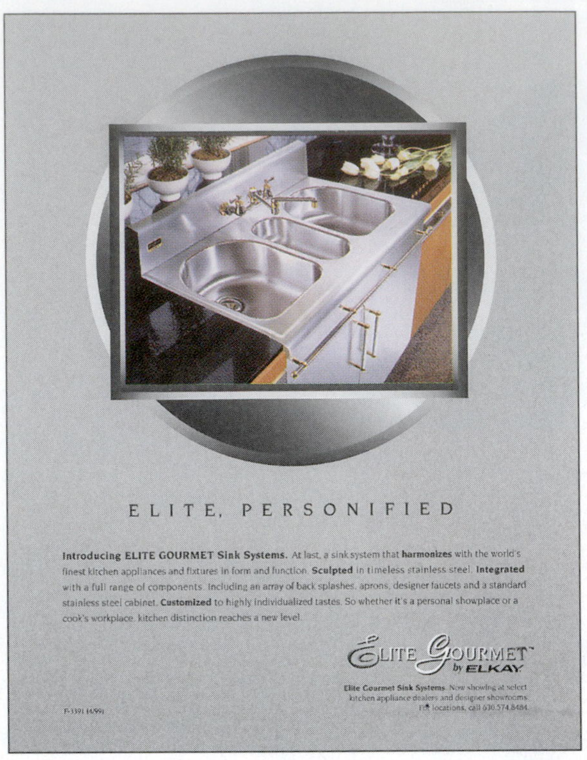

price and value, or they may attempt to educate buyers about less obvious features that contribute to a product's quality, appeal, and uniqueness. In Figure 11.4, Elkay attempts to distinguish its sinks from those of other manufacturers by focusing on design and customization.

ELITE, PERSONIFIED
Introducing ELITE GOURMET Sink Systems. At last, a sink system that **harmonizes** with the world's finest kitchen appliances and fixtures in form and function. **Sculpted** in timeless stainless steel. **Integrated** with a full range of components. Including an array of back splashes, aprons, designer faucets and a standard stainless steel cabinet. **Customized** to highly individualized tastes. So whether it's a personal showplace or a cook's workplace, kitchen distinction reaches a new level.
ELITE GOURMET™ by ELKAY
Elite Gourmet Sink Systems. Now showing at select kitchen appliance dealers and designer showrooms.
locations, call 630.574.8484
F-3391 (4/99)

Other shopping products seem heterogeneous because of basic differences among them. Examples include furniture, physical-fitness training, vacations, and clothing. Differences in features often separate competing heterogeneous shopping products in the minds of consumers. Perceptions of style, color, and fit can all affect consumer choices.

Specialty Products **Specialty products** offer unique characteristics that cause buyers to prize those particular brands. They typically carry high prices, and many represent well-known brands. Examples of specialty goods include Hermès scarves, Gucci leather goods, Ritz-Carlton resorts, Tiffany jewelry, and Rolls-Royce automobiles. Specialty services include professional services such as financial, legal, and medical services.

Purchasers of specialty goods and services know just what they want—and they are willing to pay accordingly. These buyers begin shopping with complete information, and they refuse to accept substitutes. Because consumers are willing to exert considerable effort to obtain specialty products, producers can promote them through relatively few retail locations. In fact, some firms, like Hermès, a designer and maker of exclusive scarves, ties, and other accessories, intentionally limit the range of retailers that carry their products to add to their cachet. In addition, the location of these shops, such as New York or Paris, adds to the mystique of the product.

Both highly personalized service by sales associates and image advertising help marketers to promote specialty items. Because these products are available in so few places, advertisements frequently list the locations or give toll-free telephone numbers that provide customers with this information.

It is important to note that in recent years some makers of specialty products, such as Coach handbags and Donna Karan clothing, have broadened their market by selling some of their goods through company-owned discount outlets. These stores attract consumers who want to own specialty items but who cannot or do not wish to pay the high prices usually associated with these goods.

Hermès, an exclusive designer of accessories such as ties, scarves, belts, and purses, enhances its product image by limiting the sale of its specialty products to a few stores in prestigious locations.

Applying the Consumer Products Classification System

The three-way classification system of convenience, shopping, and specialty goods and services helps to guide marketers in developing a marketing strategy. Consumer behavior patterns differ for the three types of purchases. For example, classifying a new food item as a convenience product leads to insights about marketing needs in branding, promotion, pricing, and distribution decisions. Table 11.1 summarizes the impact of this classification system on the development of an effective marketing mix.

The classification system, however, also poses a few problems. The major obstacle in implementing this system results from the suggestion that all goods and services must fit within one of the three categories. Some fit neatly into one category, but others share characteristics of more than one category.

For example, how would you classify the purchase of a new automobile? Before classifying the expensive good, which is sold by brand and handled by a few exclusive dealers in each city as a specialty product, consider other characteristics. Most new car buyers shop extensively among competing models and dealers before deciding on the best deal. Consider a continuum representing degrees of effort expended by consumers. At one end of the continuum, they casually pick up convenience items; at the other end, they search extensively for specialty products. Shopping products fall between these extremes. In addition, car dealers may offer services, both during and after the sale, that play a big role in the purchase decision. On this continuum, the new car purchase might appear between the categories of shopping and specialty products but closer to specialty products.

A second problem with the classification system emerges because consumers differ in their buying patterns. One person may make an emergency visit to the dentist because of a toothache, while another may extensively compare prices and office hours before selecting a dentist. But one buyer's impulse purchase does not make dental services a convenience item. Marketers classify goods and services by considering the purchase patterns of the majority of buyers.

Types of Business Products

Business buyers are professional customers. Their job duties require rational, cost-effective purchase decisions. For instance, General Mills applies much of the same purchase decision process to buy flour that Pillsbury does.

<interactive>**learning goal**

CHAPTER OBJECTIVE #3: DESCRIBE EACH OF THE TYPES OF BUSINESS GOODS AND SERVICES.

The classification system for business products emphasizes product uses rather than customer buying behavior. Business products generally fall into one of six categories for product uses: installations, accessory equipment, component parts and materials, raw materials, supplies, and business services.[8] Figure 11.5 illustrates the six types of business products.

Installations The specialty products of the business market are called **installations.** This classification includes major capital investments for new factories and heavy machinery, and for telecommunications

TABLE 11.1

Marketing Impact of the Consumer Products Classification System

	Convenience Products	Shopping Products	Specialty Products
Consumer Factors			
Planning time involved in purchase	Very little	Considerable	Extensive
Purchase frequency	Frequent	Less frequent	Infrequent
Importance of convenient location	Critical	Important	Unimportant
Comparison of price and quality	Very little	Considerable	Very little
Marketing Mix Factors			
Price	Low	Relatively high	High
Importance of seller's image	Unimportant	Very important	Important
Distribution channel length	Long	Relatively short	Very short
Number of sales outlets	Many	Few	Very few; often one per market area
Promotion	Advertising and promotion by producer	Personal selling and advertising by both producer and retailer	Personal selling and advertising by both producer and retailer

FIGURE 11.5

Classification of Business Products

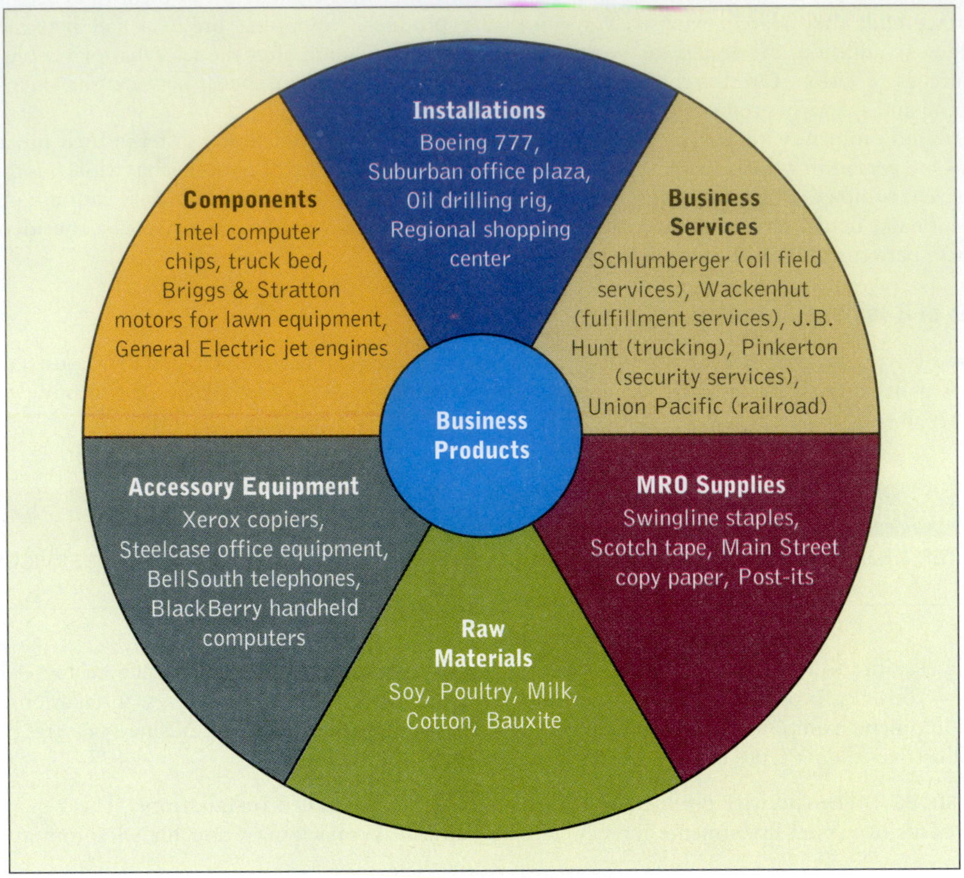

Business Products

Installations
Boeing 777, Suburban office plaza, Oil drilling rig, Regional shopping center

Business Services
Schlumberger (oil field services), Wackenhut (fulfillment services), J.B. Hunt (trucking), Pinkerton (security services), Union Pacific (railroad)

MRO Supplies
Swingline staples, Scotch tape, Main Street copy paper, Post-its

Raw Materials
Soy, Poultry, Milk, Cotton, Bauxite

Accessory Equipment
Xerox copiers, Steelcase office equipment, BellSouth telephones, BlackBerry handheld computers

Components
Intel computer chips, truck bed, Briggs & Stratton motors for lawn equipment, General Electric jet engines

systems. Purchases of Boeing 737s for Air New Zealand and locomotives for Burlington Northern are considered installations.

Since installations last for long periods of time and their purchases involve large sums of money, they represent major decisions for organizations. Negotiations often extend over several months and involve numerous decision makers. Vendors often provide technical expertise along with tangible goods. Representatives who sell custom-made equipment work closely with buying firms' engineers and production personnel to design the most satisfactory products possible.

Price typically does not dominate purchase decisions for installations. A purchasing firm buys such a product for its efficiency and performance over its useful life. The firm also wants to minimize breakdowns. Downtime is expensive because the firm must pay employees while they wait for repairs on the machine.

Installations are major investments often designed specifically for the purchasers. Effective operation may also require considerable training of the buyer's workforce along with significant after-sale service. As a result, marketers of these systems typically emphasize highly trained sales representatives, often with technical backgrounds. Advertising, if the firm employs it at all, emphasizes company reputation and directs potential buyers to contact local sales representatives.

Most installations are marketed directly from manufacturers to users. Even a one-time sale may require continuing contacts for regular product servicing. Some manufacturers prefer to lease extremely expensive installations to customers rather than selling the items outright and assign personnel directly to the lessees' sites to operate or maintain the equipment.

Accessory Equipment Only a few decision makers may participate in a purchase of **accessory equipment**—capital items that typically cost less and last for shorter periods than installations.

Although quality and service exert important influences on purchases of accessory equipment, price may significantly affect these decisions. Accessory equipment includes products such as hand tools, portable drills, small lathes, and laptop computers. Although these products are considered capital investments and buyers depreciate their costs over several years, their useful lives generally are much shorter than those of installations.

Marketing these products requires continuous representation and dealing with the widespread geographic dispersion of purchasers. To cope with these market characteristics, a wholesaler—often called an industrial distributor—contacts potential customers in its own geographic area. Customers usually do not need technical assistance, and a manufacturer of accessory equipment often can sell its products effectively through wholesalers.

Advertising is an important component in the marketing mix for accessory equipment. Lexmark's ad for its Z65 Photo printer in Figure 11.6 emphasizes the machine's speed, the quality of copies it produces, and potential savings to the business customer. Note that Lexmark sells a variety of computer printers and related products. Lexmark develops and manufacturers its own devices, thereby speeding product cycles.

FIGURE 11.6

Promoting Accessory Equipment

Resolution revolution.
The new Z65. At 4800 x 1200 dpi, it's the ultimate photo printer.
The revolution is here and the Z65 is ready to rule. Just imagine what industry-leading 5.8 megapixels and a microscopic drop size will do for your digital images. Crisp, razor-sharp color. Amazingly lifelike skin tones. Lighting fast speeds of up to 21 pages per minute. Add to that outstanding paper handling capabilities and the Z65 delivers output that's everything you can imagine. And more.
LEXMARK
Passion for printing ideas.

Component Parts and Materials Whereas business buyers use installations and accessory equipment in the process of producing their own final products, **component parts and materials** represent finished business products of one producer that actually became part of the final products of another producer. Milwaukee-based Johnson Controls has supplied automobile seats to car manufacturers for years. Now the company has teamed up with Philips Electronics to deliver in-car DVD entertainment systems. The products made and sold by these two firms become part of the completed autos sold by the auto manufacturers.[9] Some fabricated materials, such as flour, undergo further processing before becoming part of finished products. Textiles, paper pulp, and chemicals are also examples of component parts and materials.

Purchasers of component parts and materials need regular, continuous supplies of uniform-quality products. They generally contract to purchase these items for set periods of time. Marketers commonly emphasize direct sales, and satisfied customers often become regular buyers. Wholesalers sometimes supply fill-in purchases and handle sales to smaller purchasers.

Raw Materials Farm products, such as beef, cotton, eggs, milk, poultry, and soybeans, and natural products, such as coal, copper, iron ore, and lumber, constitute **raw materials.** These products resemble component parts and materials in that they actually become part of the buyers' final products.

Most raw materials carry grades determined according to set criteria, assuring purchasers of the receipt of standardized products of uniform quality. As with component parts and materials, vendors commonly market raw materials directly to buying organizations, typically according to contractual terms. Wholesalers are increasingly involved in purchasing raw materials from foreign suppliers.

Price is seldom a deciding factor in a raw materials purchase since terms are often set at central markets, determining virtually identical exchanges among competing sellers. Purchasers buy raw materials from the firms they consider best able to deliver the required quantities and qualities.

Supplies If installations represent the specialty products of the business market, operating supplies are its convenience products. **Supplies** constitute the regular expenses that a firm incurs in its daily operations. These expenses do not become part of the buyer's final products.

Supplies are also called *MRO items* because they fall into three categories: (1) maintenance items, such as brooms, filters, and light bulbs; (2) repair items, such as nuts and bolts used in repairing equipment; and (3) operating supplies, such as fax paper, Post-it notes, and pencils.

A purchasing manager regularly buys operating supplies as a routine job duty. Wholesalers often facilitate sales of supplies due to the low unit prices, the small order size, and the large number of potential buyers. Since supplies are relatively standardized, heavy price competition frequently keeps costs under control. However, a business buyer spends little time making decisions about these products. Exchanges of products frequently demand simple telephone or EDI orders or regular purchases from a sales representative of a local wholesaler.

Business Services The **business services** category includes the intangible products that firms buy to facilitate their production and operating processes. Examples of business services are financial services, leasing and rental services that supply equipment and vehicles, insurance, security, legal advice, and consulting. Many service providers sell the same services—telephone, gas, and electric, for example—to both consumers and organizational buyers, although service firms may maintain separate marketing groups for the two customer segments.

FIGURE 11.7

Business Services: A Storage Management Solution

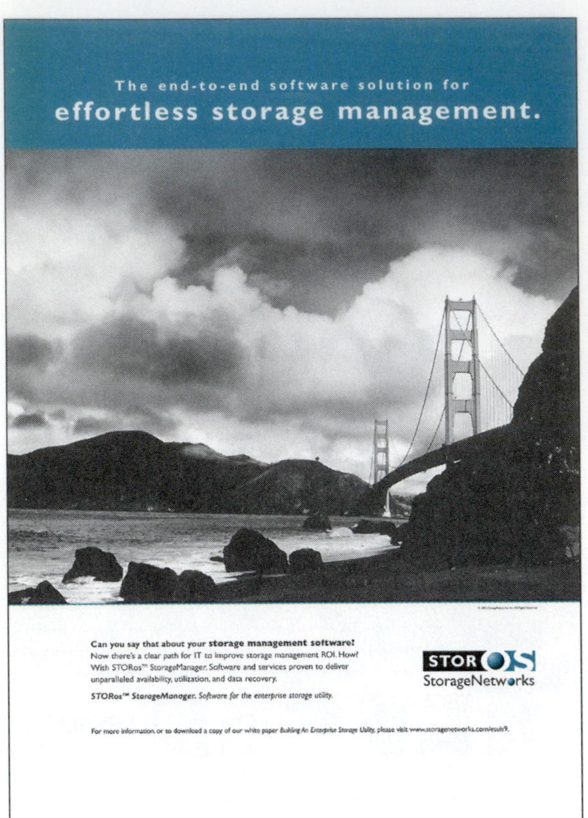

Organizations also purchase many adjunct services that assist their operations but are not essentially a part of the final product. Akamai Technologies serves customers such as CNN.com and MarthaStewart.com by helping their Web pages avoid bottlenecks on the Internet. Akamai accomplishes this by developing alliances with other hardware and software vendors and ISPs in order to provide an entire spectrum of Internet business services.[10] When so many businesses lost their computer data in the attacks on New York's World Trade Center, firms began to turn to data storage companies such as StorageNetworks, advertised in Figure 11.7, to protect valuable data.

Price often strongly influences purchase decisions for business services. The buying firm must decide whether to purchase a service or provide that service internally. This decision may depend on how frequently the firm needs the service and the specialized knowledge required to provide it.

Purchase decision processes vary considerably for different types of business services. For example, a firm may purchase window-cleaning services through a routine and straightforward process similar to that for buying operating supplies. By contrast, a purchase decision for highly specialized environmental engineering advice requires complex analysis and perhaps lengthy negotiations similar to those for purchases of installations. This variability of the marketing mix for business services and other business products is outlined in Table 11.2.

The buying and selling of business products often involves alliances among different types of firms. As mentioned earlier, Johnson Controls formed a relationship with Philips Electronics in order to deliver in-car DVD systems. Akamai Technologies has relationships with 750 hardware and software vendors in order to provide services to its customers. Equity Office Properties, a real estate firm that leases offices and buildings to businesses, has formed partnerships with other companies to offer its tenants telecom services, full-service business suites including mailrooms and copy centers, office furniture, and fitness clubs.[11]

<interactive>**exercise**

'NET EX: CUSTOMER SERVICE

QUALITY AS A PRODUCT STRATEGY

No matter how a product is classified, nothing is more frustrating to a customer than having a new item break after just a few uses, or having it not live up to expectations. The portable phone that hisses static at you unless you stand still, the seam that rips out of the new jacket, the plastic wrap that tears or sticks to itself instead of to the bowl of leftovers, aren't life-altering experiences, but they do leave an impression of poor quality that likely will lead you to make different purchases in the future. Then there's the issue of quality in service—the department store that seems to have no salespeople or the computer help line that leaves you on hold for 20 minutes.

<interactive>**learning goal**

CHAPTER OBJECTIVE #4: DISCUSS HOW TOTAL QUALITY MANAGEMENT (TQM) IS IMPLEMENTED.

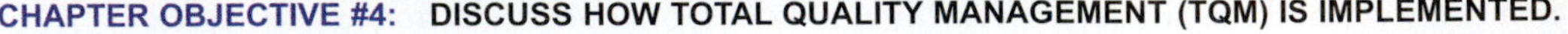

Quality is a key component to a firm's success in a competitive marketplace, so few aspects of product strategy have attracted as much attention during the past two decades as the quality of the firm's output. The result of these efforts to create and market goods and services equal to any in the world has been a movement referred to as **total quality management (TQM).** It asks all employees in a firm to continually improve products and work processes with the goal of achieving customer satisfaction and world-class per-

TABLE 11.2

Marketing Impact of the Business Products Classification System

FACTOR	INSTALLATIONS	ACCESSORY EQUIPMENT	COMPONENT PARTS AND MATERIALS	RAW MATERIALS	SUPPLIES	BUSINESS SERVICES
Organizational Factors						
Planning time	Extensive	Less extensive	Less extensive	Varies	Very little	Varies
Purchase frequency	Infrequent	More frequent	Frequent	Infrequent	Frequent	Varies
Comparison of price and quality	Quality very important	Quality and price important	Quality important	Quality important	Price important	Varies
Marketing Mix Factors						
Price	High	Relatively high	Low to high	Low to high	Low	Varies
Distribution channel length	Very short	Relatively short	Short	Short	Long	Varies
Promotion method	Personal selling by producer	Advertising	Personal selling	Personal selling	Advertising by producer	Varies

formance. In a total quality organization, marketers develop products that people want to buy; engineers design items to work the way customers want to use them; production workers build quality into everything they produce; salespeople deliver what they promise customers; information systems' experts apply technology to ensure that customer orders are filled correctly and on time; and financial specialists help to determine prices that give customers value.

The quality movement started in the U.S. during the 1920s as an attempt to improve product quality by improving the manufacturing process itself. Walter Shewhart, a physicist at AT&T Bell Laboratories, pioneered an innovative approach called *statistical quality control,* which employed statistical techniques to locate and measure quality problems on production lines. W. Edwards Deming, a statistician who worked with Shewhart, helped to popularize Shewhart's quality control methods in the U.S. and abroad. Deming encouraged managers to view their organizations as systems that direct the knowledge and skills of all employees toward improving quality. Managers are responsible for communicating the goals of total quality management to all staff members and for encouraging workers to improve themselves and take pride in their work.

Of course, achieving maximum quality is easier said than done. At one electric utility, the top 350 business customers are served by six people in the customer service department. The next level of 700 customers are served by six more employees, and the "bottom" layer of 30,000 customers are handled by just two customer service representatives. At this company, it's almost impossible to provide top-quality service.[12] To achieve quality, support must come from top management in the form of resources and staff.

Worldwide Quality Programs

During the 1980s, the quality revolution picked up speed in U.S. corporations. The campaign to improve quality found leadership in large manufacturing firms like Ford, Xerox, and Motorola that had lost market share to Japanese competitors. Smaller companies that supplied parts to large firms then began to recognize quality as a requirement for success. Today, a commitment to quality has spread to service industries, not-for-profit organizations, government agencies, and educational institutions.

As part of the national quality improvement campaign, Congress established the Malcolm Baldrige National Quality Award in 1987 to recognize excellence in quality management. Named after late Secretary of Commerce Malcolm Baldrige, the award is the highest national recognition for quality that a U.S. company can receive. The award works toward promoting quality awareness, recognizing quality achievements of U.S. companies, and publicizing successful quality strategies.

The quality movement is very strong in European countries. The European Union's *ISO 9002* (formerly ISO 9000) standards define international criteria for quality management and quality assurance. These standards were developed by the International Standards Organization in Switzerland to ensure consistent quality among products manufactured and sold throughout the nations of the European Union (EU).

Many European companies now require suppliers to complete ISO certification as a condition of doing business with them. To become ISO certified, a company must undergo an on-site audit that includes an inspection of the firm's facilities to ensure that documented quality procedures are in place and that all employees understand and follow those procedures. Meeting ISO requirements is an ongoing process, typically covering a 14-month period, during which periodic audits verify conformance. Once granted certification, the firm must frequently ensure that its suppliers are also ISO certified. ISO 9002 is clearly a basic requirement for firms doing business in Europe. Competitors in non-EU countries, concerned over the threats of exclusion from this huge market, have moved quickly to implement ISO 9002 standards.

The Role of Benchmarking in Quality

Many quality-conscious businesspeople rely on an important tool called *benchmarking* to set performance standards. This method for creating a world-class marketing operation seeks to identify how business leaders achieve superior marketing performance levels in their industries and to develop a system for continuously comparing and measuring performance against outstanding performers. The technique involves learning how the world's best goods and services are designed, produced, and marketed. The purpose of benchmarking is to achieve superior performance that results in a competitive advantage in the marketplace.

<interactive>learning goal

CHAPTER OBJECTIVE #5: EXPLAIN THE ROLE BENCHMARKING PLAYS IN ACHIEVING CONTINUOUS IMPROVEMENT.

A typical benchmarking process involves three main activities: identifying processes that need improvement, comparing internal processes against similar activities of industry leaders, and implementing changes for better quality. As Figure 11.8 shows, the process continuously repeats itself since vigilant companies continue to search for and identify areas that need improvement, even after implementing changes. This ongoing devotion helps these firms to ensure that they remain market leaders.

Benchmarking requires two types of analyses: internal and external. Before a company can compare itself with another, it must first analyze its own activities to determine strengths and weaknesses. This establishes a baseline for comparison. External analysis involves gathering information about the benchmark partner to find out why the partner is perceived as the best. A comparison of the results of the analysis provides an objective basis for making improvements.

In recent years, General Motors has used benchmarking and other strategies to dramatically improve quality and productivity in its auto manufacturing processes. CEO Rick Wagoner relied on a successful program called Work Out, developed by General Electric. (Note that benchmarking can take place across different industries.) Wagoner renamed the program Go Fast and began to use it to reengineer manufacturing processes and break through logjams in decision making. At Go Fast meetings, engineers, designers, and other managers discuss how to fix defects in manufacturing and engineering, helping GM to improve the quality of its processes and automobiles, as illustrated in Figure 11.9. In just a couple of years, managers have held thousands of Go Fast meetings and trained 25,000 employees in the quality improvement process.[13]

FIGURE 11.8

The Benchmarking Process

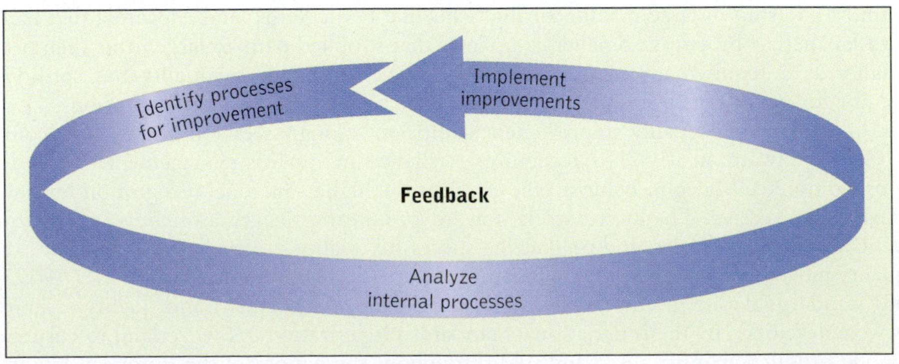

DEVELOPMENT OF PRODUCT LINES

Few firms today market only one product. A typical firm offers its customers a **product line,** that is, a series of related products. The Clorox Company has many product lines, one of which is the Glad Products line, illustrated in Figure 11.10. Other items in the line include freezer, sandwich, and food storage bags; food wraps; ovenware; and containers.[14]

<interactive>**learning goal** 

CHAPTER OBJECTIVE #6: EXPLAIN WHY FIRMS DEVELOP LINES OF RELATED PRODUCTS RATHER THAN MARKETING INDIVIDUAL ITEMS.

By developing comprehensive product lines as opposed to concentrating solely on individual products, firms benefit in four ways. The motivations for marketing full product lines include the desire to grow, optimal use of company resources, enhancing the company's position in the market, and exploiting the product life cycle. Large companies such as Clorox have the resources to develop and market an entire mix of product lines, which may or may not be related to one another. The following paragraphs examine each of the first three reasons. The final reason, exploiting the product life cycle, is discussed in the next section, which focuses on strategic implications of the product life cycle concept.

FIGURE 11.9

Chevy Blazer: Improved Quality as a Result of Benchmarking

Introducing Chevy Blazer LT with OnStar.* The most comprehensive standard security package in its class.*
Good news for you and all your traveling companions. Blazer LT now has OnStar,† plus lots of other features you can be comfortable with: a CD player, 8-way power driver seat, antilock disc brakes, Autotrac and more. What a specially equipped way to have a little security in an insecure world. From Chevrolet, the most dependable, longest-lasting trucks on the road.** chevrolet.com
BLAZER
LIKE A ROCK

Desire to Grow

A company limits its growth potential when it concentrates on a single product, even though the company may have started that way, as retailer L.L. Bean did with its single style of work boots called Maine Hunting Shoes. Now the company sells a complete line of work boots for men, women, and children, not to mention other types of boots, along with apparel, outdoor and travel gear, home furnishings, and even products for pets. In 2002 the company, which has grown into a large mail-order and online retailer with a flagship store in Freeport, Maine, celebrated its 90th anniversary. It is unlikely that the company would have grown to its current size if Leon Leonwood Bean had stuck to manufacturing and selling a single style of his Maine Hunting Shoes.[15]

Enhancing the Company's Position in the Market

A company with a line of products often makes itself more important to both consumers and marketing intermediaries than a firm with only one product. A shopper who purchases a tent often buys related camping items. As just described, L.L. Bean now offers a wide range of products so that consumers can completely outfit themselves for outdoor activities or travel. They can purchase hiking boots, sleeping bags and tents, duffel bags, and clothing for their adventures. Few would know about Bean if the company only sold its original boots. Business buyers often expect a firm that manufactures a particular product to offer related items as well.

Optimal Use of Company Resources

By spreading the costs of its operations over a series of products, a firm may reduce the average production and marketing costs of each product. Hospitals have taken advantage of idle facilities by adding a variety of outreach services. Many now operate health and fitness centers that, besides generating profits themselves, also feed customers into other hospital services. For example, a blood pressure check at the fitness center might result in a referral to a staff physician.

THE PRODUCT MIX

A company's **product mix** is the assortment of product lines and individual product offerings that the company sells. The right blend of product lines and products allows a firm to maximize sales opportunities within the limitations of its resources. Marketers typically measure product mixes according to width, length, and depth.

<interactive>**learning goal**

CHAPTER OBJECTIVE #7: IDENTIFY THE MAJOR PRODUCT MIX DECISIONS THAT MARKETERS MUST MAKE.

Product Mix Width

The width of a product mix refers to the number of product lines the firm offers. As Table 11.3 shows, Clorox offers a broad line of retail consumer products in the U.S. market. Clorox also has products designed for professional users. Some ten different product lines are offered: laundry additives; household cleaners; automotive care; charcoal; insecticides; bags, wraps, and containers; cat litter; dressings and sauces; water filtration; and home fireplaces. Contrast this width with that of Colgate-Palmolive: oral care, personal care, household surface cleaners, fabric care, and pet food.

Product Mix Length

The length of a product mix refers to the number of different products a firm sells. Table 11.3 shows 42 separate Clorox products ranging from Clorox and Formula 409 to Armor All, Black Flag, and Hidden Valley dressings. By comparison, Colgate-Palmolive offers only nine major brands in the U.S. market. Some of Colgate's leading brands are Colgate, Palmolive, Mennen, Ajax, and Fab. The firm has other brands targeted at selected foreign markets.

Product Mix Depth

Depth refers to variations in each product that the firm markets in its mix. For instance, Clorox sells Glad, Glad-Lock, and Gladware in its bags, wraps, and containers line. Formula 409 and Formula 409 carpet cleaner are included among its household-cleaners line. Similarly, Colgate-Palmolive offers Hill's Prescription Diet and Hill's Science Diet in its pet food line.

To evaluate a firm's product mix, marketers look at the effectiveness of all three elements—width, length, and depth. Has the firm ignored a viable consumer segment? It may improve performance by increasing product line depth to offer a product variation that will attract the new segment. Can the firm achieve economies of scale in its sales and distribution efforts by adding complementary product lines to the mix? If so, a wider product mix may seem appropriate. Does the firm gain equal contributions from all products in its portfolio? If not, it may decide to lengthen or shorten the product mix to increase revenues.

FIGURE 11.10

Promoting One Item in Glad's Product Line

Product Mix Decisions

Establishing and managing the product mix has become an increasingly important marketing task. In the 1980s, many large firms added depth, length, and width to their product mixes without fully considering the consequences of expansion. Recently many of these same firms had to contend with unprofitable product lines and products. Retailers could not carry the full range of this merchandise, and consumers felt overwhelmed by their choices. A number of companies decided to eliminate poor sellers and focus on a few key products.

Other firms, however, seek to expand their product mixes. This is especially true for newer and smaller firms seeking to grow. Often, firms purchase product lines from other companies that want to narrow their product mixes. Other firms expand their offerings by acquiring entire companies through mergers or acquisitions. Recently, Sears, Roebuck & Company acquired the mail-order firm Lands' End in order to re-establish its general mail-order presence. Sears originally started as a mail-order firm, but stopped publishing its "Big Book" in recent years. Instead of starting it back up again, the firm decided to acquire Lands' End. Some firms, like Swiss Army, must expand their mix out of necessity, as described in the "Solving an Ethical Controversy" Interactive Example.

TABLE 11.3

Clorox's Mix of U.S. Retail Consumer Products

Laundry Additives	Automotive Care	Bags, Wraps, and Containers	Dressings and Sauces
Clorox	*Armor All*	*Glad*	*Hidden Valley*
Clorox 2	*No. 7*	*Glad-Lock*	*K.C. Masterpiece*
Stain Out	*Rain Dance*	*Gladware*	*Kitchen Bouquet*
Household Cleaners	*Rally*	**Cat Litter**	**Water Filtration**
Clorox toilet bowl cleaner	**Charcoal**	*EverClean*	*Brita*
Clorox Clean-Up	*Kingsford*	*EverFresh*	**Home Fireplace**
Formula 409	*BBQ Bag*	*Jonny Cat*	*Crackling HearthLogg*
Formula 409 carpet cleaner	*Match Light*	*Scoop Away*	*HearthLogg*
Liquid-Plumr	**Insecticides**	*Fresh Step*	*StarterLogg*
Lestoil	*Black Flag*	*Fresh-Step Scoop*	
Pine Sol	*Roach Motel*	*Perfomax*	
Soft Scrub	*Combat*		
S.O.S.			

Source: *Clorox Company Annual Report,* p. 21, accessed at Clorox Web site, http://www.clorox.com, June 11, 2002.

RIGHT/WRONG: SOLVING AN ETHICAL CONTROVERSY—SWISS ARMY LOOKS IN NEW DIRECTIONS

A firm should assess its current product mix for another important reason: to determine the feasibility of a line extension. A *line extension* develops individual offerings that appeal to different market segments while remaining closely related to the existing product line. Coach, a manufacturer of luxury leather handbags, belts, wallets, and briefcases, recently decided to extend its offerings to include such products as leather and wood director's chairs, leather headbands, and leather picture frames. Chic pet owners can even purchase leather dog collars and jackets for their canine friends. Coach's decision to expand its product mix came from a reassessment of its entire mission. "Once we redefined ourselves from a house of leather to a lifestyle accessories brand, everything else fell into place," explains CEO Lew Frankfort.[16]

The marketing environment also plays a role in a marketer's evaluation of a firm's product mix. In the case of Coach, the social-cultural environment had shifted so that consumers were looking for more casual, contemporary styles than Coach had been offering. In addition, the company wanted to attract younger customers. "I received a wake-up call that the classic world of Coach needed transformation," said Frankfort.[17]

Careful evaluation of a firm's current product mix can also help marketers in making decisions about brand management and new-product introductions. Chapter 12 will examine the importance of branding, brand management, and the development and introduction of new products.

THE PRODUCT LIFE CYCLE

Products, like people, pass through stages as they age. Successful products progress through four basic stages: introduction, growth, maturity, and decline. This progression, known as the **product life cycle,** is depicted in Figure 11.11 along with examples of products that currently fit into each stage. Notice that the product life cycle concept applies to products or product categories within an industry, not to individual

FIGURE 11.11

Stages in the Product Life Cycle

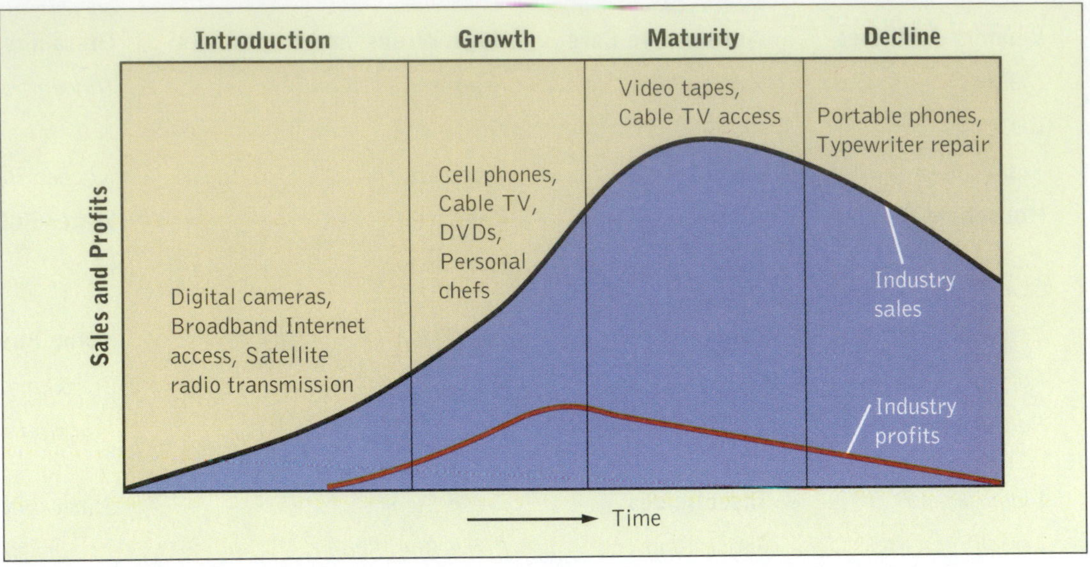

brands. Also, some products may move rapidly through the product life cycle, while others pass slowly through the four stages.

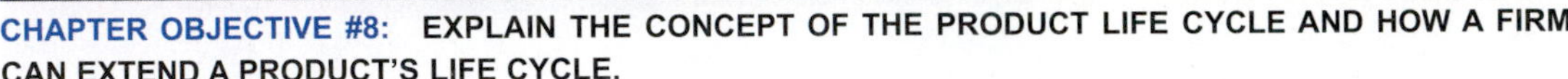

CHAPTER OBJECTIVE #8: EXPLAIN THE CONCEPT OF THE PRODUCT LIFE CYCLE AND HOW A FIRM CAN EXTEND A PRODUCT'S LIFE CYCLE.

Introductory Stage

During the early stages of the product life cycle, a firm works to stimulate demand for the new market entry. Products in the introductory stage often bring new technical features to a product category. Since the product is unknown to the public, promotional campaigns stress information about its features. Additional promotions directed toward distribution channel members try to induce these members to carry the product. In this phase, the public becomes acquainted with the item's merits and begins to accept it.

Technical problems are common during the introductory stage as companies fine-tune product design. This is especially true of new technologies, such as the wireless Web. When it was introduced, the idea of using wireless phones and hand-held computers to check e-mail and perform other tasks on the Internet sounded like a sure hit. But the reality proved to be less promising. The equipment was hard for the average consumer to figure out, connections were often cut, and tiny handheld screens were just too hard too read. In addition, services that were once free began to carry charges. Although Sprint and Verizon claimed to have 1 million and 750,000 wireless Web subscribers respectively only months after beginning to offer the services, industry watchers noted that the companies had raised consumers' expectations too high, too early, and could not yet deliver the level of service that they promised.[18]

Financial losses are common during the introductory stage as the firm incurs considerable costs associated with heavy promotion and extensive research-and-development costs. However, by finding the correct formula for consumer trial and acceptance during the introductory stage, a business lays the groundwork for future profits, as Research in Motion did (see "Marketing Hits" Interactive Example). Firms can then focus on recovering their costs and on beginning to earn profits as the new product moves into the second phase of its life cycle—the growth stage.

<interactive>example

MARKETING HIT: CUSTOMERS PICK BLACKBERRIES

Growth Stage

Sales volume rises rapidly during the growth stage as new customers make initial purchases and early buyers repurchase the product, such as DVD players, as described in the "Marketing Hits" Interactive Example. Word-of-mouth reports and mass advertising encourage hesitant buyers to make trial purchases. The growth stage usually begins when a firm starts to realize substantial profits from its investment.

MARKETING HIT: DVD SALES ROCKET THROUGH THE GROWTH STAGE

However, the growth stage may also bring new challenges for marketers. Inevitably, success attracts competitors, who rush into the market with similar offerings. An item that built enviable market share during the introductory stage may suddenly lose sales to competitive products. To compete effectively, a firm may need to make improvements and changes to a product during this stage. Additional spending on promotion and distribution may also be necessary.

Maturity Stage

Sales of a product category continue to grow during the early part of the maturity stage, but eventually they reach a plateau as the backlog of potential customers dwindles. By this time, many competitors have entered the market, and the firm's profits begin to decline as competition intensifies.

At this stage in the product life cycle, differences between competing products diminish as competitors discover the product and promotional characteristics most desired by customers. Available supplies exceed industry demand for the first time. Companies can increase their sales and market shares only at the expense of competitors, so the competitive environment becomes increasingly important.

In the maturity stage, heavy promotional outlays emphasize any differences that still separate competing products, and brand competition intensifies. Some firms try to differentiate their products by focusing on attributes such as quality, reliability, and service. The 70-year-old Zippo Manufacturing Company found itself head-to-head against competition in the form of disposable lighters, so the company decided to rejuvenate its product by investing in a new ad campaign with the tagline, "Zippo. For Real," as illustrated in Figure 11.12. Zippo marketers wanted consumers to consider the quality and value of its long-lasting product, as opposed to its throwaway competitors. "We wanted to equate that long-lasting relationship with other things in life," explained Bill Garrison, group creative director for the Blattner Brunner advertising agency that developed the new campaign.[19]

As competition intensifies, competitors tend to cut prices to attract new buyers. Although a price cut may seem the easiest method for boosting purchases, it is also one of the simplest moves for competitors to duplicate. Reduced prices decrease revenues for all firms in the industry, unless the lower prices stimulate enough new purchases to offset the loss in revenue on each unit sold. Interestingly, Zippo decided not to reduce its prices. Consumers can purchase a Zippo lighter for around $12.95 for conventional models, or splurge for a collectible style at $3,000. Competing disposables run around $2.[20]

FIGURE 11.12

Investing in Retaining Market Share by Extensive Promotion during the Maturity Stage

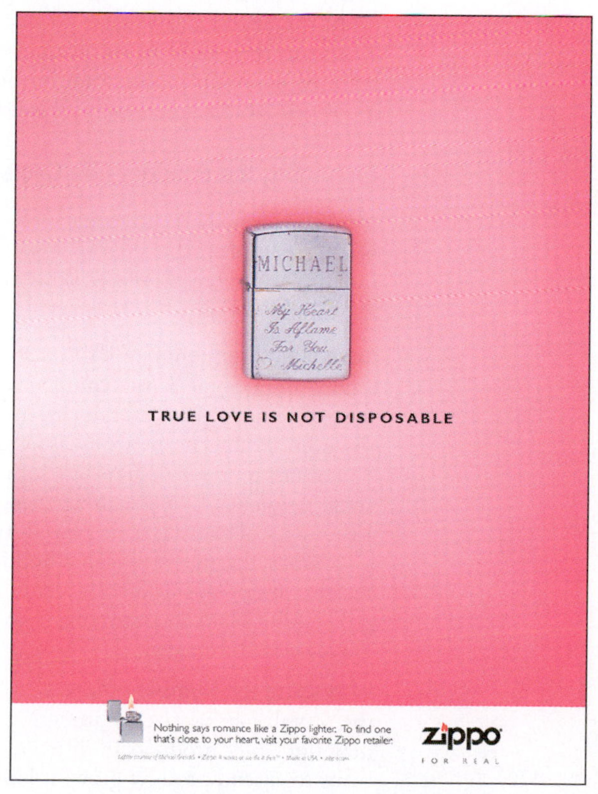

MICHAEL
My Heart Is Aflame For You Michelle
TRUE LOVE IS NOT DISPOSABLE
Nothing says romance like a Zippo lighter. To find one that's close to your heart, visit your favorite Zippo retailer.
Zippo
FOR REAL

Decline Stage

In the final stage of a product's life, innovations or shifts in consumer preferences bring about an absolute decline in industry sales. The color television replaced original black and white TVs; now high-definition TV is nipping at the heels of conventional color TVs. Dial telephones became touch-tone phones, which evolved to portable phones, which are now increasingly being replaced by cell phones. Notice that the decline stage of an old product often coincides with the growth stage for a new entry.

In addition to promoting "contests" to select new M&M colors, Mars offers holiday versions of its M&Ms candy.

As sales fall, profits for the product category decline, sometimes actually becoming negative. This change forces firms to cut prices further in a bid for the dwindling market. Companies gradually drop the declining items from their product lines and search for alternatives. The next section discusses potential strategies for actually extending the life cycle of a product.

The traditional product life cycle differs from fad cycles. Fashions and fads profoundly influence marketing strategies. *Fashions* are currently popular products that tend to follow recurring life cycles. Women's apparel and accessories provide the best examples. After more than a decade out of fashion, the miniskirt became stylish again recently. Small, wire-rimmed sunglasses, popular during the late 1960s, became fashionable again decades later. Often the fashion is reintroduced with a different name. Bell-bottom pants that were popular in the 1960s and 1970s are now called flares; diamond tennis bracelets (made fashionable by tennis star Chris Evert) are now referred to as line bracelets.

In contrast, *fads* are fashions with abbreviated life cycles. Most fads experience short-lived popularity and then quickly fade, although some maintain residual markets among certain segments. The average clothing fad is popular for a few months, after which customers abandon it for the next fad.

STRATEGIES FOR MANAGING THE PRODUCT LIFE CYCLE

A variety of factors in the marketing environment, including the strength or weakness of the economy, increased competition, and technological innovation can affect the way a product moves through its life cycle. Knowledge of the life cycle itself can provide useful guidance for marketing strategy decisions. Marketers can anticipate that sales and profits will assume a predictable pattern throughout the life cycle stages, so they can shift promotional emphasis from product information in the early stages to brand promotion in the later ones. Such insight helps marketers to focus on maximizing sales and profits at each stage through appropriate promotional efforts.

At the introductory stage, a firm's marketing efforts should emphasize the goal of stimulating demand. The focus then shifts to cultivating selective demand in the growth period. Extensive market segmentation helps to maintain momentum in the maturity period. During the decline stage, the emphasis returns to increasing primary demand. Chapter 12 will cover new-product strategies in more detail.

Extending the Product Life Cycle

Marketers usually try to extend each stage of the life cycles for their products as long as possible. They can often accomplish this goal if they take action early in the maturity stage. Product life cycles can stretch indefinitely as a result of decisions designed to increase the frequency of use by current customers, increase the number of users for the product, find new uses, or change package sizes, labels, or product quality.

Increasing Frequency of Use During the maturity stage, the sales curve for a product category reaches a maximum point as the competitors exhaust the supply of potential customers who previously had not made purchases. However, if current customers buy more frequently than they formerly did, total sales will rise even though no new buyers enter the market.

For instance, consumers buy some products during certain seasons of the year. Marketers can boost purchase frequency by persuading these people to try the product year-round. Many ski resorts advertise the advantages of visiting their areas during the summer—for the scenery, hiking, and golf. Marketers may try to connect the use of seasonal holiday products to additional occasions throughout the year. During the summer months, Butterball—traditionally known for its Thanksgiving turkeys—advertises "turkey on the grill." And Mars Incorporated comes out with special-edition M&Ms for different holidays, including Halloween and Easter.

Increasing the Number of Users A second strategy for extending the product life cycle seeks to increase the overall market size by attracting new customers who previously have not used the product. Marketers may find their products in different stages of the life cycle in different countries. This difference can help firms to extend product growth. Items that have reached the maturity stage in the U.S. may still be in the introductory stage somewhere else.

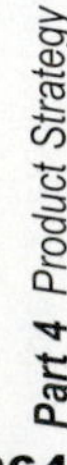

In recent years, the Walt Disney Company has spent time and money on advertising its theme parks to attract adults, in addition to young families. Television commercials portray empty nesters taking off to Disney World for a second honeymoon once their children are grown. And the dairy industry's "Got Milk?" campaign is aimed at all sorts of nontraditional milk drinkers—anyone other than children or pregnant women—in an attempt to increase the number of people who drink milk.

For more than a decade, the dairy industry has featured celebrities wearing a milk "moustache" in its advertising efforts.

Finding New Uses Still another strategy for extending a product's life cycle is to identify new uses for it. New applications for mature products include oatmeal as a cholesterol-reducer, mouthwash as an aid in treating and preventing plaque and gum disease, and antacids as a calcium supplement. The Web sites of some manufacturers such as Kraft Foods provide information on new recipes and uses for their products.

Changing Package Sizes, Labels, or Product Quality Many firms try to extend their product life cycles by introducing physical changes in their offerings. Food marketers have brought out small packages designed to appeal to one-person households and extra large containers for customers who want to buy in bulk. Other firms offer their products in convenient packages for use away from home or for use at the office.

The wine industry is well-known for relying on packaging and labeling to attract consumers to its mature products. Upstate New York–based Constellation Brands, the fourth largest winemaker in the world—E. & J. Gallo is the largest—recently introduced a line of fruit-flavored wines under its Arbor Mist label. The wines, such as a Chardonnay with a peach flavor, come in gently curved, frosty bottles that have attracted a whole new group of wine drinkers, according to some retailers.[21]

Product Deletion Decisions

To avoid wasting resources promoting unpromising products, marketers must sometimes prune product lines and eliminate marginal products. Marketers typically face this decision during the late maturity and early decline stages of the product life cycle. Periodic reviews of weak products should justify either eliminating or retaining them.

A firm may continue to carry an unprofitable item in order to provide a complete line for its customers. For example, while most grocery stores lose money on bulky, low-unit-value items such as salt, they continue to carry these items to meet shopper demand.

Shortages of raw materials sometimes prompt companies to discontinue production and marketing of previously profitable items. Alcoa discontinued making its brand of aluminum foil due to such a shortage. A firm may even drop a profitable item that fails to fit into its existing product line. Some of these products return to the market carrying the names of other firms that purchase the brands from the original manufacturers. One marketer tried to build an entire business on this idea. Ian R. Wilson founded Aurora Foods in 1995, persuading investors that he could make a hit by buying up a dozen "orphan" food brands—items that other food companies no longer wanted—such as Mrs. Butterworth's syrup, Mrs. Paul's frozen fish, and Lender's frozen bagels. But it turned out that the market had already turned away from many of these products for a variety of reasons; for instance, consumers were gravitating away from frozen bagels and toward fresh-baked ones. In addition, supermarkets grant shelf space based on the current strength of brands, and these products had already declined to the point that their originators had chosen to delete them by selling them to Aurora, which later began to falter.[22]

Some food industry experts do say that products deleted by their original companies might sell well on the Internet. A Web site called hometownfavorites.com currently offers 400-some products, including Brer Rabbit Molasses and My-T-Fine Pudding. Shelf space for these products is not a problem, and the site can offer these products to a loyal following.[23]

STRATEGIC IMPLICATIONS OF MARKETING IN THE 21ST CENTURY

Marketers who want their businesses to succeed will continue to develop new goods and services to satisfy their customers. They will engage in continuous improvement activities, including benchmarking when necessary. And they will continually evaluate their company's mix of products. Corning, the number-one glassmaker in the U.S., is a good example of such a firm. Corning has long had a tradition of inventing new manufacturing processes that produce top-quality items at low cost. This constant quest is true of its fiber-manufacturing process, in which Corning currently holds 40 to 50 percent of worldwide sales. The company also relies on constant innovation for growth. In one recent year, 84 percent of Corning's revenues came from products that had not existed four years before. In fact, company officials like to say that their goal is to keep making Corning's own products obsolete, instead of constantly coming up with new items in the product line designed to anticipate and fulfill customers' needs.[24]

Just like the marketers at Corning, marketers everywhere are constantly developing new and better products that fit their firm's overall strategy. They will come up with ways to extend the lives of certain products and will be able to recognize and delete those that no longer meet expectations.

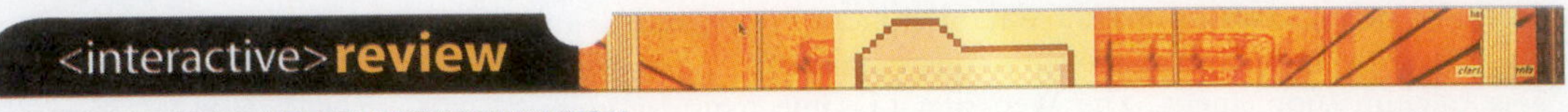

FLASH CHAPTER REVIEW PRESENTATION

<interactive>video case

FOSSIL IS A REMINDER OF GOOD TIMES

endofchaptermaterial

- Summary of Chapter Objectives
- Chapter Outline
- Key Terms
- Review Questions
- Projects and Teamwork Exercises
- 'netWork
- Crossword Puzzles
- Case 11.1: Satellite Radio—A New Product Hits the Air Waves

Take the Post-Test to assess your overall understanding of the key ideas in this chapter. The Post-Test provides a comprehensive selection of exam-style questions addressing the main topics and concepts of the chapter. At the completion of each Post-Test, you will receive a score and instructive feedback on how you answered each question, and a direct link to the part of the chapter addressed in the question. Take the Post-Test as often as you need to—a record of your progress for each attempt is kept for you to revisit and gauge your improvement. And each Post-Test is randomly generated, so every attempt is new.

Post-Test

CHAPTER 12

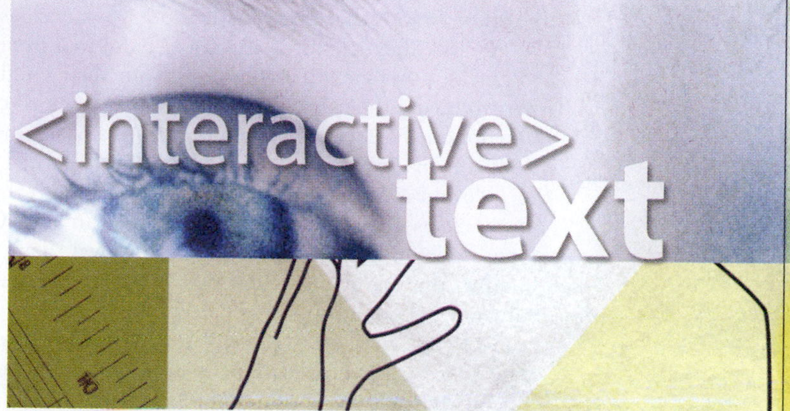

Category and Brand Management, Product Identification, and New-Product Planning

Chapter Objectives

1. Explain the benefits of category and brand management.
2. Identify the different types of brands.
3. Explain the strategic value of brand equity.
4. Discuss how companies develop strong identities for their products and brands.
5. Describe the strategies for new product development.
6. Describe the consumer adoption process.
7. List the stages in the process for developing new products.
8. Discuss the relationship between product safety and product liability.

Pre-Test

Take the Pre-Test to assess your initial knowledge of the key ideas in this chapter. The Pre-Test provides exam-style questions addressing the main topics and concepts of the chapter. At the completion of each Pre-Test, you will receive a score and instructive feedback on how you answered each question, and a direct link to the part of the chapter addressed in the question. Take the Pre-Test as often as you need to—a record of your progress for each attempt is kept for you to revisit and gauge your improvement.

REDOX PUTS A NEW SPIN ON OLD BRANDS

Some people credit—or blame—Procter & Gamble for creating a whole genre of entertainment called *soap operas* when its Oxydol brand detergent began sponsorship of the popular *Ma Perkins* radio show in 1933. The *Ma Perkins* show is long gone, and P&G watchers thought the old brand Oxydol was gone as well when its retail sales tumbled from $64 million to $5.5 million. P&G decided to unload what it thought was a worn-out brand. But soap operas are alive and well, and so, it turns out, is Oxydol.

Two Gen-Xers, Todd Wichmann and Richard Owen, were looking to start their own business. In fact, they happened to be working for Procter & Gamble when the company decided to sell Oxydol. So they quit their jobs and convinced their former employer to sell the brand to their new venture, called Redox Brands. Two months later, with a bit more cash raised from investors, the duo picked up BIZ bleach as well. Suddenly, they were in the detergent business. Now they had to figure out how to revitalize two languishing brands that many of their peers—as well as younger consumers—had never even heard of.

At first, they tried introducing Oxydol as a premium brand, hoping to appeal to baby boomers who might be nostalgic about products from their childhood. They relied on packaging to spark memories, reintroducing the original bull's-eye box. They also convinced cataloguer Restoration Hardware to feature Oxydol on the cover of its catalog and to stock it in its 106 stores. The strategy flopped. When they conducted focus groups, Wichmann and Owen learned that baby boomers had long since developed loyalties to Tide and other top-selling brands. They weren't interested in switching, especially since Oxydol cost just as much as their favorites. But Wichmann and Owen learned another bit of valuable information: Consumers in their twenties weren't yet loyal to any particular brand, and they weren't particularly interested in the brands that their parents (baby boomers) were purchasing. In addition, these younger consumers were not as budget-minded as their parents.

So Redox marketers went to work fast. They ordered new packaging—green bottles with labels reading: "Don't freak. Help conquer your most extreme dirt, not to mention laundrophobia." A large "X" pops out of Oxydol's name, alluding to Generation Xers, people born between 1979 and 1994, and younger. Then they began to work on ads featuring a mud-soaked dirt biker.

Revitalizing an old brand for a new generation has its risks. But Wichmann and Owen are confident of their strategy. "You've got so many laundry detergent brands, they're falling off the grocery store shelves," asserts Owen. "Yet not one of them is aimed at the demographic we're going after." Wichmann adds, "Every single one of those brands is focused on moms 35 and older with kids. But over the last decade, a very large group of Gen-X people are coming into the focus of marketing." And if Redox has its way, they'll all be wearing very, very clean clothes.[1]

CHAPTER OVERVIEW

Brands play a huge role in our lives. We try certain brands for all kinds of reasons, on recommendations from friends or because we remember colorful advertisements. We develop loyalty to certain brands and product lines through category management for varying reasons as well—quality of a product, price, and habit are a few examples. This chapter examines the way companies make decisions about developing and managing the products and product lines that they hope will become necessities to consumers. Developing and marketing a product and product line are costly propositions. To protect its investment and maximize the return on it, a business and category manager must carefully nurture both existing and new products.

This chapter focuses on two critical elements of product planning and strategy. First, it looks at how firms build and maintain identity and competitive advantage for their products through branding. Second, it focuses on the new product planning and introduction process, often influenced greatly by a category manager. Effective new product planning and meeting the profit responsibility that a category manager has for a product line require careful preparation. The needs and desires of consumers change constantly, and the successful companies are those that manage to keep up with—or stay just ahead of—those changes. Even the founders of Redox Brands had to plan their strategy for revitalizing a brand that had languished on the shelves. And when they learned something vital about their potential customers, they had to move quickly.

MANAGING BRANDS FOR COMPETITIVE ADVANTAGE

Think of the last time you went shopping for groceries. As you moved through the store, chances are your recognition of various brand names influenced many of your purchasing decisions. Perhaps you chose Colgate toothpaste over competitive offerings or loaded Heinz ketchup into your cart instead of the store brand. Walking through the snack food aisle, you might have reached for Smartfood popcorn or Lay's potato chips without much thought.

<interactive>**learning goal**

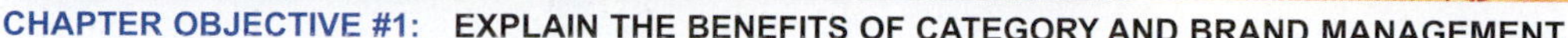

CHAPTER OBJECTIVE #1: EXPLAIN THE BENEFITS OF CATEGORY AND BRAND MANAGEMENT.

Marketers recognize the powerful influence on customer behavior that creating and protecting a strong identity for products and product lines has. Branding is the process of creating that identity. A **brand** is a name, term, sign, symbol, design, or some combination that identifies the products of one firm while differentiating these products from competitors' offerings. For decades, brawny Mr. Clean has represented the cleansing strength of his household cleaner. Even as new scents and colors are added to the product line, the image of Mr. Clean is clearly represented on every bottle, as illustrated in Figure 12.1.

As you read this chapter, consider how many brands you are aware of—both those you are loyal to and those you have never tried, or have tried and abandoned. Table 12.1 shows some selected brands, brand names, and brand marks. Buyers respond to branding by making repeat purchases of the same product because they identify the item with the name of its producer. One buyer might derive satisfaction from an ice cream bar with the brand name Dove; another might derive the same satisfaction from one with the name Ben & Jerry's.

> **Briefly Speaking**
>
> The Internet is all about branding. It's more important here than it is offline. People have to remember your name and type it in. There are no Golden Arches or Coke cans to remind them.
>
> *Mark Brier*
> *Amazon.com executive*

Brand Loyalty

Brands achieve widely varying consumer familiarity and acceptance. While a snowboarder might insist on a Burton snowboard, the same consumer might show little loyalty to particular brands in another product category such as tissues. Marketers measure brand loyalty in three stages: brand recognition, brand preference, and brand insistence.

Brand recognition is a company's first objective for newly introduced products. Marketers begin the promotion of new items by trying to make these items familiar to the public. Advertising offers one effective way for increasing consumer awareness of a brand. Wendy's introduced its new Garden Sensations salads with advertisements such as the one in Figure 12.2, which shows an enticing fresh salad with the Wendy's name below it. Or a company might create a character like Tommy Bahama, as described in the "Marketing Hits" Interactive Example.

<interactive>**example**

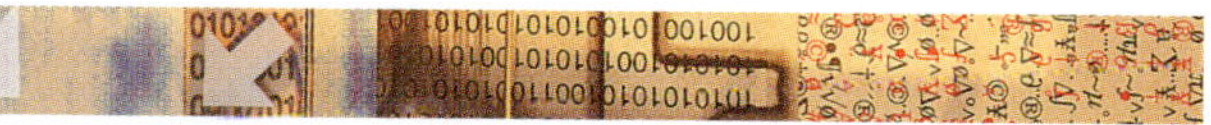

MARKETING HIT: WHO IS TOMMY BAHAMA, AND WHERE DOES HE LIVE?

Other strategies for creating brand recognition include offering free samples or discount coupons for purchases. Once consumers have used a product, seen it advertised, or noticed it in stores, it moves from the unknown to the known category, which increases the probability that those consumers will purchase it.

At the second level of brand loyalty, **brand preference,** buyers rely on previous experiences with the product when choosing that product, if available, over competitors' products. Recently, several competitors in the meat industry have launched major advertising campaigns designed to create brand preference for their precooked entrees. Although the meat industry historically has not enjoyed the benefits of branding that other food categories have, "We're convinced this is the future, and it may be a $1 billion category in the next five years," predicts Jim Schloss of one of Smithfield Foods' subsidiaries. IBP (part of Tyson Foods), the country's leading beef processor, is promoting its new line of precooked pork and beef under the brand name Thomas E. Wilson. The product line, which includes an Italian-seasoned pork roast, achieved the number one brand spot in all refrigerated entrees in its test markets. The firm followed its test marketing with a national advertising campaign.[2]

FIGURE 12.1

Promoting a Well-Known Brand

The freshness of the seasons. The strength of Mr. Clean®
Mr. Clean now brings you Seasons' Freshness™. An antibacterial cleaner with four great scents.
Spring Garden, Summer Citrus, Sparkling Apple and Invigorating Breeze.
They'll remind you of your favourite season. Any time of the year.
Mr. Clean

TABLE 12.1

Selected Brands, Brand Names, and Brand Marks

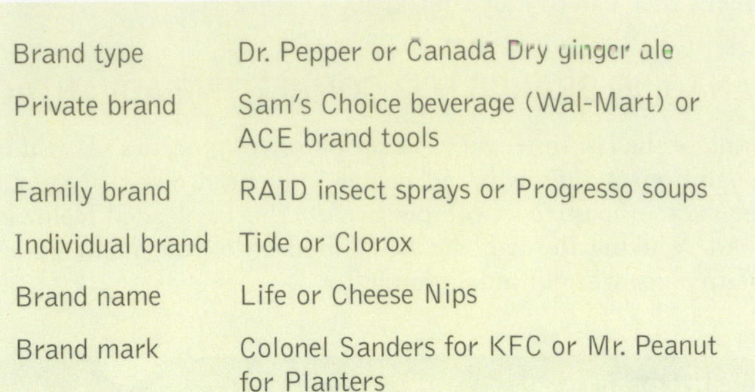

Brand type	Dr. Pepper or Canada Dry ginger ale
Private brand	Sam's Choice beverage (Wal-Mart) or ACE brand tools
Family brand	RAID insect sprays or Progresso soups
Individual brand	Tide or Clorox
Brand name	Life or Cheese Nips
Brand mark	Colonel Sanders for KFC or Mr. Peanut for Planters

Brand insistence, the ultimate stage in brand loyalty, leads consumers to refuse alternatives and to search extensively for the desired merchandise. A product at this stage has achieved a monopoly position with its consumers. Although many firms try to establish brand insistence with all consumers, few achieve this ambitious goal. Companies that offer specialty or luxury goods and services, such as Tiffany diamonds or Rothschild wine, are more apt to achieve this status than those that offer mass goods and services.

Types of Brands

Companies that practice branding classify brands in several ways: private, manufacturer's (national), family, and individual brands. In making branding decisions, firms must weigh the benefits and disadvantages of each type of brand.

<interactive>**learning goal**

CHAPTER OBJECTIVE #2: IDENTIFY THE DIFFERENT TYPES OF BRANDS.

Some firms, however, sell their goods without any efforts at branding. These items are called **generic products.** They are characterized by plain labels, little or no advertising, and no brand names. Common categories of generic products include food and household staples. These no-name products were first sold in Europe at prices as much as 30 percent below those of brand name products. This product strategy was introduced in the U.S. a quarter century ago. The market shares for generic products increase during economic downturns but subside when the economy improves. However, many consumers do request generic substitutions for certain brand-name prescriptions at the pharmacy whenever possible.

Manufacturers' Brands versus Private Brands Manufacturers' brands, also called *national brands,* define the image that most people form when they think of a brand. A **manufacturer's brand** refers to a brand name owned by a manufacturer or other producer. Well-known manufacturers' brands include Kodak, Pepsi Cola, and Heinz. In contrast, many large wholesalers and retailers place their own brands on the merchandise they market. The brands offered by wholesalers and retailers are usually called *private brands* (or private labels). Although some manufacturers refuse to produce private label goods, most regard such production as a way to reach additional market segments. Wal-Mart offers many private label products at its stores, including its Sam's Choice cola. In addition, Information Resources Inc. estimates that Wal-Mart accounted for three-quarters of the private-label sales growth in nonfood categories in one recent year.[3]

Private brands and generic products expand the number of alternatives available to consumers. As Figure 12.3 illustrates, True Value hardware stores sells its own brand of paint called E-Z Kare. Sears sells its own brands under the names of Craftsman, Kenmore, Diehard, and Canyon River Blues. Shaw's supermarkets have their own Signature line of groceries.

FIGURE 12.2

Salads: A New Line of Wendy's Food Offerings

FIGURE 12.3

Use of Private Brands by True Value Stores

The growth of private brands has paralleled that of chain stores in the U.S., most of the growth occurring since the 1930s. Manufacturers not only sell their well-known brands to stores but also put the store's own label on these products. Such leading manufacturers as Westinghouse, Armstrong Rubber, and Heinz generate ever-increasing percentages of their total incomes by producing goods for sale under retailers' private labels.

One arena in which private label branding is gaining new ground is personal computers. After watching sales of big-name PCs stumble, retailers such as Best Buy and RadioShack have begun stocking their shelves with their own private-label computers—and watching them sell. Best Buy started by selling a line of PCs designed for teenagers who mostly play games. The PCs come in fluorescent colors instead of black or silver, and the kids are attracted to them. The computers are just as expensive as brand-name PCs, but they do come with fancy components. Ted Waitt, founder of Gateway, refers to Best Buy as one of his biggest competitors. "Best Buy moved a lot of those [private label] products very quickly," he notes. "They can drive a lot of share with that model."[4]

Captive Brands The nation's major discounters—such as Wal-Mart, Target, and Kmart—have come up with a spin-off of the private-label idea. So-called *captive brands* are national brands that are sold exclusively by a retail chain. Captive brands typically provide better profit margins than private labels. Kmart's captive brands include Martha Stewart paints, linens, and home furnishings. Similarly, Wal-Mart sells General Electric small appliances, even though these items are actually made by other manufacturers.

Family and Individual Brands A **family brand** is a single brand name that identifies several related products. For example, KitchenAid markets a complete line of appliances under the KitchenAid name, and Johnson & Johnson offers a line of baby powder, lotions, plastic pants, and baby shampoo under one name. All Pepperidge Farm products, from bread to rolls to cookies, carry the Pepperidge Farm name.

A manufacturer may instead choose to market a product under an *individual brand,* which uniquely identifies a product itself, rather than promoting it under the name of the company or under an umbrella name covering similar items. Lever Brothers, for example, markets Aim, Close- Up, and Pepsodent toothpastes; All and Wisk laundry detergents; Imperial margarine; Caress, Dove, Lifebuoy, and Lux bath soaps; and Shield and Lever 2000 deodorant soaps. PepsiCo's Quaker Oats unit markets Aunt Jemima breakfast products, Gatorade beverages, and Celeste Pizza. Individual brands cost more than family brands to market because the firm must develop a new promotional campaign to introduce each new product to its

FIGURE 12.4

An Addition to a Family Brand—Kool-Aid Jammers

target market. Distinctive brands are extremely effective aids in implementing market segmentation strategies, however.

On the other hand, a promotional outlay for a family brand can benefit all items in the line. For example, a new addition to the Kool-Aid line, shown in Figure 12.4, gains immediate recognition as part of the well-known family brand. Family brands also help marketers to introduce new products to both customers and retailers. Since supermarkets stock thousands of items, they hesitate to add new products unless they are confident they will be in demand.

Family brands should identify products of similar quality, or the firm risks harming its overall product image. If Rolls Royce marketers were to place the Rolls name on a low-end car or a line of discounted clothing, they might severely tarnish the image of the luxury car line. Conversely, Lexus, Infiniti, and Mercedes-Benz put their names on luxury sport-utility vehicles to capitalize on their reputations and to enhance the acceptance of the new models in a competitive market.

Individual brand names should, however, distinguish dissimilar products. PepsiCo's Quaker Oats division markets dog food under the Ken-L Ration brand name and cat food under Puss 'n Boots. Kimberly-Clark markets two different types of diapers under its Huggies and Pull-Ups names. Procter & Gamble offers fruit drinks under its Sunny Delight name, laundry detergent under Cheer, and dishwasher soap under Cascade.

Brand Equity

As individuals, we often like to say that our strongest asset is our reputation. The same is true of organizations. A brand can go a long way toward making or breaking a company's reputation. A strong brand identity backed by superior quality offers important strategic advantages for a firm. First, it increases the likelihood that consumers will recognize the firm's product or product line when they make purchase decisions. Second, a strong brand identity can contribute to buyers' perceptions of product quality. Branding can also reinforce customer loyalty and repeat purchases. A consumer who tries a brand and likes it will likely look for that brand on future store visits. All of these benefits contribute to a valuable form of competitive advantage called brand equity.

<interactive>**learning goal**

CHAPTER OBJECTIVE #3: EXPLAIN THE STRATEGIC VALUE OF BRAND EQUITY.

Brand equity refers to the added value that a certain brand name gives to a product in the marketplace. Brands with high equity confer financial advantages on a firm because they often command comparatively large market shares and consumers may pay little attention to differences in prices. Studies have also linked brand equity to high profits and stock returns.

In global operations, high brand equity often facilitates expansion into new markets. Currently, Coca-Cola is the most valuable—and most recognized—brand in the world.[5] Similarly, Disney's brand equity allows it to market its goods and services in Europe and Japan—and now China. What makes a global brand powerful? According to Interbrand Corp., a division of Omnicom Group, which measures brand equity in dollar values, a strong brand is one that has the power to increase a company's sales and earnings. A global brand is generally defined as one that sells at least 20 percent outside of its home country, as Coca-Cola does. Interbrand's top ten global brands include Microsoft, Disney, McDonald's, and AT&T.[6]

The global advertising agency Young & Rubicam (Y&R) developed another brand equity system called the *Brand Asset Valuator.* Y&R interviewed more than 90,000 consumers in 30 countries and collected information on over 13,000 brands to help create this measurement system. According to Y&R, a firm builds brand equity sequentially on four dimensions of brand personality. These four dimensions are differentiation, relevance, esteem, and knowledge:

- *Differentiation* refers to a brand's ability to stand apart from competitors. Brands like Porsche and Victoria's Secret stand out in consumers' minds as symbols of unique product characteristics.
- *Relevance* refers to the real and perceived appropriateness of the brand to a big consumer segment. A large number of consumers must feel a need for the benefits offered by the brand. Brands with high relevance include AT&T and Hallmark.
- *Esteem* is a combination of perceived quality and consumer perceptions about the growing or declining popularity of a brand. A rise in perceived quality or in public opinion about a brand enhances a brand's esteem. But negative impressions reduce esteem. Brands with high esteem include Starbucks and Honda.
- *Knowledge* refers to the extent of customers' awareness of the brand and understanding of what a good or service stands for. Knowledge implies that customers feel an intimate relationship with a brand. Examples include Jell-O and Band-Aid.[7]

FIGURE 12.5

Brands That Have Received the Good Housekeeping Seal

Brand equity can actually be assisted by outside organizations that endorse a product. The Good Housekeeping Seal signifies to consumers that a product has been tested by a staff of independent evaluators at *Good Housekeeping* who are willing to apply the Good Housekeeping Consumers' Refund or Replacement Policy to the product.[8] Although not all advertisers in *Good Housekeeping* magazine have received the seal, many have. Figure 12.5 showcases the advertisers who had received the seal in a recent year. Consumers who are familiar with the seal—which is a brand itself—often feel more comfortable purchasing products that have been tested by an independent organization.

Unfortunately, even brands with high equity can lose their luster for a variety of reasons. It may be because of perceived or real defects in a product that become public knowledge, as in the case of the Bridgestone/Firestone tires installed on Ford's Explorer SUVs. Or it may be because of a court battle, as in the case of Microsoft's antitrust struggles. In fact, although Microsoft sits in the number two spot on Interbrand's list of most valuable global brands, some analysts assert that it could easily have soared to the top spot without the court battles.[9]

The Role of Category and Brand Management

Because of the tangible and intangible value associated with strong brand equity, marketing organizations invest considerable resources and effort in developing and maintaining these dimensions of brand personality. Traditionally, companies assign the task of managing a brand's marketing strategies to a *brand manager.* Recently, companies have been reevaluating the effectiveness of brand management and changing the system in a variety of ways. General Motors has decided to eliminate brand managers in favor of marketing director positions, largely because of duplication. The company found that it was spending time, money, and effort in separate divisions to come up with essentially the same car.[10]

Today, major consumer goods companies have adopted a strategy called **category management,** in which a category manager oversees an entire product line. Unlike traditional product managers, category managers have profit responsibility for their product group. These managers are assisted by associates usually called "analysts." Part of this shift was initiated by large retailers, who realized they could benefit from the marketing muscle of large grocery and household goods producers like Kraft and Procter & Gamble.

As a result, producers began to focus their attention on in-store merchandising instead of mass-market advertising. A few years ago, Kraft reorganized its sales force so that each representative was responsible for a retailer's needs, instead of pushing a single brand. Kraft now has a "customer manager" for each major grocery chain in a city or region. Technology also plays a role in Kraft's strategy. A software application called Three-Step Category Builder allows managers to tear apart a product category, analyze all its related data, and create a new management plan in two days. The software presents the plan in a few easy-to-read charts that the manager can show to the retailer. "It shouldn't take more than 15 minutes to explain," says Christopher Hogan, technology chief of Kraft's sales division. Kraft then recommends everything from which products the retailer should carry to where they should be positioned.[11]

PRODUCT IDENTIFICATION

Organizations identify their products in the marketplace with brand names, symbols, and distinctive packaging. Almost every product that is distinguishable from another gives buyers some means of identifying it. Sunkist Growers, for instance, stamps its oranges with the name Sunkist. Iams stamps a paw print on all of its pet food packages. For nearly 100 years, Prudential Insurance Co. has used the Rock of Gibraltar as its symbol. Choosing how to identify the firm's output represents a major strategic decision for marketers.

CHAPTER OBJECTIVE #4: DISCUSS HOW COMPANIES DEVELOP STRONG IDENTITIES FOR THEIR PRODUCTS AND BRANDS.

Brand Names and Brand Marks

What's in a name? According to researchers, a name plays a central role in establishing brand and product identity. The American Marketing Association defines a **brand name** as the part of the brand consisting of words or letters that form a name that identifies and distinguishes the firm's offerings from those of its competitors. The brand name is, therefore, the part of the brand that people can vocalize. Firms can also identify their brands by brand marks. A *brand mark* is a symbol or pictorial design that distinguishes a product. In Figure 12.6, "French's" is the brand name of the mustard; the red flag and white lettering are the brand mark that distinguish this mustard from those made by other companies.

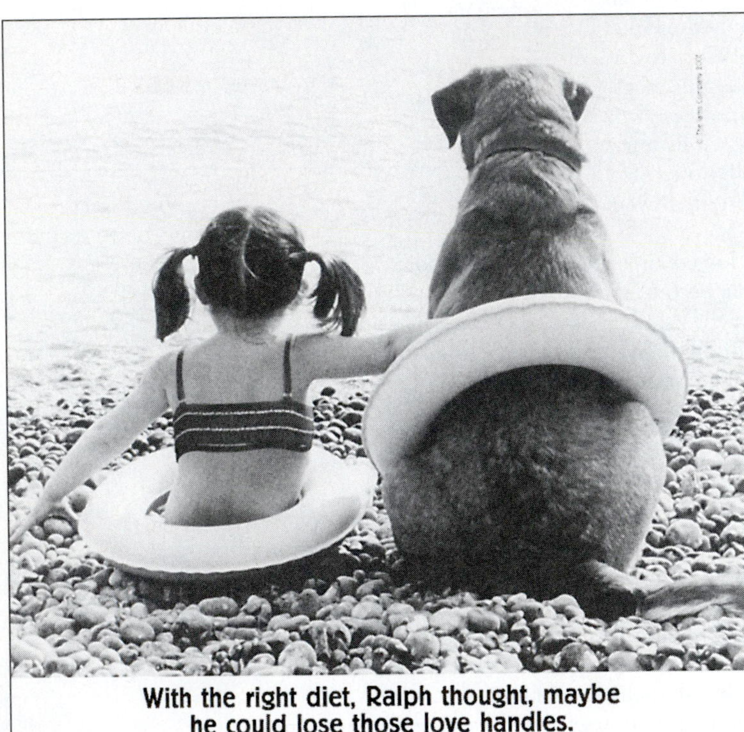

With the right diet, Ralph thought, maybe he could lose those love handles.
Like people, dogs can have weight issues too. Iams Less Active Formula turns fat into energy to help trim unnecessary pounds. Gradually.
Contact us at www.iams.com or 1-800-525-4267
Less Active
IAMS
The result? More healthy years for your dog. And perhaps, a little less embarrassment at the beach.
IAMS
Good for Life

Iams identifies its products with a paw print on every package.

Effective brand names are easy to pronounce, recognize, and remember. Short names, such as Nike, Ford, and Bounty, meet these requirements. Marketers try to overcome problems with easily mispronounced brand names by teaching consumers the correct pronunciations. For example, early advertisements for the Korean car maker Hyundai explained that the name rhymes with *Sunday.*

A brand name should also give buyers the correct connotation of the product's image. The name Lunchables for Oscar Mayer's prepackaged lunches suggests a convenient meal that can be eaten anywhere. Discover suggests a credit card that allows treasure hunting. Chevy's Trail Blazer represents adventure and ruggedness.

A brand name must also qualify for legal protection. The Lanham Act of 1946 states that registered trademarks must not contain words or phrases in general use, such as *automobile* or *suntan lotion.* These generic words actually describe particular types of products, and no company can claim exclusive rights to them.

Marketers feel increasingly hard-pressed to coin effective brand names, as multitudes of competitors rush to stake out brand names for their own products. Some companies register names before they have products to fit the names in order to stop competitors from using them.

When a class of products becomes generally known by the original brand name of a specific offering, the brand name may become a descriptive generic name. If this occurs, the original owner loses exclusive claim to the brand name. The generic names nylon, aspirin, escalator, kerosene, and zipper started as brand names. Other generic names that were once brand names include cola, yo-yo, linoleum, and shredded wheat.

Marketers must distinguish between brand names that have become legally generic terms and those that seem generic only in many consumers' eyes. Consumers often adopt legal brand names as descriptive names. Jell-O, for instance, is a brand name owned exclusively by General Foods, but many consumers casually apply it as a descriptive name for gelatin desserts. Similarly, many people use the term Kleenex to refer to facial tissues. English and Australian consumers use the brand name Hoover as a verb for vacuuming. Xerox is such a well-known brand name that people frequently—though incorrectly—use it as a verb to mean photocopying. To protect its valuable trademark, Xerox Corp. has created advertisements explaining that Xerox is a brand name and registered trademark and should not be used as a verb.

'NET EX: LEVERAGING A BRAND NAME

Trademarks

Businesses invest considerable resources in developing and promoting brands and brand identities. The high value of brand equity encourages firms to take steps in protecting the expenditures they invest in their brands.

A **trademark** is a brand for which the owner claims exclusive legal protection. A trademark should not be confused with a trade name, which identifies a company. The Coca-Cola Company is a trade name, but Coke is a trademark of the company. Some trade names duplicate companies' brand names. For example, Stride Rite is the children's shoe brand name of Stride Rite Corporation.

Protecting Trademarks Trademark protection confers the exclusive legal right to use a brand name, brand mark, and any slogan or product name abbreviation. It designates the origin or source of a good or service. The multicolored butterfly for MSN shown in Figure 12.7 is a trademarked symbol.

Frequently, trademark protection is applied to words or phrases, such as *Bud* for Budweiser or *the Met* for the New York Metropolitan Opera. For example, the courts upheld Budweiser's trademark in one case, ruling that an exterminating company's slogan "This Bug's for You" infringed on Budweiser's rights.

FIGURE 12.6

A Brand Name (French's) and a Brand Mark (the French's Flag)

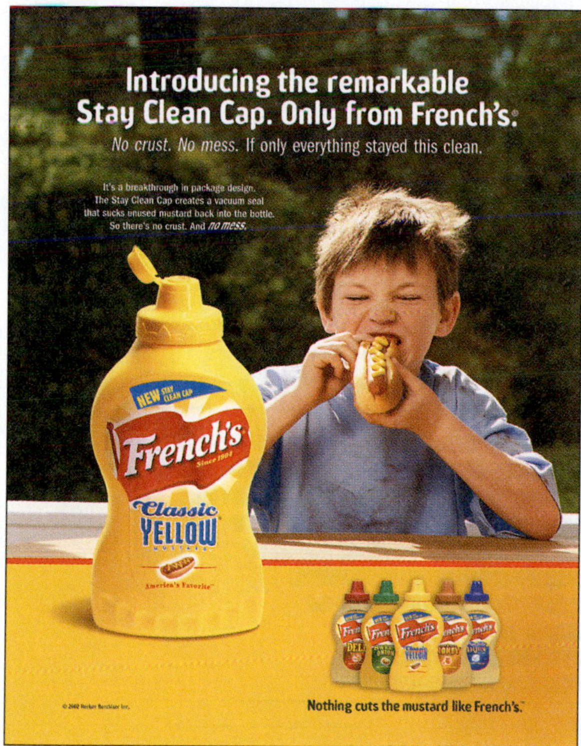

FIGURE 12.7

The Butterfly Trademark Used by MSN

The leaping jaguar figure is part of Jaguar's distinctive and distinguished trade dress.

Firms can also receive trademark protection for packaging elements and product features such as shape, design, and typeface. U.S. law has fortified trademark protection in recent years. The Federal Trademark Dilution Act of 1995 gives a trademark holder the right to sue for trademark infringement even if other products using its brand are not particularly similar or easily confused in the minds of consumers. The infringing company does not even have to know that it is diluting another's trademark. The act also gives a trademark holder the right to sue if another party imitates its trademark.

The Internet may be the next battlefield for trademark infringement cases. Some companies are attempting to protect their trademarks by filing infringement cases against companies using similar Internet addresses.

Trade Dress Visual cues used in branding create an overall look sometimes referred to as *trade dress.* These visual components may be related to color selections, sizes, package and label shapes, and similar factors. For example, McDonald's golden arches, Merrill Lynch's bull, and the yellow of Shell's seashell are all part of these products' trade dress. A combination of visual cues may also constitute trade dress. Consider a Mexican food product that uses the colors of the Mexican flag: green, white, and red. The leaping jaguar figure that adorns the front of a Jaguar as well as brand name is part of the trade dress for Jaguar cars.

Trade dress disputes have led to numerous courtroom battles. In one widely publicized case, Kendall-Jackson Vineyards and Winery sued Ernest & Julio Gallo Winery Inc., claiming that the bottle design used for Gallo's Turning Leaf Chardonnay was too similar to its Kendall's Vintner's Reserve chardonnay bottle. Kendall-Jackson lost in court, but this case suggests the importance that firms assign to trade dress.[12]

Developing Global Brand Names and Trademarks

International marketers face a particularly acute problem in selecting brand names and trademarks; an excellent brand name or symbol in one country may prove disastrous in another. Iranian detergent producer Paxan Corp., for example, might have a hard time marketing its laundry detergent Barf to English-speaking countries. (In Iran, *barf* means "snow.")[13] A firm marketing a product in multiple countries must also decide whether to use a single brand name for universal promotions or tailor names to individual countries. Most languages contain *o* and *k* sounds, so *okay* has become an international word. Most languages also have a short *a;* so Coca-Cola, Kodak, and Texaco work as effective brands abroad. Figure 12.8 shows the most popular global brand names, as reported by marketing research company ACNielsen. World events may also intervene in marketing efforts, as Yum! learned in the "Marketing Hits" Interactive Example.

FIGURE 12.8

The World's Most Popular Brands

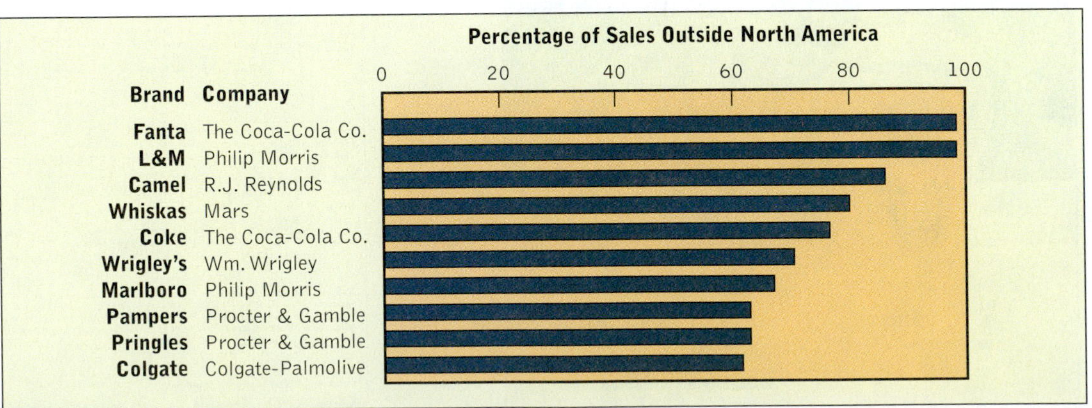

Source: Data from ACNielsen in "Which Brands Travel Best?" *Time,* November 26, 2001, p. B10.

<interactive>**example**

MARKETING HIT: YUM! SATISFIES GLOBAL APPETITES BY ADAPTING TO LOCAL TASTES

Trademarks that are effective in their home countries may do less well in other cultures. Perhaps the world's most dubious brand name at the moment is attached to a line of clothing recently launched by one of Osama bin Laden's relatives, Yeslam Binladin. Yeslam Binladin applied for trademark protection for the "Bin Ladin" clothing label in Switzerland several months before the tragedies of September 11, 2001. In spite of the events, he decided to push ahead with his line. Yeslam is from a different branch of the family (the surnames are spelled slightly differently), and the Saudi family is well respected in the Middle East, where it controls a $5 billion construction conglomerate, the Saudi Binladin Group. So Yeslam hopes to counteract negative impressions of the Bin Ladin brand name with a positive one. The clothing line will appear first in the Arab world, then in Europe, and much later in the U.S. Yeslam wants to donate a portion of the profits from the clothing line to a charitable foundation in Switzerland. Gaining worldwide acceptance for the label will be an uphill battle. "It's not that the sins of the fathers should fall on the shoulders of the children, or that one brother should be blamed for the actions of another," explains Mario Boselli, head of Italy's fashion trade organization. "But I can't see how someone could ever try to exploit this type of notoriety."[14]

Packaging

A firm's product strategy must address questions about packaging. Like its brand name, a product's package can powerfully influence buyers' purchase decisions.

Firms are applying increasingly scientific methods to their packaging decisions. Rather than experimenting with physical models or drawings, more and more package designers work on special computer graphics that create three-dimensional images of packages in thousands of colors, shapes, and typefaces. Another computer system helps firms design effective packaging by simulating the displays shoppers see when they walk down supermarket aisles. Companies conduct marketing research to evaluate current packages and to test alternative package designs. Kellogg, for example, tested its Nutri-Grain cereal package—as well as the product itself—before launching the product into the market.

A package serves three major objectives: (1) protection against damage, spoilage, and pilferage; (2) assistance in marketing the product; and (3) cost effectiveness. Let's briefly consider each of these objectives.

Protection against Damage, Spoilage, and Pilferage The original objective of packaging was to offer physical protection for the merchandise. Products typically pass through several stages of handling between manufacturing and customer purchases, and a package must protect the contents from damage. Furthermore, packages of perishable products must protect the contents against spoilage in transit and in storage until purchased by the consumer. The American Plastics Council developed an advertising campaign to promote the benefits of using plastics in food packaging, asserting that plastic bottles, wraps, and containers reduce the chance of food contamination and that tamper-resistant plastic seals provide product safety assurance.

Fears of product tampering have forced many firms to improve package designs. Over-the-counter medicines are sold in tamper-resistant packages covered with warnings informing consumers to not purchase merchandise without protective seals intact. Many grocery items and light-sensitive products are packaged in tamper-resistant containers as well. Products in glass jars, like spaghetti sauce and jams, often come with vacuum-depressed buttons in the lids that pop up the first time the lids are opened.

Likewise, many packages offer important safeguards for retailers against pilferage. Shoplifting and employee theft cost retailers several billion dollars each year. To limit this activity, many packages feature oversized cardboard backings too large to fit into a shoplifter's pocket or purse. Efficient packaging that protects against damage, spoilage, and theft is especially important for international marketers, who must contend with varying climatic conditions and the added time and stress involved in overseas shipping.

Assistance in Marketing the Product The proliferation of new products, changes in consumer lifestyles and buying habits, and marketers' emphasis on targeting smaller market segments have increased the importance of packaging as a promotional tool. Many firms are addressing consumer concerns about protecting the environment by designing packages with minimal amounts of biodegradable and recyclable materials. To demonstrate serious concern regarding environmental protection, Procter & Gamble, Coors, McDonald's, BP Chemical, and other firms have created ads that describe their efforts in developing environmentally sound packaging.

In a grocery store where thousands of different items compete for notice, a product must capture the shopper's attention. Marketers combine colors, sizes, shapes, graphics, and typefaces to establish distinctive trade dress that sets their products apart from the products of their competitors. Packaging can help to establish a common identity for a group of items sold under the same brand name. Like the brand name, a package should evoke the product's image and communicate its value. Some companies patent their package designs, which may play crucial roles in consumers' brand insistence.

Packages can also enhance convenience for the buyers. Pump dispenser cans, for example, facilitate the use of products ranging from mustard to insect repellent. Squeezable bottles of honey and ketchup make the products easier to use and store. Packaging provides key benefits for convenience foods such as meals and snacks packaged in microwavable containers, juice drinks in aseptic packages, and frozen entrees and vegetables packaged in single-serving portions. Beverage manufacturers have gone to great lengths to accommodate the needs of consumers. First, scientists videotaped consumers drinking from bottles, then made plaster molds of their hands. Researchers discovered that an average gulp took in 6.44 ounces of fluid and that half the people studied would rather sip liquid through a pop-up top than guzzle it from an open container. The results are new, sleeker, hourglass-shaped bottles that are easy to grip and drink from. Within six months of introducing its new bottles, Gatorade saw a 25 percent jump in sales. "We think of our bottles as sports equipment," explains a Gatorade marketing manager. Other beverage producers, including Dannon, Nestlé, and Snapple, have developed similar, ergonomically designed bottles; these companies claim a double-digit increase in sales, as well.[15]

Some firms increase consumer utility with packages designed for reuse. Empty peanut butter jars and jelly jars have long doubled as drinking glasses. Parents can buy bubble bath in animal-shaped plastic bottles suitable for bathtub play. Packaging is a major component in Avon's overall marketing strategy. The firm's decorative, reusable bottles have even become collectibles.

Cost-Effective Packaging Although packaging must perform a number of functions for the producer, marketers, and consumers, it must do so at a reasonable cost. Sometimes changes in the packaging can make packages both cheaper and better for the environment. Compact disc manufacturers, for instance, once packaged music CDs in two containers, a disk-sized plastic box inside a long, cardboard box that fit into the record bins in the stores. Consumers protested against the waste of the long boxes, and the recording industry finally agreed to eliminate the cardboard outer packaging altogether. Now CDs come in just the plastic cases, and stores display them in reusable plastic holders to discourage theft.

Labeling Labels were once a separate element that was applied to a package; today, it is an integral part of a typical package. Labels perform both promotional and informational functions. A **label** carries an item's brand name or symbol, the name and address of the manufacturer or distributor, information about the product's composition and size, and recommended uses. The right label can play an important role in attracting consumer attention and encouraging purchase.

Consumer confusion and dissatisfaction over such incomprehensible descriptions as giant economy size, king size, and family size led to the passage of the Fair Packaging and Labeling Act in 1966. The act requires that a label offer adequate information concerning the package contents and that a package design facilitate value comparisons among competing products.

The Nutrition Labeling and Education Act of 1990 imposes a uniform format in which food manufacturers must disclose nutritional information about their products. In addition, the Food and Drug Administration (FDA) has mandated design standards for nutritional labels that provide clear guidelines to consumers about food products. The FDA has also tightened definitions for loosely used terms like light, fat free, lean, and extra lean, and it mandates that labels list the amounts of fat, sodium, dietary fiber, calcium, vitamins, and other components in typical servings. The fast-food industry has long been plagued with labeling challenges. Not long ago, McDonald's faced a new one. For over a decade, the company has advertised that its famous french fries were cooked in "100 percent vegetable oil." However, in a recent statement, the company admitted that some additional flavoring used in the fries contains "a miniscule amount of beef extract." Several consumers who are vegetarians subsequently filed suit against the company in Seattle, alleging that McDonald's had engaged in deceptive marketing practices in its labeling. The lawsuit sought financial compensation and class-action status for all vegetarian consumers who have eaten McDonald's fries since 1990 thinking that they were receiving nonanimal foods.[16]

Labeling requirements differ elsewhere in the world. In Canada, for example, labels must give information in both French and English. The type and amount of information required on labels also varies among nations. International marketers must carefully design labels to conform to the regulations of each country in which they operate and market their merchandise.

The *Universal Product Code (UPC)* designation is another very important aspect of a label or package. Introduced in 1974 as a method for cutting expenses in the supermarket industry, UPCs are numerical bar codes printed on packages. Optical scanner systems read these codes, and computer systems recognize items and print their prices on cash register receipts. Virtually all packaged grocery items carry the UPC bars. While UPC scanners are costly, they permit both considerable labor savings over manual pricing and improved inventory control. The Universal Product Code is also a major asset for marketing research. However, many consumers feel frustrated when only a UPC is placed on a package without an additional price tag, because they do not always know how much an item costs if the price labels are knocked off the shelf.

Co-Branding and Co-Marketing

Co-branding joins together two strong brand names, perhaps owned by two different companies, to sell a product. The automotive world is packed with co-branded vehicles. A quick tour of car dealerships would reveal The North Face edition of the Chevy Avalanche, the Eddie Bauer edition of the Ford Explorer, the Lexus special Coach edition of the ES 300 sedan, and even the Bugs Bunny Chevrolet Venture minivan, complete with video screen. Subaru of America has also teamed up with L.L. Bean Inc. in a multiyear co-branding agreement that makes Subaru the official car of the outdoor retail giant, featured at L.L. Bean stores and in its catalogs. For its part, L.L. Bean has become the official outfitter to Subaru, which will sell Bean's outdoor clothing with Subaru branding at Subaru auto dealerships. Subaru currently sponsors events such as the Subaru Gorge Games in Oregon, in which L.L. Bean will participate. "L.L. Bean is a natural partner for Subaru, as both companies provide outdoor enthusiasts with products that enhance their lives," says Bill Cyphers, vice president for marketing at Subaru.[17]

In a co-marketing effort, two organizations join together to sell their products in an allied marketing campaign. Perhaps you've seen a Reebok logo on a college campus scoreboard or stopped in at the Burger King booth at the campus food court. More and more schools are forming co-marketing relationships with commercial firms, including brands such as Nike, Powerade, Coca-Cola, Fidelity Investments, and Barnes & Noble. The University of Massachusetts even has a relationship with the Boston Celtics. Although these relationships are becoming increasingly common, it has been a decade since Boston University opened a food court with vendors such as Burger King and Starbucks, and negotiated with Barnes & Noble to add the bookseller's logo to the name of the Boston University bookstores. Both the food court—whose revenues doubled from $2.5 million to $5.2 million in one year—and the bookstore have been huge successes. The practice has its critics, but so far students seem to appreciate having access to the brands they like.[18]

Brand Extensions

Some brands become so popular that companies carry these products over to unrelated products in pursuit of marketing advantages. The strategy of attaching a popular brand name to a new product in an unrelated product category is known as **brand extension.** Readers should not confuse this practice with *line extensions,* which refers to new sizes, styles, or related products. A brand extension, in contrast, carries over from one product nothing but the brand name. In establishing brand extensions, companies hope to gain access to new customers and markets by building on the equity already established in their existing brands.

The Bic brand of ballpoint pens became popular, after which the late French entrepreneur Marcel Bich launched his successful line of Bic disposable razors and Bic utility lighters. But brand extensions run considerable risk of brand dilution, as Bich discovered. Brand dilution occurs when a firm introduces too many brand extensions, some of which might not succeed. You've probably never even heard of "fannyhose," a Bic brand of hosiery launched in the 1970s, or Bic sailboards. But Bich's biggest blunder was probably Parfum Bic, a drugstore fragrance introduced in 1989 with a $20 million marketing campaign. The perfume sat on the shelves for so long that Bich finally pulled it out of the stores a year later, taking an $11 million loss.[19]

Brand Licensing

A growing number of firms have authorized other companies to use their brand names. This practice, known as *brand licensing,* expands a firm's exposure in the marketplace, much as a brand extension does. The brand name's owner also receives an extra source of income in the form of royalties from licensees, typically from 4 to 8 percent of wholesale revenues.

Major League Baseball has long been engaged in successful brand licensing. Hats, trading cards, and electronic games—not to mention baseballs, bats, and gloves with the MLB logo—have all been popular at retail outlets. Rawlings makes the baseballs, Russell Athletic and Majestic Apparel make clothing, Topps produces trading cards, and New Era puts out headwear. Altogether there are about 20 top licensees currently working with the MLB organization.[20]

Brand experts note several potential problems with licensing, however. Brand names do not transfer well to all products. If a licensee produces a poor-quality product or an item ethically incompatible with the original brand, the arrangement could damage the reputation of the brand.

NEW PRODUCT PLANNING

As its offerings enter the maturity and decline stages of the product life cycle, a firm must add new items to continue to prosper. Regular additions of new products to the firm's line helps to protect it from product obsolescence.

New products are the lifeblood of any business, and survival depends on a steady flow of new entries. Some new products may implement major technological breakthroughs. Other new products simply extend existing product lines. In other words, a new product is one that either the company or the customer has not handled before. Only about 10 percent of new product introductions bring truly new capabilities to people who are completely unfamiliar with them. But who should get credit for product innovations? The "Solving an Ethical Controversy" Interactive Example discusses this issue.

<interactive>**example**

RIGHT/WRONG: SOLVING AN ETHICAL CONTROVERSY—WHOSE IDEA IS IT ANYWAY?

Product Development Strategies

A firm's strategy for new product development varies according to its existing product mix and the match between current offerings and the firm's overall marketing objectives. The current market positions of products also affect product development strategy. Figure 12.9 identifies four alternative development strategies: market penetration, market development, product development, and product diversification.

<interactive>**learning goal**

CHAPTER OBJECTIVE #5: DESCRIBE THE STRATEGIES FOR NEW PRODUCT DEVELOPMENT.

A *market penetration strategy* seeks to increase sales of existing products in existing markets. Firms can attempt to extend their penetration of markets in several ways. They may modify products, improve product quality, or promote new and different ways to use products. Packaged goods marketers often pursue this strategy to boost market share for mature products in mature markets. Product positioning often plays a major role in such a strategy.

Product positioning refers to consumers' perceptions of a product's attributes, uses, quality, and advantages and disadvantages relative to competing brands. Marketers often conduct marketing research studies to analyze consumer preferences and to construct product positioning maps that plot their products' positions in relation to those of competitors' offerings.

A *market development strategy* concentrates on finding new markets for existing products. Market segmentation, discussed in Chapter 8, provides useful support for such an effort. Bank of America has succeeded in developing a new market by targeting Asian residents in San Francisco with special television commercials aimed at Chinese, Koreans, and Vietnamese consumers. Mott's Inc. has focused on building loyal customers among Asian Americans, particularly for its Mott's Juice, Hawaiian Punch, and Clamato juice drinks.[21]

The strategy of *product development* refers to the introduction of new products into identifiable or established markets. A few years ago, Nike decided to enter the golf market by creating a new division called Nike Golf and introducing its first new golf products—branded golf balls. Although the company stumbled at first by targeting casual and budget-oriented players, the firm's marketers quickly changed gears and went after more skilled players who were willing to purchase premium balls. Today, Nike Golf lays claim to somewhere between 8 and 10 percent of the entire golf ball market of $800 million. With that success, the company decided to introduce its golf clubs, which it spent two years developing. Nike began by offering drivers, and later introduced a complete range of clubs.[22]

Firms may choose to introduce new products into markets in which they have already established positions to try to increase overall market share. These new offerings are called *flanker brands.* Smucker's flanks its famous jams and jellies with dessert products such as its Magic Shell toppings, illustrated in Figure 12.10.

Finally, a *product diversification strategy* focuses on developing entirely new products for new markets. Some firms look for new target markets that complement their existing markets; others look in completely new directions. The Sara Lee Corporation doesn't just sell pound cakes and other desserts. The company has grown so diversified that it offers a vast array of branded products, from Wonderbras to Kiwi shoe polish to Endust furniture polish and Chock Full O' Nuts coffee. However, the firm had become so fragmented over the years that one of the first moves CEO C. Steven McMillan made when he took over was to sell off disparate brands, vowing to concentrate on its core businesses: food, underwear, and household products.[23]

FIGURE 12.9

Alternative Product Development Strategies

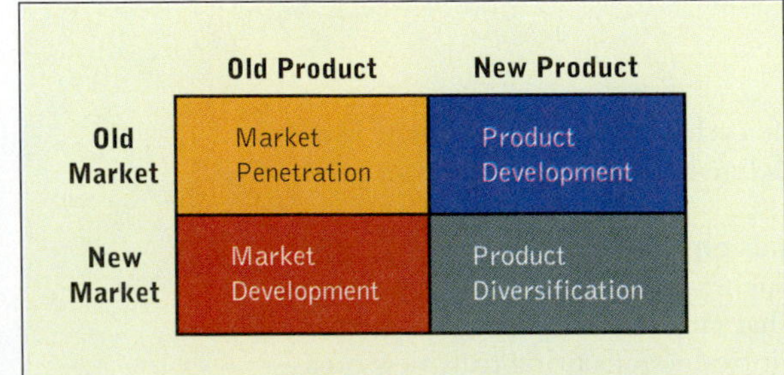

Old Product
New Product
Old Market
Market Penetration
Product Development
New Market
Market Development
Product Diversification

Marketers need to consider *cannibalization* in picking a new product strategy. Any firm wants to avoid investing resources in a new product introduction that will adversely affect sales of existing products. A product that takes sales from another offering in the same product line is said to cannibalize that line. A firm can accept some loss of sales from existing products if the new offering will generate sufficient additional sales to warrant the firm's investment in its development and market introduction.

The Consumer Adoption Process

Consumer purchases also influence decisions regarding a new product offering. In the **adoption process,** consumers go through a series of stages from learning about the new product to trying it and deciding whether to purchase it regularly or to reject it. These stages in the consumer adoption process can be classified as the following:

1. *Awareness.* Individuals first learn of the new product, but they lack full information about it.
2. *Interest.* Potential buyers begin to seek information about it.
3. *Evaluation.* They consider the likely benefits of the product.
4. *Trial.* They make trial purchases to determine its usefulness.
5. *Adoption/Rejection.* If the trial purchase produces satisfactory results, they decide to use the product regularly.[24]

<interactive>**learning goal**

CHAPTER OBJECTIVE #6: DESCRIBE THE CONSUMER ADOPTION PROCESS.

Marketers must understand the adoption process to move potential consumers to the adoption stage. Once marketers recognize a large number of consumers at the interest stage, they can take steps to stimulate sales by moving these buyers through the evaluation and trial stages. Johnson & Johnson enhanced the evaluation and trial of its disposable contact lenses by offering free trial pairs to consumers. America Online mails its Internet-access software and offers a free one-month membership to computer owners who are not AOL members. From time to time you may receive free samples of breakfast cereals, snack foods, cosmetics, or shampoos in the mail. These companies are encouraging you to try their products in the hope that you will eventually adopt these products.

Adopter Categories

Consumer innovators are people who purchase new products almost as soon as these products reach the market. Other adopters wait for additional information and rely on the experiences of initial buyers before making trial purchases. Consumer innovators welcome innovations in each product area. Some computer users, for instance, rush to install new software immediately after each update becomes available. Some physicians, as well, pioneered the uses of new pharmaceutical products for their AIDS patients. Some fans bought season tickets before the NFL Browns came back to Cleveland.

A number of studies about the adoption of new products have identified five categories of purchasers based on relative times of adoption. These categories, shown in Figure 12.11, are consumer innovators, early adopters, early majority, late majority, and laggards.

The *diffusion process* brings acceptance of new goods and services by the members of the community or social system. Figure 12.11 shows a normal distribution over the course of this process. A few people adopt at first, then the number of adopters increases rapidly as the value of the innovation becomes apparent. The adoption rate finally diminishes as the number of potential consumers who have not adopted, or purchased, the product diminishes. Typically, innovators make up the first 2.5 percent of buyers who adopt the new product; laggards are the last 16 percent to do so. Figure 12.11 excludes those who never adopt the innovation.

FIGURE 12.10

From Jellies to Ice Cream Toppings: Smucker's Promotes Flanker Brands

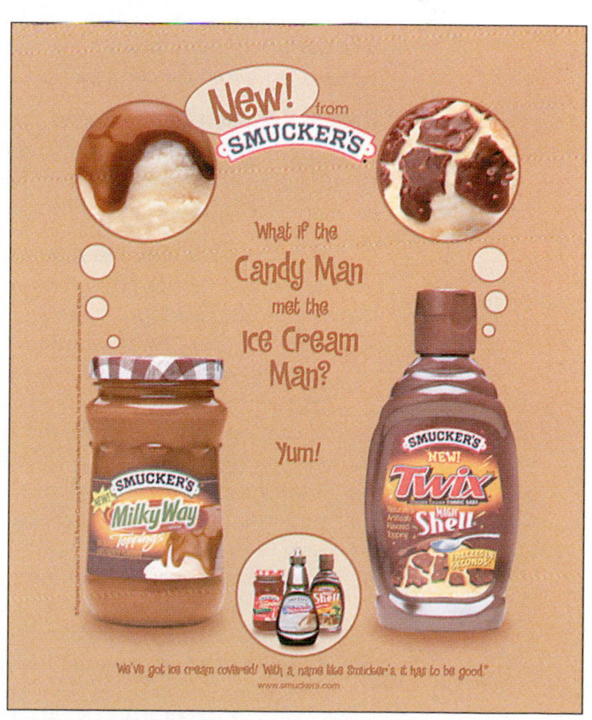

Identifying Early Adopters

It's no surprise that identifying consumers or organizations who are most likely to try a new product can be vital to a product's success. By reaching these buyers early in the product's development or introduction, marketers can treat these adopters as a test market, evaluating the product and discovering suggestions for modifications. Since early purchasers often act as opinion leaders from whom others seek advice, their attitudes toward new products

FIGURE 12.11

Categories of Adopters Based on Relative Times of Adoption

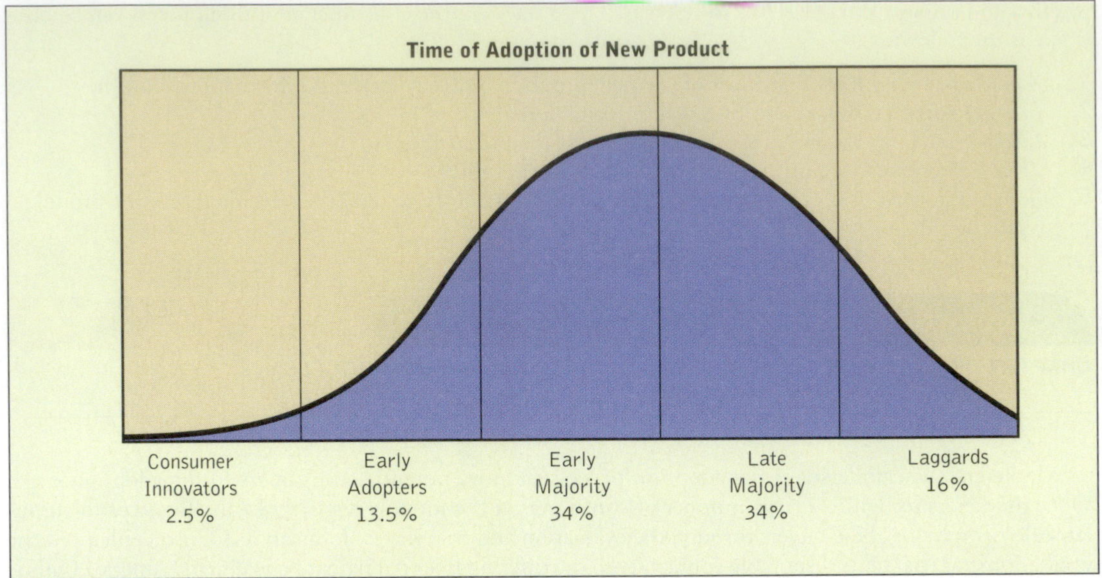

quickly spread to others. Acceptance or rejection of the innovation by these purchasers can help forecast its expected success. Several auto companies, including Honda and Ford, have developed gasoline-electric vehicles for the consumer market. These hybrid vehicles use a combination of gasoline and electric batteries to get superior gas mileage and send fewer exhaust emissions into the air. But although Honda and Ford got their vehicles to market first, Toyota tried an entirely different marketing approach in attempting to gain a competitive edge anyway. While Honda and Ford targeted environmentalists and consumers who are concerned about clean air, Toyota aimed its first promotional efforts at consumer innovators and early adopters. The ads for its new Prius mentioned its environmentally friendly features, but they focused on consumers who wanted to be the first on their block to have one of these unique cars.[25]

A large number of studies have established the general characteristics of first adopters. These pioneers tend to be younger, have higher social status, are better educated, and enjoy higher incomes than other consumers. They are more mobile than later adopters and change both their jobs and addresses more often. They also rely more heavily than later adopters on impersonal information sources; more hesitant buyers depend primarily on company-generated promotional information and word-of-mouth communications.

Rate of Adoption Determinants Frisbees progressed from the product introduction stage to the market maturity stage in a period of six months. By contrast, the U.S. Department of Agriculture tried for 13 years to convince corn farmers to use hybrid seed corn, an innovation capable of doubling crop yields. Five characteristics of a product innovation influence its adoption rate:

1. *Relative advantage.* An innovation that appears far superior to previous ideas offers a greater relative advantage—reflected in terms of lower price, physical improvements, or ease of use—and increases the product's adoption rate.
2. *Compatibility.* An innovation consistent with the values and experiences of potential adopters attracts new buyers at a relatively rapid rate. Investors who are already comfortable with making transactions online would probably be attracted to Lycos's LiveCharts, which offers live, real-time streaming charts showing the activity of stocks.
3. *Complexity.* The relative difficulty of understanding the innovation influences the speed of acceptance. In most cases, consumers move slowly in adopting new products that they find difficult to understand or use. Farmers' cautious acceptance of hybrid seed corn illustrates how long an adoption can take.
4. *Possibility of trial use.* An initial free or discounted trial of a good or service means that adopters can reduce their risk of financial or social loss when they try the product. A coupon for a free item or a free night's stay at a hotel can accelerate the rate of adoption.
5. *Observability.* If potential buyers can observe an innovation's superiority in a tangible form, the adoption rate increases. In-store demonstrations or even advertisements that focus on the superiority of a product, like the one for Ford's Quality Checked Pre-owned Program in Figure 12.12, can encourage buyers to adopt a product.

Marketers who want to accelerate the rate of adoption can manipulate these five characteristics at least to some extent. An informative promotional message about a new allergy drug could help consumers overcome their hesitation in adopting this complex product. Effective product design can emphasize a product's advantages over the competition. Everyone likes to receive something for free, so giving away small samples of a new product lets consumers try it at little or no risk. In-home demonstrations or trial home placements of items such as furniture or carpeting can achieve similar results. Marketers must also make positive attempts in ensuring the innovation's compatibility with adopters' value systems.

FIGURE 12.12

Ford: Focusing on Observability through a Quality Checklist

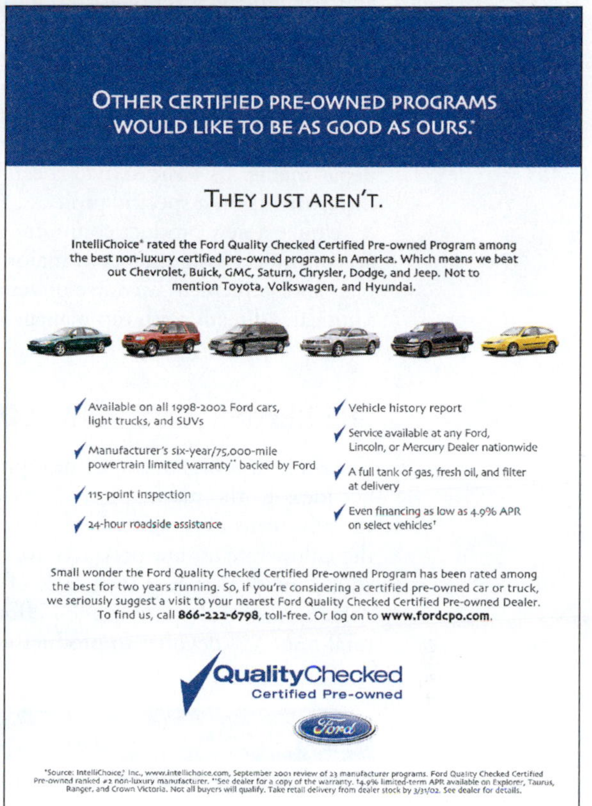

Organizing for New Product Development

A firm needs to be organized in such a way that its personnel can stimulate and coordinate new product development. Some companies contract with independent design firms to develop new products. Many assign product-innovation functions to one or more of the following entities: new product committees, new product departments, product managers, and venture teams.

New Product Committees The most common organizational arrangement for activities in developing a new product is to center these functions in a new product committee. This group typically brings together experts in such areas as marketing, finance, manufacturing, engineering, research, and accounting. Committee members spend less time conceiving and developing their own new product ideas than reviewing and approving new product plans that arise elsewhere in the organization. The committee might review ideas from the engineering and design staff, or perhaps from marketers and salespeople who are in constant contact with customers.

Since members of a new product committee hold important jobs in the firm's functional areas, their support for any new product plan likely foreshadows approval for further development. However, new product committees in large companies tend to reach decisions slowly and maintain conservative views. Sometimes members may compromise so they can return to their regular responsibilities.

New Product Departments Many companies establish separate, formally organized departments to generate and refine new product ideas. The departmental structure overcomes the limitations of the new product committee system and encourages innovation as a permanent, full-time activity. The new product department is responsible for all phases of a development project within the firm, including screening decisions, developing product specifications, and coordinating product testing. The head of the department wields substantial authority and typically reports to the chief executive officer, chief operating officer, or a top marketing executive.

Product Managers

A *product manager* is another term for a brand manager, a function mentioned earlier in the chapter. This marketing professional supports the marketing strategies of an individual product or product line. Procter & Gamble, for instance, assigned its first product manager in 1927, when it made one person responsible for Camay soap.

Product managers set prices, develop advertising and sales promotion programs, and work with sales representatives in the field. In a company that markets multiple products, product managers fulfill key functions in the marketing department. They provide individual attention for each product and support and coordinate efforts of the firm's sales force, marketing research department, and advertising department. Product managers often lead new product development programs, including creation of new product ideas and recommendations for improving existing products.

However, as mentioned earlier in the chapter, companies such as Procter & Gamble and General Mills have either modified the product manager structure or done away with it altogether in favor of a category management structure, based on small teams. Category managers have profit and loss responsibility, which is not characteristic of the product management system. This change has largely come about because of customer preference, but it can also benefit a manufacturer by avoiding duplication of some jobs and competition among the company's own brands and its managers.

Venture Teams A *venture team* gathers a group of specialists from different areas of an organization to work together in developing new products. The venture team must meet criteria for return on investment, uniqueness of product, serving a well-defined need, compatibility of the product with existing technology, and strength of patent protection. Although the organization sets up the venture team as a temporary entity, its flexible life span may extend over a number of years. When purchases confirm the commercial potential of a new product, an existing division may take responsibility for that product, or it may serve as the nucleus of a new division within the company or of an entirely new company.

Some marketing organizations differentiate between venture teams and task forces. A new-product task force assembles an interdisciplinary group working on temporary assignment through their functional departments. Its basic activities center on coordinating and integrating the work of the firm's functional departments on a specific project.

Unlike a new product committee, a venture team does not disband after every meeting. Team members accept project assignments as major responsibilities, and the team exercises the authority it needs to both plan and implement a course of action. To stimulate product innovation, the venture team typically communicates directly with top management, but it functions as an entity separate from the basic organization.

THE NEW-PRODUCT DEVELOPMENT PROCESS

Once a firm is organized for new product development, it can establish procedures for moving new product ideas to the marketplace. Developing a new product is often time-consuming, risky, and expensive. Usually, firms must generate dozens of new product ideas to produce even one successful product. In fact, the failure rate of new products averages 80 percent. Products fail for a number of reasons, including inadequate market assessments, lack of market orientation, poor screening and project evaluation, product defects, and inadequate launch efforts. And these blunders cost a bundle: firms invest nearly half of the total resources devoted to product innovation on products that become commercial failures.

<interactive>**learning goal**

CHAPTER OBJECTIVE #7: LIST THE STAGES IN THE PROCESS FOR DEVELOPING NEW PRODUCTS.

A new product is more likely to become successful if the firm follows a six-step development process: (1) idea generation, (2) screening, (3) business analysis, (4) development, (5) test marketing, and (6) commercialization. Of course, each step requires decisions about whether to proceed further or abandon the project. And each step involves a greater financial investment.

Traditionally, most companies have developed new products through phased development, which follows the six-step process in an orderly sequence. Responsibility for each phase passes first from product planners to designers and engineers, to manufacturers, and finally to marketers. The phased development method can work well for firms that dominate mature markets and can develop variations on existing products. But with rapid changes in technology and markets, many companies feel pressured to speed up the development process.

After a decade of flops and near-successes, several competitors—large and small—are racing to get their version of the "smart box" to consumers' televisions as fast as possible. Satellite companies have been developing receivers with hard drives so that digital movies and programs can be beamed right into subscribers' TV sets. Cable companies are fighting back with their own style of smart box. But it's the Moxi Digital software that has industry watchers watching even more closely. With Moxi, TV watchers can use a single remote to surf through galaxies of digital media feeds and capture whatever they want. "It's one box and one remote control, and no cables," boasts Moxi founder Steve Perlman. "That's a revolution!"[26]

This time pressure has encouraged many firms to implement parallel product development programs. These programs generally consist of teams with experts from design, manufacturing, marketing, and sales who carry out development projects from idea generation to commercialization. Venture teams, discussed earlier, follow this parallel development model. This method can reduce the time needed to develop products because team members work on the six steps concurrently rather than in sequence. Wyeth was able to bring its antidepressant Effexor to market in just two years—half the usual time it takes to develop and launch such a drug—by using such a team.[27]

Whether a firm pursues phased development or parallel product development, all phases can benefit from planning tools and scheduling methods such as the program evaluation and review technique (PERT) and the critical path method (CPM). These techniques, originally developed by the U.S. Navy in connection with construction of the Polaris missile and submarine, map out the sequence of each step in a process and show the time allotments for each activity. Detailed PERT and CPM flowcharts help marketers to coordinate all activities entailed in the development and introduction of new products.

In introducing its golf clubs described earlier in the chapter, Nike followed its own patented business strategy that included a systematic product introduction, extensive endorsement by golf tour professionals—including phenom Tiger Woods—and a new product budget of up to $100 million, with a $35 million marketing budget. Those numbers illustrate the importance of planning.[28]

Idea Generation

New product development begins with ideas from many sources: the sales force, suggestions from customers, research-and-development specialists, competing products, suppliers, retailers, and independent inventors. Some top executives are beginning to recognize the value of keeping their eyes, ears, and minds open to ideas from employees at all levels of the firm. Susan Lyne, president of ABC Entertainment, says, "My top priority is getting the younger, creative people at the network to feel comfortable speaking up. . . . We need to find the gaps in our schedule, identify categories of viewers that we're missing, and force everyone to address those needs as we read the material coming in."[29]

Screening

Screening separates ideas with commercial potential from those that cannot meet company objectives. Some organizations maintain checklists of development standards in determining whether a project should be abandoned or considered further. These checklists typically include such factors as product uniqueness, availability of raw materials, and the proposed product's compatibility with current product offerings, existing facilities, and present capabilities. The screening stage may also allow for open discussions of new product ideas among different parts of the organization.

Business Analysis

A product idea that survives the initial screening must then pass a thorough business analysis. This stage consists of assessing the new product's potential market, growth rate, and likely competitive strengths. Marketers must evaluate the compatibility of the proposed product with organizational resources.

Concept testing subjects the product idea to additional study prior to its actual development. This important aspect of a new product's business analysis represents a marketing research project that attempts to measure consumer attitudes and perceptions about the new product idea. Focus groups and in-store polling can contribute effectively to concept testing. When Kolcraft Enterprises learned that its customers wanted a more rugged mode of transporting babies than the traditional baby stroller it had been manufacturing, the company actually licensed the Jeep brand name from DaimlerChrysler and came out with a heavy-duty stroller modeled after the parents' SUVs.[30]

The screening and business analysis stages generate extremely important information for new product development because they (1) define the proposed product's target market and customers' needs and wants and (2) determine the product's financial and technical requirements. Firms that are willing to invest money and time during these stages tend to be more successful at generating viable ideas and at creating successful products.

Development

Financial outlays increase substantially as a firm converts an idea into a physical product. The conversion process is the joint responsibility of the firm's development engineers, who turn the original concept into a product, and of its marketers, who provide feedback on consumer reactions to the product design, package, color, and other physical features. Many firms implement computer-aided design systems to streamline the development stage, and prototypes may go through numerous changes before the original mock-up reaches the stage of a final product.

Test Marketing

As discussed in Chapter 7, many firms test market their new product offerings to gauge consumer reaction. After a company has developed a prototype, it may decide to test market it to gauge consumer reactions under normal conditions. Test marketing's purpose is to verify that the product will perform well in a real-life business environment. If the product does well, the company can proceed to commercialization. If it flops, the company can decide to fine-tune certain features and reintroduce it or pull the plug on the project altogether. Industries that rely heavily on test marketing are snack foods, automobiles, and movies. Of course, even if a product tests well and reaches the commercialization stage, it may still take a while to catch on with the general public, as has been the case of inventor Dean Kamen's Segway Human Transporter, a gyroscopic scooter that Kamen hopes will change individual transportation.[31]

Commercialization

When a new product idea reaches the commercialization stage, it is ready for full-scale marketing. Commercialization of a major new product can expose the firm to substantial expenses. It must establish marketing strategies, fund outlays for production facilities, and acquaint the sales force, marketing intermediaries, and potential customers with the new product.

When Nike was ready to launch its drivers, wedges, and irons, the company unveiled them at the PGA Merchandise Show in Orlando, Florida. Several golf pros, including John Cook, Michael Campbell, and David Duval used the clubs in successful tournament play. And Nike signed a multimillion-dollar endorsement deal with golf star Tiger Woods.[32] All of this was part of the commercialization process.

PRODUCT SAFETY AND LIABILITY

A product can fulfill its mission of satisfying consumer needs only if it ensures safe operation. Manufacturers must design their products to protect users from harm. Products that lead to injuries, either directly or indirectly, can have disastrous consequences for their makers. *Product liability* refers to the responsibility of manufacturers and marketers for injuries and damages caused by their products. Chapter 3 discussed some of the major consumer protection laws that affect product safety. These laws include the Flammable Fabrics Act of 1953, the Fair Packaging and Labeling Act of 1966, the Poison Prevention Packaging Act of 1970, and the Consumer Product Safety Act of 1972.

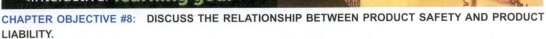

CHAPTER OBJECTIVE #8: DISCUSS THE RELATIONSHIP BETWEEN PRODUCT SAFETY AND PRODUCT LIABILITY.

Federal and state legislation play a major role in regulating product safety. The Poison Prevention Packaging Act requires drug manufacturers to place their products in packaging that is child resistant yet accessible to all adults, even ones who have trouble opening containers. The Consumer Product Safety Act created a powerful regulatory agency—the Consumer Product Safety Commission (CPSC). This agency has assumed jurisdiction over every consumer product category except food, automobiles, and a few other products already regulated by other agencies. The CPSC has the authority to ban products without court hearings, order recalls or redesigns of products, and inspect production facilities. It can charge managers of negligent companies with criminal offenses. The CPSC is especially watchful of products aimed at babies and young children. In one unanimous vote, the agency resolved to warn parents about potential safety problems with infant bath seats made by such companies as Safety 1st that could slip into the water or topple over if a child were to be left unattended.[33] In another case, the CPSC fined Costco $1.3 million in civil penalties to settle charges that the retailer had violated a federal law by failing to report hundreds of injuries and even a death related to its Options 5 high chair as well as several other defective products.[34]

The federal Food and Drug Administration (FDA) must approve food, medications, and health-related devices such as wheelchairs. The FDA can also take products off the market if concerns arise about the safety of these products.

The number of product liability lawsuits filed against manufacturers has skyrocketed in recent years. Although many such claims reach settlements out of court, juries have decided on many claims, sometimes awarding multimillion-dollar settlements. This threat has led most companies to step up efforts to ensure product safety. Safety warnings appear prominently on the labels of such potentially hazardous products as cleaning fluids and drain cleaners to inform users of the dangers of these products, particularly to children. Changes in product design have reduced the hazards posed by such products as lawn mowers, hedge trimmers, and toys. Product liability insurance has become an essential element for any new or existing product strategy. Premiums for this insurance have risen alarmingly, however, and insurers have almost entirely abandoned some kinds of coverage.

Regulatory activities and the increased number of liability claims have prompted companies to sponsor voluntary improvements in safety standards. Safety planning is now a vital element of product strategy, and many companies now publicize the safety planning and testing that go into the development of their products, as illustrated by the ad for Toyota in Figure 12.13.

STRATEGIC IMPLICATIONS OF MARKETING IN THE 21ST CENTURY

Marketers who want to see their products reach the marketplace successfully have a number of options for developing them, branding them, and developing a strong brand identity among consumers and business customers. The key is to integrate all of the options so that they are compatible with a firm's overall business and marketing strategy, and ultimately the firm's mission. Thus, as marketers consider ideas for new products, they need to be careful not to send their companies in so many different directions as to dilute

FIGURE 12.13

Publicizing Safety Planning and Testing at Toyota

TODAY
Produce virtual crash dummy
TOMORROW
Reduce actual crash injuries
TOYOTA
He can't talk, he can't walk, he can't drive a car. Yet he could be the most important "person" in the world of automotive safety testing today. He's THUMS, the world's first virtual human for crash testing.
Developed by Toyota engineers, THUMS can provide a microscopic look at the injuries real people are likely to sustain in a car accident. By analyzing data from THUMS' 80,000 cyberparts, engineers can now zero in on skin, bones, ligaments and tendons — something they were never able to do before.
Although currently only an experiment, technologies like THUMS may one day be used to supplement Toyota's existing safety programs, to make our cars even safer for real human beings. Safer cars—thanks to one very smart dummy.
www.toyota.com/tomorrow

the identities of their brands, making it nearly impossible to keep track of what their companies do well, as in the case of the Sara Lee Corporation. Category management can help companies develop a consistent product mix with strong branding, while at the same time meeting the needs of customers. Looking for ways to extend a brand without diluting it or compromising brand equity is also an important marketing strategy. Even though Sara Lee CEO C. Steven McMillan sold off 15 of the corporation's unrelated businesses, he also purchased the breadmaker Earthgrains, which quadrupled the company's bakery operations and was compatible with Sara's Lee's core food operations.[35]

Finally, marketers must continue to work to produce high-quality products that are also safe for all users. Even though Costco has been plagued with safety problems in some of its products, the organization has made efforts to turn things around. Upon recommendation from the CPSC, the company hired safety expert Mark Evanko to oversee issues related to product hazard analysis, safety testing, and quality control. Evanko vowed to improve the system.[36]

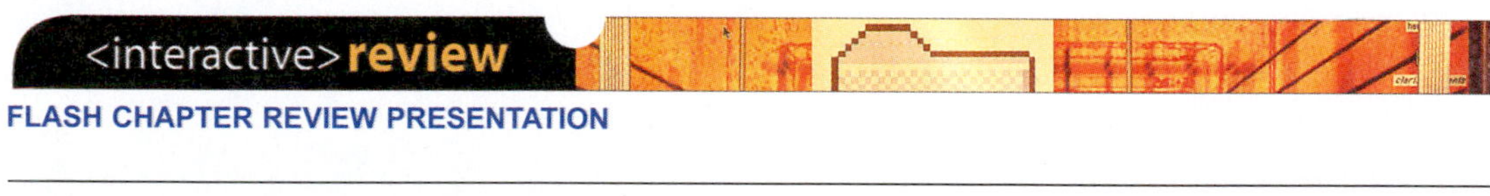
<interactive>review

FLASH CHAPTER REVIEW PRESENTATION

<interactive>video case

STRIDE RITE KEEPS ITS BRANDS IN STEP

<interactive>game

QUIZ BOWL

<interactive>**video case**

KRISPY KREME CONTINUING VIDEO CASE: THE KRISPY KREME BRAND

endofchaptermaterial

- **Summary of Chapter Objectives**
- **Chapter Outline**
- **Key Terms**
- **Review Questions**
- **Projects and Teamwork Exercises**
- **'netWork**
- **Crossword Puzzles**
- **Case 12.1: How Samsung Polished Its Global Brand**

Take the Post-Test to assess your overall understanding of the key ideas in this chapter. The Post-Test provides a comprehensive selection of exam-style questions addressing the main topics and concepts of the chapter. At the completion of each Post-Test, you will receive a score and instructive feedback on how you answered each question, and a direct link to the part of the chapter addressed in the question. Take the Post-Test as often as you need to—a record of your progress for each attempt is kept for you to revisit and gauge your improvement. And each Post-Test is randomly generated, so every attempt is new.

Post-Test

PART 5

Pricing Strategy

CHAPTER 13

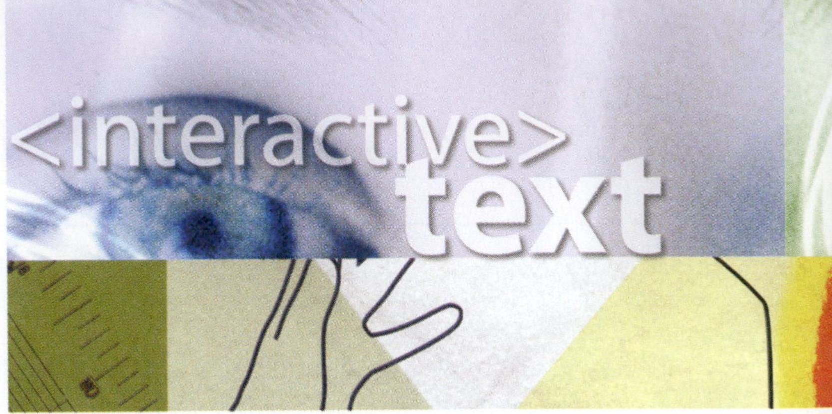

Price Determination

Chapter Objectives

1. Outline the legal constraints on pricing.
2. Identify the major categories of pricing objectives.
3. Explain price elasticity and its determinants.
4. List the practical problems involved in applying price theory concepts to actual pricing decisions.
5. Explain the major cost-plus approaches to price setting.
6. List the chief advantages and shortcomings of using breakeven analysis in pricing decisions.
7. Explain the superiority of modified breakeven analysis over the basic breakeven model and the role of yield management in pricing decisions.
8. Identify the major pricing challenges facing online and international marketers.

Pre-Test

Take the Pre-Test to assess your initial knowledge of the key ideas in this chapter. The Pre-Test provides exam-style questions addressing the main topics and concepts of the chapter. At the completion of each Pre-Test, you will receive a score and instructive feedback on how you answered each question, and a direct link to the part of the chapter addressed in the question. Take the Pre-Test as often as you need to—a record of your progress for each attempt is kept for you to revisit and gauge your improvement.

WHY PUGET POWER SWITCHED TO TIME-OF-DAY PRICING

In 300,000 Seattle-area homes, consumers are watching the clock. At 9 P.M., when off-peak electricity rates kick in, a nightly ritual of household chores begins. On go washing machines, dishwashers, and other high-energy appliances. Timers crank up hot-water heaters or the air conditioning. By 6 A.M., thermostats are down again and dishwashers are silenced for the day.

It's all part of a pilot scheme by Puget Sound Energy to level out the daily demand surges that inflate energy costs and, in the worst cases, lead to blackouts. Energy consumers who confine electricity use to times of day when power is cheapest are rewarded with lower rates. The Rader family, for instance, has cut monthly bills by a fifth—just by adding a timer to the hot water heater and keeping the dishwasher and washing machine off when electricity costs more.

The idea is simple—charge more for power used during demand surges and give customers a price break during off-peak hours, when power costs the utility less. It's the same approach that long-distance and cellular phone companies have used for years by charging more for calls during business hours than in the evenings or on weekends.

Electricity can cost a utility 10 times more from 6 to 10 A.M. and from 5 to 9 P.M., when more people are at home. During hot- or cold-weather extremes, when the air conditioning or heating is on at full blast, overuse leads to the risk of blackouts. During such high-use periods, utilities typically supply added electricity demand by purchasing it in costly spot markets. They also increase capacity by building new power plants—and the cost finds its way onto monthly utility bills. By using price incentives to level out demand, Puget Sound Energy management seeks to avoid these costs and pass the savings along to consumers.

Sophisticated cellular meters that transmit data on usage minute by minute have replaced antiquated door-to-door meter readings. In addition to eliminating the expense of visual meter readings, the new system provides the utility—and the customer—with a real-time picture of power peaks and valleys. Once consumers are aware of real-cost savings that they can achieve on a daily basis with minimal effort, many change their usage patterns. In addition to limiting appliance use to off-peak periods, they might, for example, stockpile cooling by adjusting the thermostat. Puget Sound Energy executives estimate that, if rolled out on a national basis, these variable-demand programs could save utilities up to $15 billion annually and eliminate the need for 200 additional power plants over the next 10 years.

While Puget Sound Energy marketers insist that price-break incentives can change consumers' power-usage habits and lead to energy conservation, state regulators are slow to change traditional rate structures. Critics claim that time-of-day savings discriminate against some householders—like the elderly—who often find it difficult to shift energy use, while benefiting no one as much as the utilities themselves. Although off-peak programs may succeed in leveling out demand, they do little to reduce it. To effectively lower energy consumption, for instance, customers would need to unplug their hot tubs, not just limit their use to off-peak hours. Variable-rate programs are also open to abuse by utilities who may conserve supply only to sell it off during hot- or cold-weather peaks to the highest bidder. Moreover, computer networks and automated metering systems are a huge capital investment for utilities. The cost—as well as the savings—will find its way back to the consumer.

Following a successful six-month pilot program, regulators approved Puget Sound's plans to extend its variable-rate pricing program. Nine out of ten households reported that they had improved their power-use habits, while half reported saving money by shifting their usage patterns to take advantage of less costly off-peak rates. Puget is now expanding into the B2B sector by piloting a similar incentive program to 20,000 business customers.[1]

CHAPTER OVERVIEW

As Puget Sound Energy's experience with off-peak discounts shows, price has a powerful impact on consumer spending behavior. One of the first questions shoppers ask is, "How much does it cost?" Marketers understand the critical role that price plays in the consumer's decision-making process. From lipstick and perfume to automobiles and gasoline to donuts and coffee, marketers must develop strategies that price products to achieve their firms' objectives.

Briefly Speaking

Price is what you pay. Value is what you get.

Warren Buffett (b. 1930) American investor

As a starting point for examining pricing strategies, consider the meaning of the term *price*. A **price** is the exchange value of a good or service—in other words, it represents whatever that product can be exchanged for in the marketplace. Price does not necessarily involve money. In earlier times, the price of an acre of land might have been 20 bushels of wheat, three head of cattle, or one boat. Even though the barter process continues to be used in some transactions, in the 21st century price typically refers to the amount of funds required to purchase a product.

Prices are both difficult to set and dynamic; they shift in response to a number of variables. A higher-than-average price can convey an image of prestige, while a lower-than-average price may connote good value. Price can also powerfully affect a company's overall profitability and market share.

This chapter discusses the process of determining a profitable but justifiable (fair) price. The focus is on management of the pricing function, including pricing strategies, price-quality relationships, and pricing in various sectors of the economy. The chapter also looks at the effects of environmental conditions on price determination, including legal constraints, competitive pressures, and changes in global and online markets.

PRICING AND THE LAW

Pricing decisions are influenced by a variety of legal constraints imposed by federal and state governments. The next time you pull up to a gas station, consider where each dollar goes. Almost 50 percent is taken up in federal, state, local, and excise taxes. Tariffs—taxes levied on the sale of imported goods and services—often make it possible for firms to set prices on domestically produced goods well above world market levels. To shield the ailing U.S. steel industry and protect American jobs, the Bush administration imposed tariffs of up to 30 percent on steel imports, driving up the price of steel at home. The tariffs led to protests not only from foreign producers who were cut out of the U.S. market but from American manufacturers across a range of industries who are reliant on low-cost steel to make their products.[2] Tariffs on foodstuffs have a similar effect on price, resulting, for example, in higher prices for bananas in Europe than in the U.S.

<interactive>learning goal

CHAPTER OBJECTIVE #1: OUTLINE THE LEGAL CONSTRAINTS ON PRICING.

An industry where the legal environment has a powerful impact on price is the firearms sector. Following a rash of public shootings—including several on school grounds by teenagers—antigun activists pressured Congress to pass tough restrictions regulating handgun ownership and sales. At the same time, survivors, families of victims, and even cities filed lawsuits against handgun manufacturers, which added to their costs. But consumer fears for personal safety following the terrorist attacks of September 11 led to increased handgun sales, and the added demand pushed retail prices up almost 10 percent.[3]

Pricing is also regulated by the general constraints of U.S. antitrust legislation, as outlined in Chapter 3. The following sections review some of the most important pricing laws for contemporary marketers.

Robinson-Patman Act

The **Robinson-Patman Act** (1936) typifies Depression-era legislation. Known as the Anti-A&P Act, it was inspired by price competition triggered by the rise of grocery store chains—in fact, the original draft was prepared by the U.S. Wholesale Grocers Association. Enacted in the midst of the Great Depression, when legislators viewed chain stores as a threat to employment in the traditional retail sector, the act was intended primarily to save jobs.

The Robinson-Patman Act was technically an amendment to the Clayton Act, enacted 22 years earlier, that had applied only to price discrimination between geographic areas, which injured local sellers. Broader in scope, Robinson-Patman prohibits price discrimination in sales to wholesalers, retailers, and other producers. It rules that differences in price must reflect cost differentials and prohibits selling at unreasonably low prices in order to drive competitors out of business. Supporters justified the amendment by arguing that chain stores might secure substantial discounts from suppliers, while small, independent stores would continue to pay regular prices.

Price discrimination, where some customers pay more than others for the same product, dates back to the very beginnings of trade and commerce. Today, however, technology has added to the frequency and complexity of price discrimination, as well as the strategies marketers adopt to get around it. For example, marketers may encourage repeat business by inviting purchasers to become "preferred customers," entitling them to average discounts of 10 percent. As long as companies can demonstrate that their price discounts and promotional allowances do not restrict competition, they avoid penalties under the Robinson-Patman

Act. Direct-mail marketers frequently send out catalogs of identical goods but with differing prices. Zip-code areas that traditionally consist of high spenders get the high-price catalogs, while price-sensitive zip-code customers get a low-price catalog. Victoria's Secret, Staples, and Simon & Schuster are among the hundreds of companies that employ legal price discrimination strategies. Amazon.com's recent experiments with so-called dynamic pricing—a method of using random price differentials to test the market—brought protests that the e-tailer was unfairly customizing its pricing according to consumer characteristics.[4]

Firms accused of price discrimination often argue that they set price differentials to meet competitors' prices and that cost differences justify variations in prices. When a firm asserts that it maintains price differentials as good-faith methods of competing with rivals, a logical question arises: What constitutes good-faith pricing behavior? The answer depends on the particular situation.

A defense based on cost differentials works only if the price differences do not exceed the cost differences resulting from selling to various classes of buyers. Marketers must then justify the cost differences; indeed many authorities consider this provision one of the most confusing areas in the Robinson-Patman Act. Courts handle most charges brought under the act as individual cases. Therefore, domestic marketers must continually evaluate their pricing actions to avoid potential Robinson-Patman violations.

Unfair-Trade Laws

More than 20 states supplement federal legislation with their own **unfair-trade laws,** which require sellers to maintain minimum prices for comparable merchandise. Enacted in the 1930s, these laws were intended to protect small specialty shops, such as dairy stores, from the loss-leader pricing tactics, in which chain stores might sell certain products below cost to attract customers. Typical state laws set retail price floors at cost plus some modest markup.

Although most unfair-trade laws have remained on the books for the past 70 years, marketers had all but forgotten them until recent years. Then in 1993, Wal-Mart, the nation's largest retailer, was found guilty of violating Arkansas's unfair-trade law for selling drugs and health-and-beauty aids below cost. The lawsuit filed by three independent drugstore owners accused the mass merchandiser of attempting to drive them out of business through predatory pricing practices. Wal-Mart appealed and the decision was overturned, but similar lawsuits have been filed in several other states, all seeking to end the chain's low-price marketing strategy.

The "Marketing Misses" Interactive Example explains what happened when Wal-Mart tried to flex its below-cost pricing muscle in the highly regulated German retail market.

MARKETING MISS: WAL-MART REQUIRED TO RAISE PRICES IN GERMANY

Fair-Trade Laws

The concept of fair trade has affected pricing decisions for decades. **Fair-trade laws** allow manufacturers to stipulate minimum retail prices for their products and to require dealers to sign contracts agreeing to abide by these prices.

Fair-trade laws assert that a product's image, determined in part by its price, is a property right of the manufacturer. Therefore, the manufacturer should have the authority to protect its asset by requiring retailers to maintain a minimum price. Exclusivity is one method manufacturers use to achieve this. By severely restricting the number of retail outlets that carry their figurines, Lladro can coordinate the prices charged by retail partners and discourage price discounting, which might adversely affect the company's image. The Lladro collection, shown in Figure 13.1, is one example of the figurines available only through fine stores like Macy's, Burdines, and a few other premier outlets.

Like the Robinson-Patman Act, fair-trade legislation has its roots in the Depression era. In 1931, California became the first state to enact fair-trade legislation. Most other states soon followed; only Missouri, the District of Columbia, Vermont, and Texas failed to adopt such laws.

A U.S. Supreme Court decision invalidated fair-trade contracts in interstate commerce, and Congress responded by passing the Miller Tydings Resale Maintenance Act (1937). This law exempted interstate fair-trade contracts from compliance with antitrust requirements, thus freeing states to keep these laws on their books if they so desired.

Over the years, fair-trade laws declined in importance as discounters emerged and price competition gained strength in marketing strategy. These laws became invalid with the passage of the Consumer Goods Pricing Act (1975), which halted all interstate enforcement of resale price maintenance provisions, an objective long sought by consumer groups.

PRICING OBJECTIVES AND THE MARKETING MIX

The extent to which any or all of the four factors of production—natural resources, capital, human resources, and entrepreneurship—are employed depends on the prices that those factors command. An individual firm's prices and the resulting purchases by its customers determine the company's revenue, influencing the profits it earns. Overall organizational objectives and more specific marketing objectives guide the development of pricing objectives, which in turn lead to development and implementation of more specific pricing policies and procedures.

<interactive>**learning goal**

CHAPTER OBJECTIVE #2: IDENTIFY THE MAJOR CATEGORIES OF PRICING OBJECTIVES.

A firm might, for instance, set a major overall goal of becoming the dominant producer in its domestic market. It might then develop a marketing objective of achieving maximum sales penetration in each region, followed by a related pricing objective of setting prices at levels that maximize sales. These objectives might lead to the adoption of a low-price policy implemented by offering substantial price discounts to channel members.

Price affects and is affected by the other elements of the marketing mix. Product decisions, promotional plans, and distribution choices all impact the price of a good or service. For example, products distributed through complex channels involving several intermediaries must be priced high enough to cover the markups needed to compensate wholesalers and retailers for services they provide. Basic so-called "fighting brands" are intended to capture market share from higher-priced, options-laden competitors by offering relatively low prices to entice customers to give up some options in return for a cost savings.

While pricing objectives vary from firm to firm, they can be classified into four major groups: (1) profitability objectives, (2) volume objectives, (3) meeting competition objectives, and (4) prestige objectives. Not-for-profit organizations as well as for-profit companies must consider objectives of one kind or another when developing pricing strategies. Table 13.1 outlines the pricing objectives marketers rely on to meet their organization's overall goals.

FIGURE 13.1

Protecting Brand Image by Avoiding Price Discounting

Profitability Objectives

Marketers at for-profit firms must set prices with profits in mind. Even not-for-profit organizations realize the importance of setting prices high enough to cover expenses and provide a financial cushion to cover unforeseen needs and expenses. As the Russian proverb goes, "There are two fools in every market: One asks too little, one asks too much." For consumers to pay prices that are either above average or below average, they must be convinced they are receiving fair value for money.

Economic theory is based on two major assumptions. It assumes, first, that firms will behave rationally and, second, that this rational behavior will result in an effort to maximize gains and minimize losses. Some marketers estimate profits by looking at historical sales data; others use elaborate calculations based on predicted future sales. It has been said that setting prices is an art, not a science. The talent lies in a marketer's ability to strike a balance between desired profits and the customer's perception of a product's value.

Marketers should evaluate and adjust prices continually to accommodate changes in the environment. The technological environment, for example, forces Internet marketers to respond quickly to competitors' pricing strategies. New search capabilities performed by shopping bots (described in Chapter 5) allow customers to compare prices locally, nationally, and globally in a matter of seconds.

Intense price competition—sometimes conducted even when it means forgoing profits altogether—often results when rival manufacturers battle for leadership positions in new product categories. Recently, Microsoft—which has yet to turn a profit on its Xbox video game—planned to disclose a deep price cut to revive flagging sales. Sony stole its thunder by announcing that the retail price of

TABLE 13.1

Pricing Objectives

OBJECTIVE	PURPOSE	EXAMPLE
Profitability objectives	■ Profit maximization ■ Target return	Low introductory interest rates on credit cards with high standard rates after 6 months
Volume objectives	■ Sales maximization ■ Market share	Dell's low-priced PCs increase market share and sales of services
Meeting competition objectives	■ Value pricing	Price wars among major airlines
Prestige objectives	■ Lifestyle ■ Image	High-priced luxury autos such as Ferrari and watches by Rolex
Not-for-profit objectives	■ Profit maximization ■ Cost recovery ■ Market incentives ■ Market suppression	High prices for tobacco and alcohol to reduce consumption

its PlayStation 2 would drop by a third, a move that Microsoft quickly matched. Meanwhile, Nintendo announced that it would undercut both products by pricing its Game Cube at $50 less than rival technologies.[5]

Profits are a function of revenue and expenses:

$$\text{Profits} = \text{Revenue} - \text{Expenses}.$$

Revenue is determined by the product's selling price and number of units sold:

$$\text{Total Revenue} = \text{Price} \times \text{Quantity Sold}.$$

Therefore, a profit maximizing price rises to the point at which further increases will cause disproportionate decreases in the number of units sold. A 10 percent price increase that results in only an 8 percent cut in volume will add to the firm's revenue. However, a 10 percent price hike that results in an 11 percent sales decline will reduce revenue.

Economists refer to this approach as *marginal analysis.* They identify **profit maximization** as the point at which the addition to total revenue is just balanced by the increase in total cost. Marketers must resolve a basic problem of how to achieve this delicate balance when they set prices. Relatively few firms actually hit this elusive target. A significantly larger number prefer to direct their effort toward more realistic goals.

Consequently, marketers commonly set **target-return objectives**—short-run or long-run goals usually stated as percentages of sales or investment. The practice has become particularly popular among large firms in which other pressures interfere with profit-maximization objectives. Target-return objectives offer several benefits for marketers in addition to resolving pricing questions. For example, these objectives serve as tools for evaluating performance. They also satisfy desires to generate "fair" profits as judged by management, stockholders, and the public.

Volume Objectives

Some economists and business executives argue that pricing behavior actually seeks to maximize sales within a given profit constraint. In other words, they set a minimum acceptable profit level and then seek to maximize sales (subject to this profit constraint) in the belief that the increased sales are more important than immediate high profits to the long-run competitive picture. Such a company continues to expand sales as long as its total profits do not drop below the minimum return acceptable to management.

In the continuing battle to maintain its online image as American's online store, Amazon.com decided to intensify the battle with smaller rivals with a special offer. Internet shoppers placing orders over $99 were provided with free shipping, a considerable savings particularly for bulky, heavy items. The promotion shown in Figure 13.2 describes the new offer, an alternative to a price cut, that Amazon marketers anticipate will in time cover the cost of the upfront offer over time with increased sales volume.

Sales maximization can also result from nonprice factors such as service and quality. Marketers increased sales for Dr. Scholl's new shoe insert, Dynastep, by advertising heavily in magazines. The ads explained how the Dynastep insert would help relieve leg and back pain. Priced around $14 per insert—twice as

FIGURE 13.2

Absorbing Shipping Expenses as a Pricing Tool to Achieve Volume Objectives

much as comparable offerings—Dynastep ran over its competitors to become number one in its category.

And the box said,
"Let me be free."
amazon.com
INTRODUCING
FREE SHIPPING
ON ORDERS OVER $99
Use Super Saver Shipping. Some restrictions apply. See Web site for details.

Another volume-related pricing objective is the *market-share objective*—the goal set for controlling a portion of the market for a firm's good or service. Dr. Scholl's was able to increase its market share to 29 percent by focusing on the benefits of Dynastep. The company's specific goal may be to maintain its present share of a particular market, or to increase its share, for instance, from 10 percent to 20 percent. Volume-related objectives such as sales maximization and market share play an important role in most firms' pricing decisions.

The PIMS Studies Market-share objectives may prove critical to the achievement of other organizational objectives. High sales, for example, often mean more profits. The **Profit Impact of Market Strategies (PIMS) project,** an extensive study conducted by the Marketing Science Institute, analyzed more than 2,000 firms and revealed that two of the most important factors influencing profitability were product quality and market share. Marketing campaigns with ads like the one in Figure 13.3 help to enhance profitability for PepsiCo's Pepsi soft drinks. Battling industry leader Coca-Cola worldwide, Pepsi's second-place global ranking is currently approaching the market leader as a strong and growing competitor. As one of two leaders in the soft-drink industry, PepsiCo marketers do not focus on low price in their consumer promotions, but rather on emphasizing values such as the pleasure derived from consuming the product. Numerous studies confirm the link between market share and profitability.

The relationship between market share and profitability is evident in PIMS data that reveal an average 32 percent return on investment (ROI) for firms with market shares above 40 percent. In contrast, average ROI decreases to 24 percent for firms whose market shares are between 20 and 40 percent. Firms with a minor market share (less than 10 percent) generate average pretax investment returns of approximately 13 percent.[6]

The relationship also applies to a firm's individual brands. PIMS researchers compared the top four brands in each market segment they studied. Their data revealed that the leading brand typically generates after-tax ROI of 18 percent, considerably higher than the second- ranked brand. Weaker brands, on average, fail to earn adequate returns.

Marketers have developed an underlying explanation of the positive relationship between profitability and market share. Firms with large shares accumulate greater operating experience and lower overall costs relative to competitors with smaller market shares. Accordingly, effective segmentation strategies might focus on obtaining larger shares of smaller markets and on avoiding smaller shares of larger ones. A firm might achieve higher financial returns by becoming a major competitor in several smaller market segments than by remaining a relatively minor player in a larger market.

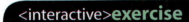

'NET EX: PROFIT IMPACT OF MARKET STRATEGIES (PIMS) PROJECT

Meeting Competition Objectives

A third set of pricing objectives seeks simply to meet competitors' prices. In many lines of business, firms set their own prices to match those of established industry price leaders.

Price is a pivotal factor in the ongoing competition between long-distance telephone services and wireless carriers. When cellular companies began offering huge bundles of "use-anytime" minutes with free long-distance service, MCI rolled out its Select 200 program—offering customers 200 minutes of long-distance calling time, with no monthly fees, taxes, or surcharges attached. In its efforts to stem defections of customers to wireless services, AT&T recently offered unlimited long-distance calling at a flat rate of $19.95 a month—but only between households served by AT&T. Since, from the customer's perspective, long-distance companies and cellular companies offer a service that is in many respects interchangeable, neither class of carrier could continue operations unless they came close to matching each other's prices.[7]

Pricing objectives tied directly to meeting prices charged by major competitors deemphasize the price element of the marketing mix and focus more strongly on nonprice variables. Pricing is a highly visible component of a firm's marketing mix and an easy and effective tool for obtaining a differential advantage over competitors. It is, however, a tool that other firms can easily duplicate through price reductions of their own. Airline price competition of recent years exemplifies the actions and reactions of competitors in this marketplace. Rather than emphasizing the lowest fares of any carrier, most airlines choose to compete by offering convenient arrival and departure times, enhanced passenger comfort with more room between each row, an attractive frequent-flyer program, and customer-focused alliances with automobile rental, lodging, and other partners. Some airlines even returned to providing passenger meals on long flights, a practice that had previously been discontinued in a cost-cutting effort. Even when price increases are needed to remain profitable, an announced price hike by one airline will be implemented only if its major competitors match the new price. Because price changes directly affect overall profitability in an industry, many firms attempt to promote stable prices by meeting competitors' prices and competing for market share by focusing on product strategies, promotional decisions, and distribution—the non-price elements of the marketing mix.

Lands' End, a Sears catalog and online retail subsidiary, focuses on such nonprice elements. The copy-intensive ad in Figure 13.4 describes the benefits of the product, the range of colors and styles, the company's excellence in customer service, and its easy-ordering system, as well as price. While low price is a key attraction, the emphasis on other product and customer-service benefits sets Lands' End apart.

Value Pricing When discounts become normal elements of a competitive marketplace, other marketing-mix elements gain importance in purchase decisions. In such instances, overall product value, not just price, determines product choice. In recent years, a new strategy—**value pricing**—has emerged that emphasizes the benefits a product provides in comparison to the price and quality levels of competing offerings. This strategy typically works best for relatively low-priced goods and services.

Laundry detergents are a good example of value pricing. The label on Dash detergent proclaims *Value Price,* while Arm & Hammer's label assures customers that it *Cleans Great—Value Price, Too!* Yes detergent announces *Great Value!,* while Ultra Rinso claims *Super Value,* and the back label on Ultra Trend boasts that it offers *hard-working performance at a reasonable price.* The label on another detergent, All, simply advises customers to *Compare & Save.*

Value-priced products generally cost less than premium brands, but marketers point out that *value* does not necessarily mean *inexpensive.* The challenge for those who compete on value is to convince customers that low-priced brands offer quality comparable to that of a higher-priced product. An increasing number of alternative products and private-label brands has resulted in a more competitive marketplace in recent years. Pampers Premium baby diapers, like many Procter & Gamble brands, is premium priced, often selling at twice the price of rival store-brands. Luvs, a low-end P&G brand, costs 30 percent less. In a no-growth market marked with signs that shoppers are switching to lower-priced competition, P&G recently began to phase out Pampers Premium in favor of a product intended to deliver discernable extra value. Baby Stages—also priced at the high end of the market—is designed for specific stages during a child's first two years: extra absorbency for newborns, stretchy sides for crawlers, and pull-up pants for toddlers.[8]

Value pricing is perhaps best seen in the personal computer industry. In the past few years, PC prices have collapsed, reducing

FIGURE 13.3

Increasing Market Share and Profitability by Emphasizing Product Quality and "The Joy of Pepsi"

In the extremely price-competitive category of laundry products, Purex invites customers to make value comparisons—"Don't waste money on dirt."

Briefly Speaking

A thing is worth whatever the buyer will pay for it.

Publilius Syrus (1st century B.C.) Latin mimographer

the effectiveness of traditional pricing strategies intended to meet competition. In fact, PCs priced at under $600 are now the fastest-growing segment of the market. This category now accounts for almost 20 percent of PCs sold in stores. Industry leaders like Dell, Hewlett-Packard/Compaq, and Gateway cannot continue to cut prices, so they are adding features such as increased memory and 3-D graphic accelerator cards that increase speed. Dell has even launched a home-installation plan to offset tumbling prices in the PC market.[9] The "Marketing Hits" Interactive Example demonstrates how marketers are able to build a perception of value into a readily available resource: water.

<interactive>**example** 

MARKETING HIT: HOW PEPSICO IS MAKING A KILLING WITH AQUAFINA BOTTLED WATER

Prestige Objectives

The final category of pricing objectives, unrelated to either profitability or sales volume, is prestige objectives. Prestige pricing establishes a relatively high price to develop and maintain an image of quality and exclusiveness that appeals to status-conscious consumers. Such objectives reflect marketers' recognition of the role of price in creating an overall image of the firm and its product offerings.

Prestige objectives affect the price tags of such products as Waterford crystal, Alfa Romeo sports cars, Omega watches, and Tiffany jewelry. When a perfume marketer sets a price of $135 or more per ounce, this choice reflects an emphasis on image far more than the cost of ingredients. Analyses have shown that ingredients account for less than 5 percent of a perfume's cost. Thus, advertisements for Joy that promote the fragrance as the "costliest perfume in the world" use price to promote product prestige.

In contrast to low-price strategies used by marketers of economy cars, ads for Jaguar tout exclusivity and target wealthy clientele. Appearing in upscale magazines such as *Smithsonian,* the ad in Figure 13.5 states: "Follow the Leader is only fun if you're the leader."

In the business world, private jet ownership imparts an image of prestige, power, and high price tags—too high for most business travelers to consider. Recognizing that cost is the primary factor that makes jet ownership prohibitive, companies like Flight Options and NetJets have created an alternative—fractional ownership. The companies target firms whose executives travel periodically rather than year round. Instead of buying a preowned plane, they take a share in a new jet. Fractional ownership companies account for almost half the backlog of orders at the five major manufacturers of business jets.[10]

FIGURE 13.4

Lands' End: Implementing the Pricing Objective of Meeting Competition

PRICING OBJECTIVES OF NOT-FOR-PROFIT ORGANIZATIONS

Pricing typically is a key element of the marketing mix for not-for-profit organizations. Pricing strategy can help these groups to achieve a variety of organizational goals:

1. *Profit maximization.* While not-for-profit organizations by definition do not cite profitability as a primary goal, there are numerous instances in which they do try to maximize their returns on single events or a series of events. A $1,000-a-plate political fundraiser is a classic example.
2. *Cost recovery.* Some not-for-profit organizations attempt to recover only the actual cost of operating the unit. Mass transit, toll roads and bridges, and publicly supported colleges are common examples. The amount of recovered costs is often dictated by tradition, competition, or public opinion.
3. *Market incentives.* Other not-for-profit groups follow a lower-than-average pricing policy or offer a free service to encourage increased usage of the good or service. Seattle's bus system offers free service in the downtown area in an attempt to reduce traffic congestion, encourage retail sales, and minimize the effort required to access downtown public services.
4. *Market suppression.* Price can also discourage consumption. High prices help to accomplish social objectives independent of the costs of providing goods or services. Illustrations include tobacco and alcohol taxes (the so-called "sin taxes"), parking fines, tolls, and gasoline excise taxes.

METHODS FOR DETERMINING PRICES

Marketers determine prices in two basic ways—by applying the theoretical concepts of supply and demand and by completing cost-oriented analyses. During the first part of the previous century, most discussions for price determination emphasized the classical concepts of supply and demand. During the last half of the 20th century, however, the emphasis shifted to a cost-oriented approach. Hindsight reveals certain flaws in both concepts.

Treatments of this subject often overlook another concept of price determination—one based on the impact of custom and tradition. **Customary prices** are retail prices that consumers expect as a result of tradition and social habit. Candy makers have attempted to maintain traditional price levels by considerably reducing product size. Similar practices have prevailed in the marketing of soft drinks as bottlers attempt to balance consumer expectations of customary prices with the realities of rising costs.

Wm. Wrigley Jr. Co., manufacturer of such chewing gum standards as Juicy Fruit, Doublemint, and Big Red, took advantage of the weakness in the industry's customary pricing strategy by introducing a smaller-quantity pack at a lower price. While competitors continued to offer only seven-piece packs for 35 cents, Wrigley priced its five-piece packs at 25 cents. To spur impulse buying, the company prominently displayed the price on the package. The strategy was so successful that within two years of its inception, Wrigley discontinued selling seven-stick gum packs.

At some point, someone has to set initial prices for products. In addition, competitive moves and cost changes necessitate periodic reviews of price structures. The remaining sections delve into the issue of price determination. This section also considers how marketers can most effectively integrate the concepts to develop realistic pricing systems.

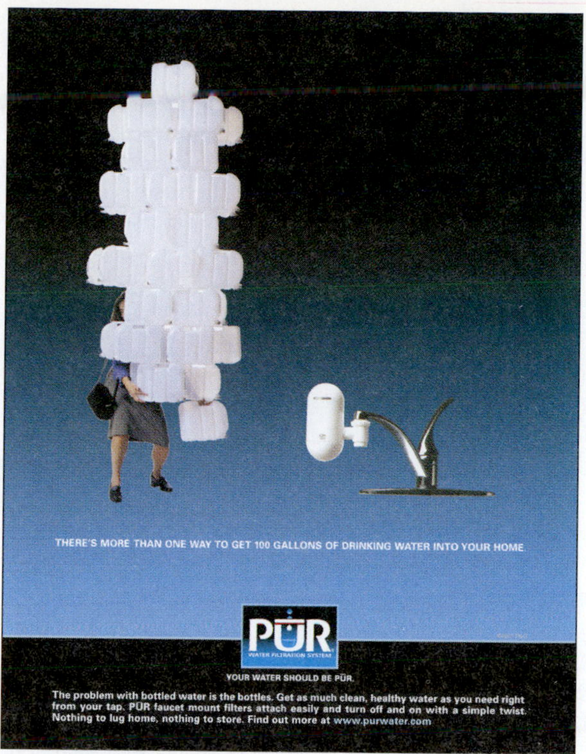

This message is intended to be a wake-up call to consumers who have become accustomed to buying bottled water—a reminder that water can be obtained practically free from a tap. PŪR offers healthy and great-tasting filtered water at one-tenth the cost of bottled water.

PRICE DETERMINATION IN ECONOMIC THEORY

Microeconomics suggests a way of determining prices that assumes a profit-maximization objective. This technique attempts to derive correct equilibrium prices in the marketplace by comparing supply and demand. It also requires more complete analysis than actual business firms typically conduct.

Demand refers to a schedule of the amounts of a firm's product that consumers will purchase at different prices during a specified period. *Supply* refers to a schedule of the amounts of a good or service that will be offered for sale at different prices during a specified time period. These schedules may vary for different types of market structures. Businesses operate and set prices in four types of market structures: pure competition, monopolistic competition, oligopoly, and monopoly.

Pure competition is a market structure with so many buyers and sellers that no single participant can significantly influence price. Pure competition presupposes other market conditions, as well: homogeneous products and ease of entry for sellers due to low start-up costs. The agricultural sector exhibits many characteristics of a purely competitive market, making it the closest actual example.

Monopolistic competition typifies most retailing and features large numbers of buyers and sellers. These diverse parties exchange heterogeneous, relatively well-differentiated products, giving marketers some control over prices.

Relatively few sellers compete in an *oligopoly.* Each seller may affect the market, but no single seller controls it. High start-up costs form significant barriers to entry for new competitors. Each firm's demand curve in an oligopolistic market displays a unique kink at the current market price. Because of the impact of a single competitor on total industry sales, competitors usually quickly match any attempt by one firm to generate additional sales by

FIGURE 13.5

Emphasizing Exclusivity as Part of Jaguar's Prestige Pricing

reducing prices. Price cutting in such industry structures is likely to reduce total industry revenues. Oligopolies operate in the petroleum refining, automobile, and tobacco industries.

The availability of alternative air transportation in the form of such discount carriers as Southwest Airlines and Frontier Airlines forces established air carriers to maintain competitive airfares—or risk losing business to the upstarts. For example, before JetBlue and Southwest launched their first coast-to-coast flights from Washington to Los Angeles, transcontinental flights were the domain of bigger, higher-fare airlines. If these alternatives disappear, prices will probably rise.[11]

A *monopoly* is a market structure where only one seller of a product exists and for which there are no close substitutes. Antitrust legislation has nearly eliminated all but temporary monopolies, such as those created through patent protection. The "Solving an Ethical Controversy" Interactive Example explores how pharmaceutical companies protect their pricing policies through the exercise of patents. Regulated industries, such as utility companies, constitute another form of monopoly. The government allows regulated monopolies in markets in which competition would lead to an uneconomical duplication of services. In return for such a license, government reserves the right to regulate the monopoly's rate of return.

RIGHT/WRONG: SOLVING AN ETHICAL CONTROVERSY—WHAT'S A FAIR PRICE FOR PRESCRIPTION DRUGS?

The four types of market structures are compared in Table 13.2 on the following bases: number of competitors, ease of entry into the industry by new firms, similarity of competing products, degree of control over price by individual firms, and the elasticity or inelasticity of the demand curve facing the individual firm. Elasticity—the degree of consumer responsiveness to changes in price—is discussed in more detail in a later section.

Cost and Revenue Curves

Marketers must set a price for a product that generates sufficient revenue to cover the costs of producing and marketing it. A product's total cost is composed of total variable costs and total fixed costs. *Variable costs* change with the level of production (such as human resource and raw materials costs), while *fixed costs* remain stable at any production level within a certain range (such as lease payments or insurance costs). *Average total costs* are calculated by dividing the sum of the variable and fixed costs by the number of units

TABLE 13.2

Distinguishing Features of the Four Market Structures

	TYPE OF MARKET STRUCTURE			
CHARACTERISTICS	**PURE COMPETITION**	**MONOPOLISTIC COMPETITION**	**OLIGOPOLY**	**MONOPOLY**
Number of competitors	Many	Few to many	Few	No direct competitors
Ease of entry into industry by new firms	Easy	Somewhat difficult	Difficult	Regulated by government
Similarity of goods or services offered by competing firms	Similar	Different	Can be either similar or different	No directly competing goods or services
Control over prices by individual firms	None	Some	Some	Considerable
Demand curves facing individual firms	Totally elastic	Can be either elastic or inelastic	Kinked; inelastic below kink; more elastic above	Can be either elastic or inelastic
Examples	2000-acre ranch	Gap stores	Shell	Duke Energy

produced. Finally, *marginal cost* is the change in total cost that results from producing an additional unit of output.

The demand side of the pricing equation focuses on revenue curves. Average revenue is calculated by dividing total revenue by the quantity associated with these revenues. Average revenue is actually the demand curve facing the firm. Marginal revenue is the change in total revenue that results from selling an additional unit of output. Figure 13.6 shows the relationships of various cost and revenue measures; the firm maximizes its profits when marginal costs equal marginal revenues.

Table 13.3 illustrates why the intersection of the marginal cost and marginal revenue curves is the logical point at which to maximize revenue for the organization. Although the firm can earn a profit at several different prices, the price at which it earns maximum profits is $22. At a price of $24, $66 in profits are earned—$4 less than the $70 profit at the $22 price. If a price of $20 is set to attract additional sales, the marginal costs of the extra sales ($7) are greater than the marginal revenues received ($6), and total profits decline.

The Concept of Elasticity in Pricing Strategy

Although the intersection of the marginal cost and marginal revenue curves determines the level of output, the impact of changes in price on sales varies greatly. In order to understand why it fluctuates, it is necessary to understand the concept of elasticity.

<interactive>learning goal

CHAPTER OBJECTIVE #3: EXPLAIN PRICE ELASTICITY AND ITS DETERMINANTS.

Elasticity is the measure of responsiveness of purchasers and suppliers to price changes. The price elasticity of demand (or elasticity of demand) is the percentage change in the quantity of a good or service demanded divided by the percentage change in its price. A 10 percent increase in the price of eggs that results in a 5 percent decrease in the quantity of eggs demanded yields a price elasticity of demand for eggs of 0.5. The price elasticity of supply of a product is the percentage change in the quantity of a good or service supplied divided by the percentage change in its price. A 10 percent increase in the price of shampoo that results in a 25 percent increase in the quantity supplied yields a price elasticity of supply for shampoo of 2.5.

Consider a case in which a 1 percent change in price causes more than a 1 percent change in the quantity supplied or demanded. Numerically, that means an elasticity greater than 1.0. When the elasticity of demand or supply is greater than 1.0, that demand or supply is said to be elastic. If a 1 percent change in

FIGURE 13.6

Determining Price by Relating Marginal Revenue to Marginal Cost

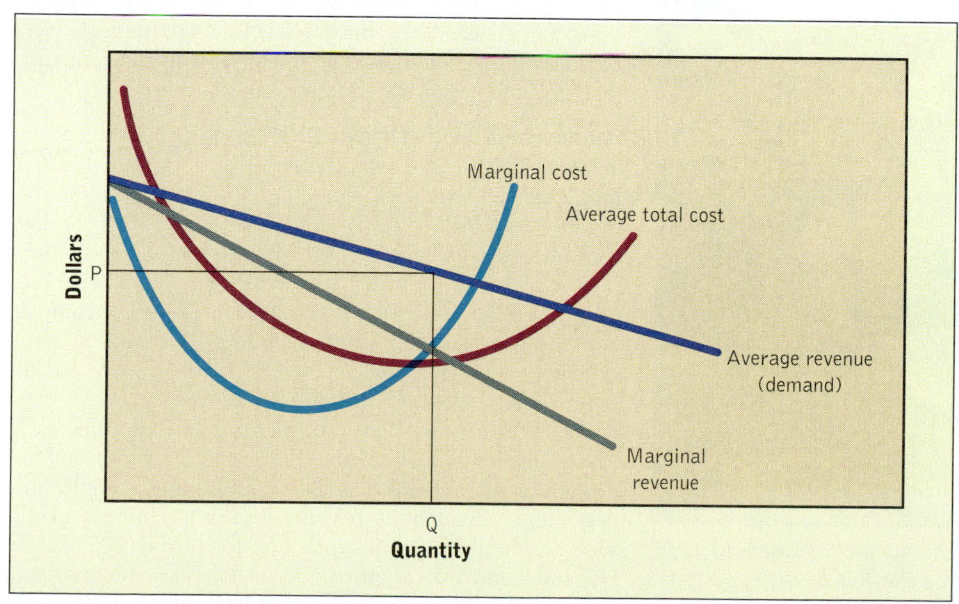

TABLE 13.3

Price Determination Using Marginal Analysis

PRICE	NUMBER SOLD	TOTAL REVENUE	MARGINAL REVENUE	TOTAL COSTS	MARGINAL COSTS	PROFITS (TOTAL REVENUE MINUS TOTAL COSTS)
—	—	—	—	—	—	($50)
$34	1	$34	$34	57	$7	(23)
32	2	64	30	62	5	2
30	3	90	26	66	4	24
28	4	112	22	69	3	43
26	5	130	18	73	4	57
24	6	144	14	78	5	66
22	7	154	10	84	6	70
20	8	160	6	91	7	69
18	9	162	2	100	9	62
16	10	160	(2)	110	11	50

price results in less than a 1 percent change in quantity, a product's elasticity of demand or supply will be less than 1.0. In that case, the demand or supply is called *inelastic*. For example, the demand for cigarettes is relatively inelastic; research studies have shown that a 10 percent increase in cigarette prices results in only a 4 percent sales decline.

The U.S. Postal Service, the subject of Case 13.1, uses promotional messages like this to rally support for policy changes—such as recent price increases—that affect users of its mail services.

In countries such as Argentina or Brazil, where the annual inflation rate has been known to top 100 percent, prices on almost all products have risen accordingly. These higher prices have led to elastic demand for some items, such as houses and cars; many of the cars on Argentina's roads are over 10 years old, and the nation's housing market is severely depressed. For other products, demand has been inelastic; families continue to buy food because, after all, they need to eat. However, even if they do not affect demand, inflationary prices can alter consumers' buying patterns. Lower-income Brazilians, for instance, buy all the food items they can afford when they get each paycheck.

Determinants of Elasticity Why is the elasticity of supply or demand high for some products and low for others? What determines demand elasticity? One major factor influencing the elasticity of demand is the availability of substitutes or complements. If consumers can easily find close substitutes for a good or service, the product's demand tends to be elastic. For example, the relatively inelastic demand for motor oil reflects its role as a complement to a more important product, gasoline. The end-of-chapter case explores pricing decisions at the U.S. Postal Service, including the effect of rate hikes on consumer demand.

As increasing numbers of buyers and sellers complete their business transactions online, the elasticity of a product's demand is drastically affected. Take large discounters, for example. Small businesses and individual do-it-yourselfers shop Home Depot for tools, such as wheelbarrows; parents look for birthday gifts at Toys "R" Us; and homeowners go to Circuit City for new refrigerators or stoves. Today, however, the Internet lets consumers contact product manufacturers and service providers directly, often giving them better selections and prices for their efforts. Wheelbarrows, for instance, were once sold at almost identical prices at a relatively small number of retail outlets (inelastic demand). Today's shoppers can pick up a wheelbarrow at dozens of different locations—traditional hardware stores, plant nurseries, home-improvement centers, discount stores, and even some department stores. No longer does one wheelbarrow fit all—the product comes in different sizes, colors, and materials to match the specific needs of different users. The availability of different models and different prices for each combine to create a market characterized by demand elasticity.

Elasticity of demand also depends on whether a product is perceived as a necessity or a luxury. The Four Seasons chain of luxury hotels and resorts enjoys such a strong reputation for service, comfort, and exclusiveness that it has become a favorite among affluent individual travelers and business professionals. The combination of personal service and exclusiveness attracts a select group of upscale travelers who consider reservations at Four Seasons hotels essential components of their trips to Atlanta or Tokyo. Because its accommodations are viewed as a necessity, not a luxury, sales remain strong despite rising room rates.

Most people regard high-fashion clothes, such as a $2,000 Armani suit, as luxuries. If prices for designer outfits increase, people can respond by purchasing lower-priced substitutes instead. In contrast, medical and dental care are considered necessities, so price changes have little effect on the frequency of medical or dental visits.

However, under the continuing influence of higher prices, some products once regarded as necessities may be dismissed as luxuries, leading to decreasing demand. Formerly booming personal computer sales have shown little or no growth in recent years. As home movies make the expensive conversion from VHS to DVD, many consumers choose to wait rather than spend the extra money for a DVD player and discs. In Figure 13.7, leading U.S. consumer electronics retailer Best Buy works hard to persuade potential buyers that a next-generation digital camera is a necessity rather than a luxury.

FIGURE 13.7

Promoting Digital Cameras as Necessities to Stimulate Demand and Lessen the Product's Price Elasticity

Elasticity also depends on the portion of a person's budget that he or she spends on a good or service. People no longer really need matches. They can easily find good substitutes. Nonetheless, the demand for matches remains very inelastic because people spend so little on them that they hardly notice a price change. In contrast, the demand for housing or transportation is not totally inelastic, even though they are necessities, because both consume large parts of a consumer's budget.

Elasticity of demand also responds to consumers' time perspectives. Demand often shows less elasticity in the short run than in the long run. Consider the demand for home air conditioning. In the short run, people pay rising energy prices because they find it difficult to cut back on the quantities they use. Accustomed to living with specific temperature settings and dressing in certain ways, they prefer to pay more during a few months out of the year than to explore other possibilities. Over time, though, with global warming becoming a real and present danger, they may find ways to economize. They can better insulate their homes, or plant shade trees.

Sometimes the usual patterns do not hold true, though. Alcohol and tobacco, which are not necessities but do occupy large shares of some personal budgets, are also subject to inelastic demand.

Elasticity and Revenue The elasticity of demand exerts an important influence on variations in total revenue as a result of changes in the price of a good or service. Assume, for example, that San Francisco's Bay Area Rapid Transit (BART) officials are considering alternative methods of raising more money for the city budget. One possible method for increasing revenues would be to change rail pass fares for BART commuters. But should the city raise or lower the price of a pass? The correct answer depends on the elasticity of demand for subway rides. A 10 percent decrease in fares should attract more riders, but unless it stimulates more than a 10 percent increase in riders, total revenue will fall. A 10 percent increase in fares will bring in more money per rider, but if more than 10 percent of the riders stop using the subway, total revenue will fall. A price cut will increase revenue only for a product with elastic demand, and a price increase will raise revenue only for a product with inelastic demand. BART officials seem to believe that the demand for rapid rail transit is inelastic; they raise fares when they need more money for the city budget.

Practical Problems of Price Theory

Marketers may thoroughly understand price theory concepts but still encounter difficulty applying them in practice. What practical limitations interfere with price setting?

<interactive>**learning goal**

CHAPTER OBJECTIVE #4: LIST THE PRACTICAL PROBLEMS INVOLVED IN APPLYING PRICE THEORY CONCEPTS TO ACTUAL PRICING DECISIONS.

First, many firms do not attempt to maximize profits. Economic analysis is subject to the same limitations as the assumptions on which it is based—for example, the proposition that all firms attempt to maximize profits. Second, it is difficult to estimate demand curves. Modern accounting procedures provide managers with a clear understanding of cost structures, so managers can readily comprehend the supply side of the pricing equation. But they find it difficult to estimate demand at various price levels. Demand curves must be based on marketing research estimates that may be less exact than cost figures. Although the demand element can be identified, it is often difficult to measure in real-world settings.

PRICE DETERMINATION IN PRACTICE

The practical limitations inherent in price theory have forced practitioners to turn to other techniques. *Cost-plus pricing,* the most popular method, uses a base-cost figure per unit and adds a markup to cover unassigned costs and to provide a profit. The only real difference among the multitude of cost-plus techniques is the relative sophistication of the costing procedures employed. For example, a local apparel shop may set prices by adding a 45 percent markup to the invoice price charged by the supplier. The markup is expected to cover all other expenses and permit the owner to earn a reasonable return on the sale of clothes.

<interactive>**learning goal**

CHAPTER OBJECTIVE #5: EXPLAIN THE MAJOR COST-PLUS APPROACHES TO PRICE SETTING.

In contrast to this rather simple pricing mechanism, a large manufacturer may employ a complex pricing formula requiring computer calculations. However, this method merely adds a more complicated procedure to the simpler, traditional method for calculating costs. In the end, someone still must make a decision about the markup. The apparel shop and the large manufacturer may figure costs differently, but they are remarkably similar in completing the markup side of the equation.

Cost-plus pricing often works well for a business that keeps its costs low, allowing it to set its prices lower than those of competitors and still make a profit. American discounter Wal-Mart keeps costs low by buying most of its inventory directly from manufacturers and relying on wholesalers and other intermediaries only in special instances like localized items. This strategy has helped the discounter in its rise to become the world's largest retailer.

Alternative Pricing Procedures

The two most common cost-oriented pricing procedures are the full-cost method and the incremental-cost method. *Full-cost pricing* uses all relevant variable costs in setting a product's price. In addition, it allocates those fixed costs that cannot be directly attributed to the production of the specific item being priced. Under the full-cost method, if job order 515 in a printing plant amounts to .000127 percent of the plant's total output, then .000127 percent of the firm's overhead expenses are charged to that job. This approach allows the marketer to recover all costs plus the amount added as a profit margin.

The full-cost approach has two basic deficiencies. First, there is no consideration of competition or demand for the item. Perhaps no one wants to pay the price the firm has calculated. Second, any method for allocating overhead (fixed expenses) is arbitrary and may be unrealistic. In manufacturing, overhead allocations often are tied to direct labor hours. In retailing, the square footage of each profit center is sometimes the factor used in computations. Regardless of the technique employed, it is difficult to show a cause-effect relationship between the allocated cost and most products.

One way to overcome the arbitrary allocation of fixed expenses is with *incremental-cost pricing,* which attempts to use only those costs directly attributable to a specific output in setting prices. Consider a small-scale manufacturer with the following income statement:

Sales (10,000 units at $10)		$100,000
Expenses:		
Variable	$50,000	
Fixed	40,000	90,000
Net Profit		$ 10,000

Suppose the firm is offered a contract for an additional 5,000 units. Since the peak season is over, these items can be produced at the same average variable cost. Assume that the labor force would otherwise be working on maintenance projects. How low should the firm price its product in order to get the contract?

Under the full-cost approach, the lowest price would be $9 per unit. This figure is obtained by dividing the $90,000 in expenses by an output of 10,000 units. The incremental approach, on the other hand, could permit any price above $5, which would significantly increase the possibility of securing the additional contract. This price would be composed of the $5 variable cost associated with each unit of production plus a $.10-per-unit contribution to fixed expenses and overhead. With a $5.10 proposed price, the income statement now looks like this:

Sales (10,000 at $10; 5,000 at $5.10)		$125,500
Expenses:		
Variable	$75,000	
Fixed	40,000	115,000
Net Profit		$ 10,500

Profits thus are increased under the incremental approach.

Admittedly, the illustration is based on two assumptions: (1) the ability to isolate markets such that selling at the lower price will not affect the price received in other markets, and (2) the absence of legal restrictions on the firm. The example, however, does illustrate that profits can sometimes be enhanced by using the incremental approach.

Breakeven Analysis

Breakeven analysis is a means of determining the number of goods or services that must be sold at a given price to generate sufficient revenue to cover total costs. Figure 13.8 graphically depicts this process. The total cost curve includes both fixed and variable segments, and total fixed cost is represented by a horizontal line. Average variable cost is assumed to be constant per unit as it was in the example for incremental pricing.

The breakeven point is the point at which total revenue just equals total cost. In the example in Figure 13.8, a selling price of $10 and an average variable cost of $5 result in a per-unit contribution to fixed cost of $5. The breakeven point in terms of units is found by using the following formula, where the per-unit contribution equals the product's price less the variable cost per unit:

$$\text{Breakeven Point (in units)} = \frac{\text{Total Fixed Cost}}{\text{Per-Unit Contribution to Fixed Cost}}$$

$$\text{Breakeven Point (in units)} = \frac{\$40{,}000}{\$5} = 8{,}000 \text{ units}$$

The breakeven point is found with the following formula:

$$\text{Breakeven Point (in dollars)} = \frac{\text{Total Fixed Cost}}{1 - \frac{\text{Variable Cost per Unit}}{\text{Price}}}$$

$$\text{Breakeven Point (in dollars)} = \frac{\$40{,}000}{1 - (\$5/\$10)} = \frac{\$40{,}000}{0.5} = \$80{,}000$$

Once the breakeven point has been reached, sufficient revenues will have been obtained from sales to cover all fixed costs. Any additional sales will generate per-unit profits equal to the difference between the product's selling price and the variable cost of each unit. As Figure 13.8 reveals, sales of 8,001 units (1 unit above the breakeven point) will produce net profits of $5 ($10 sales price less per-unit variable cost of $5). Once all fixed costs have been covered, the per-unit contribution will become the per-unit profit.

FIGURE 13.8

Breakeven Chart

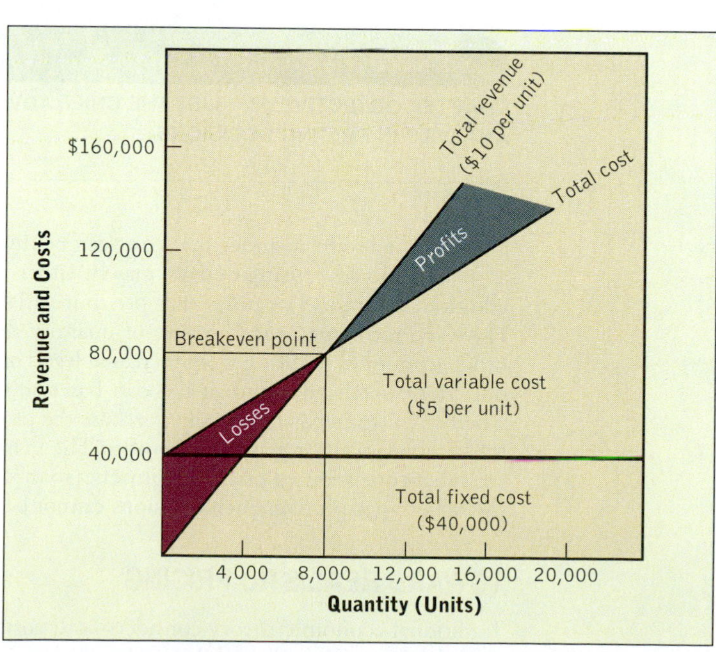

Thomas Lipsky knew enough about breakeven analysis to convince himself that he could start a record label—and make money. With limited financing and even less clout in the music business, the Raleigh, North Carolina–based concert promoter knew he would not be signing hot groups like the Backstreet Boys, who can sell 1.2 million copies of a new CD in a single week. So he signed the only acts he could afford: 1980s rock groups like Slaughter and Warrant that featured gaudy guitar solos and oversized stage theatrics. Even though Slaughter had sold 3 million albums in 1990, they quickly fell off the charts—and Lipsky had much more modest expectations for the Las Vegas–based group.

The key to making money was contained within the breakeven formula. Slaughter already owned a recording studio, so the $100,000 advance Lipsky shelled out went into the band members' pockets. Another $150,000 was spent on promotion, much of which went to retailers to persuade them to stock his product. Lipsky's record company makes a gross profit of $5 per disc, so he starts making money once an album sells more than 50,000 copies. Even though the advances are meager, the band goes along with it because (1) nobody else is beating down their doors to record them, and (2) the new albums make it easier to convince concert promoters to book them for tours. Lipsky is happy; the band rocks; and breakeven analysis shows how profits can be gleaned from modest sales by shrewd marketers who can control overhead.[12]

Target Returns Although breakeven analysis indicates the sales level at which the firm will incur neither profits nor losses, most firms' managers include a targeted profit in their analyses. In some instances, management sets a desired dollar return when considering a proposed new product or other marketing action. A retailer may set a desired profit of $250,000 in considering whether to expand to a second location. In other instances, the target return may be expressed in percentages, such as a 15 percent return on sales. These target returns can be modified as follows:

$$\text{Breakeven Point (including specific dollar target return)} = \frac{\text{Total Fixed Cost} + \text{Profit Objective}}{\text{Per-Unit Contribution}}$$

$$\text{Breakeven Point (in units)} = \frac{\$40{,}000 + \$15{,}000}{\$5} = 11{,}000 \text{ units}$$

If the target return is expressed as a percentage of sales, it can be included in the breakeven formula as a variable cost. Suppose the marketer in the preceding example seeks a 10 percent return on sales. The desired return is $1 for each product sold (the $10 per-unit selling price multiplied by the 10 percent return on sales). In this case, the basic breakeven formula will remain unchanged, although the variable cost per unit will be increased to reflect the target return, and the per-unit contribution to fixed cost will be reduced to $4. As a result, the breakeven point will increase from 8,000 to 10,000 units:

$$\text{Breakeven Point} = \frac{\$40{,}000}{\$4} = 10{,}000 \text{ units}$$

Evaluation of Breakeven Analysis Breakeven analysis is an effective tool for marketers in assessing the sales required for covering costs and achieving specified profit levels. It is easily understood by both marketing and nonmarketing executives and may help them decide whether required sales levels for a certain price are in fact realistic goals. However, it has its shortcomings.

<interactive>**learning goal**

CHAPTER OBJECTIVE #6: LIST THE CHIEF ADVANTAGES AND SHORTCOMINGS OF USING BREAKEVEN ANALYSIS IN PRICING DECISIONS.

First, the model assumes that costs can be divided into fixed and variable categories. Some costs, such as salaries and advertising outlays, may be either fixed or variable depending on the particular situation. In addition, the model assumes that per-unit variable costs do not change at different levels of operation. However, these may vary because of quantity discounts, more efficient utilization of the workforce, or other economies resulting from increased levels of production and sales. Finally, the basic breakeven model does not consider demand. It is a cost-based model and does not directly address the crucial question of whether consumers will actually purchase the product at the specified price and in the quantities required for breaking even or generating profits. The marketer's challenge is to modify the breakeven analysis and the other cost-oriented pricing approaches to incorporate demand analysis. Pricing must be examined from the buyer's perspective. Such decisions cannot be made by considering only cost factors.

TOWARD REALISTIC PRICING

Traditional economic theory considers both costs and demand in determining an equilibrium price. The dual elements of supply and demand are balanced at the point of equilibrium. In actual practice, however, most pricing approaches are largely cost oriented. Since purely cost-oriented approaches to pricing violate the marketing concept, modifications that will add demand analysis to the pricing decision are required.

Consumer research on such issues as degree of price elasticity, consumer price expectations, existence and size of specific market segments, and buyer perceptions of strengths and weaknesses of substitute products is necessary for developing sales estimates at different prices. Because much of the resulting data involves perceptions, attitudes, and future expectations of present and potential customers, such estimates are likely to be less precise than cost estimates.

The Modified Breakeven Concept

The breakeven analysis method illustrated in Figure 13.8 assumes a constant $10 retail price regardless of quantity. But what happens at different retail prices? As Figure 13.9 shows, a more sophisticated approach called **modified breakeven analysis** combines the traditional breakeven analysis model with an evaluation of consumer demand.

<interactive>**learning goal**

CHAPTER OBJECTIVE #7: EXPLAIN THE SUPERIORITY OF MODIFIED BREAKEVEN ANALYSIS OVER THE BASIC BREAKEVEN MODEL AND THE ROLE OF YIELD MANAGEMENT IN PRICING DECISIONS.

Table 13.4 summarizes both the cost and revenue aspects of a number of alternative retail prices. The $5 unit variable cost and the $40,000 total fixed cost are based on the costs utilized in the basic breakeven model. The expected unit sales for each specified retail price are obtained from marketing research. The table contains the information necessary for calculating the breakeven point for each of the five retail price alternatives. These points are shown in Part A of Figure 13.9.

The data shown in the first two columns of Table 13.4 represent a demand schedule that indicates the number of units consumers are expected to purchase at each of a series of retail prices. As Part B of Figure 13.9 shows, these data can be superimposed onto a breakeven chart to identify the range of feasible prices for the marketer to charge.

Figure 13.9 reveals that the range of profitable prices exists from a low of approximately $8 ($TR_4$) to a high of $10 ($TR^2$), with a price of $9 ($TR_3$) generating the greatest projected profits. Changing the retail price produces a new breakeven point. At a relatively high $15 ($TR_1$) retail price, the breakeven point is 4,000 units; at a $10 retail price, it is 8,000 units; and at the lowest price considered, $7 ($TR_5$), it is 20,000 units.

FIGURE 13.9

Modified Breakeven Chart: Parts A and B

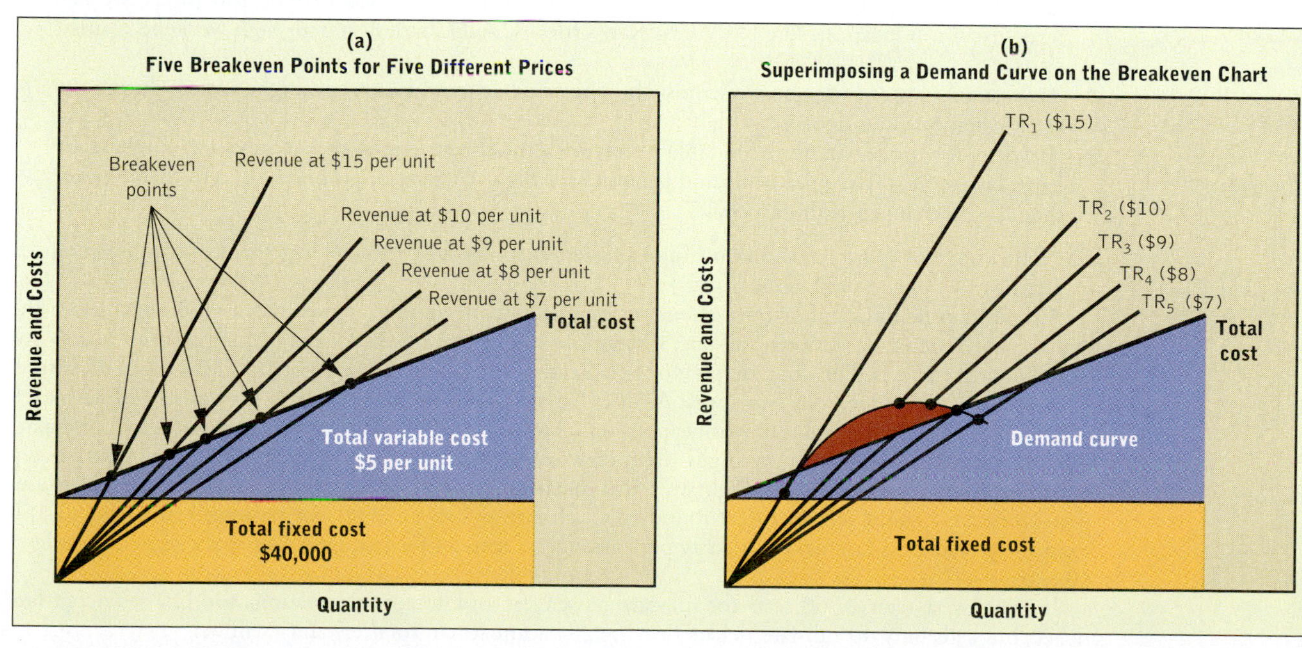

TABLE 13.4

Revenue and Cost Data for Modified Breakeven Analysis

	REVENUES		COSTS				
PRICE	QUANTITY DEMANDED	TOTAL REVENUE	TOTAL FIXED COST	TOTAL VARIABLE COST	TOTAL COST	BREAKEVEN POINT (NUMBER OF SALES REQUIRED TO BREAK EVEN)	TOTAL PROFIT (OR LOSS)
$15	2,500	$37,500	$40,000	$12,500	$52,500	4,000	$(15,000)
10	10,000	100,000	40,000	50,000	90,000	8,000	10,000
9	13,000	117,000	40,000	65,000	105,000	10,000	12,000
8	14,000	112,000	40,000	70,000	110,000	13,334	2,000
7	15,000	105,000	40,000	75,000	115,000	20,000	(10,000)

The contribution of modified breakeven analysis is that it forces the marketer to consider whether the consumer is likely to purchase the number of units of a good or service required for achieving breakeven at a given price. It demonstrates that a large number of units sold does not necessarily produce added profits, since—other things equal—lower prices are necessary for stimulating additional sales. Consequently, it is important to consider both costs and consumer demand in determining the most appropriate price.

Yield Management

When most of a firm's costs are fixed over a wide range of outputs, the primary determinant of profitability will be the amount of revenue generated by sales. **Yield management** strategies allow marketers to vary prices based on such factors as demand, even though the cost of providing those goods or services remains the same. For example, sports teams like the San Francisco Giants charge more for weekend games, while the Colorado Rockies raise ticket prices based on the crowd-pleasing power of visiting teams. In the public sector, the Port Authority of New York and New Jersey recently experimented with variable pricing, charging more to cross the George Washington bridge at peak rush hours.[13]

Similar yield management strategies typify the marketing of such goods and services as the following:

- *Theater tickets*—lower prices in the afternoons to offset low demand and higher prices in the evening when demand rises
- *Lodging*—lower prices off season and higher prices during peak season periods; low-priced weekend rates (except in locations like Las Vegas, New Orleans, and Charleston with high weekend tourist visits)
- *Auto rental*—lower prices on weekends when business demand is low and higher prices during the week when business demand is higher
- *Airfares*—low prices on nonrefundable tickets with travel restrictions such as advance-purchase and Saturday-night stay requirements and penalties for flight changes; high prices on refundable tickets that can be changed without penalty

The following example from the airline industry demonstrates how yield management maximizes revenues in situations where costs are fixed.[14]

Airlines constantly monitor reservations on every flight. Beginning approximately 330 days before the flight, space is allocated between full-fare, discount-fare, and free tickets for frequent flyers who qualify for complimentary tickets. This allocation is monitored and adjusted at regular intervals until the actual departure.

Assume, for example, that Northwest Airlines has scheduled a 180-seat plane as Flight 1480 with an 8 a.m. departure from Memphis to Minneapolis on October 23. When Flight 1480 leaves its gate for departure, all costs associated with the flight (fuel, crew, and other operating expenses) are fixed. The pricing that maximizes revenues on this flight will also maximize profits. An examination of past sales indicates that Northwest could sell 40 to 60 round-trip, full-fare tickets at $600 per passenger and 100 to 150 round-trip restricted-fare tickets at $200 per passenger. Demand for frequent-flyer space should be at least 10 seats.

If Northwest reserves 60 seats for full-fare passengers and accepts reservations for 110 restricted-fare tickets but sells only 40 full-fare tickets (leaving 20 vacant seats), total revenues will be:

Revenues = (40 × \$600) + (110 × \$200) = \$46,000

On the other hand, if Northwest's pricing decision makers want to reduce vacancies, they might decide to reduce the number of full-fare tickets to 20 and increase the restricted-fare tickets to 150. If the plane leaves the gate at full capacity, the flight will generate the following total revenues:

Revenues = (20 × \$600) + (150 × \$200) = \$42,000

In the intensively competitive, global marketplace for credit cards, American Express frequently features cardholding celebrities in its international promotions. This ad features two award-winning filmmakers—producer Brian Grazer and former child star and successful director Ron Howard—who have collaborated on such memorable pictures as Academy Award–winning A Beautiful Mind. *Since foreign revenues from U.S.-made films often match or even exceed domestic revenues, American Express expects to recoup the endorsement fees paid through increased U.S. and international revenues.*

Instead of rigidly maintaining the allocations established nearly a year before the flight, Northwest will use yield management to maximize the revenue per flight. In this example, the airline initially holds 60 full-fare seats and accepts reservations for up to 110 restricted-fare seats. Thirty days before the October 23 departure, updated computer projections indicate that 40 full-fare seats are likely to be sold. The allocation is now revised to 40 full-fare and 130 restricted-fare tickets. A full flight leaves the gate and revenues are:

Revenues = (40 × \$600) + (130 × \$200) = \$50,000

Applying yield management for the Memphis–Minneapolis flight increases revenues by at least \$4,000 over the inflexible approach of making advance allocations and failing to adjust them based on passenger reservations and other data.

GLOBAL ISSUES IN PRICE DETERMINATION

It is equally important for a firm engaging in global marketing to use a pricing strategy that reflects its overall marketing strategy. Prices must support the company's broader goals, including product development, advertising and sales, customer support, competitive plans, and financial objectives.

<interactive>learning goal

CHAPTER OBJECTIVE #8: IDENTIFY THE MAJOR PRICING CHALLENGES FACING ONLINE AND INTERNATIONAL MARKETERS.

In general, there are five pricing objectives that firms can use to set prices in global marketing. Four of these are the same pricing objectives that we discussed earlier in the chapter: profitability, volume, meeting competition, and prestige. In addition, international marketers work to achieve a fifth objective: price stability.

In the global arena, marketers may choose profitability objectives if their company is a price leader that tends to establish international prices. Profitability objectives also make sense if a firm is a low-cost supplier that can make a good profit on sales.

Volume objectives become especially important in situations where nations lower their trade barriers to expose domestic markets to foreign competition. As the European Union lowered economic barriers between countries, for instance, competition for customers soared. A recent trend has been mergers of European firms to form larger companies that can achieve volume objectives. As one economist notes, "Merger activity [is] a way to get economies of scale." Carrefour, France's version of Wal-Mart, recently acquired a former European competitor to become the world's second-largest retailer behind the Arkansas-based discount giant.

Increased competition in Europe has also spurred firms to work toward the third pricing objective of meeting competitors' prices. Dutch corporation Philips Electronics offers U.S.-style coupons that give buyers 10 to 15 percent discounts off kitchen appliances. Aldi and Lidl, two German-owned food retailers, have opened discount outlets in France, forcing native French stores such as Carrefour to reduce prices. Automaker Fiat once boasted a 54 percent share of the Italian car market; its share has since dropped significantly due to inroads from competitively priced Ford of Europe, Inc. Fiat has fought back by offering $1,600 rebates and zero-interest financing on certain models.

Prestige is a valid pricing objective in international marketing when products are associated with intangible benefits, such as high quality, exclusiveness, or attractive design. The greater a product's perceived benefits, the higher its price can be. Marketers must be aware, however, that cultural perceptions of quality can differ from one country to the next. Sometimes items that command prestige prices in the U.S. are considered run-of-the-mill in other nations; sometimes products that are anything but prestigious in America seem exotic to overseas consumers. American patrons, for instance, view McDonald's restaurants as affordable fast-food eateries, but in China they are seen as fashionable and relatively expensive.

The fifth pricing objective, price stability, is desirable in international markets although it is difficult to achieve. Wars, terrorism, economic downturns, changing governments and political parties, and shifting trade policies can alter prices. An example is the computer industry. A few years ago, U.S. computer manufacturers sold their products in Europe for 30 to 50 percent more than U.S. prices. Today, greater competition within the European Union has forced computer prices down until they average only 10 percent higher than the U.S. prices, barely enough to cover manufacturers' costs in retooling machines for the local market. Falling prices have slashed profits for both American and European manufacturers, including IBM, Hewlett-Packard, and Olivetti.

Price stability can be especially important for producers of commodities—goods and services that have easily accessible substitutes that other nations can supply quickly. Countries that export international commodities, such as wood, chemicals, and agricultural crops, suffer economically when their prices fluctuate. A nation such as Nicaragua, which exports sugar cane, can find that its balance of payments changes drastically when the international price for sugar shifts. This makes it vulnerable to stiff price competition from other sugar cane producers.

In contrast, countries that export value-oriented products, rather than commodities, tend to enjoy more stable prices. Prices of electronic equipment and automobiles tend to fluctuate far less than prices of sugar cane or bananas.

STRATEGIC IMPLICATIONS OF MARKETING IN THE 21ST CENTURY

This chapter has focused on traditional pricing concepts and methods—principles that are critical to all marketing strategies, especially in e-commerce. Consumers can now compare prices quickly, heightening the already intense competitive pricing environment. The Web allows for prices to be negotiated on the spot and anything can be auctioned. From airline tickets to automobiles, the Web allows consumers to name their price.

While Internet shopping has not resulted in massive price cutting, it has increased the options available for consumers. Online price comparison engines, known as shopping bots, promise to help consumers find the lowest price for any good or service. Reverse auctions offered by sites like priceline.com, which allows customers to submit the highest price they are willing to pay for airline tickets, could conceivably be extended to other types of goods.[15]

Electronic delivery of music, books, and other goods and services will only lead to further price reductions. E-commerce has smoothed out the friction of time, which kept pricing relatively static. Microsoft cofounder Bill Gates recently gave a futuristic view of what he sees as a "friction-free economy." The current obsession with time and the ability to measure it will change perceptions and pricing of tangible goods. Goods and services are no longer made before they are ordered and their prices will no longer be fixed; instead, prices will shift up and down.

While at least in the short term consumers are enjoying the benefits of competitive online pricing, retailers worry as they watch their profit margins disappearing. The giant discount warehouse Costco, for example, offers housewares, furniture, and even office supplies delivered to your door through its discounted Web site. Meanwhile, Buy.com goes a step further. The online superstore recently announced plans to price goods at wholesale—wiping out any profit margin and depending entirely on on-site advertising for revenues. 16 While there is no obvious blueprint for success, pricing strategies at Costco and Buy.com derive from a similar way of thinking: Spend generously to win new customers, offer the lowest prices possible, and then give them superior customer services to keep them loyal.

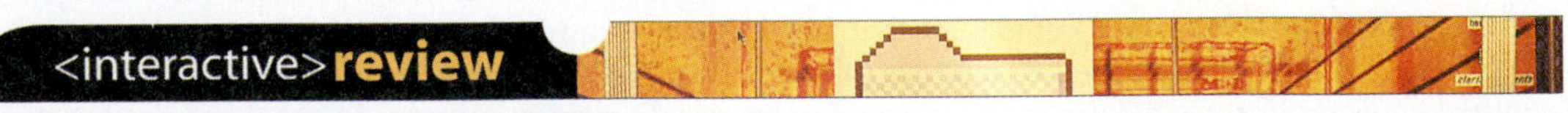

FLASH CHAPTER REVIEW PRESENTATION

<interactive>video case

CYBEX INTERNATIONAL WHIPS PRICING INTO SHAPE

endofchaptermaterial

- Summary of Chapter Objectives
- Chapter Outline
- Key Terms
- Review Questions
- Projects and Teamwork Exercises
- 'netWork
- Crossword Puzzles
- Case 13.1: U.S. Postal Service Fights Chronic Financial Losses by Raising Prices for First-Class Mail

Take the Post-Test to assess your overall understanding of the key ideas in this chapter. The Post-Test provides a comprehensive selection of exam-style questions addressing the main topics and concepts of the chapter. At the completion of each Post-Test, you will receive a score and instructive feedback on how you answered each question, and a direct link to the part of the chapter addressed in the question. Take the Post-Test as often as you need to—a record of your progress for each attempt is kept for you to revisit and gauge your improvement. And each Post-Test is randomly generated, so every attempt is new.

Post-Test

CHAPTER 14

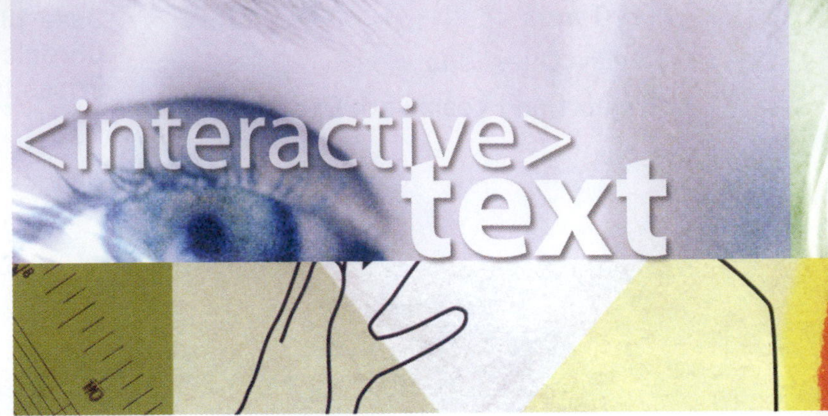

Managing the Pricing Function

Chapter Objectives

1. Compare the alternative pricing strategies and explain when each strategy is most appropriate.
2. Describe how prices are quoted.
3. Identify the various pricing policy decisions that marketers must make.
4. Relate price to consumer perceptions of quality.
5. Contrast competitive bidding and negotiated prices.
6. Explain the importance of transfer pricing.
7. Compare the three alternative global pricing strategies.
8. Relate the concepts of cannibalization, bundle pricing, and bots to online pricing strategies.

ZERO-PERCENT FINANCING REVS UP AUTO SALES

Several star-crossed economic factors foretold a rotten year in the auto industry. The "R" word (whispered recession) was heard everywhere as signs of a slowdown spread. Workers were laid off by companies large and small. When people lose their jobs—or worry that they may be next in line to receive pink slips—they are much less likely to buy major items such as autos. And once the events of September 11 took place, demand for new cars nearly dried up.

What could automakers do to counteract sagging demand in a sluggish economy, in a country that had just been attacked on its own soil? The answer came from basic economics: Slash prices to stimulate sales. The chosen method? Zero-percent loans. Since most new-car buyers finance part of the purchase, free financing is perceived as a deep discount in the overall price they pay to get behind the wheel. When General Motors ran its "Keep America Rolling" campaign, consumers flocked to dealerships to take advantage of no-interest loans for up to five years on nearly every GM vehicle. Ford and DaimlerChrysler followed with similar offers, perhaps fearing that they'd lose out. As a result, when car sales were tallied at the end of the year, 2001 was the second best auto sales year in history. Automakers sold 17.2 million cars and trucks that year, compared with the all-time record of 17.4 million. The downside was, of course, that the price cuts took a deep slice out of profits. What happened next?

As the zero-percent offers ran their course at the end of the year, sales began to lag again. Some industry experts feared that the "loan wars" simply reinforced a vicious cycle in which consumers would buy when there were special incentives to do so and back off when the incentives were removed. Carmakers were, in effect, borrowing sales from the future, and genuine expansion in demand for the new vehicles was never really created. "It's a nightmare," said one industry watcher.

But General Motors—which had reaped most of the benefits from the interest-rate incentive programs—was not about to be caught flat-footed. When its zero-percent loan offer expired, GM began offering a new incentive to car buyers: $2,002 rebates for its 2002 models. The company called this program "GM Overdrive," and for a while GM did seem to be in overdrive to create demand for its products. Then Ford, despite a major shake-up at the top and heavy cost cutting across its operations, sought to stall GM's program with its larger $2,500 discount and more cut-rate finance programs. Chrysler, in a move to emphasize value rather than add fuel to the incentives-driven price war, extended its "Home for the holidays" free, 10-year, 100,000-mile engine and transmission warranty (which previously had been sold as an extra option). Meanwhile, competitors from Europe and Asia continued to take big bites out of the Big Three's market share.

By summer, as the new model year approached, automakers began to dial up the costly deals once more. The auto marketers were forced to conclude that price-cutting had spurred short-term sales, while sapping GM profits and resulting in financial losses at Ford. But the Big Three automakers, still plagued with excess capacity, are reluctant to risk further market share erosion to imports. GM, Ford, and Chrysler continue to spend an average of $2,288 per car on incentives—well above such foreign competitors as Honda (about $470 per vehicle) and Toyota ($572). Some industry analysts estimate that, without incentives, GM's current 29 percent market share would shrink to 25 percent. These analysts were not surprised when the nation's largest automaker announced that zero-percent financing would also apply to its 2003 models. DaimlerChrysler quickly followed suit for its Chrysler models, but Ford—already operating in the red—resisted.[1]

Pre-Test

Take the Pre-Test to assess your initial knowledge of the key ideas in this chapter. The Pre-Test provides exam-style questions addressing the main topics and concepts of the chapter. At the completion of each Pre-Test, you will receive a score and instructive feedback on how you answered each question, and a direct link to the part of the chapter addressed in the question. Take the Pre-Test as often as you need to—a record of your progress for each attempt is kept for you to revisit and gauge your improvement.

CHAPTER OVERVIEW

As U.S. auto marketers will attest, setting prices is not a one-time decision, nor is it a routine or standard practice. Considered as much an art as a calculated scientific process, pricing is a dynamic function of the marketing mix. While about half of all companies change prices once a year or less frequently, one in ten does so every month. Online companies, who face enormous price pressures, often adjust prices daily. Some even negotiate prices on the spot.

Companies translate pricing objectives into pricing decisions in two major steps. First, someone must accept responsibility for making pricing decisions and administering the resulting pricing structure. Second, someone must set the overall pricing structure—that is, basic prices and appropriate discounts for channel members, quantity purchases, and geographic and promotional considerations.

The decision to make price adjustments is directly related to demand. Most businesses slowly change the amounts they charge customers, even when they clearly recognize strong demand. Instead of raising prices, they may choose to scale down customer service or add fees to cover added costs. They may also wait to raise prices until they see what their competitors will do. (Few businesses want the distinction of being the first to charge higher prices.) Since many businesses base their prices on manufacturing costs rather than consumer demand, they may wait for increases in their own costs before responding with price changes. These increases generally emerge more slowly than changes in consumer demand. Finally, since many business executives believe that steady prices will help to preserve long-term relationships with customers, they are reluctant to raise prices even when strong demand probably justifies the change.

Chapter 13 introduced the concept of price and its role in the economic system and marketing strategy. This chapter examines various pricing strategies and price structures, such as reductions from list prices and geographic considerations. It then looks at the primary pricing policies, including psychological pricing, price flexibility, product-line pricing, and promotional pricing, as well as price/quality relationships. Competitive and negotiated prices are discussed, and one section focuses entirely on transfer pricing. Finally, the chapter concludes by describing important factors in pricing goods and services for online and global markets.

Briefly Speaking

What is a cynic? A man who knows the price of everything and the value of nothing.

Oscar Wilde (1854–1900) Irish poet, playwright, and novelist

PRICING STRATEGIES

The specific strategies that firms use to price goods and services grow out of the marketing strategies they formulate to accomplish overall organizational objectives. One firm's marketers may price products to attract customers across a wide range; another group of marketers may set prices to appeal to a small segment of a larger market; still another group may simply try to match competitors' price tags. In general, firms can choose from three pricing strategies: skimming, penetration, and competitive pricing. The following sections look at these choices in more detail.

<interactive>**learning goal**

CHAPTER OBJECTIVE #1: COMPARE THE ALTERNATIVE PRICING STRATEGIES AND EXPLAIN WHEN EACH STRATEGY IS MOST APPROPRIATE.

Skimming Pricing Strategy

Derived from the term "skimming the cream," **skimming pricing strategies** are also known as *market-plus pricing*. They involve the intentional setting of a relatively high price compared with the prices of competing products. Although some firms continue to utilize a skimming strategy throughout most stages of the product life cycle, it is more commonly used as a market entry price for distinctive goods or services with little or no initial competition. Such was the case with early Polaroid cameras, the first videocassette recorders, and the introduction of electric toothbrushes. More recently, in the marketing of personal computers and DVD players, early high prices were followed by rapid declines as competitors flooded the marketplace.

A company may practice a skimming strategy in setting a market-entry price when it introduces a distinctive good or service with little or no competition. Canon released its new S600 bubble-jet printer with a clever "Out of the Blue" ad campaign focusing on an innovative product feature—individual ink tanks that let users replenish a single color without having to throw away an entire cartridge. This money-saving feature alone allowed Canon to price the printer at the top of the market.[2]

Improvements in existing products may allow firms to change from other pricing structures to a skimming strategy. Following a failed attempt to hike prices for its fleece apparel, Polartec modified its products by using fabrics to offer enhanced wind resistance. By bringing something new to the market for which consumers were willing to pay more, Polartec improved its chances that its new price structure would be successful.[3]

Skimming strategies are often used by marketers of high-end goods and services. For instance, the ad for the Weber gas grill and outdoor oven in Figure 14.1 makes no mention of price. While the product is backed by a warranty, the firm's marketers play up the notion that the Weber name is the only quality guarantee buyers will ever need.

In some cases, a firm may maintain a skimming strategy throughout most stages of a product's life cycle. The jewelry category is a good example. For example, even though relatively stable prices of gold bullion allow discounters such as Service Merchandise to offer high-karat jewelry for just a couple of hundred dollars, prestige brands like Tiffany or Cartier are able to command prices in excess of $5,000 for similar pieces. Exclusivity and craftsmanship justify the pricing—and the price, once set, never falls. Van Cleef & Arpels, featured in Figure 14.2, uses a skimming pricing strategy for its distinctive jewelry collections. Similarly, in the industrial sector, high-end Canadian steelmaker Dofasco Inc. was able to ride out an industry slump that dragged down rivals while keeping its prices up. The company focused on customized products for which price is not the main consideration.

Sometimes maintaining a high price through the product's life cycle works and sometimes it does not. Consider, for example, the entertainment industry. From Disney World to Six Flags and from Cirque du Soleil to movie theaters, admission prices for popular entertainment have soared in recent years. The cost of rock concert tickets has climbed by a third and the average ticket to an NBA game has gone up by almost 20 percent. Broadway attractions top $100 a seat, and fans can pay as much as $450 each for a VIP package to see Madonna, the Eagles, or the Rolling Stones in concert. Even a family outing to a nearby museum with a special exhibit can cost $20 or more per person—not including parking. Prices have, in fact, gone so high that many people have decided to stay home. As consumers reeled with sticker shock, concert grosses plummeted 35 percent in a single year. At Disney, attendance was off by 8 percent. Crowds at baseball parks, too, are steadily thinning out across the nation.

FIGURE 14.1

Weber: Distinctive Grills Marketed with a Skimming Pricing Strategy

don't let your kitchen stove see you reading this.
weber
EVERYTHING YOU DO IN YOUR OVEN, YOU CAN DO IN A WEBER® GAS GRILL. BECAUSE IT PROVIDES PRECISE HEAT CONTROL. NOT TO MENTION, IT'S CONSTRUCTED FROM THE HIGHEST-QUALITY U.S. STEEL AND BACKED BY A WARRANTY YOU'LL PROBABLY NEVER NEED. LIFE'S NOT PERFECT. THAT'S WHY WE STRIVE TO MAKE PRODUCTS THAT ARE.
genesis® gas grill and outdoor oven
weber
www.weber.com™
© 2002 Weber-Stephen Products Co. The Weber name, logo, url, and kettle grill configuration are registered U.S. trademarks

Despite the risk of backlash, a skimming strategy offers several benefits. First, it allows a manufacturer to quickly recover its research-and-development (R&D) costs. Pharmaceutical companies, who fiercely protect their patents on new drugs, justify high prices because of astronomical R&D costs—an average of 16 cents of every sales dollar, compared with 8 cents for computer makers and 4 cents in the aerospace industry. To protect their brand names from competition from lower-cost generics, drug makers frequently make small changes to their products, enabling them to extend their patents. Eli Lilly, for example, hopes to move patients to a newly patented weekly-dosage Prozac antidepressant, while Schering-Plough is seeking approval for a reformulation of its blockbuster antiallergy drug Claritin.[4]

A skimming strategy also offers a second benefit. It allows a firm to maximize revenue from a new product before competitors enter the field. In many industries, increasing competition eventually drives down initially high prices, as with television sets, digital watches, and pocket calculators.

A skimming pricing strategy is also a useful tool for segmenting a product's overall market on price. For a significant new product innovation, a relatively high price conveys an image of distinction, helping the product to appeal to buyers with low sensitivity to price. Over 50 years ago, the ballpoint pen was a dramatic breakthrough in writing instruments—and a highly visible one. Wealthy consumers with high discretionary incomes were willing to spend as much as $20 on the innovation. Today the best-selling ballpoint pens are priced at less than $1.

A final advantage of a skimming strategy is that it permits marketers to control demand in the introductory stages of a product's life cycle and then adjust productive capacity to match changing demand. A low initial price for a new product risks problems if demand outstrips the firm's production capacity, resulting in consumer and retailer complaints and possibly permanent damage to the product's image. Excess demand occasionally leads to poor-quality products, as the firm strives to satisfy consumer desires for the product with inadequate production facilities.

During the late growth and early maturity stages of its life cycle, a product's price typically falls for two reasons: (1) the pressure of competition and (2) the desire to expand its market. Figure 14.3 shows that 10 percent of the market would buy Product X at $10.00, and another 20 percent would buy at a price of $8.75. Successive price declines expand the firm's market and meet challenges posed by new competitors.

FIGURE 14.2

Van Cleef & Arpels: Skimming Strategy for Products for Which Price Is Not a Key Consideration

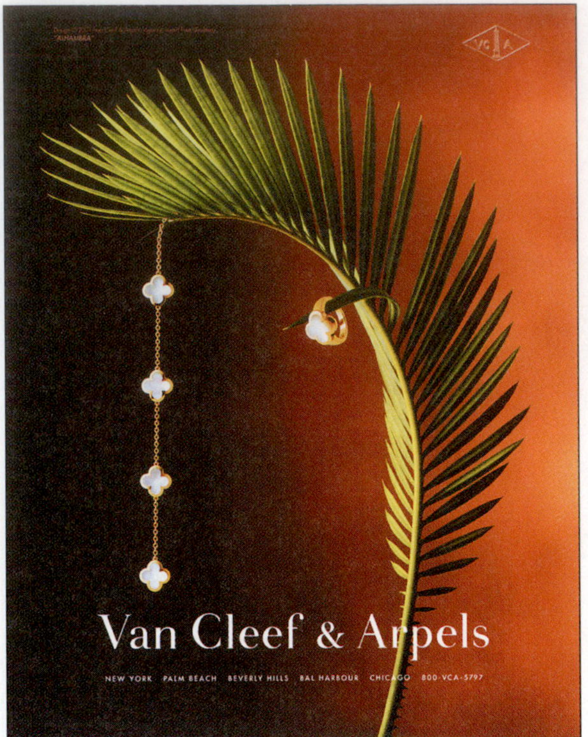

A skimming strategy has one chief disadvantage: It attracts competition. Potential competitors see innovative firms reaping large financial returns and decide to enter the market. This new supply forces the price of the original product even lower than its eventual level under a sequential skimming procedure. However, if patent protection or some other unique proprietary ability allows a firm to exclude competitors from its market, it may continue a skimming strategy for a relatively long period. Gillette marketers took out 35 patents to stave off competition for its Mach3 shaving system. When the top-selling product had been on the market less than three years, Gillette was ready with a new and improved Mach3 Turbo.[5]

Penetration Pricing Strategy

A **penetration pricing strategy** sets a low price as a major marketing weapon. Marketers often price products noticeably lower than competing offerings when they enter new industries characterized by dozens of competing brands. Once the product achieves some market recognition through consumer trial purchases stimulated by its low price, marketers may increase the price to the level of competing products. Marketers of consumer products such as detergents often use this strategy. A penetration pricing strategy may also extend over several stages of the product life cycle as the firm seeks to maintain a reputation as a low-price competitor.

A penetration pricing strategy is sometimes called *market-minus pricing* when it implements the premise that a lower-than-market price will attract buyers and move a brand from an unknown newcomer to at least the brand-recognition stage or even to the brand-preference stage. Since many firms begin penetration pricing with the intention of increasing prices in the future, success depends on generating many trial purchases.

Should competitors view the new product as a threat, marketers attempting to use a penetration strategy often discover that rivals will simply match their prices. Even though about 40 percent of the population currently uses cell phones, the U.S. is five years behind Japan and many parts of Northern Europe, where usage tops 50 percent. And in at least one country—Finland—cell phone usage has hit the 75 percent mark. But even as U.S. cell phone usage has soared, worries that price cuts for cell phones will immediately be matched by the growing number of competing service providers have resulted in cell phone prices remaining fairly stable while competitors decided to focus on lower fees, increased time and geographic limits, and improved customer service.[6]

Discount air carriers like AirTran, America West, JetBlue, and Southwest continually face the problem of having their prices matched by larger competitors. As a result, they often compete with major carriers by offering not just low prices, but a combination of attractive airfares, high customer service levels, and routes that are often underserved by the majors. Aided by flight purchase guarantees from local businesses seeking improved air service, AirTran has established routes to minor markets such as Myrtle Beach, SC, and Biloxi, MS.[7]

FIGURE 14.3

Price Reductions to Increase Market Share

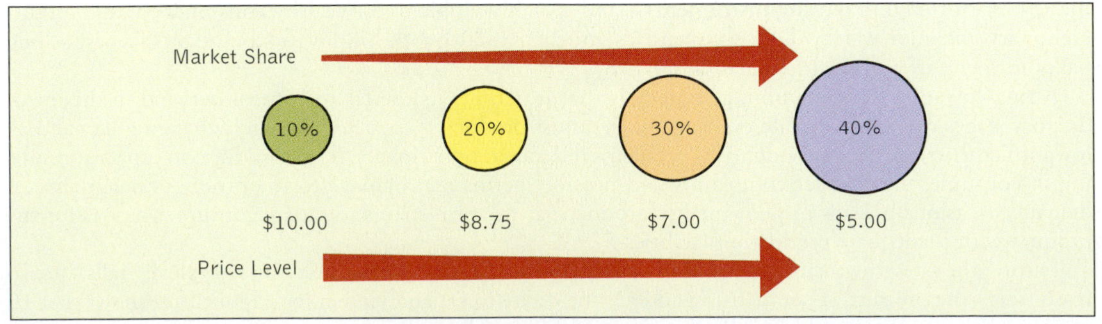

Retailers may use penetration pricing to lure shoppers to new stores. Strategies might take such forms as zero interest charges for credit purchases at a new furniture store, two-for-one offers for dinner at a new restaurant, or an extremely low price on a single product purchase for first-time customers to get them to come in and shop.

Penetration pricing works best for goods or services characterized by highly elastic demand. Large numbers of highly price-sensitive consumers pay close attention to this type of appeal. The strategy also suits situations in which large-scale operations and long production runs result in low production and marketing costs. Finally, penetration pricing may be appropriate in market situations in which introduction of a new product will likely attract strong competitors. Such a strategy may allow a new product to reach the mass market quickly and capture a large share prior to entry by competitors. Research shows that about 25 percent of companies use penetration pricing strategies on a regular basis.

Everyday Low Pricing Closely related to penetration pricing is *everyday low pricing (EDLP),* a strategy devoted to continuous low prices as opposed to relying on short-term, price-cutting tactics such as cents-off coupons, rebates, and special sales. EDLP can take two forms. In the first, retailers like Wal-Mart compete by consistently offering consumers low prices on a broad range of items. Through its EDLP policy, Lowe's offers not only to match any price the consumer sees elsewhere but to take off an additional 10 percent. The Lowe's EDLP strategy is featured in the firm's promotion shown in Figure 14.4.

In many cases, the EDLP pricing strategy is used by the manufacturer in dealing with channel members. Manufacturers may seek to set stable wholesale prices that undercut offers that competitors make to retailers, offers that often rise and fall with the latest trade promotion deals. Many marketers reduce the list prices on a number of products while simultaneously reducing promotion allowances to retailers. While reductions in allowances mean that retailers may not fund in-store promotions, such as shelf merchandising and end-aisle displays, the manufacturers hope that stable low prices will stimulate sales instead. During the 1990s, Procter & Gamble initiated a program that led to many dramatic price cuts on some of its products such as detergents, paper towels, and disposable diapers. Recently, R. J. Reynolds used EDLP to fend off deeply discounted cigarette imports. Reynolds cut the prices of its own deep-discount brands, Monarch and Best Value. For other brands, retailers received an extra 70 cents per pack from RJR as an incentive to stock more of its higher-tier brands instead of cheaper cigarettes. In addition, participating retailers are encouraged to price RJR's deep-discount cigarettes below or on a par with rivals.[8]

Some retailers oppose EDLP strategies. Grocery stores, for instance, operate on "high-low" strategies that set profitable regular prices to offset losses of frequent specials and promotions. Other retailers believe that EDLP will ultimately benefit both sellers and buyers. Supporters of EDLP in the grocery industry point out that it already succeeds at two of the biggest competitors, Wal-Mart and warehouse clubs. Marketing theorists express differing opinions about the prospects of EDLP emerging as a dominant pricing strategy.

One popular myth of pricing is that a low price is a sure sell. Low prices are an easy means of distinguishing the offerings of one marketer from other sellers, but such moves are easy to counter by competitors. Unless overall demand is price elastic, overall price cuts will mean less revenue for all firms in the industry. In addition, low prices may generate an image of questionable quality. As 19th-century critic John Ruskin put it, "There is hardly anything in the world that some men can't make a little worse and sell a little cheaper, and the people who consider price only are this man's lawful prey." The astute marketer should evaluate both the benefits derived from low-price strategies and the costs involved before launching an EDLP strategy.

Competitive Pricing Strategy

Although many organizations rely heavily on price as a competitive weapon, even more implement **competitive pricing strategies.** These organizations try to reduce the emphasis on price competition by matching other firms' prices and concentrating their own marketing efforts on the product, distribution, and promotion elements of the marketing mix. As pointed out earlier, while price offers a dramatic means of achieving competitive advantage, it is also the easiest marketing variable for competitors to match. In fact, in industries with relatively homogeneous products, competitors must match each other's price reductions to maintain market share and remain competitive.

Briefly Speaking

Cutting prices is usually insanity if the competition can go as low as you can.

Michael E. Porter (b. 1947) American educator

FIGURE 14.4

Lowe's: Succeeding with an Everyday Low Pricing Strategy

FIGURE 14.5

The Coca-Cola Company's Dasani Bottled Water: Building Market Share by Emphasizing Non-Price Marketing Mix Elements

Retailers like Home Depot and Lowe's both use price-matching strategies, assuring consumers they will meet—and beat—competitors' prices. Grocery chains such as Safeway, Winn-Dixie, and Raley's often compete with seasonal items: watermelons, soft drinks, and hot dogs in the summer; apples, hot chocolate, and turkeys in the winter. As soon as one store lowers the price of an item like turkey, the rest follow suit.

Even when marketers sell relatively heterogeneous products, they continue to analyze the prices of major competing offerings and ensure their own prices do not markedly differ. When IBM entered the personal computer market, its marketing efforts emphasized the versatility and power of its machines. However, the firm's marketers also quickly pointed out to potential customers that each PC in the line carried a competitive price.

Under competitive pricing, a price reduction results in financial effects throughout an industry as other firms match the drop. Unless the lower prices can attract new customers and expand the overall market enough to offset the loss of per-unit revenue, the price cut will leave all competitors with less revenue. Research shows that nearly two-thirds of all firms set prices using competitive pricing as their primary pricing strategy.

Web marketing is typically associated with penetration pricing strategies due to the inroads that book, music, and air travel sales have made using low, negotiable prices with razor-thin profit margins. However, online marketers are discovering that such customer benefits as selection, quick order fulfillment, and easy returns are also important decision criteria. Customers drawn to a Web site with lots of perks and lavish customer service are likely to pay full price for more individualized, high-ticket items like brand-name apparel and accessories. Amazon.com, for example, frequently charges more than its cut-price competitors. Although now defunct e-discounter Books.com consistently charged less for the same commodity products, its market share never rose above 2.2 percent. Having gained not only brand awareness but the trust of online shoppers, Amazon stayed way ahead.[9]

By pricing products at the general levels of competitive offerings, marketers largely negate the price variable in their marketing strategies. They must then emphasize nonprice variables to develop areas of distinctive competence and attract customers. Consider the bottled water market. While some firms currently marketing bottled water to a thirsty public emphasize price as a primary component of their marketing mixes, when global bottlers Coca-Cola and PepsiCo decided to launch their Dasani and Aquafina brands, they chose to emphasize product quality, the brands' easy availability due to saturation coverage of the marketplace, and considerable promotion focusing on the products' attributes. Although their prices are higher than those of the smaller competitors, both companies chose to align their prices with well-known brands like Evian and Poland Springs. As Figure 14.5 illustrates, the Dasani ad emphasizes fresh taste, enjoyment, and high-quality fresh water. And even though both brands were latecomers to the competitive fray, both have enjoyed considerable sales success.

PRICE QUOTATIONS

The choice of the best method for quoting prices depends on many industry conditions, including competitive trends, cost structures, and traditional practices, along with the policies of individual firms. This section examines the reasoning and methodology behind price quotation practices.

<interactive>**learning goal**

CHAPTER OBJECTIVE #2: DESCRIBE HOW PRICES ARE QUOTED.

Most price structures are built around *list prices*—the rates normally quoted to potential buyers. Marketers usually determine list prices by one or a combination of the methods discussed in Chapter 13. The sticker price on a new automobile is a good example: It shows the list price for the basic model and then adds the prices of options.

T-shirts offer another familiar example of list prices. About 1 billion of them are bought in the U.S. each year, generating sales revenues of $10 billion. Many of the most lucrative sales involve T-shirts sporting images of musical groups or sports stars and event dates. But where does the money go when you purchase a concert T-shirt at a list price of $25? Figure 14.6 supplies the answers. Although 54 percent of the $25 list price goes for production costs, the $7.50 licensing fee paid to the recording artist accounts for nearly half of the total. The remaining 46 percent is paid to the retailer (the concert arena) and to concert vendors.

Reductions from List Price

The amount that a consumer pays for a product—its *market price*—may or may not equal the list price. Discounts and allowances sometimes reduce list prices. A list price often defines a starting point from which discounts set a lower market price. Marketers offer discounts in several classifications: cash, trade, and quantity discounts.

Cash Discounts Consumers, industrial purchasers, or channel members sometimes receive reductions in price in exchange for prompt payment of bills; these price cuts are known as *cash discounts.* Discount terms usually specify exact time periods, such as 2/10, net 30. This notation means that the customer must pay within 30 days, but payment within 10 days entitles the customer to subtract 2 percent from the amount due.

Cash discounts represent a traditional pricing practice in many industries. They fulfill legal requirements, provided that all customers can take the same reductions on the same terms. Sellers originally instituted such discount practices to improve their own liquidity positions, reduce their bad-debt losses, and cut collection expenses. Whether these advantages outweigh the relatively high cost of capital that sellers incur by offering cash discounts depends on the need for liquidity as well as alternative sources (and costs) of funds.

Trade Discounts Payments to channel members for performing marketing functions are known as *trade discounts,* or functional discounts. Later chapters discuss the services performed by various channel members and the related costs. A manufacturer's list price must incorporate the costs incurred by channel members in performing required marketing functions and expected profit margins for each member.

Trade discounts initially reflected the operating expenses of each category, but they have become more or less customary practices in some industries. The Robinson-Patman Act allows trade discounts as long as all buyers in the same category, such as all wholesalers or all retailers, receive the same discount privileges.

Figure 14.7 shows how a chain of trade discounts works. In the first instance, the trade discount is "40 percent, 10 percent off list price" for wholesalers. In other words, the 40 percent discount on the $40 product is the trade discount the retailer receives to cover operating expenses and earn a profit. The wholesaler receives 10 percent of the $24 price to retailers to cover expenses and earn a profit. The manufacturer receives $21.60 from the wholesaler for each order.

FIGURE 14.6

The Take on a $25 T-Shirt

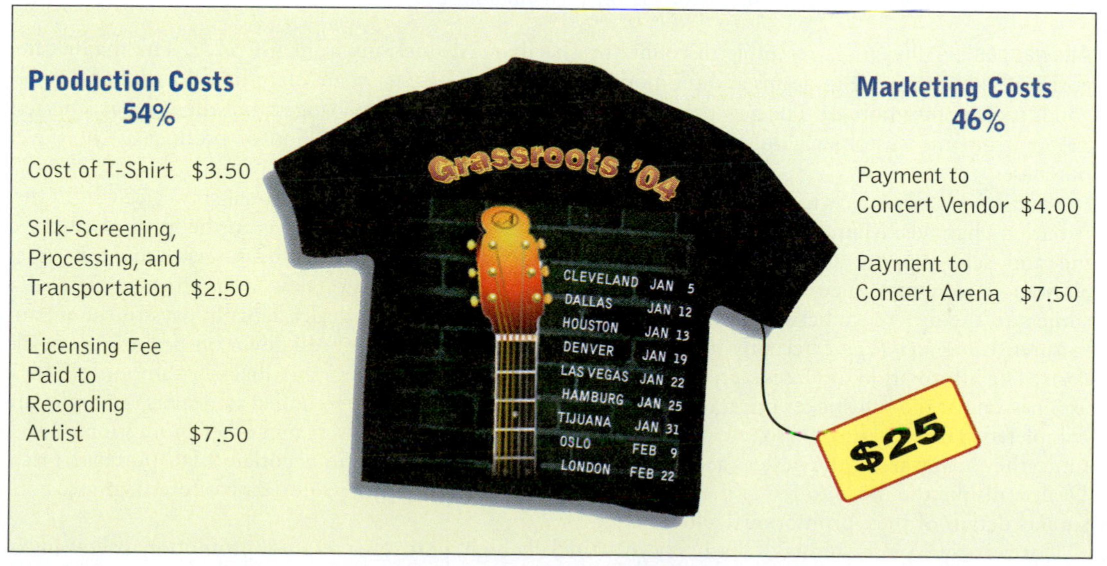

FIGURE 14.7

Chain of Trade Discounts

"40 PERCENT, 10 PERCENT OFF" TRADE DISCOUNT						
List Price	−	Retail Trade Discount	−	Wholesale Trade Discount	=	Manufacturer Proceeds
$40	−	$16 ($40 × 40%)	−	$2.40 ($24 × 10%)	=	$21.60 ($40 − $16 − $2.40)

"45 PERCENT" TRADE DISCOUNT				
List Price	−	Retail Trade Discount	=	Manufacturer Proceeds
$40	−	$18 ($40 × 45%)	=	$22 ($40 − $18)

In the second example, the manufacturer and retailer decide to bypass the wholesaler. The producer offers a trade discount of 45 percent to the retailer. In this instance, the retailer receives $18 for each product sold at its list price, and the manufacturer receives the remaining $22. Either the retailer or the manufacturer must assume responsibility for the services previously performed by the wholesaler, or they can share these duties between them.

Quantity Discounts Price reductions granted for large-volume purchases are known as *quantity discounts.* Sellers justify these discounts on the grounds that large orders reduce selling expenses and may shift some costs for storage, transportation, and financing to buyers. The law allows quantity discounts, provided they are applied on the same basis to all customers.

Quantity discounts may specify either cumulative or noncumulative terms. *Cumulative quantity discounts* reduce prices in amounts determined by purchases over stated time periods. Annual purchases of at least $25,000 might entitle a buyer to a 3 percent rebate, while purchases exceeding $50,000 would increase the refund to 5 percent. These reductions are really patronage discounts, since they tend to bind customers to a single supply source.

Noncumulative quantity discounts provide one-time reductions in the list price. For example, a firm might offer the following discount schedule for a product priced at $1,000 per unit:

1 unit	List: $1,000
2–5 units	List less 10 percent
6–10 units	List less 20 percent
Over 10 units	List less 25 percent

Many businesses have come to expect quantity discounts from suppliers. Ignoring these expectations can create competitive trouble for a firm. When United Parcel Service (UPS) balked at providing quantity discounts for large clients such as DuPont, it created an opportunity for competitors. One rival, Roadway Package System, lured several UPS customers by offering discounts to a wide range of organizational clients.

Marketers typically favor combinations of cash, trade, and volume discounts. For example, catalogers like Oriental Trading Co., specializing in novelty products, and Current, Inc., specializing in stationery supplies, offer customers discounts according to how much they purchase. They typically place time limits on when such discounts are applicable for each catalog. In addition, Current includes free samples of seasonally timed greeting cards for customers on their mailing list.

Allowances Allowances resemble discounts by specifying deductions from list price. The major categories of allowances are trade-ins and promotional allowances. *Trade-ins* are often used in sales of durable goods such as automobiles. The new product's basic list price remains unchanged, but the seller accepts less money from the customer along with a used product—usually the same kind of product as the buyer purchases.

Promotional allowances reduce prices as part of attempts to integrate promotional strategies within distribution channels. Manufacturers often return part of the prices that buyers pay in the form of advertising and sales-support allowances for channel members. Automobile manufacturers frequently offer allowances to retail dealers to induce them to lower prices and stimulate sales. In an effort to alert consumers to the difference between a car's sticker price and the price the dealer actually pays to the manufacturer, *Consumer Reports* recently began selling car and truck buyers a breakdown on dealers' wholesale costs. The information discloses secret dealer profits such as manufacturers' "holdbacks"—amounts as high as 3 percent of the full sticker price, or $750 on a $25,000 car—that are refunded to dealers after sales are completed. The breakdown also reveals allowances for the dealers' advertising and other promotional costs. Once they are aware of the dealer's actual cost, car buyers are better able to negotiate a fair purchase price. Dealers dislike the move to reveal their markups, arguing that no other retail sector is forced to give consumers details of their promotional allowances.[10]

For years, the price of music CDs has been artificially high, partly as a result of promotional allowances. Major record companies paid fees to stores that agreed not to advertise their CDs below set prices. Known as *minimum advertised pricing (MAP),* the policy, in effect, raised prices per CD by \$1 to \$2 across the board, eliminating competition. Under pressure from the Federal Trade Commission, major companies such as Bertelsmann, Sony, and EMI recently agreed to discontinue MAP allowances.[11]

Rebates In still another way to reduce a consumer's cost, marketers may offer a *rebate*—a refund of a portion of the purchase price. Rebates have appeared most prominently in automobile promotions by manufacturers eager to move models during periods of slow sales. However, firms have also offered rebates for sales in product categories ranging from appliances and sports equipment to grocery products and toiletries. Bed manufacturer Sealy has successfully used rebates to move consumers up its product line, offering the biggest rebates for its top-priced mattresses.

Internet companies like Upromise.com offer rebates that can be funneled into savings plans to pay for future college tuition. By purchasing products at participating retailers—including 15,000 grocery stores across the U.S., as well as major companies like ExxonMobil and AT&T, consumers can earn from 3 to 5 percent back for college when they buy any of the thousands of participating items, from Coca-Cola and Pop Tarts to Keebler cookies and Huggies diapers. Since the program is folded into existing loyalty card programs at grocery stores, consumers need to do nothing more than register, and Upromise keeps track of spending and credits their accounts.[12]

'NET EX: REBATES

Geographic Considerations

Rare is the 21st-century business whose operations are not affected by geographic considerations. In industries dominated by catalog and online marketers, these factors weigh heavily on the firm's ability to deliver orders in a cost-effective manner at the right time and place. In other instances, geographic factors affect the marketer's ability to receive additional inventory quickly in response to demand fluctuations. And although geographic considerations strongly influence prices when costs include shipping heavy, bulky, low-unit-value products, they can also affect lightweight, lower-cost products. The "Marketing Misses" Interactive Example explains the complexity of adjusting online pricing to cover shipping costs.

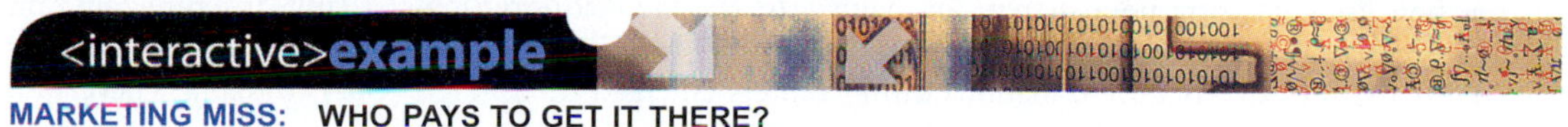

MARKETING MISS: WHO PAYS TO GET IT THERE?

Buyers and sellers can handle transportation expenses in several ways: (1) The buyer pays all transportation charges, (2) the seller pays all transportation charges, or (3) the buyer and the seller share the charges. This decision has major effects on a firm's efforts to expand its geographic coverage to distant markets. How can marketers compete with local suppliers in distant markets who are able to avoid the considerable shipping costs that their firms must pay? Sellers can implement several alternatives for handling transportation costs in their pricing policies.

FOB Pricing **FOB (free on board) plant,** or *FOB origin,* prices include no shipping charges. The buyer must pay all freight charges to transport the product from the manufacturer's dock. The seller pays only to load the merchandise aboard the carrier selected by the buyer. Legal title and responsibility pass to the buyer after the seller's employees load the purchase and get a receipt from the representative of the common carrier.

Many marketing intermediaries, such as Virginia-based General Medical Corp., sell only on FOB plant terms to downstream channel members. These distributors believe that their customers have more clout than they do in dealing with carriers. They prefer to assign transportation costs to the channel members in the best positions to negotiate the most cost-effective shipping terms.

Sellers may also quote prices as **FOB origin-freight allowed,** or **freight absorbed.** These terms permit buyers to subtract transportation expenses from their bills. The amount such a seller receives for its product varies with the freight charged against the invoice. This alternative is popular among firms with high fixed costs because it helps them to expand their markets considerably by quoting the same prices regardless of shipping expenses.

Uniform-Delivered Pricing When a firm quotes the same price, including transportation expenses, to all buyers, it adopts a **uniform-delivered price** policy. Such a pricing structure is the exact opposite of FOB origin pricing. This system resembles the pricing structure for mail service, so it is sometimes called *postage-stamp pricing.* The price quote includes a transportation charge averaged over all of the firm's customers, meaning that distant customers actually pay a smaller share of shipping costs while nearby customers pay what is known as phantom freight (the amount by which the average transportation charge exceeds the actual cost of shipping).

Zone Pricing **Zone pricing** modifies a uniform-delivered pricing system by dividing an overall market into different zones and establishing a single price within each zone. This pricing structure incorporates average transportation costs for shipments within each zone as part of the delivered price of goods sold there; by narrowing distances, it reduces but does not eliminate phantom freight. The primary advantage of zone pricing comes from easy administration methods that help a seller to compete in distant markets. The U.S. Postal Service's parcel rates depend on zone pricing.

Zone pricing helps explain why gasoline can cost more in one suburb than it costs in a neighborhood just two or three miles down the road. One way in which refinery companies boost profits is by mapping out areas based on formulas that factor in location, affluence, or simply what the local market will bear. Dealers are then charged different wholesale prices, which are reflected in the prices paid at the pump by customers. In response to recent upswings in the price of gasoline, many dealers are now pushing to make zone pricing illegal or at least establish rules for fair use. As drivers shop around for cheaper gas, stations in high-price zones are unable to compete. Ironically, it is the local dealer, not just the oil company, that consumers suspect of price gouging.[13] The "Solving an Ethical Controversy" Interactive Example examines a legal loophole in Europe's trade laws that allows for a form of zone pricing from country to country.

RIGHT/WRONG: SOLVING AN ETHICAL CONTROVERSY—FAIR PLAY ACROSS BORDERS

Basing-Point Pricing In **basing-point pricing,** the price of a product includes the list price at the factory plus freight charges from the basing-point city nearest the buyer. The basing point specifies a location from which to calculate freight charges—not necessarily the point from which the goods are shipped. In either case, the actual shipping point does not affect the price quotation. Such a system seeks to equalize competition between distant marketers since all competitors quote identical transportation rates. Few buyers would accept a basing-point system today, however.

The best-known basing-point system for many years was the Pittsburgh-plus pricing structure common in the steel industry. Steel buyers paid freight charges from Pittsburgh regardless of where the steel was produced. As the industry matured, manufacturing centers emerged in Chicago; Gary, Indiana; Cleveland; and Birmingham, Alabama. Still, Pittsburgh remained the basing point for steel pricing, forcing a buyer in Atlanta that purchased steel from a Birmingham mill to pay phantom freight from Pittsburgh.

PRICING POLICIES

Pricing policies contribute important information to buyers as they assess the firm's total image. A coherent policy provides an overall framework and consistency that guides day-to-day pricing decisions. Formally, a *pricing policy* is a general guideline that reflects marketing objectives and influences specific pricing decisions.

<interactive>learning goal

CHAPTER OBJECTIVE #3: IDENTIFY THE VARIOUS PRICING POLICY DECISIONS THAT MARKETERS MUST MAKE.

Decisions concerning price structure generally tend to focus on technical, detailed questions, but decisions concerning pricing policies cover broader issues. Price structure decisions take the firm's pricing policy as a given, from which they specify applicable discounts. Pricing policies have important strategic effects, particularly in guiding competitive efforts. They form the basis for more practical price-structure decisions.

Firms implement variations of four basic types of pricing policies: psychological pricing, price flexibility, product-line pricing, and promotional pricing. Specific policies deal effectively with various competitive situations; the final choice depends on the environment within which marketers must make their pricing decisions.

Psychological Pricing

Psychological pricing applies the belief that certain prices or price ranges make products more appealing to buyers than others. No research offers a consistent foundation for such thinking, however, and studies often report mixed findings. Nevertheless, marketers practice several forms of psychological pricing. Chapter 13 discussed one—prestige pricing. Two more psychological pricing techniques include odd pricing and unit pricing.

In *odd pricing,* marketers set prices at odd numbers just under round numbers. Many people assume that a price of $4.95 appeals more strongly to consumers than $5.00, supposedly because buyers interpret it as $4.00 plus change. Odd pricing originated as a way to force clerks to make change, thus serving as a cash-control device. Odd pricing remains a common feature of contemporary price quotations.

Some producers and retailers practice odd pricing but avoid prices ending in 5, 9, or 0. These marketers believe that customers view price tags of $5.95, $5.99, or $6.00 as regular retail prices, but they think of an amount like $5.97 as a discount price.

Unit pricing states prices in terms of some recognized unit of measurement (such as grams and liters) or a standard numerical count. Unit pricing arose to improve convenience when consumer advocates complained about the difficulty of comparing the true prices of products packaged in different sizes. These advocates thought that posting prices in terms of standard units would help shoppers make better-informed purchases. Some supermarket chains have come to regard unit pricing as a competitive tool, and they feature it extensively in advertising. However, unit pricing has not improved consumers' shopping habits as much as supporters originally envisioned that it would. Instead, research shows that standard price quotes most often affect purchases only by relatively well-educated consumers with high earnings.

With gasoline prices soaring way above $1.60 per gallon in some states, it is interesting to compare its unit price with that of other products. As Table 14.1 demonstrates, most other products command far higher unit prices than gasoline!

Price Flexibility

Marketing executives must also set company policies that determine whether their firm will permit **price flexibility**—that is, the decision of whether to set one price that applies to every buyer or permit variable prices for different customers. Generally, one-price policies suit mass-selling marketing programs, whereas variable pricing is more likely to be applied in marketing programs based on individual bargaining. In a large department store, customers do not expect to haggle over prices with retail salespeople. Instead, they expect to pay the amounts shown on the price tags. Generally, customers pay less only when the retailer replaces regular prices with sale prices or offers discounts on damaged merchandise.

Traditionally, car buyers have come to expect variable pricing policies from dealers. During the 1990s, however, when Saturn marketers chose to stray from the norm with a nonnegotiable pricing policy on its vehicles, many other automakers such as Ford and Honda were attracted to its success and followed suit. While the trend toward nonnegotiable pricing did not last long, manufacturers have begun using the Internet to deliver pricing information to potential customers. Ford, GM, and Toyota offer Web sites that allow car buyers to price out models with the options they require, along with lists of actual cars on nearby lots. The sites also provide suggested retail prices—customers can e-mail dealerships to check how much they are charging. However, while checking out pricing online may allow customers a stronger negotiating position, the prices are not fixed.

TABLE 14.1

Unit Price of Gasoline Compared with Other Products

Product	Price per Container	Price per Gallon
Gasoline	—	$1.50 and higher
Coors Light	$5.19 per six-pack	$9.23
Ozarka Natural Spring Water	69 cents for 8 oz.	$11.04
Crest toothpaste	$2.98 for 6.2 oz.	$62.00
OPI Nail Lacquer	$6 for 1/2 oz.	$1,536.00
Ralph Lauren's Romance fragrance	$60 for 3.4 oz.	$2,252.00
Estee Lauder Resilience Lift Eye Crème	$42.50 for 1/2 oz.	$10,880.00

The telecommunications industry, on the other hand, has moved toward flat-rate pricing strategies. Rather than charge different rates for different times of the day, AT&T and MCI offer a one-rate nationwide plan. Yet while flat rates may mean that customers pay as little as five cents a minute for long-distance calls, their phone bills are still rising. A grab bag of access fees and service charges ups the ante. Second-line charges, portability fees, rural service fees, and federal excise taxes are just a few of the mandatory monthly charges. In addition, customers may decide to pay more for options such as call waiting, caller ID, or call forwarding. As the whole package of service costs continues to rise, increasing numbers of customers are cutting the wire and going cellular.[14]

While variable pricing adds some flexibility to selling situations, it may conflict with provisions of the Robinson-Patman Act. It may also lead to retaliatory pricing by competitors, and it may stir complaints among customers who find that they paid higher prices than necessary.

Product-Line Pricing

Since most firms market multiple product lines, an effective pricing strategy must consider the relationships among all of these products instead of viewing each in isolation. **Product-line pricing** is the practice of setting a limited number of prices for a selection of merchandise. For example, a clothier might offer three lines of men's suits—one priced at $475, a second at $625, and the most expensive at $795. These price points help the retailer define important product characteristics that differentiate the three product lines and contribute to customer choices to trade up or trade down.

Retailers practice extensive product-line pricing. In earlier days, five-and-dime variety stores exemplified this technique. It remains popular, however, because it offers advantages to both retailers and customers. Shoppers can choose desired price ranges and then concentrate on other product variables such as colors, styles, and materials. Retailers can purchase and offer specific lines in limited price categories instead of more general assortments with dozens of different prices.

Most airlines divide their seating areas on international flights according to product-line pricing. These flights offer a certain percentage of discount, business-class, first-class, and coach-price seats on each flight. On an overseas flight, for instance, the industry averages about 18 percent business-class seats. A round-trip, business-class ticket from Houston to Paris on Continental Airlines costs almost twice the regular coach fare and several times more than the discount fare.

A potential problem with product-line pricing is that once marketers decide on a limited number of prices to use as their price lines, they may have difficulty making price changes on individual items. Rising costs, therefore, force sellers to either change the entire price-line structure, which results in confusion, or cut costs through production adjustments. The second option opens the firm to customer complaints that its merchandise is not what it used to be. Frito Lay, which competes in the highly price-sensitive snack foods category, recently responded to rising costs not by raising its prices but by shrinking the size of its packages. Such silent price hikes, achieved in the form of "package shrink," have also been implemented by marketers of candy, coffee, and diapers.

Promotional Pricing

In **promotional pricing,** a lower-than-normal price is used as a temporary ingredient in a firm's selling strategy. Some promotional pricing arrangements form part of recurrent marketing initiatives, such as a shoe store's annual "buy one pair, get the second pair for one cent" sale. Another example would be "7 CDs for 1 cent." This artificially low price attracts customers who must then agree to purchase a set number of CDs within a specified time limit. Another firm may introduce a promotional model or brand with a special price to begin competing in a new market.

Leader Pricing and Loss Leaders Retailers rely most heavily on promotional pricing. In one type of technique, stores offer **loss leaders**—goods priced below cost to attract customers who, the retailer hopes, will also buy other, regularly priced merchandise. Loss leaders can form part of an effective marketing program, but—as pointed out in the previous chapter—states with unfair-trade laws prohibit the practice.

Retailers frequently use a variant of loss-leader pricing called *leader pricing.* To avoid violating minimum-markup regulations and to earn some return on promotional sales, they offer so-called leader merchandise at prices slightly above cost. Among the most frequent practitioners of this combination pricing/promotion strategy are supermarkets and mass merchandisers such as Wal-Mart and Target. Retailers sometimes treat private-label products (like Sam's Choice colas at Wal-Mart stores) as leader merchandise since prices of the store brands average 5 percent to 60 percent less than those of comparable national brands. While store brand goods generate lower per-unit revenues than national brands would produce, higher sales volume will probably offset some of the difference, as will related sales of high-margin products like toiletries and cosmetics.

The personal computer industry provides an excellent example of this trend in pricing. Just a decade ago, PCs cost up to $5,000. At first, prices tumbled because of production economies and high demand. But the industry became embroiled in a brutal price war that saw Dell Computer Corp. not only slash PC prices to under $400 but also throw in free printers, free Internet access, and free delivery. Working on razor-thin profit margins, competitors struggled to match Dell's plunging prices. Apple Computer focused on product image and caught buyers' eyes with the attractive iMac design. Both Apple and IBM realigned their operations to provide services they could bundle along with the basic PC offerings. Compaq and Hewlett-Packard consolidated in order to compete. The economic slowdown at the beginning of this century, combined with a saturated U.S. market and consumer expectations of low prices, set the stage for long-term problems ahead.[15] The "Marketing Hits" Interactive Example explains Dell's aggressive pricing strategy.

interactive>example

MARKETING HIT: DELL'S LOW-PRICE STRATEGY DOMINATES PC MARKET

Marketers should anticipate two potential pitfalls when making a promotional pricing decision:

1. Some buyers are not attracted by promotional pricing.
2. By maintaining an artificially low price for a period of time, marketers may lead customers to expect it as a customary feature of the product. In the airline industry, for example, pervasive ticket discounting has taught consumers to expect to pay prices below full fare. As a result, airlines are losing money because many travelers will fly only if they can get discounted fares.

Price-Quality Relationships

One of the most thoroughly researched aspects of pricing is its relationship to consumer perceptions of product quality. In the absence of other cues, price serves as an important indicator of a product's quality to prospective purchasers. Many buyers interpret high prices as signals of high-quality products.

CHAPTER OBJECTIVE #4: RELATE PRICE TO CONSUMER PERCEPTIONS OF QUALITY.

The relationship between price and perceived quality provides a widely used tool for contemporary marketers. Figure 14.8 shows the Land Rover, a vehicle known around the globe for its dependability,

FIGURE 14.8

Relationship between Price and Perceived Quality

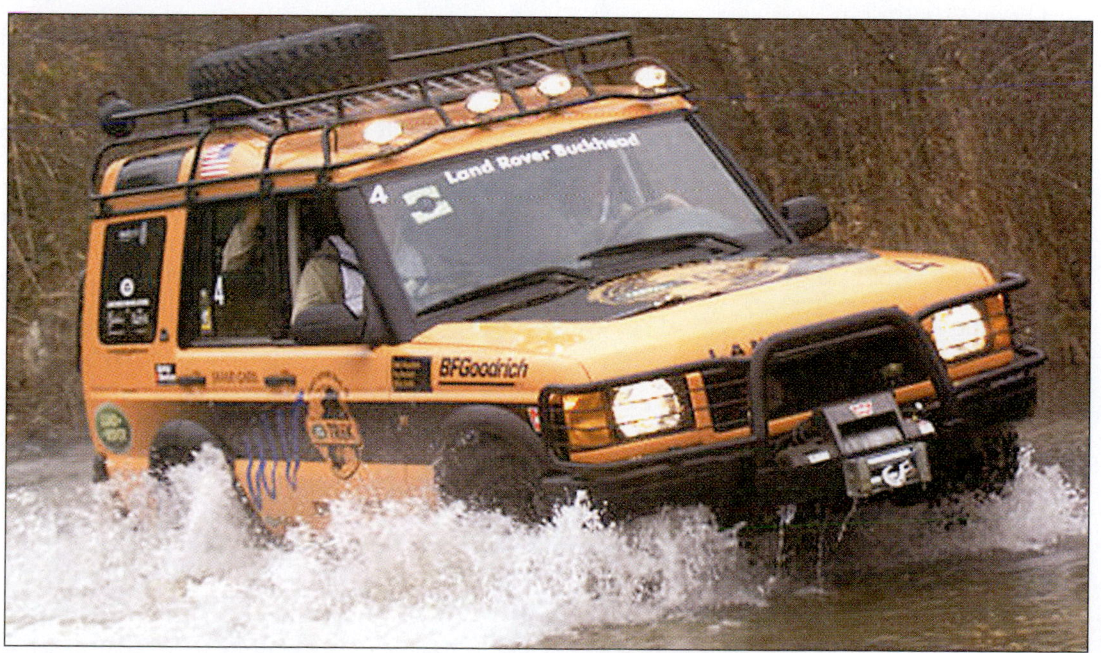

performance, and price. Instead of attempting to justify its price, Land Rover instead focuses on being the logical choice for a trek across Africa.

The recent recession obviously took its toll on upscale brand sales, but premium products have also proven they are able to withstand ups and downs. Wineries in the Pacific Northwest have discovered a growing market niche. In recent years, increasing numbers of consumers have traded up from cheaper California wines, priced from $3 to $6, weakening demand at the low end of the market. Although they are not ready to plunk down $80 for a top vintage wine, shoppers are willing to pay anything from $7 to $30 a bottle at wine shops or grocery stores. With a reputation for high-quality grapes, Washington State wineries continue to sell well, despite lackluster demand in the industry overall.[16]

Probably the best statement of the price-quality connection is the idea of price limits. Consumers define certain limits within which their product-quality perceptions vary directly with price. A potential buyer regards a price below the lower limit as too cheap, and a price above the higher limit seems too expensive. This perception holds true for both national brands and private-label products.

In some South American and Asian countries, hyperinflation occurring during the past 10 years has left consumers little relationship between price and quality. In Brazil during the mid-1990s, for example, a consumer could buy a deluxe ice cream sundae or two kitchen blenders for 950 cruzados ($15). Moreover, prices for a single product also varied tremendously from store to store. As a result, a consumer could end up paying anywhere from 2 cruzados ($.03) to 21 cruzados for a pencil eraser.

COMPETITIVE BIDDING AND NEGOTIATED PRICES

Many government and organizational procurement departments do not pay set prices for their purchases, particularly for large purchases such as U.S. Department of Defense orders for MREs (Meals Ready to Eat) to replace those used by troops assigned to Afghanistan and other isolated areas. Instead, they determine the lowest prices available for items that meet specifications through *competitive bidding*. This process consists of inviting potential suppliers to quote prices on proposed purchases or contracts. Detailed specifications describe the good or service that the government agency or business organization wishes to acquire. One of the most important procurement tasks is to develop accurate descriptions of products that the organization seeks to buy. This process generally requires the assistance of the firm's technical personnel, such as engineers, designers, and chemists.

<interactive>**learning goal**

CHAPTER OBJECTIVE #5: CONTRAST COMPETITIVE BIDDING AND NEGOTIATED PRICES.

Ford Motor Co. has been particularly successful in supplying state and government agencies with auto models that meet their price and performance specifications. At present, 85 of every 100 U.S. police cars are Crown Victorias.

In some cases, business and government purchasers negotiate contracts with favored suppliers instead of inviting competitive bids from all interested parties. The terms of such a contract emerge through offers and counteroffers between the buyer and the seller.

Where only one supplier offers a desired product or where projects require extensive research and development, buyers and sellers often set purchase terms through negotiated contracts. In addition, some state and local governments permit their agencies to skip the formal bid process and negotiate purchases under certain dollar limits—say $500 or $1,000. This policy seeks to eliminate economic waste that would result from obtaining and processing bids for relatively minor purchases.

Negotiating Prices Online

Many people see today's cyberworld as one big auction site. Whether it is toys, art, or automobiles, there seems to be an online auction site to serve every person's needs—buyer and seller alike. Auctions are the purest form of negotiated pricing. As Figure 14.9 shows, buyers and sellers electronically communicate ask and bid prices until a mutually agreed-upon price is set.

Ticket sales are an online auction favorite. Whether it is a Broadway show, a NASCAR race, a trip to the zoo, or an OzzFest concert, you can find tickets online. Tickets.com catalogs the dates, times, and locations of everything from concerts to museum exhibits. It recently tied in with the Advantix ticketing system, opening up a sales site for sports venues. In addition, Tickets.com also functions as a reseller through its own online auctions.

THE TRANSFER PRICING DILEMMA

A pricing problem peculiar to large-scale enterprises is the determination of an internal **transfer price**—the price for moving goods between **profit centers,** which are any part of the organization to which revenue and controllable costs can be assigned, such as a department. As companies expand, they tend to decentralize management and set up profit centers as a control device in the newly decentralized operation.

<interactive>**learning goal**

CHAPTER OBJECTIVE #6: EXPLAIN THE IMPORTANCE OF TRANSFER PRICING.

In a large company, profit centers might secure many needed resources from sellers within their own organization. The pricing problem thus poses several questions: What rate should profit center A (maintenance department) charge profit center B (production department) for the cleaning compound used on B's floors? Should the price be the same as it would be if A did the work for an outside party? Should B receive a discount? The answers to these questions depend on the philosophy of the firm involved.

Transfer pricing can be complicated, especially for multinational organizations. The government closely monitors transfer pricing practices because these exchanges offer easy ways for companies to avoid paying taxes on profits. Recent Congressional investigations of the trend for U.S. firms to incorporate in Bermuda have focused on U.S. tax savings made possible by transfer pricing rates used between the firm's production location (U.S.) and its home country (Bermuda), even though no production takes place in Bermuda.

Figure 14.10 shows how this type of pricing manipulation might work. Suppose that a South Korean VCR manufacturer sells its machines to its U.S. subsidiary for distribution to dealers. Although each unit costs $50 to build, the manufacturer charges the distributor $150. In turn, the distributor sells the VCRs to retailers for $200 each. This arrangement gives the South Korean manufacturer a $100 profit on each machine, on which it pays taxes only in South Korea. Meanwhile, the American distributor writes off $50 for advertising and shipping costs, leaving it with no profits—and no tax liability.

GLOBAL CONSIDERATIONS AND ONLINE PRICING

Throughout the text and especially in Chapter 5, we have seen the impact of the Internet on every component of the marketing mix. This chapter has touched on the outer edges of the Internet's influence on pricing practices. Remember that every online marketer is inherently a global marketer who must understand the wide variety of internal and external conditions that affect global pricing strategies. Internal influences include the firm's goals and marketing strategies; the costs of developing, producing, and marketing its products; the nature of the products; and the firm's competitive strengths. External influences include general conditions in international markets, especially those in the firm's target markets, regulatory limitations, trade restrictions, competitors' actions, economic events, and the global status of the industry.

Traditional Global Pricing Strategies

In general, a company can implement one of three export pricing strategies: a standard worldwide price, dual pricing, or market-differentiated pricing. Exporters often set standard worldwide prices, regardless of their target markets. This strategy can succeed if foreign marketing costs remain low enough that they do not affect overall

FIGURE 14.9

Online Auctions: Purest Form of Negotiated Pricing

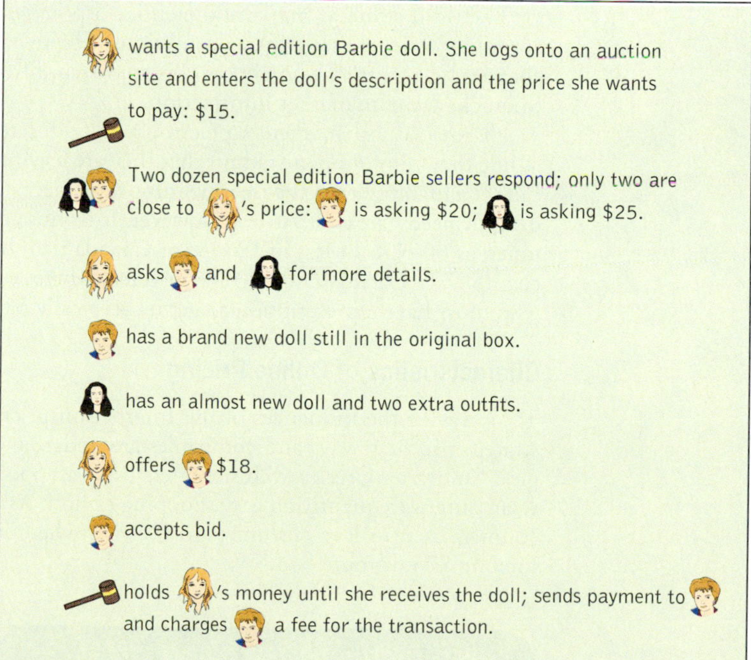

wants a special edition Barbie doll. She logs onto an auction site and enters the doll's description and the price she wants to pay: $15.
Two dozen special edition Barbie sellers respond; only two are close to 's price: is asking $20; is asking $25.
asks and for more details.
has a brand new doll still in the original box.
has an almost new doll and two extra outfits.
offers $18.
accepts bid.
holds 's money until she receives the doll; sends payment to and charges a fee for the transaction.

FIGURE 14.10

Transfer Pricing to Escape Taxation

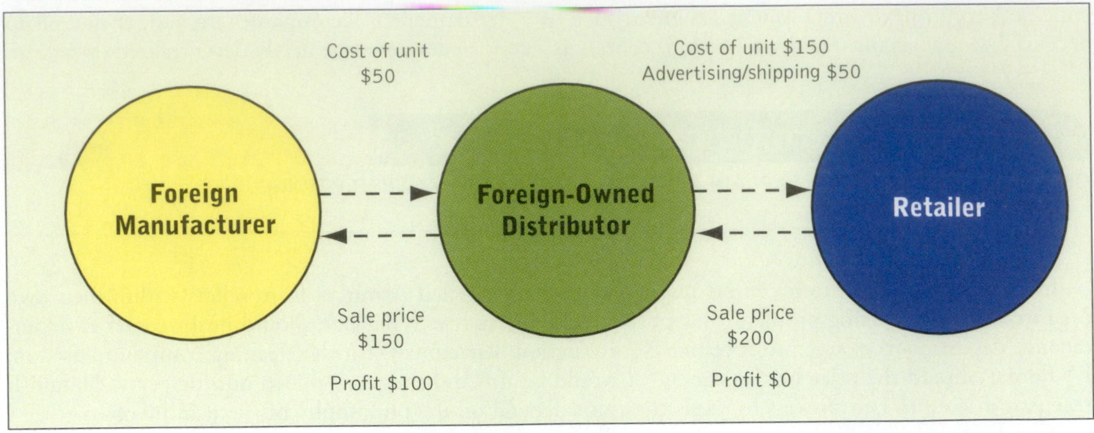

costs or if their prices reflect average unit costs. A company that implements a standard pricing program must monitor the international marketplace carefully, however, to make sure that domestic competitors do not undercut its prices.

<interactive>**learning goal**

CHAPTER OBJECTIVE #7: COMPARE THE THREE ALTERNATIVE GLOBAL PRICING STRATEGIES.

The dual pricing strategy distinguishes prices for domestic and export sales. Some exporters practice cost-plus pricing to establish dual prices that fully allocate their true domestic and foreign costs to product sales in those markets. These prices ensure that an exporter makes a profit on any product it sells, but final prices may exceed those of competitors. Other companies opt for flexible cost-plus pricing schemes that allow marketers to grant discounts or change prices according to shifts in the competitive environment or fluctuations in the international exchange rate.

The third strategy, market-differentiated pricing, makes even more flexible arrangements to set prices according to local marketplace conditions. The dynamic global marketplace often requires frequent price changes by exporters who choose this approach. Effective market-differentiated pricing depends on access to quick, accurate market information.

Pharmaceutical marketers practice market-differentiated pricing in their global marketing strategies. While they cannot openly admit that they are levying a North American surcharge on the drug, marketers can set a high price on the treatment for wealthier patients in America while charging pennies for the same drug in needy areas of Africa. However, it is more difficult to understand why some drugs are priced as much as 60 percent less in Europe or Canada than in the U.S. A month's supply of Claritin, for example, costs $17 in Canada and $13 in Australia, where it is available over the counter. American consumers—who must have a prescription to get it—typically pay $62.[17]

Characteristics of Online Pricing

To deal with the influences of the Internet on pricing policies and practices, marketers are applying old strategies in new ways and companies are updating operations to compete with new electronic technologies. Coldwater Creek's Web site offers time-strapped professional women who may not be able to visit its retail outlets frequently an easy shopping option. As the ad in Figure 14.11 shows, a limited-time cash discount is used to lure customers to the site, where it can be applied against purchases of quality apparel totaling $75 or more.

<interactive>**learning goal**

CHAPTER OBJECTIVE #8: RELATE THE CONCEPTS OF CANNIBALIZATION, BUNDLE PRICING, AND BOTS TO ONLINE PRICING STRATEGIES.

The Cannibalization Dilemma However, by pricing the same products differently online, companies run the risk of **cannibalization.** The new twist to an old tactic is that companies are self-inflicting price cuts by creating competition among their own products. By building new e-businesses designed to compete head-on with the parent company, marketers are hoping to survive the transition from bricks-and-mortar to electronic storefronts on the Web. Online securities trading company e.Schwab cannibalized its parent Charles Schwab when it offered online investors a flat $29.95 transaction fee. Traditional clients, who were still being charged $65 per trade, demanded and received the same flat fee.[18]

Books-A-Million, the nation's third-largest bookstore chain, sells its Top 20 best-sellers at 40 percent below list price. But click on the company's Web site, and you can buy the same book at discounts of 46 percent or more. Why sell books online at a lower price than you charge at the store? Books-A-Million's head of online marketing supplies two reasons:

- It provides an additional channel to reach book buyers who do not regularly patronize their local Books-A-Million as well as those purchasers who live in areas with no BAM retail stores.
- It also represents a defensive move, since the company would rather have the business—even at extremely low margins—than lose it to Amazon.com.

FIGURE 14.11

Using Cash Discounts to Attract Shoppers as an Online Pricing Strategy

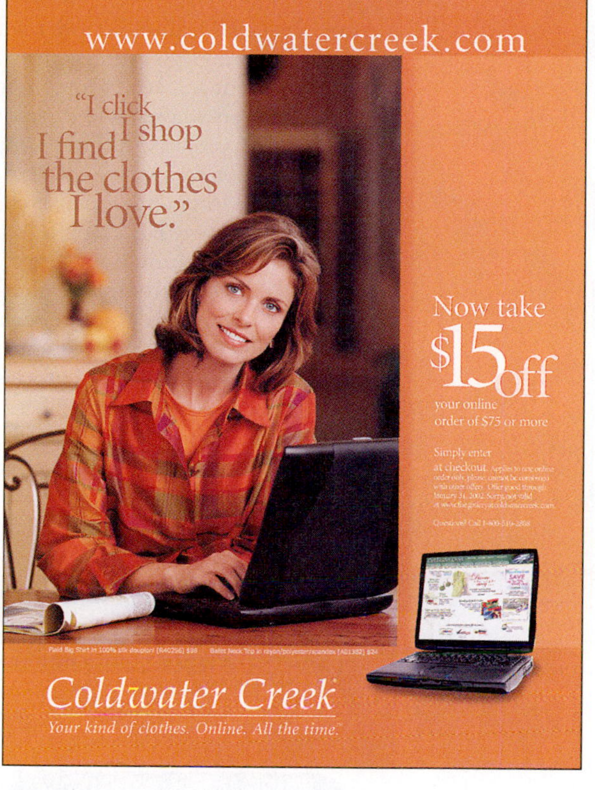

Use of Shopping Bots A second characteristic of online pricing is the use of search programs called *bots* or *shopbots*—derived from the word "robots"—that act as comparison shopping agents. As Chapter 5 explained, bots search the Web for a specific product, then print out a list of sites that offer the best prices. In online selling, bots force marketers to keep prices low. However, marketing researchers report that almost 4 of every 5 online shoppers will check out several sites before buying, and price is not the only variable they consider when making a purchase decision. For example, service quality and support information are powerful motivators in the decision process. Also, while price is an important factor with products such as books and CDs, it is not as important with complex or highly differentiated products, such as real estate or investment banking. Brand image and customer service often outweigh price in these purchase decisions. In an attempt to protect its proprietary server resources, the popular portal Google recently decided to wall off sections of its site from other search bots. As a result, a search for "L.L. Bean" performed through a link to Google from any other search engine will come up empty. The same search that goes directly through google.com will bring up 20 pages of references.[19]

Bundle Pricing

As marketers have watched e-commerce weaken their control over prices, they have modified their use of the price variable in the marketing mix. Whenever possible, they have moved to an approach called **bundle pricing,** where customers acquire a host of goods and services in addition to the tangible products they purchase. In Dallas, SBC Communications' customers can purchase a full-service bundle for $137 a month. This entitles the household to two telephone lines; DirectTV satellite television; discounted local toll calling, wireless calling, and dial-up Internet services; inside wire maintenance on both lines; and 13 add-on features such as voice mail and caller ID. The personal computer industry has proven the feasibility of almost giving away products that require installation, hookups, and ongoing maintenance. In the face of intense price competition for PCs, these firms generate earnings by supplying software, Internet access, e-mail, and downloaded pay-per-view entertainment. A full year's worth of America Online service is now bundled into the purchase of computers from Gateway, while Dell offers AOL free for six months. The bundling is part of a deliberate strategy to increase long-term use, since AOL is counting on the possibility that a high percentage of free users will become paying customers once the trial period is up.[20]

STRATEGIC IMPLICATIONS OF MARKETING IN THE 21ST CENTURY

Over the years, price was arguably the marketing variable least likely to be used as a source of competitive advantage. Even in industries where the discounting phenomenon resulted in radical changes in customer service levels, marketers gradually moved away from this competitive weapon. In moves consistent with discussion of the wheel of retailing theory in upcoming Chapter 16, minimal-service, low-priced operations added services, and prices began to creep up. Some retailers—including giants like Wal-Mart, the world's largest retailer with major international expansion currently taking place in Brazil, China, Germany, and South Korea—continue to use price as a major (but not sole) feature. But firms who use price to attract and retain customers cannot be ignored, and the risk of dangerous, money-losing price wars in such industries is ever present. Not surprisingly, then, many marketers drift toward developing marketing mixes that feature nonprice competition.

But technology has forever changed these markets. The traditional geographic monopolies that permitted inefficient marketers to continue in business are being destroyed by lower-priced, big-selection mass merchandisers whose rapid expansion now places them within a few miles of most shoppers, and they operate in fields as diverse as office supplies and pet food, sporting goods and books, toys and pharmaceuticals.

In addition to the new breed of high-volume marketers featuring unsurpassed selection and major price savings, the Internet has delivered competition to the homes and offices of even the most geographically isolated shoppers. For example, a customer in Kansas might want to purchase an individually carved and painted walking cane from Kenya or an ornamental fan from Kyoto. Not a problem—the Web connects buyers and sellers around the globe. Similarly, the cost of shipping an overnight FedEx package from New York to California is no more than shipping it to a nearby city.

Not only is it possible to escape the boundaries of time and space on the Internet, but price is no longer a constant in the marketing process. With the increasing number of auction sites and new search technologies like bots, customers now have more power to control the prices of goods and services. Consumers can find the lowest prices on the market, and they can also negotiate prices for many of the products they buy.

What marketers must continue to do to remain successful in the 21st century is offer value—good prices for quality goods and services—and superior customer service. These factors are the critical success factors in marketing in the new millennium.

<interactive>review

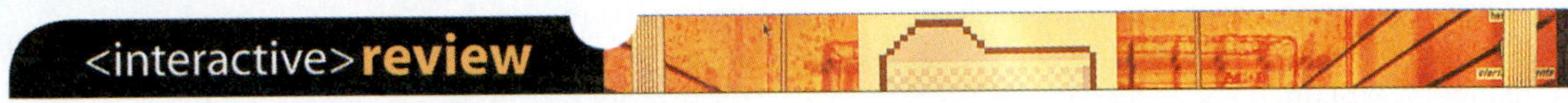

FLASH CHAPTER REVIEW PRESENTATION

<interactive>video case

BOMBARDIER LETS PRICES SOAR

<interactive>game

QUIZ BOWL

<interactive>video case

KRISPY KREME CONTINUING VIDEO CASE: KRISPY KREME—VALUE IN EVERY BITE

endofchaptermaterial

- Summary of Chapter Objectives
- Chapter Outline
- Key Terms
- Review Questions
- Projects and Teamwork Exercises
- 'netWork
- Crossword Puzzles
- Case 14.1: CQC Dental Makes a Price Increase Easier to Swallow

Take the Post-Test to assess your overall understanding of the key ideas in this chapter. The Post-Test provides a comprehensive selection of exam-style questions addressing the main topics and concepts of the chapter. At the completion of each Post-Test, you will receive a score and instructive feedback on how you answered each question, and a direct link to the part of the chapter addressed in the question. Take the Post-Test as often as you need to—a record of your progress for each attempt is kept for you to revisit and gauge your improvement. And each Post-Test is randomly generated, so every attempt is new.

Post-Test

PART 6

Distribution Strategy

CHAPTER 15

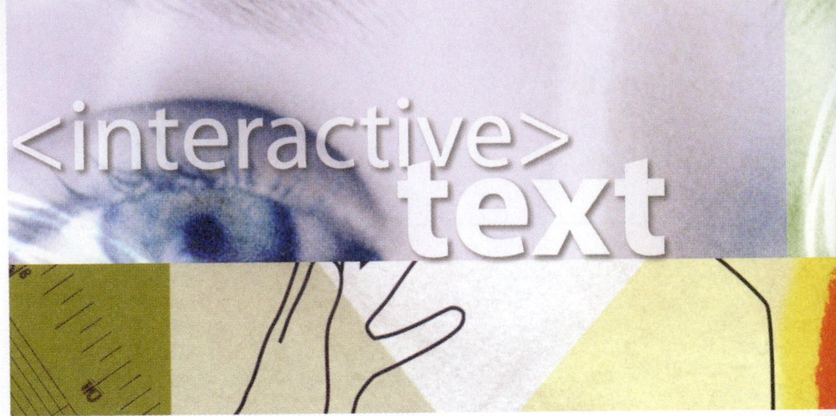

Marketing Channels, Logistics, and Supply Chain Management

Chapter Objectives

1. Describe the roles that marketing channels and logistics play in marketing strategy.
2. Describe the various types of distribution channels available to marketers.
3. Outline the major channel strategy decisions.
4. Describe the concepts of channel management, conflict, and cooperation within the marketing channel.
5. Identify and compare the major components of a physical distribution system.
6. Outline the suboptimization problem in logistics.
7. Compare the major transportation alternatives on the basis of speed, dependability, cost, frequency of shipments, availability in different locations, and flexibility in handling products.
8. Discuss how transportation intermediaries and combined transportation modes can improve physical distribution.

MARINE PROCUREMENT, THE WAL-MART WAY

In the military operation to take over Kandahar Airport during the war in Afghanistan, U.S. Marines carried everything they needed on their backs. Yet sending in troops and sustaining them in hostile territory required Marine logisticians to take care of hundreds of details. Today, the military relies on supplies of all kinds—from food to medical equipment to tank fuel and computer parts. With the revolution in high-tech weapons and computer-guided systems, you'd think methods for procuring the supplies would be equally high-tech. But until recently, the U.S. Marine Corps's system for distributing items to its 173,000 troops did not keep up with the times. All supplies, regardless of their strategic importance, were ordered using the same processes. The ordering scheme encompassed more than 200 different computer systems in use worldwide, and most of them were incompatible with each other. This electronic "Rat's Nest," as Marine technology crews called it, forced soldiers to phone or fax their requests for supplies and created a situation in which it wasn't unusual for an order to take a week to cross from one side of a military base to the other. Errors and waste were commonplace. During the Persian Gulf War, for instance, tons of supplies were stockpiled in an "Iron Mountain" near the front lines. Since no one could keep track of what was in the containers, many items were never used.

Private industry, in the meantime, was developing strategies to save time, cut costs, and boost productivity—all by improving the logistics by which parts and raw materials were delivered to manufacturers just when they were needed and not a moment too soon, or too late. The Marines knew that their system could get better.

So, a 10-year logistics initiative has recently begun in the corps to improve the way in which 10,000 different items pass through 30 distribution centers to reach 450 units around the world. Among the program's goals are the use of the latest computer technology to assist the distribution process, the reduction of many layers of paperwork to a single step, and the elimination of a huge "just-in-case" inventory consisting of a 60-day supply of nearly everything.

"We're in the middle of a revolution," says Lt. Gen. Gary S. McKissock, deputy commander for installations and logistics. That isn't a military revolution. It's an effort to reduce inventory by half, save up to $200 million, and shift about 2,000 troops out of logistics and into the jobs they were trained for. And the Marines aren't in it alone. Consultants from Sapient Corp. and a team from Pennsylvania State University have studied the Marine Corps's supply systems, figuring out what works and what doesn't and recommending improvements —like not stockpiling items that are easy to find, such as office supplies.

Change is expensive, and in the military, budget constraints always have to be kept in mind. But the Marines have also been studying companies like Wal-Mart and United Parcel Service, both known for their ability to move goods quickly and efficiently. They are also looking at Unilever Group and Swissair for ways to improve relationships with suppliers, a key factor in ensuring ready access to hard-to-get items. Caterpillar Inc. has also offered advice about upgrading warehousing and inventory tracking tools.

It will take a few more years to whittle down the number of information technology systems to a manageable 30 to 50 and link them all together. When that is done and the other improvements to the corps's supply logistics are in place, the U.S. Department of Defense plans to roll out the Marines' best practices to the other branches of the armed services. Then it should be just as easy to get a case of bottled water across a base as it is to ship an aircraft engine around the world.[1]

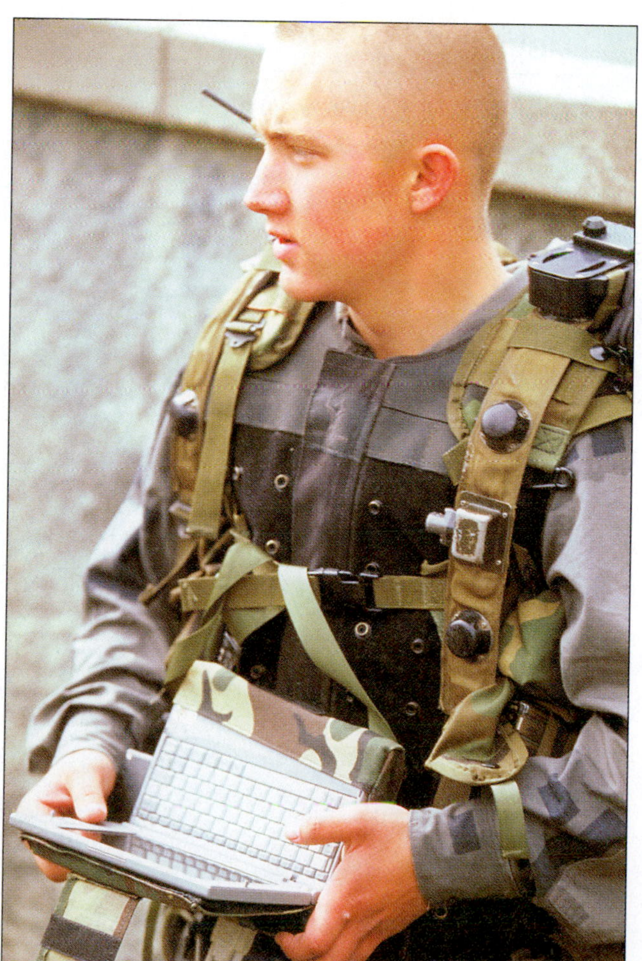

CHAPTER OVERVIEW

Distribution—moving goods and services from producers to customers—is an important marketing concern. Although good design and creative promotion may motivate

Pre-Test

Take the Pre-Test to assess your initial knowledge of the key ideas in this chapter. The Pre-Test provides exam-style questions addressing the main topics and concepts of the chapter. At the completion of each Pre-Test, you will receive a score and instructive feedback on how you answered each question, and a direct link to the part of the chapter addressed in the question. Take the Pre-Test as often as you need to—a record of your progress for each attempt is kept for you to revisit and gauge your improvement.

consumers to purchase a product, these practices are useless if consumers cannot actually buy the product when and where they want it. Distribution strategy has two critical components: marketing channels and logistics.

<interactive>**learning goal**

CHAPTER OBJECTIVE #1: DESCRIBE THE ROLE THAT MARKETING CHANNELS AND LOGISTICS PLAY IN MARKETING STRATEGY.

A **marketing,** or **distribution, channel** is an organized system of marketing institutions and their interrelationships that promote the physical flow and ownership of goods and services from producer to consumer or business user. The choice of marketing channels should support the firm's overall marketing strategy. By contrast, **logistics** refers to the process of coordinating the flow of information, goods, and services among members of the marketing channel. Efficient logistical systems support customer service, enhancing customer relationships—an important goal of any marketing strategy.

A key aspect of logistics is physical distribution, which covers a broad range of activities aimed at efficient movement of finished goods from the end of the production line to the consumer. Although some marketers use the terms *transportation* and *physical distribution* interchangeably, these terms do not carry the same meaning. Physical distribution extends beyond transportation to include such important decision areas as customer service, inventory control, materials handling, protective packaging, order processing, transportation, warehouse site selection, and warehousing.

Well-planned marketing channels and effective logistics provide ultimate users with convenient ways for obtaining the goods and services they desire. This chapter discusses the activities, decisions, and marketing intermediaries involved in managing marketing channels and logistics. Chapter 16 looks at other players in the marketing channel: retailers, direct marketers, and wholesalers.

FIGURE 15.1

Marketing Channels: Linking Buyers and Sellers

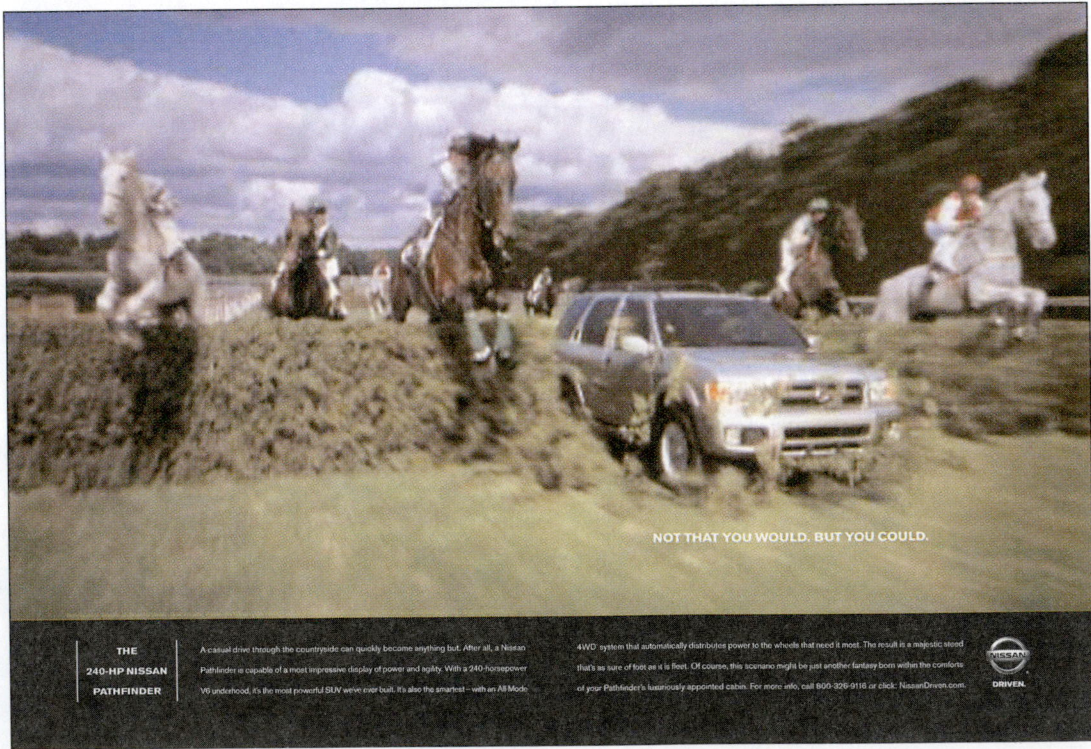

THE ROLE OF MARKETING CHANNELS IN MARKETING STRATEGY

A firm's distribution channels play a key role in its marketing strategy because these channels provide the means by which the firm moves the goods and services it produces to ultimate users. Channels perform four important functions. First, they facilitate the exchange process by cutting the number of marketplace contacts necessary to make a sale. Suppose you want to buy a new SUV. You see an ad for the Nissan Pathfinder like the one in Figure 15.1. The ad prompts you to check Nissan's Web site, where you will be able to find out more about the car and connect with a local dealer. You can also call a toll-free number to make the same connection. The dealer forms part of the channel that brings you, a potential buyer, and Nissan, the seller, together to complete the exchange process.

Distributors adjust for discrepancies in the market's assortment of goods and services via a process known as sorting, the second channeling function. A single producer tends to maximize the quantity it makes of a limited line of goods, while a single buyer needs a limited quantity of a wide selection of merchandise. Sorting alleviates such discrepancies by channeling products to suit both the buyer's and the producer's needs.

The third function of marketing channels involves standardizing exchange transactions by setting expectations for products, and it involves the transfer process itself. Channel members tend to standardize payment terms, delivery schedules, prices, and purchase lots among other conditions.

Finally, marketing channels facilitate searches by both buyers and sellers. Buyers search for specific goods and services to fill their needs, while sellers attempt to learn what buyers want. Channels bring buyers and sellers together to complete the exchange process.

Literally hundreds of distribution channels carry products today, and no single channel best serves the needs of every company. Instead of searching for the best channel for all products, a marketing manager must analyze alternative channels in light of consumer needs to determine the most appropriate channel or channels for the firm's goods and services.

Marketers must remain flexible, however, since channels, like so many marketing variables, may change. Today's ideal channel may prove inappropriate in a few years. As an example, for many years flowers were sold exclusively through independent specialty shops. During the past decade, however, consumer shopping habits have changed as customers started to look for convenience and one-stop shopping. Increasingly, consumers decided to buy flowers in supermarkets, over the telephone, or through the Internet. Consequently, florist services are now available via a variety of marketing channels.

The following sections examine the diverse types of channels available to marketers. The chapter looks at the decisions marketers must make to develop an effective distribution strategy that supports their firm's marketing objectives.

Briefly Speaking

You can do away with middlemen, but you can't do away with the functions they perform.

American business saying

TYPES OF MARKETING CHANNELS

The first step in selecting a marketing channel is determining which type of channel will best meet both the seller's objectives and the distribution needs of customers. Figure 15.2 depicts the major channels available to marketers of consumer and business goods and services.

<interactive>**learning goal**

CHAPTER OBJECTIVE #2: DESCRIBE THE VARIOUS TYPES OF DISTRIBUTION CHANNELS AVAILABLE TO MARKETERS.

Some channel options involve several different *marketing intermediaries.* A marketing intermediary (or *middleman*) is an organization that operates between producers and consumers or business users. Retailers and wholesalers are both marketing intermediaries. A retail store owned and operated by someone other than the manufacturer of the products it sells is one type of marketing intermediary. A *wholesaler* is an intermediary that takes title to the goods it handles and then distributes these goods to retailers, other distributors, or sometimes end consumers.

A short marketing channel involves few intermediaries. By contrast, a long marketing channel involves many intermediaries working in succession to move goods from producers to consumers. In general, business products tend to move through shorter channels than consumer products due to geographical concentrations and comparatively few business purchasers. Service firms market primarily through short channels because they sell intangible products and need to maintain personal relationships within their channels. Not-for-profit organizations also tend to work with short, simple, and direct channels. Any marketing intermediaries in such channels usually act as agents, such as independent ticket agencies or fundraising specialists.

FIGURE 15.2

Alternative Marketing Channels

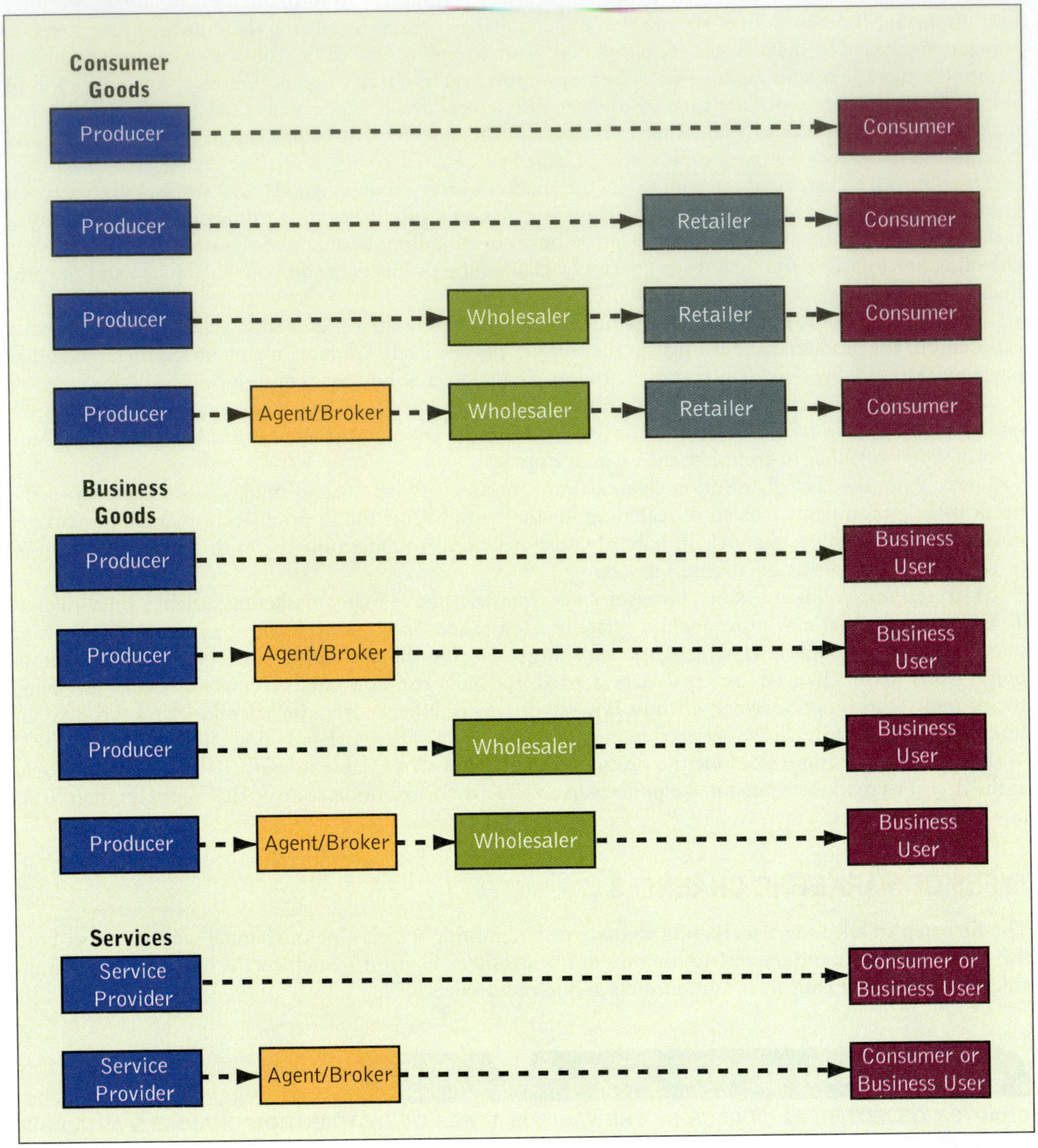

Direct Selling

The simplest and shortest marketing channel is a direct channel. A **direct channel** carries goods directly from a producer to the business purchaser or ultimate user. This channel forms part of *direct selling,* a marketing strategy in which a producer establishes direct sales contact with its product's final users. Direct selling is an important option for goods that require extensive demonstrations in convincing customers to buy.

Direct selling plays a significant role in business-to-business marketing. Most major installations, accessory equipment, and even component parts and raw materials are sold through direct contacts between producing firms and final buyers. Firms that market products to other businesses often develop and maintain large sales forces to call on potential customers.

Direct selling is also important in consumer goods markets. Direct sellers, such as Mary Kay, Amway, and Avon, sidestep competition in store aisles by developing networks of independent dealers that sell their products direct to consumers. Even the Avon Web site, shown in Figure 15.3, links customers to one of the company's 30,000 sales reps, operating in their own localities. Avon kiosks in shopping malls, too, are operated by local reps, maintaining a simple, direct channel between the "Avon lady" and her customers.[2]

FIGURE 15.3

Avon's Web Site: Connecting Consumers Directly with Avon Representatives

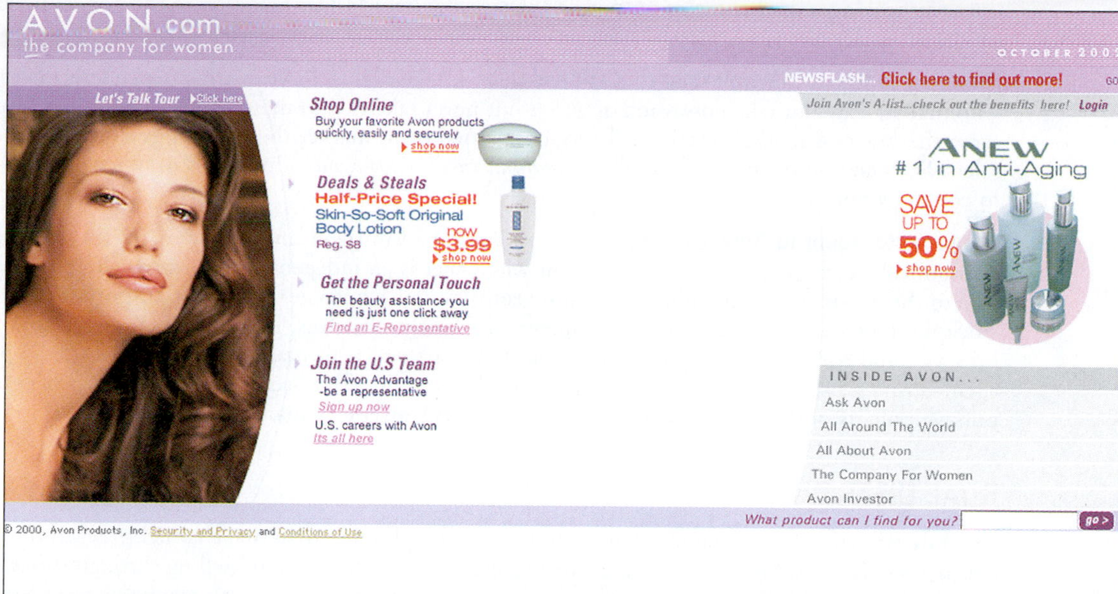

A traditional direct selling strategy is the so-called party plan, popularized by Tupperware and others. Recent hits include candle parties, cookware parties, and basket parties. The seller recruits someone to invite friends to her home, where the seller demonstrates goods and encourages guests to make purchases. Longaberger Basket, which started as a one-store operation in Dresden, Ohio, now markets products from more than 7,000 designers through basket parties run by 70,000 independent sales associates. Other direct sellers have used party plans to sell everything from lingerie to popcorn.[3]

Dell Computer Corp. sells computers and computer parts directly to companies, government agencies, and consumers. Dell builds computers to customer specifications, configured for processor speed, hard drive size, and monitor type. Michael Dell founded the company as a 19-year-old college student when he realized how difficult it was to track down parts for his own computer system. By buying parts from manufacturers, assembling them, and selling directly to customers, Dell is able to cut overhead and save customers money at the same time. Today, Dell sells more than $31.2 billion worth of computers each year via telephone and the Internet. Recent expansions into network servers, storage, and communications equipment promise continued rapid growth. Case 15.1 at the end of the chapter features Dell Direct.[4]

Channels Using Marketing Intermediaries

Although direct channels allow simple and straightforward marketing, they do not always move goods from producers to consumers efficiently. Some products serve geographically dispersed markets or large numbers of potential end users. Other categories of goods rely heavily on repeat purchases. The producers of these goods may find more efficient, less expensive, and less time-consuming alternatives to direct channels by using marketing intermediaries. This section considers five channels that involve marketing intermediaries.

Producer to Wholesaler to Retailer to Consumer The traditional channel for consumer goods proceeds from producer to wholesaler to retailer to user. This method carries goods between small retailers and literally thousands of small producers with limited lines. Small producers with limited financial resources rely on the services of wholesalers as immediate sources of funds and as marketers to hundreds of retailers that will stock their output. Small retailers draw on wholesalers' specialized buying skills, which ensure balanced inventories of goods produced in various regions of the world. The wholesaler's sales force promotes the producer's output to its customers. In addition, many manufacturers employ field sales representatives to service retail accounts. These representatives serve as sources of marketing information, but actual sales are typically handled by wholesalers.

Producer to Wholesaler to Business User Similar characteristics in the organizational market often attract marketing intermediaries to operate between producers and business purchasers. The term *industrial distributor* commonly refers to intermediaries in the business market that take title to the goods.

Producer to Agent to Wholesaler to Retailer to Consumer When many small companies serve a market, a unique intermediary—the agent—performs the basic function of bringing buyer and seller together. An agent may or may not take possession of the goods but never takes title. The agent merely represents a producer by seeking a market for its output or a wholesaler (which does take title to the goods) by locating a source of supply.

Producer to Agent to Wholesaler to Business User Like agents, brokers are independent intermediaries who may or may not take possession of goods but never take title to these goods. Agents and brokers also serve the business market when small producers attempt to market their offerings through large wholesalers. Such an intermediary, often called a *manufacturers' representative,* provides an independent sales force to contact wholesale buyers.

Producer to Agent to Business User For products sold in small units, only merchant wholesalers can economically cover the markets. A merchant wholesaler is an independently owned wholesaler that takes title to the goods. By maintaining regional inventories, this wholesaler achieves transportation economies, stockpiling goods and making small shipments over short distances. For a product with large unit sales, however, and for which transportation accounts for a small percentage of the total cost, the producer-agent-business user channel is usually employed. The agent in effect becomes the producer's sales force, but bulk shipments of the product reduce the intermediary's inventory management function.

DUAL DISTRIBUTION

Dual distribution refers to movement of products through more than one channel to reach the same target market. Talbot's, for instance, has a three-pronged distribution system, selling through stores, catalogs, and the Internet. Marketers usually adopt this distribution strategy either to maximize their firm's coverage in the marketplace or to increase the cost effectiveness of the firm's marketing effort. For instance, automobile parts manufacturers promote products through both direct sales forces and independent jobbers. The cost-effectiveness goal, on the other hand, might lead a manufacturer to assign its own sales force to sell in high-potential territories while relying on manufacturers' representatives (independent, commissioned salespeople) in lower volume areas.

Starbucks, which once relied on its franchised coffee-shop network, now offers its whole-bean coffees through grocery stores. The ad in Figure 15.4 invites coffee drinkers to take the distinctive taste of Starbucks home with them.

FIGURE 15.4

Starbucks' Dual Distribution Strategy

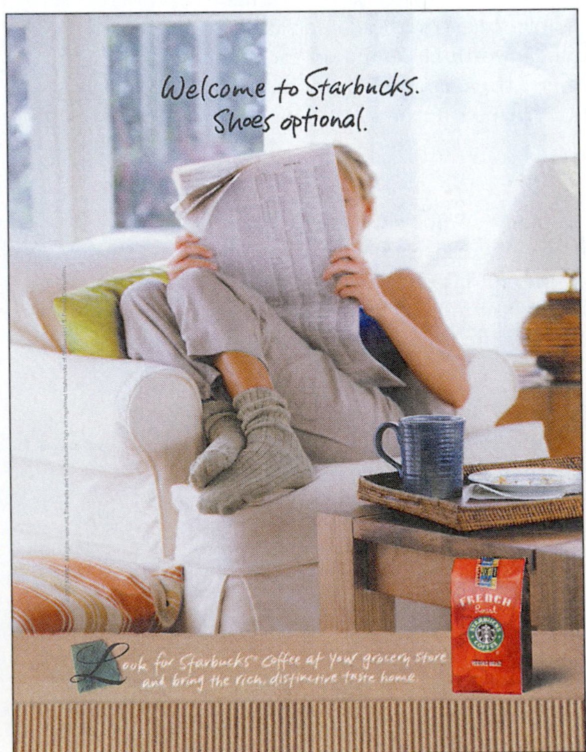

REVERSE CHANNELS

While the traditional concept of marketing channels involves the movement of goods and services from producer to consumer or business user, marketers should not ignore *reverse channels*—channels designed to return goods to their producers. Reverse channels have gained increased importance with rising prices for raw materials, spreading availability of recycling facilities, and passage of additional conservation laws. For instance, consumers pay refundable deposits on bottled products in states like Maine, Michigan, and Oregon. New Jersey requires businesses and households to separate their trash to aid recycling.

Some reverse channels move through the facilities of traditional marketing intermediaries. In states that require bottle deposits, retailers and local bottlers perform these functions in the soft-drink industry. For other products, manufacturers establish redemption centers, develop systems for rechanneling products for recycling, and create specialized organizations to handle disposal and recycling. Other reverse channel participants include community groups that organize cleanup days and develop recycling and waste disposal systems.

Reverse channels also handle product recalls and repairs. Registration of car owners allows manufacturers to send proper notification in the event of recalls. For example, an automobile recall notice might advise owners of potential problems that may need correcting at their dealerships. Similarly, reverse channels have carried some items to manufacturers' repair centers. The warranty for a small appliance might direct the owner to return a defective unit to the dealer for repairs within 90 days after the sale and to the factory after that period. Such reverse channels are a vital element of product recall and repair procedures.

CHANNEL STRATEGY DECISIONS

Marketers face several strategic decisions in choosing channels and marketing intermediaries for their products. Selecting a specific channel is the most basic of these decisions. Marketers must also resolve questions about the level of distribution intensity, the desirability of vertical marketing systems, and the performance of current intermediaries.

<interactive>**learning goal**

CHAPTER OBJECTIVE #3: OUTLINE THE MAJOR CHANNEL STRATEGY DECISIONS.

Selection of a Marketing Channel

Consider, for example, the following questions: What characteristics of a franchised dealer network make it the best channel option for a company? Why do operating supplies often go through both agents and merchant wholesalers before reaching their actual users? Why would a firm market a single product through multiple channels? Marketers must answer many such questions in choosing marketing channels.

A variety of factors impact the selection of a marketing channel. Some channel decisions are dictated by the marketplace in which the company operates. In other cases, the product itself may be a key variable in picking a marketing channel. Finally, the marketing organization may set limits or offer opportunities related to specific distribution channels.

Market Factors Channel structure reflects a product's intended markets, either for consumers or business users. Business purchasers usually prefer to deal directly with manufacturers (except for routine supplies or small accessory items), but most consumers make their purchases from retailers. Marketers often sell products that serve both business users and consumers through more than one channel.

Other market factors also affect channel choice, including the market's needs, its geographical location, and its average order size. To serve a concentrated market with a small number of buyers, a direct channel offers a feasible alternative. To serve a geographically dispersed potential market in which customers purchase small amounts in individual transactions—the conditions in the consumer goods market—distribution through marketing intermediaries makes sense.

Product Factors Product characteristics also guide the choice of an optimal marketing channel strategy. Perishable goods, such as fresh produce, beverages, and fashion products with short life cycles, typically move through short channels.

One way that the Coca-Cola Company sells its beverages is through vending machines, a relatively short channel. Vending machine sales account for 10 percent of the company's unit volume in the U.S. To maximize customer convenience, the firm is exploring radio-frequency identification in which office workers can swipe a key chain in front of a machine to buy a can of pop instead of using change. Meanwhile, United Artists, which operates 206 theaters, is testing vending machines that cook frozen pizzas from Kraft Foods in less than 90 seconds.[5]

Complex products, producers of custom-made installations, and computer equipment are often sold directly to ultimate buyers. In general, relatively standardized items pass through comparatively long channels. For another generalization, low product unit values, such as a pack of Post-it notes shown in Figure 15.5, call for long channels.

Organizational Factors Companies with adequate financial, management, and marketing resources feel little need for help from intermediaries. A financially strong manufacturer can hire its own sales force, warehouse its own goods, and grant credit to retailers or consumers. A weaker firm must rely on marketing

FIGURE 15.5

Post-it Notes: A Simple Product with a Long Distribution Channel

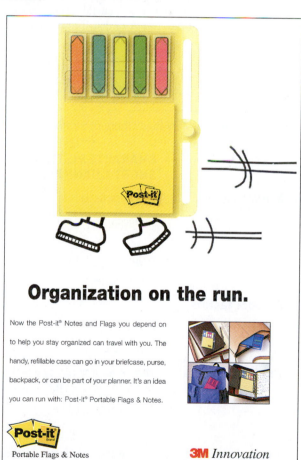

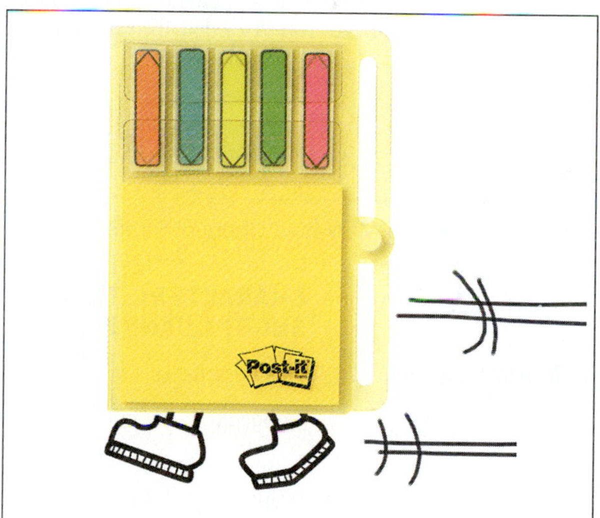

Organization on the run.

Now the Post-it® Notes and Flags you depend on to help you stay organized can travel with you. The handy, refillable case can go in your briefcase, purse, backpack, or can be part of your planner. It's an idea you can run with: Post-it® Portable Flags & Notes.

Portable Flags & Notes

3M Innovation

For more information, visit our website at: http://www.post-it.com/flags or call 1-800-854-4266

© 2000, 3M. Post-it is a registered trademark of 3M.

intermediaries for these services. In one exception, a large retail chain may purchase all of a manufacturer's output, bypassing independent wholesalers. A production-oriented firm may need the marketing expertise of intermediaries to offset its own lack of such skills.

A firm with a broad product line can usually market its products directly to retailers or business users since its own sales force can offer a variety of products. High sales volume spreads selling costs over a large number of items, allowing returns from direct sales. Single-product firms often view direct selling as unaffordable.

The manufacturer's desire for control over marketing of its product also influences channel selection. To ensure aggressive promotion by retailers, producers often choose the shortest available channels. To distribute a new product, the producer may have to implement an informative advertising campaign before independent wholesalers will agree to handle the campaign.

Businesses that explore new marketing channels must be careful to avoid antagonizing their channel intermediaries. Lids Corporation, a mall retailer of hats and caps, sought a means of offering 7,000 non-store items to mall buyers without alienating sales associates. The company installed point-of-sale kiosks—with a Web site hook-up—inside its stores. Salespeople guide in-store customers around the site and earn commissions on purchases initiated inside the store.[6]

Competitive Factors Some firms feel compelled to develop new marketing channels to remedy inadequate promotion of their products by independent marketing intermediaries. In one popular alternative, a manufacturer might add a direct sales force or set up its own retail distribution network (a move discussed later in the chapter). Table 15.1 summarizes the factors that affect the selection of a marketing channel and examines the effect of each on the channel's overall length.

Determining Distribution Intensity

Another key channel strategy decision is the intensity of distribution. *Distribution intensity* refers to the number of intermediaries through which a manufacturer distributes its goods. The decision about distribution intensity should ensure adequate market coverage for a product. Adequate market coverage varies depending on the goals of the individual firm, the type of product, and the consumer segments in its target market. In general, however, distribution intensity varies along a continuum with three general categories: intensive distribution, selective distribution, and exclusive distribution.

TABLE 15.1

Factors Influencing Marketing Channel Strategies

	CHARACTERISTICS OF SHORT CHANNELS	CHARACTERISTICS OF LONG CHANNELS
Market factors	Business users	Consumers
	Geographically concentrated	Geographically dispersed
	Extensive technical knowledge and regular servicing required	Little technical knowledge and regular servicing not required
	Large orders	Small orders
Product factors	Perishable	Durable
	Complex	Standardized
	Expensive	Inexpensive
Producer factors	Manufacturer has adequate resources to perform channel functions	Manufacturer lacks adequate resources to perform channel functions
	Broad product line	Limited product line
	Channel control important	Channel control not important
Competitive factors	Manufacturing feels satisfied with marketing intermediaries' performance in promoting products	Manufacturer feels dissatisfied with marketing intermediaries' performance in promoting products

Intensive Distribution An **intensive distribution** strategy seeks to distribute a product through all available channels in a trade area. M&M Mars, for example, implements an intensive distribution strategy, placing its products in supermarkets, chain stores, vending machines, and drugstores. Producers of convenience goods try to saturate their markets, enabling purchasers to buy their products with minimum efforts. Usually, an intensive distribution strategy suits items with wide appeal across broad groups of consumers. Examples of goods distributed through this strategy include soft drinks, candy, gum, and cigarettes.

Selective Distribution In another market coverage strategy, **selective distribution,** a firm chooses only a limited number of retailers in a market area to handle its line. This arrangement helps to control price cutting since relatively few dealers handle the firm's line. By limiting the number of retailers, marketers can reduce total marketing costs while establishing strong working relationships within the channel. Moreover, selected retailers often agree to comply with the company's strict rules for advertising, pricing, and displaying its products. *Cooperative advertising,* in which the manufacturer pays a percentage of the retailer's advertising expenditures and the retailer prominently displays the firm's products, can be utilized for mutual benefit, and marginal retailers can be avoided. Where service is important, the manufacturer usually provides training and assistance to dealers it chooses.

Exclusive Distribution When a producer grants exclusive rights to a wholesaler or retailer to sell its products in a specific geographical region, it practices **exclusive distribution,** an extension of selective distribution. The automobile industry provides the best example of exclusive distribution. A city with a population of 40,000 may have a single Mazda or Ford dealer. Exclusive distribution agreements also govern marketing for some major appliance and apparel brands.

Marketers may sacrifice some market coverage by implementing a policy of exclusive distribution. As compensation, however, they often develop and maintain an image of quality and prestige for the product. In addition, exclusive distribution limits marketing costs since the firm deals with a smaller number of accounts. In exclusive distribution, producers and retailers cooperate closely in decisions concerning advertising and promotion, inventory carried by the retailers, and prices.

In recent years, carmakers have sought to gain tighter control over the sales process, traditionally the dealerships' domain. DaimlerChrysler initiated its Five Star program, through which it rewards dealers who meet its sales training, customer service, and relationship management objectives by sharing some marketing costs and awarding special recognition. Despite initial resistance from dealers who resented being told how to run their businesses, more than half of all Chrysler dealers are now certified. Ford's best practice system, Blue Oval, is similar but offers cash incentives in the form of an additional 1.25 percent discount off wholesale prices.[7]

Legal Problems of Exclusive Distribution Exclusive distribution presents potential legal problems in three main areas: exclusive dealing agreements, closed sales territories, and tying agreements. Although none of these practices is illegal per se, all may break the law if they reduce competition or tend to create monopolies.

As part of an exclusive distribution strategy, marketers may try to enforce an *exclusive dealing agreement,* which prohibits a marketing intermediary (a wholesaler or, more typically, a retailer) from handling competing products. Producers of high-priced shopping goods, specialty goods, and accessory equipment often require such agreements to assure total concentration on their own product lines. Such contracts violate the Clayton Act only if the producer's or dealer's sales volumes represent a substantial percentage of total sales in the market area. While exclusive dealing is legal for companies first entering a market, such agreements violate the Clayton Act if used by firms with a sizable market share seeking to bar competitors from the market.

Producers may also try to set up *closed sales territories* to restrict their distributors to certain geographical regions. Although the distributors gain protection from rival dealers in their exclusive territories, they sacrifice any opportunities in opening new facilities or marketing the manufacturers' products outside their assigned territories. The legality of a system of closed sales territories depends on whether the restriction decreases competition. If so, it violates the Federal Trade Commission Act and provisions of the Sherman Act and the Clayton Act.

The legality of closed sales territories also depends on whether the system imposes horizontal or vertical restrictions. Horizontal territorial restrictions result from agreements between retailers or wholesalers to avoid competition among sellers of products from the same producer. Such agreements consistently have been declared illegal. However, the U.S. Supreme Court has ruled that vertical territorial restrictions—those between producers and wholesalers or retailers—may meet legal criteria. The ruling gives no clear-cut answer, but such agreements likely satisfy the law in cases where manufacturers occupy relatively small parts of their markets. In such instances, the restrictions may actually increase competition among competing brands; the wholesaler or retailer faces no competition from other dealers carrying the manufacturer's brand, so it can concentrate on effectively competing with other brands.

The third legal question of exclusive dealing involves *tying agreements,* which allow channel members to become exclusive dealers only if they also carry products other than those that they want to sell. In the apparel industry, for example, an agreement might require a dealer to carry a comparatively unpopular line of clothing to get desirable, fast-moving items.

BMW North America expanded its channels to include its Financial Services division. The company started with vehicle financing for its autos and motorcycles, and it has now branched into personal banking for the BMW driver, offering such services as credit cards, certificates of deposit, and money market accounts.

Tying agreements violate the Sherman Act and the Clayton Act when they reduce competition or create monopolies that keep competitors out of major markets. For this reason, the courts prohibited International Salt Company from selling salt as a tying product with leases of its patented salt-dispensing machines for snow and ice removal. The Supreme Court ruled that such an agreement unreasonably reduced competition among sellers of salt.

Who Should Perform Channel Functions?

A fundamental marketing principle governs channel decisions: Some member of the channel must perform certain central marketing functions; channel members can shift responsibility, but they cannot eliminate those functions. Although independent wholesalers perform many of these functions for manufacturers, retailers, and other wholesaler clients, other channel members could fulfill these roles instead. Manufacturers might, for example, bypass wholesalers by establishing regional warehouses, maintaining field sales forces, serving as sources of information for retail customers, or arranging details of financing. Carmakers, for example, who have long operated credit units that offer new-car financing, have even opened their own banks. Within a year of opening, BMW's bank signed up 25,000 customers.[8] Rather than fill the intermediary function themselves, manufacturers might push responsibility for some functions through the channel to retailers or ultimate purchasers. Large retailers face the same choices, but the principle remains the same: Channel members can eliminate an intermediary only when someone else performs its channel functions.

An independent intermediary earns a profit in exchange for providing services to manufacturers and retailers. This profit margin is low, however, ranging from 1 percent for food wholesalers to 5 percent for durable goods wholesalers. Manufacturers and retailers could reap these profits, or they could market directly and reduce retail prices—but only if they could perform the channel functions and match the efficiency of the independent intermediaries.

To grow profitably in a competitive environment, an intermediary must provide better service at lower costs than manufacturers or retailers can provide for themselves. In this case, consolidation of channel functions can represent a strategic opportunity for a company.

The $5 million pawnshop industry, at first suspicious that availability of used products over the Internet would damage sales, has discovered that the opposite is true. Pawnshops like California-based Desert Jewelry Mart use online auction site eBay as an intermediary in selling hard-to-move merchandise such as buffalo teeth, muskrat skulls, or some Native American jewelry. By selling online through eBay, Desert Jewelry has tripled its revenues.[9]

CHANNEL MANAGEMENT AND LEADERSHIP

Distribution strategy does not end with the choice of a channel. Manufacturers must also focus on channel management by developing and maintaining relationships with the intermediaries in their marketing channels. Positive channel relationships encourage channel members to remember their partners' goods and market them. Manufacturers also must carefully manage the incentives offered to induce channel members to promote their products. This effort includes weighing decisions about pricing, promotion, and other support efforts that the manufacturer performs.

CHAPTER OBJECTIVE #4: DESCRIBE THE CONCEPTS OF CHANNEL MANAGEMENT, CONFLICT, AND COOPERATION WITHIN THE MARKETING CHANNEL.

Increasingly, marketers are managing channels in partnership with other channel members. Effective cooperation allows all channel members to achieve goals that they could not achieve on their own. Keys to successful management of channel relationships include the development of high levels of coordination, commitment, and trust between channel members.

Not all channel members wield equal power in the distribution chain, however. The dominant and controlling member of a marketing channel is called the **channel captain.** This firm's power to control a channel may result from its control over some type of reward or punishment to other channel members, such as granting an exclusive sales territory or taking away a dealership. Power might also result from contractual arrangements, specialized expert knowledge, or agreement among channel members about their mutual best interests. Central Steel & Wire Company controls the distribution of its products through its Performance Assured service system. The company provides on-time delivery by operating its own fleet of delivery trucks and helps customers reduce their inventory costs by offering just-in-time and distributor managed inventory programs.

Channel Conflict

Channel captains often must work to resolve channel conflicts. Marketing channels work smoothly only when members cooperate in well-organized efforts to achieve maximum operating efficiencies, yet channel members often perform as separate, independent, and even competing forces. Too often, marketing institutions see only one step forward or backward along a channel. They think about their own suppliers and customers rather than about vital links throughout the channel. Two types of conflict—horizontal and vertical—may hinder the normal functioning of a marketing channel.

Horizontal Conflict Horizontal conflict sometimes results from disagreements among channel members at the same level, such as two or more wholesalers or two or more retailers, or among marketing intermediaries of the same type, such as two competing discount stores or several retail florists. With 1,675 dealerships nationwide, farm equipment manufacturer Deere & Company has run into conflicts with its dealer network. Dealers complain that high saturation—48 dealers in a 35-mile radius in Ohio, for example—along with a downturn in the farming industry has reduced their ability to achieve market share. Not only must they compete against other manufactures, but too many Deere dealers are chasing after the same customers.[10]

More often, horizontal conflict causes sparks between different types of marketing intermediaries that handle similar products. An independent retail druggist competes with discount houses, department stores, convenience stores, mail-order houses, and Internet sites, all of which may buy identical branded products from a single producer. Varied consumer preferences have drawn products into multiple channels and numerous rival outlets.

Consider the experiences of furniture manufacturer American Leather. One of its retailers set up a Web site offering Internet-only discounts to consumers outside its exclusive territories, sparking fury among rival dealers. At first, the company reacted by forbidding retail partners to use its brand name or image for e-commerce. But this solution was far from ideal because it closed off the company from sales and promotion opportunities through fast-growing Internet channels. It also frustrated dealers who had developed costly Web sites of their own. Instead, American Leather updated its own Web site with detailed product information and a "dealer locator" system that directed customers to local stores. The company also stepped up its advertising in consumer magazines and newspapers in an effort to drive customers first to the site and from there to retail outlets. Within a year, sales from the same dealer base were up by 40 percent.[11]

Vertical Conflict Vertical relationships also cause frequent and often severe conflict. Channel members at different levels find many reasons for disputes, as when retailers develop private brands to compete with producers' brands or when producers establish their own retail stores or create mail-order operations that compete with retailers. Producers may annoy wholesalers and retailers when they attempt to bypass these intermediaries and sell directly to consumers. In one well-publicized case, Levi Strauss suspended attempts to sell over its own Web site following complaints from enraged retailers. In another, a Chicago area carpet dealer attempted to set up a reverse auction site—Carpetshopping.com—that allowed customers to purchase any brand of carpet at discount prices. Customers fed their requirements into the site, and then dealers offered bids to fulfill the sales. The lowest bidder won the right to strike a deal with the customer. Fearful that Internet discounts would drive down prices at retail, the three largest carpet manufacturers—which account for 80 percent of the $26 billion market—demanded that Yahoo! close down the offending Web site. The biggest of the three revoked the dealer's exclusive license.[12]

In other instances, retailers may anger suppliers by requesting concessions suppliers believe are unfair. The "Solving an Ethical Controversy" Interactive Example explains the practice of *slotting fees,* or *slotting allowances* (discussed in Chapter 11), in which retailers demand payment for granting new products coveted shelf space. In other instances, retailers take unexpected deductions from payments to manufacturers to cover damaged or defective goods. Although retailers allege deductions like these cover essential costs that belong with the producers, manufacturers claim retailers are using their power as channel captains to reduce the cost of goods.

<interactive>example

RIGHT/WRONG: SOLVING AN ETHICAL CONTROVERSY—SECRET COSTS OF SHELF SPACE

The Grey Market Another type of channel conflict results from activities in the grey market. As U.S. manufacturers license their technology and brands abroad, they sometimes find themselves in competition in the U.S. market against versions of their own brands produced by overseas affiliates. These *grey goods,* or *parallel goods,* enter U.S. channels through the actions of foreign distributors. While licensing agreements usually prohibit foreign licensees from selling in the U.S., no such rules inhibit their distributors.

A decade ago, the grey market became a problem for U.S. firms in the electronics field. It then spread to such products as flashlight batteries, photographic film, packaged goods, and the apparel industry. Some manufacturers have protested against this practice, but retailers can still legally buy goods through the grey market because the Supreme Court has ruled that products made under legitimate licenses can legally enter the market regardless of their countries of origin.

Because of the disproportionately high cost of medications in the U.S., many consumers turn to Canada to fill prescriptions. Internet sites like unitedhealthalliance.com forward a medical history along with a doctor's prescription to a Canadian pharmacy. Once a Canadian doctor reviews the order, the drugs are shipped directly to the patient's home in the U.S. Although it is technically illegal to import drugs, authorities have made exceptions for "personal use." Recently, the U.S. Senate backed a bill that would allow reimportation of U.S. drugs from Canada. Although the ultimate fate of the bill is uncertain, widespread support exists for this measure.[13]

Achieving Channel Cooperation

The basic antidote to channel conflict is effective cooperation among channel members. Cooperation is best achieved when all channel members regard themselves as components of the same organization. Achieving this kind of cooperation is the primary responsibility of the dominant member—the channel captain—which must provide the leadership necessary to ensure the channel's efficient functioning.

VERTICAL MARKETING SYSTEMS

Efforts to reduce channel conflict and improve the effectiveness of distribution have led to the development of vertical marketing systems. A **vertical marketing system (VMS)** is a planned channel system designed to improve distribution efficiency and cost effectiveness by integrating various functions throughout the distribution chain.

A vertical marketing system can achieve this goal through either forward or backward integration. In *forward integration,* a firm attempts to control downstream distribution. For example, a manufacturer might buy a retail chain that sells its products. *Backward integration* occurs when a manufacturer attempts to gain greater control over inputs in its production process. A manufacturer might buy the supplier of a raw material the manufacturer uses in the production of its products. Backward integration can also extend the control of retailers and wholesalers over producers that supply them.

A VMS offers several benefits. First, it improves chances for controlling and coordinating the steps in the distribution or production process. It may lead to the development of economies of scale that ultimately saves money. A VMS may also let a manufacturer expand into profitable new businesses. However, a VMS also involves some costs. A manufacturer assumes increased risk when it takes control of an entire distribution chain. Manufacturers may also discover that they lose some flexibility in responding to market changes.

Marketers have developed three categories of VMSs: corporate systems, administered systems, and contractual systems. These categories are outlined in the sections that follow.

Corporate Systems

Where a single owner runs organizations at each stage of the marketing channel, it operates a **corporate marketing system.** The "Marketing Hits" Interactive Example explains one company's success in marketing lifestyle products through company-owned stores and tightly controlled independent retailers. Phillips Auctioneers, shown in Figure 15.6, restricts its channels to company-owned salesrooms in the U.S., the U.K., and Switzerland, supplemented by representatives in 15 countries. A Web site connects potential customers with sales representatives.

MARKETING HIT: COACH BUILDS A WORLD-CLASS ACCESSORY BUSINESS WITH A CORPORATE MARKETING CHANNEL

FIGURE 15.6

Channel Leadership

Administered Systems

An **administered marketing system** achieves channel coordination when a dominant channel member exercises its power. Even though Goodyear sells its tires through independently owned and operated dealerships, Goodyear controls the stock that these dealerships carry. Other examples of powerful channel captains leading administered channels include McKesson, Sears, and Wal-Mart.

Contractual Systems

Instead of common ownership of intermediaries within a corporate VMS or the exercising of power within an administered system, a **contractual marketing system** coordinates distribution through formal agreements among channel members. In practice, three types of agreements set up these systems: wholesaler-sponsored voluntary chains, retail cooperatives, and franchises.

Wholesaler-Sponsored Voluntary Chain A wholesaler-sponsored voluntary chain represents an attempt by an independent wholesaler to preserve a market by strengthening its retail customers. To enable independent retailers to compete with outlets of rival chains, the wholesaler enters into a formal agreement with retailers to use a common name, maintain standardized facilities, and purchase the wholesaler's products. Often, the wholesaler develops a line of private brands to be stocked by the members of the voluntary chain.

IGA (Independent Grocers' Alliance) Food Stores is a good example of a voluntary chain. Other wholesaler-sponsored chains include Associated Druggists, Sentry Hardware, and Western Auto. Since a single advertisement promotes all the retailers in the trading area, a common store name and similar inventories allow the retailers to save on advertising costs.

Retail Cooperative In a second type of contractual VMS, a group of retailers establish a shared wholesaling operation to help them compete with chains. This is known as a retail cooperative. The retailers purchase ownership shares in the wholesaling operation and agree to buy a minimum percentage of their inventories from this operation. The members typically adopt a common store name and develop common private brands. Ace Hardware is an example of a retail cooperative.

Franchise A third type of contractual vertical marketing system is the franchise, in which a wholesaler or dealer (the franchisee) agrees to meet the operating requirements of a manufacturer or other franchiser. Franchising is a huge and growing industry. Twenty years ago, Subway had 134 franchises and McDonald's had 5,749; today, Subway has almost 17,000 franchises and McDonald's boasts more than 30,000 outlets worldwide. Over 3,000 U.S. companies distribute goods and services through systems of franchised dealers, and numerous firms also offer franchises in international markets. The total number of franchise units tops 250,000, and it continues to rise. The five fastest growing franchise categories are photo processing, human resource training, children's businesses, computer services, and maintenance companies.

Franchise owners pay anywhere from several thousand dollars to hundreds of thousands of dollars to purchase their franchises. Typically, they also pay a royalty on sales to the franchising company. In exchange for these initial and ongoing fees, the franchise owner receives the right to use the company's brand name as well as services such as training, marketing, advertising, and volume discounts. Franchise fees for top brands are shown in Figure 15.7.

Major franchise chains justify the steep price of entry since it allows new businesses to hitch onto winning brands. But if the brand enters a slump or the corporation behind the franchise makes poor strategic decisions, franchisees feel the pain. In recent years, Burger King, the number two fast-food chain, made moves that negatively influenced the revenues of franchisees. Troubles began when the company withdrew its longstanding 99-cent Whopper promotion, depriving owners of a powerful tool for drawing diners into their restaurants. A series of movie tie-ins with some box-office busts exacerbated the problem. Plans to overhaul restaurant designs and kitchen operations—at a cost to owners of $250,000 per store—enraged franchisees. Recently, Burger King has scaled back remodeling plans and strengthened menu choices. Tie-ins with recent hit movies have improved the outlook for franchisees. Even so, a Los Angeles–based owner of 140 Burger King franchises claims to have lost millions of dollars because of corporate-mandated policies.[14]

Briefly Speaking

There are no problems we cannot solve together, and very few we can solve by ourselves.

Lyndon B. Johnson (1908–1973) 36th president of the United States

THE ROLE OF LOGISTICS IN DISTRIBUTION STRATEGY

Pier 1 imports its eclectic mix of items from 600 vendors in 55 countries, and more than 80 percent come from small companies. If high-demand items or seasonal products are late into its warehouses or are shipped in insufficient quantities, the company misses opportunities to deliver popular shopping choices at its 700 retail stores and risks losing ground to competitors such as Pottery Barn and Crate & Barrel.

This situation illustrates the importance of logistics. Careful coordination of Pier 1's supplier network, its shipping processes, and its inventory control is the key to its continuing success. Yet while rival merchandisers manage to sell through inventory at a rate of three times a year, Pier 1's turnover rate is not much better than two turns a year. In a recent year, this meant the company paid for $34 million worth of goods that—due to inventory logjams—did not make it onto retail shelves. To improve its processes, Pier 1's logistics team is implementing an electronic monitoring system that will track goods as they move from the point of origin into retail outlets. If sales of a particular product in a particular region move faster than anticipated, the company will be able to divert shipments of goods to undersupplied warehouses. The system will also improve storage-space allocation and labor assignments, making for better efficiencies in unpacking containers and moving goods out to retail stores while demand is still high.[15]

Effective logistics requires proper management of the supply chain (also known as the value chain). As discussed in Chapter 6, the *supply chain* is the complete sequence of suppliers that contribute to the creation and delivery of merchandise. The supply chain begins with the raw-material inputs for the manufacturing process of a product and then proceeds to the actual production activities. The final link in the supply chain is the movement of finished goods through the marketing channel to customers. Each link of the chain benefits the consumers as goods move from raw materials through manufacturing to distribution. The value chain encompasses all activities that enhance the value of the finished goods, including design, quality manufacturing, customer service, and delivery. Customer satisfaction results directly from the perceived value of a purchase to its buyer. To manage the supply chain, businesses must look for ways to add and maximize customer value in each activity they perform.

FIGURE 15.7

Costs of Acquiring Top Franchise Brands

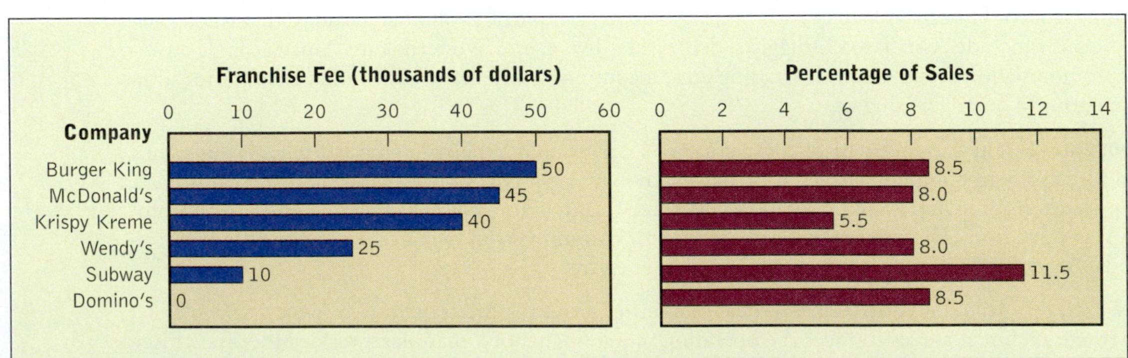

Source: Data from companies; Kessev Finance, in Daniel Kruger, "Carrying the Flame," *Forbes*, December 24, 2001, p. 65.

As Pier 1's experience makes clear, logistical management plays a major role in giving customers what they need when they need it. Therefore, logistical management plays a central role in the supply chain. Another important component of this chain, *value-added service,* adds some improved or supplemental service that customers do not normally receive or expect.

Enterprise Resource Planning

Software is an important aspect of logistics management and the supply chain. Consider the case of Mott's, the applesauce people. Their ideal production plan is developed from enterprise resource planning (ERP) software sold by SAP, the largest German software producer. An *enterprise resource planning system* is an integrated software system that consolidates data from among the firm's units. Roughly two-thirds of ERP system users are manufacturers that are concerned with production issues such as sequencing and scheduling.

As valuable as it is, ERP and its related software aren't always perfect. For example, ERP failures were blamed for Hershey's inability to fulfill all of its candy orders during a recent Halloween period, when a fall-off in sales was blamed on a combination of shipping delays, inability to fill orders, and partial shipments while candy stockpiled in warehouses. The nation's major retailers were forced to shift their purchases to other candy vendors.[16]

Enterprise Resource Planning software has been a very valuable integrated software tool for many companies. Unfortunately, Hershey Foods had some difficulties fulfilling their orders during the time they were implementing their ERP system.

Logistical Cost Control

In addition to enhancing their products by providing value-added services to customers, many firms are focusing on logistics for another important reason: to cut costs. Distribution functions currently represent almost half of a typical firm's total marketing costs.

Historically, cost-cutting efforts have focused on economies in production. These attempts began with the Industrial Revolution, when the emerging science of management emphasized efficient production and a continual drive to decrease production costs and improve the output levels of factories and production workers. Managers, however, now recognize that production efficiency leaves few easy opportunities for further cost savings. Increasingly, managers are looking for possible cost savings in their logistical functions.

To reduce logistical costs, businesses are reexamining each link of their supply chains to identify activities that do not add value for customers. By eliminating, reducing, or redesigning these activities, they can often cut costs and boost efficiency.

Third-Party Logistics Some companies try to cut costs and offer value-added services by outsourcing some or all of their logistics functions to specialist firms. The *third-party (contract) logistics firms* specialize in handling logistical activities for their clients. The Wallace Company, whose W.I.N. total print management Web site is featured in Figure 15.8, is a leading provider of comprehensive print-related activities to Fortune 1,000 companies. Wallace's Total Print Management (TPM) strategy dramatically reduces customers' process costs for printing, shipping, distribution, storage, and payment of all printing needs.

Recently, TRW Aeronautical Systems won a contract to provide supply chain management systems to South African Airways Technical. The third-party logistics firm will manage overhaul and repair of avionics and engine control parts for a fleet of Boeing jets.[17]

Through such outsourcing alliances, producers and logistical service suppliers cooperate in developing innovative, customized systems that speed goods through carefully constructed manufacturing and distribution pipelines. Although many companies have long outsourced transportation and warehousing functions, today's alliance partners use similar methods to combine their operations.

PHYSICAL DISTRIBUTION

A firm's physical distribution system is an organized group of components linked according to a plan for achieving specific distribution objectives. It contains the following elements:

1. *Customer service.* What level of customer service the distribution activities should support.
2. *Transportation.* How the firm should ship its products.
3. *Inventory control.* How much inventory the firm should maintain at each location.
4. *Protective packaging and materials handling.* How the firm can efficiently handle goods in the factory, warehouse, and transport terminals.
5. *Order processing.* How the firm should handle orders.
6. *Warehousing.* Where the distribution system will locate stocks of goods. The number of warehouses the firm should maintain.

FIGURE 15.8

W.I.N.: Third-Party Print Management Firm

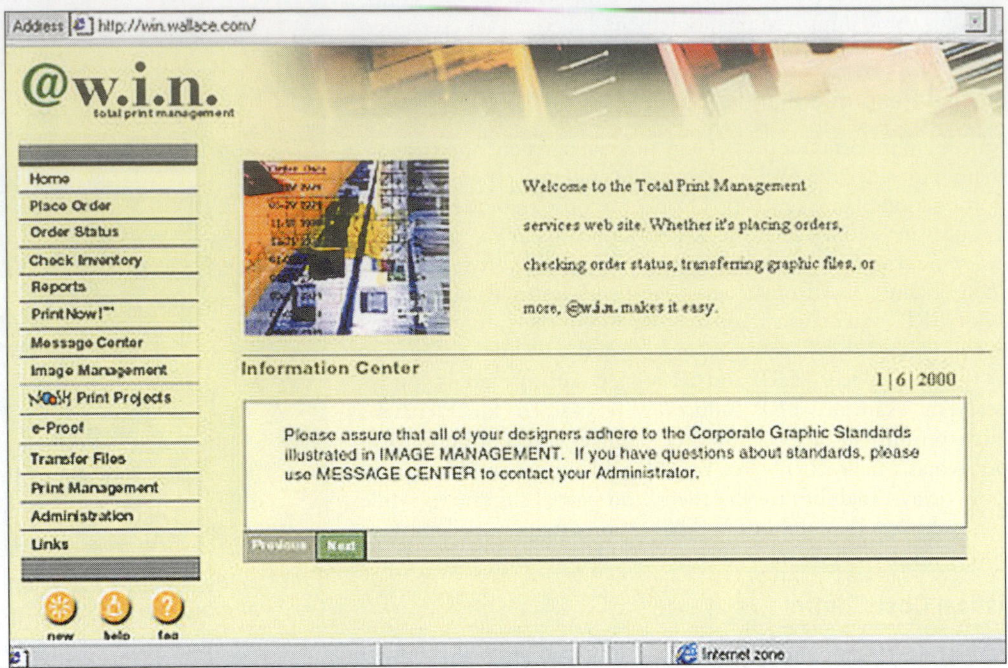

<interactive>**learning goal**

CHAPTER OBJECTIVE #5: IDENTIFY AND COMPARE THE MAJOR COMPONENTS OF A PHYSICAL DISTRIBUTION SYSTEM.

All of these components function in interrelated ways. Decisions made in one area affect relative efficiency in others. The physical distribution manager must balance each component so that the system avoids stressing any single aspect to the detriment of overall functioning. For example, a firm might decide to reduce transportation costs by shipping its products by inexpensive—but slow—water transportation. However, slow deliveries would likely force the firm to maintain high inventory levels and to raise inventory holding costs, such as warehousing expenses. This mismatch between system elements often leads to increased production costs.

<interactive>**exercise**

'NET EX: CUSTOMER-DRIVEN PRODUCTION

The Problem of Suboptimization

Logistics managers seek to establish a specified level of customer service while minimizing the costs of physically moving and storing goods from their production point to their ultimate purchasers. Marketers must first agree on their customer service priorities and then seek to minimize the total costs of moving goods to buyers—all while meeting customer service goals. To meet customer service levels at minimum costs, marketers must mesh all physical distribution elements together rather than setting up independent arrangements. Marketers do not always achieve this goal, however.

<interactive>**learning goal**

CHAPTER OBJECTIVE #6: OUTLINE THE SUBOPTIMIZATION PROBLEM IN LOGISTICS.

Suboptimization results when the managers of individual physical distribution functions attempt to minimize costs, but the impact of one task on the others leads to less than optimal results. A frequently used analogy describes a football team composed of many talented players who hold individual records in different aspects of the game. Unfortunately, though, these personal accomplishments fail to result in a winning team if the players do not cooperate and score more points than their opponents.

Suboptimization may cause problems in physical distribution when marketers judge each logistics activity by its ability to achieve its own objectives, some of which may work at cross-purposes with other goals. Suboptimization becomes particularly likely when a firm introduces a new product that may not fit easily into its current physical distribution system. Businesspeople often focus on certain adjustments to their systems without anticipating related problems that eventually arise.

Effective management of the physical distribution function requires some cost trade-offs. By accepting relatively high costs in some functional areas in order to cut costs in others, managers can minimize their firm's total physical distribution costs. Of course, any reduction in logistical costs should support progress toward the goal of maintaining customer service standards.

Briefly Speaking

Timely service, like timely gifts, is doubled in value.

George MacDonald (1824–1905) Scottish novelist, poet, and clergyman

Customer Service Standards

Customer service standards state goals and define acceptable performance for the quality of service that a firm expects to deliver to its customers. For example, one firm might set a customer service standard that calls for the shipment of 95 percent of all orders within 48 hours after the receipt of the orders and the shipment of all orders within 72 hours. Many e-tailers survive through their ability to ship within hours of receiving an order.

Designers of a physical distribution system begin by establishing acceptable levels of customer service. These designers then assemble physical distribution components in a way that will achieve this standard at the lowest possible total cost. As shown in Figure 15.9, this overall cost breaks down into five components: (1) transportation, (2) warehousing, (3) customer service/order processing, (4) administrative costs, and (5) inventory control.

Transportation

As noted in Table 3.1 in Chapter 3, the transportation industry has been largely deregulated. Deregulation has been particularly important for motor carriers, railroads, and air carriers. Many transporters are now free to develop unique solutions to shippers' needs. Before deregulation, no truck carrier served all 48 contiguous U.S. states. Today, more than 4,000 carriers have that authority. In addition, the trucking industry now operates far more efficiently than it did under government regulation; many carriers have reduced empty mileage by two-thirds.

Typically adding 10 percent to the cost of a product, transportation and delivery expenses represent the largest category of logistics-related costs for most firms.[18] Also, for many items—particularly perishable ones such as fresh fish—transportation makes a central contribution to satisfactory customer service.

Many logistics managers have found that the key to controlling their shipping costs is careful management of relationships with shipping firms. Freight carriers set two basic rates: class and commodity rates. A *class rate* is a standard rate for a specific commodity moving between any pair of destinations. A carrier may charge a lower *commodity rate,* sometimes called a *special rate,* to a favored shipper as a reward for either regular business or a large-quantity shipment. Railroads and inland water carriers frequently reward customers in this way.

In addition, the railroad and motor carrier industries sometimes supplement this rate structure with negotiated, or contract, rates. In other words, the two parties finalize terms of rates, services, and other variables in a contract.

Classes of Carriers Freight carriers are classified as common, contract, and private carriers. Common carriers, often considered the backbone of the transportation industry, provide transportation services as for-hire carriers to the general public. The government still regulates

FIGURE 15.9

Allocation of Physical Distribution Expenditures

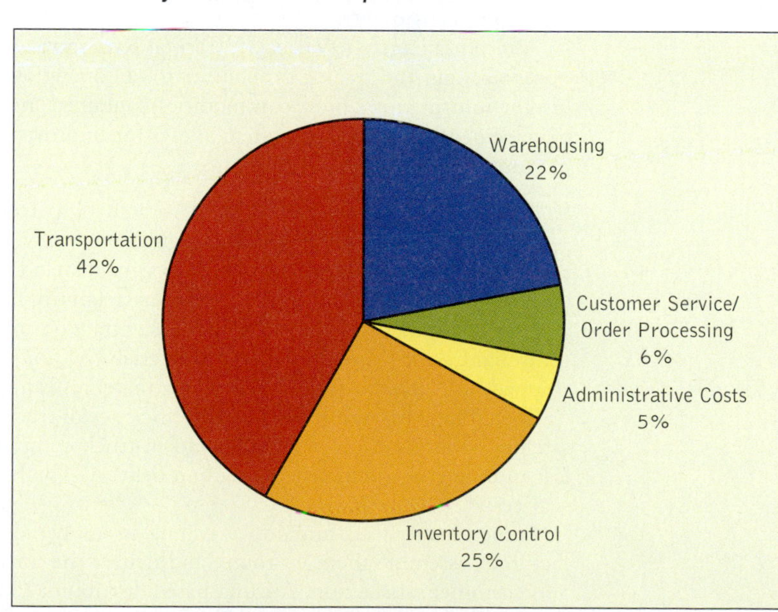

Source: These 2003 estimates were provided by Dr. Julie Gentry, Logistics Faculty, University of Arkansas–Fayetteville.

their rates and services, and they cannot conduct their operations without permission from the appropriate regulatory authority. Common carriers move freight via all modes of transport.

Contract carriers are for-hire transporters that do not offer their services to the general public. Instead, they establish contracts with individual customers and operate exclusively for particular industries, most commonly the motor freight industry. These carriers operate under much looser regulations than common carriers.

Private carriers do not offer services for hire. These carriers provide transportation services solely for internally generated freight. As a result, they observe no rate or service regulations. The Interstate Commerce Commission (ICC), a federal regulatory agency, permits private carriers to operate as common or contract carriers as well. Many private carriers have taken advantage of this rule by operating their trucks fully loaded at all times.

Major Transportation Modes Logistics managers choose among five major transportation alternatives: railroads, motor carriers, water carriers, pipelines, and air freight. Each mode has its own unique characteristics. Logistics managers select the best options for their situations by matching the situation features to their specific transportation needs.

<interactive>**learning goal**

CHAPTER OBJECTIVE #7: COMPARE THE MAJOR TRANSPORTATION ALTERNATIVES ON THE BASIS OF SPEED, DEPENDABILITY, COST, FREQUENCY OF SHIPMENTS, AVAILABILITY IN DIFFERENT LOCATIONS, AND FLEXIBILITY IN HANDLING PRODUCTS.

Railroads—The Nation's Leading Transporter Railroads continue to control the largest share of the freight business as measured by ton-miles. The term *ton-mile* indicates shipping activity required to move 1 ton of freight 1 mile. Thus, a 3-ton shipment moving 8 miles equals 24 ton-miles. Rail shipments quickly rack up ton-miles because this mode provides the most efficient way for moving bulky commodities over long distances. For instance, rail carriers generally transport huge quantities of coal, chemicals, grain, nonmetallic minerals, lumber and wood products, and automobiles.

The railroads have improved their service standards through a number of innovative concepts, such as unit trains, run-through trains, *intermodal* (piggyback) operations, and double-stack container trains. Unit trains carry much of the coal, grain, and other high-volume commodities shipped, running back and forth between single loading points (such as a mine) and single destinations (such as a power plant) to deliver a single commodity. Run-through trains bypass intermediate terminals to speed up schedules. They work similar to unit trains, but a run-through train may carry a variety of commodities.

In piggyback operations, highway trailers and containers ride on railroad flatcars, thus combining the long haul capacity of the train with the door-to-door flexibility of the truck. A double-stack container train pulls special rail cars equipped with bathtub-shaped wells so they can carry two containers stacked on top of one another. By nearly doubling train capacity and slashing costs, this system offers enormous advantages to rail customers.

A recent alliance between GE Capital Rail Services and logistics software company IntelliTrans introduces tracking and tracing capabilities to rail operations. Through easy Web access, manufacturers can get instant information about commodities contained in rail cars en route and integrate the data into their management systems. The system allows for improved production planning, inventory control, and supply forecasting.[19]

Motor Carriers—Flexible and Growing About 80 percent of all goods in the U.S. ride on trucks at some point. The trucking industry has grown dramatically over recent decades and is expected to grow by 25 percent in the next 10 years to keep up with demand.[20] Trucking offers some important advantages over the other transportation modes, including relatively fast shipments and consistent service for both large and small shipments. Motor carriers concentrate on shipping manufactured products, while railroads typically haul bulk shipments of raw materials. Motor carriers, therefore, receive greater revenue per ton shipped, since the cost for shipping raw materials is higher than for shipping manufactured products.

Technology has also improved the efficiency of trucking. Many trucking firms now track their fleets via satellite communications systems, and in-truck computer systems allow drivers and dispatchers to make last-minute changes in scheduling and delivery. The Internet is also adding new features to motor carrier services.

Some private fleets function as rolling assembly plants that pick up semifinished products from manufacturers, assemble them en route, and deliver the finished goods to customers, increasing overall service and customer satisfaction. Arizona-based distributor Pinacor, for example, partners with New Jersey–based Lucent Technologies to perform final testing and configuration of Lucent's telecommunications systems.

Oceangoing container ships, such as the Carsten Maersk Sealand ship shown here, are behemoths. Rows of containers are piled 17 across and 14 deep—so many that if they were placed end to end they would reach 27 miles. Why so large? Their size helps cut shipping costs for customers.

Pinacor's ability to assume these final manufacturing steps reduces product lead time dramatically, from an average of 30 to 45 days to about 10 days. Other distribution companies, like Gates/Arrow, have broadened their roles to offer ordering, shipping, and tracking solutions for companies such as Hewlett-Packard and Intel Corp.[21]

Water Carriers—Slow but Inexpensive Two basic types of transport methods move products over water: inland or barge lines and oceangoing, deep-water ships. Barge lines efficiently transport bulky, low unit value commodities such as grain, gravel, lumber, sand, and steel. A typical lower Mississippi River barge line may stretch more than a quarter-mile across.

Oceangoing ships carry a growing stream of containerized freight between ports around the world. Large ships also operate on the Great Lakes. New supertankers from global companies like Maersk Sealand are the size of three football fields, almost doubling the capacity of other vessels. At full capacity, the ships can cut the cost of shipping a container across the Pacific by a fifth.[22] Shippers that transport goods via water carriers incur very low costs compared with the rates for other transportation modes. Standardized modular shipping containers maximize savings by limiting loading, unloading, and other handling.

Pipelines—Specialized Transporters Although the pipeline industry ranks third after railroads and motor carriers in ton-miles transported, many people scarcely recognize its existence. More than 214,000 miles of pipelines crisscross the U.S. in an extremely efficient network for transporting natural gas and oil products. Oil pipelines carry two types of commodities: crude (unprocessed) oil and refined products, such as gasoline, jet fuel, and kerosene. In addition, one so-called slurry pipeline carries coal in suspension after it has been ground up into a powder and mixed with water. The Black Mesa Pipeline, owned by Union Pacific, moves the coal 290 miles from northern Arizona into southern Nevada.

Although pipelines offer low maintenance and dependable methods of transportation, a number of characteristics limit their applications. They have fewer locations than water carriers, and they can accommodate shipments of only a small number of products. Finally, pipelines represent a relatively slow method of transportation; liquids travel through this method at an average speed of only 3 to 4 miles per hour.

Air Freight—Fast but Expensive International water carriers still transport many low value products or heavy mass-market goods such as automobiles, but more and more international shipments travel by air. The significant growth in shipping volume handled by air carriers will probably continue as freight carriers seek to satisfy increased customer demand for fast delivery. Although 80 percent of the world's overnight air deliveries take place in the U.S., international demand for overnight air-freight service is soaring by 18 percent every year. Already more than 1.3 million 24-hour deliveries are made daily outside the U.S.[23]

FIGURE 15.10

UPS: Air Freight—Fast but Expensive

The photo in Figure 15.10 was taken during the ceremony celebrating UPS's inaugural flight into China, the most recent member of the World Trade Organization. The company now offers express carrier service six days a week to mainland China.

Table 15.2 compares the five transportation modes on several operating characteristics. Although all shippers judge reliability, speed, and cost in choosing the most appropriate transportation methods, they assign varying importance to specific criteria when shipping different goods. For example, while motor carriers rank highest in availability in different locations, shippers of petroleum products frequently choose the lowest ranked alternative, pipelines, for their low cost. Examples of the types of goods most often handled by the various transport modes include the following:

- *Railroads.* Lumber, iron and steel, coal, automobiles, grain, chemicals
- *Motor carriers.* Clothing, furniture and fixtures, lumber and plastic products, food products, leather and leather products, machinery
- *Water carriers.* Fuel, oil, coal, chemicals, minerals, petroleum products
- *Pipelines.* Oil, diesel fuel, jet fuel, kerosene, natural gas
- *Air carriers.* Flowers, technical instruments and machinery, high-priced specialty products, direct-to-consumer e-commerce goods

Freight Forwarders and Supplemental Carriers Freight forwarders act as transportation intermediaries, consolidating shipments to gain lower rates for their customers. The transport rates on less-than-truckload (LTL) and less-than-carload (LCL) shipments often double the per-unit rates on truckload (TL) and carload (CL) shipments. Freight forwarders charge less than the highest rates but more than the lowest rates. They profit by consolidating shipments from multiple customers until they can ship at TL and CL rates. The customers gain two advantages from these services: lower costs on small shipments and faster delivery service than they could achieve with their own LTL and LCL shipments.

<interactive>**learning goal**

CHAPTER OBJECTIVE #8: DISCUSS HOW TRANSPORTATION INTERMEDIARIES AND COMBINED TRANSPORTATION MODES CAN IMPROVE PHYSICAL DISTRIBUTION.

In addition to the transportation options reviewed so far, a logistics manager can also ship products via a number of auxiliary, or supplemental, carriers that specialize in small shipments. These carriers include bus freight services, United Parcel Service, FedEx, DHL International, and the U.S. Postal Service.

TABLE 15.2

Comparison of Transport Modes

MODE	SPEED	DEPENDABILITY IN MEETING SCHEDULES	FREQUENCY OF SHIPMENTS	AVAILABILITY IN DIFFERENT LOCATIONS	FLEXIBILITY IN HANDLING	COST
Rail	Average	Average	Low	Low	High	Average
Water	Very slow	Average	Very low	Limited	Very high	Very low
Truck	Fast	High	High	Very extensive	Average	High
Pipeline	Slow	High	High	Very limited	Very low	Low
Air	Very fast	High	Average	Average	Low	Very high

Intermodal Coordination Transportation companies emphasize specific modes and, as a result, serve certain kinds of customers, but they sometimes combine their services to give shippers the service and cost advantages of each. Piggyback service, mentioned in the section on rail transport, is the most widely used form of intermodal coordination. *Birdyback service,* another form of intermodal coordination, sends motor carriers to pick up a shipment locally and deliver that shipment to local destinations, while an air carrier takes it between airports near those locations. *Fishyback service* sets up a similar intermodal coordination system between motor carriers and water carriers.

Intermodal transportation generally gives shippers faster service and lower rates than either mode could match individually because each method carries freight in its most efficient way. However, intermodal arrangements require close coordination between all transportation providers.

Recognizing this need, multimodal transportation companies have formed to offer combined activities within single operations. Piggyback service generally joins two separate companies—a railroad and a trucking company. A multimodal firm provides intermodal service through its own internal transportation resources. Shippers benefit because the single service assumes responsibility from origin to destination. This unification prevents arguments over which carrier delayed or damaged a shipment.

Multimodal transportation options allowed DaimlerChrysler to avert a parts crisis following the terrorist attacks of September 11, which suspended air freight and brought mass disruptions to road transportation. Like other carmakers, the company relied on just-in-time supply of auto parts—an inventory control system that works only if trucks, trains, boats, and planes carrying assembly-line parts all run precisely on schedule. Following the attacks, DaimlerChrysler went into crisis mode, airlifting supplies from production points to assembly plants. When the government closed U.S. airspace, the company instigated an expedited truck service, in which two-person teams of truckdrivers made nonstop highway driving possible. The company worked to persuade U.S. customs officials to keep trucking routes open between Detroit and Windsor, Ontario, and to add more inspectors to ease congestion at checkpoints. Canadian Pacific Railroad Co. set up an emergency shuttle service to transport goods through road-traffic logjams.[24]

Warehousing

Products flow through two types of warehouses: storage and distribution warehouses. A storage warehouse holds goods for moderate to long periods in an attempt to balance supply and demand for producers and purchasers. For example, controlled atmosphere—also called *cold storage*—warehouses in Yakima and Wenatchee, Washington, serve nearby apple orchards. By contrast, a distribution warehouse assembles and redistributes goods, keeping them moving as much as possible. Many distribution warehouses or centers physically store goods for less than 24 hours before shipping them on to customers.

Logistics managers have attempted to save on transportation costs by developing central distribution centers. A manufacturer located in Philadelphia, for example, could send direct shipments to customers in the Illinois-Wisconsin-Indiana area, but if each customer placed small orders, the shipper would pay high transportation charges. Instead, it might send a single, large, consolidated shipment to a break-bulk center—a central distribution center that breaks down large shipments into several smaller ones and delivers them to individual customers in the area. Many Internet retailers use break-bulk distribution centers. UPS Logistics manages the entire fulfillment process for several companies, receiving and stocking inventory, picking, packing, and then shipping to customers. For Nike.com, UPS Logistics handles far more than shipping. Its employees provide customer service at Nike's 800 number, and the company maintains an inventory of shoes and clothing in its warehouses and exchanges or extends credit for returned goods.[25]

Automated Warehouse Technology Logistics managers can cut distribution costs and improve customer service dramatically by automating their warehouse systems. Although automation technology represents an expensive investment, it can provide major labor savings for high-volume distributors such as grocery chains. A computerized system might store orders, choose the correct number of cases, and move those cases in the desired sequence to loading docks. This kind of warehouse system reduces labor costs, worker injuries, pilferage, fires, and breakage.

Mother's Work, a $366 million maternity-apparel company, uses a sophisticated warehouse-automation system to sort, pick, pack, label, ship, and replenish inventory of up to 140,000 items each day. Its assembly-line sorting process allows pickers to select from more than 12,000 products in a range of sizes, colors, and styles. The software checks and double-checks all orders before they are routed onto trucks and out to stores. Computer-generated inventories, integrated with retail point-of-sale terminals, allow for easy identification of fast- or slow-moving items at each outlet.[26]

Warehouse Locations Every company must make a major logistics decision when it determines the number and locations of its storage facilities. Two categories of costs influence this choice: (1) warehousing and materials handling costs and (2) delivery costs from warehouses to customers. Large facilities offer economies of scale in facilities and materials handling systems; per-unit costs for these systems decrease as volume increases. Delivery costs, on the other hand, rise as the distance from warehouse to customer increases.

Warehouse location also affects customer service. Businesses must place their storage and distribution facilities in locations from which they can meet customer demands for product availability and delivery times. They must also consider population and employment trends. For example, the rapid growth of metropolitan areas in the southern and western U.S. has caused some firms to open more distribution centers to these areas. The "Marketing Hits" Interactive Example describes the importance of location in today's e-commerce environment, where fast delivery is essential.

MARKETING HIT: HITCHING A RIDE ON THE MIDNIGHT EXPRESS

Inventory Control Systems

Inventory control captures a large share of a logistics manager's attention because companies need to maintain enough inventory to meet customer demand without incurring unneeded costs for carrying excess inventory. Some firms attempt to keep inventory levels under control by implementing just-in-time (JIT) production, discussed in Chapter 10.

Companies like Costco have shifted responsibility—and costs—for inventory control from retailers back to individual manufacturers. Costco gives Kimberly-Clark access to individual store sales data. Kimberly-Clark uses the information to track inventory levels of its diapers and other products and replenish stocks as needed. Vendor-managed inventory (VMI) systems like this are based on the assumption that suppliers are in the best position to spot understocks or surpluses, cutting costs along the supply chain that can be translated into lower prices at the checkout.[27]

Order Processing

Like inventory control, order processing directly affects the firm's ability to meet its customer service standards. A company may have to compensate for inefficiencies in its order processing system by shipping products via costly transportation modes or by maintaining large inventories at many expensive field warehouses.

Order processing typically consists of four major activities: (1) conducting a credit check; (2) keeping a record of the sale, which involves recordkeeping tasks such as crediting a sales representative's commission account; (3) making appropriate accounting entries; and (4) locating orders, shipping them, and adjusting inventory records. A *stockout* occurs when an order for an item is not available for shipment. A firm's order processing system must advise affected customers of a stockout and offer a choice of alternative actions.

As in other areas of physical distribution, technological innovations improve efficiency in order processing. Many firms are streamlining their order processing procedures by using e-mail and the Internet.

Outdoor gear retailer REI, for example, pushes customers toward Web ordering, its least costly fulfillment channel, in its catalogs, store receipts, signs, mailers, and membership letters.[28]

FIGURE 15.11

Providing Critical Customer Service for Online Sales

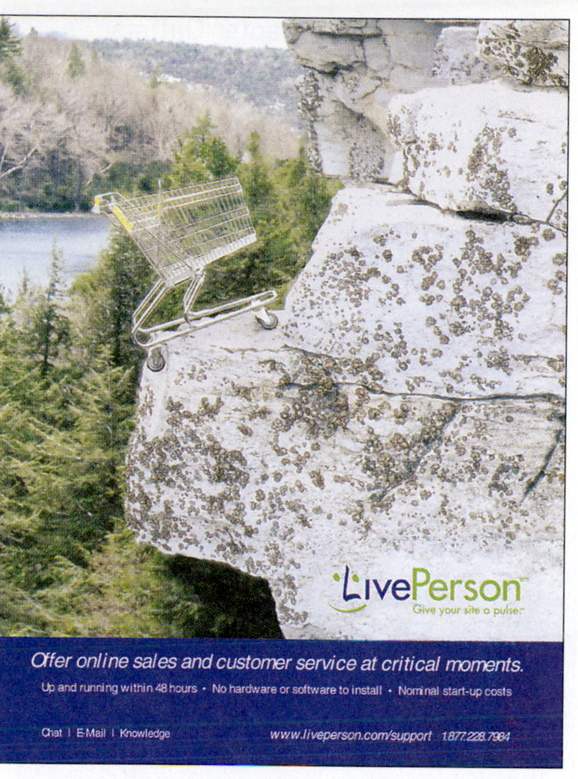

Protective Packaging and Materials Handling

Logistics managers arrange and control activities for moving products within plants, warehouses, and transportation terminals, which together compose the *materials handling* system. Two important concepts influence many materials handling choices: unitizing and containerization.

Unitizing combines as many packages as possible into each load that moves within or outside a facility. Logistics managers prefer to handle materials on pallets (platforms, generally made of wood, on which goods are transported). Unitizing systems often lash materials in place with steel bands or shrink packaging. A shrink package surrounds a batch of materials with a sheet of plastic that shrinks after heating, securely holding individual pieces together. Unitizing promotes efficient materials handling because each package requires minimal labor to move. Securing the materials together also minimizes damage and pilferage.

Logistics managers extend the same concept through *containerization*—combining several unitized loads. A container of oil rig parts, for example, can be loaded in Tulsa and trucked to Kansas City, where rail facilities place the shipment on a high-speed, run-through train to New York City. There, the parts are loaded on a ship headed to Saudi Arabia.

In addition to the benefits outlined for unitizing, containerization also markedly reduces the time required to load and unload ships. Containers limit in-transit damage to freight because individual packages pass through few handling systems en route to purchasers.

STRATEGIC IMPLICATIONS OF MARKETING IN THE 21ST CENTURY

Several factors, not the least of which is today's burgeoning e-commerce environment, are driving changes in channel development, logistics, and supply chain management. As the Internet continues to revolutionize the ways in which manufacturers deliver goods to ultimate consumers, marketers must find ways to promote cooperation between existing dealer, retailer, and distributor networks while harnessing the power of the Web as an alternative channel. This system demands not only delivery of goods and services faster and more efficiently than ever before but also superior service to Web-based customers. Companies like Liveperson.com, featured in Figure 15.11, can provide personalized customer service to e-commerce operations.

In addition, increased product proliferation—grocery stores typically stock almost 50,000 different items—demands logistics systems that can manage multiple brands delivered through multiple channels. And those channels must be finely tuned to identify and rapidly rectify problems such as retail shortfalls or costly overstocks. The trend toward leaner retailing, in which the burden of product tracking and inventory control is switching from retailers to manufacturers, means that to be effective, logistics and supply chain systems must result in cost savings.[29]

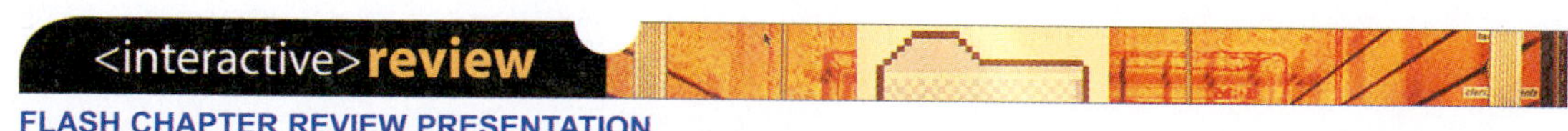

FLASH CHAPTER REVIEW PRESENTATION

<interactive>video case

IPSWICH SHELLFISH DELIVERS FRESH LOBSTER

endofchaptermaterial

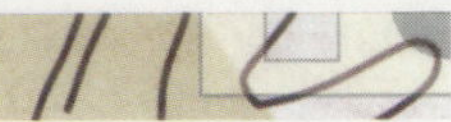

- Summary of Chapter Objectives
- Chapter Outline
- Key Terms
- Review Questions
- Projects and Teamwork Exercises
- 'netWork
- Crossword Puzzles
- Case 15.1: Dell Direct? Well, Not Always

Take the Post-Test to assess your overall understanding of the key ideas in this chapter. The Post-Test provides a comprehensive selection of exam-style questions addressing the main topics and concepts of the chapter. At the completion of each Post-Test, you will receive a score and instructive feedback on how you answered each question, and a direct link to the part of the chapter addressed in the question. Take the Post-Test as often as you need to—a record of your progress for each attempt is kept for you to revisit and gauge your improvement. And each Post-Test is randomly generated, so every attempt is new.

Post-Test

CHAPTER 16

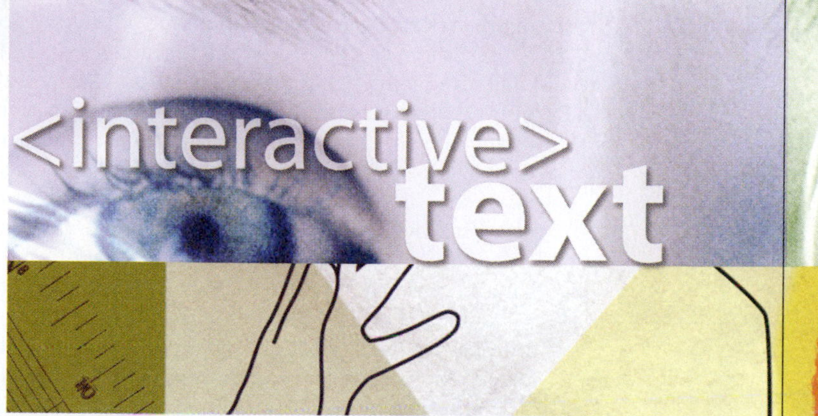

Direct Marketing and Marketing Resellers: Retailers and Wholesalers

Chapter Objectives

1. Explain the wheel of retailing.
2. Explain how retailers select target markets.
3. Show how the elements of the marketing mix apply to retailing strategy.
4. Explain the concepts of retail convergence and scrambled merchandising.
5. Identify the functions performed by wholesaling intermediaries.
6. Identify the major types of independent wholesaling intermediaries and the situations appropriate for each.
7. Compare the basic types of direct marketing and nonstore retailing.
8. Explain ways in which the Internet has altered the wholesaling, retailing, and direct marketing environments.

Pre-Test

Take the Pre-Test to assess your initial knowledge of the key ideas in this chapter. The Pre-Test provides exam-style questions addressing the main topics and concepts of the chapter. At the completion of each Pre-Test, you will receive a score and instructive feedback on how you answered each question, and a direct link to the part of the chapter addressed in the question. Take the Pre-Test as often as you need to—a record of your progress for each attempt is kept for you to revisit and gauge your improvement.

RAZZLE DAZZLE RETAIL

Mirror, mirror, on the wall, who's the fairest of them all? The elite shopper at Prada's new flagship store in Manhattan, of course! The Milan fashion house has created a magnificent showcase for its luxury brand in the well-heeled Soho shopping district. Although the store is elegantly appointed, featuring Italian marble, zebrawood, and walls of glass, its sleek décor is only part of the attraction. Hidden behind the architecture lies futuristic technology designed to amaze and delight the Prada shopper.

As the customer walks through the door, a smiling sales associate, discreetly holding a sophisticated scanning device, greets her by name and a personalized tour begins. Each garment she approaches is equipped with a radio-frequency tag. At the touch of a button, the sales associate calls up data on sizes and colors or matching accessories. On video monitors that move around the store on a system of tracks and pulleys, the shopper can view fashion-show clips of supermodel Cindy Crawford as she sashays down the runway wearing the selected garment. In an instant, the sales associate can even call up the designer's original sketches.

The shopper steps inside the dressing room, and here the fun really begins. A smart-reader automatically scans garment tags to display related images and information on an easy-to-use touch screen. A record of every item goes to the customer's personal account, giving the store a complete picture of her fashion preferences. Magic mirrors—actually a semitransparent liquid crystal display, complete with hidden cameras—allow her a full-circle view of herself in each garment. If she wants the approval of friends before she buys, she can push a button and the outer wall of the dressing room goes transparent. If she wishes, she can instantly modify her order—silk instead of cotton? A lighter shade? Matching shoes? If she's still undecided, it's easy to access her personal account from home—the customer can view each item again, search for accessories, and send a message to her sales associate to place her order.

While rival fashion houses have long established an online presence, Prada's $20 million investment in Internet technology has a different purpose from other haute couture sites. Rather than using the Net to reduce costs by limiting interactions with sales associates, Prada leverages its high tech to pamper its clients, delivering the ultimate in customer service. Not only does technology enrich the shopper's in-store experience, but it allows her access to one of high-fashion's ultra-chic labels from home. Of course, Prada reaps enormous benefits, too. Features like dressing-room scanners, for instance, are far more than high-tech gizmos—they allow the fashion house a firsthand view not only of what big-spending shoppers buy but of what they try on and then decline.

How much does it cost to do business with the world's elite shoppers? "The right amount," quips Prada chairman, Patrizio Bertelli. Yet while sales at Prada topped $1.5 billion last year—more than double the revenues of just three years earlier—it remains to be seen whether the company's splashy entry onto the Web and into one of Manhattan's hottest shopping spots will pay off. High-fashion rivals like Gucci, Hermes, and Louis Vuitton are spending tens of millions of dollars on their own world-class stores from New York and Los Angeles to Paris, London, and Milan. Planned before the stock market swooned, during a period when more consumers felt affluent, the glitzy stores are opening their doors at a time when there may no longer be enough big spenders to go around. Still, Prada's confidence remains high. The company plans to duplicate its Manhattan flagship at prime locations in Los Angeles, San Francisco, and Tokyo. Its 150 boutiques worldwide will also incorporate some of its high-tech gadgetry.[1]

CHAPTER OVERVIEW

Prada's Web-enabled flagship store is just one example of the convergence of Internet retailing with brick-and-mortar stores. In exploring how today's retailing sector operates, this chapter introduces many more examples that explain the combination of activities involved in selling goods to ultimate consumers. Then the chapter discusses the role of wholesalers and other intermediaries who deliver goods from the manufacturers into the hands of retailers. Finally, the chapter looks at nonstore retailing. Direct marketing, a channel consisting of direct communication to consumers or business users, is a major form of nonstore retailing. It includes not just direct mail and telemarketing but direct-response advertising, infomercials, and Internet marketing. The chapter concludes by looking at a less pervasive but growing aspect of nonstore retailing, automatic merchandising.

> **Briefly Speaking**
>
> When I walk into a grocery store and look at all the products you can choose, I say, "My God! No king ever had anything like I have in my grocery store today."
>
> *Bill Gates (b. 1954) founder, Microsoft Corp.*

RETAILING

Retailers are the marketing intermediaries who are in direct contact with ultimate consumers. **Retailing** describes the activities involved in selling merchandise to ultimate consumers. Retail outlets serve as contact points between channel members and ultimate consumers. In a very real sense, retailers represent the distribution channel to most consumers since a typical shopper has little contact with manufacturers and virtually no contact with wholesaling intermediaries. Retailers determine locations, store hours, quality and quantity of salespeople, store layouts, merchandise selections, and return policies—factors that often influence the consumers' images of the offerings more strongly than consumers' images of the products themselves. Both large and small retailers perform the major channel activities: creating time, place, and ownership utilities.

Retailers act as both customers and marketers in their channels. They sell products to ultimate consumers, and at the same time they buy from wholesalers and manufacturers. Because of their critical location in their channels, retailers often perform a vital feedback role. They obtain information from customers and transmit that information to manufacturers and other channel members.

Evolution of Retailing

The development of retailing illustrates the marketing concept in operation. Retailing continues to satisfy changing consumer wants and needs.

<interactive>**learning goal**

CHAPTER OBJECTIVE #1: EXPLAIN THE WHEEL OF RETAILING.

Early retailing in the U.S. can be traced to the establishment of trading posts, such as the Hudson Bay Company, and to pack peddlers who carried their wares to outlying settlements. The first type of retail institution, the general store, stocked a wide range of merchandise that met the needs of an isolated community or rural area. Supermarkets appeared in the early 1930s in response to consumers' desire for lower prices. In the 1950s, discount stores delivered lower prices in exchange for reduced services. The emergence of convenience food stores in the 1960s satisfied consumer demand for fast service, convenient locations, and expanded hours of operation. The development of off-price retailers in the 1980s and 1990s reflected consumer demand for brand-name merchandise at prices considerably lower than those of traditional retailers. In recent years, Internet-enabled retailing has increased in influence and importance.

A key concept, known as the **wheel of retailing,** attempts to explain the patterns of change in retailing. According to the wheel of retailing, a new type of retailer gains a competitive foothold by offering customers lower prices than current outlets charge and maintains profits by reducing or eliminating services. Once established, however, the innovator adds more services, and its prices gradually rise. It then becomes vulnerable to new low-price retailers that enter with minimum services—and so the wheel turns. The retail graveyard is littered with former giants like W.T. Grant and Montgomery Ward, as well as such merchandisers as the original Sears catalog and catalog retailers such as Service Merchandise. Kmart, the topic of the "Marketing Misses" Interactive Example, is a current question mark.

Many major developments in the history of retailing appear to fit the wheel's pattern. Early department stores, chain stores, supermarkets, discount stores, hypermarkets, and catalog retailers all emphasized limited service and low prices. Most of these retailers gradually increased prices as they added services.

Some exceptions disrupt this pattern, however. Suburban shopping centers, convenience food stores, and vending machines never built their appeals around low prices. However, the wheel pattern has been a good indicator enough times in the past to make it an accurate indicator of future retailing developments.

<interactive>example

MARKETING MISS: THE NATION'S LARGEST RETAIL BANKRUPTCY

RETAILING STRATEGY

Like manufacturers and wholesalers, a retailer develops a marketing strategy based on the firm's goals and strategic plans. The organization monitors environmental influences and assesses its own strengths and weaknesses in identifying marketing opportunities and constraints. A retailer bases its key decisions on two fundamental steps in the marketing strategy process: (1) selecting a target market and (2) developing a retailing mix to satisfy the chosen market. The retailing mix specifies merchandise strategy, customer service standards, pricing guidelines, target market analysis, promotion goals, location/distribution decisions, and store atmosphere choices. The combination of these elements projects a desired *retail image*—consumers' perceptions of the store and the shopping experience it provides. Retail image communicates the store's identity to consumers as, say, an economical, a high-value, or a prestigious outlet. Crate & Barrel, for instance, featured in Figure 16.1, counts on its trendy, contemporary image to draw affluent, style-conscious consumers. All components of retailing strategy must work together to create an image that appeals to the store's target market.

Once unbeatable for snappy, casual fashions at reasonable prices, Gap Inc. has recently floundered. In an attempt to appeal to younger customers, the retailer replaced its popular basic jeans and khakis with hip, gimmicky apparel. Following a drop-off in same-store sales, Gap switched back to its old formula—but not before losing market share to rivals like Target.[2]

Selecting a Target Market

A retailer starts to define its strategy by selecting a target market. The size and profit potential of a target and the level of competition for its business influence this decision. Retailers pore over demographic, geographic, and psychographic profiles to segment markets. In the end, most retailers identify their target markets in terms of certain demographics.

Kmart's failed attempt to match Wal-Mart's low pricing strategy head on by reviving its Blue Light Special contributed to the bankruptcy of one of the nation's largest retailers.

FIGURE 16.1

Crate & Barrel Creating a Contemporary Retail Image

<interactive>**learning goal**

CHAPTER OBJECTIVE #2: EXPLAIN HOW RETAILERS SELECT TARGET MARKETS.

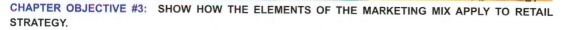

The importance of identifying and targeting the right market is dramatically illustrated by the erosion of department store retailing. While mall anchor stores like Sears and JCPenney fight to hold on to customers, stand-alone store Target, known for its chic but cheap casual clothes, has solidified its niche. The store attracts style-conscious consumers with fashionable lines under its own designer labels, like cosmetics from Kashuk, apparel from Mossimo Giannulli, and sleek kitchenware from Michael Graves. The trendy but affordable lines draw shoppers with conservative tastes away from traditional department stores.[3]

Deep-discount chains like Family Dollar Stores or Dollar General, with their so-so locations and low-price merchandise crammed into narrow aisles, target low-income shoppers. Attracted by cents-off basics like shampoo, cereal, or laundry detergent, customers typically pick up higher margin goods—toys or chocolates—on their way to the checkout.[4]

By appealing to women, hardware chain Lowe's hopes to hammer arch-rival Home Depot. Wide aisles, clean presentation, friendly service, and a broad selection of high-end merchandise, such as Laura Ashley paints, have boosted the store's popularity with female shoppers, who now account for half of all customers.[5]

After identifying a target market, a retailer must then develop marketing strategies to attract these chosen customers to its stores. The following sections discuss tactics for implementing different strategies.

Merchandising Strategy

A retailer's merchandising strategy guides decisions regarding the items it will offer. A retailer must decide on general merchandise categories, product lines, specific items within lines, and the depth and width of its assortment. Target stores, for example, offer customers a wide variety of merchandise, from apparel to personal care, home décor, and automotive products. But to compete as the upscale alternative to Wal-Mart, Target has rolled out a chain of combination food and general merchandise stores called SuperTarget. Bringing fashion to food, the retailer has expanded its categories. Its *planogram*—a computerized diagram of how to exhibit selections of merchandise within each store—now includes gourmet brand pastas and sauces, produce, and fresh-baked goods.[6]

<interactive>**learning goal**

CHAPTER OBJECTIVE #3: SHOW HOW THE ELEMENTS OF THE MARKETING MIX APPLY TO RETAIL STRATEGY.

To develop a successful merchandise mix, a retailer must weigh several priorities. First, it must consider the preferences and needs of its previously defined target market, keeping in mind that the competitive environment influences these choices. The retailer must also consider the overall profitability of each product line and product category.

Category Management As mentioned in Chapter 12, a popular merchandising strategy is *category management,* in which a category manager oversees an entire product line and is responsible for the profitability of the product group. Category management seeks to improve the retailer's product category performance through more coordinated buying, merchandising, and pricing.[7] Rather than focusing on the performance of individual brands, such as Flex shampoo or Kleenex tissue, category management evaluates performance according to each product category. Laundry detergent, skin-care, and paper goods, for example, are each viewed as individual profit centers, and the category manager supervises the performance and growth of the entire group. Those that underperform are at risk, regardless of the strength of individual brands. To improve their profitability, for example, some department stores have narrowed their traditionally broad product categories to eliminate high-overhead, low-profit lines like toys, appliances, and furniture.

Ateeco Inc., a family-owned business specializing in ethnic foods such as the Polish pierogi, targets tiny categories that the giant food marketers leave unserved. To win freezer space, the company presents marketing research that proves its products are profitable. In-store demonstrations and samplings introduce pierogies—a child-friendly food as well as a mainstay of Polish cuisine—to customers. While Ateeco virtually owns the category, its success may tempt companies with deeper pockets—such as Kraft, Nestlé, or ConAgra Foods—to introduce new brands, forcing Ateeco to devise new strategies to keep its market share.[8]

Briefly Speaking

Consumers are statistics. Customers are people.

Stanley Marcus (1905–2002) American merchant

The Battle for Shelf Space As discussed in Chapter 15, large-scale retailers are increasingly taking on the role of channel captain within many distribution networks. Some have assumed traditional wholesaling functions, while others dictate product design and specifications to manufacturers. The result is a shift in power from the manufacturers of top-selling brands to the retailer who makes them available to customers.

Adding to the pressure is the increase in the number of new products and variations on existing products. To identify the varying items within a product line, retailers refer to a specific product offering as a **stockkeeping unit (SKU).** Within the skin-care category, for example, each facial cream, body moisturizer, and sunscreen in each of a variety of sizes and formulations is a separate SKU. The proliferation of new SKUs has resulted in a fierce battle for space on store shelves.

Increasingly, major retailers, such as Wal-Mart, Sears, and JCPenney, make demands in return for shelf space. They may, for example, seek pricing and promotional concessions from manufacturers as conditions for selling their products. Retailers also routinely require that manufacturers participate in their electronic data interchange (EDI) and quick-response systems. Manufacturers unable to comply may find themselves unable to penetrate the marketplace.

Slotting allowances, described in Chapter 11, are just one of the range of nonrefundable fees retailers receive from manufacturers to secure shelf space for new products. A manufacturer can pay a retailer as much as $25,000 per item just to get its new products displayed on store shelves.[9] Other fees include failure fees (imposed if a new product does not meet sales projections), annual renewal fees (a "pay to stay" inducement for retailers to continue carrying brands), trade allowances, discounts on high-volume purchases, survey fees for research done by the retailers, and even fees to allow salespeople to present new items.

Customer Service Strategy

Some stores build their retailing strategy around heightened customer services for shoppers. Gift wrapping, alterations, return privileges, bridal registries, consultants, interior design services, delivery and installation, and perhaps even electronic shopping via gift-ordering machines in airports are all examples of services that add value to the shopping experience. A retailer's customer service strategy must specify which services the firm will offer and whether it will charge customers for these services. Those decisions depend on several conditions: store size, type, and location; merchandise assortment; services offered by competitors; customer expectations; and financial resources.

The basic objective of all customer services focuses on attracting and retaining target customers, thus increasing sales and profits. Some services—such as convenient rest rooms, lounges, and complimentary coffee—enhance shoppers' comfort. Other services are intended to attract customers by making shopping easier and faster than it would be without the services. Some retailers, for example, offer child-care services for customers to ease the burden of shopping. At Kroger's supermarket chain, featured in Figure 16.2, a self-scanning device allows customers to avoid the cashier's line, and the wait involved, by checking out their own groceries.

FIGURE 16.2

Self-Scanners: Avoiding the Wait in the Checkout Line

A customer service strategy can also support efforts in building demand for a line of merchandise. Debra's Natural Gourmet, a Concord, Massachusetts, healthful-food-and-lifestyle store, employs a personal touch to entice customers. The store solicits advice and referrals from 35 health practitioners and shares its findings with its customers. Through in-store workshops and a monthly newsletter with tips on everything from healthful diets to antiaging treatments, the store nurtures an ongoing relationship with its customers. It even employs a registered nurse to make sure its natural remedies will not interfere with customers' routine medications.[10]

Wal-Mart, described in Chapter 13 as a major user of everyday low pricing, also employs price reductions to eliminate slow-moving items and leftover seasonal merchandise such as these shoes available during the spring selling season.

Pricing Strategy

As we discussed in Chapters 13 and 14, prices reflect a retailer's marketing objectives and policies. They also play a major role in consumers' perceptions of a retailer. Consumers realize, for example, that when they enter a Gucci boutique in Milan, New York, or Tokyo, they will find such expensive products as $275 suede pumps and $1,500 boar-hide briefcases. Customers of the retail chain Everything's $1.00 expect a totally different line of merchandise; true to the name, every product in the store bears the same low price.

Markups and Markdowns The amount that a retailer adds to a product's cost to set the final selling price is the **markup.** The amount of the markup typically results from two marketing decisions:

1. *The services performed by the retailer.* Other things being equal, stores that offer more services charge larger markups to cover their costs.
2. *The inventory turnover rate.* Other things being equal, stores with a higher turnover rate can cover their costs and earn a profit while charging a smaller markup.

A retailer's markup exerts an important influence on its image among present and potential customers. In addition, the markup affects the retailer's ability to attract shoppers. An excessive markup may drive away customers; an inadequate markup may not generate sufficient income to cover costs and return a profit. Retailers typically state markups as percentages of either the selling prices or the costs of the products.

Marketers determine markups based partly on their judgments of the amounts that consumers will pay for a given product. When buyers refuse to pay a product's stated price, however, or when improvements in other products or fashion changes reduce the appeal of current merchandise, a retailer must take a **markdown.** The amount by which a retailer reduces the original selling price—the discount typically advertised for a sale item—is the markdown. Markdowns are sometimes used to evaluate merchandisers. For example, a department store might base its evaluations of buyers partly on the average markdown percentages for the product lines for which they are responsible.

Location-Distribution Strategy

Retail experts often cite location as a potential determining factor in the success or failure of a retail business. A retailer may choose to locate at an isolated site, in a central business district, or in a planned shopping center. The location decision depends on many conditions, including the type of merchandise, the retailer's financial resources, characteristics of the target market, and site availability.

In recent years, many localities have become saturated with stores. As a result, some retailers have reevaluated their location strategies. A chain may close individual stores that do not meet sales and profit goals. Kmart, for example, plans to close hundreds of its suburban locations to focus on better performing, high-density, urban populations.[11]

Other retailers have experimented with nontraditional location strategies. McDonald's now operates stores in hospitals, military bases, amusement parks, train stations, and gasoline stations. As described in the "Solving an Ethical Controversy" Interactive Example, even the world's largest big-box retailer is diverging from its suburban megastore formula by testing small-format outlets in urban markets.

Briefly Speaking

The universe is really big. It's even bigger than Wal-Mart.

Richard Belzer (b. 1944) American comedian

<interactive>**example**

RIGHT/WRONG: SOLVING AN ETHICAL CONTROVERSY—WAL-MART ON THE MARCH

Locations in Planned Shopping Centers Over the past several decades, retail trade has shifted away from traditional downtown retailing districts and toward suburban shopping centers. A **planned shopping center** is a group of retail stores designed, coordinated, and marketed as a unit to shoppers in a geographical trade area. Together, the stores provide a single convenient location for shoppers as well as free parking. They facilitate shopping by maintaining uniform hours of operation, including evening and weekend hours.

There are four main types of planned shopping centers. The smallest, the *neighborhood shopping center*, most often consists of a supermarket and a group of smaller stores, such as a drugstore, a dry cleaner, a small appliance store, and perhaps a hair-styling salon. This kind of center provides convenient shopping for 5,000 to 50,000 shoppers who live within a few minutes' commute. It contains 5 to 15 stores, and the product mix is usually confined to convenience goods and some shopping goods.

A *community shopping center* serves 20,000 to 100,000 people in a trade area extending a few miles from its location. It contains anywhere from 10 to 30 retail stores, with a branch of a local department store or some other large store as the primary tenant. In addition to the stores found in a neighborhood center, a community center probably encompasses more stores featuring shopping goods, some professional offices, a branch bank, and maybe a movie theater or supermarket. Community shopping centers typically offer ample parking, and tenants often share some promotion costs. With the advent of stand-alone big-box retailers, some community shopping centers have declined in popularity.

A *regional shopping center* is a large facility with at least 400,000 square feet of shopping space. Its marketing appeal usually emphasizes one or more major department stores with the power to draw customers, supplemented by as many as 200 smaller stores. A successful regional center needs a location within 30 minutes' driving time of at least 250,000 people. A regional center—or a superregional center like Minnesota's Mall of America—provides a wide assortment of convenience, shopping, and specialty goods, plus many professional and personal service facilities.

A *power center*, usually located near a regional or superregional mall, brings together several huge specialty stores, such as Toys "R" Us, Home Depot, or Bed, Bath, and Beyond, as stand-alone stores in a single trading area. Rising in popularity during the 1990s, power centers offered value because they were able to underprice department stores while providing a huge selection of specialty merchandise. Heated competition from cost-cutter Wal-Mart and inroads from more upscale discounters like Target and Kohl's have now reduced the drawing power of these centers.

Recently, a fifth type of planned center has emerged, known as a *lifestyle center*. This retailing format seeks to offer a combination of shopping, entertainment, and restaurants in an attractive environment. At 300,000 square feet, the centers are large, but they seek to offer the intimacy and easy access of neighborhood retailing with a fashionable cachet. Here, there are no big anchor stores but rather a mix of just the right upscale tenants—Williams-Sonoma, Eddie Bauer, or Restoration Hardware, for instance. Movie theaters and fine dining complete the mix. About 50 lifestyle centers are currently operating around the nation.[12]

Retail analysts believe that the "malling of America" has reached the saturation point. There are 20 square feet of retail space per capita, up by more than a third over a 15-year period. As upscale shoppers migrate to newer lifestyle centers or to the Internet, the malls have begun to shift away from traditional department store anchors. Some are turning to high-traffic draws like Target or Kohl's, but this puts specialty retailers like Gap or Banana Republic in a tough spot. Taking their lead from the popularity of lifestyle centers, others seek to com-

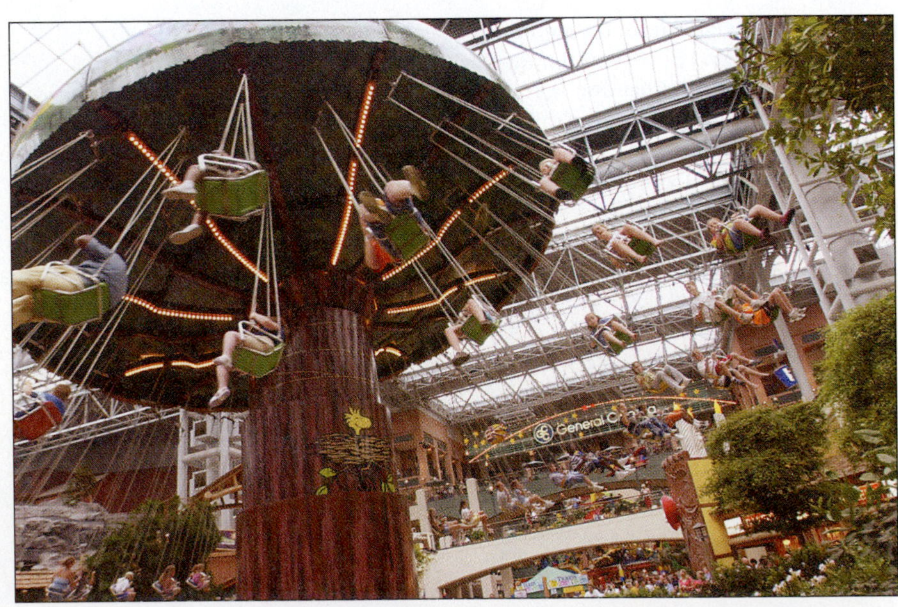

In some instances, major malls can even become tourist destinations. Mall of America attracts more than 40 million people a year, making it Minnesota's top tourist attraction. The mall has 520-plus stores, 86 restaurants and food shops, 9 nightclubs, 15 movie screens, and more—like this Camp Snoopy amusement park.

bine shopping with entertainment; malls are adding carousels, rock-climbing walls, movie theaters, and large food courts. For example, Mall of America promotes its shopping center as a "shopping and fun destination," complete with an amusement park, a spa, an aquarium, and nightclubs and restaurants. Still others, such as the Market Place Mall in Champaign-Urbana, Illinois, emphasize customer service: well-padded playgrounds for toddlers, comfortable lounges for their parents, and luxurious restrooms equipped with infant changing rooms and nursing rooms with rocking chairs. Some malls hire concierges to help customers locate hard-to-find gifts and order theater tickets; others may offer valet parking, gift-wrap services, and parking-lot shuttle buses.[13]

Promotional Strategy

To establish store images that entice more shoppers, retailers use a variety of promotional techniques. Through its promotional strategy, a retailer seeks to communicate to consumers information about its stores—locations, merchandise selections, hours of operation, and prices. If merchandise selection changes frequently to follow fashion trends, advertising is typically used to promote current styles effectively. In addition, promotions help retailers to attract shoppers and build customer loyalty.

Innovative promotions can pay off in unexpected ways. Consider the opening of a new flagship store in New York's Times Square by Toys "R" Us. The store opened its door prior to the Christmas shopping season. An estimated 25 percent of retail revenue comes from the holiday shopping season, and for toys, the number is even greater. Bigger-than-life attractions, like the 60-foot indoor Ferris wheel, make this a "must-see" store with huge word-of-mouth advertising potential. Timed to coincide with the rejuvenation of Toys "R" Us outlets—remodeled stores, branded merchandise, and a customer service training initiative—the flagship helped reposition the retailer away from its discount roots.[14]

National retail chains often purchase advertising space in newspapers, on radio, and on television. Like many retail chains, Best Buy promotes its stores through advertising circulars in local and regional Sunday newspapers, as shown in Figure 16.3. Other retailers are experimenting with promoting over the Internet. Sometimes a well-chosen store location aids promotion; this is why dollar stores like California-based 99¢ Only Stores tend to locate on major streets leading to a large competitor, such as a Wal-Mart.

Retailers also try to combine advertising with in-store merchandising techniques that influence decisions at the point of purchase. 7-Eleven's drive to recast itself as a popular stop for teens on the go led to choice placement for trendy new products like its Slurpees and prepaid cellular phones. In-store point-of-purchase displays feature the latest hot teen products.[15]

A retail salesperson plays a vital role in conveying a store image to consumers and in persuading shoppers to buy. To serve as a source of information, a salesperson must possess extensive knowledge regarding credit policies, discounts, special sales, delivery terms, layaways, and returns. To increase store sales, the salesperson must persuade customers that the store sells what those customers need. To this end, salespeople should receive training in selling up and suggestion selling.

FIGURE 16.3

Best Buy's Advertising Circulars in Sunday Newspapers

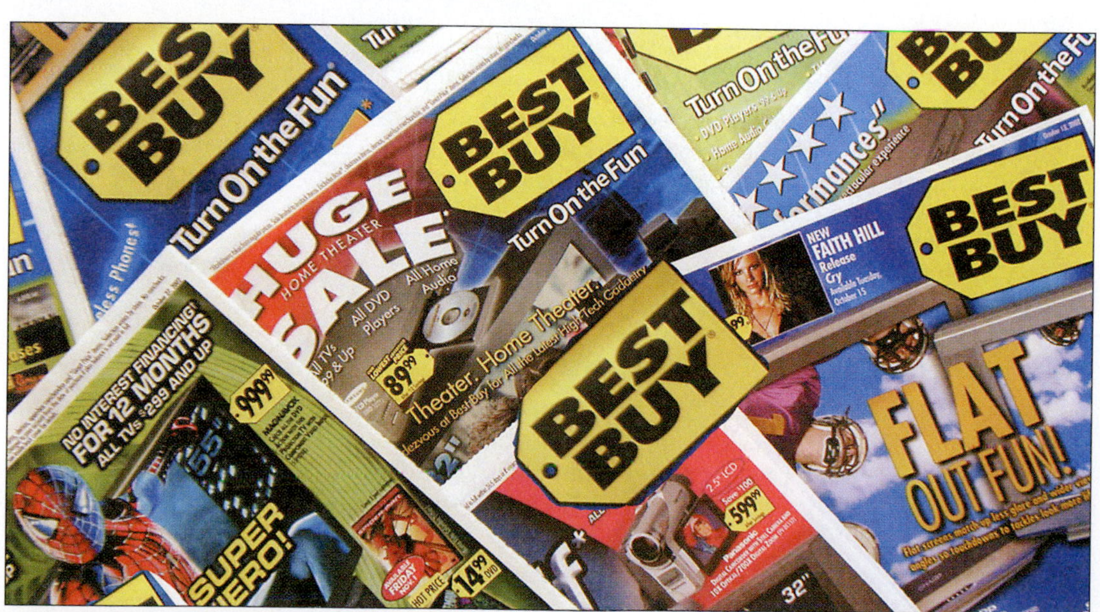

By *selling up,* salespeople try to persuade customers to buy higher priced items than originally intended. For example, an automobile salesperson might convince a customer to buy a more expensive model than the car that the buyer had initially considered. Of course, the practice of selling up must always respect the constraints of a customer's real needs. If a salesperson sells customers something that they really do not need, the potential for repeat sales dramatically diminishes.

Another technique, *suggestion selling,* seeks to broaden a customer's original purchase by adding related items, special promotional products, or holiday or seasonal merchandise. Here, too, the salesperson tries to help a customer recognize true needs rather than unwanted merchandise. Beauty advisors in upscale department stores are masters of suggestion selling. Estee Lauder's 8,800 beauty advisors receive 100 hours of training in their first year and annual follow-up classes. A 150-page training guide covers everything from icebreakers to "link selling"—a lip-liner pencil to go with that new lipstick?—to follow-up calls.[16]

Just as knowledgeable and helpful sales personnel can both boost sales and set retailers apart from competitors, poor service influences customers' attitudes toward a retailer. Increasing customer complaints about unfriendly, inattentive, and uninformed salespeople have prompted many retailers to intensify their attention to training and motivating salespeople.

Store Atmospherics

While store location, merchandise selection, customer service, pricing, and promotional activities all contribute to a store's consumer awareness, stores also project their personalities through *atmospherics*—physical characteristics and amenities that attract customers and satisfy their shopping needs. Atmospherics include both a store's exterior and interior décor.

A store's exterior appearance, including architectural design, window displays, signs, and entryways, helps to identify the retailer and attract its target market. The Saks Fifth Avenue script logo on a storefront and McDonald's golden arches are exterior elements that readily identify these retailers. Other retailers design eye-catching exterior elements aimed at getting customers' attention. Life-size cartoon figures seem poised in midflight over the entrance to the Warner Brothers outlet in the Horton Plaza Shopping Center in San Diego, drawing customer interest.

The interior décor of a store should also complement the retailer's image, respond to customers' interests, and most important, induce shoppers to buy. Interior atmospheric elements include store layout, merchandise presentation, lighting, color, sounds, scents, and cleanliness. At Sam's Club or Costco, for instance, merchandise is stacked high on pallets to emphasize the chains' rock-bottom pricing and no-frills approach and to encourage customers to buy in bulk. Low, low prices and unexpected deals on selected upscale merchandise draw customers in.[17]

When designing the interior and exterior of a store, the fact that many people shop for reasons other than just purchasing needed products must be taken into account. Other common reasons for shopping include escaping the routine of daily life, avoiding weather extremes, fulfilling fantasies, and socializing with family and friends. Retailers expand beyond interior design to create welcoming and entertaining environments that draw shoppers. To cater to teens, Nordstrom needed to rethink multiple aspects of the store environment and product placement. New, hip fashions are located right by the doors and are visible from the mall; music summons teen shoppers inside, where they no longer need to pass through housewares to get to their stuff.[18]

TYPES OF RETAILERS

Since new types of retailers continue to evolve in response to changes in consumer demand, a universal classification system for retailers has yet to be devised. Certain differences do, however, define several categories of retailers: (1) forms of ownership, (2) shopping effort expended by customers, (3) services provided to customers, (4) product lines, and (5) locations of retail transactions.

Most retailing operations fit in different categories. A 7-Eleven outlet may be classified as a convenience store (category 2) with self-service (category 3) and a relatively broad product line (category 4). It is both a store-type retailer (category 5) and a member of a chain (category 1).

Classification of Retailers by Form of Ownership

Perhaps the easiest method for categorizing retailers divides retailers by ownership structure, distinguishing between chain stores and independent retailers. In addition, independent retailers may join wholesaler-sponsored voluntary chains, band together to form retail cooperatives, or enter into franchise agreements with manufacturers, wholesalers, or service-provider organizations. Each type of ownership has its own unique advantages and strategies.

Chain Stores *Chain stores* are groups of retail outlets that operate under central ownership and management and handle the same product lines. Chains have a major advantage over independent retailers in economies of scale. Volume purchases allow chains to pay lower prices than their independent rivals must pay. Since a chain may encompass hundreds of retail stores, it can afford advertising layout specialists, sales training, and sophisticated computerized systems for merchandise ordering, inventory management, forecasting, and accounting. Also, the large sales volume and wide geographical reach of a chain may enable it to advertise in a variety of media, including television and national magazines.

Independent Retailers The U.S. retailing structure supports a large number of small stores, many medium-size stores, and a small number of large stores. Even though only 12 percent of the almost 2.7 million retail establishments earn annual sales of $1 million or more, those large operators account for almost three-quarters of all retail sales in the U.S. On the other hand, over half of all stores generate yearly sales below $500,000. According to the Department of Commerce, independent retailers account for about 43 percent of all retail sales.

Independent retailers compete with chains in a number of ways. The traditional advantage of independent stores is friendly, personalized service. Cooperatives offer another strategy for independents. For instance, cooperatives like Ace Hardware and Valu-Rite Pharmacies help independents compete with chains by providing volume buying power as well as advertising and marketing programs.

Classification by Shopping Effort

Another classification system is based on the reasons consumers shop at particular retail outlets. This approach categorizes stores as convenience, shopping, or specialty retailers.

Convenience retailers focus their marketing appeals on accessible locations, long store hours, rapid checkout service, and adequate parking facilities. Local food stores, gasoline stations, and dry cleaners fit in this category.

Shopping stores typically include furniture stores, appliance retailers, clothing outlets, and sporting goods stores. Consumers usually compare prices, assortments, and quality levels at competing outlets before making purchase decisions. Consequently, managers of shopping stores attempt to differentiate their outlets through advertising, window displays, in-store layouts, well-trained and knowledgeable salespeople, and appropriate merchandise assortments.

Specialty retailers combine carefully defined product lines, services, and reputations in attempts to convince consumers to expend considerable effort to shop at their stores. Examples include Neiman-Marcus, Lord & Taylor, and Nordstrom.

'NET EX: CONVENIENCE AS A RETAILING STRATEGY

Classification by Services Provided

Another category differentiates retailers by the services they provide to customers. This classification system consists of three retailer types: self-service, self-selection, or full-service retailers.

Target illustrates a self-service store, while Kroger grocery stores and A&P Future Stores are examples of self-selection stores. Both categories sell convenience goods that people can purchase frequently with little assistance. By contrast, full-service retailers, like Saks Fifth Avenue, featured in Figure 16.4, focus on fashion-oriented merchandise, backed by a complete array of customer services.

Classification by Product Lines

Product lines also define a set of retail categories and the marketing strategies appropriate for firms within those categories. Grouping retailers by product lines produces three major categories: specialty stores, limited-line retailers, and general merchandise retailers.

Specialty Stores A *specialty store* typically handles only part of a single product line. However, it stocks this portion in considerable depth or variety. Specialty stores include a wide range of retail outlets: Examples include fish markets, grocery stores, men's and women's shoe stores, and bakeries. Although some specialty stores are chain outlets, most are independent small-scale operations. They represent perhaps the greatest concentration of independent retailers who develop expertise in one product area and provide narrow lines of products for their local markets.

Specialty stores should not be confused with specialty products. Specialty stores typically carry convenience and shopping goods. The label *specialty* reflects the practice of handling a specific, narrow line of merchandise. For example, Lady Foot Locker is a specialty store that offers a wide selection of name-brand athletic footwear, apparel, and accessories made specifically for women.

Limited-Line Retailers Customers find a large assortment of products within one product line or a few related lines in a *limited-line store.* This type of retail operation typically develops in areas with a large enough population to sufficiently support it. Examples of limited-line stores are IKEA (home furnishings and housewares) and Levitz (furniture). These retailers cater to the needs of people who want to select from complete lines in purchasing particular products.

FIGURE 16.4

Saks Fifth Avenue: Providing a Full-Service Environment for Its Stylish Offerings

A unique type of limited-line retailer is known as a *category killer.* These stores offer huge selections and low prices in single product lines. Stores within this category—for example, Borders Books; Bed, Bath, and Beyond; and Home Depot—are among the most successful retailers in the nation. Popular in the 1990s, category killers at first took business away from general merchandise discounters, which were not able to compete in selection or price. Recently, however, expanded merchandise and aggressive cost cutting by warehouse clubs and by Wal-Mart have turned the tables. Competition from Internet companies that are able to offer unlimited selection and speedy delivery has also taken customers away. While they still remain a powerful force in retailing, category killers are not invulnerable.[19]

General Merchandise Retailers *General merchandise retailers,* which carry a wide variety of product lines that are all stocked in some depth, distinguish themselves from limited-line and specialty retailers by the large number of product lines they carry. The general store described earlier in this chapter is a primitive form of a general merchandise retailer. This category includes variety stores, department stores, and mass merchandisers such as catalog retailers, discount stores, off-price retailers, and hypermarkets.

Variety Stores A retail outlet that offers an extensive range and assortment of low-price merchandise is called a *variety store.* Less popular today than they once were, many of these stores have evolved into or given way to other types of retailers such as discount stores. The nation's variety stores now account for less than 1 percent of all retail sales. However, variety stores remain popular in other parts of the world. Many retail outlets in Spain and Mexico are family-owned variety stores.

Department Stores A *department store* gathers a series of limited-line and specialty stores under one roof. By definition, this large retailer handles a variety of merchandise, including men's, women's, and children's clothing and accessories; household linens and dry goods; home furnishings; and furniture. It serves as a one-stop shopping destination for almost all personal and household products. Chicago's Marshall Field's is a classic example.

Department stores built their reputations by offering wide varieties of services, such as charge accounts, delivery, gift wrapping, and liberal return privileges. As a result, they incur relatively high operating costs, averaging about 45 to 60 percent of sales.

Department stores have faced intense new competition over the past several years. Relatively high operating costs have left them vulnerable to retailing innovations such as discount stores, catalog merchandisers, and hypermarkets. In addition, department stores' traditional locations in downtown business districts suffered from problems associated with limited parking, traffic congestion, and population migration to the suburbs.

Department stores have fought back in a variety of ways. Many have closed certain sections, such as electronics, in which high costs kept them from competing with discount houses and category killers. They have added bargain outlets, expanded parking facilities, and opened major branches in regional shopping centers. They have attempted to revitalize downtown retailing in many cities by modernizing their stores, expanding store hours, making special efforts to attract the tourist and convention trade, and serving the needs of urban residents.

Retailers like Macy's constantly try to stop the slide by reinventing the department store, experimenting with different layouts, store-branded merchandise, and adding amenities like child care, day spas, and e-mail stations for customers. Sears recently stated that it no longer wanted to be classified as a department store at all, but it has yet to find a profitable niche of its own.[20]

Mass Merchandisers Mass merchandising has made major inroads into department stores' sales by emphasizing lower prices for well-known brand-name products, high product turnover, and limited services. A *mass merchandiser* often stocks a wider line of items than a department store but usually without the same depth of assortment within each line. Discount houses, off-price retailers, hypermarkets, and catalog retailers are all examples of mass merchandisers.

- ***Discount Houses*** A *discount house* charges low prices and offers fewer services. Early discount stores sold mostly appliances. Today, they offer soft goods, drugs, food, and furniture.

  By eliminating many of the "free" services provided by traditional retailers, these operations can keep their markups 10 to 25 percent below those of their competitors. Some of the early discounters have since added services, stocked increasingly prestigious name brands, and boosted their prices. In fact, many now resemble department stores. Kohl's, for instance, defies classification. The store offers centralized checkouts at more than one entrance and distinctive black mesh shopping carts. Departments are staffed by knowledgeable personnel—jewelry and cosmetics counters offer personal assistance, for example. The widespread success of Kohl's—with sales up by 10 percent when rival retailers reported losses—has inspired mall-based department stores like JCPenney to experiment by cutting back on some aspects of one-on-one customer service.[21]

  A discount format that is gaining strength is the warehouse club. Costco and Wal-Mart's Sam's Club are the largest warehouse clubs in the U.S. These no-frills, cash-and-carry outlets offer consumers access to name-brand products at deeply discounted prices. Selection at warehouse clubs includes everything from gourmet popcorn to fax machines to peanut butter to luggage and sunglasses, sold in vast warehouselike settings. Attracting business away from almost every retailing segment, warehouse clubs now even offer fresh food and gasoline. Customers must be members to shop at warehouse clubs.[22]
- ***Off-Price Retailers*** Another version of a discount house is an *off-price retailer.* This kind of store stocks only designer labels or well-known brand-name clothing at prices equal to or below regular wholesale prices and then passes the cost savings along to consumers. While many off-price retailers are located in outlets in downtown areas or in freestanding buildings, a growing number are concentrating in *outlet malls*—shopping centers that house only off-price merchandise by many retailers.

  Inventory at off-price retailers changes frequently as buyers take advantage of special price offers from manufacturers selling excess merchandise. Off-price retailers such as Loehmann's, Marshall's, Stein Mart, and T.J. Maxx also keep their prices below those of traditional retailers by offering fewer services. Off-price retailing has been well received by today's shoppers.
- ***Hypermarkets and Supercenters*** Another innovation in discount retailing is the creation of *hypermarkets*—giant one-stop shopping facilities that offer wide selections of grocery and general merchandise products at discount prices. Store size determines the major difference between hypermarkets and supercenters. Hypermarkets typically fill up 200,000 or more square feet of selling space, about a third larger than most *supercenters.* At Meijer stores, for example, Michigan, Ohio, and Indiana consumers can buy food, hardware, soft goods, building materials, auto supplies, appliances, and prescription drugs in locations averaging 245,000 square feet. When consumers finish shopping, Meijer customers can visit a restaurant, beauty salon, barber shop, bank branch, or bakery within the facility. Fred Meyer on the West Coast is another hypermarket approach. By contrast, the supercenter format is used by Wal-Mart, Kmart, and Target.
- ***Showroom and Warehouse Retailers*** Showroom retailers send direct mail to their customers and sell the advertised goods from showrooms that display samples. Back-room warehouses fill orders for the displayed products. Low prices are important to catalog store customers. To keep prices low, these retailers offer few services, store most inventory in inexpensive warehouse space, limit shoplifting losses, and handle long-lived products such as luggage, small appliances, gift items, sporting equipment, toys, and jewelry.

- ***Classification of Retail Transactions by Location*** Although most retail transactions occur in stores, nonstore retailing serves as an important marketing channel for many products. In addition, both consumer and business-to-business marketers rely on nonstore retailing to generate orders or requests for more information that may result in future orders.

  Direct marketing is a broad concept that includes direct mail, direct selling, direct response retailing, telemarketing, Internet retailing, and automatic merchandising. The last sections of this chapter will consider each type of nonstore retailing.

Retail Convergence and Scrambled Merchandising

Many traditional differences no longer distinguish familiar types of retailers, rendering any set of classifications less useful. **Retail convergence,** whereby similar merchandise is available from multiple retail outlets distinguished by price more than any other factor, is blurring distinctions between types of retailers and the merchandise mix they offer. A few years ago, a customer looking for a fashionable coffeepot might have headed straight for Williams-Sonoma or Starbucks. Today, she's just as likely to pick one up at Target or Wal-Mart, where she can check out new spring fashions and stock up on paper goods. Gap is no longer pitted only against Eddie Bauer or American Eagle Outfitters but against designer-label brands at department stores and Kohl's, too. Grocery stores compete with Wal-Mart.[23]

CHAPTER OBJECTIVE #4: EXPLAIN THE CONCEPTS OF RETAIL CONVERGENCE AND SCRAMBLED MERCHANDISING.

Scrambled merchandising—in which a retailer combines dissimilar product lines in an attempt to boost sales volume—has also muddied the waters. Drugstores not only fill prescriptions but offer cameras, cards, housewares, magazines, and even small appliances. Convenience retailer 7-Eleven recently began offering such services as bill payment, payroll check cashing, money wiring, and ticket purchasing through in-store terminals hooked up to the Web. Goods ordered through the system are delivered to the store for later pick-up.[24]

WHOLESALING INTERMEDIARIES

Recall from Chapter 15 that several distribution channels involve marketing intermediaries called **wholesalers.** These firms take title to the goods they handle and sell those products primarily to retailers or to other wholesalers or business users. They sell to ultimate consumers only in insignificant quantities if at all. **Wholesaling intermediaries,** a broader category, includes not only wholesalers but also agents and brokers, who perform important wholesaling activities without taking title to goods.

Functions of Wholesaling Intermediaries

As specialists in certain marketing functions, as opposed to production or manufacturing functions, wholesaling intermediaries can perform these functions more efficiently than producers or consumers. The importance of these functions results from the utility they create, the services they provide, and the cost reductions they allow.

<interactive>learning goal

CHAPTER OBJECTIVE #5: IDENTIFY THE FUNCTIONS PERFORMED BY WHOLESALING INTERMEDIARIES.

Creating Utility Wholesaling intermediaries create three types of utility for consumers. They enhance time utility by making products available for sale when consumers want to purchase them. They create place utility by helping to deliver goods and services for purchase at convenient locations. They create ownership (or possession) utility when a smooth exchange of title to the products from producers or intermediaries to final purchasers is complete. Possession utility can also result from transactions in which actual title does not pass to purchasers, as in rental-car services.

Providing Services Table 16.1 lists a number of services provided by wholesaling intermediaries. The list clearly indicates the marketing utilities—time, place, and possession utility—that wholesaling intermediaries create or enhance. These services also reflect the basic marketing functions of buying, selling, storing, transporting, providing market information, financing, and risk taking.

TABLE 16.1

Wholesaling Services for Customers and Producer-Suppliers

SERVICE	BENEFICIARIES OF SERVICE: Customers	BENEFICIARIES OF SERVICE: Producer-Suppliers
Buying Anticipates customer demands and applies knowledge of alternative sources of supply; acts as purchasing agent for customers.	✓	
Selling Provides a sales force to call on customers, creating a low-cost method for servicing smaller retailers and business users.		✓
Storing Maintains warehouse facilities at lower costs than most individual producers or retailers could achieve. Reduces risk and cost of maintaining inventory for producers.	✓	✓
Transporting Customers receive prompt delivery in response to their demands, reducing their inventory investments. Wholesalers also break bulk by purchasing in economical carload or truckload lots, then reselling in smaller quantities, thereby reducing overall transportation costs.	✓	✓
Providing Marketing Information Offers important marketing research input for producers through regular contacts with retail and business buyers. Provides customers with information about new products, technical information about product lines, reports on competitors' activities and industry trends, and advisory information concerning pricing changes, legal changes, and so forth.	✓	✓
Financing Grants credit that might be unavailable for purchases directly from manufacturers. Provides financing assistance to producers by purchasing products in advance of sale and by promptly paying bills.	✓	✓
Risk Taking Evaluates credit risks of numerous, distant retail customers and small business users. Extends credit to customers that qualify. By transporting and stocking products in inventory, the wholesaler assumes risk of spoilage, theft, or obsolescence.	✓	✓

Of course, many types of wholesaling intermediaries provide varying services, and not all of them perform every service listed in the table. Producer-suppliers rely on wholesaling intermediaries for distribution, which also entails the selection of firms that offer the desired combinations of services. In general, however, the critical marketing functions listed in the table form the basis for any evaluation of a marketing intermediary's efficiency. The risk-taking function affects each service of the intermediary.

Synnex Information Technologies of Fremont, California, markets computer-related products and peripherals, and it also offers warehousing and trucking capabilities that help lower overhead for retail customers. Inventory management, next-day delivery, financing, and technical service support are among the menu of services the company offers.[25]

Lowering Costs by Limiting Contacts When an intermediary represents numerous producers, it often cuts the costs of buying and selling. The transaction economies are illustrated in Figure 16.5, which shows five manufacturers marketing their outputs to four different retail outlets. Without an intermediary, these exchanges create a total of 20 transactions. Adding a wholesaling intermediary reduces the number of transactions to 9.

For example, United Stationers is a wholesaler of everything from paper clips to fax machines to discount chains, independent stores, and Internet resellers. While big-box retailers buy in bulk directly from manufacturers, they are able to order low-volume specialty goods faster and more efficiently from United Stationers. Through Web-enabled ordering, mom-and-pop stores have access to more than 35,000 items, delivered either to the store or directly to customers overnight. Positioning itself as a one-stop warehousing, logistics, and distribution network, the company recently expanded beyond its office-products roots by establishing a new janitorial supply unit.[26]

FIGURE 16.5

Transaction Economics through Wholesaling Intermediaries

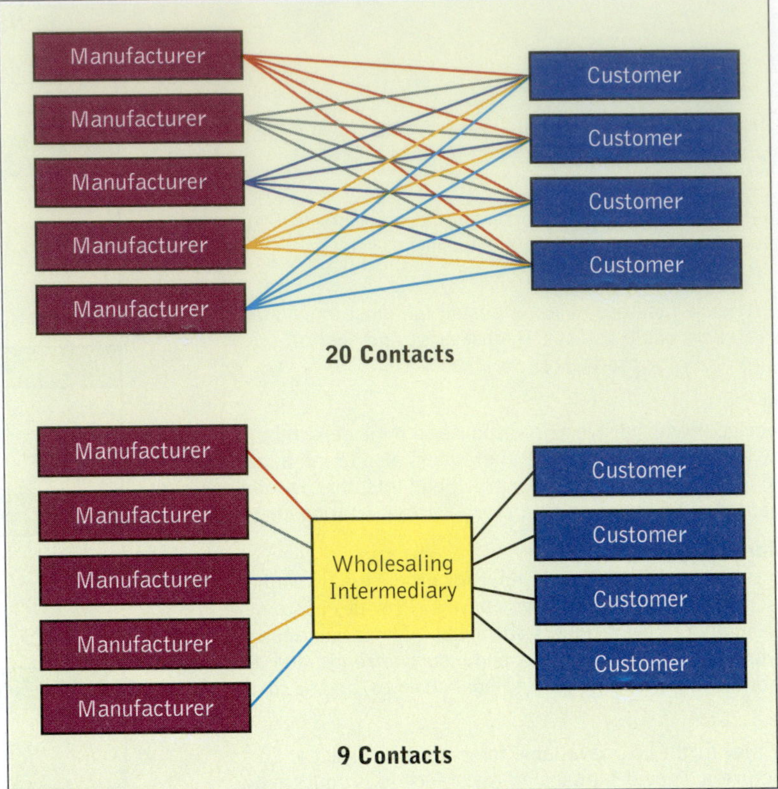

Types of Wholesaling Intermediaries

Various types of wholesaling intermediaries operate in different distribution channels. Some provide wide ranges of services or handle broad lines of goods, while others specialize in individual services, goods, or industries. Figure 16.6 classifies wholesaling intermediaries by two characteristics: ownership and *title flows* (whether title passes from manufacturer to wholesaling intermediary). The three basic ownership structures are as follows: (1) manufacturer-owned facilities, (2) independent wholesaling intermediaries, and (3) retailer-owned cooperatives and buying offices. The two types of independent wholesaling intermediaries are merchant wholesalers, which take title of the goods, and agents and brokers, which do not.

<interactive>**learning goal**

CHAPTER OBJECTIVE #6: IDENTIFY THE MAJOR TYPES OF INDEPENDENT WHOLESALING INTERMEDIARIES AND THE SITUATIONS APPROPRIATE FOR EACH.

Manufacturer-Owned Facilities Several reasons lead manufacturers to distribute their goods directly through company-owned facilities. Some perishable goods need rigid control of distribution to avoid spoilage; other goods require complex installation or servicing. Some goods need aggressive promotion. Goods with high-unit values allow profitable sales by manufacturers directly to ultimate purchasers. Manufacturer-owned facilities include sales branches, sales offices, trade fairs, and merchandise marts.

A *sales branch* carries inventory and processes orders for customers from available stock. Branches provide a storage function like independent wholesalers and serve as offices for sales representatives in their territories. They are prevalent in marketing channels for chemicals, commercial machinery and equipment, motor vehicles, and petroleum products.

A *sales office*, in contrast, does not carry inventory, but it does serve as a regional office for a manufacturer's sales personnel. Locations close to the firm's customers help limit selling costs and support active

FIGURE 16.6

Major Types of Wholesaling Intermediaries

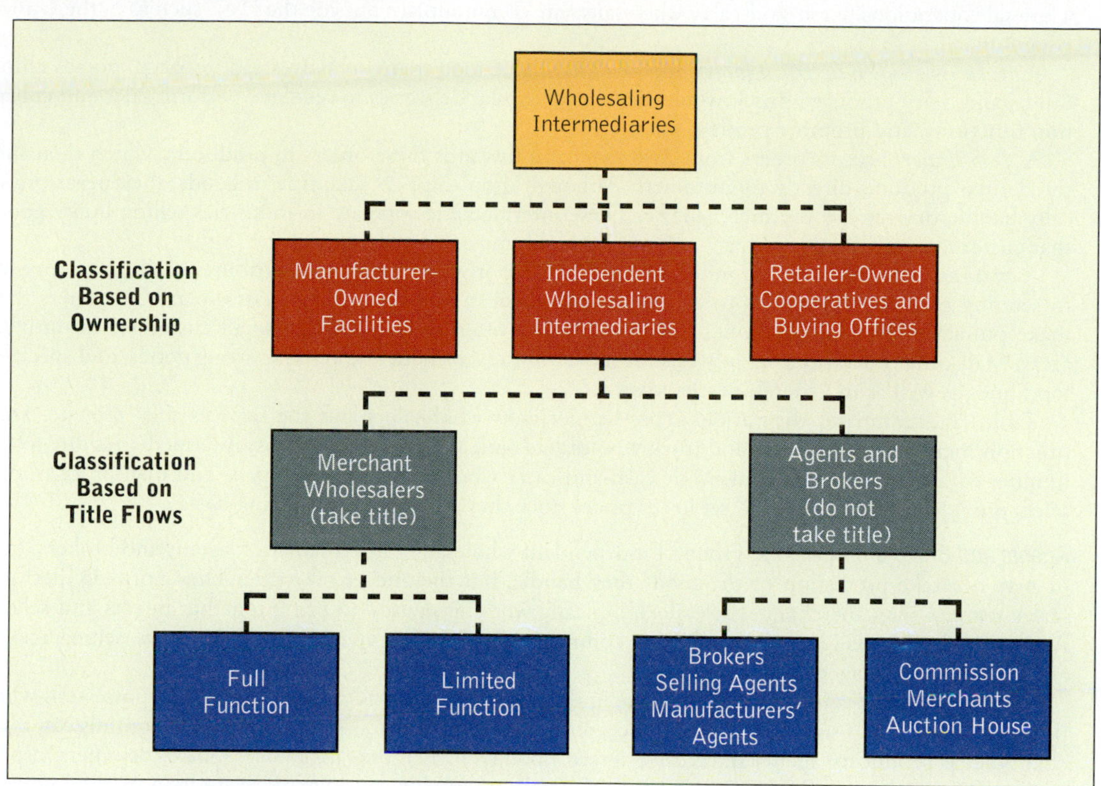

customer service. For example, numerous sales offices in the Detroit suburbs serve the area's automobile industry.

A *trade fair* (or trade exhibition) is a periodic show at which manufacturers in a particular industry display their wares for visiting retail and wholesale buyers. For example, the Internet World Conference sponsors an enormous trade exhibition that brings together over 600 companies to demonstrate their latest Internet technology.

A *merchandise mart* provides space for permanent showrooms and exhibits, which manufacturers rent to market their goods. One of the world's largest merchandise marts is Chicago's Mart Center, a 7-million-square-foot complex that hosts more than 30 seasonal buying markets each year.

Independent Wholesaling Intermediaries Many wholesaling intermediaries are independently owned. These firms fall into two categories: merchant wholesalers and agents and brokers.

Merchant Wholesalers A *merchant wholesaler* takes title to the goods it handles. Merchant wholesalers account for roughly 60 percent of all sales at the wholesale level. Further classifications divide these wholesalers into full-function or limited-function wholesalers, as indicated in Figure 16.6. Synnex, mentioned in the previous section, is a merchant wholesaler.

A full-function merchant wholesaler provides a complete assortment of services for retailers and business purchasers. Such a wholesaler stores merchandise in a convenient location, allowing customers to make purchases on short notice and minimizing inventory requirements. The firm typically maintains a sales force that calls on retailers, makes deliveries, and extends credit to qualified buyers. Full-function wholesalers are common in the drug, grocery, and hardware industries. In the business-goods market, full-function merchant wholesalers (often called *industrial distributors*) sell machinery, inexpensive accessory equipment, and supplies.

A *rack jobber* is a full-function merchant wholesaler who markets specialized lines of merchandise to retailers. A rack jobber supplies the racks, stocks the merchandise, prices the goods, and makes regular visits to refill shelves.

Limited-function merchant wholesalers fit into four categories: cash-and-carry wholesalers, truck wholesalers, drop shippers, and mail-order wholesalers. Limited-function wholesalers serve the food, coal, lumber, cosmetics, jewelry, sporting goods, and general merchandise industries.

A *cash-and-carry wholesaler* performs most wholesaling functions except for financing and delivery. Although feasible for small stores, this kind of wholesaling generally is unworkable for large-scale grocery stores. Today, cash-and-carry operations typically function as departments within regular full-service wholesale operations. Cash-and-carry wholesalers are commonplace outside the U.S., such as in the United Kingdom.

A *truck wholesaler,* or *truck jobber,* markets perishable food items such as bread, tobacco, potato chips, candy, and dairy products. Truck wholesalers make regular deliveries to retailers, perform sales and collection functions, and promote product lines.

A *drop shipper* accepts orders from customers and forwards these orders to producers, which then ship the desired products directly to customers. Although drop shippers take title to goods, they never physically handle or even see the merchandise. These intermediaries operate in industries selling bulky goods that customers buy in carload lots, such as coal and lumber.

A *mail-order wholesaler* is a limited-function merchant wholesaler who distributes catalogs as opposed to sending sales representatives to contact retail, business, and institutional customers. Customers then make purchases by mail or phone. Such a wholesaler often serves relatively small customers in outlying areas. Mail-order operations mainly exist in the hardware, cosmetics, jewelry, sporting goods, and specialty food lines as well as in general merchandise.

Table 16.2 compares the various types of merchant wholesalers and the services they provide. Full-function merchant wholesalers and truck wholesalers rank as relatively high-cost intermediaries due to the number of services they perform, while cash-and-carry wholesalers, drop shippers, and mail-order wholesalers provide fewer services and set lower prices since they incur lower operating costs.

Agents and Brokers A second group of independent wholesaling intermediaries, agents and brokers, may or may not take possession of the goods they handle, but they never take title. They normally perform fewer services than merchant wholesalers, typically working mainly to bring together buyers and sellers. Agents and brokers fall into five categories: commission merchants, auction houses, brokers, selling agents, and manufacturers' agents.

Commission merchants, who predominate in the markets for agricultural products, take possession when producers ship goods such as grain, produce, and livestock to central markets for sale. Commission merchants act as producers' agents and receive agreed-upon fees when they make sales. Since customers inspect the products and prices fluctuate, commission merchants receive considerable latitude in marketing decisions. The owners of the goods may specify minimum prices, but the commission merchants sell these goods at the best possible prices. The commission merchants then deduct their fees from the sales proceeds.

An auction house gathers buyers and sellers in one location and allows potential buyers to inspect merchandise before submitting competing purchase offers. Auction house commissions typically reflect specified percentages of the sales prices of the auctioned items. Auctions are common in the distribution of tobacco, used cars, artworks, livestock, furs, and fruit. The Internet has led to a new type of auction house that connects customers and sellers in the online world. A well-known example is eBay, which auctions a wide variety of products in all price ranges. Another example, Sotheby's, featured in Figure 16.7, offers high-end items such as jewelry, paintings, and furniture to Internet bidders.

Brokers work mainly to bring together buyers and sellers. A broker represents either the buyer or the seller, but not both, in a given transaction, and the broker receives a fee from the client when the transac-

TABLE 16.2

Comparison of the Types of Merchant Wholesalers and Their Services

		LIMITED-FUNCTION WHOLESALER			
SERVICE	**Full-Function**	**Cash-and-Carry**	**Truck**	**Drop Shipper**	**Mail-Order**
Anticipates customer needs	✓	✓	✓	—	✓
Carries inventory	✓	✓	✓	—	✓
Delivers	✓	—	✓	—	—
Provides market information	✓	Rarely	✓	✓	—
Provides credit	✓	—	—	✓	Sometimes
Assumes ownership risk by taking title	✓	✓	✓	✓	✓

tion is completed. Intermediaries that specialize in arranging buying and selling transactions between domestic producers and foreign buyers are called *export brokers.* Brokers operate in industries characterized by large numbers of small suppliers and purchasers, such as real estate, frozen foods, and used machinery. Since they provide one-time services for sellers or buyers, they cannot serve as effective channels for manufacturers seeking regular, continuing service. A firm that seeks to develop a more permanent channel might choose instead to use a selling agent or manufacturer's agent.

A *selling agent* typically exerts full authority over pricing decisions and promotional outlays, and it often provides financial assistance for the manufacturer. Selling agents act as independent marketing departments because they can assume responsibility for the total marketing programs of client firms' product lines. Selling agents mainly operate in the coal, lumber, and textiles industries. For a small, poorly financed, production-oriented firm, such an intermediary might prove the ideal marketing channel.

While a manufacturer may deal with only one selling agent, a firm that hires **manufacturers' agents,** commonly known as manufacturers' reps, often delegates marketing tasks to many of these agents. Such an independent salesperson may work for a number of firms that produce related, noncompeting products. Manufacturers' reps are paid on a commission basis, such as 6 percent of sales. Unlike selling agents, who may contract for exclusive rights to market a product, manufacturers' agents operate in specific territories. They may develop new sales territories or represent relatively small firms and those firms with unrelated lines.

When inventor Jane McKittrick first launched Earth Bud-Eze, an innovative range of tools that eased the strains of many gardening tasks, the products—sold largely at state fairs—were modestly successful. But when McKittrick enlisted the expertise of Marshall Associates, a manufacturers' rep group with extensive contacts in the hardware and gardening markets, sales skyrocketed. The start-up product line was even able to penetrate mass merchants nationwide.[27]

FIGURE 16.7

An Internet-based Auction Site

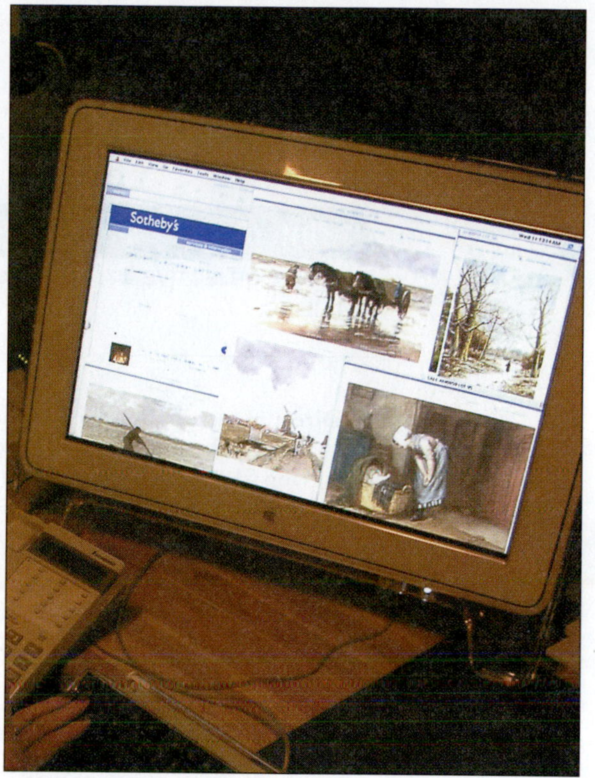

The importance of selling agents in many markets has declined because manufacturers want better control of their marketing programs than these intermediaries allow. In contrast, the volume of sales by manufacturers' agents has more than doubled and now accounts for 37 percent of all sales by agents and brokers. Table 16.3 compares the major types of agents and brokers on the basis of the services they perform.

Retailer-Owned Cooperatives and Buying Offices

Retailers may assume numerous wholesaling functions in an attempt to reduce costs or provide special services. Independent retailers sometimes band together to form buying groups that can achieve cost savings

TABLE 16.3

Services Provided by Agents and Brokers

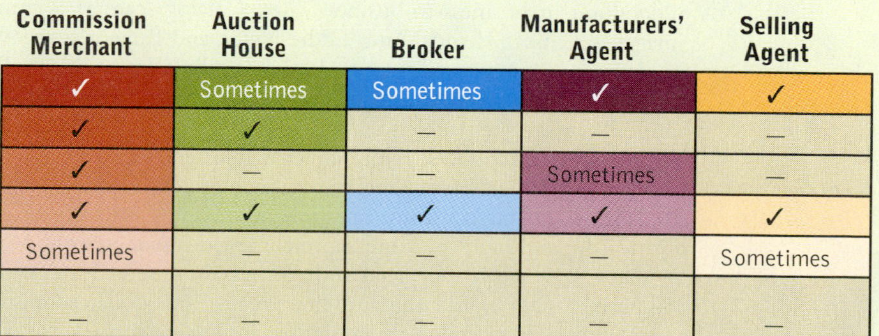

SERVICE	Commission Merchant	Auction House	Broker	Manufacturers' Agent	Selling Agent
Anticipates customer needs	✓	Sometimes	Sometimes	✓	✓
Carries inventory	✓	✓	—	—	—
Delivers	✓	—	—	Sometimes	—
Provides market information	✓	✓	✓	✓	✓
Provides credit	Sometimes	—	—	—	Sometimes
Assumes ownership risk by taking title	—	—	—	—	—

through quantity purchases. Other groups of retailers establish retailer-owned wholesale facilities by forming cooperative chains. Large chain retailers often establish centralized buying offices to negotiate large-scale purchases directly with manufacturers.

DIRECT MARKETING AND OTHER NONSTORE RETAILING

Although most retail transactions occur in stores, nonstore retailing is an important marketing channel for many products. As well as sales, both consumer and business-to-business marketers rely on nonstore retailing to generate leads or requests for more information that may result in future orders.

<interactive>**learning goal**

CHAPTER OBJECTIVE #7: COMPARE THE BASIC TYPES OF DIRECT MARKETING AND NONSTORE RETAILING.

Direct marketing is a broad concept that includes direct mail, direct selling, direct-response retailing, telemarketing, Internet retailing, and automatic merchandising. Direct and interactive marketing expenditures top $190 billion a year, a figure that is expected to rise at the rate of 6.5 percent a year until 2006.[28] The last sections of this chapter will consider each type of nonstore retailing.

Direct Mail

Direct mail is a major component of direct marketing. It comes in many forms, ranging from sales letters, postcards, brochures, booklets, catalogs, and house organs (periodicals issued by organizations) to video and audio cassettes. Both not-for-profit and profit-seeking organizations make extensive use of this distribution channel.

Direct mail offers several advantages such as the ability to select a narrow target market, achieve intensive coverage, send messages quickly, choose from various formats, provide complete information, and personalize each mailing piece. Response rates are measurable and higher than other types of advertising. In addition, direct mailings stand alone and do not compete for attention with magazine articles and television programs. On the other hand, the per-reader cost of direct mail is high, effectiveness depends on the quality of the mailing list, and some consumers object strongly to direct mail, considering it to be "junk mail."

Direct mail marketing relies heavily on database technology in managing lists of names and in segmenting these lists according to the objectives of the campaign. Recipients get targeted materials, often personalized with their names within the ad's content. The "Marketing Misses" Interactive Example shows what can happen when personalized pitches like these misfire.

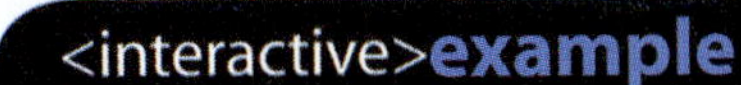

MARKETING MISS: PROZAC BY MAIL

Catalogs are a popular form of direct mail, with more than 10,000 different consumer specialty mail-order catalogs—and thousands more for business-to-business sales—finding their way to almost every mailbox in the U.S. In a typical year, mail-order catalogs generate almost $40 billion in consumer sales and $24 billion in business-to-business sales. Catalogs can be a company's only or primary sales method. Spiegel, L.L. Bean, Lands' End, Eddie Bauer, and Patagonia are well-known examples. Brick-and-mortar retailers like Bloomingdale's and Macy's also distribute catalogs. Web retailers, too, have discovered that catalogs stimulate sales. Exotic goods e-tailer eZiba.com used a catalog to expand its customer base beyond young, Web-savvy clientele to older shoppers. Amazon has recently mailed a catalog of home and garden products, while Yahoo! is testing direct-mail offers for its range of premium pay services.[29]

New technologies are changing catalog marketing. Today's catalogs can be updated quickly, providing consumers with the latest information and prices. CD-ROM catalogs allow marketers to display products in three-dimensional views and can include video sequences of product demonstrations. Following terrorist scares in which letters laced with anthrax were sent through the mail, direct marketers responded by combining e-mail marketing and direct mail. E-mails alerted customers that catalogs or direct mail packages were coming through the postal service, easing concerns over mail from unknown sources.[30]

Direct Selling

Through direct selling, manufacturers completely bypass retailers and wholesalers. Instead, they set up their own channels to sell their products directly to consumers. Avon, the Fuller Brush Company, Dell

Computer, and party-plan marketers like Tupperware are all direct sellers. This channel was discussed in detail in Chapter 15.

Direct-Response Retailing

Customers of a direct-response retailer can order merchandise by mail or telephone, by visiting a mail-order desk in a retail store, or by computer or fax machine. The retailer then ships the merchandise to the customer's home or to a local retail store for pickup. Shown in Figure 16.8, Lactaid offers free samples via direct response by telephone or to its Web site.

Many direct-response retailers rely on direct mail, such as catalogs, to create telephone and mail-order sales and to promote in-store purchases of products featured in the catalogs. Additionally, some firms, such as Lillian Vernon, make almost all of their sales through catalog orders. Mail-order sales have grown about 10 percent a year in recent years, about twice the rate of retail store sales.

Direct-response retailers are increasingly reaching buyers through the Internet and through unique catalogs. Lillian Vernon supplements its general merchandise catalogs with specialty catalogs of children's products and personalized gifts. Jackson and Perkins holiday season catalogs offer a variety of plants for gift giving. Signals advertises merchandise with tie-ins to Public Broadcasting Service programs.

Direct-response retailing also includes home shopping, which runs promotions on cable television networks to sell merchandise through telephone orders. One form of home shopping has existed for years—the late-night commercials that run for at least 30 minutes. Such products as K-Tel Records and Veg-O-Matic vegetable slicers have been featured on these commercials. More recently, TV networks like Home Shopping Network have successfully focused exclusively on providing shopping opportunities. Programming ranges from extended commercials to call-in shows to game-show formats. Shoppers call a toll-free number to buy featured products, and the retailer ships ordered goods directly to their homes.

Telemarketing

Telemarketing refers to direct marketing conducted entirely by telephone. It is the most frequently used form of direct marketing. It provides marketers with a high return on their expenditures, an immediate response, and the opportunity for personalized two-way conversations. Telemarketing is discussed in further detail in Chapter 19.

Internet Retailing

Internet-based retailers sell directly to customers via virtual storefronts on the Web. They usually maintain little or no inventory, ordering directly from vendors to fill customer orders received via their Web sites. In recent years, conventional retailers have anxiously watched the rise—and then the demise—of Internet-based retailers. During the dot.com bust, 130 e-tailers failed. Even early successes like Ezshop, an online home furnishings retailer, eventually ran aground. Traditional retailers, using the Web to support brick-and-mortar stores, have had much better staying power. Gap, Best Buy, and Lands' End, for example, have succeeded in extending their expertise to the Web. Office Depot credits its success to its solid brand name, its low-cost buying strategies, and most important, its extensive distribution network—customers can pick up purchases they initiate on the Web at local Office Depot outlets.[31] Chapter 5 discussed Internet retailing and other forms of e-commerce in more detail.

FIGURE 16.8

A Direct Response Marketer

Enjoy dairy, not the discomfort.
Try Lactaid for FREE.
Lactaid Ultra
If dairy foods cause you cramps, gas and bloating, take LACTAID® Supplements with your first bite of dairy and help prevent the symptoms before they start.
Call 1-800-LACTAID for your FREE 6-count pack of LACTAID® Ultra, to help you enjoy dairy without the consequences.
Enjoy dairy again.
www.lactaid.com
Call 1-800-LACTAID for a FREE 6-count pack of Lactaid Ultra.

Automatic Merchandising

The world's first vending machines dispensed holy water for five-drachma coins in Egyptian temples around 215 b.c. This retailing method has grown rapidly ever since; today, about 4.7 million vending machines sell approximately $25 billion in convenience goods to Americans.

While in the past U.S. vending machines have been limited to snacks, soft drinks, and lottery tickets, Japanese consumers use automatic merchandising for everything from fresh sushi to new underwear. Recently, U.S. marketers have begun to realize the potential of this underused marketing tool. As technological advances and credit-card payments make it easier to sell high-cost items, vending machines offering $15 movie soundtracks are popping up in movie-theater lobbies, while Underwear to Go offers boxer shorts in pop-up aluminum cans.[32] The end-of-chapter case explains that automated merchandising is just one way in which marketers seek to keep pace with today's 24/7 society.

STRATEGIC IMPLICATIONS OF MARKETING IN THE 21ST CENTURY

As the Internet revolution steadily becomes a way of life—both for consumers and for the businesses marketing goods and services to them—technology will continue to transform the ways in which retailers, wholesalers, and direct marketers connect with customers.

<interactive>learning goal

LEARNING OBJECTIVE #8: EXPLAIN WAYS IN WHICH THE INTERNET HAS ALTERED THE WHOLESALING, RETAILING, AND DIRECT MARKETING ENVIRONMENTS.

In the retail sector, the unstoppable march toward lower and lower prices has forced retailers from Saks Fifth Avenue to dollar stores to reevaluate everything from their logistics and supply networks to their profit margins. Many have used the power of the Internet to strengthen such factors as store image, the merchandising mix, customer service, and the development of long-term relationships with customers.

Though manufacturers first anticipated that Internet technology would enable them to bypass such intermediaries as wholesalers and agents, bringing them closer to the customer, the reality is quite different. Successful wholesalers have been able to establish themselves as essential links in the supply, distribution, and customer service network. By leveraging technology, they have been able to carve out new roles, providing such expert services as warehousing or fulfillment to multiple retail clients.

The Internet has empowered direct marketers by facilitating ever more sophisticated database segmentation. Traditional catalog and direct mail marketers have integrated Internet sites, Web advertising, and e-mailing programs into a cohesive targeting, distribution, and repeat-buying strategy.

Briefly Speaking

If you're not doing Internet business, then you're in the Dark Ages, and you're going to be left behind.

John Chambers (b. 1948) CEO, Cisco Systems

<interactive>review

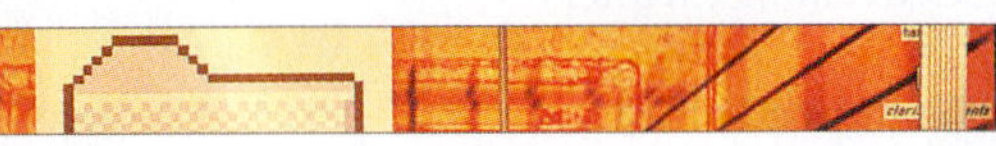

FLASH CHAPTER REVIEW PRESENTATION

<interactive>video case

NEIMAN MARCUS TAKES CARE OF ITS CUSTOMERS

<interactive>game

QUIZ BOWL

<interactive>video case

KRISPY KREME CONTINUING VIDEO CASE: KRISPY KREME'S DISTRIBUTION STRATEGY

endofchaptermaterial

- Summary of Chapter Objectives
- Chapter Outline
- Key Terms
- Review Questions
- Projects and Teamwork Exercises
- 'netWork
- Crossword Puzzles
- Case 16.1: Retail Rocks Around the Clock

Take the Post-Test to assess your overall understanding of the key ideas in this chapter. The Post-Test provides a comprehensive selection of exam-style questions addressing the main topics and concepts of the chapter. At the completion of each Post-Test, you will receive a score and instructive feedback on how you answered each question, and a direct link to the part of the chapter addressed in the question. Take the Post-Test as often as you need to—a record of your progress for each attempt is kept for you to revisit and gauge your improvement. And each Post-Test is randomly generated, so every attempt is new.

Post-Test

PART 7

Promotional Strategy

CHAPTER

17

Integrated Marketing Communications

Chapter Objectives

1. **Discuss how integrated marketing communications relates to the development of an optimal promotional mix.**
2. **Describe the communication process and how it relates to the AIDA concept.**
3. **Discuss how the promotional mix relates to the objectives of promotion.**
4. **Identify the different elements of the promotional mix and explain how marketers develop an optimal promotional mix.**
5. **Discuss the role of sponsorships and direct marketing in integrated marketing communications.**
6. **Contrast the two major alternative promotional strategies.**
7. **Explain how marketers budget for and measure the effectiveness of promotion.**
8. **Discuss the value of marketing communications.**

TERRORISM—AND TIMING—UPSET THE NISSAN ALTIMA IMC STRATEGY

Nissan North America had big marketing plans. The Japanese automaker had made major improvements to its product line, including completely overhauling the Altima and Maxima models and repositioning them to overtake competing cars from Toyota and Honda. As part of the overall promotional mix, Nissan authorized a $100 million campaign that included print and TV advertising, as well as direct mail, built around the theme "The Cure for the Common Car."

During the year prior to the launch, Nissan marketers had identified American households matching precisely their new target market, households they were confident had high purchase potential. Each target household received a series of mailings and sales promotional items—brochures, a compact disc, and offers of expensive gifts in return for visiting a nearby showroom and taking a test drive. All of these mailed pieces carried the cure for the common car theme. Then came the final promotional piece—an offer for a free test drive. However, this direct mailing was unfortunately timed. Designed to look like an oversized prescription bottle and carrying the words "Active Ingredient: The Stuff You Asked For" on its label, the mailing arrived in October 2001—right at the height of the post-September 11 anthrax scare. Strange letters with the deadly white powder had already shut down post offices and government agencies around the country and frightened many citizens into opening their mail with gloves—when they opened it at all.

Nissan immediately cut the mailing short when complaints arose and company marketers realized what they had inadvertently done. The company immediately sent a letter of apology to all those who had received the mailing. The Altima went on to become a huge sales success, but an otherwise ingenious marketing strategy was damaged by events beyond Nissan's control.

Nissan was not the only car company whose marketing communications were affected by the anthrax scare. In late September 2001, American Honda, the U.S. unit of Honda Motor Co., mailed brochures containing attractive financial rebate offers to 89,000 potential car buyers in Indiana, Kentucky, Michigan, and Ohio. In keeping with the mailing's theme, "Have a cup of coffee on us," the mailing contained a packet of coarse brown granules that rattled when shaken. It seemed like just the kind of thing postal authorities had warned consumers to watch for—yet it contained nothing more than ground coffee. "Obviously, it was dreamed up in advance of everything that has happened," a Honda spokesperson said at the time. "It's something we'd certainly rethink for the future."

Such incidents make many marketers flinch, but using a variety of communication avenues to reach consumers is still a viable—and competitive—marketing strategy. It is important for marketers to stay in touch with current events and consumers' attitudes about certain types of promotional efforts—and to accept that some things are simply out of their control, as was the anthrax scare.[1]

Pre-Test

Take the Pre-Test to assess your initial knowledge of the key ideas in this chapter. The Pre-Test provides exam-style questions addressing the main topics and concepts of the chapter. At the completion of each Pre-Test, you will receive a score and instructive feedback on how you answered each question, and a direct link to the part of the chapter addressed in the question. Take the Pre-Test as often as you need to—a record of your progress for each attempt is kept for you to revisit and gauge your improvement.

CHAPTER OVERVIEW

Three of the four components of the marketing mix—product, pricing, and distribution strategies—were discussed in previous chapters. The following three chapters in Part 7 analyze the fourth marketing mix variable—promotion. **Promotion** is the function of informing, persuading, and influencing the consumer's purchase decision.

This chapter introduces the concept of integrated marketing communications, briefly describes the elements of a firm's promotional mix—personal and nonpersonal selling—and explains the characteristics that determine the success of the mix. Next, the chapter identifies the objectives of promotion and describes the importance of developing promotional budgets and measuring the effectiveness of promotion. Finally, the chapter discusses the importance of the business, economic, and social aspects of promotion. Chapter 18 covers advertising, sales promotion, and the other nonpersonal selling elements of the promotional mix. Chapter 19 completes this part of the book by focusing on personal selling.

Throughout this book, special emphasis has been given to

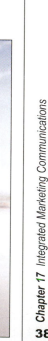

new information that focuses on how technology is changing the way marketers approach communication, the transmission of a message from a sender to a receiver. Consumers receive **marketing communications**—messages that deal with buyer-seller relationships—from a variety of media, including television, magazines, and the Internet. Marketers can broadcast an ad on the Web to mass markets or design a customized appeal targeted to a small market segment. Each message the customer receives from any source represents the brand, company, or organization. A company needs to coordinate all these messages so the consumer doesn't completely tune them out.

To prevent this loss of attention, marketers are turning to **integrated marketing communications (IMC),** which coordinate all promotional activities—media advertising, direct mail, personal selling, sales promotion, and public relations—to produce a unified, customer-focused promotional message. IMC is a broader concept than marketing communications and promotional strategy. It uses database technology to refine the marketer's understanding of the target audience, segment this audience, and select the best type of media for each segment.

This chapter shows that IMC involves not only the marketer but also all other organizational units that interact with the consumer. Marketing managers set the goals and objectives of the firm's promotional strategy in accordance with overall organizational objectives and marketing goals. Based on these objectives, the various elements of the promotional strategy—personal selling, advertising, sales promotion, direct marketing, publicity, and public relations—are formulated into an integrated communications plan. This plan becomes a central part of the firm's total marketing strategy to reach its selected market segments. The feedback mechanism, including marketing research and field reports, completes the system by identifying any deviations from the plan and suggesting improvements.

Briefly Speaking

The codfish lays
ten thousand eggs,
The homely
hen lays one.
The codfish
never cackles
To tell you what
she's done.
And so we scorn
the codfish,
While the humble hen we
prize.
Which only goes
to show you
That it pays to
advertise.

Anonymous

INTEGRATED MARKETING COMMUNICATIONS

Stop and think for a moment about all the marketing messages you receive in a single day. You click on the television for the morning news, and you see plenty of commercials. Listen to the car radio on the way to work or school, and you can sing along with the jingles. You get catalogs, coupons, and flyers in the mail. People even leave promotional flyers stuck under your car's windshield wiper while it sits in the parking lot. When you log on to your computer, you're deluged with banner and pop-up ads and even e-mail from marketers. Even an annoying phone call during dinner from a telemarketer is a message. Marketers know that you are receiving many types of communication. They know they need to compete for your attention. So they look for ways to reach you in a coordinated manner through integrated marketing communications.

<interactive>**learning goal**

CHAPTER OBJECTIVE #1: DISCUSS HOW INTEGRATED MARKETING COMMUNICATIONS RELATES TO THE DEVELOPMENT OF AN OPTIMAL PROMOTIONAL MIX.

Successful marketers use the marketing concept and relationship marketing to develop customer-oriented marketing programs. The customer is also at the heart of integrated marketing communications. An IMC strategy begins not with the organization's goods and services but with consumer wants or needs and then works in reverse to the product, brand, or organization. It sends receiver-focused rather than product-focused messages.

Rather than separating the parts of the promotional mix, IMC looks at these elements from the consumer's viewpoint: as information about the brand, company, or organization. Even though the messages come from different sources—sales presentations, TV, radio, newspaper, billboards, direct mail, coupons, public relations, the Internet, and online services—consumers may perceive them as "advertising" or a "sales pitch." IMC broadens promotion to include all the ways a customer has contact with an organization, adding to traditional media and direct mail such sources as packaging, store displays, sales literature, and online and interactive media. Unless the organization takes an integrated approach to present a unified, consistent message, it may send conflicting information that confuses consumers. Figure 17.1 illustrates how several organizations—including a television network, a manufacturer, and a major retailer—joined together to create a unified marketing message about family first aid and products that can help consumers have a safe summer.

Today's marketing environment is characterized by many diverse markets and media, creating both opportunities and challenges. The success of any IMC program depends on identifying the members of an audience and understanding what they want. Without good current information about existing and potential customers, their purchase histories, needs, and wants, marketers may send the wrong message. But they cannot succeed simply by improving the quality of the messages or by sending more of them. IMC must not only deliver messages to intended audiences but also gather responses from them. Databases and interactive marketing are important IMC tools that help marketers collect information from customers and then segment markets according to demographics and preferences. Marketers can then design specialized communications programs to meet the needs of particular segments.

Art museums often face an uphill battle when it comes to attracting more visitors. It's even harder, sometimes, for television networks to get viewers to sit down and watch programming about art. But A&E Network met the challenge in promoting its special "Biography" series, *The Impressionists,* with a successful IMC campaign. Working in conjunction with the Civic Entertainment Group in New York, A&E contacted dozens of art museums around the country, whose regular customers matched the demographic profiles of A&E's viewers. A&E then supplied the museums with a "Fundraiser in a Box" promotional kit, complete with a 20-minute preview of the series, a customized press release and invitations, a handbook for producing fundraising events (with special tips on French catering and music), a coupon for purchasing cheese and crackers, and two cases of Turning Leaf wine supplied by Gallo Wines. The museums loved it—and so did their visitors, who then tuned in to watch *The Impressionists.* A&E reported a viewing audience of 2.7 million households, which was 32 percent higher than its prime time average for that month.[2]

The increase in media options provides more ways to give consumers product information; however, it can also create information overload. Marketers have to spread available dollars across fragmented media markets and a wider range of promotional activities to achieve their communication goals. Mass media such as TV ads, while still useful, are no longer the mainstays of marketing campaigns. In 1960, a company could reach about 90 percent of U.S. consumers by advertising on the three major TV networks. Today, these network ads reach fewer than 60 percent. Audiences are also more fragmented. So to reach desired groups, organizations are turning to niche marketing by advertising in special-interest magazines; by purchasing time on cable TV channels to target consumers with sports, family, science, history, comedy, and women's interests; by reaching out through telecommunications like the Internet; and by sponsoring events and activities. Without an IMC program, marketers frequently encounter problems within their own organizations because separate departments have authority and responsibility for planning and implementing specific promotional mix elements.

The coordination of an IMC program frequently produces a competitive advantage based on synergy and interdependence among the various elements of the promotional mix. With an IMC strategy, marketers can create a unified personality for the product or brand by choosing the right elements from the promotional mix to send the message. At the same time, they can develop more narrowly focused plans to reach specific market segments and choose the best form of communication to send a particular message to a specific target audience. IMC provides a more effective way to reach and serve target markets than less coordinated strategies.

Importance of Teamwork

IMC requires a big-picture view of promotion planning, a total strategy including all marketing activities, not just promotion. Successful implementation of IMC requires that everyone involved in every aspect of promotion—public relations, advertising, personal selling, and sales promotion—function as a team. They must present a consistent, coordinated promotional effort at every point of customer contact with the organization. This way, they save time, money, and effort. They avoid duplication of efforts, increasing marketing effectiveness and reducing costs.

Teamwork involves both in-house resources and outside vendors. It involves marketing personnel; members of the sales force who deal with wholesalers, retailers, and organizational buyers; and customer service representatives. A firm gains nothing from a terrific advertisement featuring a toll-free telephone number that has unhelpful, surly operators on the other end. The company must train its representatives to send a single positive message to consumers and also to solicit information for the firm's customer database. Excedrin Migraine, featured in Figure 17.2, will have a successful promotional

FIGURE 17.1

Joint Integrated Marketing Promotion by ABC's Good Morning America, Band-Aid, and Target.

FIGURE 17.2

Excedrin Migraine: Using Free Samples, a Web Site, and a Toll-free Number in an IMC Effort

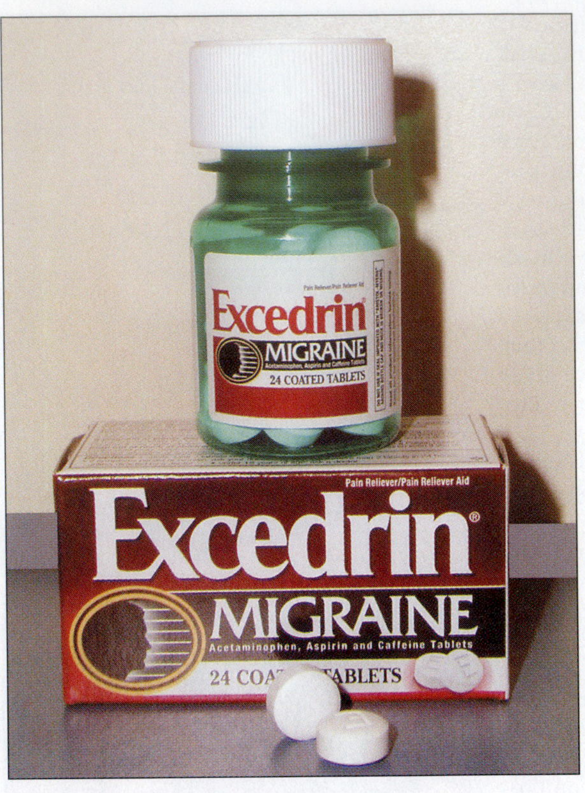

message if consumers can quickly receive the free sample offered and can easily access information at the Web site or via the toll-free number.

IMC also challenges the traditional role of the advertising agency. A single agency may no longer fulfill all of a client's communications requirements, including traditional advertising and sales promotions, interactive marketing, database development, direct marketing, and public relations. To best serve client needs, an agency must often assemble a team with members from other companies.

Role of Databases in Effective IMC Programs

With the growth of the Internet during the last 10 years, marketers have been given the power to gather more information faster and to organize it more easily than ever before in history. By sharing this detailed knowledge appropriately among all relative parties, a company can lay the foundation for a successful IMC program.

The move from mass marketing to a customer-specific marketing strategy—a characteristic of online marketing—requires not only a means of identifying and communicating with the firm's target market but also information regarding important characteristics of each prospective customer. As discussed in Chapter 6, organizations can compile different kinds of data into complete databases with customer information, including names and addresses, demographic data, lifestyle considerations, brand preferences, and buying behavior. This information provides critical guidance in designing an effective IMC strategy that achieves organizational goals and finds new opportunities for increased sales and profits.

Direct sampling is another method frequently used to quickly obtain customer opinions regarding a particular firm's goods and services. If you've ever received a free sample of bath soap, aspirin, or even a newspaper in your mailbox, you've been the recipient of direct sampling. Companies such as Illinois-based Snyder Communications use databases to target these promotions to certain consumers for companies. They might target a particular ethnic audience, such as Hispanic consumers, or they might target a particular age group, such as aging baby boomers.

THE COMMUNICATIONS PROCESS

When you have a conversation with someone, do you wonder whether the person understood your message? Do you worry that you might not have heard the person correctly? Marketers have the same concerns—when they send a message to an intended audience or market, they want to make sure it gets through clearly and persuasively. That is why the communications process is so important to marketing. The top portion of Table 17.1 shows a general model of the communications process and its application to promotional strategy. The *sender* acts as the source in the communications system as he or she seeks to convey a *message* (a communication of information, advice, or a request) to a receiver. An effective message accomplishes three tasks:

1. It gains the receiver's attention.
2. It achieves understanding by both receiver and sender.
3. It stimulates the receiver's needs and suggests an appropriate method of satisfying them.

The table also provides several examples of promotional messages. Although the types of promotion may vary from a highly personalized sales presentation to such nonpersonal promotions as television advertising and dollar-off coupons, each goes through every stage in the communications process.

CHAPTER OBJECTIVE #2: DESCRIBE THE COMMUNICATION PROCESS AND HOW IT RELATES TO THE AIDA CONCEPT.

The three tasks just listed are related to the **AIDA concept** (attention-interest-desire-action), the steps consumers take in reaching a purchase decision. First, the promotional message must gain the potential

TABLE 17.1

Relating Promotion to the Communications Process

TYPE OF PROMOTION	SENDER	ENCODING BY SENDER	CHANNEL	DECODING BY RECEIVER	RESPONSE	FEEDBACK
Personal selling	IBM e-solutions networking system	Sales presentation on new applications of system	IBM sales representative	Office manager and employees discuss sales presentation and those of competing suppliers.	Order is placed for IBM e-solutions system installation.	Customer asks about a second system for subsidiary company.
Dollar-off coupon (sales promotion)	Kellogg's Special K cereal	Coupons prepared by Kellogg's marketing department and advertising agency	Coupon insert in Sunday newspaper	Newspaper reader sees coupon for Special K cereal and saves it.	Special K is purchased by consumer using coupon.	Kellogg researchers see increase in market share.
Television advertising	Styx River Water World	Advertisement developed by Styx River's advertising agency featuring the new park rides	Network television ads during program with high percentages of viewers under 20 years old	Teens and young adults see ad and decide to try out the new park.	Water World tickets are purchased.	Customers purchase season ticket packages for Water World.

consumer's attention. It then seeks to arouse interest in the good or service. At the next stage, it stimulates desire by convincing the would-be buyer of the product's ability to satisfy his or her needs. Finally, the sales presentation, advertisement, or sales promotion technique attempts to produce action in the form of a purchase or a more favorable attitude that may lead to future purchases.

The message must be *encoded,* or translated into understandable terms, and transmitted through a communications channel. *Decoding* is the receiver's interpretation of the message. The receiver's response, known as *feedback,* completes the system. Throughout the process, *noise* can interfere with the transmission of the message and reduce its effectiveness.

The marketing manager is the message sender in Table 17.1. He or she encodes the message in the form of sales presentations, advertising, displays, or publicity releases. The *channel* for delivering the message may be a salesperson, a public relations outlet, or an advertising medium. Decoding is often the most troublesome step in marketing communications because consumers do not always interpret promotional messages in the same way that senders do. Since receivers usually decode messages according to their own frames of reference or experiences, a sender must carefully encode a message in a way that matches the frame of reference of the target audience. Consumers today receive many sales messages through many media channels. This communications traffic can create confusion as noise in the channel increases. Consumers choose to process only a few messages each, and ignored messages waste communications budgets. Marketers for Sharp, a leading producer of copiers and electronics products, wanted to convey the message that their new wireless device delivers clear communication and computing capabilities to users—wherever they happen to be. So they juxtaposed an image of the source of a creative idea—the sandcastle—with the tagline "be brilliant" above the business message being sent on the device and the words "be sharp." A simple glance at the ad, shown in Figure 17.3, tells consumers that the Zaurus mobile tool delivers accurate, unrestricted communication, allowing people to maintain their wireless connections, even at the beach.

The AIDA concept is also vital to online marketers. It is not enough to say a Web site has effective content or high response rates. Marketers must know just how many "eyeballs" are looking at the site, how often they come to view a message, and what they are examining. Most important, they must find out what consumers do besides just look. The bottom line is that if nobody is responding to a Web site, it might as well not exist. According to Bill White, vice president of sales for financial services site The Motley Fool,

FIGURE 17.3

Sending a Clear Marketing Message

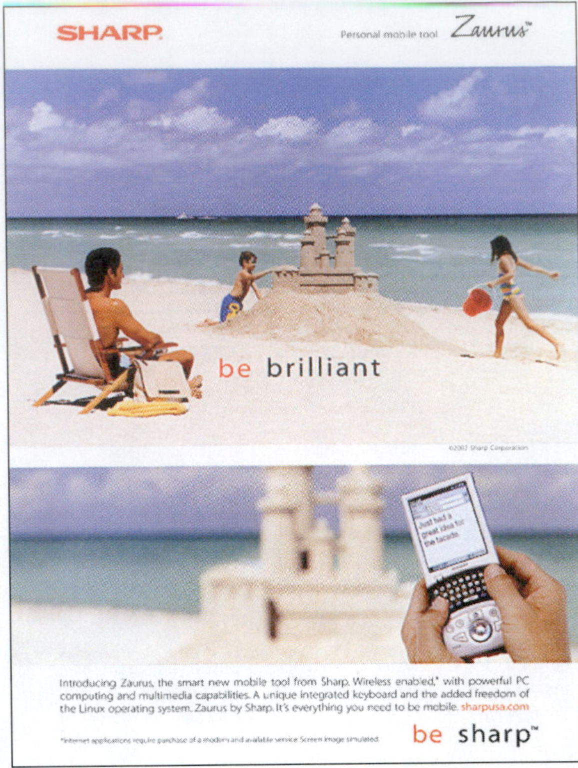

FIGURE 17.4

Collecting Feedback on Promotional Effectiveness by Using Contests

"A few years ago, advertisers just wanted to get on the Internet. Today it's all about return on investment (ROI)."[3] Experts advise attracting users' attention by including people in advertisements and other communications in addition to new content and formats. Marketers at iwon.com alternate the sizes of their customers' ads, as well as balancing the types of ads that appear on the site. Ad sales increased 37 percent during the following year as a result of greater response to varying messages.[4]

Feedback, the receiver's response to the message, provides a way for marketers to evaluate the effectiveness of the message and tailor their responses accordingly. Feedback may take the form of attitude changes, purchases, or nonpurchases. In some instances, organizations use promotion to create favorable attitudes toward their goods or services in the hope of future purchases. Other promotional communications have the objective of directly stimulating consumer purchases. Marketers using infomercials that urge the viewer to call a toll-free number to place orders for music collections, the latest fitness fad, or other products can easily measure the success of their objective by counting the number of calls they receive that result in orders.

A few years ago, marketers at Mars Inc., one of the nation's largest candy makers, launched a novel promotional campaign inviting consumers to vote on a new color to include in packages of M&M® chocolate candies. Even though colors on each candy shell are flavorless, maintaining purchaser interest of the brand (first introduced in 1941) was essential in maintaining high sales levels—and extensive promotions were used to urge consumers to participate in a series of color-naming contests. The ad shown in Figure 17.4 illustrates a recent contest in which global participants were asked to choose from among pink, purple, and aqua. (Purple won.) Comparisons of participation rates over time assisted marketers in assessing the effectiveness of each promotion.

Even nonpurchases may serve as feedback to the sender. Failure to purchase may result from ineffective communication in which the receivers do not believe or remember the message. Alternatively, the message may have failed to persuade the receiver that the firm's goods or services are superior to those of its competitors. Marketers frequently gather feedback through such techniques as marketing research studies and field sales reports.

Noise represents interference at some stage in the communications process. It may result from disruptions such as transmissions of competing promotional messages over the same communications channel, misinterpretation of a sales presentation or advertising message, receipt of the promotional message by the wrong person, or random events such as people conversing or leaving the room during a television commercial. Noise can also result from distractions within an advertising message itself.

Noise can be especially problematic in international communications. Disruption often results from too many competing messages. Italian television channels, for instance, broadcast all advertisements during a single half-hour slot each night. Noise might stem from differences in technology, such as a bad telephone connection, or from poor translations into other languages. Nonverbal cues, such as body language and tone of voice, are important parts of the communication process, and cultural differences may lead to noise and misunderstandings. For example, in the U.S., the round o sign made with the thumb and first finger means "okay." However, in Mediterranean countries, it means "zero" or "the worst." A Tunisian interprets this same sign as "I'll kill you," and to a Japanese it means "money."

Perhaps the most misunderstood language for U.S. marketers is English. It is often said that the 74 English-speaking nations are separated by a common language. The following examples illustrate how easy it can be for marketers to make mistakes in English-language promotional messages:

- *Underpants:* pants (Britain), underdaks (Australia)
- *Police:* bobby (Britain), garda (Ireland), Mountie (Canada), police wallah (South Asia)
- *Porch:* stoep (South Africa), gallery (Caribbean)
- *Bar:* pub (Britain), hotel (Australia), boozer (Australia, Britain, New Zealand)
- *Bathroom:* loo (Britain), dunny (Australia), lav (Britain, South Africa)
- *Ghost or monster:* wendigo (Canada), duppy (Caribbean), taniwha (New Zealand)
- *Barbecue:* braai (South Africa), barbie (Australia)
- *Pickup truck:* bakkie (South Africa), ute (Australia), utility vehicle (New Zealand)

Faulty communications can be especially risky on a global level, where noise can lead to some interesting misinterpretations. Here are three recent international examples:

- *On a sign in a Bucharest hotel lobby:* The lift is being fixed for the next day. During that time, we regret that you will be unbearable.
- *From a Japanese information booklet about using a hotel air conditioner:* Cooles and Heates: If you want just condition of warm in your room, please control yourself.
- *In an Acapulco hotel:* The manager has personally passed all the water served here.

Briefly Speaking

That's the kind of ad I like: facts, facts, facts.

Samuel Goldwyn (1882–1974) American motion-picture producer

OBJECTIVES OF PROMOTION

What specific tasks should promotion accomplish? The answers to this question seem to vary as much as the sources consulted. Generally, however, marketers identify the following objectives for promotion:

1. Provide information to consumers and others.
2. Increase demand.
3. Differentiate a product.
4. Accentuate a product's value.
5. Stabilize sales.

<interactive>learning goal

CHAPTER OBJECTIVE #3: DISCUSS HOW THE PROMOTIONAL MIX RELATES TO THE OBJECTIVES OF PROMOTION.

Provide Information

The traditional function of promotion was to inform the market about the availability of a particular good or service, as described in the "Marketing Hits" Interactive Example about JetBlue Airways. In fact, marketers still direct much of their current promotional efforts at providing product information for potential customers. An advertisement for a musical performance typically provides information about the performer, time, and place. A commercial for a theme park offers information about rides, location, and admission price. Information can also help differentiate a product from its competitors by focusing on its features or benefits.

MARKETING HIT: UP, UP, AND AWAY WITH JETBLUE

In addition to traditional print and broadcast advertising, marketers often distribute a number of high-tech, low-cost tools to give consumers product information. One such tool, the information-packed videocassette, is currently used for products ranging from cosmetics to automobiles to exercise equipment. In fact, one college recently sent videos to alumni in an attempt to increase attendance at their upcoming reunion. A 10-minute video costs about $1.50 to duplicate and send (not including production costs), compared with $8 or more for a full-color brochure. Consumers are more likely to regard the video as a novelty that stands out from other promotions, so they are less likely to throw out the cassette. In fact, 9 of every 10 recipients take the time to view them. In some cases, response rates are as high as 49 percent and returns on investment exceed 1,000 percent. These figures translate into substantial profits for companies involved in video promotions.

Many companies also send CDs containing software that provides information about or sampling of a product or service. Music companies and Internet service providers such as AOL are regular users of this promotional technique.

FIGURE 17.5

EarthLink: Focusing on Increased Market Share by Differentiating Its Service

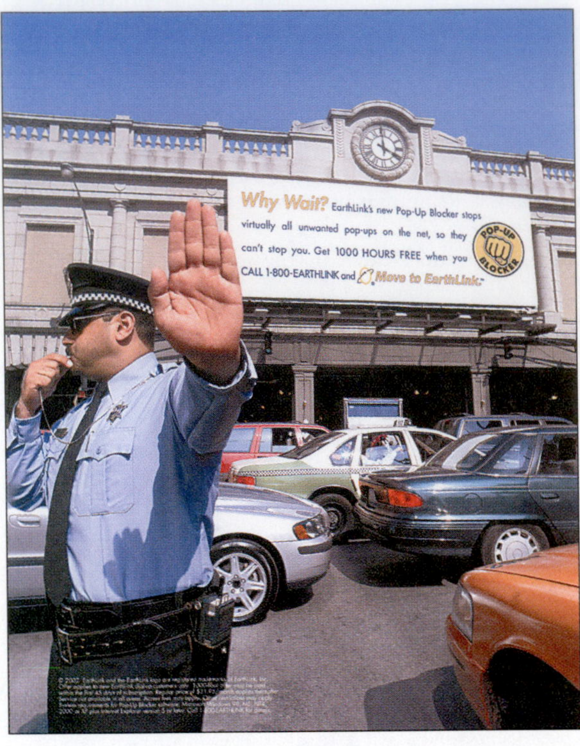

Increase Demand

Most promotions pursue the objective of increasing demand for a good or service. Some promotions are aimed at increasing *primary demand,* the desire for a general product category such as HDTVs or DVD players. This type of promotion is more typical for marketers who decide to expand overseas, creating new markets for their products in other parts of the world. When Procter & Gamble first introduced its Pampers disposable diapers in Hungary, most parents were using overpants with paper inserts to diaper their babies. So early Pampers television ads focused on generating interest in the novel product.

More promotions, however, are aimed at increasing *selective demand,* the desire for a specific brand. Denny's restaurant chain decided to stimulate selective demand for its food and service by offering free kids' meals every night. During the promotion, two children under the age of 10 years received a free dinner with each adult entree purchased. The kids' meals cost the restaurant only about 50 cents to give away but could bring in about $14 worth of business when the parents each ordered a meal. In addition, Denny's tailored to kids' tastes by offering mini–corn dogs and dinosaur-shaped chicken nuggets in an effort to create a preference for Denny's among children.[5]

Differentiate the Product

A frequent objective of the firm's promotional efforts is *product differentiation.* Homogeneous demand for many products results when consumers regard the firm's output as virtually identical to its competitors' products. In these cases, the individual firm has almost no control over marketing variables such as price. A differentiated demand schedule, in contrast, permits more flexibility in marketing strategy, such as price changes.

Surveys focusing on the Internet experience often list pop-up ads as the most annoying online experience. So marketers at Atlanta-based EarthLink came up with an idea: offer subscribers software to block them. Although the 4.9 million subscribers to the USA's No. 3 Internet service provider sound like small change in an industry dominated by industry giant AOL, EarthLink based its recent market growth strategy on offering a solution to the estimated 4.8 billion ads that pop up on computer screens worldwide every month. As Figure 17.5 shows, EarthLink combines its Pop-Up Blocker feature with 1,000 hours free to new subscribers.[6]

Accentuate the Product's Value

Promotion can explain the greater ownership utility of a product to buyers, thereby accentuating its value and justifying a higher price in the marketplace. This objective benefits both consumer and business products. A firm's promotional messages must build brand image and equity and at the same time deliver a "call to action." Advertising typically offers reasons why a good or service fits into the consumer's lifestyle. Today, consumers everywhere value their time; the challenge for marketers is to demonstrate how their products will make their life better.

Best Western and Shell recently teamed up in a "Sleep and Win" promotion in which Best Western hotel guests received a scratch-and-win card offering one of 15 Jaguars and Ford Explorers, free or discounted room nights, or gas redeemable at more than 10,000 Shell stations. Ramada countered with a "Getaway for Life Sweepstakes" in which guests staying at Ramada Inns had a chance to win an annual week-long vacation at any Ramada for life.[7]

Stabilize Sales

For the typical firm, sales are not uniform throughout the year. Sales fluctuations may result from cyclical, seasonal, or irregular demand. Stabilizing these variations is often an objective of promotional strategy. Coffee sales, for example, follow a seasonal pattern, with purchases and consumption increasing during the winter months. To stimulate summer sales of Sanka brand decaffeinated coffee, General Foods created ads that include a recipe for instant iced coffee, promoting it as a refreshing, caffeine-free summer beverage. Hotels and motels often seek to supplement high occupancy during the week from business travelers by promoting special weekend packages with lower room rates. Some firms sponsor sales contests during slack periods that offer prizes to sales personnel who meet goals.

ELEMENTS OF THE PROMOTIONAL MIX

Like the marketing mix, the **promotional mix** requires a carefully designed blend of variables to satisfy the needs of a company's customers and achieve organizational objectives. The promotional mix works like a subset of the marketing mix, with its product, pricing, distribution, and promotion elements. With the promotional mix, the marketers attempt to blend various elements optimally to achieve promotional objectives. The components of the promotional mix are personal selling and nonpersonal selling, including advertising, sales promotion, direct marketing, public relations, and guerilla marketing.

<interactive>**learning goal**

CHAPTER OBJECTIVE #4: IDENTIFY THE DIFFERENT ELEMENTS OF THE PROMOTIONAL MIX AND EXPLAIN HOW MARKETERS DEVELOP AN OPTIMAL PROMOTIONAL MIX.

Personal selling, advertising, and sales promotion usually account for the bulk of a firm's promotional expenditures. However, direct marketing, guerilla marketing, sponsorships, and public relations also contribute to integrated marketing communications. Later sections of this chapter examine the use of guerilla marketing, sponsorships, and direct marketing, and Chapters 18 and 19 present a detailed discussion of the other elements. This section defines the elements and discusses their advantages and disadvantages.

'NET EX: PROMOTIONAL MIX

Personal Selling

Personal selling is the oldest form of promotion, dating back as far as the beginning of trading and commerce. Traders vastly expanded both market sizes and product varieties as they led horses and camels along the Silk Road from China to Europe roughly between 300 B.C. and A.D. 1600, conducting personal selling at both ends. Personal selling may be defined as a seller's promotional presentation conducted on a person-to-person basis with the buyer. This direct form of promotion may be conducted face to face, over the telephone, through videoconferencing, or through interactive computer links between the buyer and seller. Today, about 14 million people in the U.S. are employed in personal selling, and the average sales call costs about $300.

Nonpersonal Selling

Nonpersonal selling includes advertising, sales promotion, direct marketing, and public relations. Advertising and sales promotion are usually regarded as the most important forms of nonpersonal selling. About one-third of marketing dollars pay for media advertising, and two-thirds fund trade and consumer sales promotions.

Advertising **Advertising** is any paid, nonpersonal communication through various media about a business firm, not-for-profit organization, product, or idea by a sponsor identified in a message that is intended to inform or persuade members of a particular audience. It is a major promotional mix component for thousands of organizations. Mass consumption and geographically dispersed markets make advertising particularly appropriate for marketing goods and services using the same promotional messages to large audiences.

Advertising primarily involves the mass media, such as newspapers, television, radio, magazines, and billboards, but also includes electronic and computerized forms of promotion such as Web commercials, videotapes, and video screens in supermarkets. The rich potential of the Internet as an advertising channel to reach millions of people one at a time has attracted the attention of companies large and small, local and international.

Product Placement *Product placement* is a form of nonpersonal selling in which the marketer pays a motion picture or television program owner a fee to display his or her product prominently in the film or show. The practice gained attention more than two decades ago in the movie *E.T.: The Extraterrestrial* when E.T. dropped Reese's Pieces behind himself to mark a path. Product sales for Reese's Pieces candies went through the roof. (Interestingly, this was not the moviemakers' first choice of candy; Mars turned down the opportunity to have its M&Ms appear in the film.) Fees charged to marketers for such placements have grown significantly since then, and most studios employ specialists to market them to relevant product suppliers.

Sales Promotion **Sales promotion** consists of marketing activities other than personal selling, advertising, and public relations that stimulate consumer purchasing and dealer effectiveness. This broad category includes displays, trade shows, coupons, contests, samples, premiums, product demonstrations, and various nonrecurring, irregular selling efforts. Sales promotion provides a short-term incentive, usually in combination with other forms of promotion, to emphasize, assist, supplement, or otherwise support the objectives of the promotional program. Restaurants, including those that serve fast food, often place certain items on the menu at a lower price "for a limited time only." Advertisements may contain coupons for free or discounted items for a specified period of time. Or companies may conduct sweepstakes for prizes such as new cars or vacations, which may even be completely unrelated to the products the companies are selling.

Movies are famous for sales promotions and tie-ins, which combine such products and toys and games with characters and themes from hit films. Disney's recent animated hit *Monsters, Inc.,* shown in Figure 17.6, attracted $80 million in promotional tie-ins from PepsiCo, McDonald's, and Kellogg. PepsiCo ran advertisements featuring the *Monsters, Inc.* characters, McDonald's ran promotions offering action figures and puzzles for Happy Meal customers, and Kellogg included a movie-branded spoon inside its cereal boxes.[8]

However, many companies that used to be involved with sales promotions, advertising, and tie-ins with movies are finding that they no longer get the return they were hoping for. Taco Bell, which lost money on promotions tied to recent releases in the six-film *Star Wars* movies, recently decided to abandon movie characters and focus its promotion on featuring expanded menu offerings. "It's less risky than tying in with a movie that may or may not be a hit—or might not help your product, even if it is," explains vice president Amy Sherwood.[9]

Sales promotion geared to marketing intermediaries is called *trade promotion.* Companies actually spend about as much on trade promotion as on advertising and consumer-oriented sales promotion combined. Trade promotion strategies include offering free merchandise, buyback allowances, and merchandise allowances along with sponsorship of sales contests to encourage wholesalers and retailers to sell more of certain products or product lines.

Direct Marketing Another element in a firm's integrated promotional mix is **direct marketing,** the use of direct communication to a consumer or business recipient designed to generate a response in the form of an order (direct order), a request for further information (lead generation), or a visit to a place of business to purchase specific goods or services (traffic generation). While many people equate direct marketing with direct mail, this promotional category also includes telephone marketing (telemarketing), direct-response advertising and infomercials on television and radio, direct-response print advertising, and electronic media.

FIGURE 17.6

Sales Promotions Tied to Movies

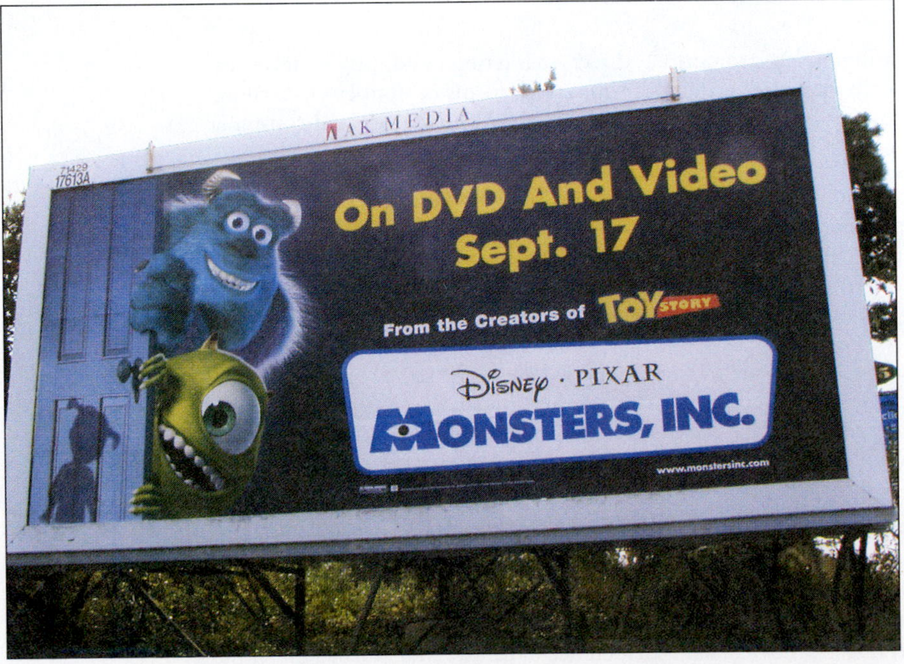

Public Relations and Publicity **Public relations** refer to a firm's communications and relationships with its various publics. These publics include customers, suppliers, stockholders, employees, the government, the general public, and the society in which the organization operates. Public relations programs can conduct either formal or informal contacts. The critical point is that every organization, whether or not it has a formally organized program, must be concerned about its public relations.

Publicity is an important part of an effective public relations effort. It can be defined as nonpersonal stimulation of demand for a good, service, person, cause, or organization through unpaid placement of significant news about it in a published medium or through a favorable presentation of it through radio, television, or the stage. Compared with personal selling, advertising, and even sales promotion, expenditures for public relations are usually low in most firms. Since companies do not pay for publicity, they have less control over the publication by the press or electronic media of good or bad company news. But this often means that consumers find this type of news source more believable than if the information were disseminated directly by the company. Of course, bad publicity can damage a company's reputation and diminish brand equity. Continental Tire, aware of the severe damage to the Bridgestone/Firestone brands following a series of accidents involving Ford Explorers when the tread separated from the tire and alerted to a heightened risk of tread separation, recently spent little time deciding to recall half a million tires installed as original equipment on Ford SUVs.[10]

Sometimes bad publicity is just a matter of bad luck, as happened to Major League Baseball's Houston Astros and the city of Houston. When the team and city needed to raise additional funds for their state-of-the-art, gleaming new ballpark, they offered the naming rights to another company—an increasingly common practice. So when one of Houston's largest employers agreed to write a check for $30 million for the naming rights for a 30-year period, MLB and Houston fans breathed a sigh of relief. The glitch? The newly named field would be called Enron Field. The agreement was canceled by all parties following the Enron bankruptcy, and the Astros signed a $100 million, 28-year deal with Minute Maid (a unit of Coca-Cola) to rename the field Minute Maid Park.[11]

Guerilla Marketing Guerilla marketing is a relatively new approach used by marketers whose firms are underfunded for a full marketing program. Many of these firms can't afford the huge costs involved in the orthodox media of print and broadcasting, so they need to find an innovative, low-cost way to reach their market. But some large companies, like PepsiCo, engage in guerilla marketing as well, as described in the "Marketing Hits" Interactive Example. The results can be funny and outrageous—even offensive to some people. But they almost always get consumers' attention. Some guerilla marketers stencil their company and product names anywhere graffiti might appear. Marketers for Yoo-hoo, the chocolate milk drink (whose parent companies didn't want to spend valuable dollars on promoting the product) served Yoo-hoo in consumers' own shoes at their booth during a rock concert. The American Legacy Foundation decided to circulate its antismoking message—which it refers to as a "brand" called Truth—with a mobile program. Trucks outfitted with DJ decks, computer games, and Web access stopped at beaches, concerts, and skate parks, where they sent out teams armed with "Infect Truth" viral kits containing T-shirts, stickers, and bandannas. Truth teams weren't clean-cut geeks or baby boomers, either. They were rappers, boarders, skaters, and musicians—all of them ex-smokers delivering the harsh message of smoking's damage to the body. During the tour, Truth trucks reached more than 4 million teens, 850,000 of whom actually interacted with team members.[12]

MARKETING HIT: GUERILLA MARKETING—PEPSI'S CODE RED

As Table 17.2 indicates, each type of promotion has both advantages and shortcomings. Although personal selling entails a relatively high per-contact cost, it wastes less effort than do nonpersonal forms of promotion such as advertising. Personal selling often provides more flexible promotion than the other forms because the salesperson can tailor the sales message to meet the unique needs—or objections—of each potential customer.

The major advantages of advertising come from its ability to create instant awareness of a good, service, or idea; build brand equity; and deliver the marketer's message to mass audiences for a relatively low cost per contact. Major disadvantages of advertising include the difficulty in measuring its effectiveness and high media costs. Sales promotions, by contrast, can be more accurately monitored and measured than advertising, produce immediate consumer responses, and provide short-term sales increases. Direct marketing gives an action-oriented choice, permits narrow audience segmentation and customization of communications, and produces measurable results. Public relations efforts such as publicity frequently offer substantially higher credibility than other promotional techniques. Guerilla marketing efforts can be innovative—and highly effective—at a low cost to a company, as long as the tactics are not too outrageous, but it is more difficult to reach people. The marketer must determine the appropriate blend of these promotional mix elements to effectively market the firm's goods and services.

SPONSORSHIPS

One of the hottest trends in promotion during the past 10 years offers marketers the ability to integrate several elements of the promotional mix. Commercial sponsorships of an event or activity apply personal selling, advertising, sales promotion, and public relations in achieving specific promotional goals. These sponsorships link events with sponsors and with media ranging from TV and radio to print and the Internet, billions of dollars in business worldwide.

TABLE 17.2

Comparison of the Six Promotional Mix Elements

	PERSONAL SELLING	ADVERTISING	SALES PROMOTION	DIRECT MARKETING	PUBLIC RELATIONS	GUERILLA MARKETING
Advantages	Permits measurement of effectiveness Elicits an immediate response Tailors the message to fit the customer	Reaches a large group of potential consumers for a relatively low price per exposure Allows strict control over the final message Can be adapted to either mass audiences or specific audience segments	Produces an immediate consumer response Attracts attention and creates product awareness Allows easy measurement of results Provides short-term sales increases	Generates an immediate response Covers a wide audience with targeted advertising Allows complete, customized, personal message Produces measurable results	Creates a positive attitude toward a product or company Enhances credibility of a product or company	Is low cost Attracts attention because it is innovative Is less cluttered with competitors trying the same thing
Disadvantages	Relies almost exclusively upon the ability of the salesperson Involves high cost per contact	Does not permit totally accurate measurement of results Usually cannot close sales	Is nonpersonal in nature Is difficult to differentiate from competitors' efforts	Suffers from image problem Involves a high cost per reader Depends on quality and accuracy of mailing lists May annoy consumers	May not permit accurate measurement of effect on sales Involves much effort directed toward non-marketing-oriented goals	May not reach as many people If the tactics are too outrageous, they may offend some people

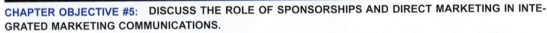

<interactive>**learning goal**

CHAPTER OBJECTIVE #5: DISCUSS THE ROLE OF SPONSORSHIPS AND DIRECT MARKETING IN INTEGRATED MARKETING COMMUNICATIONS.

Sponsorship occurs when an organization provides cash or in-kind resources to an event or activity in exchange for a direct association with that event or activity. The sponsor purchases two things: (1) access to the activity's audience and (2) the image associated with the activity. Sponsorships typically involve advertising that includes direct mail, sales promotion, and personal selling at the event itself. They also involve relationship marketing, bringing together the event, its participants, and the sponsoring firms. Marketers underwrite varying levels of sponsorships depending on the amount their companies wish to spend and the types of events.

Sponsorship Spending

Global marketers have flocked to sponsorships as a means of reaching an increasingly segmented audience to leverage the equity of sports and entertainment properties. In addition, an army of e-commerce firms found sponsorships to be a quick way to enhance—and in many cases, initiate—brand awareness. Sponsorships also provide a platform through which sports and entertainment properties can expand their programs and attract new partners. Even utilities and pharmaceutical firms that sell over-the-counter medication and prescription drugs are also increasing their activities. In a recent year, more than 60 companies spent more than $10 million on sponsorships. Philip Morris is the largest sponsor with over $145 million in sponsorship commitments. Anheuser-Busch is second and General Motors is third, followed by The Coca-Cola Company and rival PepsiCo. Total sponsorship spending more than tripled over the past 10 years to almost $10 billion.[13]

Nowhere is sponsorship more prevalent than at sports events. Total spending for sports marketing in one recent year was $35 billion; about $6.4 billion of that was devoted to sponsorships. One of the biggest deals of the year was among CBS, the National Collegiate Athletic Association, and The Coca-Cola Company. In the $500 million agreement, the Coca-Cola brand appeared on everything from the NCAA championships to CBS broadcasts of the "March Madness" basketball finals.

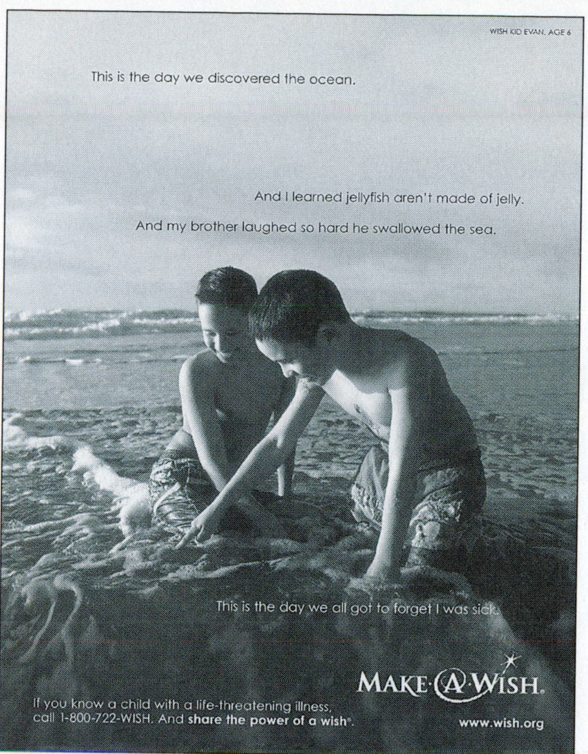

WISH KID EVAN, AGE 6
This is the day we discovered the ocean.
And I learned jellyfish aren't made of jelly.
And my brother laughed so hard he swallowed the sea.
This is the day we all got to forget I was sick.
MAKE-A-WISH.
If you know a child with a life-threatening illness, call 1-800-722-WISH. And share the power of a wish®.
www.wish.org

The Make-A-Wish Foundation® grants the wishes of children with life-threatening illnesses to enrich their lives with hope, strength, and joy. The Foundation is funded by numerous corporate sponsorships, which are described on the Foundation's Web site at http://www.wish.org.

Growth of Sponsorships

Commercial sponsorship of sporting and cultural events is not a new phenomenon. Aristocrats in ancient Rome sponsored gladiator competitions and chariot races featuring teams that were often supported financially by competing businesses. Over 2,000 years ago, wealthy Athenians underwrote drama, musical, and sporting festivals. Craft guilds in 14th-century England sponsored plays (occasionally insisting that the playwrights insert "plugs" for their lines of work in the scripts). In the U.S. during the 1880s, streetcar companies commonly sponsored local baseball teams.

Sponsorship as a promotional alternative has grown rapidly over the past three decades. During this period, corporate sponsorship spending has increased faster than promotional outlays for advertising and sales promotion. Several factors have influenced the growth of commercial sponsorships:

- Government restrictions on tobacco and alcohol advertising and the growing reluctance of newspaper and magazine publishers to accept print ads for alcoholic beverages and tobacco products have led marketers to seek alternative promotional media.
- Escalating costs of traditional advertising media make commercial sponsorships cost-effective marketing tools.
- Additional opportunities resulting from diverse leisure activities, as well as the increasing array of sporting events featured on television and in newspapers and magazines, allow marketers to target specific audiences.
- Greater media coverage of sponsored events allows sponsors to gain greater exposure for their money.
- Global marketers recognize sponsorship as an effective way to reach an international audience in a manner that is universally understood.
- The proven effectiveness of a sponsorship that is properly planned and executed can buy productive marketing contacts. Sponsorships also represent alternatives to the increased clutter associated with advertising and direct mail.

It is important to note that today's sponsorships cover a broad base, including events and programs that fall into the category of social responsibility. Companies and nonprofit organizations may sponsor reading programs, child-care programs, programs to help small or minority-owned businesses get started, as well as humanitarian programs like the Make-A-Wish Foundation® and cultural events such as free classical concerts.

How Sponsorship Differs from Advertising

Even though sponsorship spending and traditional advertising spending represent forms of nonpersonal selling, their differences outnumber their similarities. Chief among these differences are the sponsor's degree of control versus that of advertising, the nature of the message, audience reaction, and measurements of effectiveness.

Marketers have considerable control over the quantity and quality of market coverage when they advertise. Sponsors, on the other hand, must rely on signs to present their messages. Also, they have little control of sponsored events beyond matching the audiences to profiles of their own target markets. In addition, sponsorship is a mute, nonverbal medium since the message is delivered in association with an activity possessing its own personality in the eyes of its audience. By contrast, a traditional advertisement allows the marketer to create an individual message containing an introduction, a theme, and a conclusion.

Audiences react differently to sponsorship as a communications medium than to other media. The sponsor's investment provides a recognizable benefit to the sponsored activity that the audience can appreciate. As a result, sponsorship is often viewed more positively than traditional advertising. Some marketers have tried to take advantage of this fact by practicing *ambush marketing,* in which a firm that is not an official sponsor tries to link itself to a major international event, such as the Olympics or a concert tour by a

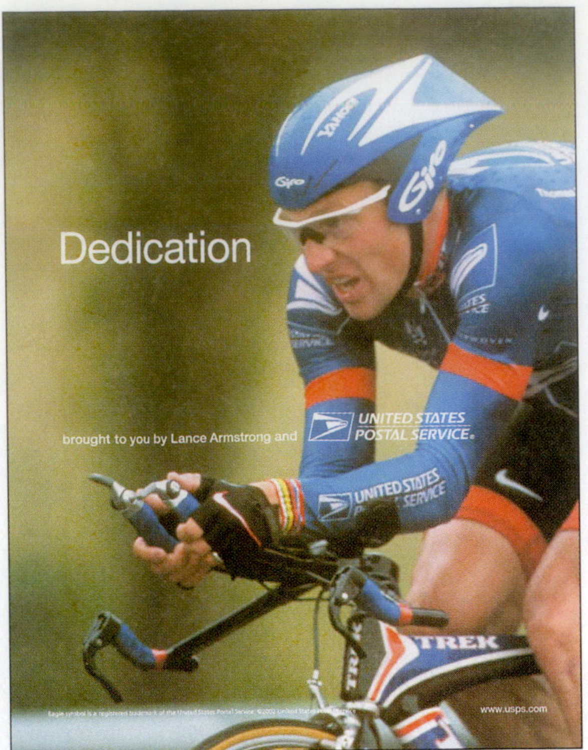

Dedication
brought to you by Lance Armstrong and
UNITED STATES POSTAL SERVICE
www.usps.com

Faced with growing competition from UPS and overnight delivery companies like Airborne, DHL, and FedEx, the U.S. Postal Service decided to sponsor the start-up U.S. cycling team almost a decade ago to deliver the theme that the former monopoly should be everyone's first choice as a source of fast, dependable service. Then along came team member and cancer survivor Lance Armstrong. With four Tour de France victories, Armstrong gives USPS steady but silent publicity with the postal service logo emblazoned on his jersey.

musical group. While it might be tempting to assume that smaller firms with limited marketing budgets would be most likely to engage in this type of marketing, this is not always the case. At a recent World Cup soccer match, television cameras panned hordes of cheering spectators wearing caps bearing the Samsung logo. Samsung was not the official sponsor for the match; its competitor Philips Electronics was.[14] While passing out logo-bearing hats is not illegal, some ambush practices clearly are. If a nonsponsor used the Olympic rings in an advertisement, the ad would be illegal. Famed guerilla marketer Schirf Brewing Co. of Park City, Utah, was priced out of any sponsorship possibilities at the Salt Lake City winter games, so it adorned its sales manager's Chevy Blazer with signs advertising its Wasatch beer as "The *Unofficial* Beer of the 2002 Winter Games." Although the unamused U.S. Olympic Committee and official beer sponsor, Anheuser-Busch, quickly responded with a cease-and-desist order, Wasatch generated millions in free publicity from the stunt.[15]

Assessing Sponsorship Results

To assess the results of sponsorships, marketers utilize some of the same techniques by which they measure advertising effectiveness. However, the differences between the two promotional alternatives often necessitate some unique research techniques as well. A few corporate sponsors attempt to link expenditures to sales. Kraft General Foods, for example, evaluates the effectiveness of its NASCAR sponsorship by comparing Country Time lemonade sales in the races' primary southeastern U.S. markets with sales in other markets. Other sponsors measure improved brand awareness and image as effectiveness indicators; they conduct traditional surveys before and after the events to secure this information. Still other sponsors measure the impact of their event marketing in public relations terms. Typically, a researcher will count press clippings featuring a sponsor's name or logo and then translate this number into equivalent advertising costs.

Despite the impressive visibility of special events like soccer's World Cup and football's Super Bowl, these events do not necessarily lead directly to increased sales. Marketers want their brands to be associated with characteristics of the sporting event such as speed, accuracy, precision, and teamwork.

DIRECT MARKETING

Few promotional mix elements are growing as fast as direct marketing. Overall media spending for direct marketing initiatives such as interactive electronic media, direct mail, telemarketing, infomercials, and direct-response advertising totals more than $1.7 trillion a year.[16] Both consumers and business-to-business marketers rely on this promotional mix element to generate orders or sales leads (requests for more information) that may result in future orders. Direct marketing also helps to increase store traffic (visits to the store or office to evaluate and perhaps purchase the advertised goods or services).

Direct marketing opens new international markets of unprecedented size. Electronic marketing channels have become the focus of direct marketers, and Web marketing is international marketing. Even direct mail and telemarketing will grow outside the U.S. as commerce becomes more global. Consumers in Europe and Japan are proving to be responsive to direct marketing. But most global marketing systems remain undeveloped, and many are almost dormant. The growth of international direct marketing is being spurred by marketing operations born in the U.S.

Direct marketing communications pursue goals beyond creating product awareness. Marketers want direct marketing to persuade people to place an order, request more information, visit a store, call a toll-free number, or respond to an e-mail message. In other words, successful direct marketing should prompt consumers to take action. Since direct marketing is interactive, marketers can tailor individual responses to meet consumers' needs. They can also measure the effectiveness of their efforts more easily than with advertising and other forms of promotion. Direct marketing is a very powerful tool that helps organizations to win new customers and enhance relationships with existing ones.

The growth of direct marketing parallels the move toward integrated marketing communications in many ways. Both respond to fragmented media markets and audiences, growth in customized products, shrinking network broadcast audiences, and the increasing use of databases to target specific markets. Lifestyles also play a role because today's busy consumers want convenience and time savings.

Databases are an important part of direct marketing. Using the latest technology to create sophisticated databases, a company can select a narrow market segment and find good prospects within that segment based on desired characteristics. Marketers can cut costs and improve returns on dollars spent by identifying those customers who are most likely to respond to messages and by eliminating others from their lists who are not likely to respond. In fact, mining information about customers is a trend boosted by the growth of e-commerce. DNA software from Austin, Texas–based Smart Technologies can create profiles of customers, suppliers, and business partners by analyzing their movements on a Web site.

FIGURE 17.7

Direct Marketing Sales by Media Category

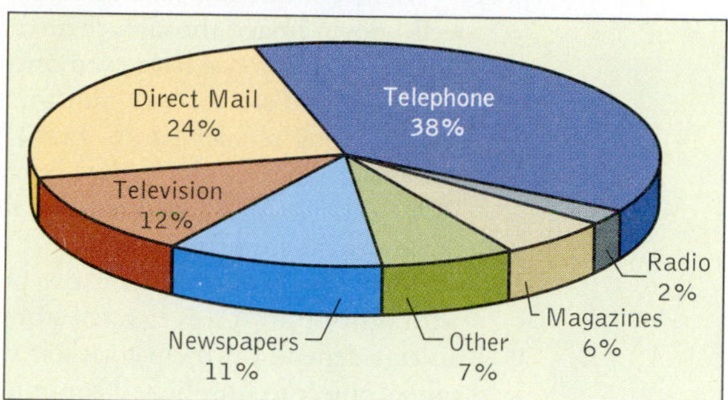

Direct Marketing Communications Channels

As Figure 17.7 indicates, direct marketing uses many different media forms. Each works best for certain purposes, although marketers often combine two or more media in one direct marketing program. A company can start with telemarketing to screen potential customers and then follow up by sending more material by direct mail to interested consumers.

Direct Mail

As the amount of information about consumer lifestyles, buying habits, and wants continues to mount, direct mail has become a viable channel for identifying a firm's best prospects. Marketers gather information from internal and external databases, surveys, personalized coupons, and rebates that require responses. **Direct mail** is a critical tool in creating effective direct-marketing campaigns. It comes in many forms, ranging from sales letters, postcards, brochures, booklets, catalogs, and house organs (periodicals issued by organizations) to video and audio cassettes.

Direct mail offers advantages such as the ability to select a narrow target market, achieve intensive coverage, send messages quickly, choose from various formats, provide complete information, and personalize each mailing piece. Figure 17.8 shows the power of direct mail to "target new customers and their wallets and keep existing ones coming back for more."

FIGURE 17.8

Promoting the Benefits of Direct Mail

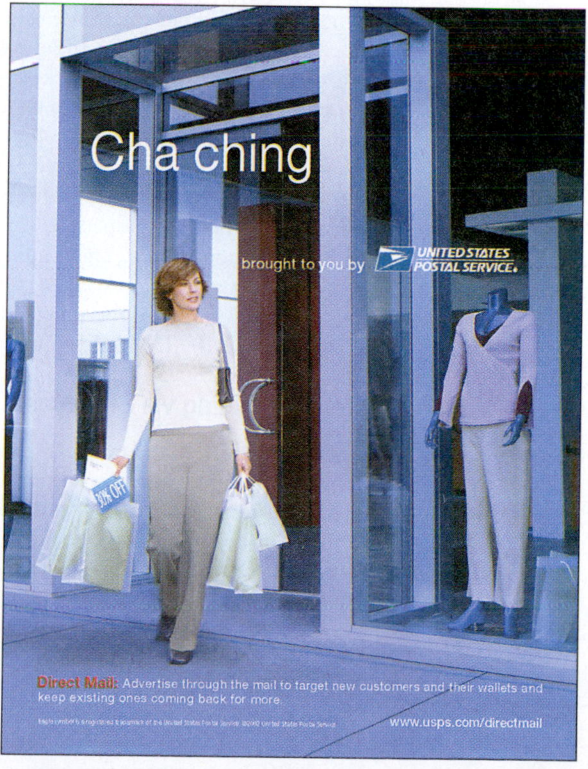

Response rates are measurable and higher than other types of advertising. In addition, direct mailings stand alone and do not compete for attention with magazine articles and television programs. On the other hand, the per-reader cost of direct mail is high, effectiveness depends on the quality of the mailing list, and some consumers object strongly to what they consider "junk mail."

As mentioned earlier in the opening vignette on Nissan's IMC campaign, the recent anthrax scare caused a real disruption in many direct mail marketing efforts. According to a survey conducted by the Direct Marketing Association, one-third of all consumers were now treating their mail with at least some suspicion. Some companies, such as the B2B software maker Commerce One, decided to abandon its traditional direct mail programs in favor of e-mail and telemarketing. "Normally we would have used direct mail," explained vice president Bill Fraine. "But I don't think people are opening their mail." Although the anthrax scare that followed the September 11 terrorist attacks disrupted the direct mail portion of the Nissan Altima IMC campaign, marketers at Foot-Smart turned the problem into an opportunity. With the assistance of Caroline Ernst, director of e-commerce at the health-care products firm, they contacted customers in advance to alert them that the new Foot-Smart catalog was in the mail. As a result of this advance message, Foot-Smart saw a 20 percent increase in sales.[17]

Catalogs Catalogs have been a popular form of direct mail in the U.S. for more than 100 years. More than 10,000 different consumer, specialty, mail-order catalogs—and thousands more for business-to-business sales—find their way into almost every U.S. mailbox. In a typical year, they generate over $57 billion in consumer sales and $36 billion in business-to-business sales. On any given day, you might find a catalog from Patagonia, Crate & Barrel, Office Depot, Title IX, or Birkenstock in your mailbox. Catalogs fill so many segments that you could probably order just about anything you need for any facet of your life from a catalog.

Many companies, such as Sears and its new Lands' End subsidiary, built their businesses and created a well-known image through their catalogs. More recently, however, catalog companies have expanded into Web sites, and some have even opened retail stores to increase sales and market share. (Sears discontinued its catalog in favor of its retail stores but continued to use specialty catalogs and later bought Wisconsin-based catalog retailer Lands' End.) Sophisticated electronic technologies are changing catalog marketing. Today's catalogs can be updated quickly, providing consumers with the latest information and prices. CD-ROM catalogs allow marketers to display products in three-dimensional views and include video sequences of product demonstrations.

Many Americans still refuse to purchase from a catalog, but others—such as those who live in rural areas with little or no access to retail stores or busy professionals who do not have time to spend wandering store aisles—depend on them for their shopping needs. Although many consumers like to receive direct mail, others object to unsolicited communications. Many catalog companies do not understand their customers' needs and wants but, instead, send loads of catalogs to millions of people whether or not they want them. The 21st-century consumer is time-pressed and overloaded with information. To help consumers escape the barrage of mail stuffed into their boxes, the Direct Marketing Association established its Mail Preference Service. This consumer service sends name removal forms to people who do not wish to receive direct-mail advertising.[18]

Telemarketing

Any person whose dinner has been interrupted by a sales call can attest that telemarketing is the most frequently used form of direct marketing. It provides marketers with a high return on their expenditures, an immediate response, and the opportunity for personalized two-way conversations. *Telemarketing* refers to direct marketing conducted entirely by telephone. It can be classified as either outbound or inbound contacts. Outbound telemarketing involves a sales force that uses only the telephone to contact customers, reducing the cost of making personal visits. The customer initiates inbound telemarketing, which typically provides a toll-free number for customers to use at their convenience to obtain information and/or make purchases. Like direct mail, telemarketing taps into databases to target calls based on customer characteristics like family income, number of children, and home ownership. For example, income is an important criterion for banks that use telemarketing to solicit new credit-card customers.

Telemarketing is gaining importance in the marketing strategies of many firms; revenues from phone sales, now at $600 billion annually, are expected to grow about 9 percent per year. New predictive dialer devices improve telemarketing's efficiency and reduce costs by automating the dialing process to skip busy signals and answering machines. When the dialer reaches a human voice, it instantaneously puts the call through to a salesperson. This technology is often combined with a print advertising campaign that features a toll-free number for inbound telemarketing.

Business-to-business telemarketing is on the rise as well. Marketers at Xerox and long-distance telephone companies use telemarketing to develop sales leads. Because recipients of both consumer and business-to-business telemarketing calls often find them annoying, the Federal Trade Commission passed a Telemarketing Sales Rule in 1996. The rule cracks down on abusive telemarketing practices by establishing allowed calling hours and regulating call content. Companies must clearly disclose details of any exchange policies, maintain lists of people who do not want to receive calls, and keep records of telemarketing scripts, prize winners, customers, and employees for two years. While designed to protect customers against fraud—with losses estimated in excess of $40 billion, almost 10 percent of telemarketing-generated revenues—the rule also helps improve the image of telemarketers. Consumers can cut down on undesirable sales calls by requesting that the DMA Telephone Preference Service put them on the "do not call" list.[19]

Direct Marketing via Broadcast Channels

Broadcast direct marketing can take three basic forms: brief direct-response ads on television or radio, home shopping channels, and infomercials. Direct-response spots typically run 30, 60, or 90 seconds and include product descriptions and toll-free telephone numbers for ordering. Often shown on cable television and independent stations and tied to special-interest programs, broadcast direct marketing usually encourages viewers to respond immediately by saying that they will receive a special price or a gift if they call within a few minutes of an ad's airing. Radio direct-response ads also provide product descriptions and addresses or phone numbers to contact the sellers. Radio actually proves expensive compared with other direct marketing media, and listeners may not pay close enough attention to catch the number or may not be able to write it down because they are driving a car, which accounts for a major portion of radio listening time.

Home shopping channels like Quality Value Convenience (QVC), Home Shopping Network (HSN), and ShopNBC represent another type of television direct marketing. Broadcasting around the clock, these channels offer consumers a variety of products, including jewelry, clothing, skincare, home furnishings, computers, cameras, kitchen appliances, and toys. In essence, home shopping channels function like on-air catalogs. The channels also have Web sites that consumers can browse through to make purchases. In both cases, customers place orders via toll-free telephone numbers and pay for their purchases by credit card.

Infomercials are 30-minute or longer product commercials that resemble regular television programs. Because of their length, infomercials do not get lost as easily as 30-second commercials can, and they permit marketers to present their products in more detail. But they are usually shown at odd hours, and people often watch only portions of them—think of how many times you have channel-surfed past an infomercial for Bow-flex, Victoria Principal's skincare line, or Ronco's rotisserie. Infomercials do provide toll-free telephone numbers so viewers can order products or request more information. Although infomercials incur higher production costs than prime-time 30-second ads on national network TV, they generally air on less expensive cable channels and in late-night time slots on broadcast stations.

Electronic Direct Marketing Channels

Anyone who has ever logged on to the Web is abundantly aware of the growing number of commercial advertisements that now clutter their computer screen. Web advertising is a recurring theme throughout this text, alluding to its importance as a component of the promotional mix. In fact, Chapter 5 explained the vital role e-commerce now plays in contemporary marketing practices. In one recent year, Web companies sold $1 billion in advertising, and that number grows with each new application of electronic technology.

Web advertising, however, is only one component of electronic direct marketing. E-mail direct marketers have found that traditional practices used in print and broadcast media are easily adapted to electronic messaging. Experts agree that the basic rules for online direct marketing mirror those of traditional practices. Any successful offline direct marketing campaign can be applied to e-mail promotions.

Electronic media deliver data instantly to direct marketers and help them to track customer buying cycles quickly. As a result, they can place customer acquisition programs online for about 50 to 80 percent less than the cost of traditional programs. In the early years of the Internet, the most predominant products for direct marketers were books, music CDs, wine, and gourmet foods. Today, however, there seems to be no limit to the variety of goods and services available to online shoppers. In fact, consumer-to-consumer sales through auction sites are becoming the most popular avenue for direct online sales.

Other Direct Marketing Channels

Print media like newspapers and magazines do not support direct marketing as effectively as do Web marketing and telemarketing. However, print media and other traditional direct marketing channels are still critical to the success of all electronic media channels. Magazine ads with toll-free telephone numbers enhance inbound telemarketing campaigns. Companies can place ads in magazines or newspapers, include reader-response cards, or place special inserts targeted for certain market segments within the publications.

Kiosks provide another outlet for electronic sales. Dell Computer, the nation's largest PC marketer, recently began placing kiosks at malls so consumers could touch, see, and try out different configurations of its computers. However, because the company builds customized computers to order, until recently consumers had to place their orders by phone or online. In an about-face from its traditional exclusive direct sales approach, Dell recently decided to expand its market share by selling to dealers. In addition to marching directly onto the turf long dominated by Hewlett-Packard and IBM, Dell hopes to capture a sizable share of the $3 billion-a-year so-called "white box" market, the no-name computers put together with parts from various suppliers and tailored to a customer's specific needs.[20]

DEVELOPING AN OPTIMAL PROMOTIONAL MIX

By blending advertising, personal selling, sales promotion, and public relations to achieve marketing objectives, marketers create a promotional mix. Since they can refer to no quantitative measures to determine the effectiveness of each mix component in a given market segment, the choice of an effective mix of promotional elements presents one of marketers' most difficult tasks. Several factors influence the effectiveness of a promotional mix: (1) the nature of the market, (2) the nature of the product, (3) the stage in the product life cycle, (4) the price, and (5) the funds available for promotion.

Nature of the Market

The marketer's target audience has a major impact on the choice of a promotion method. When a market includes a limited number of buyers, personal selling may prove a highly effective technique. However, markets characterized by large numbers of potential customers scattered over sizable geographical areas may make the cost of contact by personal salespeople prohibitive. In such instances, extensive use of advertising often makes sense. The type of customer also affects the promotional mix. Personal selling works better in a target market made up of industrial purchasers or retail and wholesale buyers than in a target market consisting of ultimate consumers. Similarly, pharmaceutical firms use large sales forces to sell prescription drugs directly to physicians and hospitals, but they advertise to promote over-the-counter drugs for the consumer market. When a prescription drug receives FDA approval to be sold over the counter, the drug firm must switch its promotional strategy from personal selling to consumer advertising.

As people have grown tired of cola drinks over the last few years, the Coca-Cola Co. and PepsiCo have had to come up with new ways to appeal to consumers. Both companies are still big media spenders—in one recent year, Coca-Cola spent $194 million, and PepsiCo came in at $125 million. PepsiCo has run a highly successful series of splashy ads with pop star Britney Spears and Austin Powers creator Mike Myers and did promotional tie-ins with the hit movie *Monsters Inc.* Its Atlanta-based rival poured out ads to support its sponsorships at the Olympics and created nostalgic ads for the holiday season. Still, baby boomers and seniors aren't drinking the amount of cola they once did, so the cola giants are focusing on younger target markets. Both companies are now focusing on their bottled water brands Aquafina and Dasani, and both have a stable of noncarbonated drinks that are doing well. PepsiCo has created a 100-person sales force to sell its noncarbonated drinks, such as Gatorade and Lipton iced teas.[21]

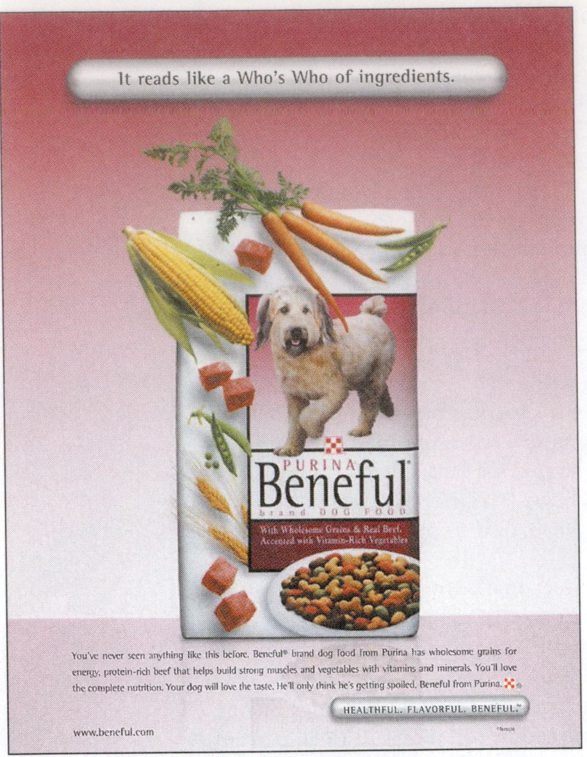

It reads like a Who's Who of ingredients.
PURINA
Beneful
brand DOG FOOD
You've never seen anything like this before. Beneful® brand dog food from Purina has wholesome grains for energy, protein-rich beef that helps build strong muscles and vegetables with vitamins and minerals. You'll love the complete nutrition. Your dog will love the taste. He'll only think he's getting spoiled. Beneful from Purina.
HEALTHFUL. FLAVORFUL. BENEFUL.
www.beneful.com

With its "Healthful. Flavorful. Beneful" ad, Ralston Purina develops advertising based on the nature of the product—promoting its healthy ingredients.

Nature of the Product

A second important factor in determining an effective promotional mix is the product itself. Highly standardized products with minimal servicing requirements usually depend less on personal selling than do custom products with technically complex features and/or requirements for frequent maintenance. Consumer products are more likely to rely heavily on advertising than are business products. Ralston Purina has launched a $34 million television and print advertising campaign to promote its new Beneful dry dog food. Nestlé, Purina's parent company, wants to establish Beneful as a premium line of pet food priced between the value brands and the highest priced brands such as Procter & Gamble's Iams.[22]

Promotional mixes vary within each product category. In the B2B market, for example, installations typically rely more heavily on personal selling than does marketing of operating supplies. In contrast, the promotional mix for a convenience product is likely to involve more emphasis on manufacturer advertising and less on personal selling. On the other hand, personal selling plays an important role in the promotion of shopping products, and both personal and nonpersonal selling are important in the promotion of specialty goods. A personal-selling emphasis is also likely to prove more effective than other alternatives in promotions for products involving trade-ins.

Stage in the Product Life Cycle

The promotional mix must be tailored to the product's stage in the product life cycle. In the introductory stage, heavy emphasis on personal selling helps to inform the marketplace of the merits of the new good or service. Salespeople contact marketing intermediaries to secure interest in and commitment to handling the offering. Trade shows frequently inform and educate prospective dealers and ultimate consumers.

Marketers of new products may need to work closely with customers to answer questions and adjust promotional mixes as needed. Advertising and sales promotion at this stage create awareness and stimulate initial purchases. As the good or service moves into the growth and maturity stages, advertising gains relative importance in persuading consumers to make purchases. Marketers continue to direct personal-selling efforts at marketing intermediaries in an attempt to expand distribution. As more competitors enter the marketplace, advertising begins to stress product differences to persuade consumers to purchase the firm's brand. In the maturity and early decline stages, firms frequently reduce advertising and sales promotion expenditures.

Mature products often require creative promotions to keep the product in the mind of the consumer. That's the case with Coke and Pepsi, as described earlier. During the fall and winter before PepsiCo launched its Britney Spears ads, the company conducted one of the most successful advertising campaigns in its 103-year existence. Run in partnership with Yahoo!, the company set up a Web site called Pepsistuff.com, where consumers could log on and enter a code found under the caps of 1.5 billion Pepsi bottles. Each code was worth 100 points, redeemable for prizes such as sporting apparel and DVDs. The only requirement was that participants provide their name, e-mail address, zip code, and date of birth—all to be used in future marketing efforts. The Web site greeted 3.5 million registered visitors, and national sales of Pepsi's single-serve bottles rose 5 percent during the promotion. And at the end, Pepsi marketers had a database to use in further efforts.[23]

Price

The price of the good or service is the fourth factor that affects the choice of a promotional mix. Advertising dominates the promotional mixes for low-unit-value products due to the high per-contact costs in personal selling. These costs make the sales call an unprofitable tool in promoting lower value goods and services. Advertising, in contrast, permits a low promotional expenditure per sales unit because it reaches mass audiences. For low-value consumer goods, such as chewing gum, soft drinks, and snack foods, advertising is the most feasible means of promotion. Even shopping products like the Westinghouse ceiling fan advertised in Figure 17.9 can be sold at least partly on the basis of price—in this case, the money saved by purchasing and installing the fan without having to hire an electrician. On the other hand, consumers of high-priced items like luxury cars expect lots of well-presented information. High-tech direct marketing promotions like videocassettes, CD-ROMs, fancy brochures, and personal selling appeal to these potential customers.

FIGURE 17.9

Promotion Based on Price

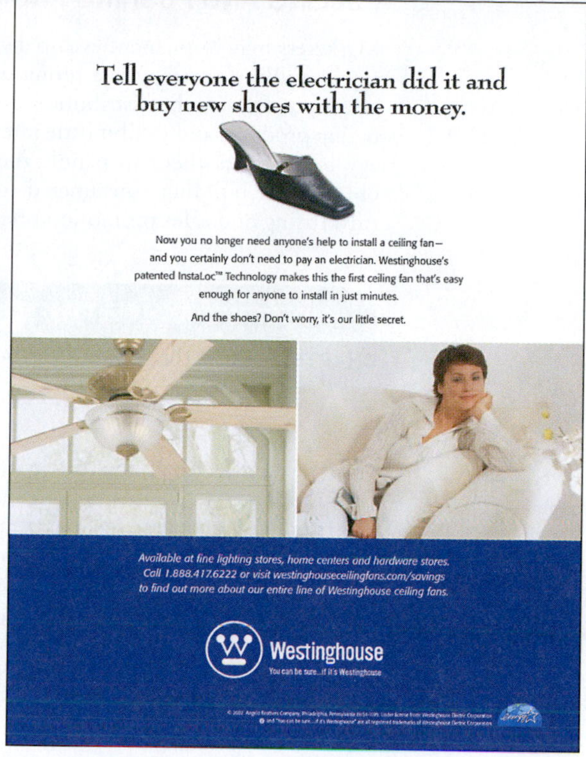

Tell everyone the electrician did it and buy new shoes with the money.
Now you no longer need anyone's help to install a ceiling fan– and you certainly don't need to pay an electrician. Westinghouse's patented InstaLoc™ Technology makes this the first ceiling fan that's easy enough for anyone to install in just minutes.
And the shoes? Don't worry, it's our little secret.
Available at fine lighting stores, home centers and hardware stores. Call 1.888.417.6222 or visit westinghouseceilingfans.com/savings to find out more about our entire line of Westinghouse ceiling fans.
Westinghouse
You can be sure...if it's Westinghouse

Funds Available for Promotion

A real barrier in implementing any promotional strategy is the size of the promotional budget. A single 30-second television commercial during the Super Bowl telecast costs an advertiser $2 million. While millions of viewers may see the commercial, making the cost per contact relatively low, such an expenditure exceeds the entire promotional budgets of thousands of firms, which is how guerilla marketing got its start. And if a company wants to hire a celebrity to advertise its goods and services, try these numbers: Basketball star Michael Jordan earns about $45 million a year in endorsement deals, and singer Ricky Martin gets at least $3 million to perform at private corporate parties (which are designed to promote company products).[24] Table 17.3 summarizes the factors that influence

TABLE 17.3

Factors Influencing Choice of Promotional Mix

	EMPHASIS	
	PERSONAL SELLING	**ADVERTISING**
Nature of the market		
Number of buyers	Limited number	Large number
Geographic concentration	Concentrated	Dispersed
Type of customer	Business purchaser	Ultimate consumer
Nature of the product		
Complexity	Custom-made, complex	Standardized
Service requirements	Considerable	Minimal
Type of good or service	Business	Consumer
Use of trade-ins	Trade-ins common	Trade-ins uncommon
Stage in the product life cycle	Often emphasized at every stage; heavy emphasis in the introductory and early growth stages in acquainting marketing intermediaries and potential consumers with the new good or service	Often emphasized at every stage; heavy emphasis in the latter part of the growth stage, as well as the maturity and early decline stages, to persuade consumers to select specific brands
Price	High unit value	Low unit value

the determination of an appropriate promotional mix: nature of the market, nature of the product, stage in the product life cycle, and price.

PULLING AND PUSHING PROMOTIONAL STRATEGIES

Marketers may implement essentially two promotional alternatives: a pulling strategy and a pushing strategy. A **pulling strategy** is a promotional effort by the seller to stimulate final-user demand, which then exerts pressure on the distribution channel. When marketing intermediaries stock a large number of competing products and exhibit little interest in any one of them, a firm may have to implement a pulling strategy to motivate them to handle the product. In such instances, this strategy is implemented with the objective of building consumer demand so that consumers will request the product from retail stores. Advertising and sales promotion often contribute to a company's pulling strategy.

<interactive>**learning goal**

CHAPTER OBJECTIVE #6: CONTRAST THE TWO MAJOR ALTERNATIVE PROMOTIONAL STRATEGIES.

In contrast, a **pushing strategy** relies more heavily on personal selling. Here the objective is promoting the product to the members of the marketing channel rather than to final users. To achieve this goal, marketers employ cooperative advertising allowances, trade discounts, personal selling efforts by salespeople, and other dealer supports. Such a strategy is designed to gain marketing success for the firm's products by motivating representatives of wholesalers and/or retailers to spend extra time and effort promoting the products to customers. About half of manufacturers' promotional budgets—$30 million a year—pays for cash incentives to get retailers to stock their products.

While pulling and pushing strategies are presented here as alternative methods, few companies depend entirely on either one. Most firms combine the two methods. Skechers' IMC strategy combines pushing and pulling strategies aimed at both retailers who purchase the company's trendy shoes for their stores and the ultimate consumers. Consumers can see television commercials and print ads in many magazines. To push its products, the company once spent $5 million on a lavish display at a national footwear trade show, including lasers, dancers, and a 30-foot-high transparent wall that displayed tens of thousands of shoes.[25]

Timing also affects the choice of promotional strategies. The relative importance of advertising and selling changes during the various phases of the purchase process. Prior to the actual sale, advertising usually is more important than personal selling. However, one of the primary advantages of a successful advertising program is the support it gives the salesperson who approaches the prospect for the first time. Selling activities are more important than advertising at the time of purchase. Personal selling provides the actual mechanism for closing most sales. In the postpurchase period, advertising regains primacy in the promotional effort. It affirms the customer's decision to buy a particular good or service and reminds him or her of the product's favorable qualities by reducing any cognitive dissonance that might occur.

The promotional strategies used by auto marketers illustrate this timing factor. Car, truck, and SUV makers spend heavily on consumer advertising to create awareness before consumers begin the purchase process. At the time of their purchase decisions, however, the personal-selling skills of dealer salespeople provide the most important tools for closing sales. Finally, advertising frequently maintains postpurchase satisfaction by citing awards such as *Motor Trend's* Car of the Year and results of J.D. Power's customer-satisfaction surveys to affirm buyer decisions.

BUDGETING FOR PROMOTIONAL STRATEGY

Promotional budgets may differ not only in amount but also in composition. Business-to-business marketers generally invest larger proportions of their budgets in personal selling than in advertising, while the reverse is usually true of most producers of consumer goods. Cannondale Associates, a leading U.S. sales and marketing consulting firm, conducts an annual survey of trade promotion spending in different industries. Figure 17.10 provides an estimate of how consumer packaged goods manufacturers will allocate their promotional budgets in 2005.

<interactive>**learning goal**

CHAPTER OBJECTIVE #7: EXPLAIN HOW MARKETERS BUDGET FOR AND MEASURE THE EFFECTIVENESS OF PROMOTION.

Evidence suggests that sales initially lag behind promotional expenses for structural reasons—funds spent filling up retail shelves, boosting low initial production, and supplying buyer knowledge. This fact produces a threshold effect in which few sales may result from substantial initial investments in promotion. A second phase might produce sales proportionate to promotional expenditures—the most predictable range. Finally, promotion reaches the area of diminishing returns where an increase in promotional spending fails to produce a corresponding increase in sales.

For example, an initial expenditure of $40,000 may result in sales of 100,000 product units for a consumer goods manufacturer. An additional $10,000 expenditure may generate sales of 30,000 more units, and another $10,000 may produce sales of an additional 35,000 units. The cumulative effect of the expenditures and repeat sales will have generated increasing returns from the promotional outlays. However, as the advertising budget moves from $60,000 to $70,000, the marginal productivity of the additional expenditure may fall to 28,000 units. At some later point, the return may actually become zero or negative as competition intensifies, markets become saturated, and marketers employ less expensive advertising media.

FIGURE 17.10

Allocation of Promotional Budgets for Consumer Packaged Goods

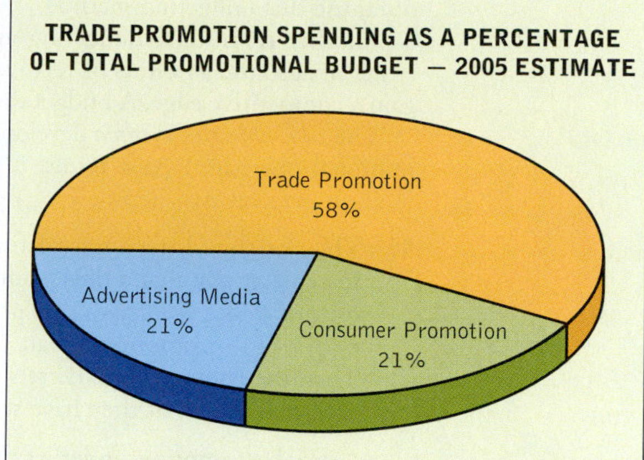

Source: Data from Donnelley Marketing and Accenture Analysis, "Capturing and Sustaining Value Opportunities in Trade Promotion," accessed at the Accenture Web site, September 6, 2002, http://www.accenture.com.

The ideal method of allocating promotional funds would increase the budget until the cost of each additional increment equals the additional incremental revenue received. In other words, the most effective allocation procedure increases promotional expenditures until each dollar of promotional expense is matched by an additional dollar of profit. This procedure—referred to as marginal analysis—maximizes the input's productivity. The difficulty arises in identifying the optimal point, which requires a precise balance between marginal expenses for promotion and the resulting marginal receipts. Traditional methods for creating a promotional budget include the percentage-of-sales and fixed-sum-per-unit methods, along with techniques for meeting the competition and achieving task objectives. Each method is briefly examined in Table 17.4.

The *percentage-of-sales method* is perhaps the most common way of establishing promotional budgets. The percentage can be based on sales either from some past period (such as the previous year) or forecasted for a future period (the current year). While this plan is appealingly simple, it does not effectively support

TABLE 17.4

Promotional Budget Determination

METHOD	DESCRIPTION	EXAMPLE
Percentage-of-sales method	Promotional budget is set as a specified percentage of either past or forecasted sales.	"Last year we spent $10,500 on promotion and had sales of $420,000. Next year we expect sales to grow to $480,000, and we are allocating $12,000 for promotion."
Fixed-sum-per-unit method	Promotional budget is set as a predetermined dollar amount for each unit sold or produced.	"Our forecast calls for sales of 14,000 units, and we allocate promotion at the rate of $65 per unit."
Meeting competition	Promotional budget is set to match competitor's promotional outlays on either an absolute or relative basis.	"Promotional outlays average 4 percent of sales in our industry."
Task-objective method	Once marketers determine their specific promotional objectives, the amount (and type) of promotional spending needed to achieve them is determined.	"By the end of next year, we want 75 percent of the area high-school students to be aware of our new, highly automated fast-food prototype outlet. How many promotional dollars will it take, and how should they be spent?"

the achievement of basic promotional objectives. Arbitrary percentage allocations can't provide needed flexibility. In addition, sales should depend on promotional allocation rather than vice versa.

The *fixed-sum-per-unit method* differs from budgeting based on a percentage of sales in only one respect: It allocates a predetermined amount to each sales or production unit. This amount can also reflect either historical or forecasted figures. Producers of high-value consumer durable goods, such as automobiles, often use this budgeting method.

Another traditional budgeting approach, *meeting competition*, simply matches competitors' outlays, either in absolute amounts or relative to the firms' market shares. But this method doesn't help a company gain a competitive edge. A budget that is appropriate for one company may not be appropriate for another.

The *task-objective method* develops a promotional budget based on a sound evaluation of the firm's promotional objectives. As a result, it attunes its allocation of funds to modern marketing practices. The method involves two steps:

1. The firm's marketers must define realistic communication goals that they want the promotional mix to achieve. Say that a firm wants to achieve a 25 percent increase in brand awareness. This step quantifies the objectives that promotion should attain. These objectives in turn become integral parts of the promotional plan.
2. Then the company's marketers determine the amount and type of promotional activity required for each objective that they have set. Combined, these units become the firm's promotional budget.

A crucial assumption underlies the task-objective approach: Marketers can measure the productivity of each promotional dollar. That assumption explains why the objectives must be carefully chosen, quantified, and accomplished through promotional efforts. Generally, budgeters should avoid general marketing objectives such as, "We want to achieve a 5 percent increase in sales." A sale is a culmination of the effects of all elements of the marketing mix. A more appropriate promotional objective might be, "We want to achieve an 8 percent response rate from a targeted direct-mail advertisement."

Promotional budgeting always requires difficult decisions. Still, recent research studies and the spread of computer-based models have made it a more manageable problem than it used to be.

MEASURING THE EFFECTIVENESS OF PROMOTION

It is widely recognized that part of a firm's promotional effort is ineffective. John Wanamaker, a successful 19th-century retailer, observed the following: "I know half the money I spend on advertising is wasted, but I can never find out which half."

Evaluating the effectiveness of a promotion today is a far different exercise in marketing research than it was even a few decades ago. For years, marketers depended on store audits conducted by large organizations like A.C. Nielsen. Other research groups conducted warehouse withdrawal surveys. These research studies were designed to determine whether sales had risen as a direct result of a particular promotional campaign. In the 1980s, the introduction of scanners and automated checkout lanes completely changed marketing research. For the first time, retailers and manufacturers had a tool to obtain sales data quickly and efficiently. The problem was that the collected data was used for little else than determining how much of which product was bought at what price and at what time.

By the 1990s, marketing research entered another evolutionary period with the advent of the Internet. Now marketing researchers can delve into each customer's purchase behavior, lifestyle, preferences, opinions, and habits. All of this information can also be obtained in a matter of seconds. The next section explains the impact of electronic technologies on measuring promotional effectiveness. However, marketers today still depend on two basic measurement tools: direct sales results tests and indirect evaluations.

Most marketers would prefer to use a *direct sales results test* to measure the effectiveness of promotion. Such an approach would reveal the specific impact on sales revenues for each dollar of promotional spending. This type of technique has always eluded marketers, however, due to their inability to control other variables operating in the marketplace. A firm may receive $20 million in additional sales orders following a new $1.5 million advertising campaign, but the market success may really have resulted from price increases for competing products rather than from the advertising outlays.

Marketers often encounter difficulty isolating the effects of promotion from those of other market elements and outside environmental variables. *Indirect evaluation* helps researchers to concentrate on quantifiable indicators of effectiveness, such as recall (how much members of the target market remember about specific products or advertisements) and readership (size and composition of a message's audience). The basic problem with indirect measurement is the difficulty of relating these variables to sales. Will the fact that many people read an ad lead directly to increased sales?

Marketers need to ask the right questions and understand what they are measuring. Promotion to build sales volume produces measurable results in the form of short-term returns; brand-building programs, however, and efforts to generate or enhance consumers' perceptions of value in a product, brand, or organization cannot be measured over the short term.

Measuring Online Promotions

The latest challenge facing marketers is how to measure the effectiveness of electronic media. Early attempts at measuring online promotional effectiveness involved counting hits (user requests for a file) and visits (pages downloaded or read in one session). But as Chapter 5 explained, it is not how many times a Web site is visited, but how many people actually buy something. Traditional numbers that work for other media forms are not necessarily relevant indicators of effectiveness for a Web site. For one thing, the Web combines both advertising and direct marketing. Web pages effectively integrate advertising and other content, such as product information, that may be the page's main feature. For another consideration, consumers generally choose the advertisements they want to see on the Net, whereas traditional broadcast or print media automatically expose consumers to ads.

One way that marketers measure performance is by incorporating some form of direct response into their promotions. This technique also helps them to compare different promotions for effectiveness and rely on facts rather than opinions. Consumers may say they will try a product in response to a survey question yet not actually buy it. A firm may send out three different direct mail offers in the same promotion and compare response rates. An offer to send for a sample may generate a 75 percent response rate, coupons might show a 50 percent redemption rate, and rebates might appeal to only 10 percent of the targeted group.

The two major techniques for setting Internet advertising rates are *cost per impression* and *cost per response (click-throughs).* Cost per impression is a measurement technique that relates the cost of an ad to every thousand people who view it. In other words, anyone who sees the page containing the banner or other form of ad creates one impression. This measure assumes that the site's principal purpose is to display the advertising message. Cost per response is a direct marketing technique that relates the cost of an ad to the number of people who click on it. Measurement based on click-throughs assumes that those who actually click on an ad want more information and, therefore, consider the ad valuable. Both rating techniques have merit. Site publishers point out that click-through rates are influenced by the creativity of the ad's message. Advertisers, on the other hand, point out that the Web ad has value to those who click on it for additional information.

THE VALUE OF MARKETING COMMUNICATIONS

The nature of marketing communications is changing as new formats transform the traditional idea of an advertisement or sales promotion. Sales messages are now placed subtly, or not so subtly, in movies and television shows, blurring the lines between promotion and entertainment and changing the traditional definition of advertising. Messages show up on stadium turnstiles, buses, and even police cars.

<interactive>**learning goal**

CHAPTER OBJECTIVE #8: DISCUSS THE VALUE OF MARKETING COMMUNICATIONS.

Despite new tactics by advertisers, promotion has often been the target of criticism. Some people complain that it offers nothing of value to society and simply wastes resources. Others criticize that promotion encourages consumers to buy unnecessary products that they cannot afford. Many ads seem to insult people's intelligence or offend their sensibilities, and they criticize the ethics—or lack thereof—displayed by advertisers and salespeople. Many consumers would agree that the value of cigarette advertising is limited at best; in fact, many would consider it unethical to promote smoking in this way.

New forms of promotion are considered even more insidious because marketers make pitches that do not look like paid advertisements. Many of these complaints cite true problems. Some salespeople use unethical sales tactics. Some product advertising hides its promotional nature or targets consumer groups that can least afford the advertised goods or services. Many television commercials do, in fact, contribute to the growing problem of cultural pollution. One area that has sparked both criticism and debate is promotion aimed at children, as discussed in the "Solving an Ethical Controversy" Interactive Example.

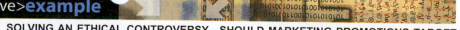

RIGHT/WRONG: SOLVING AN ETHICAL CONTROVERSY—SHOULD MARKETING PROMOTIONS TARGET CHILDREN?

While promotion can certainly be criticized on many counts, it also plays a crucial role in modern society. This point is best understood by examining the social, business, and economic importance of promotion. The AARP message in Figure 17.11 provides valuable information to seniors who are taking prescription drugs.

Social Importance

Criticisms of promotional messages as tasteless and lacking any contribution to society sometimes ignore the fact that our social framework provides no commonly accepted set of standards or priorities for these judgments. We live in a varied economy characterized by consumer segments with differing needs, wants, and aspirations. What one group finds tasteless may be quite appealing to another. But diversity is one of the benefits of living in our society because it offers us many choices and opportunities. Promotional strategy faces an averaging problem that escapes many of its critics. The one generally accepted standard in a market society is freedom of choice for the consumer. Consumer buying decisions eventually determine acceptable practices in the marketplace, which is why consumers who criticize cigarette ads may also agree that it is acceptable for them to appear.

Promotion has also become an important factor in campaigns aimed at achieving social objectives, such as stopping drug abuse or supporting national parks. Advertising agencies donate their expertise to creating *public service announcements (PSAs)* aimed at promoting these causes, as illustrated by the Ad Council message in Figure 17.12 on afterschool programs.

Promotion performs an informative and educational task crucial to the functioning of modern society. As with everything else in life, what is important is how promotion is used rather than whether it is used.

Business Importance

Promotional strategy has become increasingly important to both large and small business enterprises. The well-documented, long-term increase in funds spent on promotion certainly attests to management's faith in the ability of promotional efforts to encourage attitude changes, brand loyalty, and additional sales. It

FIGURE 17.11

Using Promotion to Provide Valuable Information for Product Users

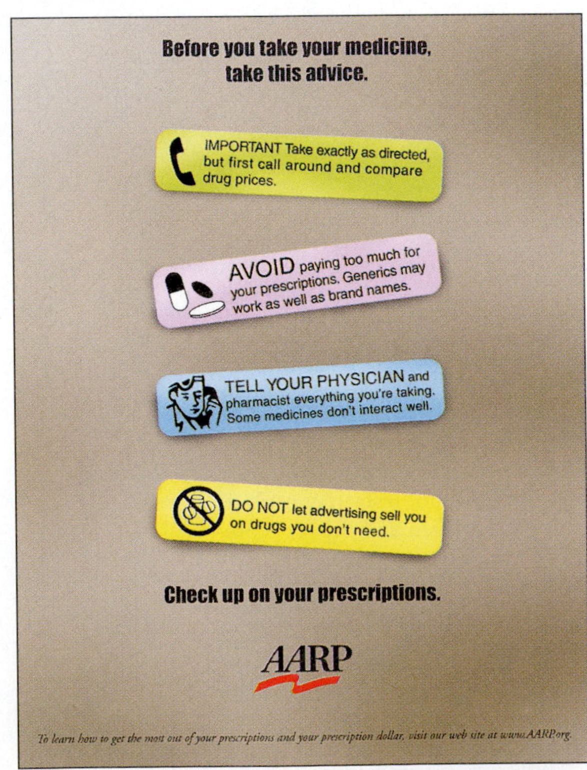

FIGURE 17.12

Promotional Message Addressing an Important Social Concern

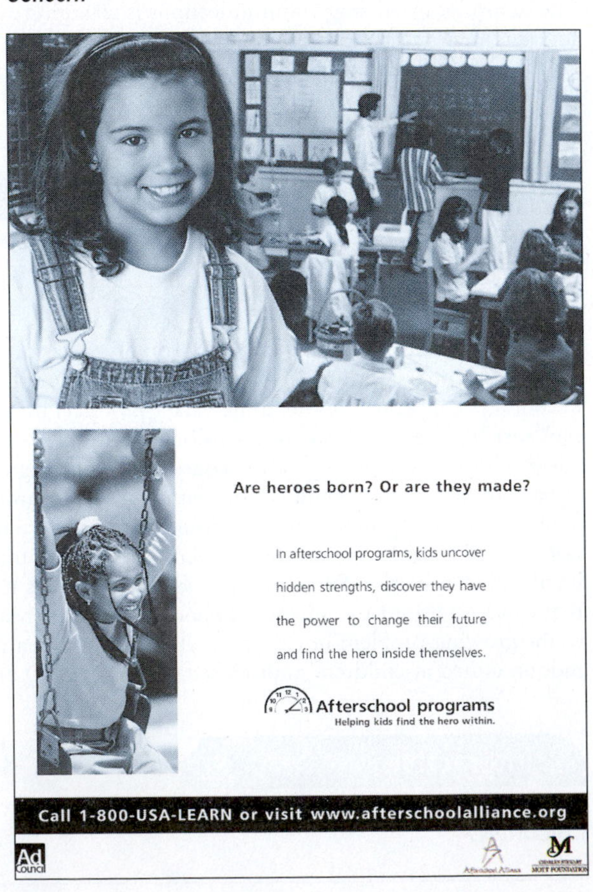

is difficult to conceive of an enterprise that would not attempt to promote its good or service in some manner. Most modern institutions simply cannot survive in the long run without promotion. Business must communicate with its publics.

Nonbusiness enterprises also recognize the importance of promotional efforts. The U.S. government spends about $300 million a year on advertising and ranks 36th among all U.S. advertisers. The Canadian government is the leading advertiser in Canada, promoting many concepts and programs. Religious organizations have acknowledged the importance of promotional channels to make their viewpoints known to the public at large.

Economic Importance

Promotion has assumed a degree of economic importance, if for no other reason than because it provides employment for thousands of people. More important, however, effective promotion has allowed society to derive benefits not otherwise available. For example, the criticism that promotion costs too much isolates an individual expense item and fails to consider its possible beneficial effects on other categories of expenditures.

Promotional strategies increase the number of units sold and permit economies of scale in the production process, thereby lowering the production costs for each unit of output. Lower unit costs allow lower consumer prices, which in turn make products available to more people. Similarly, researchers have found that advertising subsidizes the information contents of newspapers and the broadcast media. In short, promotion pays for many of the enjoyable entertainment and educational opportunities in contemporary life as it lowers product costs.

STRATEGIC IMPLICATIONS OF MARKETING IN THE 21ST CENTURY

With the incredible proliferation of marketing messages in the media, today's marketers—who are also consumers themselves—must find new ways to reach customers without overloading them with unnecessary or unwanted communications. Guerilla marketing has emerged as an effective strategy for large and small companies, but ambush marketing has raised ethical concerns. Product placement has gained in popularity, but if movies and television shows become jammed with brands, marketers will have to find yet another venue for their messages. In addition, it is difficult to overstate the impact of the Internet on the promotional mix of 21st-century marketers. Small companies are on the Web, and big businesses are there as well. Even individual entrepreneurs have found a lucrative new launch pad for their enterprises. But even though cyberspace marketing has been effective in business-to-business transactions and, to a lesser extent, for some types of consumer purchases, a major source of Internet revenues is advertising. The Net has ads for almost every good or service imaginable. In fact, Web companies sell over $1 billion in advertising each year.

Integrating marketing communications into an overall consumer-focused strategy that meets a company's promotional and business objectives has become more and more critical in the busy global marketplace. Chapter 18 will examine specific ways marketers can use advertising, sales promotion, and public relations to convey their messages; then Chapter 19 will discuss personal selling and sales-force management in the same manner.

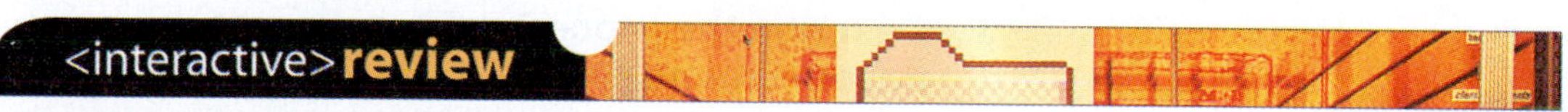

FLASH CHAPTER REVIEW PRESENTATION

<interactive>**video case**

CHERRY CAPITAL AIRPORT KEEPS PEOPLE FLYING

endofchaptermaterial

- **Summary of Chapter Objectives**
- **Chapter Outline**
- **Key Terms**
- **Review Questions**
- **Projects and Teamwork Exercises**
- **'netWork**
- **Crossword Puzzles**
- **Case 17.1: Elvis Is Alive and Well—in Graceland**

Take the Post-Test to assess your overall understanding of the key ideas in this chapter. The Post-Test provides a comprehensive selection of exam-style questions addressing the main topics and concepts of the chapter. At the completion of each Post-Test, you will receive a score and instructive feedback on how you answered each question, and a direct link to the part of the chapter addressed in the question. Take the Post-Test as often as you need to—a record of your progress for each attempt is kept for you to revisit and gauge your improvement. And each Post-Test is randomly generated, so every attempt is new.

Post-Test

CHAPTER 18

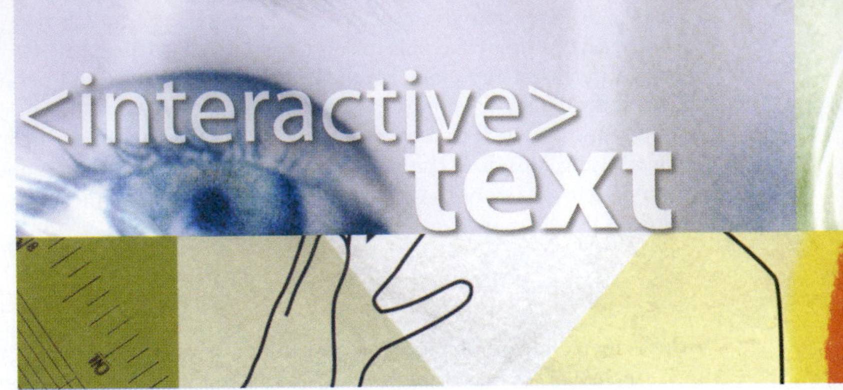

Advertising, Sales Promotion, and Public Relations

Chapter Objectives

1. **Identify the three major advertising objectives and the two basic categories of advertising.**
2. **List the major advertising strategies.**
3. **Describe the process of creating an advertisement.**
4. **List and compare the major advertising media.**
5. **Outline the organization of the advertising function and the role of an advertising agency.**
6. **Identify the principal methods of sales promotion.**
7. **Explain the roles of cross promotions, public relations, publicity, and ethics in an organization's promotional strategy.**
8. **Explain how marketers assess promotional effectiveness.**

DELL'S UNLIKELY ADVERTISING HERO

Spot him on TV and he makes you a little uneasy, reminding you of someone who, 20 years from now, might be one of those CEOs and accounting types featured on the TV news in handcuffs and forced by FBI agents to take the "perp walk" in front of news cameras. Others see him as sort of a surfer dude, but with a geeky streak. He wears slouchy clothes and ethnic jewelry and has scruffy hair. He looks like he just rolled out of bed. He's probably visited the principal's office a few times during his high school career. But he's smart. In fact, "Steven," as he's called in the highly popular—and highly effective—Dell Computer ads, gives parents expert advice on what kind of computer they should buy for their kids. He knows computer lingo. But he can also turn around and quip, "Dude, you're gettin' a Dell." And Steven isn't afraid to make a fool of himself: During Dell's Christmas ad campaign, he dressed up in a green elf suit to pitch the firm's $899 desktop computer.

Steven the Dell Guy is really Benjamin Curtis, a college acting student in his early twenties who was hired by Dell's advertising agency, Lowe Worldwide, to appeal to younger customers. He has succeeded—and reached other age groups as well. Although the PC market has barely been treading water during the past three years, Dell has doubled its share of the market to 17 percent, thanks largely to the Steven ads, which seem to be a hit with both men and women. "I would choose a Dell over a Gateway because Steven is cuter than Gateway's cow," says Libby Marie LeForce, a 17-year-old student from Arizona. Chas McAvoy, a 35-year-old Web site designer, recommends Dell computers to his clients. "I am much more aware of the company because of the commercials," he notes. A recent *USA Today*/Harris Poll survey reported that 30 percent of women and 23 percent of men liked the ads a lot, while overall 30 percent thought the ads were "very effective."

In fact, the job of an effective advertising campaign is to create awareness among consumers, to provide information about a good or service, and to persuade them to buy. Steven seems to be able to do all three, which is why Charles Smulder of technology research firm Gartner Group observes that the campaign is "icing on the cake of a business model that [Dell] carefully crafted and used successfully to take market share away from the competition." Dell usually targets second-time computer buyers with direct marketing methods while first-time buyers seek advice and guidance at retail stores. The Steven campaign creates awareness and a desire for the Dell brand.

The ad campaign has been so effective that Dell spokesperson Curtis has received offers for other acting jobs. But the Steven character is so ingrained in consumers' minds that he sometimes worries he will be typecast. "People look at me and stare," he says. "I have been training in theater for years, not to be typecast as a surfer dude." Still, his upbeat character has struck a chord with nontechnical consumers, and it's hard to complain about success.[1]

Pre-Test

Take the Pre-Test to assess your initial knowledge of the key ideas in this chapter. The Pre-Test provides exam-style questions addressing the main topics and concepts of the chapter. At the completion of each Pre-Test, you will receive a score and instructive feedback on how you answered each question, and a direct link to the part of the chapter addressed in the question. Take the Pre-Test as often as you need to—a record of your progress for each attempt is kept for you to revisit and gauge your improvement.

CHAPTER OVERVIEW

From the last chapter, you already know that the nonpersonal elements of promotion include advertising, sales promotion, and public relations. Thousands of organizations rely on nonpersonal selling in developing their promotional mixes and integrated marketing communications strategies. While advertising is the most visible form of nonpersonal promotion, marketers spend three times as much on sales promotion, and they often use them together to create effective promotional campaigns. Television is probably the most obvious medium for nonpersonal selling dollars. But theater advertising is a major ad component in Europe, and Regal Entertainment, the large U.S. movie theater chain, took in $70 million in on-screen advertising in just one year during a recent test.[2]

Marketers seeking excitement for new-product launches have recently paid as much as $3 million to have the Rolling Stones perform at a single event. Kraft Foods recently moved away from its traditional TV advertising for its back-to-school sales push in favor of sponsoring 'tween idol Aaron Carter's 30-city summer tour. The singer, a favorite of older children and preteens, was recently voted No. 1 Pop Star in a *Tiger Beat* poll. The marketer of such popular snacks as Oreos, Post cereals, Ritz crackers, Cheese Nips, and Kraft Cheese Singles mined kids' obsession with music and fame with an instant-win "Be a Pop Star" game with five grand prize trips to Los Angeles to meet Carter and make a demo CD.[3]

This chapter begins with a discussion of the types of advertising and explains how advertising is used to achieve a firm's objectives. It then considers alternative advertising strategies and the process of creating an advertisement. Next, we provide a detailed look at various advertising media channels, from television and radio to print advertising and direct mail to outdoor and interactive media. Sales promotion, the second major type of nonpersonal advertising, is explained with detailed discussions of both consumer-oriented and trade promotions. The chapter then focuses on the importance of public relations, publicity, and cross promotions in e-commerce. Alternative methods of measuring the effectiveness of both online and offline nonpersonal selling are examined. We conclude the chapter by exploring current ethical issues relating to nonpersonal selling.

Briefly Speaking

If you think advertising doesn't pay—we understand there are 25 mountains in Colorado higher than Pikes Peak. Can you name one?

Anonymous

ADVERTISING

Twenty-first century advertising is closely related to integrated marketing communications (IMC) in many respects. While IMC involves a message dealing with buyer-seller relationships, **advertising** involves paid nonpersonal communication through various media with the purpose of informing or persuading members of a particular audience. Advertising is used by marketers to reach target markets such as business firms, not-for-profit organizations, or individuals identified in the message.

While the ability of the Internet to make every marketer a global marketer has become a truism, America remains home to most of the world's leading advertisers. General Motors, Procter & Gamble, AOL Time Warner, Philip Morris, and DaimlerChrysler are five of the top advertisers in the world, each spending more than $1 billion—an average of almost $3 million a day—on advertising. Although advertising spending totals over $200 billion each year, belt tightening by businesses facing declining revenues during the recent recession resulted in a 6.5 percent drop in ad spending during a recent 12-month period. But spending flattened the following year and, by 2003, was once again on the increase.[4]

Advertising spending varies among industries as well as companies. The cosmetic industry is widely known for pouring dollars into advertising, as is the auto manufacturing industry. In fact, total auto ad spending amounts to nearly $15 billion a year. Other industries, such as aviation manufacturing, spend far less—a mere $48 million annually.

As previous chapters have discussed, the emergence of the marketing concept, with its emphasis on a companywide consumer orientation, boosted the importance of integrated marketing communications. This change, in turn, expanded the role of advertising. Today, a typical consumer is exposed to hundreds of advertising messages each day. Advertising provides an efficient, inexpensive, and fast method of reaching the ever-elusive, increasingly segmented consumer market. Its current role rivals those of sales promotion and personal selling. In fact, advertising has become a key ingredient in the effective implementation of the marketing concept.

Types of Advertising

Advertisements fall into two broad categories: product advertising and institutional advertising. **Product advertising** is nonpersonal selling of a particular good or service. This is the type of advertising the average person usually thinks of when talking about most promotional activities. **Institutional advertising,** in contrast, promotes a concept, an idea, a philosophy, or the goodwill of an industry, company, organization, person, geographical location, or government agency. This term has a broader meaning than *corporate advertising,* which is typically limited to nonproduct advertising sponsored by a specific profit-seeking firm.

<interactive>**learning goal**

CHAPTER OBJECTIVE #1: IDENTIFY THE THREE MAJOR ADVERTISING OBJECTIVES AND THE TWO BASIC CATEGORIES OF ADVERTISING.

Institutional advertising is often closely related to the public-relations function of the enterprise. The ad in Figure 18.1 featuring the Statue of Liberty attempts to encourage visitors to return to the beauty and excitement of New York. Its ultimate objective is to increase overall spending by visitors to the state rather than increase market share for a specific brand.

Objectives of Advertising

Marketers use advertising messages to accomplish three primary objectives: to inform, to persuade, and to remind. These objectives may be used individually or, more typically, in conjunction with each other. For example, an ad for a not-for-profit agency may inform the public of the existence of the organization and at the same time persuade the audience to make a donation, join the organization, or attend a function.

Informative advertising seeks to develop initial demand for a good, service, organization, person, place, idea, or cause. The promotion of any new market entry tends to pursue this objective because marketing success at this stage often depends simply on announcing availability. Therefore, informative advertising is common in the introductory stage of the product life cycle.

Persuasive advertising attempts to increase demand for an existing good, service, organization, person, place, idea, or cause. Persuasive advertising is a competitive type of promotion suited to the growth stage and the early part of the maturity stage of the product life cycle.

Reminder advertising strives to reinforce previous promotional activity by keeping the name of a good, service, organization, person, place, idea, or cause before the public. It is common in the latter part of the maturity stage and throughout the decline stage of the product life cycle. Nabisco's Triscuits have been around for a long time; the packaged-good company's marketers continue to advertise as a means of reminding consumers of the heartiness of the crackers.

Figure 18.2 illustrates the relationship between advertising objectives and the stages of the product life cycle. Informative advertising tends to work best during the early stages, while reminder advertising is effective later on. Persuasive advertising, if done well, can be effective through the entire life cycle.

Traditionally, marketers stated their advertising objectives as direct sales goals. A more current and realistic standard, however, views advertising as a way to achieve communications objectives, including informing, persuading, and reminding potential customers of the product. Advertising attempts to condition consumers to adopt favorable viewpoints toward a promotional message. The goal of an ad is to improve the likelihood that a customer will buy a particular good or service. In this sense, advertising illustrates the close relationship between marketing communications and promotional strategy.

To get the best value for a firm's advertising investment, marketers must first determine what that firm's advertising objectives are. Effective advertising can enhance consumer perceptions of quality in a good or service, leading to increased customer loyalty, repeat purchases, and protection against price wars. In addition, perceptions of superiority pay off in the firm's ability to raise prices without losing market share.

FIGURE 18.1

An Example of Institutional Advertising

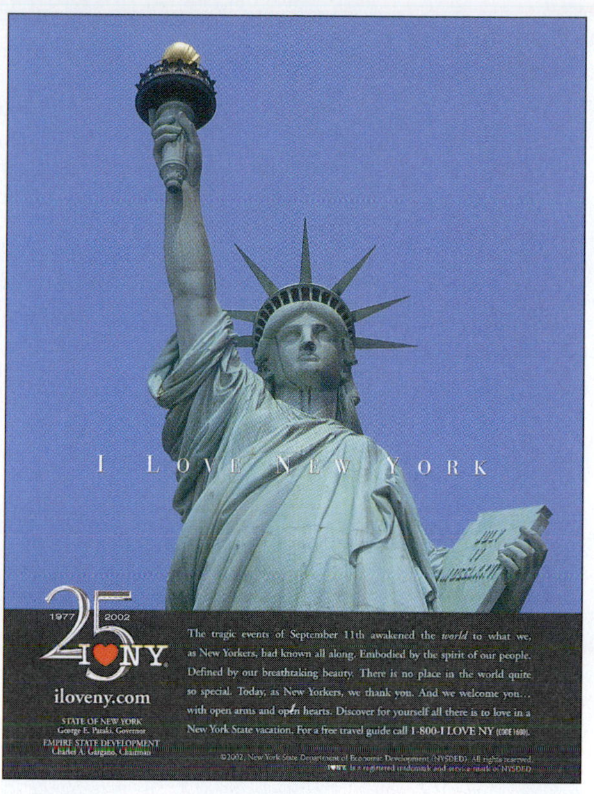

FIGURE 18.2

Advertising Objectives in Relation to Stage in the Product Life Cycle

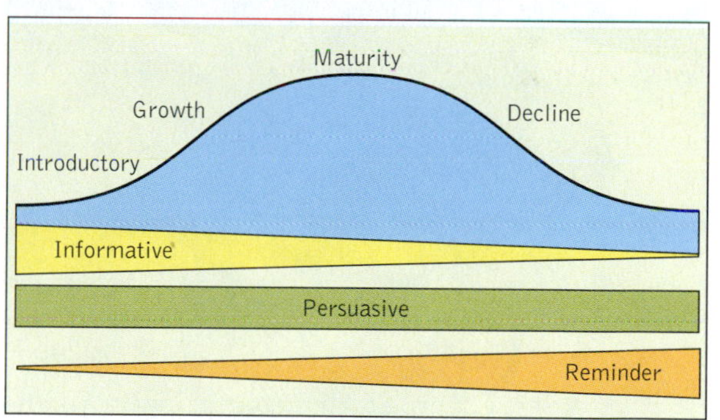

ADVERTISING STRATEGIES

If the primary function of marketing is to bring buyers and sellers together, then advertising is the means to an end. Effective advertising strategies accomplish at least one of three tasks: informing, persuading, or reminding consumers. The secret to success in choosing the best strategy is developing a message that best positions a firm's product in the audience's mind. Among the advertising strategies available for use by 21st century marketers are comparative advertising and celebrity advertising, as well as decisions about global and interactive ads. Channel-oriented decisions such as retail and cooperative advertising must also be devised.

<interactive>**learning goal**

CHAPTER OBJECTIVE #2: LIST THE MAJOR ADVERTISING STRATEGIES.

Marketers often combine several of these advertising strategies to ensure that the advertisement accomplishes set objectives. As markets become more segmented, the need for personalized advertising increases. The next sections describe strategies that contemporary marketers develop to reach their target markets.

Comparative Advertising

Firms whose goods and services are not the leaders in their markets often favor **comparative advertising,** a promotional strategy that emphasizes advertising messages with direct or indirect comparisons to dominant brands in the industry. By contrast, market leaders seldom acknowledge in their advertising that competing products even exist, and when they do, they usually do not point out any benefits of the competing brand.

Struggling desktop computer maker Gateway recently launched an advertising campaign for its new Profile PC by showing it alongside Apple Computer's iMac to demonstrate their similar appearance and then touting Gateway's advantage in price, performance, and software selection. Print ads and TV commercials urged consumers to "Think Smarter," a phrase borrowed from Apple's long-running "Think Different" tag line.[5]

A generation ago, comparative advertising was not the norm; in fact, it was frowned on. But the Federal Trade Commission now encourages comparative advertising. Regulators believe such ads keep marketers competitive and consumers better informed about their choices. Generally speaking, where there is competition through advertising, prices tend to go down because people can shop around. This benefit has proved increasingly true for online consumers, who now use bots to help find the best prices on goods and services.

Briefly Speaking

In good times people want to advertise; in bad times they have to.

Bruce Barton (1886–1967) American advertising executive

Celebrity Testimonials

A popular technique for increasing advertising readership in a cluttered promotional environment and improving overall effectiveness of a marketing message involves the use of celebrity spokespeople. About one of every five U.S. ads currently includes celebrities. This type of advertising is also popular in foreign countries. In Japan, 80 percent of all ads use celebrities, both local and international stars. U.S. celebrities featured in Japanese ads include actors Harrison Ford for Kirin Beer, Jodie Foster for Keri Cosmetics and Latte Coffee, and Paul Newman for Evance watch stores. Japanese consumers view foreign stars as images more than actual people, which helps marketers to sell products. They also associate American stars with quality.

Marketers at tractor and lawn-equipment giant John Deere chose a strong comparative advertising campaign to position its little-known Sabre entry-level lawn tractor against the popular Sears Craftsman tractor. In addition to detailed copy emphasizing Sabre's advantages over its rival at Sears, the comparative ad included the John Deere Web address, toll-free number for additional information, and a comparison chart for the two models.

Both the number of celebrity ads and the dollars spent on those ads have increased in recent years. Professional athletes are among the highest paid product endorsers, raking in millions per year. They appear in advertisements for a wide variety of products, many having little or nothing to do with sports. Basketball great Michael Jordan earns more than $30 million annually as a spokesperson for underwear maker Hanes and for his MJ clothing line. Practically everyone has seen former boxer George Foreman in ads for Salton's Lean Mean Fat-Reducing Grilling Machine. And golfing phenom Tiger Woods has lucrative deals with dozens of products, ranging from telecommunications and credit card giants to Buick automobiles, in addition to his $40 million agreement with Nike Golf.

One advantage of associations with big-name personalities is improved product recognition in a promotional environment filled with hundreds of competing 15- and 30-second commercials. Advertisers use the term *clutter* to describe this situation. As e-commerce continues to soar, one inevitable result has been the increase in advertising clutter as companies rush to sell their goods and services online. But marketers need to remember that an effective online site must have meaningful content and helpful service.

Another advantage to using celebrities occurs when marketers are trying to reach consumers of another culture. Blockbuster Video and McDonald's have hired Hispanic stars to attract Hispanic consumers to their stores. Actress Daisy Fuentes appears in ads for McDonald's, while John Leguizamo and Hector Elizondo advertise for Blockbuster. "We see lots of new companies going into the Hispanic market who have never advertised before, and one way is hiring celebrities," explains Raul Mateu, a vice president at the William Morris talent agency. "It seems like an easy way of getting instant credibility in the marketplace is using [the celebrity's] equity."[6]

A celebrity testimonial generally succeeds when the celebrity is a credible source of information for the product being promoted. The most effective ads of this type establish relevant links between the celebrities and the advertised goods or services, such as the models and actresses who endorse Revlon cosmetics, as described in the "Marketing Hits" Interactive Example. Note that in the examples listed earlier, even though many of the products are not sports related, they do make a link to the celebrity—likable boxing champion George Foreman seems like a person who enjoys eating. Several studies of consumer responses show that celebrities improve the product's believability, recall of the product, and brand recognition. Celebrity endorsements also create positive attitudes, leading to greater brand equity.

<interactive>**example**

MARKETING HIT: REVLON WANTS TO BE UNFORGETTABLE

However, a celebrity who endorses too many products may create marketplace confusion. Customers may remember the celebrity but not the product or brand; worse, they might connect the celebrity to a competing brand. Another problem can arise if a celebrity is involved in a scandal or has trouble with the law, as marketers do not want their products associated with a negative image. Kmart merchandisers worried about a shopper backlash harming sales of their highly successful Martha Stewart product line when allegations of insider stock trading by the nation's decorating diva became the subject of a congressional investigation.[7]

Some advertisers try to avoid such problems by using cartoon characters as endorsers. Snoopy, a character in the popular *Peanuts* comic strip and long-running TV animated programs, has appeared in MetLife ads for years. Some advertisers may actually prefer cartoon characters because the characters can never say anything negative about the product, they do exactly what the marketers want them to do, and they cannot get involved in scandals. The only drawback is high licensing fees; popular animated characters often cost more than live celebrities. Companies may create their own cartoon characters, which eventually become celebrities in their own right as a result of many appearances in advertisements, as is the case with the Keebler elves.

In recent years, marketers have begun to consider celebrities as marketing partners rather than pretty or famous faces who can sell goods and services. Tiger Woods has been active in developing Nike's golf gear and apparel. Former supermodel Claudia Schiffer not only agreed to endorse a signature line of PalmPilots, but she also assisted in positioning the hand-held computers in the electronics market by selecting fashionable colors and her own favorite software programs. Of course, George Foreman actually uses the grills he advertises. "George has been very active in the marketing of his grills and genuinely believes in them," says Jake Fuller, an equity research analyst at Credit Suisse First Boston in New York. The grills served up $375 million in sales for Salton in one year.[8]

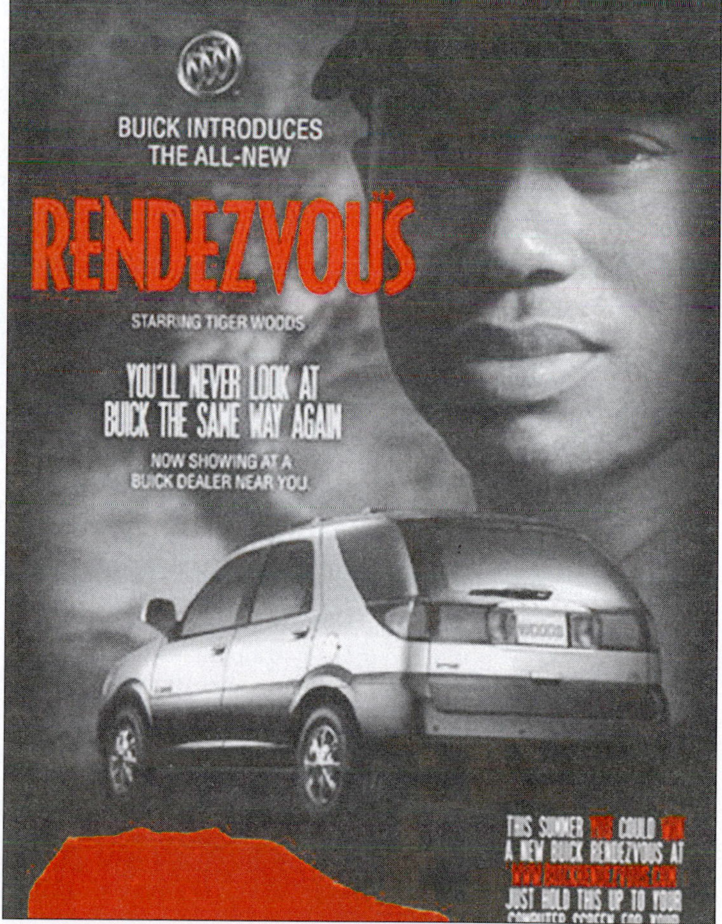

Tiger Woods, easily the most recognizable golfer in the PGA, has numerous endorsement deals. One of his most successful campaigns has been for Buick.

Retail Advertising

Most consumers are confronted daily with **retail advertising,** which includes all advertising by retail stores that sell goods or services directly to the consuming public. While this activity accounts for a sizable portion of total annual advertising expenditures, retail advertising varies widely in its effectiveness. One study showed that consumers often respond with suspicion to retail price advertisements. Source, message, and shopping experience seem to affect consumer attitudes toward these advertisements.

Many retail stores view advertising as a secondary activity, although that is changing. Except for the giants like electronics retailer Best Buy, illustrated in Figure 18.3, retailers rarely use independent advertising agencies, perhaps because of the expense associated with agencies. Instead, store managers may accept responsibility for advertising in addition to

FIGURE 18.3

Retail Advertising Used to Inform and Persuade Shoppers to Patronize Electronics Retailer Best Buy

their other duties. Management can begin to correct this problem by assigning one individual the sole responsibility and authority for developing an effective retail advertising program.

A retailer often shares advertising costs with a manufacturer or wholesaler in a technique called **cooperative advertising.** For example, an apparel marketer may pay a percentage of the cost of a retail store's newspaper advertisement featuring its product lines. Cooperative advertising campaigns originated to take advantage of the media's practice of offering lower rates to local advertisers than to national ones. Later, cooperative advertising became part of programs to improve dealer relations. The retailer likes the chance to secure advertising that it could not run otherwise. Cooperative advertising can create vertical links, as when a manufacturer and retailer coordinate their resources. It can also involve firms at the same level of the supply chain. In a horizontal arrangement, a group of retailers—for example, all the Ford dealers in the northeastern U.S.—might pool their resources.

Interactive Advertising

Millions of advertising messages float across idle—and active—computer screens in homes and offices around the country every day. Net surfers play games that are embedded with ads from the site sponsors. Companies offer free e-mail service to people willing to receive ads with their personal messages. Video screens on grocery carts display ads for shoppers to see as they wheel down the aisles of grocery stores.

Since marketers realize that two-way communications provide more effective methods for achieving promotional objectives, they are interested in interactive media. *Interactive advertising* involves two-way promotional messages transmitted through communication channels that induce message recipients to participate actively in the promotional effort. Achieving this involvement is the difficult task facing contemporary marketers. Although interactive advertising has become nearly synonymous with e-commerce and the Web, it also includes other formats such as kiosks in shopping malls. Multimedia technology, the Internet, and commercial online services are changing the nature of advertising from a one-way, passive communication technique to more effective, two-way marketing communications. Interactive advertising creates dialogue between marketers and individual shoppers, providing more materials as the user asks. The advertiser's challenge is to gain and hold consumer interest in an environment where these individuals control what they want to see.

Interactive advertising changes the balance between marketers and consumers. Unlike the traditional role of advertising—providing brief, entertaining, attention-catching messages—interactive media provide information to help consumers throughout the purchase and consumption processes. In a sense, it becomes closer to personal selling as consumers receive immediate responses to questions or requests for more information about goods and services. Interactive advertising provides consumers with more information in less time to help them make necessary comparisons between available products.

Successful interactive advertising adds value by offering the viewer more than just product-related information. An ad on the Web can do more than promote a brand; it can create a company store, provide customer service, and offer additional content.

Most firms deliver their interactive advertising messages through proprietary online services and through the Web. In fact, online ad spending is estimated at $6 billion per year. Top high-tech Internet spenders include Microsoft and IBM. Of the eight largest Internet spenders not based in information technologies, four are auto firms—General Motors, Ford, Toyota, and Honda. The other four include CBS Sportsline, Disney, Visa, and Amazon.[9]

CREATING AN ADVERTISEMENT

Marketers spend about $200 billion a year on advertising campaigns in the U.S. alone. With so much money at stake, they must create effective, memorable ads that increase sales and enhance their organizations' images. They cannot afford to waste resources on poor ads that fail to capture consumers' attention, communicate a message effectively, and lead to a purchase, donation, or other positive action for the organization.

<interactive>**learning goal**

CHAPTER OBJECTIVE #3: DESCRIBE THE PROCESS OF CREATING AN ADVERTISEMENT.

Research helps marketers create better ads by pinpointing goals that an ad needs to accomplish, such as educating consumers about product features, enhancing brand loyalty, or improving consumer perception of the brand. These objectives should guide the design of the ad. Marketers can also discover what appeals to consumers and can test ads with potential buyers before committing funds for a campaign.

Marketers sometimes face specific challenges as they develop advertising objectives for services. They must find a creative way to fill out the intangible images of most services and successfully convey the benefits that consumers receive. Also, they may have to find a strategy for advertising in a way that turns a negative event into a positive one, as in the case of life insurance.

Translating Advertising Objectives into Advertising Plans

Once a company defines its objectives for an advertising campaign, it can develop its advertising plan. Marketing research assists managers in making strategic decisions that guide choices in technical areas such as budgeting, copywriting, scheduling, and media selection. Posttests, which will be discussed in greater detail later in the chapter, measure the effectiveness of advertising and form the basis for feedback concerning possible adjustments. The elements of advertising planning are shown in Figure 18.4. The most experienced marketers know the importance of following even the most basic steps in the process, such as market analysis.

As Chapter 8 explained, positioning involves developing a marketing strategy that aims to achieve a desired position in a prospective buyer's mind. Marketers use a positioning strategy that distinguishes their good or service from those of competitors. Effective advertising then communicates the desired position by emphasizing certain product characteristics, such as performance attributes, price/quality, competitors' shortcomings, applications, user needs, and product classes.

Advertising Messages

The strategy for creating a message starts with the customer benefits a product offers and moves to the creative concept phase, in which marketers strive to bring an appropriate message to consumers using both visual and verbal components. Marketers work to create an ad with meaningful, believable, and distinctive appeals—one that stands out from the clutter and escapes "zapping" by the television remote control.

Usually, ads are not created individually but as part of specific campaigns. An **advertising campaign** is a series of different but related ads that use a single theme and appear in different media within a specified time period. The series of Gateway Computer ads, aimed at capturing market share from the Apple iMac, represents an advertising campaign.

In developing a creative strategy, advertisers must decide how to communicate their marketing message. They must balance message characteristics, such as the tone of the appeal, the extent of information provided and the conclusion to which it leads the consumer, the side of the story the ad tells, and its emphasis on verbal or visual primary elements.

Should the tone of the advertisement focus on a practical appeal such as price, or should it evoke an emotional response of, say, fear, humor, or fantasy? In recent years, marketers have relied increasingly on fear appeals. Ads for insurance, cars, health-care products, and even certain foods imply that incorrect buying decisions could lead to illness, injury, or other bad consequences. Even ads for business services imply that if a company doesn't purchase the advertised services, its competitors will move ahead or valuable information may be lost.

Pharmaceutical companies spend nearly $2 billion a year on advertising, much of which is directed toward consumers' fears—whether fear of hair loss, fear of allergies, or fear of heart attacks. These drug advertisements have flourished in both print and broadcast media after the Food and Drug Administration

FIGURE 18.4

Elements of the Advertising Planning Process

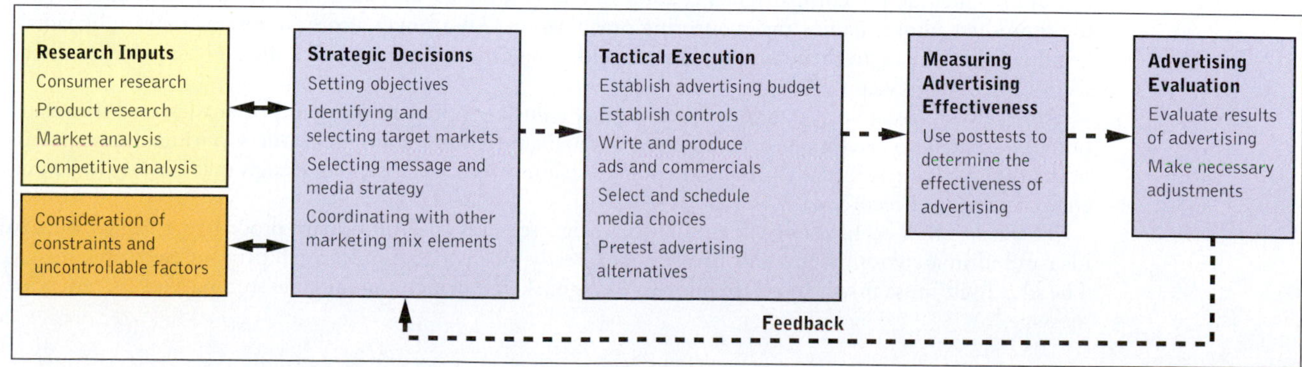

FIGURE 18.5

Elements of a Typical Ad

lifted a ban on prescription drug advertising on television. Such ads have become a key component of marketers' pulling channel strategies. Typical ads encourage readers and viewers to ask their doctors whether the medication should be prescribed for their medical needs.

Fear appeals can backfire, however. Viewers are likely to practice selective perception and tune out statements they perceive as too strong or not credible. Some analysts believe that viewer/reader backlash will eventually occur due to the amount of prescription drug advertising based on fear appeals.

A humorous ad seeks to create a positive mood related to a product. Humor can improve audience awareness and recall and enhance the consumer's favorable image of the brand. After all, if the ad makes the consumer feel good, then the product may as well. But advertising professionals differ in their opinions of the effectiveness of humorous ads. Some believe that humor distracts attention from brand and product features; consumers remember the humor but not the product. Humorous ads, because they are so memorable, may lose their effectiveness sooner than ads with other kinds of appeals. In addition, humor can be tricky because what one group of consumers finds funny may not be funny at all to another group. Men and women sometimes have a different sense of humor, as do people of different ages. This distinction may become even greater across cultures.

Developing and Preparing Ads

The final step in the advertising process—the development and preparation of an advertisement—should flow logically from the promotional theme selected. This process should create an ad that becomes a complementary part of the marketing mix with a carefully determined role in the total marketing strategy. Preparation of an advertisement should emphasize features like its creativity, its continuity with past advertisements, and possibly its association with other company products.

What immediate tasks should an advertisement accomplish? Regardless of the chosen target, an advertisement should (1) gain attention and interest, (2) inform and/or persuade, and (3) eventually lead to a purchase or other desired action. It should gain attention in a productive way; that is, it should instill some recall of the good or service. Otherwise, it will not lead to buying action.

Gaining attention and generating interest—cutting through the clutter—can be a formidable task. Stimulating buying action is often difficult because an advertisement cannot actually close a sale. Nevertheless, if an ad gains attention and informs or persuades, it probably represents a worthwhile investment of marketing resources. Too many advertisers fail to suggest how audience members can purchase their products if they desire to do so. Creative design should eliminate this shortcoming.

When Starbucks decided to expand its market by offering its premium coffee in retail stores, it developed a series of ads to inform customers of its availability in non-Starbucks outlets. The ad in Figure 18.5 shows the four major elements of this print advertisement: headline, illustration, body copy, and signature. Headlines and illustrations (photographs, drawings, or other artwork) should work together to generate interest and attention. Body copy serves to inform, persuade, and stimulate buying action. The signature, which may include the company name, address, phone number, Web address, slogan, trademark, or simply a product photo, names the sponsoring organization. An ad may also have one or more subheads—headings subordinate to the main headline that either link the main headline to the body copy or subdivide sections of the body copy.

After advertisers conceive an idea for an ad that gains attention, informs and persuades, and stimulates purchases, their next step involves refining the thought sketch into a rough layout. Continued refinements of the rough layout eventually produce the final version of the advertisement design that is ready to be executed, printed, or recorded.

The creation of each advertisement in a campaign requires an evolutionary process that begins with an idea and ultimately results in a finished ad that is ready for distribution through print or electronic media. The idea itself must first be converted into a thought sketch, which is a tangible summary of the intended message.

Advances in technology allow advertisers to create novel, eye-catching advertisements. Innovative computer software packages now allow artists to merge multiple images to create a single image with a natural, seamless appearance. Computer-generated images appeal to younger, computer-literate consumers.

Creating Interactive Ads

Web surfers want engaging, lively content that takes advantage of the medium's capabilities and goes beyond what they find elsewhere. Increasingly, Web ads are competing with television ads by enhancing their content with video and audio clips. But this orientation overlooks the Web's major advantages: offering speed, providing information, exchanging input through two-way communications, offering self-directed entertainment, and allowing personal choice.

The growing number of new ways to advertise on the Web attest to the rapidly changing environment marketers encounter on the Internet and in e-commerce in general. Web ads have grown from information-based home pages to innovative, interactive channels for transmitting messages to cyberaudiences, including banners, pop-ups, keyword ads, advertorials, and interstitials. In fact, many online ads now closely resemble television commercials.

Advertising banners were the trendsetters in online advertising, allowing customers to quickly access a company's goods and services through other Web site links. *Banners,* advertisements on a Web page that link to an advertiser's site, are the most common type of advertising on the Web. They can be free of charge or cost thousands of dollars per month depending on the amount of hits the site receives. Online advertisers often describe their Internet ads in terms of "richness," referring to the degree to which new technologies—such as streaming video, 3-D animation, Java script, and interactive capabilities—are implemented in the banners.

Banners have evolved into a more target-specific technique for Internet advertising with the advent of missiles, which are messages that appear on the screen at exactly the right moment. When a customer visits the site of Company A's competitor, a missile can be programmed to appear on the customer's monitor that allows the customer to click on a direct link to Company A's site, which many people may feel is a questionable practice.

Keyword ads are an outcropping of banner ads. Used in search engines, keyword ads appear on the results page of a search, specific to the term being searched. Advertisers pay search engines to target their ads and only display the banners when users search for relevant keywords, allowing marketers to target specific audiences. For example, if a user searched on the term "digital camera," keyword ads might appear for electronic boutiques or camera shops that sell digital cameras and film.

Banner designs that have also evolved into larger advertising squares that closely resemble advertisements in the telephone Yellow Pages are called *advertorials.* An advertorial on the *Forbes* Web site costs about $25,000 a month. Advertisers quickly expanded on these advertorials with *interstitials*—ads that appear in between Web pages of related content. Interstitials appear in a separate browser window while the user waits for a Web page to download. Then there are pop-ups, as described in the "Solving an Ethical Controversy" Interactive Example, which are little advertising windows that appear in front of the top window of a user's computer screen, and "pop-unders," which appear under the top window. All of these ads are more aggressive than banners, forcing consumers to take action to eliminate them from their screens, which is the source of controversy discussed in the Interactive Example.[10] Many users complain that interstitials, like pop-ups and missiles, are intrusive and unwanted. Interstitials are more likely to contain large graphics and streaming presentations than banner ads and therefore are more difficult to ignore than typical banner ads. And despite complaints, some studies show that users are more likely to click on interstitials than banners.

RIGHT/WRONG: SOLVING AN ETHICAL CONTROVERSY—WHAT TO DO ABOUT POP-UP ADS?

Web site developers can now add 3-D effects to their sites, a capability that provides new opportunities for advertisers. For example, graphics can show products in lifelike representations. Retailers can create 3-D stores where visitors can take a stroll through the virtual aisles viewing merchandise on display; Web sites need no longer provide their information in cataloglike formats.

MEDIA SELECTION

One of the most important decisions in developing an advertising strategy is the selection of appropriate media to carry a firm's message to its audience. The media selected must be capable of accomplishing the communications objectives of informing, persuading, and reminding potential customers of the good, service, person, or idea being advertised.

<interactive>**learning goal**

CHAPTER OBJECTIVE #4: LIST AND COMPARE THE MAJOR ADVERTISING MEDIA.

Research identifies the ad's target market to determine its size and characteristics. Advertisers then match the target characteristics with the media best able to reach that particular audience. The objective of media selection is to achieve adequate media coverage without advertising beyond the identifiable limits of the potential market. Finally, cost comparisons between alternatives should determine the best possible media purchase.

Table 18.1 compares the major advertising media by noting their shares of overall advertising expenditures. It also compares the advantages and disadvantages of each media alternative. *Broadcast media* include television (network and cable) and radio. Newspapers, magazines, outdoor advertising, and direct mail represent the major types of print media. Electronic media include the Internet and kiosks.

Television

Television—network and cable combined—accounts for almost one of every four advertising dollars spent in the U.S. The attractiveness of television advertising is that marketers can reach local and national markets. Whereas most newspaper advertising revenues come from local advertisers, the greatest share of tele-

TABLE 18.1

Comparison of Advertising Media Alternatives

MEDIA OUTLET	PERCENTAGE OF TOTAL*	ADVANTAGES	DISADVANTAGES
Broadcast			
Network television	17	Mass coverage; repetition; flexibility; prestige	High cost; temporary message; public distrust; lack of selectivity
Cable television	8	Same strengths as network TV; less market coverage since not every viewer is a cable subscriber	Same disadvantages as network, TV, although cable TV ads are considerably more targeted to specific viewer segments
Radio	8	Immediacy; low cost; flexibility; targeted audience; mobility	Short life span; highly fragmented audience
Print			
Newspapers	19	Tailored to individual communities; ability to refer back to ads	Short life span
Direct mail	19	Selectivity; intense coverage; speed; flexibility; opportunity to convey complete information; personalization	High cost; consumer resistance; dependence on effective mailing list
Magazines	5	Selectivity; quality image reproduction; long life; prestige	Lack of flexibility
Outdoor	2	Quick, visual communication of simple ideas; link to local goods and services; repetition	Brief exposure; environmental concerns
Electronic			
Internet	3	Two-way communications; flexibility; link to self-directed entertainment	Poor image reproduction; limited scheduling options; difficult to measure effectiveness

*An estimated 20 percent is spent on a variety of miscellaneous media, including Yellow Pages listings, business papers, transit displays, point-of-purchase displays, cinema advertising, and regional farm papers.
Source: Data from "Advertising Boom in U.S. Ended in '01," *Advertising Age*, May 13, 2002, p. 24.

vision advertising revenues comes from companies that advertise nationally. The newest trend in television advertising is virtual ads—banner-type logos and brief messages that are superimposed onto television coverage of sporting events so that they seem to be a part of the arena's signage but cannot be seen by anyone attending the game. Then there are streaming headlines run by some news stations, which are paid for by corporate sponsors whose names and logos appear within the news stream. Another trend in television advertising is the abbreviated spot—15- and 30-second spots—that costs less to make and buy and is too quick for most viewers to zap with their remote controls.

In the past decade, cable television's share of ad spending and revenues has grown tremendously. Satellite television has contributed to increased cable penetration, which almost three-fourths of all Americans now have installed in their homes. In response to declining ratings and soaring costs, network television companies like NBC, CBS, ABC, Fox, and Warner Bros. (WB) are refocusing their advertising strategies with a heavy emphasis on moving onto the Net to capture younger audiences.

As cable audiences grow, programming improves, and ratings rise, advertisers are compelled to earmark more of their advertising budgets to this medium. In fact, cable was the only advertising medium—other than direct mail—to actually grow in the advertising downturn that accompanied the recent recession.[11] Cable advertising offers marketers access to more narrowly defined target audiences than other broadcast media can provide. The great variety of special-interest channels devoted to subjects such as cooking, history, home and garden, health, and golf attract specialized audiences and permit niche marketing.

Television advertising offers the advantages of powerful impact, mass coverage, repetition of messages, flexibility, and prestige, as described in the "Marketing Hits" Interactive Example about Monster.com. Its disadvantages include loss of control of the promotional message to the telecaster (which can influence its impact), high costs, high mortality rates for commercials, and some public distrust. Compared with other media, television can suffer from lack of selectivity since specific TV programs may not reach consumers in a precisely defined target market without a significant degree of wasted coverage. However, the growing specialization of cable TV channels can help to resolve the problem.

MARKETING HIT: MONSTER.COM DOES A GOOD JOB ADVERTISING

Finally, it is important to note that some types of products are actually banned from television advertising. Tobacco goods, such as cigarettes, cigars, and smokeless tobacco, fall into this category. Ads for alcoholic beverages are not allowed on network television, but companies such as Anheuser-Busch have done very well with their commercials on cable channels and independent stations permitting them.

Radio

Radio advertising has always been a popular media choice for up-to-the-minute newscasts and for targeting advertising messages to local audiences. But in recent years, radio has become one of the fastest growing media alternatives. As more and more people find they have less and less time, radio provides immediate information and entertainment at work, at play, and in the car. In addition, as e-commerce continues to push the growth in global business, more people are traveling abroad to seek out new markets. For these travelers, radio, because many radio stations are airing over the Internet, is a means of staying in touch with home—wherever that may be. Marketers frequently use radio advertising to reach local audiences. But in recent years, it plays an increasingly important role as a national—and even global—listening favorite. Thousands of online listeners use the Internet to beam in on radio stations from almost every city—tuning in on an easy- listening station in London, a top-40 Hong Kong broadcaster, or a chat show from Toronto. Other listeners equip their vehicles with satellite radio to maintain contact with hometown or destination stations during long trips.

Radio ad revenues in the U.S. are slightly larger than those for cable television. Advertisers like the chance to reach people while they drive because they are a captive audience. With an increase in commuters, this market is growing. Stations can adapt to local preferences by changing format, such as going from country and western to an all-news or rock-and-talk radio. The variety of stations allows advertisers to easily target audiences and to tailor their messages to those listeners. Other benefits include low cost, flexibility, and mobility. Disadvantages include fragmentation, the temporary nature of messages, and a lack of research information as compared with television.

While most radio listening is done at home, in cars, or with headset-equipped portables, technology has given birth to Net radio. Web-cast radio allows customers to widen their listening times and choices through their computers. The potential for selling on this new channel is great. A listener can simply "click here to purchase the song you're hearing." Other goods are easily adapted to click-and-sell possibilities.

Newspapers

Newspaper advertising continues to dominate local markets, accounting for $44 billion of annual advertising expenditures. In addition to retail advertisements, classified advertising is an important part of newspaper revenues.

Newspapers' primary advantages start with flexibility because advertising can vary from one locality to the next. Newspapers offer community prestige since readers recognize they have deep impacts on their communities. "Newspapers provide the kind of touch points for people to get the depth behind the broad premise laid out in other media," says Chris Wall, creative director for ad agency Ogilvy & Mather. "Creative people have always liked newspapers. And newspapers have gotten much better technology in the past fifteen years."[12] Newspapers allow intensive coverage for ads. In a typical location, a single newspaper reaches 90 percent of the homes. "One thing we know is that media you can target geographically should do better," observes Jon Mandel, comanaging director of MediaCom. "The closer you can get to the point of sale, especially in a recessionary environment, the better off you're going to be."[13] Readers control their exposure to the advertising message, unlike television or radio advertising messages, and can refer back to newspaper ads.

According to a survey by the Newspaper Association of America and the American Society of Newspapers, consumers rely on newspapers as their primary source of advertising information for a variety of goods and services. Survey participants reported referring to newspapers for information on new cars 52 percent of the time (compared with television 15 percent of the time). Consumers shopping for home appliances also favor newspapers over television (53 percent versus 10 percent), as well as those looking for personal computers (37 percent versus 8 percent).[14]

Newspaper advertising does have some disadvantages: a short life span, hasty reading (the typical reader spends about 40 minutes reading the newspaper), and relatively poor reproduction quality, although that is changing as technology improves.

Magazines

Advertisers divide magazines into two broad categories: consumer magazines and business magazines. These categories are also subdivided into monthly and weekly publications. The four top magazines in the U.S. in order of their ad revenue ranking are *TV Guide, People, Sports Illustrated,* and *Time.* Of these four, only *TV Guide* is not owned by AOL Time Warner.

The primary advantages of magazine advertising include the following: selectivity in reaching precise target markets, quality reproduction, long life, the prestige associated with some magazines, and the extra services that many publications offer. The primary disadvantage is that magazines lack the flexibility of newspapers, radio, and television.

Media buyers study circulation numbers and demographics information for various publications to choose placement opportunities and to negotiate rates. The same advertising categories have claimed the title for big spenders for several years running. Automotive, retail, and movies and media advertising have held their first, second, and third places, respectively, each year and have continued to show strong growth percentages. Advertisers seeking to promote their products to target markets can reach them by advertising in the appropriate magazines.

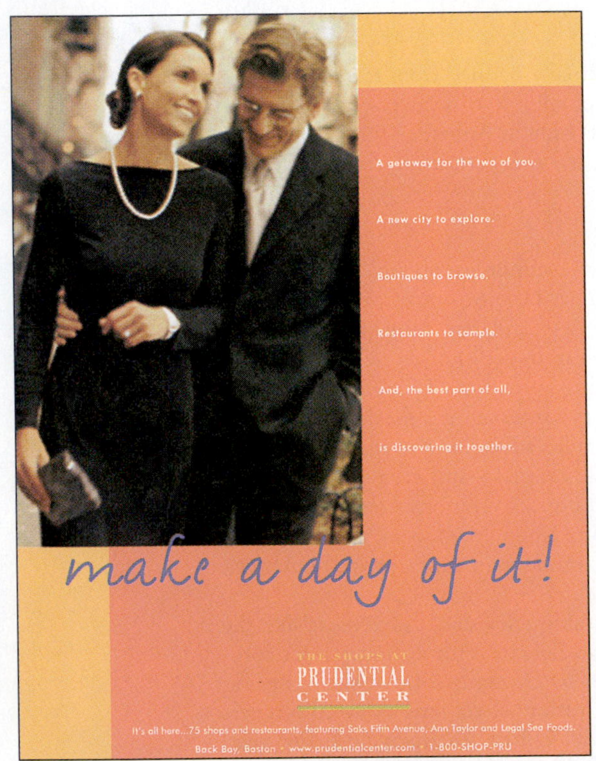

A getaway for the two of you.
A new city to explore.
Boutiques to browse.
Restaurants to sample.
And, the best part of all,
is discovering it together.
make a day of it!
THE SHOPS AT
PRUDENTIAL
CENTER
It's all here...75 shops and restaurants, featuring Saks Fifth Avenue, Ann Taylor and Legal Sea Foods.
Back Bay, Boston • www.prudentialcenter.com • 1-800-SHOP-PRU

Marketers for The Shops at Prudential Center, Boston's upscale high-fashion group of 75 shops and restaurants, pooled their advertising media dollars and selected Yankee Magazine for their advertisement. The magazine, widely circulated in New England, enjoys a readership of affluent consumers residing in the Northeast.

Direct Mail

As discussed in Chapter 16, direct mail advertising consists of sales letters, postcards, leaflets, folders, booklets, catalogs, and house organs (periodicals published by organizations to cover internal issues). Its advantages come from direct mail's selectivity, intensive coverage, speed, formal flexibility, completeness of information, and personalization. Disadvantages of direct mail include high cost per reader, dependence on the quality of mailing lists, and some consumers' resistance to it.

The advantages of direct mail explain its widespread use. Although nearly half of the direct mail sent to consumers is discarded immediately, Americans spend about $200 billion each year from these promotions. Data are available on previous purchase patterns and preferred payment methods, as well as household characteristics such as number of children or seniors. Direct mail accounts for about 19 percent of total advertising expenditures.[15]

The downside to direct mail is clutter, otherwise known as junk mail. So much advertising material is stuffed into people's mailboxes every day that the task of grabbing consumers' attention and evoking some interest is daunting to direct mail advertisers. Three of every five respondents to a survey about "things most likely to get on consumers' nerves" rated junk mail at the top—above telemarketing, credit-card fees, and the fine print on billing statements.

Outdoor Advertising

Outdoor advertising, perhaps the oldest and simplest media business around, represents just over 2 percent of total advertising spending.[16] Traditional outdoor advertising takes the form of billboards, painted bulletins or displays (such as those that appear on the walls of buildings), and electric spectaculars (large, illuminated, and sometimes animated signs and displays). But advertisers are finding new places to put their messages outdoors. You might find an advertising message stenciled guerilla-style on the base of a traffic light or the back of a park bench. A section of highway might be mowed and cleaned up by a local real estate company or restaurant, with a sign implanted where passersby can easily see it. All of these are outgrowths of outdoor advertising. Ironically, the Internet has breathed new life into outdoor advertising. "All the clutter online has actually created a huge push for more and more billboards," comments Diane Cimini, executive vice president for marketing at the Outdoor Advertising Association of America.[17]

This form of advertising has the advantages of immediate communication of quick and simple ideas, repeated exposure to a message, and strong promotion for locally available products. Outdoor advertising is particularly effective along metropolitan streets and in other high-traffic areas.

But outdoor advertising, just like every other type, is subject to clutter.[18] It also suffers from the brevity of exposure to its messages by passing motorists. Driver concerns about rush-hour safety and limited time also combine to limit the length of exposure to outdoor messages. As a result, most such ads use striking, simple illustrations, short selling points, and humor to attract people interested in products like beer, vacations, local entertainment, and lodging. As Figure 18.6 shows, Diamond Trading Companies marketers decided the affluent New York commuter market represented a good target market for their firm's diamonds and used billboards to deliver this message.

A third problem involves public concern over aesthetics. The Highway Beautification Act of 1965, for example, regulates the placement of outdoor advertising near interstate highways. In addition, many cities have local ordinances that set regulations on the size and placement of outdoor advertising messages. Critics have even labeled billboard advertising as "pollution on a stick."

New technologies are helping to revive outdoor advertising, offsetting the huge drop that resulted from limitations on ads for tobacco and alcohol products. Technology livens up the billboards themselves with animation, large sculptures, and laser images. Digital message signboards can display winning lottery numbers or other timely messages like weather and traffic reports. The best-known digital signboard in the U.S. is in New York's Times Square. And very soon, certain billboards will be able to "beam" messages to consumers' cell phones as they drive past.

France spends the greatest amount on outdoor advertising—nearly 12 percent of total ad spending, compared with 6 percent for Europe as a whole and 4 percent for the U.S. But recent changes in advertising policy brought about by the European Union may disallow France's ban on TV advertising, which could shift revenues away from outdoor advertising. Retailers in France are eagerly awaiting the outcome.[19]

FIGURE 18.6

Outdoor Advertising for a Luxury Product

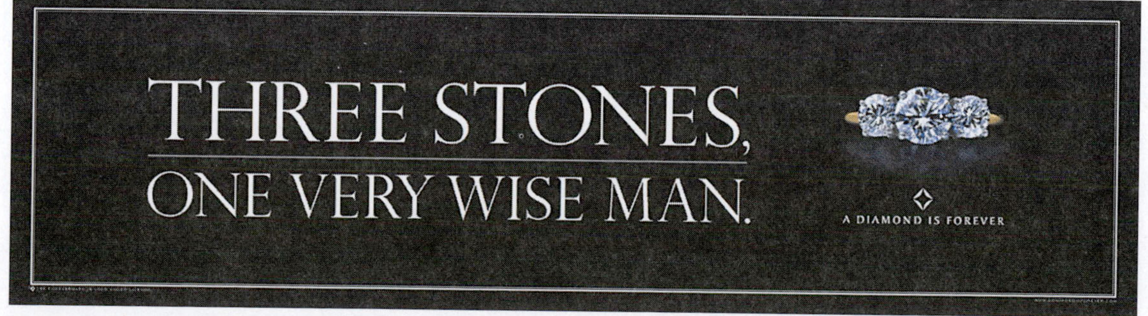

THREE STONES,
ONE VERY WISE MAN.
A DIAMOND IS FOREVER

Interactive Media

Interactive media—especially the Internet—are growing up. A recent survey conducted by the Online Publishers Association revealed that 57 percent of consumers prefer to find out about new products online, 43 percent report that the Internet contains advertising that is rich in information, and 42 percent feel that online advertising helps them decide what products to buy.[20] Not surprisingly, interactive advertising budgets are being beefed up at a growing number of companies. Five years ago, Adidas America viewed online advertising as nothing more than static banner ads, allocating a mere 2 percent of its total marketing budget to online ads. Today, however, Adidas is changing its strategy to increase its customer base via the Internet. Competing shoemaker Reebok is currently spending 10 to 15 percent more on online advertising than it did two years ago. At AT&T, online advertising spending has reached nearly 10 percent of the company's total advertising budget. "We've learned how to better use the medium," says Jeff Bauer, media director for AT&T Business. "We're moving beyond the banner and placing greater emphasis on interactivity with the creative message." By 2005, total online advertising is expected to hit $14 billion.[21]

Other Advertising Media

As consumers filter out appeals from traditional as well as Internet ads, marketers need new ways to catch their attention. In addition to the major media, firms use a vast number of other vehicles to communicate their messages. Transit advertising includes ads placed both inside and outside buses, subway trains and stations, and commuter trains. Some firms place ads on the roofs of taxicabs, on bus stop shelters and benches, on entertainment and sporting event turnstiles, in public restrooms, and even on parking meters. About half of the 23,000 U.S. movie theaters accept commercials. Movie-theater ads have proved especially effective for targeting young people aged 12 to 24 years.

Ads also appear on T-shirts, inlaid in store flooring, in printed programs of live-theater productions, and as previews on movie videocassettes. Directory advertising includes the familiar Yellow Pages in telephone books, along with thousands of business and industry directories. Some firms pay to have their advertising messages placed on hot-air balloons, blimps, banners behind airplanes, and on scoreboards at sporting events. Other companies have their own advertising vehicles, called mobile marketing squads. Yahoo! and Dreyer's Grand Ice Cream pay to have their logos placed on autos via a San Francisco–based company called Autowraps. Autowraps then hires drivers based on their regular driving routes and occupations, paying them a monthly fee for the use of the outside of their vehicles as advertising space. Shopping bags have long been great spots for advertising retail stores, but now the space is for sale. "With bagvertising, we place your company name, logo or Web address on minimum orders of 100,000 paper bags that we give away to about 500 stores," explains Moses Abughosh, president of Smart Bags.[22]

MEDIA SCHEDULING

Once advertisers have selected the media that best match their advertising objectives and promotional budget, attention shifts to *media scheduling*—setting the timing and sequence for a series of advertisements. A variety of factors influence this decision as well. Sales patterns, repurchase cycles, and competitors' activities are the most important variables.

Seasonal sales patterns are common in many industries. An airline might reduce advertising during peak travel periods and boost its media schedule during low travel months. Repurchase cycles may also play a role in media scheduling—products with shorter repurchase cycles will more likely require consistent media schedules throughout the year. Competitors' activities are still other influences on media scheduling. A small firm may avoid advertising during periods of heavy advertising by its rivals.

Advertisers use the concepts of reach, frequency, and gross rating points to measure the effectiveness of media scheduling plans. *Reach* refers to the number of different people or households exposed to an advertisement at least once during a certain time period, typically four weeks. *Frequency* refers to the number of times an individual person is exposed to an advertisement during a certain time period. By multiplying reach times frequency, advertisers quantitatively describe the total weight of a media effort, which is called the campaign's *gross rating point.*

Recently, marketers have questioned the effectiveness of reach and frequency to measure ad success online. The theory behind frequency is that the average advertising viewer needs a minimum of three exposures to a message to get it. For Web surfers, the "wear-out" is much quicker, hence the greater importance of building customer relationships through advertisements.

A media schedule is typically created in the following way. Say an auto manufacturer wants to advertise a new model designed primarily to appeal to professional consumers in their 30s. The model would be introduced in November with a direct mail piece offering test drives. Outdoor, newspaper, and magazine advertising would support the direct mail campaign but also follow through the winter and into the spring and summer. The newspaper ads might actually be cooperative, for both the manufacturer and local dealers. Early television commercials might air during a holiday television special in mid-December, and then one or more expensively produced, highly creative spots would be first aired during the Super Bowl in late

January. Another television commercial—along with new print ads—might be scheduled for fall clearance sales as the manufacturer gets ready to introduce next year's models. This example illustrates how marketers might plan their advertising year for just one product.

ORGANIZATION OF THE ADVERTISING FUNCTION

Although the ultimate responsibility for advertising decision making often rests with top marketing management, organizational arrangements for the advertising function vary among companies. A producer of a technical industrial product may interact with one person within the company, who works primarily to write copy for submission to trade publications. A consumer goods company, on the other hand, may staff a large department with advertising specialists.

<interactive>**learning goal**

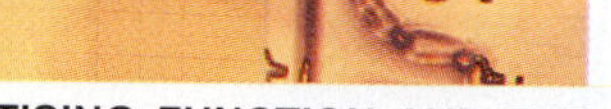

CHAPTER OBJECTIVE #5: OUTLINE THE ORGANIZATION OF THE ADVERTISING FUNCTION AND THE ROLE OF AN ADVERTISING AGENCY.

The advertising function is usually organized as a staff department reporting to the vice president (or director) of marketing. The director of advertising is an executive position with the responsibility for the functional activity of advertising. This position requires not only a skilled and experienced advertiser but also an individual who communicates effectively within the organization. The success of a firm's promotional strategy depends on the advertising director's willingness and ability to communicate both vertically and horizontally. The major tasks typically organized under advertising include advertising research, design, copywriting, media analysis, and in some cases, sales and trade promotion.

Advertising Agencies

Most large companies in industries characterized by large advertising expenditures will hire an independent **advertising agency,** a firm whose marketing specialists assist advertisers in planning and preparing advertisements. Advertising is a huge, global industry. Ranked by worldwide gross income, Japan's Dentsu is the world's largest advertising agency. McCann-Erickson Worldwide, based in New York, is second largest.[23]

Most large advertisers cite several reasons for relying on agencies for at least some portion of their advertising. Agencies typically employ highly qualified specialists who provide a degree of creativity and objectivity that is difficult to sustain in a corporate advertising department. Some also manage to reduce the cost of advertising by allowing the advertiser to avoid many of the fixed expenses associated with maintaining an internal advertising department.

Figure 18.7 shows a hypothetical organization chart for a large advertising agency. Although job titles may vary among agencies, the major functions may be classified as creative services; account services; marketing services, including media services, marketing research, and sales promotion; and finance and management.

SALES PROMOTION

Sales promotion, those marketing activities other than personal selling, advertising, and publicity that enhance consumer purchasing and dealer effectiveness, accounts for double the promotional dollar outlays of advertising. Like advertising, these activities trace their roots to the far reaches of antiquity. Examples of both sales promotion and advertising have been found among the ruins of Pompeii and Ephesus. In the U.S., Adolphus Busch gave away samples of his beer and a pocket knife as a premium in 1880. Ten years later, Procter & Gamble exchanged watch-chain charms for Ivory soap wrappers. In 1895, Grape Nuts cereal marketers were the first to offer a coupon on the box (for a one-cent discount off the purchase price), and in 1914, Ford Motor Co. offered a rebate of $50 for each $490 Model T. Marketers spend over $250 billion annually on such consumer and trade sales promotion activities as coupons, sampling, displays, trade shows and exhibitions, demonstrations, and various nonrecurrent promotional efforts.

<interactive>**learning goal**

CHAPTER OBJECTIVE #6: IDENTIFY THE PRINCIPAL METHODS OF SALES PROMOTION.

FIGURE 18.7

Advertising Agency Organizational Chart

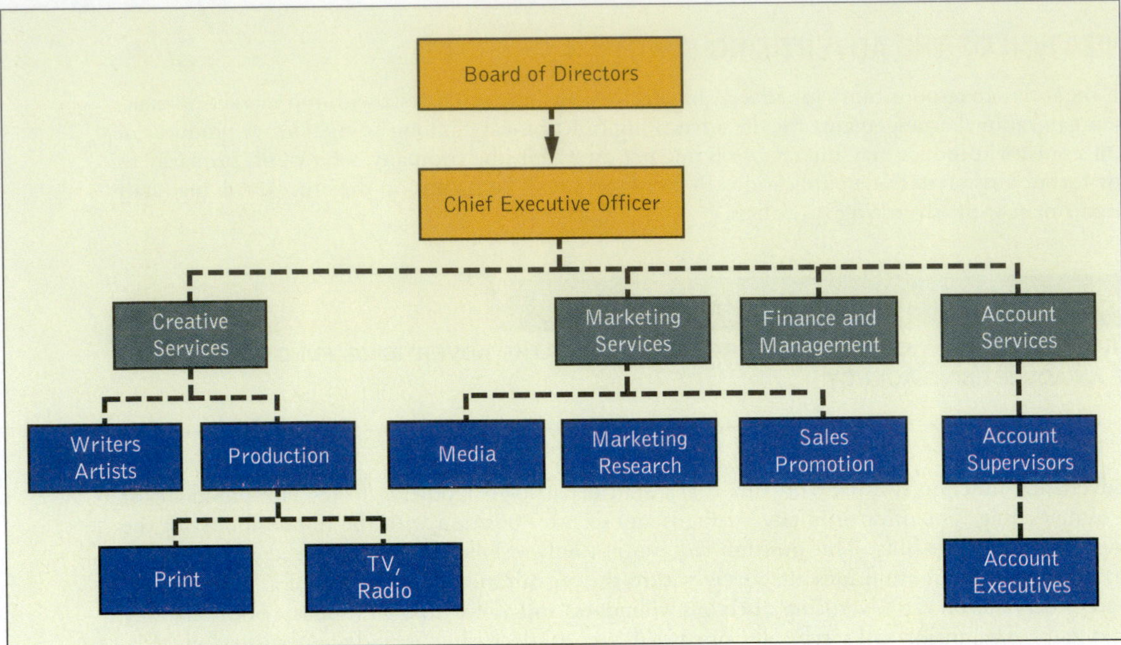

Sales promotion techniques were originally intended as short-term incentives aimed at producing immediate consumer buying responses. Traditionally, these techniques were viewed as supplements to other elements of the firm's promotional mix. Today, however, marketers recognize them as integral parts of many marketing plans, and the focus of sales promotion has shifted from short-term to long-term goals of building brand equity and maintaining continuing purchases. A frequent-flyer program enables an airline to build a base of loyal customers where it had none before. A frequent-stay program allows a chain of hotels to attract regular guests.

Both retailers and manufacturers use sales promotions to offer consumers extra incentives to buy. Rather than emphasizing product features to make consumers feel good about their purchases, these promotions are likely to stress price advantages. The general objectives of sales promotion are to speed up the sales process and increase sales volume. Through a consumer promotion, a marketer encourages consumers to try the product, use more of it, and buy it again. The firm also hopes to foster sales of complementary products and increase impulse purchases.

Because sales promotion is so important to a marketing effort, an entire promotion industry exists to offer expert assistance in its use, just as an entire advertising industry offers similar services for advertisers. These companies, like advertising agencies, provide other firms with assistance in promoting their goods and services.

Sales promotion complements advertising, and marketers often produce their best results when they combine the two. Ads create awareness, while sales promotions lead to trial or purchase. Promotions encourage immediate action because they impose limited time frames. For example, cents-off coupons and rebates have expiration dates. In addition, sales promotions produce measurable results, making it relatively easy for marketers to evaluate their effectiveness.

It is important to understand what sales promotions can and cannot do. They can encourage interest from salespeople and consumers for both new and mature products, help introduce new products, encourage trial and repeat purchases, increase usage, neutralize competition, and reinforce advertising. On the other hand, sales promotions cannot overcome poor brand images, product deficiencies, or poor training for salespeople. While sales promotions increase volume in the short term, they often lead to lower profits.

Sales promotion techniques may serve all members of a marketing channel. In addition, manufacturers may use trade promotion methods to promote their products to resellers. A single promotional strategy may combine more than one option, but probably no promotional strategy has ever used all of them in a single program. While the different types are not mutually exclusive, promotions generally are employed selectively. Sales promotion techniques include the following consumer-oriented promotions: samples, bonus packs, premiums, coupons, price-off deals, refunds, contests, sweepstakes, and specialty advertising. Trade-oriented promotions include trade allowances, point-of-purchase advertising, trade shows, dealer incentives, and training programs.

Consumer-Oriented Sales Promotions

In the $85 billion promotion industry, marketers use all types of sales promotions, including games, contests, sweepstakes, and coupons to persuade new and existing customers to try their products. Consumer-oriented sales promotions encourage repurchases by rewarding current users, boosting sales of complementary products, and increasing impulse purchases. These promotions also attract consumer attention in the midst of advertising clutter. Table 18.2 lists the most popular consumer promotion techniques for firms using this element of the promotional mix.

TABLE 18.2

Seven Most Popular Consumer Promotion Techniques

TECHNIQUE	PERCENTAGE OF MARKETERS WHO USE IT
Coupons in retail ads	90
In-store coupons	88
Refunds	85
Electronic in-store displays	83
Samples of established products	78
Premiums	75
Sweepstakes	70

It's important for marketers to use sales promotions selectively because if they are overused, consumers begin to expect price discounts, which ultimately diminish brand equity. The following sections briefly describe the various forms of consumer-oriented sales promotions.

Coupons and Refunds *Coupons,* the most widely used form of sales promotion, offer discounts on the purchase price of goods and services. Consumers can redeem the coupons at retail outlets, which receive a handling fee from the manufacturer. The $5 billion coupon industry has been somewhat clipped in recent years due to more complex accounting rules that make couponing less attractive to some marketers, as well as the growing clout of retailers. But coupons are still popular among consumers and many marketers, who allocate roughly 15 percent of their marketing budgets to the practice. Although nearly 300 billion coupons are issued in a typical year, fewer than 5 billion are actually redeemed.[24]

Mail, magazines, newspapers, package insertions, and increasingly, the Internet are the standard methods of distributing coupons. Free-standing inserts (FSIs) in certain magazines and Sunday newspapers account for nearly 75 percent of all coupons distributed. In one recent year, Kraft Foods launched a magazine-style FSI, called *Food and Family,* distributed by NewsAmerica and Meredith Publishing. The insert was dropped in nationally to newspapers each month and contained eight pages of recipes, tips on food storage and serving, and family-friendly tips or other information that featured Kraft brands such as Oscar Mayer, Kraft Macaroni & Cheese, and Post cereals. The first insert carried six coupons from such brands as Tombstone pizza, DiGiorno pasta, and Minute Rice. "We wanted to do something that stands out [and carries] our equity message of helping families connect over food," explained Wendy Kritt, director of corporate and consumer promotions.[25]

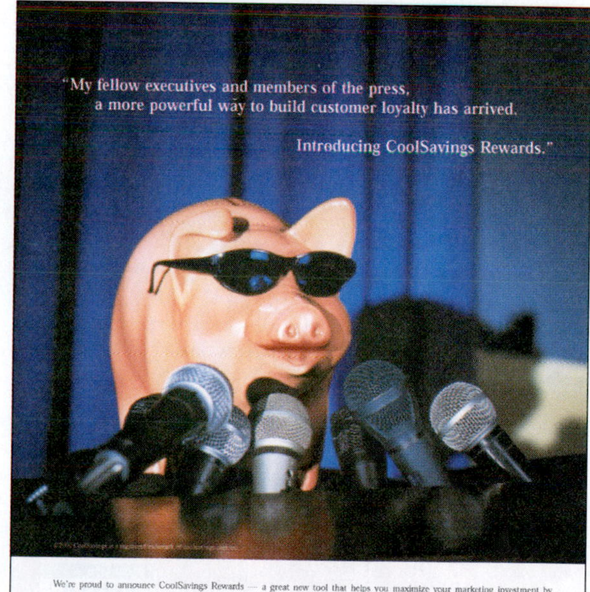

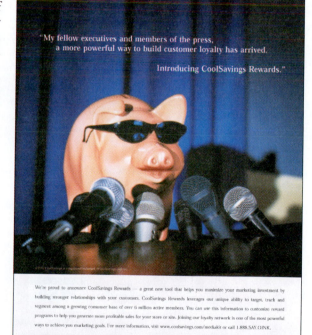

Shoppers seeking coupons can turn to such Web sites as CoolSavings.com, where they can access and print out coupons and be linked to sites of the manufacturer or retailer.

Refunds, or rebates, offer cash back to consumers who send in proof of purchasing one or more products. Refunds help packaged goods companies to increase purchase rates, promote multiple purchases, and reward product users. Although many consumers find the refund forms too bothersome to complete, plenty still take the time and energy to do so. "Rebates are tried and true," says Roy Spencer, general manager of the Promotion Fulfillment Center. Computer hardware, software, and sporting goods companies have been increasing their rebate programs in recent years.[26]

Samples, Bonus Packs, and Premiums Marketers are increasingly adopting the "try it, you'll like it" approach as an effective means of getting consumers to try and then purchase their goods and services. *Sampling* refers to the free distribution of a product in an attempt to obtain future sales. Samples may be distributed door-to-door, by mail, via demonstrations in stores or at events, or by including them in packages with other products.

Sampling produces a higher response rate than most other promotions. About three-quarters of the consumers who receive samples try them, and total annual spending on this sales promotion technique has reached $1.12 billion.[27] A recent survey showed that

92 percent of consumers preferred receiving free samples rather than coupons. With sampling, marketers can target potential customers and be certain that the product reaches them. Sampling provides an especially useful way to promote new or unusual products because it gives the consumer a direct product experience.

One of the disadvantages of sampling is the high cost. Not only must the marketer give away small quantities of a product that might otherwise have generated revenues through regular sales, but the market is also, in effect, closed for the time it takes consumers to use up the samples. In addition, the marketer may encounter problems in distributing the samples. Hellman's marketers annoyed consumers instead of pleasing them when the firm distributed sample packets of Italian and French salad dressing in home-delivered copies of *The New York Times*. Many of the packets burst when the papers hit the driveways.

A *bonus pack* is a specially packaged item that gives the purchaser a larger quantity at the regular price. For instance, Camay soap offered three bars for the price of two, and Salon Selectives often increases the size of its shampoos and conditioners for the same price as regular sizes.

Premiums are items given free or at reduced cost with purchases of other products. For example, Pantene frequently attaches a purse-size bottle of hairspray to the sides of its other hair-care products. Premiums have proven effective in motivating consumers to try new products or different brands. A premium should have some relationship with the product or brand it accompanies, though. A home-improvement center might offer free nail aprons to its customers, for example.

Contests and Sweepstakes Firms often sponsor contests and sweepstakes to introduce new goods and services and to attract additional customers. *Contests* require entrants to solve problems or write essays, and they may also require proofs of purchase. A recent contest by Irish brewer Guinness gave a pub in Ireland to the author of a winning essay. *Sweepstakes,* on the other hand, choose winners by chance, so no product purchase is necessary. They are more popular with consumers than contests because they do not take as much effort for consumers to enter. Marketers like them, too, because they are inexpensive to run and the number of winners is predetermined. With some contests, the sponsors cannot predict the number of people who will correctly complete the puzzles or gather the right number of symbols from scratch-off cards.

Not surprisingly, contests and sweepstakes have become more sophisticated and creative with the advent of the Internet. The mall-based hat retailer Lids came up with a promotion in which customers received a special game piece with their receipts each time they bought a hat. Then they went home to their computers, logged on to lids.com, and held the game piece up to the computer screen to see if they'd won a prize.[28] With the recent rash of court rulings and legal restrictions, the use of contests requires careful administration. Any firm contemplating using this promotional technique should engage the services of online promotion specialists such as WebStakes or NetStakes.

A recent Visa sales promotion contest offering cardholders a chance to win free purchases by using their Visa cards. Every time cardholders used their Visa cards for a purchase, they were automatically entered in the contest.

Specialty Advertising The origin of specialty advertising has been traced to the Middle Ages, when artisans gave wooden pegs bearing their names to prospects, who drove them into the walls at home to serve as convenient hangers for armor. In more modern times, corporations began putting their names on a variety of products in the late 1800s, as newspapers and print shops looked for ways to make more money from their presses.

Specialty advertising is a sales promotion technique that places the advertiser's name, address, and advertising message on useful articles that are then distributed to target consumers. Marketers give out more than $8 billion worth of specialty advertising items each year. Wearable products, including T-shirts, baseball caps, and jackets, are the most popular products, accounting for nearly a third of distributor sales. Writing instruments, glassware, and calendars are other popular forms of specialty advertising.

Advertising specialties help to reinforce previous or future advertising and sales messages. Consumers like these giveaways, which generate stronger responses to direct mail, resulting in three times the dollar volume of sales compared with direct mail alone. Companies use this form of promotion to highlight store openings and new products, motivate salespeople, increase visits to trade show booths, and improve customer relationships.

Trade-Oriented Promotions

Sales promotion techniques can also contribute effectively to campaigns aimed at such channel members as retailers and wholesalers. *Trade promotion* is sales promotion that appeals to marketing intermediaries rather than to consumers. Marketers use trade promotion in push strategies by encouraging resellers to stock new products, continue to carry existing ones, and promote both effectively to consumers. As discussed earlier, the typical firm actually spends half of its promotional budget on trade promotion—as much money as it spends on advertising and consumer-oriented sales promotions combined. Successful trade promotions offer financial incentives. They require careful timing and attention to costs and are easy to implement by retailers. These promotions should bring quick results and improve retail sales.

Trade Allowances Among the most common trade promotion methods are *trade allowances*—special financial incentives offered to wholesalers and retailers that purchase or promote specific products. These offers take various forms. A *buying allowance* gives retailers a discount on goods. They include *off-invoice allowances* through which retailers deduct specified amounts from their invoices or receive free goods, such as one free case for every ten ordered, when they order certain quantities. When a manufacturer offers a *promotional allowance,* it agrees to pay the reseller a certain amount to cover the costs of special promotional displays or extensive advertising that features the manufacturer's product. The goal is to increase sales to consumers by encouraging resellers to promote effectively.

As mentioned in previous chapters, some retailers require vendors to pay a special slotting allowance before they agree to take on new products. These fees guarantee so-called slots, or shelf space, in the stores for new items. This practice is common in large supermarket chains. Retailers defend these fees as essential to cover the added costs of carrying the products, such as redesigning display space and shelves, setting up and administering control systems, managing inventory, and taking the risks inherent in stocking new products. The fees can be sizable, from several hundred dollars per store to many thousands of dollars for a retail chain and millions of dollars for nationally distributed products. Naturally, this puts smaller food manufacturers at a disadvantage. The controversy has resulted in recent congressional inquiries to determine whether they constitute unfair methods of competition.

Point-of-Purchase Advertising A display or other promotion located near the site of the actual buying decision is known as **point-of-purchase (POP) advertising.** This method of sales promotion capitalizes on the fact that buyers make many purchase decisions within the store, so it encourages retailers to improve on-site merchandising. They directly benefit the retailer by creating special displays designed to stimulate sales of the item being promoted.

Free-standing POP promotions often appear at the ends of shopping aisles. On a typical trip to the supermarket, you might see a POP display for Disney videos, sunscreen, or Kodak film. Warehouse-style retailers such as Home Depot and Sam's Club, along with Staples and Wal-Mart, all use POP advertising displays frequently. Electronic kiosks, which allow consumers to place orders for items not available in the store, have begun to transform the POP display industry, as creators of these displays look for ways to involve consumers more actively as well as entertain them.[29]

Trade Shows To influence resellers and other members of the distribution channel, many marketers participate in *trade shows.* These shows are often organized by industry trade associations, perhaps as part of these associations' annual meetings or conventions. Vendors who serve the industries are invited to appear at the shows to display and demonstrate their products for members. Every year, over 4,300 different shows in the U.S. and Canada draw more than 1.3 million exhibitors and 85 million attendees. One of the biggest trade shows is Comdex, the information technology show held in Las Vegas each November. Roughly 220,000 people attend the show. Each year, workers arrange 7,000 chairs, lay enough carpet to cover 21 football fields, and hang 2,500 banners around town advertising Comdex. At the opening gala, Microsoft CEO Bill Gates delivers his "state of the industry" speech. The following day, corporate executives, electronics manufacturers, and computer resellers pour through the display aisles evaluating 10,000 new products offered by the show's 2,100 exhibitors.

Because of the expense involved in trade shows like Comdex, a company must assess the value of such a show on several criteria, such as direct sales, any increase in product awareness, image building, and any contribution to the firm's marketing communications efforts. Trade shows give especially effective opportunities to introduce new products and to generate sales leads. Some types of shows reach ultimate consumers as well as channel members. Home, recreation, and automobile shows, for instance, allow businesses to display and demonstrate home improvement, recreation, and other consumer products to entire communities.

Dealer Incentives, Contests, and Training Programs Manufacturers run dealer incentive programs and contests to induce retailers and their salespeople to increase sales and to promote products. These channel members receive incentives for performing promotion-related tasks and can win contests by reaching sales goals. Manufacturers may offer major prizes to resellers such as trips to exotic places. *Push money* is another incentive that gives retail salespeople cash rewards for every unit of a product they sell. This benefit increases the likelihood that the salesperson will try to convince a customer to buy the product rather than a competing brand.

For more expensive and highly complex products, manufacturers often provide specialized training for retail salespeople. This background helps salespeople explain features, competitive advantages, and other information to consumers. Training can be provided in several ways: A manufacturer's sales representative can conduct training sessions during regular sales calls, or the firm can distribute sales literature and videocassettes.

PUBLIC RELATIONS

Chapter 17 defined public relations as the firm's communications and relationships with its various publics, including customers, employees, stockholders, suppliers, government agencies, and the society in which it operates. Organizational public relations efforts date back to 1889, when George Westinghouse hired two people to publicize the advantages of alternating-current electricity and to refute arguments for direct-current systems.

<interactive>**learning goal**

CHAPTER OBJECTIVE #7: EXPLAIN THE ROLES OF CROSS PROMOTIONS, PUBLIC RELATIONS, PUBLICITY, AND ETHICS IN AN ORGANIZATION'S PROMOTIONAL STRATEGY.

Public relations is an efficient, indirect communications channel through which a firm can promote products, although it serves broader objectives than those of other components of promotional strategy. It is concerned with the prestige and image of all parts of the organization. Today, public relations plays a larger role than ever within the promotional mix, and it may emphasize more marketing-oriented information. In addition to its traditional activities, such as surveying public attitudes and creating a good corporate image, PR also supports advertising in promoting the organization's goods and services.

Approximately 160,000 people work in public relations in both the not-for-profit and profit-oriented sectors. Some 1,800 public relations firms currently operate in the U.S. In addition, thousands of smaller firms and one-person operations compete to offer these services.

Public relations is in a period of major growth as a result of increased public pressure on industries regarding corporate ethical conduct and environmental and international issues. International expenditures on public relations are growing more rapidly than those for advertising and sales promotion. Many top executives are becoming more involved in public relations as well. The public expects top managers to take greater responsibility for company actions than they have accepted in the past. Those who refuse are widely criticized, censured, and even arrested. Tobacco manufacturer Philip Morris has long been the target of criticism for allegedly creating advertisements that appeal to young people. While strongly denying these allegations, the company decided to create its Youth Smoking Prevention campaign, designed to be aired in school classrooms through Primedia. The tag line of one of the ads read, "Reflect confidence—think don't smoke." But antitobacco activists continued to blast these efforts as "one more attempt to get kids when they say they're not trying to reach kids."[30]

The PR department is the link between the firm and the media. It provides press releases and holds news conferences to announce new products, the formation of strategic alliances, management changes, financial results, or similar developments. The PR department may issue its own publications as well, including newsletters, brochures, and reports. Such new innovations as the Segway personal transporter and Crest's WhiteStrips received tremendous boosts when their PR managers placed them on popular TV shows. The Segway transporter was demonstrated on *Good Morning America* and WhiteStrips on Rosie O'Donnell's former syndicated TV talk show.[31]

A PR plan begins much like an advertising plan, with research to define the role and scope of the firm's overall public relations and current challenges. Next come strategic decisions on short-term and long-term goals and markets, analysis of product features, and choices of messages and media channels—or other PR strategies such as speaking engagements or contests—for each market. Plan execution involves developing messages highlighting the benefits that the firm brings to each market. The final step is to measure results.

The Internet has actually changed some PR planning, as PR representatives now have more direct access to the public instead of having their messages filtered through journalists and the news media. This direct access gives them greater control over their messages.[32]

Marketing and Nonmarketing Public Relations

Nonmarketing public relations refers to a company's messages about general management issues. When a company makes a decision that affects any of its publics, input from public relations specialists can help to smooth its dealings with those publics. A company that decides to close a plant would need advice on how to deal with the local community. Other examples include a company's attempts to gain favorable public opinion during a long strike or an open letter to Congress published in a newspaper during congressional debates on a bill that would affect a particular industry. Although some companies organize their public relations departments separately from their marketing divisions, PR activities invariably affect promotional strategies.

In contrast, *marketing public relations (MPR)* refers to narrowly focused public relations activities that directly support marketing goals. MPR involves an organization's relationships with consumers or other groups about marketing concerns and can be either proactive or reactive.

With proactive MPR, the marketer takes the initiative and seeks out opportunities for promoting the firm's products, often including distribution of press releases and feature articles. For example, companies send press releases about new products to newspapers, television stations, and relevant consumer, business, and trade publications. It is a powerful marketing tool since it adds news coverage that reinforces direct promotion activities.

Reactive MPR responds to an external situation that has potential negative consequences for the organization. Examples of reactive MPR are responses to product tamperings, such as the deaths caused by cyanide in Tylenol (1982) and Sudafed (1991) capsules. Prompt corrective action and strong PR campaigns from Johnson & Johnson and Burroughs Wellcome, respectively, prevented these situations from becoming disasters. On the other hand, both Ford and Bridgestone/Firestone fumbled in their attempts to blame each other for injuries and deaths caused by defective tires. More recently, several major airlines have used MPR to try to attract more flying customers after the tragedies of September 11, 2001.

Publicity

The aspect of public relations that is most directly related to promoting a firm's products is **publicity,** nonpersonal stimulation of demand for a good, service, place, idea, person, or organization by unpaid placement of significant news regarding the product in a print or broadcast medium. It has been said that if advertising is the hammer, publicity is the nail. It creates credibility for the advertising to follow. Firms generate publicity by creating special events, holding press conferences, and preparing news releases and media kits. Many firms, such as Starbucks and Wal-Mart's Sam's Club, have built their brands with virtually no advertising. Pharmaceutical products including Viagra and Prozac became worldwide brands with relatively little advertising, although advertising now supports them.

While publicity generates minimal costs compared with other forms of promotion, it does not deliver its message entirely free of cost. Publicity-related expenses include the costs of employing marketing personnel assigned to create and submit publicity releases, printing and mailing costs, and related expenses.

Firms often pursue some publicity to promote their images or viewpoints. Other publicity efforts involve organizational activities such as plant expansions, mergers and acquisitions, management changes, and research-and-development programs. A significant amount of publicity, however, provides information about goods and services, particularly new goods and services.

Because many consumers consider news stories to be more credible than advertisements as sources of information, publicity releases are often sent to media editors for possible inclusion in news stories. The media audiences perceive the news as coming from the communications media, not the sponsors. The information in a publicity release about a new good or service can provide valuable assistance for a television, newspaper, or magazine writer, leading to eventual broadcast or publication. Publicity releases sometimes fill voids in publications, and at other times, they become part of regular features. In either case, they offer firms valuable supplements to paid advertising messages.

CROSS PROMOTION

In recent years, marketers have begun to combine their promotional efforts for related products using a technique called *cross promotion,* in which marketing partners share the cost of a promotional campaign that meets their mutual needs—an important benefit in an environment of rising media costs. Relationship marketing strategies like comarketing and cobranding, discussed in earlier chapters, are forms of cross promotion. Marketers realize that these joint efforts between established brands provide greater benefits in return for both companies; investments of time and money on such promotions will become increasingly important to many partners' growth prospects.

The entertainment industry is one of the most prominent users of cross promotion. Movie studios frequently partner with fast-food chains. Consider a cartoon show called *SpongeBob SquarePants,* which has achieved a loyal following among fans of all ages—and brand equity—with very little advertising. Aired by Nickelodeon, the show quickly became the No.1 children's show on television. Now Nickelodeon has a variety of cross promotional deals, from license agreements with toy manufacturers to a deal with Kraft Foods to place SpongeBob on the cover of its macaroni and cheese boxes and to offer "ocean blue" colored cheese sauce inside, as shown in Figure 18.8.[33]

MEASURING PROMOTIONAL EFFECTIVENESS

Each element of the promotional mix represents a major expenditure for a firm. Although promotional prices vary widely, advertisers typically pay a fee based on cost to deliver the message to viewers, listeners, or readers—the so-called *cost per thousand (CPM).* Billboards are the cheapest way to spend advertising dollars, with television and some newspapers the most expensive. So while price is an important factor in media selection, it is by no means the only one—or all ads would appear on billboards!

<interactive>**learning goal**

CHAPTER OBJECTIVE #8: EXPLAIN HOW MARKETERS ASSESS PROMOTIONAL EFECTIVENESS.

Because promotion represents such a major expenditure for many firms, they need to determine whether their campaigns accomplish appropriate promotional objectives. Companies want their advertising agencies and in-house marketing personnel to demonstrate how promotional programs contribute to increased sales and profits. Marketers are well aware of the number of advertising messages and sales promotions that consumers encounter daily, and they know that these people practice selective perception and simply screen out many messages.

By measuring promotional effectiveness, organizations can evaluate different strategies, prevent mistakes before spending money on specific programs, and improve their promotional programs. As the earlier discussion of promotional planning explained, any evaluation program starts with objectives and goals; otherwise, marketers have no yardstick against which to measure effectiveness. However, determining whether an advertising message has achieved its intended objective is one of the most difficult undertakings in marketing. Sales promotions and direct marketing are somewhat easier to evaluate because they evoke measurable consumer responses. Like advertising, public relations is also difficult to assess on purely objective terms.

Measuring Advertising Effectiveness

Measures to evaluate the effectiveness of advertising, while difficult and costly, are essential parts of any marketing plan. Without an assessment strategy, marketers will not know whether their advertising achieves the objectives of the marketing plan or whether the dollars in the advertising budget are well spent. To answer these questions, marketers can conduct two types of research. *Media research* assesses how well a particular medium delivers the advertiser's message, where and when to place the advertisement, and the size of the audience. Buyers of broadcast time base their purchases on estimated Nielsen rating points, and the networks have to make good if ratings do not reach promised levels. Buyers of print advertising space pay fees based on circulation. Circulation figures are independently certified by specialized research firms.

FIGURE 18.8

SpongeBob SquarePants and Macaroni & Cheese: Cross Promotion between Nickelodeon and Kraft Foods

The other major category, *message research,* tests consumer reactions to an advertisement's creative message. Pretesting and posttesting, the two methods for performing message research, are discussed in the following sections.

Pretesting To assess an advertisement's likely effectiveness before it actually appears in the chosen medium, marketers often conduct *pretesting.* The obvious advantage of this technique is the opportunity to evaluate ads when they are being developed. Marketers can conduct a number of different pretests, beginning during the concept phase in the campaign's earliest stages when they have only rough copy of the ad and continuing until the ad layout and design are almost completed.

Pretesting employs a variety of evaluation methods. Focus groups can discuss their reactions to mock-ups of ads using different themes, headlines, or illustrations. To test magazine advertisements, the Batten, Barton, Durstine & Osborn ad agency cuts ads out of advance copies of magazines and then inserts the ads it wants to test. Interviewers later check the impact of the advertisements on readers who receive free copies of the revised magazines. Another ad agency, McCann-Erickson, uses a *sales conviction test* to evaluate magazine advertisements. Interviewers ask heavy users of a particular item to pick one of two alternative advertisements that would convince them to purchase it.

To screen potential radio and television advertisements, marketers often recruit consumers to sit in a studio and indicate their preferences by pressing two buttons, one for a positive reaction to the commercial and the other for a negative reaction. Sometimes, proposed ad copy is printed on a postcard that also offers a free product; the number of cards returned represents an indication of the copy's effectiveness. *Blind product tests* are also frequently used. In these tests, people are asked to select unidentified products on the basis of available advertising copy.

Mechanical devices offer yet another method of assessing how people read advertising copy. One mechanical test uses a hidden camera to photograph eye movements of readers. The results help advertisers to determine headline placement and copy length. Another mechanical approach measures the galvanic skin response—changes in the electrical resistance of the skin produced by emotional reactions.

Posttesting *Posttesting* assesses advertising copy after it has appeared in the appropriate medium. Pretesting generally is a more desirable measurement method than posttesting because it can save the cost of placing ineffective ads. However, posttesting can be helpful in planning future advertisements and in adjusting current advertising programs.

In one of the most popular posttests, the *Starch Readership Report* interviews people who have read selected magazines to determine whether they observed various ads in them. A copy of the magazine is used as an interviewing aid, and each interviewer starts at a different point in the magazine. For larger ads, respondents are also asked about specifics, such as headlines and copy. All such *readership tests,* also called recognition tests, assume that future sales are related to advertising readership.

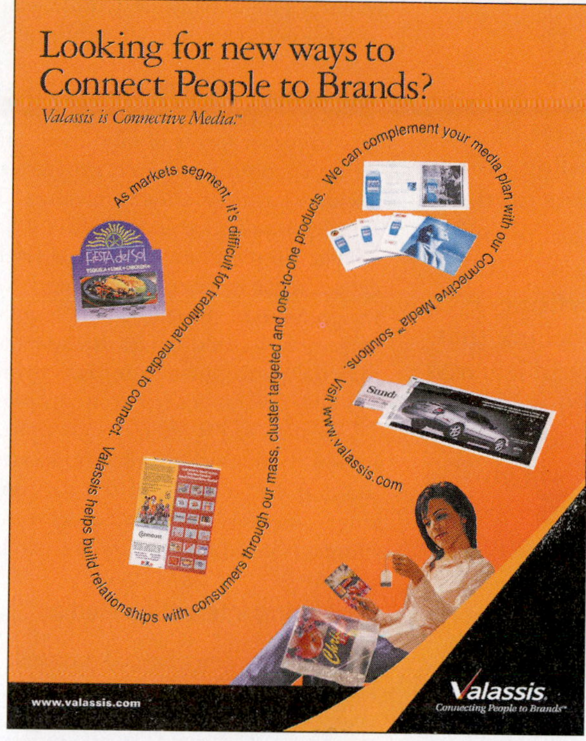

Newspaper sampling is often effective because consumers take time to read the paper and examine its contents. Inclusion of samples may result in additional attention from recipients than would be the case for other sampling delivery systems.

Unaided recall tests are another method of posttesting the effectiveness of advertisements. Respondents do not see copies of the magazine after their initial reading but must recall the ads from memory. Burke Research Corp. conducts telephone interviews the day after a commercial has aired on television to test brand recognition and the advertisement's effectiveness. Another unaided recall test is adWatch, a joint project of *Advertising Age* magazine and the Gallup Organization. It measures ad awareness by telephone polling that asks each consumer to name the advertisement that first comes to mind of all the ads he or she has seen, heard, or read in the previous 30 days.

Inquiry tests are another popular form of posttest. Advertisements sometimes offer gifts—generally product samples—to people who respond to them. The number of inquiries relative to the advertisement's cost forms a measure of its effectiveness.

Split runs allow advertisers to test two or more ads at the same time. Although advertisers traditionally place different versions in newspapers and magazines, split runs on cable television systems frequently test the effectiveness of TV ads. With this method, advertisers divide the cable TV audience or a publication's subscribers in two: Half view advertisement A and the other half view advertisement B. The relative effectiveness of the alternatives is then determined through inquiries or recall and recognition tests.

Regardless of the exact method they choose, marketers must realize that pretesting and posttesting are expensive efforts. As a result, they must plan to use these techniques as effectively as possible.

Measuring Sales Promotion Effectiveness

Because many sales promotions, especially consumer-oriented techniques, result in direct consumer responses, marketers can relatively easily track their effectiveness. As with other elements in the promotional mix, marketers must weigh the cost of the promotion against the benefits. They can measure the redemption rate of cents-off coupons, for example, and coupons often carry printed codes indicating their sources to let manufacturers and retailers know which media provide the highest redemption rates. To evaluate sampling, one of the most popular types of consumer promotions, marketers want to know how effectively it induces consumers to actually buy the product once they try the sample. Studies have shown that sampling does promote trial purchases. Newspaper samples seem to do particularly well at generating brand awareness and trial. "It breaks through the clutter, because it reaches people when they have time on their hands," explains Tom Butler of the Sunflower Group.[34] Still, marketers have found no definitive answers about whether sampling helps the rate of repurchase. Sweepstakes and contest entries can also be tracked.

Some trade promotions—allowances, contests, and dealer incentives, for example—give easily measurable results like sales increases or heavier customer traffic. Other promotions, however, like trade shows and training programs, may require more subjective judgments of the first results, such as greater product awareness and knowledge, while sales gains will take longer to show up.

Measuring Public Relations Effectiveness

As with other forms of marketing communications, organizations must measure PR results based on their objectives both for the PR program as a whole and for specific activities. In the next step, marketers must decide what they want to measure. This choice includes determining whether the message was heard by the target audience and whether it had the desired influence on public opinion.

The simplest and least costly level of assessment involves outputs of the PR program: whether the target audience received, paid attention to, understood, and retained the messages directed to them. To make this judgment, the staff could count the number of media placements and gauge the extent of media coverage. They could count attendees at any press conference, evaluate the quality of brochures and other materials, and pursue similar activities. Formal techniques include tracking publicity placements, analyzing how favorably their contents portrayed the company, and conducting public opinion polls.

To analyze PR effectiveness more deeply, a firm could conduct focus groups, interviews with opinion leaders, and more detailed and extensive opinion polls. The highest level of effectiveness measurement looks at outcomes: Did the PR program change people's opinions, attitudes, and behavior? PR professionals measure these outcomes through before-and-after polls (similar to pretesting and posttesting) and more advanced techniques like psychographic analysis, cluster analysis, and communicants audits.

Briefly Speaking

We grew up founding our dreams on the infinite promise of American advertising. I still believe that one can learn to play the piano by mail and that mud will give you a perfect complexion.

Zelda Fitzgerald (1900–1948) American artist, dancer, and writer

Evaluating Interactive Media

Marketers employ several methods to measure how many users view Web advertisements: hits (user requests for a file), impressions (the number of times a viewer sees an ad), and clickthroughs (when the user clicks on the ad to get more information). However, some of these measures can be misleading. Because each page, graphic, or multimedia file equals one hit, simple interactions can easily inflate the hit count, making it less accurate. To increase effectiveness, advertisers must give viewers who do click through their site something good to see. Successful Web campaigns use demonstrations, promotions, coupons, and interactive features.

Internet marketers price ad banners based on cost per thousand (CPM). Web sites that sell advertising typically guarantee a certain number of impressions—the number of times an ad banner is downloaded and presumably seen by visitors. Marketers then set a rate based on that guarantee times the CPM rate.

Although the Web does not yet have a standard measurement system, a number of companies like I/Pro, NetCount, and Interse offer different Web tracking and counting systems. At least two auditing services, Audit Bureau of Verification Services and BPA International, are currently in operation. Nielsen NetRatings rates Internet sites based on the number of different visitors they receive.

ETHICS IN NONPERSONAL SELLING

Chapter 3 introduced the topic of marketing ethics and noted that promotion is the element in the marketing mix that raises the most ethical questions. People actively debate the question of whether marketing communications contribute to better lives. The final section of this chapter takes a closer look at ethical concerns in advertising, sales promotion, and public relations.

Advertising Ethics

Even though laws allow certain types of advertising, many promotions still may involve ethical issues. One area of controversy is advertising aimed at children. To woo younger consumers, especially teens and those in their twenties, advertisers make messages as different from advertisements as possible; they design ads that seem more like entertainment.

Liquor advertising on television is another controversial area. Beer marketers advertise heavily on television and spend far more on advertising in print and outdoor media than do marketers of hard-liquor brands. Some members of Congress want much stricter regulation of all forms of liquor advertising on television and other media. This change would restrict ads in magazines with a 15 percent or more youth readership to black-and-white text only. Critics decry advertisements with messages implying that drinking the right beer will improve a person's personal life or help to win a sports contest. Many state and local authorities are considering more restrictive proposals on both alcohol and tobacco advertising.

In cyberspace ads, it is often difficult to separate advertising from editorial content since many sites resemble magazine and newspaper ads or television infomercials. Another ethical issue surrounding advertising online is the use of *cookies,* small text files that are automatically downloaded to a user's computer whenever a site is visited. Each time the user returns to that site, the site's server accesses the cookie and gathers information: What site was visited last? How long did the user stay? What was the next site visited? Marketers claim that this device helps them determine consumer preferences and argue that cookies are stored in the user's PC, not the company's Web site. The problem is that cookies can and do collect personal information without the user's knowledge. Lawsuits were recently filed by several consumers against Netscape for use of its SmartDownload program. In another case, Mattel apologized for adding a data-gathering program to more than 100 titles of its educational programs for children.[35]

'NET EX: ADVERTISING AND CHILDREN

Puffery and Deception *Puffery* refers to exaggerated claims of a product's superiority or the use of subjective or vague statements that may not be literally true. A company might advertise the "most advanced system" or claim that its product is "most effective" in accomplishing its purpose.

Exaggeration in ads is not new. Consumers seem to accept advertisers' tendencies to stretch the truth in their efforts to distinguish their products and get consumers to buy. This inclination may provide one reason that advertising does not encourage purchase behavior as successfully as sales promotions do. A tendency toward puffery does raise some ethical questions, though: Where is the line between claims that attract attention and those that provide implied guarantees? To what degree do advertisers deliberately make misleading statements?

The Uniform Commercial Code standardizes sales and business practices throughout the U.S. It makes a distinction between puffery and any specific or quantifiable statement about product quality or performance that constitutes an "express warranty," which obligates the company to stand behind its claim. General boasts of product superiority and vague claims are puffery, not warranties. They are considered so self-praising or exaggerated that the average consumer would not rely on them to make a buying decision.

A quantifiable statement, on the other hand, implies a certain level of performance. For example, tests can establish the validity of a claim that a brand of long-life light bulbs outlasts three regular light bulbs.

Ethics in Sales Promotion and Public Relations

Both consumer and trade promotions can also raise ethical issues. Sales promotions provide opportunities for unscrupulous companies to take advantage of consumers. Companies may not fulfill rebate and premium offers or may mislead consumers by inaccurately stating the odds of winning sweepstakes or contests. Trade allowances, particularly slotting allowances, have been criticized for years as a form of bribery.

Several public relations issues open organizations to criticism. Various PR firms perform services for the tobacco industry; publicity campaigns defend unsafe products. Also, marketers must weigh ethics before they respond to negative publicity. For example, do firms admit to problems or product deficiencies, or do they try to cover them up? It should be noted that PR practitioners violate the Public Relations Society of America's Code of Professional Standards if they promote products or causes widely known to be harmful to others.

STRATEGIC IMPLICATIONS OF MARKETING IN THE 21ST CENTURY

Greater portions of corporate ad budgets will migrate to the Web in the near future. In the five years since consumer Web advertising began, Web ad expenditures have seen a 753 percent increase.[36] Currently, North America leads the world in Internet advertising by a wide margin: nearly $20 billion, as opposed to nearly $2 billion by European advertisers.[37] This trend means that marketers must be increasingly aware of the benefits and pitfalls of Internet advertising. But they should not forget the benefits of other types of advertising as well.

Promotion industry experts agree that e-commerce broadens marketers' job tasks, though many promotional objectives still remain the same. Today, advertisers need 75 different ways to market their products in 75 countries in the world and innumerable market segments. In years to come, advertisers also agree that channels will become more homogeneous while markets become more fragmented.

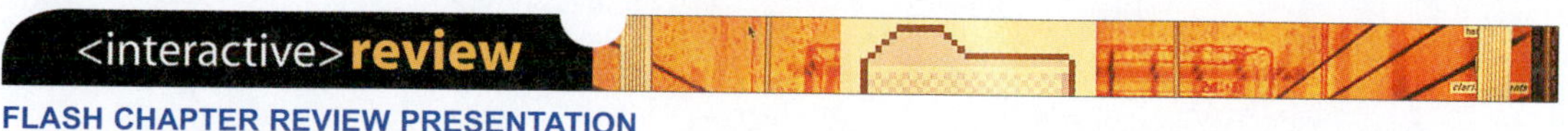

FLASH CHAPTER REVIEW PRESENTATION

<interactive>video case

OXYGEN MEDIA AND MULLEN ADVERTISING TEAM UP FOR WOMEN'S PROGRAMMING

---

endofchaptermaterial

- Summary of Chapter Objectives
- Chapter Outline
- Key Terms
- Review Questions
- Projects and Teamwork Exercises
- 'netWork
- Crossword Puzzles
- Case 18.1: JCPenney Learns Some Tough Advertising Lessons

Take the Post-Test to assess your overall understanding of the key ideas in this chapter. The Post-Test provides a comprehensive selection of exam-style questions addressing the main topics and concepts of the chapter. At the completion of each Post-Test, you will receive a score and instructive feedback on how you answered each question, and a direct link to the part of the chapter addressed in the question. Take the Post-Test as often as you need to—a record of your progress for each attempt is kept for you to revisit and gauge your improvement. And each Post-Test is randomly generated, so every attempt is new.

Post-Test

CHAPTER 19

Personal Selling and Sales-Force Management

Chapter Objectives

1. Explain the conditions that determine the relative importance of personal selling in the promotional mix.
2. Contrast over-the-counter selling, field selling, telemarketing, and inside selling.
3. Describe each of the four major trends in personal selling.
4. Identify the three basic sales tasks.
5. Outline the steps in the sales process.
6. Describe the sales manager's boundary-spanning role.
7. List and discuss the functions of sales-force management.
8. Discuss the role of ethics in personal selling and sales-force management.

Pre-Test

Take the Pre-Test to assess your initial knowledge of the key ideas in this chapter. The Pre-Test provides exam-style questions addressing the main topics and concepts of the chapter. At the completion of each Pre-Test, you will receive a score and instructive feedback on how you answered each question, and a direct link to the part of the chapter addressed in the question. Take the Pre-Test as often as you need to—a record of your progress for each attempt is kept for you to revisit and gauge your improvement.

TEAM SELLING SUCCEEDS AT PARAMOUNT

How're the renewals, Mark?" asks *Entertainment Tonight* host Mary Hart, as she walks onto the set and greets Paramount sales executive Mark Dvornik. Renewals, in TV sales-speak, are the television stations that have signed on to air the popular entertainment news show into the next decade. And make no mistake, Hart and cohost Bob Goen are a big part of the sales team who have made *Entertainment Tonight* the No. 1 syndicated show in its category. Industry analysts identify *ET* as a top money earner, bringing in over $100 million a year in licensing fees alone. With an easy smile, an uncanny ability to remember names and faces, and an instant rapport with station managers, Hart is as focused on sales as everyone else at Paramount—from President Joel Berman down through the ranks.

Team selling is the first order of business at Paramount, and with good reason. The 210 television markets in the U.S. pay billions of dollars each year to a small group of syndication companies whose upper echelon includes Paramount, Fox, Columbia TriStar, WB, and MGM. It's an extremely tight market with a limited number of customers, particularly considering that each show can be sold to only one station in each market. And a deal in Nashville, for example, could have a domino effect in other markets. Perhaps the buyer has sister stations in other major markets; playing hardball with price might cut the show not only out of Nashville but out of Chicago, Boston, and Los Angeles, too. Coordination and cooperation are key. Paramount's highly trained 23-member sales force starts each week with intensive planning meetings, setting out goals for each TV market. Then a grueling travel schedule begins. Each rep makes regular visits to about 70 clients, spread over 12 to 15 cities, to sell rights to everything from *Star Trek* to *I Love Lucy* to *Cheers,* as well as a roster of new shows. Since the sales cycle can take years to complete, building relationships and staying close to the client are key. On the road, daily conference calls involving top company execs, including Dvornik, keep everyone apprised of even the smallest developments that can affect sales.

To prevent the possibility of turf wars that are created as a result of commission-based systems, Paramount's sales reps are salaried employees who receive bonuses when sales goals are achieved. In multimarket deals, every success hinges on another, and there is no room to fly solo. National and regional sales meetings, in addition to weekly or daily teleconferences, build team rapport. Through intensive role playing in which they simulate aggressive sales situations, sales reps sharpen their selling skills. An open dialogue with top management invites them to make recommendations to improve the selling process. A "Deal of the Week" program awards recognition for the hardest fought and best won sales. For *Entertainment Tonight,* Mary Hart is often the first to congratulate reps on a new renewal—and she's always ready to do extra radio interviews or customized promos to help clinch a deal in cities where the show is struggling.

Despite its fast pace and its complexity, selling at Paramount is not all work and no play. Executives make it fun for their staff. In launching the sitcom *Becker,* starring Ted Danson as a New York doctor, all salespeople and top management dressed in hospital whites and stethoscopes to makes sales calls. That stunt—along with creative licensing deals that make the show easier to buy in uncertain economic times—pushed *Becker* into half of the nation's TV markets more than a year before it went on the air.[1]

CHAPTER OVERVIEW

Personal selling at Paramount focuses on the customer, on building a relationship that will in time lead to ongoing sales. Chapters 17 and 18 explained how increased emphasis on customer relationships has trans-

formed traditional concepts of promotion and the promotional mix in achieving marketing objectives. In exploring personal selling strategies, this chapter gives special attention to the relationship-building opportunities that the selling situation presents.

Personal selling is the process of a seller's person-to-person promotional presentation to a buyer. The sales process is essentially interpersonal, and it is basic to any enterprise. Accounting, engineering, human resource management, production, and other organizational activities produce no benefits unless a seller matches the needs of a client or customer. The 15 million people employed in sales occupations in the U.S. testify to the importance of selling. While the average firm's advertising expenses may represent from 1 to 3 percent of total sales, personal selling expenses are likely to equal 10 to 15 percent. This makes personal selling the single largest marketing expense in many firms.

Briefly Speaking

A salesperson is someone who sells goods that won't come back to customers who will.

Anonymous

<interactive>**learning goal**

CHAPTER OBJECTIVE #1: EXPLAIN THE CONDITIONS THAT DETERMINE THE RELATIVE IMPORTANCE OF PERSONAL SELLING IN THE PROMOTIONAL MIX.

Personal selling is a primary component of a firm's promotional mix in certain well-defined conditions:

1. Customers are geographically concentrated.
2. Individual orders account for large amounts of revenue.
3. The firm markets goods and services that are expensive, technically complex, or require special handling.
4. Trade-ins are involved.
5. Products move through short channels.
6. The firm markets to relatively few potential customers.

Table 19.1 summarizes the factors that influence the importance of personal selling in the overall promotional mix based on four variables: consumer, product, price, and marketing channels.

THE EVOLUTION OF PERSONAL SELLING

Selling has been a standard business activity for thousands of years. The earliest peddlers sold goods in which they had some type of ownership interest after manufacturing or importing them. They viewed selling as a secondary activity. Selling later became a business function in its own right. In 18th-century America, peddlers sold directly to farmers and settlers of the vast territories to the west. In the 19th century, salespeople called drummers sold to both consumers and marketing intermediaries. These early sellers sometimes used questionable sales practices and techniques and earned undesirable reputations for themselves and their firms. Negative stereotypes persist today. To some people, the term *salesperson*

TABLE 19.1

Factors Affecting the Importance of Personal Selling in the Promotional Mix

VARIABLE	CONDITIONS THAT FAVOR PERSONAL SELLING	CONDITIONS THAT FAVOR ADVERTISING
Consumer	Geographically concentrated	Geographically dispersed
	Relatively low numbers	Relatively high numbers
Product	Expensive	Inexpensive
	Technically complex	Simple to understand
	Custom made	Standardized
	Special handling requirements	No special handling requirements
	Transactions frequently involve trade-ins	Transactions seldom involve trade-ins
Price	Relatively high	Relatively low
Channels	Relatively short	Relatively long

FIGURE 19.1

Multiple Sales, Service, and Information Options Offered to T. Rowe Price Clients

conjures up unpleasant visions of Arthur Miller's antihero Willy Loman in the classic American play *Death of a Salesman:*

> Willy is a salesman. . . . He don't put a bolt to a nut. He don't tell you the law or give you medicine. He's a man way out there in the blue, riding on a smile and a shoe shine. And when they start not smiling back—that's an earthquake.

But selling is far different today than in its early years. Far from the fast-talking, joke-telling, back-slapping caricatures in some novels and comic strips, today's salesperson is highly trained. Sales professionalism has been aptly defined as a "a customer-oriented approach that employs truthful, nonmanipulative tactics to satisfy the long-term needs of both the customer and the selling firm."[2] Professional salespeople are problem solvers who focus on satisfying the needs of customers before, during, and after sales are made. Armed with knowledge about their firm's goods or services, those of competitors, and their customers' business needs, salespeople pursue a common goal of creating long-term relationships with customers.

Personal selling is a vital, vibrant, dynamic process. As domestic and foreign competition increases emphasis on productivity, personal selling is taking on a more prominent role in the corporate marketing mix. Salespeople must communicate the subtle advantages of their firms' goods and services over those of competitors. The salesperson's role has changed from persuader to consultant and problem solver. In addition, mergers and acquisitions, along with a host of new products and promotions, have expanded the scope and complexity of many selling jobs.

As discussed in Chapter 6, relationship marketing affects all aspects of an organization's marketing function, including personal selling and sales-force management. This transition involves marketers in both internal and external relationships and forces them to develop different sales skills. Instead of working alone, many salespeople now unite their efforts in sales teams. The customer-focused firm wants its salespeople to form long-lasting relationships with buyers by providing high levels of customer service, rather than going for quick sales. Even the way salespeople perform their jobs is changing. Growing numbers of companies are integrating communications and computer technologies into the sales routine. These trends are covered in more detail later in the chapter.

Personal selling is an attractive career choice for today's college and university students. Approximately 60 percent of all marketing graduates choose sales jobs as their first marketing positions, in part because they see attractive salaries and career potentials. The Bureau of Labor Statistics projects that jobs in selling and marketing occupations requiring a college degree will show faster than average rates of growth compared with all occupations during the next 10 years. A sales background provides visibility for the individual and serves as an excellent route to the top of the corporate hierarchy. Many corporations are headed by executives who began their careers in sales.

THE FOUR SALES CHANNELS

Personal selling occurs through several types of communication channels: over-the-counter selling, field selling, telemarketing, and inside selling. Each of these channels includes both business-to-business and direct-to-customer selling. Although telemarketing and online selling are lower cost alternatives, their lack of personal interaction with prospective customers often makes them less effective than personalized, one-to-one field selling and over-the-counter channels. In fact, many organizations use a number of different channels. The ad in Figure 19.1, for example, invites T. Rowe Price customers to receive personalized investment information by meeting one-on-one with an investment advisor, talking with a trained phone representative, or going online.

<interactive>**learning goal**

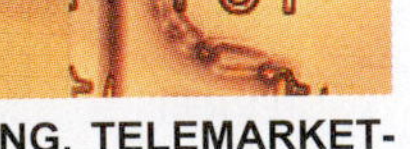

CHAPTER OBJECTIVE #2: CONTRAST OVER-THE-COUNTER SELLING, FIELD SELLING, TELEMARKETING, AND INSIDE SELLING.

Over-the-Counter Selling

The most frequently used sales channel, **over-the-counter selling,** typically describes selling in retail and some wholesale locations. Most over-the-counter sales are direct-to-customer, although wholesalers serve business customers. Customers typically visit the seller's location on their own initiative to purchase desired items. Some visit their favorite stores because they enjoy shopping and consider it a type of leisure activity. Others come in response to many kinds of invitations, including direct mail appeals, personal letters of invitation from store personnel, and advertisements for sales, special events, and new-product introductions. From the electronics-product salesperson at Circuit City to the diamond purveyor at Tiffany's, this type of selling typically involves providing product information and arranging for completion of sales transactions.

Before the advent of big chain retailers and discount stores, it was not unusual for local retailers to know their customers by name or to be familiar with their tastes and preferences. Today, in a back-to-the-future trend, similar one-on-one sales tactics are paying off for astute marketers. Top direct marketers like Lands' End, for example, use sophisticated database technology to identify callers and any recent purchases made. This customer recognition helps build strong relationships in over-the-counter sales as well. Starbucks is a successful model of how over-the-counter selling builds relationships by creating an enjoyable and satisfying experience for customers. Starbucks emphasizes "one customer, one partner, one cup at a time." Customers are willing to pay premium prices for Starbucks coffee because they are buying more than just coffee—it's the personal touch that keeps them coming back.

Other marketers are trying to re-create the personalized, one-to-one experience of over-the-counter selling on the Internet, but for most, success remains elusive. Though many have experimented with Web-driven sales, most banks, for instance, still rely heavily on face-to-face selling for insurance sales. Customer referral, followed by one-on-one meetings between insurance reps and potential customers, is the method most likely to result in a sale. Banks use their Web sites mainly to educate customers about insurance, not to close sales.[3]

Field Selling

Field selling involves making sales calls on prospective and existing customers at their businesses or homes. Some situations involve considerable creative effort, such as in-home sales of encyclopedias and insurance or industrial sales of major computer installations. Often the salesperson must convince customers first that they need the good or service and then that they need the particular brand the salesperson is selling. Field sales of large industrial installations also often require considerable technical expertise.

Largely because it involves travel, field selling is considerably more expensive than other selling options. Figure 19.2 shows the average cost of sales calls across a range of industries. B2B sales calls, because of the sophistication or technical nature of products and the level of expertise needed to communicate to potential buyers, top the list.

In fairly routine field selling situations, such as calling on established customers in industries like food, textiles, or wholesaling, the salesperson may basically act as an order taker who processes regular customers' orders. Field selling may involve regular visits to local stores or businesses, or it may involve many days and nights of travel, by car or plane, every month. Salespeople who travel a great deal are frequently labeled

FIGURE 19.2

Cost of a Sales Call by Industry

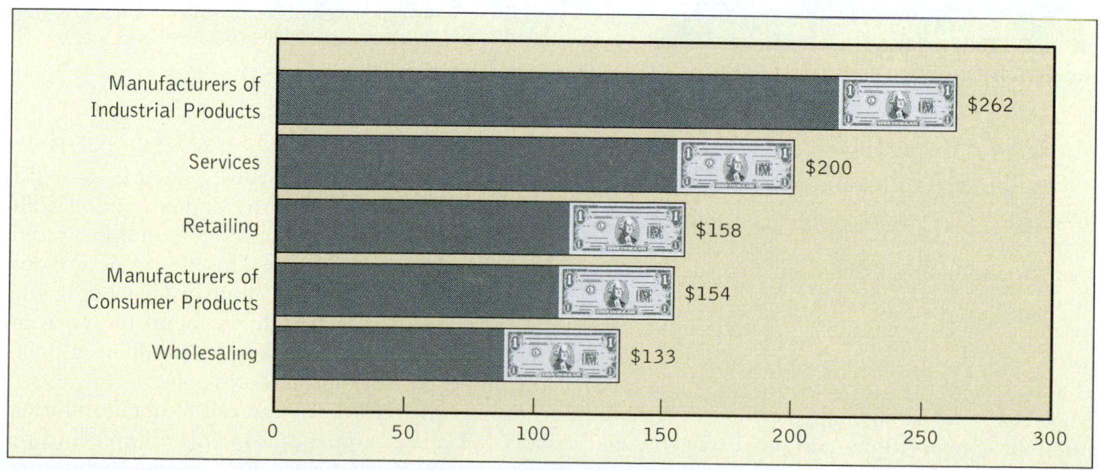

Source: Sales data reported in "Cost of a Call Survey," *Sales & Marketing Management,* September 2000, p. 82.

road warriors. A recent study found that it costs an average of $215 per day to keep a salesperson on the road. More than half the money is eaten up in hotel costs.[4] As technology seeps into every modern business transaction, marketers have adapted their personal selling techniques to take advantage of electronic communications channels, including voice mail, e-mail, and the Internet.

Avon, whose 3 million independent sales reps worldwide built a business on door-to-door selling, has explored several alternative sales methods to counter the fact that changes in consumer lifestyles—two-career couples, for example—means that fewer and fewer consumers are home to open the door. Recognizing that its reps are the backbone of the company, Avon is experimenting with retail kiosks run by local Avon representatives in shopping malls. A Web site, focused on the "eRepresentative," allows salespeople who sell online to earn commissions of up to 25 percent for orders shipped direct or up to 50 percent for orders delivered to the customer in person.[5] The "Marketing Hits" Interactive Example demonstrates how high-energy field selling helped revitalize flagging brands at Newell Rubbermaid.

<interactive>**example**

MARKETING HIT: SALES PRO BOUNCES BACK

Telemarketing

Telemarketing, a channel in which the selling process is conducted by phone, serves two general purposes—sales and service—and two general markets—business-to-business and direct-to-customer. As noted in Chapter 16, both inbound and outbound telemarketing are forms of direct marketing.

Outbound telemarketing involves a sales force that relies on the telephone to contact customers, reducing the substantial costs of personal visits to customers' homes or businesses. Technologies such as predictive dialers, autodialing, and random-digit dialing increase chances that telemarketers will reach customers at home. Predictive dialers weed out busy signals and answering machines, nearly doubling the number of calls made per hour. Autodialing allows telemarketers to dial numbers continually; when a customer answers the phone, the call is automatically routed to a live sales agent. Random-digit dialing allows telemarketers to reach unlisted numbers and blocks caller ID.[6] The effectiveness of telemarketers is evaluated on various bases, including total calls made per hour or per shift, revenue per sale or per hour, and profitability. In general, outbound telemarketing calls geared toward men get the best responses between 7 P.M. and 9 P.M., whereas women tend to respond more favorably to telemarketers between 10 A.M. and 4 P.M.

As demonstrated in the "Solving an Ethical Controversy" Interactive Example, a major drawback of telemarketing is that the majority of customers don't like it. Surveys indicate that up to 60 percent of consumers are so bothered by intrusive calls to their homes that they will not listen to a telephone sales presentation. The Telephone Consumer Protection Act of 1991 requires companies to keep a list of people who request not to receive telemarketing calls and to refrain from calling again. Also, the Federal Trade Commission's Telemarketing Sales Rules restrict all but calls from charities or political organizations to daytime and early evening hours (not after 9 P.M.). In addition to federal regulations, telemarketers have also become the focus of state legislation. Twenty-three states currently have "do not call" laws with high fines for offenders. In Indiana, fines are as high as $25,000 every time a company calls anyone on its no-call list.[7]

RIGHT/WRONG: SOLVING AN ETHICAL CONTROVERSY—DO NOT CALL!

Why, then, is outbound telemarketing such a popular sales technique? Companies like it because it is cost-effective and it works. An average telemarketing call costs $5, compared with hundreds of dollars for a field sales call. Despite the annoyance of receiving unsolicited calls, some people do respond. In a recent year, 185 million U.S. consumers made a purchase via outbound telephone calls. The effectiveness of outbound telemarketing as a sales technique is further evidenced by the size of the industry. Generating sales of more than $660 billion a year, consumer and business-to-business telemarketing accounts for 6 percent of GDP. Consumer sales alone are expected to grow by 8 percent a year, exceeding $400 billion in 2006. The industry also employs close to 6 million people, mainly entry-level and minority jobs.[8]

Inbound telemarketing typically involves a toll-free number that customers can call to obtain information, make reservations, and purchase goods and services. When a customer calls in on a toll-free line, the caller can be identified and routed to the sales agents with whom he or she has done business before, creating a human touch not possible before. This form of selling provides maximum convenience for customers who initiate the sales process. Many large catalog merchants, like The Sharper Image, Lillian Vernon, and Lands' End, keep their inbound telemarketing lines open 24 hours a day, 7 days a week. In fact, you can even call L.L. Bean on Christmas Day to place an order! Other catalog retailers maintain reputations for superior customer service and marketing ideas. Williams-Sonoma, a kitchen and culinary cataloguer, for instance, satisfies its customers by guaranteeing that any product defect will be corrected or repaired using genuine parts from the manufacturer or with a new product.

> **Briefly Speaking**
>
> You don't want your daughter to marry a telemarketer.
>
> *Matt Mattingley*
> *Director, American Teleservices Association*

Inside Selling

The role of many of today's telemarketers is a combination of field selling techniques applied through inbound and outbound telemarketing channels with a strong customer orientation, called **inside selling.** Inside sales reps perform two primary jobs: They turn opportunities into actual sales, and they support technicians and purchasers with current solutions. Inside sales reps do far more than read a canned script to unwilling prospects. They perform a dynamic selling function that goes beyond taking orders to solving problems, providing customer service, and selling. eTapestry.com, an Indianapolis-based application service provider for nonprofit organizations, is one of many companies that successfully combines selling approaches. eTapestry's inside salespeople do far more than run down leads; they close major deals over the phone—some worth more than a quarter-million dollars. The team is made up of former outside sales pros. With revenues that exceed $3 million a year, eTapestry finds its inside reps more cost effective and easier to manage than an outside sales force.[9]

A successful inside sales force relies on close working relationships with field representatives to solidify customer relationships. In the printing industry, for example, the increasing complexity of the printing process has led to a need for more detailed coordination and internal management than in the past. Across the industry, the traditional role of customer service has evolved to incorporate account development and resource management responsibilities. Increasingly, sales reps and customer service personnel work together in teams, providing the inside backup that allows the salesperson to spend more time focusing on new business.[10]

Integrating the Various Selling Channels

Figure 19.3 illustrates how firms are likely to blend alternative sales channels—from over-the-counter selling and field selling to telemarketing and inside selling—to create a successful cost-effective sales organization. Existing customers whose business problems require complex solutions are likely to be best served by the traditional field sales force. Other current customers who need answers but not the same handholding as the first group can be served by inside sales reps who call on them as needed. Over-the-counter sales reps serve existing customers by supplying information and advice and completing sales transactions. Telemarketers are often used to contact prospective customers and to attempt to win back previous clients who are currently purchasing from competitors. In some instances, telemarketers attempt to complete the sale; in other, more complex selling situations, they turn promising sales leads over to the field sales force for follow-up.

Georgia-based Omnibus Solutions, a $120 million company that provides new and refurbished computer servers, employs 15 inside and 25 outside sales reps. Cost-effective inside salespeople handle specific customer needs, and the outside team concentrates on building long-term relationships. The ability of outside reps to cross-sell multiple products due to the customer intelligence they glean from face-to-face selling situations is vital to the company's success.[11]

RECENT TRENDS IN PERSONAL SELLING

In today's complex business environment, effective personal selling requires different strategies than salespeople used in the past. Rather than selling one-on-one, it is now the norm to sell to teams of corporate

FIGURE 19.3

Alternative Sales Channels for Serving Customers

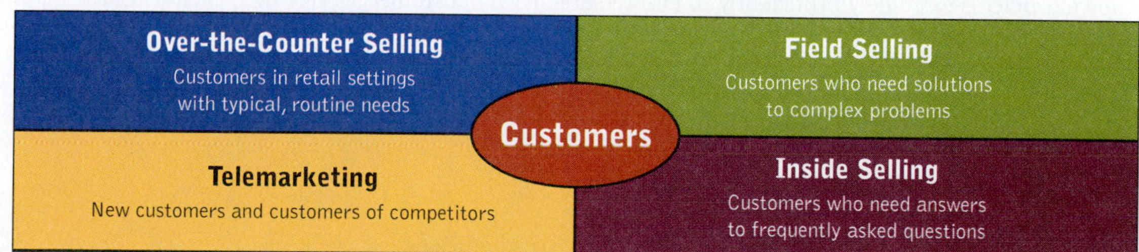

representatives who make up the client firm's decision-making units. In particular, in business-to-business sales situations involving technical products, customers expect salespeople to answer technical questions—or bring along someone who can. They also want representatives who understand technical jargon and can communicate using sophisticated technological tools. Patience is also a requirement for personal selling because the sales cycle, from initial contact to closing, may take years. The average industrial sale takes at least four sales calls to close, and the larger and more expensive the equipment, the longer it takes.

<interactive>**learning goal**

CHAPTER OBJECTIVE #3: DESCRIBE EACH OF THE FOUR MAJOR TRENDS IN PERSONAL SELLING.

To address these concerns, companies rely on four major personal selling approaches: relationship selling, consultative selling, team selling, and sales-force automation. Together, these methods are changing the sales function at companies of all sizes.

Relationship Selling

As competitive pressures mount, more firms are emphasizing **relationship selling,** a technique for building a mutually beneficial relationship with a customer through regular contacts over an extended period. Such buyer-seller bonds become increasingly important as companies cut back on the number of suppliers and look for companies that provide high levels of customer service and satisfaction. Salespeople must also find ways to distinguish themselves and their products from competitors. To create strong, long-lasting relationships with customers, salespeople must meet buyers' expectations. Table 19.2 summarizes the results of several surveys that indicate what buyers expect of professional salespeople.

The success of tomorrow's marketers depends on the relationships they build today, in both the business-to-customer and business-to-business markets. Merrill Lynch recently refocused its 10,000-plus U.S. brokers on a relationship selling approach. For years, the company had tried to compete with low-cost brokerages like Charles Schwab by matching their cheap trading fees. Recently, the company redirected its brokers to concentrate only on wealthy clients with $1 million or more to invest. Investors with more modest assets are now handled by call centers. The firm's expert salespeople work only with its best customers. The change not only has cut costs but positions Merrill Lynch for faster growth, as brokers are able to offer more sophisticated advice to fewer but more profitable clients.[12] While it is far from abandoning its low-cost trade positioning, Charles Schwab also seeks a personal relationship between its sales professionals and top investors.

Relationship selling is equally important in business-to-business sales. ProSlide Technology sells water rides to amusement parks, but a closer look reveals that the company's success is centered on the ability of its sales force to customize each customer's order. New attractions like the CanonBOWL, an exhilarating water ride that allows parents to ride with children, are created by asking customers what they want and delivering both quality products and premium customer service. Rather than depend on repeat sales from

TABLE 19.2

What Buyers Expect from Salespeople

Buyers prefer to do business with salespeople who:

- Orchestrate events and bring to bear whatever resources are necessary to satisfy the customer
- Provide counseling to the customer based on in-depth knowledge of the product, the market, and the customer's needs
- Solve problems extremely proficiently to ensure satisfactory customer service over extended time periods
- Demonstrate high ethical standards and communicate honestly at all times
- Willingly advocate the customer's cause within the selling organization
- Create imaginative arrangements to meet buyers' needs
- Arrive well-prepared for sales calls

established customers, ProSlide works to shape and reshape relationships with each order a customer places. As a result, over 70 percent of ProSlide's business comes from the same customers.[13]

Consultative Selling

The once-popular "good-old boy" sales style—getting chummy with customers, buying them a meal or a drink, giving the standard sales presentation, applying pressure, and expecting to get the sale on that basis—is rapidly going the way of the dinosaur. Field representatives and inside sales reps require sales methods that satisfy today's cost-conscious, knowledgeable buyers. One such method, **consultative selling,** involves meeting customer needs by listening to customers, understanding—and caring about—their problems, paying attention to details, and following through after the sale. It works hand in hand with relationship selling in building customer loyalty. Anne M. Mulcahey, president of Xerox Corp., is an advocate of consultative selling. A 25-year veteran saleswoman, Mulcahey insists on putting the company's resources and expertise behind its sales force. A hugely popular, high-energy manager, she promises to fly anywhere, anytime to help salespeople close tough deals.[14]

As rapid technological changes drive business at an unprecedented pace, selling has become more complex, often changing the role of salespeople. At Zeks Compressed Air Solutions, for instance, sales representatives have a background in engineering. With the job title Application Engineer, they bring technical proficiency to the sales situation. The change in title has helped the company overcome resistance to sales calls, since the expertise offered brings extra value to the customer-seller relationship.[15]

Online companies have instituted consultative selling models to create long-term customers. Particularly for complicated, high-priced products that require installation or specialized service, Web sellers must be able to quickly communicate the benefits and features of their products. They accomplish this through consultative selling. In its ad featured in Figure 19.4, software vendor SAP uses a consultative selling approach to promote its sophisticated customer relationship management software mySAP—after all, customer service should concern more than one department.

Similar to consultative selling, *cross-selling*—offering multiple products or services to the same customer—is another technique that capitalizes on a firm's strengths. It costs a bank five times more to acquire a new customer than to cross-sell to an existing one. Moreover, research shows that the more a customer buys from an institution, the less likely that person is to leave.

Wells Fargo uses cross-selling to sell twice as many financial products to its clients than its competing institutions are able to achieve. As well as training in cross-selling, bank staff receive generous incentives for sending checking-account customers, for example, to the credit-card department.[16]

Team Selling

One of the latest developments in the evolution of personal selling is **team selling,** in which the salesperson joins with specialists from other functional areas of the firm to complete the selling process. Teams can be formal and ongoing or created for a specific short-term selling situation. Some salespeople have hesitated to embrace the idea of team selling. Although some salespeople prefer working alone, others believe that team selling brings better results. Customers often prefer the team approach, which makes them feel well served. Another advantage of team selling is the formation of relationships between companies rather than between individuals.

In sales situations that call for detailed knowledge of new, complex, and ever-changing technologies, team selling offers a distinct competitive edge in meeting customers' needs. In most computer software B2B departments, up to a third of the sales force is composed of technically trained, nonmarketing experts such as engineers or programmers. A salesperson continues to play the lead role in most sales situations, but technical experts bring extra value to the sales process. Some companies establish permanent sales-and-tech teams that conduct all sales presentations together; others, like software vendor ClientSoft, have a pool of engineers or other professionals who are on call for different client visits.[17]

CDW Computer Centers, the largest direct seller of Hewlett-Packard, IBM, Microsoft, Toshiba, and other top-name computer industry brands, relies on team selling to serve its 600,000 consumer and business customers. Each customer is provided with a highly trained account manager who serves as the team leader of a group of specialists dedicated to finding solutions to buyers' needs. In a typical day, more than 700 systems are custom configured for CDW customers. Customers can receive continuing lifetime technical support by visiting the CDW extranet or by calling a toll-free telephone number to speak with factory-trained technicians.[18]

In some cases, team selling brings in help from outside the company. AT&T, for example, works with PeoplePC to form a team-selling partnership to serve Delta Airlines. Through their Wired Workplace Program, the two companies provide free Internet access and free PCs for home-based Delta employees. This unique solution helps AT&T create a competitive advantage.

In any team-selling situation, preparation is the key to performing well. At Sun Microsystems, team members gather frequently in any way they can to share information—via e-mail, conference calls, and

FIGURE 19.4

SAP: Consultative Selling for Sophisticated Products

face-to-face meetings. Each team member reaches out to insiders at the client company to gather insights that can help them leapfrog over the competition. Good preparation, along with a clear designation of team leader, helps avoid in-team conflicts that can hamper the overall sales efforts.[19]

Sales-Force Automation

A major trend in personal selling is **sales-force automation (SFA)**—the application of new technologies to the sales process. Broadly used, the term refers to the use of everything from pagers and Web-browsing cell phones, to voice and electronic mail, to laptops and notebook computers. More narrowly used, it refers to the use of computers by salespeople for activities beyond the use of word processors, spreadsheets, and connections to order-entry systems.

With SFA tools, both large and small companies can increase their efficiency and spend more time on client acquisition and retention. The benefits of SFA include improvements in the quality and effectiveness of sales calls because of improved access to information; low selling, printing, and training costs; improved product launches; and attentive customer service. Sales reps at Old World Christmas, a supplier of Christmas ornaments, now use hand-held devices to speed order processing. The devices scan UPC bar codes on products and e-mail orders to headquarters. The scanner can then be hooked to a printer to give the customer instant, accurate written confirmation of pricing. The company's old, cumbersome order processing system has been reduced to just seconds using the new electronic sales aid.[20]

Other companies have integrated telephony with the Internet to provide both team selling and consultative selling online. Wrigley, the Chicago chewing-gum company, for example, uses software created by SAP to operate in real time online. Sales representatives can collaborate on sales projects, bringing in experts as needed to strengthen their sales presentations. They can also use the software to get instant access to marketing or customer data, receive detailed product information, or download competitive data—all of which can be incorporated into customized sales presentations.[21]

SFA usage differs sharply by industry: Food, beverage, and pharmaceutical industries are using sophisticated third-generation systems, whereas many apparel companies have not yet moved to SFA. Software for sales-force automation also falls into several categories depending on its intended use. Most salespeople use basic productivity and general-purpose programs such as word processors, e-mail, and spreadsheets. Some programs help to organize prospect lists and to remind salespeople to make follow-up calls. More expensive systems may integrate order processing and other types of information.

Fujitsu puts technology into sales reps' hands. Its touch-screen PC displays product lines, places orders, checks inventory, and more.

SALES TASKS

Today's salesperson is more concerned with establishing long-term buyer-seller relationships and with helping customers select the correct products for meeting their needs than with simply selling whatever is available. Where repeat purchases are common, the salesperson must be certain that the buyer's purchases are in his or her best interest; otherwise, no future sales will be made. The seller's interests are tied to the buyer's in a symbiotic relationship.

<interactive>**learning goal**

CHAPTER OBJECTIVE #4: IDENTIFY THE THREE BASIC SALES TASKS.

Not all selling activities are alike. While all sales activities assist the customer in some manner, the exact tasks that are performed vary from one position to another. Three basic sales tasks can be identified: (1) order processing, (2) creative selling, and (3) missionary sales. These tasks form the basis for a sales classification system.

Most sales personnel do not fall into a single category. Instead, they often perform all three tasks to some extent. A sales engineer for a computer firm may be doing 50 percent missionary sales, 45 percent creative selling, and 5 percent order processing. Most selling jobs, however, are classified on the basis of the primary selling task performed.

A major consideration for most businesses is improving productivity throughout their operations, and sales-force productivity is no exception. With the climbing costs of travel and compensation for experienced salespeople, each sales rep must spend time efficiently and effectively to raise productivity.

Order Processing

Order processing, which can involve both field selling and telemarketing, is most often typified by selling at the wholesale and retail levels. For instance, a Pepsi-Cola route salesperson who performs this task must take the following steps:

1. *Identify customer needs.* The route salesperson determines that a store has only 7 cases left in stock when it normally carries an inventory of 40 cases.
2. *Point out the need to the customer.* The route salesperson informs the store manager of the inventory situation.
3. *Complete (write up) the order.* The store manager acknowledges the need for more of the product. The driver unloads 33 cases, and the manager signs the delivery slip.

Order processing is part of most selling positions. It becomes the primary task in situations where needs can be readily identified and are acknowledged by the customer. Even in such instances, however, salespeople whose primary responsibility involves order processing will devote some time convincing their wholesale or retail customers to carry more complete inventories of their firms' products or to handle additional product lines. They also are likely to try to motivate purchasers to feature some of their firms' products, increase the amount of shelf space devoted to their products, and improve product location in the stores.

Sales-force automation is easing order-processing tasks. In the past, salespeople would write up an order on the customer's premises but spend much time later, after the sales visit, completing the order and transmitting it to headquarters. Today, many companies have automated order processing. With portable computers and state-of-the-art software, the salesperson can place an order on the spot, directly to headquarters, thus freeing up valuable time and energy. Computers have even eliminated the need for some of the traditional face-to-face contacts for routine reorders.

Creative Selling

When a considerable amount of analytical decision making is involved in purchasing a good or service, the salesperson must use **creative selling** techniques to solicit an order. In contrast to the order-processing task, which deals mainly with maintaining existing business, creative selling generally is used to develop new business either by adding new customers or by introducing new goods and services. New products often require a high degree of creative selling. The salesperson must first identify the customer's problems and needs and then propose a solution in the form of the good or service being offered. Creative selling techniques are used in over-the-counter selling, field selling, telemarketing, and inside selling.

As more and more companies consolidate and the number of buyers for a product or service shrinks, creative selling approaches are increasingly necessary to win the sale. Take the case of Blue Barn Interactive, a New York–based online community developer. Blue Barn inked a $250,000-a-year deal to deliver online solutions to a Web division representing three major cable television brands. To get close to a sale, Blue Barn offered to begin work on a trial basis. Before the contract was final, the cooperative Web division disappeared in a cost-cutting move, and each of the three cable companies took control of its own Web content. Blue Barn had invested heavily in a deal—and a buyer—that vanished overnight into thin air. Rather than walk away, Blue Barn reinvented its sales approach. Representatives courted each of the three cable companies to start building relationships and find out where the eventual buy-in would be. Blue Barn also went directly to the CEO overseeing all three brands' Web content. A renewed presentation explained how the product fit in with the new overall initiative and with each company's specific needs. The multilevel approach paid off, and Blue Barn was at last able to make a deal. Later, the company found that the three brand managers—with whom they could have pursued contracts individually—were laid off or transferred due to further consolidations.[22] The "Marketing Hits" Interactive Example describes some of the ways top reps craft creative selling solutions for their clients.

MARKETING HIT: SELLING SAP SOFTWARE IN A ROTTEN ECONOMY.

Missionary Selling

Missionary selling is an indirect approach to sales. Salespeople sell the firm's goodwill and provide their customers with information and technical or operational assistance. For example, a toiletries company salesperson may call on retailers to check on special promotions and overall product movement, even though a wholesaler takes orders and delivers merchandise. Large pharmaceutical companies are the most aggressive of missionary sales operations. Through extensive gift-giving, wining and dining, free seminars, and other incentives, teams of sales reps typically court doctors (the indirect customer) in the hope of persuading them to prescribe a particular brand to patients. They also inundate doctors with glossy product literature. Here, the doctor is clearly the decision maker, even though the transaction is not complete until the patient hands the prescription over to a pharmacist.[23] And increasingly, they rely on a flurry of direct-to-consumer ads for new medications like Allegra that can be purchased only with a prescription. The pharmaceutical marketers urge consumers to consult their doctors as a first step in a diagnosis—and to request a free sample of the product.

Missionary sales may involve both field selling and telemarketing. Many aspects of team selling can also be seen as missionary sales, as when technical support salespeople help design, install, and maintain equipment; when they train customers' employees; and when they provide information or operational assistance. For example, Harris InfoSource, a Cleveland-based corporate communications company, compiles and markets databases profiling U.S. manufacturers and their decision makers. Recently, the firm has branched into services research, too. Harris's salespeople gather leads from such sources as trade shows and field sales activities and follow up with missionary sales strategies. After each trade show, between two and three people from Harris's internal sales staff call on the leads, looking for customers who need accurate, in-depth sales lead information. The Harris selling approach begins at the trade show booth and continues with follow-up letters, phone calls, and sales calls.[24]

THE SALES PROCESS

If you have worked in a retail store or simply sold candy or wrapping paper to raise money for your band, swim team, or other organization, you will recognize some of the activities involved in the sales process, even if you did not think of them as such. Personal selling encompasses the following sequence of activities: (1) prospecting and qualifying, (2) approach, (3) presentation, (4) demonstration, (5) handling objections, (6) closing, and (7) follow-up.

<interactive>**learning goal**

CHAPTER OBJECTIVE #5: OUTLINE THE STEPS IN THE SALES PROCESS.

As Figure 19.5 indicates, these steps follow the attention-interest-desire-action concept (AIDA) discussed in Chapter 17. Once a sales prospect has been qualified, an attempt is made to secure his or her attention. The presentation and demonstration steps are designed to generate interest and desire. Successful handling of buyer objections should arouse further desire. Action occurs at the close of the sale.

Salespeople modify the steps in this process to match their customers' buying processes. For instance, the Girl Scout whose Aunt Ada buys boxes and boxes of Girl Scout Thin Mint cookies every year probably needs no presentation. She could just call her aunt and tell her that cookies are on sale. She might also remind her aunt how grateful she is for her order each year and highlight the new cookies in the hope that

FIGURE 19.5

The AIDA Concept and the Personal Selling Process

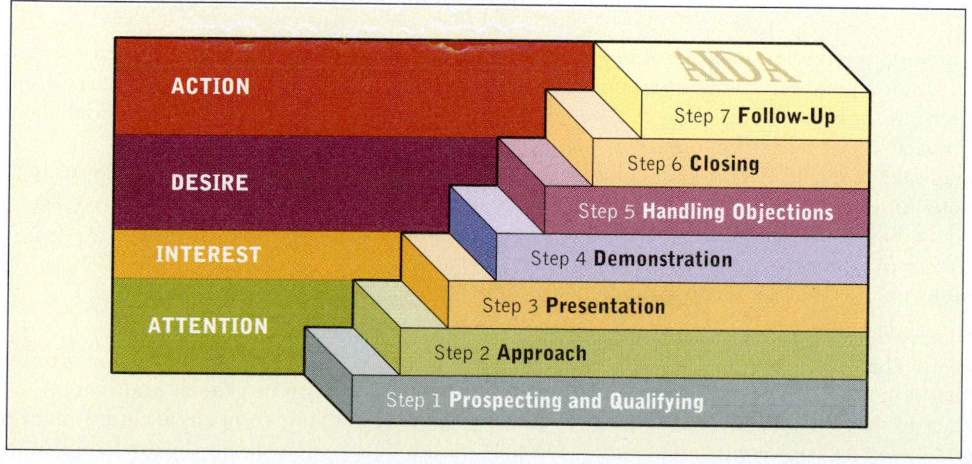

she will also order some of those. If every other house has a girl selling the cookies, the scout may need to join with other members of her troop to find new customers in different locations, such as the lobby of local grocery stores.

Prospecting and Qualifying

Prospecting, the process of identifying potential customers, is difficult work involving many hours of diligent effort. Leads about prospects may come from many sources: computerized databases, trade show exhibits, previous customers, friends and neighbors, other vendors, nonsales employees in the firm, suppliers, and social and professional contacts. Although a firm may emphasize personal selling as the primary component of its overall promotional strategy, direct mail and advertising campaigns are also effective in identifying prospective customers. Technology consulting firm The Meta Group credits a prospecting initiative with boosting revenues by $1.5 million. The company ran a series of real-time informational teleconferences for potential customers. Participants were invited to complete a poll, providing details on their organizations and their consulting needs. The conferences increased sales lead flow by 600 percent.[25]

New sales personnel may find prospecting frustrating because they usually receive no immediate payback. But selling is frequently a numbers game, and for many salespeople, sales numbers start with prospecting. Without successful prospecting, future sales growth is limited to current accounts. Prospecting is a continuous process because of the inevitable loss of some customers over time, as well as the emergence of new potential customers or first-time prospects.

Recently, salespeople have turned to the Internet in their efforts to identify prospective customers. Auto marketers, for instance, offer Internet shoppers an array of promotional incentives, including coupons off the purchase price, gift certificates, savings bonds, sweepstakes, and games. Once consumers sign up for the incentives, they are often asked for information about themselves and their preferences. Auto marketers use this information to track and communicate with customers in ways they could not do offline. Some companies report successes in turning respondents to Web giveaways into real customers, but others are less enthusiastic about prospecting on the Internet. In a recent survey of auto dealers, more than half rated the quality of Internet leads as poor or very poor.[26]

Qualifying—determining that the prospect really is a potential customer—is another important sales task. Not all prospects are qualified to make purchase decisions. A person with an annual income of $25,000 may wish to own a $200,000 house, but his or her ability to actually become a customer is questionable.

Qualifying can be a two-way street. The sales representative determines that the prospect has the authority and the resources to make the purchase decision. Likewise, prospects must agree that they are candidates for the goods or services being offered. If either of those conditions is not met, then further contact is not likely to lead to a sale and will be a waste of time for both salesperson and prospect. To keep costs under control, many firms engage in telemarketing for both prospecting and qualifying. Telemarketers and inside sales reps pass on qualified leads to field salespeople, who can concentrate on prospects most likely to buy.

Approach

Once the salesperson has identified a qualified prospect, he or she collects all available, relevant information and plans an *approach*—the salesperson's initial contact with the prospective customer. Information about the prospect can provide invaluable help to ease the initial contact for telemarketers, inside sales reps, and field salespeople. Salespeople can gather information from secondary sources—magazine or newspaper articles—or from the prospect's own published literature—annual reports, press releases, and even Internet sites. In collecting information, the salesperson must be sensitive to the issue of invading the prospect's privacy. A sales professional does not use unethical tactics to obtain personal information about a prospect.

Information gathering makes *precall planning* possible. A salesperson who has gathered relevant information about a prospect can make an initial contact armed with knowledge about the prospect's purchasing habits; his or her attitudes, activities, and opinions; and common interests between the salesperson and the prospect. This preparation often provides key help for winning an account.

Retail salespeople usually cannot conduct precall planning, but they can compensate by asking leading questions to learn more about the purchase preferences of buyers. Business marketers have access to far more data than retail sellers, and they should review it before scheduling the first sales contact. Marketing research studies often provide invaluable information that serves as the basis of a sales approach. Answering the following questions can help salespeople complete effective precall planning:

- Who are the audience members and what jobs do they perform each day?
- What is their level of knowledge? Are they already informed about the idea you are going to present?
- What do they want to hear? Do they want detailed, technical jargon or general information?
- What do they need to hear? Do they need to know more about your company or more about the good or service your company provides? Do they need to know more about the availability and cost of your product or more about how your product actually works?

Presentation

The salesperson gives the sales message to a prospective customer in a *presentation.* The seller describes the product's major features, points out its strengths, and concludes by citing illustrative successes. One popular form of presentation is a "features-benefits" framework wherein the seller's objective is to talk about the good or service in terms that are meaningful to the buyer. The salesperson relates product features to customer needs and explains benefits of those features, rather than relating technical specifications.

The presentation should be well organized, clear, and concise, and it should emphasize the positive. Printed sales support materials (charts, product literature, market research, product reviews), charts designed on a laptop computer, and audiovisual aids such as videotapes enhance the clarity and effectiveness of presentations. The level of preparation depends on the type of call. For a routine sales call, up-to-date product knowledge and information about the prospect may be sufficient. When the salesperson is competing with several other companies for an account, a major presentation requires in-depth preparation and rehearsals to ensure that everything goes perfectly. Flexible presentations are nearly always needed to match the unique circumstances of each purchase decision. Proper planning and sensitivity to the customer's reactions are an important part of tailoring a presentation to each prospective customer.

Increasingly, presentations are going high-tech. Computer-based multimedia presentations are considered the next wave in sales-force automation. With a multimedia-ready laptop or a larger PC or LCD projection computer, salespeople can bring color, animation, video, audio, and interactivity—as well as the latest product and pricing information—to their presentations. CNN Headline News salespeople previously used ordinary PowerPoint presentations to sell ads to cable operators. But when the company recently decided to change the look and feel of the Atlanta-based 24-hour cable news network, executives knew their sales force would need multimedia presentation materials that matched the network's more modern cutting-edge look. Presentations now include audio and video clips and high-tech graphics.[27]

'NET EX: IMPROVING YOUR SALES PRESENTATIONS

Demonstration

One important advantage of personal selling over most advertising is the ability of salespeople to provide a *demonstration* of the good or service to the potential buyer. As shown in Figure 19.6, Canon's new ink jet printers have individual ink tank systems, allowing customers to replace a single color rather than an entire cartridge when they are "out of blue." The ad for this new product invited customers to check out the Canon ink jet Web site at http://consumer.usa.canon.com/printers/index.html or to call a toll-free number for further information.

But a static magazine advertisement or even a quasi-demonstration of a product in action on a television screen is a far cry from the real thing. A demonstration ride in a new automobile, for example, allows the prospect to become involved in the presentation. It awakens customer interest in a way that no amount of verbal presentation can.

More firms use new technologies to make their demonstrations more effective. Multimedia interactive demonstrations are now common. Sales representatives for magazines such as *Forbes* and *Newsweek,* for instance, use data stored on CD-ROM or interactive laser discs to demonstrate the magazine's demographics and circulation patterns. These presentations use full-color video and sound, along with animation, statistics, and text, to demonstrate how a prospective client's ad will appear.

The key to a good demonstration—one that gains the customer's attention, keeps his or her interest, is convincing, and stays in the customer's memory—is planning. The salesperson should check and recheck all aspects of the demonstration prior to its delivery.

Handling Objections

A vital part of selling involves handling objections. *Objections* are expressions of sales resistance by the prospect, and it is reasonable to expect them: "Well, I really should check with my spouse." "Perhaps I'll stop by next week." "I like everything except the color." Objections typically involve the product's features, its price, and services to be provided by the selling firm. A sales professional uses each objection as a cue for providing additional information for the prospect. In most cases, an objection such as "I don't like the color of the interior" is really the prospect's way of asking what other choices or product features are available. A customer's question reveals an interest in the product and gives the seller an opportunity to expand a presentation by supplying additional information. For instance, testimonials from satisfied customers may be effective in responding to product objections. Also, providing a copy of the warranty and the dealer's service contract may resolve the buyer's doubts about customer service.

FIGURE 19.6

Demonstration—Critical Step for Buyers Purchasing a New Color Copier

During this stage of the selling process, salespeople often are confronted with objections concerning competitors' products. Professional salespeople avoid criticizing the competition. Instead, they view objections as an opportunity to provide more information about the good or service. Often this requires conducting extra behind-the-scenes research. Sales-force automation can help sales representatives handle certain objections by making needed information immediately available. In just a few moments, the salesperson can confirm for the customer that the amount and type of a certain product are in stock and can be quickly shipped, for example.

Overcoming objections in the marketplace starts with a "we can do it" attitude. When Marshall Maguire, national sales manager for New Jersey–based RMB Miniature Bearings, heard that more and more customers were using price as an objection to purchase, he refused to let reps negotiate. RMB produced a commodity-type product—foreign-made bearings could be bought at a fraction of the price. To avoid reducing margins, Maguire insists that reps emphasize the value of the product to the customer—RMB offers vastly superior customer service and customization to the client's needs. Overcoming objections by offering value rather than low price allows the company to keep a reasonable profit margin and stay in business.[28]

Closing

The moment of truth in selling is the *closing*—the point at which the salesperson asks the prospect for an order. If the sales representative has made an effective presentation based on applying the product to the customer's needs, the closing should be the natural conclusion. However, a surprising number of sales personnel find it difficult to actually ask for an order. Nearly 80 percent of salespeople fail to close when the buyer is ready, and many customers are ready to close much earlier than the salesperson is.

To be effective, salespeople must learn when and how to close a sale. Commonly used methods of closing a sale include the following:

1. The "if I can show you . . ." technique first identifies the prospect's major concern in purchasing the good or service and then offers convincing evidence of the offering's ability to resolve it. ("If I can show you how the new heating system will reduce your energy costs by 25 percent, would you be willing to let us install it?")
2. The alternative-decision technique poses choices for the prospect in which either alternative is favorable to the salesperson. ("Will you take this sweater or that one?")
3. The SRO (standing-room-only) technique warns the prospect that a sales agreement should be concluded now because the product may not be available later or an important feature, such as price, will soon be changed.

4. Silence can be used as a closing technique, since a discontinuance of a sales presentation forces the prospect to take some type of action (either positive or negative).
5. An extra-inducement close offers special incentives designed to motivate a favorable buyer response. Extra inducements may include quantity discounts, special servicing arrangements, or layaway options.

Figure 19.7 suggests several low-pressure phrases salespeople may use to move smoothly from the presentation to the close, wrapping up a deal.

FIGURE 19.7

Low-Pressure Closing Phrases

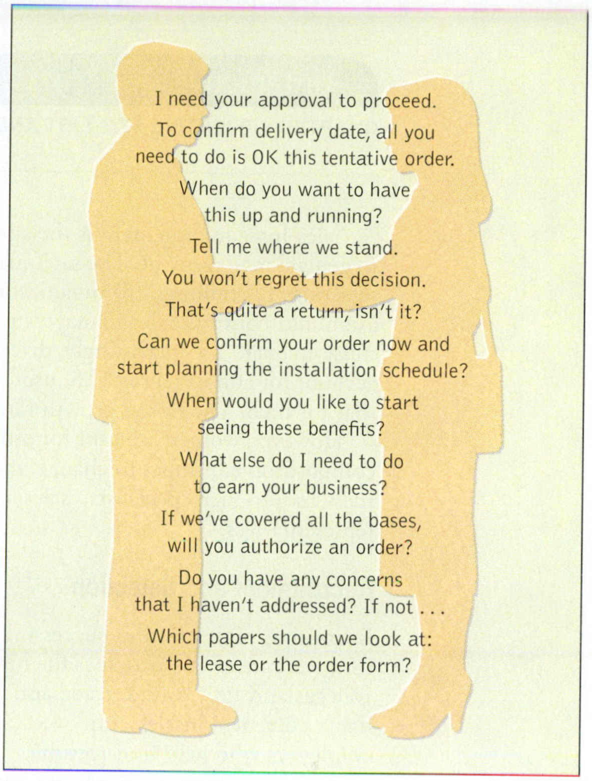

I need your approval to proceed.

To confirm delivery date, all you need to do is OK this tentative order.

When do you want to have this up and running?

Tell me where we stand.

You won't regret this decision.

That's quite a return, isn't it?

Can we confirm your order now and start planning the installation schedule?

When would you like to start seeing these benefits?

What else do I need to do to earn your business?

If we've covered all the bases, will you authorize an order?

Do you have any concerns that I haven't addressed? If not . . .

Which papers should we look at: the lease or the order form?

Source: "Hot Closing Phrases," *The Competitive Advantage*, 2001, p. 3, adapted from Terry L. Booton, *Cracking New Accounts*.

Follow-Up

The word *close* can be misleading, since the point at which the prospect accepts the seller's offer is where much of the real work of selling begins. In today's increasingly competitive sales environment, the successful salesperson seeks to ensure that today's customers will be future purchasers. It is not enough to close the sale and move on. Relationship selling requires the salesperson to reinforce the customer's purchase decision and make sure that the company delivers high-quality goods or services on schedule. Salespeople must also ensure that customer service needs are met and that satisfaction results from all of a customer's dealings with the company. Otherwise, another company may get the next order.

These postsale activities, which often determine whether a person will become a repeat customer, constitute the sales *follow-up*. Whenever possible, the sales representative should contact customers to find out whether they are satisfied with their purchases. This step allows the salesperson to psychologically reinforce the customer's original decision to buy. It also gives the seller an opportunity to correct any sources of discontent with the purchase and to secure important market information and make additional sales, as well.

Follow-up helps to strengthen the bond salespeople try to build with customers in relationship selling. Automobile dealers, for example, often keep elaborate records of their previous customers so that they can promote new models to individuals who already have shown a willingness to buy from them. Some auto dealers assign representatives from their service departments to call several days after a customer's appointment to make sure the customer is satisfied with the work. Proper follow-up is a logical part of the selling sequence.

MANAGING THE SALES EFFORT

The overall direction and control of the personal selling effort are in the hands of sales managers, who are organized on a hierarchical basis. For example, in a typical geographical sales structure, a district or divisional sales manager might report to a regional or zone manager, and these people, in turn, may report to a national sales manager or vice president of sales.

<interactive>**learning goal**

CHAPTER OBJECTIVE #6: DESCRIBE THE SALES MANAGER'S BOUNDARY-SPANNING ROLE.

Sales managers perform a **boundary-spanning role** in that they link the sales force to other elements of the internal and external environments. The internal organizational environment consists of top management, other functional areas in the firm, and other internal information sources. The external environment includes trade groups, competitors, customers, suppliers, and regulatory agencies.

The sales manager's job requires a unique blend of administrative and sales skills depending on the specific level in the sales hierarchy. Sales skills are very important for first-level sales managers since these managers must train and directly lead the sales force. But as people rise in the sales management structure, they require more managerial skills and fewer sales skills to perform well. Over 60 percent of a typical salesperson's time is devoted to prospecting, face-to-face selling, and travel. The typical time allocations for a salesperson are shown in Figure 19.8.

As with other promotional activities, personal selling requires effective planning and strategic objectives, including such strategies as selling existing products to new customers, selling new products, servicing customer accounts to enhance retention and satisfaction, and expanding customer relationships by selling more products to existing customers.

<interactive>learning goal

CHAPTER OBJECTIVE #7: LIST AND DISCUSS THE FUNCTIONS OF SALES-FORCE MANAGEMENT.

Sales-force management is the administrative channel for sales personnel; it links individual salespeople to general management. The sales manager performs seven basic managerial functions: (1) recruitment and selection, (2) training, (3) organization, (4) supervision, (5) motivation, (6) compensation, and (7) evaluation and control. Sales managers perform these tasks in a demanding and complex environment. They must manage an increasingly diverse sales force that includes more women and minorities. Women account for almost half of U.S. professional salespeople, and their numbers are growing at a faster rate than that for men. The fastest growth rate is among salespeople of Hispanic and Asian descent.

However, women account for only one of every four business-to-business salespeople. As the workforce composition continues to change, more people will be needed to fill a growing number of selling positions such as product specialists, sales consultants, telemarketers, and customer service and sales support representatives.

Recruitment and Selection

Recruiting and selecting successful salespeople are one of the sales manager's greatest challenges. The turnover rate of salespeople is the highest of all white-collar professions. Sources of new salespeople include colleges and universities, trade and business schools, sales and nonsales personnel in other firms, and the firm's current nonsales employees. A growing number of companies are offering bonuses and perks for employees who help find recruits.

Not all of these methods are equally productive. One problem area involves the reluctance of some high-school guidance counselors and college instructors to promote the advantages of a selling career to students. But in fact, a successful sales career offers satisfaction in all of the following five areas that a person generally considers when deciding on a profession:

1. *Opportunity for advancement.* Studies have shown that successful sales representatives advance rapidly in most companies. Advancement can come either from within the sales organization or laterally to a more responsible position in some other functional area of the firm.

FIGURE 19.8

How Salespeople and Sales Managers Spend Their Time

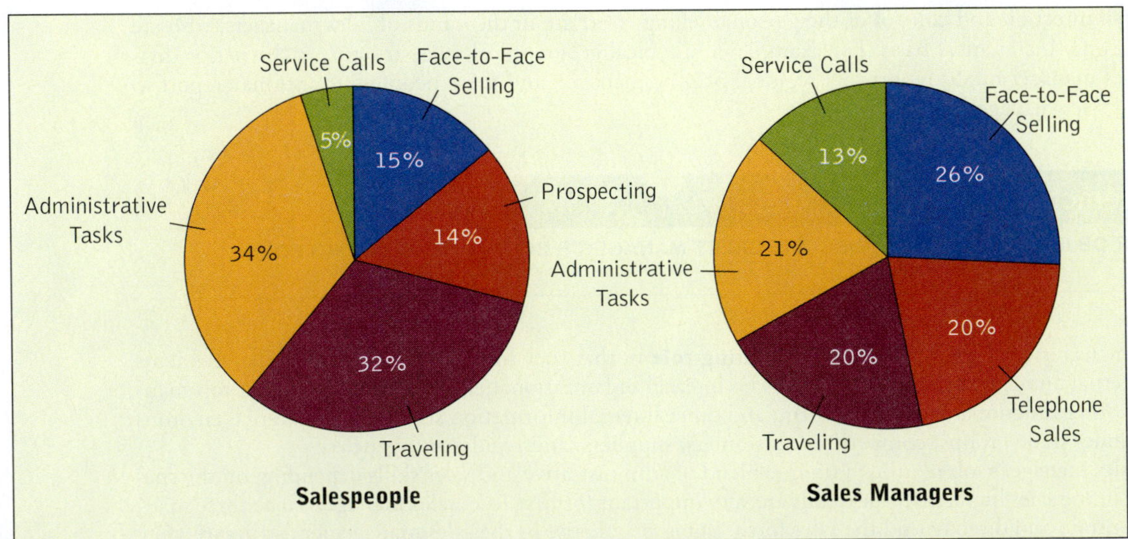

Source: Salesperson time allocations reported in "How Salespeople Spend Their Time," *Sales & Marketing Management,* March 1998, p. 96.

2. *High earnings.* The earnings of successful salespeople compare favorably with those of successful people in other professions. The average top-level consumer goods salesperson can earn more than $75,000 per year.
3. *Personal satisfaction.* A salesperson derives satisfaction from achieving success in a competitive environment and from helping customers satisfy their wants and needs.
4. *Job security.* Contrary to what many students believe, selling provides a high degree of job security. Experience has shown that economic downturns affect personnel in sales less than they do people in most other employment areas. In addition, there is a continuing need for good sales personnel.
5. *Independence and variety.* Salespeople most often operate as "independent" businesspeople or as managers of sales territories. Their work is quite varied and provides an opportunity for involvement in numerous business functions.

Careful selection of salespeople is important for two reasons. First, the selection process involves substantial amounts of money and management time. Second, selection mistakes are detrimental to customer relations and sales-force performance and are costly to correct, as well.

A seven-step process typically is used in selecting sales personnel: application, screening interview, in-depth interview, testing, reference checks, physical examination, and analysis and hiring decision. An application screening is followed by an initial interview. If the applicant looks promising, an in-depth interview is conducted. During the interview, sales managers look for personal characteristics like enthusiasm, good organizational skills, ambition, persuasiveness, the ability to follow instructions, and sociability.

Next, the company may use testing in its selection procedure, including aptitude, intelligence, interest, knowledge, and personality tests. One testing approach gaining in popularity is the assessment center. This technique, which uses situational exercises, group discussions, and various job simulations, allows the sales manager to measure a candidate's skills, knowledge, and ability. Assessment centers enable managers to see what potential salespeople can do rather than what they say they can do. After testing applicants, companies check their references to ensure that job candidates have represented themselves accurately. A physical examination is usually included before the final analysis and hiring decision.

Briefly Speaking

I couldn't believe that God meant a woman's brain to bring 50 cents on the dollar.

Mary Kay Ash (1918–2001) Founder, Mary Kay Cosmetics (on her 1963 decision to start her own company after her male assistant at a direct-sales company was promoted at twice her salary)

Training

To shape new sales recruits into an efficient sales organization, managers must conduct an effective training program. The principal methods used in sales training are on-the-job training, individual instruction, in-house classes, and external seminars.

Popular training techniques include instructional videotapes, lectures, role-playing exercises, slides, films, and interactive computer programs. Simulations can help salespeople improve their selling techniques. Another key area for training is sales-force automation (SFA). However, salespeople who are not very computer literate can balk when presented with SFA tools. Many firms supplement their training by enrolling salespeople in executive development programs at local colleges and by hiring specialists to teach customized training programs. In other instances, sales reps attend courses and workshops developed by outside companies.

Construction Information Systems, a company that provides building contractors with information on jobs sent out to bid via the Internet, is a fast-growing business that credits its success to its sales-training process. Concentrated sessions at regular intervals focus on precall planning, through which reps learn to set goals for every call they make, prospecting skills, questioning skills that encourage customers to express their business needs, and role playing, in which reps work through difficult sales challenges.[29]

Ongoing sales training is also important for veteran salespeople. Much of this type of training is conducted by sales managers informally. A standard format is for the sales manager to travel with a field sales representative periodically and then critique the person's work. Sales meetings, training tapes, classes, and seminars are other important forms of training for experienced personnel.

Mentoring is a key training tool at many organizations. Sealed Air Corporation, a New Jersey company, offers a sales mentoring program that cuts training costs, fosters loyalty, and helps groom future managers. Top sales performers spend three years coaching new or underperforming salespeople in their territories. While the trainee sets up calls and takes the lead in sales pitches, the mentor provides help and encouragement along the way. Microsoft uses mentoring as a means of helping women and minority personnel develop their careers, and communications and electronics designer Agilent Technologies' mentor program—open only to those who excel—mixes people from different functions in the company to give future managers a broader view of operations.[30]

Organization

Sales managers are responsible for the organization of the field sales force. General organizational alignments, which are usually made by top marketing management, may be based on geography, products, types of customers, or some combination of these factors. Figure 19.9 presents a simplified organizational chart illustrating each of these alignments.

FIGURE 19.9

Basic Approaches to Organizing the Sales Force

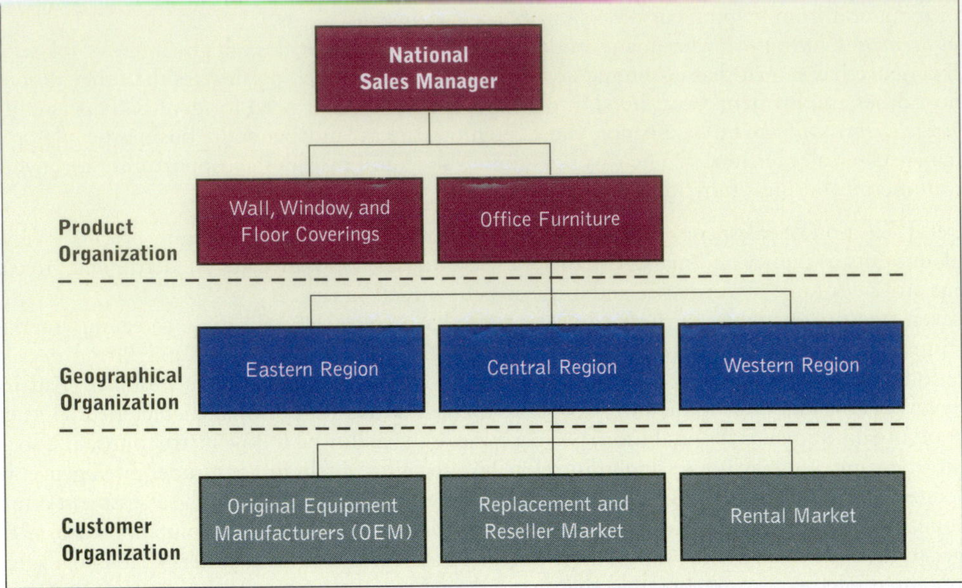

A product sales organization should have specialized sales forces for each major category of the firm's products. This approach is common among industrial product companies that market large numbers of similar but separate products of a very technical or complex nature that are sold through different marketing channels.

Firms that market similar products throughout large territories often use geographical specialization. For example, multinational corporations may have different sales divisions in different continents. Geographical organization may be combined with one of the other organizational methods. However, companies are moving away from using territorial sales reps as they adopt customer-focused sales forces. When confronted with a sales territory problem, Stephen Wald, CEO of apparel manufacturer Naturally Knits, had to devise a plan that would settle a dispute between two of his salespeople. The problem arose when one sales rep lost a lucrative account when the territories in his district were reconfigured. Wald knew the importance of maintaining positive relationships between the salesperson and the customer—even though the customer was now located in another sales rep's territory. The company, therefore, added a "cherry-picking clause" that spells out exceptions to the home-territory rule. This reorganization saved two multimillion-dollar accounts that came to the company through relationships developed long-distance by reps outside their territories.[31]

Customer-oriented organizations use different sales-force strategies for each major type of customer served. Some firms assign separate sales forces for their consumer and organizational customers. Others have sales forces for specific industries, such as financial services, educational, and automotive. Sales forces can also be organized by customer size, with a separate sales force assigned to large, medium, and small accounts.

A growing trend among firms using a customer-oriented organizational structure is the **national accounts organization.** This structure, designed to strengthen a firm's relationship with large and important customers, assigns senior sales managers or sales teams to major accounts in each market. Organizing by national accounts helps sales representatives develop cooperation between departments to meet customer needs. The classic example of a national account selling situation is the relationship between Wal-Mart and its major vendors. Clorox, Colgate, Coleman, H.J. Heinz, Johnson & Johnson, Kraft, and Nestlé are just seven of the growing number of companies that have set up sales offices near Wal-Mart's Bentonville, Arkansas, headquarters. Doing so places dedicated sales resources close to this key account.

A decade ago, the Boise Cascade office products sales force had a regional organization, and large customers were required to deal with a different sales representative in each region. The system was inefficient, resulting in additional selling expenses for Boise Cascade and complicating the purchasing process for buyers. "Our corporate customers were telling us that we were a very good provider on a regional basis, but they wanted us to meet their strategic needs," says Tom VanHootegem, director of national accounts. In response, Boise created a formal national account management program that today includes 23 national account managers who call on approximately 600 accounts worth $250,000 in annual revenues. This reorganization has boosted total revenues to over $1 billion in just six years.[32]

As companies expand their market coverage across national borders, they may use a variant of national account sales teams. These global account teams may be staffed by local sales representatives in the countries in which a company is operating. In other instances, the firm selects highly trained sales executives from its domestic operations. In both instances, training is critical to the success of a company's global sales force. End-of-chapter Case 19.1 explains some of the challenges presented by the international marketplace.

The individual sales manager also has the task of organizing the sales territories within his or her area of responsibility. Factors such as sales potential, strengths and weaknesses of available personnel, and workloads are considered in territory allocation decisions.

Supervision

A source of constant debate among sales managers concerns the supervision of the sales force. It is impossible to pinpoint the exact amount of supervision that is correct in each situation since the individuals involved and the environments in which they operate vary. However, a concept known as *span of control* helps provide some general guidelines. Span of control refers to the number of sales representatives who report to first-level sales managers. The optimal span of control is affected by such factors as complexity of work activities being performed, ability of the individual sales manager, degree of interdependence among individual salespeople, and the extent of training each salesperson receives. A 6-to-1 ratio has been suggested as the optimal span of control for first-level sales managers supervising technical or industrial salespeople. In contrast, a 10-to-1 ratio is recommended if sales representatives are calling on wholesale and retail accounts.

Motivation

The sales manager's responsibility for motivating the sales force cannot be taken lightly. Because the sales process involves problem solving, it often leads to considerable mental pressures and frustrations. Sales often result only after repeated calls on customers and may involve a long completion period, especially with new customers and complex technical products. Efforts to motivate salespeople usually take the form of debriefings, information sharing, and both psychological and financial encouragement. Appeals to emotional needs, such as ego needs, recognition, and peer acceptance, are examples of psychological encouragement. Monetary rewards and special benefits, such as club memberships, are types of financial incentives. Well-managed incentive programs can motivate salespeople and improve customer service. They typically include leisure trips or travel, gifts, recognition dinners, plaques and awards, and cash.[33] Figure 19.10 illustrates a range of gifts from Sharper Image, positioned as rewards to motivate salespeople.

However, not all incentive programs are effective in motivating employees. Poorly planned programs—for example, those that have targets set too high, are poorly publicized, allow only the top performers to

FIGURE 19.10

Sales Incentives from the Sharper Image

participate, or feature trips that do not include spouses—can actually have an adverse effect. Companies should not expect these programs to solve all their sales problems.

Sales managers can improve sales-force productivity by understanding what motivates individual salespeople. They can gain insight into the subject of motivation by studying the various theories of motivation developed over the years. One theory that has been applied effectively to sales-force motivation is **expectancy theory,** which states that motivation depends on the expectations an individual has of his or her ability to perform the job and on how performance relates to attaining rewards that the individual values.

Sales managers can apply the expectancy theory of motivation by following a five-step process:

1. Let each salesperson know in detail what is expected in terms of selling goals, service standards, and other areas of performance. Rather than setting goals just once a year, many firms do so on a semi-annual, quarterly, or even monthly basis.
2. Make the work valuable by assessing the needs, values, and abilities of each salesperson and then assigning appropriate tasks.
3. Make the work achievable. As leaders, they must inspire self-confidence in their salespeople and offer training and coaching to reassure them.
4. Provide immediate and specific feedback, guiding those who need improvement and giving positive feedback to those doing well.
5. Offer rewards that each salesperson values. JD Edwards, an e-business solutions provider, runs a twice-yearly customer satisfaction survey. Questions include ratings for employee integrity and overall satisfaction. Salespeople must score at a certain level or forfeit compensation amounting to between 75 and 125 percent of total bonuses earned that year.[34]

Compensation

Because monetary rewards are an important factor in motivating subordinates, compensating sales personnel is a critical matter for managers. Sales compensation can be based on a commission plan, a straight-salary plan, or some combination of these options. Bonuses based on end-of-year results are another popular form of compensation. The increasing popularity of team selling has also impelled companies to set up reward programs to recognize performance of business units and teams. Today, about one in four companies reward business-unit performance.

A *commission* is a payment tied directly to the sales or profits that a salesperson achieves. For example, a salesperson might receive a 5 percent commission on all sales up to a specified quota and a 7 percent commission on sales beyond that point. This approach to sales compensation is increasingly popular. But while commissions reinforce selling incentives, they may cause some sales-force members to shortchange nonselling activities, such as completing sales reports, delivering sales promotion materials, and performing normal account servicing. Commission programs can also backfire. Some retailers, such as Sears and electronics chain Highland Superstores, modified their compensation systems after discovering that salespeople were being too aggressive or recommending unnecessary services.

A salary is a fixed payment made periodically to an employee. A firm that bases compensation on salaries rather than commissions might pay a salesperson a set amount every week. A company must balance benefits and disadvantages in paying predetermined salaries to compensate managers and sales personnel. A straight salary plan gives management more control over how sales personnel allocate their efforts, but it reduces the incentive to expand sales. As a result, many firms develop compensation programs that combine features of both salary and commission plans.

Because good salespeople are both hard to find and expensive to train, sales managers want to do what they can to encourage productive workers to stay with their firms. Incentive plans that favor experienced sales representatives tend to provide fewer benefits for new representatives who are not yet fully productive. Some companies, therefore, have developed interim compensation plans for new recruits, such as a straight salary for a given period of time or a commitment that the salesperson will not earn less than a certain amount but can earn more during his or her training period.

The typical U.S. sales representative earns $54,000 in salary with average bonuses and commission of a further $26,000. Figure 19.11 shows total sales compensation figures for various levels of sales personnel. Total compensation packages vary according to industry, with the finance, insurance, and real estate industries coming out on top, followed closely by general services. They also vary according to years of experience in sales.[35]

Evaluation and Control

Perhaps the most difficult tasks required of sales managers are evaluation and control. Sales managers are responsible for setting standards and choosing the best methods for measuring sales performance. Sales volume, profitability, and investment return are the usual means of evaluating sales effectiveness. They typically involve the use of **sales quotas**—specified sales or profit targets that the firm expects salespeople to achieve. For example, a particular sales representative might be expected to sell $720,000 in territory 27 during a given year. In many cases, the quota is tied to the compensation system. SFA has greatly improved

FIGURE 19.11

Annual Pay for Sales Representatives and Sales Managers

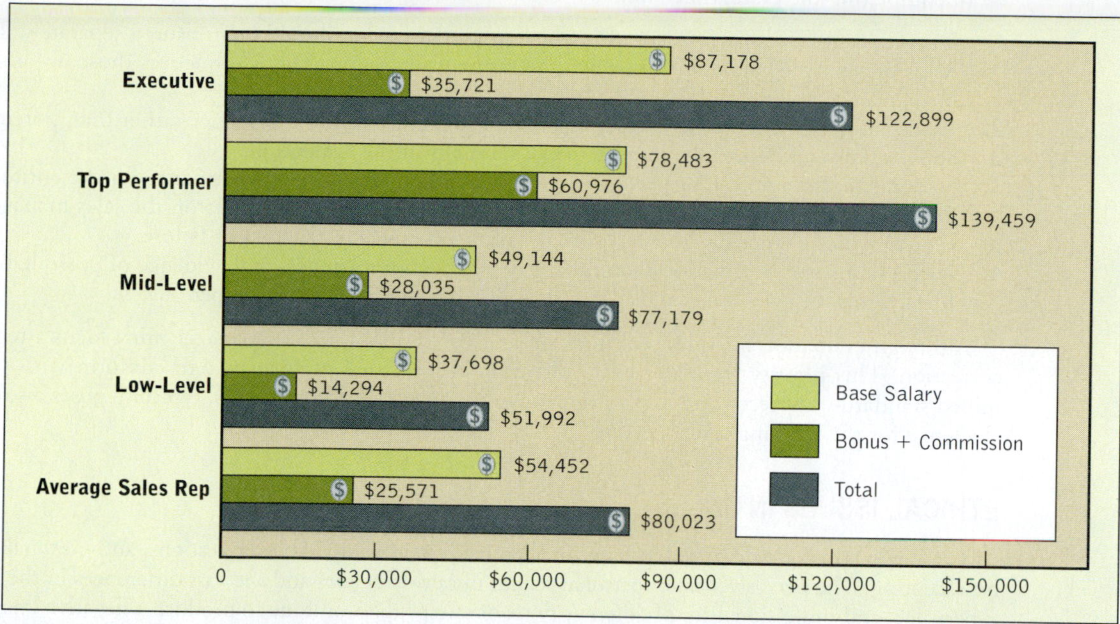

Source: Christine Galea, "2002 Salary Survey," *Sales & Marketing Management,* May 2002, p. 32.

the ability of sales managers to monitor the effectiveness of their sales staffs. Databases enable sales managers to break out revenue by salesperson, by account, and by geographical area.

In addition to sales quotas, other measures such as customer satisfaction, profit contribution, share of product-category sales, and customer retention are also coming into play. The changes are the result of three factors:

1. An increasingly long-term orientation that results from greater use of total quality management and customer relationship building efforts.
2. The realization that evaluations based on sales volume alone can lead to overselling and excessive inventory problems that work against customer relationship building
3. The need to encourage sales representatives to develop new accounts, provide customer service, and emphasize new products. A concentration on sales quotas tends to focus salespeople's attention on short-term selling from which they can generate the most sales today.

Regardless of the key elements in the evaluation program, the sales manager must follow a formal system of decision rules. Such a system supplies information to the sales manager for action. This input helps the sales manager to answer three general questions.

First, where does each salesperson's performance rank relative to the predetermined standards? This comparison should fully consider the effect of uncontrollable variables on sales performance. Preferably, each adjusted rank should be stated as a percentage of the standard. This system simplifies evaluation and facilitates converting various ranks into a single composite index of performance.

The second evaluation question asks about the salesperson's strong points. One way to answer this question is to list areas of the salesperson's performance in which he or she has surpassed the respective standard. Another way is to categorize a salesperson's strong points in three areas of the work environment:

1. *Task, or technical ability.* This strength appears in knowledge of the products (end uses), customers, and company, as well as selling skills.
2. *Process, or sequence of work flow.* This strength pertains to actual sales transactions—the salesperson's application of technical ability and interaction with customers. Managers frequently measure process performance based on personal observation. Other measures are sales calls and expense reports.
3. *Goal, or end results (output) of sales performance.* Sales managers usually state this aspect of the salesperson's work environment in terms of sales volume and profits.

The third evaluation question asks about the weaknesses or negatives in the salesperson's performance. The manager should categorize these faults as carefully as the salesperson's strong points. The sales manager should explain candidly, but kindly, the employee's weak areas. Because few people like to hear this part of an evaluation and consequently tend to listen with only "half an ear," the manager should make sure the employee understands any performance problems that he or she needs to correct and ways the manager will measure progress. The manager and employee should then establish specific objectives for improvement and set a timetable for judging the employee's improvement.

In completing the evaluation summary, the sales manager should follow a set procedure:

1. Each aspect of sales performance for which a standard exists should be measured separately. This helps prevent the halo effect, in which the rating given on one factor influences those on other performance variables.
2. Each salesperson should be judged on the basis of actual sales performance rather than potential ability. This emphasizes the importance of rankings in the evaluation.
3. Sales managers should judge each salesperson on the basis of sales performance for the entire period under consideration rather than for the particular incidents. As an evaluator, the sales manager should avoid reliance on isolated examples of the salesperson's success or failure.
4. Each salesperson's evaluation should be reviewed for completeness and evidence of possible bias. Ideally, this review would be made by the sales manager's immediate superior.

Although evaluation includes both revision and correction, the sales manager must focus attention on correction. This priority translates into a drive to adjust actual performance to conform with predetermined standards. Corrective action, with its obviously negative connotations, typically poses a substantial challenge for the sales manager.

ETHICAL ISSUES IN SALES

As the previous chapter discussed, promotional activities raise many ethical questions, and personal selling is no exception. The pervasiveness of personal selling in our daily lives and the vast differences in the training, experience, and professionalism of different types of salespeople combine to produce a negative image of the profession for many. Plays like *Death of a Salesman,* television shows, and movies reinforce this poor image.

<interactive>**learning goal**

CHAPTER OBJECTIVE #8: DISCUSS THE ROLE OF ETHICS IN PERSONAL SELLING AND SALES-FORCE MANAGEMENT.

Today's highly paid, highly professional salesperson knows that long-term success is based on building and maintaining mutually satisfying relationships with clients. Still, the stereotype lingers. A recent Gallup poll offered still more evidence of how much people dislike certain types of salespeople. Car salespeople ranked at the bottom of a list of professionals with high levels of honesty and ethics. Advertising execs and insurance reps ranked below average, too.[36]

Some people believe that ethical problems are inevitable because of the very nature of the sales function. They simply do not trust someone who by making a sale will personally benefit from the interaction. Responding to the high level of distrust among car buyers, some dealerships have initiated a videotape strategy that involves taping all final sales transactions. There are four main objectives: to make sure that customers fully understand what they are buying, to prevent finance and insurance staff from overselling extras or misleading customers, to ensure all extras are offered with every purchase, and to handle customer claims of dishonesty or mistreatment. While videotaping customers has raised issues of consumer privacy, dealers consider that the tapes benefit car buyers by providing an accurate record of transactions.[37]

Thousands of companies are working to overcome the stigma associated with sales careers and to educate the general public about the contributions of today's sales professionals. It is to their advantage to do so because salespeople generate the firm's revenue, link the company to the customer, and provide valuable product information to customers and members of the marketing channel as well as supplying feedback for the producer. By recruiting highly ethical, educated individuals and by training them in relationship selling techniques, companies develop sales forces able to win the customer's respect and trust. By stressing consultative selling techniques, sales professionals meet customer needs without resorting to unethical behavior. In addition, sales managers create an ethical sales environment by doing the following:

- Promoting ethical awareness during training programs, sales meetings, and sales calls
- Making sure that all employees—salespeople and other company personnel—know that the firm opposes unethical conduct
- Establishing control systems to monitor ethical conduct

Ethical Dilemmas

Despite management efforts to foster ethical behavior, from time to time, salespeople may find themselves in situations with their employers, fellow employees, and customers that involve ethical dilemmas. Among

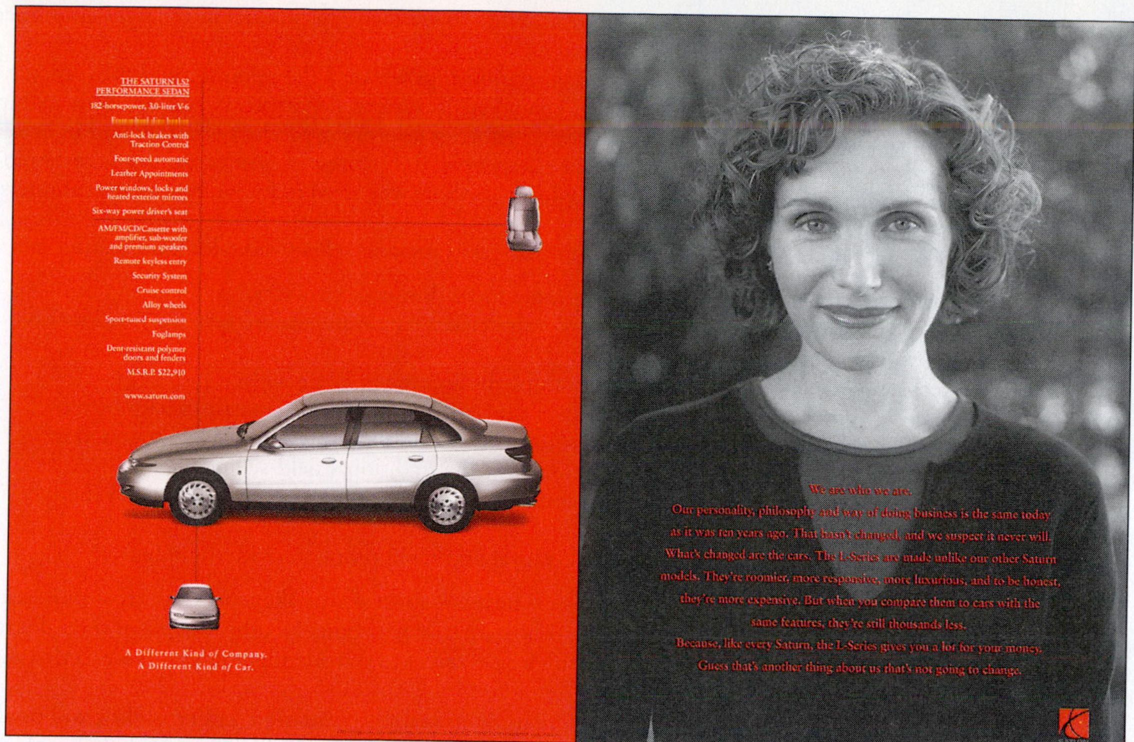

Saturn built a business on improving the car buyer's perceptions of the new-car purchase experience. Its no-hassle pricing policies sought to attract buyers who might not quite trust other dealerships.

the ethical breaches that occur between salespeople and their employers are improper use of company assets and cheating. Use of a company car for personal purposes is one such possibility; padding expense reports is another. A salesperson might resort to deception in an attempt to win a sales contest, such as holding on to orders until a contest begins or shipping unordered merchandise to customers, which will not be returned until after the contest ends.

Sexual harassment is another problem faced by many sales representatives. An Ohio State University study reported that about 30 percent of business-to-business saleswomen—and about 20 percent of salesmen—have experienced unwanted sexual advances from customers.

Another type of unethical conduct involves using bribes to secure a sale. While gifts such as pens and tickets to sporting events are accepted business practices, they can be misused. Since expensive gifts may be considered a form of bribery, many firms prohibit their employees from accepting any gift from a sales representative.

Customer demand for cash kickbacks represents another ethical dilemma. Suppose, for example, a copy-machine salesperson calls on an important business customer who is planning to order new copiers for most of his company's departments. The purchasing manager offers her the account if she will share half of her commission with him. Although she knows this is illegal and she has signed her company's strong code of ethical conduct, she also wants the sale.

In cases like this, possible options include going along with the unethical request, ignoring the request, confronting the person, or reporting the behavior. Experts recommend telling the purchasing manager that the representative wants to gain the buyer's business without resorting to such tactics. If the purchasing agent refuses to move forward on these terms, the salesperson should report the incident to a manager, who should then speak to the customer representative's supervisor. Companywide codes of ethics should help guide salespeople with such situations and should aim to protect all parties.

STRATEGIC IMPLICATIONS OF MARKETING IN THE 21ST CENTURY

Today's sales forces are a new breed of businesspeople. Richly nourished in a tradition of sales, their roles are strengthened even further through technology. However, as many companies are discovering, nothing can replace the power of personal selling in generating sales and in building strong, loyal customer relationships.

Selling has experienced a series of evolutionary stages, each building on the strengths of previous ones. Whereas salespeople of the early 1900s were familiar with customers' lifestyles as well as their occupational needs, the mid-1900s moved selling from a one-to-one environment to a process of providing goods and services to massive numbers of people who remained largely anonymous. In the past decade, however, database technology and the Internet have again enabled salespeople to satisfy the needs of individual customers, often through teamwork and partnerships. Instead of eliminating many of the processes performed by a salesperson, electronic technologies enhance the ability to sell the right product to the right consumer at the right time.

Salespeople today are a critical link in developing relationships between the customer and the company. They communicate customer needs and wants to coworkers in various departments and divisions within an organization, enabling a cooperative, companywide effort in improving product offerings and in better satisfying individuals within the target market. For salespeople, the greatest benefit of electronic technologies is the ability to share knowledge when it is needed with those who need to know, including customers, suppliers, and employees.

A number of environmental pressures have led to changes in personal selling and sales-force management:

- Buyers are more sophisticated, demanding more rapid, low-cost transactions.
- Customer and supplier data are linked via computerized data warehousing systems that identify optimal consumer characteristics.
- New technology makes alternative, low-cost distribution methods possible.
- Automatic inventory reorder processes reduce the need for face-to-face meetings with buyers.
- Computer databases, telecommunication sales, catalogs, and the Internet provide transaction mediums at much lower costs per transaction than the traditional field-selling channel.
- Product life cycles are accelerating, with products moving more rapidly into and out of the marketplace.
- Customers in some market segments are less loyal and more prone to switch suppliers.

Recognizing the long-term impact of keeping satisfied buyers—those who make repeat and cross-purchases and provide referrals—versus dissatisfied buyers—who generally tell about 11 other people of their dissatisfaction—organizations are increasingly training their sales forces to provide superior customer service and rewarding them for increasing satisfaction levels.

Where skills of the last century's salesperson were likely to include persuasion, selling ability, and product knowledge, the 21st-century sales professional is more likely to possess communication skills, problem-solving skills, and knowledge of products, customers, industries, and applications. Last century's salesperson tended to be self-driven; today's sales professional is more likely to be a team player as well as a customer advocate who serves his or her buyers by solving problems.

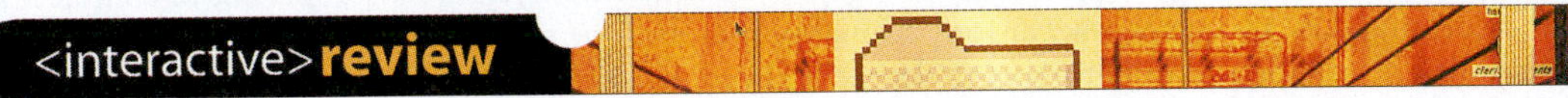

<interactive>review

FLASH CHAPTER REVIEW PRESENTATION

<interactive>video case

CONCEPT2 ROWS TO SUCCESS

<interactive>game

QUIZ BOWL

<interactive>video case

KRISPY KREME CONTINUING VIDEO CASE: KRISPY KREME COMMUNICATES SWEET NOTHINGS

endofchaptermaterial

- Summary of Chapter Objectives
- Chapter Outline
- Key Terms
- Review Questions
- Projects and Teamwork Exercises
- 'netWork
- Crossword Puzzles
- Case 19.1: The Complex World of Overseas Sales

Take the Post-Test to assess your overall understanding of the key ideas in this chapter. The Post-Test provides a comprehensive selection of exam-style questions addressing the main topics and concepts of the chapter. At the completion of each Post-Test, you will receive a score and instructive feedback on how you answered each question, and a direct link to the part of the chapter addressed in the question. Take the Post-Test as often as you need to—a record of your progress for each attempt is kept for you to revisit and gauge your improvement. And each Post-Test is randomly generated, so every attempt is new.

Post-Test

PROLOGUE

1. Julie Rawe, "Young & Jobless," *Time*, June 6, 2002, pp. 36–39; Stephanie Armour, "Young Job Seekers Get Squeezed Out," *USA Today*, January 29, 2002, p. B1.
2. Joanne Gordon, "Battle of the Boards," *Forbes*, August 12, 2002, p. 50.
3. Diya Gullapalli, "Who Says Interns No Longer Get Any Perks?" *The Wall Street Journal*, July 30, 2002, pp. B1, B8.
4. Reported in Louis E. Boone, *Quotable Business, 2nd ed.* New York: Random House, 1999, p. 103.
5. Daniel Eisenberg, "The Coming Job Boom," *Time*, May 6, 2002, p. 41.
6. Christine Galea, "2002 Salary Survey," *Sales & Marketing Management*, May 2002, p. 34.

CHAPTER 1

1. Erin Strout, "Keep Them Coming Back for More," *Sales & Marketing Management*, February 2002, p. 51; Daniel Gross, "Public Trust," *U.S. Airways Attache*, December 2001, pp. 15, 17; "Want Loyalty? Treat Them Like Royalty," *Brandweek*, August 13, 2001, p. 26; Susan Greco, "Fanatics!," *Inc.*, April 30, 2001, pp. 37–47.
2. David M. Szymanski and David H. Henard, "Customer Satisfaction: A Meta-Analysis of the Empirical Evidence," *Journal of the Academy of Marketing Science*, Winter 2001, vol. 29, no. 1, pp. 16–35.
3. Erik Hedegaard, "The Osbournes—America's First Family," *Rolling Stone*, May 9, 2002, pp. 33–36; Edna Gundersen, Bill Kennedy, and Ann Oldenburg, "'The Osbournes' Find a Home in America's Living Rooms," *USA Today*, April 19, 2002, pp. A1, A2.
4. David Finnigan, "Toy Kingpins Find Reluctant Buyers with Showroom Virtually Quiet," *Brandweek*, February 18, 2002, pp. 11–12; Seth M. Siegel, "The Quietest Toy Fair," *Brandweek*, February 11, 2002, pp. 23–24.
5. Joseph P. Guiltinan and Gordon W. Paul, *Marketing Management*, 6th ed. (New York: McGraw-Hill, 1996), pp. 3–4.
6. Betsy McKay, "In a Water Fight, Coke and Pepsi Try Opposite Tacks," *Wall Street Journal*, April 18, 2002, pp. A1, A8.
7. Advertisement, copyright 2001, New York Stock Exchange.
8. Zachary Schiller, "Make It Simple," *Business Week*, September 9, 1996, p. 102.
9. Paul A. Herbig, *Handbook of Cross-Cultural Marketing* (New York: The International Business Press, 1998), pp. 96–100.
10. Robert J. Keith, "The Marketing Revolution," *Journal of Marketing*, January 1960, p. 60.
11. Laura Hillenbrand, *Seabiscuit: An American Legend* (New York: Random House, 2001), pp. 3–6.
12. Robert J. Keith, "The Marketing Revolution," *Journal of Marketing*, January 1960, p. 60.
13. Theodore Levitt, *Innovations in Marketing* (New York: McGraw-Hill, 1962), p. 7.
14. Steven Rosenbush, "Armstrong's Last Stand," *BusinessWeek*, February 25, 2001, pp. 88–96.
15. Ann Marsh, "Ryder System," *Forbes*, May 21, 2001, p. 106.
16. Steve Rosenbrush, "Armstrong's Last Stand," *Business Week*, February 25, 2001, pp. 88–96.
17. Jacquelyn Lynn, "Hidden Resources," *Entrepreneur*, January 2000, p. 102.
18. Betsy Spethmann, "Charity Begins at the Home Page," *Promo*, February 2000, p. 52.
19. Ibid., p. 50.
20. Michael M. Phillips, "Taking Stock: Top Sports Pros Find a New Way to Score: Getting Equity Stakes," *Wall Street Journal*, April 18, 1997, pp. A1, A8.
21. Roy Hoffman, "A Conversation with Jimmy Buffett," *Mobile Register*, April 21, 2002, pp. E1, E5; James Brady, "In Step with Jimmy Buffett," *Parade*, April 28, 2002, p. 22.
22. John Rofe, "Giants Take Pauses for Causes," *Sports Business Journal*, April 23–29, 2001, p. 10.
23. Andy Brumer, "Coca-Cola Steps up for Woods' Charity," *Sports Business Journal*, April 29, 2001, p. 10.
24. "Consumers Care About Causes," *Sales & Marketing Management*, June 1999, p. 74; and Linda I. Nowak, "Cause Marketing Alliances: Corporate Associations and Consumer Responses," *Proceedings of the Winter Educators Conference*, St. Petersburg, FL: American Marketing Association, February 1999.
25. Hilary Cassidy, "An Olympic Moment," *Brandweek*, October 29, 2001, pp. 1, 8.
26. Anne Marie Chaker, "Red Cross Will Use the Entire $564 Million of Liberty Fund for September 11 Victims, Relief," *The Wall Street Journal*, November 15, 2001, **http://wsjclassroomedition .com**.
27. Louis E. Boone and David L. Kurtz, *Recession and the Terrorist Attacks on America* (Mason, OH: South-Western Publishing, 2002).
28. Gene D. Cohen, "c=me," *Modern Maturity*, March–April 2000, p. 43.
29. Mylene Mangalindan, "Yahoo Says Its Online Sales Volume Jumped 86 %," *The Wall Street Journal*, December 27, 2001, p. B2; Chris Pentila, "Wholesell Changes," *Entrepreneur*, May 2002, pp. 48–49.
30. Laura Bly, "Budget Car Rental Joins Online Name-Your-Price Fray," *USA Today*, June 4, 1999, p. A1.
31. Steve Jarvis, "A Whirlwind of Technologies May Sweep up Marketers," *Outlook 2002*, January 7, 2002, p. 8.
32. Ibid.
33. Ibid.
34. Scott McCartney, "Flight of Fancy," *The Wall Street Journal*, February 4, 2002, p. A1.
35. "Forbes Magnetic 40," *Forbes*, May 21, 2001, p. 100.
36. Michael McCarthy, "Anti-Smoking Ad Stirs Up Super Bowl," *USA Today*, January 25, 2002, p. B7.
37. Alan Byrd, "Where NFL Leads, Many Sports Follow," *Street & Smith's Sports Business Journal*, January 4–10, 1999, p. 21.
38. "Shell Gives Students a Head Start," from a special report of the Shell Oil Company, *Fortune*, November 9, 1998, pp. S7–S8.

CHAPTER 2

1. Steven Levy, "The Skinny: AOL's Suit," *Newsweek*, February 4, 2002, p. 9; Julia Angwin, "Netscape Goes One More Round," *The Wall Street Journal*, January 24, 2002, p. B1; Julia Angwin, Nicholas Kulish, and Rebecca Buckman, "AOL Sues Microsoft over Netscape in Case That Could Seek Billions," *The Wall Street Journal*, January 23, 2002, p. B1; Eryn Brown, "Just Another Product Launch," *Fortune*, November 12, 2001, pp. 102–108; Steven Levy, "Shooting with Live Ammo," *Newsweek*, August 13, 2001, pp. 32, 34; Catherine Yang et al., "AOL vs. Microsoft," *BusinessWeek*, August 13, 2001, pp. 28, 30.
2. Kathy Mulady, "Nordstrom Way Is Legendary in Shopping," *Seattle P-I.com*, June 26, 2001, **http://seattlep-i.nwsource.com**; Ron Lieber, "She Reads Customers' Minds," *Fast Company*, February 2001, **http://www.fastcompany.com**.
3. Louise Lee and Nanette Byrnes, "More Than Just a Bad Patch at the Gap," *BusinessWeek*, February 11, 2002, p. 36.
4. "Office Depot's E-Diva," *BusinessWeek Online*, August 6, 2001, **http://www.businessweek.com**.
5. Bass Pro Shops promotional brochure, Bass Pro Shops, Springfield, Missouri.
6. Company Web site, **http://www.maldenmills.com**, accessed March 8, 2002.
7. Darrell Rigby, "Smart Managing/Best Practices, Careers, and Ideas: What's Today's Special at the Consultant's Cafe?" *Fortune*, September 7, 1998, p. 162.
8. Derek F. Abell, "Strategic Window," *Journal of Marketing*, July 1978, pp. 21–26; and John K. Ryans and William L. Shanklin, *Strategic Planning: Concepts and Implementation* (New York: Random House, 1985), p. 11.
9. Stephanie N. Mehta, "Cisco Fractures Its Own Fairy Tale," *Fortune.com*, May 14, 2001, **http://www .fortune.com**.
10. Presentation by Maxine Clark, St. Louis, March 2002.
11. Genaro C. Armas, "Black, Hispanic Populations Nearly Equal," *Mobile Register*, March 8, 2001, p. A9.
12. Bob Woods, "Hispanic Marketing Can Be Eventful," *Promo*, May 2000, pp. 25–26.
13. "Women on Their Way," Wyndham Hotels Web site, **http://www.wyndham.com**, accessed January 3, 2003; Katherine Conrad, "Hoteliers Cashing in with Women Business Travelers," *East Bay Business Times*, March 8, 2002, **http://eastbay.bizjournals.com**.
14. Gary Hamel, "Smart Mover, Dumb Mover," *Fortune*, September 3, 2001, pp. 191–192.
15. Peter Newcomb, "Sony," and Jody Yen, "Georgia-Pacific Group," in "Forbes Magnetic 40," *Forbes*, May 21, 2001, pp. 84, 86.
16. John G. Spooner, "EMachines Shows Off Latest PC Fashions," *C/Net News.com*, April 10, 2002, **http://news.com.com**.

17. Kathryn Kranhold, "Sotheby's Chief Is Convicted of Price-Fixing," *The Wall Street Journal*, December 6, 2001, p. B1; Noelle Knox, "Former Chairman of Sotheby's Convicted," *USA Today*, December 6, 2001, p. B1.
18. Emily Thornton, "Enviro-Cars: The Race Is On," *Business Week*, February 8, 1999, pp. 74–76.
19. Andrew Gillies, "General Mills," in "Forbes Magnetic 40," *Forbes*, May 21, 2001, p. 86.
20. Scott Thurm, "The Ultimate Weapon," *The Wall Street Journal*, April 17, 2000, p. R18.
21. L.L. Bean Web site, **http://www.llbean.com**, accessed May 10, 2002; William Symonds, "Paddling Harder at L. L. Bean," *Business Week*, December 7, 1998, pp. 48–49.
22. Eryn Brown, "Just Another Product Launch," *Fortune*, November 12, 2001, p. 104.
23. Alex Taylor III, "Eat Our Dust," *Fortune*, June 11, 2001, p. 151.
24. John Bissell, "Top of the Mind: No. 1 Means Little in Fast Times," *Brandweek*, March 22, 1999. p. 28.
25. A meta-analysis of 48 studies revealed a positive relationship between market share and profitability. See David M. Szymansky, Sundarwaj G. Bharadgaj, and P. Rajan Varadarajan, "An Analysis of the Market Share-Profitability Relationship," *Journal of Marketing*, July 1993, pp. 1–18.

CHAPTER 3

1. Marilyn Adams, "Despite Losses, Delta Remains Optimistic About Its Future," *USA Today*, April 26, 2002, pp. B1, B2; "Airline Industry Still Smarting from September 11," The Associated Press, February 22, 2002, AP Online; Christopher Elliott, "Plane Truths about Flying," *The Washington Post*, February 18, 2002, p. A23.
2. "Top 10 Scams on the Information Highway," *U.S. News & World Report*, November 13, 2000, p. 16; Paul Keegan, "Online Auctions: From Seedy Flea Markets to Big Business," *Upside*, July 1999, pp. 70–80; Kip Cheng, "eBay: Best Virtual Marketing," *Adweek*, June 28, 1999, p. 42.
3. Larry Margasak, "UPS Flexed Political Muscle to Win First Flights to China," *Mobile Register*, April 11, 2001, p. B6; Charles Haddad, "How UPS Delivered through the Disaster," *BusinessWeek*, October 1, 2001, p. 66.
4. "MasterCard and Hotel Reservations Announce Strategic Alliance," *Card News*, February 20, 2002; "Love at First Site," *Art & Auction*, July/August 1999, p. 7.
5. "Go to Jail," *Forbes*, May 29, 2000, p. 62.
6. G. Pascal Zachary, "Let's Play Oligopoly!" *The Wall Street Journal*, March 8, 1999, p. B1.
7. David Pringle, "Motorola Hopes Early Push in 3G Market Yields Gains," *The Wall Street Journal*, March 28, 2002, p. B4; Jennifer Tanaka, "Design: The Coolest Cell Phone Wins," *Newsweek*, February 25, 2002, p. 9; Maureen Tkacik, "Hey Dude, This Sure Isn't the Gap—Pink Fur Pants, Tongue Rings Draw 'Alternative' Teens to Hot Topic's Mall Stores," *The Wall Street Journal*, February 12, 2002, p. B1.
8. Paulo Prada and Bruce Orwall, "A Certain 'Je Ne Sais Quoi' at Disney's New Park," *The Wall Street Journal*, March 12, 2002, p. B1.
9. Gardiner Harris, "Back to the Lab," *The Wall Street Journal*, January 29, 2002, p. A1.
10. Amy Tsao, "Fiorina's Stereotype-Smashing Performance," *BusinessWeek*, April 3, 2002, **http://www .businessweek.com**; Kristine Ellis, "Sharing Best Practices Globally," *Training*, July 2001.
11. Faith Keenan and Spencer E. Ante, "The New Teamwork," *BusinessWeek*, February 18, 2002, **http://www.businessweek.com**.
12. Dori Jones Yang, "Leaving Moore's Law in the Dust," *U.S. News & World Report*, July 10, 2000, p. 37.
13. Michael Gartenburg, "Enough Is Enough with Microsoft Case," *Computerworld*, March 25, 2002, p. 25; Joseph Nocera, "Witnesses in Wonderland," *Fortune*, March 1, 1999, pp. 168–180.
14. "DotCons," *Entrepreneur*, March 2001, p. 24; John Rendleman, "FTC Steers Clear of Internet Regulation—For Now," *Informationweek*, October 9, 2000. See also **http://www.ftc.gov/bcp/conline/edcams/dotcon**.
15. Elizabeth Crowley and Glenn R. Simpson, "Citicorp Joins Up with Secret Service to Fight E-Fraud," *The Wall Street Journal*, March 16, 2000, p. A12.
16. Dana James, "Deregulation Growing by Fits and Starts," *Marketing News*, June 5, 2000, p. 10.
17. Bryan Gruly and Rebecca Smith, "Anatomy of a Fall: Keys to Success Left Kenneth Lay Open to Disaster," *The Wall Street Journal*, April 26, 2002, pp. A1, A5; "AGL Chief Sees Deregulation Reform in Georgia," Reuters Limited, January 28, 2002.
18. William Glanz, "Bankruptcies Climb to Record Levels in 2001," *The Washington Times*, February 20, 2002.
19. Tully, "From Bad to Worse."
20. Jeannine Aversa, "Unemployment Rate Hits 6 Percent," Associated Press, downloaded from AOL.com, May 3, 2002.
21. Joan Raymond, "The Jaws of Victory," *Newsweek*, March 18, 2002, p. 38P.
22. Betsy Shiffman, "Still Want to Teach the World to Sing?" *Forbes*, January 16, 2002; Brian Zajac, "Yankee Travelers," *Forbes*, July 27, 1998, p. 162.
23. "High Powered Alliance Demonstrates Wireless Internet Services in China," *Direct Marketing*, August 2000, p. 12.
24. Marc L. Songini, "Phillips Gives Petroleum Blending Software the Gas," *Computerworld*, March 18, 2002, p. 19.
25. Anita Hamilton, "Why Hybrids Are Hot," *Time*, April 29, 2002, pp. 52–53.
26. Daniel Fisher, "When the National Nanny Does Your Laundry," *Forbes*, July 9, 2001, p. 64.
27. Kerry A. Dolan and Quentin Hardy, "The Challenge from China," *Forbes*, May 13, 2002, pp. 73–76.
28. Gaston F. Ceron, "Online Brokerage Firms Face Pinched Earnings," *The Wall Street Journal*, July 16, 2001, p. B8; Charles Gasparino and Rebecca Buckman, "Facing Internet Threat, Merrill to Offer Trading Online for Low Fees," *The Wall Street Journal*, June 1, 1999, pp. A1, A10.
29. Scott Woolley, "Steal This Movie," *Forbes*, February 18, 2002, p. 66.
30. "Dieste Multicultural Shop of Year," *Advertising Age*, January 14, 2002, p. S-8.
31. Leslie E. Royal, "Make 'Lemon Law' Lemonade," *Black Enterprise*, May 2001, p. 150; Lawrence Lindner, "Whole Grains, Half Truths; You Must Know the Code to Tell the Whole Wheat from the Chaff," *The Washington Post*, July 31, 2001, p. F1.
32. O. C. Ferrell, John Fraedrich, and Linda Ferrell, *Business Ethics* (Boston, MA: Houghton Mifflin Company, 2002), pp. 85–86; David Barboza, "Tyson Fosters Ties to Officials but Is Unable to Avoid Scrutiny," *The New York Times*, January 1, 2002, p. C1.
33. Jim Carroll, "Significant Drop in Teen Smoking Is Recorded in U.S.," *The Wall Street Journal*, December 20, 2001, **http://www.wsj.com**; Corinne Economaki, "Still Smokin' at the Track," *Brandweek*, March 22, 1999, pp. 20–22; Robert D. Deutsch, "A Eulogy for Joe Camel," *Brandweek*, May 3, 1999, pp. 29, 32.
34. Larry Dobrow, "Tread Carefully on Privacy," *Advertising Age*, October 29, 2001, **http://www .adage.com**; Megan Santosus, "The Price Is Right," *CIO Enterprise*, June 15, 1999, p. 24.
35. "DoubleClick Settles Online-Privacy Suits, Plans to Ensure Protections, Pay Legal Fees," *The Wall Street Journal*, April 1, 2002, p. B8.
36. Eilene Hu, "What That Seal of 'Approval' Really Means," *McCall's*, November 1998, p. 152.
37. Brandon Copple, "Bake Off," *Forbes*, April 16, 2001, p. 305.
38. Cindy Starr, "Pharmaceutical Advertising Barrage Lures Consumers, Worries Doctors," Scripps Howard News Service, February 2, 2002; Devika Sennik, "Influence of Direct to Consumer Pharmaceutical Advertising and Patients' Requests on Prescribing Decision," *British Medical Journal*, February 2, 2002.
39. Laura Johannes and David Armstrong, "Why Some Dialysis Patients Take $12-a-Day Drug Instead of Tums," *The Wall Street Journal*, June 26, 2001, p. B1.
40. Donna Rosato, "New Travel Sites under Scrutiny on Ticket Costs," *USA Today*, May 24, 2000, p. 1B; Ira Teinowitz, "Web Ad Disclosures Examined," *Advertising Age*, May 24, 1999, p. 48.
41. "Schering-Plough Corp.: U.S. Attorney Begins Issuing Subpoenas in Pricing Probe," *The Wall Street Journal*, April 1, 2002, p. C5.
42. Karen Lowry Miller, "The Pill Machine," *Newsweek*, November 19, 2001, p. 46.
43. Joel Dreyfuss, "Planned Obsolescence Is Alive and Well," *Fortune*, February 15, 1999, p. 192.
44. Bob Garfield, "Inspiration and Urge-to-Serve Mark the Best of Ad Council," *Advertising Age*, April 29, 2002, p. C2.
45. Michelle Kessler, "PC Makers Soon May Be Forced to Recycle," *USA Today*, February 26, 2002, p. B1.
46. Christopher Tkaczyk, "Recycling," *Fortune*, April 1, 2002, p. 36; Laura Cohn, "The Nuclear Waste Debate: All Over but the Shouting?" *BusinessWeek*, December 10, 2001, p. 43; John T. Maybury, "Your Wedding Band May Have Once Lived in a Computer," *Forbes ASAP*, February 22, 1999, p. 20.
47. Arlene Weintraub and Laura Cohn, "A Thousand-Year Plan for Nuclear Waste," *BusinessWeek*, May 6, 2002, pp. 94, 96.
48. Geoffrey A. Fowler, "Green Sales Pitch Isn't Moving Many Products," *The Wall Street Journal*, March 6, 2001, p. B1.
49. "The Nation's CEOs Look to the Future," National Institute of Science and Technology, **http:// www.quality.nist.gov**, June 16, 1999.

CHAPTER 4

1. Lisa Bertagnoli, "E-Marketing Tricky in Europe," *Marketing News*, July 16, 2001, p. 19; Patrick Thibodeau, "Bush Rejects EU Privacy Plan," *ComputerWorld*, April 2, 2001, **http://www.computer world.com**; Brandon Mitchener, "Border Crossings," *The Wall Street Journal*, November 22, 1999, pp. R41.
2. Margret Johnson, "Report: U.S. Hi-Tech Exports Now Largest Segment," IDG News Service, March 13, 2000, **http://www.idg.net**; Eric S. Hardy, "An Almost Perfect World," *Forbes*, July 26, 1999, pp. 160–161.
3. Wendy Zellner et al., "How Well Does Wal-Mart Travel?" *BusinessWeek*, September 3, 2001, pp. 82, 84.
4. "About New York Metro Weddings," company Web site, **http://www.NewYorkMetroWeddings .com**, accessed January 13, 2003; Scott S. Smith, "The Vow Factor," *Entrepreneur*, February 2001, **http://www.entrepreneur.com**.
5. Ad for Hilton HHonors Worldwide, copyright 2002 Hilton HHonors Worldwide.
6. "IDC Predicts Worldwide Internet Services Revenues Will Surge Past $78 million in 2003," *NetScorecard*, **http://www.netscorecard.com**, accessed June 9, 1999.

7. "Finance Site the Stickiest Online," **http://cyberatlas.internet.com**, February 28, 2002; Michael Pastore, "Branches Still Rule Banking in Europe," **http://cyberatlas.internet.com**, November 19, 2001.
8. "REI Opens First International Store in Tokyo," *Sports Trend,* June 2000, p. 6.
9. Business Latin America, "Two U.S. Fast Food Chains Expand Locally," Yahoo Finance, biz.yahoo.com, February 23, 2002; "Arby's to Open 102 Restaurants in Britain," *Mobile Register,* July 11, 1999, p. 6B.
10. Mark Tatge, "Burgertory," *Forbes,* June 11, 2001, p. 76; and Jonathan Asher, "Global Branding: Same, but Different," *Brandweek,* April 9, 2001, p. 25.
11. Jack Neff, "Test in Paris, France, Launch It in Paris, Texas," *Advertising Age,* May 31, 1999, p. 26; and Jack Neff, "P&G Marks First with U.S. Test of Swiffer," *Advertising Age,* July 12, 1998, p. 32.
12. "World Population Profile: 1998 Highlights," U.S. Census Bureau, **http://www.census.gov**, accessed April 11, 2002.
13. Daniel Fisher, "Gone Flat," *Forbes,* October 15, 2001, p. 79.
14. Betsy McKay, "Pepsi and Coke Roll Out Flavors to Boost Sales," *The Wall Street Journal,* May 7, 2002, pp. B1, B4; "The Coca-Cola Co.," *Hoover's Online* company capsule, **http://www.hoovers.com**, accessed April 26, 2002.
15. John A. Byrne, "Today, Mexico. Tomorrow . . . ," *BusinessWeek,* April 10, 2000, p. 184.
16. Mercedes M. Cardona, "J&J Readies U.S. Intro of Leading French Brand," *Advertising Age,* July 12, 1999, p. 57.
17. David Woodruff, "For French Retailers, a Weapon against Wal-Mart," *The Wall Street Journal,* September 27, 1999, p. B1.
18. Miriam Jordan, "Marketing Gurus Say: In India, Think Cheap, Lose the Cold Cereal," *The Wall Street Journal,* October 11, 1996, p. A7.
19. Reuters Limited, "Nokia Looks to Dominate Sales in China," *CNet Asia,* February 26, 2002, asia.cnet.com; Andrew Tanzer, "China Goes Wireless," *Forbes,* July 26, 1999, pp. 60–63.
20. Geri Smith et al., "A Wrong Turn?" *BusinessWeek,* January 21, 2002, pp. 42–44; Tony Smith, "Argentina Devalues Peso, Drops Peg to Dollar," *Mobile Register,* January 7, 2002, p. A7.
21. Colleen Barry, "Euro Currency Begins in Europe," *Mobile Register,* January 1, 2002, p. A11; and "Europeans Make Change to Euro," *USA Today,* December 26, 2001, p. 3B.
22. Lalita Khosla, "You Say Tomato," *Forbes,* May 21, 2001, p. 36.
23. Desa Philadelphia, "And What Does It Mean in Farsi?" *Time Global Business,* November 2001, pp. B16–17; David Lieberman, "I'd Like to Buy a Vowel, Drivers Say," *USA Today,* August 9, 2001, p. B3; Sally McGrane, "Cultural Web Faux Pas," *Forbes ASAP,* February 21, 2000, p. 28.
24. *Marketing News,* July 3, 2000, p. 15; "Projected Growth of Online Population," *Mobile Register,* June 25, 2000, p. 6A; "The Web Is Truly Worldwide," *Global Insights,* June 1999, pp. 1–2.
25. "Europe to Demand Strict Molecular Characterisation for GMOs?" the Institute of Science in Society press release, May 21, 2002, **http://www.biotech-info.net**; Amy Bowdler and Emily Felt, "GMO's Exporters Should Follow the Debate," *Insight,* Summer 1999, pp. 1–2.
26. Anne Neville, "France's Shopping Frenzy: All's Well That Sells Well," *Mobile Register,* February 25, 1999, p. 3D.
27. Dexter Roberts et al., "Days of Rage," *BusinessWeek,* April 8, 2002, pp. 50–51.
28. Lisa Bertagnoli, "E-Marketing Tricky in Europe," *Marketing News,* July 16, 2001, p. 19.
29. Michael Plogell and Felix Hofer, "No-Nos in Europe," *Promo,* April 2000, p. 23.
30. Antoaneta Bezlova, "McDonald's Arches Outlawed in Beijing," *USA Today,* March 5, 2002, p. 7B.
31. "Landmark Trade Agreement Sets Vietnam on Course Toward Reform," *Mobile Register,* July 15, 2000, p. 6B.
32. Martin Crutsinger, "Canadian Timber Slapped with Tariff," *USA Today,* August 13, 2001, p. B3.
33. James Cox, "Tariffs Shield Some U.S. Products," *USA Today,* May 6, 1999, pp. B1, B2.
34. Andrew Tanzer, "The Great Quota Hustle," *Forbes,* March 6, 2000, p. 124.
35. James Bennett, "To Clear the Air with Europe, U.S. Waives Some Sanctions," *The New York Times,* May 19, 1998, **http://www.nytimes.com**, accessed July 27, 1999.
36. Aaron Bernstein, "Backlash," *BusinessWeek,* April 24, 2000, pp. 38–48.
37. Paul Geitner, "World Trade Organization Hands Major Loss to U.S.," *Mobile Register,* January 15, 2002, p. B5.
38. "USWA Challenging NAFTA Constitutionality in Lawsuit," *Fair Trade Watch,* **http://www.fairtradewatch.org**, accessed July 27, 1999; David C. Datelle, "NAFTA's Effect on U.S. Jobs," *Progressive Policy Institute,* **http://www.ppionline.org**, accessed July 28, 1999.
39. Jim Rogers, "Running on Empty," *Worth,* January/February 2002, pp. 55–56; Traci Carl, "Mexican Stand-off on Trade," *The Morning News,* August 22, 2001, p. 3C; Geri Smith, "Is the Magic Starting to Fade?" *BusinessWeek,* August 6, 2001, pp. 42–43; Charles J. Whalen et al., "NAFTA's Scorecard: So Far, So Good," *BusinessWeek,* July 9, 2001, p. 54.
40. Geri Smith et al., "Betting on Free Trade," *BusinessWeek,* April 23, 2001, pp. 60, 62.
41. Geri Smith et al., "Mexico Pulls Off Another Trade Coup," *BusinessWeek,* February 7, 2000, p. 56.
42. Lambeth Hochwald, "Are You Smart Enough to Sell Globally?" *Sales & Marketing Management,* July 1998, pp. 53–55.
43. Jay Green and Ken Belson, "The Mariners Catch a Tsunami," *BusinessWeek,* June 25, 2001, pp. 98–99.
44. "Foreign Direct Investment Is on the Rise around the World," *The New Economy Index,* accessed April 26, 2002, **http://www.neweconomyindex.org**; Russell B. Scholl, "The International Investment Position of the United States at Year-end 1998," *Survey of Current Business,* U.S. Bureau of Economic Analysis, July 1999, pp. 4, 7.
45. Stephen Baker, "Why Europe Keeps Gobbling Up U.S. Companies," *BusinessWeek,* June 18, 2001.
46. Lisa Bertagnoli, "Middle East Muddle," *Marketing News,* July 16, 2001, pp. 1, 9.
47. Herb Greenberg, "Does Tyco Play Accounting Games?" *Fortune,* May 6, 2002, pp. 83–86; Peter Marsh, "Tyco Searches for Directors in Europe and Asia," *Financial Times,* July 16, 2001, **http://news.ft.com**.
48. Jonathan Asher, "Global Branding: Same, but Different," *Brandweek,* April 9, 2001, p. 25.
49. William Echikson and Dean Foust, "For Coke, Local Is It," *BusinessWeek,* July 3, 2000, p. 122.
50. Ibid.
51. "The Best Global Brands," *BusinessWeek,* August 5, 2002, pp. 92–96.
52. Juliana Korentang, "SonicNet Tunes into Youth Music Worldwide," *Ad Age International,* June 1999, p. 29.
53. Venture Safenet Inc. Web site, **http://www.vsnet.com**, accessed January 12, 2003.
54. Stephen Baker, "Why Europe Keeps Gobbling up U.S. Companies," *BusinessWeek,* June 18, 2001, p. 56.

CHAPTER 5

1. "December Rakes in E-Commerce Dough," CyberAtlas, accessed at the CyberAtlas Web site, **http://cyberatlas.internet.com**, April 5, 2002; Robert Hof and Heather Green, "How Amazon Cleared That Hurdle," *BusinessWeek,* February 4, 2002, pp. 60–62; Jon Swartz, "E-Tailers Ring Up a Record Holiday Week," *USA Today,* December 27, 2001, p. B3; Mylene Mangalindan, "Yahoo Says Its Online Sales Volume Jumped 86%," *The Wall Street Journal,* December 27, 2001, p. B2; Jeanette Brown et al., "Shoppers Are Beating a Path to the Web," *BusinessWeek,* December 24, 2001, p. 41; Jon Swartz, "Retailers Discover Leap to Web's a Doozy," *USA Today,* December 18, 2001, p. B3; Allen Wan, "Microsoft Having Xmas to Remember," *CBS Market Watch,* accessed at the CBS Market Watch Web site, **http://cbs.marketwatch.com**, December 18, 2001.
2. CyberAtlas, accessed from the CyberAtlas Web Site, **http://cyberatlas.internet.com**, April 15, 2002.
3. Robert Hof, "Don't Cut Back Now," *BusinessWeek,* accessed at the *BusinessWeek* Web site, **http://www.businessweek.com**, March 30, 2002.
4. Neoforma, accessed from the Neoforma Web site, **http://www.neoforma.com**, April 8, 2002.
5. CyberAtlas, accessed from the CyberAtlas Web site, **http://cyberatlas.internet.com**, April 8, 2002.
6. Lisa Bowman, "Disney Wins Round in Movie-Trailer Case," CNET News, accessed from the CNET Web site, **http://www.cnet.com**, April 9, 2002.
7. "Top of the Week," *U.S. News & World Report,* April 15, 2002, p. 15.
8. CyberAtlas, accessed from the CyberAtlas Web site, **http://cyberatlas.internet.com**, April 9, 2002.
9. CIO Web Business, accessed from the CIO Web site, **http://www.cio.com**, March 29, 2002.
10. CIO Web Business, accessed from the CIO Web site, **http://www.cio.com**, March 30, 2002.
11. Lands' End, accessed from the Lands' End Web site, **http://www.landsend.com**, April 12, 2002; Dell Computer, accessed from the Dell Computer Web site, **http://www.dell.com**, April 12, 2002; *USA Today,* accessed from the *USA Today* Web site, **http://www.usatoday.com**, April 12, 2002; Farm.com, accessed from the Farm.com Web site, **http://www.farm.com**, April 12, 2002.
12. **http://cyberatlas.internet.com**, accessed April 22, 2002.
13. "H.J. Heinz Company Case Study," **http://www.freemarkets.com**, accessed March 27, 2002.
14. **http://cyberatlas.internet.com**, accessed April 22, 2002.
15. Alex Salkever and Olga Kharif, "Business' Killer App: The Web," *BusinessWeek,* **http://www.business week.com**, accessed April 15, 2002.
16. IBM, accessed from the IBM Web site, **http://www.ibm.com**, April 15, 2002.
17. Robert Hof et al., "The 'Click Here' Economy," *BusinessWeek,* **http://www.businessweek.com**, accessed April 15, 2002.
18. Alex Salkever and Olga Kharif, "Business' Killer App: The Web."
19. "Falling in Gov," *Entrepreneur,* March 2002, pp. 58–63.
20. Anne D'Innocenzio, "2nd Chance for Customizing," Associated Press, **http://www.ap.org**, accessed April 15, 2002.
21. HistoryBuff.com, **http://www.historybuff.com**, accessed April 17, 2002.

22. Robyn Greenspan, "Customer Service Is Key to Travelers," http://cyberatlas.internet.com, accessed April 17, 2002.
23. Amy Tsao, "Where Retailers Shop for Savings," *BusinessWeek*, http://www.businessweek.com, accessed April 17, 2002.
24. AutoNetwork.com, http://www.autonetwork.com, accessed April 17, 2002.
25. http://cyberatlas.internet.com, accessed April 22, 2002.
26. Ibid.
27. Ibid.
28. Marcia Stepanek, "None of Your Business," *BusinessWeek*, http://www.businessweek.com, accessed March 28, 2002.
29. Ibid.
30. "Privacy Groups Ask for Investigation of Amazon.com," ZDNet News, http://www.zdnet.com, accessed March 29, 2002; Nick Wingfield, "Amazon Clarifies Customer Info Policy," *Wall Street Journal*, http://www.zdnet.com, accessed March 29, 2002.
31. Nick Wingfield, "Amazon Clarifies Customer Info Policy."
32. "PrivaSeek E-Wallet Protects Privacy," *PC World*, http://www.pcworld.com, accessed March 21, 2002.
33. http://www.cyberatlas.com, accessed April 22, 2002.
34. Source: U.S. Department of Commerce, http://www.doc.gov, accessed April 17, 2002.
35. "Irrelevance through Constant Consumer Analysis," Jupiter Media Metrix, http://www.jmm.com, accessed April 17, 2002.
36. Ibid.
37. About Dell Computer, accessed at the Dell Web site, http://www.dell.com, April 22, 2002.
38. http://cyberatlas.internet.com, accessed April 22, 2002.
39. J. William Gurley, "The One Internet Metric that Really Matters," Fortune, http://www.fortune.com, accessed March 29, 2002.
40. "Success Story: Lexmark International," WebCriteria, http://www.webcriteria.com, accessed March 18, 2002.

CHAPTER 6

1. Lara Lee, "Hogging the Market," *Sales & Marketing Management*, April 2002, p. 70; Jonathan Fahey, "Love into Money," *Forbes*, January 7, 2002, p. 60; and Missy Sullivan, "High-Octane Hog," *Forbes*, September 10, 2001, p. 8. See also http://www.harley-davidson.com.
2. Lawrence A. Crosby and Sheree L. Johnston, "CRM and Management," *Marketing Management*, January/February 2002, p. 10.
3. Cara B. DiPasquale, "CRM: Navigate the Maze," *Advertising Age*, October 29, 2001, p. s1.
4. Wendy Cole, "Suddenly Loyalty Is Back in Business," *Time* Bonus Section: Your Business, December 2001, pp. Y13–16.
5. Veronica Agosta, "Nat City Takes Customer Focus to the Airwaves," *American Banker*, March 19, 2002, p. 1.
6. Karen Norman Kennedy, Felicia G. Lask, and Jerry R. Goolsby, "Customer Mind-Set of Employees throughout the Organization," *Journal of the Academy of Marketing Science*, Spring 2002, Vol. 30, No. 2, pp. 159–71; and Cole, "Suddenly Loyalty Is Back in Business."
7. Alan J. Liddle, "Internal Marketing As Important to Success at Pleasing Customers," *Restaurant News*, October 29, 2001, p. 60; and Jennifer Koch Laabs, "Optimas 2001—General Excellence: Thinking Outside the Box at The Container Store," *Workforce*, March 2001, pp. 35–38.
8. Mary Naylor and Susan Greco, *How to Keep the Customers You Want—and Say "Good-bye" to the Ones You Don't* (New York: McGraw-Hill, 2002).
9. Andy Cohen, "Look Who's Cooking Now," *Sales & Marketing Management*, December 2001, pp. 31–35.
10. Mary Jo Bitner, "Building Service Relationships: It's All About Promises," *Journal of the Academy of Marketing Science*, Fall 1995, pp. 246–251.
11. Cynthia Crossen, "The Big Power Crunch—Hot Selling Point: Guaranteed Cost of Utility Bills," *The Wall Street Journal*, May 9, 2001, p. B1.
12. Ron Zemke, "Training Top 100: FedEx," *Training*, March 2002, p. 67.
13. Leonard L. Berry, "Relationship Marketing of Service-Growing Internet, Emerging Perspectives," *Journal of the Academy of Marketing Science*, Fall 1995, p. 240.
14. "Deals and Discounts," *The New York Times*, March 17, 2002, p. 3.
15. Edmund O. Lawler, "Fine Line Between Added Value, Spam," *Advertising Age*, October 29, 2001, p. s4.
16. Bernard Stamler, "The Web Doesn't Sell Cars, But Lets Buyers Build Their Own," *The New York Times*, September 26, 2001, p. H10.
17. Lawler, "Fine Line between Added Value, Spam."
18. Richard Levey, "Tracking May Avoid Customer Defections," *Direct*, September 1, 1998, p. 50.
19. "Marriott Rewards Introduces Elite Membership and Benefits," Marriott News Release, April 27, 2000, http://www.marriott.com.
20. Mike Koller, "Harrah's Rewards Gamblers," *Internetweek*, October 8, 2001, pp. 10–11.
21. Greenberg, "Chrysler Group Maps Out Tactical Ventures into Alternative Marketing"; and Kate Fitzgerald, "Events a Big 1st Step," *Advertising Age*, October 29, 2001, p. s4.
22. Jeff Howe, "Ready for Prime Time," *Adweek*, September 10, 2001, p. Q10.
23. Steve Jarvis, "Net to the Rescue," *Marketing News*, February 18, 2002, p. 9.
24. Lawrence A. Crosby and Sheree L. Johnson, "CRM and Management," *Marketing Management*, January/February, 2002, p. 10; and Cara B. DiPasquale, "CRM: Navigate the Maze," *Advertising Age*, October 29, 2001, pp. s1–2.
25. Carleen Hawn, "The Man Who Sees Around Corners," *Forbes*, January 21, 2002, p. 72.
26. Ibid.
27. Kathleen Cholewka, "CRM: The Failures Are Your Fault," *emanager*, January 2002, pp. 23–24.
28. Hawn, "The Man Who Sees Around Corners."
29. David Finnigan, "The Biz," *Brandweek*, April 8, 2002.
30. Henry Canaday, "Is Bigger Better?" *Selling Power*, April 1999, pp. 64–65.
31. Joanne Cleaver, "Subtle Net Pitch Works for Seniors," *Marketing News*, July 19, 1999, pp. 1, 7.
32. Howard Millman, "Easy EDI for Everyone," *InfoWorld*, August 17, 1998, pp. 38–39.
33. Heather Harreld, "Supply Chain Collaboration," *InfoWorld*, December 24, 2001, pp. 22–25.
34. Harreld, "Supply Chain Collaboration."
35. Howard Millman, "Easy EDI for Everyone," *InfoWorld*, August 17, 1998, pp. 38–39.
36. "SkyTeam Gets on Board with $18 M Effort," *Brandweek*, April 11, 2002.

CHAPTER 7

1. Hillary Chura, "The New Normal," *Advertising Age*, March 11, 2002, p. 1; Greg Johnson, "Funny Ads Make Comeback," *Los Angeles Times*, January 10, 2002, http://www.latimes.com; Lisa Sanders, "Agencies Study a New America," *Advertising Age*, November 26, 2001, p. 3; Michael McCarthy, "Southwest Ads' Quick Return Works," *USA Today*, November 26, 2001, http://www.usatoday.com; Marc Gunther, "Ad Libbing," *Fortune*, October 29, 2001, pp. 111–116; Greg Hassell, "After Attacks, Firms Seek a More Sensitive Touch," *Houston Chronicle*, September 27, 2002, http://www.chron.com.
2. Gilbert A. Churchill, Jr., *Basic Marketing Research*, 4th Ed. (Fort Worth, TX: Harcourt, Inc., 2001), pp. 12–13.
3. Jack Honomichl, "Colossal Changes," *Marketing News*, August 13, 2001, p. H2.
4. Sandra Yin, "The Nose Knows," *American Demographics*, February 2002, p. 14.
5. "Spies Like Us," *Inc.*, August 1998, p. 45.
6. Ibid.
7. Stephanie Thompson, "Wal-Mart Tops List for New Food Lines," *Advertising Age*, April 29, 2002, pp. 4, 61.
8. Jerry W. Thomas, "Skipping MR a Major Error," *Marketing News*, March 4, 2002, p. 50.
9. Bob Edwards, "Analysis: Businesses Eagerly Anticipating the Release of U.S. Census Numbers," interview with Ross DeVal, Milken Institute, *Morning Edition* (National Public Radio), March 7, 2001.
10. "Census Bureau Breaks New Ground with Release of DVD Products," *US Newswire*, February 6, 2001.
11. Jack Neff, "Rivals Shut Out Wal-Mart," *Advertising Age*, August 27, 2001, p. 8; and Kevin Murphy, "Opening the Gates," *Executive Edge*, February–March 1999, p. 13.
12. Matt Michell, "The Internet as a Market Research Tool," *Public Relations Tactics*, March 2002, p. 6; Theano Nikitas, "Your Customers Are Talking. Are You Listening?" *Ziff Davis Smart Business*, February 2002, p. 50.
13. Deborah Szynal, "Big Bytes," *Marketing News*, March 18, 2002, p. 3.
14. Steve Jarvis, "Sum of the Parts," *Marketing News*, January 21, 2002, p. 1.
15. Theano Nikitas, "Your Customers Are Talking. Are You Listening?" *Ziff Davis Smart Business*, February 2002, p. 50; Claire Tristram, "Mining for Meaning," *Technology Review*, July/August 2001, p. 3.
16. Linda Moss, "A Constant Companion," *Broadcasting & Cable*, February 11, 2002.
17. Melanie Wells, "New Ways to Get into Our Heads," *USA Today*, March 2, 1999, pp. 1B–2B.
18. Michael McCarthy, "Stalking the Elusive Teenage Trendsetter," *The Wall Street Journal*, November 18, 1998, pp. B1, B10.
19. Alicia Clegg, "Seen and Heard," *Marketing Week*, April 19, 2001, p. 53; Stephen B. Wilcox, "Ethnography as a Product Development Tool," *Appliance Manufacturer*, July 2001, p. 58.
20. Steve Jarvis, "CMOR Finds Survey Refusal Rate Still Rising," *Marketing News*, February 4, 2002, p. 4.
21. "TRU Announces Launch of First Teen Online Offer," Teenage Research Unlimited Press Release, April 19, 2001; and McCarthy, "Stalking the Elusive Teenage Trendsetter."
22. Kenneth Wade, "Focus Groups' Research Role Is Shifting," *Marketing News*, March 4, 2002, p. 47.
23. Sylvia Marino, "Survey Says!" *Econtent*, April 2002, pp. 32–36.
24. Tedra Meyer, "Circuit City Seeks Customer Feedback Online," *Twice*, August 6, 2001, p. 17.
25. Dana James, "This Bulletin Just In," *Marketing News*, March 4, 2002, p. 45.
26. Anni Layne Rodgers, "More Than a Game," *Fast Company*, May 2002, p. 46; Heather Green, "Tracking Who Surfs Where," *BusinessWeek*, April 27, 1998, p. 78.

27. Richard Natale, "Audiences Return to Movies," *Los Angeles Times*, October 1, 2001, **http://www.latimes.com**.
28. Jim Kirk, "Wait Nearly Over for U.S. Rollout of Low-Carb Beer," *Chicago Tribune*, May 2, 2002, S3, p. 3.
29. Carol Power, "Citi Wireless Test to Go Global," *American Banker*, January 6, 2000, p. 1.
30. Wesley Sprinkle, "In Sync with Customers," *Bests Review*, April 2002.
31. Gary H. Anthes, "The Search Is On," *ComputerWorld*, April 15, 2002, pp. 54–56.
32. Carol Krol, "Data Warehouse Generates Surprises, Leads for Camelot," *Advertising Age*, January 4, 1999, p. 20.
33. Peter J. Howe, "Verizon to Test 10-Cent Pay Phones in the Boston Area," *The Boston Globe*, January 31, 2001, **http://www.boston.com/globe**.
34. Thomas, "Skipping MR a Major Error."

CHAPTER 8

1. "PRWeek Awards 2002," *PRWeek*, **http://www.prweekus.com**, accessed April 19, 2002; Debbie Becker, "The 'Lady' Golf Ball Also Suits Men to a Tee," *USA Today*, August 2, 2001, p. 12C; "This Lady Is a Champ for Precept," *The Columbus Dispatch*, April 8, 2001, **http://www.dispatch.com**.
2. Jean Halliday, "Toyota Leads in Hispanic Niche," *Advertising Age*, July 3, 2000, p. 16.
3. Samar Farah, "What Women Want," *Metro*, February 14, 2002, p. 11 [originally published in the *Christian Science Monitor*].
4. Ibid.
5. John Henry, "State, Area Demographics Give Marketing Clues," *Northwest Arkansas Business Journal*, January 21, 2002, p. 18.
6. Sonia Reyes, "Betty Crocker Says *Hola!* in TV Ads, Twin Entries, Seeking Authenticity," *Brandweek*, May 22, 2000, p. 4.
7. "The Customization Bandwagon," *Sporting Goods Business*, April 16, 2001, p. 12.
8. Roger Simon and Angie Cannon, "An Amazing Journey," *U.S News & World Report*, August 6, 2001, p. 13.
9. U.S. Census Bureau Web site, **http://www.census.gov/population/www/pop-profile/stproj.html**, May 2, 2002.
10. "Metropolitan Areas and Primary Metropolitan Statistical Areas," **http://www.itl.nist.gov/fipspubs/fip8-6-3.htm**, accessed April 19, 2002.
11. Ibid.
12. Ibid.
13. Haya El Nasser, "Out-of-State Moves Are Up for Second Year," *USA Today*, May 31, 2001, p. 3A.
14. "Domino's," company capsule, *Hoover's Online*, **http://www.hoovers.com**, accessed May 2, 2002; Mark Hammond, "GIS Lands on the Map," *PC Week*, January 4, 1999, p. 1.
15. Samar Farah, "What Women Want."
16. "Do Gender-Specific Razors Differ?" *Fortune*, November 12, 2001, p. 48.
17. Ibid.
18. Sally Beatty, "Oxygen Media, After Long Lag, Shows New Life," *The Wall Street Journal*, December 21, 2001, p. B1.
19. Roger Simon and Angie Cannon, "An Amazing Journey."
20. Ibid.
21. Robert N. Anderson, "United States Life Tables," *National Vital Statistics Reports*, Vol. 47, No. 28, Centers for Disease Control and Prevention, December 13, 1999, **http://www.cdc.gov**.
22. "Longer Life for 50-Plus Americans," *AARP Bulletin*, November 2001, p. 4.
23. "Done Deals," *mm*, January/February 2002, p. 13.
24. Paul Campbell, "State Population Projections," U.S. Census Bureau, **http://www.census.gov/population/www/pop-profile/stproj.html**, accessed May 26, 2002.
25. Ibid; and Roger Simon and Angie Cannon, "Amazing Journey."
26. Bob Woods, "Hispanic Marketing Can Be Eventful," *Promo*, May 2000, pp. 25–26, 35–36.
27. Wilfred Masumura, "Money Income," U.S. Census Bureau, **http://www.census.gov/population/ www/pop-profile/moninc.html**, March 9, 2000.
28. "Work," *Advertising Age*, March 4, 2002, p. 28.
29. Foxwoods Resort & Casino Web site, **http://www.foxwoods.com**, accessed May 8, 2002.
30. Roger Simon and Angie Cannon, "Amazing Journey."
31. Ibid.
32. Ibid.
33. Jean Halliday, "GayRide," *Advertising Age*, February 25, 2002, p. 18.
34. **http://www.sric-bi.com/vals**, March 9, 2000.
35. **http://www.yankelovich.com**, March 9, 2000.
36. Roper ASW, **http://www.roper.com**, accessed May 7, 2002; Tom Miller, "Global Segments from Strivers to Creatives," *Marketing News*, July 20, 1998, p. 11.
37. Scott Kirsner, in "Best of the Best 2002," *Fast Company*, May 2002, pp. 92–100.
38. Alison Overholt, "New Leaders, New Agenda," *Fast Company*, May 2002, p. 52.
39. *Chronicle*, WCVB-TV, May 7, 2002.
40. Tony Case, "Triumph of the Niche," *Spring Magazines*, March 4, 2002, pp. SR4–SR8.
41. Laurie Freeman, "Small, Smaller, Smallest," *Marketing News*, September 24, 2001, p. 17.
42. Ibid.
43. Ibid.

CHAPTER 9

1. Lou Dobbs, "Road Map for Recovery," *Money*, January 2002, p. 45; Betsy Streisand, "The Comfort Zone," *U.S. News & World Report*, November 19, 2001, p. 39; "Consumers in Crisis Explored by Unity Marketing," *Business Wire*, September 18, 2001, **http://www.findarticles.com**.
2. Robert Sharoff, "Diversity in the Mainstream," *Marketing News*, May 21, 2001, p. 14.
3. Tobi Elkin, "Sony Marketing Aims at Lifestyle Segments," *Advertising Age*, March 18, 2002, p. 72.
4. John U. Bacon, "A Yen for Pork," *Time Global Business*, October 2001, p. B18.
5. Nancy Coltun Webster, "Teens Under Watchful Eye," *Advertising Age*, September 18, 2000, p. s23.
6. Charles Schwab & Co., **http://www.schwab.com**, accessed May 16, 2002; Jennifer Gore, "Ethnic Marketing May Become the Norm," *Bank Marketing*, September 1998, p. 12.
7. Patricia Sellers, "The Business of Being Oprah," *Fortune*, April 1, 2002, pp. 52–53.
8. John Henry, "State, Area Demographics Give Marketing Clues," *Northwest Arkansas Business Journal*, January 21, 2002, p. 18; Laurie Freeman, "Fast-Food's Battleground," *Advertising Age*, September 18, 2000, p. s20.
9. Robert Sharoff, "Diversity in the Mainstream," *Marketing News*, May 21, 2001, p. 13.
10. Sharoff, "Diversity in the Mainstream."
11. Roger Simon and Angie Cannon, "An Amazing Journey," *U.S. News & World Report*, August 6, 2001, pp. 15, 18.
12. Carole Paquette, "Drive-Throughs," *Mobile Register*, April 22, 2001, p. 2J.
13. Marci McDonald, "Call It Kid-fluence," *U.S. News & World Report*, July 30, 2001, pp. 32–34.
14. Ibid.
15. Ibid.
16. Gregory L. White, "Battling the Inferior-Interior Complex," *The Wall Street Journal*, December 3, 2001, p. B1.
17. These categories were originally suggested in John A. Howard, *Marketing Management: Analysis and Planning* (Homewood, IL: Richard D. Irwin, 1963).
18. Robert Sharoff, "Diversity in the Mainstream," *Marketing News*, May 21, 2001, p. 1.
19. Marci McDonald, "Call it 'Kid-fluence,'" *U.S. News & World Report*, July 30, 2001, p. 34.

CHAPTER 10

1. Eric Young, "Web Marketplaces That Really Work," *Fortune/CNET Tech Review*, Winter 2002, pp. 78–86; Neil Weinberg, "B2B Grows Up," and Alberto Vilar, "B2B: The Best Is Yet to Be," *Forbes Best of the Web*, September 10, 2001, pp. 18–21.
2. Robert A. Hamilton, "Budget Plan Has Billions for the State," *The New York Times*, February 10, 2002, p. 4.
3. Frederick E. Webster Jr. and Yoram Wind, "A General Model for Understanding Organizational Buying Behavior," *Marketing Management*, Winter/Spring 1996, pp. 52–57.
4. The market orientation of resellers is discussed in Thomas L. Baker, Penny M. Simpson, and Judy A. Siguaw, "The Impact of Suppliers' Perceptions of Reseller Market Orientation on Key Relationship Constructs," *Journal of the Academy of Marketing Science*, 27, Winter 1999, pp. 50–57.
5. B2B E-Commerce Headed for Trillions," **http//:www.cyberatlas.internet.com**, March 6, 2002.
6. Michael D. Hutt and Thomas W. Speh, *Business Marketing Management*, 8th Edition (Mason, OH: South-Western Publishing, 2004).
7. "Small Business 2001," *Inc. Magazine*, May 29, 2001, p. 16.
8. **http://www.census.gov/epcd/www/naics.html**; and **http://www.census.gov/naics**, downloaded February 1, 2003.
9. Gordon A. Wyner, "Segmentation Architecture," and Gerald E. Smith, "Segmenting B2B Markets with Economic Value Analysis," *Marketing Management*, March/April 2002, p. 6 and p. 35.
10. Spencer S. Hsu, "Federal Spending in Region Surged," *The Washington Post*, April 21, 2001, p. E1.
11. Jim Mateja, "Ford Suppliers Coming to First-of-Kind Campus," *Chicago Tribune*, May 16, 2002, S3, p.1.
12. Sean Callahan, "China Calling," *BtoBonline*, March 11, 2002, **http://www.btobonline.com**.
13. Jon E. Hilsenrath, "Globalizations Persists in Precarious New Age," *The Wall Street Journal*, December 31, 2001, p. A1.
14. John Pletz and Kirk Ladendorf, "Quick Fix Unlikely for PC Chip Producers, Research Firm Finds," *Knight/Ridder, Tribune Business News*, August 9, 2001.
15. "MasterCard Rolls Out Interoperable API for Storing Personal Data on Smart Cards," *Card News*, May 1, 2002, p. 1.
16. Patrick Burnson, "Just Too Critical," *World Trade*, April 2002, p. 8.

17. Diane Rezendes Khirallah, "Affiliated Computer Near Outsourcing Deal with P&G," *InformationWeek*, July 8, 2002, http://www.informationweek.com; Elliot Spagat, "P&G Narrows Outsourcing Candidates," *The Wall Street Journal*, May 14, 2002, p. B16.
18. Robyn Greenspan, "Companies Look Outside Themselves," May 3, 2002, http://www.cyberatlas.internet.com.
19. Desiree De Myer, "Combat the Downside of Outsourcing Sprint," *Ziff Davis Smart Business*, May 1, 2002, p. 47.
20. Bob Frances, "Gold Winner: Color My World, Boise," *Brandweek*, March 18, 2002, p. R17.
21. References for the organizational buying process incorporate several stages. Arthur Hughes, "Building Profits with Relationship Marketing," *Direct*, January 1999, pp. 49–52, reflects use in stages 1, 2, 3, 4.
22. Betsy McKay, "Pepsi Is Set to Become the Cola of Choice for United Airlines, *The Wall Street Journal*, March 25, 2002, p. A3.
23. Hughes, "Building Profits with Relationship Marketing."
24. Hutt and Speh, Business Marketing Management.
25. Don Green, "Count on Strong Relationships," *Paperboard Packaging*, November 2001, p. 8.
26. Hsu, "Federal Spending in Region Surged."
27. Shane Harris, "The Only Game in Town," *Government Executive*, December 2001, pp. 16–26; and Edward Robinson, "The Pentagon Finally Learns How to Shop," *Fortune*, December 21, 1998, pp. 174–182.
28. Allan V. Burman, "Buying Better All the Time," *Government Executive*, December 2001, p. 72.
29. John H. Cushman, "The Government Shops on the Web, Too," *The New York Times*, March 29, 2000, p. H31.
30. Harris, "The Only Game in Town."
31. Matt Forney, "Cultural Revolution: Taiwan Breaks Free of China Syndrome," *The Wall Street Journal*, July 27, 1999, pp. A1, A12.

CHAPTER 11

1. Nicholas Von Hoffman, "The New iMac," *Architectural Digest*, July 2002, pp. 48, 51; Jon Swartz, "Latest iMac a Boost to Staid Industry," *USA Today*, February 21, 2002, p. 3B; Peter Lewis, "Apple Jacks It Up," *Fortune*, February 18, 2002, pp. 139–140; Stephen H. Wildstrom, "Finally, a No-Hassle, No-Strain Computer," *BusinessWeek*, February 11, 2002, p. 22; Edward C. Baig, "Apple's iMac Is Flat-Out Powerful and Pretty," *USA Today*, February 6, 2002, p. 7D.
2. Concept first introduced by G. Lynn Shostack, "Breaking Free from Product Marketing," *Journal of Marketing*, April 1977, p. 77; and John M. Rathmell, "What Is Meant by Services?" *Journal of Marketing*, October 1980, pp. 32–36.
3. "How Marriott Never Forgets a Guest," *BusinessWeek*, February 21, 2000, p. 74.
4. U.S. Census Bureau, *1997 Economic Census: Advance Summary Statistics for the United States*, http://www.census.gov/epcd/www/advanc1a.htm, accessed June 3, 2002.
5. Catharine P. Taylor, "Buck Stops Here; Doctors, and Their Rx Pads, at the Forefront of DTC," *Advertising Age Special Report on Direct-to-Consumer Marketing*, May 27, 2002, pp. S-2, S-8.
6. Melissa Campanelli, "Gotta Have It!" *Entrepreneur*, April 2001, p. 49.
7. Brandon Copple, "Shelf-Determination," *Forbes*, April 15, 2002, pp. 131–142.
8. Michael D. Hutt and Thomas W. Speh, *Business Marketing Management*, Eighth Edition (Mason, OH: South-Western, 2004).
9. Ben Berentson, "Johnson Controls," *Forbes*, May 21, 2001, p. 70.
10. Karen Bannon, "Akamai Technologies," *Forbes*, May 21, 2001, p. 94.
11. Katherine Bruce, "Equity Office Properties," *Forbes*, May 21, 2001, p. 100.
12. Diane Brady, "Why Service Stinks," *BusinessWeek*, October 23, 2000, p. 119.
13. Alex Taylor III, "Finally GM Is Looking Good," *Fortune*, April 1, 2002, pp. 69–74.
14. *The Clorox Company 2001 Annual Report*, p. 21, accessed at Clorox Web site, http://www.clorox.com, June 11, 2002.
15. *L.L. Bean Catalog*, Summer 2002, p. 4.
16. Lorrie Grant, "Coach Bags Old Ideas," *USA Today*, April 24, 2001, p. B5.
17. Ibid.
18. Dori Jones Yang, "Wireless but Useless," *U.S. News & World Report*, May 7, 2001, pp. 32–33.
19. Cara Beardi, "Zippo's Eternal Flame," *Advertising Age*, August 13, 2001, p. 4.
20. Ibid.
21. William Erickson et al., "Wine War," *BusinessWeek*, September 3, 2001, p. 57.
22. Devon Spurgeon, "The Hard Life of Orphan Brands," *The Wall Street Journal*, April 13, 2001, p. B1.
23. Ibid.
24. Bill Shepherd, "Wizards of Light," *Worth*, July/August 2001, pp. 61–64.

CHAPTER 12

1. Redox Brands, Inc., http://www.redoxbrands.com, accessed January 26, 2003; Richard Curtis, "The X Factor," *Cincinnati Business Courier*, June 6, 2001, http://cincinnati.bizjournals.com; Jim Hopkins, "Partners Turn Decrepit Detergent into Boffo Start-Up," *USA Today*, June 20, 2001, http://www.usatoday.com; Matthew Swibel, "Spin Cycle," *Forbes*, April 2, 2001, p. 118; Mike Boyer, "Quick Labels Boost Soap Maker," *The Cincinnati Enquirer*, January 19, 2001, http:/ enquirer.com.
2. Joseph Agnese, "Tyson Rules the Roost," *BusinessWeek Online*, July 1, 2002, http://www.businessweek.com; Stephanie Thompson, "Meat Gets Branded," *Advertising Age*, September 24, 2001, p. 6.
3. Jack Neff, "Private Party at Wal-Mart," *Advertising Age*, October 29, 2001, p. 8.
4. Gary McWilliams, "Retailers Create Own-Label PCs as Brand Names Dwindle," *The Wall Street Journal*, May 3, 2002, p. B1.
5. Gerry Khermouch, Stanley Holmes, and Moon Ihlwan, "The Best Global Brands," *BusinessWeek*, August 6, 2001, p. 50.
6. Ibid.
7. "What Is Brand Asset Valuator? Brand Development Findings," http://www.yr.com/knowledge/what2.php, March 22, 2000.
8. "The Good Housekeeping Seal," *Good Housekeeping*, May 2002, p. 14.
9. Gerry Khermouch, Holmes and Ihlwan, "The Best Global Brands," p. 53.
10. David Welch, "GM Brand Managers Get the Boot," *BusinessWeek*, April 22, 2002, p. 14.
11. Brandon Copple, "Shelf-Determination," *Forbes*, April 15, 2002, pp. 131–142.
12. The concept of trade dress is examined in Michael Harvey, James T. Rothe, and Laurie A. Lucas, "The 'Trade Dress' Controversy: A Case of Strategic Cross-Brand Cannibalization," *Journal of Marketing Theory and Practice*, 6, Spring 1998, pp. 1–15. The *Kendall-Jackson v. Gallo* case is discussed in "Jury Clears E&J Gallo-Winery in Lawsuit Over Bottle Design," *The Wall Street Journal*, April 7, 1997.
13. Paxan Company Web site, http://www.iran-export.com/exporter/company/PAXAN, accessed July 9, 2002.
14. Deborah Ball, "Osama Relative Fashions Apparel Bin Ladin Line," *The Wall Street Journal*, June 17, 2002, p. B1.
15. Olga Kharif, "Getting a Grip on Consumer Tastes," *BusinessWeek*, July 16, 2001, p. 12.
16. Steve Jarvis, "French Fried," *Marketing News*, June 4, 2001, p. 3.
17. Anita Lienert, "Wheels Sport New Labels," The Detroit News, April 25, 2001, http://detnews.com; Jean Halliday, "L.L. Bean, Subaru Pair for Co-Branding," Advertising Age, February 21, 2000, p. 21.
18. James Martin and James E. Samuels, "Campus Scoreboards Tell Us More Than the Score," *Boston Business Journal*, Spring 2002.
19. "Ballpoint Perfume," *Forbes*, July 3, 2000, p. 154.
20. "Uniforms, New Ball MLB's Big Stories," *Sports Trend*, June 2000, p. 30.
21. Gerry Kermouch, "An Almost Invisible $1 Trillion Market," *BusinessWeek*, June 11, 2001, p. 151.
22. Chuck Stogel, "It's Easier Being Green," *Brandweek*, January 28, 2002, pp. 16, 18, 20.
23. Julie Forster, "Sara Lee: Changing the Recipe—Again," *BusinessWeek*, September 10, 2001, pp. 125–126.
24. Everett M. Rogers and F. Floyd Shoemaker, *Communication of Innovation* (New York: Free Press, 1971), pp. 135–157. Rogers later relabeled his model as an innovation-decision process. He called the five steps knowledge, persuasion, decision, implementation, and information. See Everett M. Rogers, *Diffusion of Innovations*, 3rd ed. (New York: Free Press, 1983), pp. 164–165.
25. Reuters Limited, "Toyota's Prius First to Get $2,000 Tax Deduction OK," *Forbes*, August 12, 2002, http://www.forbes.com; Jeff Green, "Attention Techies and Assorted Geniuses: Toyota Prius Wants You," *Brandweek*, May 15, 2000, p. 113.
26. Devin Leonard, "The Most Valuable Square Foot in America," *Fortune*, April 1, 2002, pp. 118, 120, 124.
27. Wyeth Web site, http://www.wyeth.com, accessed August 14, 2002; Rob Wherry, "No Worries," *Forbes*, July 23, 2001, p. 168.
28. Chuck Stoge, "It's Easier Being Green," *Brandweek*, January 28, 2002, p. 16.
29. Alison Overholt, "New Leaders, New Agenda," *Fast Company*, May 2002, p. 54.
30. Wendy Cole, "SUV Strollers," *Time*, January 29, 2001.
31. John Heilimann, "Reinventing the Wheel," *Time.com*, December 2, 2001, http://www.time.com.
32. E. Michael Johnson, "The Swoosh Swoops In," *Golf Digest*, January 25, 2002, http://www.golfdigest.com.
33. Amanda Spake, "Bath Seats Demand a Watchful Eye," *U.S. News & World Report*, June 11, 2001, p. 67.
34. Jayne O'Donnell, "Costco's History Reads Like Recipe for Recalls," *USA Today*, April 4, 2001, p. B1.
35. Julie Forster, "Sara Lee: Changing the Recipe—Again," *BusinessWeek*, September 10, 2001, pp. 125–126.
36. Jayne O'Donnell, "New Safety VP Plans Quality Improvements," *USA Today*, April 4, 2001, p. B1.

CHAPTER 13

1. Peter Huber, "The Four-Hour Energy Crisis," *Forbes*, September 17, 2001; Fred Bayles, "Savings Seen in Hour of Energy Use," *USA Today*, July 16, 2001; Lee Hochberg, "Time-of-Day Pricing," Online NewsHour, June 22, 2001, http://www.pbs.org/newshour; WUTC OKs Extension, Expansion of Puget Sound Energy's Time-of-Day Program, press release, Puget Sound Energy, September 26,

2001; and David Wright, "An Incentive to Conserve," http://abcnews.com, August 6, 2001.

2. Richard S. Dunham and Paul Magnusson, "Those Steel Tariffs Look Anything But Ironclad," *BusinessWeek*, May 6, 2001, p. 45.
3. Al Baker, "Steep Rise in Gun Sales Reflects Post-Attack Fears," *The New York Times*, December 16, 2001, p. A1.
4. Paul Krugman, "What Price Fairness?" *The New York Times*, October 4, 2000, p. A35.
5. Byron Acohido, "Will Microsoft's Xbox Hit the Spot?" *USA Today*, June 4, 2002, pp. B1, B2; Todd Wasserman, "Playing to Win," *Brandweek*, May 20, 2002, pp. 1, 8; Tobi Elkin, "Video-Game Makers Heat Up Competition," *Advertising Age*, May 20, 2002, pp. 3, 157.
6. Robert D. Buzzell and Frederick D. Wiersema, "Successful Share Building Strategies," *Harvard Business Review* (January–February 1981), pp. 135–144.
7. Jon Van, "AT&T to Offer Unlimited Long Distance Calling Plan with Certain Limits," *Chicago Tribune*, February 7, 2002.
8. Emily Nelson, "Bottom Line," *The Wall Street Journal*, December 27, 2001, p. A1.
9. Michelle Kessler, "PC Makers Jump into House Call Business," *USA Today*, May 10, 2002, p. B1.
10. Joe Sharkey, "Life Can Be Pretty Good Five Miles Up," *The New York Times*, May 14, 2002, p. C7.
11. Barbara De Lollis, Chris Woodyard, and Marilyn Adams, "Savvy Travelers Fly for Less," *USA Today*, April 21, 2002.
12. Peter Kafka, "Rock On," *Forbes*, September 20, 1999, p. 142.
13. David Leonhardt, "Tiptoeing Toward Variable Pricing," *The New York Times*, May 12, 2002.
14. See James L. McKenney, *Stouffer Yield Management System, Harvard Business School Case 9-190-193* (Boston: Harvard Business School, 1994); and Anirudh Dhebar and Adam Brandenburger, *American Airlines, Inc: Revenue Management, Harvard Business School Case 9-190-029* (Boston: Harvard Business School, 1992).
15. David P. Hamilton, "E-Commerce: The Price Isn't Right," *The Wall Street Journal*, February 12, 2001, p. B1.
16. Ibid.

CHAPTER 14

1. Jerry Flint, "Money Isn't Everything," *Forbes*, August 12, 2002, p. 80; Sholnn Freeman, "Detroit Renews Price War on SUVs, Trucks," *The Wall Street Journal*, June 5, 2002, p. D1; Kathleen Kerwin, "0% Financing: A Risky Addiction," *BusinessWeek*, January 14, 2002, pp. 86–87; Karl Greenberg, "Carmakers Build Up from Zero," *Brandweek*, January 7, 2002, p. 5; Earle Eldridge, "2001 Car Sales Rank 2nd Best Ever," *USA Today*, January 4, 2002, p. B1.
2. "Canon News," downloaded from http://www.canon.com, January 22, 2003; see also Karl Greenberg, "Canon Fires Off $20M in Colorful Launch for Money-Saving Printer," *Brandweek*, April 9, 2001, p. 6.
3. "Polartec Windbloc Series," downloaded from http://www.polartec.com, January 22, 2003.
4. "Prescription Drug Pricing, Utilization, and Spending," downloaded from http://aspe.os.dhhs.gov/health/reports/drugstudy, January 22, 2003; "Court Agrees to Review State Regulation of Drug Pricing," downloaded from http://www.washingtonpost.com, June 28, 2002.
5. Jack Neff, "$100 Million-Plus Push Seen for Gillette Razors," *Advertising Age*, February 25, 2002, p. 1.
6. Nara Schoenberg, "Cell Phone Use Expected to Grow, Mature in America," *Mobile Register*, July 29, 2002, p. D1.
7. Marilyn Adams, "Airlines' Balance of Power Shifts," *USA Today*, July 30, 2002, pp. B1, B2.
8. "Domestic Tobacco Pricing," downloaded from http://www.tobacco.org/news, January 23, 2003.
9. "Amazon.com and Dynamic Pricing on the Internet," downloaded from http://faculty-gsb.stanford.edu/groseclose/Papers/amazon.pdf, January 24, 2003; see also Kevin Newman, "Amazon.com Admits to Variable Pricing," downloaded from http://abcnews.go.com/onair/worldnewstonight/wnt000927_amazonpricing_feature.html, January 24, 2003.
10. "Dealer Holdbacks: What Are They and What Do They Do?" downloaded from http://www.carbuytip.com/dealer-holdbacks.html, January 23, 2003.
11. "The New 'Digital Economics' of the Music Industry," downloaded from http://64.33.34.112/.WWW/digecon.html, January 24, 2003.
12. Justin Pope, "Tuition from Grocery Rebates," *Chicago Sun Times*, May 5, 2002, p. 41.
13. "A Primer on Gasoline Prices," downloaded from http://www.eia.doe.gov/pub/oil_gas/petroleum/analysis_publications/primer_on_gasoline_prices/html/petbro.html, January 25, 2003; "How Gas Prices Work," downloaded from http://www.howstuffworks.com/gas-price.html, January 24, 2003.
14. "Telephone Service Pricing," downloaded from http://indian.vinu.edu/telecomm/links.htm, January 25, 2003.
15. "PC Makers Ready for Price War," downloaded from http://www.newsfactor.com/perl/story/ 7591.html, January 25, 2003.
16. Frank Vinlaun, "Washington State Wineries Thrive in 'Premium' Niche," *The Seattle Times*, April 19, 2002, p. B7.
17. "AIDS Drug Makers Slash Prices for Third World," downloaded from http://abcnews.go.com/sections/living/DailyNews/aidsdrugs_africa0511.html, January 26, 2003.
18. "Product Preannouncement, Market Cannibalization, and Price Competition," downloaded from http://netec.mcc.ac.uk/BibEc/data/Papers/fthecsucp98-136.html, January 25, 2003.
19. Brian McWilliams, "Google Turns Away Robots from Its Front Door," *News Bytes*, March 28, 2002.
20. Julia Angwin, "More Subscribers to AOL Get Online Free," *The Wall Street Journal*, March 14, 2002.

CHAPTER 15

1. "Marine Corps News, 26th MEU, Marines Demand, Supply Delivers," http://192.156.19.108/marinelink/mcn2000.nsf/main5/A81508058DE1676B85256B4200515210?opendocument, accessed on March 15, 2003; "U.S. Marine Corps: Modernizing Military Logistics," Sapient Web site, http://www.sapient.com, accessed on March 15, 2003; Faith Keenan, "The Marines Learn New Tactics—from Wal-Mart," *BusinessWeek*, December 24, 2001, p. 74.
2. Ann D'Innocenzio, "Avon Calling on a New Retail Plan," *Mobile Register*, May 13, 2001, p. 3F.
3. Richard Roeper, "Oh for the Simpler Days of Tupperware Parties," *Chicago Sun Times*, May 1, 2002.
4. Michael Schrage, "The Dell Curve," *Wired*, October 7, 2001, http://www.wired.com.
5. Cathleen Egan, "Vending Machine Technology Matures, Offering Branded Foods, Convenience," *The Wall Street Journal*, December 13, 2001, p. B13.
6. Dan Hanover, "Channel Conflict? Put a Lid on It," *Sales & Marketing Management*, March 2000, p. 86.
7. Mark McMaster, "Shifting Gears," *Sales & Marketing Management*, August 2001, pp. 43–48.
8. Pallavi Gogoi, "What's Next—The Bank of Burger King?" *BusinessWeek*, June 18, 2001, p. 150.
9. Dean Foust, "Ebay, A Hock Shop's Best Friend," *BusinessWeek*, July 30, 2001, p. 10.
10. Brandon Copple, "Plowed Under," *Forbes*, February 21, 2000, p. 56.
11. Bob Duncan, "First, Do No Harm," *Inc Tech*, accessed at the *Inc.* Web site, http://www.inc.com, August 4, 2002.
12. Ann Stuart, "Not Dead Yet," *Inc Tech*, accessed at the *Inc.* Web site, http://www.inc.com, August 4, 2002; Mark Tatge, "Rug Burns," *Forbes*, March 5, 2001, pp. 58–60.
13. "U.S. Senate Backs Canada Drug Reimports," Reuters Limited, July 17, 2002, http://ca.news.yahoo.com; Debra Rosenberg, "Getting Their Fill," *Newsweek*, June 24, 2002, p. 25.
14. Josh Kosman, "TPG, Goldman Sachs Want Burger King Their Way," *TheDeal.com*, April 9, 2002, http://tdnycprodwww01.thedeal.com; Daniel Kruger, "Carrying the Flame," *Forbes*, December 24, 2001, pp. 64–65.
15. Victoria Murphy, "The Logistics of a Dinner Plate," *Forbes*, January 21, 2002, pp. 96–97.
16. Ed Pasahow, "How Can You Improve the Odds for Successful ERP Implementation," *Digital Systems Report*, Spring 2000, pp. 24–26.
17. John Gorsuch, "Examining the Links," *Overhaul & Maintenance*, April 20, 2002, p. 38.
18. Special Advertising Section, *BusinessWeek*, June 26, 2000.
19. "Partnerships," GE Capital rail services Web sites, http://www.ge.com/capital/rail, accessed August 28, 2002; "GE Pursues e-Fulfillment from All Angles," *BusinessWeek*, June 26, 2000.
20. "The Lifelong Lure of the Open Road," *US News & World Report*, February 18, 2002, p. 48.
21. Warren S. Hersch, "Midrange Distributors' Role Broadens in E-Commerce World," *Computer Reseller News*, accessed at the CRN Web site, http://www.crn.com, August 4, 2002.
22. "The New Wave in Giant Ships," *Fortune*, November 12, 2001, p. I182 I-P.
23. Andrew Tanzer, "Warehouses That Fly," *Forbes*, accessed at the *Forbes* Web site, http://www.forbes.com, August 4, 2002.
24. Jeffrey Ball, "Chrysler Averts a Parts Crisis," *The Wall Street Journal*, September 24, 2001, p. B1.
25. Philip Siekman, "New Victories in the Supply-Chain Revolution," *Fortune*, accessed at the *Fortune* Web site, http://www.fortune.com, August 4, 2002.
26. Siekman, "New Victories."
27. Emily Nelson and Ann Zimmerman, "Kimberly-Clark Keeps Costco in Diapers, Absorbing Costs Itself," *The Wall Street Journal*, September 7, 2000, p. A1.
28. "Web Trails," *Forbes Best of the Web*, December 3, 2001, p. 15.
29. Mark Henricks, "No Long-Term Parking," *Entrepreneur*, January 2002, pp. 83–85.

CHAPTER 16

1. Michael Moyer, "At Prada's New Store, the Coolest Thing Isn't the Merchandise," *Popular Science*, http://www.popsci.com, accessed January 15, 2003; D.C. Denision, " 'Smart' Stats: Business at the Speed of a Fastball," *The Boston Globe*, May 19, 2002,

http://www.boston.com/globe; Jeanette Brown, "Prada Gets Personal," *BusinessWeek e.biz*, March 18, 2002, pp. 8–9; Teri Agins and Deborah Ball, "Designers Spend Millions on Elegant Megastores," *The Wall Street Journal*, August 21, 2001.

2. Jean Scheidnes, "Retailers Woo Youth Dollars with Discount Denim," *Forbes*, August 23, 2002, **http://www.forbes.com**; and Louise Lee, "Can Gap Put It All Together Again?" *BusinessWeek*, August 14, 2000, pp. 58–60.
3. Anne D'Innocenzio, "Designer Names Helping Target Offer Cheap Chic," *Mobile Register*, March 16, 2002, p. B7; and Teri Agins, "Todd Does Target," *The Wall Street Journal*, April 11, 2002, p. B1.
4. "Family Dollar Reports Record Third Quarter and First Three Quarters Sales and Earnings; and Announces Plans to Open 575 New Stores in Fiscal 2003," Family Dollar Stores press release, *PR Newswire*, June 25, 2002; and Chad Terhune, "In Modest Times, Dollar Stores Remain Upbeat," *The Wall Street Journal*, December 22, 2000, pp. B1, B4.
5. Aixa M. Pascual, "Lowe's Is Sprucing Up Its House," *BusinessWeek*, June 3, 2002, pp. 56–58.
6. SuperTarget Web site, accessed January 4, 2003, **http://www.target.com**; and Calmetta Y. Coleman, "Target's Aim: 'Bring Fashion to Food' on a National Scale," *The Wall Street Journal*, March 1, 2000, p. 4.
7. Kristof De Wulf, "Retail Category Strategy Varies by the Store," *Marketing News*, September 10, 2001, p. 22.
8. Donna Fenn, "Leveraging Local Intelligence," *Inc.*, August 2001, pp. 54–56.
9. Chana R. Schoenberger, "Ca-Ching!" *Forbes*, June 12, 2000, pp. 84–85.
10. D. M. Osborne, "The Store That Stark Built," *Inc.*, August 2001, p. 46.
11. Alexander R. Moses, "Analysts: Rivals Hold Key to Kmart Closures," *Mobile Register*, January 24, 2002, p. B6.
12. Dean Starkman, "The Mall, Without the Haul," *The Wall Street Journal*, July 25, 2001, p. B1.
13. Alice Z. Cuneo, "What's in Store?" *Advertising Age*, February 25, 2002, pp. 30–31.
14. Nanette Byrnes and Christopher Palmeri, "A Showstopper on Broadway," *BusinessWeek*, December 24, 2001, p. 54; "NetWorth Datebook," *Worth*, December 2001, p. 50; and Steven T. Goldberg, "Retailing's Comeback Kid," *Kiplinger's*, November 2001, p. 60.
15. "7-Eleven to Cast Itself as New Teen Heaven," *Brandweek*, April 2, 2001, pp. 1, 8.
16. Emily Nelson, "The Art of the Sale," *The Wall Street Journal*, January 11, 2001, p. B1.
17. Wendy Zellner, "Warehouse Clubs: When the Going Gets Tough," *BusinessWeek*, July 16, 2001.
18. Katherine Hobson, "Miracle on 34th Street," *U.S. News & World Report*, November 26, 2001, pp. 44–45.
19. William M. Bulkeley, "Cut Down to Size: Category Killers Go from Lethal to Lame in Less Than a Decade," *The Wall Street Journal*, March 9, 2000, p. B1.
20. Hobson, "Miracle on 34th Street."
21. Lorrie Grant, "Department Stores Ring Up Centralized Checkouts," *USA Today*, June 6, 2002, p. 5B.
22. Zellner, "Warehouse Clubs: When the Going Gets Tough."
23. Cuneo, "What's in Store?"
24. "Products & Services," 7-Eleven Web site, **http://www.7-Eleven.com/products**, accessed September 4, 2002; and Benjamin Fulford, "I Got It @ 7-Eleven," *Forbes*, April 3, 2000, p. 53.
25. Russell Flannery, "Happy in the Middle," *Forbes*, April 1, 2002, p. 62.
26. "United Stationers Opens New State-of-the-Art Distribution Center in Denver," United Stationers' press release, June 25, 2001; and Ashlea Ebeling, "Paper Tiger," *Forbes*, February 21, 2000, pp. 71–74.
27. Don Debelak, "Farmers' Market," *Entrepreneur*, February 2002, p. 104.
28. Cara B. Dipasquale, "Direct Marketing Rose 3.6% in '01," *Advertising Age*, June 10, 2002, p. 8.
29. Tobi Elkin, "Yahoo! Increases Direct Marketing," *Advertising Age*, April 22, 2002, p. 20; and Ellen Neuborne, "Coaxing with Catalogs," *BusinessWeek e.biz*, August 6, 2001, p. EB6.
30. Deborah Szynal, "Anthrax and You," *Marketing News*, April 29, 2002, pp. 1, 4.
31. Office Depot Web site, **http://www.officedepot.com**, accessed January 5, 2003; Jon Swartz, "E-Tailers Turn Net Profits," *USA Today*, December 13, 2000, pp. 1B–2B; and David Rocks, "Why Office Depot Loves the Net," *BusinessWeek e.biz*, September 27, 1999, pp. EB66–68.
32. JapanScan Market Report, "Automatic Vending Machines in Japan," January 2002, **http://www.foodindustryjapan.com/automatic_vending.htm**; Tim Sanford, "Vending and Beyond," *Vending Times*, March 25–April 24, 2001, **http://www.vendingtimes.com**.

CHAPTER 17

1. Andy Cohen, "Rethinking Direct Mail," *Sales & Marketing Management*, December 2001, p. 14; Jane M. Von Bergen, "Anthrax Scare Might Hurt Direct Marketing Business," *Amarillo Globe-News*, November 6, 2001, **http://www.amarillonet.com**; Micheline Maynard, "Anthrax Scare Trips Up Some Mail Companies," *The New York Times*, October 28, 2001, college3nytimes.com.
2. Dale Buss, "Art of Gaining Impressions," *Brandweek*, March 18, 2002, p. R14 ("Reggie Awards").
3. Betsy Cummings, "Making It Click," *Sales & Marketing Management*, April 2002, p. 21.
4. Ibid., p. 22.
5. Bruce Horovitz, "Kids Eat Free as Chains Vie for Business," *USA Today*, April 9, 2001, p. B2.
6. Jon Swartz, "EarthLink Joins Movement to Kill Pop-Up Ads," *USA Today*, August 20, 2002, p. B1; "EarthLink Will Offer Subscribers Software to Block Pop-Up Ads," *The Wall Street Journal*, August 20, 2002, p. B6.
7. Mike Beirne, "Hoteliers Take Different Roads to Travelers," *Brandweek*, June 10, 2002, p. 4.
8. David Finnigan, "Disney's Search for Treasure," *Brandweek*, August 12, 2002, pp. 1, 8.
9. Ronald Grover and Gerry Khermouch, "The Trouble with Tie-ins," *BusinessWeek*, June 3, 2002, p. 63.
10. David Kiley, "Half a Million Tires Recalled, Most on Ford SUVs," *USA Today*, August 20, 2002, p. B2.
11. Kenneth Hein, "Here's Chocolate in Your Eye," *Brandweek*, Nov. 12, 2001, p. 26.
12. Kenneth Hein, "Here's Chocolate in Your Eye," and Mike Beirne, "Butt-Kicking Big Tobacco," *Brandweek*, Nov. 12, 2001, pp. 26, 28.
13. Lisa M. Keefe, "*Still* Brought to You by . . . ," *Marketing News*, October 22, 2001, p. 3; data from IEG Inc., Chicago.
14. Gabriel Kahn, "Soccer's FIFA Cries Foul as Ambushers Crash World Cup," *The Wall Street Journal*, June 20, 2002, p. B1.
15. Donna Fenn, "Honeys, Hand Me a Polygamy Porter," *Inc.*, August 2002, pp. 94–97.
16. Direct Marketing Association, **http://www.the-dma.org**, accessed January 27, 2003.
17. Laird Harrison, "You've Got Ads!" *Time Bonus Section—Inside Business*, January 2002, p. Y7.
18. Direct Marketing Association, **http://www.the-dma.org**, accessed January 28, 2003.
19. Ibid.
20. Gary McWilliams, "In About-Face, Dell Will Sell PCs to Dealers," *The Wall Street Journal*, August 20, 2002, pp. B1, B4.
21. Kenneth Hein, "Memo from the Front," *Brandweek*, February 11, 2002, p. 38.
22. Sonia Reyes, "Purina Plots Poaching Protective Pooch Pals," *Brandweek*, August 27, 2001, p. 7.
23. John Gaffney, "Case Study: Corn Syrup, Britney, the Web, and Thou," *Business 2.0*, August 2001, **http://www.business2.com**.
24. Mark Hyman, "Betting That His Airness Will Soar Again," *BusinessWeek*, October 1, 2001, p. 72; "Rent-a-Celeb," *BusinessWeek*, July 9, 2001, p. 10.
25. Melanie Wells, "Sole Survivors," *Forbes*, August 6, 2001, pp. 62–68.

CHAPTER 18

1. Todd Wasserman, "Services Fill the Gap as Dell's Dude Reigns," Brandweek, June 17, 2002, p. S35; Lorrie Lynch, "Who's News," *USA Weekend*, February 1–3, 2002, p. 2; Michael McCarthy, "Goofy Dell Guy Exudes Star Power," *USA Today*, January 14, 2002, p. 5B; Suzanne Veronica, "Another Advertising Star Is Born as Viewers Embrace Dell Pitchman," *The Wall Street Journal*, January 10, 2002, pp. B1, B4.
2. Dorothy Pomerantz, "Coming Distractions," *Forbes*, June 10, 2002, p. 50.
3. Stephanie Thompson, "Kraft Eschews TV for Pop Star Promo," *Advertising Age*, August 12, 2002, p. 11.
4. Anna Bernasek, "Is This Where the Economy Is Headed?" *Fortune*, September 2, 2002, pp. 85–90; William Spain, "Ad Spending Almost Flat in First Half," downloaded from **http://www.CBS.MarketWatch.com**, August 26, 2002; Robert J. Coen, "Advertising Boom in U.S. Ended in '01," *Advertising Age*, May 13, 2002, p. 24.
5. Gary McWilliams, "Gateway Barks Right Up Apple's Tree in New Ad Campaign," *The Wall Street Journal*, August 26, 2002, pp. B1, B4.
6. Laurel Wentz, "Marketers Turn to Celebrities to Lure Hispanic Consumers," *Advertising Age*, May 13, 2002, p. 20.
7. Christopher H. Schmitt, "Earth to Martha: Forget the Doilies. You're in Big Trouble," *U.S. News & World Report*, July 1, 2002, pp. 26–27.
8. Betsy Cummings, "Star Power," *Sales & Marketing Management*, April 2001, pp. 52–56.
9. Coen, "Advertising Boom in U.S. Ended in '01."
10. Jon Swartz, "EarthLink Joins Movement to Kill Pop-Up Ads," *USA Today*, August 20, 2002, p. B1; Tobi Elkin, "'Intrusive' Pop-Ups Get Closer Scrutiny after iVillage Block," *Advertising Age*, August 5, 2002, p. 6.
11. Coen, "Advertising Boom in U.S. Ended in '01."
12. Tony Case, "The Last Mass Medium?" *Newspapers*, April 30, 2001, pp. SR13–SR14.
13. Ibid.
14. Ibid.
15. Coen, "Advertising Boom in U.S. Ended in '01."
16. Ibid.
17. Charles Pappas, "Ad Nauseum," *Advertising Age*, July 10, 2000, p. 16.
18. Ibid.
19. Erin White, "Outdoor Ads May Get Indoor Rival," *The Wall Street Journal*, July 17, 2002, p. B10.
20. Scott Hays, "Has Online Advertising Finally Grown Up?" *Advertising Age*, April 1, 2002, p. C1.

21. Ibid.
22. Charles Pappas, "Ad Nauseum."
23. "Agency Report," *Advertising Age*, April 22, 2002, p. S-2.
24. Jack Neff, "Coupons Get Clipped," *Advertising Age*, November 5, 2001, p. 1.
25. "Back to Basics," *Industry Report—Promo Magazine*, May 2000, p. A20.
26. "Virtual Satisfaction," *Industry Report—Promo Magazine*, May 2000, p. A26.
27. "Give and Take," *Industry Report—Promo Magazine*, May 2000, p. A36.
28. "Getting Labeled," *Industry Report—Promo Magazine*, May 2000, p. A8.
29. "Retailment Today," *Industry Report—Promo Magazine*, May 2000, p. A16.
30. Bonnie Tsui, "Philip Morris Coverup: No-Smoke Ads Hit Books," *Advertising Age*, September 4, 2000, p. 12.
31. Jack Neff, "Ries' Thesis: Ads Don't Build Brands, PR Does," *Advertising Age*, July 15, 2002, pp. 14–15.
32. Steve Jarvis, "How the Internet Is Changing the Fundamentals of Publicity," *Marketing News*, July 17, 2000, p. 6.
33. Suzanne C. Ryan, "Soak Up the Fun!" *Boston Sunday Globe*, July 7, 2002, p. L1.
34. "Give and Take," *Industry Report—Promo Magazine*.
35. Maxine Lans Resky, "Just Posting Cookie Agreement Not Enough," *Marketing News*, September 24, 2001, p. 12.
36. "U.S. Ad Expenditures by Type of Media, 1997–2001," *Marketing News*, July 2, 2001, p. 11.
37. "Worldwide Internet Advertising Spending, by Region," *Marketing News*, July 2, 2001, p. 13.

CHAPTER 19

1. Ron Donoho, "Prime-Time Sellers," *Sales & Marketing Management*, February 2002, pp. 26–29; Suzanne Ault, "ET, the Business behind the Buzz," *Broadcasting & Cable*, July 2, 2002, p. 14; Steve McClellan, "Creative Deals for Becker," *Broadcasting & Cable*, June 24, 2002, p. 23; see also *Entertainment Tonight* Web page, **http://www.etonline.com**.
2. Thomas N. Ingram, Raymond W. LaForge, Charles H. Schwepker, Jr., Ramaon A. Avila, and Michael R. Williams, *Sales Management: Analysis and Decision Making*, 5th ed. (Mason, OH: South-Western, 2004).
3. Trevor Thomas, "FIIA Study Finds Banks Favor One-on-One Selling for Insurance," *National Underwriter*, May 6, 2002, p. 41.
4. Andy Cohen, "Costs on the Road," *Sales & Marketing Management*, April 2001, p. 11.
5. "Welcome to Avon's Home Page," **http://avon.avon.com/**, accessed January 16, 2003.
6. John J. Miller, *National Review online*, May 30, 2002, **http://www.nationalreview.com**.
7. Brian P. Murphy, "Giving Cold Calls the Cold Shoulder," *BusinessWeek*, July 2, 2001, p. 12.
8. "The Direct Marketing Association Responds to the Federal Trade Commission's Proposed Changes to the Telemarketing Sales Rule," Direct Marketing Association press release, April 19, 2002, **http://www.the-dma.org**.
9. Kimberly L. McCall, "The Ins and Outs," *Sales & Marketing Management*, March 2002, pp. 87–88.
10. Dick Gorelick, "The Changing Sales Rep-CSR Relationship, *American Printer*, June 2001, p. 108.
11. McCall, "The Ins and Outs."
12. Emily Thornton, "'Reengineering' at Merrill Lynch," *BusinessWeek*, August 6, 2001, p. 31.
13. Tim O'Brien, "Kahuna Lagoon Makes a Splash at Camelbeach," *Amusement Business*, May 20, 2002, p. 6.
14. Pamela L. Moore, "She's Here to Fix the Xerox," *BusinessWeek*, August 6, 2001, p. 47.
15. Gabrielle Birkner, "Who Says Titles Don't Matter?" *Sales & Marketing Management*, July 2001, p. 14.
16. Nick Pachetti, "A Tough Sell," *Money*, June 2002, p. 138.
17. Steve Jarvis, "Double Teamed," *Marketing News*, March 18, 2002, pp. 1, 7.
18. L. Biff, "Customers Still Want Expert Advice," *Bank Marketing*, May 2002, p. 41.
19. Ellen Neuborne, "Tag Team Pitches," *Sales & Marketing Management*, March 2002, p. 57.
20. Gabrielle Birkner, "In the Field: Closing Deals Quickly," *Sales & Marketing Management*, September 2001, p. 22.
21. Jennifer Maselli, "Wrigley Sales Rep Pitch in Real Time," *InformationWeek*, January 14, 2002, p. 51.
22. Mark McMaster, "The Incredible Shrinking Customer Base," *Sales & Marketing Management*, July 2001, pp. 65–66.
23. Scott Hensley, "More Than Ads, Drug Makers Rely on Sales Reps," *The Wall Street Journal*, March 14, 2002, pp. B1, B6.
24. "Harris InfoSource: The Gold Standard in Sales & Marketing for over 30 Years," **http://www.hoovers.com/store/reports**, accessed January 17, 2003.
25. Kathleen Cholewka, "What's Old Is New Again," *Sales & Marketing Management*, June 2002, p. 20.
26. Julie Cantwell, "Dealers Unhappy with Internet Sales Leads," *Automotive News*, March 25, 2002, p. 37.
27. "Multimedia Information Services," **http://viswiz.gmd.de/MultimediaInfo/**, accessed January 18, 2003.
28. Mark McMaster, "Ask S&M," *Sales & Marketing Management*, May 2001, p. 74.
29. Ian Gelenter, "Train Sales Reps to Reach the Next Sales Plateau," *Selling*, November 2001, p. 9.
30. Kathleen Cholewka, "Motivating Mentors," *Sales & Marketing Management*, June 2002, p. 61.
31. "Back to the Future Naturally with Hemp Clothing," **http://www.hemp-sisters.com/**, accessed January 18, 2003.
32. "Boise," **http://www.endgame.org/boise.html**, accessed January 18, 2003.
33. "2001 Salary Survey," *Sales & Marketing Management*, May 2001, p. 50.
34. "IBM and JD Edwards," downloaded from **http://www.ibm-jdedwards.com**, January 18, 2003.
35. Christine Galea, "2002 Salary Survey," *Sales & Marketing Management*, May 2002, p. 32.
36. Kathleen Cholewka, "Survey Says: Some Sales Execs Are Liars," *Sales & Marketing Management*, February 2001, p. 18.
37. Earle Eldridge, "More Car Dealers Now Videotape Sales," *USA Today*, July 3, 2001, p. B1.

A

accelerator principle Disproportionate impact of changes in consumer demand on business market demand.
accessory equipment Capital items that typically cost less and last for shorter periods of time than installations.
acculturation Degree to which newcomers adapt to a culture.
administered marketing system VMS that achieves channel coordination when a dominant channel member exercises its power.
adoption process Stages that consumers go through in learning about a new product, trying it, and deciding whether to purchase it again.
advertising Any paid, nonpersonal communication through various media about a business firm, not-for-profit organization, product, or idea by a sponsor identified in a message that is intended to inform or persuade members of a particular audience.
advertising agency Firm whose marketing specialists assist advertisers in planning and preparing advertisements.
advertising campaign Series of different but related ads that use a single theme and appear in different media within a specified time period.
advertorial Large advertising square on Web pages, which resembles an ad seen in the Yellow Pages.
affinity marketing Marketing effort sponsored by an organization that solicits responses from individuals who share common interests and activities.
AIDA concept Explanation of steps through which an individual reaches a purchase decision: attention, interest, desire, and action.
AIO statements Items on lifestyle surveys that describe various activities, interests, and opinions of respondents.
ambush marketing Attempt by a firm that is not an official sponsor of an event or activity to link itself to the event or activity.
application service providers (ASPs) Outside companies that specialize in providing both the computers and the application support for managing information systems of business clients.
approach Salesperson's initial contact with a prospective customer.
Asch phenomenon Impact of groups and group norms on individual behavior, as described by S. E. Asch. People often conform to majority rule, even when majority rule goes against their beliefs.
atmospherics Combination of physical characteristics and amenities that contribute to a store's image.
attitudes Person's enduring favorable or unfavorable evaluations, emotions, or action tendencies toward some object or idea.
average total costs Costs calculated by dividing the sum of the variable and fixed costs by the number of units produced.

B

banner Advertisement on a Web page that links to an advertiser's site.
basing-point pricing System used in some industries during the early 20th century in which the buyer paid the factory price plus freight charges from the basing-point city nearest the buyer.
benchmarking Method of measuring quality by comparing performance against industry leaders.
blind product test Test of advertising effectiveness in which participants are asked to select unidentified products on the basis of available advertising copy.
bonus pack Sales promotion technique consisting of a specially packaged item that gives the purchaser a larger quantity at the regular price.
boomers People born between the years of 1946 and 1965.
bot Search program that checks hundreds of Web sites, gathers and assembles information, and brings it back to the sender.
bottom line Business jargon referring to the overall profitability of an organization.
boundary-spanning role Role performed by a sales manager in linking the sales force to other elements of the organization's internal and external environments.
brand Name, term, sign, symbol, design, or some combination that identifies the products of one firm while differentiating them from the competition's.
brand equity Added value that a brand name gives to a product in the marketplace.
brand extension Strategy of attaching a popular brand name to a new product in an unrelated product category.
brand insistence Consumer refusals of alternatives and extensive search for desired merchandise.
brand licensing Firm's authorization of other companies to use its brand names.
brand manager Marketer who supports a specific brand.
brand mark Symbol or pictorial design that distinguishes a product.
brand name Part of a brand consisting of words or letters that form a name that identifies and distinguishes a firm's offerings from those of its competitors.
brand preference Consumer reliance on previous experiences with a product to choose that product again.
brand recognition Consumer awareness and identification of a brand.
breakeven analysis Pricing technique used to determine the number of products that must be sold at a specified price in order to generate enough revenue to cover total cost.
broadband technology Extremely high speed, always-on Internet connection.
broadcast media Television (network and cable) and radio.
broker Agent wholesaling intermediary who does not take title to or possession of goods in the course of its primary function, which is to bring together buyers and sellers.
bundle pricing Offering two or more complementary products and selling them for a single price.
business cycle Pattern of differing stages in the level of economic activity of a nation or region. Although the traditional cycle includes the four stages of prosperity, recession, depression, and recovery, most economists believe that future depressions can be prevented through effective economic policies.
business products Goods and services purchased for use either directly or indirectly in the production of other goods and services for resale.
business services Intangible products that firms buy to facilitate their production and operating processes.
business-to-business marketing (B2B) Organizational purchases of goods and services to support production of other products, for daily company operations, or for resale.
buyer Person who has the formal authority to select a supplier and to implement the procedures for securing a good or service.
buyer partnership Relationship in which a firm purchases goods or services from one or more providers.
buyer's market Market in which there are more goods and services than people willing to buy them.
buying allowance Promotional incentive that gives retailers a discount on goods.
buying center Participants in an organizational buying action.

C

cannibalization Loss of sales of an existing product due to competition from a new product in the same line.
captive brand National brands that are sold exclusively by a retail chain.
cash discount Price reduction offered to a consumer, business user, or marketing intermediary in return for prompt payment of a bill.
category killer Store that offers huge selections and low prices in single product lines.
category management Product management system in which a category manager—with profit and loss responsibility—oversees a product line.
cause marketing Identification and marketing of a social issue, cause, or idea to selected target markets.
channel Medium through which a message is delivered.
channel captain Dominant and controlling member of a marketing channel.
click-through rate The percentage of people presented with a Web banner ad who click on it.
closed sales territory Exclusive geographic selling region of a distributor.
closing Stage of personal selling where the salesperson asks the customer to make a purchase decision.
cluster sample Probability sample in which researchers select geographic areas or clusters, and all of the chosen individuals within this area become respondents.
cognitive dissonance Imbalance among a person's knowledge, beliefs, and attitudes.
cohort effect Tendency of members of a generation to be influenced and bound together by events occurring during their key formative years—roughly 17 to 22 years of age.
commercial market Individuals and firms that acquire products to support, directly or indirectly, production of other goods and services.
commission Incentive compensation directly related to the sales or profits achieved by a salesperson.
commission merchant Agent wholesaling intermediary who takes possession of goods shipped to a central market for sale, acts as the producer's agent, and collects an agreed-upon fee at the time of the sale.
common market Extension of a customs union by seeking to reconcile all government regulations affecting trade.
comparative advertising Advertising strategy that emphasizes messages with direct or indirect promotional comparisons between competing brands.
competitive environment Interactive process that occurs in the marketplace among marketers of directly competitive products, marketers of products that can be substituted for one another, and marketers competing for the consumer's purchasing power.
competitive pricing strategy Pricing strategy designed to deemphasize price as a competitive variable by pricing a good or service at the general level of comparable offerings.
competitive strategy Methods through which a firm deals with its competitive environment.
component parts and materials Finished business products of one producer that actually become part of the final products of another producer.
concentrated marketing Focusing marketing efforts on satisfying only one market segment; also called *niche marketing.*
concept testing Method for subjecting a product idea to additional study before actual development, by involving consumers through focus groups, surveys, in-store polling, and the like.
consolidated metropolitan statistical area (CMSA) Urban area that includes two or more PMSAs.
consultative selling Meeting customer needs by listening to them, understanding—and caring about—their problems, paying attention to details, and following through after the sale.
consumer behavior Buying behavior of individuals who will use the goods and services they purchase.
consumer innovator People who purchase new products almost as soon as the products reach the market.
consumer orientation Business philosophy incorporating the marketing concept that emphasizes first determining unmet consumer needs and then designing a system for satisfying them.
consumer products Products bought by ultimate consumers for personal use.
consumer rights As stated by President Kennedy in 1962, the consumer's right to choose freely, to be informed, to be heard, and to be safe.
consumerism Social force within the environment designed to aid and protect the consumer by exerting legal, moral, and economic pressures on business and government.
containerization Process of combining several unitized loads into a single, well-protected load for shipment.
contest Sales promotion technique using games that require entrants to solve problems or write essays to win prizes.
contractual marketing system VMS that coordinates channel activities through formal agreements among channel members.
controlled experiment Scientific investigation in which a researcher manipulates a test group (or groups) and compares the results with those of a control group that did not receive the experimental controls or manipulations.
convenience products Goods and services that consumers want to purchase frequently, immediately, and with minimal effort.
convenience retailer Store that appeals to customers on accessible location, long hours, rapid checkout, and adequate parking.
convenience sample Nonprobability sample selected from among readily available respondents.
conversion rate The percentage of visitors to a Web site who make a purchase.
cookie Controversial technique for collecting information about online Web site visitors in which a small text file is automatically downloaded to a user's computer to gather such data as length of visit and the site visited next.
cooperative advertising Strategy in which a retailer shares advertising costs with a manufacturer or wholesaler.
core competencies Activities that a company performs well, and that customers value and competitors find difficult to duplicate.
corporate marketing system A VMS in which a single owner operates the entire marketing channel.
corporate Web site Web site that seeks to build customer goodwill and supplement other sales channels rather than to sell goods and services.
cost per impression (CPM) Measurement technique that relates the cost of an ad to every thousand people who view it.
cost per response (also called *click-throughs*) Direct marketing technique that relates the cost of an ad to the number of people who click on it.
cost per thousand (CPM) Calculation of the cost to deliver a message to each 1,000 viewers, listeners, or readers.
cost-plus pricing Practice of adding a percentage of specified dollar amount (markup) to the base cost of a product to cover unassigned costs and to provide a profit.
countertrade Form of exporting whereby goods and services are bartered rather than sold for cash.
coupons Form of sales promotion that offers discounts on the purchase price of goods and services.
creative selling Personal selling involving situations in which a considerable degree of analytical decision making on the buyer's part results in the need for skillful proposals of solutions for the customer's needs.
creativity Human activity that produces original ideas or knowledge, frequently by testing combinations of ideas or data to produce unique results.
critical thinking Process of determining the authenticity, accuracy, and worth of information, knowledge, claims, and arguments.
cross promotion Promotional technique in which marketing partners share the cost of a promotional campaign that meets their mutual needs.
cross-selling Selling of multiple, often unrelated products and services to the same customer, based on knowledge of that customer's needs.
cue Any object in the environment that determines the nature of a consumer's response to a drive.
culture Values, beliefs, preferences, and tastes handed down from one generation to the next in a society.
cumulative quantity discount Price discount determined by amounts of purchases over stated time periods.

customary prices Traditional prices that customers expect to pay for certain goods and services.
customer-based segmentation Dividing a business-to-business market into homogeneous groups based on buyers' product specifications.
customer behavior Buying behavior of individual consumers as well as organizational buyers.
customer relationship management (CRM) Combination of strategies and tools that drive relationship programs, reorienting the entire organization to a concentrated focus on satisfying customers. Leveraging technology, CRM integrates all stakeholders into a company's product design and development, manufacturing, marketing, sales, and customer service processes.
customer satisfaction Extent to which customers are satisfied with their purchased goods or services.
customer service standard Statement of goals and acceptable performance for the quality of service that a firm expects to deliver to its customers.
customs union Establishment of a free-trade area plus a uniform tariff for trade with nonmember unions.
cybermall Group of virtual stores planned, coordinated, and operated as a unit for online shoppers.

D

data mining Process of searching through customer databases to detect patterns that guide marketing decision making.
database marketing Use of software to analyze marketing information, identifying and targeting messages toward specific groups of potential customers.
decider Person who chooses a good or service, although another person may have the formal authority to do so.
decoding Receiver's interpretation of a message.
Delphi technique Qualitative sales forecasting method that gathers and redistributes several rounds of anonymous forecasts until the participants reach a consensus.
demand Schedule of the amounts of a firm's product that consumers will purchase at different prices during a specified time period.
demarketing Process of reducing consumer demand for a good or service to a level that the firm can supply.
demographic segmentation Dividing an overall market into homogeneous groups based on variables such as gender, age, and income.
demonstration Opportunity for the customer to try out or otherwise see how a product or service works before purchase.
department store Large store that handles a variety of merchandise, including clothing, household goods, appliances, and furniture.
deregulation movement Opening of markets previously subject to government control.
derived demand Demand for a business product that results from demand for a consumer product.
differentiated marketing Marketing strategy to produce several products and promote them with different marketing mixes designed to satisfy smaller segments.
diffusion process Process by which new goods or services are accepted in the marketplace.
digital tools Electronic technologies used in e-commerce, including fax machines, computer modems, telephones, and CD-ROMS.
direct channel Marketing channel that moves goods directly from a producer to the business purchaser or ultimate user.
direct mail Communications in the form of sales letters, postcards, brochures, catalogs, and the like conveying messages directly from the marketer to the customer.
direct marketing Direct communications, other than personal sales contacts, between buyer and seller, designed to generate sales, information requests, or store or Web site visits.
direct sales results test Method for measuring the effectiveness of promotion based on the specific impact on sales revenues for each dollar of promotional spending.
direct selling Strategy designed to establish direct sales contact between producer and final user.
discount house Store that charges low prices but may not offer services such as credit.
discretionary income Money people have available to spend after buying necessities such as food, clothing, and housing.
distribution intensity Number of intermediaries through which a manufacturer distributes its goods.
distribution strategies Planning that ensures that consumers find their products in the proper quantities at the right times and places.
drive Any strong stimulus that impels a person to act.
drop shipper Limited-function merchant wholesaler who accepts orders from customers and forwards these orders to producers, which then ship directly to the customers who place the orders.
dual distribution Network that moves products to a firm's target market through more than one marketing channel.
dumping Controversial practice of selling a product in foreign market at a price lower than what it receives in the producer's domestic market.

E

economic environment Factors that influence consumer buying power and marketing strategies, including stage of the business cycle, inflation, unemployment, income, and resource availability.
80/20 principle Principle stating that 80 percent of a product's revenues come from 20 percent of its total customers.
elasticity Measure of responsiveness of purchasers and suppliers to a change in price.
electronic bulletin board Specialized online service that provides information on a specific topic or area of interest.
electronic commerce (e-commerce) Targeting customers by collecting and analyzing business information, conducting customer transactions, and maintaining online relationships with customers by means of computer networks.
electronic data interchange (EDI) Computer-to-computer exchanges of invoices, orders, and other business documents.
electronic exchanges Online marketplaces that bring buyers and sellers together.
electronic marketing (e-marketing) Strategic process of creating, distributing, promoting, and pricing goods and services to a target market over the Internet or through digital tools.
electronic signature Electronic approval of a document that has the same status as a written signature.
electronic storefront Online store where customers can view and order merchandise much like window shopping at traditional retail establishments.
embargo Complete ban on the import of specified products.
employee satisfaction Employee's level of satisfaction for his or her company and the extent to which that loyalty or lack of loyalty is communicated to external customers.
encoding Translating a message into understandable terms.
end-use application segmentation Segmenting a business-to-business market based on how industrial purchasers will use the product.
Engel's laws Three general statements based on Engel's studies of the impact of household income changes on consumer spending behavior.
enterprise resource planning (ERP) system Software system that consolidates data from among a firm's units.
environmental management Attainment of organizational objectives by predicting and influencing the competitive, political-legal, economic, technological, and social-cultural environments.
environmental scanning Process of collecting information about the external marketing environment in order to identify and interpret potential trends.
ethnocentrism Tendency to view one's own culture as the norm.
ethnography Observational research method developed by social anthropologists; also known as interpretive research or "going native."
European Union (EU) Customs union that is moving in the direction of an economic union by adopting a common currency, removing trade restrictions, and permitting free flow of goods and workers throughout the member nations.
evaluative criteria Features that a consumer considers in choosing among alternatives.
event marketing Marketing of sporting, cultural, and charitable activities to selected target markets.

everyday low pricing (EDLP) Pricing strategy of continuously offering low prices rather than relying on such short-term price cuts as cents-off coupons, rebates, and special sales.
evoked set Number of alternatives that a consumer actually considers in making a purchase decision.
exchange control Method used to regulate the privilege of international trade among importing organizations by controlling access to foreign currencies.
exchange function Buying and selling functions of marketing.
exchange process Activity in which two or more parties give something of value to each other to satisfy perceived needs.
exchange rate Price of one nation's currency in terms of other countries' currencies.
exclusive dealing agreement Arrangement between a manufacturer and a marketing intermediary that prohibits the intermediary from handling competing product lines.
exclusive distribution Distribution of a product through one wholesaler or retailer in a specific geographical region.
expectancy theory Theory developed by management author Victor Vroom stating that motivation depends on an individual's expectations of his or her ability to perform a job and how that performance relates to attaining a desired reward.
exploratory research Process of discussing a marketing problem with informed sources both within and outside the firm and examining information from secondary sources.
exponential smoothing Quantitative forecasting technique that assigns weights to historical sales data, giving the greatest weight to the most recent data.
exporting Marketing domestically produced goods and services in foreign countries.
extended problem solving Situation that results when brands are difficult to categorize or evaluate, and usually involves lengthy external searches.
external customer People or organizations that buy or use another firm's goods or services.
external marketing Marketing efforts that a company directs toward customers, suppliers, and other parties outside the organization.
extranet Secure network accessible through a Web site by external customers or organizations for electronic commerce. It provides more customer-specific information than a public site.

F

facilitating functions Functions that assist the marketer in performing the exchange and physical distribution functions.
fads Fashions with abbreviated life cycles.
fair-trade laws Statutes enacted in most states that once permitted manufacturers to stipulate a minimum retail price for their product.
family brand Single brand name that identifies several related products.
family life cycle Process of family formation and dissolution.
fashions Currently popular products that tend to follow recurring life cycles.
feedback Receiver's response to a message.
field selling Sales presentations made at prospective customers' homes or businesses on a face-to-face basis.
first-mover strategy Concept that advocates that the company that is first to offer a product in a marketplace will be the long-term winner.
fixed costs Costs that remain stable at any production level within a certain range (such as lease payments or insurance costs).
fixed-sum-per-unit method Method of promotional budgeting in which a predetermined amount is allocated to each sales or production unit.
FOB (free on board) plant Price quotation that does not include shipping charges; also called FOB origin.
FOB origin-freight allowed or freight absorbed Price quotation system that allows the buyer to deduct shipping expenses from the cost of purchases.
focus group Marketing research procedure that typically brings together 8 to 12 individuals to discuss a given subject.
follow-up Post sales activities that often determine whether an individual who has made a recent purchase will become a repeat customer.
foreign licensing Agreement that grants foreign marketers the right to distribute a firm's merchandise or to use its trademark, patent, or process in a specified geographic area.
franchise Contractual arrangement in which a wholesaler or retailer agrees to meet the operating requirements of a manufacturer or other franchiser.
free-trade area Region in which participating nations agree to the free trade of goods among themselves, abolishing tariffs and trade restrictions.
Free Trade Area of the Americas (FTAA) Proposed free trade area stretching the length of the entire Western hemisphere and designed to extend free trade benefits to additional nations in North, Central, and South America.
frequency Number of times an individual is exposed to an advertisement during a certain time period.
frequency marketing Frequent buyer or user marketing programs that reward customers with cash, rebates, merchandise, or other premiums.
friendship, commerce, and navigation (FCN) treaties International agreements that deal with many aspects of commercial relations among nations.
full-cost pricing Pricing method that uses all relevant variable costs in setting a product's price and also allocates those fixed costs that cannot be directly attributed to the production of the specific item being priced.
full-service research supplier Customized service that provides all the steps in the marketing research process.

G

gatekeeper Person who controls the information that all buying center members will review.
General Agreement on Tariffs and Trade (GATT) International trade accord that has helped reduce world tariffs.
general merchandise retailer Store that carries a wide variety of product lines, stocking all of them in some depth.
generic products Products characterized by plain labels, no advertising, and no brand names.
geographic information system (GIS) System that places data in a spatial format, on a map.
geographic segmentation Dividing an overall market into homogeneous groups based on their locations.
global marketing strategy Standardized marketing mix with minimal modifications that a firm uses in all of its domestic and foreign markets.
global sourcing Contracting to purchase goods and services from suppliers worldwide.
good Tangible product that customers can see, hear, smell, taste, or touch.
goods-services continuum Spectrum along which goods and services fall according to their attributes, from pure good to pure service.
green marketing Production, promotion, and reclamation of environmentally sensitive products.
grey good Product manufactured abroad under license from a U.S. firm and then sold in the U.S. market in competition with that firm's own domestic output.
gross rating point Total weight of a media effort, which is determined by multiplying reach times frequency.
guerilla marketing Innovative, low-cost marketing schemes designed to get consumers' attention in unusual ways.

H

high-involvement purchase decision Buying decision that evokes high levels of potential social or economic consequence.
home shopping channel Television direct marketing in which a variety of products are offered and consumers can order them directly by phone or online.
hypothesis Tentative explanation for some specific event.

I

import quotas Trade restriction that limits the number of units of certain goods that can enter a country for resale.
importing Purchasing foreign goods, services, and raw materials.

inbound telemarketing Sales method in which prospects call a toll-free number to obtain information, make reservations, and purchase goods and services.
incremental-cost pricing Pricing method that attempts to use only those costs directly attributable to a specific output in setting prices.
indirect evaluation Method for measuring promotional effectiveness by concentrating on quantifiable indicators of effectiveness such as recall and readership.
individual brand Single brand that uniquely identifies a product itself.
inflation Rising prices caused by some combination of excess consumer demand and increases in the costs of one or more factors of production.
influencer Typically technical staff such as engineers who affect the buying decision by supplying information to guide evaluation of alternatives or by setting buying specifications
infomercial Paid 30-minute product commercial that resembles a regular television program.
informative advertising Promotion that seeks to develop initial demand for a good, service, organization, person, place, idea, or cause.
infrastructure A nation's basic system of transportation networks, communication systems, and energy facilities.
inquiry tests Posttests that measure the number of inquiries relative to an advertisement's cost.
inside selling Performing the functions of field selling but avoiding travel-related expenses by relying on phone, mail, and electronic commerce to provide sales and product service for customers on a continuing basis.
installations Business products that are major capital investments.
instant messaging E-mail service that allows for the immediate exchange of short messages between online users.
institutional advertising Promotion of a concept, idea, philosophy, or goodwill of an industry, company, organization, person, geographical location, or government agency.
integrated marketing communications (IMC) Coordination of all promotional activities to produce a unified, customer-focused promotional message.
intensive distribution Distribution of a product through all available channels.
interactive advertising Two-way promotional messages transmitted through communication channels that induce message recipients to participate actively in the promotional effort.
interactive marketing Buyer-seller communications in which the customer controls the amount and type of information received from a marketer through such channels as the Internet, CD-ROMS, interactive toll-free telephone numbers, and virtual reality kiosks.
interactive television (iTV) Television service package that includes a return path for viewers to interact with programs or commercials by clicking their remote controls.
intermodal service Combination of transport modes such as rail and highway carriers (piggyback), air and highway carriers (birdyback), and water and air carriers (fishyback) to improve customer service and achieve cost advantages.
internal customer Employees or departments within an organization that depend on the work of another employee or department to perform tasks.
internal marketing Managerial actions that help all members of the organization understand and accept their respective roles in implementing a marketing strategy.
Internet (or Net) Worldwide network of interconnected computers that lets anyone with access to a personal computer send and receive images and data anywhere.
Internet service provider (ISP) Organization that provides access to the Internet via a telephone or cable television network.
interstitial Ad that appears between Web pages of related content.
intranet Internal corporate network that allows employees within an organization to communicate with each other and gain access to corporate information.
ISO (International Standards Organization) 9000 certification Internationally recognized standards that ensure a company's goods and services meet established quality levels.
ISO 9002 International quality standards developed by the International Standards Organization in Switzerland to ensure consistent quality among products manufactured and sold throughout the nations of the European Union (EU).

J

joint demand Demand for a business product that depends on the demand for another business product used in combination with the first item.
jury of executive opinion Qualitative sales forecasting method that considers the sales expectations of various executives.
just-in-time (JIT)/just-in-time II (JIT II) Inventory practices that seek to boost efficiency by cutting inventories to absolute minimum levels. With JIT II, suppliers' representatives work at the customer's facility.

K

keyword ad Web advertisement that appears on the results page of a search, specific to the term being searched.

L

label Branding component that carries an item's brand name or symbol, the name and address of the manufacturer or distributor, information about the product, and recommended uses.
lateral partnership Strategic relationships that extend to external entities but involve no direct buyer-seller interactions.
leader pricing Variant of loss-leader pricing in which marketers offer prices slightly above cost to avoid violating minimum-markup regulations and earn a minimal return on promotional sales.
learning Immediate or expected changes in consumer behavior as a result of experience.
lifetime value of a customer Revenues and intangible benefits, such as referrals and customer feedback, that a customer brings to the seller over an average lifetime, less the amount the company must spend to acquire, market to, and service the customer.
limited-line store Retailer that offers a large assortment within a single product line or within a few related product lines.
limited problem-solving Situation in which the consumer knows the evaluative criteria for a product, but has not applied the criteria to assess a new brand.
line extension Development of individual offerings that appeal to different market segments while remaining closely related to the existing product line.
list price Established price normally quoted to potential buyers.
logistics Process of coordinating the flow of information, goods, and services among members of the distribution channel.
loss leader Product offered to consumers at less than cost to attract them to stores in the hope that they will buy other merchandise at regular prices.
low-involvement purchase decision Routine purchase that poses little risk to the consumer, either socially or economically.

M

mail-order wholesaler Limited-function merchant wholesaler who distributes catalogs instead of sending sales representatives to contact customers.
mall intercept Interviews conducted randomly in shopping centers.
manufacturers' agent Agent wholesaling intermediary who represents a number of manufacturers of related but noncompeting products and who receives a commission on each sale.
manufacturer's brand Brand name owned by a manufacturer or other producer.
marginal analysis Method of analyzing the relationship between costs, sales price, and increased sales volume.
marginal cost Change in total cost that results from producing an additional unit of output.
markdown Amount by which a retailer reduces the original selling price of a product.
market Group of people or institutions with sufficient purchasing power, authority, and willingness to buy.
market attractiveness/business strength Portfolio analysis technique that rates SBUs according to the attractiveness of their markets and their organizational strengths.

market development strategy Strategy that concentrates on finding new markets for existing products.
market penetration strategy Strategy that seeks to increase sales of existing products in existing markets.
market price Price that a consumer or marketing intermediary actually pays for a product after subtracting any discounts, allowances, or rebates from the list price.
market segmentation Division of the total market into smaller, relatively homogeneous groups.
market share/market growth matrix Framework that places SBUs in a chart that plots market share against market growth potential.
market-share objective Volume-related pricing objective in which the goal is to achieve control of a portion of the market for a firm's good or service.
market test Quantitative forecasting method that introduces a new product, price, promotional campaign, or other marketing variable in a relatively small test-market location in order to assess consumer reactions.
marketing Process of planning and executing the conception, pricing, and distribution of ideas, goods, services, organizations, and events to create and maintain relationships that will satisfy individual and organizational objectives.
marketing communications Messages that deal with buyer-seller relationships.
marketing concept Company-wide consumer orientation with the objective of achieving long-run success.
marketing decision support system (MDSS) Marketing information system component that links a decision maker with relevant databases and analysis tools.
marketing distribution channel System of marketing institutions that promotes the physical flow of goods and services, along with ownership title, from producer to consumer or business user.
marketing ethics Marketers' standards of conduct and moral values.
marketing information system (MIS) Planned, computer-based system designed to provide managers with a continuous flow of information relevant to their specific decisions and areas of responsibility.
marketing intermediary (middleman) Wholesaler or retailer that operates between producers and consumers or business users.
marketing mix Blending of the four strategy elements—product, pricing, distribution, and promotion—to fit the needs and preferences of a specific target market.
marketing myopia Management's failure to recognize the scope of its business.
marketing planning Implementing planning activities devoted to achieving marketing objectives.
marketing public relations (MPR) Narrowly focused public relations activities that directly support marketing goals.
marketing research Process of collecting and using information for marketing decision making.
markup Amount that a retailer adds to the cost of a product to determine its selling price.
mass merchandiser Store that stocks a wider line of goods than a department store, usually without the same depth of assortment within each line.
materials handling Set of activities that move production inputs and other goods within plants, warehouses, and transportation terminals.
media research Advertising research that assesses how well a particular medium delivers an advertiser's message, where and when to place the advertisement, and the size of the audience.
media scheduling Setting the timing and sequence for a series of advertisements.
meeting competition Method of promotional budgeting that simply matches competitors' outlays.
merchant wholesaler Independently owned wholesaling intermediary who takes title to the goods that it handles; also known as an industrial distributor in the business-goods market.
message Communication of information, advice, or a request by the sender to the receiver.
message research Advertising research that tests consumer reactions to an advertisement's creative message.
metropolitan statistical area (MSA) Freestanding urban area with a population in the urban center of at least 50,000, and a total MSA population of 100,000 or more.
micromarketing Targeting potential customers at a basic level, such as zip code.
mission Essential purpose that differentiates one company from others.
missionary selling Indirect type of selling in which specialized salespeople promote the firm's goodwill among indirect customers, often by assisting customers in product use.
modified breakeven analysis Pricing technique used to evaluate consumer demand by comparing the number of products that must be sold at a variety of prices in order to cover total cost with estimates of expected sales at the various prices.
modified rebuy Situation in which a purchaser is willing to reevaluate available options for repurchasing a good or service.
monopolistic competition Market structure involving a heterogeneous product and product differentiation among competing suppliers, allowing the marketer some degree of control over prices.
monopoly Market structure in which a single seller dominates trade in a good or service for which buyers can find no close substitutes.
motive Inner state that directs a person toward the goal of satisfying a need.
MRO items Business supplies that include maintenance items, repair items, and operating supplies.
multidomestic marketing strategy Application of market segmentation to foreign markets by tailoring the firm's marketing mix to match specific target markets in each nation.
multinational corporation Firm with significant operations and marketing activities outside its home country.
multiple sourcing Spreading purchases among several vendors.

N

national account selling Promotional effort in which a dedicated sales team is assigned to a firm's major customers to provide sales and service needs.
national accounts organization Organizational arrangement that assigns sales teams to a firm's largest accounts.
need Imbalance between a consumer's actual and desired states.
new-task buying First-time or unique purchase situation that requires considerable effort by the decision makers.
9/11 Generation People in their formative years at the time of the September 11 terrorist attacks.
noise Any stimulus that distracts a receiver from receiving a message.
noncumulative quantity discount Price reduction granted on a one-time-only basis.
nonmarketing public relations Organizational messages about general management issues.
nonpersonal selling Promotion that includes advertising, sales promotion, direct marketing, and public relations—all conducted without being face-to-face with the buyer.
nonprobability sample Arbitrary grouping that produces data unsuited for most standard statistical tests.
norms Values, attitudes, and behaviors that a group deems appropriate for its members.
North American Free-Trade Agreement (NAFTA) Accord removing trade barriers among Canada, Mexico, and the United States.
North American Industrial Classification System (NAICS) Classification used by NAFTA countries to categorize the business marketplace into detailed market segments.

O

objection Expression of sales resistance by the prospect.
odd pricing Pricing policy based on the belief that a price ending with an odd number just under a round number is more appealing—for instance, \$9.97 rather than \$10.
off-invoice allowance Promotional incentive through which retailers deduct specified amounts from their invoices or receive free goods.
oligopoly Market structure, like those in the steel and telecommunications industries, in which relatively few sellers compete, and

where high start-up costs form barriers to keep out new competitors.

opinion leaders Trendsetters who are likely to purchase new products before others in a group and then share their experiences and opinions via word of mouth.

order processing Selling, mostly at the wholesale and retail levels, that involves identifying customer needs, pointing them out to customers, and completing orders.

organization marketing Marketing by mutual-benefit organizations, service organizations, and government organizations intended to influence others to accept their goals, receive their services, or contribute to them in some way.

outbound telemarketing Sales method in which sales representatives place phone calls to prospects and try to conclude the sale over the phone.

outsourcing Using outside vendors to produce goods and services formerly produced in-house.

over-the-counter selling Personal selling conducted in retail and some wholesale locations in which customers come to the seller's place of business.

P

partnership Affiliation of two or more companies that assist each other in the achievement of common goals.

penetration pricing strategy Pricing strategy involving the use of a relatively low entry price compared with competitive offerings; based on the theory that this initial low price will help secure market acceptance.

percentage-of-sales method Way of establishing a promotional budget in which a dollar amount is based on a percentage of past or projected sales.

perception Meaning that a person attributes to incoming stimuli gathered through the five senses.

perceptual screen Filtering process through which all inputs must pass in a person's mind.

person marketing Marketing efforts designed to cultivate the attention, interest, and preference of a target market toward a person (typically a political candidate or celebrity).

personal selling Interpersonal influence process involving a seller's promotional presentation conducted on a person-to-person basis with the buyer.

persuasive advertising Promotion that attempts to increase demand for an existing good, service, organization, person, place, idea, or cause.

physical distribution function Transportation and distribution of goods and services.

place marketing Marketing efforts to attract people and organizations to a particular geographic area.

planned obsolescence Intentional design, manufacture, and marketing of products with limited durability.

planned shopping center Group of retail stores planned, coordinated, and marketed as a unit.

planning Process of anticipating future events and conditions, and of determining the best way to achieve organizational goals.

point-of-purchase (POP) advertising Display or other promotion located near the site of an actual buying decision.

political-legal environment Component of the marketing environment consisting of laws and interpretations of laws that require firms to operate under competitive conditions and to protect consumer rights.

political risk assessment (PRA) Units within a firm that evaluate the political risks of the marketplaces in which they operate as well as proposed new marketplaces.

population (universe) Total group that researchers want to study.

pop-up ads Advertising messages that appear unsolicited as windows on a computer screen.

positioning map Graphic depiction of consumers' perceptions of competing products within an industry.

POSSLQ Abbreviation for unmarried "people of the opposite sex in the same living quarters."

postage-stamp pricing System for handling transportation costs under which all buyers are quoted the same price, including transportation expenses. Also known as *uniform-delivered price.*

posttesting Research that assesses advertising effectiveness after it has appeared in the appropriate medium.

precall planning Use of information collected during the prospecting and qualifying stages of the sales process and during previous contacts with the prospect to tailor the approach and presentation to match the customer's needs.

premium Sales promotion technique in which an item is provided free or at a reduced cost with the purchase of other products.

presentation Describing a product's major features and relating them to a customer's problems or needs.

pretesting Research that evaluates an ad during its development stage.

price Exchange value of a good or service.

price flexibility Pricing policy permitting variable prices for goods and services.

pricing policy General guidelines based on pricing objectives and intended for use in specific pricing decisions.

pricing strategy Methods of setting profitable and justifiable prices.

primary data Information collected for the first time.

primary demand Desire for a general product category.

primary metropolitan statistical area (PMSA) Urbanized county or set of counties with social and economic ties to nearby areas.

private brand Brand offered by a wholesaler or retailer.

probability sample Sample that gives every member of the population a chance of being selected.

product Bundle of physical, service, and symbolic attributes designed to satisfy a customer's wants and needs.

product advertising Nonpersonal selling of a particular good or service.

product development Introduction of new products into identifiable or established markets.

product differentiation When consumers regard a firm's products as different in some way from those of competitors.

product diversification strategy Developing entirely new products for new markets.

product liability Responsibility of manufacturers and marketers for injuries and damages caused by their products.

product life cycle Progression of a product through introduction, growth, maturity, and decline.

product line Series of related products offered by one company.

product-line pricing Practice of setting a limited number of prices for a selection of merchandise and marketing different product lines in each of these price levels.

product manager Marketers who support an individual product or product line; also called a brand manager.

product mix Assortment of product lines and individual product offerings that a company sells.

product placement Form of promotion in which a marketer pays a motion picture or television program owner a fee to display a product prominently in the film or show.

product positioning Consumers' perceptions of a product's attributes, uses, quality, and advantages and disadvantages relative to competing brands.

product-related segmentation Division of a population into homogeneous groups based on characteristics of their relationships to the product.

product strategy Decisions about what goods or services a firm will offer its customers; also includes decisions about customer service, packaging, brand names, and the like.

production orientation Business philosophy stressing efficiency in producing a quality product, with the attitude toward marketing that "a good product will sell itself."

profit center Any part of an organization to which revenue and controllable costs can be assigned.

Profit Impact of Market Strategies (PIMS) project Research that discovered a strong positive relationship between a firm's market share and its return on investment.

profit maximization Point at which the additional revenue gained by increasing the price of a product equals the increase in total costs.

promotion Communication link between buyers and sellers. Function of informing, persuading, and influencing a consumer's purchase decision.

promotional allowance Promotional incentive in which the manufacturer agrees to pay the reseller a certain amount to cover the costs of special promotional displays or extensive advertising.
promotional mix Subset of the marketing mix in which marketers attempt to achieve the optimal blending of the elements of personal and nonpersonal selling to achieve promotional objectives.
promotional pricing Pricing policy in which a lower-than-normal price is used as a temporary ingredient in a firm's marketing strategy.
prospecting Personal selling function of identifying potential customers.
protective tariff Taxes designed to raise the retail price of an imported product to match or exceed that of a similar domestic tariff.
psychographic segmentation Division of a population into groups that have similar psychological characteristics, values, and lifestyles.
psychological pricing Pricing policy based on the belief that certain prices or price ranges make a good or service more appealing than others to buyers.
public relations Firm's communications and relationships with its various publics.
public service announcements (PSAs) Advertisements aimed at achieving socially oriented objectives by focusing on causes and charitable organizations.
publicity Nonpersonal stimulation of demand for a good, service, place, idea, person, or organization by unpaid placement of significant news regarding the product in a print or broadcast medium.
puffery Exaggerated claims of a product's superiority, or the use of subjective or vague statements that may not be literally true.
pulling strategy Promotional effort by the seller to stimulate final-user demand, which then exerts pressure on the distribution channel.
pure competition Market structure characterized by homogeneous products in which there are so many buyers and sellers that none has a significant influence on price.
push money Promotional incentive that gives retail salespeople cash rewards for products they sell.
pushing strategy Promotional effort by the seller directed to members of the marketing channel rather than final users.

Q

qualifying Determining that a prospect has the needs, income, and purchase authority necessary for being a potential customer.
qualitative forecasting Use of subjective techniques to forecast sales.
quantitative forecasting Use of techniques based on numerical data developed through statistical analysis.
quantity discount Price reduction granted for a large-volume purchase.
quick response merchandising Just-in-time strategy that reduces the time a retailer must hold merchandise in inventory, resulting in substantial cost savings.
quota sample Nonprobability sample divided to ensure representation of different segments or groups in the total sample.

R

rack jobber Full-function merchant wholesaler who markets specialized lines of merchandise to retail stores.
raw materials Natural resources such as farm products, coal, copper, or lumber, which become part of a final product.
reach Number of different individuals or households exposed to an advertisement at least once during a certain time period.
readership test Test of advertising effectiveness based on the assumption that future sales are related to advertising readership; also called *recognition test.*
rebate Refund of a portion of the purchase price, usually granted by the product's manufacturer.
reciprocity Policy to extend purchasing preference to suppliers that are also customers.
reference groups Groups whose value structures and standards influence a person's behavior.
refund Sales promotion technique in which consumers who send in proof of purchasing one or more products are offered cash to reduce the total price paid; also called a *rebate.*
reinforcement Reduction in drive that results from a proper response.
relationship marketing Development and maintenance of long-term, cost-effective relationships with individual customers, suppliers, employees, and other partners for mutual benefit.
relationship selling Regular contacts over an extended period to establish a sustained seller-buyer relationship.
reminder advertising Advertising that reinforces previous promotional activity by keeping the name of a good, service, organization, person, place, idea, or cause before the public.
repositioning Changing the position of a product within the minds of prospective buyers relative to the positions of competing products.
research design Master plan for conducting marketing research.
reseller Marketing intermediaries that operate in the trade sector.
response Individual's reaction to a set of cues and drives.
retail advertising All advertising by retail stores that sell goods or services directly to the consuming public.
retail convergence The coming together of shoppers, goods, and prices, resulting in the blurring of distinctions between types of retailer and the merchandise mix they offer.
retailing Activities involved in selling merchandise to ultimate consumers.
revenue tariff Taxes designed to raise funds for the importing government.
reverse channel Channel designed to return goods to their producers.
Robinson-Patman Act Federal legislation prohibiting price discrimination that is not based on a cost differential; also prohibits selling at an unreasonably low price to eliminate competition.
role Behavior that members of a group expect of individuals who hold specific positions within that group.
routinized response behavior Type of rapid consumer problem solving in which the consumer has already set evaluative criteria and identified available options.

S

sales analysis In-depth evaluation of a firm's sales.
sales conviction test Test of advertising effectiveness in which participants evaluate two alternative ads and choose the one that best convinces them to make a purchase.
sales-force automation (SFA) Applications of computer and other technologies to make the sales function more efficient and competitive.
sales force composite Qualitative sales forecasting method based on the combined sales estimates of the firm's salespeople.
sales forecast Estimate of company revenue for a specified future period.
sales orientation Business assumption that consumers will resist purchasing nonessential goods and services with the attitude toward marketing that only creative advertising and personal selling can overcome consumers' resistance and convince them to buy.
sales promotion Marketing activities other than personal selling, advertising, and public relations that stimulate consumer purchasing and dealer effectiveness.
sales quota Level of expected sales for a territory, product, customer, or salesperson against which actual results are compared.
sampling Sales promotion technique in which a product is distributed at no cost in an attempt to encourage trial use by potential customers to stimulate future sales.
scrambled merchandising Retailing practice of combining dissimilar product lines to boost sales volume.
search engine A tool to help online users find specific Web sites and pages.
secondary data Previously published information.
selective demand Desire for a specific brand.
selective distribution Distribution of a product through only a limited number of channels.
self-concept Person's multifaceted picture of himself or herself.
seller partnership Relationship involving long-term exchanges of goods or services in return for cash or other valuable consideration.
seller's market Market in which there are more buyers for fewer goods and services.

selling agent Agent wholesaling intermediary responsible for the entire marketing program of a firm's product line.
sender Source of the message communicated to the receiver.
service Intangible task that satisfies the needs of consumer and business users.
shaping Process of applying a series of rewards and reinforcements to permit more complex behavior to evolve over time.
shopping products Products that consumers purchase after comparing competing offerings.
simple random sample Basic type of probability sample in which every individual in the relevant universe has an equal opportunity of selection.
skimming pricing strategy Pricing strategy involving the use of a high price relative to competitive offerings.
slotting allowances Money paid to retailers to guarantee prominent display.
slotting fee See *slotting allowances.*
smart card Multipurpose card embedded with computer chips that store personal and financial information, such as credit card data, health records, and driver's license number.
social-cultural environment Component of the marketing environment consisting of the relationship between the marketer and society and its culture.
social responsibility Marketing philosophies, policies, procedures, and actions that have the enhancement of society's welfare as a primary objective.
sole sourcing Purchasing a firm's entire stock of a product from just one vendor.
span of control Approach to supervision of sales personnel based on the number of representatives who report to first-level sales managers.
specialty advertising Sales promotion technique that places the advertiser's name, address, and advertising message on useful articles that are then distributed to target consumers.
specialty products Products that offer unique characteristics that cause buyers to prize those particular brands.
specialty retailer Store that combines carefully defined product lines, services, and reputation to convince shoppers to spend considerable shopping effort there.
split run Method of testing alternate ads by dividing a cable TV audience or a publication's subscribers in two, using two different ads, and then evaluating the relative effectiveness of each.
sponsorship When an organization provides cash or in-kind resources to an event or activity in exchange for a direct association with that event or activity.
spreadsheet analysis Analysis that lays out a rigid grid of columns and rows that organize numerical information in a standardized, easily understandable format.
status Relative position of any individual member in a group.
stockkeeping unit (SKU) Specific offering within a product line such as a specific size of liquid detergent.
straight rebuy Recurring purchase decision in which a customer repurchases a good or service that has performed satisfactorily in the past.
strategic alliance Partnerships in which two or more companies combine resources and capital to create competitive advantages in a new market
strategic business units (SBUs) Key business units within diversified firms.
strategic planning Process of determining an organization's primary objectives and adopting courses of action that will achieve these objectives.
strategic window Limited periods during which the key requirements of a market and the particular competencies of a firm best fit together.
stratified sample Probability sample constructed to represent randomly selected subsamples of different groups within the total sample.
subcontracting Contractual agreements that assign the production of goods or services to local or smaller firms.
subcultures Groups with their own distinct modes of behavior.
subliminal perception Subconscious receipt of incoming information.
suboptimization Condition that results when individual operations achieve their objectives but interfere with progress toward broader organizational goals.
subsidy Government financial support of a private industry.
supercenter Large store, smaller than a hypermarket, that combines groceries with discount store merchandise.
supplies Regular expenses that a firm incurs in its daily operations.
supply Schedule of the amounts of a good or service that firms will offer for sale at different prices during a specified time period.
supply (value) chain Sequence of suppliers that contribute to the creation and delivery of a good or service.
survey of buyer intentions Qualitative sales forecasting method that samples opinions among groups of present and potential customers concerning their purchase intentions.
sweepstakes Sales promotion technique using games in which prize winners are chosen by chance.
switchless reseller Telecommunications company with no lines or equipment that buys blocks of long-distance time from major carriers and resells it by the minute at a discount.
SWOT analysis Analysis that helps planners compare internal organizational strengths and weaknesses with external opportunities and threats.
syndicated service Organization that regularly provides standardized data to all customers.
systems integration Centralization of the procurement function within an internal division or as a service of an external supplier.

T

tactical planning Planning that guides the implementation of activities specified in the strategic plan.
target market Group of people toward whom the firm decides to direct its marketing efforts, and ultimately its goods and services.
target-return objective Short-run or long-run pricing objectives of achieving a specified return on either sales or investment.
tariff Tax levied against imported goods.
task-objective method Development of a promotional budget based on evaluation of the firm's promotional objectives.
team selling Selling situation in which several sales associates or other members of the organization are recruited to assist the lead sales representative in reaching all those who influence the purchase decision.
technological environment Applications to marketing of knowledge based on discoveries in science, inventions, and innovations.
telemarketing Promotional presentation involving the use of the telephone on an outbound basis by salespeople or on an inbound basis by customers who initiate calls to obtain information and place orders.
test-marketing Method that involves introducing a new product in a specific area and then observing its degree of success.
third-party (contract) logistics firm Company that specializes in handling logistics activities for other firms.
time-based competition Strategy of developing and distributing goods and services more quickly than competitors.
total quality management (TQM) Movement that asks all employees in a firm to continually improve products and work processes with the goal of achieving customer satisfaction and world-class performance.
trade allowance Promotional incentive offered to wholesalers and retailers who purchase specific products.
trade discount Payment to a channel member or buyer for performing marketing functions; also known as a functional discount.
trade dress Visual components that contribute to the overall look of a brand.
trade-in Credit allowance given for a used item when a customer purchases a new item.
trade industry Retailers or wholesalers that purchase products for resale to others.
trade promotion Sales promotion that appeals to marketing intermediaries rather than consumers.
trade show Show organized by industry trade associations in which vendors are invited to appear in order to display and demonstrate their products for association members.

trademark Brand for which the owner claims exclusive legal protection.

transaction-based marketing Buyer and seller exchanges characterized by limited communications and little or no ongoing relationship between the parties.

transfer price Cost assessed when a product is moved from one profit center in a firm to another.

trend analysis Quantitative sales forecasting method that estimates future sales through statistical analyses of historical sales patterns.

truck wholesaler Limited-function merchant wholesaler who markets perishable food items; also called a truck jobber.

tying agreement Arrangement that requires a marketing intermediary to carry items other than those they want to sell.

U

unaided recall tests Posttests in which respondents do not see copies of an ad after its original reading, but must recall it from memory.

undifferentiated marketing Marketing strategy to produce a single product and market it to all customers; also called *mass marketing.*

unemployment Proportion of people in the economy who are actively seeking work but do not have jobs.

unfair-trade laws State laws requiring sellers to maintain minimum prices for comparable merchandise.

uniform-delivered price Pricing system for handling transportation costs under which all buyers are quoted the same price, including transportation expenses. Sometimes known as *postage-stamp pricing.*

unit pricing Pricing policy in which prices are stated in terms of a recognized unit of measurement or a standard numerical count.

unitizing Process of combining individual materials into large loads for easy handling.

Universal Product Code (UPC) Numerical bar code system used to record product and price information.

unsought products Products marketed to consumers who may not yet recognize any need for them.

utility Want-satisfying power of a good or service.

V

VALS2 System that divides consumers into eight psychographic categories: actualizers, fulfilleds, believers, achievers, strivers, experiencers, makers, and strugglers.

value analysis Systematic study of the components of a purchase to determine the most cost-effective approach.

value pricing Pricing strategy emphasizing benefits derived from a product in comparison to the price and quality levels of competing offerings.

variable costs Costs that change with the level of production (such as labor and raw materials costs).

vendor analysis Assessment of supplier performance in areas such as price, back orders, timely delivery, and attention to special requests.

vendor-managed inventory (VMI) Inventory management system in which the seller—based on an existing agreement with a buyer—determines how much of a product is needed.

venture team Group of specialists from different areas of an organization who work together in developing new products.

vertical marketing system (VMS) Planned channel system designed to improve distribution efficiency and cost effectiveness by integrating various functions throughout the distribution chain.

W

Web kiosk Small, free-standing computer, often located in a store, that provides consumers with Internet connections to a firm and its goods and services.

wheel of retailing Hypothesis that each new type of retailer gains a competitive foothold by offering lower prices than current suppliers charge, and maintains profits by reducing or eliminating services.

wholesaler Channel intermediary that takes title to goods it handles and then distributes these goods to retailers, other distributors, or B2B customers.

wholesaling intermediary Comprehensive term that describes wholesalers as well as agents and brokers.

wireless technology Technology that allows communications connections without wires.

World Trade Organization (WTO) Organization that replaces GATT, overseeing GATT agreements, making binding decisions in mediating disputes, and reducing trade barriers.

World Wide Web Collection of resources on the Internet that offers easy access to text, graphics, sound, and other multimedia resources.

Y

yield management Pricing strategy that allows marketers to vary prices based on such factors as demand, even though the cost of providing those goods or services remains the same; designed to maximize revenues in situations such as airfares, lodging, auto rentals, and theater tickets, where costs are fixed.

Z

zone pricing Pricing system for handling transportation costs under which the market is divided into geographic regions and a different price is set in each region.

Prologue 1 AP Topic Gallery
Prologue 2 "©2002 Principal Financial Services, Inc. Used with permission. Depicted are trademarks and registered trademarks of Principal Financial Services, Inc."
Prologue 3 "Courtesy, 6FigureJobs, a Workstream, Inc. Company"
Prologue 4 ©Giry Daniel/CORBIS Sygma
Prologue 5 ©Susan Van Etten
Opening Vignette 1 "Courtesy, Fulton Street Market"
Figure 1.1 "©Reuters NewMedia, Inc./CORBIS"
Figure 1.2 Image used with permission of the New York Stock Exchange.
Figure 1.4 ©Susan Van Etten
Figure 1.5 "©2002 City Harvest. Special thanks to the NY Giants. Photo: David Leach. Agency: Foote, Cone & Belding."
Unnumbered 1.1 ©Susan Van Etten
Unnumbered 1.2 Source: San Antonio Convention & Visitors Bureau
Unnumbered 1.3 ©2002 Corporate Angel Network
Unnumbered 1.4 ©Athens 2004; Photo by Allsport
Figure 1.6 "Courtesy, General Motors"
Figure 1.7 Reprinted by permission of Duke Energy Corporation. All rights reserved.
Unnumbered 1.5 "Courtesy, General Motors"
Unnumbered 1.8 ©Roy Zipstein. Used by permission of Expedia.com
Figure 1.9 "Courtesy, Stride Rite Shoes"
Figure 1.11 Reprinted with permission of The Timberland Company. Timberland and ⊕ are trademarks or registered trademarks of The Timberland Company. ©2001 The Timberland Company. All rights reserved.
Opening Vignette 2 "©Reuters NewMedia,Inc./CORBIS"
Figure 2.1 "©2002 Nordstrom, Inc."
Unnumbered 2.1 ©2002 Bass Pro Shops
Figure 2.2 ©Susan Van Etten
Figure 2.4 ©Mark Laita. Used by permission of Apple.
Unnumbered 2.3 "Courtesy, Latina Magazine"
Figure 2.6 "Courtesy of Nestle USA, Inc."
Figure 2.7 AP Topic Gallery
Figure 2.8 ©Susan Van Etten
Opening Vignette 3 ©AP/Wide World Photos
Figure 3.2 ©Susan Van Etten
Figure 3.3 ©Susan Van Etten
Figure 3.4 "Courtesy, Toyota"
Figure 3.5 "Courtesy, General Motors"
Figure 3.6 "Courtesy, Council for Biotechnical Information"
Figure 3.7 "©2002, Quaker Oats Company. Used by permission."
Figure 3.12 "Photo appears courtesy of Keep America Beautiful, Inc."
Unnumbered 3.1 "Courtesy, United Parcel Service."
Unnumbered 3.2 "Courtesy, Boca Foods Company"
Unnumbered 3.3 ©AP/Wide World Photos
Unnumbered 3.4 ©Peter Turnley/CORBIS
Unnumbered 3.5 ©Susan Van Etten
Unnumbered 3.6 "©2002. Used by permission of HotJobs.com, Ltd."
Unnumbered 3.7 ©Susan Van Etten
Unnumbered 3.8 ©2002 Scott Lowden Photography for Home Depot
Unnumbered 3.9 ©AP/Wide World Photos
Opening Vignette 4 "©2002. Lands' End, Inc. Used with permission."
Unnumbered 14.1 ©Susan Van Etten
Figure 4.2 "Courtesy, ©United States Postal Service"
Figure 4.3 "The creative part of Hitachi's Global Brand Campaign is courtesy of Hitachi America, Ltd."
Figure 4.4 "Courtesy, Korean Investment Service Center"
Unnumbered 4.2 AP Topic Gallery
Unnumbered 4.3 Used with permission from McDonald's Corporation.
Unnumbered 4.4 ©2002 Rolex
Unnumbered 4.5 ©Leo Burnett USA
Opening Vignette 5 Courtesy of Amazon.com
Figure 5.3 "Courtesy, Bank of America"
Figure 5.5 ©Susan Van Etten
Figure 5.9 ©TRUSTe
Figure 5.13A Courtesy of Amazon.com
Figure 5.13B ©2002 Nokia.
Opening Vignette 6 ©Eric Butler
Figure 6.3A AP Topic Gallery
Figure 6.3B AP Topic Gallery
Figure 6.4 Courtesy Toyota and Team One Advertising
Figure 6.6 "Courtesy, Amazon.com"
Figure 6.7 "Courtesy, Marriott Rewards"
Unnumbered 6.1 "Priority Club is a registered trademark of Six Continents Hotels, Inc. Used by permission."
Unnumbered 6.2 ©Jack Gruber/USA TODAY
Unnumbered 6.3 "Courtesy, PeopleSoft, Inc."
Unnumbered 6.4 "The advertisement within this book is reprinted by arrangement with Sears, Roebuck and Co. and is protected under copyright. No duplication is permitted"
Unnumbered 6.5 ©2002 Bax Global
Opening Vignette 7 Courtesy of Southwest Airlines
Figure 7.1 "Courtesy, Roper Starch"
Figure 7.2 Courtesy Cunningham Research
Figure 7.5 "Courtesy, Ipsos-ASL, Inc."
Figure 7.6 "©2002 C & R Research Services, Inc."
Figure 7.7 "Used by permission, FocusVision Worldwide, Inc."
Figure 7.8 "Courtesy, NOP World"
Unnumbered 7.1 ©Susan Van Etten
Unnumbered 7.2 "Courtesy, U.S. Air Force Reserve"
Unnumbered 7.3 "©Decision Analyst, Inc."
Opening Vignette 8 "©Fletcher, Martin & Ewing Advertising Agency for PreceptMC Lady Golf Ball"
Figure 8.1 Courtesy of Toyota
Figure 8.2 ©Susan Van Etten
Unnumbered 8.1 ©Lowe's Companies Inc.
Unnumbered 8.2 ©Mitchell Gerber/CORBIS
Unnumbered 8.4 "©Wendy's International, Inc."
Unnumbered 8.3 ©Susan Van Etten
Figure 8.5 ©Unilever Bestfoods North America. Used with permission.
Unnumbered 8.5 ©Dave G. Houser/CORBIS
Unnumbered 8.6 Image courtesy of Dodge
Figure 8.6 ©2002 Cessna Aircraft Company. Used by permission.
Figure 8.8 Courtesy of Mastercard and McCann-Erickson.
Unnumbered 8.7 ©Susan Van Etten
Figure 8.9 ©Susan Van Etten
Figure 8.11 "The advertisement within this book is reprinted by arrangement with Sears, Roebuck and Co. and is protected under copyright. No duplication is permitted"
Unnumbered 8.8 Used by permission of Old Sturbridge Village.
Unnumbered 8.9 ©Susan Van Etten
Opening Vignette 9 ©Michael Newman/PhotoEdit Inc.
Figure 9.1 "Courtesy of Nestle USA, Inc."
Figure 9.2 ©Susan Van Etten
Unnumbered 9.1 "©2002 Charles Schwab & Co., Inc. All rights reserved."
Unnumbered 9.2 "Courtesy, Sears/Kang & Lee Advertising"
Unnumbered 9.3 "The Phoenix Companies, Inc."

Figure 9.4 "©Daren Rees, Photographer; Virginia Museum of Transportation. Used by permission of Mercedes-Benz©2002"
Figure 9.6 ©Susan Van Etten
Unnumbered 9.4 "Courtesy, Quaker Oats Company"
Figure 9.7 ©Susan Van Etten
Figure 9.8 ©2002 Olive Garden. Used by permission.
Unnumbered 9.5 ©Whirlpool
Figure 9.9 ©Susan Van Etten
Figure 9.1 AP Topic Gallery
Figure 9.11 ©2002 American Airlines. Used by permission.
Unnumbered 9.6 Used by permission of Ford Motor Company.
Opening Vignette 10 ©Scott Goldsmith
Figure 10.1 ©J. Beam Photography
Figure 10.3 ©Xerox Corporation.
Figure 10.4 ©2002 Intel Corporation
Figure 10.5 "Courtesy, ADP, Inc."
Figure 10.6 "AppGate, Inc. ©2002/Concept and Creation by NIX Design"
Figure 10.8 ©2002 Cessna Aircraft Company. Used by permission.
Figure 10.10 "Courtesy, Steelcase, Inc."
Figure 10.11 "Courtesy, GSA."
Figure 10.12 AP Topic Gallery
Unnumbered 10.1 "Courtesy, U.S.A."
Unnumbered 10.2 "Provided compliments of InFocus, the market leader in digital projections."
Unnumbered 10.3 ©Siemens Corporation
Opening Vignette 11 ©Susan Van Etten
Figure 11.2 ©Veterinary Pet Insurance
Unnumbered 11.2 Advertisement reproduced with permission of Hershey Foods Corporation.
Figure 11.4 "©Elkay Manufacturing ad by Marketing Support, Inc."
Unnumbered 11.3 ©Susan Van Etten
Figure 11.6 "Courtesy, Lexmark"
Figure 11.7 "Courtesy, Storage Networks, Inc."
Figure 11.9 "Courtesy, General Motors"
Figure 11.10 ©2002. The Glad Products Co. Used with permission.
Figure 11.12 ©Zippo Manufacturing Company
Unnumbered 11.4 "TM®M&M'S is a registered trademark of Mars, Incorporated and its affiliates. It is used with permission. Mars, Incorporated is not associated with South-Western Publishing. Advertisement printed with permission of Mars, Incorporated. ©Mars, Inc. 3003"
Unnumbered 11.5 AP Topic Gallery
Opening Vignette 12 "©2002 Redox Brands, Inc"
Figure 12.1 ©The Proctor & Gamble Company. Used by permission.
Figure 12.2 "Courtesy, Wendy's."
Figure 12.3 "Courtesy, ©Truserv Corporation"
Unnumbered 12.1 ©Susan Van Etten
Figure 12.4 ©Susan Van Etten
Figure 12.5 "©Good Housekeeping, Hearst Communications, Inc."
Unnumbered 12.3 Courtesy of the Iams Company
Figure 12.6 "©2002 Reckitt Benckiser, Inc. Used by permission."
Figure 12.7 AP Topic Gallery
Unnumbered 12.4 ©2002 Jaguar Car North America
Figure 12.10 ©The J.M. Smucker Company
Figure 12.12 "Used by permission of Ford Motor Company and Intellichoice, Inc."
Figure 12.13 "Courtesy, Toyota"
Opening Vignette 13 ©Roger Ressmeyer/CORBIS
Figure 13.1 ©J. Beam Photography
Figure 13.2 Courtesy of Amazon.com
Figure 13.3 ©Pepsi-Cola company
Figure 13.4 "©2002. Lands' End, Inc. Used with permission."
Unnumbered 13.1 Courtesy Dial Corporation.Purex
Figure 13.5 ©2002 Jaguar Car North America
Unnumbered 13.2 Courtesy PUR Water Filters
Unnumbered 13.3 "Courtesy, ©United States Postal Service"
Figure 13.7 "Courtesy, Best Buy Advertising"
Unnumbered 13.4 Reprinted with permission from American Express Company
Opening Vignette 14 ©Deborah Davis/PhotoEdit
Figure 14.1 "©2002 Weber-Stephen Products, Inc."
Figure 14.2 ©2002 Mark Laita for Van Cleef & Aroels
Figure 14.4 "Courtesy, Lowe's Company, Inc."
Figure 14.5 ©Susan Van Etten
Figure 14.8 AP Topic Gallery
Figure 14.11 "©2002 Cold Water Creek, Inc."
Opening Vignette 15 "©Mark Richards/PhotoEdit, Inc."
Figure 15.1 ©Nissan 2002. Nissan and the Nissan logo are registered trademarks of Nissan.
Figure 15.3 ©2002 Avon. Used by permission.
Figure 15.4 ©2002 Starbucks Coffee Company and NYASC. All rights reserved.
Figure 15.5 ©2002 Post-it Flags from 3M
Figure 15.6 ©Susan Van Etten
Figure 15.8 AP Topic Gallery
Figure 15.10 AP Topic Gallery
Figure 15.11 "©2002 Live Person, Inc. Used by permission."
Unnumbered 15.1 ©Terri Miller/e-visual communications
Unnumbered 15.2 ©Susan Van Etten
Unnumbered 15.3 ©Macduff Everton
Opening Vignette 16 ©James Leynse/CORBIS/SABA
Figure 16.1 ©2002 Crate & Barrel; photo: ©Alan Shortall
Figure 16.2 ©Christopher Glass/York Daily Record
Figure 16.3 "Courtesy, Best Buy Advertising"
Figure 16.4 ©Susan Van Etten
Figure 16.7 ©Susan Van Etten
Figure 16.8 ©2002 Johnson & Johnson
Unnumbered 16.1 ©Susan Van Etten
Unnumbered 16.2 "Courtesy, Wal-Mart Stores, Inc."
Unnumbered 16.3 ©Dawn Villella
Opening Vignette 17 "Courtesy, Nissan North America"
Figure 17.1 ©2002 Johnson & Johnson and ABC News
Figure 17.2 ©Susan Van Etten
Figure 17.3 Courtesy Sharp Electronics Corporation
Figure 17.4 "TM®M&M'S and GLOBAL COLOR VOTE are trademarks of Mars, Incorporated and its affiliates. They are used with permission. Mars, Incorporated is not associated with South-Western Publishing. Advertisement printed with permission of Mars, Incorporated. ©Mars, Inc. 2002."
Figure 17.5 ©2002 Earthlink. Used by permission.
Figure 17.6 ©Susan Van Etten
Unnumbered 17.1 ©2002 Make-A-Wish Foundation. Used by permission.
Unnumbered 17.2 "Courtesy, ©United States Postal Service"
Figure 17.8 "Courtesy, ©United States Postal Service"
Unnumbered 17.3 "Provided by Nestle Purina PetCare, ©Nestle"
Figure 17.9 Used by permission of Angelo Brothers Company
Figure 17.11 "Courtesy, AARP"
Figure 17.12 "Courtesy, Afterschool Alliance"
Opening Vignette 18 ©Susan Van Etten
Figure 18.1 ©2002 NYSDED The I Love New York logo is a registered mark of NYSDED.
Unnumbered 18.1 ©Susan Van Etten
Unnumbered 18.2 AP Topic Gallery
Figure 18.3 ©Susan Van Etten
Figure 18.5 ©2002 VISA
Unnumbered 18.4 ©2002 Boston Properties
Figure 18.6 "©2002 Diamond Trading Company and J. Walter Thompson, USA, Inc."
Unnumbered 18.6 "©Cool Savings, Inc."
Unnumbered 18.7 ©2002 Starbucks Coffee Company and NYASC. All rights reserved.
Figure 18.8 ©Susan Van Etten
Unnumbered 18.9 "Courtesy, Valassis"
Opening Vignette 19 ©AP/Wide World Photos
Figure 19.1 "Courtesy, T. Rowe Price. Printed by permission. Photo: ©2002 Eliot Crowley/NK Reps; Models: Courtesy of Kayo/Samantha Group and Bridget Ho/KSA"
Figure 19.4 "Courtesy, SAP"
Figure 19.6 ©Susan Van Etten
Figure 19.10 ©2002 The Sharper Image. Used by permission.
Unnumbered 19.1 ©Fujitsu PC Corporation
Unnumbered 19.2 "©2002 Agilent Technologies, Inc. Reproduced with Permission, Courtesy Agilent Technologies, Inc."
Unnumbered 19.3 ©Courtesy Saturn Division of General Motors

NAME AND COMPANY INDEX

Page numbers followed by i refer to interactive examples

SUBJECT INDEX

T

U

V

W

Y

Z